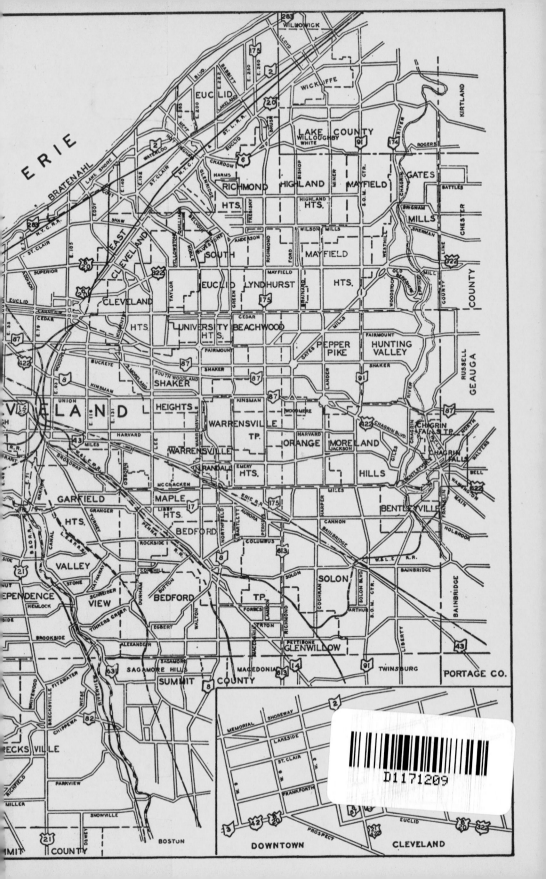

CLEVELAND

The Making of a City

Moses Cleaveland and the Terminal Tower

PERRY CRAGG, CLEVELAND NEWS

CLEVELAND

The Making
of a City

BY

WILLIAM GANSON ROSE

CLEVELAND AND NEW YORK

THE WORLD PUBLISHING COMPANY

Published by THE WORLD PUBLISHING COMPANY

2231 WEST 110TH STREET · CLEVELAND 2 · OHIO

WP

TO

THE YOUTH OF TODAY

WHO WILL BUILD

THE CITIES OF TOMORROW

THIS BOOK IS DEDICATED

I like to see a man proud of the place in which he lives; I like to see a man live in it so that his place will be proud of him.

LINCOLN

CLEVELAND

Born of the pathfinder's daring,
  Godly and thrifty his clan,
Deep through the wilderness faring,
  Blazing his way in the van;
Forest and thicket surrounding,
  Here by the freshwater sea,
Fortune smiled down on thy founding,
  Town of a million to be!

Low on this rock of foundation
  Budded the flower of thy name;
Now all the winds of creation
  Carry and scatter its fame.
Toilers from distant lands drifting,
  Seeking the land of the free,
Helped in thy mighty uplifting,
  Town of a million to be!

Countless the wheels thou art turning,
  Moving the engines of trade,
Countless the furnace fires burning,
  Countless the goods thou hast made.
Progress, the soul of thy story,
  Guiding thy spirited way,
Voices the hymn of thy glory,
  Town of a million today!

W. R. ROSE

THE

Western Reserve Historical Society

IS GRATIFIED TO BE A SPONSOR

OF THIS VOLUME

DESIGNED TO FURTHER THE

EDUCATIONAL AND HISTORICAL INTERESTS

OF THE

City of Cleveland

AND THE

Western Reserve

INTRODUCTION

SOME cities are born great, many achieve greatness, and possibly a
few have greatness thrust upon them. Some cities have natural advantages upon which they fail to capitalize; some have meager opportunities, yet climb to glorious heights.

What are the factors that contribute to the development of a great city,
and what are the destructive forces that retard growth and progress? These
and a thousand other questions can be answered by a study, not of the
theory of city-building, but of the actual making of a city.

The people of Cleveland, representing forty-eight nationalities, have developed an unsurpassed teamwork as proved in civic and national campaigns. They enjoy higher education in six universities and colleges within
the county limits; they root for their home teams in the mammoth Stadium;
they set attendance records when Metroplitan Opera comes to town, and they
fill magnificent Severance Hall when their Cleveland Orchestra plays.

Cleveland's achievements are due, not to natural advantages alone, but
to vision, resourcefulness, hard work, and civic spirit. Clevelanders believe
that a city is not merely a place where people exist and houses are built,
but that a city is a living, pulsing institution with heart and soul and
character.

What makes a city? Its people under leadership. Why do they volunteer
time, effort, and money to the task? Pride in the home town—faith in the
city's future—insurance that the next generation and the next may enjoy
the dividends earned by their unselfish investments.

The making of a city is one of the most fascinating stories of the ages.
This volume deals with a cosmopolitan city of everyday people—a place
blessed with advantages and at times fraught with reverses—a typical American city, capitalizing upon opportunities, overcoming obstacles, never satisfied, believing in quality rather than size, and in health as the first wealth.
Cleveland is proud of its industrial and commercial standing; it finds gratification in attaining eminence in creativeness, culture, and co-operation.

It is hoped that the story of Cleveland, its romance and its business, may
suggest practical ideas for the upbuilding of other cities, for the making of
better cities is the making of a greater America.

This story is told by William Ganson Rose, who was born in Cleveland,
and has always worked for its advancement. He believes that the admonition
of the old Greek philosopher, "Know thyself," has another practical application—know thy city. His breadth of interests and his many associations

3

make him the logical authority to trace the forward march of people and institutions in their making of a city—Cleveland.

Within these covers, also, is the history of the Western Reserve, that great expanse of territory stretching over northern Ohio for 120 miles from Pennsylvania's western boundary, with Cleveland as the major city. Noble vision and courageous effort are revealed on page after page as the story unfolds. Rich in heritage and productivity, the progress of the many thriving urban and rural communities in this great empire, is indeed enlightening and entertaining.

The author's aim has been to show the steady development of ideas and institutions, and the many factors that have contributed to sound, substantial progress. This is not merely a chronological account of events. It is rather a story of many-sided community life, revealing the significance of trends and reforms, as influenced by national and local circumstances, natural resources, and opportunities.

WILLIAM G. MATHER
CHARLES A. OTIS

ACKNOWLEDGMENTS

CLEVELAND has been called "the city of co-operation," and the spirit of teamwork manifested by a legion of Clevelanders made this volume and its preparation a pleasant task. The history of the teamwork given by institutions and individuals would of itself make a book. Unfortunately, there is not space to call them by name and express thanks to them individually; but they can find gratification in the fact that they have helped to preserve permanently the story of the city they love.

Certain institutions were called upon frequently, and their intelligent response smoothed the way through a maze of names, dates, events, statistics, and technical information, seemingly without end: the Cleveland Public Library, Municipal Reference Division of City Hall, Cleveland Chamber of Commerce, Western Reserve Historical Society, and Cleveland Board of Education. To the many able and patient members of the staffs in these outstanding organizations go sincere thanks.

Acknowledgment is made to these capable historians: Colonel Charles Whittlesey, James H. Kennedy, Samuel P. Orth, Harriet Taylor Upton, Gertrude Van Rensselaer Wickham, Elroy McKendree Avery, William R. Coates, Wilfred Henry Alburn and Miriam Russell Alburn, Leo Weidenthal, S. J. Kelly, Ella Grant Wilson, Archer H. Shaw, F. Leslie Speir, Elbert J. Benton, and Mary Scott Thayer. Their writings were of fundamental assistance in the preparation of this book.

For the executive direction of the major part of the work and for invaluable aid in organizing and editing the collected data, first thanks are due to Mrs. Lillian C. Brown. During the long period of developing the volume, she made a contribution of discriminating research and inspiring helpfulness. Of the many tireless workers on the staff, special assignments were faithfully handled by Jean Hudson, Frances B. Mehlek and Josephine S. Birt.

For securing the financial assistance that made the publication possible, Charles A. Otis was responsible. He suggested the book as a memento of the Cleveland Sesquicentennial Celebration of 1946, and upon his invitation the following Clevelanders became underwriters:

Cleveland Foundation

James A. Bohannon	Ben F. Hopkins	John Sherwin
George Gund	William G. Mather	Mrs. Windsor T. White
Leonard C. Hanna, Jr.	William Ganson Rose	B. D. Zevin

Contributors to special research were:

The Cleveland Electric Illuminating Company	The M. A. Hanna Company
Diesel Engine Division	J. J. McIntyre
General Motors Corporation	The May Company
Samuel H. Halle	The Sherwin-Williams Company
	The Standard Oil Company of Ohio

Mr. Otis was helpful in many ways from the inception of the history until it went to the printer. It was another evidence of "Mr. Cleveland's" interest in civic enterprise.

A vast amount of research was required in assembling the material contained in this volume. Material was gleaned from a large number of histories, public records and documents, reports, tracts and annals, newspaper files, manuscripts, historical papers and journals, and authoritative sources of every conceivable kind. Painstaking original research was undertaken in the examination of hundreds of individual histories of business and industrial companies, social and cultural institutions, schools, colleges and churches. Every effort was made to promote accuracy of statement, but it was found that in some instances even accepted authorities failed to agree upon certain facts. If mistakes crept into the pages, it should be remembered that "to err is human."

Contents

Illustrations

CLEVELAND

The Making of a City

HOW TO USE THIS BOOK

Cleveland: The Making of a City is designed to trace the growth and development of the district, decade by decade, from pioneer days. Beginning with Chapter 2, an editorial account gives a general picture of conditions, locally and nationally, followed by ten years of chronology. This treatment, it is believed, will give the reader a new appreciation of Cleveland's steady advance from settlement to city, and from city to metropolitan district.

An early-day system of identifying streets continued in effect until 1906, when the change was made from names to numbers. Old-time names are used consistently until the change, and a list of early streets with their present-day equivalents is given in the Appendix.

To facilitate an understanding of certain historical items in terms of present-day institutions or locations, appropriate data appears within parentheses.

Pioneering companies and those that have made large contributions to industrial progress, are presented in story form. Other companies, fifty or more years old, appear at the approximate time of their founding. In the Appendix is a list of manufacturers, according to size, compiled by the Cleveland Chamber of Commerce.

Stories of companies, schools, churches, and other institutions have often been written into several decades to show significant progress or to stress an important influence in establishing a trend or era. Reference to the Index will give a continuous account.

The comprehensive index was planned as a ready-reference key to the factual history and prepared by Mrs. Lillian C. Brown.

CHAPTER 1

Cleveland—Born Great

UNDER a sheet of ice a mile thick lay the site of the City of Cleveland more than 20,000 years ago. Vast glaciers covered much of North America, including two-thirds of what became the State of Ohio. Eventually the ice field melted away, leaving hills and valleys, rivers and small lakes, and a clear evidence of natural advantages that played an important part in the march of civilization.

The glaciers helped to shape the Great Lakes, a mighty influence upon Cleveland's growth and progress. They were responsible for the natural setting of the Erie Canal through the Mohawk Valley, and for the Portage Lakes that largely determined the location of the Ohio Canal. Another heritage was fertile soil that made Ohio surpassingly rich in agricultural products.

The district owes much to its geologic past. No wonder Dr. J. Paul Goode, eminent student of natural resources, said, "Cleveland was born great." Later he predicted that some day Cleveland, Chicago, and Milwaukee, because of their locations on the Great Lakes, would be numbered among the foremost of the world's business centers.

Who were the first inhabitants of this area? Discoveries have indicated that men lived here during the glacial period, evidence having been found in the form of stone implements and other relics left in terraces formed by the glaciers. Some authorities believe these people later became the Eskimos of the polar regions.

The advent of the Mound Builders, a later race, is variously placed between six and twelve centuries ago. Their mysterious entrance into history and their veiled exit from human records are matters that research has been unable to explain. Ohio has many evidences of their early civilization in the form of earthen mounds built for various purposes—village sites, fortifications, and burial grounds; also relics, consisting of tools, utensils, and fabrics. In Cleveland, the two best-known mounds were discovered at what became the southeast corner of Euclid and East 9th Street and at East 53rd Street near Woodland, while others were found in Newburgh and in the Cuyahoga River valley to the south. Some students believe that the Mound Builders were the ancestors of historic Indian tribes.

With the coming of the red men, the wilderness that became Ohio was a hunting ground of migrating, warfaring tribes. In the north, the most prominent were the Wyandots, Hurons, Ottawas, Neutral Nation, Andastes, Iroquois, and Eries, for whom Lake Erie was named. The Eries developed great power and gained control of the southern shore of the lake from Sandusky Bay to the site of Buffalo. Their kin, the Iroquois, however, became their bitter enemies, and organized smaller tribes into the mighty Five Nations to oppose them.

In the middle of the Seventeenth Century came a merciless war; and the Iroquois, with their allies, superior in numbers, practically exterminated the

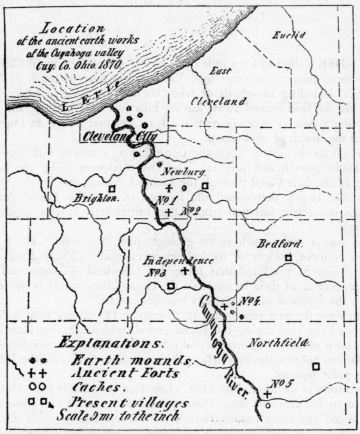

Map by Colonel Charles Whittlesey showing location of earth mounds left by the Mound Builders in the northern section of the Cuyahoga Valley. The results of Colonel Whittlesey's interesting surveys are preserved in the Western Reserve Historical Society.

Eries to become masters of northeastern Ohio. Early in the Eighteenth Century, the Five Nations became the Six Nations when the Tuscarora came north. The Cuyahoga River was the boundary line between the Iroquois and the Hurons. The Indians engaged in fur trading along the southern shores of Lake Erie, finding customers among venturesome French and English traders.

In 1772, David Zeisberger and John Heckewelder, Moravian missionaries, built Gnadenhutten and Schoenbrunn villages for friendly Christian Indians on the Tuscarawas River. The ninety inhabitants were brutally massacred in 1782 by irresponsible whites, and acts of revenge by furious Indians of several tribes followed.

Hoping to establish a new colony, and believing that the bitter conflicts were over, Zeisberger and Heckewelder founded a settlement called Pilgerruh, meaning Pilgrim's Rest, in May, 1786, near the junction of the Cuyahoga River and Tinker's Creek. A chapel and log cabins were built, and the few residents engaged in agriculture. Indians and hostile whites interfered, and the new project was given up. The Moravians left a map and a description of the area which are preserved by the Western Reserve Historical Society.

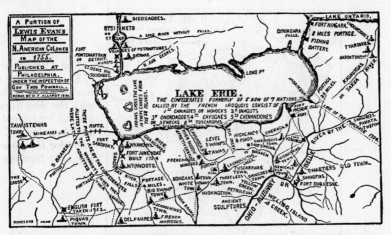

This map, made by Lewis Evans, one of the first American geographers to study the Great Lakes, was published in 1755 in Philadelphia and was printed by Benjamin Franklin and D. Hall.

Scattered whites are said to have lived in isolated clearings west of the Cuyahoga, but they did not establish a settlement. Tradition states that in 1786, agents of the Northwestern Fur Company, identified with the Astor family, built a trading post of hewn timbers on the west side of the river near the mouth. The Astor House was Cleveland's most famous relic, leading a migratory existence until it was razed in the 1920s.

The Indians were not the sole claimants to northeastern Ohio. The Cabots, who stumbled against Newfoundland's bleak shore, led England to claim North America. The French, because of their explorations and discoveries, considered themselves the rightful owners. Connecticut, Massachusetts, New York, and Virginia had vague claims under early charters granted by English kings. These monarchs, through geographical ignorance or political expediency, made their gifts with little consideration for boundary lines, and often one king gave what his predecessor had already given.

In 1662, the State of Connecticut persuaded Charles II of England, whose

knowledge of liqueur was said to have been greater than his understanding of geography, to grant her a vast territory of western land for her
questionable title deed. It lay between the parallels which bounded the
State, and extended "from sea to sea." Ownership was a confused issue to be
settled only after the Thirteen States had agreed to relinquish disputed lands
to the Federal Government so that they might be admitted to the Con-
federation as new states. Connecticut, which waived part of her claim on
September 14, 1786, reserved a tract in what became northeastern Ohio as
compensation for her comparatively small size. This area, known as the
Western Reserve, extended southward from the lake to the forty-first parallel
of north latitude, and continued westward 120 miles from the Pennsylvania
line. It was frequently called New Connecticut.

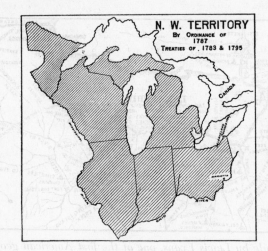

*The Ordinance of
1787 establishing the
Northwest Territory
was the first funda-
mental act passed by
an American Con-
gress for the govern-
ing of a territory.*

The Ordinance of 1787, passed on July 13 by the Congress of Confedera-
tion, provided machinery for government in the Northwest Territory. This
vast area, appended to the Thirteen States, was originally bounded by the
Ohio River on the south, the Mississippi on the west, the Great Lakes on
the north and Pennsylvania and Virginia on the east. The Ordinance of
1787 was a significant achievement, setting the form by which subsequent
western territories were created and later admitted into the Union, marking
the beginnings of western expansion and increasing the powers of the
Federal Government. Arthur St. Clair, scholarly soldier, was chosen governor, and the seat of government was established at Marietta, Ohio, on July
15, 1788. Slavery was prohibited within the Territory.

In May, 1792, Connecticut set apart 500,000 acres of the western end of the
Reserve for the benefit of citizens who had suffered losses by fire or otherwise during the Revolution, and the area was commonly known as the
"Fire Lands" (Erie and Huron counties). The remaining tract of about
3,000,000 acres was offered for sale by the General Assembly in May, 1795,
and the proceeds provided Connecticut with a permanent school fund.

Citizens of the State, organized as the Connecticut Land Company, purchased the unsurveyed Western Reserve lands, sight unseen, for $1,200,000, or 40 cents an acre, the individual members receiving quitclaim deeds. There were forty-nine original shareholders, who gave mortgages for their interests, payment to become due in five years:

Joseph Howland and Daniel L. Coit	$ 30,461
Elias Morgan	51,402
Caleb Atwater	22,846
Daniel Holbrook	8,750
Joseph Williams	15,231
William Love	10,500
William Judd	16,256
Elisha Hyde and Uriah Tracey	57,400
James Johnston	30,000
Samuel Mather, Jr.	18,461
Ephraim Kirby, Elijah Boardman and Uriel Holmes, Jr.	60,000
Samuel Griswold	10,000
Oliver Phelps and Gideon Granger, Jr.	80,000
William Hart	30,462
Henry Champion II	85,675
Asher Miller	34,000
Robert C. Johnson	60,000
Ephraim Root	42,000
Nehemiah Hubbard, Jr.	19,039
Solomon Cowles	10,000
Oliver Phelps	168,185
Asahel Hathaway	12,000
John Caldwell and Peleg Sanford	15,000
Timothy Burr	15,231
Luther Loomis and Ebenezer King, Jr.	44,318
William Lyman, John Stoddard and David King	24,730
Moses Cleaveland	32,600
Samuel P. Lord	14,092
Roger Newberry, Enoch Perkins and Jonathan Brace	38,000
Ephraim Starr	17,415
Sylvanus Griswold	1,683
Joseb Stocking and Joshua Stow	11,423
Titus Street	22,846
James Bull, Aaron Olmstead and John Wyles	30,000
Pierpoint Edwards	60,000

For convenience in business transactions, the interests of the land company were placed in the hands of three trustees—John Caldwell, John Morgan, and Jonathan Brace. Management rested with a board of directors, with an office in Hartford. On the board were Oliver Phelps, Henry Champion II, Moses Cleaveland, Samuel W. Johnson, Ephraim Kirby,

Samuel Mather, Jr., and Roger Newberry, all men of prominence in their home state. Ephraim Root became secretary. It was decided by the investors that the Indian claims should be "extinguished," and that 16,000-acre townships should be speedily laid out and surveyed in lots suitable for sale and settlement. A sawmill and grist-mill were to be erected in each township at company expense to attract settlers.

General Moses Cleaveland, a shareholder and a man of courage and wide experience, was selected as superintendent of the Western Reserve surveying party. His commission, issued on May 12, 1796, read in part as follows:

> We the Board of Directors of said Connecticut Land Company, having appointed you to go on to said land as superintendant over the Agents and Men sent on to survey & make Locations on said Land to make and enter into friendly negotiations with the Natives who are on said Land or contiguous thereto and may have any pretended claim to the same and secure such friendly intercourse amongst them as will establish peace, quiet & Safety to the survey & settlement of said Lands . . . not ceded by the natives under the authority of the United States . . .

Vested in the General were broad powers to act and transact business, to make contracts, and to draw on the company treasury as necessity required.

Moses Cleaveland was a man of action, and early in June his officers and men had been organized for the expedition at Schenectady. The surveying party included:

> General Moses Cleaveland, superintendent
> Augustus Porter, principal surveyor and deputy superintendent
> Seth Pease, astronomer and surveyor
> Amos Spafford, John Milton Holley, Richard M. Stoddard and Moses
>   Warren, surveyors
> Joshua Stow, commissary
> Theodore Shepard, physician

Employees of the Company

Joseph Tinker, boatman	Titus V. Munson	Michael Coffin
George Proudfoot	Charles Parker	Thomas Harris
Samuel Forbes	Nathaniel Doan	Timothy Dunham
Stephen Benton	James Halket	Shadrach Benham
Samuel Hungerford	Olney F. Rice	Wareham Shepard
Samuel Davenport	Samuel Barnes	John Briant
Amzi Atwater	Daniel Shulay	Joseph Landon
Elisha Ayres	Joseph M'Intyre	Ezekiel Morly
Norman Wilcox	Francis Gray	Luke Hanchet
George Gooding	Amos Sawtel	James Hamilton
Samuel Agnew	Amos Barber	John Lock
David Beard	William B. Hall	Stephen Burbank
	Asa Mason	

James Kingsbury

Moses Cleaveland

Samuel Huntington

Dr. David Long

Leonard Case, Jr.

Levi Johnson

Alfred Kelley

Nathan Perry, Jr.

Leonard Case, Sr.

Map of the Connecticut Western Reserve, made by Seth Pease in 1798, preserved by the Western Reserve Historical Society.

Accompanying the party were Elijah Gun and his wife, Anna, who were to have charge of company stores at Conneaut; Job Phelps Stiles and his wife, Tabitha Cumi; Nathan Chapman and Nathan Perry, who provided the surveyors with fresh meat and traded with the Indians. Thirteen horses and some cattle were transported with the expedition. Employees were enlisted in company service "as in the army, for two years, providing it took so long."

After a hazardous journey down swift streams and through uncharted wilderness, the surveyors reached Buffalo Creek on June 22. Here General Cleaveland held diplomatic meetings with the Mohawk and Seneca representatives of the mighty Six Nations. After shrewd persuasion, the Indians relinquished their claim to the lands east of the Cuyahoga River in exchange for 500 pounds New York currency, two beef cattle, and 100 gallons of whisky.

Proceeding westward on June 27, the expedition reached Conneaut Creek on the evening of July 4. Raising the new flag of the new nation, the place was christened Port Independence with gunfire salute. Thus Independence Day was celebrated for the first time on the Reserve. At a feast of pork and beans, six spirited toasts were drunk, the first three being proposed to the President of the United States, the State of New Connecticut, and the Connecticut Land Company.

The erection of a cabin headquarters, called "Stow's Castle" in honor of the commissary manager, was begun the next day. It was a nondescript structure of "uncouth appearance such as to provoke the laughter of the builders and the ridicule of the Indians."

General Cleaveland's preparations for permanent settlement stirred the Massasagoes, an Indian tribe in the vicinity, and they summoned him for an explanation. After considerable discussion, an understanding was reached, with the assurance that they should not be disturbed in their possessions. The pipe of friendship and peace was presented to Cleaveland by Chief Paqua in exchange for wampum, trinkets, and whisky valued at a total of about $25 to seal the agreement. This friendly meeting forestalled future requests for charity and gratuities, especially for "fire water."

The land-company employees having been separated into groups to expedite the surveying of the Western Reserve, Moses Cleaveland and his party journeyed westward on the lake in an open bateau. With him were Commissary Stow, probably the Stileses, and hardy men numbering a boatload. One historian claims that the explorers started up the Chagrin River by mistake, believing it to be the Cuyahoga; and upon discovering their error, their leader named the river Chagrin. This story, however, is discredited by maps made before the Revolution, on which the name Chagrin appears. There is also a disputed report that early French traders named the stream Chagrin after having suffered a misfortune near its mouth. The probable source of the name is Shagrin or Shaguin, Indian names meaning "clear water."

The final stage of the historic journey to the mouth of the Cuyahoga River was uneventful; and General Moses Cleaveland little dreamed that he was nearing the site of a city that was destined to achieve greatness.

CHAPTER 2

The Founding

1796-1799

WHILE I was in New Connecticut I laid out a town on the bank of Lake Erie, which was called by my name, and I believe the child is now born that may live to see that place as large as Old Windham."

With these words, General Moses Cleaveland reported in part to the directors of the Connecticut Land Company upon the success of his expedition to the Western Reserve. It has been observed that the founder was a man of vision, for Cleveland passed Windham, Connecticut—a town of 2,700 persons in 1790—well within the predicted time.

From the start, Cleveland was a commercial proposition. The land company had real estate to sell, and the promoters were anxious to realize a return on their investment as speedily as possible. Moses Cleaveland, shareholder, who was commissioned to survey the Western Reserve lands, was also directed to establish a "capital" city. Why did he choose the Cuyahoga River site as the location for the principal city of the Western Reserve?

Robert Shackleton, at one time a Clevelander, said in his *Book of Philadelphia* (Wm. Penn Publishing Corp.): "Before ever a single cabin was erected where the great city of Cleveland now stands, when there was no road but an Indian trail and while the mouth of the Cuyahoga was but a sandbar, Benjamin Franklin, from his study of conditions, pointed out the site of the future Cleveland as the place at which an important city was to arise." It is possible that the Connecticut pathfinder and surveyor had heard of Franklin's remarkable prophecy.

Cleaveland's men were capable engineers and practical planners, endowed with courage and endurance. The survey of 1796 was made under the direction of Augustus Porter, superintendent, who had the technical assistance of Amos Spafford and Seth Pease, makers of the first two maps of Cleveland. These maps, similar in most respects, initiated a city plan with right-angle streets of noble width, and that inestimable blessing, the Public Square.

In the fall, the surveyors departed. The founder had done his work wisely and well; but when he returned to Connecticut, he resumed his law practice, never again to visit the settlement on the lake. When he died ten years later, the little colony bearing his name was slowly taking substantial form.

Early in 1797, a second expedition was organized, with the Rev. Seth Hart, head of the party, and Seth Pease, chief surveyor. By fall, the exploration of the Reserve was concluded, Cleveland street lines were determined and lots were laid out. The surveyors left a rich heritage in the form of a goodly waterfront, forests of sturdy timber, a curving stream, and wide stretches of level land backed by a gentle ridge.

The year 1797 witnessed the arrival of the first settlers—Elijah Gun, Lorenzo Carter, Ezekiel Hawley, and James Kingsbury with their families. Despite privations, disease, and danger, the pioneers sought opportunity at the frontier, ax in one hand, rifle in the other, *Bible* and spelling book in the saddle bags. They came prepared for a bitter struggle to provide food, clothing, and shelter with the crude implements at hand. Hardships tried the toughest New England souls, but with patient hands the seed was planted that would flower into the future city.

Seth Pease, maker of the second map of Cleveland.

Cleveland's industry began with a blacksmith shop, a sawmill, and a grist-mill. At the grist-mill there was a market for grain grown on the primitive farms, easing the local food problem.

The political boundaries of Jefferson County were created, and Cleveland was located within its limits. Steubenville was the county seat, but there was an absence of civil and military government for several years.

The years from the founding through 1799 tested the courage and confidence of the sturdy little band of pioneers, and proved their loyalty to the new "capital" of the Western Reserve in which they had built their cabin homes. Growth and progress were dreams the early settlers determined to achieve, and they were building better than they knew.

1796

General Moses Cleaveland, representing the Connecticut Land Company, proceeded westward from Conneaut on the lake with a small company, including Joshua Stow, commissary chief, and young Job Phelps Stiles and

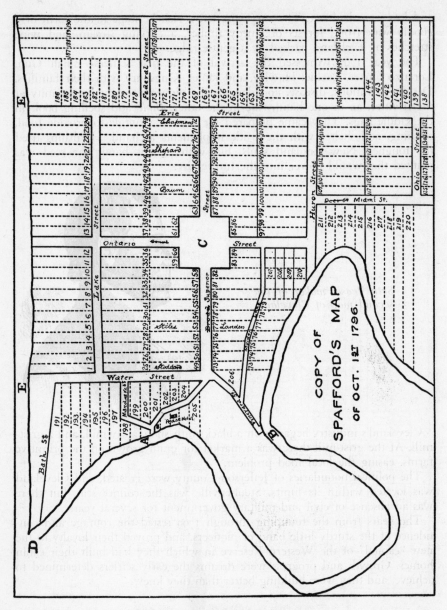

FIRST MAP OF CLEVELAND

On the original, preserved by the Western Reserve Historical Society, Amos Spafford wrote "Original Plan of the Town and Village of Cleveland, Ohio, October 1, 1796."

A marks lower landing on the river; B, upper landing; C, Public Square; D, mouth of river; E, Lake Erie.

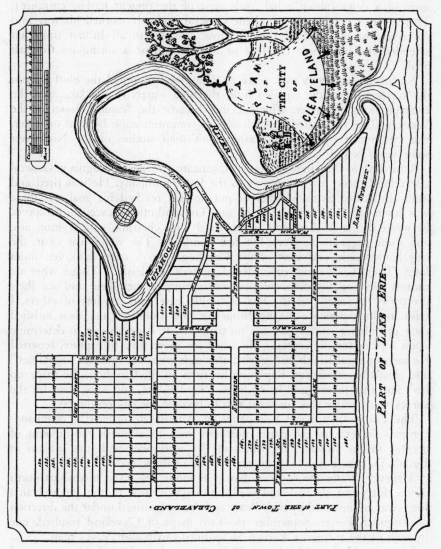

Second map of Cleveland. Made by Seth Pease in 1796.

his wife, Tabitha Cumi Stiles, seventeen. In an open boat they followed the densely forested shore line until they reached the Cuyahoga—"crooked water," which they entered on July 22. The mouth of the river was in the form of a delta (about a half mile west of the present harbor entrance). There were several outlets, and the General probably worked his way into the river through one of these narrow passages to an Indian trail that ascended the hill (near the foot of St. Clair) past a spring on the east bank.

No formal ceremony took place as Cleaveland mounted the bluff to scan the surroundings—the wooded hills, the blue waters of the lake, and the swamps along the river. This site that became the "capital" town of the Western Reserve, located strategically for communication by land or water, was envisioned by George Washington's map studies of the Northwest some years before.

Returning to Port Independence—Conneaut Creek—on August 5, General Cleaveland made his first report to the home company. He was tired and quite undecided as to whether or not he had reached his goal, yet there was much to be said in favor of the site. The land offered excellent prospects, he wrote, being level on top and covered with chestnut, oak, walnut, ash, and some sugar-maple trees, but few hemlocks. The water was clear, the clay banks high, and west of the Cuyahoga was a steep bank ten miles long. Then Cleaveland unburdened himself fearlessly: "Those who are meanly envying the compensation and sitting at their ease and see their prosperity increasing at the loss of health, ease, and comfort of others, I wish might experience the hardships for one month; if not then satisfied their grumbling would give me no pain . . . It is impossible to determine upon a place for the capital." He asked for more time to explore, reported his men in good health and spirits, although without "sauce or vegetables," and closed his statement. Rejoining his men on the Cuyahoga, he made up his mind that there could be no better "capital" site, and soon plans for the survey were under way for what was to become the city on the lake.

The Connecticut Land Company, on August 26, ordered a chain-and-compass traverse of the entire northern area, to establish the amount of acreage in the Reserve, regardless of the agreement with the Indians at Buffalo that there was to be no survey west of the Cuyahoga.

A survey of the site of town No. 7 in range 12—seven townships north of the forty-first parallel and twelve townships west of the Pennsylvania line—was commenced by Seth Pease and Amos Spafford under the direction of Augustus Porter, September 16. Two maps of Cleveland resulted, one by each of the surveyors, known as Spafford's map and Pease's map.

Surveyors Holley—Hawley or Holly, Shepard, and Spafford commenced to run their lines in the township around Cleveland on September 22. Cleveland Township was one of six designated to be sold and not divided among the company's stockholders, as was the case in many Reserve towns. The plan, at first, was to sell only a quarter of each township, and, accordingly, on September 28, Porter, chief surveyor, proposed a method of achievement, which was later confirmed, and is described in Crisfield Johnson's *History of Cuyahoga County*:

> City lots Number 58 to 63 inclusive, and 81 to 87 inclusive, comprising all the lots bordering on the Public Square, and one more, were to be reserved for public purposes, as were also 'the point of land west of the town' (which we take to be the low peninsula southwest of the viaduct), and some other portions of the flats if thought advisable. Then Mr. Porter proposed to begin with lot number one, and offer for sale every fourth number in succession throughout the towns, on these terms. Each person who would engage to become an actual settler in 1797 might purchase one town lot, one ten or twenty-acre lot, and one hundred-acre lot, or as much less as he might choose; settlement, however, to be imperative in every case. The price of town lots was to be fifty dollars; that of ten-acre lots three dollars per acre; that of twenty-acre lots two dollars per acre; and that of hundred-acre lots a dollar and a half per acre. The town lots were to be paid for in ready cash; for the larger tracts twenty per cent was to be paid down, and the rest in three annual installments with annual interest.

The land east of the river (later a portion of Cuyahoga County) was claimed by Washington County of the Northwest Territory. A civil township had not yet been organized, for the question as to whether legal jurisdiction was held by the territory or the land company had not been settled. The area west of the river belonged to Wayne County, of which Detroit was the seat; and although the company had purchased the pre-emption rights, the Indians' claims had not been satisfied, and the red men remained in possession.

In late summer, General Cleaveland's surveyors, chain bearers, and technicians threatened to quit unless more profitable arrangements were made. They had found their work tedious, the swamps dangerous, and the food scarce. On September 30, forty-one of them settled for equal shares in township No. 8 in the 11th range, each man pledging faithful service to the company to the end of the year, and subscribing to a colonization agreement. The township was called Euclid, honoring the great mathematician, patron saint of the surveyor's art, upon the suggestion of Moses Warren. The next year, David Dille, first settler in the township, built his cabin. In 1836, he erected the historic Dille home, that after a century still stood sturdy and proud.

Spafford endorsed his first field map, "Original Plan of the Town and Village of Cleveland, Ohio, October 1, 1796" (map preserved by the Western Reserve Historical Society). Pease, who compiled the official report of the survey, attached to it a map endorsed, "A Plan of the City of Cleaveland." Both maps reserved space for the Public Square, described 220 two-acre lots with numbers, and determined the street plan. Spafford's map, drawn on foolscap sheets pasted together, showed changes in certain street names and gave the names of a few lot owners. Lots other than those reserved for public use were priced at $50 each, subject to immediate settlement. Beginning at the lake, the boundary line ran southward (East 14th) to a section of lots south of Ohio Street (Central Avenue), thence along the river to Vineyard Lane and the junction of Superior and Water streets, and westward to the river, which it followed to the lake. Streets were 99 feet wide, with the exception of Superior Street, which was 132 feet in width. This was practical planning of the city's center that was to remain basically the same down through the years.

The first Cleveland plan was designed to facilitate sales and distribution of real estate, following a mechanical pattern of uniformly shaped lots facing

Cleveland under the Hill—1797. Left to right, on the east bank of the Cuyahoga River, surveyors' cabin, or "Pease's Hotel"; surveyors' log storehouse; Lorenzo Carter's first cabin.

the streets in a similar fashion. Envisioning future expansion, General Cleaveland made plans to plot the immediate outlying land in 10-acre lots, and the rest of the township in 100-acre lots, instead of larger tracts.

Although the founder intended to give the settlement the name of the river, his associates successfully urged him to bestow upon it his own name. It is interesting to note that Spafford spelled Cleveland without the "a" in the first syllable when identifying his map.

There was nothing novel about the plan of the Public Square, the center of the "capital" of the Reserve, as Surveyor Pease laid it out. Crossroads and adjoining "commons" were typical New England planning; and although many American communities began with open centers, few were able to retain them.

The Public Square contained 4.4 acres of land—38 by 40 rods, with 2 rods greater north and south than east and west. Surrounding streets and sidewalks made up the plot, variously defined as 9½ and 10 acres. Cost of the area to the land company was $1.76; in 1946 it was valued at $4,320,000, and was definitely not for sale.

During the summer, the surveyors had built a cabin, labeled "Pease's Hotel," and a storehouse for supplies near the river. They also erected a cabin for the Stiles family on lot 53 (West 6th near Superior). In about mid-October, winter threatened, urging plans for departure. By the eighteenth, the surveying party had gone, and General Cleaveland never again visited the town that bore his name. Six of his employees had faith in the settlement's future, and arranged for the purchase of lots.

Seed wheat, brought from a settlement on the Genesee River in New York State, was sowed in the fall on a 6-acre clearing at Conneaut, east of the creek, by land-company employees. It produced the first crop of grain grown by civilized men on the Western Reserve.

Only a footpath led down to the mouth of the Cuyahoga where the surveyors' cabins had been empty for a month. Three people remained in the settlement in a lonely cabin built by the surveyors (1410 West 11th Street), the first family dwelling in Cleveland—the Stileses, and Joseph Landon, who soon moved on. A new boarder, Edward Paine, traded with the Ottawa, Delaware, and Chippewa Indians west of the river, and he later founded Painesville. A small camp of friendly Senecas lived "under the hill" (Erie Depot site). This was Cleveland on that first Thanksgiving, as the pioneer population of three persons prepared to face the first winter in the wilderness.

The first adventurer to seek a new home for his family in the Reserve of his own volition was James Kingsbury, aged twenty-nine. He had come to Conneaut from Alsted, New Hampshire, with his wife, Eunice Waldo Kingsbury, and three small children, arriving soon after the surveyors. The story of their first six months in Conneaut is typical of pioneer courage and fortitude.

Dwindling supplies and an absence of game presaged starvation for the family. In November, Kingsbury set out for New Hampshire to secure provisions, expecting to be gone a month or so. There he was stricken with fever. Anxiety for his family urged him to start home sooner than advisable; and when he reached Buffalo on December 3, he was almost exhausted. Pushing forward the next day with his Indian guide into the wilds, he was overtaken with snow that fell for three weeks without intermission, until, in places, it was up to his chin. His horse died on the way, but determination spurred him on, and it was Christmas Eve when he reached his cabin.

Meantime, friendly Indians had brought Mrs. Kingsbury meat until they could no longer brave the winter storms. Her husband's thirteen-year-old nephew cared for the oxen and a cow, and tried to comfort the pioneer mother in her loneliness and despair when she gave birth to the first white child born on the Reserve before the father returned. Soon fever attacked his wife, their food was almost gone, and James Kingsbury, forgetful of his own weakness, set out with a hand-sled for Erie, where he obtained a bushel of wheat, which when cracked and boiled stayed starvation. Upon the death of the cow from the effects of eating the browse of oak trees, the baby's chance for life decreased daily, and the child died in January. The family endured near-starvation, and for two weeks Mrs. Kingsbury was scarcely conscious. Late in February or early in March the bitter winter relaxed, and Kingsbury was able to bring down a solitary pigeon with a well-aimed shot. The nourishing broth kindled a spark that started the long climb to health in the frail, tired body of his wife.

1797

The first white child born in Cleveland was Charles Phelps Stiles, son of Job Phelps and Tabitha Cumi Stiles. The date was January 23.

At a meeting of the Connecticut Land Company held in January, a committee was appointed on behalf of the stockholders to investigate the "very great expense of the company during the first year, the causes which have prevented the completion of the surveys; and why the surveyors and agents have not made their reports." The expedition had cost about $14,000. Directors and trustees were required to urge the Legislature to create a county comprising all of the Western Reserve. An assessment of $5 per share was ordered on the 400 shares of company stock, Daniel Holbrook, Moses Warren, Jr., Seth Pease, and Amos Spafford constituting a committee of partition. A committee was also appointed to inquire into the conduct of the directors of the company; a decision reached in February exonerated the management.

Making his report to the directors at Hartford, Connecticut, on January 28, Augustus Porter stated that the Western Reserve contained 3,450,753 acres, exclusive of the islands in Lake Erie, and including Sandusky Bay. Deducting 500,000 acres for the "Fire Lands," the company had about 50,000 acres less than supposedly purchased. His report was questioned, but upon examination no error could be found. Naturally, the thrifty New Englanders were indignant upon learning that they had really paid 40 cents an acre for a vast tract that never existed.

A second expedition to the Western Reserve was authorized under the superintendence of an Episcopalian clergyman, the Rev. Seth Hart. Whether the appointment was offered to General Moses Cleaveland is not known; but if it was, he declined. Cleaveland, a lawyer and a man of important responsibilities in Connecticut, remained a member of the company's board of directors until his death in 1806.

Seth Pease, chief surveyor, set out for Schenectady on April 3 to organize the new party. Running short of funds, he was assisted financially by Thomas Mather of Albany, New York, whose credit enabled him to purchase supplies. Two months were required to round up men, boats, and equipment, and on May 26 the surveying party reached Conneaut.

Familiar names of members of the first expedition are noticed in the roll of seventy-one employees under Hart and Pease—Richard M. Stoddard, Moses Warren, Amzi Atwater, Joseph Landon, Amos Spafford, Warham Shepard—or Wareham Shepard, Theodore Shepard—or Shepherd, Na-

thaniel Doan, Ezekiel Morley—or Morly, Joseph Tinker, David Beard, and
Charles Parker. At Conneaut they found the James Kingsburys in "a low
state of health," and they learned that the Elijah Gun—or Gunn—family
had moved on "to Cuyahoga," the second family to make Cleveland its home.

Lorenzo Carter, thirty, and his brother-in-law, Ezekiel Hawley—Holley
or Holly, arrived in May from Vermont with their families. Carter erected
a pretentious log cabin with a garret on the east bank of the river (foot of
St. Clair) on a tract near the surveyors' hut. Travelers were welcomed to a
meal, a bed, and a drink of good New England rum. Carter was a man of
action and energy. He soon built a boat, launched a ferry at the foot of
Superior Street, and laid in a stock of goods for trade with the Indians.
Carter, a Baptist, was Cleveland's first permanent settler.

*Lorenzo Carter, first permanent
settler and most versatile Clevelander of the early days.*

The first boat of the second surveying expedition landed at the storehouse
on the Cuyahoga on the afternoon of June 1. As the other boats came in,
they brought news of tragedy, the drowning of David Eldridge, one of the
party, as he attempted to ford the Grand River on horseback on June 3.
Rev. Hart conducted the first religious service in Cleveland the next day
at the burial in the first cemetery on the east side of Ontario (north of
Prospect). The plot was surrounded by briars and bushes. Virgin forests
crowded in, and a little to the south on Ontario was a large mound, said to
be the work of the Mound Builders.

Headquarters were set up, company stores were examined, and land was
cleared for a vegetable garden that was enclosed with the first fence built
in Cleveland. Early in June the expedition was organized into groups that
would continue exploring and surveying the Western Reserve. Full and
interesting field books and memoranda of Pease and his men show the
progress of the work, as described by Elbert Jay Benton in his *Cultural
Story of an American City—Cleveland*:

The eyes of the explorers were especially open for good waterpower for flour mills and saw mills. The Salt Springs on the Mahoning were tested and described. A burning spring of natural gas aroused no more than a passing curiosity. Considerable more work was done in the survey of Cleveland, marking out the street lines and laying out the ten acre and hundred acre lots around the projected town. The ten acre lots were located east of the town lots, extending from those which faced Erie on Ninth Street to 55th Street. Beyond these lay the one hundred-acre lots. Three radiating roads were platted through the ten acre lots. For many years these were on paper only. North Highway led north-eastward parallel to the Lake, to become St. Clair Avenue later. Center Highway was marked out eastward, and within a few years cleared as the road to the township of Euclid . . . the road to Euclid should in time be known as Euclid Avenue. A third, South Highway, was platted in 1797 southeast from the junction of Ontario and Huron, a road to Kinsman, Ohio—and with equal logic called Kinsman Road, to be changed later to Woodland. The radiating roads would cut the ten-acre lots into varying sizes, increasing in acres as the distance from the square increased and as the value decreased. In effect the plan equalized the value of the lots and simplified the problem of the company's agents in selling them.

James Kingsbury and his family accompanied the surveyors when they moved from Conneaut to Cleveland. They lived for a time in a deserted log trading cabin west of the river (near Main and Center streets)—reputedly the Astor House—until a new cabin was built (Federal Building site).

Gilman—or Gillman—Bryant, with his father, David Bryant, reached Cleveland in June, and gave a pen picture of the Indians. Encamped on the west side of the river were from sixty to eighty families, and Bryant was invited to partake of a feast, with boiled dog as the principal course. He reported that the red men were pious in their way, and frequently offered sacrifices and prayers to Manitou, asking for a good crop of corn and other blessings. In the spring they packed their skins, sugar, bear oil, honey, and jerked venison, and paddled their canoes back into the woods. The Bryants quarried grindstones from the Vermilion ledges for shipment to the east by boat.

The first wedding was performed in Carter's cabin on July 4. Chloe Inches, Mrs. Carter's household helper, became the bride of William Clement, who pursued her from Ontario. Rev. Hart officiated. The bride and groom left the settlement on their honeymoon and never returned. This seems to be the last record of the good reverend's clerical ministrations.

Edward Paine opened the first dry-goods store. His stock of bright-colored calicoes and trinkets brought a traffic line of curious but friendly Indians. Pierre Meloche—or Maloch, a Frenchman, came to Cleveland during the year and remained until about 1808.

Their work finished, the surveyors departed in October, and the land was ready to be divided among the stockholders. Townships had been platted, five miles square. As shown on Surveyor Pease's map, Cleveland Township appeared as a large, irregular tract of 25,242 acres, located in range 12, tiers 7 and 8 (parts of East Cleveland, Cleveland and Newburgh townships).

To the early trail-blazers who kept history-making diaries and notes with painstaking care, some of them mere boys in their teens, Cleveland is greatly indebted. Enduring months of merciless weather, the rigors of the wilderness, privations of food and comfort, and malarial afflictions that cost the lives of several men, the Western Reserve was established, and soon adventuresome families would settle its fertile acres.

On December 11, the Kingsburys moved again, this time to a higher, healthier location away from the swamps—the ridge southeast of Cleveland (Woodhill Road) on the line from what became Doan's Corners (East 105th Street). This was the beginning of Newburgh—or Newburg—settlement. The move to the suburbs had begun.

Jefferson County was created out of Washington County, the new district including the Western Reserve that lay east of the Cuyahoga and the old portage path, an Indian trail that led to the Tuscarawas River. Steubenville became the county seat.

Colonization was taking hold on the Mahoning at Youngstown, Canfield, and Poland, and in other parts of the Reserve. Alexander Harper purchased 16,000 acres, a township, and the settlement became Harpersfield. Likewise, isolated areas were being opened up by brave frontiersmen.

1798

The new survey of the Reserve having been completed, the land was divided among the stockholders of the Connecticut Land Company in January. Recognizing the pioneering spirit of the first settlers, the proprietors gave them land in compensation: To Tabitha Cumi Stiles, wife of the first settler, one city lot, a 10-acre lot, and a 100-acre lot; to Anna Gun, wife of Elijah Gun, a 100-acre lot; to the Kingsburys, a 100-acre lot and an additional 100 acres, honoring them as parents of the first white child born on the Western Reserve; to Nathaniel Doan, one city lot on which he was to reside as blacksmith. To those who would build grist-mills to provide flour for the settlers, bounties were offered.

Narrow paths, marked by blazed trees, and a few old Indian trails constituted the highways. One led from Buffalo to Detroit along the lake, and another from the Ohio River, via the portage, to the mouth of the Cuyahoga, where the Indians had a ferry. Traders traveled between the French and English trading posts, and from their pack-horse stores the pioneers obtained goods and provisions. Families seeking new frontiers needed all the courage, self-reliance, and resourcefulness they could muster as they journeyed for months in heavy, springless wagons, behind plodding horses or oxen, along hazardous trails and across swollen streams, with danger lurking on every hand.

The land-company's committee, appointed to "enquire into the expediency of laying and cutting out roads on the Reserve," recommended on January 30 that a road be opened from the Pennsylvania line to Cleveland. Work began within a few months on the first recorded highway in the Western Reserve—the "Old Girdled Road." It passed through Conneaut, Sheffield, Plymouth, Austinburg, Harpersfield, Trumbull in Ashtabula County, thence to Thompson in Geauga County, and through Leroy and Concord in Lake County westward to Cleveland (Euclid Avenue). Its course was marked and its name was derived from encircling cuts or girdles through tree bark.

Nathaniel Doan—or Doane, surveyor, opened Cleveland's first industrial plant, his blacksmith shop on the south side of Superior Street near Bank, on a lot granted to him by the land company. It was apparent that the company considered the services of a doctor, a lawyer, and a preacher dispensable; but a blacksmith they must have. Doan kept the company's pack-horses shod, and he also fashioned tools.

During the late summer and fall, almost every person in the colony was attacked by fever and ague. There was no physician, and an infusion of barks was the only medicine. The families of Kingsbury and Gun, who fared better than the rest, gave untiring attention to the afflicted, supplying food and necessities.

To escape the pestilence, Stiles moved his family out on the ridge near the Kingsbury home, and Elijah Gun followed. The Stiles, however, remained only a few years, then returned to the East. Cleveland's population was certainly on the down-grade. Joseph Landon and Stephen Gilbert, surveyors, returned, cleared ground, and sowed wheat. A cornfield of several acres had been planted by Lorenzo Carter on Water Street. The unhealthful "Flats" were soon abandoned to commerce and industry, and the upper lands were converted into farms.

Samuel Mather, Jr., a member of the board of directors of the land company, traveled on horseback to New Connecticut, visited Cleveland, and stopped at Carter's cabin. Upon his return to the East, he increased his property investments as evidence of his faith in the new territory. He was to be "the only stockholder whose family would be directly and in a large way identified with the history of Cleveland."

Samuel Dodge, twenty-one, settled in Cleveland after his long journey from New Hampshire. He was the first carpenter. Nathan Chapman, who had supplied meat to the first surveying expedition, returned to make the settlement his home.

Rodolphus—or Rudolphus—Edwards, a new arrival in the autumn, settled with his family on a 300-acre tract on Butternut Ridge (Woodland Hills, on Steinway Avenue west of Woodhill Road). Here he built a cabin east of the "fever and ague line."

The claim is made that David Abbott built the first grist-mill on the Reserve in the fall (Willoughby). A mill at the forks of Indian Run, between Youngstown and Canfield, is also said to have been operating within the year.

Turhand Kirtland, agent for the land company, was sent to Cleveland to investigate the lagging sale of land tracts. Although prices were reduced, it was difficult to interest buyers. Competition had arisen from rival companies, especially in central New York and southern Ohio, where markets and trade routes were available, land titles were clear, and government had been established. The sale of large holdings was being pushed by owners —state, federal, and private—and many new proprietors, unable to pay, barely escaped debtor's prison. The company's list of shareholders changed frequently. Shares were passed on to members of families and to others to ease the financial burden, and a complete list cannot be determined.

1799

Out on the Euclid Road, Nathaniel Doan bought land for a home at $1 per acre, and in January he built a cabin tavern (northwest corner of Euclid and East 107th, continuously serving hotel purposes, Fenway Hall site). He added a store, and served as justice of the peace, postmaster, and clergyman. The community needed saleratus, so Doan built a plant and started production. A blacksmith shop completed his group plan of buildings. Farms were prospering, and the new road from Doan's Corners to Newburgh was a popular thoroughfare. Doan died in his tavern in 1815.

Warm weather came with February, and "pinks and other flowers bloomed." In the spring, William Wheeler Williams—also known as Wheeler W. Williams and William W. Williams—and Major Ezra Wyatt erected a combined sawmill and grist-mill, the first in the neighborhood and probably the third in the Western Reserve, on the Mill Creek falls (Broadway near Warner Road). Williams had received as a bounty a 100-acre lot, the iron for the grist-mill, and $150 in money. Wyatt was the actual builder, and Williams was the owner and miller. Two great mill stones were laboriously cut and shaped for them by David and Gilman Bryant, and it is said that they ground 20 bushels of wheat a day. Cleveland's manufacturing greatness had germinated. Now the laborious "stump mortar" method of milling grain into coarse meal could be forgotten in the "luxury of bolted flour" made from home-grown wheat.

David Hudson, owner of a portion of the township that bore his name, and several companions, of Goshen, Connecticut, founded a settlement early in June that they called Hudson, honoring the pioneer. After surveying the land, building temporary log houses, and cutting roads, Hudson, two men, and his son departed for the East. New recruits joined Hudson and his family when they started back to the Reserve, arriving in May, 1800. Among them was Heman Oviatt, brother of Benjamin Oviatt, one of the original "proprietors" of the township, who opened a trading post. A log schoolhouse was built, with George Pease as the first teacher. A frame house erected by Hudson in 1806 was the first frame dwelling in what later became Summit County. The ancestral home was well preserved a century later in the quaint residential community that had cherished its traditions as a "bit of New England-in-the-west," unspoiled by industry. Hudson was incorporated as a village in 1837.

Ebenezer Sheldon and his family selected a site southeast of Cleveland in June for their wilderness home. When Major Amos Spafford stopped at the Sheldon home the next year, they discussed the future of the area, and Sheldon proposed that this new settlement be called Aurora in honor of Spafford's daughter. The Taylor family were early settlers.

New arrivals in Cleveland this year were Richard H. Blinn—or Blin—and a Mr. Gallup. The Hawleys had sought refuge out on the ridge with the other pioneers, and until April, 1800, the Carters were the only white family in Cleveland. There were now ten families in Newburgh, a hamlet that was given its start by ravenous Cleveland mosquitoes. The heights extended to Doan's Corners and the Buffalo Road. Soon a main highway and coach road opened to Pittsburgh (Broadway), and Newburgh looked forward to pre-eminent prosperity. From Mill Creek and the 40-foot "Cataract" falls could be developed the greatest water power in the frontier area. Curiously, citizens never decided conclusively upon the spelling of the village name, and for a century and a half Newburgh appeared with or without the "h." Likewise, Pittsburgh toyed with the "h" until the eighties, when it was adopted. The community had taken the population lead away from Cleveland, which was soon called "a small village six miles from Newburgh."

Prosperous James Kingsbury hauled timbers for the first frame house in Newburgh to Williams' sawmill during the winter. A spring freshet, however, carried away the dam, and the mill was shut down for a time. Determined to finish his house, Kingsbury erected his own mill on Kingsbury's Run and completed the job.

Three of the Kingsbury children and two of the Hawleys' became lost on their way from the Stiles home on Christmas Day. Lorenzo Carter, while on his way home from hunting, found them in a dark hollow.

CHAPTER 3

Stout-Hearted Men
1800-1809

CLEVELAND turned the century corner with little prospect of turning another, her population having moved to Newburgh's healthier heights or back to the East. Only seven courageous souls were left in the trading-post settlement.

The history of a city is the story of its people. Cleveland's early years were shaped by courageous men, the best that New England had to offer. The ability to swing an ax, outwit the cunning Indian, bring down game with a trusty rifle, and maintain equilibrium in spite of potent raw whisky, proved the mettle of the frontiersman. From the trees of the forest he built his cabin home, fashioned its furnishings and utensils, and secured his fuel. Having laboriously cleared a parcel of land and planted it with seeds from the homeland, a meager crop of essential foods and grains would result if the weather was favorable. Nothing was wasted; of necessity pioneer resourcefulness put everything to use. There was work for every member of the family. Clothing was the product of the spinning wheel or was made of the hide of an animal. Grain was pounded into meal before the advent of the grist-mill. Tallow candles and whale-oil lamps furnished illumination. Salt was a luxury that came from Onondaga or from Pittsburgh, and sold for $20 a barrel; but it could be secured at the "Salt Springs," nine miles west of Youngstown, by boiling down the saline waters. Wild honey and maple sugar were a great blessing to the homemaker.

At the opening of the decade, the Western Reserve became established legally, and shortly afterward the State of Ohio was created. Indian tribes reluctantly gave up their claims to Ohio lands, and new proprietors assumed responsibility for their real-estate purchases in the Reserve.

Trailways were widened to accommodate clumsy wagons making their way to the frontier, and new roads were planned. Mail service was inaugurated, bringing the outside world a little closer to Cleveland. The port on the Cuyahoga was officially opened when Lorenzo Carter built the first schooner for lake trading, launching Cleveland's shipbuilding industry.

An iron furnace was established near Youngstown, and the roots of industry found fertile soil in the territory that was to become a great industrial empire.

Suveyor Spafford refined his earlier map of Cleveland as the foundation for future real-estate development. Although the land west of the Cuyahoga

River had not been opened for settlement, a few adventuresome families moved into the wilderness, one of them Negro.

During this period, the first schoolhouse opened on the Reserve, and private classes were organized in Newburgh and in Carter's cabin in Cleveland.

While it is generally understood that the pioneers were endowed with courage, hospitality, and frontier chivalry, the law was needed in Cleveland, as elsewhere. In New England, the church and state were closely connected; political and religious castes dominated society. The first emigrants were mostly men desiring to escape from the old conservatism; and fired by a wave of land speculation that was sweeping the East, a relaxing of moral influences no doubt resulted. At any rate, missionary observations declared emphatically that "some were much inclined to infidelity," "were careless about religious affairs" and "appear very stupid." Living on a high, moral plane, the spiritual ambassador's judgment meant that "all that which was not directly religious needed his condemnation." He did not seem to take into account the fact that the pioneers "came here to improve their fortunes and not to spread the gospel."

Early-day families cherished a home library that consisted of the *Bible,* an almanac, and perhaps *Pilgrim's Progress*; but they were careful to put aside their reading when an Indian came to visit. The tribesmen believed that books inspired the white men to claim their lands; and the report that a settler had been seen with a volume had been known to create an uprising.

In order to carry the gospel to Congregationalists and Presbyterians who were building hewn-log outposts in the Western Reserve, the Connecticut Missionary Society raised money and secured missionaries, and the New York Presbytery provided the administration by which churches were established. The Rev. Joseph Badger, Congregational minister and Revolutionary War veteran, was the first missionary on the Reserve and the first to represent this famous Plan of Union.

Leaving the refinements of comfortable home life in the East, frontier women were called upon to endure not only a primitive domestic life in crude cabin homes, but they endured the stern pioneer fathers as well. Economic problems were narrowed to a lonely struggle against Nature for existence; and devoting themselves wholeheartedly to the care of their large families, they went bravely on. Meals were prepared from coarse foods, and venison and game were roasted on a spit before the open fire. Clothes were made from animal hides or homespun, produced patiently at the spinning wheel. Neighbors were few and far between, and there was a longing for the community life that had been enjoyed back home. Friendly Indians, however, often invited themselves in to enjoy the fireside, and perhaps to catch a nap, with quiet indifference to household affairs. Somehow there was time to pass along to the children fragmentary and elementary bits of learning from memory or from a few well-thumbed books. At dusk, the tired pioneer mother put her little brood to sleep in homemade beds of round spruce poles bound with elm bark. Tomorrow would be just another day.

As the decade closed, there were unmistakable signs that Cleveland was assuming the stature of a village as a handful of stout-hearted men molded its destiny upon a foundation of New England character and culture.

1800

Sarah Doan, daughter of Nathaniel Doan, was the teacher of the first school in Newburgh (9213 Miles Avenue). Books were scarce. Letters of the alphabet were pasted on one side of a wooden paddle, the multiplication table on the other, and it was passed from hand to hand for study. Pay of $10 a month in produce was considered excellent.

On April 28, President John Adams signed the bill by which New Connecticut—the Western Reserve—came under jurisdiction of the United States, at the same time establishing the validity of Connecticut land title.

By Act of Congress, the Northwest Territory was divided on May 7 by a line running due north from the Kentucky River mouth. The eastern division retained the name of the Northwest Territory, with Chillicothe as the capital, and the western division became the Territory of Indiana.

Trumbull County was created on July 10 and named for Jonathan Trumbull, the governor of Connecticut. It included the Western Reserve, the "Fire Lands" and Sandusky islands, and Warren was chosen as the county seat. A larger population and the preponderance of Federalists there, it is said, dictated the selection, inciting the bitterness of Cleveland and Youngstown at having been rejected. The few settlers, however, had little time for the weighty matters of government. They were far too busy building cabins and clearing lands for farms.

At the first Court of Quarter Sessions of Trumbull County, held between Ephraim Quinby's corn cribs in Warren, August 25, James Kingsbury of Cleveland was appointed judge by General St. Clair, governor of the territory. The court, said to be the first formal governmental agency to be established in the Western Reserve, was attended by five justices of the quorum, namely, John Young, Turhand Kirtland, Camden Cleaveland—a brother of Moses Cleaveland, James Kingsbury, Eliphalet Austin, and their associates, justices of the peace. In their hands rested the entire civil jurisdiction of the county.

At the five-day court session, Amos Spafford, David Hudson, Simon Perkins, John Minor, Aaron Wheeler, Edward Paine, and Benjamin Davidson were appointed to divide Trumbull County into townships, establishing limits and boundaries. Accordingly, eight townships were created: Warren, Youngstown, Hudson, Vernon, Richfield, Middlefield, Painesville, and Cleveland, the latter embracing the area east of the Cuyahoga River (later Cuyahoga County), all of the Indian country from the river to the west line of the Reserve, and Chester, Russell, and Bainbridge (in Geauga County).

A committee of the court chose a room in Quinby's log house as temporary jail quarters for the county, and made him the jailer. During the earlier years there had been no form of local government, either civil or military. In Cleveland, Lorenzo Carter was the "law" to Indians and whites alike. He and Stephen Gilbert were appointed the first constables for Cleveland Township.

The first resident physician on the Reserve was Dr. Moses Thompson, twenty-four, who settled at Hudson in the summer. He had studied under the best doctors in Connecticut. His practice extended over the wide area from Lake Erie to Coshocton, and he traveled on horseback. For his livelihood, however, he turned to his farm and his dairy. Here the vast cheese-making industry in Summit, Trumbull, Geauga, and Ashtabula counties had its beginning.

Amos Spafford and David Clark, surveyors, who had brought their families from Vermont, were joined by Lorenzo Carter in protest to Judge Turhand Kirtland against the high price of Cleveland lots. All things considered, the judge recommended a reduction, which before long was set at $25 per lot with time to pay. Clark built on the west side of Water Street, and later opened a store. Samuel Jones and Alexander Campbell, who erected a crude trading post and did business with the Indians, were also newcomers this year.

Pioneers found a ready market for superfluous grain. Fermentation products and liquor were produced in the first distillery, a second-hand plant brought from Virginia in the fall by David and Gilman Bryant. They operated their "still" along the edge of the Cuyahoga at the foot of Superior Street. The capacity was two quarts of raw spirits a day. This potent product served as an essential commodity in the household for medicinal purposes, as coin in commerce and trade, and as a pacifying influence over uneasy Indians.

Riding into the colony from Charlton (Willoughby) on October 7, Samuel Huntington, thirty-four, nephew of Samuel Huntington, signer of the Declaration of Independence, found three families in Cleveland. After a short expedition by boat along the lake, he departed for Marietta, where meetings were held with Governor Arthur St. Clair and authorities of the Northwest Territory. Returning to Connecticut, he made plans to bring his family to Cleveland.

A settlement consisted of isolated farms, and strong township government was not possible for some time. The sheriff and local officials, appointed by the governor, conducted the business of the county. By Governor St. Clair's order, the first election was held in the Reserve at Warren on October 14, under the territorial system, to determine a representative from Trumbull County to the Territorial Legislature. The sheriff of the county, assembling the electors by proclamation, presided, and counted forty-two votes of the electors. Of these, Edward Paine received thirty-eight and was declared elected.

1801

The first schoolhouse in the Western Reserve was built at Warren, a small, single-story, log structure, with one door and five greased-paper windows. A fireplace provided too much heat for some pupils and too little for others. Students sat on benches facing the wall, and a shelf ran around the room on which they propped their few books. When called upon to recite, the scholar whirled about and responded, reversing the process when finished. William H. McGuffey applied for a teaching position in this school when he had completed college, but was rejected when he failed to pass the examination. His chagrin, he said later, was an incentive to further study that led to his success as a great educator.

Timothy Doan, brother of Nathaniel Doan, brought his family from Herkimer County, New York, to Euclid in the spring. He purchased 320 acres of land for a little more than $1 an acre. The Doans' new log house was ready in November. For several years the children's only playmates were Indians camped nearby.

In the early summer, Samuel Huntington's party traveled by oxcart from Connecticut to Cleveland. Amos Spafford built for Huntington a pretentious blockhouse on the bluff, south of Superior (overlooking Erie Depot). While he was a lawyer, the profession in these early days could not be lucrative, with county court at a distance and few litigants. Soon after Huntington's arrival, Governor St. Clair appointed him lieutenant colonel of the Trumbull County Militia, in command of the Reserve's territorial troops.

A mail route was established in the Western Reserve, extending from Pittsburgh to Warren, via Youngstown. Fortnightly deliveries were made on foot through the dense forests.

Elisha Norton opened a store in Carter's cabin, where Indian squaws traded for gaudy yard-goods and trinkets, while the warriors narrowed their wants to whisky.

The Rev. William Wick, thirty-three-year-old Presbyterian missionary, began his ministry to a newly organized congregation at Youngstown, Ohio, on July 1. This was the beginning of the First Presbyterian Church, the first church body on the Western Reserve; and in 1946, it continued to serve under its original name. A "preacher of considerable force, somewhat more polished than most of his brethren," Rev. Wick rose to positions of leadership in the denomination. He was "the first permanent laborer" on the Reserve, dividing his time with the Hopewell church until his death at the age of forty-seven.

The Fourth of July was celebrated with the first "grand ball," held in Carter's cabin "under the hill." The elite of the community were there: twelve women and twenty men, dancing to the rhythm of Samuel Jones' squeaky fiddle, the first violin brought to Cleveland. A beverage of maple sugar, hot water, and whisky refreshed the merry-makers and limbered the fiddler's elbow. Powder horns, rifles, and shotguns adorned the ballroom. In a letter written by Gilman Bryant, dated in 1857, he gives an entertaining account of that memorable evening:

I waited on Miss Doan, who had just arrived at the Corners, four miles east of town. I was then about seventeen years of age, and Miss Doan about fourteen. I was dressed in the then style—a gingham suit—my hair queued with one and a half yards of black ribbon, about as long and as thick as a corncob, with a little tuft at the lower end; and for the want of pomatum, I had a piece of candle rubbed on my hair, and then as much flour sprinkled on, as could stay without falling off. I had a good wool hat, and a pair of brogans that would help to play "Fisher's Hornpipe," or "Hie, Bettie Martin," when I danced. When I went for Miss Doan I took an old horse; when she was ready I rode up to a stump near the cabin, she mounted the stump and spread her under petticoat on "old Tib" behind me, secured her calico dress to keep it clean, and then mounted on behind me. I had a fine time!

The Rev. Joseph Badger, a Congregationalist minister, had come to the Western Reserve as the first missionary late in 1800. He traveled on horseback, preaching and praying with families and such groups as would assemble to hear him, bringing the gospel to Cleveland on August 18, when he lodged with Lorenzo Carter. After a time he moved on. During the year, he presented a petition to the "General Assembly of the Territory of the United States Northwest of the River Ohio" asking that a charter be granted for a college to be located in the Reserve; but there was not enough enthusiasm to plant a new Yale in New Connecticut, and the petition was denied.

Samuel Dodge built the first frame barn in Cleveland, 30 by 40 feet, for Samuel Huntington, in back of the lawyer's house on Superior near Bank Street. Huntington could not pay for it at the time, and he deeded to Dodge a 20-acre strip of land bordering on the Buffalo Road (Euclid on both sides of East 17th).

The first Congregational church on the Reserve was organized by the Rev. Joseph Badger at Austinburg, Ohio, on October 24. In the following February, he and his family set out from New England by wagon, completing the journey to their new home in sixty days. Eliphalet Austin, village founder, and Badger's devoted wife, Sibyl, were of tremendous help to the clergyman in establishing his missionary headquarters. On a salary of seven dollars a week paid by eastern sponsors, and later reduced to six dollars, Badger rode his circuit, organizing churches and schools and ministering to the pioneers. After a time, his work was directed to the Indians along the Maumee River, with no provision for a missionary to take his place in the Reserve. Taking the task upon herself, Mrs. Austin courageously headed eastward on horseback, pushing alone for four weeks through the forests. In time, she returned with the Rev. Giles H. Cowles and his family, and a notable pastorate of twenty-one years began that was the foundation of the deeply rooted First Congregational Church, which grew up with the Reserve.

Cleveland's streets and lanes were re-surveyed by Amos Spafford in November, and the principal corners were marked with oak posts. His new map became the official early-Cleveland authority for fixing the lot and street lines and determining land titles.

In a letter to Moses Cleaveland dated November 15, Samuel Huntington wrote of his migration to Cleveland from Connecticut: "I have moved my Patriarchal Caravan through the wilderness to this Canaan. I was nine days on the Journey, with two Waggons, ten oxen, three horses, seven Cows and eighteen persons in my Retinue. We slept seven nights in the open air (after leaving the settlements in New York State)." A significant statement appears later: "We have now here about 200 Indians going up the Cuyahoga . . . They have a jealousy of my coming here, owing to a story that has been propagated amongst them, that I am raising Soldiers to drive them out of the country. I have had a great number of Workmen here who they think are Soldiers in Disguise."

1802

Aside from financial interests in their Western Reserve holdings, the new proprietors exerted practically no direct influence over the region except to give their names to townships and towns. Elbert Jay Benton in the *Cultural Story of an American City—Cleveland* observes:

> They undoubtedly represented the wealth and culture of Connecticut . . .
> Sixty-five of the proprietors of 1802, 33 percent, were alumni of Yale College, not to forget two graduates of Harvard College and one from the College of New Jersey. But it was culture transmitted indirectly, through members of their families, and over a long time. The company missed every opportunity to stamp on the record any direct cultural influence. In Southern Ohio the Ohio Company at Marietta and the Symmes interests on the Miami had made the promotion of religion and education and free labor a part of the company's objectives. The Connecticut Company assumed that these matters would be taken care of by the settlers.

The Ohio Compact of 1802, however, encouraged settlement, and gave to the Western Reserve pioneers educational assistance comparable with that given earlier to settlements in the southern part of the State. From the sale of public lands, 5 per cent of the receipts were to be spent by the Federal Government on road-building; and in each township a section of land was to be set aside for school purposes. In return, purchasers of public lands were to be exempt from taxation for five years.

The first election in Cleveland Township, ordered by the Trumbull

County Court of Quarter Sessions, was held at James Kingsbury's home on April 5. Officers chosen were Rodolphus Edwards, chairman; Nathaniel Doan, town clerk; Amos Spafford, Timothy Doan, and William W. Williams, trustees; Samuel Hamilton and Elijah Gun, appraisers of houses; Ebenezer Ayrs, lister; Samuel Huntington, Nathaniel Doan, and Samuel Hamilton, supervisors of highways; William W. Williams and Samuel Huntington, overseers of the poor; Lorenzo Carter and Nathan Chapman, fence viewers; Ezekiel Hawley and Richard Craw, constables.

On April 30, Congress authorized a convention to form a state constitution for Ohio, if it were the will of the people to seek admission to the Union. Samuel Huntington of Cleveland and David Abbott of Charlton (Willoughby) represented Trumbull County at Chillicothe, where the convention opened on November 1. On the 29th, Ohio's constitution was adopted, with power vested in the people. Some historians declare that Ohio became part of the Union on this latter date. Voters were required to pay road tax, which could be paid by work.

Arthur St. Clair, governor of the Northwest Territory, had lost much of his popularity by maintaining staunch opposition to statehood. He contended that the pioneers were neither capable nor worthy of self-government, and at the same time he realized that such achievement meant the end of his position as territorial head. His pro-state adversaries had sought his removal from office for some time; but although President Jefferson recognized the potential strength of the proposed state, if admitted under the Republican banner, he refused to unseat the governor. It was to be expected, therefore, that when St. Clair rode into Chillicothe astride a good horse and dressed in regimental finery, he would receive only brief courtesy. With Jefferson's sanction, the governor addressed the convention, uttering remarks that ultimately forced the chief executive to dismiss him. Once a dashing British officer, St. Clair was now a broken, impoverished old man. He retired to Pennsylvania, where he died in 1818.

Ezekiel Hawley, constable, reported the first census of Cleveland Township on June 3: seventy-six free male inhabitants of twenty-one or over. Apparently women and children were considered unimportant in the count.

Travel on the Buffalo—or Euclid—Road (Euclid Avenue) was hazardous. Ruts and stumps obstructed the oxcart trail that led to Buffalo, and wild animals roamed its borders. A swamp covered a large area (Euclid to Scovill and East 40th to East 55th). It is said that Samuel Huntington was making his way through the swampy forest one night on horseback, when a wolf pack attacked him. Beating frantically with his umbrella and urging his horse to top speed, he was able to outdistance the ravenous beasts and reach the village in safety.

In a report to the Connecticut Land Company, Samuel Huntington stated that the Williams grist-mill, in operation for about three years, was not serving the community properly. It is interesting to note that he purchased the land on which the dam and mill were located, and probably the mill, also, and from that time the Newburgh establishment became an important factor in pioneer living.

A medicine man, variously called Menompsy, Nobsy, Menobsy or Menopsy, of the Chippewa or Ottawa tribe, was stabbed to death in 1802 or 1803 by Big Son, a Seneca, to avenge the death of his squaw who failed to recover despite the "healer's" ministrations. "Fire water" is said to have figured prominently in the first murder in the village, and Cleveland came close to real trouble with the Indians. The opposing tribesmen demanded that Big Son be surrendered to them, and only Lorenzo Carter's negotiations, fortified with whisky and eloquence, restored peace.

Cleveland's first school was held in Carter's "front room." Here Anna Spafford instructed the youngsters of the settlement in the simplest forms of book knowledge.

Upon payment of four dollars, Lorenzo Carter and Amos Spafford were each licensed by the court at Warren in August to keep a tavern. In September, Carter purchased 23½ acres of land—12 acres fronting on St. Clair (east of West 9th), and an irregular parcel on Superior Street, Union Lane, and the river. Here he built the first frame house in Cleveland on the hill west of Water Street and north of Superior Lane. When it was almost finished, fire destroyed it, and on the site Carter erected a blockhouse the same year. This was the famous Carter Tavern. A spacious living room, kitchen, and two bedrooms constituted the first floor, with a large chimney in the center. Several rooms and an attic were upstairs. With lumber from Detroit, a local carpenter built furniture for the first hotel in Cleveland.

Returning from his missionary journey to Detroit in the fall of 1801, the Rev. Joseph Badger had stopped at Hudson, Ohio, "where he found material from which to organize a church." In September, 1802, he organized the First Congregational Church with a charter membership of thirteen, headed by David Hudson. It was the second Congregational church on the Western Reserve.

Expansion to the east is reflected in the disposition of a 1,200-acre virgin-forest tract (centering at about the southwest corner of Euclid and East 71st) purchased this year by a syndicate for $13,333. Four years later, 105 acres were sold for $330; and in 1818, 72 acres brought $114. Forty-one acres were sold in 1832 for $431. At a foreclosure sale in 1850, Thomas Bolton purchased 145 acres for $11,675, and this land became the Bolton estate. About 9 acres (corner of Euclid and East 71st) changed hands in 1917 for over $350,000.

In order that all the Western Reserve property should be in private hands, a draft was made of the six reserved townships on December 28. Ninety-six parcels constituted all these lands east of the Cuyahoga, except a few city lots in Cleveland. The original owners of Cleveland lots by draft, or first purchase, included Samuel Huntington, Caleb Atwater, Lorenzo Carter, Ephraim Root, Elijah Boardman and others, Ezekiel Hawley, David Clark, Joseph Howland, Charles Dutton, James Kingsbury, Samuel W. Phelps, Joseph Perkins and others, Austin & Huntington, Wyles and others, Judson Canfield and others, Samuel P. Lord, Jr., William Shaw, Samuel Parkman, John Bolls and others, Asher Miller, Ephraim Stow and others, Martin Sheldon and others, Amos Spafford, Oliver Phelps, and Richard W. Hart and others.

1803

On February 19, Congress declared that the eastern portion of the Northwest Territory, south of Lake Erie, had become Ohio, the seventeenth state of the Union, by virtue of its adoption of a constitution. This broke up the Territory. The first General Assembly met on March 1, and Edward Tiffin of Chillicothe became governor. Samuel Huntington of Cleveland, senator from Trumbull County and first president of the Ohio Legislature, took his seat as one of the first judges of the Supreme Court. At the same time, he was supervisor of highways.

James Kingsbury's home was chosen as election headquarters for a township meeting in the spring. The results were Amos Spafford, chairman; Nathaniel Doan, town clerk; Amos Spafford, James Kingsbury, and Timothy Doan, trustees; James Kingsbury and James Hamilton, overseers of the poor; Rodolphus Edwards, Ezekiel Hawley, and Amos Spafford, fence viewers; Elijah Gun and Samuel Huntington, appraisers of houses; James Kingsbury, lister; William Elivin, James Kingsbury, and Timothy Doan, supervisors of highways, and Rodolphus Edwards, constable. Twenty-one votes were cast in Cleveland's first election after Ohio became a state.

The electors met again in June at Kingsbury's residence and chose Amos Spafford and Timothy Doan as the first justices of the peace.

The Pittsburgh-Warren mail route was extended to Cleveland, via Austinburg and Painesville, returning via Hudson and Tappanville (Ravenna). Bold carriers, such as Joseph Burke and his two sons, traveled the 150-mile route in ten days to two weeks, bringing news from New York. These postmen braved Indian trails, dense forests, and swollen streams on foot.

John Walworth, prominent farmer in Painesville Township, was one of the founders of the first Masonic lodge in northern Ohio, organized at Warren.

Meeting again at Kingsbury's home on October 11, the township voters elected Benjamin Tappan, senator, and David Abbott and Ephraim Quinby, representatives in the General Assembly.

The Legislature granted to the Erie Literary Society a charter for an academy at Burton for the "education of pious, indigent young men for the ministry" in the Presbyterian and Congregational churches. Sponsors and trustees lived in all parts of the Western Reserve, including John Walworth from Painesville Township and the Rev. Joseph Badger, who had failed to secure a charter in 1801. The Seminary of Learning was launched in 1805 in its building on the square in Burton. It was ahead of its time, however, and support was inadequate. Fire destroyed the building in 1810; and although it was rebuilt ten years later, the project was not considered successful and was abandoned in a few years.

Newcomers to Euclid Township were John Shaw, Thomas McIlrath, John Ruple, Garrett Thorp, and William Coleman. The next year Shaw brought his bride, Sarah McIlrath Shaw, to live on the tract that he had purchased (north of Euclid and east of Shaw Avenues, East Cleveland). While John Shaw farmed for a living, he was a firm believer in education, and taught school part of the time. His wife's consuming passion was the church; and having inherited considerable money, she gave to charity with a sympathetic understanding.

In the wilderness east of Cleveland (northwest corner of Euclid and Superior), Alexander McIlrath established a tavern and a general store. His brother, Abner, enlarged it in the thirties, and it became the social center of the community, pioneers coming from miles around to take part in coon hunts and "pigeon shoots." Early Clevelanders recall that a bear was kept chained to a tree outside the hostelry. The McIlrath Tavern was torn down in 1890.

1804

Not long before, Missionary Thomas Robbins had denounced the people of Cleveland as "rather loose in principles and conduct." Religious conviction had taken root, however, as evidenced by a pledge of the people of five townships:

> We do by these presents bind ourselves, our heirs, executors, and administrators firmly, to pay the sums annexed to each of our names, without fraud or delay, for the term of three years, to the Rev. Giles Cowles, the pay to be made in wheat, rye, corn, oats, potatoes, mess-pork, whisky, etc., the produce of farms, as shall be needed by the said Mr. Cowles and family, together with chopping, logging, fencing, etc. We agree, likewise, should any contribute anything within said term of three years toward the support of the said Mr. Cowles, it shall be deducted according to the sum annexed to each man's name. We likewise agree that the preaching in each town shall be in proportion to what each town subscribes for said preaching.

Cash was scarce, but these earnest folk had assured the minister to their spiritual needs that "thou shalt not want."

A "town tax" of $10 was ordered at the April town meeting.

Early in the year, Captain Elijah Wadsworth of Canfield was appointed in charge of the fourth division of the Ohio Militia, constituting northeastern Ohio. On May 7, Cleveland's first military company, officially the second brigade of the fourth division, was organized. Lorenzo Carter was elected captain; Nathaniel Doan, lieutenant; and Samuel Jones, ensign. The little village felt safer from the threat of British invasion and Indian attack, as the little company marched to the spirited rhythm of fife and drum, relics of Revolutionary days. In August, Carter became a major.

Oliver Culver, surveyor, arrived in Cleveland with a boatload of salt, dry goods, liquors, tobacco, and merchandise with which he opened a store. Transportation from Black Rock (near Buffalo), where he embarked, was three dollars per barrel. In a short time he left the settlement.

1805

Historic Indian trails joined east of Cleveland and were still in use (Euclid and East 107th, where a large boulder marking the junction was dedicated on the lawn of the Western Reserve Historical Society's former building, November 10, 1938). The Lake Shore Trail (following Euclid Avenue) crossed the Mahoning Trail, which led from the lakeshore inland (to Niles, Ohio).

Free trade with Canada no longer existed, when the collection district of Erie was established. John Walworth of Painesville Township was appointed collector of the port at the mouth of the Cuyahoga. Two landings were provided for transportation by water, which was carried on in open boats, sturdy, well-built bateaux that bravely weathered the fiercest gale. At the foot of Vineyard Lane was the "upper landing" for up-river business. Lake trade used the "lower landing," where Mandrake and Union lanes came to the river (St. Clair Avenue).

Missionary labors of the Shakers, "the United Society of Believers in Christ's Second Appearing," began in Ohio in Warren County. The members were known for their religious zeal, evidenced in their occupational life, along with strong co-operative methods of a communal character. They were spiritualists, who believed in the equality of the sexes and forbade marriage. Strong passions, deep convictions, and rigid beliefs characterized these simple folk, who at times showed marked indifference to laws not of their making. They were called Shakers or Jerkers, for in their religious frenzy they jerked their bodies violently in strange ecstasy. Severely plain dress was prescribed, and for the most part the Shakers were farmers, cabinet-makers, and weavers. Unfortunate children were gathered in and reared as Shakers.

Elisha Norton became Cleveland's first postmaster on April 1, upon commission of Gideon Granger, seventh United States Postmaster General. Granger was interested in lands west of the Cuyahoga River, and when visiting Cleveland this year, he prophesied that "within fifty years an extensive city will occupy these grounds and vessels will sail directly from this point into the Atlantic Ocean." This was one of the earliest predictions looking toward the Great Lakes-to-the-sea movement.

Indians regarded a total eclipse of the sun on June 16 as an expression of the Great Spirit's displeasure that they were about to relinquish their lands to the white men.

David Abbott built the *Cuyahoga Packet* on the Chagrin River (Willoughby), a 20-ton schooner that sailed the lake until it was captured by the British.

Samuel Huntington, a man of influence, moved from his aristocratic log house and took up residence at the Newburgh mill. The ever-present threat of malaria from the swampy Cleveland lowlands may have prompted the change. He moved to Painesville Township shortly afterward.

Indian tribes west of the Cuyahoga were summoned to Fort Industry on the Maumee River (Toledo) to attend a council of several days. Colonel Charles Jewet, commissioner of the United States, General Henry Champion of the Connecticut Land Company, and I. Mills of the Fire Lands Company conducted the council. On July 4, the Indians signed away title to lands in northwestern Ohio, whereby they were to receive from the government an annual payment of $13,760 forever. Money to close the transaction was brought from Pittsburgh through Warren and Cleveland by Lyman Potter, Josiah W. Brown, John Lane, James Staunton, Major Lorenzo Carter, and Jonathan Church. A barrel of whisky was opened to celebrate the signing of the treaty. It is said that the Indians parted with their lands reluctantly, and many of them wept.

At about this time, Charles Miles, Sr., arrived in Newburgh from Hudson, where he had purchased a large tract. There were six sons, the "Miles brothers." Samuel and Theodore operated a general store at Superior and Seneca streets, the latter being a prominent citizen in Newburgh Township for many years. The second son, Erastus, married Laura, daughter of Lorenzo Carter, and they lived at Carter's Tavern in Cleveland until the pioneer's death in 1814.

With lumber sawed in his mill, James Kingsbury began building a frame house in Newburgh. Chimney bricks were made on his land. In the large room upstairs, dances were held, and the Cleveland Masonic lodge met here, Kingsbury being a devoted member. The new apple orchard commenced to bear the next year.

On December 31, the State Legislature created Geauga County from a part of Trumbull County, including lands which later became Cuyahoga County. A Court of Common Pleas and a Board of County Commissioners were established.

1806

John Walworth became postmaster of Cleveland on January 1. Postal receipts during the first quarter of the year amounted to $2.83. The first Post Office was located in the upper part of a frame building on the north side of Superior Street near Water Street. In April, the Walworth family moved to Cleveland from Painesville Township. Judge Samuel Huntington had become interested in Walworth's holdings of a vast tract on the Grand River. A trade was arranged in 1807 whereby the judge exchanged his 300 acres between Huron and Erie streets and the river, where he had a farm, for the Grand River property. During this year, President Jefferson appointed Walworth inspector of revenue for the port of Cuyahoga, and Governor Tiffin made him associate judge of the Court of Common Pleas for a seven-year term "if he shall so long behave well." Walworth's small frame office on Superior Street (parking lot west of Hotel Cleveland) thus housed the city, county, and federal authority in Cleveland, and later the only attorney and physician occupied space there. His name is perpetuated in Cleveland streets and in Walworth Run, where he had a farm.

In a spring storm, a sailing vessel foundered off shore (Lakewood), and the only survivor was Ben, a fugitive slave. Major Carter, who did not believe in slavery, nursed him back to health, but could not legally resist the Negro's two owners who eventually arrived from Pittsburgh to take him back. The three started out on horseback, and in the hills (Independence) two woodsmen, said to be Carter's men, halted them, and ordered Ben to dismount and go his way. After seeking refuge in the forest for a time, the Negro escaped safely to Canada. This might be termed Cleveland's first social case record.

A bounty of $400 was paid to James and Daniel Heaton for the erection of the first iron furnace in the Reserve, on the Mahoning River, a short distance northwest of Youngstown on the site of Niles, where bog iron ore was available. The ability of pioneers to purchase stoves, large kettles and cast articles for home use from local factories stimulated settlement of the area.

Samuel Cozad, Jr., came to Cleveland with his family and built their cabin on land extending east from Doan's Corners (Adelbert College site to Lake View Cemetery). His sons acquired property on the north side of Euclid (including Wade Park). Samuel III built his home on a 100-acre tract (beginning at Euclid and East 107th). As a young man, Cozad's son, Newell Samuel, determined that some day a portion of the beautiful woodland should be preserved in its natural state as a park. For years he labored diligently, until financial reverses overcame him; yet he lived to see Jeptha H. Wade make Wade Park a reality.

The Connecticut Land Company employed Abraham Tappan—or Tappen—and others to survey the land west of the river, as well as that lying beyond (Elyria and Lorain and slightly westward).

Aside from that gleaned from the family's few treasured volumes, such elementary education as could be had by the young was provided in a handful of private schools of the kind launched this year in October by ambitious Asael Adams, twenty, of Canterbury, Connecticut. In a log house near the foot of Superior Street he commenced to fulfill his contract, whereby he was to earn ten dollars a month, "to be paid in money or wheat at the market price, whenever such time may be that the school doth end," provided the citizens supplied benches and sufficient fire-wood for comfort. He further agreed "to keep six hours in each day, and to keep good order." Samuel Huntington, James Kingsbury, W. W. Williams, George Kilbourne, Susannah Hammil, Elijah Gun, and David Kellogg were among his patrons.

A continuous shifting of the earth's upper strata, and the encroachment of the lake upon the shore in the vicinity of Cleveland is illustrated by an event recorded by Colonel Charles Whittlesey in the *Early History of Cleveland,* published in 1867:

In 1806 or 1807, Amos Spafford sent his hired man, with a yoke of oxen to plow a patch of ground on the margin of the lake, which must have been not far from the Marine Hospital (then at the foot of E. 12th). At noon, the man chained his team to a tree, fed them, and went home to dinner. Returning in the afternoon, his oxen were no where to be seen. Proceeding to the edge of the bank, the man discovered them still attached to the tree, quietly chewing their cuds, but the ground on which they stood had sank between twenty and thirty feet, carrying with it some of the new furrows, the trees and the oxen. Thus a belt of land about twelve and one half rods in width—nearly 200 feet—was lost, along the entire front of the city.

Whittlesey, a geologist, estimated that at this rate the lake would have undermined the Public Square in about five hundred years.

As early as 1796, Nathan Perry, Sr., had come to Ohio and purchased 1,000 acres of land at 50 cents an acre (in Lake County). He now bought two parcels in Cleveland (five acres bounded by Superior, St. Clair, West 6th, and West 9th; and a larger tract later known as the Horace Perry farm at Broadway and East 22nd). Other holdings were acquired along the Black River (Lorain). Perry became one of the first county judges in Cleveland. He died in 1813.

Moses Cleaveland, trail-blazer to the Western Reserve and founder of the city that bore his name, died on November 16 and was buried in Canterbury, Windham County, Connecticut, his birthplace. The second son of Aaron and Thankful Paine Cleaveland, he was born on January 29, 1754. According to Harvey Rice, the name Cleaveland—or Cleveland—appears to be "of Saxon origin and was given to a distinguished family in Yorkshire, England, prior to the Norman conquest. The family occupied a large landed estate which was peculiarly marked by open fissures in its rocky soil, styled 'clefts' or 'cleves' by the Saxons and by reason of the peculiarity of the estate its occupants were called 'Clefflands,' which name was accepted by the family." It is said that Samuel Cleaveland of Leicestershire, England, had a son, Moses, who migrated to America in 1635 and became the ancestor of the Cleavelands and Clevelands of New England origin. For several years he lived in Boston. Some of his descendants moved to Canterbury, Connecticut, where Aaron, son of Joseph Cleaveland, was born in 1727. Aaron and Thankful Paine married in 1748; and, being "persons of refinement," they sent their son, Moses, to Yale, where he was graduated in 1777. Then he studied law and began practicing in his home town. He became captain of a company of sappers and miners in government service in 1779; but after several years, he returned to law. Cleaveland served several years in the Connecticut Legislature and was a prominent Mason. He married Esther Champion, "a young lady of rare accomplishments," in 1794, and they had two sons and two daughters. Two years later, he was commissioned as brigadier general of the Connecticut Militia, and was selected by the Connecticut Land Company to head the exploration to the Western Reserve, where he had invested in lands to the extent of $32,600. According to an early historian, the founder of the City of Cleveland "wore such a sedate look that strangers often took him for a clergyman. He had a somewhat swarthy complexion, which induced the Indians to believe him akin to their own race . . . He was of medium height, erect, thick-set, and portly, and was of muscular limbs and his step was of a military air." Having selected the site for the "capital" of the Western Reserve in the fall of 1796, he returned to Canterbury and the legal profession.

1807

The last division of the Western Reserve lands was made on January 5, the drawing taking place at Hartford, Connecticut. The area extending along the west border of the Cuyahoga to the lake was drawn by Samuel P. Lord and others. A survey was commenced soon afterward, and the lots were offered for sale. Lord's son, Richard, and his son-in-law, Josiah Barber, undertook to develop the property.

The Legislature created Portage, Ashtabula, and Cuyahoga counties on February 10, the last named to "embrace so much of the county of Geauga as lay west of the ninth range of townships."

The first white settlers are said to have moved into the lands west of the Cuyahoga River (Lakewood) this year. John Haberton chose a high Rocky River bank for his home, and William McConkey settled in the lowland.

Enterprising citizens devised an ingenious scheme by which the Ohio Legislature authorized "The Cuyahoga and Muskingum Navigation Lottery" for "improving the navigation between Lake Erie and the river Ohio through the Cuyahoga and Muskingum." Although lotteries were publicly approved and much the fashion, an elaborate ticket sale staged in the East failed to produce enough subscribers who would gamble five dollars for the good of improved transportation. After numerous postponements the money was refunded. Influential men were identified with the management—Samuel Huntington, Amos Spafford, John Walworth, Lorenzo Carter, James Kingsbury, Timothy Doan, and Turhand Kirtland.

Through "union" effort, the Presbyterians and Congregationalists established churches and missions throughout the Western Reserve. On August 27, five families organized the "Plan of Union" Church in Euclid (later First Presbyterian Church of East Cleveland). The Rev. William Wick, missionary, was in charge at the founding. Tradition states that the first service was held in Andrew McIlrath's barn; another story says that charter members gathered in the home of Nathaniel Doan at Doan's Corners. The church came under the care of the Hartford Presbytery on March 15, 1810. When the new log house of worship was erected the same year on Nine Mile Creek, it was the first church building in the Cleveland vicinity and one of the earliest in the Reserve. Among those in the early congregation were the Doan, Cozad, McIlrath, Shaw, Ruple, and Dille families. This pioneer endeavor is affectionately called "the Grandmother of us all," for in it were the roots of spiritual power from which stemmed religious consciousness and growth.

In the first service following the organization of the Plan of Union Church, the Rev. William Wick remarked solemnly that some had indulged in the "unscriptural, vain and vicious practice of dancing." When he called for public acknowledgment "of this sin," two men and two women stood. One young woman, Sarah McIlrath Shaw, wife of John Shaw, admitted that she had danced at the ball given in Doan's Tavern months before, but she could see no sin in it. Her staunch refusal to repent led to ostracism from the church of which she was a charter member. She later expressed regret, the church record states, "and agreed that the committee might make such use of her acknowledgment as they should judge most fitting for the glory of God and the advantage of the church."

1808

Before the road-building era, much of the goods and merchandise was carried in canoes or sturdy boats. Cleveland's shipbuilding industry was inaugurated when the 30-ton *Zephyr* was built for lake trading by Lorenzo Carter. The first vessel launched at Cleveland had an ethereal name, despite its rude, flat-bottomed design. To proud citizens, who made a big occasion of the christening, it was the last word in sailing craft. Furs and Cleveland-made grindstones could now be traded in the East for much-needed salt, iron, leather, groceries, and dry goods.

Philo Taylor and his family reached the mouth of Rocky River by boat in April, and settled on the land chosen for their new home (Clifton Park lagoon, Lakewood). Taylor had spent about a year clearing the forest when he learned that plans for a town site, to be known as Granger City, were under way and included his property. Despite his title claim by verbal agreement, he was forced to yield; and although he was compensated for his investment, he angrily cursed the mouth of the river and moved to Dover, where he established his home. The little Rocky River settlement's hopes of future greatness were blighted from the start, as Cleveland's lead outdistanced it.

The Cleveland-to-Erie mail route was established this year. John Metcalf, the carrier, averaged about thirty miles a day on foot, bearing a satchel with from five to seven pounds of mail.

One of the earliest newspapers in the State was the *Ohio Patriot*, that began publication in Lisbon, southwest of Youngstown. As Cleveland had no paper, legal advertisements of the settlement and of Cuyahoga County appeared in its columns.

Young Nathan Perry, Jr., who had spent four years in the camp of Chief Red Jacket of the Senecas while his father acquired lands in the Reserve, came to Cleveland this year and built a store and dwelling on the northeast corner of Superior and Water streets. The store was considered an improvement over the early trading post that catered largely to Indians, and Perry thus claims the distinction as the first established merchant. A brick store and dwelling built some years later in the same location was a landmark for a long time.

A tall, thin man, who wore bowed spectacles over a rather sharp nose, walked into Cleveland beside his wagon, in which rode his wife and five daughters. Abram—or Abraham—Hickox had journeyed from Waterbury, Connecticut, and he was to become Cleveland's famous blacksmith. Over the door of his shop (west of the Rockefeller Building) were the words, "Uncle Abram Works Here." As creator and mender, he was an essential citizen. He was a patriotic enthusiast, and on the Fourth of July he roused the populace at dawn with ringing blows from his anvil. Hickox was the village sexton, and for many years he supervised the burial of the dead.

Samuel Huntington was elected governor of Ohio on December 12. At the end of the term he retired to his farm in Painesville Township. He was a founder of Fairport, laid out in 1812, and died in 1817 of injuries sustained while supervising repairs to the road from his estate (on Fairport Road) to the harbor.

Peter Chardon Brooks, stockholder in the Connecticut Land Company, offered to the commissioners a tract of land as the county seat of Geauga County on condition that they give the settlement his middle name, Chardon. The offer was accepted this year. Norman Canfield erected the first building in the village, a three-room log tavern. Merrick Pease and his family came from Connecticut in 1810; and two years later, General Edward Paine moved his family to Chardon and erected a large log house that served as the first court house. Samuel King, a Negro named Anthony Carter, and Aaron Canfield raised homes for their families in the wilderness within a few years. In the early 1820s or 1830s, Fowler's Mill began grinding meal and flour from grain grown in the countryside, as it was in 1946. Located in the heart of the maple-sugar country, the Maple Festival was originated in 1926, when Chardon became the Maple Capital of Ohio.

1809

The list of shareholders of the Connecticut Land Company had expanded considerably, indicating increasing interest in the development of New Connecticut. As soon as possible, the company passed on to the proprietors the managerial responsibilities, and relinquished title and control entirely. Land allotments varied from a section to larger areas comprising several townships of approximately 16,000 acres each. Samuel Mather, Jr., and William Hart jointly owned four townships, and Mather himself owned four more. The combined tracts amounted to 155,629 acres, and their investment was $53,629. Not many of the proprietors settled on the new lands, but rather sent agents or family members to do the pioneering.

A few proprietors, however, played a large part in the economic and cultural advance of the section of the Reserve in which they were interested: David Hudson in Hudson, Turhand Kirtland in Poland, Samuel Huntington in Painesville, Eliphalet Austin in Austinburg, Simon Perkins in Warren, and Solomon Griswold in Windsor. New communities were sometimes founded by members of a stockholder's family, as was Liberty in Trumbull County, settled in 1800 by Paine and Camden Cleaveland, brothers of the founder of Cleveland. Henry Newberry, son of General Roger Newberry, proprietor, joined William Wetmore and Joshua Stow, stockholders, in founding Cuyahoga Falls. The latter gave his name to the new settlement of Stow. John Stark Edwards, son of Pierpont—or Pierpoint—Edwards, assumed his father's interests at Warren, and became influential in the southeastern Reserve. David Root, founder of Rootstown, was a brother of Ephraim Root. Elyria was founded by Heman Ely, son of Justin Ely, whose name was identified with that of the township. Henry H. Coit, son of Daniel L. Coit, settled on his father's holdings between Doan's Corners and Euclid.

Opposite St. Clair Street on the west side of the Cuyahoga River, where the Indians had a ferry, a trail led across the marshes up to the hill past the old log trading cabin and the springs, to a clearing (crossing of West 25th and Detroit). Here the red men practiced games, held pow-wows, and when "fire water" was on hand, had a lively time. The trail continued westward to Rocky River, Sandusky, and Detroit.

A road from Cleveland to the mouth of the Huron River was made possible by appropriation of the Legislature, and Lorenzo Carter, Nathaniel Doan, and Ebenezer Murray of Mentor supervised the work. The highway followed the ridge along the lakeshore, and was later known as the Milan State Road and the Detroit Road. (Detroit Avenue was its beginning.)

The first Negro settler chose the virgin land west of the river for his home. Early in the spring, George Peake—Peak, Peek, or Peeke, eighty-seven, and his family made their way westward to the mouth of a small stream (Rocky River, Lakewood), and following it about a mile southward, the pioneer and his two oldest sons, George, Jr., and Joseph, built a log house. They are credited with being the first to follow the new Cleveland-Huron Road.

A mail route was opened between Cleveland and Detroit this year. About once every two weeks, a carrier made the journey on foot over the Indian trail along the lake to Sandusky, thence to the Maumee River basin and on to his destination. Speedier delivery on horseback came in 1811.

Allen Gaylord bought 50 acres in Newburgh (Woodland Hills Road near Miles Avenue), and on May 7 he married Philena, twenty-eight, daughter of Elijah and Anna Gun. Captain Gaylord became a man of prominence in Cleveland and Newburgh.

Two schooners of five or six tons were launched: the *Sally* by Joel Thorp—or Thorpe—and the *Dove* by Alex Simpson. The foundation of Cleveland's shipbuilding greatness was taking form.

This year witnessed the departure of Seneca, good friend of the pioneers, and he never returned. Edward Paine leaves a record of the conduct and character of the red man who frequented the neighborhood and who was called Stigwanish by his tribesmen, which in English means Standing Stone. "In him there was the dignity of the Roman, the honesty of Aristides, and the benevolence of Penn," Paine affirmed. "He was never known to ask a donation, but would accept one as he ought, but not suffer it to rest here. An appropriate return was soon to be made. He was so much of a teetotaler as to abjure ardent spirits, since in a drunken spree, he had aimed a blow at his wife with a tomahawk, and split the head of his child which was on her back."

With the arrival of Levi Johnson, twenty-four, from Herkimer County, New York, a career of outstanding usefulness as a builder began in Cleveland. Near the Public Square Johnson built his cabin. A man of versatility in his trade, he accomplished all kinds of construction from public buildings to schooners and lighthouses.

Stanley Griswold, who settled at Doan's Corners this year, had filled offices of public service elsewhere, and his experience qualified him to become clerk of Cleveland Township within a short time. When a vacancy occurred in the United States Senate, Governor Samuel Huntington appointed Griswold to fill the unexpired term, and he was soon on his way to Washington.

Cleveland and Newburgh had been engaged in a dispute for the honor of being made the seat of Cuyahoga County. Newburgh, healthful and thriving, had increased her population and claimed superior advantages. Although a committee of the Legislature selected Cleveland this year for its position at the mouth of the Cuyahoga, the rival community bitterly contested the action for more than a decade.

Amos Spafford was elected to the State Legislature from Geauga County. Upon his appointment as collector of the port for the district of Miami, he moved to Perrysburg the next year.

The report from the port of Cuyahoga to the United States Treasury showed that the total value of goods, wares, and merchandise exported to Canada from April to October was $50. The growing business of commerce and the Post Office apparently influenced the erection of a new frame building for the collector-postmaster's headquarters.

CHAPTER 4

Coming of Leaders
1810-1819

WITH a population of about fifty-seven courageous souls, Cleveland started a new decade with discouraging prospects for the future. Hardy pioneers had built their few primitive dwellings with crude hand-made tools, and through patient endeavor had been able to keep the settlement alive. There was no church, no schoolhouse, no meeting place. Illness was prevalent, due in part to the swamp lands, and there was no doctor to attend the sick. There were legal problems and no attorney to solve them.

Then fortune smiled, and Dr. David Long, the first physician, and Alfred Kelley, the first lawyer, came with their talents to lend a hand. Samuel Williamson, business and professional leader, and Leonard Case, banker, brought specialized experience that was fundamental to the establishment of the colony on the lake.

Although few in numbers, Cleveland's men of influence were awake to opportunities, urging practical new developments to meet growing needs. Natural resources were put to work, new enterprises were begun, and vision and initiative were reflected in ambitious efforts to expand commerce and industry. The sound advance of the early days, that quickened with the years, was due in large measure to their character, initiative, and confidence.

A bank was incorporated and tanneries went into operation, but farming provided the livelihood for most of the settlers. Taverns and general stores sprang up as trade and traffic grew. Civil government was established and townships were organized. Church congregations began to assemble, and there was an awakening to the necessity for educational opportunities. A library association was formed. Having reached the stature of a village, Cleveland received a charter of incorporation from the Ohio Legislature. Log cabins gave way to frame and brick construction, and the assessed value of the "capital" city of the Western Reserve was more than $20,000!

The need for a newspaper was met by enthusiastic editors. Editor Logan of the *Register*, the Jeffersonian journal, and politically independent Howe of the *Herald* tried desperately to keep their readers informed with news gleaned from the columns of exchange papers. Sensational stories and heated political discussions were welcomed at the frontier, regardless of stale headlines. Local news had no place in the papers at first, as it was generally broadcast thoroughly by the well-known grapevine in the small community. In the advertisements, however, can be traced the growth and development of the village, as well as the habits and customs of the people.

Newburgh citizens pointed with pride to their progress and natural advantages, fully expecting to maintain an increasing population lead over mosquito-infested Cleveland. Doan's Corners was flourishing on the road to Newburgh. Lands had been placed on the market west of the Cuyahoga River, and pioneers were pushing back the wilderness to make room for a cabin and a patch of a farm. Mail routes and trailways broadened their lines to keep pace with stimulated passenger and freight service into the district. The first steamboat on Lake Erie stopped at Cleveland on its maiden voyage late in the decade, and a stage line opened to Champion (Painesville).

The War of 1812 seriously disturbed the little community and resulted in economic depression; but courageous leadership guided the citizens through the troubled times, and essential industries and institutions gained a foothold.

Cleveland followed the usual plan of city development—a little settlement, a hamlet, a village. Its people joined for protection, sympathy, betterment and gain. Came the road, the crude highway, the unpaved street. The trail deepened to a rut—a rut hollowed by the tumbrel of progress. Beside it men pitched their tents, raised humble dwellings, and rested from their wanderings. Among the early evidences of progress is the street, the epitome of daily life; tragedy stalks through it, comedy minces by, love and life enter it, and death knocks at every door.

The early Cleveland planners knew the importance of streets, and they laid them out with visions of homes and businesses that would eventually line them. They gave the name Euclid to one street that brought lasting fame to the community.

The Public Square was a cow pasture studded with stumps and underbrush, but it had begun to attain importance as the center of the settlement. Footpaths crossed under the tall trees, disappearing in the adjacent forest. Small boys used it as a playground. Here horses were given their workouts, and wandering swine turned up the turf with their snouts. Civic pride lay dormant indeed.

As the decade closed, daring New Englanders were on their way to the western frontier—not a land of milk and honey, but of hills and valleys clothed with sturdy timber; uplands bearing an abundance of nuts, berries, wild plums, crabapples, and mountain grapes, and marshes producing fox grapes. Sassafras, medicinal barks, and herbs were plentiful, and the sugar maples oozed their sweetness in early spring. The forests abounded in game, and the waters teemed with fish. Nature was a good provider. In this new world, the head of the family cleared ground for a cabin to shelter his loved ones, and built a lean-to for his oxen. A pitifully small collection of furniture, utensils and provisions, with perhaps a little money, were the extent of his earthly goods as he and his family began life anew in the Promised Land.

1810

Lands beyond the Cuyahoga were offered for sale, and Major Lorenzo Carter and his son, Alonzo, purchased a tract on the west side of the river near the mouth. Here the latter farmed, keeping the Red House Tavern and a small warehouse. Elijah Gun operated a ferry between this point and the foot of Superior Street on the east side. It was the only means of public transportation across the river.

In the unbroken forest in township 7, range 11, Daniel Warren built a cabin for his wife and two small children in early January. Moses Warren, his father, followed with two sons, William and Moses, Jr., five years later, and Warrensville had its beginning. Township government was established in 1816.

In February, Zanesville became the seat of government of Ohio. During the 1811-12 session of the Legislature, however, Columbus was selected as the permanent state capital. Suitable buildings were completed by 1816, and in the meantime the central government convened at Chillicothe.

On May 1, the judicial existence of Cuyahoga County began, when the Court of Common Pleas was organized and the first county officers were inaugurated: Benjamin Ruggles, presiding judge; Nathan Perry, Sr., Augustus Gilbert, and Timothy Doan, associate judges. Huron County was attached to Cuyahoga for administrative purposes. The officials were elected by the Legislature, and under the constitution, the court had common-law and chancery jurisdiction. While it was essential that the presiding judge should be "learned in the law," his associates were usually respected men of prominence in the community.

The first session of the Court of Common Pleas was held on June 5 in the new store of Elias and Harvey Murray on the south side of Superior Street (adjoining Hotel Cleveland site). The first officers of Cuyahoga County were Peter Hitchcock of Geauga, prosecuting attorney, succeeded by Alfred Kelley in November; John Walworth, clerk and recorder; Smith S. Baldwin, sheriff; Jabez Wright and Nathaniel Doan, county commissioners; Asa Dille, treasurer, and Samuel S. Baldwin, surveyor. Typical of the early court cases were those of Daniel Miner, who conducted a ferry across Rocky River, fined twenty-five cents for selling a gill of whisky for six cents without a license; Thomas McIlrath, prosecuted for trading a quart of whisky for three raccoon skins; and Erastus Miles, indicted for selling liquor to the Indians. Law and order in Cleveland had been fully established.

The Murray store deserves more than passing interest. For three years it housed county officials. During the War of 1812, it was converted into a hospital for wounded soldiers. Then, having been restored to its original purpose, it was soon recognized as "one of the local mercantile features," and served until it was razed in 1855.

Joshua Stow, of the Moses Cleaveland party of 1796, and his nephew, Alfred Kelley, of Oneida County, New York, rode into town with Jared

P. Kirtland in the summer. Kelley found quarters in Walworth's small frame office, his companions remaining only for a visit. Kirtland's father, Turhand Kirtland, was agent for the Connecticut Land Company at Poland in Trumbull County at this time, and Stow had large land tracts in the Reserve. On November 7, his twenty-first birthday, Kelley was admitted to the bar and hung out his shingle, the first practicing attorney in Cleveland. Almost continuously from 1814 to 1822, he represented Cuyahoga County in the General Assembly. Daniel and Jemima Stow Kelley, his father and mother, and their sons, Datus, Irad, Joseph Reynolds, and Thomas, new settlers from Connecticut, joined him during the next several years.

When Dr. David Long, twenty-three, the first resident physician, arrived in June from Hebron, New York, the nearest doctor was in Hudson. After having studied medicine with an uncle, a country doctor, Dr. Long had been enrolled for about four months in the College of Physicians and Surgeons in New York City during the winter before coming to Cleveland. He found office space with Alfred Kelley, and the two young men were destined to make great contributions to Cleveland.

Lorenzo Carter erected the first log warehouse on Union Lane at about this time, and Murray & Bixby built the *Ohio*, a 60-ton vessel, which became part of Commodore Perry's fleet.

Under the existing judicial system, the Supreme Court of Ohio held its annual sessions in the several counties. It first convened in Cuyahoga County in August this year. Producing their commissions, William W. Irwin and Ethan A. Brown organized the court and appointed John Walworth as clerk.

Elias Cozad laid the cornerstone of his tannery at Doan's Corners, the first to be built in the district later known as Cleveland. Trappers brought him raw furs of wolves, foxes, bears, and squirrels, which, when tanned and dressed, provided leather for makers of boots and shoes in the community. At about the year-end, Samuel and Matthew Williamson, newcomers from Pennsylvania, also built a tannery in Cleveland on lot No. 202 near a spring. Samuel brought his family with him, his oldest child, named Samuel, then being only two years old. Matthew was a bachelor brother. Samuel, the elder, became familiarly known as the "judge," having served as an associate judge of the Court of Common Pleas. The first Williamson home was located on Water Street near Superior Lane.

According to Charles Whittlesey, historian, the population of Cleveland this year was fifty-seven. Although a "United States census," compiled more than a century later, placed the figure at 300, this probably included the village and its environs. The larger figure cannot be substantiated by research relating to the inhabitants within the confines of Cleveland. In Cuyahoga County there were 1,459 people, according to the census, the smallest county total in Ohio.

1811

A public well on Bank Street near Superior, eight feet across, with a wheel and two buckets, afforded the first water supply for fire-fighting. Every family had a well. However, when rain water failed for washing, Benhu Johnson hauled lake water with his horse and wagon, selling it at 25 cents a load of two barrels. Soap could be had at a shilling a gallon at Jabez Kelley's soap-and-candle factory, a log structure on Superior Street near the river.

Only a few primitive houses fronted on Superior between the river and the Public Square, with an occasional temporary dwelling in the woods. The river outlet was sometimes completely barred with sand, so that men could walk across and scarcely wet their feet. The sand-bar continued to be a menace for more than a decade, when the citizens demanded practical harbor improvements.

Ohio was divided into five medical districts by the Legislature, each district being entitled to three censors, who acted as examiners or licensers of applicants who desired to practice medicine. The next year, the state was re-divided into seven districts, with Cuyahoga County in the sixth.

Dr. David Long married Juliana Walworth, daughter of John Walworth, in April, and they lived in the Huntington blockhouse, where a daughter, Mary Helen, was born. Later they moved into a new brick house facing Bank Street. There were neither roads nor bridges, and the good doctor traveled through the wilds, answering "hurry-up" calls from isolated cabins located as much as eight and ten miles apart. He was reputed to be the best physician and surgeon in the region. In the early 1830s, the Longs moved into a finer stone house on Superior Street (west of Hotel Cleveland site). Here the doctor expanded his income by operating a notions and dry-goods store. A characteristic advertisement offered 800 barrels of salt, 10 tons of plaster, and 50 buffalo robes for sale.

Elijah Russell, eldest son of Jacob Russell of Connecticut, came to Ohio to inspect his father's holdings. In the spring he returned to the frontier with his brother, Ralph, and they cleared land (Warrensville area), planted corn, and built a log house; then they went back to Connecticut to assist in moving the family. Jacob Russell and the families of his brother, Elisha, and a brother-in-law, Hart Risley, made the journey in the autumn. Elijah Russell moved his family the following summer, arriving in Cleveland on August 31, 1813.

A larger and more elaborate house was built by Levi Johnson for Rodolphus Edwards (at Woodhill and Buckeye roads), of timbers and hand-sawed boards. It was the famous Buckeye Tavern, later the Pioneer, where Cleveland society revelled and danced. In 1883, the tavern was converted into a dwelling by Rodolphus Edwards, Jr., and it was a landmark for many years.

Sixteen of the eighteen families in the village met in July to form the first library association, among those present being the households of Alfred Kelley, Lorenzo Carter, Nathan Perry, John Walworth, Dr. David Long, and Samuel Williamson. The initial fee was five dollars, and the annual membership fee, one dollar. Dr. Long was appointed librarian. Most popular books in the scanty prized collection were *Don Quixote,* Goldsmith's *History of Greece,* and Scott's *Lay of the Last Minstrel.* The library project was short-lived, failing to survive the coming war period.

At an all-day meeting in Harvey Murray's new store, August 23, the Free Masons, the first fraternal order in Cleveland, organized with thirteen members. Dispensation having come from Lewis Cass, grand master of Ohio, Samuel Huntington, deputy grand master who had been grand master of the Grand Lodge of Ohio in 1809, installed the officers. Abraham Bishop was the first master. A man of some means, he had built the first sawmill in Euclid Township, was the township's first treasurer and the supervisor of highways. A charter in the name of Concord Lodge No. 15 was granted on January 9, 1812. As the village grew, leading men in and around Cleveland became members, meeting in taverns, halls, public buildings, and private homes.

Charles Dutton sold to Turhand Kirtland two acres of land on the Public Square (Marshall Building site, northwest corner of Superior, and adjoining sites) for $30. Kirtland evidently considered it a poor investment, and he resold the land to Jacob Coleman, Jr., in 1813 for $30. Coleman profited when he sold it to William Coleman in 1815 for $55, but the latter sold the corner—28 feet on Superior and 66 feet on the Square—to Leonard Case, Sr., for $200. In 1908, W. G. Marshall leased the land (Marshall Building site) for ninety-nine years at $12,000 a year.

Datus Kelley and his bride reached Cleveland in mid-October. They kept house for a short time in a new warehouse at the mouth of the river, then purchased a farm at $3.18 per acre (about a mile west of Rocky River on the lake).

In a clearing east of Cleveland Village (East 55th Street), Nathan Chapman built his shanty. His nearest neighbors were at the Public Square.

A Canadian named Granger was one of the first to settle west of the river. He located on a high bluff (near Riverside Cemetery) that became known as "Granger's Hill," and here he lived until 1815, when he and his son, Samuel, moved on.

Eight persons signed the charter of a Congregational church organization in Lee, Massachusetts—Jedediah Crocker and wife; Lydia Hall, wife of Moses Hall; Kate Crosby, wife of Jedediah Crosby; Jonathan Smith and wife; and Abner Smith and wife. Journeying to Dover, Ohio, the new Reserve settlement, during the year, they continued to worship as the Congregational Church of Dover, the first church of the denomination in Cuyahoga County. Congregational churches were organized in the Brecksville settlement in 1816, in Strongsville in 1817, and in Olmstead Township in 1835. The little log church at Dover, built in 1822, burned, and members met in the town house until it was replaced. A rift in the church family came in 1840 over the slavery question, but the wound healed. The church increased slowly in numbers, its roots reaching deep into family life for miles around. In 1946, located at 2519 Dover Center Road, it continued as a vital force in the community, then known as Westlake, under the leadership of the Rev. Harold W. Freer, called as pastor in 1945.

Seth Paine, agent for Robert Breck, Massachusetts merchant, was the first settler on the proprietor's lands, covering about half of Brecksville Township, organized in 1814. After him came Lemuel Bourne and his bride, and pioneering families, among them those of Wolcott, Bagley, Newell, Hoadley, Adams, Bradford, Waite, Johnston, Rice, Barnes, Wilcox, Hunt, Snow, and Oakes. Robert Breck never lived on his land; and after his death in 1830, his sons, Theodore, John Adams, and Dr. Edward, claimed their inheritance and settled in Brecksville. Here they lived for many years. The Village of Brecksville was not officially formed, however, until 1921.

Although his stay was short, William King was the first settler of Independence, described as township 6, range 12, in the original Western Reserve survey. Among early permanent settlers were the Comstock, Wood, Morton, and Johnson families. Records prior to 1834, including those of township organization, were destroyed, and origin of the township is unknown. Incorporation of Independence Village was not effected until 1914.

George Peake purchased 103 acres of land in the area that became Rockport (Lakewood-Rocky River) on December 31, and farmed and worked for the settlers that soon claimed the district. His invention of a hand-operated mill for grinding grain was hailed as a vast improvement over the mortar-and-pestle type. Peake was a highly respected citizen, and died at the age of 105.

1812

Religious power had begun to manifest itself on the Reserve, and about twenty church organizations had been formed in or near Hudson, Youngstown, Austinburg, Warren, Poland, Canfield, Euclid, Burton, Tallmadge, Chardon, Aurora, North Springfield, Fredericksburg, Rootstown, Dover, and Mantua. By 1820, the number had grown to about sixty. Many of the settlers were discouraged and homesick, and welcomed the fellowship and cooperation of the little church circle.

James Fish, first permanent white settler in the territory that became Brooklyn, moved his family into an eighteen-dollar log cabin in May, after having spent the winter in Newburgh. It is said that while clearing his 80-acre tract (on both sides of Denison Avenue), he encountered a section infested with rattlesnakes. After a narrow escape, he exclaimed, "What a smart idea it was in God Almighty to put bells on them things!" Moses and Ebenezer Fish, cousins, arrived shortly afterward. Fish Street honored the family name.

The family burial lot on the Fish farm became the oldest public cemetery west of the Cuyahoga (part of Scranton Road Cemetery). James Fish deeded it to trustees of a school district and it fell into neglect. Owners of the lots, however, acting as the Brooklyn Cemetery Association and successors of the North Brooklyn Association, later assumed maintenance responsibility. On the Fish family monument appear the names of Elisha and Mary Will-cox, parents of the wife of James Fish, and the inscription states that the father died in 1788. This raises an interesting question without an answer —were the remains brought from New England? The grave of James Fish is said to lie under Scranton Road near the cemetery.

Thomas D. Webb, twenty-eight, was editor of the first newspaper in the Western Reserve, with the pompous title, *The Trump of Fame*. The first issue appeared on June 9 in Warren, which had been his home since 1807, when he arrived from Windham, Connecticut. The pioneer publication consisted of four small pages printed from minute type. There was little controversial copy, no local news, and only scanty editorials. Eastern papers were combed for material; and although the columns were stale when they reached the subscriber, they were welcomed. Four years later, the editor was able to secure the letters "V" and "W," and the paper became known by the dignified title, *Western Reserve Chronicle* (later the *Warren Tribune Chronicle*).

Levi Johnson commenced the erection of Cuyahoga County's first Court House and Jail this year, on the northwest corner of the Public Square. A town pump and watering trough were popular meeting places here. Johnson was chosen as the first county coroner this year, and he was the first deputy sheriff.

On a gallows erected by Levi Johnson near the partially completed Court House, the Indian O'Mic—also called Poccon, John O'Mic, O'Mick, and Omic—was hanged on June 24 as penalty for his part in murdering two white trappers near Sandusky and stealing their furs. Because of his great courage and his influence with the Indians, Lorenzo Carter had custody of the prisoner. Cleveland's entire population witnessed O'Mic's murder trial and execution, the first in Cuyahoga County. It was marked with a certain dramatic quality, intended as an example of the speed and finality of the white-man's justice.

Co-operative study among medical practitioners in Cleveland is said to have begun when Dr. Long invited Western Reserve physicians to observe the O'Mic execution. Many came, and that night, it is related, they opened the grave in a severe storm, removed the body and dissected it. Dr. Long retained the skeleton, and Cleveland physicians used it in teaching medical students.

The untimely end of O'Mic held more than idle curiosity for some of the citizens at the Public Square that June day, as evidenced by the statement of Mrs. David Long, preserved in history:

I knew John O'Mic and his father very well. John was not a bad Indian towards the whites. When we were children at Painesville, we used to play together on the banks of the Grand river, at my father's old residence, which we called Bloomingdale . . . O'Mic's father came to our house, on Water street, a short time before the execution. We were very much afraid of the

Indians then. I was alone, and my babe was sleeping in the cradle. He took up a gun which was in the room, in order to show me how Semo killed himself, after he had been arrested. I thought he was going to kill me or my baby, in revenge for his son. I seized the child and ran up Water street towards Mr. Williamson's, screaming pretty hard, I suppose. O'Mic followed after me, trying to explain what he meant. Mr. Williamson caught the child, and we all went to Major Carter's house, which was on the corner of Superior street and Union lane. Major Carter had a short talk with O'Mic, who explained what he meant, and we all had a hearty laugh. O'Mic had lived near Painesville. I was in the crowd on the square when O'Mic was to be hung, and I suddenly thought, "Why should I wish to see my old play-fellow die?" I got out of the crowd as quickly as possible and went home.

News of the outbreak of war with Great Britain on June 18 reached Cleveland by courier on June 28. As the settlement was near the western battle grounds, there was great fear of British and Indian attack. Women and children were hastily moved inland for security, leaving about thirty men on guard with flintlock guns. Mrs. George Wallace, Mrs. John Walworth, and Mrs. David Long, however, refused to leave their homes. When reminded that she could not fight, Mrs. Long replied that she "could nurse the sick or wounded—encourage and comfort those who could fight; at any rate she would not, by her example, encourage disgraceful flight." Farms and shops felt the manpower shortage as the war progressed, and most of the men were drafted into the Cleveland and Newburgh militias. An anti-war party in New England had followers in the village, but the pioneers were too close to danger to join in opposing the agitation. Near-panic resulted, after families had begun to return to their homes, when paroled soldiers wrapped in blankets were mistaken for Indians as they arrived in Cleveland.

A Negro who enlisted for war duty from Cleveland was William H. Jackson, about fifteen years old. The exact date of his arrival in the settlement is not known, but it is believed that he and his mother were freed by their slave owner in Kings County, New York, May 6, 1803. Jackson was buried in Woodland Cemetery at the age of eighty-two.

Shipbuilding on the lakes received its first impetus from the War of 1812. While Commodore Perry's fleet was built largely in Erie, three of his ships were constructed on the Cuyahoga River (near Akron). William Coggswell, son of a veteran English ship owner, helped bring the ships down to Cleveland, where they were equipped with sails. On the way, Coggswell brought a porcupine on board one of the schooners, and the sailors were so impressed with the courageous beast that the *Portage* became the *Porcupine*. This ship, with the *Tigress* and *Trippe,* sailed away to join Perry at Presque Isle (near Erie). By 1816, small shipyards were to be found in leading ports, and Vermilion, Sandusky, and especially Huron became rivals of Cleveland in the boat-building industry.

Reports of fertile land west of the river induced James Nicholson to trade

160 acres in Conneaut for land on which he built his cabin (Waterbury and Detroit, Lakewood). Upon his return from the War of 1812, he purchased an additional 160-acre tract and built a larger cabin. A white colonial house erected in 1835 (13335 Detroit Avenue), was Lakewood's oldest residence in the 1940s. The names of Nicholson's grandsons, Lewis and Clarence, were given to Lewis Drive and Clarence Avenue; and Grace Avenue was named for their sister. Other families that helped to lay the foundations in the area were the Deans, the Turners, the Van Benscoters, the Nicholses, and the Kedneys.

One of the oldest cemeteries in the Western Reserve is a plot overlooking the valley of Nine Mile Creek (adjoining First Presbyterian Church of East Cleveland). The first grave was made this year for Susannah Barr, wife of the pastor of the Plan of Union Church, the Rev. Thomas Barr. Here were buried John Shaw (for whom Shaw High School was named), Andrew McIlrath, and Enoc Murray, the first Mason to settle in the Western Reserve. Soldiers and stout-hearted men and women found a last resting place in this obscure corner.

George Wallace opened a tavern on the south side of Superior Street, west of Seneca. Superior was the only street that had been cleared. Water Street was hardly more than a path.

An 18-acre tract of land on the Buffalo Road (near East 14th) was purchased by Samuel Phelps of Painesville for $2 to pay delinquent taxes, "there being no other persons who would pay taxes for a less quantity than eighteen acres on said lots."

Upon the death of his father, John Walworth, Ashbel W. Walworth became postmaster and collector of the port on October 25. He was the first letter carrier, delivering the mail—three or four letters—from his hat at his convenience.

1813

One of the earliest west-side settlers was Nathan Alger. The first grave in Alger Cemetery (16711 Lorain) was made for his remains on January 21 of this year. On his tombstone is a neighborly inscription:

> My friends, I'm here, the first to come,
> And in this place, for you there's room.

Captain Stanton Sholes, United States Army, reached Carter's Tavern on May 10 with his company to establish a military post to protect the village. He was a man of action, and soon the building of Fort Huntington, a stockade, was under way on the high lakefront ground near the foot of Seneca Street (Fort Huntington Park). A small army hospital was erected about June 1 to care for the sick and wounded, the first in Cleveland. Not "a nail, a screw, or iron latch or hinge" was about the 40 by 20-foot building. The floor was of chestnut bark, and two tiers of bunks were filled with clean straw. At the close of the war, the hospital was abandoned. Major Jessup was in command of the fort that was never put to attack and siege, but was used largely as a guardhouse for soldiers under arrest. Later several militia companies made it their headquarters. In July, General William Henry Harrison, in command of the Northwestern Army, visited the fort with Colonel Samuel Huntington, army paymaster and former governor of Ohio, for whom the defense was named. Their coming attracted visitors from all parts of the Reserve.

Cleveland's strategic location made it an important base for supplies and troop movement, so that there was constant fear of enemy invasion. On June 19, the settlement was disturbed by the appearance of several British ships on the horizon, and a landing was considered probable. Household goods were hastily packed, ready for evacuation of women and children. The contents of Carter's warehouse were moved several miles up the river. Militias mobilized, and an old swivel, muzzle-loading cannon was dragged from the fort to the river mouth on its heavy wagon wheels. The ships approached to within a mile and a half of shore, then suddenly disappeared, as a violent rain storm broke upon them.

Levi Johnson's men were working on the first Court House on the Public Square on September 10 when the report of cannon, signaling the Battle of Lake Erie, brought the population of Cleveland running to the high banks of the lake (foot of West 6th and West 9th). Johnson shouted, "Three cheers for Perry. If his fleet wins, the lake will be free from the British." The band of loyal Clevelanders joined him. For three long hours the battle continued. Then came a time when there was only the sound of the heavy cannon— the small reports had ceased. "Perry had the big guns," exclaimed Johnson. "The battle is won by Perry and the Americans!" Back to their homes went the little Cleveland company. News soon came of the historic Battle of Lake Erie fought seventy miles away at Put-in-Bay. Young Commodore Oliver Hazard Perry commanded the Americans from his famous flagship, the *Lawrence,* in this battle of the wooden ships, one of the bloodiest in history. The turning point in the second war with Great Britain had come with Perry's famous words, "We have met the enemy and they are ours!" The commodore sent his victory dispatch to General William Henry Harrison at Detroit by Rufus Wright, later a well-known Cleveland innkeeper, who made the perilous journey through wild country "filled with British hirelings and bloodthirsty Indians." After the battle, the commodore and General Harrison were entertained in the home of their friend, Judge James Kingsbury in Newburgh, and the Masons of the community met them in special session. Several weeks before the famous battle, Perry had sought Kingsbury's counsel as to the strategy he should follow. The judge replied decisively, "Why, sir, I would fight!" A cannon captured from the British was mounted on the Public Square in 1872.

Four days after the Battle of Lake Erie, the first printed account of Perry's victory off Put-in-Bay appeared in Warren's pioneer newspaper, *The Trump of Fame.* Perry's courier had left immediately for Washington with news dispatches for the War Department, having been on the road three days when he reached Warren on horseback. Here he rested for the night; and from his eye-witness account, the enterprising editor gave to the world on September 14 the first major newspaper "scoop" on the Reserve.

During this year or the next, Levi Johnson built the schooner *Ladies' Master* near his home in the woods (Euclid near East 4th). It was hauled to the river by ox teams rounded up from the neighborhood. Johnson and Tom Rummage commenced their lake careers by fitting out a little schooner, loading it with rations and running the British blockade to feed American troops near Detroit. Rummage died of cholera, leaving two seafaring sons, Solon and Harvey. Early in shipping history, Captain Harvey sailed a schooner loaded with black-walnut timber from Cleveland to Germany in a month's time—a fine record. An impressive Rummage home was built on Johnson's wooded boatyard site.

Meetings of Cleveland Township officials had been held in private homes until the first Court House was completed this year in late summer. The first floor of the two-story, log building housed jail cells for delinquent debtors and provided a living room for the sheriff. The courtroom upstairs was also the scene of social gatherings and town meetings. Tallow dips provided the light, and a large, wood-burning stove the heat. The little red structure is variously reported to have cost $500 and $700 to build. It was torn down in 1830, when a new Court House replaced it.

1814

Culture, education, and entertainment centered largely in the home. Praiseworthy attempts to make possible the latter may be better understood by I. A. Morgan's account of a social event arranged by the Rev. Stephen Peet at the log house of Samuel Dille, "on the road from Newburgh to Cleveland." Here the populace assembled from miles around, and "witnessed the performance of the 'Conjurer' taken from the *Columbian Orator*; the 'dissipated Oxford Student,' also taken from the same book; 'Brutus and Cassius,' taken from the *American Preceptor*; and several other pieces. The various parts were conceded by the critics there to have been performed in admirable style . . . After the performance, my father, mother, two sisters and myself returned home, a distance of a mile and a half on the family horse. Two adults and three plump children, six to twelve years of age, might now be considered a rather large load to carry, and five on a horse, as may be supposed, would now render a cavalcade somewhat uncouth in appearance on the streets of Cleveland." The clergyman also conducted a school in Newburgh.

Lorenzo Carter, frontiersman, community leader, and tavernkeeper, the most versatile of the early settlers, died in his tavern in February, aged forty-seven, afflicted with a wasting disease. His grave is in the Erie Street

Cemetery, and his wife, Rebecca, is buried beside him. The Carter Tavern was leased by Phineas Shepherd—Shephard or Shepard.

Levi Johnson built the schooner *Pilot*. Twenty-eight yoke of oxen were required to drag the craft from the Johnson boatyard to the river. This year also saw the erection of the first brick building, a store on Superior Street, built by Irad Kelley and his brother, Joseph Reynolds Kelley.

On his land extending from Water Street to the river, Alfred Kelley "began the construction of a stone house on the bluff overlooking Lake Erie" (near West Ninth and Lakeside) for his parents, according to the *Kelley Family History*. His mother died before it was finished. This was Cleveland's first stone house, and, for years, the finest in town. It was not as pretentious, however, as homes elsewhere in the Reserve, where greater New England wealth was to be found, and where commerce and industry had gained a foothold.

In May, the Court of Common Pleas had been in existence for four years, during which time 109 civil suits were entered, most of them being petitions for the partition of lands. Only seven lawyers appear on the record in this period—Alfred Kelley, Thomas D. Webb, Robert B. Parkman, Samuel W. Phelps, Peter Hitchcock of Geauga, who preceded Kelley as prosecuting attorney, John S. Edwards, and D. Redick. During the war years, there was little activity in the courts.

Ozias Brainard of Connecticut had been living with his family west of the river (Denison Avenue) for a year when a train of six wagons, drawn by ten horses and six oxen, arrived. From Connecticut had come four more Brainards with their families—Asa, Stephen, Enos, and Warren, also the families of Elijah Young and Isaac Hinckley. Their enthusiasm for the frontier had inspired them to exchange their home lands for those offered for sale in the new territory west of the Cuyahoga River. Hinckley stopped to rest in Euclid, but the others pushed on to Cleveland. The news of their coming was alarming to the Cleveland Township trustees, who feared the "avalanche" of immigrants to be a band of paupers that would burden them for support. A constable set out to warn the caravan; and it was not until Alonzo Carter vouched for the newcomers that they were allowed to proceed. Isaac Hinckley carved a farm out of 360 acres of wilderness "a mile from anybody" (Schaaf Road district). Later came the Gates, Sears, Storers, Aikens, Fosters, Kroehles, and Poes to Brooklyn Township.

Isaiah W. Fish, son of James Fish, was the first white child born west of the river, on May 9.

With the arrival of Dr. Donald McIntosh, Cleveland had two physicians. Although an able practitioner, he was restless and quick-tempered, and frequently risked his reputation at the expense of being a "good fellow."

Alfred Kelley made a map of the village based upon Spafford's map of 1801, indicating on it the buildings in existence. It is interesting to note that a street crossing had not yet been introduced in the center of the Public Square. Some years later, Charles Whittlesey added shore lines to the map and showed important changes in the river entrance, based upon surveys beginning in 1796.

In a clearing on his 17-acre tract east of the Square (Euclid and East 79th), Timothy Watkins built a cabin for his family and laid out a farm. Watkins' Tavern, erected on the Euclid Road, was the half-way house between the Public Square and Doan's Corners, and it served until 1867. To the south, a brook trickled merrily through the woods known as Watkins Glen.

Newburgh Township was organized on October 15, and included practically all of township 7, range 12, in the Western Reserve. The first township officers were Erastus Miles, first clerk; Giles Barnes, Charles Miles, and Daniel Marvin, trustees. Gaius Burke, one-legged and one-armed, was constable of the justice court—Newburgh's first policeman. Burke was elected county treasurer in 1827 and served until 1832. Newburgh produced many of Cleveland's most influential families, among them the Morgans, Wightmans, Peets, Hubbells, Baldwins, Hamiltons, Warners, Whites, Dilles, Gilberts, and Ingersolls.

An 85-acre tract of land in Euclid Township was purchased by Paul P. Condit, of Morristown, New Jersey. Felled timbers were converted into Farmer's Inn, sometimes called the Condit House. It provided a "spell" for the traveler until 1859, when its days of public service ended.

A charter of incorporation as a village was granted to Cleveland—spelled "Cleveland"—by the Ohio Legislature on December 23, largely through Alfred Kelley's efforts. At this time there were thirty-four dwellings and business places. Existing streets were Superior, Water, and Bank, the latter two merely wagon roads. Stores and most of the homes faced on Superior.

1815

Phinney Mowrey—Plinney Mowry or Mowery—was erecting his tavern in May at the southwest corner of Superior Street and the Public Square. It was a small log structure, situated on lot No. 82, which he had purchased from Samuel Huntington for $100 in 1812. Taverns and hotels were located here continuously through the years (Hotel Cleveland site). A spring near the barn was a favorite meeting place.

Noble H. Merwin was favorably impressed upon his visit to Cleveland, and built a log warehouse at the corner of Superior and Merwin streets this year. The next year he brought his family from Connecticut, and his career of business importance began. Merwin Street in the "Flats" bears his name.

Under the new charter, the first officials of the newly incorporated Village of Cleveland held a quiet election on June 5. Of the twelve male voters, nine received offices: Alfred Kelley, president, twenty-five years old; Horace Perry, recorder; Alonzo Carter, treasurer; John A. Ackley, marshal; George Wallace and John Riddle, assessors; Samuel Williamson, David Long, and Nathan Perry, Jr., trustees. Government was administered in a small frame building on Superior Street that had been erected by John Walworth. In the following March, Alfred Kelley resigned, and his father, Daniel Kelley, was appointed president. He served four successive terms. Trustees were empowered to pass and enforce ordinances, lay out streets, and operate as a council. The charter defined the village limits from Erie Street west to the river, and from Huron Street north to the lake.

Village tap rooms were still echoing *Perries Victory on Lake Erie,* a triumphant ballad of twenty verses, when George Wallace purchased Spafford's Tavern on June 13, and named it the Wallace House. Michael Spangler purchased Wallace's tavern and operated it as Spangler's Inn.

Phineas Shepherd made a home for his family in the new land west of the river (near St. John's Church, Church Avenue and West 26th).

In October, the village trustees laid out a number of streets to be known as St. Clair—named for General Arthur St. Clair, first governor of the Northwest Territory, Bank, Seneca, Wood, Bond, and Euclid. Diamond Street was to encompass the Square. These new streets were not shown on the early maps of Cleveland. Euclid Street was surveyed the next year. It extended from the Square to Huron Street. Its name was inspired, no doubt, by the little settlement of surveyors to the east; but as late as 1825, it was known as the Buffalo Road. When broad Superior Street was laid out parallel with the lake, it was expected to be the main thoroughfare; but as trade and traffic expanded, it deferred to Euclid.

Robert Harper brought his bride to Shandy Hall, their new home nestled under locust trees (about a mile east of Unionville). In June, 1798, his father, Colonel Alexander Harper, with a party of twenty-five including his family, had claimed extensive lands in the area, where he established a home (on Johnny Cake Ridge). The pioneer died on September 10, 1798, having survived the campaigns of the Revolutionary War and the rigors of two years and eight months as a prisoner of the British. He had named the new settlement Harpersfield after the old home in New York State. Colonel Harper was buried in a hollowed-out log in Unionville's little cemetery, which was later beautified and given to the town by members of the Norton family. His is the oldest marked grave in the Western Reserve. Additions to Shandy Hall were built in 1826, and seventeen rooms were fully equipped "with all that a good home of Jackson's time possessed," from French wallpaper to a priceless grand piano brought by oxcart from the ancestral home in Harpersfield, New York. The Harper house was occupied continuously for 120 years by the builder's family. When Mrs. Fred R. White, Laurence Harper Norton, president of the Western Reserve Historical Society, and Robert Castle Norton inherited Shandy Hall from their father, David Z. Norton, they secured the assistance of George W. Bierce in restoring the homestead. The treasure-house was later placed under the care of the society as a public museum.

Serenus Burnett settled on the Chagrin River in township 7, range 10, of the Western Reserve. Within a few years, Jesse Kimball, Rufus Parsons, John White, Theron White, Amos Boynton, and Thomas King were clearing farm land. In 1820, Orange Township was created, containing both townships 6 and 7. It later became the townships of Solon and Orange. Chagrin Falls was formed from portions of these subdivisions and Geauga County in 1845. It was first called Morensi, and later named Chagrin Falls, originating in an Indian name meaning clear water.

1816

"Cleaveland never would amount to anything because the soil was too poor," observed a visitor, and he moved on toward Newburgh where he spent the night. Indeed, the area from Doan's Corners to the Public Square showed pitiful signs of settlement, according to Captain Lewis Dibble, who declared many years later:

> On leaving Doan's Corners, one would come in a little time to a cleared farm. Then down about where A. P. Winslow now lives (Euclid and E. 71st) a man named Curtis had a tannery. There was only a small clearing, large enough for the tannery and a residence. There was nothing else but woods until Willson avenue was reached, and there a man named Bartlett had a small clearing, on which there was a frame house, the boards running up and down. Following down the line of what is now Euclid avenue, the next sign of civilization was found at what is now Erie street, where a little patch of three or four acres had been cleared, surrounded by a rail fence . . . I don't remember any building between that and the Square, which was already laid out, but covered with bushes and stumps.

Superior Street west of the Square was almost cleared, and teams could travel Euclid Road and part of Ontario Street. Water Street, Union and Vineyard lanes were mere paths. Mandrake Lane, Seneca and Bank streets, Ontario north of the Square, Superior to the east, and Erie, Bond, and Wood streets were still in the woods. Cleveland-Newburgh traffic had created a road out by Ontario Street.

Ashbel W. Walworth was appointed corporation clerk in January, with well-defined orders not to "issue any amount of bills greater than double the amount of the funds in his hands."

On the wooded river bank near the foot of Eagle Street, Levi Johnson had built the schooner *Neptune,* 65 tons, launching it this spring. It later engaged in the fur trade.

The assessed value of Cleveland real estate was $21,065, including the entire plat surveyed in 1796. A tax of one-half of one per cent was laid on all lots in the township.

The first application for divorce was filed this year. From 1820 to 1835, thirty suits were entered, but a large number were settled out of court.

The capital of the State of Ohio was moved from Chillicothe to Columbus.

John S. Strong headed a small party that settled Strongsville Township, No. 5, range 14, in the Western Reserve survey. They represented two influential land owners—Oliver Ellsworth of Connecticut and Governor Caleb Strong of Massachusetts. In March, John Hilliard and his small family took up residence, followed by the Whitney, Haynes, Porter, Gilbert, Nichols, Goodwin, Cole, Avery, Bennett, Hall, and Smith families, early settlers who sought the Strongsville highlands. The first township election was held in 1818. The mill built by Strong in about 1821 was acquired by Cornelius Roy years later, and continued in the family. Ahijah Haynes, Sr., pioneer, built a homestead in 1830 that decade after decade was preserved by his descendants.

Lack of a central bank made it difficult to finance the War of 1812, and the end of the conflict found the country flooded with unsound currency and its financial system in chaos. Despite arguments of unconstitutionality, enough support was secured to charter a new institution for twenty years, and the Second National Bank of the United States was established this year. Cleveland was to have a branch in the proposed new Commercial Bank of Lake Erie.

Leonard Case "wrote a good hand and was a good accountant," and Judge James Kingsbury recommended that he be brought to Cleveland from Warren, Ohio, to be cashier of the new bank. Case came in June, as the first bank in the village was being organized. His salary was $800 annually. He was born in 1786 in Westmoreland County, Pennsylvania, the son of Meshach Case, a poor frontier farmer. His parents brought their large family to Warren Township in 1800. In 1801, Leonard suffered from extreme outdoor exposure leading to an illness that left him a cripple and in pain during his lifetime. This was, however, no handicap to his ambition. He served as confidential clerk to General Simon Perkins, land agent for the Connecticut Land Company in 1807, and studied law in his spare time. During the War of 1812, he collected delinquent taxes. When Case came to Cleveland, he brought a valuable knowledge of the Western Reserve gained in the Warren tax office; and besides serving as cashier of the bank, he practiced law and dealt in real estate.

A fierce blizzard raged in the East, commencing June 17, and people froze to death. On August 30, another heavy storm swept through, and freak weather reigned throughout "the year without a summer." Ohio's frost-bitten crops yielded small return.

There were fifty members in the little Plan of Union church founded by the Presbyterians and Congregationalists in Euclid Township, admitted by a stern session after strict evaluation of past actions, present beliefs, and rigid promises for future conduct. Having outgrown the crude log cabin, a white frame meeting house of New England architecture was erected this year in its place, the first in the county. The Rev. Thomas Barr was pastor until 1820. Ministers from Cleveland supplied the pulpit until 1825, when the Rev. Stephen Peet was ordained. In 1828, the First Presbyterian Society of Euclid (later First Presbyterian Church of East Cleveland) was organized. Staunch leaders of the caliber of the Rev. William H. Beecher, brother of the famed pulpit orator, the Rev. Henry Ward Beecher, guided the congregation through eventful years.

Levi Johnson was soon to have competition, now that Philo Scovill had come to Cleveland. He was the son of Timothy Scoville—who retained the "e," and he had come from his home in Buffalo with his talents of carpenter and joiner. Notwithstanding, he became interested in the drug and grocery business, which proved disappointing and unprofitable. Building a sawmill with Thomas O. Young on Big Creek, near Cleveland's southern limits, was more to his liking; and, once it was operating successfully, he commenced to take building contracts. There was business enough in the growing village for both Johnson and Scovill, and they prospered. Scovill Avenue is a monument to this pioneering family.

Quicksand and storms put an end in a short time to the first pier, built by the Cleveland Pier Company. Leading businessmen headed this pioneer harbor development.

The Commercial Bank of Lake Erie was incorporated by John H. Strong, Samuel Williamson, Philo Taylor, George Wallace, David Long, Erastus Miles, Seth Doan, and Alfred Kelley. It opened for business on August 6 in the parlor of a house at the northeast corner of Superior and Bank streets. Alfred Kelley was president, and Leonard Case, cashier.

Mindful of the need for education of the young, twenty-seven of Cleveland's prominent citizens subscribed almost $200, in amounts ranging from $2.50 to $20, to erect a small school building in a grove of oak trees on St. Clair Street near Bank (Lincoln Hotel site). It was a typical early-day school, "one story, the size about 24 by 30, chimney at one end, door at the corner near the chimney, the six windows of twelve lights each placed high; it being an old notion that children should not look out to see anything." This was Cleveland's first schoolhouse.

A two-acre parcel, sublot 84, at the southwest corner of the Public Square (portion of the Higbee store site) was purchased by Samuel Huntington for $1.12. In 1819, it was sold for $45; and on September 21 of the same year, the purchase price was $300. The property changed hands again in 1834 for $630.

Carter's warehouse had been undermined and washed away by high waters, and at about this time Leonard Case and Captain William Gaylord built the first frame warehouse in Cleveland, a little north of St. Clair Street on the river. Dr. David Long and Levi Johnson built another in the neighborhood "not long afterwards," and John Blair erected still another. Commerce was growing steadily.

Daniel Kelley was appointed postmaster on October 22, and at the same time served as president of the village.

Rufus Wright paid Gideon Granger $300 for three-quarters of an acre of land on the west bank of Rocky River (Westlake Hotel site). Here he built a large frame tavern from stout timbers cut from the thick woodland. The twin-gabled, squat structure with its wide porch was a welcome resting place for travelers for decades, and the location served hotel purposes continuously through the years.

Despite the claim that there were but two Christians in Cleveland, devout religious effort manifested itself this year. The house of Phineas Shepherd, west of the river, was selected as the meeting place on November 9 "for the purpose of nominating officers for a Protestant Episcopal Church" in Cleveland. Timothy Doan was chosen moderator, and Charles Gear, clerk; wardens elected were Phineas Shepherd and Abraham Scott; Timothy Doan, Abram Hickox, and Jonathan Pelton, vestrymen; Dennis Cooper, reading clerk. The meeting adjourned "till Easter Monday next." This congregation became known as Trinity Parish of Cleveland, one of the earliest Episcopal churches organized west of the Alleghenies.

1817

Cleveland's trustees voted on January 13 to assume an interest in the new school building on St. Clair Street, declaring that the subscribers should be

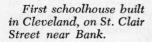

First schoolhouse built in Cleveland, on St. Clair Street near Bank.

refunded their money from "the treasury of the corporation at the end of three years from and after the 13th of June, 1817." The village thus became the sole owner of its first schoolhouse, and at the same time manifested a glimmer of interest in the importance of education. Admission, however, was not "free, except to a few who were too poor to pay tuition. The town gave the rent of the house to such teachers as were deemed qualified, subjecting them to very few conditions. They were left to manage the school in all respects just as they pleased. It was, in short, a private and not a public school." Unmarried men of the village were compelled to pay the tuition of the poor, which was considered an equitable arrangement. Religious services were held in the schoolhouse regularly, "Judge Kelley offering prayer, a young man read the sermon, and my mother led the singing," related George B. Merwin in *Recollections*.

Cleveland was having trouble making ends meet, and additional revenue was sought by taxing every horse in the township 50 cents, and every head of horned cattle 25 cents. Those persons likely to become a burden on the community were notified to leave town. Solving the problem of poor relief was as simple as that at the time.

An unstable money market prevailed, and small change became so scarce in Cleveland that the trustees issued corporation scrip or "shinplasters" to the amount of $100, and running in value from 6¼ cents to 50 cents. These due bills, intended to relieve the situation, were pressed into use for personal obligations, as well, leading to much confusion. Silver dollars were cut into nine pieces and half dollars into five, each passing for a shilling; and a Spanish peseta, worth 18¾ cents, went also for a shilling. The Commercial Bank of Lake Erie was unable to withstand the troubled times, and it failed in 1820. The village felt the blow for years.

At a vestry meeting held on March 2 in the Court House, a congregation called "Trinity Parish of Cleaveland, Ohio" was formed, and it was resolved that the persons present were attached to the Protestant Episcopal Church of the United States. Those present at the meeting held on November 9, 1816, were declared in attendance officially, together with John Wilcox, Alfred Kelley, Irad Kelley, Thomas M. Kelley, Noble H. Merwin, David Long, D. C. Henderson, Philo Scovill, the Rev. Roger Searle—or Searl—of Plymouth, Connecticut, and others. The little congregation could not afford to pay a minister for the first few years, and the services were conducted by laymen at the Court House, the schoolhouse, or members' homes. In the spring, Rev. Searle reported that the infant parish represented thirteen families and eleven communicants.

Job Doan replaced his father's log tavern at Doan's Corners (Fenway Hall site) with a new structure. It was cut in two, years later, and moved to Cedar Avenue, east of East 100th Street, where after more than a century it was still serving as a residence.

One of Cleveland's earliest industrial products was the burr millstone, quarried in the Mill Creek area around Newburgh and cut by Abel R. Garlick on Bank Street. Millstones were soon shipped in quantities.

In the summer, Alfred Kelley and his bride left Lowville, New York, where they were married, in a new carriage that he had purchased in Albany. Setting out for Cleveland, they found traveling difficult upon reaching Buffalo. As the schooner lying at anchor was not ready to sail, they took a side trip to Niagara Falls, returning to find that the vessel had caught a favorable breeze and was on her way. Getting back in the rig, they started on the seven-day journey. Sometimes the newlyweds had to walk, but they finally reached their new home—ahead of the schooner! This was the first carriage in Cleveland. It set a pace for ambitious citizens, and was in great demand at public functions.

Leonard Case and Elizabeth Gaylord were married at the home of her brother-in-law, Captain William Stowe in Portage County on September 28. Case borrowed Alfred Kelley's carriage to bring his bride to Cleveland. Until 1826 they lived in a frame house at Bank and Superior streets, which also housed the Commercial Bank of Lake Erie. Then they moved to their new home at the northeast corner of Superior and the Square, which also served as Case's business headquarters.

When Irad Kelley became postmaster on December 31, he moved the Post Office to his brick store on the south side of Superior Street opposite Bank. Receipts for the year amounted to $500, and the postmaster retained one-fourth as compensation and expense for rent, fuel, and clerk hire. The privilege of franking letters was considered a valuable asset to the chief of the office. Postage was never less than five cents, and twenty-five cents was charged for distances beyond 300 miles.

1818

The Commercial Coffee House on the north side of Superior Street, west of the Square, was the depot for the rumbling Conestoga wagons that labored from Pennsylvania into Cleveland loaded with nails, iron, and heavy freight, and drawn by four- to eight-horse teams. The arrival of a fleet of the brightly painted land frigates was the signal for the community to assemble and get a glimpse of the latest shipments from the East. The drivers were professionals, receiving large salaries and dressing in furs and fine clothing. Their horses were geared with heavy harness, trimmed with bells, fur, and gleaming brass. The name Conestoga, or "stogie," also identified the strong black cigars, a foot in length to provide the drivers with a long, steady smoke as they pushed their teams overland.

Some of Cleveland's taverns afforded space for business purposes, at the same time catering to transient guests. They were considered as landmarks in the location of homes and commercial institutions.

In bitter February, Ahimaaz Sherwin left Middlebury, Vermont, with his wife and baby daughter in a large sleigh drawn by two farm horses, bound for the western frontier. Taverns were widely scattered, and for ten days the temperature was below zero. From Buffalo, they journeyed on the frozen lake, breaking through the ice near Dunkirk. On the eighteenth day, they reached Job Doan's tavern, at Euclid and Doan streets, where they found warmth and rest. Sherwin purchased 15 acres of land on Euclid (at East 96th). Here he built a humble home, and his parents from Vermont joined the family. In about 1820, he moved to Cleveland and established a carpenter shop at his residence. He was one of Cleveland's pioneer builders.

The record speaks for Ara Sprague, who relates his impressions of Cleveland upon his arrival in April:

> I arrived a few weeks after the first census—of the village—had been taken. Its population was, at that time, but one hundred and seventy-two souls; all poor, and struggling hard to keep soul and body together. Small change was very scarce. They used what were called "corporation shinplasters" as a substitute. The inhabitants were mostly New England people, and seemed to be living in a wilderness of scrub oaks. Only thirty or forty acres had

been cleared. Most of the occupied town lots were fenced with rails. There were three warehouses on the river; however, very little commercial business was done, as there was no harbor at that time. All freight and passengers were landed on the beach by lighter and smaller boats. To get freight to the warehouses, which were a quarter of a mile from the beach, we had to roll it over the sand.

Faced with this menace to shipping progress, the villagers petitioned Congress for channel improvements, but without avail.

There were three practicing physicians in the village, with the arrival of Dr. Israel Town. Later he opened a drug store, and announced free professional service to prospective patients who purchased their medical requirements from him.

A circuit-riding Methodist preacher, who traveled northern Ohio, gathered together eight followers west of the river—Seth Brainard, Moses Fish, William Brainard, Ebenezer Fish, and their wives, and organized the first Methodist Church society (later Brooklyn Memorial Methodist Church) in May. The log town hall (West 25th and Denison) was their place of worship. A class formed in Newburgh this year did not survive. Then members formed a class at Euclid Creek three years later. In 1822, itinerant ministers began preaching in Cleveland.

Brooklyn Township was organized on June 1, embracing territory west of the river, excepting a farm owned by Alfred Kelley. This area later became Ohio City, West Cleveland, early Brooklyn Village, Brighton (South Brooklyn), Linndale, Brooklyn Heights, Brooklyn Village, and Lakewood. The first four were ultimately annexed to Cleveland, the others continuing to exist as independent municipalities. Corn was a principal product, and the name Egypt was proposed; but agreement finally settled on Brooklyn.

Dorcas Hickox, sister of Abram Hickox, Cleveland's blacksmith, taught the first school in Brooklyn during the summer in the house of James Fish. A log schoolhouse was later built on David Brainard's farm.

Mars Wagar, a student of Latin and Greek and a skilled writer, also had a background of mathematics and surveying. He was influenced to settle in Avon this year, and two years later he purchased 160 acres on Detroit Street (east of Warren Road) for $7 an acre. Later he bought 111 acres on the west of his tract, and acquired 12 acres (along Belle Avenue) in trade for a yoke of oxen valued at $84. (The third Wagar homestead was razed to make way for the Bailey Company store, Detroit Avenue and Warren Road.) Mars and Wagar avenues in Lakewood perpetuated the pioneer's name.

The burden of taxes rested heavily on the citizens, as assessments were levied for road, poor relief, corporation, and state purposes. Tax gatherers, it was affirmed, handled all the currency of the country.

The first recorded ordinance, enacted in June, provided that "if any person shall shoot or discharge any gun or pistol within said village, such person so offending shall, upon conviction, be fined in any sum not exceeding five dollars, nor under fifty cents, for the use of the said village."

On July 4, liberty-loving Americans saluted their new flag, authorized by

Congress, with thirteen horizontal stripes and a union of twenty stars. Henceforth, a new star was to be added for every new state.

Twenty-one boats entered or cleared the Cleveland port for Buffalo and Detroit during the week of July 8-13. Cargoes consisted of household furniture, stoneware, salt, groceries, dry goods, whisky, livestock, pork, flour, butter, grindstones, and tallow.

Cleveland's story of growth and promise had reached beyond the Atlantic; and when the schooner *American Eagle* arrived from Buffalo on July 22, it brought "six families of Irish, forty-seven passengers, three months from Ireland." The steady stream of foreign-born that followed exerted a lasting influence on the character and development of their new home.

The first newspaper, *The Cleaveland Gazette and Commercial Register,* a weekly and rarely on time, was published in a small structure on the north side of Superior just west of Public Square (220 Superior, N.W.). The editor, publisher, and entire staff was Andrew Logan of Beaver, Pennsylvania, who brought a well-worn hand press and type with him by wagon. The first issue appeared on July 31, a four-page, four-column paper that sold for two dollars per year, if paid in advance, or three dollars otherwise. Headlines screamed "Shocking Murder" and "The Sea Serpent Again!" A featured quotation was Paine's "Where liberty dwells, there is my country." Editor Logan's first editorial characterized his consuming passion for liberty "as laid down by the Declaration of Independence and secured by the Constitution, and the sovereignty of the people." News of struggles against tyranny in Mexico, South America, and Spain was given great prominence; and domestic news centered in an attack on the United States Bank, recently chartered and viciously opposed by the paper, the building of the Erie Canal, and the invasion of Florida. The name of the paper was soon condensed to *Cleaveland Register.* In March, 1820, the brave little publication succumbed to its competitor and the paper shortage. The plant was advertised for sale, and Logan became the first village inspector, operating the new hay scales.

Richard and Samuel Lord and Josiah Barber, of the firm of Lord & Barber, realtors, came to Brooklyn this year. Barber built his pioneer home on a bluff overlooking the river valley, the high, steep banks of Cleveland, Newburgh, and Brooklyn rising around it. Later a brick dwelling replaced the log house. Barber Avenue was named for this west-side leader.

General stores had sprung up in a surprising number, engaging in friendly competition. As there was practically no money in circulation, country produce was accepted by the merchants in payment for goods. Elisha Taylor moved into his new store opposite the Commercial Coffee House in December, and offered a typical line of goods for sale: groceries, dry goods, paints, dyestuffs, drugs and medicine, crockery, glass, and chinaware.

Price French had purchased 50 acres of forest-land in Rockport, from the Connecticut Land Company (north of Detroit Avenue, Lakewood), and to this wilderness he brought his wife and six children. At the conclusion of the War of 1812, in which he served as captain, his older brother, Lord French of England, died; but Price French frowned on the title and remained at the western frontier. French Avenue was named for him.

Leonard Case advertised 90 acres of land in Warrensville for cash, salt, flour, whisky, wheat, or rye. This notice characterized the trade of the times.

A regular stage line commenced operation on August 11, leaving Cleveland every Thursday for Chagrin (Willoughby), Mentor, and Painesville. The eighteen-hour trip included putting up for the night at Chagrin. The public was urged to ride the springless wagon with its plain board seats, and, after all, the *Register* declared, the canvas-topped mail coach afforded greater comfort than horseback. When the traveler climbed aboard, he reached for a leather strap fastened to the side of the coach that was standard equipment. With his life in the balance, he hung on, as the stage swayed and jostled mile after mile in the dust or mud; there was always one or the other. Strap-hanging was the style long before the advent of streetcars.

Clevelanders lined the bluff overlooking the lake and crowded along the bank of the river as the *Walk-in-the-Water* entered the port on August 25. The elegant little steamer, the first on Lake Erie, was named for an Indian chief who had served with the Americans after the War of 1812, and helped

The Walk-in-the-Water, first steamboat on Lake Erie.

to make the boilers for his namesake at Black Rock (near Buffalo). This was her maiden voyage from Black Rock to Detroit, a trip that required nine or ten days. She traveled at from eight to ten miles an hour, and accommodated 100 cabin passengers with a large number in the steerage. Tonnage is variously reported at from 240 to 342. As the sidewheeler approached, a field piece fired a salute from the shore. After a cheer for Captain Job Fish and his crew, a group of the populace were permitted to go aboard. The fare from Black Rock to Cleveland, including board, was $10. The proud vessel was driven ashore near Buffalo in November, 1821, and wrecked.

In the morning, citizens assembled near the Commercial Coffee House on September 18 to learn why "all the strangers were in town." It developed that a meeting had been called to select a slate of candidates in the coming elections. Some of the thirty-six delegates—two from each town in the county—had brought women and children to shop, and the stores were thriving on the "rushing business." At the political pow-wow in the Coffee House, Elias Lee was chairman of the meeting, and the following candidates were recommended for office: Ethan A. Brown for governor; General Peter Hitchcock for congressman; John Campbell for state senator, and Philo

Taylor for sheriff. In this small assembly, Cleveland's great convention business had its beginning.

A supplementary treaty with the Wyandot, Shawnee, Seneca, and Ottawa tribes, effected October 17, permitted the Indians to hold as reserves about 160 sections of land, with an addition to their annuities of $3,500. All claims to the fee of the lands reserved to them were relinquished. The tract of Ohio land to which the Indian title was extinguished by the treaty amounted to about 6,000,000 acres.

The newspaper of November 10 mentioned a stage performance, the *Theater Royal*, at the Shakespeare Gallery, No. 1 Superior Street, once a week, admission $1. This was a high price in the period of hard times.

Eager to raise bigger and better crops, enterprising farmers met at the home of James Hillman in Warren on December 22 to organize the first Agricultural Society in the Western Reserve. Three years later a "Cattle Show and Fair" was held in the vicinity of Warren. It opened with "a plowing match," and included horse races.

The popular sport with the men was hunting, and large numbers turned out, particularly for the big holiday hunt. Three hundred took part in an event at Chagrin (Willoughby) that netted two elk, seventy-five deer, twenty-three bears, seventeen wolves, and ten turkeys.

This year witnessed the arrival in Cleveland of Reuben Wood, Vermont lawyer, who was to experience a distinguished career at the bar and in public office; Ahaz Merchant, surveyor and engineer, who laid out the most important allotments in what was to become Ohio City, a portion of Brooklyn Township; Orlando Cutter, who opened a store with a $20,000 stock of merchandise—a big store in those days; Samuel Cowles, businessman and attorney; Levi Sargent—or Sargeant—with his family that included his young son, John H., who was to gain prominence as a civil engineer and railroad builder.

1819

Farming was the principal occupation around Cleveland, and the soil yielded good corn, grains, and produce. Invention of labor-saving machinery was encouraged, the latest equipment being a machine that operated 20 flails, threshed 100 sheaves an hour and was worked by a horse. The cost of a cow and her year's "keeping" was estimated at $33; and a four-year-old stray horse, a natural trotter, was valued at $18.

· Rockport Township, created on February 24, was bounded by Brooklyn Township on the east, Middleburgh Township on the south, Dover Township on the west, and the lake on the north. Colonel O. J. Hodge, historian, relates that as the first election day approached, the outcome was pretty well determined. The candidates played safe, however, and provided a jug of free whisky. The spirits produced an unanimous victory, and until 1827 the "jug ticket" won. Then Datus Kelley staged a one-man temperance campaign that abolished the practice.

Court week opened on May 18, and the village was entertained with a wax museum in the ballroom of the Navy House operated by Dr. Donald McIntosh. Featured were Washington, founder of the Republic; Monroe, the President; Commodore Decatur; an Indian warrior; and a Baltimore belle. Admission 25 cents, and half price for children.

The *Savannah,* first American steamboat to cross the Atlantic, left Savannah on May 22 and reached Liverpool June 20 on her historic voyage. River men were laying plans for finer Cleveland-built vessels that would some day travel the trade routes of the world.

Transportation charges were high for eastern goods, and there was antagonism toward foreign products. This resulted in a newspaper campaign to encourage home industries. It was not until a decade later, however, that manufacturing had its start. Community needs were supplied by the journeyman and apprentice form of labor.

The Erie Canal was on the way to reality, and the subject of canals for Ohio dominated conversation and politics. The entire state was stirred, and the next year the Legislature authorized the appointment of commissioners with power to employ technical assistance to study the practicability of the canal project and make surveys. Benjamin Tappan, Alfred Kelley of Cleveland, Thomas Worthington, Ethan A. Brown, Jeremiah Morrow, Isaac Minor, and Ebenezer Buckingham were appointed in 1822. Kelley was a firm believer in the inland waterway, and gave his best years and his brilliant efforts to the cause.

State authority was exercised in local affairs, and prohibited the sale of more than 50 cents worth of liquor "to any resident of the county where a tavern is kept or within ten miles of it." Tavern keepers faced a fine of $50 and suspension of license for four months if there was rioting, revelling, or drunkenness. Peace-loving citizens welcomed the laws that would "secure the slumbers of the sober part of the community from the din and vociferations of the midnight fry," a local paper stated.

Leather was Joel Scranton's stock in trade when he came to Cleveland this year; and his schooner-load of the highly essential commodity was the basis of his fortune. Scranton was a man of wisdom and keen merchandising ability. He purchased the "Scranton Flats," west of the river, and Scranton Road bears his name.

With $3 in his pocket, John Blair, new arrival from Maryland, speculated in pork. He was lucky, and soon opened a produce and commission business on the river. Building a warehouse this year, he competed with Giddings and Merwin in the purchase of wheat.

The "dandy" of the day dressed himself according to strict propriety. His hat brim was six inches wide, and a green or black ribbon was the style. The coat buttoned under the chin, had no pockets, sleeves hid the fingers, and any color was correct, excepting drab. The white or black vest was two inches longer than the coat, showing a strip in front when the coat was buttoned. A white-cambric or black-silk cravat was proper. Pantaloons, cut cossack or meal-sack pattern, reached within eight inches of the ankle, hanging in folds from the hips. Short boots laced before, and a watch chain of gold, black ribbon, or braided hair completed the costume.

The Sunday School movement had spread beyond the mountains, and in June, the first religious school was formed. Elisha Taylor, of the Plan of Union Church in Euclid (East Cleveland), was the superintendent, and Moses White, a Baptist layman, served as secretary. For some time, about forty pupils attended. This pioneer organization developed into the First Presbyterian Church of Cleveland (Old Stone Church).

Presbyterian missionaries organized a church in Brooklyn under the Plan of Union principle on July 25 with six members: Amos Brainard, Isaac Hinckley and wife, James Smith and wife, and Rebecca Brainard. The Revs. William McLean and S. J. Bradstreet of the First Presbyterian Church of Cleveland first served in the pulpit. Records reveal stern discipline of church officers in the forties. A deacon and his wife were expelled from the church for their belief in "universal salvation." Another deacon was admonished because of "rumors" that he used "very profane language." A good anti-slavery resolution forbidding invitation of a slave-holder to the pulpit and refusing a welcome to him at the Communion table was lost in debate. Years of hardship marked the first four decades of the church's "Presbygational" existence, when meetings were held in the town house and in homes of the community. Although fostered by the Presbyterians, it was incorporated as the First Congregational Society of Brooklyn (later Archwood Congregational Church); a Congregational meeting was recorded in early March, 1831. Official union with the Cleveland Congregationalists did not come, however, until 1867.

The first issue of the *Cleaveland Herald*, with the "a" in the masthead, appeared on October 19 without a single subscriber. Eber—or Eben—D. Howe encountered many difficulties in publishing his new paper in the Z. Willes & Company plant that had been moved from Erie to Cleveland on Superior Street. Mails were carried on horseback weekly from Buffalo, Pittsburgh, Columbus, and Sandusky. Printing paper was brought by wagon from Pittsburgh, sometimes arriving too late for publication deadlines. In two years, the subscription list had grown to 300, scattered over the Western Reserve, except Trumbull County. Howe traveled 30 miles on horseback between Cleveland and Painesville, delivering the weekly in all kinds of weather, and with his tin horn announced the arrival of the latest news—usually 40 "news" days from Europe and ten days from New York. After two years, he left the *Herald* and moved to Painesville, where he established the *Telegraph*. Cleveland's second newspaper claimed to be independent of politics, but in 1832 it favored Democracy or "Jacksonianism," causing displeasure among the Cleveland Whigs. The *Herald* became a daily in 1835 and supported the Whigs. In 1819, Ohio had thirty-three papers, located in the most populous districts.

Noble H. Merwin, Nathan Perry, and William Gaylord were appointed on November 22 to study ways and means for strict enforcement of an act requiring inspection of wheat and rye flour, buckwheat meal, Indian corn, biscuit, butter, hogs, lard, pork, and beef. Flagrant violations must be penalized, they declared.

CHAPTER 5

Beginning of Canal Commerce
1820–1829

DESPITE roads of "extreme badness," frontiersmen continued to make their way laboriously to the Western Reserve, where the ring of the ax echoed through the timberland, and self-reliance and resourcefulness were man's greatest assets.

Cleveland was emerging from the log-cabin stage. Houses were small structures, for the most part, with an occasional brick dwelling, located between Superior and Lake streets and Ontario and the river. Commerce and industry had not yet provided the wealth that made possible fine residences such as were found in other parts of the Reserve. Stumps dominated the Public Square, and forests rimmed it to the east. Euclid Street was a narrow thoroughfare through the woods, and only a few streets were entirely cleared. Yet an enthusiastic observer described it as "a pretty place nested upon a high bluff." Land in the "Flats" brought $7 per acre. Indians lived along the river.

In 1820, the village ranked fourteenth in the Western Reserve, with a population of 606, according to the United States census. The metropolis of Ohio was Cincinnati, numbering 9,642; Chillicothe was second with 2,426; and Zanesville, third, with 2,052. Detroit had reached 1,422, and Youngstown was not far behind, having just passed the thousand mark; Washington, 13,247; Philadelphia, 63,802; and New York, 123,706. Ohio's population was 581,434, and that of Cuyahoga County, 6,328.

The little Cleveland community was making some progress despite retarding economic influences. Trading was difficult, due to the great variety of paper money in circulation and the constant change in value. It was not unusual to see a man leave for market with a cow, and return with bartered purchases ranging from cast iron, salt, and utensils to whisky. Swindlers flourished by counterfeiting and issuing notes on non-existent banks. Lists of delinquent taxes in the newspaper reflected hard times and tragic failures.

Canal commerce was inaugurated in the middle of the decade, when the Erie Canal opened in New York State, and its many benefits in facilitating trade soon inspired a feverish demand for waterways in Ohio. The success of the Ohio Canal stands as a monument to the foresight and ability of Alfred Kelley, who was instrumental in selecting Cleveland as the northern terminus. This new form of inland transportation had inched its way toward Newark as the decade closed. New markets were being opened, increasing wealth, broadening sectional feeling, and starting Cleveland on its way to future greatness.

Thousands of workers were employed in building the Ohio Canal, and, as Cleveland grew, so did its problems of government and welfare. Irish and Germans had begun to crowd into the village, many of them political refugees from abroad, bringing strange languages and customs along with the best learning and culture the homeland had to offer. Near the river mouth on the West Side the Irish settled, while the Germans located on Superior and Garden streets and along Lorain Street west of the river. Wages were low, averaging about $8 for twenty-six "dry" working days.

The Ohio Canal followed the east side of the Cuyahoga Valley as it approached Cleveland, terminating at the river, where docks and warehouses had already been established. This valley, known as the "Flats," was Cleveland's cradle of industry, forming a natural dividing line between the eastern and western highlands. Farms flourished on the heights, residential districts developed, and business and commerce gained a foothold. Deep ravines and gullies formed the physical boundaries between the early communities. Kingsbury Run was the line between early Cleveland and Newburgh. Big Creek Valley became the boundary between Cleveland and Brooklyn on the west, and later Doan Brook would separate Cleveland and Glenville. Highways followed the ridges, and the ravines would become the routes of railroads.

As Cleveland gathered industrial strength, a campaign was launched to attract new industries. It advertised steam power at "trifling expense," power from the canal for mill purposes, and an "abundance" of iron ore. "No safer nor more profitable investment of capital" could be found. The twenties saw the establishment of primitive plants for making axes and tools, French burr millstones, hats, castor oil, gilt and mahogany-framed looking glasses, lumber, tin, sheet and iron products, chairs, guns, and castings.

Super-selling was required to dispose of the first load of coal brought to Cleveland. Wood was plentiful and cheap, and finicky housewives refused to use the dirty, black fuel; but industry found it superior, and soon coal was firing the foundries and steamboats that broadened the lines of the lake city's commerce and trade. Realizing the potential importance of Cleveland's strategic location as a shipping center by lake and by canal, harbor improvements were undertaken, and the first steamboat was launched.

Local merchants were now handling products of sister cities, and profiting by lower prices and shorter distances. From Pittsburgh came printers' supplies and glass; from Cincinnati, pottery; from Steubenville, fine-quality woolens, and iron came from the Canton and Youngstown area.

A mushroom growth had begun to develop as canal-building progressed. The tavern bowed to a new hotel. Merchants did a thriving business in goods and wares shipped from the East to the new frontier market. As the population grew, Cleveland boundaries were extended and court facilities were enlarged. Fire protection was inaugurated, and a public market was established.

The authorities, however, were not prepared for the rising tide of opportunity seekers that were arriving by all manner of transportation; and as the decade closed, they were already confronted with serious problems of health, housing, and management.

Among the newcomers during this period were John W. Willey, John W. Allen, and Sherlock J. Andrews, lawyers who gave distinguished public service; and Peter M. Weddell, Richard Hilliard, and Richard Winslow, influential businessmen. They were men of unusual ability, whose wise leadership guided the community through years of economic chaos and unhealthy growth. With the coming of Harvey Rice, education had a champion not only in Cleveland but throughout the State.

A few cultural institutions had taken root in Cleveland, and the citizens were manifesting greater interest in private schools. Forums and debates on topics of the times provided inspiring and valuable means of entertainment and enlightenment.

Prosperity brought with it increased worldliness, and followers of the faith raised their voices against the curse of whisky and in defense of the enslaved. Trinity, Cleveland's first house of worship, was built by the Episcopalians. Other denominations, weak in numbers, threaded their way to meeting, in log cabin or public hall, by oxcart or horseback. In Hudson, Ohio, staunch Presbyterians and Congregationalists had founded a new institution that was to be guided by "the four basic controlling ideas of religion, morality, law observance, and education." Here Western Reserve University had its beginning.

The regions from which Cleveland's early settlers came are revealed by Mrs. Gertrude VanRensselaer Wickham in *Pioneer Families of Cleveland*. Slightly over half had a New England background; one-third were directly from Connecticut, and one-third from New York and Pennsylvania. Many families in other parts of the Reserve came from Connecticut. Dr. Frederick C. Waite characterized the times by "trinitarian congregationalism in religion, democracy in government, agriculture as the major occupation and frugality in personal affairs." Yale College manifested its influence in the services of itinerant missionaries and college instructors for many years.

Near the end of the decade, neighbors raised a sawmill without accident, without disputes, without profanity, and without ardent spirits, a report that was certainly worthy of public print. The desire to lend a hand brought out the community for miles around when there was a house, a barn, or a more pretentious building to be raised. Organized effort cut the timber, erected the scaffolding, and stayed with the job until the last nail was in place. Meantime, the women prepared a feast for the hungry builders, and made the most of the occasion by exchanging bits of gossip. This was a great day for young and old in the building of co-operative enterprise and friendly helpfulness. Together the citizens labored through pestilence in their battle with the wilderness. They were respectful and proud as they joined in displaying their accomplishments at the first fair, held on the Public Square. Cleveland was founded upon unselfish, united effort.

1820

The census of Cleveland showed a population of 606. Compared with the following, it was one of the smallest towns in the Western Reserve: Ashtabula, 929; Austinburg, 720; Brooklyn (Ohio City), 348; Burton, 506; Canfield, 787; Chagrin Falls, 733; Elyria, 174; Euclid, 809; Hudson, 491; Huron, 651; Jefferson, 150; Black River (Lorain), 354; Madison, 931; Newburgh, 756; Norwalk, 579; Painesville, 1,257; Perry, 614; Poland, 990; Ravenna, 418; Sandusky, 243; Tallmadge, 742; Warren, 340; and Youngstown, 1,025.

Dr. Donald McIntosh had purchased Mowrey's Tavern on the Public Square for $4,500, and on January 25 he sold it to Leonard Case. In 1822, Case deeded it to Thomas Hartford for $810. It was known as the Cleveland House or Cleveland Hotel.

Horace Perry was elected president of the village this year. He was succeeded in 1821 by Reuben Wood. Leonard Case served until 1825, when he failed to qualify on his election, and Eleazur Waterman, the recorder, became president ex officio. At this point the record is defective, but it is assumed that Waterman continued to serve until 1828, when poor health forced him to resign. Oirson Cathan, son-in-law of Lorenzo Carter, became president in May of that year; Dr. David Long in 1829; Richard Hilliard, 1830-31; John W. Allen, 1832-35. Twelve votes were cast for Alfred Kelley in 1815; in 1835, Allen received 106, which is a fair indication of village growth.

The Episcopal Church, called Trinity, had been in existence for about two years when the vestry adopted a resolution on Easter-Monday declaring "that it is expedient in future to have the clerical and other public services of the Episcopal Church in Trinity Parish, heretofore located in Cleveland, held in Brooklyn ordinarily, and occasionally in Cleveland and Euclid, as circumstances may seem to require." The majority of the members were residents of Brooklyn.

Men's clothing was colorful, and elaborately tailored, as exemplified by the newspaper description of Joseph Smith, who disappeared in April, on his way to Painesville, where he was to exchange a load of castings for merchandise. Smith wore a light-drab great-coat without a cape, lined with red flannel; a black domestic coat with long skirts and metal buttons; a vest; loose, deep-green pantaloons; thick shoes; and new felt hat. Also missing was his boy, who wore a faded black great-coat; butternut-colored coat; light, striped swansdown vest; blue pantaloons; and fur cap.

Forums and debates emerged in the community. Lively themes provided heated pros and cons, such as "Ought Females of Full Age to have an equal share with Males in the Government of the Nation?," "Is Love a Stronger Passion than Hatred?," and "Do National Manufactures contribute more to the wealth of a Nation than National Commerce?."

Blanchard's visiting troupe of entertainers gave the first professional theatrical performance in Cleveland in Mowrey's Tavern (Hotel Cleveland site) on May 23. The sensational event drew an audience from miles around, and the players performed nightly for a week, their features being *The Purse Won the Benevolent Tar,* and *The Mountaineers.* Admission was the high price of 50 cents, and 25 cents for children.

Herschel Foote opened the Cleaveland Book Store in June, and promptly advertised "a general assortment of books and stationery" to "the inhabitants of the Western Reserve." Book titles related largely to theology, histories of foreign countries, travel in distant lands, and strange phenomena. As was the case with the newspapers, there was nothing relating to the Western Reserve or of local interest. A deal with a publisher or a paper mill may have prompted this advertisement: "Rags! Rags! Two cents per pound, in books, will be given for rags."

Gunfire at sunrise announced the celebration of Independence Day. A procession started from Merwin's Hotel at ten o'clock, led by martial music. Officials, citizens, and strangers participated. At the Court House, the Declaration of Independence was read, and Alfred Kelley delivered an oration that filled four columns of the paper next day. At a banquet in the evening, twenty-three scheduled and ten volunteer toasts were proposed after the cloth was removed. Liberty was precious and inspiring to the pioneers.

Horace J. Hulbert opened the first bindery in Cleveland early in July in the rear of Nathan Perry's store. Here he bound books and periodicals.

The first stage set out for Columbus in the summer, and in the autumn, another line started to Norwalk, inaugurating rapid transit to the south. Wagon lines were established to Pittsburgh and Buffalo in 1821. In bad weather, "The traveler was sure to be called on to go on foot a large portion of the time, and was often expected to shoulder a rail and carry it from mudhole to mudhole to pry out the vehicle in which he was, in theory, supposed to be riding." The mail was soon carried by stage.

In August, trustees enacted legislation to clean up the village. Owners who allowed their swine to run at large were fined $1 to $3; wandering geese rated penalties of not less than fifty cents; cattle permitted to roam during January, February, and March meant $1 fine for each offense. A pound was established for stray animals, with levies for maintenance. Butchering within the village limits was subject to a $50 fine, unless the platform "was kept well washed and cleansed so no unhealthy smell may arise." "Every dog, hound, cur, or spaniel was to be registered with the village recorder." Horse racing, shouting, disorderly conduct, and resisting arrest were outlawed. Strict measures regulated the licensing of public amusements. Fines of from $5 to $15 were to be imposed on householders for each month's delay in providing their fireplaces with adequate "good leather fire bucket" protection. Fire hazards were great in these early days, when practically everything in the home was made of wood, and a spark from a blazing fireplace might easily bring destruction. Fires must be well secured after nine o'clock in the evening under penalty of $50 fine. Juvenile delinquency may have prompted the law which made "all parents, guardians or masters of any child, children, infants or wards punishable for their children's offenses against the village."

With the village "inspector" rested the responsibility of enforcing many of the new laws enacted by the trustees. History is hazy, but Andrew Logan is credited with being the first inspector, and at the same time the operator of the new hay scales.

The village authorities advertised on August 15 that they would receive bids to dig and stone a public well near Bank and Superior streets, the diameter to be ten feet at the bottom and six feet at the top.

Elisha Taylor's Bible class met in the Court House on September 19 and organized the First Presbyterian Church of Cleveland (later Old Stone Church). Signing the charter were Elisha Taylor and his wife Ann, Samuel I. Hamlen, Philip B. Andrews, Mrs. Sophia L. Perry, Mrs. Bertha Johnston, Sophia Walworth, Mrs. Mabel Howe, Henry Baird and his wife Ann, Rebecca Carter, Juliana Long, Isabella Williamson, Harriet Howe, and Robert Baird and his wife Nancy. When the Rev. Randolph Stone was engaged as pulpit supply, fifty-seven men signed the subscription list for his support. The Rev. William McLean came to the pulpit in 1822, followed by the Rev. Stephen J. Bradstreet, who served until 1830. For more than a decade, the congregation, poor in earthly goods but rich in spirit, worshiped in the Court House and in public meeting halls.

A dancing school was opened in October for ladies and gentlemen, with tuition at $5 per quarter.

Fifty feet of land on Superior Street (east of West 9th) was purchased by Timothy Scoville from Nathan Perry for $300. In 1830, Scoville sold it to his son, Philo, for double the figure.

The Isaac Hinckleys in Brooklyn Township had new neighbors this year, when Edwin Foote claimed 640 acres of adjoining land that had been awarded him for surveying the area. Together they controlled a large, fertile tract (north and south of Schaaf Road, from about West 11th Street to the top of Schaaf Road hill) that was gradually reduced to smaller farms. When a German named Schaaf moved into the district (Brookpark and Schaaf roads), the turnpike assumed his name because of the large number of his children who traveled it.

Two runaway slaves, Martin and Sam, had escaped from their owner at Clarksburg, Virginia, and were captured by Joseph Keeler (in Independence), who claimed the $500 reward. While trying to return them, he was arrested at Hudson upon a kidnaping charge and the Negroes were released. On November 6, he was tried in Cleveland before Judge George Tod. Alfred Kelley was prosecuting attorney, and Samuel Cowles and Reuben Wood represented the defense. At the end of the spectacular two-day trial, Keeler was found guilty. This was the first trial of a slave-hunter in Cleveland.

A twenty-eight-page missionary drama entitled *Catherine Brown, the Converted Cherokee* was signed "Written by a Lady," and recognition of Cleveland's first author is lost forever. The pamphlet was printed on the presses of Z. Willes & Company and sold for 12½ cents.

The price of flour was about $2.50 per barrel; wheat, 37 cents per bushel; corn, 25; rye, 31; oats, 18; hay, $6 per ton; beans, 50 cents per bushel; butter, 8 cents per pound; cheese, 6; pork, 3½; beef, 4; sugar, 5; whisky, 20 cents per gallon. Storekeepers accepted pork, whisky, and beeswax in payment of merchandise, with special preference for "ginseng with the curls taken off."

1821

Private subscription schools provided educational opportunities for those who could afford them. State legislation relating to education was confined to the passage of bills authorizing the incorporation of seminaries, religious, and educational organizations, and arranging for the lease of school land. It was not until this year that village and township trustees were authorized to establish public schools by levying taxes. Local taxpayers, however, resisted another burden, and for many years private schools carried the load. There were no citizens of wealth in Cleveland; and the institutions that were established were supported from the modest means of public-spirited pioneers, interested in educational advancement.

The township tax amounted to $86.02.

In his dealings as land agent, Leonard Case was obliged to take over two-acre lot No. 63 (Federal Building site) in settlement of a debt. Reluctantly he paid $266.50 for it. In 1826 he moved his family into the beautiful Case homestead that he had built on the property. In 1856, the Federal Government purchased 199 feet on the Square and 105 feet on Superior Avenue for $30,000 for the site of a Federal Building.

Gypsum, or plaster of paris, was discovered on the government lands bordering Sandusky Bay, and Clevelanders could expect to pay a cheaper price for this essential product.

An election or appointment to public office was equivalent to a draft, and a fine was imposed upon a man who declined to serve. When Peter M. Weddell refused an appointment as overseer of the poor, he was fined $2. Weddell had first come to Cleveland in 1802, a fatherless Kentucky lad of fourteen, used to hardship. He found work in a general store, and five years later became a partner. When the senior partner died, young Peter went to Newark, Ohio, for a time. He married Sophia Perry, daughter of Nathan Perry, Sr., and returning to Cleveland, he opened a store on Superior Street. Keen in business matters, Weddell had a talent for making money, and in 1823 he built a pretentious dwelling and store on the northwest corner of Superior and Bank streets. His mercantile business became one of the largest in Ohio.

A Connecticut citizen, by name Dr. Hand, put his impressions of Cleveland into letters which he wrote to his brother at home. He was particularly impressed with women's dress in the Western Reserve, as shown by his comments:

Caps are little worn by the women except on Sabbaths or other high days, and they are such as worn long ago, as I can remember. As to the bonnets,

I will describe them as well as I can. I have seen three or four imported from New York of the Dunstable kind, and quite in fashion, and as to the rest, they are something like a parson's wig, and it would hardly be considered as idolatry to worship them as they were in the likeness of nothing on earth. The stuff of which they are made is every kind of cloth from silk to flannel. I have just seen one made of yellow flannel quilted and trimmed with fur of muskrat, and it is made to set close to the head answering the purpose of an ordinary skull cap. Some are made of chambray and trimmed with scarlet, crimson, green, or any colored ribbons. Some are white trimmed with any of the vast varieties which can be made by a composition of all of the colors of the rainbow.

Departing from his report on caps and bonnets, the doctor continued:

The gowns worn by women as dress gowns in winter are either light-colored calico, or new domestic flannel of any color which may please the wearer. Crapes, silks, or even bombazetts, are seldom seen on the Reserve, although there are a few which are occasionally worn by the wealthiest people. The dress of misses on gala days is in many instances a yellow flannel frock, with a small ruffle, sometimes of muslin; but more frequently of colored cotton stuff with one of the above described bonnets and a stout pair of cowhide shoes.

Commenting in an offhand manner, Dr. Hand wrote:

The men generally dress in homespun cloth and in many cases appear quite decent on days of exhibition. It is much the custom here to overlay pantaloons on the seat and the inside and front of the legs with sheepskin. A small part of the community, both male and female, dress with some good degree of taste and neatness.

Farmers took pride in their agricultural achievements, some of their produce assuming gigantic proportions, on testimony of the *Herald*. Major E. Taylor grew a radish 3 feet long, 20 inches in greatest circumference, and weighing 11¼ pounds when stripped for market. The largest pumpkin of the season measured 6 feet, 10 inches in circumference, and weighed 131½ pounds. Whether or not these figures are exaggerations, in later years the fertile soil of Cuyahoga County produced the largest and most concentrated greenhouse area in the United States.

1822

"This morning throws us into the year 1822, sans ceremony," announced an editorial in the *Herald* of January 1, "and there is not really felt any hesitancy in entering it with all and singular every token of benevolence that the most unbounded philanthropy can dictate. . . . Our Country has run ahead of her income; acknowledges her financial deficiencies, and has committed her credit to the ordeal of such as have been willing to put it to the test, but she holds high expectations of her future destinies; means to continue steadfast at the watchtower in view of better times, and intends to live to see a return of the golden days of prosperity." Reporting on the latest state legislation, a letter dated in Columbus, December 16, 1821, declared that the bill reducing the pay of members to $2 per day had passed the House; the governor's salary was fixed at $1,000; salaries of the auditor and secretary of state were reduced to $200 each, and the state treasurer's salary to $300. From the column devoted to the "weekly corrected bank-note exchange," it was learned that Pennsylvania banks were all sound; and that there was not a single bank in Ohio whose notes were quoted at par, Ohio bank notes being discounted at from one per cent to as high as 75 per cent. Crowded into the advertising section were the public notices of the few business houses offering their stocks in exchange for cash, pork, flour, whisky, and essential commodities. Local news was pitifully scarce, and in these cramped little ads, weighted with type, was the story of Cleveland's forward march. Having reported the news of the world to its readers, the *Herald* disclosed its poor financial health in a sentimental New Year poem:

> Does the mechanic cease to fret
> Over the long unsettled debt
> Due from the rich delinquent?
> Can printers yet escape from care
> And hope for punctual payment where
> Their labor and their ink went?

Then followed an urgent and realistic appeal to the editor's delinquents: "Wood! Subscribers to this paper who wish to pay in wood must deliver it soon."

Real-estate transactions reveal the meager education of some of the early justices, and their struggle to phrase and spell in keeping the public records. Job Doan, esteemed and a credit to his office, witnessed a deed as follows: "Personly appeared John Gould and his wife, Philinda Gould, she being examing separate and a part from Her Husband. They acknowledg the with in Instrument to be there free act before me at Cleveland This 26th day of Jany, A.D. 1822." Justices were now permitted to draw marriage covenants and perform the nuptial ceremony.

John W. Willey, twenty-five, New Hampshire lawyer, towered head and shoulders in importance above the newcomers to Cleveland this year. He was to become outstanding in his profession, and a leader in municipal, judicial, and legislative affairs.

On Giddings Street there was a private school—a block log house, 15 by 20 feet, with five windows and a six-foot fireplace. George Watkins, son of Timothy Watkins, attended this school. He relates that "We wrote with a goose quill, and every morning the master set our copies and mended our pens. We had school but three months in the winter."

Noble H. Merwin, river man, built and launched the 44-ton schooner *Minerva* at the foot of Superior Street in March. Her chain, fashioned on a Cleveland anvil, was one of the first products of home industry. To test its strength, it was fastened to a butternut tree, and the strain of twelve yoke of oxen parted it. "When she was launched," George B. Merwin relates, "I stood on the heel of her bowsprit, and as she touched the water, christened her, by giving her my mother's name, 'Minerva' and broke a gallon jug of whisky over her bows, as was the custom on similar occasions in those times. She was dispatched to Mackinac, loaded with provisions, for the garrison on that island, and made the round trip in four weeks, which at that time was regarded as a wonderful achievement."

The Cleveland Academy, opened in 1822, stood on St. Clair Street opposite the first schoolhouse.

Ulysses Simpson Grant was born at Point Pleasant on the Ohio River on April 27. He was to become the eighteenth President of the United States.

Noble H. Merwin purchased the Wallace House on June 1, and in its place built a two-story frame tavern with a grand name, the Mansion House, a favorite for twenty years. Fire destroyed it in 1835, when the south side of Superior Street was reduced to ruins.

In June, local merchants inaugurated a price war that lasted through the year. Nathan Perry fired the opening gun with an advertisement of new goods from New York offered on "better terms." Orlando Cutter purchased large space to herald "New Goods" of as good quality and equally cheap. The battle went on for months. Cutter failed to survive the price-cutting campaign, and sold out the following spring.

The Cleveland Academy opened on June 26 on the north side of St. Clair Street, nearly opposite the first schoolhouse, under the direction of the Rev. William McLean. His prices per twelve-week term were: Reading, spelling, and writing, $1.75; grammar and geography, $1 additional; Greek, Latin, and the higher mathematics for a grand total of $4. The brick building was about 45 by 25 feet, and had a handsome spire. Two schoolrooms occupied the lower story of the little building with its proud bell tower, and the upper floor was used for religious services, lectures, and public purposes.

Wolves roamed the neighboring forests and preyed upon farmers' stock. To encourage extermination, the Legislature offered a bounty of $3 for the scalp of a grown wolf, and $1.50 for each scalp of animals under six months.

Isaac Warren, an original stockholder in the Connecticut Land Company, settled this year in Rockport Township on the land he had purchased (Warren Road and Madison Avenue, Lakewood). In 1824, Warren Road was laid out.

At about this time, Ralph Russell, Warrensville farmer, established a Shaker colony, known as North Union (in Shaker Heights), after having become a follower when he visited the sect near Warren. In its most prosperous days, from 1840 to 1858, the Cleveland society numbered about two hundred, and owned approximately 1,400 acres of land. They were a respected, energetic, peaceful people, and farmers came from miles around to have their grain ground in the Shaker mills. The Shakers' establishments included a grist-mill, a sawmill, a woolen factory, a woodenware works, a tannery, a linseed-oil mill, and a broom factory. In *This Cleveland of Ours,* Wilfred H. Alburn gives a comprehensive story of the Shakers.

Rutherford Birchard Hayes, born at Delaware, Ohio, on October 4, became the nineteenth President of the United States.

A reward of $30 was announced by Seth Doan, Cleveland sheriff, for the apprehension of Stockwell S. Hillibert, who escaped from the county jail in the little log Court House on the Public Square. The fugitive, who had been awaiting trial for passing counterfeit money, was arrested in December in New York State.

One of the early newspapers in the Western Reserve was the *Sandusky Clarion* (later *Sandusky Register-Star-News*), founded this year, edited and published by David R. Campbell. It became a daily in 1848, and was a charter member of the Associated Press.

The new lower bridge across the Cuyahoga River was completed this year, a "free bridge," of sturdy whitewood timbers. Citizens subscribed to it in labor or in produce—50 cents per bushel for wheat, 25 cents for corn, 25 cents per gallon for whisky, and $7 per thousand feet of lumber. This floating structure could be drawn aside, allowing boats to pass on the river. It was Cleveland's first bridge.

1823

The *Traveler's Guide or Pocket Gazetteer of the United States,* published by Jedidiah Morse, D.D., and Richard Morse, A.M., gave a quick picture of the "capital" town of the Western Reserve: "Cleveland—post town and capital of Cuyahoga County, O., at the mouth of the Cuyahoga River, on Lake Erie, 54 miles N.W. Warren, 150 miles N.E. Columbus, 60 miles E. Sandusky, 180 miles W. Buffalo, 131 miles N.W. Pittsburgh. Population 606 (1820 figures). It has a bank. It is favorably situated for trade and is one of the principal places for embarkation on the lake."

This was the era of road-building. A growing demand for improved public highways resulted in action by the State toward laying out a "free road" from Cleveland to the Ohio River in Columbiana County. The stage-road to the southwest was converted to a turnpike by private interests—one of the best highways in Ohio; and the following year, another state road was laid out, running from Cleveland (along Kinsman) through Warrens-ville and Orange. These wagon and stage roads were primitive indeed, but the traveling public was obliged to use them until the advent of the railroad.

Progress in the East inspired citizens to meet on March 29 at the Court House to establish the Cuyahoga County Agricultural Society. Farmers' prosperity was reflected in the development of Cleveland business generally. Flour had sold for $2.50 per barrel in a slow market not so long before; now it brought from $5 to $5.25 and moved rapidly, principally to Buffalo. The raising of hemp was introduced on farms in the locality.

Leonard Case was responsible for an ordinance regulating the planting of shade trees on village streets, and starting the Forest City on the way to fame. Case was the first auditor of Cuyahoga County. While serving in the State Legislature, he was a champion of the canals, and he drafted the first bill providing for taxation of Ohio lands according to their value.

With the establishment of a paper mill in Brooklyn, the *Herald* purchased a supply and on May 29 printed the publication on the first paper made in the Western Reserve. To have paper so close at hand was a great boon to printers. The *Herald* editor indulged in the making of printing ink on the side, and produced a good quality with local ingredients to sell at 50 cents per pound.

Dutch immigrants erected a distillery for producing gin and brandy, which was followed by a series of breweries and some thirteen tanneries. The first legitimate chemical product was "saleratus"—bicarbonate of soda, a food-leavening agent, and a commercial alkali for soap-making. It was produced from wood ashes by West Side manufacturers.

There was wisdom in Richard Hilliard's decision to abandon school-teaching in New York State and come to Cleveland. Here, as a young merchant in his late twenties, he built up a large dry-goods and grocery business that was profitable, and enabled him to build a brick block on Water Street at the corner of Frankfort. Until his death in 1856, Hilliard was one of Cleveland's leading figures.

Job Doan and associates, acting as "The Society for a Publick Burying Ground in the East Part of Cleaveland near Job Doan's Esqr.," purchased about an acre and a half of land from John F. Strong (northwest corner of Euclid and East 105th) for $40 this year. Stately elms bordered the property, and for many years the north end was used as a cemetery, while the south portion served as a village common. In 1895, a frontage of 118.5 feet on Euclid at the corner was purchased by the Euclid Avenue Congregational Church at a tax sale for $1,021.02. Ten years later, after H. Clark Ford had laboriously cleared the title at considerable expense, the Cleveland Trust Company paid $40,000 for the parcel.

A news item announced that the Christmas sport would be "to expose to the aim of our sharpshooters a few dozen geese, pigs, dunghill fowls, etc. Pigs at 350 feet, 9 cents a shot, dinner for all and spirits at a low rate."

1824

Newspapers carried an advertisement of a commission of the Presbyteries of the Western Reserve, for 60 acres on which to found a college for the education of young men for the ministry, as the Burton Academy did not meet educational requirements. Cleveland passed up the opportunity. Hudson's citizens, however, offered a high, healthful location and subscribed $7,500, while David Hudson, the village founder, gave $2,142 and 160 acres of land for the future home of Western Reserve College (later Adelbert College of Western Reserve University). A charter with broad powers was secured in 1826, and support came largely from the Presbyterian and Congregational churches.

Redistricting of the State took place from time to time until now there were twenty medical units, with Cuyahoga and Medina counties in the nineteenth medical district. From three to five censors were elected in each district to approve applications of those who wished to practice, and to deal with vendors of high-powered patent medicines and cure-alls.

The first convention drawing delegates to Cleveland from outside the county was held in May for the purpose of organizing "qualified physicians and surgeons" of the nineteenth district. Dr. Donald McIntosh, physician and proprietor of the Navy House, is acknowledged as the first Clevelander to influence a convention to meet in the village. Impressed with their welcome, the society returned for most of its sessions until 1832, when it faded from history. Leaders in medical affairs in Cleveland were Drs. David Long, N. H. Manter, George W. Card, Bela B. Clark, and John M. Henderson. Dr. McIntosh lost his life when thrown from a racing horse in 1834.

Levi Johnson and the Turhooven brothers launched the *Enterprise*, about 220 tons, the first steamboat built in Cleveland, just below the foot of St. Clair Street. The vessel carried merchandise from Buffalo to Cleveland and lake towns. Johnson's lake experience gained during the War of 1812, led to realization of the need for improved facilities. Primitive craft, joined with wooden pins, did not meet the demands of increasing lake commerce. There was great need for shipbuilders and caulkers as the new industry kept pace with the city's trade expansion.

Harvey Rice of Massachusetts, twenty-four-year-old graduate of Williams

College, was a poor boy who worked his way through school. He and his traveling companion were rowed into Cleveland from a sailing vessel on September 24, and landed at the foot of Union Lane at midnight. Shouldering their trunks, they groped their way in the darkness to Spangler's tavern, where they lodged. "Entering the bar room, which was lighted by a solitary candle," Rice relates, "we stumbled over several teamsters who lay fast asleep on the floor laboriously engaged in complimenting the landlord with a nasal serenade. This was the first musical concert that I attended in Cleveland." In the morning, Rice spent a half hour surveying the Public Square, "begemmed with stumps" with here and there a house nestled among the trees around it. Then he traveled down St. Clair Street to the Academy. The next day he was appointed principal and teacher of classics. Chemistry and natural and moral philosophy were added to the course of study, and "vulgar arithmetic" continued to be taught. Rice abandoned teaching in 1826 for the law profession, and through his pioneering educational plans he became known as the father of Ohio's free public schools.

Rufus and Jane Pratt Dunham, of Mansfield, Massachusetts, purchased 13¾ acres of land facing Euclid Road for $147, and here they built their log home (Dunham Tavern site).

At the northeast corner of a 100-acre lot, wooded and extending to the lake, Nathan Perry, Jr., built the Perry House (the center portion of the historic house at 2157 Euclid Avenue, with its quaint porch, entrance, and cupola. As the family grew, it expanded with their needs.). Here the Indians brought furs to Perry, often spending the night bundled in blankets before his friendly fire. Traveling musicians were his guests, and from a balcony they played for the famous Cleveland parties.

1825

The Cuyahoga River emptied into the lake at a point west of what later became the harbor entrance. A low sandbar ran out from the eastern shore of the lake, and the depth of the water at the river mouth was only 3 or 4 feet; but after crossing the bar, the depth was 15 feet. By an Act of Congress passed on March 3, $5,000 was appropriated for the building of a pier at Cleveland as a solution to the navigation problem; but the 600-foot-long jetty brought no relief, as sand continued to fill in as rapidly as before. In 1827, an additional $10,000 was provided, and a new and more direct channel was opened at a point where a bend of the river carried it near to the lake shore. A dam was built across the river, opposite the south end of the experimental pier. When high water came, men with spades and teams with scrapers dug a trench across the isthmus from the river to the lake. With the first break in the outlet, the force of the water came into play and the work was about done. An eastern pier, built parallel to the first, increased the velocity of the current and scoured away the bar. Through the river-straightening process, 8 acres of Cleveland—part of the

Carter farm—were thrown into what became Ohio City. This old river bed was rich in soil, rushes, bullfrogs, and game. By 1840, $75,000 had been used in harbor improvement to good advantage.

Asa Brainard baked the brick for the first brick house in Brooklyn Township, built this year (Scranton Road and West 25th Street). It was the popular stopping point for drovers who brought their herds to the Cleveland markets. The tavern was later modernized with a handsome three-story front and pillared porches. Grace Hospital took quarters in the rear. The tavern finally became a rooming house, then a night club, and it was razed in 1937.

Cleveland's newspaper had grown in importance and page size. At the expense of news from South America, advertising space was increased not only through the patronage of local merchants, but also those of Newburgh, Medina, Euclid, Elyria, Tappanville (Ravenna), and Buffalo, who saw in the village a market newly created by the steamboat and the advent of the canal.

Canal, Michigan, Champlain, and a portion of Seneca streets were laid out. Paving was believed unnecessary, as the coarse native gravel and sand afforded quick drainage of the heaviest rainfall, according to a local newspaper. A tax of one-fourth of one percent was levied on all village property this year.

Largely through Alfred Kelley's efforts, Cleveland was selected as the northern terminus of the Ohio Canal. Rival towns wanted the canal badly, and the commissioners found great difficulty in compromising with the many interests. Five natural routes were available, and two major canals were finally recommended. One was a 309-mile route starting at Cleveland and following the Cuyahoga Valley to Massillon, Coshocton, Newark, Chillicothe, to Portsmouth on the Ohio River, to be known as the Ohio Canal. This choice was inspired by the large natural reservoir of water in the Portage Lakes. A second route, to be known as the Miami and Erie Canal, was planned from Toledo to Cincinnati, to serve the western part of the State.

The first shovelful of earth was turned by Governor DeWitt Clinton of New York, on Licking Summit, just west of Newark, on July 4, marking the beginning of construction of the Ohio Canal. Prior to the inauguration, an impressive reception was staged at the Mansion House in Cleveland for the governor and dignitaries. Warehousing and forwarding men, however, were gloomy as they realized what this new competition in transportation would do to overland hauling of wheat, pork, flour, potash, and produce by wagon.

Spirited citizens advanced a step beyond the militia and organized the "Light Horse" Troop, the first mounted cavalry unit. It disbanded in the early thirties.

A few equestrian acts were staged for the citizens in a three-day event that opened on September 29. It had no menagerie and no band, but it was called a circus, Cleveland's first.

The Erie Canal was opened on October 26, a monument to the perseverance of Governor DeWitt Clinton. The first boat left Buffalo and reached New York City, November 4. Cleveland celebrated the epochal event with a "grand dinner." Soon Cleveland merchants were inviting their patrons to purchase "cassimers and sattinettes, changeable lute strings, silk and tabby velvets, Marseils, Swansdown, Toitonette, Valentia, Florentine and elegant figured silk vestings, Denmark, Sattin Prunell, white kid and Morroco shoes" . . . "for Ready Pay Only." Freight rates dropped to one-tenth their former figure. One barrel of salt had cost four barrels of flour before the canal opened; now one barrel of flour was worth ten of salt. Mail went by stage and canal to New York in five days, and eastern and import markets were brought within reach of Cleveland.

Painted houses were coming into vogue, and on October 27 Thomas Tyler advertised his services and his shop on Ontario Street. Painting of tavern signs, regimental colors, and Masonic "transparencies" could be had by calling upon Jarvis F. Hanks. He was also a portrait painter of some repute, for he is known to have painted "Uncle" Abram Hickox, Truman P. Handy, and Peter M. Weddell. There were few pictures and art objects in the early homes—those brought from the East, or produced by itinerant painters, wood carvers, and stonecutters. It was several decades before the fine arts would have a place in community living.

A rumor that the village was "sickly" resulted in an investigation by a "respectable physician" into the health of the community. His findings, published in November, indicated that there were twelve deaths per thousand population in the twelve-month just closed, six of which were children under a year and a half. Only one death was caused by fever, although the season had been warm and sultry.

Two sons of Connecticut joined the ranks of the law profession this year—John W. Allen, twenty-three, who studied with Judge Samuel Cowles; and Sherlock J. Andrews, twenty-four-year-old son of a physician, who became associated with the judge. From Rhode Island came Samuel Starkweather, twenty-six, to study law. His exceptional talents and unusual powers of oratory soon brought him into the limelight. Ahead of these young lawyers were distinguished careers of public service. Another arrival was that of Melancthon Barnett, merchant, whose son, James, became one of Cleveland's most useful citizens.

In December, a bakery opened, where loaf bread, cakes, and Boston and butter crackers could be purchased.

1826

With the coming of Irish immigrants to work on the canal, there was need of the ministrations of a Catholic priest. Upon the direction of the Rt. Rev. Edward Fenwick, bishop of Cincinnati, the Dominican Fathers in Perry County sent the Rev. Thomas Martin on a visit to the village in the autumn. Later he was succeeded by the Very Rev. Stephen T. Badin, the first priest ordained in the United States. Mass was said in private homes.

Immigrants from the Isle of Man in the Irish Sea were arriving in Cleveland. William Kelley of Newburgh was prominent in the clan, which was to include names of distinction and achievement. Among them were the Collister, Corlett, Quayle, Ramsey, Kerruish, Gill, Creer, Teare, and Christian families.

In the "Hall Room" of the Navy Hotel, managed by Dr. Donald McIntosh, an ardent Mason, Webb Chapter No. 14, Royal Arch Masons, was organized on January 18. The second Masonic body in Cleveland, it was named in honor of Thomas Smith Webb, chairman of the initial proceedings when Freemasonry was brought into existence in Boston in 1797. Webb established the Grand Chapter of Ohio, October 21, 1816. The local chapter received its charter on January 11, 1827.

Disappointment and hardship sharpened the determination and resourcefulness of the founders of Western Reserve College (later Adelbert College of Western Reserve University) at Hudson, as they labored to provide education for their sons in the "art of right living." There had been considerable debate as to whether to locate the new college in Cleveland or in Hudson, the latter being chosen when a campus site was offered. Cleveland was voted down by arguments that the village was unhealthful, and that the presence of so many rowdy lake sailors would be a bad influence on young students. Besides, Hudson was a day's journey closer by stage to flourishing Pittsburgh.

The trustees of Western Reserve College, earnest and hard-working pioneers, were men of vision: David Hudson—who gave Hudson Village its name, Elizur Wright, Joshua B. Sherwood, Henry Brown, Simeon Woodruff, Zalmon Fitch, John Seward, Harvey Coe, Benjamin Fenn, Harmon Kingsbury, the Rev. Stephen J. Bradstreet of the First Presbyterian Church (Old Stone) in Cleveland, Caleb Pitkin, and William Hanford. When a large quantity of building brick proved inferior, they purchased facilities for making their own material. First-quality chimney brick, however, was hauled from Cleveland by oxcart. When funds were exhausted, they challenged poverty and sacrifice, and raised the required amount. When they learned that the charter failed to provide for theological training, they rode to Columbus in bitter winter and achieved their purpose.

On April 26 the trustees of Western Reserve College laid the cornerstone of Middle College, the first building of the proud new "Yale of the West," located in a typical New England campus setting. The first three students were admitted in December to the college for men, and they were instructed in an academy at Tallmadge until the new building was ready in 1827. A preparatory school was established as indispensable (later Western Reserve Academy).

To meet the demands of stagecoach business, Philo Scovill built the Stage House on Superior Street (712 Superior, N.W.), soon afterward named the Franklin House, in honor of Benjamin Franklin. It was a white frame structure, the first three-story building in the Western Reserve. Finding the cost greater than he had anticipated, Scovill offered to sell for $300, but there were no buyers. His popularity can be measured by his election as county commissioner in 1827, when he received more votes than David Long. For nearly a quarter century he was owner-manager of the hotel, his wife's good housekeeping adding to a reputation for "neatness and sumptuous fare." Traveling showmen used the Franklin, and an early feature presented a museum of curiosities including "quadrupeds, birds, fishes, insects, minerals, and mussels"—admission 25 cents, children half price. The ambitious collectors advertised in the local press for a weasel and a pelican in "a state fit of preservation." The Franklin House was Cleveland's largest tavern, the headquarters for the various stage lines centered in the village under Levi Sartwell, genial stage manager. Lake captains and itinerant lawyers favored it.

In April, a new stage was operating regularly twice a week between Pittsburgh and Cleveland. The mail coach, advertised as comfortable, closed and drawn by four horses, traveled the 104-mile distance between Cleveland and Erie on a daily schedule, with the fare $3. Buffalo was 40 hours away, and passage for the 200-mile trip cost $6. Some of the lines, however, collected fares according to the weight and size of the passenger. The arrival of the stagecoach was the signal for townfolk to put on their best clothes and be on hand to greet newcomers and await mail. Wild cheers went up as the team pulled to a halt. With considerable importance, the driver stepped down from his high seat, and well-shaken passengers alighted to stretch tired limbs, brush off the dust, and smooth out wrinkles.

Discussion of the location of a new church in the Trinity Parish produced rivalry between Brooklyn and Cleveland, and the matter was settled in favor of the latter at the Ninth Annual Convention of the diocese held June 7. In the fall, the Rev. Silas C. Freeman of Virginia was engaged as rector at an annual salary of $500, to be paid partially by the Norwalk church, with which he was to divide his time.

In a room in the Franklin House, S. Hardyear, traveling dentist, "inserted artificial teeth, in most cases without pain." Thus read his advertisement on July 28. False teeth of porcelain or mineral were being used, and fillings were made from gold, lead, or tin.

At about this time, Newton E. Crittenden arrived and opened the first jewelry store in a small brick building next to the Franklin House. He offered such luxuries as watches, perfume, and plain and twisted-hair rings and necklaces. His five-hundred-dollar stock of goods was obtained on credit. In 1868, he moved into a fine Euclid Street home, with a long, successful record of mercantile experience behind him.

David H. Beardsley moved to Cleveland from Lower Sandusky (Fremont), where he served as a judge and a member of the Legislature. In 1827, he was appointed collector for the Ohio Canal at Cleveland, serving for many years with a highly creditable record. Nicholas Dockstader, also a newcomer, soon became the leading hat, cap, and fur dealer in town, yet he had time for public service along many lines.

Joseph Triskett came to Rockport Township with his father and brothers this year. They cleared 50 acres from the wilderness (bordering on Triskett Road).

As the owner of the property occupied by the Ontario Street burying ground took action to gain possession for building purposes, Leonard Case and civic-minded men purchased about 10 acres of land "far out of town" on Erie Street, south of Prospect, for the City Cemetery (later Erie Street Cemetery). Title was passed to the Village of Cleveland with the understanding that the land be used for burial purposes. The first interment was that of Minerva M., daughter of Moses and Mary White, who was laid away in September, 1827. Remains of the pioneers buried in the original cemetery (at Ontario and Prospect) were removed to Erie Street.

On the eastern portion of land acquired for the Erie Street Cemetery, a "township poorhouse" was built to accommodate elderly patients and those afflicted with chronic disease. This was the beginning of City Hospital.

The first hall consecrated to Masonic purposes and owned by Cleveland Masons was dedicated December 27. Concord Lodge and Webb Chapter had united in an unusual building plan whereby Brother Marvin Oviatt, merchant and first secretary of the chapter, built a third story to his new block at the northwest corner of Superior and Water streets as a Masonic Hall for $956, title being vested in the Masons. A keystone cemented in the doorway was symbolic of brotherly affection. Widespread antagonism to Freemasonry and secret societies resulted from the mysterious disappearance of William Morgan in western New York this year, giving rise to the Anti-Masonic Party. Lodges began to deteriorate under the heat of flagrant persecution; and in 1829, the Cleveland Masons had lapsed into a "period of repose" that continued for a decade. The Methodist Society took over the hall.

1827

The first plant in the county worthy to be called a manufactory was started in a workshop in the "Flats" (southeast corner of Detroit Avenue, N.W., at the drawbridge). Seven years later it became the Cuyahoga Steam Furnace Company. Its output consisted of cast and wrought iron work, the pig iron used being brought from a blast furnace in Dover.

The First Presbyterian Society of Cleveland (later Old Stone Church) was incorporated on January 5. Samuel Cowles was president; David H. Beardsley, secretary; and Peter M. Weddell, treasurer. Although composed chiefly of Congregationalists and organized by Congregational ministers, the church was Presbyterian in government, and became the Mother of Cleveland Presbyterianism. Six years later, the Ladies' Missionary Society was organized and began its influential service that was to become worldwide.

James S. Clark—or Clarke—had established a rental agency, and on April 6 listed stores for rent on Superior and Ontario streets, on the river, and in the business section, as well as dwellings on Water, Bank, and Euclid streets.

Peter M. Weddell, Edmund Clark, and George Stanton organized The

Cleaveland & New York Line, a "commission, storage and transportation business." Their warehousing interests and connections with lake and Hudson River steam navigation prepared them to "ship expeditiously," so they advertised.

The first Methodist society of Cleveland, which became the First Methodist Church, was formed, with the Revs. John Crawford and Cornelius Jones in charge. Founders were Mrs. Grace Johnson, Andrew Tomlinson, Eliza Worley, Elizabeth Southworth, Job Sizer and wife, Elijah Peet and wife, and Lucinda Knowlton. The Cleveland circuit comprised Cuyahoga, Lake, Geauga, and Summit counties, and a part of Ashtabula and Portage. Cleveland was made a permanent station in 1830, and the Rev. George McCaskey became pastor. The congregation met in public places until 1841.

The question of slavery was discussed publicly for the first time in the county at a meeting of the Cuyahoga County Colonization Society in the Academy. Its followers believed that the Government should buy the slaves and send them back to Africa, the theory being that many slave-holders would free their bondsmen if assured they would be sent out of the country. Samuel Cowles was president, and prominent citizens were members. With overwhelming opposition of the Abolitionists, the society soon faded out.

Harmon Kingsbury and the Rev. Randolph Stone edited the first religious weekly published in Cleveland, the *Western Intelligencer*. It appeared on July 21 and was discontinued in 1830.

A log church was built by the Brooklyn Methodist Church Society (later Brooklyn Memorial Church), and it was finished in June (northeast corner West 25th and Denison). In January, the membership had reached fifty-seven. A Sunday School had been organized with twenty-one members, and Ebenezer Fish was the first superintendent. In 1849, a one-story frame sanctuary was erected on the original site, serving until 1881. During the pastorate of the Rev. W. Arthur Smith in 1911, it was replaced by a two-story brick house of worship at West 25th and Archwood. The Rev. William J. Hodder was pastor in 1946.

On July 4, the first canal boat navigated 37 miles and passed through forty-one locks of the Ohio Canal from Akron to Cleveland. As the two northernmost locks were not yet completed, the mule-drawn packet bearing Governor Allen I. Trimble and members of the canal commission was met by a welcome party aboard the *Pioneer*, 6 miles from the village. A great day of celebration heralded the new era of transportation progress.

An epidemic of typhoid fever swept over Cleveland in midsummer, originating in the canal area and aggravated by unhealthful and unsanitary conditions. In less than two months, seventeen deaths occurred. Cleveland's first charitable activities on anything like a mass scale began when provisions were distributed to families of canal workers, who appealed to citizens for help. According to Ara Sprague, "A terrible depression of spirits and stagnation of business ensued. The whole corporation could have been bought for what one lot would now cost on Superior street. For two months I gave up all business; went from house to house to look after the sick and their uncared-for business. People were generally discouraged and anxious to leave," but the desire to achieve progress and improvement kept them in Cleveland to help build a city.

A tract of 100 acres southeast of Cleveland (Woodland Hills Park) was purchased for $400 this year. In 1918, 86 acres were bought for real-estate development at $216,000.

The Newburgh Literary Society was incorporated on December 14. It was a substantial organization, and the first evidence of determined literary effort.

Horse racing had already become a popular sport on the Water Street speedway, from Superior to the north end of the street. Purses of from $25 to $100 for quarter-mile contests attracted crowds from the county.

Alfred Greenbrier, a distinguished-appearing mulatto from Kentucky, purchased a farm (vicinity of Bridge Avenue), where he engaged in the breeding of fine horses and cattle. His horses furnished speedy transportation for fugitive slaves. Stock raising was an important industry attracting eastern buyers.

1828

When a tax of two mills on the dollar was levied, and the trustees set aside $200 "to put the village in proper order," the citizens challenged such waste, demanding to know "what on earth the trustees could find in the village to spend two hundred dollars on."

Cleveland's smoke nuisance had its beginning when Henry Newberry brought the first load of coal to Cleveland, mined from his land on the banks of the Cuyahoga at Tallmadge near the canal. He peddled it door to door, offering it for sale to housewives; but they spurned the dirty, black stuff in favor of cheap, clean wood. Finally, Philo Scovill was induced to try burning the new-fangled fuel in his barroom grate, and blacksmiths began using it. In this new product was the future greatness of industry and commerce, and the fortunes of Cleveland men. John Ballard & Company commenced to operate a small iron foundry in the spring.

Noah Webster's famous *Elementary Spelling Book* was studied diligently in pioneer homes where children could not attend school. Where there were schools, it was a fundamental text-book, and inspired thrilling spelling matches. At the age of seventy Webster published his *American Dictionary of the English Language* this year. The volumes made a lasting contribution to educational and cultural advance.

Yearning for higher education was revealed in the formation of the Twinsburg Literary Institute, which prepared "any young people" for college. It continued for more than sixty years, and at one time had an enrollment of three hundred students.

The first pretentious map of the United States, published by John Cary in London this year, slighted Ohio. The Western Reserve was ignored, as were all the lakeshore towns, excepting Sandusky. Gnadenhutten and several small places were shown, but Cincinnati and Cleveland, the coming cities of the West, did not appear.

The first court session was held in the new eight-thousand-dollar, two-story, brick Court House, surmounted by a wooden dome, on the southwest quarter of the Square facing the lake. Here public and social gatherings were held. Four years later a stone jail, with three cells and living quarters for the sheriff, was erected at the rear, fronting on Champlain Street. It was familiarly known as "the Blue Jug." The bitter struggle that had been waged between Newburgh and Cleveland for location of the county building was ended.

Newburgh erected a brick town hall on the site of its first school (9213 Miles Avenue), and it served at one time as the meeting place of town-

The second Court House, opened in 1828, served as the community center.

ship officials, a schoolhouse, and a church. It ceased to be used for public purposes around 1860, and was converted into a dwelling. On an adjacent lot, Edward Taylor built a frame house in 1832. The two landmarks continued in service through the years.

Ebenezer Williams, Disciples minister and former Universalist, was preaching at this time to scattered Disciples in the vicinity of Newburgh. No converts were gained, however, until 1832, when William Hayden held a meeting and John Hopkinson was inspired to join. In the following year, Colonel John Wightman and his wife, Eliza Everett, with several others, responded to the preaching of Williams and Hayden. The Disciples of Christ in Ohio were an outgrowth of a "reform" movement within the churches of the Mahoning Baptist Association. In 1830, a formal separation took place, and each congregation became a Church of Christ, independent of the others.

A Sunday School, started this year near Doan's Corners by Mrs. Sally Mather Hale in her home (site of entrance to Flora Stone Mather College), was the forerunner of a Presbyterian church founded in 1843 (later Euclid Avenue Congregational Church). In the early thirties, Benjamin F. Rouse began another Bible school in a stone shop to the east.

1829

John Kilbourn of Columbus wrote a book advertising Ohio for circulation in the East. His boost for Cleveland stated, "Cleveland, the seat of justice of Cuyahoga County, will in time become one of the most important." He

Trinity in 1829, the first church erected within the boundaries of Cleveland.

credited the village with 168 dwelling houses, 13 mercantile stores, 15 warehouses, 4 drug stores, 1 book and stationery store, 9 groceries, 6 taverns, and about 1,000 inhabitants.

Cleveland was growing in importance as a meat-producing center, and its products were reaching the New York markets. Two establishments were slaughtering 1,400 hogs weekly, and 50,000 pounds of ham were cured during the winter.

When Daniel Worley became postmaster on April 15, he moved the delivery office to the north side of Superior Street in Miller's Block, between Seneca and Bank streets. In the rear was the Custom House. Aaron Barker became postmaster on March 2, 1839; Benjamin Andrews on September 6, 1842; and Timothy P. Spencer on April 11, 1845.

Small private schools were opened from time to time, many of them of short duration. J. Mills announced a college-preparatory course in his

"Select School" on Ontario Street, and a dancing school taught the cotillion, mazurka, waltz, and Spanish dance.

The Rev. Silas C. Freeman's money-raising efforts in the East on behalf of a new church home for Trinity Parish were successful, and a site was secured (southeast corner of St. Clair and West 3rd). Trinity Parish of Cleveland had been incorporated in 1828, with Josiah Barber, Phineas Shepherd, Charles Taylor, Henry L. Noble, Reuben Champion, James S. Clarke, Sherlock J. Andrews, Levi Sargeant, and John W. Allen, wardens and vestrymen. Trinity Church, "the first house devoted to the worship of God in the present City of Cleveland," was consecrated on August 12 by Bishop Philander Chase. It was a frame structure, costing $3,070, surmounted by four belfry pinnacles bearing weathercocks of sheet-iron, so heavy that the winds could not turn them and they had to be removed. The little white church with the green blinds was Cleveland's first religious center. Trinity joined with Grace Church in Chagrin (Willoughby) and St. James in Painesville in an arrangement whereby Rev. Freeman traveled a 228-mile circuit on horseback every month. He resigned at the end of the year, having served since 1825. The Rev. William N. Lyster, a deacon, who opened a Sunday School with about thirty scholars, was placed in charge of the parish for a time. It is said that he was the first minister in the West to wear a surplice.

The first fire engine was purchased at a cost of $285. Trustees who voted for it were defeated for re-election. Many citizens firmly declared that buckets were good enough. The new officials repudiated the note for a substantial balance owing on the engine, and when it came due, judgment was rendered and the bill was paid. Early the next year, a volunteer fire company was organized in the community.

When young George Worthington rode into Cleveland on horseback, immigrants were arriving at the rate of about six hundred in a fortnight to work on the canal. He found them poorly equipped with tools, and here was his opportunity. Turning his horse back toward Cooperstown, New York, he borrowed $500 from his brother and purchased an assortment of implements in the East, shipping his stock by Erie Canal to Buffalo, thence by schooner to Cleveland. The supply sold quickly, he doubled his money, and bought more stock with which he opened the first store of The Geo. Worthington Company (Superior and West 10th). In 1835, he bought out his competitor and moved to the corner of Water Street. Business came from northern Ohio, but Worthington had to go after it through good weather and bad on horseback, delivering his wares by oxcart, until the first successful railroad came.

Cleveland's first fair, a two-day event that opened on October 30, was held in the Public Square and the Court House under the auspices of the Cuyahoga County Agricultural Society. Livestock was tethered in the Square, and prizes of from $1 to $5 were given for the best brood mares and stallions. In the First Presbyterian Church (Old Stone) the ladies exhibited needlework, quilts, and home products. Silkworm culture was the rage, and farmers were planting acres of mulberry trees, hoping to establish a stable industry.

Mrs. David Long received a five-dollar prize for a pair of stockings she had made from local silk. Mrs. Mary L. Severance took the prize for silk twist. A Mrs. Brainard of Brooklyn received an award for eight shades of silk, for which she had produced both the silk and the dyes. James Houghton entered the best half acre of mulberry trees. The industry of the little silkworm proved disappointing, however, and the craze died with it; but the fair became an annual event of great importance in the life of the community.

Entries in the daily-sales book of Peter M. Weddell from November 2, 1829, to October 31, 1831, provide an interesting and revealing picture of the times. The first item in the journal, kept by young Dudley Baldwin, reads: "George G. Hills, per self, To 2½ lbs tobacco 12½c; nails, per James 10 lbs. at 5¢; goods for Miss Bidwell, $1.82; goods for self $1.19." On November 29, 1829, John W. Willey was charged with 36 gallons of whisky at 28 cents a gallon; while Reuben Wood, who must have been a fine dresser, bought 3¾ yards of blue suiting cloth for $26.25 and trimmings for $4.87. He later spent $3 for a Valencia vest, and purchased 25 quills and a quire of writing paper. Dudley Baldwin's purchases indicated that the social season was about to open: "blue suiting and trimmings for $6.64; paid $5.00 for having the suit made and bought a pair of pumps for a dollar and a half." Sometimes the entries show the need of a spelling teacher; for example, "1 barl flower, 1 vest patron, 2 yds. bumbasette, 2 led pencils, 1 pare speck-tickles, 2 yards ribband, 1 parisoll, 1 lb beeswacks, 1 yard bonnanett." There was a great deal more than merchandising involved in the following entry: "Lucind Coldwell By hur Bill skooling Horace to dat Sep. 13, is $1.75."

No doubt Jonathan Pearse grumbled when he paid the tax bill in December on his 100-acre tract of land in Newburgh (Harvard Avenue and Independence Road). Assessments on his property, valued at $505, amounted to $4.69, of which 76 cents was for personal tax.

The village fathers decided that Cleveland needed more room in which to grow, and in December, the General Assembly made possible the extension of boundary lines. All the land was annexed "from the southerly line of Huron street down the river to a point westerly of the junction of Vineyard lane with the road leading from the village to Brooklyn, thence west parallel with said road to the river, and down the river to the old village line." Canal Street was laid out this year.

The first public market was established on Ontario Street south of the Square, and regulated by city ordinance. Receipts for the year following were $27.50. The familiar neighborhood butcher with his cart and tinkling bell set up shop in a shed, where stalls were offered at auction to the highest bidder. Fresh meats could be sold daily except Sunday, and vegetables and other items could be sold on Wednesday and Saturday.

Philip Cody and his wife, Lydia Martin Cody, native New Englanders, were past middle age when they came to Cleveland from Canada with their family about this time, making their home at Doan's Tavern for a year. Then Cody began to buy property in the vicinity. Shortly after 1831, he purchased a 63-acre tract on Euclid (near East 83rd). In the ancestral home that stood for many years, eleven children were raised.

CHAPTER 6

A Boom Town Becomes a City
1830-1839

AN ERA of prosperity had begun in Ohio and the nation in 1825, marked by great public improvements. The National Road was stretching westward from Wheeling to Columbus and beyond. Dirt roads were being converted into turnpikes, increasing the speed and safety of multiplying stage lines. With brave hearts and unquenchable faith, families moved slowly to the frontier to claim cheap land and map promising trails of progress. The growing influence of the new West strengthened Jacksonian democracy.

The population of Cleveland in 1830, according to the United States census, was 1,075, and of Cuyahoga County, 10,373. The area of the village was about two-thirds of a square mile. Immigrants were arriving in increasing numbers to work on the canal, and housing had become a problem.

The Irish were making their homes on the West Side near the river mouth. William Murphy, who came in 1830, was one of the earliest, followed by the Evans family, Arthur Quinn, John Smith, the Sanders family, Joseph Turney, Hugh Buckley, Sr., Father John Dillon, Father Patrick O'Dwyer, Hugh Blee, Patrick Smith, the Cahill, Conlan and Whelan families, Captain Michael C. Frawley, Michael Feely, Michael Gallagher, Father Peter McLaughlin, and others who were prominent in the colony.

The Germans began to come in 1830, settling along Lorain Street on the West Side, and in the vicinity of Superior and Garden streets to the east. They were industrious folk, skilled in their trades, many of them political refugees, bringing with them a background of the cultural arts. The earliest families were the Silbergs, butchers; the families of Neeb, Kaiser, Denker, and Borges, tailors and clothiers; Wigman, mason contractor; Schiele, gardener; and the Diemers, Fingers, Rissers, and Freys. They were followed by the Wanglein, Laisy, Steinmeir, Hessenmueller, Henninger, Ehringer, Schaaf, and Umbstaetter families. Pioneering Carl Scheekley, John Krehbiehl, Fritz Hoffman, Gregor Dietz, and John Denzer sought opportunity and freedom in Cleveland, far from the political oppression of their old-world fatherland.

Young men, many of them in their early twenties, were coming to Cleveland from New England and the East, endowed with energy and talent that were soon translated into responsible leadership in the city suffering from growing pains.

The canal era in Ohio had begun in 1825. Ohio real estate at that time was valued at $45,000,000 and personal property at $14,000,000; yet $16,-000,000 was spent by the State for two canals: the Ohio Canal, connecting Cleveland and Portsmouth on the Ohio River, and the Miami and Erie Canal, joining Toledo and Cincinnati—to provide transportation at the rate of three to four miles per hour!

Clevelanders were more or less indifferent to the Ohio Canal at first, some of them being perfectly satisfied to "Give it to Painesville or Black River (Lorain)," who wanted it badly. The lakes to the south of Cleveland, and the Cuyahoga and Tuscarawas rivers were the deciding factors, however, and the canal reached its southern goal in 1832, the total cost of construction and repairs to December 1 being $4,244,539.64.

The Ohio Canal contributed greatly to the industry and wealth of farmers and townsmen in a wide territory bordering it, augmenting trade and increasing opportunities in many directions. Akron, Massillon, and other villages sprang to life, benefiting from canal commerce and water power; existing towns increased in population and trade. Products of farm and mine could now reach markets that were opened and expanded by lowered transportation costs. Prior to the canal era, it cost $5 to ship a barrel of flour 150 miles; charges on carrying a cord of wood 20 miles were $3. Commodities commanded higher prices for the producer. Formerly, wheat sold in interior Ohio for 20 to 30 cents a bushel; now it brought from 50 to 75 cents.

The importance of canal navigation is traced in a cargo of goods shipped by water from New York to Dayton: New York to Buffalo via the Erie Canal, on the lake to Cleveland, Ohio Canal to Portsmouth, Ohio River to Cincinnati, and Miami Canal to Dayton, a distance of 1,100 miles in a record time of twenty days at a cost of $17.25 per ton!

Cleveland's fame spread far and wide with the opening of the canal. Strategic location on lake and inland water route made the village an exchange point for goods from the south and east as well as for export. Long lines of overland wagons and heavy passenger traffic by waterways taxed housing facilities. Vessels crowded the river, light and heavy vehicles filled the unpaved streets, and pedestrians wormed their way around bags, barrels, and boxes on the sidewalks. Real-estate values rose at an alarming rate, and rents were high.

Newcomers were met at the docks by smooth-talking promoters with beautiful city plans on paper, urging them to buy. Inflationary prosperity was manifested in new taverns and hotels, commercial blocks, stores, tenement buildings, and extended boundary lines. Cleveland, a boom town, was riding the crest of the wave!

Canal boats were operated by private individuals and companies, subject to tolls charged by the canal builder. The boat or packet was between 70 and 80 feet long, about 14 feet wide, and was usually drawn by two horses, tandemwise, on one of which the driver was seated. There was space for freight, cabins in front, and a saloon or dining room at the rear. Berths for ladies and children were in the cabins. The crew consisted of the captain, two energetic steersmen, two young drivers, and the cook, who worked "all of the time." Canal travel was safe and popular, especially in fair weather, when passengers lounged on the top deck, leisurely enjoying the wooded hillsides, the shadowy mysteries of the canal, and the twinkling lights in isolated houses.

"Missing the boat" was not necessarily a disaster. The passenger merely hired a rig and galloped to the nearest bridge across the canal, waited for the boat and climbed aboard. The expression, "low bridge," is said to have originated when the skipper warned passengers riding on top of the packet to prepare to recognize the three- or four-foot clearance between bridge and boat.

After completing the Ohio Canal, the State seems to have abandoned the burden of laying out state roads, and gave to private corporations the right to improve certain roads and charge tolls. Stock in the company was usually purchased by the State. Turnpike and plank-road companies sprang up over night all over Ohio, building a network called The Farmers Railway. By 1870, the companies had almost all disappeared, leaving upkeep to the counties.

Reports of railroad progress in the East incited emphatic expressions for and against the new development. Pessimists pointed to the hazards that accompanied wood-burning engines, their stacks belching great glowing coals along with the smoke. Goggles saved the eyes from cinders, but passengers' protective coats and hats were not always adequate, they declared. "Oversets" were not uncommon, when a strip of strap-iron on top of a wooden rail became loose. There was little enthusiasm here for the iron horse. Speed by stage or canal was good enough, despite irksome winter isolation.

On the other hand, Cleveland leaders were spurred to action, and they began planning rail connections with Pittsburgh and Cincinnati. In the face of many protests from the citizenship, forward-looking businessmen took their first steps in the long, uphill climb to bring the railroad to Cleveland. At the same time, local promoters were laying wooden rails for a streetcar line motivated by horsepower that was ahead of its time.

Horses were replacing oxen as beasts of burden as the urge for speed increased. Fine farms around Cleveland boasted the best breeds. Those who wished to travel on business or for pleasure could hire saddle horses, gigs, sulkies, and hacks at a number of local livery stables.

There was always room for one more rider on the patient family nag when ladies chose to do a bit of shopping. It was considered quite proper for two buxom females to mount one horse, jog to town with perhaps a basket of eggs and a pail of butter, and trade for their family needs at the general store. The one-horse principle served equally well when a young sprout took his best girl to a sociable. Starched and smiling, she stood on the mounting block; and with a sprightly leap, born of experience, she settled herself on the horse behind her escort, arranged yards of skirts and petticoats, and clung to him with genuine pleasure.

This was a period of city-making. Under the first state constitution, municipalities were chartered by special act, and the legislative mill produced abundantly. The City Council was the supreme authority. Three members were elected from each of three wards, with as many aldermen as there were wards, the mayor amounting to little more than a head magistrate. The marshal, his deputy or deputies, and the city treasurer were elected annually. Public and private corporations were also chartered by special act. This led to the issuance of charters and legislation designed to please grasping politicians and fanciful law-makers.

In the race for incorporation as a city in 1836, little Ohio City won over Cleveland by two days. Since early in the decade, hostile relations prevailed between the new municipalities as they elected wise leaders to establish government, to regulate, restrict and reform, and to lay the foundations of orderly development.

City management, however, did not rest entirely with the office holders. The Court House rang as citizens settled vital issues in democratic town-meeting debate. Community spirit raised a brigade of fire-fighting volunteers and a salvage corps, preserved law and order, tracked down horse thieves, launched cultural societies, cheered on Independence Day, and returned thanks to Almighty God at Thanksgiving time for blessings received.

The business district of the new City of Cleveland fronted on the river, where steamers, schooners, and canal boats exchanged imported commodities for products of local industry. The river bank was a thriving center of forwarding and commission warehouses, ship chandlers, merchants, and artisans. Stores lined steep, unpaved Superior hill, and there were a few brick buildings of several stories on the street beyond. A flagged sidewalk had been laid in front of the bank at the corner of Bank Street, where a town pump stood. At the southwest corner of the Public Square stood the Court House; the new Presbyterian Church had been built at the northwest corner of Ontario Street, the First Baptist Church at the southeast corner of Seneca and Champlain streets, and at Seneca and St. Clair was Trinity Church. Pigs roamed at will, and cows browsed contentedly.

Despite Cleveland's forward strides, the city bore the marks of a frontier village. Log houses were still in existence, although frame houses were plentiful, and there was an occasional brick building. Facing the Square were the modest residences of Richard Winslow, Leonard Case, Charles M. Giddings, Elijah Bingham, William Lemen, Dr. Erastus Cushing, and John W. Allen. Water, Seneca, Bank, St. Clair, and Lake streets constituted the principal residential section, but Michigan Street was considered more fashionable.

The woods were being pushed back slowly along unpaved and unlighted Euclid Street, deeply scarred by the wheels of lumbering stages. Men of vision and influence, however, had employed prominent architects to build new homes here of classical and colonial design: Samuel Williamson (easterly portion of Williamson Building site), Sherlock J. Andrews, George Hoadley, Harvey Rice, Ahaz Merchant, Lyman Kendall, Samuel Cowles, and Truman P. Handy. Beyond Erie Street lived Thomas Kelley, Henry H. Dodge, and Nathan Perry, Jr. A Virginia rail fence lined the north side of Euclid from Bond almost to Erie Street. Groves of sturdy timber stood on Erie between Superior and Prospect streets and between St. Clair and the lake. A paint shop, shoemaker, blacksmith, wagon-maker, carpenter, and joiner represented the extent of trade, and thirty-five vacant lots, valued at about five dollars a foot front, were not considered a promising investment.

The Euclid Road, as it was also called, was increasing in importance, affording the most popular route from Cleveland to Buffalo. In 1832, it was recognized by the Legislature as a public highway. As street systems developed, and Cleveland and Ohio City stretched their boundaries, communicative progress demanded that waterways and ravines should be bridged. Yet when a bridge was raised to join the east and west sides of the Cuyahoga, a pitched battle delayed co-operative effort until the early fifties.

It was easy to start a newspaper. A small printing press, some type, a printer, a little capital, and a lot of enthusiasm were all that were necessary. It might be an instrument of partisan or political power, a champion of religion, slavery, or free thought; frontier democracy could provide ample excuse for another paper. When Cleveland became a city, there was an overabundance of newspapers, the majority of them short-lived.

There was a consciousness of the need for higher education, and itinerant schoolmasters established a number of private schools in Cleveland. Many of them existed only a short time, and are recorded only in newspaper notices and directories. Schools for special instruction in writing, ciphering, and bookkeeping, penmanship, art, and music were opened by professional men beginning about the middle of the decade. The meager tuition for poor children was paid by the village until free schools were established by the frugal city fathers of the new municipality in rented quarters.

Academies, seminaries, and colleges prospered in the Western Reserve from 1830 to 1850. They were generally private schools in the form of stock companies, often operating under state charters and endowed by gifts of land or money. The extent of their popularity is indicated by their locations: Akron, Ashtabula, Aurora, Austinburg, Berea, Brighton, Brooklyn, Canfield, Chagrin Falls, Chardon, Chesterland, Cleveland, Collamer, Conneaut, Cuyahoga Falls, Farmington, Geneva, Hiram, Hudson, Huron, Kingsville, Kinsman, Kirtland, Madison, Mechanicsville, Milan, New Lyme, Norwalk, Oberlin, Painesville, Parkman, Poland, Richfield, Rome, Strongsville, Tallmadge, Twinsburg, Unionville, Wadsworth, Warren, Wayne, Willoughby, and Youngstown.

Before a cheery fire in the plain little wooden "Ark" on the Public Square, the Case brothers and their friends talked of science and cultural things that would someday influence the life of their city far beyond their most cherished hopes.

The Western Reserve was fertile ground for revivalists and reformers. Fear and loneliness had lived day and night with the settlers from the time they left their eastern homes. There was little gaiety, only occasional dances, entertainments, and cultural events, but no festivals. Stern New Englanders considered it pagan to celebrate Christmas. There was plenty of time to meditate on the soul; but with aching joints and a deranged liver to aggravate the body, it was no wonder that some of the pioneers submitted to the hypnotic influences of fiery new doctrines.

The arrival of a missionary or an impelling preacher was the signal for the community to awaken to a consciousness of sin, self, and personal shortcomings. This was a day of fierce revivals, jerkings, and shakings, when camp-meeting conversions took on highly emotional form. Swayed by fanaticism, people were persuaded to believe in revelations, dreams, and prophesies of the millennium. Thus Mormonism, the Shakers, Second Adventists, and Oberlin Covenanters arose, while, at the same time, vicious attacks temporarily exhausted the strength of the Masonic order.

Temperance, slavery, and reform were heated subjects fanned by the sensational fire of isms and emotional doctrines. Church members were called upon to make decisions on these vital controversial issues, with the result that inevitably congregations began to divide. The Presbyterian General Assembly concluded that radicalism had invaded the synod of the Western Reserve. Consequently, the Plan of Union that had inspired co-operative effort of Presbyterians and Congregationalists since 1801, was repudiated in 1837.

Saloons were doing a land-office business. Raw corn whisky and fiery liquors were on a par with beans and butter in many family larders. Sunday was just another day in the week, with business as usual. There was little incentive to practice religious doctrines and pious living in the rough pioneer village; yet from three churches in 1830, the number grew to eight congregations in 1837. The prosperity of the early thirties put more money in the hands of church members, who spent some of it to build churches, pay ministers' salaries, and establish Sunday School missions. Nevertheless, the faith and patience of even the most courageous man of God must have been sorely tried many times as he sought earnestly to inspire moral uplift and save wayward souls.

Welfare work began in the ministry of early charities to boatmen and sailors who had failed to plan for slack seasons in lake and canal commerce, and to those who had suffered from misfortune or disaster.

Few physicians in the Western Reserve had enjoyed a medical education. Knowledge and experience were generally gained as an apprentice to a practitioner during the early part of the century; and, armed with a certificate, the student began at once to practice. Bleeding, emetics, blisters, calomel, antimony, and the like were relied upon by pioneer men of medicine to produce a patient's recovery. Ethics of the day permitted physicians to hold public office, engage in business, advertise their services, and bear their share of community responsibilities. Cleveland had a number of flourishing drug stores that also sold groceries and commodities. The prescription business had hardly begun. Physicians purchased their drug supplies, mixed vile-tasting remedies, and passed them on to their patients for better or for worse.

Eastern entertainers and novel exhibitions traveled a circuit that included Cleveland, but appearances were infrequent. Entertainment facilities were poor and inadequate. Three public halls were mentioned in the first directory, seating several hundred people each. They were located on the upper floors of commercial blocks, and could be reached by climbing narrow stairs. Despite feeble light, poor ventilation, smoking stoves, and uncomfortable chairs and benches, capacity crowds attended lectures and debates, entertainments, and concerts. Apollo Hall, on the third floor of the Merwin Building on Superior Street near Water, gained popularity later as a theater. Concert Hall, three flights above Handerson's drug store on Superior Street, catered to music lovers. Liberty Hall, on the third floor of the Hancock Block, at Superior and Seneca streets, echoed to lively literary and debating programs.

Recreation took the form of picnics, hunting and fishing expeditions, berry-picking and nut-gathering socials, singing in the schoolhouse, square dances, occasional concerts, and lectures. Children amused themselves with pom-pom-pullaway, duck-on-a-rock, shinny, one-old-cat—in which baseball originated, anthony ("anty") over, and marbles. The entire community joined in house-raisings, husking bees, and wood-chopping contests.

The City of Cleveland was little more than a year old, but according to the first *Directory of Cleveland and Ohio, For the Years 1837-38,* it was entitled to call itself a manufacturing city. In it were four iron foundries and steam-engine manufactories; three soap-and-candle factories, two breweries, one sash factory, two rope walks, one stoneware pottery, two carriage shops, and two millstone factories in full operation. There were two banks, five insurance companies, and four newspapers; the Post Office, connecting with eight mail routes; Custom House, ten hotels, and three coffee houses; eight church congregations, a hospital, theater, and four public open-air markets; a "free" school and numerous cultural organizations. The medical profession was represented by twenty-four physicians and surgeons; two surgical dentists were offering their services, and forty-six attorneys were expounding the law. Six stage lines and a number of forwarding lines on the canal and the lake connected Cleveland with the outside world.

A small paragraph in the directory showed the remarkable population growth since early in the decade: 1831—"not more than" 1,100; 1832—1,500; 1833—1,900; January, 1834—3,323; November, 1834—4,250; and August, 1835 —5,080. "The number of inhabitants in the city of Cleveland at present (1837) exceeds nine thousand," estimated the publisher, "and judging from the rapid increase of that number, and the flattering prospects of this infant city, we anticipate its being doubled in less than three years." Editor MacCabe's prophetic figures never had a chance to materialize. Even as he computed them, depression had struck; and, as the decade closed, Cleveland's population barely passed the six-thousand mark.

Lake commerce was fundamental to Cleveland's growth. Steamboats carrying freight and passengers were multiplying on Lake Erie, and in 1830 the Government built a lighthouse at the port. Cabin fare from Buffalo to Cleveland in 1836 was $5; steerage, $2.50. Gradually, luxuries in the form of fabrics, furnishings, and foods were arriving from the East. In 1837, "lemons, raisins, figs" were abundantly advertised, and a few years later, Connecticut shad. Lake trout and whitefish had always been abundant in season. Over thirty sidewheelers were operating in 1839, most of them stopping at Cleveland.

Shipping and exchange constituted the principal commercial activity of the city. Manufacturing was still in the primitive stage. Until the canal era, Cleveland depended upon the farmers of the county for its business; now a vast fan-shaped agricultural area was opening up, and increasing commerce and trade reflected the benefits to the city on the lake.

The decade of the thirties witnessed the founding of three establishments that were still in existence in 1946: Strong Cobb & Company, 1833; Hamlin Finance Company, 1834; and J. H. Brown & Son, Inc., 1837.

Rumors of war were thick in 1837. Some two thousand "patriots" crossed the river at Detroit and took Fort Malden from the Canadian garrison. A Mexican cruiser fired upon an American merchant brig. In Florida, an Indian uprising was in progress. In the midst of these threats and the turmoil of emotional and economic confusion came financial panic, retarding the training and progress that the two young military companies in Cleveland expected to make.

Good management and the sale of public lands had squared the nation's obligations, and in 1835-36, its people owed not a cent of public debt!

Speculative enthusiasm and promises to pay, however, were brought sharply to task with the Panic of 1837. President Andrew Jackson's "specie circular" of July 11, 1836, forbade the Treasury to receive anything but gold and silver in payment of public lands; and as state banks did not have adequate specie to redeem their notes, the inflationary boom in the West collapsed. By the end of May, 1837, all banks had suspended specie payment and many failed. As a result of the depression, the Government went into the business of borrowing—only $336,000, but the long upward climb to the astronomical billions of a century later had begun.

While the canal era brought great commercial and industrial progress to Cleveland and the State, it hastened the financial crisis of '37. To satisfy local interests throughout Ohio, branches of canals were constructed in a network of more than a thousand miles. A fantastic period of borrowing brought about passage of the Plunder Act in 1838, committing the State to assist any private company that would build either a canal, railroad, or turnpike, by subscribing one-third of the capital stock of the company. Repeal of the act in 1840 saved Ohio from bankruptcy, but some of the other states that faced the same conditions were not so fortunate. The early canal days were indeed scandalous.

Cleveland and Ohio City suffered from the hard times, and the Bank of Cleveland closed, leaving only the pioneer Commercial Bank. Land and building investors lost heavily. Public improvements were postponed. Currency became worthless; and coin, especially silver, was so scarce that it was difficult to "make change." "Shinplaster" due bills appeared, often poorly printed, acknowledging obligations and leading to much confusion.

High prices prevailed, as shown in a letter written by Theodore Breck to his brother, John, in Northampton, Masachusetts, on April 20, 1839: "Flour is worth $7.50 per bbl.; hay, $8.00 per ton; pork, $22.00 per bbl.; beef, $6.00; corn, $1.00 per bushel; oats, 50 cents; potatoes, $1.00; oxen per yoke, $80.00 to $100.00."

Shandy Hall, built in 1815, was in excellent condition in 1946 when it was given as a museum to the Western Reserve Historical Society by the Norton family. CLEVELAND PICTURE COLLECTION, CLEVELAND PUBLIC LIBRARY.

The Astor House was the oldest building in Cleveland when it was destroyed in 1923. It was said to have been a trading post for fur traders before Moses Cleaveland arrived in 1796. STANLEY L. MᶜMICHAEL COLLECTION, CLEVELAND PUBLIC LIBRARY.

Cuyahoga County's first Court House and Jail, completed in 1813, from a painting in the Western Reserve Historical Society Museum.

The grist-mill, built by the Shakers in 1845, was the only stone building in the Colony. It was destroyed by its owner, Charles Reader, in 1886.

Curtis Cramer was a Shaker trustee at various times.

Clymena Minor was an eldress of the Shaker Society.

The neglected home of the East family as it appeared ten years after the Shakers departed.

PICTURES ON THIS PAGE COURTESY WESTERN RESERVE HISTORICAL SOCIETY

Cleveland's neighbors followed the growth of the lake city intently and sometimes jealously. The *Erie Gazette* observed in 1838, "Cleveland has had its day, and reached the zenith of its popularity . . . Erie (Pennsylvania) is progressing steadily and surely to greatness and importance, while the mushroom city of Cleveland is retrograding almost as rapidly as it sprang up." The *Herald* replied that there were no stores for rent in the city, and nine large warehouses had been erected during the year.

Nathan Perry and one hundred and ninety-seven fellow citizens, representing two-thirds of Cleveland's taxable property, protested in 1839 against an extravagant administration and excessive taxation. The City Council had too many arbitrary powers, they declared, and Cleveland was in danger of bankruptcy. Naturally, this sweeping charge further delayed public improvements. The "period of purging and sobering" continued until 1842.

1830

Having come under the influence of Thomas and Alexander Campbell, religious reformers who were recruiting converts in Mahoning, Portage, and Geauga counties, young Sidney Rigdon joined them and became a popular and powerful orator. For some time he had been preaching in the vicinity of Kirtland, Mantua, and Hiram. In his discourses he prophesied wonders that were strangely related to the Indian mounds and lost races, and he announced that a revealing book would soon explain the mysteries. His remarks were based upon a manuscript that he had read a few years earlier. In the fall of this year, the first copy of the *Book of Mormon* to reach Ohio fell into his hands. It contained translations from certain golden plates purported to enclose an ancient record, and was the foundation for Rigdon's sermon at a Campbellite meeting in Kirtland. Thus Mormonism was preached in the State for the first time. The minister and his wife were immersed as Mormons, and the Campbellites were incensed at Rigdon's desertion from their beliefs. The day of miracles had come for those who became followers of the new faith, preached the dramatic and pleading clergyman, and many joined under his frenzied spell. In these highly emotional meetings, people were overcome with convulsions and strange emotions, jabbering insanely in what were believed to be ancient tongues inspiring power and discernment.

A "Free School," established in Cleveland this year, was supported by subscription, "for the education of male and female children of every religious denomination." It was predominantly a Sunday School.

In "a large and respectable" group of citizens, meeting at the Court House on March 31, the temperance movement had its beginning. A drive was directed at "fifteen to twenty grog shops." This County Temperance Society inspired the comment that there was no "common drunkard" in the village.

Early in the year, an ordinance was passed regulating markets. Fresh meats could be sold every weekday, and vegetables and "other articles" could be offered only on Wednesdays and Saturdays. Business ended at 10 A.M. in the market on Ontario Street south of the Square. "Monopolizing" of stalls was prohibited. A village seal was adopted, and a tax of one-half mill on the dollar was ordered on city property.

Railroad passenger service started in the United States on May 24, when the Baltimore & Ohio Railroad Company began running a "brigade" of horse-drawn cars on a 14-mile line from Ellicott's Mills, Maryland, to Baltimore. On August 25, Peter Cooper's *Tom Thumb* demonstrated its ability on the Baltimore & Ohio tracks between Baltimore and Ellicott's Mills, pushing a small, open car with eighteen passengers aboard. It was the first successful American-built steam locomotive; and while it swallowed the dust of a racing gray mare, it moved steadily toward its goal—the Ohio River and Lake Erie.

Five sidewheelers were carrying passengers between Buffalo and Detroit via Cleveland. An occasional explosion called attention to the "devilish contraption," and some travelers preferred horseback, fearing that a side-wheel would fall off, creating abrupt finality.

The *Herald* announced with pride on June 24, that "now the traveller to the South, instead of providing himself with a fleet horse, a carbine and a brace of pistols and toiling weeks in the forest to reach a point on the Ohio where he might take a Flat Boat, can take the Telegraph Line (of stagecoaches) at Cleveland and in four days sit down in Cincinnati, and in ten more bring him to New Orleans." An elegant coach with a team of prancing horses dominated newspaper advertisements, but there was little comfort in a journey over rutted roads, intolerably dusty in the dry season, indescribably muddy, and often impassable when wet. Travel many times became more burdensome than walking, yet it continued to be popular.

Navigation was opened on the Ohio Canal from Lake Erie to Newark on July 10, a total of 174 miles, and Cleveland was flourishing under the impact of this new form of transportation. Large quantities of flour and wheat were coming from the south to be exchanged for salt and essential merchandise. Mechanics were in great demand, and cash was offered for their services.

The Western Seamen's Friend Society was established as a Protestant mission and lodge for destitute sailors. It was the first Cleveland society to receive charitable donations.

The Rev. James McElroy became "minister in charge" of Trinity Church, giving three-fourths of his time to the parish and receiving a salary of $450. A six-hundred-pound bell was placed in the church belfry.

The first president of Western Reserve College, founded in 1826, was elected this year—Charles Backus Storrs, ardent Abolitionist, who served from 1830 until his death in 1834. His faculty of five members gave heroic service in return for pitifully small salaries, paid most of the time in farm produce or merchandise. Storrs was succeeded by George Edmond Pierce, who guided the school's destiny through twenty-one perilous years. A theological department, established in 1830, was abandoned in 1852; a professorship of chemistry was created in 1837. The college was a progressive institution, experimenting in co-operative education, manual education, and co-education. It admitted Negroes long before the Civil War. Students were required to attend services in the chapel which they erected on the campus in 1831. The Sabbath was religiously observed, although in a strict sense the institution, forerunner of Adelbert College of Western Reserve University and Western Reserve Academy, was considered undenominational.

Western Reserve College was indeed fortunate in securing men of character and achievement for its early faculties. The first tutor in chemistry, Elizur Wright, Jr., later became a newspaperman, campaigning against fraudulent insurance practices. He drew the tables upon which modern life insurance is predicated, devised the first paid-up policy, and earned the title, "father of life insurance." Nathan Perkins Seymour, professor of Greek and Latin languages from 1840 to 1870, was undoubtedly one of the leading scholars of his time. His son became a professor at Yale, and his grandson, its president. Charles Augustus Young, professor of mathematics and natural philosophy, 1856-66, was the author of an important series of mathematical text-books. Samuel St. John taught chemistry, mineralogy, and geology, 1838-52, and was one of the first lecturers on chemistry.

Levi Johnson's shipbuilding career had closed, and this year he completed Cleveland's first lighthouse for the United States Government at a cost of $8,000. It was a brick tower, erected on a bluff at Main and Water streets. Johnson also erected a lighthouse at Cedar Point and set the channel buoys in Sandusky Bay. Later, he built 700 feet of the east pier for the Government in Cleveland. On "Lighthouse Hill" Johnson built his fine home (northeast corner of Lake and West 9th). One of Cleveland's most useful citizens, he died a wealthy man in 1871 at the age of eighty-six.

There was a ready market for the product of Ebenezer Duty's labors. In his small yard he was molding clay forms and sun-baking them into brick, a substantial step in the building industry of the village. His son, Andrew, applied for a patent on a brick-making machine in 1832. The art descended to a great-grandson, Spencer M.

Captain Jared Clark looked over 100 acres at the Public Square and Ontario Street, offered to him for $10 per acre, but turned them down as inferior farm land. Going south to Brecksville, he purchased 200 acres for $5 an acre. Euclid Street property (near East 4th) was now selling at $2 per foot.

John P. Spencer came to Rockport this year and commenced to clear his 125-acre farm in the southwestern section of the township. A country highway later bore his name—Spencer Road in Rocky River.

Eastern entertainers brought stark tragedy and amusing comedy to the boards of local halls. Sensational chemical and scientific exhibitions were well patronized. Collections of birds, animals, and curiosities, an Egyptian mummy in its coffin, a gory wax works, trained-animal acts, and the periodic visit of the circus delighted the citizens.

Louisa Lane, child dancer, appeared in the village with her parents and the famous Madame Celeste, danseuse and pantomimist. Many years later, as Mrs. John Drew, "the grand old lady of the American stage," she recalled her childhood appearance. "I remember the village with its pretty rose gardens leading down to the lake. There were only four of us in the company. I do not remember whether it was in Cleveland or Buffalo that we had such a time to secure an orchestra. I believe the only talent was a solitary Negro who could play a fiddle and all he could play was *Yankee Doodle* and *Hail Columbia*."

Selling their property in New York, Benjamin and Rebecca Cromwell Rouse, agents for the American Sabbath School Union of Philadelphia, reached their frontier post in Cleveland on October 17. They rented a house on Superior Street for $91 a year, fitting the front room as a book depository from which religious literature was dispensed. Prominent women met in the Rouse home and assisted Mrs. Rouse with her evangelistic work. It is said that male "sinners" of Cleveland observed that "there is more religion in Rouse's windows than in the whole village besides." From this small effort grew the women's union gospel work of Cleveland. Benjamin Rouse organized Trinity Sunday School in 1830, and the First Baptist and First Methodist Episcopal Sunday Schools in 1833. Purchasing land on the northwest corner of Superior Street and the Square (Marshall Building site), he built a small two-story building with his residence above and store space for rental below.

Thieves were helping themselves to all kinds of property, particularly horses, and citizens organized in self-defense. On November 23, farmers of the county formed the Union Club for the Detection of Horse Thieves at the Spangler Tavern, with Datus Kelley, chairman of the meeting. The first officers were Charles M. Giddings, commandant, and Gordon Fitch, secretary.

A little group of colored folk, fugitive slaves from the deep South who were jubilant in freedom from their masters, met on an early winter evening in a house near the corner of Bolivar and Erie streets to form the first Negro religious body in Cleveland, St. John's African Methodist Episcopal Church. The Rev. William Paul Quinn, an itinerant preacher, had called them together into a prayer group, where they could manifest freely their impassioned spiritual emotions. The general Negro population, however, showed no interest, and it was not until 1848 that the church appeared in the city records.

The Cleveland Insurance Company was granted a perpetual charter with power to operate both an insurance and banking business. Capital was $500,000. It was devoted entirely to banking until 1861, when reorganization solely as an insurance company was effected. The company was one of many in the nation that failed to survive losses sustained in the great Chicago fire of 1871. Eastern insurance companies opened offices in Cleveland as the city grew.

There were a number of important arrivals in Cleveland this year. George Hoadley was elected justice of the peace, and "decided over twenty thousand cases," few being appealed and none reversed. He served as mayor of Cleveland from 1846 to 1848, moving to Cincinnati the next year. His son, George, who spelled his family name without the "e," was elected governor of Ohio in 1883. Seth A. Abbey became city marshal and judge of the Police Court. Abbey Avenue was named for him. His son, Henry G., became a leading figure in Cleveland. Norman C. Baldwin joined Noble H. Merwin in the commission business. He was a member of the firm of Giddings, Baldwin & Company that owned one of the first regular steamship lines on the lake. In later years, Baldwin turned to banking and real estate. Richard Winslow brought with him both capital and energy, and opened a wholesale grocery store on Superior Street opposite Union Lane. His imposing residence facing the Public Square (May Company site) was built by Levi Johnson, and reflected his business success. Winslow's future lay in building lake vessels. S. H. Sheldon opened a drug store on Detroit Street, Brooklyn, and later turned to the grocery business.

1831

The first issue of the *Cleveland Advertiser* appeared on January 6 without the "a" in "Cleveland." Madison Kelley, editor, and Henry Bolles produced the weekly that first championed the Whig Party and later supported the Democrats. The paper changed hands several times. John W. Allen was one of its editors. In January, 1835, it located above the Post Office, and in 1836, it became a daily.

When Milo H. Hickox came to Cleveland from Rochester he was shocked at the high price asked for a room—$1 a month. Writing to a friend, he commented, "Everything that we want to live upon commands cash and a high price. Mechanics' wages are low. Journeymen get from $10 to $20 per month and board; I get nine shillings and six pence per day, and board myself. I have the best of work . . . There are between fifteen and twenty grogshops, and they all live."

Only one course in natural science was offered by the Ashtabula School of Science and Industry that opened to male and female students this year at Mechanicsville, Ohio. It was a self-help school, and students were required to work two or three hours a day. This greatly assisted parents who were obliged to stretch their finances to educate their children. In 1835 the school and the building were moved to Austinburg, Ohio, and became the Grand River Institute.

The first Shakespearean performance was given in the little brick Court House by Gilbert & Trowbridge. In lumber wagons and oxcarts the pioneers came from as far as Doan's Corners to see the showfolks present the drama, and they liked it.

A boom in land speculation originated this year that produced virtual war between Cleveland and Brooklyn. It began in Brooklyn, when the Buffalo Company and the New Harbor Company, made up of Buffalo and Brooklyn investors, purchased the Carter farm between the Cuyahoga and the old river bed, consisting of about 80 acres. They laid it out in lots and streets —Centre, Main, and others—and put it on the market for anyone who could pay one-fourth of the purchase price in cash. Lots changed hands over and over at inflated prices that reached $250 a foot front in 1836. A distillery built on a mound in the vicinity further inflated the spirits of the investors, and gave the name of Whisky Island to the district.

Prospect Street, first named Cuyahoga Street, was laid out this year from Ontario to Erie.

In the early thirties, Dr. David Long built a substantial stone house at the southwest corner of Seneca and Superior streets. Here his daughter, Mary H., seventeen, became the bride of Solomon L. Severance, a young merchant, in 1833. He died five years later, leaving her with two sons, Louis H. and Solon L. The doctor maintained an office at Superior and Erie streets. In 1836 he moved to a farm on Kinsman Street, where he built a fine stone house with classic columns, that he sold to Erastus Gaylord in 1845 (St. Ann's Maternity Hospital site). In his brick house built to the west (Woodland and Longwood avenues), Dr. Long died in 1851, and Cleveland lost one of its most valuable citizens. Long Street, cut through the doctor's pasture, and Longwood Avenue were named in his honor.

John M. Hughes, a brewer in the "Flats," was a passenger on the *DeWitt Clinton* when it made its trial run from Albany to Schenectady, August 9. It was the first steam locomotive to operate on the 17-mile Mohawk & Hudson Railroad, pioneer unit of the New York Central System, hauling three converted stagecoaches on strap-type rails over a 12½-mile course in less than an hour. Despite enthusiasm for the new venture, it was believed impossible for the road to survive competition of the palatial steamers operating between New York and Albany. Besides, the physical difficulties of constructing a railroad were colossal.

A Methodist class of nineteen members was organized at Doan's Corners by the Rev. Milton Colt, who established the first Methodist Sunday School in Cleveland Village. Meetings were held by the Methodist Church Society of East Cleveland in the stone schoolhouse until 1837, when their first sanctuary was erected. They shared it occasionally with the Presbyterians, and some of the good Methodist brethren protested at the desecration by Jarvis F. Hanks' fiddle, despite his claim that it had been converted. A brick church was completed in 1870 on the original site in the heart of the flourishing East End community. The congregation became known as the Euclid Avenue Methodist Church, and in 1920 it joined with Epworth Memorial as the Epworth-Euclid Church.

A four-day series of revival meetings, bordering on the fanatical, was held in August, leaving in its wake "maniacs, family broils, neighborhood disturbances, assaults and misdemeanors." As a result, a citizens' committee was appointed to caution leaders against such vigorous religious demonstrations.

James Abram Garfield was born on November 19 in a log cabin in Cuyahoga County (Jackson and SOM Center roads, Orange Township). A replica of the humble birthplace of the twentieth President of the United States stands on the grounds of "Lawnfield," the Garfield home in Mentor (maintained by the Western Reserve Historical Society).

1832

James S. Clark razed the Cleveland House on the Public Square, and a larger, three-story hotel took its place in the early winter. Lorenzo A. Kelsey, wealthy and cultured, managed it for a short time in 1837. Meetings, balls, and public functions made the Cleveland the bright spot on the Square. In 1842, James W. Cook, proprietor, officially joined the "drys," banning the sale of liquors. There could be no doubt of his stand when he renamed the hotel the Cleveland Temperance House.

Having paid its liabilities after the financial crash in 1820, amounting to less than ten thousand dollars due the Treasurer of the United States, the Commercial Bank of Lake Erie was reorganized, opening its doors on April 2. Leonard Case was president, and Truman P. Handy, cashier. It is related that through the influence of George Bancroft, eminent historian, capital of $200,000 was provided to make re-opening of the bank possible. Bancroft sent Handy to Cleveland, where he became one of the city's great bankers. The new directors were Leonard Case, Samuel Williamson, Edward Clark, Peter M. Weddell, Heman Oviatt, Charles M. Giddings, John Blair, Alfred Kelley, David King, James Duncan, Roswell Kent, T. P. Handy, and John W. Allen. Upon expiration of the charter in 1842, the bank's affairs were placed in the hands of Handy, Henry B. Payne, and Dudley Baldwin, special commissioners, who made final disposition. The remaining assets were distributed in June, 1845.

The first boat traveled the entire length of the Ohio Canal from Cleveland to Portsmouth on the Ohio River, a distance of about 309 miles. The Cleveland terminus was on the river near the foot of Superior Street.

The *Cleaveland Herald* dropped the "a" from its masthead on May 1, and, consistent with common usage, was henceforth known as the *Cleveland Herald*. One reason historians give for the change is that the letters in a new font of type were too wide for the space, and the compositor did the expedient thing—cut the "a." Another story states that the publisher received a stock of paper too narrow to accommodate the name of the newspaper in the heading, and to solve the difficulty, the "a" was dropped as superfluous. A third story relates that the "a" in the title type was broken, and there being none to replace it, the shortened form of spelling was used. Records of Cleveland Township show the "a" in general use until about this time. Newspaper advertisements were being dramatized with crude, impersonal woodcut illustrations.

The first piano was brought to the village by the town brewer, and crowds gathered to hear this newest wonder. Short-term singing schools, church music, and an occasional brass band, imported for special occasions, constituted the gamut of early-day music.

An epidemic of Asiatic cholera was raging in Quebec and Montreal, and panic spread throughout the Great Lakes region. With the arrival in Cleveland of a troop boat from the Black Hawk War came the scourge that found fertile soil in the village that was without sanitation and health facilities. Dr. David Long appointed the first Board of Health, on June 24, consisting of Drs. E. W. Cowles, Joshua Mills and Oran St. John, Silas Belden and Charles Denison (latter two were not doctors); Dr. S. J. Weldon and Daniel Worley were added later. They were to take all necessary health measures in combating the disease. Vessels were quarantined and inspected. A "pest house"—Cleveland's second hospital—was set up on Whisky Island. A village hearse, harness, and bier were purchased. A system of smallpox vaccinations was adopted, and free inoculations were offered to those unable to pay. About fifty deaths resulted in Cleveland. News that Black Hawk and his warriors had sacked Fort Dearborn (Chicago) added to the fears of the stricken village.

Charles Whittlesey, of Connecticut, twenty-four-year-old West Point graduate who had seen service in the Black Hawk War, resigned from the army and opened a law office in Cleveland this year. While he soon acquired an interest in local newspapers, he was to become best known for his geological surveys and historical writings.

An ordinance established sidewalk lines on July 11: on Superior Street, 16½ feet wide; on 6-rod streets, 12 feet; on 4-rod streets, 10 feet; and on other streets, lanes and alleys, as might be designated. Trespassing on a sidewalk with a vehicle meant a fine up to $20. The luxury of new sidewalks was drowned, however, in taxpayers' grumbling, when they learned that a tax of two mills on the dollar had been levied.

When the Mestayer theatrical troupe disbanded in Cleveland through inability to make ends meet, the managers of the company presented comic shows in Seth A. Abbey's new tavern at the corner of Ontario and Michigan streets (Higbee store site) to earn enough money to leave town. Here vaudeville in Cleveland had its beginning. During a performance, Dan Marble made his debut in a sketch and songs, starting him on the road to fame as a great comedian.

Rufus Dunham owned a 140-acre farm that stretched northward from Euclid (to Hough), and this year he replaced his log cabin with a larger log structure called Dunham Tavern (6709 Euclid).

The first Baptist meeting in Cleveland was held on November 19 at the Academy.

Christian families, who had united in a Sunday School, met on December 31 and organized the First Congregational Church of Newburgh, under the direction of the Rev. Stephen Peet of Euclid. Charter members were Edward and Theodosia Taylor, James and Sarah Ashwell, James and Elizabeth Southam, John and Amy Righter, John and Amy Stair, and Elizabeth Stair. They worshiped for a time in the town hall and in the schoolhouse. The Rev. John Keys supplied the pulpit, and was succeeded by the Rev. Matthew Fox, the first pastor. The church became Presbyterian in government in 1840 as the First Presbyterian Church of Newburgh. Willing sacrifice and earnest effort made possible the dedication of a little white meeting house in 1845 at Woodland Hills and Gorman Street. During the pastorate of the beloved Rev. Eleroy Curtis, a new brick edifice was dedicated in 1872 on Miles Park that became known as the Miles Park Presbyterian Church (9114 Miles Park). The Rev. Arthur C. Ludlow, who served from 1887 to 1923, was its best-known minister. He was not only an able pastor, but he was a writer and speaker of importance; and under his ministry, the church became a leader in the denomination in northern Ohio. The Rev. Peter Macaulay, pastor in 1946, had come to the pulpit in 1927.

1833

A hole was cut in the ice on January 13, and four persons were baptized in Lake Erie in the first baptismal service of the Baptist faith in Cleveland.

Seventeen devout Baptists organized the First Baptist Society on February 16, the charter members including Moses White, Benjamin and Rebecca C. Rouse, John Seaman, Horatio Ranney, Leonard and Sophia Stockwell, John and Harriet Malvin, and others. The Rev. Richard Taggart was the first pastor, and services were held in the Academy. At great sacrifice, a meeting house was provided in 1836 costing $13,000. Deacon Brewster Pelton, who lived in Euclid, was moved to mortgage his farm for $2,000 to provide his contribution, although neighbors questioned his judgment. John Seaman, William T. Smith, Loren Prentiss, and earnest families rejoiced when the brick sanctuary was dedicated at the southeast corner of Seneca and Champlain streets. It was said to be the finest church in Ohio, surmounted by the first steeple in Cleveland, a 150-foot spire having at its base a clock and a belfry.

A bill passed by the Legislature in February encouraged the organization of fire companies, and forty-five volunteer citizens banded together as the Live Oak Company, under John G. McCurdy, foreman, to defend Cleveland against the fire menace. Purchase of a hand-pumping engine, called Live Oak No. 1, bolstered their spirits and cost the village $700. Headquarters were on Superior Street, just west of Water Street.

Cleveland had found its place in "the age of lyceums." In February the Cleveland Lyceum was incorporated by Sherlock J. Andrews, John W. Allen, Orville B. Skinner, James S. Clark, Irad Kelley, John Barr, Leonard Case, Edward Baldwin, Richard Hussey, James L. Conger, and Thomas M. Kelley. Henry H. Dodge was recording secretary. Amusements were few at this time and there was a craving for knowledge. Young men of the community sought mutual improvement and entertainment in cultural organizations, where they exchanged the few books and magazines and settled the questions of the day. The lyceum flourished for about ten years, expanding its activity to present lecture courses and imported speakers.

In February the newly incorporated Cleveland Library Company commenced soliciting funds for a subscription library, the first in the village. It struggled through the panic of '37 and perished about 1840.

Thomas Burnham decided to abandon his occupation as master of a freight boat running on the Champlain Canal from Whitehall to Albany,

New York, and with his young wife started to Cleveland. Their journey discloses the common modes of transportation at this time. From Glens Falls to Saratoga they traveled by team. Here they boarded the railroad for Schenectady. The cars on this line resembled stagecoaches, ran on strap rails, and were drawn by three horses driven tandemwise. At Schenectady, the Burnhams took passage for Buffalo on the Erie Canal, thence to Cleveland on the steamer *Pennsylvania,* which stopped at every port, taking four days and nights for the trip. Burnham took charge of a Brooklyn Township school at Washington and Pearl streets.

The Black Hawk War was over. Black Hawk, famous Indian chief, had been subdued; and, in government custody, was peacefully observing eastern cities and the white man's progress. On his way back to the West, he asked to visit his mother's grave on the Cuyahoga's bank. Alone in a canoe, he paddled up the river to a bluff overlooking the valley (from the southeast corner of Riverside Cemetery), where he remained a while, and it is said there were tears in his eyes when he returned. It is believed that Black Hawk was born in the neighborhood of Cleveland.

John A. Foote—or Foot, son of Samuel A. Foote, governor of Connecticut, came to Cleveland this year. His father had won distinction in the United States Senate, having introduced an historic resolution relating to public lands that prompted the famous Webster-Hayne debate. Foote, a Yale graduate, formed a law partnership with Sherlock J. Andrews that continued for a number of years, and he gave liberally in service to his city and state.

In June, the Cleveland Water Company was incorporated by Philo Scovill and others to provide water for the village, but little seems to have been achieved beyond the charter stage.

Cleveland's growth demanded an expansion of street facilities. River Street was laid out from Superior to Union Lane, and Meadow, Spring, and Lighthouse streets were planned this year.

Jonathan Goldsmith, well-known Painesville architect, built the first imposing house on Euclid Street (site of Taylor's department store) for Samuel Cowles this year. The three-story, brick residence, built "way out" of town, was the show place of the community.

A steamer that arrived in Cleveland on about July 1 brought Stephen A. Douglas, twenty, equipped with letters of introduction to "gentlemen of that place." He was most fortunate in receiving the offer of Sherlock J. Andrews, distinguished lawyer, to study law in his office, and "with increased spirit and zeal" young Douglas went to work. In a few days, however, he was attacked with a fever that lasted four months. In spite of the doctor's predictions, he recovered, but with the urge to move westward, where he later embarked on his famous career as legislator and statesman.

The *Herald* reported that to July 1, two hundred and thirty ships had arrived in the harbor, and the docks were "thronged with passengers." A great deal of freight was being handled, and the canal was prospering. During the week of July 20, fifty-two vessels arrived with heavy cargoes, twenty-four having come via the Welland Canal and eleven from Canadian ports on Lake Erie.

Joseph Smith and fifty families had come from New York to join the Mormon colony at Kirtland, Ohio, in 1831. Inspired by vision and prophecy, the "saints" sold their farms, stock, and goods to provide $40,000—a large sum in those days—with which to build a place of worship for the Church of Jesus Christ of Latter-day Saints. The cornerstone of the three-story, stone structure, 80 by 60 feet, was laid in July of this year. A belfry surmounted the building, which was an architectural confusion. Pews were hand-carved, and great windows reached to the ceiling. The faithful toiled unceasingly to fulfill their mission, and at night stood guard with their guns against opposition that had developed in the vicinity as a result of their fanatical behavior and strange practices. On March 27, 1836, the Temple was dedicated. Kirtland became a thriving town under the leadership of Brigham Young, who became one of the twelve apostles in 1835. In February, 1834, he married Mary Ann Angell, a Kirtland girl, who became the second of his twenty-six wives. Large business developments were undertaken, and the elders became involved in such financial difficulties that they were forced to leave Kirtland. On July 6, 1838, "vision and prophecy" guided 515 men, women and children out of the community, westward in 58 wagons, and with them they took a large number of cows. A goodly number of the sect that did not join Young's caravan formed the Reorganized Church of Jesus Christ of the Latter-day Saints. For many years, the Mormon property remained in the name of Joseph Smith or his family. The Kirtland Academy was later installed in the abandoned Temple; and the Western Reserve Teachers' Seminary trained teachers here. The blue exterior of the first Mormon temple in the United States had grayed by 1946, but the shrine of a courageous people remained firm and strong, the meeting place of the Mormon congregation in Kirtland.

Datus and Irad Kelley purchased the westerly half of Cunningham's Island, north of Sandusky in Lake Erie, at $1.50 per acre, continuing to buy until they owned the entire island of about three thousand acres. They opened the famous stone quarries, and Datus moved his family there. A community was established, with a school, dock, hotel, and town hall. Kelley Island became famous for its red cedar, vineyards, and peach orchards. Mark Twain once wrote, "You can't fool me with Kelley Island wine; I can tell it from vinegar every time—by the label on the bottle."

Theater audiences had outgrown the little Court House, and Samuel and William Cook erected the first theater building at about this time on the corner of Superior at Union Lane. It was a two-story, frame structure, with stores on the first floor, and an auditorium on the second, about 70 by 50 feet, poorly equipped.

John Stair, newcomer from England, opened a private school in Newburgh, and wrote home on August 16 to say that he regarded Cleveland as "an increasing place," and "for the size of it, the prettiest town I have seen in America." He reported interest in the fine arts, and observed that "this is a poor man's country . . . Situations for single men are very scarce, except as bartenders at taverns, clerks, etc." Turkeys were being marketed at 50 cents each; roasting pigs, 25 cents; mutton, beef, pork, veal, 2 to 4 cents per pound; butter, 9 cents; cheese, 6 cents. "Many raise all they eat, with few exceptions, such as tea, coffee, etc. They raise their own wool and flax which are spun and woven by the women for clothing, so that a farmer is the most independent person in the country." Stair paid 25 cents to post his letter.

Benjamin Harrison, twenty-third President of the United States, was born at North Bend, Ohio, on August 20.

Carpentering was the trade of Admiral Nelson Gray, who arrived this year. He was joined in 1835 by his brother, Nicholas A., and a year later by his youngest brother, Joseph William, both bent on teaching school. After a time, the trio opened a college-preparatory academy on Euclid Street, west of Erie, but the project soon faded. J. W. then entered the law office of Henry B. Payne and Hiram V. Willson, and in about a year was qualified to practice. However, clients were slow in seeking the new attorney, and he found that writing partisan articles for the *Advertiser* helped to fill his free time and satisfy his interest in politics.

Handerson & Punderson opened a retail drug store on lower Superior Street that was the leading establishment for many years. Lewis Handerson, one of the proprietors, was the uncle of Dr. Henry E. Handerson, who became one of Cleveland's best-known physicians. Concoctions that lined the shelves were carefully mixed by the partners: elixir, paregoric, Hungary water, soap liniment, Bateman's drops, Windham pills, milk of roses, verbena extract, chlorine tooth wash, cold cream, cream of lilies, and so on. Dragon's-blood, sassafras, opodeldoc, gum arabic, quicksilver, opium, camphor, proof-spirit, turpentine, ginger, gentian, vitriol, cinnamon, sulphur, and arsenic were in demand. Prescriptions were filled according to physicians' recipes. Household items, such as sealing wax, bug bane, amalgam, lacquer and varnish, black ink, jujube paste, congress water, and shoe blacking were also handled. One of the earliest proprietary medicine concerns, it was the forerunner of Strong Cobb & Company.

Ten Ohio City Methodists met in the home of Nathaniel Burton and formed a Methodist society, holding services in homes and in the Vermont Street schoolhouse. A building fund started by William Warmington provided a sanctuary on Church and Hanover streets that was leveled by a storm in 1836 before entirely completed. The basement was ready for use a year later, but not until nine years passed was the little Hanover Street Methodist Church dedicated. Abolition sentiments ruffled the calm of the membership; and, in 1849, the innovation of a choir shocked about ten members into demanding their letters. The York Street and Hanover Street congregations united in 1866, and a new church home was dedicated in 1870 at the northeast corner of what later became Franklin and West 32nd Street. The Rev. James Erwin was pastor. The two-ton church bell, a replica of the Liberty Bell, only larger, crashed through two floors to the basement after a time. It was rehung and rang for the first time announcing the Armistice ending World War I. The pew in which President William McKinley worshiped in 1896 was inscribed with his name. Trinity Church, 1894, and Garden Avenue Church, 1898, were the offspring of the Franklin Boulevard Methodist Church, whose pastor in 1946 was the Rev. Wilbur B. Meiser. Time dealt unkindly with the little pioneer church, built in 1836, and at the turn of the century it was being used as a livery stable.

A statement published in September indicated that in eight years Cleveland exports had increased from $50,000 to $2,000,000; and imports, from $130,640 to $4,700,000. New York and Pennsylvania markets were looking to the thriving village for a greater volume of its products.

"A Sunday School was organized in 1833 or 1834," wrote Samuel H. Mather in a discussion of early Cleveland schools, "a kind of mission or ragged school. The children, however, were found so ignorant that Sunday School teaching as such, was out of the question. The time of the teacher was obliged to be spent in teaching the children how to read. To remedy this difficulty and make the Sunday School available, a day school was started. It was supported by voluntary contributions, and was a charity school, in fact, to which none were sent but the very poorest people."

The Leonid shower, a brilliant meteoric display, was observed on November 12, and continued for two days with marked intensity.

James S. Clark, Edmund Clark, and Richard Hilliard laid out Cleveland Centre in December, comprising the land in Ox Bow Bend, the first curve of the Cuyahoga River, and offered town lots for sale at inflated prices. This was an elaborate piece of city planning. A geometric street pattern centered at Gravity Place, the east landing on the river. From it radiated China, Russia, British, French, and German streets, although not until several decades later was there a Chinese or a Russian in Cleveland. Of the streets, three became important: Columbus Street carried east-and-west traffic until the era of bridge-building; Merwin Street served the shipping and warehousing industry along the river until the sixties; Commercial Street was preserved in the name given to the Commercial Street Hill.

The union of Presbyterians and Congregationalists, as it pertained to the training of young men at Western Reserve College in Hudson, was not satisfactory to either denomination and the founding of Oberlin Collegiate Institute (later Oberlin College) resulted in December at Oberlin, Ohio. A township was acquired and families were encouraged to settle on these lands to form a bulwark against the westward invasion of worldliness and irreligion. President Asa Mahan and Charles G. Finney, theology professor, were leaders in the international reform movement then in progress. Not only young men and women, but all colors and creeds, were admitted to Oberlin in this day of violent opposition to "joint education" and riotous debate on the Negro question. It was the first college to abolish race considerations in admission, and to give degrees to women, conferring them first in 1841. "Manual labor with study" constituted the educational system. Before the Civil War, Oberlin was a strong anti-slavery center. Early faculties were composed chiefly of New England Congregationalists, and the Oberlin theology was a modified form of Calvinism, which included the doctrine of free will. The college was named for Jean Frederic Oberlin, Strassbourg educator, a follower of the Pestalozzian system of education by manual labor.

This year saw the completion of 400 miles of the Ohio Canal and its branches. Not long afterward the waterway was opened from Cleveland to Portsmouth via Columbus, and the canal had increased to a total of 500 miles.

Canal commerce in 1833 serves as an index to economic needs of the North and South. Freight shipped out of Cleveland on the canal totaled 9,896,440 pounds of merchandise and 28,447 barrels of salt. Inbound shipments included wheat, corn, flour, tobacco, whisky, beef, butter, cheese, and 49,131 bushels of coal. The Government had sold 4,000,000 acres of land at $1 per acre, and the combination of cheap land and canal progress lengthened the lines of pioneering families seeking new homes in the West.

Until this time, early statutes governing the status of the Negro were scarcely observed, as there was little north-and-south traffic through Ohio. With the opening of the canal, however, there was a sudden consciousness of the slumbering Fugitive-Slave Law and the Ohio laws enacted in 1804 and 1807, which required registry of blacks and mulattoes, bonding that guaranteed good behavior and payment for support, and penalty for harboring escaped persons. As early as 1810, antislavery sentiment was stirring in Cleveland, and a conflict of interests was evident in 1827. It was the common understanding that no fugitive could be recovered in the village. The first school for Negroes was supported by subscription. It was opened in 1832 by John Malvin, pioneer Negro preacher, engineer, canal-boat captain, and fervent Abolitionist. Dr. David Long was president of the Cleveland Anti-Slavery Society, organized in 1833, and his son-in-law, Solomon L. Severance, was secretary.

Spectacular entertainment was provided this year by the "American Fire King," a so-called fire-eater, the Siamese Twins in a three-day appearance at the Franklin House, a circus and menagerie, a theatrical troupe, two equestrian companies, "General" Black Hawk, and a female orang-outang. Theatrical performances were rare, not more than one a year. Their runs were usually short and generally not profitable to the company.

1834

The first serious fire occurred on January 20, when the Martin C. Hill store on Superior Street burned. A loss of $12,000 was suffered on the two-story, frame building that had housed a stock of $9,000. Organized fire-fighting efforts were strengthened as a result.

The Live Oak volunteers became an organized company this year, known as Eagle No. 1, Captain McCurdy in command. A fire department was soon established, composed of Neptune No. 2, Phoenix No. 4, Forest City

Hook and Ladder Company No. 1, Hope Hose Company No. 1, and No. 3, the latter made up of boys with no official recognition.

Cleveland boundary lines were extended on February 18, annexing "All the two-acre lots east of Erie street, the tier south of Ohio street, and a parcel at the southwest corner of the original plat, which was not surveyed or laid off." At about this time, Euclid Street, now a state road, was covered with planks from Perry Street to the city limits. A "corduroy" road was built out in the woods across the swamp (East 55th Street).

The first church on the Public Square was dedicated on February 26. Land had been purchased several years before from Joel Scranton for $400 by the committee of the First Presbyterian Society of Cleveland: Samuel Williamson, Samuel Cowles, John M. Sterling, Leonard Case, Harmon

*The First Presbyterian Church was known
as the Stone Church.*

Kingsbury, Nathan Perry, Samuel Starkweather, Ashbel W. Walworth, Edmund Clark, and Peter M. Weddell. Six of these staunch pillars of the church donated $50 each, and four gave $25 each to make the purchase possible. The structure was located at the northwest corner of the Public Square and Ontario Street. It represented a long struggle to surmount many difficulties, chiefly due to the scarcity of money and material. The building was temple-like in style, with pilastered front and high steps, surrounded by a low board fence, and cost $9,500. The Rev. John Keep of Oberlin, called as pulpit supply in 1833, preached the dedicatory sermon. Before long, the eighty-four high-backed pews, and the few in the gallery, were inadequate for the congregation, and the matter of expansion became a serious question.

As the First Presbyterian Church was the first stone church in Cleveland, it came to be known as the Stone Church, or Old Stone Church, rather than for its denomination. The Rev. Samuel Clark Aiken became the first pastor in 1835, and served for twenty-six years. According to the *Annals of the Early Settlers Association,* Dr. Aiken came to Cleveland "at a time when there was much discussion in the church—'throwing many unstable men off their balance, skepticism, infidelity, mormonism and universalism, was engrossing many minds.' Dr. Aiken held on to the old conservative way, with practical wisdom. Although it was said of him he was very arbitrary in his administration, and prosy as a preacher, at any rate his sermons would not keep old John Blair awake; while sleeping, leaning against the pew door, it suddenly flew open, and he lay sprawling in the aisle, the congregation laughing audibly." Dr. Aiken took more than an active interest in Cleveland affairs, and his influence was broad and deep. Many of the men who were molding the future city were in his congregation, men of the caliber of Charles Whittlesey, Dr. Erastus Cushing, William Bingham, Dr. John Delamater, and Franklin T. Backus.

The Cleveland & Newburgh Railroad Company was incorporated on March 3 with a capital of $50,000. Aaron Barker, David H. Beardsley, Lyman Kendall, Truman P. Handy, John W. Allen, Horace Perry, and James S. Clark were the incorporators. Cleveland's first street railway, built by Ahaz Merchant, ran from the Blue Stone Quarries in Newburgh township through orchards and woods to Euclid Street at Doan's Lane. At Kennard Street it followed the middle of Euclid to the southwest corner of the Public Square, disappearing in the barn back of the Cleveland House (Hotel Cleveland site). Two horses pulled a flat car on wooden rails, and, at first, stone and lumber were hauled. Conveniences were added for passengers the next year, and Silas Merchant, driver, conductor, superintendent, and barn man, made two trips daily. He did a brisk business on July 4, 1835, when he collected $125 in fares. Cleveland's first rapid-transit venture failed to pay, however, and after several years the project was abandoned.

Levi Billings had erected a tavern on the Euclid road (between East 101st and East 105th) about 1825, and his establishment took on importance when horses on the wooden-rail, streetcar line were stabled in his barn. Soon the Billings Tavern became known as the Railroad Hotel, distinguished by a sunken garden in the front yard, laid out with "excellent taste and some knowledge of gardening." At the edge of the stable yard were three poisonous shrubs, said to have been planted by foreigners living in the hotel "to scare away witches," and they persisted in defying efforts to kill them. Nathan Post converted part of the hotel into a family residence in 1846, and here Mary Post conducted a primary school in one room, while Laura Post taught "articulation to the deaf and dumb." Charles A. Post, banker and historian, was born here in 1848. The family razed the hotel and erected a new home in 1874.

The first manufacturing concern in Cleveland, formed under a state charter, was the Cuyahoga Steam Furnace Company (Center and Detroit streets, almost under the High Level Bridge). It was founded on March 3 with a capital of $100,000. The chief stockholders were Josiah Barber,

Richard Lord, and Charles Hoyt. It was the principal plant in the region, and the first Cuyahoga Valley furnace and foundry to use steam power instead of horsepower for blowing. Here was built the first locomotive operated west of the Alleghenies, machinery for the first successful screw propeller to operate on the lakes—the *Emigrant,* castings, wrought iron work, plows, and cannon. Fire swept the shop and a finer plant was erected in 1836 that produced "more than 500 tons of castings, besides a large quantity of wrought iron, giving employment to 70 men."

The Bank of Cleveland was organized this year with a capital stock of $300,000. It was located at 7 Superior Street, according to the 1837 city directory, and its officers at that time were Norman C. Baldwin, president; Alexander Seymour, cashier; T. C. Severance, teller; H. F. Brayton, book-keeper. This was Cleveland's second bank and it closed in the panic of 1837.

The Whig anti-Jackson sentiment was bitter, and a number of political gatherings chose Cleveland to air their feelings. The outstanding convention of the year was held at the Court House on March 18, where demand was made that congressmen "adopt measures to restore the country to its unwonted prosperity." The attendance was two hundred and four, and the *Herald* stated that "never, since the organization of the county, has there been a meeting so numerously attended." Temperance, agricultural, and medical sessions met in Cleveland.

In April, Leonard Case subdivided ten-acre lot No. 1 at the southeast corner of the old city plat, and widened the Newburgh Road—formerly Pittsburgh Street—from 66 feet to 99 feet to benefit his property. Residents were so impressed with the broad thoroughfare that the name was later changed to Broadway. During the year, John M. Woolsey placed on the market the 2-acre lots south of Superior Street and west of Erie.

Brooklyn followers of the Episcopal faith organized the St. John's Episcopal Parish this year under the leadership of Josiah Barber, Phineas Shepherd, and Charles Taylor, who had been instrumental in founding the Trinity Parish in 1816. The Rev. Seth Davis became the first rector the next year, and services were held in schoolhouses and homes. The matter of prior existence is interesting as related by Elroy McKendree Avery in *A History of Cleveland and Its Environs:* "Whether Trinity Cathedral or St. John's Church is the oldest (Episcopal) congregation in Cuyahoga County is still a mooted question, but the matter was prettily stated in the congratulations sent by the church to the cathedral on the occasion of their respective centennials (November 9, 1916):

> Trinity Cathedral, Cleveland—our twin brother, born in the same log cabin, on the same day and hour, under the protecting roof of the Pioneer of Brooklyn, Phineas Shepherd. We have long since forgiven Trinity for leaving our bed and board and changing its name from Trinity, Brooklyn, to Trinity, Cleveland, as it was obliged to do when it set up housekeeping for itself . . . because its members on that side of the river became weary or afraid of crossing over to Brooklyn on Sundays on a floating bridge which sometimes floated out into the lake.

The Fourth of July was devoted to a special celebration for the children of the county, to impress upon them the great significance of the holiday. They marched from their Sunday Schools to the Presbyterian meeting house, where services were held, and thence to a grove along the lake at Bond Street. Here children and teachers enjoyed "a repast of cakes, crackers and cold water." This was the largest assembly of children that had ever been arranged, reported a local paper. The practice was continued, and it was hoped that "in a very few years, the common method of using rum and gunpowder, will be wholly abandoned."

L. L. Rice edited *The Cleveland Whig,* a weekly that appeared first on August 20. It merged with the *Daily Gazette* two years later.

Cholera returned, originating, it is said, with decaying vegetable matter in the canal bottom, which was exposed to the sun when the water had been drained after a heavy rain. A day having passed with no new cases, the *Herald* issued Cleveland's first newspaper "extra" on August 28, declaring that it was believed the epidemic "has finally disappeared." The poor suffered dreadfully; and of the hundred dead, fifty-five were buried at the city's expense. In a vain effort to save the life of Postmaster Job Doan, leading citizen of Doan's Corners, Dr. Elijah Burton, pioneer physician in Euclid Township, almost succumbed to the disease. He was the head of a famous Cleveland family of physicians.

Journeymen printers met in October to form the Cleveland Typographical Association, an auxiliary to the Columbus Society and the New York Trade Union. Its purpose was to promote "better protection of their rights and interests, by establishing prices and regular hours of labor." Within a few years it had become inactive.

Members of a flourishing circulating library and lyceum at Chagrin (Willoughby) decided that if their town were to become a great lake port it must have a railroad and an important educational institution. The railroad service came later, but a charter was secured this year for Willoughby University on Lake Erie, independent of religious ties. Samuel Wilson of Chagrin; Dr. John Handerson, prominent physician; John W. Allen of Cleveland; and Joshua R. Giddings of Jefferson, Ohio, were among the founders. A medical college was opened on November 3, the first institution offering medical education in northern Ohio, but the collegiate department never materialized. A remarkable faculty was built up that included men who became leaders in their profession: Drs. Horace A. Ackley, Amasa Trowbridge, J. Lang Cassels—or Cassells, John Delamater, Jared P. Kirtland, Noah Worcester, William M. Smith, and Daniel Piexotto, the first Jew to settle in the district, elected president of the college in 1836. The new institution was not equal to the times, however, and it struggled desperately through the Panic of 1837, until 1843, when it was moved to Cleveland. The name "Willoughby" was that of Dr. Westel Willoughby, noted physician and teacher of medicine in New York State, who had invested in lands in the district. Soon afterward, Chagrin changed its name to Willoughby.

Cleveland now had fifteen German families. Several of them met and organized the German Evangelical Protestant Church society this year.

Holsey Gates, who gave the village of Gates Mills his name in 1826, built Gates Mills Inn (part of the Chagrin Valley Hunt Club) of stout timbers cut in his sawmill. During the year, Noah Graves raised the first house in Chagrin Falls Village, which was still in use more than a century later.

In the brick schoolhouse on Vermont Street, The First Presbyterian Church of Brooklyn was organized on December 21, and forty names appeared on the charter. The Rev. John Keep of Oberlin, moderator of the meeting, was the first pastor of the church, the offspring of First Church in Cleveland. The schoolhouse sheltered the congregation until a temporary house of worship was dedicated in 1835 in the rear of a lot at the southeast corner of Detroit and State streets. While Presbyterian in name, the church was Congregational in form. In 1838, forty-four members withdrew to form a Congregational church, but the two bodies united on the "Presbygational" basis three years later, calling the Rev. S. B. Canfield to the pulpit. During the pastorate of the Rev. C. L. Watson, 1844-48, the church became practically independent of the Presbytery. The ministry of the Rev. James A. Thome, 1848-71, witnessed dedication of a brick church on the front part of the lot in 1851, and union in 1857 with the Congregationalists under the name, First Congregational Church. Grace Church was given its start in 1881, and a new building was dedicated in 1885 at the corner of Taylor Street and Franklin Avenue, during the pastorate of the Rev. H. M. Tenney. The auditorium was dedicated in 1893, during the ministry of the Rev. James W. Malcolm, prominent lecturer and writer on Lincoln. The cornerstone was laid in 1917 for a new church home to replace the old. First Church survived the trials common to its neighbor, Archwood, and proudly passed the century mark. Membership neared five hundred and fifty in 1946, when the Rev. Earl Ware Foster was serving as pastor in his third year.

1835

A group of young women of Oberlin College met to form a literary society that was one of the first formal woman's clubs of importance in the Western Reserve. It was called the Young Ladies Association of Oberlin College Institution for the Promotion of Literature and Religion. Teachers and townswomen were admitted, and the attic of Ladies' Hall was used for meetings. The room was warmed by a stove presented to the society by the young men of Oberlin. Club debates were spirited and covered a wide field of subjects, among them, "Are Sewing Societies More Productive of Evil than Good?", "Hoopskirts Are a Nuisance," "Is It Proper for Young Ladies to Make Gestures?" Of the first members, a number are mentioned for their achievement and prominence: Antoinette Brown Blackwell, the first woman to be ordained as a minister in this country; Josephine Penfield Bateham, the first foreign missionary sent out by the club; Harriet Ingraham Livingstone, whose husband was David Livingstone's brother; Sarah Blachly Bradley, missionary to Siam and mother of Dr. Dan F. Bradley of Cleveland; Helen Finney Cox, daughter of President Charles G. Finney of Oberlin and wife of Governor Jacob D. Cox; Martha Parmalee Rose, first president of Cleveland Sorosis and wife of Mayor William G. Rose; Helen Shafer, president of Wellesley College; and Harriet L. Keeler, author and educator of Cleveland.

The Cleveland Harmonic Society was organized by seven amateur instrumental performers. They stressed their passion for "good music," as evidenced by their 1839 spring concert, when twenty-six numbers were presented, including works of Haydn and Handel.

Under the direction of seven young German men, the First Evangelical Protestant congregation of Cleveland was organized on April 26. The Rev. F. J. Tanke was the first pastor at a salary of $300. According to tradition, German sailors, battling a furious Lake Erie storm years before, knelt in prayer and promised that if their lives were spared, they would erect a church to Almighty God. It is believed that the little church was built by them in 1842 at Erie and York streets, for it bore the name, Schifflein Christi, Little Boat of Christ. The congregation grew, and in 1876 the little church was sold and a new structure was built during the ministry of the Rev. C. Moench at Dodge Street and Superior Avenue, bearing the name of its predecessor. In 1923, the Schifflein Christi property was sold and plans were made to build a new church. The Rev. J. C. Hansen was pastor. Death came this year to the Rev. George Maul, pastor of the Ebenezer Evangelical Church, founded in 1904 on St. Clair Avenue (and East 73rd Street), and the two congregations joined to form the First Evangelical Church. Then followed the building of a new edifice at 841 Thornhill Drive. Trinity Evangelical Protestant Church, formed in 1874, joined in a second merger in 1929, and the Rev. Theodore Albert Kitterer, who had been pastor of Trinity, became head of the united church. It bore the historic "First" name, which upon denominational union became First Evangelical and Reformed Church.

John Shaw had prospered during his thirty-two years of farming in Euclid Township (East Cleveland). On May 1, he made a will with ample provisions for his wife, Sarah, and a bequest whereby rents and profits from ninety specified acres should be used to support an academy erected in Euclid Township at a cost of no less than two thousand dollars, including equipment. Administered by William Adams, Thomas Crosby, and Andrew Cozard, trustees, it was to be called The Shaw Academy (later Shaw High School). By this practical means, John Shaw manifested his earnest belief in education.

Stagecoaches, wagons, and lake and river vessels continued to bring scores of new families to Cleveland from the East, and Ashbel W. Walworth decided to allot part of his farm for residences. In the summer, new homes were going up on a long strip of land running from the top of the Newburgh

Road bluff (Broadway) to the Cuyahoga. Hill Street became the principal thoroughfare, and here lived the Cottrells, Bakers, Judkins, and Gunnings, overlooking the lovely river valley. A century later, the street was deserted, except for vagrants. Homes, shops, and warehouses had disappeared, and the area had fallen into disrepute.

On May 14, the *Advertiser* reviewed the building situation with pride. Stores and tenements were under construction, the latter being occupied immediately by immigrants as soon as completed. With the opening of the navigation season, eight thousand passengers left Buffalo during the first week, and many remained in Cleveland.

Dr. Erastus Cushing came to Cleveland from Massachusetts in June. He had studied in eastern medical schools, and was a student under Dr. John Delamater, renowned professor. Dr. Cushing held a medical degree, and had practiced for ten years in his home state. With these rare advantages, it was natural that he should become a leader in his profession in Cleveland. The Cushing name was to be identified prominently with medicine down through the years.

The Disciples of Christ joined in a "Yearly Meeting" of non-ecclesiastical fellowship at Colonel John Wightman's farm in Newburgh this year. Great crowds came to hear the forceful preaching of Alexander Campbell, William Hayden, A. B. Green, and M. S. Clapp. There were many converts, and a church was organized (later Miles Avenue Church of Christ). Services were held in the town hall, but there was no settled minister, and the congregation lapsed in a few years.

Seth W. Johnson opened his shipyard to repair vessels. Soon, however, he turned to shipbuilding, and in Cleveland he built the steamer *Robert Fulton,* 368 tons, and the *Constellation,* 483 tons. Prominent in the business for the next three decades were Johnson & Tisdale, Quayle & Moses—later Quayle & Martin, and Peck & Masters.

A disastrous fire wiped out twenty-two stores and offices on July 29, resulting in a loss of $45,000. The *Advertiser* announced on July 30 that henceforth the authorities would permit only brick and stone to be used in rebuilding. The first life sacrificed to fire in Cleveland was that of a domestic in a boarding house.

The first resident Catholic pastor was the Rev. John Dillon, who engaged Shakespeare Hall in the Merwin Building, near the foot of Superior Street, as a chapel for his small membership. He then moved into Mechanics Hall in the Farmers Block, and transformed it into a chapel. The young priest died of fever the following year, leaving a fund of $1,000 which he had collected toward a church building. He was succeeded by the Rev. Patrick O'Dwyer.

Interest in the theater had grown, and, in the thirties, Italian Hall was built on Water Street (1300 West 9th). It was one of the few brick buildings, with three stories and a theater on the top floor, where traveling companies gave their performances to fashionable audiences. Raised seats were a novelty.

Ahaz Merchant, surveyor and city engineer, published a "Map of Cleveland

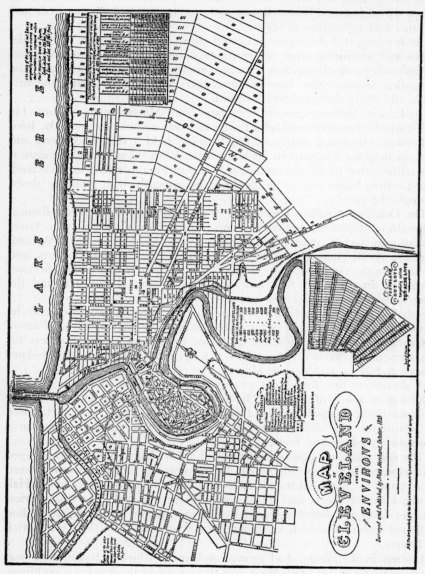

Ahaz Merchant's Map of Cleveland, 1835.

and its Environs" in October showing the street plan to date for Cleveland and Brooklyn. Elevations, location of principal points of interest, detail of ten-acre lots beyond the eastern boundary line, and clearance and tonnage figures at the port for the preceding ten-year period were recorded. High, Sheriff, Middle, Rockwell, Clinton, Lake, and Ohio streets, Lake Alley, and extensions of Prospect and Bolivar streets were new additions to the Cleveland map. Merchant Street was named for the map-maker.

Origin of some of the street names on the new map of Cleveland is interesting. Distinguished men in history or in the news were recognized; Bolivar Street, named for Simon Bolivar, famed South American liberator who died in 1830; Clinton Street for DeWitt Clinton; Columbus Street for the discoverer; Girard Street for the Philadelphia financier; Hamilton Street for the statesman. The names of men of influence related to Cleveland went up on street signs: Kinsman Street for John Kinsman, one of the original lot owners in Cleveland; Parkman Street for Samuel Parkman, also an original lot owner; Academy Street was inspired by the adjoining Academy school building; Canal Street was located near the canal; Dock Street on the wharf; the lighthouse stood on the corner of Lighthouse Street; River Street ran along the river; Meadow Street lay in the lowland near the river mouth; and Spring Street perpetuated the location of a spring that was found by the first settlers on the hillside. A small section of Cleveland streets was devoted to the names of trees: Cherry, Chestnut, Oak, Walnut, and Orange. Main Street was certainly far from being the principal street. Cross Street connected Kinsman and Pittsburgh streets, but did not cross. As Cleveland grew and new streets were opened, the names of the city's mayors, benefactors, and prominent officials appeared on the maps.

The Bethel Church was organized with nine members on October 25, an offspring of the First Presbyterian Church. It was located at Eagle and Diamond streets until the mid-century, when it made way for the Cleveland-to-Cincinnati railroad, by moving to the east side of Water Street, north of St. Clair. The "Free School" for underprivileged children was held in the basement of the church.

Dr. Benjamin Strickland, the first dentist, arrived in the village from Vermont. He was the first surgeon-dentist in Cleveland, and practiced for more than a half century.

Toward the end of the year, the Cleveland Reading Room Association was organized by voluntary subscription, with John M. Sterling, president. Periodicals, reviews, and daily papers from different parts of the country were available to about two hundred subscribers every day in the reading room, and evenings until ten o'clock.

Twelve names were signed to the charter membership roll of the First Congregational Church and Society of Parma when it was formed on November 7. The guiding spirit was Elder Hudson, physician and minister. The congregation worshiped in a schoolhouse until 1839, when they made the building of a meeting house their spare-time project. Although the church changed to Presbyterian government in 1874, twenty-four years passed before it was permitted to use the name, First Presbyterian Church of Parma. Fire destroyed the sanctuary in 1898, and a new building was erected (6155 Pearl Road). When a merger was consummated with South Presbyterian Church, organized in 1892, the name was changed to Parma South Presbyterian Church. The Rev. Howard B. Withers became pastor in 1929.

In November, at the peak of the real-estate boom, land for Clinton Park (East 17th Street near the lake) was donated to Cleveland by Lee Canfield, Sheldon Pease, and associates. It was located adjacent to their allotment of 2-acre parcels at the northeast corner of the city plat, and was the first tract preserved for park purposes in Cleveland outside of Public Square. The park was named for DeWitt Clinton, popular national figure. Residences were built around the elaborately planned grounds that were to be the fashionable retreat in the area; but the advent of the railroad and industry interfered with its bright future.

1836

As the year opened, trouble was brewing along the Cuyahoga. Arrivals from the east were shunning Cleveland and settling in the real-estate developments west of the river; new stores, warehouses, and residences studded the western hillsides, and some Cleveland families were moving to Ohio City, the name by which the settlement beyond the river was now known. Furthermore, two bills had been introduced in the Ohio Legislature—one for the incorporation of Ohio City and the other for Cleveland. Strife began as the two communities within almost a stone's throw raced for incorporation priority.

A tract of real estate was placed on the market in January by Thomas Kelley and Ashbel W. Walworth, consisting of the two-acre lots south of Ohio Street as well as 100 acres adjoining, reaching to the river. By this time, most of the original two-acre lots had been subdivided, or were in the hands of owners who improved them.

A wave of lawlessness and crime was laid at the door of the Council, many claiming that too many liquor licenses were being issued. To preserve law and order, a City Watch was established on January 3, consisting of eight volunteer companies of six men each. They policed the village from sundown to sunrise, each company serving once in four weeks.

The Mansion House site, with 40-foot frontage, was leased on February 1 by Mrs. Jane Merwin to her son, George B., and two children for an annual rental of $1,350 on a basis of about $675 per foot front. The transaction, recorded this year, is believed to be the first ninety-nine-year lease executed in Cleveland.

Benevolence and the diffusion of useful knowledge prompted the organization of the German Society of Cleveland on Washington's Birthday.

Keen competition this year resulted in a newspaper publisher's agreement to standardize prices for advertisements and subscriptions, the latter to be paid in advance.

The bill incorporating the City of Ohio was passed on March 3. Two days later, on March 5, the City of Cleveland was created, and pride mingled with chagrin and bitterness when Clevelanders, numbering nearly six thousand, learned that Ohio City, with about two thousand souls, had gained the advantage.

Cleveland boundaries were described by law as follows:

> Beginning at low water mark on the shore of Lake Erie at the most north-eastwardly corner of Cleveland, ten-acre lot number one hundred and thirty-nine, and running thence on the dividing line between lots number one hundred and thirty-nine and one hundred and forty, numbers one hundred and seven and one hundred and eight, numbers eighty and eighty-one, numbers fifty-five and fifty-six, numbers thirty-one and thirty-two, and numbers six and seven of the ten-acre lots to the south line of the ten-acre lots, thence on the south line of the ten-acre lots to the Cuyahoga River, thence down the same to the extreme point of the west pier of the harbor, thence to the township line between Brooklyn and Cleveland, thence on that line northwardly to the county line, thence eastwardly with said line to a point due north of the place of beginning, thence south to the place of beginning.

A charter was granted to the Cleveland, Columbus & Cincinnati Railroad Company (forerunner of the Big Four Route, New York Central System) on March 14. There was no practical progress during its first decade, however, as the project was caught at the start in the throes of financial chaos. In March, 1845, the charter was revived, and an act permitted the building of a road as far as Columbus, rather than to Cincinnati, as originally prescribed. Financial assistance came so slowly that failure threatened time after time; and to encourage the enterprise, the City of Cleveland voted its credit to the extent of $200,000. In 1847, Alfred Kelley, then of Columbus, accepted the presidency, and influential men lent their support. To keep the charter alive, Kelley, T. P. Handy, treasurer; J. H. Sargent, engineer; James A. Briggs, attorney; Henry B. Payne, Oliver Perry, John A. Foote, and others took to the shovel. Through one fall and winter a laborer was kept at work moving the earth on the right-of-way toward Columbus, shovel by shovel, simply to hold the charter. Frederick Harbach, Amasa Stone, and Stillman Witt agreed to build the road, taking part payment in stock. Kelley's super-selling produced sufficient finances to push his "wheelbarrow road" to its goal in 1851.

The Cleveland, Warren and Pittsburgh Railroad Company (forerunner of the Pennsylvania Railroad), also received its charter on March 14, authorizing the construction of a road from Cleveland to the Pennsylvania state line. It was destined to suffer the same financial difficulties that befell the Cleveland-to-Cincinnati road. In March, 1845, the charter was revived, and a company was organized at Ravenna on October 24, with James Stewart of Wellsville, president; A. G. Cottell—or Catlett, secretary; and Cyrus Prentiss, treasurer. The City of Cleveland subscribed $200,000 to the capital stock, but the work dragged through lack of adequate finances. There was a seven-year struggle ahead before the road would connect with Pittsburgh. The privilege of avoiding Warren was given in order to provide the most direct, practical, and convenient route to the Ohio River.

The Cleveland City Temperance Society was organized on March 15. A year later, it numbered 260 teetotalers, and claimed to be the only active society.

The first state convention held in Cleveland was that of the Carpenters' and Joiners' Benevolent Society, held "at the school house" on March 21. The Cleveland "local" was the host. A ten-hour day was adopted.

The trustees of the Village of Cleveland held their final meeting on March 21 in Brown's Hotel, formerly Abbey's Tavern. It was ordered that an election for city officials under the new charter be held in the three wards on the second Monday of April—the eleventh. The first charter is considered to be the work of John W. Willey. It is characterized by precision and certainty, reflecting the author's "clear understanding of municipal rights and duties."

The first election in Ohio City was held in March, some time before Cleveland's first election. On the evening of March 30, the officers constituting the municipal government assembled for their first meeting at the office of Ezekiel Folsom: Josiah Barber, mayor; Cyrus Williams, E. Folsom, B. F. Tyler, Norman C. Baldwin, C. E. Hill, Luke Risley, F. A. Burrows, Edgar Slaght, H. N. Ward, Edward Conklin, Richard Lord, and L. W. Benton, councilmen; Richard Lord, president of the Council; Asa Foote, treasurer; George L. Chapman, marshal; and Thomas Whelpley, recorder. They voted to rent space for a Council chamber in the Columbus Block at an annual rental of $80. Those who filled the office of mayor of Ohio City until the consolidation with Cleveland in 1854 were: Francis A. Burrows, 1837; Norman C. Baldwin, 1838-39; Needham M. Standart, 1840-41; Francis A. Burrows, 1842; Richard Lord, 1843; Daniel H. Lamb, 1844-46; David Griffith, 1847; John Beverlin, 1848; Thomas Burnham, 1849-50; Benjamin Sheldon, 1851-52, and William B. Castle, 1853-54.

Ohio City had a Franklin House, built this year at 14-16 Pearl Street. It was the political and social center of the community and the sheriff used it frequently for the sale of the property of bankrupts. After a fire in 1855 it was rebuilt "in as good style as any $1 a day house in the city." William H. Baird, proprietor in 1862, was convicted for passing counterfeit notes, and a number of other law-breakers were arrested later in the house. The Franklin was razed in 1910.

Cleveland's growth demanded increased fire protection, and Cataract No. 5 was added to the department in April.

The City of Cleveland held its first election on April 11 in the several wards: First Ward—conducted in the Court House. Richard Winslow, Seth A. Abbey, and Edward Clark, judges; Thomas Bolton and Henry H. Dodge, clerks. Second Ward—in the lower room of the Stone Church. Gurdon Fitch, Henry L. Noble, and Benjamin Rouse, judges; Samuel Williamson and George C. Dodge, clerks. Third Ward—in the Academy. John Blair, Silas

Belden, and Daniel Worley, judges; John A. Vincent and Dudley Baldwin, clerks. Historian James Harrison Kennedy observes that "the new-born city started off well, holding its first election, as it were, within the visible portals of the law, the gospel, and education."

The results of the first Cleveland election were: John W. Willey, mayor; Richard Hilliard, Nicholas Dockstader, and Joshua Mills, aldermen; George Kirk, marshal; Daniel Worley, treasurer. Councilmen: Morris Hepburn, John R. St. John, and William V. Craw, first ward; Sherlock J. Andrews, Henry L. Noble, and Edward Baldwin, second ward; Aaron T. Strickland, Archibald M. C. Smith, and Horace Canfield, third ward.

At the first meeting of the City Council of Cleveland, held April 15 in the Court House, the new officers took their oaths, including George Hoadley, justice of the peace. Sherlock J. Andrews was unanimously elected president. Henry B. Payne became city clerk and city attorney. After the "swearing-in," the important business before the officials was to establish their names on the city payroll. In August, Andrews resigned, and Joshua Mills was elected president. Payne resigned his office in October, and was succeeded by George B. Merwin. The offices of the City of Cleveland were located in the Commercial Block on Superior Street (near the entrance to Hotel Cleveland). Prior to this time, official business of the village was conducted in the Court House.

At the foot of Columbus Street, James S. Clark and his associates had built the first fixed bridge across the Cuyahoga, consisting of two covered timber spans, one on each side of a drawing span. It was 200 feet long, 33 feet wide, and about 24 feet high. A stone abutment supported it on either shore, and masonry piers at the center permitted a draw sufficient to allow a vessel of 49-foot beam to pass through. The bridge was erected at a cost of $15,000. Beyond the river, they had graded the Columbus Street hill at great expense, to connect with the Wooster and Medina turnpike. Travel would thus be facilitated to their new Cleveland Centre real-estate development and to Cleveland. At the second meeting of the City Council on April 18, Clark gave this bridge outright to Cleveland, in which his land was located, thus winning a valuable ally. The opening was a great occasion, marked with luxurious feasting on hard cider, doughnuts, apples, and coffee, climaxed with a rousing barn dance. At the same time, a tempest had begun to boil in the proverbial teapot, and the lid was blown off the next year.

Typical of the elaborate planning schemes that originated in the get-rich-quick era was that of the Ohio Railroad Company, organized at the Mansion House in Painesville, Ohio, on April 25. Among the incorporators were Eliphalet Austin, R. Harper, Heman Ely, John W. Allen, P. M. Weddell, and Charles C. Paine, men of leadership and vision. A charter was granted in the heat of the speculative period, providing for banking powers and the issuance of paper money, as well as the right to build a railroad. The plan was to build a trans-Ohio road connecting Richmond at the mouth of the Grand River and Manhattan on the Lower Maumee River, visionary cities existing only on paper. The stupendous engineering plans called for driving a double line of piles, on which rested ties and stringers and a light strap-iron rail, estimated to cost $16,000 a mile. The expense of grading would thus be saved by utilizing this elaborate "stilt" system. The company struggled until 1843, when building ceased. For many years piles remained on Lorain Street and along the ridge toward Elyria, grim reminders of about 63 miles of "stilt" road built in the air.

Fire limits were set by the City Council on May 4, embracing the village. Buildings were rented to house the fire companies: on Superior Street (west of West 9th) for No. 1; on Seneca Street for No. 2 (Blackstone Building site); on St. Clair Street for No. 4 and the Hook and Ladder Company (corner of West 4th). Wood inspectors were also appointed, and it was decreed that each cord of wood should contain 128 cubic feet. Stephen Woolverton was placed in charge of a public stand for the sale of wood at Superior and Water streets, and Samuel Brown directed operations at the yard on the Public Square near Ontario Street. An early appropriation provided for "repair or replacement of the town pump near the courthouse."

Volunteer firemen provided their uniforms and equipped their headquarters. The personal experience of George F. Marshall gives an insight into the spirit and character of these brave defenders of life and property. The department, he stated,

> was simply a concentrated man power, with willing hands and without horses or steam. It comprised a goodly share of the young blood of the city . . . men who had no other purpose in "running with the machine" than a desire to do something worthy their manhood. Of those who did not belong to that volunteer band were Joel Scranton, Philo Scovill, Benjamin Harrington, Nathan Perry, Peter M. Weddell, George Kirk, Moses White, Erastus Gaylord, Dr. Long, Levi Sartwell, Daniel Worley, Melancthon Barnett and many more like them, whose hearts were in the work, but were not fleet of foot enough to keep out of the way of the engine. . . . They could work with the same vigor to save the poor man's cottage from the flames as the rich man's palace; while on parade and drill days they would march with a more stately tread, and run with greater speed, if they but knew their sweetheart was among the spectators. . . . The "machines" were well enough for those times, but they were heavy to handle, while the streets, during one-third of the year, were nearly impassable, and the common council forbade the running of fire engines on the sidewalks.

On May 7, the Council appointed John Shier city surveyor and engineer. On the same day, the first theater license was granted by the City Council for the Dean & McKinney theater, corner Superior Street and Union Lane, upon payment of $75 for one year. *Hamlet* was presented at the first performance on May 31. In the theatrical company were Billy Forrest, one of the country's best comedians, Dean, and his daughter, Julia Dean Hayne, who became well known.

The City Council passed an ordinance on May 17 reorganizing the Fire Department, declaring that it "shall consist of a chief engineer, two assistant engineers, two fire wardens, in addition to aldermen and councilmen, and such fire engine men, hose men, hook and axe men as are, or may be, from time to time, appointed by the city council." The chief was Samuel Cook; his first assistant, Sylvester Pease; and his second assistant, Erastus Smith. Members of the department were exempt from poll tax. Council also ordered the purchase of a coat for each member of the Hook and Ladder Company. Succeeding chiefs of the volunteer department were H. L. Noble, 1837; T. Lemmon, 1838, succeeded by John R. St. John; J. L. Weatherly, 1840; M. M. Spangler, 1842; John Outhwaite, 1843; M. M. Spangler, 1844; A. S. Sanford, 1845; John Gill, 1846; M. M. Spangler, 1847; S. S. Lyon, 1848; James Bennett, 1849; M. M. Spangler, 1850-51; and Jabez W. Fitch, 1852.

Alexander Campbell, leader of the Disciples' movement, leaves an account of his journey by mail stage from Hudson to Cleveland in May:

> We spent the whole night on the road from Hudson to Bedford, a distance of only twelve miles; thus carrying the mail at the rapidity of one mile in three quarters of an hour! We had only to walk some four or five miles through mud and swamps and to abandon the coach some six or seven times to prevent upsetting and the breaking of our bones during the night watch. We mercifully, and sometimes barely escaped the disaster of being upset; and with no other detriment than mud and water and fatigue, completed our journey of forty miles in something less than a day.

Upon arriving in Cleveland, Campbell delivered several lectures against skepticism, which resulted in a three-cornered discussion in the Presbyterian Church, with Irad Kelley and Dr. Samuel Underhill supporting the opposition. At the conclusion of the controversy, which lasted for several days, the *Herald* reported:

> As is usual, both parties claim the victory. Whatever may be the effect in a moral and religious point of view, one thing is certain, the fund of valuable information upon the subjects of history, philosophy, astronomy, and indeed almost every department of natural science, which has been imparted in the course of this controversy, will not be lost on the community.

When William Tax fired a gun unlawfully on May 21, he was not only fined $2 and costs, but his name was recorded as the first person to be arrested in the new City of Cleveland.

L. L. Rice founded the *Daily Gazette* in May, and sold it to (Charles) Whittlesey & (Stoughton) Bliss on January 1, 1837. Whittlesey & (Josiah A.) Harris purchased the *Gazette* and the *Herald* in the spring, and the combination became the *Herald and Gazette.* Harris became sole owner and editor in 1838. More than three-fourths of the Whig paper was devoted to advertisements, which were the chief source of local news. The name was changed to *Herald* in 1843; and two years later, the office was moved to the Merchants Exchange.

The *Ohio City Argus,* the first newspaper published west of the river, was founded by T. H. Smead and Lyman W. Hall and commenced publication on May 26. It was printed on good-quality paper, and ran a literary column and book reviews; but it survived for only two years, and the Whigs lost another sympathetic instrument.

A statement from Mayor Willey advocating the establishment of common schools was read to the City Council on May 31, and referred to a committee consisting of Messrs. Andrews, Hilliard, and Hepburn. At this meeting, the street commissioner was directed to provide the first official ferry for public use across the Cuyahoga River.

The charter provided for the establishment of common schools, administered by a board of managers, chosen by the City Council each year. On June 9, Council ordered that a committee employ a teacher and an assistant "to continue the Free School to the end of the quarter, or until a school system for the city shall be organized, at the expense of the city." A school levy was authorized on June 22 to make possible Cleveland's first public school, that originated in a Bible school called Bethel, "under the hill."

Council directed the city marshal on June 20 to prosecute every person "retailing ardent spirits contrary to the provisions of the ordinance regulating licenses."

The cornerstone of St. John's Church (2600 Church Avenue) was laid on July 2 by the Rt. Rev. Charles McIlvaine, the second bishop of Ohio. Here the "first families" of the West Side worshiped in the white stone building they had built with their own hands. Of the eleven mayors of Ohio City, seven were communicants. The pews of the historic Episcopal church were occupied by President William McKinley, President Theodore Roosevelt, and men and women of prominence who visited Cleveland. Church Avenue derived its name from St. John's, the oldest religious structure in Cleveland in 1946.

A gun salute fired at dawn on the Public Square announced the first Fourth of July in the City of Cleveland. Visitors who had spent the night in rigs and wagons stretched themselves and prepared for the big day of celebration. In the morning, a parade formed at the Franklin House, led by the Fire Department, city officials, guests, and citizens, and marched to the Square, down to St. Clair, to Water and to Superior, to the stirring music of the visiting Eagle Circus Band. Here Revolutionary veterans joined the procession that moved to the Baptist Church, where exercises were conducted. Samuel Starkweather presided at a fine dinner that was heightened by thirteen toasts and many speeches. In the afternoon, crowds went for lake rides on the steamer *United States*.

Farmers and traveling men patronized the City Hotel, built this year on Seneca Street and said to be second to the Franklin House in its appointments. Great wooden shutters attracted attention, and a good-sized livery stable next door was a decided advantage. In 1879, David R. Hawley purchased the house to gain hotel experience. It was well known in the Midwest, attracting important meetings of its day. The hotel faded about 1890.

Settlers who had come from Massachusetts were eager to found a Unitarian church of their faith. Infrequent meetings held by the Rev. George W. Hosmer of Buffalo, later president of Antioch College, began this year and brought encouragement to the little group that included some of his personal friends. It was 1850 before formal services were conducted in a hall on Superior Street by Robert Hassell of St. Louis, who served for five months. Through the influence of Charles Bradburn, the Rev. A. D. Mayo of Massachusetts began a pastorate in 1854, the congregation now including seventy-five families with sixty members in the Sunday School. Here the First Unitarian Church had its beginning, and among the leaders were H. M. Chapin, W. P. Fogg, David Wasson, Rodney Gale, Dr. Azariah Everett, and Judge Daniel R. Tilden.

A little hotel called Spring Cottage was opened by William R. Richardson on the lakeshore in Clinton Park (near East 14th). His advertisement in the city directory the next year extolled the luxury of "a warm bath in summer." Hourly coach service conveyed patrons from the city's principal points to the "Cottage Spring Baths . . . a beautiful and pleasant retreat from heat and dust on the bank of the lake, scarce a mile from the city."

On August 21, Pollock's Intelligence Office was advertising for ten or a dozen girls to do housework.

The *DeWitt Clinton*, the newest design in canal boats, was commissioned in late summer. It was principally a freight vessel of 493 tons, built at Huron, Ohio, along the lines of the *Robert Fulton*, with a 150-foot deck and 27-foot beam. It cost $45,000. Three cabins provided fifty berths for men, thirty-three for ladies, and a large steerage.

Dr. Samuel Underhill, physician and justice of the peace, lived by standards of his own making, embracing free-thinking, unmerciful criticism, and unpredictable judgment. He delved in mesmerism, phrenology, and fanciful subjects. In order to spread atheistic doctrines and attack those whom he believed deserving of exposure to the public, he began publishing *The Cleveland Liberalist* on September 10. It later became *The Bald Eagle*, and while the weeklies were short-lived, their vicious columns left many a scar in the community. Underhill was a man ahead of his time. His advertisements in the first Cleveland directory advocated free enquiry, and announced that the paper is "Opposed to all monopolies—In favor of universal equal opportunities for knowledge in early life for every child; discourager of all pretensions to spiritual knowledge; teaches that virtue alone produces happiness; that vice always produces misery . . . that school masters ought to be better qualified, and then should have higher wages . . . that nobles by wealth are as offensive to sound democracy as nobles by birth—both are base coin;— and it inserts the other side of the question, when furnished in well written articles." Before his death, Dr. Underhill renounced atheism.

R. L. Gazlay, principal of Cleveland's "Free School," reported to the City Council that 229 children had received instruction during the quarter ending September 20 at a maintenance cost of $131.12.

The first Board of School Managers was appointed by the Council on October 5, consisting of John W. Willey, Anson Hayden, and Daniel Worley. In the following March, they urged a liberal outlay for schools and schoolhouses.

Franklin Circle, or Franklin Place, was platted by the county surveyor in October, and dedicated to the public. Farmers used it as an open-air market.

In November, the Cleveland Lyceum debated the momentous subject, "Ought the Right of Suffrage be extended to females?" Women had not yet begun to assert themselves and the negative won. Public concerts were being presented regularly by the Sacred Music Society.

The Young Men's Literary Association was organized in November, and another library and reading room were provided in the city. Charles Whittlesey was the first president. By the next year, a circulating library of eight hundred volumes had been assembled.

In the frenzy of the speculative era, the Buffalo-Brooklyn promoters and the Ohio City fathers attempted an ingenious scheme to capitalize on their new real-estate development. A channel for lake craft was cut from the old river bed to the Cuyahoga, affording a protected lake harbor, which Cleveland did not have. Docks and warehouses were built on the water front, and the elegant Ohio City Exchange Hotel was erected at Main and Centre streets, affording "the finest entertainment and hospitality in the West." To complete the big-business scheme, a ship canal was constructed from a point on the river opposite the Ohio Canal terminus through a swamp to the old river bed—Sycamore Street, on paper only, with the purpose of making the latter the real terminus of the canal. This would afford a harbor independent of Cleveland. The plan had great possibilities indeed. A year later, panic struck. The company became bankrupt, and the elaborate city plan was abandoned. James S. Clark and his associates became insolvent, and their properties were sold by the sheriff. The fine hotel struggled for a time as the Massasoit House and the Exchange Hotel; but, by 1845, factories, warehouses, and tenements had moved into the valley. When fire wiped out the hostelry, it was serving as a pail factory.

According to Cleveland's first directory, canal and lake shipping had greatly increased trade and industry during this year. Records of the Port of Cleveland showed 117,277,580 pounds of goods estimated to be worth $2,444,708.54 arrived by way of the canal at Cleveland; and 911 sailing vessels and 990 steamboats, aggregating 401,800 tons, cleared; 108 vessels were foreign. Forwarding charges to and from Cleveland during the season amounted to $685,000. The principal commodities shown on the year's export statement were 167,539 barrels of flour valued at $1,005,234.80; 464,765 bushels of wheat, $534,469.40; 392,281 bushels of corn, $215,764; 13,495 barrels of pork, $203,425.40; 3,851 hogsheads of tobacco, $192,550; and mineral-coal shipments valued at $3,492.09. Imports consisted principally of gypsum, furniture, lumber, and salt. Clevelanders were not yet aware of the rich salt deposits buried under the city, and they paid high prices for this essential product.

Based upon his past mercantile record, William Augustus Otis was "at once given rank with the foremost business men" when he arrived in Cleveland this year. Born in Massachusetts in 1794, the lineal descendant of James Otis of Revolutionary renown, he set out for Pittsburgh in 1818 where he lost his savings in an unfortunate iron business. He became a tavern-keeper and then prospered as a merchant, shipping by waterway to the New York market the first flour from the Western Reserve. Otis served two years in the State Legislature when he moved to Cleveland, where he dealt in flour,

Cleveland, 1833, from Brooklyn Hill looking east.

BELOW. *From Bank and St. Clair streets looking east.*

Cleveland, 1833, from Court House looking west.

The Mormons, members of the Church of Jesus Christ of Latter-day Saints, dedicated their temple at Kirtland, Ohio, in 1836.

A $5.00 bill issued by the Kirtland Safety Society Bank in 1837.

Joseph Smith, founder of the religious sect in 1830, came to Kirtland in 1831 and was succeeded by Brigham Young in 1847.

Pictures from LEO WEIDENTHAL COLLECTION.

pork, and potash; but later his interest turned again to iron manufacture.

Among those who came to Cleveland this year were men who were to make their mark in time to come: William Bingham, twenty, of Massachusetts, who started as a salesman for George Worthington, and became one of the leading hardware merchants of the West; Franklin T. Backus, Yale graduate, who made an enviable record as lawyer and legislator; D. W. Cross, who gained prominence as a member of the bar and as a coal operator; and Moses Kelley, recently admitted to the Rochester, New York, bar, who came to Cleveland at the call of his Harvard classmate, Thomas Bolton,

DAILY LINE OF OHIO CANAL PACKETS

Between Cleveland & Portsmouth.

DISTANCE 309 MILES—THROUGH IN 80 HOURS.

A Packet of this Line leaves Cleveland every day at 4 o'clock P. M. and Portsmouth every day at 9 o'clock A. M.

T. INGRAHAM, *Office foot of Superior-street, Cleveland,*
OTIS & CURTIS, *General Stage Office,*   *do.* } AGENTS.
G. J. LEET,   -   -   -   -   *Portsmouth,*

NEIL, MOORE & CO.'S Line of Stages leaves Cleveland daily for Columbus, via Wooster and Hebron.
OTIS & CURTIS' Line of Stages leaves Cleveland daily for Pittsburgh, Buffalo, Detroit and Wellsville.

Early transportation advertisement.

newcomer two years earlier. Bolton and Kelley formed a partnership; and as able and successful lawyers, both served their city in the Council and in other official capacities. Kelley was a member of the State Senate, 1844-45.

1837

Cleveland banks were considered well managed; but their entire capital was less than $500,000, which was equal only to the needs of river business. Forwarding merchants had paid transportation charges of $685,000 during the preceding season, and their produce purchases totaled $945,000. Businessmen had been forced to seek financial assistance outside of the city. As the year opened, Clevelanders petitioned the Legislature to charter a new bank with adequate capital to meet the needs of rapid growth. It was not until 1845 that their hopes were realized.

The Union Club was revived on January 2. It was strictly a business organization created to detect and punish horse thieves "whose daring thefts have become a menace and a serious loss to the community." Horse stealing was considered a serious offense. Having tracked down a suspect, the vigilantes warned him to leave the neighborhood; but if they could fasten the crime on him, he was turned over to the authorities. The *Herald* expressed public thanks for "labor inspired by the best motives and works tempered by discretion." The club became inactive in April, 1838, after having done a first-class clean-up job.

Jonathan Fowler opened the new Commercial Hotel at 24 Seneca Street this year. Shortly after he assumed management, the proprietor signed the pledge, and the Commercial became a temperance house. The hotel was razed in 1880 to make way for the Severance Building, which later housed the *Waechter und Anzeiger*.

"The rescuing of merchandise and furniture of every description, protecting it from improper usage, and conveying it, when expedient, to places of safety" was the lofty purpose of the Mutual Protection Society, which was formed early in the year. This was the first salvage corps, and was made up of prominent citizens.

Charles Whittlesey was appointed assistant geologist of Ohio, and working with him was Dr. Jared P. Kirtland, who was in charge of natural-history investigation. They conducted the first geological survey of Ohio, revealing rich coal and iron deposits in eastern Ohio, upon which future manufacturing greatness was built. In later years, Professor John S. Newberry, eminent scientist, stated that this early survey "did much to arrest useless expenditure of money in search for coal outside of the coal fields. . . . It is scarcely less important to let our people know what we have not, than what we have, among our mineral resources." Whittlesey surveyed the Indian mounds of Ohio in 1840.

"Some of the best young men of the place" met on Washington's Birthday to form a private military company known as the Cleveland City Guards. Military organization was completed on August 28, with Captain Timothy Ingraham in command until 1853. On the first roster of 118 men were D. W. Cross, Silas Rhodes, L. A. Stillman, Abner Brownell, Dudley C. Baldwin, T. S. Paddock, Samuel Starkweather, Harvey Rice, Henry P. Dodge, Henry B. Payne, Nathan Perry, and Thomas Bolton. The first Armory was located on the fourth floor of the Mechanics Block. Adoption of a gray, colonial-style uniform on June 7, 1838, prompted a change in name to the Cleveland Grays—or Greys. From the founding, the Grays provided trained men for military service in every conflict, at home and abroad, and served with distinction on state, civic, and official occasions. Cleveland and the Grays grew up together.

John Barr was president and Charles Whittlesey corresponding secretary of the Cleveland Lyceum, a lively organization that now had 110 members. The Cleveland Polemic Association commenced to present public debates.

The people of Cleveland expressed confidence in their first mayor by re-electing him this year by a large majority. After his second term, John W. Willey continued his outstanding career by giving admirable service as legislator and judge in the Court of Common Pleas. He died in 1841 at the age of forty-four, while serving as presiding judge of the fourteenth judicial district. Succeeding him as mayor were Joshua Mills, 1838-39; Nicholas Dockstader, 1840; John W. Allen, 1841; Joshua Mills, 1842; Nelson Hayward, 1843; Samuel Starkweather, 1844-45; George Hoadley, 1846; Josiah A. Harris, 1847; Lorenzo A. Kelsey, 1848; Flavel W. Bingham, 1849; William Case, 1850-51; Abner C. Brownell, 1852-54.

In March, Council ordered that the mayor should receive five hundred dollars for his services during the year, and that councilmen should be paid a dollar for each meeting they attended. A special committee was created to investigate the "expediency of lighting Superior street from the river to the Public Square," and to recommend the best means of paying for the installation. A dog pound was established.

The congregation had outgrown the pews of the Stone Church, and to ease the pressure, "twenty of the best families" went forth to form the Second Presbyterian Church on April 3. The Rev. Joseph Whiting was called as the first pastor. Unable to weather the panic, the earnest little flock abandoned its church-building plans, and members scattered or returned to the mother church.

Simson Thorman, twenty-six, of Bavaria, was the first Jewish resident of Cleveland. He dealt in furs, traveling as far westward as St. Louis to purchase hides and furs from the Indians. He served on the City Council, and enjoyed an influential career. Aaron Lowentritt, Isaac Alsbacher, Michael Hoffman, and Solomon Sloss, all Bavarians who had fled from Teutonic tyranny to the New World, soon joined him.

The Cleveland Female Seminary was incorporated on April 3, with Henry Sexton, Benjamin Rouse, Henry H. Dodge, A. D. Smith, and A. Wheeler as trustees. This was a private school for "young ladies."

On April 3, the Cleveland Female Orphan Asylum was incorporated largely through the effort of Trinity Church women. Mrs. Laura Willey, Mrs. Martha Kendall, Mrs. Sophia K. Ford, Mrs. Jemima B. Scovill, Mrs. Catherine Kellogg, and Mrs. Margaret Sterling were among the trustees.

Ohio City citizens became more and more incensed as they saw their trade diverted into Cleveland over the new Columbus Street Bridge. To retaliate, they avoided the structure, and determined to use only the old floating bridge at Main Street for their traffic. Cleveland Council decided to force the issue, and ordered removal of the eastern portion of the float structure, which the city owned jointly with its neighbor. An injunction intended to halt its removal came too late; the bridge was impassable.

In April, James S. Clark's organization allotted "nearly all the part of Ohio City lying south and west of the Barber & Sons' allotment" and named it Willeyville in honor of Mayor John W. Willey of Cleveland. While this move helped to build Ohio City, the citizens must have resented the name deeply. To complete their city plan, the promoters purchased a lot on Ontario Street at Prospect in Cleveland (Bailey Company site) and built the Farmers Block, a merchandising center, to draw trade from the countryside; and at the north end of Columbus Street they located the Cleveland Centre

House. The three-story hotel served until 1864, when it became a commercial block, and the next year it was moved out of the path of expanding commerce.

City Clerk George B. Merwin reported on young Cleveland's balance sheet for the first year, April 15, 1836, to March 17, 1837: Total receipts "from all sources," $16,077.53; total expenditures, $13,297.14, which included cost of a new, hand fire engine, $1,083; and "gross compensation" to Council members, $1,139. School-fund receipts from the county treasurer and the city marshal's collections totaled $2,553.32, from which was paid $301.55 to "R. L. Gazlay, for keeping free school."

The second Board of School Managers was appointed in April, consisting of Samuel Cowles, Samuel Williamson, and Philip Battell, despite the fact that a school system did not yet exist in Cleveland, nor did the city own a schoolhouse or a foot of ground on which to build one. It is estimated, however, that eight hundred children were attending schools, of which about three hundred were enrolled in the Free School maintained by the city. Leading Clevelanders, generally men who had enjoyed a liberal education, served on the early school boards, among them Samuel H. Mather, Charles Bradburn, Madison Kelley, Truman P. Handy, R. T. Lyon, Samuel Starkweather, James D. Cleveland, John Barr, Horace Benton, J. A. Thorne, Daniel P. Rhodes, and R. B. Dennis.

Truman P. Handy was president of the Cleveland Mozart Society, organized in April "for the promotion of musical science and the cultivation of a refined taste in its members, and in the community." Monthly concerts were given the next year.

To provide a beneficiary fund for disabled members of the Volunteer Fire Department, the Fireman's Insurance Company was incorporated with the blessing of city officials. The charter provided many banking privileges, but money could not be issued. Firemen served without pay, and they found it a burden to purchase stock and to provide their uniforms.

Farmers hauled their cord wood to the "wood market" at the foot of Water Street, where they waited in good and bad weather for purchasers in need of seasoned maple, hickory, oak, and ash firewood.

A momentous advertisement of the Pioneer Fast Stage Line announced, "Through in 30 hours from Cleveland to Pittsburgh." The stage ran to Wellsville, where the trip to Pittsburgh was completed by boat. Here the Good Intent Fast Mail Stage Line gave preference to those passengers who wished to continue riding for fifty-six additional hours, more or less, to Philadelphia, where connections were made for New York, Baltimore, and Washington. Daily at four in the afternoon, the Ohio Canal packet left Cleveland for Portsmouth, covering the 309-mile trip in eighty hours. It also carried the mail. Stages left daily for Buffalo, Detroit, and Cincinnati via Columbus, and one of the three lines to Pittsburgh provided mail service.

After a clean-up campaign, the northern half of the Public Square was fenced to preserve it against trespass. Pride in the city's front yard was beginning to assert itself.

In May, the poor little "township poorhouse," on the Erie Street Cemetery property on Clinton Street, received a kindlier name, City Hospital, but continued as a poorhouse. The infirmary accommodated about twenty-five people—the poor, sick, insane, and feeble-minded—and served about two hundred out-patients. Local physicians received small compensation from the public treasury for their attendant services. The building was torn down in 1851.

A resolution was offered in the Cleveland City Council on June 5 providing for the erection of markets and schoolhouses, and recommending that the city borrow $50,000 for the purpose. It was later adopted.

The first fire-insurance agency in Cleveland was the firm of Carlton & Lee. C. C. Carlton's son-in-law changed the name to James W. Lee & Company, which operated until 1940, when it was absorbed by a larger agency.

E. F. Gaylord had come to Cleveland in 1833, and his home on Ontario Street (Higbee store site) was converted into the Wright House this year by James Wright. Mark Lamb, well-known sportsman, made the place popular under his management in 1890. A little later the "new" Wright House replaced the old, upon what had been the site of Bingham & Phelps store. In 1898 the hotel went out of business.

Nathan Perry opened a street from St. Clair to Euclid and gave it his name. It is related that every morning he saddled his pony and rode from his home on Euclid Street to visit his daughter, Mrs. Henry B. Payne. A sharp bend in North Perry Street was made, so the story goes, by the Perry pony as he picked the easiest route, following the precedent of the famous cows whose wandering footpaths became the streets of Boston. On his ten-acre tract, Perry laid out a nursery where he grew shrubs, flowers, and greenhouse plants.

The 25-acre farm known as Willey Gardens on Kinsman Street was supplying the markets with fine vegetables.

The Abolitionists gained strength with the organization of the Cuyahoga County Anti-Slavery Society, formed at a meeting in the Stone Church on July 4. John A. Foote presided. J. M. Sterling, J. F. Hanks, and Solomon L. Severance, constituting a committee on constitution, reported that "the object of this society shall be the entire abolition of slavery throughout the United States and the elevation of our colored brethren to their proper rank as men." Edward Wade of Brooklyn was elected president; Samuel Freeman of Parma, Asa Cody of Euclid, John A. Foote of Cleveland, J. L. Tomlinson of Rockport, and Samuel Williamson of Willoughby, vice presidents; L. L. Rice, corresponding secretary; H. F. Brayton, recording secretary; and Solomon L. Severance, treasurer.

On July 7, the City Council passed an ordinance providing for the establishment of public schools. Suitable buildings or rooms were to be leased for school purposes and equipped with apparatus and furniture; elementary schools were to be organized and instructors secured. The school term was defined as July 24 until November 24, commencing this year, and it was provided that expenses should not exceed revenue.

Postage rates varied according to the distance the mail was carried: 6¼ cents, up to 30 miles; 10 cents, to 80 miles; 12½ cents, to 150 miles; 18¾ cents, to 400 miles; and 25 cents, over 400 miles. The charge for newspapers was one cent within 100 miles or for any distance within the state where printed; beyond 100 miles, or out of the state, 1½ cents each. Periodicals and pamphlets cost one cent a sheet within a 100-mile zone. In 1837, when the Sunday edition of a Boston newspaper was received in Cleveland the following Saturday, it was considered a great achievement.

Daniel Webster, distinguished orator, pleaded for an "assembly" of Congress, during a fleeting visit to Cleveland on July 15 while en route to the West. The appearance of the great man was discussed for days afterward.

Cleveland now had a band of its own, and it was no longer necessary to import musical talent for special occasions. The Cleveland City Band was a going concern, with eighteen members.

The American House was built on the site of the cabin-headquarters used by the second surveying party in 1797.

The City Guards, a private military organization, was formed with sixty-four members, independent of the Cleveland City Guards. It existed until 1843.

A professional horse race took place on Erie Street on August 7. Clara Fisher trotted from St. Clair to Huron Street to win in 2:47.

The American House opened on August 14 on the south side of Superior Street (west of Hotel Cleveland), and filled a crying need for hotel facilities. The city's first large hostelry, it was built by Warham J. Warner, builder of famous Euclid Avenue homes. The American was furnished "in a style of substantial comfort and luxury," and for many years it entertained Cleveland's distinguished guests. Here professional people had their headquarters, and entertainers gave theatrical performances in hotel rooms. It was the scene of colorful civic and social events. From its balcony the great and near-great delivered blazing oratory.

There were several booksellers in town when Moses G. Younglove and Edward P. Wetmore opened a wholesale and retail book-and-stationery store in the American House. The next year, Younglove bought his partner's interest and added job and news printing and publishing to the business.

In 1826, Josiah Holbrook of Derby, Connecticut, initiated a system to promote adult education through the lyceum plan. It was a great success, and spread rapidly through the country. Upon the request of John Baldwin and others, an effort was made to establish a model seminary and a lyceum village at Berea this year, as a self-improvement medium for the populace. This was Cleveland's first introduction to adult education. The experiment lasted five years and left Baldwin carrying the financial burden and facing bankruptcy. For some years, Holbrook lived in Berea and made globes and supplies for schools and associations, then he moved on to new endeavors. This was an early attempt to introduce visual education into teaching methods.

Dr. Jared P. Kirtland moved to Rockport (Lakewood) this year, where he practiced medicine, but was more widely known for horticultural experiments on his extensive farm, called "Whippoorwill." Here he built his historic home in 1839 in a setting of shrubs, fruit trees, and flowers. It was preserved through the years (14013 Detroit Avenue), together with part of the old garden and orchards. During the winter months, Dr. Kirtland taught in the Cincinnati Medical School, until 1842, when he joined the faculty of Willoughby University. He set a precedent in northern Ohio when he announced in 1843 that he had restricted his medical practice to consultation. He became Cleveland's most celebrated scientist and a leading naturalist of the country. Louis Agassiz and John Audubon, famed naturalists, were his close friends. Nevertheless, the doctor found time to assist worthy cultural movements, and was familiarly known as the "Sage of Rockport."

Commerce was expanding, and attention was turned to the lakefront again. The Lake Shore Company was incorporated, with authority to protect the lake banks from water encroachment, and permission to build wharves and piers as payment for its expenditures. Little was accomplished by the company, however, and later Charles Whittlesey was employed to drive piles at intervals along the shore. The railroads then continued the work for their own protection.

Steam was displacing sails in the harbor, when citizens heard the whistle of the new passenger boat, *Cleveland,* as it was made ready for lake traffic in the fall. This was the first vessel named for the city, and the steam whistle was an innovation on lake craft, bells and guns having been used as signals prior to this time. Built at Huron for passenger service at a cost of $85,000, the 575-ton steamer was 139 feet long, 29 feet broad, and had one hundred and twenty berths for gentlemen, twelve for ladies, and ten staterooms of three berths each. Captain Asa E. Hart commanded.

A school census taken in October revealed that there were 2,122 persons in the city between the ages of four and twenty-one. Enrollment in the public schools, however, showed only 840. School income for the year amounted to $2,830.

Joseph Hall cleared 100 acres of virgin forest in Rockport, and the street that bears his name was laid out years later. In 1874 his son, John Curtis

Hall, built a home on a section of his father's land (16913 Detroit Avenue, Lakewood). He became a banker, and married Elizabeth Rose Maile, whose parents had a farm overlooking Rocky River Valley. From this family, Maile Avenue took its name.

Ohio City was enraged at being forced to use the Columbus Street Bridge, and war broke out on the West Side, on street corners and in meetings of protest. "Two bridges or none!" became the slogan as citizens prepared to fight the "Bridge War." Their City Council ruled that the new Columbus Street Bridge was a public nuisance and must be abated. On the night of October 27, the marshal with his deputies damaged the Ohio City end with a charge of powder. Deep ditches were dug near the approaches on either side, rendering the bridge useless. Nearly a thousand citizens determined to finish the job, armed with crowbars, axes, and weapons. They received the blessing of a Presbyterian clergyman, and advanced under the leadership of C. L. Russell, Ohio City attorney.

News of the march to the bridge reached Cleveland, and Mayor Willey, backed by militia, citizens, and an old cannon, used in Fourth-of-July celebrations, set out to meet the Ohio City mob. A general free-for-all ensued, and planks were ripped up. The field piece did no damage, because Deacon House, of the Ohio City forces, bravely spiked it with an old file. Upon the arrival of the county sheriff and the Cleveland marshal, the bloody business halted, but not before men were wounded on both sides, three of them seriously.

On October 29, City Council ordered the marshal of Cleveland to guard the Columbus Street Bridge. The controversy finally reached the courts, where it was settled; but the damage had been done, and it was not until 1854 that a union of the East and the West was consummated.

The Council approved a proposal that a city directory be published, and before the end of the year Julius P. MacCabe had issued a *Directory— Cleveland and Ohio City, For the Years 1837-38*. It was pocket-size, contained one hundred and forty-four pages, and was printed by Sanford & Lott in Cleveland. Eleven pages were devoted to Cleveland history. Then followed the Cleveland city charter; historical and descriptive material relating to civic, business, and cultural institutions in the two municipalities; names and locations of eighty-eight streets, lanes, and alleys; alphabetical lists showing names and addresses of firms and individuals in Cleveland and in Ohio City as of August, 1837; an index to public officials; transportation and shipping data; a table of foreign coins and currencies and other useful information. Forty-two pages of advertisements prefaced the comprehensive directory, illustrated with crude woodcuts, many of them used several times in competitive space. This buyer's guide to goods and service presented an illuminating picture of early Cleveland—quaint shops offering macassar oil and walking canes, fur and satin beaver hats, pantaloons and suspenders, merino shawls and gauze handkerchiefs, breast pins and finger rings, diapers and "incorruptible teeth," liquors and seidlitz powders, perfumery and looking glasses, pianofortes and tombstones. A variety of business and professional notices was climaxed with the stupendous announcement:

"Carriages for hire to go to any part of the United States!" The first advertisement was that of the printers, "No. 5, Superior-Lane"; they also used the last page in the book to announce that they had "removed from 5 Superior-Lane, to 17 Superior-Street, three doors west of the Franklin-House."

A full page in the city directory described the business of Cleveland's leading merchandising firm consisting of Peter M. Weddell, Dudley Baldwin, and Peter P. Weddell:

> PETER M. WEDDELL & CO. At the old stand, on the corner of Superior and Bank Streets . . . so long and so favorably known to the public, keep constantly on hand a very extensive assortment of DRY GOODS, consisting in part of Broad Cloths, Cassimeres, Sattinets, Cotton, Linnen and Worsted Drillings . . . Summer Cloths . . . India Satins, worked Collars and Capes, dress Hk'fs and dress Shawls . . . Laces and Edgings . . . raw silk Shawls, Gothic furniture Prints . . . Flannels, English and American Calicoes, Bedticking . . . Sheeting and Shirting . . . Damask, Birdseye and Russia Diaper, Moleskins, Umbrellas, Parasols, &c. &c. . . . very choice CARPETS & RUGS, together with a carefully selected assortment of FAMILY GROCERIES. The very best of Teas, Laguira and Old Java Coffee, Sugars, Rice, Raisins, Salaeratus, Mrs. Miller's Tobacco, Honey Dew and Plug Tobacco 7 years old, Hard Soap, &c.

"Fair and honorable dealing" was assured, backed by the statement that:

> All goods not as good as recommended, will be taken back, or ample remuneration will be made; that the prices of their goods are as low as at any other store, and many articles lower than can be found at the stores generally.

Friends were invited "to make us a call, not to buy, unless they think it for their interest, but to inform themselves respecting prices, qualities, &c. &c."

A fire ordinance required that "sextons of the several churches which are now or may hereafter be furnished with bells, shall immediately on the alarm of fire repair to the several churches with which they are connected and diligently ring the bells of said churches during 20 minutes unless the fire be sooner extinguished, with penalty of $2 for every omission."

1838

Ill health distressed Leonard Case, Sr., and along in the late thirties he gradually turned his affairs over to his older son, William. Near the Case home on the Public Square (westerly half of Federal Building site) stood a small, wooden office building to which William built an addition. In the *Cultural Story of an American City—Cleveland,* Elbert Jay Benton gives a comprehensive account of the founding of an unique literary-social club in this humble structure. The "Arkites" had no constitution, bylaws, or formal organization plan, yet in their leisurely get-togethers great things were planned for Cleveland.

In 1839 a letter from Leonard, Jr., then a student at Yale, to his brother gives the first intimation that the office was something more than a place of business. "Does the office continue to be the headquarters for loafers, as usual, or is it getting to be too notorious." A letter of William's, in 1841, adds a significant point—"I have a live rattlesnake to show for the amusement of the girls, who begin to think the old office a curiosity shop." A letter from Elisha S. Sterling, dated September 8, 1849, in Paris, where he was finishing his medical studies, shows the Ark full fledged, name and all. To William Case: "I am glad to hear the city is going ahead, as it is the finest place in existence. I have no desire to live in any other, and only ask to get back again within the scent of the old 'Ark'—the greatest place, you know, in these diggings—and be again surrounded by the best of fellows."

What had happened was this: The brothers had brought together a group of companions, with similar interests, for informal meetings in their office. A common interest in natural science cemented the group, though other forms of social diversion were included—games, reading and informal discussion. The rooms gradually became a museum, with an odd variety of mounted birds, et cetera. The variety of objects suggested to some of them the name, the Ark, and the members became the Arkites.

The Arkites represented a group of men who quite unconsciously started a great cultural movement in Cleveland, more than one in fact. The original group included, besides the Case brothers, Dr. Elisha S. Sterling, Stoughton Bliss, Colonel E. A. Scovill, George A. Stanley, Bushnell White, Captain B. A. Stannard, Dr. A. Maynard, D. W. Cross, Henry G. Abbey, R. K. Winslow, J. J. Tracy, and John Coon. These are portrayed in the painting hanging over the mantle in the reference room of the library of the Historical Society, a painting ordered by William Case in 1858. The Ark was the Case brothers' club; whatever it accomplished was chiefly their achievement. But their ideas, those of William, who loved the open spaces, and of Leonard, the more studious, were sown in a fertile soil. Their influence can be traced through a contemporary natural science museum, the Kirtland Society of Natural Science, The Case Hall, The Cleveland Library Association, Case Library and Case School.

A convention drawing delegates from townships in the county met in Cleveland on January 11 "to further the cause of common school education." John W. Willey was elected president of the new county association. The encouragement of Samuel Lewis, state superintendent, and President William Holmes McGuffey of Cincinnati College contributed to its success. McGuffey's interest and his visits to Cleveland undoubtedly helped the sale of his readers in the future.

Brighton, located on the Warren Young farm in Brooklyn Township, was incorporated as a village on March 5. The act was repealed, however, in 1839, and although the community returned to the township, the territory continued to be known as Brighton for years to come.

Imprisonment for debt was abolished in Ohio by act of March 19. Leverett Johnson of Cuyahoga County introduced the legislation. Agitation for the reform originated in the Fifteenth General Assembly of 1816-17, when Andrew Kelley of Cleveland fathered the movement that failed to pass. Whittier, the poet, carried the torch in verse. The states of the Union and foreign countries followed Ohio's leadership.

The Board of School Managers made their annual report in April for the preceding winter term, from December 1 to the end of March. Eight schools had been sustained, employing three male and five female teachers, with an enrollment of 840 and an average attendance of 468. These schools were conducted in rented quarters. Of the eight, two were in the old Academy, one in the Farmers Block, one in an abandoned paint shop, and one in an old, grocery-store building. Expense for tuition was $868.62. "Schools have been wholly free and open to all within their districts legally admitted to their privileges," the report stated. "The boys and girls have been entirely separate, the former taught by male and the latter by female teachers. The teachers have been critically examined before being employed." Female teachers received $5 per week, and male teachers, $40 per calendar month.

The city's library undertakings were suffering from hard times, and an effort was made in the spring to unite the Lyceum, the Cleveland Library Company, the Cleveland Reading Room Association, and the Young Men's Literary Association. It apparently failed, with the result that shortly afterward the organizations became inactive, and the books of the libraries were distributed among members.

Steamboat racing on the lake had provoked considerable public criticism, especially from a New York gentleman whose stern observations were printed in a local paper as a warning to the operators. His experience as a passenger on the *Erie* when it raced the "luxury liner" *Buffalo* from Buffalo to Cleveland was certainly not thrilling, and he censured such recklessness in risking human life. When the "brag boat" *Erie* burned in 1841, with a loss of about 175 lives, her fate was attributed not to the strain of a heated race, but to the bursting of demijohns of spirits of turpentine placed near the boilers by painters.

Historians have found the carefully kept diary of William Case of inestimable value in fitting together the piece-work pattern of early-day life in Cleveland. An amusing account of his canal voyage to Portsmouth, consuming four days and four nights, is recorded on June 18:

At 5 P.M. we started, and at 8 arrived at *Tinker's Creek*. Shortly after leaving there the list of names was called by the Captain, so that the passengers should choose their berths in order. I had the good fortune to stand third . . . While they were undressing, the boat passed through a lock, and, striking with some force against the side, somewhat disturbed the equilibrium of those off their guard; one person in particular, who was certainly not in full dress, was thrown into the ladies' cabin rather unceremoniously by the concussion. Their cabin is only separated from the Gents by a set of curtains. In fact, there was a complete hubbub kept up all night by the passengers, some laughing, some snoring, some telling stories and some cursing their hard quarters—but all making some noise or other. Two or three times, a piercing yell came from the female dormitory when the boat had, unfortunately for their shoes and stockings, lying scattered about on the floor, shipped water by getting under the small gate while lying in the bottom of the lock, which ran on the cabin floor some inches deep. However, all passed the night safely and early in the morning several stepped ashore to see the town of *Akron*, for the packet being detained, by passing through some twenty locks, allowed us time.

The teaching of astronomy was in its infancy when Elias Loomis, professor of mathematics and natural philosophy at Western Reserve College (later Western Reserve University and Western Reserve Academy), brought astronomical instruments from Europe and erected an observatory on the campus this year. It was the third project in the country, having been preceded by one in North Carolina, built in 1830 and destroyed some years later, and one at Williams College, built in 1836. Many valuable scientific contributions originated in the little vine-clad building.

A brand-new thrill came to Cleveland on July 3, when a circus brought "a splendid menagerie" and a "great elephant saddled." Almost the entire population flocked to the grounds at the corner of Water and St. Clair streets to see the three-day exhibition. Soft drinks could be had after the big event at a Water Street drug store. Here the newest concoctions were soda-water and carbonated mead, with a choice of sarsaparilla, raspberry, strawberry, and lemon flavors.

Cleveland was fired with patriotism on the Fourth of July, some of the enthusiasm having been inspired by the City Guards on holiday parade. Faces beamed with pride as the men in blue uniforms with gold trimmings showed their strength. At a banquet in the evening, D. W. Cross, one of the Cleveland Grays, toasted the military spirit and enterprise of the Guards.

Steamboat mail service to the East began on July 31. Five days were required for the trip, and although it placed "Cleveland about two days nearer New York . . . it has become uncertain as the winds," complained a local paper in October.

On August 13, an ordinance established Wall Street, to be 60 feet wide, about 540 feet from the lake, and to extend from Water to Erie Streets (north of Lakeside). Frontier Street marked the eastern boundary line of Cleveland at this time. As the city limits expanded, however, "Frontier" was known as the farthest street to the east, so that it once identified Sterling, Case, and Willson streets.

On August 30, in accordance with the will of John Shaw, trustees of The Shaw Academy were elected: the Rev. Harvey Blodgett, president; H. H. Coit, secretary; and John Doan, treasurer. Plans were made to erect the academy on a 2½-acre plot of land set aside for the purpose by the pioneer farmer of Euclid Township (Shaw High School site, East Cleveland). The two-story, plain frame building, surrounded by a rail fence, opened in the fall. It cost $623.41, and additions were to be made later to bring the cost to the required $2,000. English grammar, geography, and the three R's were taught in the primary department, and an advanced course was intended to prepare students to become farmers, merchants, mechanics, or for college. The school was open for four terms of eleven weeks each. Tuition in the primary school was $3 a term, and in the advanced course, $4; Latin and Greek cost $5. Attendance during the early years ran as high as eighty, drawn largely from Euclid, Cleveland, Willoughby, Ohio City, Mayfield, and Medina. Boarding students lived with neighborhood families. On the rolls were the names of Baldwin, Day, Raymond, Otis, Van Tine, Tilden, Crittenden, Willey, Kendall, Dockstader, and Hoadley.

The first teacher in the female department at Shaw Academy was a Miss Lyman, a graduate of Emma Willard's Female Seminary at Troy, New York, and she came into a community prejudiced against imported teachers. Within a short time she introduced calisthenics into the classroom, and this produced wagging tongues and harsh criticism. When John Shaw's widow, familiarly known as "Aunt Shaw," heard the report, she marched down to the Academy to see for herself. What she saw was both fascinating and shocking—girls waving wands as they went through graceful routines. It was dancing, that's what it was, and she recalled the condemnation and expulsion from the church that she suffered thirty-one years before. Punishment would come from the Almighty, warned Aunt Shaw. Suddenly there was cracking overhead, and the new plaster ceiling began falling to the floor. Pupils fled in fear, but Aunt Shaw straightened herself, faced the trembling Miss Lyman, and said sternly, "Let that be a lesson to you, young woman." When, upon persuasion, the teacher abandoned the Lord's Prayer in the morning exercises, criticism was heaped upon her for having done so. School patrons were hard to please, and her career at Shaw lasted for only one winter.

Firecrackers were first used publicly in Cleveland to celebrate Perry's Victory Day, September 10.

The Mechanics Block was erected this year at the southeast corner of Ontario and Prospect streets. Aside from commercial interests, it served a variety of special purposes: first as a school and a theater; it housed the first medical college for a few years, and other mid-century educational institutions had their beginning here. This historic building continued to mark a busy corner down through the years, evolving in 1903 into the pioneer store of Richman Brothers, and it was still serving their retail trade in 1946.

The Cleveland Grays appeared on parade in full dress on November 29, and drew high praise. Their bayonets glittered, their military evolutions were exact, and their bearing in new gray uniforms was "every inch a soldier." As the years moved on, the Grays, distinctive in tall, black, bearskin shakos, took their place among the nation's finest military companies. "Pioneers" who were members of the Grays for twenty-five years or more, wore aprons and carried axes on parade.

Governor Joseph Vance having failed to proclaim a day for Thanksgiving celebration in 1837 and again this year, the staunch New Englanders of Ohio declared December 19 as the day on which they would give thanks for abundant harvests and blessings. Many of the inhabitants were reluctant to observe spirited holiday customs of the Old World at Christmas-time, feeling that to do so was a desecration of the revered event.

Entertainment during the year was novel in character, and included a menagerie, a ventriloquist, the Albino lady, an Irish giant, and a fancy glassworker's exhibition.

1839

The Cleveland Grays' social activity was inaugurated when they held their first reception and military ball on January 23 in the new American House.

On March 2, Aaron Barker became postmaster of Cleveland. He was succeeded by Benjamin Andrews on September 6, 1842, and Timothy P. Spencer on April 11, 1845.

In their April report for 1838-39, the Board of School Managers stated that the common English branches had been taught in all the schools, and that considerable progress had been made in history, the natural sciences, etc. Salaries had remained stable. The enrollment had reached 823, with an average attendance of 588; but only one-fourth of those in the city's school-age population were going to school. Even so, the schools were crowded, and the city was urged to buy land and build more buildings. Silas Belden, Henry Sexton, and Henry H. Dodge constituted the board.

The earliest Jewish settlers who came to Cleveland were immigrants from Germany and Austro-Hungary, seeking liberty and opportunity. Twenty members of the Jewish community met this year in the home of Samson Hoffman on Seneca Street and formed the Israelitic Society, their first religious organization. Under the spiritual leadership of Isaac Hoffman —or Hopferman, the organizers were Simson Thorman, chairman, Simon Newmark, Moses Alsbacher, S. L. Coleman, Gerson Strauss, Kalman Roskopf, and Samson Hoffman. Upon the death of an itinerant Jewish peddler the next year, a burial plot was purchased in Ohio City for $100 and Willett Street Cemetery had its beginning. In 1842, the small congregation was divided, and the seceding group of thirty members formed the Anshe Chesed Society with the Rev. Asher Lehman as rabbi.

With the arrival of the Huron-built "luxury liner" *Great Western* on May 9, Clevelanders thronged to see the marvel, "greater than any craft that ever floated on our fresh seas." She was 186 feet long, 781 tons, and had paddle wheels of 13½-foot radius. Her capacity for passengers and freight was larger than any boat on the lakes. On June 4 she warmed her Pittsburgh-made engine and departed for Chicago and western ports.

As directed by Council on June 19, the southern half of the Public Square was fenced, after the county commissioners fulfilled their agreement to whitewash the Court House.

An ordinance providing for the licensing of dogs was passed on June 20. "At a grove in the eastern edge of the city" (Superior and East 9th), the Cleveland Grays held their first encampment, July 3-7. They were hosts for the first time to a visiting military company, the Buffalo Guards, and a gun squad known as Fay's Battery. Drilling and a holiday parade made up the program of events. The Grays carried their new silk flag which had been presented to them by Charles M. Giddings on May 2 in a Public Square ceremony. Fireworks were used to usher in the glorious Fourth for the first time; and in the evening, "hundreds of spectators were delighted with the novelty and the romance" of a blazing finale.

Northwest section of Public Square, 1839, Cleveland Grays parading.

Nine of the Cleveland Grays formed a Gun Squad on July 6. Through their initiative they outfitted themselves with uniforms and secured an iron cannon, for which they built the carriage. They also made the caisson and their ammunition. The six-pounder shook the firmament on every possible occasion. David L. Wood was drill sergeant of the "flying artillery." In 1845, the squad left the Grays, recruited new members, secured two twelve-pound guns, and elevated Wood to the rank of captain of the new organization known as the Cleveland Light Artillery. "Young men of the best families" were in its ranks.

The Academy was purchased by the city in July for $6,000 and added to the public-school system. This was Cleveland's second school building.

Pupils of Cleveland's free schools paraded from the Public Square to the First Baptist Church on August 1 for a public examination, the questions to be asked by teachers under whom they had not studied or by prominent citizens not associated with the schools. This practice continued until 1846.

When Dr. Horace A. Ackley came to Cleveland this year, he announced his practice would be confined to surgery. He was the first Ohio physician thus to specialize. His skill became widely known, and within a decade he was the outstanding surgeon in the State. In his historical account, the *First Fifty Years of Medical Conditions in Cleveland,* Dr. Frederick C. Waite relates that "One who used more than five minutes in amputating a leg above the knee was considered a bungler . . . a few (surgeons) did it in two minutes. A student under Dr. Ackley wrote that he timed this operation by Dr. Ackley with a watch. The time was ninety seconds." Speed was vital in these early days before the use of anesthesia. Men were given large doses of whisky, and opium was administered to women and children to help them withstand the ordeal. The conscious patient was bound to a board, and strong assistants held him rigidly while the surgeon performed the operation.

Although William J. Gordon was only twenty-one years old when he came to Cleveland this year, his unusual ability inspired confidence and encouragement on the part of leading businessmen, and within a year he had established a grocery firm of his own. An orphan at the age of twelve, he left New Jersey, and in New York City he found employment as a bank clerk. Impressed with Cleveland while on a visit, he decided to make it his home. W. J. Gordon & Company, wholesale grocers, was soon the foremost firm in its field in Ohio. South of Levi Johnson's fine home, Gordon built a mansion in keeping with his influential position (1200 West 9th Street).

There was a small Negro population, "industrious, peaceable, intelligent and ambitious for improvement." School facilities were provided for three months in the year. The Colored Men's Union Society of the lyceum type was organized, and questions of the day, including colonization and abolition, were debated. A library of one hundred volumes had been accumulated.

Cleveland's first municipal market house was built this year in the center of Michigan Street at Ontario. Traffic started before sunrise on market days —Tuesdays, Thursdays, and Saturdays, and long lines of wagons loaded with all kinds of foods and commodities threaded their way to the busy shopping center. The surrounding area soon became a hay market, and farmers and dealers sold from their vehicles on the street.

"Resolved, That Corporeal Punishment is a Necessity in the Training of Children" was the lively question debated by the Cleveland Lyceum in December. The Rev. Levi Tucker and M. C. Younglove, believers in the spare-the-rod-and-spoil-the-child theory, were too much for Finlay Strong and D. W. Cross, their progressive opponents.

CHAPTER 7

Trade Trails Stretch Wide
1840-1849

UNDER the impetus of canal commerce, Cleveland had made notable strides since 1830, the population in 1840 showing an increase of more than 5.5 times. The census reported the Cleveland figure at 6,071, and that of Ohio City, 1,577. Cincinnati stood sixth among American cities with a total of 46,338, while Cleveland was forty-fifth in the nation and second in Ohio.

A breakdown of the Cuyahoga County census in 1840 shows interesting township comparisons: Cleveland Township, 7,037; Mayfield, 852; Orange, 1,114; Solon, 774; Euclid, 1,774; Warrensville, 1,085; Bedford, 2,021; Newburgh, 1,342; Independence, 754; Brecksville, 1,124; Brooklyn, 1,409; Parma, 965; Royalton, 1,051; Rockport, 1,151; Middleburgh, 339; Strongsville, 1,151; Dover, 960; Olmstead, 659. A scattered population brought the total to 26,506.

Stage lines were operating on fairly dependable schedules, as management and roads improved, and the stagecoach was still the principal means of transportation between Cleveland and the outside world. Along limited lines of travel, however, it had been replaced by the canal boat.

Marked growth and development in Ohio resulted from canal expansion. Farmers, mine operators, and manufacturers could now exchange products at a better price, not only within the State, but beyond its borders. New industries were being attracted, and Ohio was considered more desirable for settlement. Population had grown from 937,903 in 1830 to 1,519,467 a decade later, and real-estate values were climbing rapidly. The Pennsylvania & Ohio Canal, opened in 1840, provided a waterway to Pittsburgh, via Akron, where connection was established with a route to the Atlantic seaboard.

Cleveland's wealth lay in shipping and trade. The city had grown steadily in importance, and most of the 250 sailing vessels on Lake Erie in 1841 stopped at the port, their capacity varying from 50 to 350 tons. Two of the 19 ships built in lake shipyards this year originated in Cleveland. The sloop-rigged, 138-ton *Vandalia,* with cabins on deck for passengers, was launched in Oswego, New York, in 1841, fitted with a screw propeller. It was soon learned that this long, narrow, flat-bottomed, straight-sided, schoonerlike hull was better suited than the sidewheeler. Two years later, Cleveland produced its first propeller, the *Emigrant;* and within ten years, 53 propellers were sailing the lakes, all but four under 400 tons. Six thousand bushels of wheat or 2,000 bushels of wheat and 2,000 barrels of flour con-

Dealer in Bolting Cloths and Mill Furnishing generally.

From city directory, 1837

CARRIAGE & WAGON
MANUFACTORY.

Eagle Marble Works,
Opposite Miller's Block.

JACOB LOWMAN,
No. 11, 13, and 15 Vineyard Lane,
CLEVELAND, O.

From city directory, 1845

From city directory, 1845

V. SWAIN,
SAIL MAKER.

IMPORTER OF RUSSIA AND HOLLAND
SAIL DUCK,
AND RUSSIA BOLT ROPE.

SAILS, AWNINGS, AND FLAGS
of all descriptions, made to order on the shortest notice.

Advertisements for some primitive Cleveland manufacturers.

stituted the capacity of a 200-ton ship. The freight rate on wheat to Buffalo was 4 to 5 cents per bushel; flour, 16 to 18 cents per hundred pounds; pork, 25 to 28 cents per barrel.

Reports of eastern railroad ventures and the wonders of the steam age aroused Cleveland, and in 1845, engineers were surveying the proposed route between Cleveland and Cincinnati. The abandoned piles of the old Ohio Railroad took on importance. Believing that the railroad could increase business and opportunity, Cleveland voted to extend the city's credit to encourage rail projects. News went out that the lake city was on the way to greatness, and soon men of wealth and talent began to move in to share in the prosperity era. Within a decade, the day of railroad competition with lake boats, canal packets, and stagecoaches had arrived.

Products of the soil and local manufacture found a ready market. The Otis iron works was a notable addition to the small but promising industrial district. Only $557 worth of capital was needed to provide an early-day manufactory with the tools, machines, and facilities used by a single worker, laboring seventy hours a week. Skill and strength determined his production, for machines performed only 6 per cent of the work. Although earnings were small, there was little to buy and prices were high.

The decade of the forties witnessed the establishment of companies that were still in existence in 1946: Empire Plow Company, 1840; Bennett-Sharer Funeral Home, W. Bingham Company, and The Joseph & Feiss Company, 1841; Cleveland-Sandusky Brewing Corporation, and George H. Herron & Company, 1844; Barth Stamping & Machine Works, Inc., Cleveland Agency of the Mutual Benefit Life Insurance Company and The Sterling & Welch Company, 1845; Geo. H. Olmsted & Company, 1848; Northern Ohio Plating Company, Root & McBride Company, and White Music Company, Inc., 1849.

Discovery of copper and iron in southern Michigan was followed shortly by the finding of iron deposits in the Marquette Range in the Michigan peninsula. Industrial development by Cleveland capital was based upon explorations by two Cleveland scientists, Charles Whittlesey and Dr. J. Lang Cassels. According to a prominent industrialist, "The discovery of the Lake Superior iron ore has contributed more to the wealth and well-being of this Nation than has been gained from all the gold of California and Alaska."

Hard times prevailed as the decade opened, and prices were high. In 1840, flour was taken in lieu of New York exchange at $3.50 per barrel. Cheese brought 4½ cents per pound at retail; butter, 9 cents; sugar, 7½ cents; Rio coffee, 7½ to 8½ cents; eggs, 5 cents per dozen; chickens, $1 per dozen; oats, 37 to 40 cents per bushel; dried apples, $1 per bushel; spring steel, 6 cents per pound; assorted nails, 6 cents; sheet iron, 6¼ to 7½ cents; blue shirtings, 8½ to 10½ cents per yard; sheetings, 7 and 8 cents; prints, 8½ to 16 cents. A revival of business came in the summer of 1843.

Under the leadership of Alfred Kelley, a new system of branch bank operation was created in Ohio in 1845 that went a long way toward bringing order out of economic confusion. Functioning as the State Bank of Ohio, two of its twelve branches were organized in Cleveland, the Merchants Bank and the Commercial Branch Bank. In the same year, the City Bank (later The National City Bank of Cleveland) opened and began its steady march through the years. The Society for Savings began its uninterrupted career in 1849. Enterprising businessmen organized the forerunner of the Insurance Board of Cleveland in 1846; and in 1848, the Board of Trade, which fathered The Cleveland Chamber of Commerce, was created.

Dynamic J. W. Gray and his brother launched the *Plain Dealer* in 1842, supporting the Democrats in the stronghold of the Whigs. Making the most of an incident in Cleveland, young Charles Dickens pointed an accusing finger at the paper, then not a year old, giving it international publicity. Three years later, the *Plain Dealer* dared to appear as an evening daily. Its survival emphasized the quality of its leadership, and the power of the press in promoting retail business through advertising and advancing community interests. Politics, temperance, and abolition furnished live topics of news. An overabundance of newspapers created keen competition that swallowed up most of them. Late in the decade, the lines of a miraculous invention called the telegraph were extended from Pittsburgh to Cleveland. Although feeble and far from efficient, it was considered an epochal achievement by news gatherers.

Cleveland's fiftieth birthday came in 1846, and the population had passed the ten-thousand mark. Produce and shipping merchants, grocers, ship chandlers, and supply stores lined the river-front. In a bold paving experiment, broad Superior Street had been planked from the river to the Square. Neighboring downtown streets were rutted by the wheels of heavy wagons, stagecoaches, rigs, and victorias. "Hilliard & Hayes, Dry Goods and Groceries" occupied a gable-roofed building at the junction of Superior and Water streets. On the south side of Superior at the head of Bank Street stood the Merchants Exchange, next door to the American House. At the northwest corner of Bank Street, the new Weddell House was well on the way to completion. Business blocks had been erected on either side of Superior, and wooden awnings extended over the sidewalk from some of the stores. Fences enclosed the four sections of the Public Square. Oil lamps, wood stoves, and well water-buckets characterized domestic living, and made up Cleveland's public utilities.

Men went about their business in tall beaver hats, tailed coats, and wide trousers. Ladies wearing ribboned bonnets, stocks, pinched waists, billowy skirts, and neatly folded shawls made their way to the Exchange to shop. While a lady of fashion is said to have dressed simply, a complexity of voluminous skirts flapped around her ankles—a flannel petticoat, an under-petticoat, a petticoat padded to the knees, two muslin petticoats, all topped with a dress fitted with hoopskirts and a bustle. A purse was sometimes carried in the bustle. High-buttoned boots and heavy, durable stockings completed the costume.

While Euclid Street had emerged from the primitive rut, a local paper declared that the roadway was "awful." As far back as 1839, determined opposition to any expenditure that would increase taxes had been inaugurated by several prominent property owners. Regardless of its condition, Euclid Street had developed. Between the Square and Muirson Street in 1844, there were thirty-three homes, the little Wesleyan Methodist Church at Hickox Alley, a school, a carpenter shop, and thirty-four vacant lots. At one corner of the intersection with Erie was a grove, where public gatherings and picnics were held. A sand pile monopolized another corner, and two others were marked by unfenced vacant lots.

Streets were maintained by such labor as the citizenry provided. Every able man was expected to make his annual contribution, upon receiving the characteristic form notifying him to appear at a stated time and place "with a good and sufficient shovel to perform the two days labor required . . . by law."

Erection of the first public schoolhouses met with protest from shortsighted taxpayers and penurious councilmen. Nevertheless, the early champions of educational privileges established a high school, one of the first free public high schools west of the Alleghenies; and they worked long and late to lay a firm foundation upon which was built the great Cleveland public-school system of later years.

Private schools for young ladies and young men were opened by learned professors and genteel women. Miss Fitch invited children to enter her famous school that "is furnished with a set of maps." Her compelling work with children was recognized long before the kindergarten era. Select schools, seminaries, and classical schools were conducted by the well-known Miss Thayer, Professor and Mrs. J. R. Fitzgerald, W. D. Beattie, Henry Childs of Yale, Miss Cleveland, and many others. R. Fry's school for boys competed with Principal Andrew Freese's high school, inspiring an amusing inquiry among the youthful, "Are you going to Freese or Fry this year?"

The city's first medical college (later School of Medicine, Western Reserve University) was organized with an admirable faculty, the fourth institution west of the Allegheny Mountains. Physicians and surgeons of skill and training were coming to Cleveland, a city beset with health problems about which the authorities had little concern.

During the long winter months, when waterways were frozen and roads were often impassable, long work hours were replaced by leisure and social visits, as trade came virtually to a standstill; but at the first sign of spring, business and the populace thawed out together. Thus cultural interests broadened.

In the Cleveland Library Association, the city had a valuable asset, providing not only a library, but a reading room, museum, and lecture series. A collection of five hundred books in a school library marked the beginning of a vast public-library system. With the founding of the Cleveland Academy of Natural Science (later The Cleveland Museum of Natural History), the wonders of the scientific world were unfolded through lectures and a museum. Fraternal orders began to organize, adding their benevolent service to those of a few charitable societies. Music appreciation found encouragement in the influence of the German singing societies and in occasional concerts given by visiting artists. Small theaters and lecture halls presented an increasing variety of entertainment and inspiration.

Church congregations were walking through valleys of trial and tribulation as the decade opened, beset on one hand by the period of hard times, and on the other by strife and contention. Pyramiding controversies rose out of debates on slavery and temperance and the doctrine of Oberlin Perfection, climaxed by Millerism. In the excitement created by the Millerites, many converts pledged themselves to give up the *Bible* and all faith, if their predictions regarding the Second Coming of Christ proved mistaken.

In 1846, there were eighteen churches in Cleveland, including two Jewish and two Roman Catholic. New churches embodying advanced ideas were being built, now that prosperity had returned. Impressive Gothic structures were appearing, with recessed chancels or choirs, true aisles with arcades, and open-timber ceilings. A significant trend in church architecture was introduced when Grace Church mounted the tower in its new building on the corner instead of in the middle of the street-end.

The log cabin had almost disappeared in Cleveland, as finer homes were being erected, comparable with splendid achievements elsewhere in the Western Reserve. Well preserved a century later were the Kirtland homes in Poland; the Frederick Kinsman home, Warren; the Ephraim Brown house, North Bloomfield; the Hudson-Lee house, built in Hudson in 1806, one of the oldest in the Reserve; the Baldwin-Buss home, 1825; Hosford cottage, and Seymour house, also in Hudson; the Jonathan Goldsmith and Dr. John H. Mathews residences, Painesville; the Mitchell-Turner house, Milan, 1828; the Bentley Kent house, Chagrin Falls; and the Sturgis-Kennan-Fulstow, Wooster-Boalt, and Kimball-Wooster-Martin houses in Norwalk. Classic colonnaded structures of the Greek Revival and Colonial periods, they were characterized by elegantly embellished doorways with sidelights and fanlights, and grille-work ornamentation. An interesting and valuable study of many of these early homes has been recorded by I. T. Frary of Cleveland in his volume, *Early Homes of Ohio*. Plain New England meeting houses on the village greens in Hudson, Tallmadge, Claridon, Atwater, and Twinsburg were architectural gems erected by devout pioneers, as was the chapel of Western Reserve College built in 1831 in Hudson.

The location of Western Reserve towns was determined largely by water power, the canal influence or natural resources. Small streams were adequate to operate flour mills. Woolen mills, tanneries, and cheese factories were not uncommon. Gates Mills had a rake factory; Berea made grindstones; tools and stoves were manufactured in Cleveland, Akron, Cuyahoga Falls, and Franklin (Kent), and the latter made glass, while Akron produced pottery. The paper supply for Cleveland newspapers came from Ohio City and Cuyahoga Falls, and the West Side mill also made printing, writing, and wrapping paper. Shipyards were operating on almost every stream that entered the lake. Cleveland and Akron had steam-engine works. There were several iron furnaces in Youngstown, which had the first rolling mill utilizing coal as fuel. Furnaces were also established in Dover, Elyria,

Mentor, Painesville, Niles, Perry, Poland, Akron, Madison, Ashtabula, and Conneaut. Despite the variety and volume of Western Reserve production, wool and cheese were shipped in from the East; English blister steel and Pennsylvania iron and steel were imported, and Russian and Swedish iron satisfied a large part of industrial requirements.

Artificial gas added its dim and uncertain rays to the trend of Cleveland's public improvements in 1849. "Our city now looks like a living place in the night," observed the *True Democrat*. "The new gas lights give everywhere a social air, and people move about as if there was no more trouble from darkness and the evils thereof." As the year was about to close, the first wood-burning locomotive fought its way up the River Street grade, a forward step in the uphill climb to bring the railroad to Cleveland.

Cleveland had recovered from the Panic of 1837 and was enjoying the prosperity wave resulting from the Mexican War as the decade closed. Standing on the brink of the great railroad and industrial eras, it had resourceful, energetic leadership and adequate banking facilities to make the most of its opportunities. History-making inventions and developments would expand industry and create fortunes, making possible enormous strides in commerce, welfare, and culture. In the words of the friendly editor of the *Pittsburgh Business Directory,* "the city is one of the few places where we find united, great business advantages with . . . beauty of location."

1840

The Pennsylvania & Ohio Canal opened for through traffic from Akron, where it joined the Ohio Canal, to Beaver and Pittsburgh on the Ohio River, thus offering an alternate route to the Atlantic seaboard. For the first time, a market was afforded to Mahoning Valley and southeastern Ohio communities for their coal, iron, and farm produce. Philadelphia interests built the canal. The State of Ohio subscribed $450,000 of the million-dollar capital stock, which reflects a waning interest in aiding new waterway projects. In the early fifties, the Mahoning Railroad acquired control very cheaply; but tolls were excessive, canals were on the downgrade generally, and the right-of-way was converted into a railroad bed.

Watson's Hall was built by J. W. Watson this year on Superior Street (Wilshire Block site). Silas Brainard, founder of a firm of piano dealers, purchased it in 1845, changing the name to Melodeon Hall.

The Cleveland Grays Band made its first appearance on February 22.

The heated political contest of 1839-40 was the absorbing topic in Cleveland. General William Henry Harrison, of "log cabin and hard cider" fame, was the champion of staunch supporters in the Western Reserve, a stronghold of the Whigs. At the height of the opposition to President Martin Van Buren, the local Whigs organized Tippecanoe clubs, and joined the surging ranks that were rallying behind the slogan, "Tippecanoe and Tyler, too." James

A. Briggs, young Cleveland lawyer, is credited by some with having created the famous fighting words.

At a meeting of Whigs in the Court House on March 7, officers of the Tippecanoe Club of Cleveland were elected: Frederick Whittlesey, president; William A. Coleman and seventeen others, vice presidents; A. W. Walworth, treasurer; and J. L. Weatherly, secretary. On March 9, Ohio City standard-bearers organized under the leadership of F. A. Burrows.

The local clubs made plans to erect "cabins," typifying the log-cabin sentiment, on each side of the river as campaign headquarters. On the evening of March 18, east-side enthusiasts met at the American House, and, led by the Cleveland Grays, they marched to the Ohio City cabin (Detroit and West 25th) for rousing dedication ceremonies. The rough interior was decorated with strips of dried pumpkin and strings of dried peppers, and a rifle, a pouch, and powder horn hung on the wall. In one corner stood a split broom. In another was a barrel of cider that was drained in pledges to "Old Tip" and the "Union of the Whigs."

Neighboring townsmen had been hauling logs into Cleveland as their contribution toward the Whig cabin that was to be the center of the Cleveland political campaign. March 30 was rainy, but early in the morning the citizens went to work, fortified with frequent visits to the hard-cider barrel. In a short time, they had erected their headquarters building on Superior Street, adjoining the American House. Newburgh's 105-foot log was selected for a pole bearing a flag with the word "Liberty," and another sturdy timber bore a sign reading, "With Tip and Tyler we'll bust Van's biler." The cabin was 35 by 50 feet, large enough to hold several hundred people, the newspapers claimed. Flags flanked the doorway. A large stump served as a speaker's rostrum inside, and campaign insignia and implements hung on the walls. Van Buren was represented by the drawing of an eagle holding a writhing fox in its talons. A little, black bear paced restlessly at the end of a chain fastened to a crossbeam. In a corner stood a cider barrel complete with tin cup. Campaigners poured in from miles around on April 3 for the dedication that was marked by brilliant oratory and rousing songs in honor of the "people's candidates." The next day, local Whigs organized on a broader scale when they formed the Tippecanoe Club of Cuyahoga County, with Frederick Whittlesey, president; J. M. Hoyt, secretary, and A. W. Walworth, treasurer. This club continued in existence as one of the oldest Republican clubs in the United States, its membership including men of eminence in state and nation.

In order to expand public-school facilities, the city purchased two lots, one on Rockwell Street (northwest corner of East 6th) and the other on Prospect Street. Building specifications were the same—40 feet square, two stories, four rooms, and the cost was $3,500 each, including seats, fences, etc. Rockwell School was completed in the spring, and Prospect in the fall. Although 1,000 students applied for admission to the fall term, there was crowded room for only 900. The enrollment at the beginning of the winter term, December 10, was 1,041, which included Bethel School, a small school at Prospect and Ontario streets, and one on Chestnut Street. N. A. Gray,

Elizabeth Armstrong, Abby Fitch, and Louisa Kingsbury taught at Rockwell; Andrew Freese, Sophia Converse, Emma Whitney, and Sarah M. Thayer at Prospect; and George W. Yates, Louisa Snow, and Julia Butler at the Academy.

The first "salary schedule" specified $10 a week for male and $5 for female teachers. The school year consisted of forty-four weeks, with five and a half days to the week and six hours to the day. While teachers were required to keep their rooms in order and make the fires in the bulging wood stoves, attentive pupils usually assumed most of the burden. Until 1851, wood was used for fuel, and coal was used exclusively commencing in 1854. Cleveland's early teachers were earnest and hard-working; and in their organized meetings, which began in 1842, notable educational progress originated.

Primitive furniture was used in these early schools. Long, pine benches of cheap construction seated the pupils as they faced the teacher. There was a certain luxury in the smooth, splinterless seats, even if they had no backs.

Prospect Street School built in 1840; Rockwell Street School of the same architecture was built earlier in the year.

Seating expense per scholar amounted to about 50 cents. A little later, arm chairs were introduced for the primary children. The first two-seated desks were used in 1845, made from pine at a cost of from $1.50 to $1.75 each. They were supplanted by the three-legged desk, back-rest improvements, and better-grade construction.

A variety of choice greenhouse plants was offered for sale in April by Alexander Sked on Ontario between St. Clair and Lake streets. Shrubs, bulbs, and seeds for farm and garden were advertised by several dealers.

The "morus multicaulis bubble"—the craze for raising mulberry trees—had been spreading since 1837 from the Middle West eastward to the coast, because of promised profits in silk manufacture. Late in 1839, the bubble burst in New Jersey, and it is said that the high cost of labor contributed to the end of the boom. In Cleveland, however, growers held a mass meeting on April 28, this year, to draft a petition to Congress favoring a duty on foreign silk to increase their opportunities. For several years, they persisted in promoting the production of silk, despite the claim that the movement had originated to benefit a few speculative individuals. Painesville, which was to become a great rayon-producing center in the next century, was the last to acknowledge that the little silkworm's industry was a disappointment.

Although Jarvis F. Hanks offered to teach music in the public schools for a pittance, the Board of School Managers refused his proposal. Teaching of music would be illegal, they declared. One member preferred that dancing be taught. Opposition was stubborn, and music was denied the school children of Cleveland.

At a meeting in the First Presbyterian Church, a group of its members organized the First Congregational Church "for the purpose of providing another place of public worship." T. C. Severance, an incorporator of the mother church, was a leader in the new venture. The wooden house of worship erected just west of the Stone Church (Frankfort and West 3rd), dedicated in 1841, witnessed stormy scenes in the congregation's short career. Its pastor, the Rev. Charles Fitch of New England, entertained most of the isms of the time, and some of Dr. Aiken's members, who had become dissatisfied with his conservative position on the slavery question, joined the neighboring separatists. Second Adventism, Perfectionism, and tempestuous agitations retarded growth and hastened bankruptcy in 1844. The edifice was sold to the Second Presbyterian congregation for $3,671, and a number of the members returned to the First Church fold.

Temperance and liquor control had become highly controversial subjects in Council, as the record indicates. The matter of licenses had been in the legislative mill for about a year with only parliamentary debate to show for the trouble. An interesting and amusing sequence of compromises had resulted: first, an "ordinance for the suppression of dram shops"; followed by an "ordinance for the suppression or the sale of ardent spirits in less quantity than one quart"; futile attempts to strike out "one quart" and substitute "one pint," "fifteen gallons," and "a pound of bread." Reform was finally crystallized on May 6, with the passing of "an ordinance to regulate taverns, and to prohibit the sale of ardent spirits or other intoxicating liquors by a less quantity than one quart."

The four sections of the Public Square were separately enclosed with fences in the spring, and the southern half was seeded. Council ordered the street supervisor "to procure some suitable person to sink the public wells, so that they will contain at least three and one-half feet of water," the cost to be held to $35.

William Bergin built the Cataract House above the Mill Creek Falls—or cataract—in Newburgh (near 8820 Broadway). When it burned in 1850, the town raised money to rebuild. Among succeeding owners was A. H. Spencer, a schoolteacher, who bought it in 1866 and called it the Spencer House. He advertised, "amazing meals at 25 cents, clean and wholesome food! Christopher Born is one of the best cooks in northern Ohio." It eventually reverted to its original name.

Not far from the Cataract House in the forties was the Eagle House, at Miles Avenue and Broadway, with a "spring-floor" ballroom on the top floor that was a sensational achievement. Hotel stages gathered up dating couples who were eager to put spring in "pigeon-wings." Whisky, hot water, and maple sirup combined to stir the spirits, and nut cakes fried in bear grease were a special treat.

Erie Street Cemetery was replatted, and a record of lots and burials was begun. No register had been kept prior to this time.

Mould's Saloon was a grog shop extraordinary, claiming to be the "headquarters of those who love the delicacies of the season, with its strawberries and raspberries in full perfection, its ice creams and sodas which take the place of mint juleps and cobblers, its great variety of pastry, confectionery and fruit."

Lake County was created by the Legislature out of Geauga and Cuyahoga counties, and Willoughby Township no longer existed. Summit County also came into being this year.

The Rev. Peter McLaughlin became resident pastor of the Catholic Parish, and after a hard struggle the church of "Our Lady of the Lake" became a reality. It was erected at Columbus and Girard streets, midway

St. Mary's on the Flats.

between Cleveland and Ohio City, at a cost of $3,000. Although mass was said in it for the first time in October, 1839, it was not dedicated until June 7, this year. St. Mary's on the Flats, as it was familiarly known, served as the first diocesan cathedral for more than a decade. The last service was held in 1886, and two years later the pioneer church was razed.

The hero of Tippecanoe, General William Henry Harrison, made a short visit to Cleveland on June 13, stopping at the Franklin House in Ohio City. He was met at the dock by the Cleveland Grays, and, refusing a carriage, he marched with the company to the American House. Here he made an "extended speech" from the balcony to several thousand cheering admirers. This was the first presidential contest in which the candidates made speeches.

Open-air market facilities on the West Side were provided by Josiah Barber and Richard Lord, who dedicated a parcel of land for a public square at the corner of Pearl and Lorain streets. It became known as Market Square, and a wooden market house was erected in 1868.

August 25 was a great day for the Whigs in Cleveland. Tom Corwin, "wagon boy," their champion for governor, was slated to engage in an oratorical boost for the party with Thomas Ewing, "salt boiler," and Francis Granger of New York. Four miles west of the city, he was met by an escort on horseback and in wagons, the Tippecanoe Club, and the Cleveland Grays Band. Cannon boom and flag-waving heralded his approach, and for more than two hours Corwin engaged in a speech from the American House balcony to the crowd assembled in vacant lots. Reporting on the rally's great success, the *Herald* stated, "not one intoxicated person seen" during the entire day.

When Christopher Jackson built his tavern on the road to Pittsburgh (Moreland Hills Village) this year, it was a popular stopping point for stagecoach travelers on their long overland journey. Modern transportation reduced the income, and the inn became a country school and later a dwelling. It was still standing in 1946, a monument to the fine architecture of the early Western Reserve.

William A. Otis opened an iron works and began making castings. From this industrial venture, Cleveland's pioneer ironmaster forged ahead, making the name of Otis synonymous with progress and improvement.

On the banks of Big Creek (under the Brooklyn-Brighton Bridge, 3979 Pearl Road), John Tompkins built a slaughter house. In 1946, his grandson, John A. Tompkins, was handling five hundred head of livestock a week in the original building.

When Gilman Folsom contracted to dig a channel from the old river bed to the lake for $28,000, he was paid in Ohio City bonds, and his men were to receive 75 cents a day. A strike for higher wages resulted, and strikers stoned "scabs" who were willing to work for that amount.

Whigs of the county were jubilant as their candidates, Thomas Corwin for governor and William Henry Harrison for President, were swept into office. On November 19, they closed their feverish campaign of bold attacks, barbecues, songs, and demonstrations with a spirited victory celebration in Cleveland.

The federal census credited Cuyahoga County with a population of 26,506. Industry had taken a foothold, in spite of the ruinous effects of the panic. Two cast-iron furnaces, capitalized at $130,000, were producing 200 tons, consuming 1,310 tons of fuel, and employing 102 workers. The output of stone products annually was $18,822, with 28 men employed and a $2,000 capital investment. The production of pot or pearl ashes for the year was 113 tons. Manufactured machinery was valued at $43,600; hardware and cutlery, $25,000; refined metals, $31,500. The brick and lime industry manufactured products valued at $8,540 with 26 employees and $12,500 capital. Four woolen mills showed an annual production of $14,400, 18 men employed and capital of $12,400. Thirteen tanneries employed 21 men, and tanned 845 sides of sole leather and 3,680 sides of uppers; capital, $6,800. Soap manufacture totaled 113,000 pounds, and tallow candles, 82,000, with 10 workers and $4,000 capital. Two distilleries produced 80,000 gallons of whisky, and the output of 1 brewery was 50,000 gallons of beer. Six flour mills were operating, 15 grist-mills, 70 sawmills and 1 oil mill, with a combined payroll of 104 men and output valued at $183,875. Common laborers received

70 cents a day. As county industry centered largely in Cleveland and Ohio City, this report gives a comprehensive picture of the city's development up to this time.

1841

The city had become the gateway to freedom for runaway slaves who sought safety in Canada from their masters. Under the law, the slaves when arrested in Cleveland were to be turned over to their owners who took them back to bondage. An incident that occurred this year reflects Cleveland's attitude toward the great national issue. Three slaves, who were said to have escaped from New Orleans, were kidnaped by their alleged owners in Buffalo and brought to Cleveland, where they were jailed under the federal law. John A. Foote and Edward Wade, leading Abolitionists, were refused permission to visit them. Thomas Bolton, who was not an Abolitionist, was granted an interview and determined to defend them. Courageously he faced stern opposition and public opinion, and against vicious threats secured their discharge. Henceforth, Cleveland was less frequented by kidnapers.

The City Council created the office of acting school manager in March and elected Charles Bradburn, George Willey, Charles Stetson, and Madison Kelley to the Board of School Managers. In his zeal and devotion to education, Bradburn, successful merchant, gave one-fourth of his time to the schools for many years.

George Willey was born in Boston in 1821, the son of a prominent shipping merchant. After his father's death, he came to Cleveland to live with his uncle, Judge John W. Willey, who sent him to Jefferson College at Washington, Pennsylvania, where he was graduated. He studied law in his uncle's office, was admitted to the bar in 1842, and formed a law partnership in 1843 with John E. Cary. Willey was intensely interested in the progress of the public schools, and gave so much time to their pioneer struggles that his law partner protested. He successfully organized teaching systems and instruction plans that were adopted throughout the country. Cleveland's excellent public-school system is traceable to the efforts and energies of this wise and thorough leader. Most of Willey's legal work consisted of admiralty cases and patent law, and he made important contributions to maritime law. President Grant appointed him United States attorney for the northern district of Ohio. Recognized as an excellent orator, he became the city's favorite home-town lecturer, taking part in initiating cultural movements.

As a result of the economic depression, the state appropriation for the schools was reduced, and bitter opposition to public education had been aroused. Schools were crowded, but the city fathers laid aside proposals for expansion. Male teachers' salaries were cut to $32.50 per month, and female teachers had to be satisfied with $4.40 a week. In order to open two additional primary schools the next year, the school year was shortened from ten to nine months to provide the money.

Council fixed the annual salaries of city officials: mayor, $100; marshal, $300; clerk, $400; street supervisor, $400; treasurer, $200; clerk of the market, $100.

As the population multiplied, voting privileges were abused; and in 1838, election betting was prohibited legally. "To preserve the purity of elections," an act passed on March 20, this year, required electors to be twenty-one years of age, residents of Ohio for one year, and of the county, thirty days. Fraudulent voting and bribery were made prison offenses.

Early in the year, Sanford & Company, booksellers, opened the first commercial circulating library, containing five hundred volumes. Rentals were based upon the size of the volume.

Young William Bingham had spent his first five years in Cleveland clerking in George Worthington's hardware store. He had watched the oxcarts and Conestoga wagons moving westward, and listened to talk about railroads cutting in on the canal trade. He saw big schooners being built in the shipyards. Envisioning a great building era, he paid $12,933.24 for Clark & Murfey's hardware stock on April 1, and opened his store on Superior Street on the site of Abram Hickox' pioneer blacksmith shop. H. C. Blossom was Bingham's first clerk and first partner. Here W. Bingham & Company did a big business in buggy whips, curry combs, and anvils; it serviced canal boats, sold hardware to lake men, cant hooks and peavies to lumbermen, spikes to railroad builders, lunch pails and shovels to ore miners, wire and nails to builders of telegraph lines and factories. Bingham hardware and appliances went into the famous homes on Euclid Avenue.

William Henry Harrison, ninth President of the United States, had been in office only a month when he died of pneumonia on April 4. Upon hearing the news of his death, Cleveland was plunged into deep mourning. Memorial exercises were held in the Court House on April 9. The *Herald* appeared with mourning border. Vice President John Tyler became the nation's tenth President.

Antislavery dissension and panic thwarted the building plans of the little First Methodist Episcopal Church congregation; but after five years' labor, their $3,000 sanctuary was dedicated in April at the corner of St. Clair and Wood streets. This was the first Methodist church in the original boundaries of Cleveland, and from it missions and churches had their start. The Rev. D. C. Wright, the first settled pastor, was engaged in 1860. In 1865, a site was purchased at Euclid and Erie streets for a new church. Protest against the high price of $9,150 was justified by the committee in the light of 1827 real-estate figures, when a little less than two acres on the corner had sold for $64. A chapel built on Erie Street served until 1874, when a spacious $140,000 building of Sandusky limestone, with a buttressed tower and tall, cathedral windows of Munich glass, was dedicated. Gradually business encroached, and, when the property was purchased by the Cleveland Trust Company at the end of the century, the church realized about $500,000.

The stylish new omnibus, built by David Dean, Cleveland coach maker, for the Mansion House, was the city's "novelty" of May 2.

A portion of Orange Township was annexed to Geauga County, and a strip of Russell, in Geauga, was joined to Cuyahoga County. Two years later, the tract was restored to Orange.

The Ladies Fair, given by the ladies of the Episcopal Church on June 22, attracted attention, for the *Herald* had thrown out a broad hint that " a general attendance of bachelors was expected."

This year's circus featured a number of elephants, accomplished ladies, and a band.

A national movement was under way to make Independence Day the occasion for temperance demonstrations. Total Abstinence Society meetings were held, and fifteen hundred persons paraded wearing temperance-pledge badges. The *Herald* concurred editorially, stating that "The Spirit of '76 needs no stimulus from the intoxicating grape, for it was born when grape-shot rattled."

Politics, abolition, and the feminine influence inspired the launching of six newspapers this year, with weighty and enterprising titles: *The Daily Morning News, The Daily Morning Mercury, The Cleveland Gatherer, Palladium of Liberty, The Eagle-Eyed News Catcher,* and the *Mothers and Young Ladies' Guide.* Four of them discontinued before the year's end, and the others fell by the wayside shortly thereafter. In their brief span, however, the editors had helped to guide the destiny of the community, leaving a written record of inestimable value.

With the opening of The Cleveland News Room in the Franklin Building on September 8, out-of-town newspapers could now be purchased at the "news depot."

Public announcement of Daguerre's new photographic invention had been made in 1839, and on September 9, this year, Dr. Theodatus Garlick made the first daguerreotype in Cleveland in the Franklin Building.

Koch, Kauffman & Loeb opened a general store in Meadville, Pennsylvania, in September. Four years later, the business was moved to Cleveland under the name of Koch & Loeb. The firm entered the wholesale apparel field; and summer clothing, such as linen dusters and trousers, Alpaca coats, and white vests were popular items. The ready-made-clothing era had not dawned, and cloth was purchased from the mills and cut on the premises. It was then sent to small contract shops to assemble—to coat-and-overcoat shops owned largely by Bohemians; trouser shops operated mostly by Germans, and vest shops by Hungarians and Germans. Koch & Loeb were located first at 82 Superior Street, but moved shortly to the Custom House Block at Merwin and Superior. Loeb remained in the firm only a brief time. The name became Koch, Goldsmith, Joseph & Company in 1873. On September 28, 1877, John Hay, son-in-law and representative of Amasa Stone, builder, signed the agreement for construction of a building on St. Clair Street for the company. Koch retired in 1889, and about 1897, a small inside shop was started as a manufacturing experiment, the foundation for the great factory erected at 2149 West 53rd Street in 1920. The pioneering establishment became The Joseph & Feiss Company in 1907, one of the largest clothing concerns in the country. Felix S. Mayer joined the firm in 1929 and later became its president, succeeding Paul L. Feiss, who became chairman of the board.

Clumsy hulls, carrying sixty to eighty tons burden, drawn by horse and mule power, were steadily building canal traffic. The principal products received by canal this year were wheat, 1,564,421 bushels; coal, 478,370 bushels, used in local manufactories; lard, 961,161 pounds; wool, 107,805 pounds; flour, 441,425 barrels; pork, 39,200 barrels, and a steady supply of Kentucky whisky. Lumber, fish, 59,773 barrels of New York salt, and 15,164,-747 pounds of merchandise cleared the Cleveland port for the interior. Passenger arrivals in Cleveland totaled 19,492, and canal tolls as of 1840 had reached $86,851.89.

Interest in Freemasonry was revived, and Concord Lodge was reborn when Cleveland City Lodge No. 15 was organized with sixteen charter members on September 28 at a meeting in John Bennett's Coffee House in the Erie Building on the west side of Water Street, just north of Superior. Clifford Belden was the first master, and a charter was granted on October 19, 1842. The hall in the Farmers Block, rented from General H. H. Dodge, a Mason, for $50 a year, served as a meeting place until 1843, when a hall in the Merchants Exchange was leased for ten years at $100 per year. Leading men of the day were members of the order.

In a stone schoolhouse on the Euclid Road at Doan's Corners, between Republic and Doan streets, Jarvis F. Hanks, Horace Ford, and Horatio C. Ford started a school. After a continuous existence of more than a half century, the building became the nursery of the Euclid Avenue Congregational Church.

James Nicholson, James Newman, Mars Wagar, and a few followers of the Swedenborgian faith organized the Church of the New Jerusalem in Rockport, under the leadership of the Rev. McCarr of Cincinnati. Land was donated by the Wagar family (at Detroit and Andrews avenues) for the first church, erected about 1848, in the district that later became Lakewood. When the Church of the Redeemer, as it was also known, celebrated its centennial, the original structure, sheathed in modern siding, was serving proudly beside the ivy-clad brick building of more recent years. The church, a nondenominational institution, operated under a system of guest ministers, with no resident minister.

Monroe Street Cemetery was opened on November 12 on the west side of Monroe Street (and West 30th).

1842

The *Advertiser* was in financial straits when it was acquired for $1,050 in December, 1841, by the Gray brothers, Admiral Nelson, thirty-eight, and Joseph William, twenty-eight-year-old schoolteacher and lawyer. The old masthead never appeared again. Instead, a new weekly was introduced on

Peter M. Weddell

John W. Willey

Harvey Rice

Samuel E. Williamson

Sherlock J. Andrews

George Worthington

Truman P. Handy

Henry B. Payne

Dr. Jared P. Kirtland

William Bingham

William A. Otis

Hiram V. Willson

J. W. Gray

Daniel P. Rhodes

John W. Allen

William J. Gordon

Dr. John S. Newberry

James A. Garfield

January 7, this year, from the plant above the Post Office on Superior Street, under the partnership of A. N. and J. W. Gray, business manager and editor, respectively. The *Plain Dealer* was born of "democracy and modesty" and "devoted to Politics, Agriculture, Commerce, the Mechanic Arts, Foreign and Domestic Intelligence." Only two columns of the initial edition of the four-page journal contained news items, the latest date of which was December 29. Presidential messages, speeches, Congressional proceedings, European developments, and political events dominated the space. Commencing its march through the years, the *Plain Dealer* was to be pitied, launched as it was in a day of numerous short-lived, unprofitable, journalistic ventures; but to its saving credit was the dauntless courage and driving power of its editor, who laid a sturdy foundation. In its early days, it was to serve as "The Democratic voice in the wilderness of Whiggery," according to Archer H. Shaw, chief editorial writer of the paper for many years. J. W. purchased his brother's interest in 1843, and A. N. began a career related to railroad-building, when he became known as "Iron Gray." Nicholas A., a third brother, was associated with the newspaper in editorial capacities. During the Civil War, he left the Democratic Party, shocking his political travelers.

Clevelanders were suffering from "hard times," influenced by chaotic financial and economic conditions. A complicated money situation and the doubtful value of notes in circulation obstructed commerce and trade. For many, bankruptcy was imminent. To add to their troubles, there had been no real winter; rainfall had been heavy, and the mails were irregular. On February 10, an editor observed, "This has been a blue day, the bluest Cleveland ever saw." Soon afterward, the charter of the city's only bank expired, and Cleveland was without banking facilities until 1845. Exchange brokers and insurance companies were the only fiscal agencies in operation.

Upon observations taken as a result of a devastating storm that swept northern Ohio in February, Professor Elias Loomis of Western Reserve College based the calculations for weather maps completed in May, 1843. These were reduced to a single map that became the basis for the type of map used by the United States Weather Bureau.

At the request of Jeptha G. and David Nickerson, John Henry of the Disciples denomination held a meeting in Ohio City that resulted in the organization of Franklin Circle Church of Christ with twenty-nine members on February 20. They worshiped in a small building (on Vermont Avenue near West 28th), and the following year services were held in Cleveland in Apollo Hall and Empire Hall. The congregation returned to the West Side in 1846, and in 1848 they erected "God's barn." Sailors and those associated with the shipping business made up a large part of the membership, and at one time there were seven ship captains on the roster. One name stands out in the distinguished ministry of the church, that of James A. Garfield, who served from 1856 to 1858 and became President of the United States. Six pastors later became college presidents. A. R. Teachout, Cleveland businessman and philanthropist, was superintendent of the

Sunday School for twenty-five years. Jessie Brown Pounds, writer of *Beauti-ful Isle of Somewhere* and *The Way of the Cross Leads Home,* was a member of the church. Construction of the historic brick edifice on Franklin Circle began in 1874, and the dedication took place on May 13, 1883.

The widow of Samuel Cowles sold her home on Euclid Street (Taylor store site), with a frontage of 150 feet, running through to Prospect, for $7,000. In 1915, the property was valued at $6,000 per foot front.

"To visit the sick, relieve the distressed, bury the dead, and educate the orphan, to improve and elevate the character of man" was the charitable purpose of the Odd Fellows, organized this year as Cleveland Lodge No. 13 with 11 members. Meetings were held in Odd Fellows Hall on the Public Square. The oldest lodge in northern Ohio, its membership in the late seventies had reached 179. Erie Lodge, founded in 1844, met in the Odd Fellows Block at Pearl and Church streets, where it was joined by Phoenix Lodge, dating from 1854. The Odd Fellows gradually gained in numbers, Cataract Lodge being organized in 1855; Allemania, Anchor, and University, 1867; Donau, 1871; Banner, 1874; Mayflower, 1879; North Wing Encampment, 1862; and Harmonia Encampment, 1872.

Mrs. Benjamin Rouse was the guiding influence in founding the Martha Washington and Dorcas Society, devoted to care of needy children, the aged, and the sick. From this early effort came the Cleveland Protestant Orphan Asylum.

Cleveland had attracted a number of skilled physicians, but none equaled Dr. John Delamater, a newcomer this year. He had been a professor in eight medical colleges, and was recognized not only as "the best medical teacher in the United States," but he ranked among the finest physicians.

Disciples in Newburgh reorganized their church on April 21, and with twenty old and fifteen new members, the Miles Avenue Church of Christ began an influential career. John Hopkinson and Theodore Stafford were elected as elders, and David L. Wightman and John Healy, deacons. Until 1864, supply pastors officiated, among them James A. Garfield. Although he was not ordained—the Disciples believed in lay-ministry, he exercised the prerogatives of a minister by officiating at marriages, conducting funerals, and administering the ordinances of the church. Garfield was the only "minister" and the only Disciple who became President of the United States. A house of worship was erected early in the next decade. Membership in the pioneer church at 9200 Miles Avenue was 1,195 in 1946, and the Rev. Ray M. Wolford was minister.

Charles Dickens, famous English novelist not yet thirty, reached the city with his wife by steamer from Sandusky, before midnight, April 25. With a companion, he made an early tour around the city, carefully avoiding contact with the citizens, because of his indignation over a "whip England" article that he had read in the infant *Plain Dealer,* neglecting to note that it was reprinted from another paper. When curious citizens crowded on the boat at the River Street dock, Dickens was "so incensed" at this invasion of his privacy that he refused to receive Mayor Joshua A. Mills. He departed at nine in the morning to continue his American tour. Returning to England, Dickens made the Cleveland paper a target of international publicity that shrewd Editor Gray utilized to good advantage.

Dust in summer and mud after a rain characterized broad Superior Street, Cleveland's main thoroughfare. The big event of the year consisted of the planking of Superior, the first attempt at paving within the city limits. Heavy planks were laid crosswise on the street, from the Square to the river; and while smooth traveling was assured when the timbers were new, the going became worse as they loosened. When high water invaded River Street, the paving moved out with the flood. The plank road, however, was a great achievement, and now Superior "became passable at all seasons of the year."

For days at a time, Cleveland skies were darkened as millions of passenger pigeons soared overhead. The roar of their wings "sounded at the distance of miles like the heavy surges of Erie beating an iron-bound coast," it was observed. One shot could bring down many birds, and street peddlers sold them for food at less than a cent apiece.

Rufus Dunham built a more pretentious Dunham Tavern this year, a two-story frame building, and a big barn. Stout hewn timbers, fastened together with wooden pins and hand-wrought spikes, went into the buildings that were still standing in 1946 at 6709 Euclid Avenue. A lead bathtub created almost as much comment as the water tank, filled from an outside cistern by a force pump. Bedrooms were connected with the office by a call system, consisting of wires that tinkled bells. Here travelers who came by team or stage found lodging before going on to Cleveland. In the tap-room, gentlemen mingled with frontiersmen in exchanges on politics and progress, while ladies sipped port wine and frosted milk in the big center room. Trappers stored their furs in the stone smokehouse near the kitchen door, and drivers slept in the barn when the inn was filled. From time to time, dry goods and other articles were sold at the tavern, around which the community and local politics revolved. In 1853, the place was deeded to Ben and John Welch for $6,000. As stage travel was outmoded by the railroad, Dunham Tavern ceased to serve the public, and became a private home. It changed hands a number of times until 1886, when it was purchased by Dr. James A. Stephens, serving as the family residence until 1930, when the owner died.

"Novelty unparalleled! The only living Giraffe in the United States," announced the *Herald* of July 1. "The Giraffe will make a tall bow to just as many thousand visitors as choose to try to 'come the Giraffe' over him." On July 6, it was noted that the menagerie and circus was held over, as so many persons had not been able to see "the only living specimens of the giraffe, camel or leopard in the U. S."

Martin Van Buren was the first ex-President to visit Cleveland. He stopped in the city on his return from the West on July 12. A committee had joined him at the boat in Detroit, and as it neared the Cleveland harbor, a gun salute was fired from the hill near the lighthouse. Amid the cheers of the townsmen, the Cleveland Grays escorted Van Buren on parade from the Superior Street docks to the Square and back to the American House. From the balcony, he spoke of the importance of the canals in advancing transportation, and complimented the city on its greatness. Fireworks were set off as he departed for Buffalo by steamer.

Express service came to Cleveland when the first shipment of fruit was received this year. After sampling a luscious watermelon, presented to Josiah A. Harris of the *Herald* by the Cleveland agent of Hawley and Company's Express, the editor published an acknowledgment of thanks on July 13, stating that it had been "but eight days" since the melon was picked from the vine in Charleston, South Carolina. In May, fresh seafood was coming from the Atlantic, and the newspaper announced, "The Yankees are paying us off for our eggs in live lobsters." The express company offered to "forward at low rates with the utmost speed and safety, choice goods, specie, bank notes, important papers, valuable packages, etc."

Jacob Wansor was offering "bathing tubs" for sale, "with fixture attached for heating water in a few minutes." They were made in his factory, and were considered a great luxury.

For a month, John Baldwin had prayed in a grove on his farm for guidance out of the financial entanglement in which he became involved in the late thirties, while trying to promote education in the Berea community. The answer came the day he discovered sandstone, or Berea grit, in his riverbed. Hacking out a crude grindstone, he realized its great possibilities—every farm and household would need one to keep tools and utensils keen-edged. By devising a lathe, he turned out the first lathe-made grindstone, thereby increasing production, and "it was not long before my money was coming in at the rate of twenty dollars a day," related the pioneer. Baldwin leased his lands to operators, and from the fortune in stone under his large tract, a business of world proportions developed, providing broad philanthropies. John Wallace is credited with being the first actual quarry operator in the Berea district. Soon deposits of Berea grit were found elsewhere in Cuyahoga, Lorain, and Erie counties, and the making of grindstones became an important industry.

B. S. Decker became the proprietor of Doan's Tavern (Fenway Hall site), advertising it as a "Temperance House." The historic inn led a checkered career under various landlords, as the Croton House and as the Wright House, when story-telling James Wright purchased and remodeled it in 1859. Many social affairs were held here. Its popularity increased when the East Cleveland horsecar line was extended to Doan's Corners and the hotel became the end of the road. Wright sold the property to John J. Benton for $35,000 in 1871.

As the year closed, the newspapers announced that their carriers would "pay their respects to those they have served in all weathers during the past year. They anticipate a substantial response to their 'Happy New Year!'"

1843

Samuel Mather, Jr., was the only stockholder in the pioneering Connecticut Land Company whose descendants were to be of tremendous influence in the city's future. Samuel Livingston Mather, his son, came to Cleveland this year to represent his father and care for his Western Reserve holdings. He found lodging at the Franklin House; and in the Central Building, at Water and Superior streets, he began practicing law.

Fire took a toll on River Street on January 2, when it burned the warehouse of Standart, Griffith & Company, the S. Cleary & Company grocery store, and the block-and-spar shops of William Nott & Company. The steamers *Cleveland* and *New England,* ice-locked near the dock, were damaged.

A public bathing establishment, "large and commodious and fitted up in a style not surpassed west of New York," was advertised by J. L. Watson and F. White on January 25. In the rear of Watson's barber shop, "cold, warm, tepid, Russian or shower baths" could be had, and ladies were served exclusively on Friday afternoons.

William McKinley was born at Niles, Ohio, January 29, the son of a poor iron founder. He became the twenty-fourth President of the United States.

On March 29, mechanics and workmen protested against payment "in orders and store pay" in return for their labors. They claimed that since "money is the circulating medium of this country, it alone is the proper pay for the services of every class of the community." Wages during the hard times were low, but workers made no complaint. The *Plain Dealer* reported that a workmen's parade and a large mass meeting in the Square on April 5 produced results that were "partially successful."

German Lutheran families withdrew from the Schifflein Christi congregation and formed Zion Church of the Evangelical Lutheran faith, with about sixty members, under the leadership of the Rev. David Schuh. Meetings were conducted in Concert Hall on Superior Street. To preserve the religion of the fatherland and to educate their children, the Lutherans launched their first school in Cleveland in 1848, providing instruction from the first to eighth grades. A house of worship was dedicated this year on York Street between Bond and Wood. Dr. Henry C. Schwan, called as pastor in 1851, beloved and wise, was a leader in early-day denominational advance. A larger edifice on Erie Street at Bolivar served until 1903, when a new church was occupied at Sterling and Prospect, during the ministry of the Rev. C. M. Zorn. The Rev. Clarence Schuknecht came to the church in 1929, and became pastor in 1938 of Zion Lutheran Church, the oldest Lutheran congregation in the city.

Colored people of the city asked for a separate school for their children in April. Acting upon the report of the judiciary committee, the City Council voted against the petition. Nevertheless, a school for Negroes was made possible late in the year. A system for selecting public-school teachers was introduced, that provided for "thorough examination in spelling and the rudiments of the English language as contained in Webster's spelling book," and, further, that instructors "must be good readers both in prose and poetry, evince a thorough knowledge both in rules and practices of arithmetic, and furnish satisfactory evidence of good character."

William Miller, Massachusetts farmer, mathematician, religious enthusiast, and founder of the Second Adventists, known as the Millerites, had been spreading his belief that Christ's second coming was at hand. Fifty or more Cleveland people, fired with Miller's zeal, secured the Rev. Charles Fitch to lead their worship services in the Congregational Church (corner of Frankfort and West 3rd). The pastor edited and published *The Second Adventist,* a journal with comforting comments for believers and stern warnings for scoffers. In his drive for subscription he was handicapped at the start by the very method he vigorously advanced, for he preached that at any moment all worldly things might be swept away. Serial articles were out of the question. Nevertheless, the dauntless Fitch continued to circulate his paper, promising to issue the next edition if "the Lord does not appear before the day of publication." The falling of meteors in various parts of the country caused consternation; and in preparation for the Day of Judgment, the followers hurriedly built a temple of brick, round and with a circular window or skylight on top, on Wood Street near Rockwell. On the night of April 12, the appointed time, the faithful assembled in a large number arrayed in white robes, awaiting the rolling aside of the window overhead and their journey heavenward. The hour struck—nothing happened. A second date was set in 1844, but the wicked old world continued to move on its trusty axis. The Millerites disbanded in time, and the tabernacle was later razed.

German Protestant families in the Brighton community were organized into St. Luke's Church, of the Evangelical denomination, in the spring, by the Rev. C. Allard. A small schoolhouse, purchased for $80 and moved to the corner of Broadview and Schaaf roads, served as the first house of worship. A decade later, about half of the membership moved to Brighton Village, where they built a building on a site that remained the location of St. Luke's Evangelical Church (Pearl Road and Memphis Avenue) through the years. The Rev. Oscar H. Zwilling was pastor of the historic and influential church in 1946.

The first Cleveland-built steam propeller, the *Emigrant,* was launched for Pease & Allen in the shipyard of Captain George W. Jones on April 22. The 275-ton vessel cost $15,000, and was fitted with a seventy-horsepower engine built by the Cuyahoga Steam Furnace Company. This ship was the forerunner of the giant ore carriers.

There had been considerable controversy on the matter of traffic over a bridge connecting Cleveland with Ohio City. A traffic count on May 6 indicated that from morning to evening, 4,030 persons and 925 teams, wagons, and carriages made the crossing.

Members of the Disciples Church in Euclid, organized in 1830, met in a tent near the crossing of Doan Brook and Euclid Street on July 4. In attendance were the Revs. Jonas Hartzel, Matthew S. Clapp, William Hayden, and Dr. J. P. Robison. There were twenty-eight conversions, and on October 7, a new congregation was organized (later Euclid Avenue Christian Church), W. P. Hudson and Theodore Stafford being the first officers. Meetings were held in John Gardner's farmhouse (731 Ansel Road) near Doan Street, and later in the stone schoolhouse at the northwest corner of Euclid and Doan. In 1848, the first house of worship was erected on the north side of Euclid, between Doan and Republic streets. The Rev. E. H. Hawley, who came to the church in 1864, was the first resident minister. In 1867, a Gothic sanctuary was dedicated on Streator Street, and it served until 1905. During the ministry of the Rev. Jabez Hall, 1872-89, the church and city were brought into closer relationship through his cultural and civic interests. Dr. Joseph Z. Tyler's pastorate, 1892-99, was marked by tireless devotion to young people, to church expansion, and to world brotherhood. The Rev. Jacob H. Goldner, who began his fruitful service to the church in 1900, was to enjoy one of the longest Protestant pastorates in Cleveland.

Willoughby University's future was wiped out by the panic, failure of the railroad project, slow population growth in the area, and dissension in its official family. Drs. Delamater, Kirtland, Cassels, and Ackley resigned, and Dr. Starling, who owned a controlling interest, voted to move to Columbus, where he founded the Starling Medical College, which became part of Ohio State University.

At this time, thirty-eight medical colleges were operating in the United States, and only four west of the Alleghenies. As Cleveland had no medical school, the four physicians proposed that Western Reserve College in Hudson, Ohio, organize a training school in the city. Accordingly, the trustees voted on August 4 that six physicians of the Western Reserve constitute "a Committee of Examination to present to this Board the names of suitable candidates for the degree of M.D.": Drs. Delamater and Kirtland; Dr. Samuel St. John, professor of chemistry and allied subjects in Western Reserve College; Drs. Erastus Cushing and David Long of Cleveland; and Dr. George G. Baker of Norwalk. Although there was little time for advertising and recruiting students, sixty-seven enrolled for the first sixteen-week session. The first lecture was given by Dr. Kirtland in the Stone Church on November 1. A week later, classes opened in the Mechanics Block. This beginning was heartening to the new faculty that included Dean Cassels and Drs. Delamater, Kirtland, and Worcester. Application for amendment of the college charter, permitting establishment of a medical department in Cleveland, was opposed by a faction in Willoughby, and it was not until February 23, 1844, that legislation was passed.

The trustees "erected" the Medical Department of Western Reserve College (later School of Medicine of Western Reserve University) on March 20, 1844, and conferred the degree of Doctor of Medicine on eighteen men recommended by the committee on examination.

Management and finance of the Cleveland Medical College, as the new school of medicine was popularly known, were in the hands of a board of agency, headed by wealthy Leonard Case, Sr. Members were Peter M.

Weddell, John W. Allen, Samuel Starkweather, Zalmon Fitch, J. M. Woolsey, Henry B. Payne, Thomas Bolton, W. T. Warner, William A. Otis, James M. Hoyt, and Madison Miller, eminent citizens who were anxious to assist in raising the cultural and educational standards of Cleveland. Financial support came from tuition fees which were divided equally among the professors and lecturers, "it being understood that all apparatus necessary for illustrating the various departments of instruction shall be furnished by the professors and lecturers filling the same." The faculty appointed on March 20, 1844, consisted of Dr. John Delamater in charge and also professor of midwifery and diseases of women and children; Drs. Jared P. Kirtland, theory and practice of medicine; Horace A. Ackley, surgery; John Lang Cassels, materia medica; Noah Worcester, physical diagnosis and skin diseases; Samuel St. John, chemistry; and Jacob J. Delamater, son of John Delamater, lecturer on physiology. They were distinguished medical men and some of the best teachers in the country. Under Dr. Delamater's leadership, an enviable reputation was soon established; and as other institutions fell by the wayside, Reserve gained strength and became the oldest medical school operating continuously west of the Allegheny Mountains.

The *Herald* reported in September that 150 buildings had been built in Cleveland during the preceding two years. George Worthington and Isaac Taylor had erected a row of brick dwellings on St. Clair Street "with iron railings, cut stone steps and neat courts." Captain Levi Johnson's fine stone mansion had been built at the corner of Water and Lake streets, where it stood until 1909. The old Mansion House was replaced by the Atwater Block on Superior Street and Vineyard Lane, the leading business center of the city. A music hall on the third floor provided "double the capacity of any in the city."

The First United Presbyterian Church of Greater Cleveland had its beginning in the Northfield Associate Presbyterian Church, organized in October with twenty-three charter members, most of them of Scotch ancestry. The Rev. J. W. Logue was their first pastor. A frame church building, erected and equipped at a cost of $2,000 at the southwest corner of Michigan and Seneca streets, was paid for before it opened. It was replaced by an impressive brick structure, costing $7,000, on Erie Street near Prospect. The congregation grew, and in 1891 it moved eastward to a new home on East Prospect Street at Giddings.

Tailor-made overcoats could be bought in October for from $4 to $5.50; frock or dress coats, $3 to $5; pants or vests, $1 to $1.25. "Cast-off clothes taken in pay" made it easier to outfit the family for winter.

In the fall, property owners were urged to plant fruit and ornamental trees. Cleveland's fine trees would carry her fame far and wide.

John Quincy Adams' hurried visit to the city on November 11 was announced by handbills. A large audience braved a severe storm to hear him speak in a downtown church, where he was introduced by Sherlock J. Andrews. Adams was enthusiastic over the development of commerce and transportation. He departed on a long, tiresome journey to Cincinnati, where he laid the cornerstone of the Astronomical Observatory.

A Presbyterian church was organized on November 30 at Doan's Corners, the Rev. S. C. Aiken presiding. It was the outgrowth of a Sunday School started in 1828 by Mrs. Sally Mather Hale, and the roll of nineteen charter members included the names of Ford, Cozad, Walters, Cowles, Bowles, Baldwin, Clark, Coakley, and Hanks. Although eighteen were Congregationalists, one of the sisters declared that "she could not belong to any other than a Presbyterian church," and her preference prevailed in declaring church government. Cyrus Ford, Jarvis F. Hanks, and Samuel W. Baldwin were chosen as elders. Horace Ford, one of the organizers, was a leader for more than a half century, and choir director for many years. The little congregation met where it could find room, and not until 1845 did it have a settled minister in the Rev. Anthony McReynolds. Membership had reached sixty-two in 1847, when incorporation as the First Presbyterian Church of East Cleveland (later Euclid Avenue Congregational Church) was effected. Eager to have a home of their own, members shouldered a burden of $3,300 to erect a plain, two-story, brick structure, 40 by 60 feet, at the corner of Euclid and Doan streets. It was a real struggle for the faithful, some of whom worked out subscriptions at the rate of 50 cents a day; but dedication was celebrated, September 29, 1849.

The first Episcopal parish east of the river, outside of Cleveland and within the Cuyahoga County limits, was formed on December 11, when prominent families organized St. Paul's Church of the township of Euclid. Among those who signed the charter were members of the Adams, Strong, Doan, Crocker, Jaster, and Condit families. The first services were held in Shaw Academy in January, and John Doan, E. W. Slade, and Rodney Strong were elected vestrymen. Doan was licensed as the first lay reader in 1845. Construction of a modest sanctuary, started in 1846, was not completed until 1860 (at Allendale and Collamer Street). Seats were free. Lay readers served until 1853, when the church had a rector in the Rev. Thomas Corlett. The meeting house was enlarged to meet the needs of the growing congregation; and during the ministry of the Rev. Howard M. Ingham, plans were made for a new structure, completed in 1896 to replace the old. The identity of the church changed to conform to that of the community, and as St. Paul's Episcopal Church of East Cleveland, 15904 Hazel Road, it played an important part in the transition from a rural to a residential district. The pastorate of the Rev. Gerald Campbell Clarke, 1928-46, witnessed inspiring progress. Upon his death, the Rev. Francis B. Sayre, Jr., became pastor.

1844

Opening of the new engine house, built for Phoenix No. 4 on Water Street, was the occasion of a lively ceremony on January 2. In the evening, the engine was drawn through the streets by torchlight to the accompaniment of band and cannon. A banquet at the Mansion House wound up the day.

An advertisement in the *Herald* on January 3 announced bear's oil for the hair, Rio coffee at 9 cents a pound, cooking butter at 5, and beef cattle, $1.50 to $2.00 per 100 pounds. The merits of lard oil over sperm oil for lamps were argued.

N. E. Crittenden, the leading jeweler, purchased the property at the northeast corner of Ontario and Rockwell on the Public Square (Society for Savings site) at sheriff's sale for $6,000.

R. B. Dennis founded the *Ohio American,* a Liberty Party weekly, this year in Ohio City. In the plant, young Edwin Cowles, grandson of the pioneering pastor of the Western Reserve, the Rev. Giles H. Cowles, was making his first acquaintance with printer's ink, and he took over the management the next year in association with L. L. Rice, editor. M. W. Miller became the publisher in 1846. The *True Democrat,* a daily, was founded at Olmstead Falls in 1846 to further the antislavery-Whig interests. In 1848, the two papers joined forces in Cleveland under the name of the latter, and made a brave effort to further the reform influence.

Cleveland was thrilled upon learning that Samuel F. B. Morse had successfully sent the first telegraph message on May 24 over an experimental line between Baltimore and Washington. The newspapers received many inquiries as to how the miracle was performed, one of which was as follows: "I notice we are to have the telegraph soon and would like to know how they work the words along the wire. Do they twitch it?" The *Herald's* answer was short and crisp: "They do not! They holler through it!"

A local census listed 106 colored persons in Cleveland. A cross-section of twenty heads of families, who were worth on an average $2,750, reflects their thrift and industry, as reported by Harry E. Davis in *The Negro in Cleveland.*

With renewed spirit, the Second Presbyterian Church of Cleveland was organized on June 12 under a charter granted in 1837. Of the fifty-eight charter members, fifty-three had been associated with the overcrowded First Presbyterian Church, some of them pillars of the mother church, including Mr. and Mrs. T. P. Handy, Samuel H. and Emily W. Mather, Mrs. Martha Converse, Mrs. Mary H. Severance, Thomas N. Bond, Jarvis Leonard, Mrs. Francis E. Leonard, Erastus Freeman, S. I. Hamlen, Dr. and Mrs. David Long, and John L. Severance. The First Congregational house of worship on Rockwell Street was purchased for $3,671; and the Rev. Sherman B. Canfield, an Ohio City minister of dramatic power, was engaged. In 1852, an ornate, brown, sandstone edifice with brick sidewalls was erected on the south side of Superior, east of the Square (Crocker Block site), seating 850 people, the largest capacity in the city. A slender, 195-foot steeple reached skyward, and the $6,000 organ was the pride of the congregation (later Church of the Covenant).

It was announced on June 13 that there were 2,177 trees "in Public Square and upon the edge of the sidewalks" within the city limits of the Forest City, not including those in graveyards.

Firemen were often jeered and molested by citizens and bystanders. This led to feuds which sometimes broke out in open warfare. Accordingly,

Council passed an ordinance requiring the marshal and every constable to attend all fires to preserve the peace. Citizens were required to obey orders and assist in fire-fighting, under penalty of a $5 fine and imprisonment. Refusal to help draw an engine meant a $5 fine.

A five-day session of the Western Convention of Presbyterian and Congregational Ministers opened at the First Presbyterian Church on June 20. Bad roads reduced the attendance to about three hundred, but eleven states were represented. There was an appeal for church unity. A resolution proposed condemnation of slavery, and another opposed dancing as injurious to religion.

The famous *Empire,* a 260-foot passenger vessel, the first steamboat over a thousand tons and the largest in the United States, was built in Cleveland this year. It was a 1,200-ton side-wheeler, elaborately furnished, with a dining cabin on the upper deck, where service was directed by a chef. The *Empire*

The Empire, 1,200 ton side-wheeler, built in Cleveland, was the largest steamboat in the country.

was the first lake boat equipped with fire engines. Staterooms and cabins were of the latest decoration, and Leland's Band entertained as the newest attraction in seafaring travel. Buffalo was now only twelve hours and forty-four minutes away from Cleveland at a fare of $5, which Clevelanders considered excessive.

The band organized by Jack Leland was the pride of Cleveland for many years. Heading processions and parades was the handsome band wagon, built in the city, and purchased by Barnum some years later for his circus.

Robert Sanderson purchased the old Astor House from Joel Scranton, and moved it piece by piece from its original location on the west bank of the river to Hanover and Vermont streets on the West Side. Sanderson wrote that he found it "Full of hairs, from bottom to top," relics of fur-trading with the Indians. This was the oldest house in Cleveland, and the new owner used it first as a carpenter shop and then as a dwelling.

Clevelanders scoffed at the newest lakefront improvement in the form of a pier built by John G. Stockley—or Stockly—at the foot of Bank Street. When completed, however, it withstood punishment of the fiercest gales, and steamboats docked continually.

Cleveland's most famous Indian died on September 3, and funeral services were held at the Second Presbyterian Church. Joc-O-Sot, or Walking Bear, aged thirty-four, is said to have been a Sauk chief in the Black Hawk War.

He had come to Cleveland in the thirties, accompanying Dr. Horace A. Ackley on fishing and hunting trips. When the game season ended, the chief joined Dan Marble, a theatrical promoter, in what is believed to have been an effort to earn money with which to assist his tribe. They toured the country and went abroad. Joc-O-Sot was a sensation in England, and was presented to young Queen Victoria, who had a full-length portrait made of him. An old bullet wound in his lung afflicted him; he fell ill and returned to the States, bent on spending his last days at his tribal home. By the time he reached Cleveland, he could go no farther, and he died near Stockley's pier, attended by his old friend, Dr. Ackley. He was buried in Erie Street Cemetery, where friends erected a tombstone and planted corn on his grave.

Fire destroyed the Franklin House, but Philo Scovill rebuilt it and called it the New Franklin House. The handsome, five-story, brick hostelry boasted a hall and reading room with "tessellated marble floors," seventy-one bedrooms, an attic cistern that furnished "soft water for washing," and "inside window blinds, a great improvement over outside shutters." In 1852, the famous hotel had been reduced to a boarding house, and Scovill had retired. In 1855, the house was closed and converted into stores. It was relieved of obscurity in 1938, when it was torn down to make way for the Terminal development.

A library of five hundred volumes was purchased for Prospect Street School this year from the proceeds of a fair held by the pupils. Horace Mann, the famous eastern educator, selected the books that made up the first collection established in the public schools.

There were a number of musical events during the year: the Handel Society of Western Reserve College made an annual journey from Hudson. Touring musicians presented a Concert Extraordinary. Others who appeared were Madame Cinti Damoreau of the Opera Comique of Paris, Covert and Dodge, and the Misses Macomber of Boston. The Swiss Bell Ringers were regular favorites. During the year, the Cleveland Brass Band and the Quartette Club were formed. The city was advertised by the newspapers as one of the principal music centers of the West.

1845

The Brier Hill coal mines were opened near Youngstown this year by David Tod, Daniel P. Rhodes, and C. H. Andrews. Their output of fifty tons per week was brought to Cleveland by canal, where it found a market among the lake steamers.

To bring order out of the loose era of wildcat banking and easy charter-granting, the State Bank of Ohio was incorporated by the Legislature on February 24. It was largely the product of the wisdom of Senator Alfred Kelley. Under the comprehensive Ohio Bank Act, a Board of Control functioned in Columbus, and branch banks were located in twelve districts. Members of the board were chosen from the branch banks, and they supervised operation of the system and provided the branches with state currency. The act also governed the chartering of independent banks, banking operations, and the issuing of paper money. The new system prevailed until the Civil War period, when the National Bank Act took from the States some of their power.

Cleveland had reached a point where the natural water supply was considered inadequate and inefficient. With the installation of the Cleveland Centre Water Works, a major improvement was undertaken. Spring water from Willeyville hill, west of the river, was captured in a well-type receptacle of timber and brick, and piped to a 13,800-gallon reservoir. More pipes carried it for five hundred feet down the river bank to a larger pipe that lay sheltered in a timber frame on the river bottom, and delivered it to Cleveland Centre on the other side—an amazing capacity of 1,600 barrels every twenty-four hours.

Enrollment in the schools of Cleveland, as reported by School Manager Charles Bradburn in March, was 1,300 public-school students, 400 in private schools, and 800 children between the ages of four and eighteen not attending any school. As he had done in his annual report of 1844, Bradburn urged the founding of a high school; but although Council again turned a deaf ear, his deep interest in educational advancement never wavered. Teachers' salaries were restored to their former status this year. Kinsman School was built.

An experiment was tried in Prospect Street School, when the two senior sections were united, and "for the first time . . . senior classes of both boys and girls were organized." General behavior improved, and why not?

"Facilities for a thorough and practical course of instruction in every department of female education" were offered when E. Hosmer and his wife opened the Young Ladies' Institute about this time on Superior Street (near NBC Building site). Latin, algebra, geometry, composition, and music were taught, and five teachers were employed.

The Fireman's Insurance Company having been liquidated under the Ohio Bank Act, its officers, Reuben Sheldon, president, and Theodoric C. Severance, secretary, organized the City Bank of Cleveland (later The National City Bank of Cleveland). Its twenty-year charter was dated May 17, the first obtained under the provisions governing independent banks in Ohio. Sheldon was the first president, and Severance, cashier. On the board of directors were Elisha Taylor, dry-goods merchant; Moses Kelley, lawyer; and several Cleveland merchants. Capital stock of $50,000 had increased to $150,000 by 1850.

The opening of the new City Bank on July 1, in the old Fireman's quarters, marked a turning point in Cleveland commerce and fortune. Its officers were solid, dependable citizens, and good businessmen. Attendance at weekly meetings was enforced according to a bylaw, with a 50-cent fine for absence and 25 cents for a fifteen-minute tardiness. George Mygatt, a Warren and Painesville banker, became president in 1846, and was succeeded in 1850 by Dr. Lemuel Wick of the Youngstown Wicks. In September, 1848, the bank moved to 21 Superior Street near Water Street, the business center of the city. The annual payroll included the cashier's salary, $1,200 maximum; teller and bookkeeper, $1,000; president, $200 annually, in quarterly payments.

The *Plain Dealer* became an evening daily, and moved to the Merchants Exchange Building on Bank Street. For the first time, a city ordinance designated a newspaper, the *Plain Dealer,* to do the municipal printing.

Ground was broken in May at the southeast corner of St. Clair and Erie streets for the first medical building in Cleveland—a brick, four-and-a-half-story structure costing $20,000. The location was determined by proximity to the established site of the proposed United States Marine Hospital. Classes

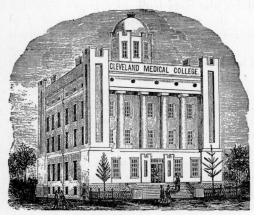

Cleveland Medical College, St. Clair and Erie streets.

began on November 4 in the new home of the Medical Department of Western Reserve College, familiarly known as the Cleveland Medical College. The faculty was a notable addition to the community, some of them taking part in cultural activities, giving lectures and contributing to an illuminating and informative newspaper column relating to causes and treatment of physical ailments. An early graduate of both the Hudson and Cleveland schools was John S. Newberry of Cuyahoga Falls, who practiced medicine in Cleveland until 1855, when his remarkable scientific career commenced. Benjamin Franklin Goodrich, pioneer of the Akron rubber industry, was a student in the medical school. Later expanding into two buildings, the school remained in this location until 1924.

The Young Men's Literary Association was revived, emphasis being placed on library rather than literary features. Its first president was William Case.

Envisioning the future of the Catholic Parish and the need for a church to the east, the Rev. Peter McLaughlin purchased from Thomas May four lots for $4,000 fronting on Superior and Erie streets. Some of his parishioners were so disturbed because he had bought land out "in the country" that he was obliged to resign a few years later. He was succeeded by the Rev. Maurice Howard.

The Canal Bank of Cleveland was organized as an independent bank with E. F. Gaylord, president; S. H. Mann, cashier; and John L. Severance, teller. Capital was $200,000. It opened in the Merchants Exchange and served canal shippers, principally.

Erection of the New England Hotel, a crescent-shaped, five-story hostelry, was begun by G. M. Atwater at the corner of Superior and Merwin streets, and completed in 1847. A rival of the city's best hotels, it had accommodations for two hundred guests and was favored by commercial men. Captain Lorenzo A. Kelsey operated it for several years. Political orators put its balcony to good use. The hotel was destroyed in the great fire of 1854.

Two branches of the new State Bank of Ohio were allotted to Cleveland. The first, the Merchants Bank, opened on June 25 in the Atwater Block and was headed by P. M. Weddell. After a long career of service, it evolved into

Lower Superior Street, 1846 (Drawn by Henry Howe).

the Mercantile National Bank. Leading businessmen served as president— Sherlock J. Andrews, T. M. Kelley, and Truman P. Handy. The second branch, the Commercial Branch Bank, also opened in the Atwater Block in January, 1846, with William A. Otis, president. Under the leadership of Handy, Dan P. Eells, Charles A. Otis, Sr., Joseph Colwell, and W. G. Mather, it ultimately became the National Commercial Bank after the turn of the century.

Under the ministrations of the Rev. Richard Bury, who had served as rector of Trinity Church since 1839, there had been such remarkable growth that Grace Church was organized on July 9, this year, in the parlor of the rectory. A brick house of worship was dedicated in 1848 at the corner of Erie and Huron streets, and the Rev. Alexander Varian was the first rector. Money to build the church was donated on condition that the seats should remain forever free. Known as the "People's Church," it was the first "free" church in Ohio. Prominent leaders were Dr. Horace A. Ackley, Moses Kelley, Thomas Bolton, and George F. Marshall. The Rev. E. W. Worthington, rector from 1887 until his death in 1906, was revered by his congregation.

Copper and iron had been discovered in commercial quantities along the south shore of Lake Superior. Charles Whittlesey and a Detroit party spent two months in the field while the scientist made valuable observations in his search for copper deposits. Without knowing it, he passed over a region that he later found to contain enough iron ore for the needs of many decades.

The first iron mine in the Lake Superior region was opened on the property of the Jackson Mining Company in the Marquette Range (near Negaunee), organized by Michigan men on July 23. Six decades later, the properties merged with The Cleveland-Cliffs Iron Company, making the history of the Cleveland company and the development of the iron-ore ranges in northern Michigan a single document.

A news item of July 24 announced a Temperance Play in Apollo Hall. "Each member of the company is a champion of temperance . . . Their manner of exhibiting to the people the way to make and become drunkards is lifelike, condensing into one evening the scenes of a lifetime." Spirited temperance plays were growing in popularity. Clevelanders found it hard to resist this powerful and sensational drama, and the theater business was greatly stimulated. Stars of the age trod the boards of the Apollo in melodrama and sentimental comedy: "Eliza Logan and her father, the Davenport girls and their father, Christie Webb, A. A. Adams, Forrest, the elder Booth, starred it right in that little old smoky hall." There were laughs aplenty when favorite comedians came to town: Dan Marble with his Yankee characters, and Barney Williams and George Holland, two funmakers.

In August, Moses C. Younglove, job printer, brought the first steam printing press to Cleveland and set it up in the *Herald* office in the Merchants Exchange. The *Plain Dealer* contracted for a share in it. It was probably the second power press west of the Alleghenies.

Now that John Baldwin's quarries in Berea assured him of financial success, he determined to keep his covenant with God. At a session of the North Ohio Conference of the Methodist Episcopal Church at Marion, Ohio, August 13, his offer to give considerable land and a building for a denominational institution of learning in Berea was accepted. Current expenses for the first year were also assured through his generosity. A charter for Baldwin Institute (later Baldwin-Wallace College) was granted during the year, and on April 9, 1846, the preparatory school opened with one hundred students in a male and female department. Rich and poor were admitted with no racial distinction. Work opportunities were found in clearing the woodlands, in the Baldwin stone quarry, and in local industry, such employment being regarded as excellent for students' total training. Holden Dwight, the first president, died during the opening year and was succeeded by Alfred Holbrook, acting president, and the Rev. Lorenzo Warner.

It was announced on August 16 that J. H. Crittendon had built Empire Hall, a spacious, public auditorium seating six hundred people, at Superior and Bank streets. The sixteen-and-a-half-foot ceiling was an innovation, as improved ventilation was badly needed.

Daguerreotypes were being made at 129 Superior Street at a cost of "from

$1.50 to $2.00 each." The business-building advertisement continued: "Ladies and gentlemen will please call and examine specimens, and after sitting for portraits if not pleased as to art and life, will be at perfect liberty to leave them. Time required in 'setting,' five to sixty seconds."

Lutheran missionaries, sent to America to gather together scattered adherents to the faith in the Middle West, joined the Ohio Synod. In a short time, however, they determined to leave it unless certain practices which they disapproved were abandoned. Their efforts failed, and at Concert Hall in Cleveland, meeting place of Zion Church, it was decided to send a delegation composed of Dr. William Sihler and the Rev. John Adam Ernst to St. Louis to confer with Lutheran pastors about the founding of a new synod. This led to subsequent meetings and founding of the Evangelical Lutheran Synod of Missouri, Ohio, and other states, April 26, 1847, in Chicago. Among the twenty-two Lutheran pastors representing four thousand parishioners, were Cleveland leaders in the denomination: Rev. Frederick C. D. Wynekeen, pastor of Trinity Evangelical Lutheran Church for many years; Dr. Henry C. Schwan, pastor of Zion Church and later elected synod president; Rev. John Adam Ernst and Rev. Frederick W. Husman, who served the South Euclid Church. A century later, the synod had grown to more than forty-seven hundred congregations with one and a half million adherents, one of the oldest and largest of the thirty-two Lutheran districts in the country.

An advertisement in the *Herald* on October 14 indicated that some citizens took their politics rather seriously. Sam Austin had offered for sale a thousand-acre tract known as "Ann Stevens' land" in Mayfield; and he purchased space to say that the "proposed sale, owing to Polk's election, dry weather and other calamities, is postponed until the same time next fall."

Cleveland had the only labor-saving machine in the West that could knead, cut, and stamp crackers ready for the oven. It reduced the price two cents per pound.

W. S. and T. S. Beckwith opened a dry-goods store on Superior Street this year. In 1850, Frederick A. Sterling found employment with the firm. W. S. Beckwith retired in 1861, and George P. Welch became associated with the enterprise in 1866. The pioneer carpet and interior-decoration house moved to Euclid Avenue in 1874, taking over the Central Rink on the south side of the Square. The firm of Beckwith, Sterling & Company became Sterling, Welch & Company in 1889. With incorporation in 1902, F. A. Sterling became president and George P. Welch, first vice president.

Thirteen devout Methodists assembled in a building at St. Clair and Water streets on November 23 to hear the first sermon preached by their minister, the Rev. E. H. Bure. This mission was the beginning of the First German Methodist Church. After several moves, a sanctuary was built on Erie Street and later exchanged for the Baptist Church at Scovill and Sterling, rebuilt and dedicated in 1894. A decade later, the congregation moved eastward again, as the community changed and the population drifted to the suburbs. In 1926, during the pastorate of Dr. Albert W. Marting, a beautiful structure was erected in Cleveland Heights, at Winsford and

Caledonia roads, for the church family which through years of transition came to be known as the Church of the Cross, one of the large Methodist churches in Greater Cleveland. The Rev. Earl R. Henderson became pastor in 1945.

Although the Cleveland Academy of Natural Science (later The Cleveland Museum of Natural History) had its origin within the friendly walls of the Ark on the Public Square, it remained for Dr. Jared P. Kirtland to make the first move toward organization. On November 24, the first meeting was held in the college, and officers were elected: Dr. Kirtland, president; Sherlock J. Andrews, first vice president; Charles W. Heard, second vice president; William D. Beattie, third vice president; William Case, Hamilton L. Smith, Henry C. Kingsley, Rufus K. Winslow, Charles Whittlesey, and Drs. Samuel St. John, J. L. Cassels, and Kirtland, curators. A room in the college was provided for a museum, and furnishings and equipment were secured through a thousand-dollar subscription campaign and festival headed by Samuel Livingston Mather, newcomer to Cleveland. The medical men then transferred to the academy their scientific collections. Lectures were given during the winter months. Prominent members of the medical profession who were members of the academy were Charles A. Terry, Jehu Brainard, Erastus Cushing, C. D. Brayton, Jacob J. Delamater, John S. Newberry, Horace A. Ackley, Elisha Sterling, Thomas G. Cleveland, and Theodatus D. Garlick. The latter was a scientist of note, who introduced fish culture into the United States. This was Cleveland's first scientific organization.

Signor Antonini, Italian opera tenor, and Ole Bull, Norwegian violinist, gave the outstanding musical performances of the year.

1846

Andrew Freese had come to Cleveland from the East in 1840 and began teaching in the Prospect Street School. His rare ability was soon recognized by the school managers, and appointment as high-school principal was made wisely. As a boy, Andrew Freese was poor, with few advantages, and it was through kindness and sincerity that he became the close friend of the underprivileged as well as students of means. He encouraged in his pupils an appreciation of good books, regularity and dependability, the importance of writing correctly and speaking with ease. On the first high-school roster were the names of boys who would achieve honor and distinction.

"Johnny," who lived down by the canal, was an example of Andrew Freese's searching and sympathetic interest. The boy came to school wearing wooden shoes. The schoolmaster soon found that he had brains, and to make it possible for him to attend, the principal bought his books. Soon Andrew Freese was going down to Johnny's miserable old house, and once he spent the night. The wind whistled through holes in the wall by his bed, but Johnny's mother covered them with a shawl, and gave thanks for their kind friend. Her boy was John P. Jackson, later of San Francisco, railroad president. In every walk of life, from the great to the lowly, from Cleveland to Hong-Kong, a legion of men and women remembered Andrew Freese, not only for his exceptional ability as an educator, but as "one who loves his fellow-men!"

Oil lamps were destined for a final trimming with the organization of the Cleveland Gas Light & Coke Company on February 6. While this new wonder was a sign of metropolitan ambition, little progress was made until late in the decade, when Moses G. Younglove assumed control.

Edward Hessenmueller launched the *Germania,* the first German news-paper in Cleveland. It continued until 1853. Hessenmueller, who came to Cuyahoga County in 1836 and moved to Cleveland in 1840, was the leading citizen of the large German population, and a prominent figure in Democratic politics and in civic movements.

The persistent efforts of a handful of citizens found practical interest on the part of Cleveland's new mayor, George Hoadley, who in his inaugural address in the spring recommended that a high school be established—an "academic department," the pupils "to be taken from our common schools according to merit. This would present a powerful stimulus to study and good conduct," he observed. "The poorest child, if possessed of talents and application, might aspire to the highest station in the republic. From such schools we might hope to issue the future Franklins of our land." On March 25, the Board of School Managers "voted to establish a high school as soon as practicable and appointed Andrew Freese, teacher, at $500 per year." Council then authorized the necessary funds.

The report for the school year 1845-46 showed thirteen schools with an enrollment of fifteen hundred pupils, four male, and thirteen female teachers. Average daily attendance, however, was only 936, and this marked shortcoming was considered detrimental to efficient and effective teaching. "Some parents as well as the children," the school managers pointed out, "seem to think that what costs nothing is worth nothing." To remedy the situation, attendance laws were passed.

A woolen mill was in operation at Doan's Corners; and about a mile to the north, I. N. Pillsbury had set up a steam carding machine in his estab-lishment to speed wool processing in dry weather. Improved manufacturing methods were constantly being sought.

The St. Andrews Society was organized, May 5, a benevolent institution "to assist Scottish immigrants who lack in worldly gear." The first officers were George Whitelaw, president; Alexander McIntosh and John McMillen, vice presidents; Robert Ford, David McIntosh, James Robertson, William Bryce, and Alexander Paton, managers; Rev. S. C. Aiken, chaplain; Dr. J. L. Cassels, physician; James Proudfoot, the painter-poet, treasurer; James Dods, secretary. Many of the sturdy Scotch newcomers became pillars of the Presbyterian denomination, and they gave liberally of their skills and abilities to industry and the professions.

President James Knox Polk signed the bill declaring war with Mexico on May 13. Company H, 15th United States Infantry, was raised jointly by

Cleveland and Cincinnati. It served on Mexican soil, taking part in major engagements, and a number of deaths resulted. In August, 1848, it was mustered out of service. Leading Cleveland newspapers were divided in their attitude toward war measures, the *Herald* identifying itself with anti-war policies, and the *Plain Dealer* urging greater enlistments and all-out support of the administration. The papers had great difficulty in securing news from the war zone, not being able to afford correspondents. Consequently, dispatches were often as much as three-weeks old when received in Cleveland.

A union of the Israelitic and Anshe Chesed societies resulted in the formation of the Israelitic Anshe Chesed Society (later Euclid Avenue Temple) on May 15 in the Farmers Block, with sixty-two members. The first president was Frederick Goldsmith. This marked the beginning of the oldest Jewish congregation in Cleveland. The spirit of the times is reflected in a transaction in which Leonard Case, non-Jewish Cleveland philanthropist, presented to the new congregation a lot on Ohio Street in exchange for one on Eagle Street. Here the first synagogue, built at a cost of $1,500, was dedicated on August 7. In the basement, children were enrolled in English, German, and Hebrew departments. The character of Cleveland Jewry was molded by rabbis of the congregation. Rabbi Gustavus M. Cohen, who filled the pulpit from 1861 until 1873, when he became rabbi emeritus, exerted an influence far beyond Cleveland. Beloved in the community was the Rev. Dr. Michaelis Machol, who ministered from 1876 until 1907, when he was made rabbi emeritus. He pioneered in promoting interfaith understanding.

The Board of School Managers engaged Silas L. Bingham as director of music in the public schools. Teaching children to sing as they were being taught to read had been widely discussed, and with much opposition. It was known that music had been introduced successfully into the Boston schools, and Lowell Mason of that city was invited to demonstrate publicly its practicability in Cleveland. Having instructed the schoolteachers briefly, and leaving a course of procedure with them, he returned home; but it was soon evident that a competent teacher must be employed to take charge. Bingham taught for a few months as an experiment, and was followed by J. H. Clark. Jarvis F. Hanks became instructor in the high school. In 1852, Bingham was re-employed, serving until 1858. Financial depression in business curtailed school expenses, and while special teachers of music and drawing were the first to be dismissed, the importance of these subjects had been fully established.

Agitation of mechanics for a ten-hour day and wages in cash had spread from Massillon to Cleveland, and on June 1 an announcement stated that "a fraternal order for mechanics protection will meet Thursday next to elect a delegate to represent the order at Buffalo." It was not until March 13, 1848, that "the mechanics combined for the mutual protection of their rights."

"One of the finest nurseries of apple trees in this vicinity was from seed saved by me and my brother, Timothy, Jr.," wrote Seth Doan. Fine orchards in Euclid and neighboring townships have their origin in seed preserved from a basket of apples purchased by Timothy in Detroit for two dollars.

The Cleveland Board of Underwriters was organized on June 22, with

Joseph L. Weatherly, president; C. C. Carlton, vice president; H. F. Brayton, treasurer; and George May, secretary. Business was conducted from Weatherly's office for two years, when desk space was provided in the new Board of Trade rooms. In 1846, the only risk against which insurance was written was that of fire. The alliance of Cleveland agents was a recognition not only of the importance of insurance, but of the necessity for reasonable regulation of the business. Voluntary organizations like the one in Cleveland laid the groundwork for the Ohio Insurance Department, founded in 1870. Identity of the board changed from time to time, and, in 1926, the corporate name became Insurance Board of Cleveland, the oldest trade organization in the city. It served to interpret the public's insurance needs to member companies, to safeguard the best interests of policyholders, to improve the business of insurance, and to promote civic and community activities, with emphasis upon fire-and-accident prevention and improvements in building construction. At the one-hundredth annual meeting in 1946, John L. Meyer was re-elected president; George W. Phypers was re-elected vice president; and S. J. Horton, executive secretary and treasurer, was named for his twenty-seventh term.

Basement rooms were rented in a church on Prospect Street (between East 8th and East 9th), and on July 13 a high school for boys (later Central High School) was opened with thirty-four students. Andrew Freese was principal, and it was one of the earliest free public high schools west of the Alleghenies. Although the rooms were miserably damp and dark, and the facilities generally inadequate, the attendance was eighty-three before the end of the year.

Numerous plunderings by horse thieves roused the citizens to action; and at a meeting in the Court House on August 29, the vigilantes organized a band that became the Cuyahoga County Anti-Horse Stealing Club, headed by Ahimaaz Sherwin. Money was raised "to be used in recovery of any horses that may be stolen from those present." The first trotting and pacing track was built this year along Woodland between Perry and Brownell streets.

Dr. J. Lang Cassels, mineralogist and medical-college professor, was sent by Cleveland men to explore the Lake Superior region for evidence of copper and silver. Learning of newly found iron deposits in the Marquette Range, he located a claim, calling it "Cleveland Mountain" (later Ishpeming) for his Cleveland backers. Dr. Cassels was one of the first to study Lake Superior iron ore, and the industry was founded upon his assays. He also made one of the earliest recorded studies on the theory of water pollution as the cause of typhoid fever.

Traffic had grown to such proportions that a new bridge was needed at Columbus Street in the "Flats"; but the memory of the bridge war a decade earlier prevented co-operation between Cleveland and Ohio City. However. the bridge had to be built, and the County built it. In 1870 an iron bridge replaced the old structure. Columbus Street was one of the leading thoroughfares.

Forty-five adherents to the faith met in the American House on October 26 and organized St. Paul's Episcopal Parish, twenty-nine of them pledging

$937 toward the first-year's support of the church. Benjamin Andrews, Moses Kelley, Oliver A. Brooks, George A. Benedict, Thomas Bolton, E. T. Sterling, D. W. Cross, and George A. Tisdale were among the founders. The Rev. Gideon B. Perry was called as the first rector, and services were held in a public hall until 1848, when a frame church was erected on the southwest corner of Sheriff and Euclid Street. Many complained it was "so far east." Before the building was completed, it burned. The entire city helped to raise funds for the handsome Gothic brick structure with a tall spire that opened in 1851. It had one of the finest organs in Cleveland. In 1858, it was consecrated, free of debt.

Elijah Peet's *Business Directory of the City of Cleveland for 1846-7* afforded a glimpse of the young community of 10,135 inhabitants and 1,814 families. Four banks flourished with a combined capital of about $750,000, and there were nineteen "Principal Hotels and Boarding Houses." The city's wealth lay in its trade and navigation. Eighty-five vessels with a total tonnage of 13,493 tons were owned in Cleveland; 638 seamen were employed. Statistics for 1845 showed exports to Canada valued at $274,375; imports, $10,581.86. Coastwise exports, $4,128,102.75; imports, $5,137,347.84. Vessel arrivals totaled 2,136; 14,895 passengers landed from Buffalo. Five vessels were built, with a total of 2,181 tons. Five stages ran daily, connecting with Pittsburgh, Columbus, Cincinnati, Detroit, and Buffalo. There were thirteen year-round public schools; seventeen teachers instructed the 1,500 children enrolled. Men teachers received $10 per week, and women, $4 to $5. Ten private schools enrolled 500 pupils. Peet's classified lists showed 18 clergymen, 47 attorneys, 31 physicians and surgeons, 28 dry-goods merchants, 87 grocers, 10 wholesale grocers, 5 hardware merchants, 7 druggists, 4 jewelers, 16 boot, shoe, and leather stores, 19 drapers and tailors, 14 dressmakers, 5 tailoresses, 4 saddle-and-harness makers, 5 carriage and wagon makers, and 8 cabinet makers. There were 4 confectioners, 6 bakers, and 4 breweries. This is a resume of Cleveland's second city directory, published with the generous financial help of the City Council, amounting to $30.

1847

Higher education came within the reach of young women when prominent Lake County citizens planned the Willoughby Female Seminary at Willoughby, Ohio. Mary Lyon, founder of the Mt. Holyoke (Massachusetts) Female Seminary in 1837, interested herself in the project and helped to select the faculty for the new school that opened this year. A destructive fire in 1856 checked its progress, but devoted founders contributed to its rebuilding in Painesville, Ohio. It reopened as Lake Erie Female Seminary (later Lake Erie College) with Lydia Sessions of the Mt. Holyoke faculty as principal.

The use of letheon, or ether, as a general anesthetic was first demonstrated publicly in Boston in October, 1846. Three months later, in mid-January this year, Dr. Horace A. Ackley amputated a leg under full anesthesia with letheon, in the Medical Department of Western Reserve College in Cleveland. On January 30, Dr. Benjamin Strickland's advertisement announced that he and a fellow surgeon-dentist would use the new anesthetic in extracting teeth.

Thomas Alva Edison, genius of electrical invention, was born at Milan, Ohio, on February 11. The humble birthplace remained standing a century later.

Charles Bradburn, George Willey, and earnest school managers who had fostered the high-school project were about to see it threatened with collapse. Taxpayers were divided as to the necessity for high-school education, many favoring common schools only. A fighting opposition led by Henry B. Payne, Harvey Rice, and John Erwin, attacked the legality of the school and the necessity for it, and Payne demanded that it be discontinued until every child should have received a thorough common-school education. The "High School Question" enlivened debates, consumed considerable newspaper space, and was a sure-fire, mass-meeting attraction for pros and cons. Bradburn, T. P. Handy, Samuel Starkweather, and William Day constituted the Board of School Managers that recommended that the Council continue the new system as the only way in which the public schools "can be made in truth what they are in name, common schools—common to all; good enough for the rich, and cheap enough for the poor—such schools as will meet the wants of all classes in the community." Council took no action, but permitted the school to continue until the following winter, when legislative enactment "authorized and required" the City Council to establish and maintain a high-school department, and levy a special tax for the purchase of land and the erection of school buildings. East St. Clair School, a grade school, was built this year.

In the spring, a class for girls was opened in the high school, and Catherine Jennings of Oberlin College was engaged as the first woman teacher at an annual salary of $250. Fourteen girls were admitted. Attendance was irregular, probably because of home duties, and on April 19 Principal Freese evidenced doubt as to the wisdom of the new policy.

The Most Rev. John Baptist Purcell, bishop of Cincinnati, petitioned the Holy See for a division of the Diocese of Cincinnati, as the rapid growth of the State now required two bishops. On April 23 of this year, the Diocese of Cleveland was created, embracing about one-third of the State, north of a line drawn at 40° 40'. The Rev. Amadeus Rappe, the "missionary of the Maumee," was consecrated as bishop at Cincinnati on October 10. A few days later, he took up his duties in Cleveland as the first bishop, serving a Catholic population estimated at ten thousand. He lived for some months in a rented house near the Haymarket (east end of Lorain-Carnegie Bridge).

The first Superior Court was created to relieve pressure in the Common Pleas Court. Sherlock J. Andrews presided during its five years of existence; it was discontinued with the revision of the judiciary system under the new state constitution.

Peter Martin Weddell, one of the best-known and most successful men in the Western Reserve, died on May 7, aged fifty-nine. A builder of business, banks, and railroads, he had accumulated wealth, and he provided generously in his will for foreign missions and benevolent societies. In his lifetime, he had aided many young men, and a number of Clevelanders owed their advancement to his generous interest. In the midst of heavily timbered land on Euclid Street (east of East 30th, extending from Payne to Central), he had built his country home, Oakland Cottage, and cleared a farm.

June 25 marked a great occasion in Cleveland, the opening of the Weddell House. Two years before, Peter M. Weddell tore down the store that had made him wealthy and laid the cornerstone of the "Astor House of the Lakes," the four-story, sandstone-and-brick hotel on the northwest corner of Superior and Bank streets, built by George P. Smith. Weddell purchased "sumptuous" furniture and furnishings in the East, and Tiffany made the

Weddell House, most famous of Cleveland's early hotels and scene of many of the city's important gatherings.

tableware. While Jerry Coon, the first tenant, had opened his jewelry store on the Superior side a year or so before, the hotel was not entirely completed until this time. The inaugural was marred, however, by the death of the pioneer merchant in May, and his son, Horace P., completed the task. A. S. Barnum became the new landlord. The crowning feature of the Weddell House was an octagonal cupola and promenade, affording citizens an extensive view of the city. Presidents and statesmen spoke from its balcony. Soldiers and poets of wealth and fame were its guests. The ballroom was the scene of colorful social gatherings and civic celebrations, and business institutions made the hotel their headquarters. A philosophical inscription in the dining room read:

> Man's life is like a winter's day;
> Some only breakfast and away;
> Others to dinner stay and are full fed;
> The oldest but sups and goes to bed.
> Long is his life who lingers out the day,
> Who goes soonest has the least to pay.

Visitors came from a distance to enjoy bountiful meals, finding common warmth and cheer before the big fireplace.

The First Universalist Church of North Olmsted originated in the church society organized in 1834 by the Rev. Harlow P. Sage. Early members represented the principal families of Olmstead Township—the Ames, Beebes, Blakes, Carpenters, Coes, Fitches, Glutzbaughs, Hands, Henrys, Huntingtons, Hurds, Kennedys, Rices, Sterns, Thompsons, Tuttles, and Underhills. Through earnest effort and sacrifice, Universalists, Methodists, and Presbyterians erected a union New England meeting-house this year in the village (near Butternut Ridge, at Lorain and Porter roads). Wooden pegs held hand-hewn logs together, and stone foundation blocks were hand-finished. Land on which the building stood was finally deeded to trustees of the First Church in 1880. A sunken stone porch and columns in the front were removed in 1881, and Sunday School rooms were added. Coe's Memorial Hall, a parish house erected in 1928 by Asher M. Coe, was a monument to his devotion to church and community. In the 1930s, the Historic American Buildings Survey of the Department of the Interior recommended that the landmark be preserved for its exceptional historic and architectural interest. Church trustees conveyed title to the Ohio Universalist Convention in 1943. In 1946, the Rev. Heber R. Robinson, pastor, was directing plans for re-dedication of the venerable house of worship, one of the oldest churches in the Western Reserve.

Patrick Smith, twenty, purchased his first dredge and began to remove mud and sand from the shallow channel of the crooked Cuyahoga on a wholesale basis. The dredge was crude, operated by horsepower, and slow progress was made. Working the river was possible for only about half the year. Five years later, Smith purchased his first steam dredge. Business of "Patrick Smith, Dredging and Contracting" expanded steadily, and six years later the equipment included four pile drivers and four dredges.

Heman B. Ely, who supervised the building of the telegraph line of the Lake Erie Telegraph Company, received authorization of the City Council in the summer to extend its Pittsburgh line through Cleveland. On August 30, the Cleveland office opened in the Weddell House; and on January 19, 1848, the line was in operation from Buffalo to Detroit and from Cleveland to Pittsburgh. Jeptha H. Wade was instrumental in the construction. The "Lake Line" became a part of the basis of the future capital of the Western Union Telegraph Company.

The superintendent, clerk, and operator of the telegraph in Cleveland was Charles Edward Wheeler, twenty-four. In a letter he stated: "I can tell you a telegraph man is quite a celebrated character. People stop and point him out. The worst part of it is that when I try to explain the principle, folks do not understand me. Most people have an idea a man has to be especially fitted by nature to enter the profession." Wheeler's equipment was a wire, a transmitter on a kitchen table, and a short, wooden shelf for patrons.

Jeptha H. Wade, portrait painter, whose future and fortune were to be linked closely with Cleveland, had become interested in the Morse telegraph and undertook to build a line from Detroit to Jackson, Michigan, center of the newly discovered iron-ore operations. Having completed it this year, he installed an instrument and inaugurated the first telegraphic service in that region.

It was reported on September 1 that "compliments" had been sent to Cincinnati via the new magnetic telegraph, a "most astonishing achievement of the human intellect." The method of communication was a great boon to the newspapers.

As early as 1822, the Methodists of Rockport had met to worship in log cabins, with William Jordan on Lorain Street, or in the homes of the Giddings, Mastick, Stearns, Spencer, Wright, Peas, Dean, and Higley families. This year, they erected a log-studded sanctuary west of the mouth of Rocky River (3300 Wooster Road). The first minister was the Rev. O. Sheldon. Through decade after decade the sturdy meeting house served a changing community that became Rocky River, but it retained its early-day identity, Rockport Methodist Church. The centennial celebration centered in plans to preserve the original pegged-log building as the wing of a new colonial-type church, to be erected under the leadership of the Rev. Howard Jay Wiant.

The township of East Cleveland was organized this year, embracing "all of the one-hundred-acre lots of the original surveyed township No. 7, north of the Newburgh line." In 1850 Judge Jacob Collamer was appointed postmaster for the district. The office not only took his name, Collamer Post Office, but the community continued, unofficially, to be identified as Collamer.

James Kingsbury, "among the last of the brave pioneers," died at his Newburgh home on December 12, aged eighty. A friendly counsellor and able leader, he served in the Ohio Legislature and held a high place in developing Cleveland and the Western Reserve.

1848

Cleveland was the center of a far-flung agricultural district when Thomas Brown founded the *Ohio Farmer,* "a family paper, devoted to agriculture, science, literature, social improvement, &c." Upon its predictions and wise counsel were based much of the farmer's planting and harvesting until the coming of the scientific age. Through its columns, farm families kept pace with new products, processes, and developments. The weekly had a number of owners and suffered hard times; but it survived and grew in circulation as a strong influence in rural life. Men who gained prominence in agriculture were identified with the paper. Walter H. Lloyd was its editor from 1923 to 1942; and L. L. Rummell, later dean of the College of Agriculture of Ohio State University and director of the Wooster Experiment Station, was a staff member for two decades. Ray T. Kelsey succeeded Lloyd as editor.

Five stages departed from the Franklin House every morning at eight o'clock "at the blast of the bugle and the crack of the driver's whip": to Buffalo, Pittsburgh via Beaver, Cincinnati via Columbus, Detroit via Toledo and Warren via Parkman. There was keen competition between the Pioneer Fast Line, the Pittsburgh Phoenix, and the Mail.

The Cleveland, Painesville & Ashtabula Railroad (later New York Central), incorporated in February, was the first step in forging the connecting link in a Chicago-to-Buffalo through route. Heman B. Ely was president, and Abel Kimball, treasurer. Although the City of Cleveland pledged its credit for a loan of $100,000 to aid the project, financing was difficult, and problems were surmounted through the executive genius of Alfred Kelley and William Case. Frederick Harbach, Amasa Stone, and Stillman Witt were employed to build the road in 1850, and, finally, in 1852, a locomotive traveled the entire length.

In order to achieve its literary ambitions, the Young Men's Literary Association was incorporated in February as the Cleveland Library Association with two hundred shares of stock at $10 each. The parent organization turned over its library, and for a few years offered an annual series of lectures. The library (later Case Library), a reading room, a museum, and a lecture series were maintained. Headquarters were in the Seneca Block (Superior and West 3rd), then in the *Herald* Building, and, in 1856, at 221 Superior Street. Leaders in the new intellectual movement were William Case and Charles Whittlesey.

Five trustees of St. John's African Methodist Episcopal Church purchased a lot on Bolivar Street, east of Erie, on February 14, for $300, three of them signing the deed with "X" marks. The Rev. S. T. Jones was the earliest resident pastor of record. Financial strength and membership grew slowly, and in 1878 a "commodious" church and parsonage were erected on Erie Street, north of Central.

"Laboring females" began airing their grievances, claiming that men were employed to do one kind of work, and that their ten-hour day produced wages of $1.25 to $1.75. On the other hand, women performed many tasks, their day was one-fourth longer, and they earned 75 cents to $1.50 a week, including board and lodging. The scale was too low, they protested.

The need for commercial education was recognized in the founding of Union College, the first of the Bryant & Stratton business-college chain, at the corner of Superior and Seneca streets. Platt R. Spencer of Geneva, Ohio, was soon employed as a writing teacher, and his Spencerian system of penmanship was taught in the nation's schools for many years. In 1887, Messrs. Spencer, Felton, and Loomis purchased the school, changing the name to Spencerian Business College (later Spencerian College). Henry T. Loomis, text-book publisher, became the head in 1895.

The Theatre Comique, built by G. Overacher on the south side of Frankfort Street, west of Bank, prospered until competition of the Academy of Music in 1853 proved disastrous. It then became a variety house, operated by Adolph Montpellier until he retired. In this theater, Clara Morris, famous actress, made her debut.

The Water Street Theater was built this year by John S. Potter, offering a choice of seats in the spacious pit, two tiers of boxes, and four private boxes. Fire destroyed the theater in 1850.

Opposition to growing interest in the theater was expressed by some of the newspapers of the day, one editor declaring that theatrical nuisances should be driven from the city and the theater turned into a house of worship. The *Herald* and the *Plain Dealer,* however, favored the trend in entertainment and encouraged it.

Music and culture gained momentum with the founding of the Frohsinn by German music-lovers. In their beer halls and singing societies, where old-world customs were preserved, these newcomers to Cleveland enjoyed fellowship and found seclusion from severity of New England traditions.

Early-day artists found it difficult to make a living. Nevertheless, occasionally there is evidence of worthy achievement. According to a New York newspaper, "Allen Smith, Jr., a Cleveland portrait painter, has been awarded one of the Art Union prizes, the subject of his painting, the *Young Mechanic.*" S. Heine had painted the Public Square in 1839; and Joseph Gregory and Julius Gollman were contemporary portrait painters.

While the existence of the first high school was assured, smoldering opposition flared at the spring election. A small plurality defeated Charles Bradburn in the race for mayor; and although the friends of the high school succeeded in electing their candidates to the Council, the old members had dropped Bradburn, the "father of the Cleveland schools," from the Board of School Managers.

Until 1852, Andrew Freese and Catherine Jennings struggled to keep the high school operating on an annual budget of $900 allowed them by the penny-pinching Council; and of that, $750 constituted their salaries. To provide needed apparatus and supplies, the boys earned the money by surveying, giving lectures, doing odd jobs, and editing a monthly paper, which they sold. They built a small brick laboratory. Seeing that the boys "could help themselves," Leonard Case, Sr., took a personal interest. On one occasion he wrote a letter "To the Boys in the Basement," enclosing a worthy donation with his regrets "that he could not attend their lectures in chemistry, being 'too lame to get up there.' "

The amazing performances of diminutive "General" Tom Thumb in May were remembered for many a day. He was then twenty-eight inches high and weighed fifteen pounds. Small boys trailed him as he paraded the streets daily with his tiny horses and miniature equipage, the gift of Queen Victoria.

Cleveland merchants met at the Weddell House on July 7 in the evening to establish the Board of Trade (later The Cleveland Chamber of Commerce). Grain-shipping interests from Cleveland to the eastern markets had become so important that there was need of handling business transactions with greater speed and efficiency. William Milford presided, and S. S. Coe was appointed secretary. The purpose of the meeting having been stated, on motion of Joseph L. Weatherly it was "Resolved: that the merchants of this city now organize themselves into an association, to be called the Board of Trade of the City of Cleveland." The first officers were Joseph L. Weatherly, president; William F. Allen, Jr., vice president; Charles W. Coe, secretary; Richard T. Lyon, treasurer. Prominent members included

Richard Hilliard, L. M. Hubby, Philo Chamberlain, Charles Hickox, Thomas Walton, S. S. Stone, R. K. Winslow, W. F. Otis, and Sheldon Pease. At first the board confined its work to the furnishing of daily market reports. The Board of Trade was the second commercial organization of its kind in Ohio and one of the earliest in the nation. It was the first to promote Cleveland's commerce and welfare. S. F. Lester was elected president in 1864, and Philo Chamberlain in 1865. Succeeding secretaries were H. B. Tuttle, 1854; C. W. Coe, 1860; H. B. Tuttle, 1862; Arthur H. Quinn, 1864; and J. C. Sage, 1865.

Wick, Otis & Brownell opened a private banking business on the corner of St. Clair and Bank streets. In the partnership were Henry Wick, Jr., Hugh B. Wick, W. A. Otis, W. F. Otis, and A. C. Brownell. The interests changed hands until 1857, when Wick owned the firm. Henry Wick & Company played a large part in the building of Cleveland until 1891, when the Wick Banking & Trust Company was organized, with Henry Wick, president; Dudley Baldwin, vice president; and D. B. Wick, treasurer and cashier. The City Trust Company took over the business in 1901, and operated for only a year.

David B. Dunham of Bedford leased the Cleveland Temperance House (Hotel Cleveland site), that had been badly damaged by fire in 1845. On the site he built a four-story brick hotel, opening it in style on July 18 as the Dunham House. It was enlarged in 1850, and W. S. Streator and H. Doolittle acquired interests.

According to the diary of James A. Garfield, the seventeen-year-old lad spent two exciting months working for his cousin aboard a Pennsylvania & Ohio canal boat during the summer. Leaving Cleveland on August 16 with a 52-ton load of copper ore, they unloaded at Pittsburgh on the twenty-eighth. On the return trip, they took aboard 60 tons of coal at Youngstown on the thirtieth, unloading at Cleveland on September 2. Young Garfield's trip was enlivened by his falling overboard fourteen times and narrowly escaping drowning, for he could not swim. He was employed to make the locks ready, see that the boat went through, trim the lamps, and serve as general handy-man, at $14 a month. During the two months, Garfield records, "we transported 240 tons of stone coal and forty tons of iron to Cleveland and 52 tons of copper ore, 150 barrels of salt, 10 thousand laths, and 1,000 feet of lumber from Cleveland to different places along the canal." A round trip to Pittsburgh took almost a month. Aside from providing an interesting account of the early experience of a notable American, the record affords illuminating insight into pioneering trade that was to give two growing industrial cities their foundations for greatness.

Lots on Bond Street, at the corner of St. Clair, were purchased this year by Bishop Amadeus Rappe. On them he built several frame houses and a large brick residence. In September he opened St. Mary's Seminary in a building that had been a stable at the rear of his home. Father Louis DeGoesbriand was the first superior, and ten theological students were enrolled. In 1850 Spring Cottage on Lake Street was purchased, affording more suitable quarters. An enlarged building, between Lake Street and

Hamilton, was ready for the occupancy of St. Mary's College in September, 1860.

On the lots purchased by Father McLaughlin for the Catholic Church at Superior and Erie streets, Bishop Rappe erected a temporary church and school. It was the Church of the Nativity, used on weekdays for classes, the first parochial school in Cleveland.

Earnest missionary efforts of Friedrich Kaufholz, a foundry foreman, brought together a little prayer group, known as the Congregation of Brethren, that raised a small house of worship on Tracy Street. The first chapel on the West Side in which services in the German language were conducted, it was dedicated on September 17. Upon the leader's death in 1859, the Rev. H. J. Ruetenik, traveling missionary, was engaged as pastor of the independent church, which united with the Reformed German denomination as the First Reformed Church. It flourished, and a new building was dedicated at Penn and Carroll streets in 1863. In the later sixties, the Second Church on the East Side was organized, due partly to Rev. Ruetenik's activities. As members were living in the South Side, forty of them were dismissed to form the nucleus of Fourth Church in 1872, which continued to serve in 1946 from its location at Woodbridge and West 32nd Street. Fifth Church, an offspring in 1876, was ministering from Hague Avenue at West 67th Street seven decades later. English services were introduced in the First Church in 1901 by the Rev. F. W. Leich. The Rev. John Sommerlatte became pastor in 1920, and he inspired plans for an impressive church home at Warren Road and Alger Avenue, Lakewood. In 1946, his vision and enthusiasm continued to guide the historic First Evangelical and Reformed Church, as it was now known.

Linda T. Guilford, trained at the Mt. Holyoke Female Seminary, arrived by boat from Buffalo in October, and two days later opened the Young Ladies Seminary in the Temperance Pavilion, formerly the Farmers Block. The new principal was fired with a keen interest in higher education for women; and with her exceptional background, young women were given opportunities almost equal with those of nearby colleges. The seminary soon moved to its own building (Osborn Building site), and the Pavilion went out of business in 1850.

Near soft-water springs in a wooded glen (Wallingford Court and East 51st) Dr. Thomas T. Seelye opened his famous Cleveland Water Cure establishment on October 9. The three-story brick sanitarium, nestled in a natural setting, developed with lovely landscaping, curving walks, and drives, was the finest in the West. Medical men frowned disapprovingly upon the pioneer hydropathic venture that was designed to serve a large number of patients. After a successful career, the doctor went to Florida in 1885, and the resort was razed.

Shaw Academy in Euclid Township (later Shaw High School) had suffered from competition of Cleveland free schools and an unfortunate succession of principals, and it had been virtually abandoned to destructive children and thievery when Joseph B. Meriam, twenty-one, and newly graduated from Western Reserve College, agreed to assume charge. The Rev.

William Beecher, president of the board of trustees and brother of Henry Ward Beecher, had promised to put the building in repair; but when Meriam arrived by stage from Hudson on October 20, nothing had been done because there was no money. Pride dictated that he invest his last few dollars in materials, and he spent the weekend making repairs with the assurance that he could have the building as a private school. Rev. Beecher's complimentary announcement to his Presbyterian congregation produced three of his own children, three from the Ezekiel Adams home, and Kate Luster for enrollment as students on Monday morning. Pupils helped with the reconstruction, and at the end of the term forty names were on the roll.

The Catholic population of Cleveland had reached four thousand, and Bishop Rappe saw the need for a second church. On the corner lot at Superior and Erie Streets, the cornerstone of St. John's Cathedral was laid on October 29.

Moses G. Younglove and John Hoyt built a paper mill in Cleveland that was the first west of the mountains to employ steam power. The Cleveland mill and others were united later as the Cleveland Paper Company, the first of that name, of which Younglove was president until 1867, when he sold his interest most profitably.

The homeopathic profession was enjoying wide acceptance, and this year the Cuyahoga County Homeopathic Society was organized. On its roster of presidents were the names of prominent Clevelanders: Drs. S. R. Beckwith, T. P. Wilson, George H. Blair, Hamilton F. Biggar, H. B. VanNorman, G. J. Jones, J. H. Stevens, David H. Beckwith, F. H. Barr, and A. L. Waltz.

An item in the *Plain Dealer* on November 9 announced a "plan to close all stores at eight o'clock instead of ten" in order that the citizens "might devote a portion of their time to mental improvement and the study of branches holding a near relation to their employment." During the winter months, when business was slow, waterways were closed, and evenings were long, lecture courses provided a profitable and inspiring way to pass the time.

More than half of Cleveland's population, estimated at 13,696, was of American birth, according to this year's city directory, which gave the first nationality analysis: United States, 8,451; Germany, 2,587; Ireland, 1,024; England, 1,007; Scotland, 176; Isle of Man, 148; Canada, 145; France, 66; Wales, 62. Poland, Prussia, Holland, and several other countries were represented by less than 10 each.

1849

Subjects taught in the schools included the alphabet, reading, spelling, intellectual arithmetic, geography, natural history, music, penmanship, grammar, and composition. The high-school course had, in addition, "intellectual algebra," physiology, chemistry, natural philosophy, bookkeeping, and geometry. The "useful and beautiful art" of drawing was introduced this year. This was the blackboard era, when entire classes marched up to the wide, long boards to display their knowledge in exercises and drills. Uniformity in school rules, texts, and study courses was attempted unsuccessfully.

Bishop Rappe consecrated St. Joseph's Cemetery on January 22. It was the first Catholic burying ground, and it comprised fifteen acres on Woodland Avenue (and East 79th).

Seabury Ford of Geauga County, who practiced extensively in the Cleveland courts, was elected governor of Ohio.

In a comprehensive "lead" article appearing March 10, the *True Democrat* complimented the city on the "good taste and neatness exhibited in the building of dwelling houses, and the proper adornment of grounds. Euclid Street is becoming one of the most beautiful avenues in the whole land." The massive stone house recently built by Henry B. Payne at the northeast corner of Euclid and North Perry streets was cited as an outstanding example of enduring architecture and elegance. In this fine, gabled residence with its stone-railed portico, railroads were planned, Civil War reconstruction was thought through, and political strategy was developed. A century of Cleveland growth and progress passed in review before the house was razed in the early 1940s. The Payne home was designed by Charles W. Heard, son-in-law of Jonathan Goldsmith, well-known Painesville architect. The homes of Charles M. Giddings and Sherlock J. Andrews were also his work.

When Charles Francis Brush was born on a farm in Euclid Township on March 17, a new source of illumination called gas had just been developed. As one of the world's foremost scientists, he was destined not only to improve gas lighting, but to outmode it through his inventive genius.

The success and benefits of the New England savings banks had captured the interest of Samuel H. Mather and Charles J. Woolson, who enlisted the practical support of leading businessmen in securing an institution for Cleveland. On March 22 the Society for Savings in the City of Cleveland was incorporated by act of the Legislature, thus creating a co-operative society, in the broadest sense—"a benevolent institution, without capital, managed by trustees without salary, in the interest of depositors only, to whom profits are paid, or for whose benefit they are accumulated and reserved." It is interesting to note the absence of the word "bank" in early savings-bank charters, their function as benevolent and not money-making institutions being interpreted as "Institutions for Savings," "Societies for Savings," and "Savings Fund Societies."

The incorporators of the Society for Savings were Nathan Brainard, James H. Bingham, James A. Briggs, Henry W. Clark, Ralph Cowles, John A. Foot, James Gardner, John H. Gorham, Lewis Handerson, Josiah A. Harris, Morgan L. Hewitt, Joseph Lyman, Samuel H. Mather, William A. Otis, Alexander Seymour, Daniel A. Shepard, and Charles J. Woolson. On June 18 the Society was organized and the first officers were elected: John W. Allen, president; Reuben Hitchcock, Dudley Baldwin, and F. W. Bingham, vice presidents; J. F. Taintor, treasurer; and S. H. Mather, secretary. The

Solon L. Severance

Charles Whittlesey

Amasa Stone

William B. Castle

Linda T. Guilford

William Case

John H. McBride

Charles A. Otis, Sr.

Andrew Freese

Clara Morris. LEO WEIDENTHAL COL-LECTION.

Joseph S. Haworth. LEO WEIDENTHAL COLLECTION.

The Academy of Music, Cleveland's early theater, at West 6th Street between Superior and St. Clair avenues.

Effie Ellsler

John A. Ellsler

trustees' names represented a who's-who of Cleveland business. A room 20 feet square in the rear of the Merchants Bank was occupied by the Society, an insurance company, and Mather for his private business. The Society paid $75 of the $400 yearly rental. Business hours were fixed at first to accommodate the treasurer, who also served as teller in the Merchants Bank. A $25-savings deposit received from Mrs. D. E. Bond on August 2 was the first transaction. At the end of the year, the books showed seventy-three depositors with deposits totaling $35,012.69.

The City Mills Store opened this year at the southwest corner of Superior and Seneca streets, later moving to the southeast corner of Frankfort and Bank, where it became Morgan, Root & Company, the principals being E. P. Morgan and Ralph R. Root. Leander and John H. McBride later purchased the Morgan interest, changing the name to Root & McBride Brothers. In 1884, the pioneer wholesale dry-goods firm moved to a traditional location on Bank Street (1250 West 6th). It incorporated in 1895 as The Root & McBride Company, with Leander McBride, president; John H. McBride, vice president and treasurer; Fred P. Root, vice president; and Herbert McBride, secretary. The institution became one of the leading wholesale dry-goods firms in the Middle West. Malcolm L. McBride became president in 1929 serving until his death in 1941 when Frederick W. Barnes succeeded him and H. Verne Reed became vice president and treasurer.

When Daniel M. Haskell became postmaster on April 11, he moved the Post Office to the *Herald* Building on Bank Street.

In May, music lovers enjoyed "a new fashioned entertainment . . . no less than an Operatic Soirée," when *La Sonnambula* and *The Daughter of the Regiment* were presented by the Manvers Operatic Company, in full costume, in Watson's Hall.

The cholera plague that was sweeping the Midwest alarmed Cleveland, and precautions were instituted by the Board of Health, consisting of A. Seymour, William Case, and John Gill. In May, a tax was levied to establish and maintain a poorhouse and hospital. Increased cemetery facilities were being planned by the newly incorporated Brooklyn Cemetery Association, and the North Brooklyn Cemetery was opened (on Scranton Avenue between Wade and Seymour).

The headline attraction of this year's circus, staged at the foot of Bank Street, was the calliope or "Appollonicon," "the most stupendous musical project of the age . . . more powerful than a band of 50 musicians, and drawn by 40 horses in procession." The *Herald* advertisement announcing the two-day event that opened June 18, also featured the Carlo Troupe of equestrians, headed by one of the leading trick clowns of Europe, and "grand Heroic and Patriotic Spectacles" of Revolutionary War days. Admission was 25 cents.

George Worthington and associates formed the Cleveland Iron Company to manufacture bar iron. The bulk of the output was sold through Worthington's hardware store.

Shiloh Baptist Church, the earliest Negro church in the denomination, originated as a mission established by the First Baptist Church. Its first pastor, the Rev. W. P. Brown, was called in 1851. The congregation grew slowly, and a house was purchased on Ohio Street near Perry as a sanctuary. In 1863 the First Church helped to acquire a house on Sterling Avenue that served as a meeting place for thirty years. Three Negro churches originated in Shiloh—Antioch, 1893; Mt. Hermon, 1903; and Messiah, 1927.

The Cuyahoga County Agricultural Society was revived this year. Fairs were held on the Kinsman Street grounds and later in Newburgh and Chagrin Falls.

The *Plain Dealer* introduced a column of news from foreign countries this year.

Cholera attacked the city, and on June 26 the first case was reported in Cleveland. A temporary hospital was provided by the Board of Health on the upper floor of the Cleveland Centre Block on the "Flats." Summarizing lengthy newspaper accounts devoted to the plague, 130 deaths were reported: 11 American-born, 49 who came from Ireland, 44 from Germany, 14 from England, 4 from Wales, 2 each from Scotland and Holland, 1 each from Norway, France, and the Isle of Man, and 1 unknown. On September 21, the *Plain Dealer* editor observed, with perhaps an ulterior motive, that in Cincinnati the death toll in one day had exceeded this number.

A number of states sent delegates to a convention in Cleveland, held on July 13, celebrating the anniversary of the passage of the Ordinance of 1787, excluding slavery from the Northwest Territory. Judge Eli Tappan presided over the sessions, and ardent enemies of slavery rallied to the "big tent on the common."

Henry Clay, accompanied by his son, stopped in Cleveland on July 28 on his way to Newport for his health. They arrived from Sandusky on the steamer *Saratoga* and were welcomed by a gun salute and an informal reception on the boat. After a carriage tour of the city, the statesman visited the Weddell House, then resumed his journey by boat to Buffalo.

"Gold in California!" The get-rich-quick fever stirred the nation, and for more than a year the newspapers printed columns about the strike and the rush westward. The largest delegation of Clevelanders left on the brig *Eureka,* built in '47 on the Black River (Lorain) by W. A. Adair & Company, Cleveland forwarding and commission merchants. Local passengers paid the $300 fare in advance, provided their own beds, bedding, and supplies, limited to one barrel-back (trunk) and ten barrels of bulk freight. Among the twenty Cleveland passengers were John P. Jones, who won wealth and distinction after a severe struggle, George Hickox, and Dr. A. S. Baldwin, trip physician. The *Eureka,* reported at 375 tons, was the first Great Lakes ship to make the trip to San Francisco. Captain William Monroe piloted "the finest vessel to sail for California," leaving on September 26. The *Eureka* was sturdy and weathered three weeks of storms in rounding the Horn. On June 19, 1850, according to the Frisco marine report, the prospectors reached port with fifty-nine passengers, seven females, aboard. Adair, the vessel's owner, had arrived by a quicker route, and had already "busted, blowed up and gone to the devil." On the return trip, the *Eureka* departed on October 26 for Panama; but she encountered misfortune at sea, and after many hardships reached a port in Mexico on January 6, 1851. The passengers deserted, and the ship was sold to satisfy passengers' accounts. Fortune-seekers suffered severe privations in travel by wagon, and a local editor reported that "Hundreds perish by the way, and thousands fall there . . . Over the new made graves the tide sweeps on." "Gold, gold— it is a humbug," he bemoaned. Nugget watch charms and fabulous stories were the reward of many disappointed adventurers who gave up and finally drifted eastward.

Clevelanders cheered the first locomotive, a wood-burning iron horse, as it coughed and labored up the River Street grade on November 3, pulling a work train of wooden flat cars on the Cleveland, Columbus & Cincinnati Railroad from St. Clair to Superior Street. The engine was built in Ohio City at the Cuyahoga Steam Furnace plant. Speed had been set at four or five miles an hour within the city limits, which would permit time for a team of horses to get out of the way. For three years, work trains hauled supplies from the docks for the road.

Comfort in travel improved somewhat with the era of the plank road. An eight-foot, planked highway was completed in November between Cleveland and Chagrin Falls, the cost being estimated at $20,000. The turnpike portion of the road, graveled and ditched, measured 40 feet wide. Toll of 2 cents a mile was charged for a two-horse, loaded wagon, and 1 cent if unloaded. An additional horse cost one-half cent a mile more, and a man on horseback could travel for 1 cent. An elaborate schedule covered tolls for animals, carriages, and the many forms of travel. Cleveland and Newburgh were now only thirty minutes apart. A plank road to Willoughby was soon followed by roads to Twinsburg, Rockport, and Wooster. Another road was built for five miles toward Elyria, and a section on Lorain Street had been begun. Planked roads ended at city limits, and horses and wagons "wallowed in the mud" through unpaved streets as they toiled into Cleveland. A bus line was running every hour between Cleveland and Ohio City, fare 6½ cents and "no credit."

The Michigan Central Railway extended its transportation to Lake Erie, operating the *Mayflower,* a 1,300-ton propeller, between Detroit, Cleveland, and Buffalo, with accommodations for eight hundred passengers along with freight. Soon the line was operating the best boats on the lake.

A little group of Czechs arrived in Cleveland, including Willi Hesky and his sister. Bernard Weidenthal came from Bohemia with his widowed mother, Mrs. Rebecca Neumann Weidenthal, and her children, Charlotte, Fannie, and Leopold; and Joseph Loewy and his daughter, Dorothea. Weidenthal purchased a residence on Woodland Avenue to which he took his bride, Dorothea Loewy. Hesky went west in early manhood, and his sister married a farmer near Sandusky.

According to the advertisements, the fireplace was on the way out, and the cooking stove was featured as a great new blessing to the meal-maker.

A gas-manufacturing plant had been built and pipes were laid to provide street lighting for Cleveland. One by one the smoky lamps were removed and the first street lights were installed, brightening Superior Street from the river to Erie, the Public Square, and Water, Merwin, and Bank streets. On December 8, the lights were turned on, and citizens gathered under the lamp posts to enjoy the novelty.

> The glory of the stars and moon
> And comets, too, may pass;
> Then let 'em go—however soon,
> For Cleveland's burning gas!

CHAPTER 8

Rails and Red Gold

1850-1859

THE DECADE opened upon an era of great economic prosperity, fostered by the influence of the Mexican War and territorial expansion. Long wagon trains were threading their way over mountain and plain to the new Far West, seeking homesteads and California gold. Arriving in Cleveland on their westward way, many of them who came overland or by waterway chose to stay, believing that the flourishing lake city offered immediate opportunity.

Industrious Germans and Irish continued to stream into Cleveland, expanding their clannish communities, holding fast to traditions even to the second generation. The Germans established a "turnverein" in 1850, and two years later a newspaper. Several Czech families, passing through on their way to the Milwaukee district in 1850, stopped to rest in Cleveland and decided to stay. They became the nucleus of an energetic, peace-loving colony, richly endowed with the culture of their homeland. The Czechs settled first in the vicinity of Hill, Cross, and Commercial streets; but, as soon as they were assured of a livelihood, they began to move to the country, their natural environment. In 1852, Hungarian immigration began with the arrival of David and Morris Black and their families. They were thrifty and religious, and near Woodland and Willson avenues they laid out a market garden, later turning to the making of ladies' cloaks and garments, an industry that was identified with the steadily growing Hungarian settlements for many years. A small Negro population of 224 was reported by the census.

Agriculture, the stagecoach, and the Ohio Canal had given many villages a healthy start, and for several decades their future was more promising than that of Cleveland. In the race for pre-eminence, however, the city's strategic position on lake and canal had given it the lead in the Western Reserve with a population of 17,034, almost thirty times the 1820 figure. Within its political boundaries lay an area of 5.381 square miles. Akron, a milling center to the south, had sprung up with the canal in 1825 and was leading inland towns outside Cuyahoga County with a total of 3,266, followed by Norwalk, 3,159; Painesville, 3,128; Madison, 2,986; Warren, 2,957; Youngstown, 2,802; Milan, 2,697; Ravenna, 2,240; Poland, 2,126; Franklin Mills (Kent), 1,749; and Elyria, 1,482. Sandusky, with 5,088 led the small but ambitious lake ports—Conneaut, Ashtabula, Sandusky, Toledo, and Black River (Lorain), the latter trailing with 659. Larger cities were awake to Cleveland's growth, and Detroit, 21,019, and Milwaukee, 20,061, sensed the threat of supremacy; but flourishing Chicago, 29,963, and Cincinnati, 115,435, were entirely content with substantial gains.

The census reported 48,099 persons in Cuyahoga County, and revealed that urban population was gaining over rural. Township figures within the county showed Bedford, 1,853; Brecksville, 1,116; Brooklyn—Ohio City, 6,375; Chagrin Falls, 1,250; Dover, 1,102; East Cleveland, 2,313; Euclid, 1,447; Independence, 1,485; Mayfield, 1,117; Middleburgh (Berea and Brook Park), 1,490; Newburgh, 1,542; Olmstead, 1,216; Orange, 1,063; Parma, 1,329; Royalton, 1,253; Solon, 1,034; Strongsville, 1,199; and Warrensville, 1,410.

"Cleveland is the most desirable town in the 'Great West' *to live in*." This profound statement was the more significant, appearing as it did in the *Cincinnati Gazette*. Commenting on his visit to the Forest City, the neighborly editor declared, "The town is clean, tasteful, elegant and healthful; for vegetables, fruit and flowers it is preeminent—for groves, parks, ornamental trees and shrubs, it is hardly surpassed by New Haven. . . . Her public and private schools are excellent; her medical college superior to any in the West, and the prevailing character of her society is educational, moral and religious. It is, therefore, 'just the spot' for the man of moderate income, to live and educate his family."

Railroad-building had been paramount in the news since 1849. After fifteen years of desperate struggle on the part of promoters, rails of iron joined Columbus and Cincinnati with Cleveland, making the latter the terminus of several great systems. In 1851, the wood-fired, brass-trimmed *Cleveland* locomotive, built in Ohio City, made her initial run from Columbus into the little frame depot on the Superior Street hill, representing a victory over public antagonism, financial misfortune, and extreme construction difficulties.

The "magical" influence of the railroad is expressed in glowing terms in the city directory of 1853. It stated:

> We have no longer an annual hybernation, but reckon time by the same almanac which serves as a guide to other civilized communities. The travel through our city has become immense; the old lumbering stage-coaches have been so entirely driven from our thoroughfares, that they are already looked upon as objects of curiosity. Our numerous and excellent hotels are constantly filled to over-flowing, and scarce one of all these arriving and departing crowds, that does not bear irrepressible testimony to the business and beauty of our city.

By 1852, three sturdy little trains were operating daily each way on the 4-foot-10-inch gauge road between Lake Erie and the Ohio River. Completion of railway lines to Cincinnati and Pittsburgh had boosted the lake city's population from 21,140 in 1851 to 25,670 a year later. Industry had made a great forward stride; the Cuyahoga Steam Furnace Company in

Ohio City was building locomotives, and Otis & Ford were producing forgings and axles.

Alfred Kelley retired as president of the Cleveland, Columbus & Cincinnati Railroad in 1853 and was succeeded by Henry B. Payne. Ohio and Indiana roads that were enduring financial struggles survived through Payne's aid of money and credit. While his policy was criticized, the revitalized lines encouraged communities and increased land values. Eventually, some of them came into their benefactor's fold.

While builders of the Cleveland & Pittsburgh railroad were not aware of the possibilities of trade in iron ore, they estimated that the line would move about a thousand tons of coal per day, a figure that was soon surpassed. In the early fifties, word went out that a trainload of coal was to be hauled into Cleveland. Four or five hundred people traveled out to the railroad shop (East 38th and Hamilton), where they joined the few company employees in cheering the first coal train—ten flat cars loaded with one hundred tons. The next morning, the papers predicted that Cleveland was "destined to become the Newcastle of America!" Superintendent John Durand of the road ventured the hope "that by three months they would be able to run in this amount of coal daily."

The Pennsylvania and Baltimore & Ohio railroads had reached the Ohio River in 1853. Ten small roads between Albany and Buffalo were consolidated the same year into the New York Central Railroad, capitalized at the staggering sum of twenty-three million dollars. Rails thus welded the East and the West.

Vague charters permitted building only to state lines, making necessary the granting of charters in various states in order to make interstate connections. Believing that the monster belching smoke and sparks would ruin their lands, farmers and property owners placed obstructions on the tracks to hinder operations. Haled into court, railroad companies found no sympathy at first in the juries.

The railroads were binding waterways and valleys of the North together. Along the lakeshore, little lines were being united in the late fifties, but safe, "through" service was retarded by the narrow-gauge policy in Ohio as against standard-gauge in Indiana and New York. Changing cars was burdensome for travelers and unpopular. It was difficult to maintain schedules, particularly in bad weather. Cars often jumped the tracks, and trains were delayed by stray animals, fallen trees, and obstructions. Night traveling was hazardous, and accidents due to washouts and threats that lurked in the darkness often brought disaster before hand brakes could be applied. As the roads slowly ironed out their problems, competition grew and petty rate wars broke out, increasing in volume until they threatened to destroy some of the roads.

Despite many hardships, the railroad developed rapidly, stimulating manufacturing and revolutionizing transportation and communication. Days of romantic stagecoach travel were numbered. The blast of the driver's horn that woke the early wilderness was replaced by the discordant whistle of the furnace-feeding engineer. As the trails of commerce shifted and the move to the cities increased, stage towns on state roads and turnpikes began to decay, taverns suffered, and weary stagecoaches were consigned to obscure mail routes between railroad towns and distant villages. Stages continued to operate regularly for some time between Cleveland and near-by points.

Canal water and power had increased the wealth and population of Ohio. Real estate in thirty-seven canal counties had risen in value from $25,000,000 in 1826 to $350,000,000 in 1859. The future greatness of Cleveland, Akron, Dayton, Columbus, Toledo, and Cincinnati had been established when these cities became canal terminals for freight shipments of mine, farm, and factory products. These were grim days for canal operators, however. Passenger traffic had succumbed to railroad competition, and canal tolls in 1859 were dwindling at an alarming rate.

The sidewheel steamer was at the height of its popularity in 1850, and Cleveland was the home of more than eighty schooners and three steamboats. Sixteen steamships were operating between Buffalo and Chicago. Handsome cabins, splendid meals, and occasional band music drew capacity crowds of four or five hundred passengers. The leading passenger line on Lake Erie was operated by the Michigan Central Railway between Detroit, Cleveland, and Buffalo. It merged locomotives and steamboats in lake-traffic business, operating a fleet of fine boats until its profitable traffic was cut off in 1858 by the Great Western Railroad, when it introduced rail transportation in Canada between Buffalo and Detroit. The Detroit & Cleveland Steam Navigation Company, founded as the decade opened, proved a striking financial success, and it was to play a leading role in the prosperity of the two flourishing cities it served. Although passenger traffic was showing a decided preference for the railroad, freight traffic in the rapidly growing industrial and agricultural lake region increased the need for lake vessels. Shipbuilding was a major industry in Cleveland, and, in 1858, freighters built in local yards opened trade routes to Europe.

In order that lake tonnage could be moved to railroad trains at Cleveland, six piers occupied by rail lines were built into the lake, east of the Cuyahoga River. Terminal operations centered here until with considerable persuasion the Government dislodged them when a larger harbor was required.

As the fifties opened, Cleveland businessmen had formulated plans to develop the new mineral country in the Lake Superior region of upper Michigan. Soon the dramatic industrial era opened, born of the vision and energy of the city's men of iron. Steam and sail plied the inland seas when the Sault Ste. Marie Canal opened in 1855, shifting trade to the lower lakes, and bringing vast natural resources within reach of Cleveland and the East. Iron ore and coal became inseparable. Boats delivering iron ore to the docks sailed away with cargoes of coal; and railroads, fired with the new fuel, exchanged their burden of coal for iron ore.

Industrial expansion was reflected in the *Cleveland Directory* of 1858, which showed that two paper mills, white-lead and copper-smelting works, furniture and melodeon manufactories, and a stove works were also making iron products. Of the 650 workers in the iron industry, 125 were producing 147 T-rails daily in the Cleveland Rolling Mill. Nevertheless, dissatisfied newspaper editors called attention to the progress of manufacturers in Youngstown, Pittsburgh, and other centers, and criticized Cleveland's leaders for depending upon outside supply and delaying the launching of furnaces in the city.

Pioneering attempts to refine coal oil, using cannel coal, were under way in 1859 when oil was discovered at Titusville, Pennsylvania, and young John D. Rockefeller was starting out in the produce and commission business. Primitive demands for tools, building materials, and necessities still engaged the large part of industry.

After two decades of feuding, Cleveland and Ohio City buried their differences in friendly alliance in 1854. To Mayor William B. Castle of the smaller city went the honor as first chief executive of the united City of Cleveland. Further strengthening the ties between East and West, a bridge was built at Main Street, another at the foot of Seneca Street, and the Center Street Bridge was rebuilt. The new water-works system, a municipal improvement long overdue, went into operation in 1856, bringing water from Lake Erie for public use. As pumps filled the city mains, the long and useful career of the well on the Public Square came to an end.

Modest homes around the Square gradually yielded as business began to move eastward from Superior Street. In 1852, the famous fifteen-year "fence war" was declared by residents against invading commerce. Two three-story, commercial blocks were erected on the northwest side in 1853, and five brick stores on the south side at a cost of twenty-five thousand dollars. A four-story, brick block at the corner of Euclid and the Square cost ten thousand dollars. A federal building rose on the site of the Leonard Case homestead at the northeast corner of Superior; and, late in the decade, construction of a new Court House began on Rockwell Street west of the Stone Church as the result of a move to keep the Public Square free of buildings and obstructions. In 1855, the First Presbyterian Church of Cleveland dedicated the Stone Church on the traditional site at the northwest corner of Ontario and the Square. It was the oldest building in the city's center in the 1940s, standing substantially as erected, except for outside modifications following a fire in 1884.

Residences filled Euclid Street, although not closely, and there was not a shop or store on it in 1850, according to recollections of James F. Ryder, veteran photographer. "I gave myself the pleasure many times of loitering past those beautiful homes and admiring them to my heart's content," he recalled. "I thanked the proprietors . . . for the pleasure they gave me . . . I could hug myself with the thought that while I could enjoy as much as the other fellow, he had to pay the taxes. It was but a short distance east from the Public Square—perhaps two miles—where rail fences in zig-zag pattern bordered the highway and a toll-gate barred the passage of teams, demanding tribute for road repairs."

Street and sidewalk improvements were initiated, and some of the principal streets were elevated to the status of "avenue." "Lake Euclid" at Erie

Street was drained, and a grading program smoothed out some of the mudholes. Street lamps burned until midnight in downtown Cleveland, excepting on moonlight nights, when moonshine was considered adequate.

Appearance of the horsecar on Cleveland streets was a step in the direction of improved traffic facilities in the growing city, realized after considerable public and official debate. A network of omnibus lines radiated from the downtown district, conveyances leaving twice a day for East Cleveland, three times daily for the West Side, and four times a day for Kinsman, Euclid, and Prospect streets.

Cleveland's retail stores centered on Superior Street west of the Square in 1850. Twenty were selling dry goods; 6, hardware; 8, drugs; 5, books. Five merchant tailors were located here, 4 of the city's 6 jewelers, 21 of its 25 clothing stores, 6 hat-and-cap stores, 21 selling boots and leather, 21 of the 22 shoe stores, and 2 vending crockery. Twenty-two of the 58 groceries were located on Superior, and four in the "uptown" district, extending from Ontario eastward to Erie Street. Wholesale trade flourished around Water, River, and Merwin streets, where there were 14 wholesale grocery houses, 5 ship chandlers, and 33 forwarding and commission houses. The residential section was moving eastward. Market gardeners, butchers, and hucksters filled the streets as well as the Michigan Street market house. Unfriendly competition resulted in efforts to reach a solution later in the decade in a market a short distance to the south at Broadway, but this plan met with antagonism.

Rents were lowered as the prosperity era leveled out. Houses within a half and three-quarters of a mile of the business center that rented for $450 per year dropped to $200 and $150 in 1854.

There were three daily newspapers and two weeklies in Cleveland in 1850. J. W. Gray of the *Plain Dealer* wielded great political power in the camp of the Democrats. Joseph A. Harris of the *Herald* was following the Whigs into the Republican fold, where Edwin Cowles had established the *Leader*. The city, a breeding ground of politics, produced prominent figures in party factions of the day.

New dailies, weeklies, and periodicals sprang up now and then, some with intriguing titles—*Dodge's Literary Museum; The Harpoon,* champion of temperance; *Scott's Soup Bowl;* and *The Spiritual Universe*. That their lives were short may be attributed to the confusing times or to ambitious printers or reporters who aspired to shape the public mind from the exalted editor's chair.

This was a high-pressure era insofar as newspaper editors were concerned. Speed in news transmission that had been increased by the "magnetic" telegraph was given further impetus by the steam railroad, which carried the mail. Well-established papers flourished as they hustled to cover the many controversial topics of the day—slavery, morality, temperance, equal rights, religion, atheism, and politics. A cultural awakening in Cleveland was reflected in increased space; and city improvements, markets, and commercial news were claiming more attention. Charles Farrar Brown's circle of readers widened as his fantastic stories in the *Plain Dealer,* signed Artemus Ward, stretched his imagination.

The power of advertising was demonstrated in continuously expanding newspaper columns. L. F. & S. Burgess called attention to Herring's fire- and burglar-proof safe, with a superior "patent powder proof lock." Their competitor, Pierce & Company, representing the World's Safe Company, claimed that "Lillie's chilled iron safe" gave the best protection. The Pierce company had diverse interests as bankers, printers, and publishers of the *Bank Note Recorder,* and were also agents for the "French pocket magnify- ing glass for detecting bogus money." Hutchinson & Palmer, druggists, had added "fine paints, glassware, groceries and wine, brandy and other liquors for medicinal purposes" to their line. W. H. Burnham advertised a shaving and hair-dressing saloon, the cleaning and repairing of clothing, and the loaning of money; while Francis Bernitz featured butter, cheese, fish, stone- ware, and nails.

Cleveland's first university was launched as the new system of liberal education was gaining favor at Brown, the University of Virginia, and a new institution, Rochester University. It gave the student freedom to follow his chosen courses to completion, and endeavored to offer opportunities in engineering, agriculture, and the arts that were not afforded in the rigidly defined curricula of established schools, particularly in church institutions, such as Oberlin, Western Reserve, Baldwin, and Hiram. While Cleveland University was established as non-sectarian, it avoided charges then current against state universities, by maintaining denominational ties through its faculty. Education was carried to the community through public lectures, and the newspapers gave generous support. Yet the school failed, despite the best leadership. Although the records have disappeared, it is reasonable to believe that when the university encountered financial extremes, land holders who speculated on its success declined or were unable to help. The principle of liberal education, however, had been born to succeed.

Seminaries and private schools had cause to fear the public schools, which now offered free instruction, excepting in communities where parochial schools existed. That the importance of free education was not appreciated is reflected in Superintendent Andrew Freese's report that 25 per cent of public-school students were absent daily. Citizens who believed firmly in education, however, met all manner of odds in encouraging its advance, and the decade witnessed not only two high schools in Cleveland, but two evening schools as well. Private institutions disappeared one by one, leaving only those incorporated and well supported by local interests.

Now that Cleveland had two medical schools, a university, homeopathic institution, Catholic cathedral, academy of natural science, natural-history museum, library, and literary and music organizations, it offered oppor- tunities that identified it as an awakened cultural center. Gaslight, plank roads, railroads, well-established banks, two-score church organizations, ex- ceptional commercial advantages, and industry with great promise attracted wealth and population.

William Case, elected mayor in 1850-51, was the first Cleveland-born citizen to attain this high position. He and his fellow "Arkites" and prominent business and professional men with broad vision shaped the foundation stones of sturdy cultural development.

Paved and lighted streets and the air of prosperity encouraged interest in year-round cultural activities. Organizations combed the country to invite the brightest names on the lecture platform to come to Cleveland; and local enthusiasm produced return engagements despite harsh criticism directed at several national figures by the press. Josiah Quincy, Henry Ward Beecher, Ralph Waldo Emerson, Horace Greeley, Edward Everett, Grace Greenwood, Horace Mann, Bayard Taylor, and James G. Dana were among those who discussed the burning questions of the day and brought illuminating wisdom and uplift to the city. Fakirs and exponents of phrenology and the stars were attracting smaller audiences as the popularity of lectures increased. Astronomy, animal life, and practical subjects were taken to the people by Cleveland's scientific and medical fraternity, which ranked with the best in the country.

Theaters shared in the flush of good times. Increased population and easy spending inspired the building of the Academy of Music, the finest playhouse of its day. The coming of John A. Ellsler touched off the spark that encouraged genuine interest in the theater. In Shakespearean and popular drama, he brought to Cleveland the leading names on the stage; and in his famous stock company, stars were born.

Although traveling was burdensome, Ole Bull, Adelina Patti, and other celebrities, discovering responsive audiences in the Midwest, made a practice of return engagements. The appearance of Jenny Lind was one of the most momentous in Cleveland's music history, for here public appreciation really began. Interest in sacred music had been inspired in churches. The spirit of German singing societies, as expressed in the brilliant Saengerfest, brought fame to Cleveland. Music teachers were gathering small classes together and giving occasional concerts.

Jarvis F. Hanks, pioneer artist, and five professional painters, including Allen Smith, Jr., and Julius Gollman, made up the art colony, along with teachers of drawing and painting in private schools and in studios. George Willey was lecturing on the fine arts, and traveling exhibitions came to Cleveland occasionally. An appreciation of art, however, was scarcely evident in the fifties.

Meetings were taking on convention proportions, as railroads began to weave their networks. Public halls were moving eastward from Water Street and St. Clair, and hotels and halls were expanding to accommodate greater crowds. The enlarged Weddell House, managed by a New York concern with an air foreign to the unpolished, untutored Western Reserve, was announcing in French its dining-room bill of fare.

With the appearance of *Harper's New Monthly Magazine, Knickerbocker's Magazine,* the *Atlantic Monthly,* the *North American Review,* and the *Century,* readers could enjoy contributions of the best authors of the day, and enrich their little worlds that had not yet begun to widen through transportation improvement. Bookstores were advertising titles related to the occult, travel, and ancient times, as well as works of foreign and American authors—Washington Irving, Grace Greenwood, Ralph Waldo Emerson, Bayard Taylor, Thoreau, Scott, Dickens, and the poets, Longfellow, Bryant, and Whittier. Polite and philosophical literature was growing in popularity.

Cleveland's general awakening was reflected in a variety of sports, some of which expanded into inter-city competitions. Horse racing had been popular since the early days; now the annual meets were attracting large crowds of fans. Yachtsmen began to organize. The St. George Cricket Club was playing teams in large cities. A fishing smack was kept busy catering to parties. The coming of the gymnasium gave rise to boxing, track, and athletic events. Billiard matches were being arranged, and a chess club was competing with distant opponents by telegraph. Pigeon shooting and a rifle-and-pistol gallery attracted the best marksmen. Skating, sleighing, and curling matches led the winter events. Sports flourished until the beginning of the Civil War.

Ferment between North and South was manifested in increased traffic of escaping slaves over the "Underground Railroad" north of the Mason-and-Dixon line. Origin of the "railroad" is obscure, but it is known to have appeared first in the late 1820s. As feeling heightened against slavery, and the cotton gin made cotton-growing more profitable, traffic of fugitives by secret passage grew. Ohio had many lines connecting the Ohio River with Lake Erie. Barns, sheds, and farmhouses of friendly Abolitionists and free Negroes constituted the stations on the hit-or-miss railway. "Conductors" smuggled escaped slaves from station to station, usually at night. Defying the stringent Fugitive-Slave Act, they held to their ideals at any cost. Salmon P. Chase of Cincinnati and Edward Wade championed the Negro's rights in Cleveland. David Hudson, pioneer of the Hudson community, was famous as a stationmaster. Owen Brown, father of John Brown, fiery foe of slavery, lived near Hudson Village. Oberlin—seat of the famous Oberlin-Wellington rescue, Vermilion, Lorain, Sandusky, Painesville, and Ashtabula were gateways to safety.

Cleveland citizens silently provided havens for frantic fugitives in their homes, and many decades later basements and secret passages in fine old residences still bore the mark of confinement in slavery days. Trembling slaves climbed the long, steep ascent to the belfry of St. John's Episcopal Church on the West Side, where they found refuge until signal flashes roused them to embark on the final lap of their journey to Canada and freedom. The city was the stamping ground for professional slave hunters. An arrangement provided for the ringing of the Stone Church bell when one of them was seen in the city, and a five-dollar reward was offered by an ardent Abolitionist to the first person making use of the alarm. That the underground movement reached major proportions is indicated by the claim that a single free Negro stationmaster helped more than a thousand runaways to freedom.

On the basis of affiliations with twenty-one congregations, about three thousand people made up the church population, as reported by the city directory of 1850. Once a strict and exacting New England community, Cleveland had undergone a profound change in its religious aspects. Denominational influence had increased with the population. From Europe had come Irish, German, and English-speaking Catholics in such numbers that Bishop Amadeus Rappe sought ministerial, educational, and charitable aid for their welfare.

Strife between Presbyterians and Congregationalists increased as anti-slavery agitation heightened. As lines became more closely defined and members were called upon to take their stand on the question, some bravely withdrew from the stern Presbytery and founded new churches on free, Congregational principles, resulting in two strong denominations.

Until 1852, churches and lodges seem to have carried on charitable efforts quietly, leaving little trace of their efforts. The railroad era, however, aroused the public to a need for organized facilities to help the homeless, the needy, and the infirm. It also brought organized hospital service and medical and dental societies, prompting the city to build a new Infirmary and manifest an interest in public health.

Young men who clerked in Cleveland stores had little time for reading and religious uplift. They worked from early morning until late evening, yet they were stirred by Lucius F. Mellen's reports of the new Young Men's Christian Association movement that had started in London in 1844, and was taking root in the United States. In their weekly prayer meeting they planned for a "Y" of their own, and the enthusiastic effort of forty members became the leaven that enriched the character and development of the city.

Bank Street—the Wall Street of Cleveland—was the center of finance, and in its growth and importance was reflected the expansion of commerce and industry. Inflation had gone hand-in-hand with careless promises and the spending spree on railroads and public improvements in the fifties. A day of reckoning came in 1857 when a large Cincinnati banking house experienced temporary panic, and failures elsewhere brought suffering and loss to the nation. A week after panic struck, the *Leader,* reporting for Cleveland, stated, "the feeling is now quite calm, comparatively . . . and things are rapidly resuming their accustomed channels." Cleveland banks came through safely. The Board of Trade, reviewing the effect on business, wrote, "We believe not one manufactory closed its doors for want of work, a few were run to their full capacity." The panic left its mark on employment, however, for in most cases "the number of employees were reduced from 25 to 50 per cent." Railroads and public-improvement projects were threatened with total loss, and, saddled with debt, it was with great difficulty that they withstood the period of business stagnation. Four independent banks, including the City Bank (later The National City Bank of Cleveland) and the Society for Savings, two state branch banks, and fourteen private banking houses were listed in the city directory of 1858.

With rich iron deposits to the north, vast coal fields to the south, untapped reserves of petroleum to the east, limestone along the lakeshore, capital, labor, management, improved transportation, and ready markets, Cleveland's future as a mighty industrial empire had been established by men whose names would ever be associated with the city's progress, among them Mather, Otis, Chisholm, Wade, and Hanna. Foundations of great fortunes had been laid that would benefit the city in many directions.

While Cincinnati reigned as the cultural and commercial queen of the West, the new era of iron ore and railroads had dawned in Cleveland. The prophetic words of the *Plain Dealer* editor in 1849 were on the way to fulfillment: "it will not be long before the flats over the Cuyahoga will be a Manchester, vying with the Iron City in the furnace blowers and dust."

1850

The demand for gas lighting exceeded the supply, as it was introduced into public buildings. When St. Paul's Church was lighted with gas, it was suggested that "all places of worship ought to be." The American House

The Herald *Building, erected in 1851, on Bank Street was the first stone-front business block in the city. The* Plain Dealer *occupied it from 1885 to 1889.*

put up warning signs, "Please do not blow out the gas!!" Street lamps operated on a "moonlight schedule," and, as late as 1861, lamps were put out at midnight. Not until 1867 did the People's Gas Light Company bring the utility to the West Side.

The Family Visitor, a weekly that appeared on January 3, was an ambitious family paper owned and edited by Drs. Jared P. Kirtland and Samuel St. John. For eight years it sought to "instruct the mind and improve the heart," bringing to the home non-partisan articles written by able authors, such as Louis Agassiz, ranging from science to the Legislature.

The *Herald* extolled the benefits of gas lighting, railroads, and plank roads on January 18. Fifty lamps were already scattered along Superior and River streets. The editor had ridden the entire ten-mile strip of railroad that was pushing toward Columbus. "Something new under heaven for Cleveland," he declared. Cleveland was a great town, concluded the newspaperman, as he lamented that she needed paved sidewalks, a pound, a seamen's home, and a house of correction.

On March 7, the Legislature authorized the City Council to establish a Board of Health with power to abate nuisances and "take such prompt and efficacious measures . . . as may be necessary" to combat infectious disease.

Construction of the new Cleveland, Columbus & Cincinnati railroad absorbed the Cleveland community, and on March 16 the City Council enjoyed an excursion over the first fifteen-mile stretch. Behind the proud little *Cleveland* locomotive, its high, expanded stack belching billows of smoke, they bounded adventurously over that distance in the remarkable time of twenty-seven minutes. Civic pride ran high, and, as a humorist observed, the locomotive was the only motive that could induce a man to leave Cleveland.

The ten-acre lots of Cleveland Township and all the unsurveyed strip along the river north and south of Kingsbury Run—nearly twice the area of the original city—was annexed on March 22. Willson Avenue, named for Hiram V. Willson, prominent lawyer, became the eastern boundary line.

The *Herald* was now a four-page daily, seven columns wide, with twenty-two columns devoted to advertisements and six to reading matter. Early in the year, A. W. Fairbanks of Toledo took an interest in the business which included printing, bookbinding, and publishing the paper. In 1857 Josiah A. Harris retired after twenty years of devoted community service. Fairbanks purchased the Benedict interest in the influential paper in 1872. Five years later, Richard C. Parsons and William F. Fogg acquired the business and organized The Herald Publishing Company. This was a short-lived venture; and, as the stock scattered, the paper deteriorated. Parsons went back to his law practice in 1880.

At a union revival meeting in the Stone Church, conducted by the Rev. Edwin H. Nevin, reformer and pronounced Abolitionist, Benajah Barker was converted. Stirred by reports that the pastor of a leading church had hid behind a column while a fugitive slave was arrested and carried to bondage, several friends joined Barker and set out to found a new church with Nevin as pastor. On March 25, this year, thirty members formed the Free Presbyterian Church—"free" of the sin of slavery—which became the Third Presbyterian Church. There were sixty-nine members in 1852 when it united with the Congregationalists and adopted the name Plymouth Church, at the suggestion of Henry Ward Beecher. An early principle opposed slaveholding as a sin and crime, declaring "this church will not fellowship slave-holders, the abettors of slavery or slave-holding churches." The round Tabernacle on Wood Street, vacated by the Millerites, was the church home until 1853, when the city's finest brick edifice, costing $20,000, was erected at the northwest corner of Euclid and Erie streets. Barker, H. B. Spelman—father of Mrs. John D. Rockefeller, and a few members who headed the building committee were unable to raise money to pay for the property, and it was sold to the First Baptist Society. The congregation rented the Wesleyan Methodist chapel until 1857, when a small church was erected on Prospect Street near Erie that served for nearly twenty years. The Rev. James C. White, second pastor, 1855-61, was a powerful and persuasive orator, and large accessions were made to the church. He was succeeded by the Rev. Samuel Wolcott, a preacher of national reputation.

Charles Whittlesey had gained wide renown as a geologist and archeologist, and his surveys of the Indian Mounds of Ohio were published by the Smithsonian Institution this year. Many of his articles on the mineral resources of the Lake Superior area had already appeared prominently. From 1847 to 1851 he was employed by the United States Government in surveying the upper peninsula of Michigan to locate mines and minerals. His vast knowledge and experience served as a great contribution to the coming industrial era.

The first stock yards took form about this time, when the Cleveland, Columbus & Cincinnati Railroad Company brought about the building of a few stock pens on Scranton Avenue (opposite Fairfield). Slaughter houses were built around the pens as well as along the river and on Walworth Run. By 1870, the Scranton yards consisted of ten open pens with a capacity of about forty cars of livestock.

The Western Reserve Eclectic Institute (later Hiram College) opened at Hiram, Ohio, this year. Built on one of the highest points in the Western Reserve, it was a cultural center of the Disciples of Christ. James A. Garfield was a student, and later principal.

Professional men were likely to be highly versatile, as evidenced by an April 14 announcement: "J. J. Walker has opened an office. . . . He practices surgery, dentistry, shaving and hairdressing, and also manufactures tooth powder and tooth tincture."

Principal Joseph B. Meriam, the trustees of Shaw Academy in Euclid Township, and "Aunt" Shaw strained every effort to provide a new building that would fulfill the terms of John Shaw's will. When housewarming day came on May 1, neighboring communities poured in to celebrate and support the fair and ice-cream festival that would help to defray the $2,800 required to pay for the new two-story, brick schoolhouse. "Aunt" Shaw, feeble and old, was carried in her rocking chair to witness the laying of the cornerstone, and tears of joy trickled down the tired face under the little lace cap as she realized that young Meriam in his enthusiasm had restored the Shaw name to a place of honor. On January 9, the next year, she died. When Meriam had built the enrollment to a hundred, he asked for a dormitory and was refused. The trustees reconsidered, but the young man had resigned to join the City Bank of Cleveland as cashier. Later he became a partner in Meriam & Morgan, makers of paraffin and one of the early oil refineries. A succession of principals followed at the academy. In 1875 the school assumed high-school rank. In 1883 the East Cleveland Board of Education leased the ground and buildings, and Shaw High School was on the way to becoming one of the finest schools of its kind in the country. The story of Shaw Academy is the story of a typical Western Reserve community, struggling heroically to achieve noble purposes for the common good.

This year witnessed practical progress in the public schools. According to the annual report for 1849-50, principals' salaries in senior schools were increased to $500 per year, and the high-school principal received $575. Operating cost for the year was $6,736.18. The Champlain Street School, a new, two-story, brick building at Champlain and Seneca streets, would be finished in the fall, and in it the wandering Bethel School would be established. A three-story building on the old Academy lot, to be finished in time for the fall term, was to be known as the West St. Clair Street School. During the year, a third story was added to Rockwell School. Teachers and pupils took great pride in the new piano they had purchased, the first piano procured for a public school. Friends donated pictures for the rooms and about four hundred books with which to start a school library at Rockwell. Fire damaged the school, and it was rebuilt in 1868. "Cleveland school buildings," a visitor observed, "are the best west of the Hudson River."

Libraries were springing into existence in Cleveland; but the chief collection consisted of about three thousand volumes that had been accumulated in a score of churches. The Cleveland Library Association collection exceeded two thousand volumes. Seamen found welcome relaxation in the Bethel Reading Room, open two evenings a week. A red signal light indicated that the library was open.

The Second Constitutional Convention met at Columbus on May 6, and Sherlock J. Andrews and Reuben Hitchcock represented Cuyahoga County. After four and a half months of earnest effort, a new instrument was submitted to the people and ratified. Ohio had learned a costly lesson. The prevailing policy of public improvements and special legislation was prohibited under the new Constitution of 1851, and only limited expenditures were permitted to maintain the state public works. Full manhood suffrage was granted to free whites, excepting idiots, insane persons, and those convicted "of an infamous crime."

During the Constitutional Convention, Dr. Norton S. Townsend, delegate from Lorain County, delivered an eloquent appeal supporting a motion to strike out the word "male" from the revised instrument. He asserted that woman was man's equal in intelligence and virtue, and therefore as well qualified as man to share in the responsibilities of government. Only seven votes joined him, but the seed had been sown that would bear fruit seventy years later.

Reuben Wood, Cleveland Democrat, was elected governor of Ohio at a salary of $1,200 per year. When his term was interrupted by the new constitution, he was re-elected by more than twice his former majority. Since 1825, when he was elected to the State Senate, Wood's stature as a political figure had grown. After serving three terms as presiding judge of the third judicial district, he was elevated to the Ohio Supreme Court in 1833, from which he resigned in 1845, having been chief justice the last three years.

Slavery had become a political rather than a moral issue, as Abolitionists gained ground enabling them to present their candidates at the elections. When Joshua R. Giddings of Jefferson, Ohio, advocate of free speech, opposed Irad Kelley of Cleveland and gained a seat in Congress on a Free-

Soil ticket in this year, there was no doubt as to the organized strength of the movement.

Champions of antislavery in Cleveland were incensed when the Fugitive-Slave Act was passed this year, providing for the return of escaped slaves to their masters. Indignation meetings were held. Leading citizens, among them Elisha Taylor, Reuben Hitchcock, Dr. Samuel C. Aiken, Samuel Williamson, John S. Newberry, George Mygatt, Judge Daniel R. Tilden, and Franklin T. Backus, denounced this legislation that extended and perpetuated human bondage. They doubled their efforts in supporting the Underground Railroad, and offered oratory and money in the bitter struggle against the vicious Kansas-Nebraska Bill.

Dissension in the Anshe Chesed Congregation resulted in formation of the Tifereth Israel Congregation (later the Temple, East 105th Street and Ansel Road) on May 26, with forty-seven charter members headed by Alexander Schwab, president. Worship was conducted in the homes of members in the early days, and Isadore Kalisch was the first rabbi. A generous contribution of Judah Touro, Jewish philanthropist, provided funds for the purchase of a lot on Huron Street, where a new Temple was dedicated in 1855.

Mrs. Thirsa Pelton cherished the idea of founding a girls' school, and purchased about seventy acres this year as a site for Pelton Park (West 14th Street). Upon her death in 1853, the grounds were fenced and locked. The people declared that the property was meant for public use, and the fence was repeatedly torn down. Bitter litigation followed in the courts, and on November 17, 1879, the city purchased the tract for $50,000, by deed from John G. Jennings. Citizens were proud of their new landscaped park, but it soon deteriorated; when it was restored in 1896, it bore a new name, Lincoln Square, later Lincoln Park.

A plat of Newburgh Village, made this year by Ahaz Merchant, county surveyor, reserved space for a park or public square. This commons was given by Theodore Miles, pioneer, and named Miles Park in his honor by ordinance of June 11, 1877.

A spectacular fire destroyed the sidewheeler *Griffith* twenty miles east of Cleveland in the early morning of June 17. Of the three hundred and twenty-six persons aboard when the boat left Buffalo, almost three hundred lost their lives. Safer construction and more rigid inspection of steam vessels resulted from the disaster.

The Cleveland Ladies Temperance Union was organized on June 27 by leading women of Cleveland. Mrs. Benjamin F. Rouse, Mrs. Josiah A. Harris, and Mrs. J. Lyman were the first directors; and Mrs. Joel Scranton, Mrs. Elisha Taylor, Mrs. Samuel Williamson, and Mrs. Samuel C. Aiken were prominent workers. More than fourteen hundred members had signed the pledge by 1853.

Thirty-seven miles of the Cleveland, Columbus & Cincinnati railroad had been completed southward as far as Wellington. On July 1 the first train left for Cleveland at 6 A.M., arriving at "8 o'clock, 30 minutes." A cheering crowd was on hand when the little brass-trimmed locomotive puffed into the wooden depot on the Superior Street hill near the New England

Hotel. The wood-burning engine moved on a pair of six-foot drivers and four front wheels. It had no cow-catcher or headlight, but it made the most of its shrill whistle. Behind the engine was a box-like car piled with wood, followed by the water tender and three forty-foot passenger cars with quaint curtains, railed platforms, and hand brakes. Twenty miles per hour was the announced speed. Patrons could get a glimpse of Berea, Olmstead, Grafton, and LaGrange en route, and a carriage met the train in Wellington to show travelers the sights. On June 29 the *Plain Dealer* had published a schedule for the two trains on the road, the first local railroad advertisement to appear in a Cleveland paper. By November the road had crept as far as Shelby, and two trains were running on weekdays.

Hecker's Band, organized this year, was in great demand at public and private functions.

The Fourth of July celebration started at sunrise with a "baby waker," a volley fired by the Cleveland Light Artillery. By nine o'clock a grand procession was forming in the Public Square. Hotels were filled, and ladies in billowy dresses and beribboned bonnets began sauntering along the streets under dainty parasols. Lemonade stands thrived on the hot day.

Cleveland bowed its head with grief upon the death of President Zachary Taylor on July 9. Memorial services were held on the twelfth; business houses closed, and flags were lowered to half mast. Mayor William Case presided at a meeting in the Square, and Reuben Wood and William Johnson delivered orations. The speakers were candidates for the governorship, Wood a Democrat, and Johnson a Whig. In a solemn military parade, a hearse upon which rested a plumed chapeau and sheathed sword was drawn by white horses, followed by a riderless mount.

Cleveland's first brick building, erected by the Kelleys in 1814 on the south side of Superior, had served as a hotel in its later years. Irad Kelley began replacing it this year with the Kelley Block, another brick structure, with stores on the first floor. The upper floor was known as the celebrated Kelley's Hall, where Clevelanders enjoyed the finest concerts and lectures of the day and the most fashionable balls. In 1863, the building took the name of the theater housed in it, Athenaeum, and it served commercial purposes for many years.

The Cleveland Iron Mining Company was organized this year, after extensive mineralogical surveys by Dr. J. Lang Cassels, its charter dating from 1853. The founders were Samuel L. Mather, John Outhwaite, Morgan L. Hewitt, Selah Chamberlain, Isaac L. Hewitt, Henry F. Brayton, and E. M. Clark. William J. Gordon was the first president. In the early fifties iron ore was hauled laboriously by mule wagon from the Lake Superior mines to Marquette, loaded in sailing vessels bound for the Soo, carried around the falls in wagons, and reloaded in ships sailing to the lower lakes, bound for Ohio and Pennsylvania furnaces. Transportation was a major problem until the Soo Canal opened in 1855, when a continuous voyage was made possible. As industry developed, the company constructed virtually everything it needed in the upper-Michigan wilderness. Timber was required for underground mine posts, and the acquisition of vast timber lands began. Railroad facilities were needed to carry ore from mine to dock, and the road later known as the Lake Superior & Ishpeming line was constructed. In 1867 the company (later The Cleveland-Cliffs Iron Company) purchased a half interest in a small freight vessel, marking the beginning of a lake fleet that numbered twenty-two freighters in the middle of the 1940s.

Annual trotting and pacing races were inaugurated with a five-day event held by the Cleveland Jockey Club at the Forest City course, a track that connected with the county fair grounds on Ohio Street (between East 9th and East 14th). The entrance fee was $5, and purses ranged from $40 to $75.

Land at the southeast corner of Ontario Street and the Public Square (Park Building site) was offered to R. H. Lodge for $1,100. In 1865, however, Joseph Tamblyn purchased the property from Horace P. Weddell for $12,000; in 1904, The Park Investment Company leased it from Tamblyn's heirs for thirty-five years at an annual rental of $17,000.

Spiritualistic meetings were being held in Henry Bingham's saloon in the basement of the American House, one of the leading bars in town. According to the *Daily True Democrat,* "many of our citizens heard and witnessed strange communications under circumstances which must have removed all doubts from the mind of the most skeptical as to the existence of any collusion between the operator and the spirit." The hotel attracted all kinds of patronage. Sleighing parties from near-by towns came to Cleveland to dine and dance at the American. Military companies, a chess club, fraternal organizations, printers, conventions, and civic groups made it their head-quarters. It also attracted its share of oddities, such as a guest who hired two men and a dray to remove his luggage, which consisted of a hat box, and who was committed on a lunacy charge; and Henderson, the barber, whose advertisement, bearing attesting signatures of customers, claimed that "he made new hair grow on their bald heads."

Bishop Amadeus Rappe invited the Ursuline Sisters of France to establish a select academy for girls in Cleveland. The Judge Samuel Cowles home on Euclid Street (Taylor's store site) was purchased, and classes opened in September. A charter was granted to the Ursuline College for women in 1871. The convent was moved to the west side of Scovill Avenue at Willson in 1893, and it remained the Mother House after the college was established on Overlook Road in the late 1920s.

Culture reached new heights with the founding of Cleveland University. Classes opened in the fall in the Mechanics Block, while construction was going ahead on the first building in University Heights (later Lincoln Heights) on the south side of the river opposite Ontario Street. Ultimately the undertaking was to be "a combined literary and charitable institution," including "a Male and Female Seminary, an Orphan Asylum, and a Retreat for aged persons," conducted on the self-supporting manual-labor plan of liberal education. The Rev. Asa Mahan left the presidency of Oberlin College to head the new university, and William Slade, later governor of Vermont, was secretary-treasurer. A class of three students, who had attended Oberlin, was graduated at the end of the first term, August 31, 1851.

The financial structure of the university was as weak as the planning was comprehensive. Despite leadership of prominent men, including Brewster Pelton of Oberlin, Harmon Kingsbury, William Case, Truman P. Handy, George Mygatt, Ahaz Merchant, Richard Hilliard, Samuel Starkweather, and James M. Hoyt, the school was dissolved after a few years. College Avenue, Literary Road, University Road, Professor Street, and Jefferson Avenue remain as reminders of a brilliant effort that was a generation ahead of its time.

In October, a school census showed that there were 4,773 persons in Cleveland between the ages of four and twenty-one. Enrollment in the public schools was 2,081, with an average daily attendance of 1,440. Twenty-five teachers were employed. In Cuyahoga County, according to the federal census, 11,601 children were attending school, 1,547 of them foreign-born.

The first winter session of the Western College of Homeopathic Medicine opened on November 4 in the Mechanics Block. An able faculty included prominent disciples of homeopathy: Drs. Edwin C. Wetherell, Charles D. Williams, Lewis Dodge, Hamilton H. Smith, Jehu Brainard, Storm Rosa, and Arthur E. Bissell. Twelve students were in the first graduating class in 1851. The institution was badly damaged in 1852 by a mob incited by stories of stolen bodies traced to the college dissecting room. At the close of the year, work was resumed in the Belvidere Building on Ohio Street near the Haymarket. Dr. Asa Mahan was elected president in March, 1853, and the name was changed to The Western Homeopathic College in 1857. Humiston Institute was purchased in 1868, and The Homeopathic Hospital College emerged in 1870, working closely with the Cleveland Protestant Hospital. Three years later, it moved into the church building formerly owned by the Congregationalists on Prospect west of Erie.

Council voted "one or more free evening schools" to "keep the youths out of mischief and teach them to improve their minds." At the same time, education was now within reach of young men and boys who were employed during the daytime. The academies were finding real competition in the public high school.

With organization of the Cleveland Mendelssohn Society in December, sacred music became a vital influence in the community. Truman P. Handy was the first president; J. L. Severance, vice president; and Jarvis F. Hanks, director of music. In 1853 membership had reached a hundred and twelve, and it seems to have been confined to pioneer stock, as it contained no Germans. An orchestra of twenty-five pieces supplemented the activity.

The canals had reached the peak of their prosperity, and their importance is reflected in the exchange of products between Cleveland and the interior during the year. Received: Coal, 2,347,844 bushels; pig iron and scrap, 7,003,438 pounds; iron and cast iron, 6,508,333 pounds; nails and spikes, 4,343,220 pounds; flour, 367,737 barrels; wheat, 1,192,559 bushels; bacon and pork, 2,284,116 pounds; wool, 2,038,195 pounds; pottersware, 1,787,814 pounds; butter, 1,339,731 pounds; lard, 1,281,368 pounds; corn, 831,704 bushels; whisky, 24,580 barrels; sundries, 6,018,366 pounds; merchandise, 1,268,444 pounds. Furniture, lumber and building materials, machinery, farm and dairy products, pot and pearl ashes, fruit, furs, hides and leather, and barrel staves and headings were also received in large quantities. Shipped: Iron and cast iron, 15,070,354 pounds; pig iron and scrap, 1,314,984 pounds; gypsum, 3,275,562 pounds; marble, 1,698,858 pounds; coffee, 1,004,411 pounds; salt, 61,468 barrels; molasses, 842,719 pounds; sugar, 833,598 pounds; Ohio saleratus, 398,953 pounds; grindstones, 332,510 pounds; pot and pearl ashes, 313,393 pounds; lumber, 7,960,018 feet; split and flat hoops, 1,947,548; shingles, 4,446,000; merchandise, 9,711,472 pounds; sundries, 7,723,591 pounds. Dairy and farm products, crockery, furniture, machinery, tobacco, hides, and leather were shipped in large amounts. Canal tolls collected at Cleveland for the year were $90,874.20. Passenger traffic totaled 10,949.

1851

Young men were holding informal prayer meetings in a law office in the Kelley Block, and, after a time, they broadened their interest to include work among the poor. Horace Benton, Dan P. Eells, Joseph B. Meriam, Solon L. Severance, E. F. Young, Lucius F. Mellen, Loren Prentiss, L. M. H. Battey, S. P. Churchill, William Gribben, and E. P. Cook were early participants. This unorganized effort fathered the Young Men's Christian Association.

"Feminists" were adding to the unrest of the period by constantly making themselves heard on the subject of equal voting rights. Their agitation, inspired by the first Woman's Rights Convention at Seneca Falls, New York, July 19, 1848, prompted a humorous editorial in the *Plain Dealer* on February 11, this year:

> Imagine a Whig husband and a Democratic wife, a free soil uncle and a hunker aunt, a liberty party cousin, a colonization nephew, a slave-holding niece and three blooming daughters who have gone over bodice and bustle to the terrified democracy and for the first time in their lives will vote in pink muslin at the next election! Imagine this group gathered around the same table, tea and muffins, graced by Mr. Garrison (William Lloyd Garrison) and Abby (Abby Kelley Foster) looking in at the window! How long would a well-built house probably stand, thus divided against itself?

The bloomer costume, introduced by fearless Mrs. Amelia Jenks Bloomer at the Woman's Rights Convention in 1848, had begun to invade Cleveland, adding to the feminine upheaval. The baggy knee trousers, representing a revolt against the hoopskirt that had been brought back into fashion, and a demand for equal rights brought down pious exhortations from the Good Book by the scornful, who declared that "woman shall not wear that which pertaineth unto a man." Most housewives gathered their voluminous, trailing skirts a little closer and went back to their knitting.

At midnight on February 18, Alfred Kelley and Mayor William Case drove the last spikes in the Cleveland, Columbus & Cincinnati railroad (later Big Four, New York Central System) at Iberia, Ohio, completing the northern half of the through railway from the lake to the Ohio River. The southern portion, from Columbus to Cincinnati, had been operating for some time.

February 21 was a day long to be remembered. At eight in the morning, a delegation of 428 citizens, officials, and dignitaries from Cincinnati and Columbus left the capital on the new Cleveland-to-Cincinnati railroad bound for Cleveland to attend a celebration of the completion of the line. Throngs gathered along the route to cheer the pioneer train as it bounded on the rough, unballasted tracks. It was drawn by a handsome, polished locomotive with flags flying and the name *Cleveland* painted in bold letters on the tender. In the evening, the engine steamed into the wooden depot on the Superior Street hill, where crowds let loose a noisy welcome in honor of "Our Railroad."

Gunfire announced Washington's Birthday and a great holiday celebrating the new railroad. City firemen led a colorful parade that ended in a public meeting at the Square, where Mayor William Case welcomed the procession from the Court House steps. C. C. Converse, president of the Ohio Senate, delivered an address, followed by Samuel Starkweather's oration and short speeches by Governor Reuben Wood, Alfred Kelley, Henry B. Payne, George E. Pugh of Cincinnati, and others. Dignitaries then returned to the depot and made a trial run to Hudson on the new Cleveland & Pittsburgh Railroad line. There was great embarrassment when food supplies ran out and some of the company were obliged to go hungry. On the return trip, the train left the tracks, and the party was late for the evening banquet at the Weddell House. A torchlight parade closed the day's events. A local editor reported that the Buckeyes from the rich valleys of the Ohio, Miami, and Scioto mingled their "congratulations with those of the Yankee Reserve upon the completion of an improvement . . . accomplishing a good work for Ohio, the value of which no figures could compute." Amasa Stone, superintendent of the Cleveland-to-Cincinnati road at a salary of four thousand dollars a year, became a director the next year and began his climb to wealth and power.

When the Cleveland-to-Hudson section of the Cleveland & Pittsburgh Railroad (later Pennsylvania) opened on February 22, John G. Stockley lost his fight to preserve the lakefront for parks and docks. "You're letting the railroad ruin the most beautiful thing we have," he protested. But the tracks remained, henceforth to complicate lakefront problems. By November the road reached Hanover (Kensington) via Ravenna; and on March 4, 1852, it was completed to Wellsville, where connections were established with Pittsburgh and the East. Rich coal and fire-clay deposits in southern Ohio were then opened.

"Churches were crowded with listeners from abroad" on Sunday morning, February 23. Governor Reuben Wood, his staff and many notables attended services at the Stone Church and listened to Dr. Samuel C. Aiken's historic sermon on the far-reaching influence of public improvements, later published by railroad officials. The text was taken from Nahum 2:4; and with vision, the good clergyman predicted that the new mode of transportation would play a great part in helping to wipe out barriers between North and South. "The railroad will be a leveller," he declared, "bringing the lowly nearer to the plane of the rich through increased means of travel. One benefit will be its auxiliary assistance to the cause of temperance, employes having to be total abstainers, if they are to be trustworthy and efficient." To those who feared that the railroad would wipe out Sabbath observance, Dr. Aiken responded: "Experience is gradually deciding in favor of remembering the Sabbath day to keep it holy. . . . Wherever the voice of the community favors it, Directors are not backward to let their men and enginery remain quiet on this day, for it is found that nothing is gained and much lost by running." On Monday morning, visitors and a Cleveland delegation left for a celebration at Columbus, eight hours and forty-five minutes to the south.

Superior Street had been paved with stone and plank and coated with sand in 1850, and it was the object of visitors' admiration during the railroad celebration. Assessments determined by the City Council, however, resulted in litigation carried to the Supreme Court, where they were upheld. By 1860 the pavement was "irreparably dilapidated" and was replenished.

The first gymnasium opened on May 2 on the top floor of the building occupied by Handerson, Punderson & Company's drug store on Superior (east of the Wilshire Building). Ladders, bars, swinging apparatus, and appliances were provided.

Construction of a new brick passenger depot was completed by the Cleveland, Columbus & Cincinnati Railroad on May 29 at the foot of Bath Street. It served as a union station for the railroads until the mid-sixties. The Cleveland-to-Cincinnati railroad carried 31,679½ fares during March, April, and May, producing revenue of $56,625.21; freight returns were $25,929.85.

Real-estate values were reviewed in a public statement on May 29:

> Lands one mile east from the court house and even to the city limits are now selling at $16 per foot, ordinary depths from main streets. On Superior street west of the square $300 per foot is freely paid. Lots on Water street range from $100 to $200 per foot its entire length; Bank street from $50 to $100. Water front lots on River street vary from $75 to $250 per foot as you approach the mouth of the river. . . . At present prices, say an average of $50 per foot, the whole city of Cleveland, as now extended, would require the entire gold receipts from California for a year at least to purchase the plat.

The new Arcade Building—the first of that name—at Superior and Vine-yard streets was purchased by J. W. Gray and its name changed to the *Plain Dealer* Building. This was the home of the paper until 1869, when it moved to Bank Street, and five years later to the Drum Block at Seneca Street and Frankfort.

The annual school report showed expansion of public-school facilities, an increase in night-school classes, new school libraries, the raising of high-school-teachers' salaries to $550 yearly, and that of the principal to $650. The teaching of American history was begun, and "professional teachers" were employed to instruct in music and drawing. The three-year high-school course included trigonometry, astronomy, mental philosophy, bookkeeping, general history, surveying, botany, elements of criticism, and logic in the third year.

The Forest City Lyceum was organized, with Albert T. Slade, president, and O. J. Hodge, librarian. It was an outgrowth of the Cleveland Lyceum, and flourished until the Civil War sapped its strength.

The Sisters of Charity had come from France this year in answer to Bishop Rappe's call for aid to minister to the sick and poor of the Cleveland Diocese. Land was purchased at Monroe and Willett streets for St. Vincent's Orphanage, and a fair provided a building fund. The asylum opened in May, 1853, to eleven children. Crowded conditions demanded enlarged facilities from time to time for the charitable institution that became known as Parmadale.

The first stone-front commercial building was erected on Bank Street by the *Herald*. It was a four-story building of brick and sandstone quarried nine miles from the city on the canal. The Post Office was located on the first floor.

Seneca O. Griswold, a student in the law office of Thomas Bolton and Moses Kelley, was admitted to the partnership, which became Bolton, Kelley & Griswold this year. Bolton had served as councilman and prosecuting attorney in the late thirties, and as alderman in 1841. He left the Democratic Party in 1848, joined the Free Soilers, and went over to the Republicans as an organizer of the party. He was elected judge of the Court of Common Pleas in 1856, serving for a decade, when he retired from active life. Kelley had been a member of the City Council and the State Senate in the forties; and, in 1849, he was selected by the Legislature to represent the city's interests in the Cleveland & Pittsburgh Railroad Company, of which he was a director. Bolton and Kelley purchased about seventy acres of the "Gidding Farm" on Euclid Street (at East 71st) at about the mid-century. Here they built identical homes in which they spent their later years. Bolton died in 1870, aged sixty-two, and the next year Kelley passed on at the age of sixty-one.

After a western tour, a Philadelphia businessman wrote this interesting criticism of Great Lakes ports in July:

> All our lake towns show promise and are now growing very fast. Some of them will overtake the largest river towns within the lives of many now living. Among the most prosperous are Cleveland, Sandusky, Toledo, Detroit, and Chicago. All afford good society. There is less form and etiquette than in the eastern towns, but I think there is more intelligence and not less real refinement. In the appearance of all there is a want of finish, as compared with older towns on the Atlantic.

A horse-drawn coach began on July 18, carrying passengers hourly from the Dunham House to Ohio City and back for a ten-cent fare.

Cleveland printers welcomed the opening of the first engraving plant on July 21. Long delays in receiving copper and steel engravings from the East had been a great handicap in getting out the news.

The first sewing machine was exhibited at the Weddell House in August. Elias Howe had invented the device in 1846, and it was soon revolutionizing the boot-and-shoe and clothing industries, despite charges that it would create unemployment. The machine turned with a crank, and sewed two hundred and fifty lock stitches a minute.

Delegates to the meeting of the American Association for the Advancement of Education came to Cleveland by stage, canal, and lake. The four-day session opened on August 19 in the First Presbyterian Church with William Case, chairman. Most of the hundred and fifty educators found lodging in private homes. The Rev. Asa Mahan, president of Cleveland University, was a prominent figure. Dominating the program was the school's system of education, which had abandoned collegiate compulsory fundamentals, and emphasized physical, mental, and moral training as essential to the development of a useful life. There was a lively debate over higher education for women.

A small house on St. Clair Street near Bond offered temporary asylum for girls of St. Mary's Orphanage, established this year by Bishop Rappe. The Ladies of the Sacred Heart of Mary, of the Sisterhood in France, were entrusted with the work, which was the first charitable undertaking of this kind established by the order in the United States. An inheritance of one of the sisters, with help from France, made possible the purchase of land for a new building on Harmon Street in 1853.

A quarter admitted the curious to see Barnum's great six-thousand-dollar exhibition of "Chinese fires, the hydro-oxygen microscope and the dissolving views," prepared in Paris and showing at the Melodeon in September.

Tallmadge coal, brought to Cleveland by canal boat, sold for two and a half dollars a ton.

After a month's preparation, Ira J. Thurston staged the first public aerial exhibition in Cleveland on October 6 when he rose from the ground at the foot of Erie Street in the balloon *Jupiter*, ending his flight in a treetop in the East Cleveland woods. Upon totaling the twenty-five-cent admissions collected from "an immense multitude," he bemoaned his loss suffered from crowds who saw the show "for free" outside the fence.

Nine Common Pleas districts were defined under the new Ohio Constitution, and Cuyahoga County made up the third subdivision of the fourth district. On October 14, Samuel Starkweather and Harvey Foote were elected judges of the court by the people; and although the Legislature increased the number to keep pace with a top-heavy docket, there were never enough officials to keep the slate clean. Thomas Bolton, James M. Coffinberry, Samuel B. Prentiss, Robert F. Paine, and Jesse P. Bishop, partner with Franklin T. Backus, early judges on the bench, were men of superior judgment. They characterized the high quality of personnel who served the people through the years.

The Probate Court was established under the new Constitution, with "jurisdiction of all probate and testamentary matters." Flavel W. Bingham was the first probate judge. He was succeeded in 1855 by Daniel R. Tilden, friend of widows and orphans. Tilden served continuously until his retirement in 1887. Henry C. White and Alexander Hadden were among those who gave conspicuous service in later years.

Clevelanders voted an emphatic "no" on October 14 to the proposed union of Cleveland and Ohio City, declaring that their neighbor would benefit from the larger city's advantages without assuming a reasonable share of the cost.

In a small room at the corner of Pearl and Turnpike streets in Ohio City, for which he paid fifty dollars a year rental, Horace Benton started his wholesale drug business. Nine years later, two brothers joined him under the name of Benton Brothers. Then followed expansion with new partners forming the firm of Benton, Meyers & Canfield. It was in 1875 that Lucien B. Hall entered the business; and in 1884, A. H. VanGorder joined him to develop Hall & VanGorder with a wide territory of sales. The Hall-VanGorder Company in 1928—its seventy-seventh year—became a division of McKesson-Robbins, Inc.

The *Plain Dealer* introduced a column of local news captioned "Spice," written by William Edward McLaren, who later left the newspaper field to join the ministry and became a bishop in the Protestant Episcopal Church. On the staff of the paper during the fifties were writers who went on to fame, among them David R. Locke, better known as Petroleum Vesuvius Nasby, author of the "Nasby Letters." Locke denounced slavery and advanced other causes through satiric propaganda in his *Toledo Blade* editorials. He later joined the *New York Evening Mail* as managing editor. J. B. Bouton of the *Plain Dealer* rose to city editor of the *Journal of Commerce* in New York. Alphonse M. Griswold became a prominent journalist, humorist, and lecturer. John H. Sargent and George M. Marshall of Cleveland made valuable contributions to the *Plain Dealer* columns through their letters written while abroad.

Musical history really began in Cleveland when Jenny Lind sang at Kelley's Hall on November 7. She had arrived at the Weddell House the night before with a troupe of fourteen people. Tickets sold quickly at from two to four dollars, and there was a fashionable capacity house. Her program included *John Anderson, My Jo,* the *Gipsy Song, Echo Song,* and her famous *Bird Song,* with which she calmed the audience when peeping spectators broke through the skylight. The Swedish Nightingale, called the greatest singer of her time, had been imported by P. T. Barnum and built into a sensational artist through ingenious publicity. Her brief but fabulous career in America closed the following May. Said Barnum, "She was a woman who would have been adored if she had had the voice of a crow."

Harvey Rice, lawyer, legislator, and keen businessman, was elected to the

State Senate this year, where he fathered the law that created free public schools in Ohio, supported by taxes rather than by voluntary subscription—schools "cheap enough for the poorest and good enough for the richest." Rice also introduced the reform-farm bill, providing for educational and moral training of delinquent boys. A wise leader, he gave liberally of his time to public welfare. His several volumes of history, biography, poems, and essays remain a valuable source of material relating to the Cleveland he knew. He died in 1891.

The Mercantile Library Association, organized on December 9 with James A. Briggs as president, originated in the Cleveland Library Association. Its membership of one hundred and fifty met in the Forest City Block on Superior Street. Through lecture courses, Clevelanders enjoyed the wisdom, eloquence, and charm of the greatest names appearing on the public platform.

A Sunday School, established in 1846 by the First Baptist Church at Eagle and Erie streets, was the nucleus of the Erie Street Baptist Church, organized in December this year by the Rev. J. Hyatt Smith with forty-three members. The meeting house on Rockwell Street was purchased from the Second Presbyterian Church and moved to the northeast corner of Erie and Ohio streets. To relieve the congregation of burdensome debt, twelve young men—John D. Rockefeller, who had joined the church in 1854, his brother, William, William and Stewart Chisholm, and others organized a society and saved the church (later Euclid Avenue Baptist Church).

As was their custom in the homeland at holiday time, Germans in the Zion Evangelical Lutheran Church set up a candle-lighted Christmas tree in their little sanctuary (Public Auditorium site). A "heathenish custom," complained hide-bound New Englanders, this "groveling before the shrubs." Not so long before, in 1847, a twenty-one-year-old German youth named August Ingard set up a Christmas tree, believed to be the first in America, in his home at Wooster, Ohio. Cleveland's tree was probably the first to appear in a church or in a ceremony. Gingerbread figures, popcorn strings, tinsel, and paper decorations were placed on the early trees with tender care.

1852

A new school building, costing $3,500, opened in January on Clinton Street, later called Brownell Street School (between Prospect and Central). It was soon overcrowded; and while the authorities debated the question, a high wind blew the roof off the building. A third story restored the roof and relieved the congestion. Children of prominent Euclid Street families received their grade-school education here.

Mrs. Benjamin Rouse and members of the early Dorcas Society took practical interest in the care of orphans, and played a large part in the founding of the Cleveland Orphan Asylum. The project was launched at a meeting in the Stone Church on January 22, its founders being John M.

Woolsey, first chairman of the board of trustees, Mrs. Sherlock J. Andrews, Mrs. Philo Scovill, Mrs. J. K. Miller, Mrs. Henry W. Clark, Mrs. Stillman Witt, Mrs. C. D. Williams, Mrs. Elisha Taylor, Mrs. George A. Benedict, Mrs. Josiah A. Harris, Mrs. Buckley Stedman, Mrs. Mary H. Severance, and Mrs. A. H. Barney. Benjamin Rouse was an early trustee. Mrs. Witt rented a house on Erie Street as a haven for unfortunate children, and, during the first year, eleven orphans received care. The asylum was incorporated in 1853, and Sherlock J. Andrews became president of the board. Mrs. Rouse was an active member of the board of managers. New and efficient methods, made possible by generous gifts and endowment, shaped a pattern for America. The asylum having outgrown its early quarters, Beech-Brook, a beautiful cottage community on suburban Lander Road, was provided in 1926 for the Cleveland Protestant Orphan Asylum, as it had become known.

John Downie came to America with his family to prospect for California gold; but his funds were exhausted when he reached Cleveland, and he found employment painting ships in Ohio City. He rented a store this year at Rockwell and Wood streets from Leonard Case for fifty dollars a year and opened a shop. Adding wallpaper to the stock, Downie & Son soon found themselves in demand as painters and decorators. The son, William, headed the business until succeeded by his son, William, who was a civic leader and a founder of Cleveland Rotary. The store moved to the Public Square, thence to Prospect; and when the firm incorporated in 1912 as William Downie Company, it was located at 9500 Edmunds Avenue. William Downie II was head of the family-owned business in the 1940s; associated with him was his son, William III. The company was the oldest painting firm in Ohio, operated continuously by the same family.

The visit of Louis Kossuth, brilliant orator and eminent Hungarian patriot, was an occasion of great moment. Upon the invitation of leading Clevelanders, he arrived January 31 and was escorted to the Weddell House by civic and military bodies. Two days later, he spoke from the balcony of the American House; and at Melodeon Hall, citizens paid three and four dollars to hear "the gallant knight," attired in a rich costume of his native land. About fifteen hundred dollars was contributed to the Hungarian-relief cause, and Hungarian aid societies were formed.

Reports that graves were being robbed to supply medical institutions with cadavers seemed to be substantiated when a portion of a body was found near the Western College of Homeopathic Medicine on February 17. A father, whose daughter's coffin had been found empty, identified the body. The news spread quickly and soon an angry mob filled the Public Square, crowded on Ontario Street to the college, and forced its way inside, spreading destruction from top to bottom. The pitiful police force was helpless, the fire hose failed to make a dent, and it took the militia to put down the riot. Long, wearisome trials of the accused disclosed that the body was that of a man, a fact that compensated not one whit for the great damage suffered by the college. This was one of the few recorded instances of mob violence in early Cleveland's history.

Members of the First Presbyterian Church of East Cleveland gathered for a crucial meeting, February 21, on the subject of a proposed change in church government, and their relation "to the sin of slavery" through connection with the General Assembly. Because the church severed its affiliation with the Presbytery, nine members dissented and two of them left the congregation, which, for the next decade, was known as the Independent Presbyterian Church. Its pastor, the Rev. C. W. Torrey, served through the critical period. In 1862, the identity became First Congregational Church of East Cleveland. Five years later, during the ministry of the Rev. Albert M. Richardson, a brick meeting house, with one hundred and twenty-four pews seating six hundred, the largest and one of the finest churches in the district, was dedicated at the southeast corner of Euclid and Logan streets on a lot given by W. S. Streator. The bell was removed from the old Doan's Corners building and hung in the new. In 1872, the name was changed to The Euclid Avenue Congregational Church of East Cleveland, and sex was eliminated from membership qualifications.

At about this time, Rufus P. Spalding retired from public life and came to Cleveland, where he engaged in law practice with Richard C. Parsons. The son of a wealthy Massachusetts doctor, Spalding was born in 1798 and educated at Yale College; he later studied law. He located in Warren, Ohio, in about 1821, later moving to Ravenna and Akron. An eloquent lawyer, he had served in the State Legislature and as judge of the Ohio Supreme Court in the forties. Spalding had been a Democrat until his party joined the advocates of slavery; he then went over to the Free Soilers, and later was an organizer of the Republican Party. He succeeded Albert G. Riddle in Congress in 1864; after re-election in 1864, he developed the Reconstruction Laws, outlining many of the important measures. Refusing a third-term nomination, he returned to Cleveland, where he was active in the social and cultural life of the city until his death in 1866.

Richard C. Parsons, law partner of Rufus P. Spalding, was born in Connecticut in 1826. Although having been admitted to the bar in 1851, he was elected to the Cleveland City Council this year, and within a few months was made president. A pioneer Republican, he served two terms in the Legislature, and was chosen speaker of the house. President Abraham Lincoln appointed him consul to Rio de Janeiro, and he later held the post of collector of internal revenue at Cleveland and was marshal of the United States Supreme Court, 1866-72. While a member of Congress, 1873-75, Parsons was instrumental in securing life-saving service for Cleveland, the lighthouse, and the launching of breakwater improvements. It is said that "his polished appearance and his patent-leather shoes" inspired defeat for re-election by the labor vote. After a brief venture in the newspaper business, he served as national-bank examiner, meanwhile continuing his law practice.

Hog owners scratched their heads when they read the marshal's notice on February 26 stating that "All persons owning hogs, are hereby notified, that the ordinance restraining the same from running at large within the city of Cleveland, will be enforced unless the same be restrained." Plainly speaking, the animals could no longer run hog-wild.

With his earnings as clerk and, later, as partner in a drug store, John Owen fulfilled the dream he had as a boy of nine, when he watched the fire-eating *Walk-in-the-Water* steam into Cleveland in 1818. He and his associates organized the Detroit & Cleveland Steamboat Line this year. They built the *Forest City,* chartered the *St. Louis* and *Sam Ward,* and took over the Detroit-Cleveland run, started two years earlier by Captain Arthur Edwards. The *May Queen* and the *City of Cleveland* were added the next year, and the business played a large part in the advance of both Cleveland and Detroit. It provided a water route from Detroit to Cleveland, and laid the foundation of one of the world's largest inland passenger and freight steamship lines. David Carter came into the firm, and in 1868 the Detroit & Cleveland Steam Navigation Company was formed. The steamers *Ocean, Morning Star,* and *R. N. Rice* were added to the fleet, the *Northwest* later replacing the *Morning Star* and the *Saginaw* taking the place of the *R. N. Rice.*

The famous Forest City House, formerly the Dunham House.

William A. Smith took over the Dunham House at the southwest corner of Superior and the Public Square on February 27. It was expanded by a four-story addition built by George P. Smith along the Square, with stores and a barber shop on the street floor. Railed porches extended above the entranceway, and an ornamental tower loomed above the high mansard roof, rising to the equivalent of six stories. This was the Forest City House, that took its name from the Forest City it served. It was one of the finest hotels in the West, the social, commercial, and historical center of the growing city. In the enlarged dining room, political clubs toasted their champions, and civic organizations furthered the city's advance. The building was later extended almost to Diebolt's Alley. Management changed a number of times, the dynasty of chin-whiskered William "Billy" Akers and S. T. Paine, beginning in 1888, standing out in the annals of Cleveland hotel history. Akers was a host out of fiction, genial and a born entertainer, with an endless fund of stories and eloquent recitations upon which to draw.

Publication of *Uncle Tom's Cabin or Life Among the Lowly,* written by

*Library of the West-
ern Reserve Histor-
ical Society on East
Boulevard.*

A Meeting at the Ark

Dr. Elisha S. Sterling	Captain B. A. Stannard	J. J. Tracy
Dr. A. Maynard	William Case	Bushnell White
D. W. Cross	Leonard Case, Jr.	E. A. Scovill
George A. Stanley	Stoughton Bliss	Rufus K. Winslow
John Coon		Henry G. Abbey

In the 1820s

In the 1830s

In the 1840s

In the 1860s

In the 1880s

In the Gay Nineties

Styles in the Nineteenth Century. CLEVELAND PICTURE COLLECTION,
CLEVELAND PUBLIC LIBRARY.

Harriet Beecher Stowe, sister of the Rev. Henry Ward Beecher, was announced on March 27, and orders were solicited at prices ranging from one to two dollars. Published by Jewett, Proctor & Worthington of Cleveland, the work was hailed as "the most beautiful, truthful, and valuable book ever written or published by an American," according to the *Daily True Democrat*. The long-awaited volume poured fresh oil on the flames of the slavery controversy.

Charles A. Otis, son of William A. Otis, pioneer ironmaster, set up a steam forge on Whisky Island with John N. Ford, a skilled mechanic from the East, to make steamboat shafts, iron castings, and axles for the railroads. Known as the Lake Erie Iron Works, a rolling mill was added early in the decade to make boiler plate. The elder Otis was a promoter of the Columbus and Pittsburgh railroads, and served as director of both for a number of years.

Dr. Leonard Hanna, his brother, Robert, and Hiram Garretson came to Cleveland from Lisbon, Ohio, and organized the wholesale grocery and commission firm of Hanna, Garretson & Company on Merwin Street. Dr. Hanna's family followed the next fall, leaving their Lisbon farm, where Marcus Alonzo Hanna was born in 1837. Having become interested in Lake Superior copper and iron, the company began operating several vessels in lake trading later in the fifties, and expanded operations to include coal mining in Ohio. Young "Mark" went to work in his father's business late in the decade. After a long illness, Dr. Hanna died in 1862, and the firm dissolved. From this small beginning, however, the diversified industrial interests of the Hanna family developed to vast proportions. Mark was a lively figure in the social set. Early in the sixties he was courting the daughter of Daniel P. Rhodes, who at first opposed a suitor of Republican politics, but later relented, and gave consent to the marriage.

Edwin B. Hale came to Cleveland and entered the private banking business of Sturgis & Hale. Having purchased his partner's interest, the firm became E. B. Hale & Company. W. H. Barriss joined him in 1859, and the business grew until it was one of the largest in Ohio. In 1891, the company was succeeded by the Marine Bank Company, of which Hale was president and Barriss, cashier.

An act of the Legislature, passed on May 3, provided for the incorporation of cities and villages. A population of twenty thousand constituted the dividing line between cities of the first and second class, and Cleveland fell short of first rating. Two trustees from each ward made up the Council, each receiving a dollar for every session. The mayor's power was restricted, and Council fixed his salary. Operation of the city had grown complex, and a board of city commissioners was created with authority over streets and bridges. The marshal, treasurer and city solicitor, and a market superintendent were elected; and added to the official family were a civil engineer, an auditor, and a complete police court, including a judge, clerk, and prosecutor.

A fourth ward was created in Cleveland, made up largely of the new district annexed to the east, and extending to Willson Avenue.

The First United Brethren Church, organized this year at Kentucky and Lorain streets, inspired the founding of several prominent United Brethren churches in the county. In 1868, it moved to an established location (West 42nd Street and Orchard Avenue). The church belonged to the Ohio German Conference until 1930, when it transferred to the East Ohio Conference. The Rev. E. F. Wegner gave stimulating leadership for twenty-two years, during which activity expanded. The Rev. James Howsare was pastor in 1946 at the time of the merger of the Evangelical and United Brethren denominations, the identity of First Church being changed to First Evangelical United Brethren Church. The Rev. D. A. Ewing later became pastor.

On lower Superior Street, between the Weddell House and the Franklin House, the site of Abram Hickox' pioneer smithy, the Johnson House had been erected by Levi Johnson. It opened in June, and commercial travelers and civic and political organizations favored it. Late in the century it had lost its prestige. In 1910 it was razed, and an addition to the Rockefeller Building rose in its place.

Although the Cleveland & Mahoning Valley Railroad Company (later Erie Railroad) had received its charter on February 22, 1848, financing seemed an impossibility. In June, 1852, the first stockholders meeting was held in Warren, Ohio, when three hundred thousand dollars had been subscribed. The directorate included able businessmen: Jacob Perkins, son of General Simon Perkins of Trumbull County, Frederick Kinsman, and Charles Smith of Warren; David Tod of Youngstown; Dudley Baldwin of Cleveland; Robert Cunningham of New Castle; and James Magee of Pittsburgh. Later having been refused aid at home and in Europe, President Perkins came forward and pledged $100,000 of his personal fortune to the venture, and the directors joined him, making the project possible. In 1857 the road reached Youngstown via Warren, opening the Mahoning Valley coal fields to Cleveland and other lake ports and dealing a mighty blow to canal commerce. Just before he passed on in 1859 in Cleveland, his home for about seven years, Jacob Perkins remarked in jest, "If I die you may inscribe on my tombstone, 'Died of the Mahoning Valley Railroad.' "

Cleveland mourned with the nation upon hearing by "magnetic telegraph" of the death of Henry Clay, "the Great Pacificator," on June 29. The remains were brought to Cleveland from Buffalo on the steamer *Buckeye State* on July 7, with a distinguished party; and as minute guns fired and bells tolled, the coffin was borne between rows of citizens to the railroad funeral car, and a committee headed by Governor Reuben Wood accompanied it to Lexington, Kentucky, for burial.

Jabez W. Fitch was appointed chief of the Volunteer Fire Department by the City Council; but William Cowen, James Hill, and Edward Hart, who succeeded him, were chosen directly by the people. Then the law was changed, and James Craw was chosen by the Council. Engine companies at this time were Eagle No. 1, Forest City No. 2, Saratoga No. 3, Phoenix No. 4, Cataract No. 5, Red Jacket No. 6, Forest City Hook and Ladder No. 1, and Hope No. 8. Slow, startling taps from the old bell on the First Baptist Church at Seneca and Champlain streets were the signal for firemen to start for the engine house, whether in a prayer meeting, at a horse race, or a-courting. The first to arrive seized the trumpet, and he was in command until the chief or an assistant came on the scene. Engines weighed from one to three tons and were dragged laboriously by ropes through sand and mud or over plank pavements. Curious citizens followed the company, and were expected to lend needed help under penalty of fine and imprisonment. Engines were operated by hand, with long levers at the sides of the machines. A stream one hundred feet high was their limit, and then only with greatest exertion. Each engine carried one hundred feet of hose. About forty firemen constituted a company. They designed and furnished their uniforms, served without pay, and were exempt from jury duty, from paying poll tax and from working on the highways. After five years of service, exemptions continued for life. They met eight times a year for drill meets, and were paid $1 each time. The chief received a salary of $150 per year, which he was expected to spend for prizes awarded at the firemen's annual ball, a brilliant affair. All companies responded to every call, and intense rivalry and jealousy resulted. This was aggravated by monthly competitive drills; but ill feeling was banished as the firemen joined in their annual celebration.

In the Democratic Convention to nominate a candidate for President of the United States, votes of Ohio delegates were all that were required to seal the nomination of Reuben Wood of Cleveland. When J. W. Gray and General H. H. Dodge, representing Cuyahoga County, failed to support him, their influence spread and Franklin Pierce was chosen. Wood had been traveling with the Hunkers in New York, a faction not approved by party leaders, Gray explained later. President Pierce appointed him consul to Valparaiso in 1853, and the next year Wood withdrew from active life, retiring to his beautiful estate on Ridge Road in Rockport Township, where he died in 1864 at the age of seventy-two.

Differences arose over the slavery question, and on July 4, a small group of members of the First Presbyterian Church of Euclid organized The Free Congregational Church of Euclid Village in a schoolhouse (near Euclid Avenue and Noble Road). Their recorded purpose was "to advance the cause of purity in our hearts and give our influence to cleanse the church, and ultimately the world, of slave holding." Charter members of the Collamer congregation included community pioneers, Asa Cady—or Cody, John Ruple, Rufus Dutton, M. S. McIlrath, William H. Coit, Jay Odell, and Andrew Wemple, said to have been "either conductors, engineers or station agents on the underground railroad." Membership began to disintegrate after the Civil War. In 1876, some members withdrew to form the Congregational Church of Collinwood. Missions at Wickliffe, Glenville, and Fairmount had been started. Affiliations with the mother church were resumed by the majority of members. On June 15, 1893, the trustees were authorized to sell the church property (at Euclid and Allendale Avenue) and transfer to the Congregational City Missionary Society the proceeds and any other property upon condition that the same be used to purchase a lot in East Cleveland and erect on it a Congregational Church building, which became the home of East Congregational Church (later East Cleveland Congregational Church) in 1900.

Resigning his connection with the Cleveland Iron Mining Company,

Henry B. Tuttle had set up an agency for the handling of Lake Superior iron ore. The first shipment of ore from the Marquette Range consisted of six barrels shipped by the Marquette Iron Company on July 7 on the schooner *Baltimore* to Tuttle in Cleveland. There were no locks at the Soo, and the ore was unloaded and sent south by rail. Although some considered it not worth the freight, "red gold" from the iron country was destined to make Cleveland one of the world's greatest producers of iron-and-steel products. George H. Ely, associated with Tuttle, later established a partnership with S. P. Ely, handling iron ore in Cleveland, and they became prominent in the business. Horace A. and Fred Tuttle ultimately joined their father, and when Willis W. Masters entered the firm in 1881, it became Tuttle, Masters & Company. Earl W. Oglebay, Wheeling industrialist, came to Cleveland in 1884, and with Horace A. Tuttle and Daniel McGarry established Tuttle, Oglebay & Company (later Oglebay, Norton & Company). Their interests centered in a new mining region later known as the Gogebic Range.

Having settled the vast estate of his father, General Simon Perkins of Trumbull County, who died in 1844, Joseph Perkins, aged thirty-three, came to Cleveland, where he became prominent in banking and business. While serving as a member of the Ohio Board of State Charities in 1867, Perkins developed a reform plan by which prisoners were classified and no longer thrown together promiscuously. He then reformed the infirmary systems of the State, greatly improving the physical and mental health of the insane. Perkins gave generously of his time and wealth to the uplift of humanity until his death in 1885. His son, Joseph, Jr., was closely identified with Cleveland's educational and cultural life.

Cleveland was growing up, and the boundaries of the open countryside were being pushed farther by new communities. This gave rise to a need for parks, and attention was turned to the Public Square. Residents whose homes fronted on the Square wanted it fenced and the street entrances closed to form "a grand central park." On July 22, a petition was introduced into Council asking that the streets be vacated; but although the law department declared it illegal, the famous "fence war" between the residents and encroaching business interests had been declared, and for fifteen years the feud continued.

P. T. Barnum's "grand colossal museum and menagerie" gave an exhibition in the city. Tradition says that the showman gave ten free tickets to prominent Bedford citizens. Train service not being available, the ten went to Cleveland on a handcar. The car was stolen while they were at the show, and they walked the ties home.

The first avenues were named this year, Case, Sawtell, Sterling, and Willson, and Superior became known also as an avenue. William Case, mayor during 1850 and 1851, led in a tree-planting movement that established Cleveland as the "Forest City." In 1855, Cedar Street became an avenue; Clinton Street was changed to Brownell; Division Street became Center Street; Second Street became Hill Street; York Street was changed to Hamilton Street; and Prospect Street on the West Side became Franklin Street.

The first issue of the *Waechter am Erie* (later *Waechter und Anzeiger*) appeared on August 2, dedicated to "the Union, the abolition of slavery and the promulgation of liberal culture." August Thieme, scholar, essayist, and journalist, was the first editor. The paper later supported the Republicans and became a daily in 1866.

Cleveland's first general hospital originated in a small brick building of St. Vincent's Orphan Asylum at Willett and Monroe streets on the West Side. On August 5, the Sisters of Charity of St. Augustine opened the doors of St. Joseph's Hospital (forerunner of St. Vincent Charity Hospital) to the community.

Cleveland's first high-school building, erected in 1852 and torn down in 1856.

Although the United States Government had purchased about nine acres of land at Erie and Lake streets for a Marine Hospital as early as 1837, construction was delayed by the administration, and it was not opened for service until this year. Surgeons appointed from civil life were in charge until 1889, when medical officers of the United States Marine Hospital Service assumed authority. The hospital cared for "sick seamen, boatmen and other navigators on the western rivers and lakes." Until 1884, the service was supported by monthly deductions from seamen's wages; support then came from tonnage taxes until 1905, when direct appropriations were made by Congress.

The reed organ, a new musical instrument made in Cleveland by Child & Bishop, later the Jewett & Goodman Organ Company, appeared in local churches.

Dr. Nathan H. Ambler established himself as a dentist at the corner of Seneca and Superior streets this year. On a large tract of land overlooking Doan Brook Valley, he built a fine stone residence. The district became known as Ambler Heights, and Ambler Road honors his name.

The High School having outgrown its quarters, a 104-foot lot was purchased by the city for $5,000 on Euclid near Erie as a site for its first home. A temporary frame building costing $1,200 was ready for occupancy in the fall, and served until 1856.

Mayflower Street School was opened this year in a little, two-room, wooden building at the corner of Orange Street. Most of the children were

Bohemian and could scarcely understand English, but they soon picked up the language in their playtime associations. Two years later, a three-story, brick building was erected to meet the growing demands of the community, and four hundred and fifty pupils were admitted. Remarkable discipline characterized Principal Palmer's school routine. He introduced the "slipper arrangement," by which slippers were worn in the schoolroom by the boys, boots having been exchanged for them in the basement. Palmer's floors were spotless! In 1869, the building was doubled in size to accommodate a thousand pupils.

The Ohio State Fair, held in Cleveland for the first time, "on the Scovill lot" on Kinsman Street, opened on September 15 for a three-day run. An advance warning went out, "Watch your railroad tickets; most people will have to eat standing up; beware of pickpockets."

General Sam Houston made a fiery speech from the balcony of the Forest City House during the State Fair, in which he pleaded the cause of his candidate for President, Franklin Pierce, Democrat. Houston was a picturesque campaigner in his broad-brimmed slouch hat and vest of wildcat skin. On the twentieth, General Winfield Scott, who headed the Whig ticket, tried to influence votes from the American House balcony, but his efforts failed to carry him to victory.

The best wheat grown in Ohio this year was produced by Thomas Hird on his East Rockport (Lakewood) farm, and he received a medal from the Ohio Board of Agriculture for his achievement. Hird was hired to manage Richard Lord's 320-acre farm in 1818 (extending from West 117th and Madison Avenue to the lake). When he married Lord's daughter, Hope, he inherited the lands. For many years, their fine home stood at Hird and Detroit avenues.

Iris Lodge No. 229, Free and Accepted Masons, was organized on October 22. Meetings were held in Iris Hall in the Forest City Block, rented for $150 per year, including light and heat. Quarters were shared with Cleveland City Lodge, which now had a membership of about sixty. Bigelow Lodge No. 243 was organized in 1853, Concordia No. 345 in 1863, and Ellsworth in 1865. Masonry was gaining slowly in strength, the Oriental Commandery, Knights Templar, having been formed in 1851. Eliadah Grand Lodge of Perfection, Ancient Scottish Rite, and Bahurim Council Prince of Jerusalem began in 1859, followed by Ariel Chapter in 1860. The Cleveland Council was organized in 1865.

Cleveland's water supply came from springs, wells, the canal, and the river. In the business district pumps had been provided for public use and for fire-fighting. Increased population, neglected sanitation, and heavy fire losses aroused the citizens, and they demanded improvements. Mayor William Case and an able committee, consisting of William J. Warner, Dr. Jared P. Kirtland, and Charles Whittlesey, made a report on October 29, after nearly two years of investigation, recommending that the lake was the only "unfailing" source of supply. Private building of a water works, they agreed, "can be carried on more economically by individuals or companies than by municipal corporations, and also better managed after construction."

Private enterprise was considered impractical in Cleveland, however, for want of adequate capital.

The first locomotive traveled the entire length of the Cleveland, Painesville & Ashtabula Railroad (later New York Central) from Cleveland eastward to the state line in November. Envisioning future needs, a double track had been laid on a 100-foot roadway, costing $15,000 per mile. T-rails, 12 to 18 feet long and made in England, had been introduced. Passenger coaches 56 feet long, the largest then in use, with eight wheels and brakes, went into service along with 26-foot freight cars, supplied with brakes. Six engines—two built in Ohio City—handled the traffic. They were 30-ton wood-burners with 6-foot drivers, the finest in Ohio. Sheds along the route furnished ample supplies of cordwood fuel. Extension of the road to Erie along the Franklin Canal Railway line was permitted when the courts overruled objections of Erie citizens. Although handicapped by varying gauges, the final link in a through route between Cincinnati and New York, via Cleveland and Buffalo, had been forged. On October 8, 1867, the company leased the Cleveland & Toledo Railroad Company. The Cleveland, Painesville & Ashtabula Railroad emerged as the Lake Shore Railway Company on June 22, 1868. It acquired the Cleveland & Toledo road in 1869, bringing the Erie-Toledo line under one corporation.

Only a country road led to the lake when St. John's Cathedral was dedicated at Superior and Erie streets on November 7. Pomp and ceremony marked the consecration of the second cathedral, seating 900. It was one of the city's finest buildings. The interior was designed by Patrick C. Keily, nationally known Gothic architect. Magnificent stained-glass windows were set in the walls, and the carved-oak altar was made in France. St. John's School for boys was constructed several years later, followed by Cathedral Hall and the school for girls in another decade. Four other parochial schools were also in existence: St. Patrick's and St. Mary's on the West Side, and St. Joseph's and St. Peter's on the East Side. Slow progress was made in early education, as Catholics were comparatively few and scattered. In 1884 St. John's Cathedral was redecorated, and four years later a new brick school building was erected.

Three brothers, Caius Cassius, Brutus Junius, and Junius Brutus Cobb, had learned the book business in the famous house of Moses C. Younglove & Company, and in 1852 they acquired the firm, which became J. B. Cobb & Company. That their father also had strong literary tendencies is evidenced by the intriguing names of his other children—Lucius Marcius, Marcius Lucius, Lucia Marcia, Cassius Caius, Marcia Lucia, and Daniel. The store on Superior Street grew, and soon there were branches in other cities. The firm was known as Cobb, Andrews & Company when it invaded residential Euclid Avenue in about 1875.

Joseph Medill came to Cleveland from Coshocton, Ohio, and established the *Daily Forest City*. The next year, it merged with the *True Democrat* under a new name, *Forest City Democrat*. Edwin Cowles became a partner and business manager, and Medill and John C. Vaughn were the editors.

Horace Mann aroused considerable comment with his middle-of-the-road lectures on *Woman* in Cleveland, December 14-15. Quoting the *Morning True Democrat,* "Neither the friends, nor the enemies, of the Woman's Rights Movement, so-called, could be altogether pleased." While the great educator devoted some of his time to an attack upon the plight of woman, the oppressed, the journal regretted that he was more intent upon "showing that God did not make woman man; that she ought not to fight, vote, preach, practice law, nor be shut up with men over night in a jury room from which her husband is excluded; and that this Woman's Rights 'school which has arisen in our day' has as 'its leader in Europe, Miss Helen Maria Weber, Esquire, who dresses like a man, with her blue dress coat, bright buttons, buff vest and biped continuations.' " Horace Mann spoke frequently to enthusiastic Cleveland audiences. In 1853 he began to put to work his pioneering plans for co-operative education when he became the first president of Antioch College. His great capacity for achievement in advancing education may be summed up in his inspiring words, "be ashamed to die until you have won some victory for humanity."

1853

Knight & Parsons' *Cleveland City Directory, 1852-3,* released on January 1, was a notable achievement. Commending the 380-page volume to the public in an introductory statement headed "Advertisement," the editors, who were local booksellers, stressed the fact that the directory was a product of Cleveland endeavor, the paper having been made in the Younglove & Hoyt mill, printing by Harris, Fairbanks & Company of the *Herald,* and a map engraved expressly for the purpose. Dr. John S. Newberry had prepared twenty editorial pages relating to the city's growth and development, compiling an historical sketch from John Barr's notes.

The trend of the times is reflected in goods and services advertised for sale in the forty-one-page yellow section of the city directory: white-ironstone ware and feather dusters, trunks and valises, agricultural implements and seeds, bird cages and umbrella stands, suspenders and cravats, gas fittings and railroad-car wheels, marble statuary and peddler's goods, saddles and horse goods, opera glasses and buffalo robes, dolls and toys, patent melodeons and daguerreotypes, steam dyeing and shawl cleaning "at the Curled-Hair Factory on the Flats," steamship services to California and Europe, and cooking, parlor, plate, and coal stoves. Six local companies and forty-three agents, largely representing eastern firms, were competing for insurance business. Six commercial banks, with a combined capital of $1,700,000, as many private banking houses, two exchange brokers and the Society for Savings were meeting the city's financial needs. There were 26 religious societies in the city, most of them agitated by the existence of 57 saloons and 105 retail grocers who also dealt in liquor. Only 360 retail stores were listed in the entire city! Although the gas age had begun, 3 companies were making lard oil; and 4, soap and candles. A page of subscribers constituted the only

Cleveland in 1853. Warehouses and commission establishments flanked the Cuyahoga River in the foreground. On the extreme right was the terminus of the Ohio Canal, and to the left was Lake Erie. Flourishing business concerns lined Superior Hill and broad Superior Avenue in the center, as far as the tree-studded Public Square in the distance. Euclid Street radiated obliquely to the right, just beyond the Court House.

reference to Ohio City, which may or may not be due to the feud of long standing. It is interesting to observe, however, that a nine-page blue section at the end of the directory advertised friendly Pittsburgh's industry and retail business. For a number of years, the directory appeared at irregular intervals.

The *Plain Dealer* commented on the free-and-easy flow of liquor, observing on January 17: "Our government lands cost $1 an acre on an average, and champagne $2 a bottle. How many a man dies in the poorhouse, who, during his lifetime, has drank a fertile township, trees and all."

The fame of Ralph Waldo Emerson, essayist and philosopher, had preceded him, and the intellectual and the curious assembled in Melodeon Hall on January 20 to hear his lecture, *The English Race*. It was presented as the ninth of the Cleveland Library Association course, arranged by the Mercantile Library Association. "The chance of hearing such a man is seldom offered," remarked an editor. A report of the event stated, "His lecture last evening was a beautiful one," while the editorial of another paper criticized carpetbagging lecturers who traveled the country reading over and over again from a few sheets of foolscap. Emerson's reception was satisfactory, for on the twenty-second he gave a second lecture on *Culture* that was instructive and "clothed in beautiful language." While the first lecture "was rather materialistic than Emersonian . . . in the latter he was more like himself," a news review stated.

"The pressing want of a Presbyterian church in the eastern portion of the city" is said to have inspired Elisha Taylor, Zalmon Fitch, George Worthington, and ten others to break away from the First Presbyterian Church, halting its building plans for several years. During a controversy as to whether or not the First Church should build a new edifice, Taylor, a founder, and his adherents met in the basement of the church on January 25 and launched the Euclid Street Presbyterian Church. Paper plans showed that a building could be provided by selling 178 pews appraised at $50,450. The southeast corner of Euclid and Brownell Street was purchased and a building erected at a cost of $60,750. Dr. Joseph B. Bittinger was called as pastor. The pretentious "church of 40 corners" greatly taxed the strength of the congregation. Time after time the courageous planners failed to reach financial goals, and it was not until 1871 that the debt was wiped out. In 1880 the word "Avenue" replaced "Street" in the church name. The pastorate of Dr. Samuel P. Sprecher, 1887-1905, was notable, as he was probably the most popular preacher of his time. In 1906, the Beckwith Memorial Church joined with Euclid Avenue; and, in 1920, a union with the Second Presbyterian Church resulted in the Church of the Covenant. Prominent in the life of the Euclid Church were Joseph Perkins, Franklin J. Slosson, Ann Walworth, Dr. H. J. Herrick, Joseph B. Meriam, Henry F. Pope, H. R. Hatch, and H. R. P. Hamilton. The old Euclid Avenue Church was razed to make way for the Hanna Building.

The Public School Library (later Cleveland Public Library) originated in a state law enacted on March 14, permitting the purchase of books for school libraries.

William Edwards, twenty-two, had been in Cleveland a year, having come from his birthplace in Springfield, Massachusetts; he found employment with W. J. Gordon, owner of the largest wholesale grocery west of the Alleghenies. This year, Treat & Edwards was organized, operating a wholesale-grocery business in a two-story frame building on River Street near the site of the great future plant at 1300 West 9th Street. The founder died in 1898, and his family continued to manage the business. From this early enterprise, the William Edwards Company developed in 1906. The founder's sons, Harry R. and Major General Clarence R.—who won distinction in World War I, were active on the board. Charles A. Otis, who had married their sister, Lucia R., became president in 1931 when General Edwards died. A year later, the company sponsored a co-operative group of independent grocers known as the Edwards Food Stores. In 1942 the William Edwards Company, the oldest food firm between New York and Chicago, was purchased by the Weideman Company, operating under direction of M. M. Cohn. Lyman F. Narten became president in 1932.

A "lightening train" was announced on March 29, to go into service between Cleveland and Cincinnati, cutting travel time to eight hours. "Every passenger train to and from this city consists of five to ten cars," observed the *Daily True Democrat*. In July, the editor reported another "lightening train" had cut the Buffalo trip to six and a half hours.

When J. W. Gray was appointed postmaster on April 1, he moved the Post Office to the *Plain Dealer* Building. With the advent of the railroad and mounting population, the volume of mail increased greatly. "Three men, three horses and two wagons are needed to bring twenty tons of mail a day from the depot," it was reported on June 27. Gray turned over the *Plain Dealer* operation to his brother, Nicholas, and others, while he fought his political enemies with a sharp pen. In 1858, he lost his office as postmaster through his devotion to Stephen A. Douglas and his compromising stand on slavery.

The election in April was of great importance, as a number of new offices were filled in accordance with the revised state constitution. Administration of city affairs was scattered in many directions, but the quality of leadership chosen seems to have precluded any serious inefficiencies that might have resulted. With the election of the first Board of Water Works Commissioners, consisting of Henry B. Payne, B. L. Spangler, and Richard Hilliard, Cleveland's major health problem was to have constructive attention. By special vote—1,230 for, and 599 against, the people authorized the city to spend $400,000 for a water works, and the officials were directed to go to work immediately.

The Cleveland Theater, under construction since 1851, was opened formally, April 16, 1853, by Manager Charles Foster of Pittsburgh. Located on the top floor of the three-story, brick building on the east side of Bank Street (1371 West 6th), it was one of the finest theaters in the country. The curtain went up on *The School for Scandal,* played by a stock company headed by Ben Maginley, later a celebrated comedian. John A. Ellsler, who had taught Joseph Jefferson the dialect for *Rip Van Winkle* when they were partners, leased the theater, which was in financial difficulties, and gave it the name of Academy of Music. He organized a stock company, one of the first dramatic schools in the nation, and gave actors their start. John McCullough began his march to stardom here as Virginius; and Lawrence Barrett, then a struggling actor, earned another chance under Ellsler. Ellsler and his wife, Effie E., were distinguished performers in the company; and his pretty red-haired daughter, Effie, Cleveland's sweetheart, became a great actress. Gas footlights in front of the red-plush curtain were lit with a taper, and the hundreds of china candles in the center chandelier were lighted from the balcony with a long rod. The stage sloped toward the audience, affording a hazard to actors who might unceremoniously tumble headlong into the orchestra pit, where a music-teacher conductor presided with his pupils. That the Academy started to go downhill may be charged to hard times or perhaps to high admissions, varying from $1 to 50 cents in the dress circle, 25 cents in the gallery, and boxes at $5 and $10. At any rate, in 1858, the Ellslers went on the road, returning at intervals with a traveling company that played to passably large audiences. Ellsler again became manager of the Academy in 1862, and a new era of sparkling music, drama, and opera began. He also managed the Opera House in Canton, where his Cleveland shows were presented. Through the stage door of the Academy passed some of America's greatest artists—Edwin Forrest, Charlotte Thompson, Edward A. Sothern, Lawrence Barrett, Joseph Jefferson, Edwin Booth, Charlotte Cushman, E. L. Davenport, Joseph Proctor, Clara Morris, Maggie Mitchell, and James Lewis, who won fame with Augustin Daly's famous stock company.

The Richman Brothers Company, founded by Henry Richman in Portsmouth, Ohio, this year, was moved to Cleveland in 1879. Richman made men's suits, trousers, and overcoats in his Water Street factory, selling products through independent dealers. As his three sons, Nathan G., Charles L., and Henry C., reached sixteen years of age, they came into the business, earning $3 a week.

Protests against mounting crime demanded more efficient policing. Only "three or four acting constables" and "half a dozen watchmen" were on duty to guard the population. On April 17, the first session of Police Court was held in a back room in the Gaylord Block on Superior Street, between Seneca and the Public Square. John Barr was the police judge; Bushnell White, prosecuting attorney; and Orlando J. Hodge, clerk. They had won their offices in a spirited political contest, the first two being victorious Whigs, and the latter a Democrat. In the first case before the court, five firemen were charged with "getting up a false alarm of fire and disturbing the peace." The culprits had been arrested and much excitement resulted, as it was understood that the volunteers were exempt from punishment, no matter how playful they became. When the judge fined all but one of the accused $5 each and costs, city firemen met in protest and the verdict was soundly denounced.

German families in Ohio City joined under the leadership of the Rev. Phillip Stempel, a learned man, in organizing the United German Evangelical Protestant Church, the pastor serving also as school teacher at a salary of $250 per year. A brick house of worship was erected in 1860 at the corner of Bridge and Kentucky streets, the traditional church site down through the years. Later known as the West Side Evangelical Church, it played a large part in the life of a changing community through broadening activities. The Rev. Walter K. Klein, the fourth pastor, came to the church in 1924. Steady growth continued, and West Side developed into one of the strongest churches in the Evangelical and Reformed denomination in Cleveland.

Euclid Street at Erie was muddy and rutted, and it was commonly called the "Frog Pond." A wit of the day erected a headboard in the street proclaiming: "Here lieth ye Street Commissioner, so called, who departed this life, May 6, 1853." Relief did not come until 1859, when a 25-foot gravel carriageway was laid from the Square to Erie Street at a cost of $776.50. The first efforts at grading and draining "Lake Euclid" had come two years before. Although an ordinance required owners to pave sidewalks, little attention was paid to it.

Omnibus service on Euclid Street was started by Ed Duty, who made two trips daily between the City Hotel and the Croton House in East Cleveland, fare ten cents. He later extended his line to Euclid Creek. By 1860, a line operated to Collamer, via St. Clair; on Kinsman, ending near Case Avenue; and on the West Side, to the Reservoir on Franklin Street.

The Bank of Commerce, chartered about 1845, opened this year in the Atwater Block with a capital of $100,000. Parker Handy, the first president, was succeeded in several years by Joseph Perkins. Reorganization as the Second National Bank was effected in 1864, and in 1870 the institution moved into the new National Bank Building. It continued for many years under a succession of able presidents—Amasa Stone, Sylvester T. Everett, Jeptha H. Wade, and G. A. Garretson. After several transitions, it emerged in 1899 as The Bank of Commerce National Association, located in the Western Reserve Building. It was the oldest unit in the merger which became the Union Trust Company in 1924.

Cleveland bankers showed the way to free the country of old Spanish coins that had been piling up. The limited amount of American silver in circulation commanded a premium of five per cent over bankable currency, and four per cent over gold. Spanish coins were widely used, but they were worn thin and were unpopular. When the banks advertised that within three months these coins would be accepted at reduced rates, they vanished in short order. As the news spread, other banks adopted the plan.

Administration of the public schools passed from the Board of School Managers to the Board of Education, created on June 1. The new board consisted of Charles Bradburn, president; Samuel H. Mather, secretary; W. D. Beattie, T. P. Handy, George Willey, Buckley Stedman, and Samuel Starkweather. One of their first acts was to elect Andrew Freese superintendent of instruction. At a salary of $1,300 a year, he supervised the schools, continued as high-school principal, examined applicants and granted certificates to qualified teachers. Freese struggled under this peculiar working and financial arrangement for three years, when he was released from high-school responsibility—with a proportionate salary reduction of $300, despite his valuable and time-taking service.

Woodland Cemetery was dedicated on June 14, and named for the fine grove of trees in it. The city had purchased about sixty acres of land from Benjamin F. Butler for $13,639.50 as the site. A sixty-foot Indian mound was preserved as a landmark. The stone entranceway with chapel and waiting room was erected in 1870.

A dozen German families banded together as St. John's Evangelical Lutheran Church, and purchased an acre of land on Mayfield Road, South Euclid, where they erected a small frame church. The Rev. H. Kuehn was pastor. In the church school the children were educated in the grammar grades. The crossroads community grew slowly, and by 1860 there were twenty families in the congregation. The Rev. John Adam Ernst, who became pastor this year, was succeeded in 1863 by the Rev. Frederick W. Husman, minister for nearly a score of years. Both were founders of the Missouri Synod. The roots of the church grew strong and deep, St. John's Lutheran Church continuing to serve on its original site, 4390 Mayfield Road. The Rev. Walter Bischoff began his long service as pastor in 1922.

Jacob H. Silverthorn moved his family to Rocky River, where he had purchased the old Wright Tavern. In the sixties the Patchen family bought the Silverthorn Tavern and remodeled it as the Patchen House. Silverthorn took over Jonathan Bowles' tavern in East Cleveland (Case School site), and until 1870 it was one of the most popular resorts in northern Ohio, famed for game dinners and champagne. In the wintertime, Silverthorn's Tavern was the destination of big bobsled parties from Cleveland.

Hundreds were turned away when P. T. Barnum lectured in National Hall, July 17, on the evils of intemperance. "He was quite as attractive as his circus," it was observed.

At about this time, P. T. Barnum's agent opened the Athenaeum, a theater on the top floor of Kelley's Block, managed by E. T. Nichols. From the start, he found keen competition in the new Academy of Music and Melodeon Hall, which were favored by the critics. The showman's great moral drama, *The Drunkard,* opened on July 18, and was an advance sell-out at 50 cents admission, "rear seats" at 25 cents. Barnum brought the Marsh family to Cleveland in his New York presentation of *Uncle Tom's Cabin,* and in fifteen nights in November more than twelve thousand people attended. Although the newspapers were obliged to acknowledge the sensational attraction, the theater failed to succeed, and Adolph Montpellier ran it as a variety house until the Theatre Comique became his consuming interest. It declined and then closed, except for special events. "General" Tom Thumb made his last appearance in Cleveland at the Athenaeum about 1870, and the building was converted into offices.

A fine retail store on Superior Street, according to Historian Orth, showed the following schedule of yearly operating expenses based on sales of $42,750 for the year and 15 per cent net profit: rent, $1,500; chief clerk, $600; assistant clerk and bookkeeper, $500; three additional clerks, $300;

insurance on stock, $300; taxes, $200; annual depreciation of stock, $2,000; proprietor's family expenses, $1,000. Only male employees were being hired, as economic necessity had not yet driven women into business.

Three companies had been organized to build certain Ohio railroads, but had hardly progressed beyond the charter stage: the Junction Railroad Company, chartered in 1846 to build a standard-gauge road from a point on the Cleveland, Columbus & Cincinnati line, within thirty miles of Cleveland, to Fremont, via Elyria and Bellevue, also a branch from Elyria to Fremont through Sandusky following the ancient Ohio Railroad right-of-way, the "stilt road"; the Toledo, Norwalk & Cleveland Railroad, incorporated in 1850 to build a narrow-gauge line from Toledo eastward via Norwalk to Grafton; and the Port Clinton Railroad Company, chartered in 1852 to build from Sandusky through Port Clinton to Toledo. On September 1, 1853, the lines were united in a new corporation, the Cleveland & Toledo Railroad Company (later New York Central). When completed, the Port Clinton, or Northern Division, came into Cleveland from the west through Whisky Island, stopping at the river bank, where its passengers were ferried across the Cuyahoga, because the city refused permission to cross the river and connect with eastbound lines. In 1856, the narrow-gauge Cleveland, Columbus & Cincinnati tracks were leased, extending the Southern Division of the Cleveland & Toledo road from Grafton to Cleveland.

Competing telegraph lines serving Cleveland, Buffalo, Milwaukee, Columbus, Cincinnati, St. Louis, Wheeling, Zanesville, Warren, and Pittsburgh were consolidated as the Speed & Wade Telegraph Lines, operating 2,515 miles of line and 104 offices, with headquarters in the American House in Cleveland. Locally, they operated as Speed's Line and Wade's Line.

Melodeon Hall was the scene of the National Woman's Rights Convention, a three-day session opening on October 5, and marked by great enthusiasm. Lucy Stone and William Lloyd Garrison, noted suffrage crusaders, were present. Godey's *Lady's Book* fanned a tempestuous attack against use of the "parasitical word 'female'" as derived from male. A local organization was set up with Frances E. Gage, president, and T. C. Severance, treasurer. The masculine population was apprehensive.

An era of strife over slavery, moral issues, and state sovereignty prevailed when the Cleveland Congregational Conference was organized on October 19, placing emphasis upon fellowship of the churches. Rapid increase in population made imperative the need of an organization that would plant new churches, and, in 1892, the Congregational City Missionary Society was created. Conference and society united in 1912 to form the Congregational Union of Cleveland.

A mission school for poor children, opened near the foot of Champlain Street by the Rev. Dillon Prosser, was one of the city's earliest charities. It originated in the outreach effort of a prayer group of young men (forerunner of YMCA). Called the Ragged School, it was reorganized in 1856 as the City Industrial School, from which the Children's Aid Society developed in 1858, with Truman P. Handy as president. So effective was its work that the City Council offered the use of a vacant schoolhouse for the education of needy children, and provided day-school teachers for a time. Mrs. Eliza Jennings gave to the society a farm on which it built a new home (10427 Detroit Avenue), and Mrs. E. G. Leffingwell, Leonard Case, Sr., and Jeptha H. Wade were among its early benefactors.

In the peaceful Chagrin Valley at the foot of the Gates Mills hill, a small community of Methodists erected a meeting house of rare Colonial beauty called the Gates Mills Methodist Episcopal Church (later St. Christopher's-by-the-River, Episcopal). Wooden-pegged floor boards were cut in Holsey Gates' mills. Much of the woodwork was carved by hand, and the pulpit was one of the finest examples of Colonial ecclesiastical architecture in the country. Gates gave $800 of the required $1,300 to build the church.

William Howard Day became editor and publisher of the first Negro newspaper, *The Aliened American*. He had come to Cleveland following graduation from Oberlin College in 1847. From 1850 to 1860 he served as a librarian for the Cleveland Library Association and a member of the staff of the *Daily True Democrat*.

St. Paul's Methodist Church was organized in Ohio City (Lorain and West 26th) under the leadership of the Rev. John Baldhauf. In 1880, the congregation moved westward, erecting a church at what became Bridge Avenue and West 44th Street. Dr. E. B. McBroom became pastor in 1945.

Ole Bull, famed violinist, appeared in Cleveland on November 28. On a return engagement, November 2, 1854, a capacity audience paid $1 admission, and heard him play their new favorite, Stephen Foster's *My Old Kentucky Home*.

A wooden drawbridge that had long been needed was built this year at Division Street, affording a natural route from downtown Cleveland to the West Side.

Trinity Church, pioneer Evangelical Lutheran congregation on the West Side, was organized this year on Jersey Street. It was the offspring of Zion Church, with the Rev. J. C. W. Lindeman, first pastor, and it became independent in 1857. Children of members attended the church grammar school. The Rev. Frederick C. D. Wynekeen, pastor for many years, had been a founder of the Missouri Synod. The German community flourished in the eighties, when there were 1,400 communicants; then the outward population shift resulted in a changing neighborhood, but Trinity remained steadfast through the years, its location taking a new address, 2031 West 30th Street, after the turn of the century. The Rev. Martin H. Sommerfeld became pastor in 1933.

Jacob Rauch began building and repairing carriages and wagons on the site of a large future factory (2168 West 25th). In 1878, Charles Rauch, son of the founder, incorporated the Rauch & Lang Carriage Company (later the Baker-Raulang Company), and custom coach-building became a specialty.

"To cherish the traditions and customs of the pioneer settlers of New England and to foster and promote a kindred spirit among their sons and daughters" was the purpose of the New England Society of Cleveland, organized on December 22. Mayor Abner C. Brownell, the first president, was succeeded by Benjamin Rouse, 1854-56, and Philo Chamberlain, 1857-58. Dinner meetings were held for a time, the last being given at the Angier House in 1859 when William Slade was president. The first secretary was Colonel William P. Fogg, who was succeeded by H. M. Chapin, 1857-69. The organization was suspended in 1869 and revived in 1894.

1854

Abolitionists who were members of the Disciples of Christ sponsored an antislavery convention in Cleveland, commencing on January 21. The constituency of the communion was about evenly divided between the North and South, and great agitation in the church was aroused. Alexander Campbell and prominent leaders opposed the Abolitionists' methods; they considered slavery to be a political issue not within the realm of the church. This meeting is the only Abolitionists' convention of record in the Disciples Church.

The Rev. Samuel C. Aiken presided over the organization meeting of the Young Men's Christian Association, February 6. A committee, including Samuel H. Mather, Presbyterian; Loren Prentiss, Baptist; L. M. H. Battey, Congregationalist; E. W. Roby, Episcopalian; and E. F. Young, Methodist, was appointed to lay founding plans. On February 28, at a meeting in the First Baptist Church, sixty members were enrolled, many of them prominent names in the city, and John S. Newberry was elected president. Through weekly prayer meetings, lectures, mission work, and a circulating library, the "Y" hoped to reach beyond the sphere of the churches, and lend moral and cultural strength to a needy community. Well-known lecturers, among them Henry Ward Beecher, Bayard Taylor, and Cassius M. Clay, were brought to Cleveland. Close co-operation existed between the new "Y" and the seven leading churches located within a mile of the Public Square. In July, association rooms were opened in Northrup & Spangler's Block at the southeast corner of Superior and Seneca streets.

The Germans' enthusiasm for music centered in the new Gesangverein, directed by Fritz Abel, which superseded the Frohsinn. Here culture of the fatherland found expression in music appreciation that was inspiring national interest.

Upon the insistence of Edwin Cowles, the *Forest City Democrat* appeared on March 16 under a new name, the *Leader,* a morning paper. A year later, he bought his partners' interests, and Medill and Vaughn joined with Cowles' brother, Alfred, in assuming control of the *Tribune* in Chicago. The *Leader* was a strong supporter of the antislavery cause; and when fearless Editor Cowles threw his weight on the side of his new champion, the Republican Party, the paper grew in influence as its owner gained stature and became a leading publisher in the West. In 1861 the *Evening Leader,* an afternoon edition, was added, and in 1868 it became the *Evening News.* Upon the death of Cowles in 1890, John C. Covert was editor for a time; he later became United States consul to Lyons, France. James B. Morrow, who succeeded him as editor, became a well-known biographer. James H. Kennedy, then on the staff, gained recognition as the author of a *History of Cleveland*.

On April 1 an incendiary fire on Seneca Street near Superior destroyed engine house No. 1, two homes and a drug store. Sparks carried the blaze to a planing mill on Michigan Street, a brewery, dwelling, paint shop, and cooper shop. The loss was $18,000.

Years of petty quarreling between the cities east and west of the river were buried in a friendly annexation election, held on April 3, that resulted in uniting Ohio City with Cleveland. The new Constitution of Ohio allowed the cities to carry through the annexation procedure on their own initiative, and commissioners were appointed to work out the details: W. A. Otis, H. V. Willson, and Franklin T. Backus for Cleveland; and William B. Castle, Needham M. Standart, and C. S. Rhodes for Ohio City.

Angier House, opened in 1854, became the Kennard House in 1866. As the Lincoln Hotel, it continued to serve patrons in the 1940s.

The Penny Post was established by Henry S. Bishop in his privately operated post office on lower Superior Street. Bishop's blue stamps, with a large "2" in the center surrounded by the words, "Bishop's City Postage, Clev'd, Ohio," sold for two cents. Employees picked up the mail from boxes located at strategic points and disposed of it through Bishop's post office. The service was so efficient and reasonable in cost that it became a real threat to federal business. In 1861 the practice was declared illegal by the United States courts.

The Board of Trade was now making daily reports after this fashion: "Wheat dull. Sales Saturday evening 13,000 bushels Chicago at $1.25." "Freight rates to New York, flour 58c, corn 12c. To Albany, corn 10c." Incoming shipments of wool, oats, starch, oil, nails, tobacco, buffalo robes, and sundries were reported. Listed as received and shipped from Cleveland were lard, sugar, cattle, pigs, sheep, coal, glass, glassware, and iron. Then the Board began reporting railroad stocks, the condition of the money market, and the arrival and departure of lake vessels.

The Angier House opened on April 17 at the southeast corner of St. Clair and Bank streets, on the site of Cleveland's first schoolhouse. This fashionable, five-story hotel was built by Ahaz Merchant and leased to Roswell P. Angier. It was "heated by the steam process," with "a reservoir on the roof for distributing water throughout the building." Visitors came from a distance to enjoy famous dinners, "the best served west of New York City." Scanning the menu printed in English, many made it their custom to order "all the way down." The hotel entertained distinguished guests and important business and social gatherings.

That the Cleveland Female Seminary was an important undertaking is evidenced by the character of the first directorate: John M. Woolsey, W. D. Beattie, Leonard Case, Jr., E. M. Sawtell, H. P. Weddell, H. V. Willson, Stillman Witt, Oliver Perry, and James M. Hoyt. In a spacious $50,000 building, erected on Kinsman Street, between Sawtell Avenue and Wallingford Court, "one of the most beautiful rural parts of the city," a boarding and day school for young ladies was opened on May 20 with one hundred and twenty pupils enrolled in the three-year course. Dr. Samuel St. Johns was installed as principal, and on the teaching staff was Linda T. Guilford. The fee of boarding students was $300 per year. The seminary was the largest private school in Cleveland, ranking with the country's finest institutions. It pointed the way to the first colleges for women and to co-educational schools, and operated until about 1883.

On June 5, the report of the committee on annexation was rendered to the councils of Cleveland and Ohio City. It provided that the City of Ohio be annexed to and constitute the eighth, ninth, tenth, and eleventh wards of Cleveland; that councilmen from these wards shall hold their seats in the augmented City Council; and that detailed provision be made for the joint liability of public property, bonds, and debts of the two cities, excepting the subscriptions to railroad stock made by each corporation. The report was adopted, and on June 10 the first meeting of the enlarged City Council was held, Richard C. Parsons being elected president. The Cleveland boundary line was thus extended beyond the Cuyahoga to the west line of original Brooklyn Township lots Nos. 49 and 50, and southward to Walworth Run. As Abner C. Brownell had been elected mayor of Cleveland for a two-year term, he continued in office; but it was agreed that the next mayor should come from the West Side. Hence, William B. Castle, Ohio City's last mayor, became chief executive of the united Cleveland in 1855.

Ohio City added 2,438 persons to the school population, 800 to the public-school attendance and 11 teachers to the staff as a result of the consolidation. The Board of Education was now increased to 11 members, of which Benjamin Sheldon was president and Samuel H. Mather, secretary. Two years later, it was reduced to 5. As chairman of the committee on schools in the City Council, Charles Bradburn was in a position to wield a great influence in public-school development. Ohio City had three school buildings, located on Penn, Vermont, and Church streets; and three large brick schoolhouses under construction on Pearl, Hicks, and Kentucky streets, which Cleveland completed at a cost of about seven thousand dollars each. Superintendent Freese began to work for uniformity of methods and text-books as well as grading and classifying of schools and pupils.

A case of cholera was reported on July 4, the first in a siege that continued until September, taking a toll of sixty-seven deaths. This was the last attack of epidemic proportions that Cleveland suffered.

The Chapin Block was erected by H. M. Chapin at the corner of Euclid and the Square (Williamson Building site), a forbidding, three-story, brown-front, commercial building. Stores occupied the street level. The third floor was given over to a "most elegant" public auditorium, with twelve hundred upholstered seats. Lectures, concerts, dances, and public and private functions were held here. It was first called Concert Hall, and later Chapin's Hall. The hot-air heating system made a name for the hall in the West. In the mid-sixties, the auditorium became known as Garrett's Hall, and stars of the entertainment world were presented until Case Hall over-shadowed it. An ice-cream parlor operated by S. W. Garrett on the street level attracted popular patronage.

A little band of members of Zion Evangelical Lutheran Church, located southeast of Cleveland in a district of farms and steel-mill workers, organized a congregation in July that took the name St. John's. They erected a small community building, and shortly after established a school. The memory of August Schefft, an early teacher whose forty years of service left a deep impress, is revered among the faithful. Unique features of a new church, erected in 1880, were exterior walls constructed of horizontally set timbers, and an exquisitely hand-carved pulpit and lectern. St. John's location, later known as Turney Road at Granger in Garfield Heights, continued un-changed through the years. The Rev. Harry C. Weidner came to the pulpit in 1911. He announced a $145,000 program in 1946 to extend the work of the church in a changing community.

The Stadler Products Company originated this year, producing commer-cial fertilizer for farmers in the Cleveland area. In 1920, a group of Cleve-landers, who saw opportunity for development in a larger territory, came into ownership, and the business spread through sections of Ohio, Indiana, and Michigan. In 1946, J. F. Johnson was president of Stadler, the oldest fertilizer company in the county, and Wesley W. Johnson was vice presi-dent and general manager.

The State Fair was held on the new fair grounds on Kinsman Street (at East 22nd), the finest in Ohio. Three halls, each 152 by 160 feet, had been built on the 20-acre tract, and stalls accommodated 300 cattle. Exhibit entries totaled 2,823, and there were 30,000 paid admissions. The State Fair Ball was a brilliant feature.

The southwest side of the Square was swept by fire on October 7, and almost a score of buildings were destroyed. Flames threatened the Court House and the First Baptist Church at Seneca and Champlain streets.

The Evangelical Association moved its Publishing House to Cleveland this year. Located on Kinsman Street, it began producing periodicals and church literature for distribution throughout the country.

A fire, originating in a livery stable on October 27, leveled the buildings on Merwin Street and the block enclosed by Superior Lane, James Street, and the railroad, with an estimated loss of $215,000. The New England Hotel—the city's largest hotel, the St. Charles Hotel, and the Commercial Exchange were destroyed. Leaping across the street, the flames blackened the walls of the Oviatt Block, consuming the Board of Trade rooms. When Oviatt's Exchange was rebuilt, the Board occupied its old headquarters. The year 1854 was marked by a number of serious fires, indicating the urgent need for improved fire protection and increased water supply.

On November 2, the *Herald* and the *Plain Dealer* contracted with a new organization, the Associated Press, to receive telegraphic reports. Market quotations were of great benefit to Cleveland business.

Uncertain value of paper money and overwhelming threat of railroad competition with the canals were largely responsible for failure of the Canal Bank of Cleveland in early November. A "run" on the bank brought out the city's population as well as a police detail to keep the peace. There was uneasiness as anxious depositors faced the probable loss of savings. Then Dr. H. C. Ackley, trustee of the new Northern Ohio Lunatic Asylum at Newburgh, stepped forward and demanded the institution's $9,000 deposit, although unmindful of his own personal account. When he was refused, the sheriff's deputies went to work, armed with sledge hammers. Despite protests, blow after blow fell on the vault until the keys were produced. The sheriff handed the doctor $400 in gold and $1,460 in bills, and the bank "exploded into thin air."

William Benedict Scofield purchased the tract of swamp land at Euclid and Erie streets. Handsome oak and black-walnut timbers were felled to make floor joists for a three-story, brick residence-hotel at the southwest corner of the intersection. Prospect Place, later remodeled as the Euclid Place Hotel, did not cater to the traveling public; but among its visitors were missionaries to the western Indian tribes, attracted by the Scofield family's religious views. William Hopkins' drug store occupied the corner of the business block on the street floor, and the location became a perennial drug-store site. The hotel landmark came down in 1901 when plans for the Schofield Building, now spelled with the "h," were under way.

The Rouse Block, Cleveland's finest office building, was erected by Benjamin Rouse on the northwest corner of Superior Street and the Square. The street floor of the four-story, gray stone structure was devoted to stores, Albertson's jewelry store occupying the corner behind "a front of costly plate glass." A newsstand and book store became a traditional institution on this site. Law firms and insurance companies occupied two upper floors, and Folsom's Mercantile College (later Spencerian College), the fourth. An ornamental iron staircase and balcony traced the Public Square wall. William Furst, barber, was a famous tenant from the eighties until 1913, when the rusty balcony came down and the building gave way to the new Marshall Building.

German Catholics west of the river organized a church under the name of St. Mary's of the Assumption, worshiping in the "church on the flats" until the new edifice at Carroll and Jersey streets was dedicated in 1865. Those east of the river founded St. Peter's congregation, from which St. Joseph's developed in 1862. Its famous church was located on Woodland at Chapel Street. St. Patrick's Church on Whitman Street was also established this year to serve a growing community of Irish Catholics. Two years later, the Immaculate Conception congregation was organized. It worshiped in a former chapel and school in the rear of the cathedral, and later in a new stone church erected at Superior and Lyman streets. St. Bridget's Parish had its beginning on Perry Street in 1858.

The William Lemen home was razed to make way for the four-story Hoffman Block at the southeast corner of the Public Square and Superior (Cuyahoga Building site). Gaylord & Company's drug store occupied the corner, and drug stores continued to flourish here through the years. The stone pillars from the beautiful old "Stone Cottage" were used in building a temple on the Lemen family lot in Lake View Cemetery.

R. B. Wheeler and E. A. Payne, music teachers, opened the Cleveland Academy of Music on November 13 in a hall in the Hoffman Block. It existed only a short time.

Education as It Should Be was the subject of Horace Greeley's lecture to a packed house in December, in which he strongly advocated the trade school. Five decades passed, however, before vocational education was introduced in Cleveland.

1855

Western Reserve College in Hudson, Ohio, (later Western Reserve University and Western Reserve Academy) had led a hand-to-mouth existence since the early days. At heart-breaking sacrifice, friends brought contributions in land, cattle, grain, implements, jewelry, household goods, and a rare assortment of commodities to keep the doors of educational opportunity open. George Edmond Pierce, president from 1834-55, rarely received his yearly $900 salary in money; and when he resigned, the college owed him thousands of dollars, in part payment of which he accepted a deed to the Oviatt farm. When the Rev. Henry L. Hitchcock succeeded him, the school was $25,000 in debt and the organization had been disrupted. The Panic of 1857 was approaching, followed by the Civil War, which took the entire faculty and student body into the service. While President Hitchcock triumphed in his singlehanded struggle to build up the financial structure of Western Reserve, it cost him his health, and he was obliged to resign in 1871. Carroll Cutler, a faculty member since 1860, succeeded him.

Isaac Cody, second son of Philip Cody of East Cleveland, had moved his family to Davenport, Iowa, where he became deeply interested in keeping Kansas a free state. On several occasions he visited Cleveland, trying to interest others in the cause. At about this time, when his son, William F., one of seven children, was nearing his tenth year, the father was seriously injured by an assailant as he discoursed on slavery. A year later, he died. Not long afterward William was sent by his mother to Cleveland, where she hoped he might obtain an education. His grandparents were no longer living, and he probably lived with relatives on the Cody lands, a large tract between Euclid and Garden Street (near East 83rd). His stay must have been short, for he was barely fourteen years old when he went to the Colorado gold mines and soon joined the Pony Express. After the Civil War, he earned the nickname "Buffalo Bill" while fulfilling a contract to supply construction camps of a western railroad with buffalo meat.

The building of the Northern Ohio Lunatic Asylum (later Cleveland State Hospital) was opened by the State in Newburgh on March 5. This was the second asylum in Ohio, the first having been located at Columbus. Two months later townsmen were shocked to learn that there were only forty-eight patients in the $190,000 building. John Gill, who had come to America from the Isle of Man in 1854, was the building contractor. His sons, John T. and Kermode F., joined him in the business, and they constructed a number of large buildings in Cleveland and in other cities.

In the spring, during the pastorate of the Rev. S. W. Adams, the congregation of the First Baptist Church moved to the impressive brick sanctuary at the northwest corner of Euclid and Erie streets, that had been purchased from the Plymouth Congregational Church. A spire rising 205 feet was added and the interior remodeled, seating a thousand people. Steady growth followed, missions were encouraged, and denominational influence extended.

Weather observations were undertaken by Professor Gustavus A. Hyde on May 1 for the United States Weather Bureau.

When Albert Shawk of Cincinnati unloaded his steam fire engine from a flat car at the foot of Water Street on May 4, he was about to demonstrate a bargain in an invention equal to four first-class hand engines. It pumped continuously for an indefinite time, and one man could easily operate it! At the Bank Street reservoir, Shawk fired the monster with cordwood and prepared to stage his exhibition before city officials and a crowd. Presently a stream of water shot higher and higher, over the Weddell House, topping the flagpole. As a cheer rose from the spectators, a chambermaid put her head out of a third-story window just in time to receive a thorough soaking. Shawk named his price, which was equal to the cost of four hand engines; but the committee shook their heads. "Too much money," they said, and not enough water in Cleveland. Besides, a steamer with one professional engineer would deal a deadly blow to the volunteer organization that served the city. Rolling up his hose, Inventor Shawk raked his fire, coupled his team, and turned their heads in the direction of the railroad station.

Thirteen acres of land were purchased for St. John's Cemetery (7000 Woodland) on May 4, and the first interment took place in 1858. Catholic priests who died while serving their parishes were buried here.

The spring term closed at the High School (later Central) with the first high-school commencement in Cleveland. Several students, however, had completed the prescribed course since the school was founded in 1846, but no class had done so. The graduates were George W. Durgin, Jr., Henry

W. Hamlen, John G. Prince, Timothy H. Rearden, Albert H. Spencer, Emeline W. Curtis, Helen E. Farrand (Mrs. Moses G. Watterson), Julia E. O'Brien (Mrs. Ashley McM. Van Duzer), Laura C. Spelman (Mrs. John D. Rockefeller), and Lucy M. Spelman, her sister. Laura C. Spelman read an essay, "I Can Paddle My Own Canoe."

The congregation had outgrown "Old Trinity," and in 1853, as the Rev. Lloyd Windsor concluded his seven-year ministry, a new house of worship was begun uptown near the southwest corner of Superior and Bond streets (west portion of *Leader* Building site). The old lot had been sold, and before disposition was made of the building, it burned in March, 1854. On May 17, 1855, the second Trinity Church was consecrated, a beautiful brick edifice with stone front. The interior was exquisitely appointed, from the Gothic doorway to the six great chandeliers. A massive, white-marble font was presented to the parish by Samuel L. Mather. The rectorship of Dr. James A. Bolles, 1854-59, was one of great devotion. The Church Home for the Sick and Friendless was opened at Scovill and Brownell streets in 1856, and a Free Chapel was consecrated. When the vestry declined to make the parish church free, Rev. Bolles resigned. The Rev. Thomas A. Starkey served as rector until 1869, and later became bishop of the Diocese of Newark.

German singing societies had united to form the Saengerbund of North America, and in 1849 they held the first Saengerfest in Cincinnati. Cleveland joined two years later. On May 28, 1855, national attention was focused on Cleveland as Saengerbund enthusiasts met in the city for the first time to hold their seventh German musical festival in Concert Hall. The Cleveland Gesangverein was represented by eighteen societies with one hundred and eighteen voices in the three-day prize competition, "patronized by a fashionable and appreciative auditory." A chorus of three hundred singers, led by Hans Balatka of Milwaukee, was a brilliant feature.

An expedition, organized by the War Department, set out this year to explore the uncharted wilds of northern California, Oregon, and the Southwest. Through the influence of Dr. John S. Newberry of Cleveland, assistant surgeon and geologist of the party, Dr. Elisha Sterling was selected as naturalist. Many of their reports represented the first authentic accounts of the tremendous resources of the West. Explorations continued until 1861. Dr. Newberry then went into war service as secretary of the western division of the United States Sanitary Commission. John Strong Newberry was born in Connecticut in 1822. About two years later, the family moved to Cuyahoga Falls, Ohio. Young Newberry was graduated from Western Reserve College in 1846, from the Cleveland Medical College in 1848, and studied in Europe. He came to Cleveland in 1850 and practiced medicine for five years. After graduating from the Cleveland Medical College, Dr. Elisha Sterling studied in Europe. An expert on fish culture and a skilled taxidermist, as well as an excellent surgeon, his name was to be found frequently as a contributor to scientific journals. He died in Cleveland in 1890, aged sixty-six.

E. M. Peck had built his first schooner, the *Jenny Lind,* and this year he joined in a partnership with I. U. Masters. They had produced fifty vessels in their yards when the firm dissolved in 1864. Peck continued in business, building several revenue cutters for the Government and some of the largest ships on the lakes.

The Ivanhoe Boat Club, Cleveland's first boating organization, was founded this year and won the Independence Day race with a Sandusky team on the Cuyahoga. River racing was abandoned several years later as commerce increased.

With the granting of university powers this year, Baldwin Institute became Baldwin University (later Baldwin-Wallace College). The Rev. John Wheeler was the first president. This college of liberal arts occupied "three spacious buildings," North and South halls and Baldwin Hall, the latter a four-story stone building housing students who desired "to board themselves." Wallace Hall, occupied the next year, was the gift of James Wallace of the board of trustees, who also deeded Public Lyceum Square to the institution. In 1868, Hulet Hall, the university chapel, was opened. It was made possible through the combined generosity of Fletcher Hulet, James Wallace, and John Baldwin. Until 1896 it served both school and community.

Conflict between market men, hucksters, and grocers had developed when hucksters began purchasing the produce of market gardeners direct, commanding high prices and cutting down the middle-men's trade. The year-old practice culminated in a "bread, meat and rent" meeting on the Public Square, August 9, when workmen organized a "protective union" to fight the monopoly. Council stepped in and passed an ordinance designed to relieve the consumer.

J. D. Garrett's plan for a breakwater was a good one, and councilmen approved it in August. It called for tight crib work, filled with stone, rising six feet above the water. Beginning at the outer end of the stone pier at the river mouth, it was to run parallel to the shore eastward, 1,000 feet out, in 15 feet of water, to a point opposite Wood Street. The district Congressman called it a visionary scheme, however, and that was the end of Citizen Garrett's plan.

One of the finest churches west of New York City was dedicated by the congregation of the First Presbyterian Church of Cleveland (Old Stone) on August 12. Built "without any extraordinary exertions or sacrifices" at a cost of $60,000, it stood on the original site of the first stone church at the northwest corner of Ontario and the Public Square.

John D. Rockefeller, a lad of sixteen, graduated from Folsom's Mercantile College (later Spencerian College) in August. Finding a job was difficult; but on September 26, Hewitt & Tuttle, commission merchants on Merwin Street, hired him to assist with bookkeeping and office work. No mention of pay was made until the last day of December, when the boy received $50 for services to date. A little brown "ledger" was one of his first purchases; and the first entry, "10 cents to the missionary cause," was indicative of thrifty living and gifts to worthy causes that exceeded a half-billion dollars during his long life. In three and one-half years with the firm, Rockefeller earned only $1,525; but his experience was to prove invaluable in future business ventures that earned great wealth for him.

The canal at Sault Ste. Marie was completed, opening to commerce 1,000 additional miles of waterway, and bringing Cleveland closer to the world's great iron region. The first cargo of iron ore, totaling 132 tons, was shipped by the Cleveland Iron Mining Company (later Cleveland-Cliffs) from the Lake Superior mines, via the Soo, bound for Cleveland. On the brigantine *Columbia,* built at Sandusky in 1842, it passed through the canal on August 14. The company's shipments for the season, amounting to 1,449 tons, constituted the waterway's ore tonnage for the year.

To circumvent the law, which permitted only one high school in Cleveland, a branch of the city high school (later Central) was organized on the third floor of the Kentucky Grade School to serve the West Side. Branch High School (forerunner of West High School) was, however, a separate school, with A. G. Hopkinson, former superintendent of the Ohio City schools, as principal. In 1861, it moved to its own building at State and Clinton streets; in 1882, into the West High School building at Bridge and Randall streets; and in 1903, to a new home on Franklin Boulevard.

Until this time, Ohio constituted a federal district, and the United States district and circuit courts convened in Columbus. Now that lake trade and maritime business had greatly expanded, a northern district was created, with Cleveland as the seat of the United States Court. President Franklin Pierce appointed Hiram V. Willson the first judge; Daniel O. Morton of Toledo, district attorney; and Jabez W. Fitch, United States marshal. The court appointed Frederick W. Green of Seneca County, clerk, and General Henry H. Dodge and Bushnell White, United States commissioners. Lewis Dibble served as bailiff for thirty years. The admiralty interests, flourishing counterfeiters, and byproducts of the Fugitive-Slave Law kept the grand jury busy and created excitement in the community.

The slavery issue had split old-line political parties, making the formation of a new party imperative. This year's campaign was of historic importance, as it was the first state contest in which the new Republican Party engaged. Dissatisfied antislavery Whigs, Free Soilers, members of the Know-Nothing Party, and Abolitionists rallied behind their candidate for governor, Salmon P. Chase of Cincinnati, who spoke in Cleveland on September 20. His great victory inspired a mammoth celebration on the night of October 13, launched by one hundred and one guns, a giant bonfire in the middle of the Square, fireworks, bands, parades, and speeches.

The City Infirmary, a brick building, was erected in Brooklyn (3395 Scranton Road) to house the insane, the sick, and the infirm poor, and to provide facilities for the instruction of medical students. In 1858 it was reported that in the Infirmary there were "187 inmates varying in age from one month to eighty years. Fifteen are insane. All of the insane women are confined in cells in straight jackets. Two wholesome meals are prepared every day . . . a very excellent and pleasant farm. At present there is no physician in attendance." After 1872 a city physician visited the institution three times a week; but it was not until 1889 that a hospital was erected by Cleveland authorities. The building was enlarged to meet growing needs, providing quarters for the Work House and the House of Correction until 1871.

Adelina Patti, a child of twelve, made her first appearance in Cleveland in Melodeon Hall on October 11.

The first American Rabbinical Conference held in the United States convened in Cleveland on October 17.

A boycott aimed by local newspapers at the Rev. Henry Ward Beecher, famous Congregational minister and lecturer, reached for the pocketbooks of Clevelanders and snapped shut all but "75 or 80" on the evening of October 24, when the "Prophet of Plymouth Church" spoke at Chapin's Hall. These few paid the fifty-cent admission to hear his discourse on *Patriotism,* unmindful of press admonitions that it was the "brassiest imposition" to ask so much. Beecher favored women's rights, but declared that females should not speak in public. As to holding public office, he observed that there were a good many "old grannies" in office, and they "might as well have real women." Cincinnati joined in the boycott; and when the admission charge was reduced to a quarter, Milwaukee and Buffalo produced full houses. The incident was discussed for weeks, and the prophecy was made in Cleveland that a repeat performance at twenty-five cents would be a great success. Beecher proved his oratorical genius on October 20, 1857, when "one of the largest crowds ever assembled in the Melodeon" heard his eloquent lecture, *The Ministration of the Beautiful;* and a capacity audience heard his *Commonwealth* the next evening. Returns from the events helped to ease the financial burden of the city's two lecture societies. For more than two decades, Beecher charmed his Cleveland audiences with brilliant discussions of the leading questions of the day.

The city's lease of the two upper floors in the new Jones Building, a brick block built by John Jones on the southwest corner of the Square, was celebrated at a banquet held in one of the lower rooms on November 14, following the meeting of City Council. Mayors who served Cleveland while the administration was located in this rented City Hall were William B. Castle, 1855-56; Samuel Starkweather, 1857-58; George B. Senter, 1859-60; Edward S. Flint, 1861-62; Irvine U. Masters, 1863-64, who died in office and was succeeded by George B. Senter; Herman M. Chapin, 1865-66; Stephen Buhrer, 1867-70; Frederick W. Pelton, 1871-72; Charles A. Otis, 1873-74.

1856

Council made a feeble step in the direction of enforced sanitation on January 10, when an ordinance creating a Board of Health also provided for the appointment of "one person and such deputies as the council may, from time to time, appoint" to be responsible for the city's health. Dr. Fred W. Marseilles, the first health officer, and his able successors attacked their problems in the name of decency and common safety; but co-operation and progress came slowly, despite realization of the need.

"You can't come it!" shouted a sleighing party of 7 four-horse teams from

Solon, Ohio, as they dashed through Twinsburg on the crusted roads. Translated into modern vernacular, this was a challenge meaning "this is a bigger crowd than Twinsburg can turn out!" Twinsburg lost no time. The next day 14 four-horse turnouts paid a call on Solon. Then Bedford stepped in with 32 teams and drove to Twinsburg bearing a cheesecloth banner with the figure of a boy, his hand to his mouth, calling out, "You can't come it." A great contest was in the making; and from Akron to Lake Erie, sleighs were recruited to swell town representations. On February 29, it took place in Bedford. Uniformed marshals, bands, and decorated sleighs and horses formed a gay procession, and Brecksville won the banner with 54 teams. The contest reached county proportions, and five thousand people came to Richfield from northern Ohio to see Summit, Cuyahoga, and Medina

First Central High School.

counties compete on March 14, when Summit won with 171 cutters. Cleveland was greatly chagrined when Cuyahoga mustered only 151. In the last contest, on March 18 at Akron, Medina County moved to first place with 185 teams and took home the banner, which it preserved for posterity.

"The finest school in the West" was built on Euclid Street west of Erie, adjacent to Mayell's drug store on the corner (Citizens Building site), as the home of the overcrowded city high school, which took the name Central. The twenty-thousand-dollar building was dedicated on April 1; and, while visitors came from miles around to see it, many taxpayers considered it "a piece of vicious extravagance." Decorative cornices were introduced in the 60 by 90-foot brick building faced with stone. On the first floor were quarters for the school superintendent and a library, and on the third was a large exhibition hall. Graduates of this early school won marked distinction in later life, among them Charles F. Brush, who made a commencement speech in 1867 on the subject of the arc light; John D. Rockefeller, Samuel Mather, Alexander E. Brown, John Long Severance, Frederick Harris Goff, and John P. Green, distinguished Negro lawyer. Central produced the beloved educator, Daniel W. Lothman, who gave forty-five years of inspiration to young Clevelanders, twenty-one of them as principal of East High School.

Thirteen telegraph companies, operating short lines in five states north of the Ohio River, were competing in their weakness when a merger as the Western Union Telegraph Company was effected on April 4. As the name implies, it was a union of western lines into one system. The initiative of Jeptha H. Wade had played a large part in the consolidation; and, having become general agent of the new company, he moved to Cleveland. The telegraph had been used in the operation of trains since 1851; and its contribution to safety and efficiency was to be of continuously increasing importance as rails reached out to the far corners of the nation. Republicans utilized the new telegraph to bring quick election returns to a political rally in Melodeon Hall for the first time this year.

In May, Dr. S. R. Beckwith organized the first privately owned hospital in Cleveland, known as the Cleveland Homeopathic Hospital (later Huron Road Hospital). The doctor was the surgeon for the railroads entering Cleveland, and hospital facilities were essential. For his purposes, he rented a two-story, frame house facing Clinton Park on Lake Street.

While pleading the antislavery cause in Cleveland, Frederick Douglass, noted Negro lecturer, an escaped slave, was permitted to stop at the Forest City House. The incident was discussed throughout the country.

Coal was first used as locomotive fuel on June 4 by the Cleveland & Pittsburgh railroad. After having consumed 9,798 pounds of coal in eleven hours and twenty-five minutes on a 101-mile run out of Cleveland, operators were convinced of its advantages and soon abandoned the use of wood.

For a dollar admission, Clevelanders enjoyed a concert by Ole Bull and Adelina Patti in Melodeon Hall. There was some regret that the great violinist included *Pop Goes the Weasel* on the program. His selections should have been of "a higher order," it was observed.

Lighthouse Street Bridge (later Willow Street Bridge) was built this year. It was replaced in 1898 by an electrically operated drawbridge.

The Jones brothers, John and David I., Pennsylvania iron men, came to Newburgh with $5,000 with which they purchased land from Alonzo Carter and erected the first rolling mill in Newburgh. Production of T-rails was started, but the partners ran out of money. Henry Chisholm and another Jones purchased the business, and in 1857 it became Chisholm & Jones. The next year Andros B. Stone, brother of Amasa Stone, acquired an interest, and the firm became Stone, Chisholm & Jones. About 150 men were employed in the mill, producing about 50 tons of railroad iron daily. A blast furnace, erected at Newburgh in 1861, was the first in what later became Cleveland. When it went into operation, the glow against the night sky brought out the Fire Department to answer the false alarm.

Henry Chisholm, twenty-eight-year-old Scotchman, had come to Cleveland in 1850 and supervised the building of a breakwater for the Cleveland & Pittsburgh Railroad at the lake terminus of the line. His work was so praiseworthy that he was kept busy building piers and docks until he entered the iron-manufacturing business.

On condition that a railroad station be erected on property at Euclid and Willson Avenue, Jared V. Willson and his wife executed a quit-claim deed for a one-dollar consideration on July 5. A little wooden building was put up by the Cleveland & Pittsburgh road at the crossing in the farm community, but almost a decade passed before a trading center began to take form.

The year-end school report, issued in July, stated that Cleveland had twenty-three school buildings with an estimated value of $150,000, including

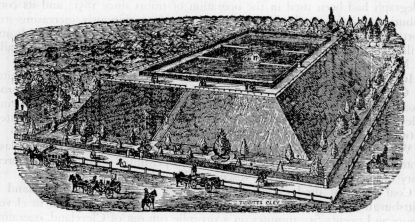

Kentucky Street Reservoir, first central pumping station.

land and equipment. The total school enrollment was 5,750, and six pupils had been graduated from each of the high schools. Greek and Latin had been introduced.

Council shelved a resolution on July 22 that contemplated construction of a tunnel, or subway, under the city from the lakeshore to the extreme southern limit of the municipality, intended primarily for use of the railroads centering in Cleveland. Had it been adopted, vexing problems concerning rights-of-way, grade crossings, and riparian rights might have been avoided, and its influence on the city's civic and industrial future can hardly be estimated.

The Federal Government purchased from Leonard Case, Sr., the Case homestead on the Public Square for $30,000 as the site for a federal building. A two-family, red-brick dwelling on Rockwell (opposite Federal Building), built in 1837 for renting purposes, was remodeled into a single house as the Case family home. In 1908, the property was acquired for the Group Plan. Leonard Street and Case Street, meeting at a bend of the Cuyahoga River, were named for Leonard Case in 1853, and Case Avenue also honored the family name.

After two years of construction, the Kentucky Street Reservoir, Cleveland's first central pumping station, opened on September 24 with a colorful celebration that attracted thirty thousand visitors. The six-acre mound was 35 feet above the level of Kentucky and Prospect streets (later Fairview Park). Spectators climbed the steps up the side for a view of the six-million-gallon wonder and the city that stretched into the countryside. The cost was $526,712.99. Water was taken from the lake through a 300-foot steel tunnel (touching shore near West 58th Street). Two large mains carried the water throughout the city. Two Cornish engines, working alternately, were the first of their kind erected west of the Alleghenies. Professional well-and-cistern cleaners saw the handwriting on the wall. Despite large-scale planning, the utility was antiquated within a decade.

As water was being let into the new city mains, a state fair was in progress in the center of the Public Square. A featured attraction was the "capacious fountain" from which thousands of visitors sampled drinking water piped from the lake. Local papers declared it was the first fountain in the State.

A market-house site (Ontario, Woodland, and Broadway) was approved in October, and part was purchased for about fifteen hundred dollars, the rest of the property being given by members of the Walworth family for market purposes. Market men condemned the site as too far uptown. Factions clashed until 1857, when the Council determined to force the issue by moving the Michigan Street market to the new Central Market site. Stubborn opposition continued to attack the project, and it found rough going.

One of the earliest Cleveland-built steamers to cross the Atlantic was the *Dean Richmond* that left Chicago for Liverpool in October.

The first hydraulic press for making bricks was set up in A. W. Duty's yards in East Cleveland. It had the amazing capacity of ten bricks a minute.

Seventy-three rooms with parlor and bath were added to the Weddell House in a $25,000 expansion program. The new four-story addition on Bank Street extended to Frankfort, where the main entrance was re-located; and two bronze lions were mounted beside the ladies' entrance on Superior. The hotel was linked with the political, business, and social progress of Cleveland until the seventies, when it began to decline.

Omnibus lines were the forerunners of the modern streetcar system. Stevens' line, connecting hotels and depots, was operating in 1856.

1857

Many were turned away from Melodeon Hall on January 29, when a capacity audience listened "attentively and quietly" to Ralph Waldo Emerson's lecture, *The Conduct of Life.* The *Herald* reporter was obviously not deeply impressed, for he stated that the subject "was treated in a transcendental sweeping, dry and orderless manner which characterizes the emanations of his mind." On one of Emerson's visits to Cleveland, his interest in education prompted him to pay an early-morning call on Central High School without warning, to see a western high school and watch the pupils at work. A telegraph line installed by the pupils, and their publication, *The School Boy,* impressed him. It was Emerson, the student, who wrote, "It matters little what your studies are; it all lies in who your teacher is."

The *Daily Review,* non-partisan morning newspaper edited by H. N. Johnson, made its appearance this year in an era of political ferment. Cleveland's first penny sheet, it labored loud and long on religion and morality, and once a week it reviewed current events. In the following April, an experiment in a Sunday edition known as the *Sunday Morning Review* concluded with the eleventh issue, a casualty due to profound observance of the Sabbath. The paper failed to survive the Civil War.

A 100-foot stream from Chief James Hill's hand-pumping engines was unable to reach the fire that spread from the roof of the Stone Church to the towering 250-foot steeple, and, like a flaming torch, it swayed and crashed across Ontario Street. Blackened stone walls remained as grim re-

Looking south from the Public Square through Ontario Street in 1862. The Square was enclosed by a fence, shutting off Ontario and Superior streets.

A balloon ascension from the Public Square.

South side of the Public Square, 1865, from a painting in the Western Reserve Historical Society.

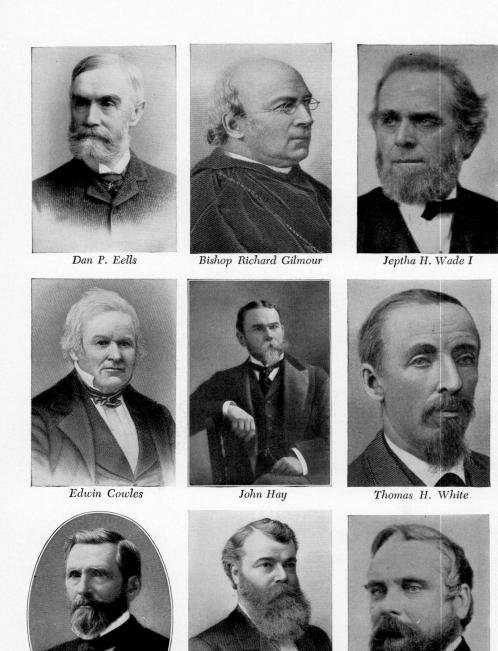

Dan P. Eells   Bishop Richard Gilmour   Jeptha H. Wade I

Edwin Cowles   John Hay   Thomas H. White

Rufus P. Ranney   Gen. John H. Devereux   Henry Chisholm

minders of the calamity suffered by the new First Presbyterian Church on March 7. Rebuilding began promptly, and the congregation worshiped in Chapin's Hall until its home was restored.

The Society for Savings needed larger quarters, and rooms built for it in the Weddell House were occupied this year. Having installed a burglar-proof safe in a brick vault, it was now prepared for safe-keeping of assets on the premises. F. W. Bingham became president in 1850 and was succeeded by William A. Otis in 1852, S. J. Andrews in 1855, and Otis, who was elected again in 1861.

The rail fences around the four sections of the Public Square had become dilapidated, and cows invaded the area to graze. The Square's residents and two thousand petitioners won a temporary victory in the "fence war" on March 24, when Council ordered that Superior Avenue and Ontario Street be vacated, and that a white double-railed fence be built around the grounds, enclosing it into a large park. On the first dark night, the fence went up, and traffic was obliged to circle the Square. Shrubs were planted and rambling walks were laid. Band concerts were given on summer evenings, and the park became a popular recreation spot. An unrelenting opposition fought the fence for a decade before it came down.

In March, Charles C. Baldwin, twenty-two-year-old graduate of the Harvard Law School, began reading law in the Cleveland office of S. B. and F. J. Prentiss, sons of Samuel Prentiss, famous Vermont senator. When he was only a babe, Baldwin's parents moved from Connecticut to Elyria, Ohio, where his father was a merchant until his death in 1847. When S. B. Prentiss was elected to the Common Pleas bench in 1867, the firm of Prentiss & Baldwin dissolved, and Baldwin later became associated with F. J. and Charles W. Prentiss. Baldwin was a corporation lawyer of unusual ability, and served on the directorate of four Cleveland banks. He was profoundly interested in the civic growth of his city, and devoted much of his time to cultural organizations. Elected circuit judge in 1884, his record on the bench reflected his keen intellect and his sterling character. He died while in office in 1895.

Cleveland police were apprehensive and helpless on April 23, as they watched a lively ball game on the Public Square; but they did nothing more—there was no law. Virtuous citizens were astonished the same day when two females appeared in the street in the fullest and most astonishing bloomer style.

The Fire Department expanded with the organization of the Alert Hose Company in this year, and the Protection Hose Company in 1858.

Rufus P. Ranney, distinguished Ohio lawyer, resigned as judge of the Ohio Supreme Court and moved to Cleveland this year, where he began practicing law with the firm of Ranney, Backus & Noble. Born in Massachusetts in 1813, his family moved to Portage County, Ohio, in 1822. Ranney received limited schooling, and with his earnings managed to attend Western Reserve College for several terms. His search for work led to Jefferson, Ohio, where he studied law in the office of the eminent legislator, Benjamin F. Wade, and became his partner. Ranney moved to Warren, Ohio; and in

1850, as a delegate to the Constitutional Convention of Ohio, he displayed in debate a brilliant knowledge of law. Later in the year he was elected to the State Supreme Court, resigning in 1856 to return to law practice. A friendly campaign for election to the Ohio Supreme Court stirred political circles in 1862, when Judge Ranney, Democrat, was chosen to run against his law partner, Franklin T. Backus, Republican. Ranney won by a majority of several thousand votes, serving until 1865, when he resigned and returned to his law office. He was unanimously elected president of the Ohio State Bar Association when it was organized in 1881. One of Ohio's greatest lawyers and jurists, Judge Ranney was widely known for his integrity and his forceful devotion to the right. Modest, unassuming, and a man of simple tastes and habits, he and his family lived in a sturdy, gabled, stone house that he built on Euclid Avenue in 1876 (later Gray Hotel, 2728 Euclid). Here he died in 1891.

Plymouth Congregational Church took the lead in a revival movement that began with daily prayer meetings at eight o'clock in the morning, chiefly for businessmen. Other churches soon began to hold services. The YMCA joined in the endeavor, and it was estimated that between two and three thousand persons worshiped every morning. Sunday Schools united in Sunday-afternoon meetings at the Second Presbyterian Church. It was believed that the "presence of an educated and cool-headed leadership exercises a restraining influence on an over-emotionalized company of people," and as a result of quiet conferences and earnest meetings, the churches greatly increased their memberships in the revival period that continued into 1858. A similar revival was held in 1866.

Cleveland Typographical Union No. 53, pioneer labor local, was organized. Following a lapse during the Civil War, it was revived, and received an international charter in 1868.

A great religious mania, born of revivalists' threats and astrologists' predictions of the end of the world, was sweeping the country and adding to the general unrest as the Panic of 1857 climaxed in August. Depression clouds had begun to gather in the nation as early as 1853, resulting from over-extended bank credit, reckless spending, and over-projection of railroads. Specie was scarce. Fortunes were wiped out. Business and industry suffered dreadfully, and sixty-five Ohio banks failed. The future of railroads and public improvements was jeopardized. Cleveland banks rode out the storm, and "business houses generally survived." Employment was hard hit, however, and in most plants, "the number of employees were reduced from 25 to 50 per cent." Tight money brought people to their senses. Common need led to better understanding between classes, and church groups began to co-operate in welfare endeavors. Unsettled times lasted until the beginning of Civil War prosperity.

Advocates of compensated emancipation met in national convention in Cleveland in August. Acknowledging that slavery was a national problem, they proposed that owners be paid $250 for the freedom of each slave, the money to be raised either by the sale of public lands or other sources of federal revenue. After airing itself, the movement died.

William S. Kerruish gave up teaching in Twinsburg, Ohio, and came to Cleveland this year to study law in the office of Ranney, Backus & Noble. In 1827 his parents had come from the Isle of Man to settle in Warrensville, Ohio, where he was born in 1831. Kerruish attended Twinsburg Institute and Western Reserve College, and was graduated from Yale in 1855. He became one of Ohio's distinguished trial lawyers; gifted with unusual speaking ability, he was in demand for public addresses. His son, Sheldon Q., was admitted to his father's firm, Kerruish & Chapman; and when George T. Chapman died in 1906, the partnership became Kerruish & Kerruish. The long career of William S. Kerruish closed with his death in 1927. His son became active head of the business, known as Kerruish, Kerruish, Hartshorn & Spooner in 1912, when George E. Hartshorn and George W. Spooner were admitted. It was one of the largest legal firms in the State.

A dozen photographic artists had opened studios in Cleveland, including Samuel Crobaugh, who was making daguerreotypes on Ontario Street in the early fifties; James F. Ryder, who won international fame; and E. Decker, who sold his thriving business to George M. Edmondson in 1863.

Franklin Circle was fenced, and a fountain and wooden pavilion were placed in it to promote beautification.

In the community of English people in the eastern part of Cleveland, the foundation for St. James Parish was laid by Trinity Church, supported by the united efforts of other Episcopal churches, resulting in a "Church Union." Samuel L. Mather of Trinity was the first senior warden, and Zenas King of St. Paul's, junior warden. A brick church was erected in 1865 at Alabama and Superior streets, and the Rev. Richard Bury, former rector of Trinity, was in charge until ill health obliged him to withdraw in 1872. The little congregation was sheltered by Trinity until 1890, when it was revived. A stone church was built on Willson Avenue at Payne, where St. James served the needs of a changing community. The Rev. Vivian A. Peterson came to the parish as rector in 1919. Canon Peterson was a leader of the Anglo-Catholic group in the Episcopal Church of America.

An overload of cattle caused the Seneca Street Bridge to collapse, and a new hand-operated wooden drawbridge took its place. A two-span iron structure replaced it in 1888.

William Howard Taft, twenty-sixth President of the United States and later chief justice of the United States Supreme Court, was born on September 15 at Cincinnati, Ohio.

A second New England Hotel was built at the northeast corner of Water and Johnson streets. It could not compete with the finer houses of the day, but it was a good second-class hotel. Wholesale business moved into the Water Street district, and the New England passed out of existence in 1900.

On October 29, Charles Farrar Brown, twenty-three, later known as Artemus Ward, was hired by J. W. Gray as commercial editor of the *Plain*

Dealer, starting at a salary of ten dollars a week. Within three weeks, the gawky tramp printer had made a place for himself on the masthead as "associate editor," and his bantering treatment of the "locals" was ranking in reader interest with the editor's eloquent analyses of politics. Brown was devoted to his mother, whom he called Caroline. They were both endowed with a rare gift of humor, and Charles delighted in teasing her. "Be respectful to your mother," she admonished one day. "Remember what the *Bible* says." "Well, I expect I ought to," he agreed, "but it is so different from the *Plain Dealer,* I don't putter with it much . . . a man cannot serve two masters, and I'm a Democrat."

Eighteen of Cleveland's twenty-two dentists were present at the organization meeting of the Northern Ohio Dental Association, announced by Drs. W. H. Atkinson, J. A. Robinson, and others. They met in Tremont Hall

Third Court House erected on the north side of the Public Square in 1857.

on November 3, and elected Dr. F. S. Slosson the first president. Dr. W. P. Horton of Cleveland was a charter member. Dr. Benjamin Strickland, who called the assembly to order, was elected president the next year, and re-elected annually for eight terms. He was Cleveland's pioneer dentist, a man of rare ability and understanding, whose long service closed with his death in 1889.

High on the roll of dentists who established their profession in Cleveland was Dr. W. H. Atkinson, who came to the city in 1853 and was Dr. Slosson's associate. Dr. Charles R. Butler was his student and later his partner. Paying tribute to Dr. Atkinson, Dr. Burton Lee Thorpe, dental historian, called him "Leader, 'Teacher of Teachers,' Prophet, and Past Grand Master Dental Enthusiast." Dr. M. L. Wright, who came in the forties, was graduated from the Cleveland Medical College. His son, M. L., and three grandsons, Harry D., Martin L., and William, chose to follow dentistry. In 1850, Dr. B. F. Robinson, the first of a family of dentists, came to Cleveland, followed by his brother, Dr. J. A., with his sons, Jere E. and William F. Dr. Lewis Buffett, newcomer in 1861, lectured at the Cleveland Medical College; and his brother, Charles, was treasurer of the Northern Ohio Dental Association for many years. Dr. D. R. Jennings practiced in Cleveland from 1872 to 1897.

The county commissioners contracted for the building of a new Court House on November 10. The official business of Cuyahoga County had expanded tremendously, and the City Council had decided to clear the Public Square of permanent buildings. Erection of a three-story stone structure, 80 by 152 feet, of simple ante-bellum dignity, was begun this year on narrow Rockwell Street at the northwest corner of the Square (west of the Illuminating Building). It was completed in 1860 at a cost of $152,500. The famous "Bridge of Sighs" connected the Court House with the jail in the rear. During the construction period, the First Baptist Church was used for court purposes.

"A great error of our present social system in America is that we have too few holidays, too few hours of relaxation from the cares of slavery of business, and too little of that social relish of existence which makes so charming the rural life of England, Germany and France. . . . We must hail the season of holidays." Thus a local editor gave vent on December 18 to weariness at keeping pace with a busy world.

1858

Cleveland's master builder, Warham J. Warner, had restored the Stone Church on the Public Square after damage by fire, and it was dedicated on January 17. Ten years later, the galleries were completed, and another graceful spire reached heavenward from the east bell tower. Within its friendly walls in the heart of the busy city, willing members gave generously of time and talents, inspiring sparks of human endeavor that developed into social, cultural, and civic movements touching the lives of Clevelanders from generation to generation. In August, 1858, the Rev. William H. Goodrich became assistant to Dr. Samuel C. Aiken, whose declining health forced retirement as pastor emeritus in 1861. Death came in 1879. Dr. Goodrich gained wide recognition as a civic leader, serving until his death in 1874.

The first of Charles Farrar Brown's famous letters introducing Artemus Ward appeared in the *Plain Dealer* of January 30. Ward, an imaginary showman, traveled about Ohio with a small sideshow, but never quite reached Cleveland. Brown's visionary young man with an annual income of $2,500, seeking a wife by mail, produced lively reading and a pile of fan mail for the author. Another of his tall stories centered on a lion that dashed headlong into a pole, the force splitting him from head to tail. The owner put the animal together, but, alas, wrong-end-to. In the *Plain Dealer,* the twisted creature cavorted to the entertainment of Artemus Ward's widening circle of readers. Patent medicines were used by Brown to add spirit to his literary efforts, and the sight of a peeping red petticoat claimed more of his attention than poking fun at politics. He dealt in extremes, whether they were intended as cutting criticism or fanciful nonsense. Where Brown's pen name originated has been debated, one authority claiming it was the name of a half-wit snake charmer who lived near Cleveland.

The Cuyahoga County Historical Society, founded in February, was the first evidence of organized interest in historical Cleveland. Leonard Case, Sr., was president; John Barr, secretary; Samuel Williamson, treasurer; and Charles Whittlesey, Ahaz Merchant, and George B. Merwin, trustees. To broaden its influence, committees were created in each township, headed by a vice president. Interest centered in collecting and preserving historical material. Thousands turned out to enjoy "grand county picnic pioneer celebrations" patterned after the county fair, where relics were exhibited along with livestock, and orators and stunt performers enjoyed a field day. While the society became a victim of the Civil War, priceless historical treasures and manuscripts had been brought to light that were handed down to the Western Reserve Historical Society in the next decade.

St. Paul's Evangelical and Reformed Church originated in a congregation organized as the Second German Evangelical Church on April 18, 1858. The Rev. J. M. Steiner was the first pastor. Affiliation with the Evangelical Synod of North America came in 1862. A church was erected on Scovill Avenue (at East 28th Street) to which a school was added. The cornerstone of a new house of worship was laid, September 11, 1921, at East 127th Street and Woodland Avenue.

The pioneer drug store of Handerson, Punderson & Company was acquired by S. E. Strong and A. C. Armstrong, who established a wholesale department and were soon supplying retail stores in four neighboring states. Their first private formula was Dr. Strong's Fever Destroyer. Ahira Cobb joined the firm in 1870, and the name became Strong, Cobb & Company. As the pharmaceutical branch developed, it gradually overshadowed other departments, so that by 1918 Strong, Cobb were manufacturing chemists, exclusively. The company became the largest "private formula" house in the United States. George Miller was made president in 1940, succeeding T. S. Strong.

W. P. Southworth, a Cleveland builder in the forties, established a grocery business this year, and surprised his competitors by inaugurating deliveries by wheelbarrow. Trade grew in his first store, at the corner of Ontario and Champlain streets, and he moved across Ontario (Park Building site), where he operated one of the leading groceries of the city. Upon his death in 1891, his son, William J., was head of the business until his death in 1907. Southworth's later moved to the Rose Building on Prospect Avenue.

The barque *D. C. Pierce* was the first Cleveland freighter to clear for Europe. It carried a cargo of staves and black-walnut timber. Ten ships followed during the year.

Four Cleveland-owned vessels, built in local shipyards, set out for Liverpool on May 29 with cargoes of wheat and black-walnut timber. City officials and the artillery arranged a noisy departure for the "Liverpool Fleet."

Twenty families were released from the Trinity Evangelical Lutheran Church on Jersey Street to organize St. Paul's Evangelical Lutheran Church in North Dover, Ohio, on June 13. The Rev. John J. Rupprecht was called as pastor to serve the congregation of fifty-three communicants and ninety-three baptized members. For a number of years, services were held in a rented church (corner of Detroit and Dover Center roads, Westlake). On weekdays the pastor conducted a school in the building. A larger sanctuary was built in 1877, and the old church served as a schoolhouse. After nearly fifty-three years of service, Pastor Rupprecht died. O. C. Yunghans became schoolmaster and organist, and the Rev. Fred Reinking, pastor, in 1911, the year in which a modern brick school was dedicated. The Rev. William J. Single succeeded Rev. Reinking upon his death in 1922.

The first iron arch and swing bridges in northern Ohio were manufactured by Zenas King, who started business this year. In 1871, the King Iron Bridge & Manufacturing Company was organized by King, Thomas A. Reeve, A. B. Stone, Charles E. Barnard, Charles A. Crumb, Dan P. Eells, and Henry Chisholm. Under Harry W. King, the founder's son, structural- and wrought-iron work was furnished for major building projects. Annual sales had reached nearly a million dollars in 1876, when the company was located at St. Clair and Wason streets. The builders had met keen criticism of competitors, but they proved the superiority of King bridges, and a nationwide business developed. By 1886, their bridges, if placed end to end, would have extended more than 150 miles.

Early in the morning of July 5—Independence Day fell on Sunday, carriages, wagons, and railroads began pouring an estimated forty thousand people into the city to observe the holiday. A subscription of $2,800 had been taken up for the celebration, the "greatest" in northern Ohio. After a parade in which three thousand participated, concluding with exercises in the Public Square, dinner was spread by Father Mathew's Total Abstinence Society. Coffee and lemonade took the place of wines and liquors. The great feature came shortly after six in the evening, when M. Godard ascended in his balloon, the *Canada,* carrying a solitary passenger. After drifting for a half hour to Olmstead, he came down in a field. The Public Square was Cleveland's first airport.

The Burnett House opened in the market district at the northeast corner of Prospect and unpaved Ontario in the Farmers Block. Weddings, reunions, and festive occasions increased its popularity, and it was soon enlarged. In 1867, it was improved and opened as the Cleveland Hotel. A series of landlords moved in and out until about 1880, when John B. White leased the hotel and named it the Prospect House. Colonel Ransom A. Gillette took it over a year later, and for more than a decade it flourished. It became the Wilmont in 1893, then the Hotel Frankfort, and in 1905 the Bailey Company acquired it, building and rebuilding until the old structure disappeared.

An attack of fever that influenced young Stephen A. Douglas to leave Cleveland in 1833 helped to shape the careers of two great national figures. Douglas eventually settled in Illinois. In the famous Lincoln-Douglas debate at Freeport, Illinois, on August 27, Douglas was forced to admit that slavery might be excluded from a territory by its citizens. Douglas' campaign for re-election to the United States Senate was successful, but Lincoln had made his mark in a fearless encounter with the champion. Staunch supporter of the Douglas political philosophies was J. W. Gray, editor of the *Plain Dealer,* whose loyalty cost him his office as Cleveland postmaster.

William Case commissioned Julius Gollman to paint "A Meeting at the Ark," showing the original "Arkites" in characteristic session (preserved in the library of Western Reserve Historical Society). The German artist received $400 for his work. Case had moved the little wooden Ark out of the way of the new government building to an adjoining location (easterly portion of Federal Building site).

A German department was inaugurated in Baldwin University (later Baldwin-Wallace College) in 1858 for the training of ministers and mission-

Going to a fire.

aries of the German Methodist Church. Its successful operation led to the opening in 1864 of German Wallace College in Baldwin Hall as a separate school, with the Rev. William Nast as president. It was the first German Methodist college in the United States. Enrollment the first year was forty students. Although the two institutions were independent in control and finances, they were intimately connected in instruction.

Rivalry was the stuff of which firemen were made, and the annual Firemen's Tournament was the big event of the year. For several days, visiting fire companies from all over Ohio—as far south as Columbus, Dayton, and Cincinnati—poured into Cleveland, bringing apparatus and bands. September 9, tournament day, opened with a parade around the Square and a short program. Contests were staged in the afternoon, each delegation fortified by the frenzied support of homefolks. Five silver trumpets, the grand awards, had stirred up the commotion. Oberlin won the first event, racing its hook-and-ladder from the Square out Superior for a quarter-mile and mounting a man on top of the ladder in one minute, twenty-six seconds. The second trumpet went to Cleveland, whose Alert Company thundered down the same course, laid 300 feet of hose, and had water running in one minute, forty-nine seconds. No. 3 went to Dayton in the first-class engine competition at Ontario and Prospect, which threw a stream just short of 195 feet. Second-class pumpers met at Erie and Euclid, and the fourth trumpet went to Cleveland with a winning stream of 194 feet. At Ontario and St. Clair, third-class pumpers fought it out, and Findlay won with a 194-foot stream. Skirmishes kept the police busy during the day, but in the evening the visitors joined with the locals in gala balls at Grays Armory and National Hall.

The problem of drainage was greatly facilitated by the topography of Cleveland, and it was not until this time that the matter of sewage received official attention. The first sewer, constructed this year, served only to drain surface water off Euclid Street. It was cut through the ridge on Sterling and Case avenues for a distance of 915 feet, and cost $952.43. This inspired the building of brick sewers and culverts in distressed areas; but benefits in the name of sanitation varied according to the funds available, and the river, lake, and brooks continued to receive the discharge until 1895.

Out of a Sunday School and prayer group, a little band of Welsh in New-burgh organized a Congregational church in the home of William Jones on Harvard Street. It had its beginning in the Jones family—David I. and his brother, John, who had erected the rolling mill, Thomas D., George M., Evan, and William. Of the fifteen original members, seven bore the name of Jones. The secretary, George M. Jones, was induced to fill the pulpit until 1864, when the Rev. W. Watkins became the first pastor, conducting services in the Welsh language. A little church built in 1860 became inade-quate, and in 1876 a new edifice was erected on Jones Avenue during the ministry of the Rev. John E. Jones. The church grew steadily as a force in the religious and social life of the clannish, hard-working Welsh people, not only in Newburgh, but in the city; and on the church directory of 1896, containing 211 names, there appeared 20 bearing the name Davies; 25, Griffiths; and 40, Jones. In later years, the church suffered from economic influences that deeply affected the life of the community; and while years of hardship were endured, it continued to serve, decade after decade, as the Jones Road Congregational Church at Broadway and Jones Road.

At a meeting in the Weddell House on November 8, the Cleveland Chess Club was organized with Leonard Case, Jr., president. Telegraph wires were installed in their room in the Waring Block, and during the winter an excit-ing game, played for almost a month, was lost to Detroit.

Oberlin College offered educational opportunities to free Negroes, and the community naturally became a haven for escaped slaves. Here a Kentucky fugitive named John Price found refuge only to be discovered by a slave-catcher. Price was cleverly abducted and taken to Wellington, Ohio, where his captors awaited a train to Columbus. News of the seizure brought a rescue mob of about a thousand who forced the kidnapers to turn over their victim. After several days in security at the home of James H. Fairchild, Oberlin professor and later president, the slave was shipped over the "underground" safely to Canada.

Thirty-seven supposed leaders in the Oberlin-Wellington rescue incident, including Oberlin professors, business and professional men, white and colored, were indicted under the Fugitive-Slave Law, and were arraigned before the United States District Court in Cleveland on December 7, where they pleaded "not guilty." Rufus P. Spalding, Franklin T. Backus, Albert G. Riddle, and Seneca O. Griswold, leading attorneys, volunteered to defend the accused. The ten-day trial was opened on April 7, 1859, by District

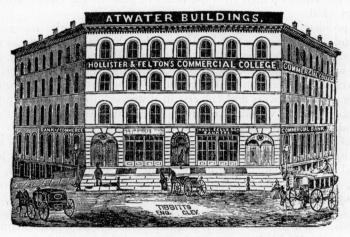

The Atwater Building as it appeared in 1858, the home of pioneer banks and other important business institutions.

Attorney George W. Belden before Judge Hiram V. Willson. Business almost ceased as citizens crowded into the Federal Building. The law clearly dictated a verdict of guilty against the major offenders, and sixty-day jail sentences were ordered with fines of $600. Protest meetings were held all over the Western Reserve, and people came from northern Ohio "by trainload and wagonload" to parade before the jail and cheer the "martyrs." Daily mass meetings were held in the Public Square, addressed by Joshua R. Giddings, Governor Salmon P. Chase, Judge Daniel R. Tilden, and leading opponents of the slave law. Professor Henry E. Peck of Oberlin, a prisoner, preached quieting sermons to his fellows and to enraged sympathizers and bystanders. While serving their sentences, prisoners produced a bi-monthly newspaper called *The Rescuer,* and prepared propaganda for release to newspapers and ministers. Professor Fitch's Oberlin Sunday School paid him a visit in jail rather than enjoy their usual picnic. The trial was widely publicized, and newsmen from large cities reported for their papers.

When the rescuers were released, they were hailed as heroes and patriots, and great crowds escorted them to their trains. Cheers, music, and prayers greeted the Oberlin party when they returned, and a banquet was served in their honor.

The Clearing House Association was organized on December 28, "to effect at one place and in the most economical and safe manner the daily exchange between the several associated banks and bankers." T. P. Handy, the first president, Lemuel Wick, and Fayette Brown, private banker, made up the executive committee. Five commercial banks and four private banking houses constituted the membership. Headquarters were in the City Bank (The National City Bank of Cleveland) for many years. The association served as little more than a medium for the exchange of checks by members until 1902, when its powers were greatly enlarged to increase its usefulness in expediting and safeguarding the city's financial interests.

A new government building was opened on the Public Square (westerly portion of Federal Building site) on December 29, during the administration of Postmaster Benjamin Harrington, appointed on June 12. It housed the Post Office, Custom House, United States courts, and federal offices. Edwin Cowles became postmaster on April 4, 1861; George A. Benedict on July 12, 1865; and John W. Allen on April 4, 1870.

1859

Rain prevented many from attending Ralph Waldo Emerson's lecture on *The Law of Success* at Melodeon Hall on January 20, arranged by the Cleveland Library Association, admission twenty-five cents. Only from the pen of that strange personality, Artemus Ward, could have come the daring, humorous criticism in the *Plain Dealer* the next morning: "He is a man of massive intellect, a great and profound thinker—but . . . his lecture last night was rather a sleepy affair. For our part . . . we had quite as lief see a perpendicular coffin behind a lecture desk as Emerson. The one would amuse as much as the other. Mr. Emerson is a great scholar—full of book learning— but, like many other great scholars, he is impractical and visionary. Let mankind adopt his ideas (Providing always that mankind can understand what his ideas are) and they would live a strange, weird life—the chaotic dream of a lunatic." Large audiences greeted the eminent lecturer several times in the sixties; and in Ward's few remaining years of life, he saw Emerson's essays and philosophies capture the attention of the great minds of his day.

Adding to his $1,000 savings a loan of $1,000 made by his father, John D. Rockefeller joined Maurice B. Clark in starting a produce commission business on River Street, March 18. Clark & Rockefeller operations soon extended into Indiana, and T. P. Handy loaned young Rockefeller $2,000 to keep pace with increasing trade. Sales the first year reached $500,000.

State legislation took the election of the Board of Education from the City Council and placed it with the voters. Charles Bradburn was president of the first board, elected on April 5. High-school courses were extended from three to four years. German was introduced during the year, but a shortage of funds hampered general progress.

Dr. C. A. Terry was the first president of the Cuyahoga County Medical Society, organized in April. Civil War years reduced it to inactivity; but in 1874 it was revived and consolidated with the Cleveland Medical Association, which had originated in the Cleveland Academy of Medicine, founded in 1867. The society's roll of presidents included leading medical men of Cleveland. In 1885 a portion of the annual dues was set aside for the purchase of medical books and journals to be placed in Case Library. This arrangement continued until a medical library association was formed in 1894.

Before Architect C. H. Heard put his plans for Case Hall on paper, William Case, who conceived the idea for a Cleveland cultural center, visited Faneuil Hall, Boston, then considered the country's civic and architectural gem, using it as a model. Case, wealthy leader in cultural and scientific affairs, had moved the historic Ark eastward on Superior (Public Library site), and erection of Case Hall began this year on Superior, just west of Wood Street, adjacent to the Federal Building. Quarters were provided for the Cleveland Library Association and the Cleveland Academy of Natural Science. William Case died of consumption in 1862 before the building was completed.

Under the new militia law, four artillery companies were formed in Cleveland, one in Brooklyn, and one in Geneva, Ohio. They were in turn organized into the 1st Regiment of Light Artillery, Colonel James Barnett commanding.

The Ohio wheat crop was ruined, cornfields had to be replanted, and a great part of the fruit failed to ripen after the "Big Frost" of June 5, when the thermometer fell to 38° in sheltered spots.

German singers came from all over the country, and a number from abroad, to compete for prizes in the eleventh Saengerfest, arranged by the North American Saengerbund, that opened on June 14 in National Hall. The Cleveland Gesangverein, represented by twenty-four societies with four hundred voices, presented *Alessandro Stradella* on the opening day, the first serious opera sung in the city, as a feature of the four-day event. First award in a prize concert on June 16 went to the Detroit Harmonie; the Buffalo Saengerbund captured the second honor.

In a local paper of July 8, Elijah Smith advertised two frame houses for rent on Water Street at $8 each per month, "supplied with water and other conveniences." Eight hundred tons of Lake Huron ice were offered for sale by the Cleveland Ice Company, and "a nice saloon" could be purchased for $300. Law & North's "coal oil factory" was at high production, "making a beautiful straw-colored oil" to be used as fuel for reading lamps. Dr. M. J. Dickerson's services ran the gamut of mid-century dentistry: "Ulcerated teeth treated, fangs and crowns filled, exposed nerves capped and saved. Also, teeth inserted in gold, silver, coralite, or vulcanite plate, or platinum plate with continuous gum, which is so much used East."

J. M. Richards built a fashionable resort hotel at the east end of the Thomas Bolton farm (northwest corner of Euclid and East 89th) that claimed to give the best service west of New York. Spring Pond House opened with a shooting match, and many ill-fated fowl, placed as targets behind a stump, met their end. Hundreds of turkeys, geese, and ducks went to the sportsmen as prizes. The house, in front of which was a circular fountain, took its name from a pond at one side, where guests bathed in summer. Swimming as a sport was hardly popular with the ladies, voluminous costumes being designed for coverage rather than for exercise. In the winter the frozen pond provided great fun for bustled women and side-whiskered escorts, and steaming oyster stew topped off many a party. About a half mile north of Spring Pond was a race track that brought profitable patronage in the racing season. The hotel served until 1878.

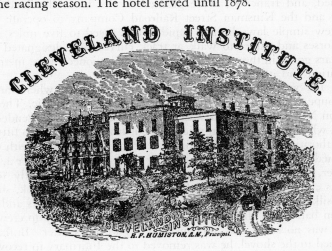

At about the time that E. L. Drake struck oil on August 27 near Titusville, Pennsylvania, three small stills were refining a smelly, tar-like oil from cannel coal in Cleveland at the rate of about a barrel daily. The country's first "oil rush" was soon under way, and refineries began to spring up in Cleveland, Pittsburgh, and on the east coast.

The plant of the Lake Erie Iron Company had been enlarged by adding a rolling mill for making bar iron, and this year it took a new name, Otis & Company. During the Civil War, it supplied the Union with railroad iron and gun-carriage axles. but when the war ended, Charles A. Otis sold his interest.

Professor Ransom F. Humiston, accomplished Cleveland teacher, organized a company and opened Cleveland Institute—or Humiston Institute—in the Cleveland University building. Students from distant states were attracted to the co-educational boarding-and-day school, and in 1867-68 there were 196 pupils enrolled. The institution prospered for a number of years, then succumbed to public-school competition, despite the superior educational opportunities it offered.

Flora Temple, the greatest trotter of her day, had equaled her mile record of 2:21½ in Cincinnati on October 7. Despite bad weather, a great crowd turned out to see her race in Cleveland. On the twenty-sixth, she won three heats from Ike Cook on a heavy track, trotting the final•mile in 2:25 and setting a record in the city.

Council rejected an ordinance in June to establish the Cuyahoga County Horse Railroad Company. Councilman Thayer protested, "It would indeed be a singular state of things if any mode of conveyance be prohibited on any street except on horseback or in ox carts." The streetcar question was debated bitterly, many taxpayers declaring that tracks would be a menace to pedestrians and existing transportation, and, further, the population was too small to support the new mode of travel. On October 25, however, opposition yielded, and franchises were granted to the East Cleveland Railway Company and the Kinsman Street Railroad Company to operate horsecar lines. A few simple laws limited rapid-transit speed to five miles an hour, ordered horses and mules to walk at track curves, and designated 300 feet between cars going in the same direction. In these pioneer lines, metropolitan transportation had its beginning.

Late in the year, grand opera returned to Cleveland when the Parodi Italian troupe gave a performance at the Academy of Music. The *Leader* reported on November 2 that it was a great success and well attended on the last night, when "the admission price was cut from one dollar to fifty cents."

City authorities approached their street-cleaning problem with an economical medium known as the chain-gang system. On November 4, the first law-breaker, "Buffalo Jim," a notorious thief, went reluctantly to work. Prosperous citizens found guilty of infraction labored with pick, shovel, or broom in silk hats and frock coats by the side of petty offenders and tramps. Heavy iron balls were chained to each member of the clean-up crew. Keeping order was no small task for the "law." Five days after "Buffalo Jim" was assigned to the shovel, he was removed to the Infirmary to recover from exertions that "brought on maladies and reduced his strength" in encounters with the police.

Many of the city's ministers opposed organization of the University Heights Congregational Church on November 13, as they feared that the thirty-four members, representing several denominations, could not live in peace and harmony. The Rev. William H. Brewster, the first pastor, served until 1868, and services were held in Humiston's Cleveland Institute. Among the early officers were John G. Jennings, Hiram V. Willson, Isaac P. Lamson, and Dr. Albert G. Hart, widely known surgeon and father of two famous sons, Hastings Hornell, penologist, and Albert Bushnell, historian. The church was independent in government until 1862, when it united with the Congregational Conference. Membership had reached 126 in 1869; and the next year a $16,000 church building was dedicated on property given by Brewster Pelton at the corner of Jennings and Howard Street during the ministry of the Rev. Thomas K. Noble. Seating capacity was increased to 700, and a $20,000 pipe organ was installed in 1877 by the flourishing congregation. Identity of the church changed in 1883 to Jennings Avenue Congregational Church, and again in 1892 to Pilgrim Congregational Church.

Many Clevelanders were aroused to bitter hatred when they learned that John Brown, of Harpers Ferry fame, was to be executed. Owen Brown had moved his family to the Hudson, Ohio, community in 1805, and his son's stormy career was followed by sympathizers and critics alike. On November 29, Judge Daniel R. Tilden presided at a Cleveland meeting where plans were made for recognition of the day of Brown's execution. Church bells in the city began tolling for a half hour on December 2 at two o'clock, as the condemned man was driven in a spring wagon to the scaffold in Charles Town, West Virginia, seated on his coffin. Flags were at half mast. The *Herald* was published with a mourning border. Melodeon Hall was draped in black when a great mass meeting assembled in the evening. It was a solemn occasion, and Judge Rufus P. Spalding was the speaker. A letter written to Judge Tilden by Brown a few days before his death was passed through the audience. The last words were, "I do not think I can better serve the cause I love so much than to die for it." When the raider's body was brought to Hudson on the way to New York City, where services were held, many Clevelanders journeyed to the ancestral home.

For nearly a half century, Alfred Kelley had devoted his tremendous ability and energy to the advancement of Cleveland and Ohio. Through his genius and firm resolve, waterways and railroads became practical realities, and both city and state were attracting industry and commerce. Through his wisdom, legislation stabilized public and private finance, and saved "the honor of the State." When Alfred Kelley died in Columbus on December 2 at the age of seventy, Ohio lost one of its greatest practical planners.

Benjamin Mastick, Asel Abels, and Andrew Kyle drafted articles of faith and by-laws for the Congregational Church of Rockport, organized this year with J. B. Allen as pastor, 1859-61. In 1861, the society became a corporate group; and in January, 1862, a building was erected near Kamm's Corners. The names of Triskett and Nichols were associated with the building enterprise. The church was related to the Cleveland Presbytery for some years until 1869, when it joined the Congregational Conference. In 1904, during the pastorate of the Rev. J. P. Riedinger, 1903-17, the name was changed to West Park Congregational Church, conforming with the name of the community, West Park, named for Benjamin West, Rockport Township pioneer. A new house of worship was erected in 1905 (at 3909 Rocky River Drive); and a parish house built in 1928 served church and community activities and became the weekly meeting place of the Kiwanis Club. The Rev. Wellington Leininger came to the pulpit in 1935. Elisha Hoffman, church member, 1882-92, was a composer of gospel songs that gained popularity after the turn of the century.

The decade of the fifties witnessed the establishment of business concerns that continued in existence in the 1940s: 1854, Cleveland Provision Company, Gerlach Company; 1856, Cleveland Agency of Berkshire Life Insurance Company; 1858, Central Publishing House, Cherry Burrell Corporation; 1859, Leopold Brothers Furniture Company, J. M. & L. A. Osborn Company.

CHAPTER 9

Heartaches and Recovery
1860-1869

THE ROMANCE of Cleveland's early artisans in primitive industry was a closed chapter. A city of commerce and trade had been established by the pioneers, and a new industrial era was commencing—a period of solid foundations, of rapid growth, and of steadily increasing civic fame. Villages and crossroads communities were decreasing in population as the decade opened. One-sixth of the American people lived in cities of eight thousand or upward in 1860, and industry was taking the lead in value of production over agriculture as the chief occupation in Ohio.

Cleveland's population had increased to 43,417, more than two and one-half times over 1850, and it represented more than half of the 78,033 inhabitants in Cuyahoga County. Within the Cleveland boundaries, from Willson Avenue on the east to Waverly Street on the west, enclosing 7.325 square miles, a notable change was taking place. More than 44 per cent of the population was of foreign origin, as compared with more than 45 per cent of Cincinnati's total of 161,044. The New England element represented a minority in Cleveland, although leaders in the professions, in business, and in industry bore the names of early-day families.

Increasing numbers of immigrants were attracted by Cleveland's prosperity—Germans, who predominated, followed by English, Irish, Scotch, and Welsh. There were 15 Czech families in the city in 1860. Nine years later there were 696, totaling 3,252, of which 1,949 were men, representing many skills and trades. Ninety men and 50 women were employed on farms, and soon they had purchased patches of ground for their simple country homes. Harvey Rice employed many Czechs on his farm, selling them land on easy terms. Thus the Croton Avenue settlement thrived until the Broadway-Willson district developed. The Czechs were music lovers, and their musicians played in theater orchestras.

From central and southern Europe were coming little groups of Hungarians. A small number of Italians arrived in 1862, settling first in the Ontario Street market district. They soon found employment in the marble works on Mayfield Road, where they started a colony known as Little Italy, a bit of the homeland, colorful with tradition and song. Improved transportation facilities and an abundance of labor and raw materials would later unite to produce a combination that swelled immigration figures and placed Cleveland in the ranks of leading American cities by the turn of the century.

The development of sectionalism in the United States, and controversies over the tariff and internal improvements had created hostility among the States. The Compromise of 1850 and enforcement of the Fugitive-Slave Law fed the fires of antislavery sentiment in the North, and with the hanging of John Brown and the trial of Lucy, the slave girl, the war clouds of rebellion were about to burst. The rise of the Republican Party had united the strength of the radicals; and the Southern States, finding themselves a minority in the hands of an antagonistic majority, seceded from the Union.

Slavery was the issue in the election of 1860. J. W. Gray had swung the Plain Dealer into compromise on the issue, following his friend, Stephen A. Douglas, while Lincoln was strongly supported by the *Leader*. The Public Square was the proving ground for many tense political demonstrations, but none that equaled the spirit of the Lincoln presidential campaigns. When Abraham Lincoln came to Cleveland on the way to his first inaugural, citizens gave him a welcome greater than that of any other city. In the November election, Cuyahoga County voted emphatically for the lawyer from Illinois.

Slavery had divided Cleveland churches, and even the ministers disagreed. Dr. Samuel C. Aiken of the Old Stone Church found it increasingly difficult to hold to the middle of the controversy. "The ultra reforms . . . Temperance, Slavery, etc.," he said, "have rendered it extremely difficult for the pastor to maintain order and harmony in his church."

Tragedy struck the nation on April 12, 1861, when Fort Sumter was attacked. Party differences were cast aside in Cleveland when President Lincoln called for volunteers. Sentiment crystallized quickly into self-denying patriotism and support of government, and there was no room for southern sympathizers. Business dwindled in stores as the city mobilized its strength. Feeling was tense as enlistment meetings were held. Families prepared for the day when their men must go off to duty, and anxious home folk prayed that the "speck of war" would be finished without the need of grapeshot and rifle bullets. Leland's Band played *The Girl I Left Behind Me* as many of the volunteers went to camp in shirt sleeves; arms and equipment were scarce. Here they had their first taste of war's privations—beans and coffee for supper and "the soft side of a pine board" for a bed.

A national economy geared to peacetime was strained as the country plunged into war. Weak banks began to fail, a list of Ohio banks published by the Federal Government in 1860 showing 10 as "broken," 23 "closed," and 31 "worthless." Cleveland banks weathered the transition. The Government was unprepared to meet the heavy demands of the military, and soon found that borrowing from the people yielded slow returns. As in past emergencies, greenbacks—unsecured treasury notes—were issued, and specie payment was suspended to protect the banks in their inability to meet demands for gold and silver. Hard money became scarce, and "shinplasters," tokens, and other substitutes began to appear, confusing values, inviting counterfeiting, handicapping business, and undermining confidence.

Laborers and salaried workers suffered as living costs outdistanced salaries and wages. In March, 1860, flour had risen to $5.50 to $6.25 per barrel; corn, 48 to 50 cents per bushel; potatoes, 30 to 40 cents; ham, 9½ to 10 cents per pound; dried beef, 10 cents; butter, 13 cents; New Orleans sugar, 7¾ to 9 cents; granulated sugar, 11 to 11¼ cents; Rio coffee, 12¼ to 14 cents; Java coffee, 16 to 17 cents; rice, 4½ to 5 cents; eggs, 12½ cents per dozen; lard oil, 85 to 88 cents per gallon; and New Orleans molasses, 46 to 50 cents. Prices had risen nearly 100 per cent by 1864, while wages increased less than 50 per cent in "The Dreadful Decade."

Schools and colleges suffered as faculty and students joined the service. Cultural activities and sports were interrupted by the war, and lecture series were curtailed. Construction halted, except in furtherance of war demands. Military control of telegraph lines was a blow to Cleveland newspapers, which were financially unable to send correspondents into the battle zones. Anson Stager of Cleveland was military superintendent of all lines and offices in the North.

Patriotism was expressed in pledges to observe rigid economy of living, and decline the purchase of foreign luxuries, such as silk or wool dress goods, shawls, expensive ribbons, feathers and flowers, carpets, liquors, cigars, and jewelry. Women worked with untiring zeal in their ministry to the sick and needy at home and to the men in battle. They organized the Ladies Aid Society, the first of its kind in the country, which became the pattern for war relief. *Old Dan Tucker, Oh, Susanna,* and *John Brown's Body* shared popularity with a new tune, *Tramp, Tramp, Tramp, the Boys are Marching,* as the people gave and gave in their heroic effort to help win the peace.

Out of the period of industrial expansion for war and the threat of inflation, there came on February 25, 1863, a reshaped banking policy in the form of the National Bank Act, providing for "a National Currency, secured by a Pledge of United States Bonds, and . . . for the Circulation and Redemption thereof." A tax on state bank notes forced state banking systems out of existence as national banks were organized under the direct supervision of the Treasury Department. In Cleveland the First National Bank was created, followed by reorganization of the Bank of Commerce as the Second National Bank, the Merchants Branch Bank as the Merchants National Bank, the Commercial Branch Bank as the Commercial National Bank, and the City Bank as The National City Bank of Cleveland. The Society for Savings alone passed through the transition as originally organized.

During the war, bank capital trebled. "One of the most remarkable features of these times," observed the *Leader* on April 1, 1863, "is the steady and rapid accumulation of savings deposits," as influenced by higher wages, soldiers' bounties, and emphasis on thrifty living. Many war veterans, however, spent bonuses and back pay carelessly and in unwise investments. In 1868, the first saving-and-loan association was established in Cleveland.

The national debt first reached billion-dollar figures after the Civil War, when the Union owed $2,755,763,000, or $77.69 per person. It was retired slowly until boosted by the Spanish-American War. The first United States income tax, levied to finance the War between the States was discontinued in 1872.

Rally 'Round the Flag and devotion to the Union produced Cleveland volunteers who fought in bloody military engagements from Bull Run to

Appomattox. Slavery was dead, but at what a cost! Thousands of lives had been lost or broken. The South lay scorched and wasted. As Cleveland gave thanks for the return of peace, word came that the hand that had signed the *Emancipation Proclamation* had been stilled by the assassin's bullet.

Chauncey M. Depew eloquently told the story of the angry crowd that gathered in Wall Street, New York City, after hearing the report of Lincoln's assassination—a crowd that threatened to wreck the financial district, believing that banking and business houses were sympathetic with the Confederates. Suddenly Congressman James A. Garfield appeared on the balcony of the Custom House and made an impassioned appeal, climaxed by these words, "God reigns and the Republic still lives!" This quieted the mob. Garfield had been elected Ohio senator in 1859, and was one of the first volunteers in the Union Army. He resigned the promise of a brilliant military career in 1863 to take a Republican seat in Congress, where he served until 1880.

Cleveland's grief was deep as her citizens gathered at their time-honored meeting place, the Public Square, to look upon the face of Abraham Lincoln, the President they loved. Their gratitude that the war was over was expressed in a huge bell, raised to the tower of the Old Stone Church, bearing the inscription:

> Cast for the First Presbyterian Church, Cleveland, Ohio
> In the Year of Peace, 1865

As battle-scarred regiments again marched down Superior Avenue, there were many gaps in the ranks, and tears mingled with rejoicing. Woefully reduced in manpower, they stooped to the task of reconstruction, resolving to bury memories of war except as they were revived in friendly organizations promoting service and fellowship, and in monuments to their brave men. Veterans and workers at home preserved comradeship in Grand Army posts, the Loyal Legion, and the Women's Relief Corps, known for many years for their charitable efforts. Interest broadened with the founding of active auxiliaries—the Ladies of the Grand Army of the Republic, Daughters of Union Veterans of the Civil War, and Sons of Union Veterans of the Civil War. Pledging themselves to national defense and security, veterans organized the Army and Navy Union in 1886, and active garrisons and auxiliaries gradually took form in Cuyahoga County.

Wealth accumulated through war industry was put to work in exploiting natural resources, and the decades following the Civil War witnessed further expansion of the West and increased immigration of workers seeking jobs in prosperous Cleveland. Railroad promoters were hastening the meeting of east-west lines in 1860, to join the seaboard with Indianapolis, Chicago, Milwaukee, St. Louis, and the fast-growing interior. In 1850 Ohio had only 299 miles of road; a decade later, roads had multiplied ten times and population had increased 2.5 times. Short-line railroads of varying gauges had sprung up to benefit small localities, and extensions developed as the importance of rail lines to commerce and industry became evident.

The network of rails, it is said, saved the Union. Completion of the broad-gauge Atlantic & Great Western Railroad (Erie) into Cleveland in 1863 not only provided a new route to the East, but increased the movement of oil from the Pennsylvania fields from the north that was to give the city supremacy over Pittsburgh.

Six railroad lines were operating daily in and out of Cleveland in 1865. Leaving Cleveland on the Cleveland-Ashtabula line at 9:50 A.M., passengers changed to the New York Central at Buffalo, and at 1 P.M. the next day reached New York City. The next year, the roads joined in erecting the "massive" Union Depot, the marvel of the age.

The year 1869 held unusual significance for Clevelanders, marking the completion of the first transcontinental railroad in the United States, laid largely along the route of Jeptha H. Wade's pioneering telegraph line that had reached the Pacific Coast in 1861. It also saw the founding of the Lake Shore & Michigan Southern trunk line, a union of disjointed roads into a main line, depending upon through traffic for its business. The Lake Shore was a great factor in city growth.

While the railroads carried the mails with greater speed, nothing had been done to improve distribution and delivery in Cleveland. Until Joseph W. Briggs devised a system of mail delivery and collection, later adopted throughout the nation, crowds waited patiently while mail was sorted.

Pioneer railroads had fostered the growth of the iron industry, and Cleveland's five foundries of the early fifties had increased to sixteen plants in 1863. The early sixties saw the founding of fifty new and highly competitive companies to exploit Michigan ore. America's first pipe line carrying crude oil, laid twelve miles long in 1859, was soon lengthened under the leadership of John D. Rockefeller, who assumed the task of bringing light to the world. Curiously, evidences of oil and gas were not new in Cleveland. Since the day that Moses Cleaveland, its founder, had given passing interest to the gaseous waters of Euclid Creek, these natural resources were hardly disturbed. Industrial progress, however, failed to receive wholehearted encouragement from the City Council, which was constantly under pressure of citizens who condemned the rolling mills as smoke nuisances and the refineries for their offensive odors.

At the close of the Civil War, there were thirty oil refineries in Cleveland, which had become the leader in coal-oil production. With a small amount of capital and a half dozen workers, a refinery could be started, its product selling for ten dollars a barrel. By 1866, the petroleum industry was in the throes of speculation, widely fluctuating prices, and careless, inefficient, and wasteful operation. Gushers burst with riches as old wells ran dry, creating overproduction one day and scarcity the next. Prices raced up and down, keeping the market in constant confusion. The oil business was doomed, declared twenty-six-year-old John D. Rockefeller, unless struggling refineries consolidated and stabilized the industry. Soon he was putting his industrial genius to work, with the aid of able Cleveland men, and the foundations of the vast Standard Oil empire were beginning to take form.

The war stimulated business of every kind, and the interdependence of industry became noticeably important. Without Grasselli chemicals, for instance, Rockefeller would have been unable to refine oil. In 1868, the Board of Trade reported fourteen rolling mills in the Cleveland area. Industrial plants were producing quantities of machinery, castings, bar iron, nails and spikes, structural iron work for bridges, railroad equipment, and stoves. The Bessemer process, introduced this year, made cheap steel possible. New enterprises were launched, some of which held continuous records of operation eight decades later. Labor unions began to make notable gains after the war, and Cleveland's industrial advance attracted the interest of labor movements.

The inter-relation of lake navigation and railroading had become a great factor in the economic development of the Great Lakes region. Water routes

Oil Refineries, 1866, at Kingsbury's Run,
the beginning of a world-wide industry.

were linked with a growing network of land routes, thus cheapening and standardizing freight and passenger rates, facilitating transfer at ports, and, in many instances, permitting a choice of routes.

The Civil War interrupted traffic between the lakes and Europe, and as the war closed, internal expansion claimed the capacity of lake fleets. "Cleveland now stands confessedly at the head of all places on the chain of lakes as a shipbuilding port," reported the *Herald* in September, 1865. Near at hand was choice Michigan and Canadian timber; and a supply of labor and materials gave the city an advantage in the building of wooden vessels. "Cleveland has the monopoly of propeller building," the *Herald* continued. "Its steam tugs are the finest on the lakes, whilst Cleveland-built sailing vessels not only outnumber all other vessels on the chain of lakes but are found on the Atlantic coast, in English waters, upon the Mediterranean and in the Baltic." Local shipyards had produced twelve large propellers during the year, aggregating 6,823 tons burden. The barge was first used in the early sixties in the lumber trade.

The horse was the king of transportation in Cleveland! Omnibus lines had flourished on city streets and served outlying towns since 1857, when they were introduced by Henry S. Stevens. Grabby carriage and hack drivers met travelers at the docks and the railroad depot, setting fares according to an estimate of the passenger's ability to pay. The newspapers called it a "most atrocious swindle."

The horsecar was still a novelty in 1860, and the *Leader* observed that citizens no longer needed "to plod the way through our almost bottomless streets nearly half the year." Horse-drawn streetcars rumbled up Euclid as far as Erie Street, turned south to Prospect, then east to the city limits, being diverted from a straight course through the strenuous efforts of the residents of upper Euclid Street. For many years, the section between Erie and Case was held sacred from streetcar traffic.

By the middle sixties, the omnibus was falling by the wayside as noisy horsecars made inroads into local transit business. While the horsecar was considered a great public institution, for every boost there was a knock; but popularity of the lines grew, leading in a few years to an epidemic of street-railway building. Pioneer lines made great contributions to city development, uniting business and industrial districts with residential areas, and influencing Cleveland to become a city of home owners.

Early streetcars were built for winter or for summer use. The cold-weather type was a ten-foot box car with a door at either end and a two-foot platform for the driver. Passengers huddled together for warmth; but the driver, who shared the elements with the horses, bundled himself in heavy clothing and earned a great deal of sympathy.

In summer, open streetcars went into service. Forty passengers could be seated back-to-back on long benches. A running board ran the length of each side of the car. In bad weather, canvas curtains were pulled down to the tops of the seats to protect the passengers. The East Cleveland line owned twenty cars, ten of the closed and ten of the open type. Daily operation called for the use of about six cars. These were increased in the morning and evening rush hours, which even then had become a problem. Cars stopped anywhere on signal. Daytime fare was five cents, night fare a dime. Runaway horses created excitement, but serious accidents were few.

Bustles posed a problem on the little horsecars. Ladies were wearing a new invention, the "tilting hoop" skirt, featuring the "duplex elliptical steel spring." A postwar model was designed to relieve the problem by fitting the bustle with covered wire springs so arranged that when the wearer sat down the bustle contracted. Prosperous men of the day hid behind beards and whiskers, and the threat of hot weather failed to alter their passion for heavy, black-broadcloth frock coats, "boiled" shirts and stovepipe hats.

The rolling mills had brought "palmy days" to Newburgh, and enterprising businessmen built a dummy railroad to bring the isolated village closer to Cleveland. Another line opened on the West Side, running to the Cliff House and the picnic grounds overlooking the Rocky River valley.

Cleveland had 182 streets, 5 avenues, and 3 alleys in 1860. Although lower Superior Street continued to be the center of commerce, business was elbowing its way into the gas-lighted Public Square. The city's center was a beauty spot in 1860. Tall shade trees cast a shadow over the entire park. There were straight and winding walks, and seats for those who would rest.

In the center, a cast-iron, circular fountain spurted refreshment of cool Lake Erie water; but later in the year, Perry's Monument moved into its place. A two-rail fence surrounded the Square until 1867, cutting off Superior and Ontario streets. The new stone Post Office, or Federal Building, faced the Square from the northeast corner of Superior. The Forest City House stood on the southwest corner at Superior on the site it would occupy for decades. It was only a matter of time before the remaining residences of well-known citizens would give way to the eastward expansion of commerce.

Superior Street extended only to Erie until 1865, when the residence of T. P. May, early merchant, was removed from its path to permit extension to the east. Fine homes built by prosperous Clevelanders east of the Public Square reflected the skill of master builders—Jonathan A. Goldsmith, Charles W. Heard, Warham J. Warner, and others. Bordering the south side, beyond the Second Presbyterian Church, were dignified residences of the Greek Revival period, erected for Henry A. Raymond, Philo Chamberlain, Frederick A. Sterling, and James Farmer.

Prospect Street and Kinsman Street, renamed Woodland Avenue in the sixties, were at the height of popularity with citizens, who entertained themselves by driving past fashionable homes on their way to the countryside. St. Clair Street continued to be well-traveled, leading to homes, gardens, and farms along the lakeshore. Modest homes on the streets around the Square were generally set on a line with the sidewalk, or a few feet back, and stone steps led up to them. They boasted basement dining rooms and kitchens in the eastern style.

Euclid Street as far as Willson Avenue was virtually "Prosperity Street." Eastward on the south side beyond St. Paul's Church at Sheriff Street was the Ursuline Convent, formerly the Judge Samuel Cowles residence, and the distinguished home of Truman P. Handy. On the north side were the fine homes of Henry Chisholm, Henry L. Gaylord, Martin B. Scott, and Lemuel Crawford. Beyond Erie wealthy residents had begun to build mansions in deep, spacious lawns—Amasa Stone, W. J. Boardman, Zalmon Fitch, Selah Chamberlain, Sr., Samuel L. Mather—later the William G. Mather home, James F. Clark—later the W. S. Tyler home, Henry H. Dodge, S. B. Prentiss, O. M. Oviatt, Lemuel Wick, and Stillman Witt. In the effusive words of the editor of the *Zanesville Times,* reprinted in the *Herald,* May 27, 1868, "The fine architectural taste of the mansions which wealth has spared no pains in perfecting, the extensive grounds, the velvet green lawns, rare flowers and plants, the fountains that adorn each residence, many of them costing their owners over $100,000 before completion, are alone worth a trip to the lake to see." The golden age of Euclid Street had begun!

Bayard Taylor, American traveler and author, visited the city frequently. He called Euclid Street the most beautiful in the world, its only rival being the Prospekt Nevsky in St. Petersburg, Russia. In a lecture before the Royal Society of Great Britain in about 1860, John Fiske described the world-famous street as "bordered on each side with a double row of arching trees, and with handsome stone houses of sufficient variety and freedom in architectural design, standing at intervals of from one to two hundred feet along the entire length of the street . . . the vistas reminding one of the nave and aisles of a huge cathedral."

Not long after his departure from Cleveland for greener pastures in the lecture field, Artemus Ward wrote a facetious tribute to Euclid Street, acknowledging it as—

> a justly celebrated thoroughfare. Some folks go so far as to say it puts it all over the well known Unter der Sauerkraut in Berlin and the equally well known Rue de Boolfrog in Paree, France. Entering by way of the Public square and showing a certificate of high moral character, the visitor, after carefully wiping his feet on the 'welcome' mat, is permitted to roam the sacred highway free of charge. The houses are on both sides of the street and seem large as well as commodious. They are covered with tin roofs and paint and mortgages, and present a truly distangy appearance. All the owners of Euclid Street homes employ hired girls and are patrons of the arts. A musical was held at one of these palatial homes the other day with singing. The soprano and the contralto were beautiful singers. The tenor has as fine a tenor voice as ever brought a bucket of water from a second-story window, and the basso sang so low that his voice at times sounded like the rumble in the tummy of a colicky whale!

While Euclid Street displayed an aristocratic air, the thoroughfare was in a state of neglect. Although a short stretch of stone pavement was intended eventually to supplant the carriageway and the old planks, a complaint was registered in 1862 that weeds were growing between the sidewalk and the street. Pavements were of poor construction, and the cost of even the best was considered extravagant. Good paving stone was brought from Buffalo, cordwood was expensive, and taxpayers were reluctant to assume increased tax burdens in the interest of improved transportation.

Rich soil to the east and west of Cleveland, not far from the Public Square, was producing fine vegetables, fruits, and flowers. Dr. Jared P. Kirtland, pioneer scientist, had developed many new varieties of fruit on his Rockport experimental farm. The craze for strawberries was sweeping in from New York, and soon almost every family had a plot. Commercial gardeners provided housewives with home-grown produce in season. At dawn they left for market with heavily loaded wagons, retailing to customers at busy intersections, or selling off the tailgate at the market stands in Cleveland. A new Central Market House that was ready for business in 1867 was hardly built in anticipation of the long years of service that it was destined to give. Antiquated and lacking in health and sanitary facilities, it continued to monopolize one of the busiest intersections in the city in the 1940s, despite decades of effort to move it.

A vigorous revival of cultural and professional interests followed the war, resulting in the founding of a number of influential organizations. Public and private library and museum projects became permanent institutions of increasing importance. Case Hall, erected by the Case family, opened in

1867 and was the city's cultural center. Theater managers made the most of postwar prosperity, and *Ten Nights in a Bar Room* drew capacity houses.

Lecture courses and the works of great authors found new competition in cheaper books and magazines as the war ended, produced by improved printing processes and lower-priced paper. The first of the dime novels appeared in the sixties.

Benjamin F. Taylor, a newspaperman who had lived in Cleveland, left enduring word pictures of the Civil War, artistic nature sketches, and delightful poems, some of which found their way into school readers. He did much of his writing in Chicago until his death in 1887. Typical camp life in the war was portrayed by a young Bedford, Ohio, artist named Archibald M. Willard, and his drawings were appearing in *Harper's Magazine*.

After her marriage to Charles E. Bolton of Cleveland at the end of the war, Sarah Knowles Bolton became widely known as the author of several volumes of poetry and numerous biographies written for young people. Both she and her husband were prominent in the temperance movement and in social-service work.

The numbers of the sick, poor, and fatherless increased as a result of the war and city growth, and a wave of welfare societies sprang up to extend helping hands. Young ladies were beginning to wonder whether it was better to brave the evils of the city or to stay on the farm within the bosom of one's family until the right man came along. Quoting from the minutes of the first annual meeting of the Women's Christian Association (YWCA), founded in the late sixties: "In the bustle and activity of the age, women are following hard after the men. Not satisfied with their quiet country homes, many of them press their way to the cities." Clothed in noble principles and sidewalk-sweeping skirts, virtuous Christian women assumed the responsibility of the welfare of the venturesome working girl.

Cleveland's importance politically attracted women of the nation who met in the city to lay plans to further the cause of woman suffrage. Under the banner of the newly formed American Woman Suffrage Association, they went out under fearless leadership to work toward their goal; but not until 1920 did they win the right to vote.

Churches were following their congregations as the population shifted with city expansion. In many of the new buildings, the simplicity of early-day design had been displaced by architectural achievements of brick and stone with rich interiors, reflecting greater wealth of the membership.

Relief from war influences was sought in athletic events. Edward Payson Weston, world-famous pedestrian, walked into Cleveland on one of his famous tours, and soon walking clubs had sprung up, and Weston fads were the rage. Not long afterward, the bone-shaking velocipede appeared.

Amateur baseball captured the interest of sports fans when the war closed, and clubs began to form in cities and towns. In the fall of 1865 the Forest City team was organized and promptly defeated by the Penfields of Oberlin. Players in the amateur clubs served without pay and were supposed to be bona-fide residents of the cities they represented. Rivalry became intense, however, players being enticed from clubs in small localities, and the practice of betting began. This created a demoralizing influence that prompted the Red Stockings, the leading amateur team of Cincinnati, organized in 1866, to declare in 1869 that henceforth it would be a professional ball club. This was a bold move, but a wise one. On the heels of Cincinnati, Cleveland reorganized the Forest City club on a professional basis. "Pro" clubs were soon springing up chiefly to meet the Cincinnati team, which in 1869 had a notable season without a defeat.

Taxpayers' resistance to public improvements began to give way in the postwar prosperity period. Control of the public schools, heretofore administered politically, was centered in the Board of Education, and plans for new buildings and more efficient management started to go forward under able superintendents. The Public School Library began to benefit through tax levies. The departments of police and fire were reorganized on a basis more nearly commensurate with the needs of the growing city. The railroad brought a need for better bridges. While the city fathers made a long step in the direction of building a City Hall, their plans were stymied. Face-lifting operations were evidenced in and around Cleveland, and in 1867 property was purchased for Lake View Park. While a few residents advocated parks in 1860, people generally were opposed. What did they want of parks when there were hundreds of acres of forest land all about them! Public pressure, rather than pride, inspired the move to round up roving animals into a pound.

The physician of the sixties was the family confidant. He made his rounds in a buggy, his appointment slate was his office assistant, and he put up his own prescriptions. Emergency patients were taken to the hospital or the surgeon's office in express wagons or in hacks. Fees depended upon ability to pay, and a charge of ten dollars was unusual, according to Dr. Hamilton F. Biggar, one of Cleveland's best-known doctors. It is related, however, that a patient who had visited the leading surgeons of Europe without benefit, sought the help of Dr. Gustave C. E. Weber in the city; and after a successful operation, a princely $1,250 was the doctor's reward.

Able medical men served on the early boards of health, yet an intolerable lack of sanitation was allowed to prevail. Many of the wells and cisterns that had been in use for years were unsafe, as refuse and seepage from backyard garbage pits contaminated the drinking water. Tenements were crowded, and people lived in damp, cramped quarters, careless in their habits and without health facilities. The health officer declared the county jail and the city prison "incurable nuisances." Contagious diseases were common and rarely reported, and isolation was a matter of the patient's choice. The city-sexton's daily newspaper statement of interments in city cemeteries represented the report on vital statistics, which, of course, was not concerned with death causes. On this basis, the death total for 1856 showed 1,257, as compared with postwar 1868, when it mounted to 1,465. The need for sewers had been recognized, but little had been done about it. A complacent city administration preferred rather to blame Cleveland's sorry plight on the "chaotic state of the health ordinance," and having done so, sat back to pull the treasury's purse strings tighter.

It should hardly be said that poor health conditions were responsible for attracting the superior talent that ministered to the afflicted. Nevertheless, the city's enviable position as a medical center was due to the able leadership of its skilled men of medicine. Suffering born of the Civil War encouraged the opening of hospitals and welfare institutions, and training-school facilities were enlarged.

As the decade closed, Cleveland's water supply was being improved by laying a larger tunnel farther into the lake. Citizens pointed with pride to the Kentucky Street Reservoir, a show place for visitors. W. R. Rose, writer on the *Plain Dealer* for many years, left a stimulating word picture of the view from the crest of the West Side water works:

> Clevelanders in those days loved their Lake Erie. In particular the throngs loved the sunsets . . . As the sun went down and a night haze swept over the lake, the lookers-on had a real picture. A great three-master, towed by a snorting little tug, would come out of the river. Sailors were aloft setting sail to catch the evening breeze. Flags were broken out. Faint shouts of command came shoreward. Then the little tug dropped its line, the great sheets were shaken loose and hauled taut and bellied to the freshening wind, and the beautiful thing took life and disappeared in the haze before our admiring eyes.

1860

The political sentiments of Abraham Lincoln, Illinois lawyer, had led him away from the Whigs to the new Republican Party, created out of opposition to the Kansas-Nebraska Bill of 1854 and already of national stature. As the party needed a convincing spokesman before the New York Republicans, James A. Briggs, Cleveland lawyer, suggested the name of his friend, Lincoln, but the committee was hesitant at first, as the rail-splitter's fame was not recognized in the East. Laying the matter before Lincoln in Springfield, Briggs persuaded him to accept; and at the Cooper Union, New York City, on February 27, this year, the national political career of the great American was launched. On the platform was Briggs in distinguished Republican company. Through his influence, the Ohio delegation supported Lincoln in the convention that first nominated him for the presidency.

Cassius M. Clay, fiery Kentucky Abolitionist, was among both friends and enemies on March 1, when he lectured on the *Causes of the Rise and Decline of this Nation*. He was the only speaker of note to bring the disputed slavery question before Clevelanders.

St. Augustine's Parish was organized to minister to Irish Catholics. A frame church, erected on Jefferson Street, served until 1896, when property formerly owned by the Congregationalists was purchased on Jennings Avenue. In 1862 English-speaking Catholics in Newburgh formed the Holy Rosary Parish, which became Holy Name in 1881.

For a striking moment, a Clevelander was the central figure in the momentous Republican National Convention, meeting in its third day in Chicago, May 18. David Kellogg Cartter, chairman of the Ohio delegation, had made notes as the third ballot progressed, and they indicated that Abraham Lincoln needed two and a half votes for nomination as the party's presidential candidate. The Buckeyes were supporting their anti-slavery champion, Salmon P. Chase, but as Lincoln gained, Chase lost. Before results of the balloting could be announced, Cartter stepped on a chair, and in a commanding voice declared, "I rise to announce the change of four votes from Ohio from Mr. Chase to Abraham Lincoln." Enemies of William H. Seward, the leading contender, were jubilant. Three states followed Ohio, and the third ballot gave the Illinois lawyer 354 votes—120 more than were needed. Cartter's career as a lawyer in Ohio began in 1846. He met Lincoln while they were serving in the Congress, from which he retired in 1853. He moved to Cleveland in 1856 and formed a law partnership with L. C. Thayer. Leaving the Democrats, he became a leader in the Republican Party. During Lincoln's administration, Cartter was rewarded with the post of minister to Bolivia. In 1863 he was appointed chief justice of the Supreme Court of the District of Columbia, in which office he died in 1887. He was buried in Lake View Cemetery.

Year after year political parties demonstrated their strength in the Public Square, both sides pleading their causes in tense party feeling. This was an historic year. Abraham Lincoln and Hannibal Hamlin had won the Republican nomination in Chicago on May 18, and Cleveland enthusiasm for "Honest Old Abe" met with regrets from surprised Seward followers. The *Leader* hung a Lincoln photograph on the office door, and stated editorially that "our standard bearer is not remarkable for beauty, as the word goes, but has an air of sturdy independence and manliness which attracts by its very singularity." Everyone was reported "in a good humor and hopeful, except the democracy, who were disturbed enough at the prospects of fighting the Chicago nominees." Democrats endorsed the Stephen A. Douglas ticket at a Public Square meeting in June. Lincoln advocates chose October 14 for an heroic torchlight rally, with William H. Seward, Tom Corwin, Governor William Dennison, Ben F. Wade, and John Sherman as headline orators. Election night in October marked the great Republican victory with an exhibition such as the Public Square had never seen. Crowds waited in suspense for the returns before campaign headquarters. When success was assured, a mammoth bonfire was built on Superior Street in front of the committee rooms, the Artillery thundered one hundred guns, church bells rang, and jubilant citizens serenaded party leaders who had labored for the towering Springfield Republican.

Adelina Patti, young Italian operatic soprano, was on the way to fame when she sang to a capacity audience in Melodeon Hall on May 31. She gave concerts in Cleveland at the height of her career and on her farewell tours, entertaining in seven languages and including the favorites, *Home, Sweet Home* and *The Last Rose of Summer*.

A breathless crowd watched the daring M. Solomon walk a rope suspended from the top of the American House to the top of the Johnson House. On his return trip, the aerialist "indulged in a few cautious gymnastic performances."

The year-end report of the public schools showed that there were 13,309 persons of school age in Cleveland: in public schools, 6,100; Catholic schools, 2,000; private Protestant schools, 200; private German schools, 250;

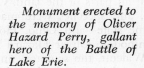

Monument erected to the memory of Oliver Hazard Perry, gallant hero of the Battle of Lake Erie.

orphan asylum, 50; not enrolled, 4,709. Superintendent Freese pointed out that buildings were too small to permit proper classification, and emphasized the need for redistricting, with a united school system as the principal goal.

The old Court House on the Public Square was sold at auction on July 28 for $60.

Henry S. Stevens, president of the East Cleveland Railway Company, broke ground on August 6 at Euclid and Willson Avenue for the first street-railway line to operate continuously in Cleveland and in the State of Ohio. Stockholders and patrons were invited to meet at the Water Street end of the route in three weeks to witness completion of the road.

The East Cleveland streetcar line was a little behind schedule, but on September 3, 3.39 miles of single track had been laid from Willson Avenue through Prospect to Bank Street, and horsecars began carrying the first passengers for a five-cent fare on the iron-strapped, wooden rails. On the 5th, Stevens' competing line, the Kinsman Street Railroad Company, opened for business from Bank Street out Kinsman (Woodland) via Superior and Erie. Dr. Azariah Everett succeeded Stevens as president.

The newest office building on the Square was the Morison Block, erected this year by David Morison, prosperous realtor. It was a narrow, three-story, wood-and-brick structure with stores on the ground floor. Morison was a man of increasing importance, who became head of a number of real-estate concerns and railway lines. He was an influential Republican, and served several terms as state senator. The block deteriorated with the years; but in the 1940s it still stood between the Marshall Building and Public Square Building, an obscure landmark, the upper floors of which were deserted. A modernized quick-lunch occupied the street level, and a towering liquor sign crowned its height—the oldest commercial building on the Public Square.

The forty-seventh anniversary of the historic battle of Lake Erie was commemorated on September 10 with the unveiling of the Perry Monument, which had been erected on a low stone foundation within a circular iron fence in the center of the Square where the first fountain had stood. Harvey Rice, who conceived the project and was chairman of the monument committee, made the presentation address before an audience estimated at a hundred thousand that had assembled from all parts of the land. George Bancroft, eminent historian, was the orator, and speeches were made by the governors of Rhode Island—Perry's home state—and Ohio. Honored guests included Oliver H. Perry, son of Commodore Oliver Hazard Perry, and a few survivors of the battle. William Walcutt, the sculptor, unveiled the statue, and Mayor George B. Senter accepted it on behalf of the city. The dedicatory ceremony was conducted by the Masons, and their regalia and that of the Wayne Guards of Erie, Pennsylvania, the Cleveland Grays, and the Light Artillery—the latter appearing in public for the first time—made a colorful spectacle. Following the dedication, a sham battle was staged on the lake for the enjoyment of thousands, with only one misfortune—the accidental drowning of an observer who fell from the pier. Receptions and gala celebrations took place in the evening, and the next morning a grand military parade was held. Cleveland's new streetcar lines were taxed to the limit carrying passengers to the Square. Reporting for the *Plain Dealer,* Artemus Ward treated the story with dignity until he came to the parade, when he injected a facetious remark to the effect that "the procession was more than two miles in length, as was the prayer of the clergyman." The monument cost $8,800, raised largely by public subscription and supplemented by Council appropriation. Sculptor Walcutt was secured by Thomas Jones & Sons, Cleveland contractors, and the eight-ton block of imported marble took shape in his studio in the city.

Perry's Victory Day, September 10, marked the opening of the Hower & Higbee store in a two-story building on Superior Street west of the Square. This was the beginning of Cleveland's first department store, founded by Edward C. Higbee and John G. Hower, with five employees. Ten years later, it moved across the street (Hotel Cleveland site) into larger quarters. In 1897, Hower died, Higbee became president, and the firm name changed to The Higbee Company five years later.

Interesting real-estate transactions took place in October. Joseph E. Sheffield purchased 100 feet of Euclid frontage by 600 feet deep (east of East 13th Street) for $24,000. John M. Sterling sold to William Bingham 22.42 acres of land on the east side of Sterling Avenue at Euclid for $26,000. Land on the south side of the Public Square (May Company site), on which two old residences stood, was valued at about $500 a foot front.

The name of Melodeon Hall was changed to Brainard's Hall this year, and later to Brainard's Opera House. In 1875, it deferred to Ellsler's celebrated Opera House on Euclid Avenue and took the name of Globe Theater. Renowned artists of the theater, the lecture platform, and the music world entertained Clevelanders from its stage.

The Artemus Ward letters earned popularity and a small increase in pay for Charles Farrar Brown, but not enough to hold their quaint, grotesque author at the *Plain Dealer*. On November 11 he severed his three-year connection to become editor of *Vanity Fair* in New York. It was at this time that he began to spell his name with a final "e"—Browne. War left its mark on the magazine; and taking his whimsical oddities to the lecture platform, he was widely acclaimed. He became the inspiring friend of Mark Twain, Bret Harte, and leading men of letters. Abraham Lincoln turned to Artemus Ward's humor for relief from the pressures of war and state.

When John C. Heenan, champion prize fighter, appeared at the Academy of Music on November 21, he was the first to introduce boxing to the theater. Having conquered Tom Sayers, he came to Cleveland's leading playhouse under the billing, "Reception Festival." Advance advertising announced, "Ladies and Gentlemen can witness the modus operandi of the Sayers fight, devoid of unpleasant features." Tickets sold quickly at 50 cents, $1 for box seats. The theater was packed. Before the curtain rose, according to S. J. Kelly's historical account years later in the *Plain Dealer*, a fight started between two men in the orchestra circle. The audience was cheering the fracas, when the curtain suddenly parted, Heenan leaped from the stage and seized a combatant in each hand. One was tossed behind the curtain and the other arrested. Heenan's theatrical appearance was an assured success.

According to the federal census of 1860, lumber and clothing headed the list of twenty-nine principal industrial classifications in Cuyahoga County in the number of establishments, the former with 50 firms employing 167 men producing products valued at $158,657; and the latter with 27 firms employing 452 men and 506 women at an annual payroll of $180,000, and producing goods valued at $621,133. Three iron, bar, and sheet-metal plants employed 374 men to produce $1,209,500 worth of products; 21 flour mills valued their output at $1,008,126; 17 machinery and engine factories, $318,-947; 9 soap-and-candle factories, $230,540; 19 boot-and-shoe firms, employing 217 men and 73 women with a payroll of $77,952, showed production valued at $222,830. Chemicals, hardware, hosiery, coal oil, sewing machines, and woolen goods represented infant industries employing 32 workers producing a combined product valuation of $39,032, of which chemicals represented $15,032. There was a total of 387 establishments in the county, employing 4,455 workers who earned $1,333,118 in wages. Capital invested amounted to $2,676,963; value of materials, $4,029,015; and value of products, $6,973,737.

1861

Federal officers, headed by Seth A. Abbey, deputy marshal, forcibly entered the home of L. A. Benton on Prospect Street on January 19 and carried away Lucy Bagby, a young mulatto servant who had escaped from her "owner" in Wheeling, West Virginia. Fearing that the angry populace would incite a riot, one hundred and fifty special deputies were employed to guard the prisoner in the Federal Building. At the hearing before United States Commissioner Bushnell White, Rufus P. Spalding made an eloquent plea that the girl be spared; but the law was plain. Double the market value was offered Lucy's master in exchange for her freedom; but he would not sell, and she went back to slavery under armed guard. She was the last slave returned to the South under the hated Fugitive-Slave Law. When the Civil War was over, Lucy married and settled in Pittsburgh. In September, 1904, she was introduced at a meeting of the Early Settlers Association in Cleveland.

The railroads had made heavy inroads into canal traffic, as shown by canal tolls collected at Cleveland in 1860 amounting to only $16,156.94. War demands were paramount, and the State leased the canals to private parties. In 1877 the Hamilton reservoir was destroyed, the lease was surrendered, and the State was obliged to take back the canals in a condition of great disrepair. Public support, however, was long in dying out, although the waterways were obviously unable to operate. Cleveland tolls in 1890 had been reduced to $6,081.96.

Cannon thundered a welcome to President-elect Abraham Lincoln as his train arrived at the Euclid Street Station at four o'clock on the afternoon of February 15. Whistles shrieked, church bells rang, and throngs cheered as the greatest parade in the city's history moved toward the Square. With stovepipe hat in hand, the gaunt man in black rode down flag-draped Euclid Street in a cold, drizzling rain in an open barouche drawn by four white horses. The Cleveland Grays, ten companies of the Light Artillery, officials in carriages, and workmen from shops and furnaces escorted Lincoln past the greatest crowd that greeted him en route to Washington. At the Weddell House thousands had assembled to hear him speak. On the balcony Lincoln was welcomed by Irvine U. Masters, president of the City Council, and Judge Sherlock J. Andrews introduced him in brilliant oratory. The towering Illinois lawyer appealed for devotion to the Constitution and the Union, and for loyalty of all to "the good old ship." He did not admit that there was a crisis in his brief, modest remarks, which he closed with "an affectionate farewell." Next morning, the Grays, under Colonel James Barnett, conducted the party to the Union Depot, and Lincoln began the next leg of

Rented quarters in the
Jones Building, above,
served the city adminis-
tration, 1855-74, until
space was available in
the Case Block in 1875.
STANLEY L. McMICHAEL
COLLECTION, CLEVELAND
PUBLIC LIBRARY.

Cleveland's monumental
City Hall, top, was dedi-
cated in 1916.

The Council Chamber of
the City Hall, an impres-
sive auditorium. CLEVE-
LAND PICTURE COLLEC-
TION, CLEVELAND PUBLIC
LIBRARY.

President Lincoln's remains rested on a catafalque on the Public Square, April 28, 1865.

One of Lincoln's earliest portraits, owned by the late William G. Taylor of Cleveland.

The locomotive Nashville *brought the funeral train to Cleveland.*

his journey to Washington and his inaugural. Twenty suites of rooms in the Weddell House had served the Lincoln party, but one room remained hallowed with the memory of the great American who had found rest for the night there. As time went on, it was reverently opened each year on the martyred President's birthday, and a memorial program was presented as a tribute by the Lincoln Society of Ohio.

Abraham Lincoln, sixteenth President of the United States, was inaugurated on March 4. John Hay, born in Salem, Indiana, in 1838, was graduated from Brown University in 1858, and practiced law in the office of his uncle, Milton Hay, Lincoln's partner. Hay was admitted to the bar this year, and went with Lincoln to Washington as one of his private secretaries. Young George C. Ashmun of Cleveland was selected to represent Ohio in the President's bodyguard. He later became a prominent physician. During the Civil War, Hay served for a time in the Army, attaining the rank of lieutenant colonel.

I. H. Carter brought a company to play in the Theatre Comique. In the boarding house where he lived, on Rockwell Street near Bond, he met precocious Clara Morrison, thirteen, who quickly became stage-struck and pleaded to go back-stage. She played "bit" parts until John A. Ellsler opened the Academy of Music, and joining the ballet, she soon became prominent. In 1869, under the name of Clara Morris, she starred in Wood's Theater, Cincinnati, and went on to fame as the great emotional actress of America.

At about this time George Cowell and his son, Herbert, started a jewelry concern known as H. Cowell & Company in the Weddell House on Bank Street, taking over the business of Royal Cowles, founded in the forties. Clocks, watches, silverware, oil-burning lamps, "pictures in fancy cases," "gold and silver cylinder watches," and notions were included in the stock. The founders having passed on, Samuel H. Cowell, a brother, operated the store; and when Addison T. Hubbard joined him, the name was changed to Cowell & Hubbard in 1879. The company moved to keep pace with its growth, and, in 1894, occupied the first floor of the new Garfield Building with a proud flourish.

The first shot of the Civil War was fired on April 12, when South Carolina moved to take Fort Sumter. On the 15th, President Lincoln called for 75,000 volunteers. In the evening, a Democrat who had joined the Republicans stood before a capacity audience in Melodeon Hall and denounced party strife. "The time has come," said Judge Rufus P. Spalding, "when every man should forget party and remember his country." Spalding's patriotic challenge brought cheering men to their feet. Torchlight parades, the marching Cleveland Grays, and speakers on street corners pushed the recruiting drive.

The Cleveland Grays were the first to leave for the war zone. On April 16 they were mustered into service as Company D, 1st Ohio Volunteer Infantry, and started for the defense of Washington. At Bull Run they were the first Union soldiers on the field and the last to leave, covering their comrades' retreat. At the end of three months' service, they re-enlisted for three years as Company E, commanded by Captain Thomas S. Paddock.

They fought at Shiloh under General Ulysses S. Grant of Ohio, and in the bloody Georgia engagements. With constant devotion to their country and to their motto, "Semper paratus"—"Always ready," the Grays at home continued to rush fresh men into uniform, raising two companies for the 84th Ohio Infantry and five for the 150th, the latter consisting almost entirely of Clevelanders.

An ordinance passed by the City Council on April 16 changed the name of the Public Square to Monumental Park, in recognition of the memorial to Commodore Perry at Superior and Ontario streets. The public argued about it for a time, then forgot it, and "Public Square" continued in common use despite the law on the statute books.

Cleveland women assembled to offer their services to the war effort on April 20, and at the meeting the Ladies Aid Society was organized. At first help was given to needy families of soldiers; but before the first week closed, the volunteers were conducting house-to-house canvasses for clothing, bedding, and supplies to relieve destitute Camp Taylor in Cleveland. A soup house was opened on Merwin Street, and farmers co-operated by supplying vegetables raised on the "soldiers' acre." The work expanded with the demands of war, and hundreds of branches were formed under a new name, The Soldiers Aid Society of Northern Ohio, which became a branch of the United States Sanitary Commission. Under the leadership of Mrs. Benjamin Rouse, president; Mary Clark Brayton, secretary, and Ellen F. Terry, treasurer, the ladies assumed the problems of relief and morale at home, in camp, and in battle. When more buildings and supplies were needed for the comfort of soldiers passing through Cleveland, some of the businessmen said that there was no money; but in a quiet tone, Mrs. Rouse declared, "It must be raised," and it was. Resourcefulness and determination marked her loving, generous spirit until her death in 1887 at the age of eighty-eight, sixteen years after her husband's death in 1871. Of the amount handled in money and supplies by the local society during four years of service, totaling $982,481.25, not a dollar was wanting and almost nothing was paid for administration. When the war ended, the organization appropriated $5,000 toward erection of the Ohio State Soldiers Home at Columbus.

Cleveland took on military importance as troops marched into Camp Taylor, hastily established in the city for preliminary training. The old fairground at Woodland and Forest Street was taken over, and recruits filed into the three halls on April 22, overflowing into tents. Brigadier General J. W. Fitch was in charge. Camp Wood was established on the Seneca Street hill in July, and two others were opened in outlying districts. The first regiments enlisted for three months. Upon reorganization, enlistments continued for the duration of the war. Thousands of recruits swarmed into Cleveland, where they were converted into fighting men, while home guards drilled to ensure the city's protection.

On April 22 six companies of the Cleveland Artillery, under Colonel James Barnett, transported six guns with caissons by rail to Columbus, where they went into service as the 1st Ohio Light Artillery. Their first three months of service were in West Virginia; and at Laurel Hill, on July 7, George H. Tillotson became the first Cleveland man to die for the Union. At Carrick's Ford, a week later, a field piece was captured; and, with the governor's sanction, it was given to Colonel Barnett. Returned veterans of the regiment were cheered wildly as they paraded Cleveland streets on July 30 with a rebel battle flag and the cannon drawn by four southern mules. The cannon was later mounted on the Public Square. After reorganization, Barnett became a general and chief of artillery on the staff of General William S. Rosecrans. The regiment was enlarged to twelve batteries that served principally in Kentucky, Tennessee, and Georgia.

The Hibernian Guards, the Zouave Light Guards, and the Sprague Cadets, local infantry units, were soon mustered into service, where they lost their identity. War laid a heavy hand upon Cleveland manpower. Fully two-thirds of the active members of the Fire Department volunteered for military duty. Professors and students laid down text-books and joined the colors, and the colleges were burdened with financial problems.

Patriotic citizens erected the first city flagpole in the Public Square in about the middle of May. The eighty-foot wooden mast was made possible by public subscription. As the war had created a heavy demand for bunting, the first flag was made of merino wool.

A jobbing business was founded by J. C. Weideman on July 1, on River Street. As the wholesale grocery prospered, the firm moved into larger quarters on Water Street in 1873, a permanent location (1240 West 9th Street) enlarged at intervals to meet growing needs. The Weideman Company, a corporation, was formed in 1889 to succeed the partnership of Weideman, Kent & Company. J. C. Weideman, the first president, served until his death in 1900. He was succeeded by his corporate co-founders, E. J. Siller and Christian Narten, whose families carried on the tradition of the enterprise. In 1942, the William Edwards Company was acquired, followed by the Summit Wholesale Grocery Company of Akron and the United Wholesale Grocery Company of Canton. Warehouses in Cleveland, Akron, Canton, and Warren were operating in the 1940s, and "Weideman Boy Brand" fine foods were being marketed in a large Midwest territory.

St. Mary's Cemetery at Burton Street and Clark Avenue was opened this year. It was used by the German and Bohemian Catholics of the West Side.

Andrew Freese asked to be relieved as superintendent of instruction of the public schools so that he might devote all of his time to teaching. Luther M. Oviatt succeeded him in August. Freese taught at Eagle School until 1868, when he returned to Central High School as principal. Ill health forced his retirement the next year, and to the pioneer schoolmaster belongs the honor of blazing the trail for an educational system that would rank with the best in later years.

Isaac A. Isaacs, who ran a clothing emporium called Union Hall on the Superior hill at Union Lane, is said to be the first advertiser to employ verse. Under the title, "The Buckeye Boys," Isaacs endeavored to capitalize upon patriotic enthusiasm:

Yes, we'll shout at Union Hall,
Where we clothe the people all . . .
And to Buckeye boys who go,
We sell clothing very low!

The first draft of men for war service began on October 1, affecting only three city wards, the others having raised their quotas. The draft threat had a curious effect upon some who were likely to be called for military service. "Men who have been wearing wigs and dyeing their whiskers, and passing for 38 or 39 years of age, have suddenly owned up to 45," it was reported, "while young bucks who have passed with the girls for 20 have shrunk to the other side of 18." As much as $700 was paid by a draftee for a substitute to enter the service; and as the practice grew, recruiting suffered.

Western Union's Jeptha H. Wade was sent to California to effect consolidation of small telegraph lines and to construct the lines eastward to Salt Lake City, Utah. As head of the Pacific Telegraph Company, he began work three months after the start of the Civil War, with a ten-year limit for completion. The nation was amazed to learn that on October 17, 1861, the final joint was made in the eastern section of the line at Fort Bridger, Utah. Brigham Young, Mormon leader, sent the first east-to-west message to Wade from Salt Lake City on that day, stating that Utah had not seceded, but was firm for the Union. The western line was completed on October 22; and the first transcontinental telegram was sent by Stephen J. Field, chief justice of California, to President Lincoln from San Francisco on October 24, expressing his state's loyalty. Thus a half-million settlers isolated on the Pacific Coast were linked with the Eastern States by this new means of communication, and the West remained in the Union during the war. The company that started with only 550 miles of wire in the forties, was making great strides toward leadership as the world's largest telegraph company.

David Tod of Youngstown was elected governor of Ohio this year. In April, 1863, he purchased the Hilliard mansion at Bond and St. Clair streets (Public Auditorium site), built at a cost of $25,000. His family lived in it little more than a year, as Tod's interests centered in Youngstown and Columbus. In 1868 Caesar Grasselli purchased the house, which was his home for a number of years. From 1906 to 1917 it was occupied, rent free, by the Associated Charities. It was also, for a time, the headquarters of the Anti-Tuberculosis League and the Visiting Nurse Association.

1862

The Soldiers Aid Society reaped $275 from admissions, and the audience laughed "at every word" of the lecture, *Children in the Wood,* given by young Artemus Ward—Charles Farrar Browne—in the Academy of Music on January 31. The famous humorist astonished his Cleveland friends when he appeared in a dress suit with his straight hair done in a mass of curls; but their amazement was soon lost in Ward's observations that he might have discussed the falsity of the saying, "Go it while you are young, for when you get old you can't." He gave his listeners funny stories and haphazard entertainment that centered around the defeat at Bull Run, then generally attributed to politician-soldiers. Victory was at hand, declared Ward, when news was received of three vacancies in the New York custom house. All the soldiers rushed to the metropolis except a musician, who "stayed to spike his fife." After Ward tucked the "babes" away for the night, without having said scarcely a word about them, an impromptu reception was given for him at the Elephant Club. His subtle nonsense centering around the Shakers and the Mormons attracted large audiences. When he presented *Among the Mormons,* he gave away complimentary tickets inscribed, "Admit the bearer and one wife."

Isaac Leisy had learned the brewer's art from his father, who came from Bavaria, and he had owned a brewery in Iowa before opening a plant in Cleveland this year, the forerunner of The Leisy Brewing Company. Leisy brewed $20,000 worth of beer in his Vega Avenue plant the first year. Business grew, and his help made possible Germania Hall and the German Home for the Aged. Just before his death in 1892, the baronial, brownstone mansion on Vega Avenue was finished, a walk leading from the front door to the brewery, so that Leisy might be near in case of emergency. Otto I. Leisy, who succeeded his father as president, built the company into the largest brewery in northern Ohio, covering eight acres of land. David B. Tarr joined Leisy in 1918, supervised the dismantling and sale of machinery and equipment in the prohibition era, and became vice president and secretary. After repeal, the brewery was re-equipped and modernized under direction of Carl Faller, who was the oldest active brewmaster in the United States when he died in 1939. Carrying on the family tradition, Herbert F. Leisy, grandson of the founder, became president-treasurer of the company. Herbert L. Noll, master brewer and vice president in charge of production, was the grandson of Peter Noll, who founded the first lager-beer brewery in Ohio.

A percussion cap exploding from a toy pistol in the hand of small Eugene Gray, son of J. W. Gray, destroyed the sight of his father's right eye on the evening of April 9, 1858. Blindness threatened the other eye, and paralysis later affected the brain of the founder and editor of the *Plain Dealer*. The death of Gray's devoted friend, Stephen A. Douglas, in June, 1861, was a great blow at a time when the editor was physically afflicted and his spirit was troubled with concern for the Union and those national principles that he had furthered with all his power. The end came for Joseph William Gray, forty-eight, on May 26, 1862, as fife and drum called volunteers to the colors on every street corner. John S. Stephenson, nephew-in-law of the late publisher, became administrator of the estate and assumed editorial direction of the *Plain Dealer*. Unqualified to conduct a Democratic daily in the face of rampant Republicanism, he made the fatal mistake of turning the paper against the national administration. Mrs. Gray petitioned the court to remove him from office, and the paper suspended publication early in March, 1865.

A mission of the Evangelical Association began its work under the Rev. S. F. Crowther, holding services in the Mayflower Presbyterian Church. It became known as the Perry Street Church when its first building was erected at Woodland and Perry Street in 1864. The congregation moved to Oakdale Street (at Steinway, S.E.) in 1886. The name was changed to Calvary, and the cornerstone of a larger building was laid at 2765 Woodhill Road in 1907. In 1941, the Rev. Victor H. Peterson was called to the pulpit of the church on the hill. Outstanding in service to the church was the record of Fred W. Ramsey, superintendent of the Sunday School since 1912; and Charles Clemens, director of social work with more than fifty years of service in 1946. When the church became known as Calvary Evangelical United Brethren Church in late 1946, membership had almost reached a thousand, representing twenty-two nationalities, and the community center was familiarly known as "a little league of nations."

Cincinnati was in danger as the Confederates advanced from Louisville and no federal troops were available. On September 10, Governor David Tod appealed to Ohio cities to mobilize volunteer defenses. Citizens left shops and farms, took up their squirrel rifles and quickly assembled such fighting equipment as was at hand. By wagon and by train the Cleveland Squirrel Hunters made their way southward. Cincinnati prepared for the surprise attack that never came. The Confederate Army turned back; perhaps its scouts had heard of the deadly aim of the squirrel-hunting marksmen. Fifteen thousand men received the official Squirrel Hunter discharge for heroic service.

Property owners on residential Euclid Street fought invasion of the horsecar, but opposition was halted on September 15 when Council authorized tracks as far east as Erie Street.

Isaac Levy and Abraham Stearn opened a toy and fancy-goods shop on Superior Avenue, known as Levy & Stearn, that became one of the best-known "toy emporiums" between New York and Chicago. In 1882 the store moved to the Parsons Block on Superior Avenue, and three years later to Euclid Avenue. It continued eastward to 1021 Euclid in 1914, when the Stearn Company was incorporated. Stearn's, purchased by Lane Bryant, Inc., of New York in 1945, was one of the largest stores in the chain. Women's ready-to-wear and accessories led in store sales.

In the fall, an oil-refining business known as Andrews, Clark & Company was formed by Samuel Andrews, the Clark brothers—Maurice B., James H., and Richard E., with John D. Rockefeller silently representing the "Company." Early in 1865, Rockefeller sold his interest in the produce-commission business of Clark & Rockefeller, purchased the oil concern, and with Andrews set up the firm of Rockefeller & Andrews. They operated a crude refinery on the south bank of Kingsbury Run, near the river and the railroad, and their office was in the Sexton Building in the "Flats" at the foot of Superior Street. By the end of the year, the refinery had ten stills of thirty-barrel capacity, and employed thirty-seven men whose monthly wages ranged from $45 to $58. Henry M. Flagler came into the firm in 1867, representing Stephen V. Harkness, whose niece Flagler had married, and who was a backer of the concern, then Rockefeller, Andrews & Flagler.

The city purchased its first steam fire engine on December 17, a shining "Silsby" costing $3,250. Two horses hauled the steamer and one the hose cart; and an engineer, two drivers, and a fireman manned the equipment. Fifty feet of hose threw a stream of water 193½ feet, "which beats the average hand machine by 60 to 70 feet." The new fire-fighter filled a crying need, as firemen joined the ranks that moved to the battlefields.

1863

The *Emancipation Proclamation,* freeing the slaves, was announced to the world on New Year's Day by a Clevelander, twenty-two-year-old Edward Rosewater, a military telegraph dispatcher in the War Department at Washington.

On February 10, the West Side Street Railroad Company received a grant to operate the first streetcar line west of the river. The route originated beside the *Plain Dealer* office at Superior and Vineyard streets, crossed the river to Detroit Street, and made a circuitous West Side journey back to its starting point. Dan P. Rhodes was president, and H. S. Stevens, secretary.

Seven Rockport families met with the Rev. C. H. Heitmeier in March and founded the Rockport Methodist Church (near 4600 West 130th Street). Until 1887, the charge was on a circuit with St. Paul's. Baldwin University students served it until 1893, when Dr. F. W. Mueller, pastor, began to hold morning services in a "wigwam" on Lorain Avenue (at West 80th Street). Late in the year, Dr. Mueller with four pastors and three laymen organized the Quarterly Conference at the Rockport Church, and united with the Bethany Church of Cleveland. In 1909, the West Park Church was organized, having been a mission under the care of J. F. Hecker, Baldwin University student. A new church was built in 1927 at West 138th Street and Fairwood Drive. In 1939, the Bethany and West Park churches merged to form the Christ Methodist Church, meeting in the West Park edifice. Membership grew to nearly fourteen hundred, and, in 1941, the Rev. Roy I. Farmer became minister.

Unrest created by the "copperheads" and Clement L. Vallandigham's campaign for governor, supported by the *Plain Dealer,* was reflected on street corners and in the public press, and some declared that the Union was doomed. On March 31, however, Brainard's Hall rang with cheers of loyalty to the Government as the Union League was organized. Clevelanders were determined to preserve the Union and continue the war "until the national flag shall float in triumph over every state now in rebellion."

Dr. Gustave C. E. Weber resigned as professor of surgery at the Cleveland Medical College and organized the Charity Hospital Medical College. He was an eminent surgeon, trained in European schools, and as dean he assembled an able faculty, including Drs. Leander Firestone, Addison P. Dutcher, M. S. Castle, Jacob Dascomb, John H. Salisbury, Robert N. Barr, William J. Scott, and Abraham Metz. In 1870 the college became the medical department of the University of Wooster. The Brownell Street School was remodeled for lecture purposes in 1873 and served until the end of the century.

Scholarly lectures of the day were targets for Artemus Ward's brand of humor; and when he originated the burlesque performance in Cleveland on April 2, his audience clamored for more. His presentation, *Sixty Minutes in Africa,* in Brainard's Hall was probably his last appearance in the city.

The First National Bank, pioneer national bank in Cleveland and the seventh in the nation, was organized on May 23, originating in the private banking house of S. W. Crittenden & Company, with capital of $300,000. George Worthington, its first president, was succeeded by William Hewitt, Philo Scovill, and James Barnett in the early years. The bank opened on Superior Street, later moving to the Perry-Payne Building.

The St. Clair Street Railroad Company was authorized on June 9 to operate a streetcar line from the north side of the Square eastward on Superior to Willson Avenue. Incorporators were R. F. Paine, Hiram Garretson, O. H. Payne, John M. Sterling, Jr., A. S. Sanford, James Pannell, and Peter Thatcher.

Quoting from a tablet in the lobby of the Federal Building on the Public Square:

> To the Honor of Joseph W. Briggs: While acting as Window Delivery Clerk at the Cleveland, Ohio, Post Office in 1863 he conceived a system of mail delivery and collection to better serve the public and with the co-operation of the local Postmaster (Edwin Cowles) acted as the first letter carrier of that city. In recognition of his special interest in this service and his success in the work, the Postmaster-General appointed him special agent for the installation of city free delivery service throughout the country, a work covering six years. He designed the first carrier uniform and was credited with the genius and perseverance which gave his service to the people. He died in Cleveland, Ohio, in 1872. Erected by the Ohio Society of New York 1921.

Free delivery of mail matter went into effect on July 1, 1863.

An ordinance was passed creating a "paid steam fire department" with a force of fifty-three men under James A. Craw, chief engineer. Cleveland now owned four steam fire engines! A colorful Fourth of July parade was arranged, featuring an Adams Express Company wagon and Clark's Forest

City Cornet Band; the new Council Committee on Fire and Water, consisting of J. D. Palmer, J. J. Benton, and William Meyer; four steam fire engines, brightly polished and drawn by sleek horses with jangling bells and canopies of flowers; and the horse-drawn Mazeppa Hook and Ladder Company. These steamers were called "black jackets," the carts being two-wheeled and the trucks small and primitive. Three of them were named for the new committeemen, and the fourth for I. U. Masters, local political figure. Some citizens still considered organized fire protection to be wasteful spending, and the Council hoped to stamp out this opposition by the gala exhibition.

Physical training and the object-lesson method of teaching were introduced in the public schools under the administration of Superintendent Oviatt, who resigned this year. He was succeeded by the Rev. Anson Smythe, ex-state commissioner of schools, at a salary of $1,800, later increased to $2,100. His efforts directed at strict classification led to overcrowding in the grades and many objections. At the same time, they revealed the urgent need for additional primary facilities; and in two years, ten new primary and secondary schools were opened.

Cleveland was host to the convention of the International Typographical Union, organized in the early fifties. The Cigar Makers Local No. 17, founded on August 1, this year, soon diminished to fifteen members and disbanded; but it was rechartered in 1879, its eighty members paying initiation fees reduced to twenty-five cents.

War demanded members of the YMCA, and it was obliged to disband. Furnishings were sold and books were placed in the care of the Cleveland Library Association. The few members at home distributed books and newspapers among soldiers.

A wooden drawbridge was built at Center Street this year, but before a decade had passed it was declared unsafe. In 1871 plans for an iron draw were under way, to cost $13,250. A steel structure built in 1900 cost $57,000.

Patrick Smith bought the *Belle King* and started a tug line, one of the first on the lakes. Ten years later, the firm of "Patrick Smith, Dredging and Contracting" boasted four tugs, and a fleet was taking form. His two sons, L. P. and J. A., were active in the business that expanded to include several schooners and steamers and the big tug *Chauncey Morgan*. "Pat" Smith served as councilman, trustee of the Board of Water Works, and county commissioner. In Council, he could be depended upon to cast his ballot for those measures "that were of the greatest value to the municipality." When he retired to his big, brick house on Washington Street, overlooking the lake (where Bulkley Boulevard leads to Edgewater Park), he was a wealthy man with a reputation for liberality to those needing help.

Small children were moved from St. Mary's Orphanage to a new home, known as St. Joseph's Orphanage (6431 Woodland), where they might have "pure country air." In 1894 the older girls were also transferred. A modern home was provided in healthful surroundings eastward on the lakeshore, at

18485 Lake Shore Boulevard, which the institution occupied in 1943 under a new name, St. Joseph's-on-the-Lake. The historic Woodland Avenue building was occupied by St. Joseph's Home for the Aged.

Cleveland celebrated "her grand Union victory"—the defeat of Clement L. Vallandigham, copperhead southern sympathizer, and the victories at Vicksburg and Gettysburg—with a rousing demonstration on the evening of October 17. Honest John Brough, governor-elect of Ohio, and Governor David Tod were borne in a fine decorated carriage in a gay parade to the Angier House, where speeches and a "glorious display" in the Public Square preceded a banquet. Brough's majority of 101,099 votes was the largest received up to that time by an Ohio governor.

Negotiations having been completed this year for lease of the Cleveland & Mahoning Railroad by the Atlantic & Great Western Railroad Company (later Mahoning Division of the Erie Railroad), immediate plans were made to lay an additional track outside the existing two tracks to provide a six-foot, broad-gauge road on which trains from the East could run. The first train arrived in Cleveland direct from New York City on November 3. On the 18th, jubilant crowds packed the Union Depot, awaiting time to board the inaugural excursion train to Meadville, Pennsylvania, over the new line. Eight passenger and four baggage cars were drawn by the handsome engine, its stack striped with patriotic colors. The crowning feature, however, was an elegantly equipped parlor car for officials, an ingenious "locomotive dwelling house." Fast trains now brought the mails westward at 40 miles per hour, carrying news from the battlefronts to anxious homefolks.

A reorganization of Stone, Chisholm & Jones, Newburgh iron-makers, resulted in the Cleveland Rolling Mill Company (later American Steel & Wire Company), incorporated on November 9 by Henry Chisholm, Andros B. Stone, Stillman Witt, Jeptha H. Wade, and H. B. Payne. The mill was a family business of the Chisholms, manned by Welsh, Irish, and Scotch workmen. Inside men and rollers received $3.50 to $7 a day, and laborers, $1.65. The first Bessemer steel in the County was blown in the Newburgh plant in 1868. Notable improvements in the Bessemer process were made by the company, and it originated methods for using steel scrap. The Cleveland Wire Mill Company was purchased in 1866 as an outlet for steel. In 1871, Chisholm, Stone, and Chicago investors organized the Union Rolling Mill Company in Chicago; and by 1875 Chisholm's investments in the industry amounted to $10,000,000. When Henry Chisholm died in 1881, he was one of the country's greatest steel men. His son, William, then became president of the Cleveland company. A central furnace was erected on the "Canal Tract" in 1881. William Garrett, mechanical genius of the company, conceived the Garrett rod mill, quintupling rolling capacity by a multiple rod-rolling development, a great contribution to wire-making. The first Garrett mill began operating in Newburgh in 1882. Mills and properties expanded, and by 1890 the company was producing 180,000 tons of steel ingots a year. A dispute arose between the management and Garrett, however, resulting in cancellation of the contract giving the company exclusive rights to the inventor's patents. Leaving Newburgh, Garrett built mills for other companies that ultimately merged in a combine which bought the Cleveland Rolling Mill Company and wiped out its identity.

There were only ten sentences in Abraham Lincoln's immortal *Gettysburg Address,* delivered at the dedication of a soldiers' national cemetery on November 19. The next day, a Cleveland paper reported, "the weather being fine, the program was carried out successfully." On the following day, an "eloquent extract" was printed from Edward Everett's two-hour-and-ten-minute oration.

War came close to Cleveland in November, when Canadian refugees and "inside" Confederates plotted to free war prisoners on Johnson's Island in Sandusky Bay, take over Federal gunboats, and bombard lake cities. The 128th Ohio Infantry, including about three hundred Cleveland men, thwarted execution of these plans by minutes.

John Wilkes Booth, dissipated star of the South who traded on his family name, had secured an engagement with the Academy of Music theatrical company through Joseph Jefferson, long a friend and associate of Manager John A. Ellsler. On November 26 he began a four-day engagement as leading man, appearing as Claude Melnotte in *The Lady of Lyons* and in Shakespearean plays supported by the stock cast. On December 5 he played his last professional engagement in the American theater in Cleveland as Charles DeMoor in *The Robbers.* Joining the Confederates soon afterward, he began his short career of plotting against the Union cause, returning once to Cleveland under the guise of business interests. Although Booth and Ellsler had joined forces in a deal involving Pennsylvania oil property, the latter was not aware of his partner's real sentiment toward the Union. After two benefit performances in New York City without pay, Booth made his final stage appearance in Washington on the evening of April 14, 1865, when he assassinated President Lincoln in Ford's Theater.

The Soldiers Home, erected by the Soldiers Aid Society, was completed on December 12 on the Union Depot pier. It served as headquarters for soldiers during the war, providing lodging and meals to 56,645 registrants. Nearly a thousand men received care in a military hospital built near the station.

1864

A partnership known as Coe, Ely & Harmon was formed on January 1 to produce railroad-car axles and heavy hex shafts, rudder frames, and major forgings for the marine trade. The firm incorporated in 1871 as the Cleveland City Forge & Iron Company, shortened some years later to Cleveland City Forge Company. Production of weldless turnbuckles and clevises began in 1882, and in 1913, the manufacture of automobile drop forgings. Ralph M. Coe became president of the company in 1923, succeeding R. A. Harmon. For many years the organization was located at 4501 Lakeside Avenue.

A part of the "Flats" in Brooklyn Township, between Walworth Run and the east bend of the river, was annexed to Cleveland on February 16.

In the fence-enclosed Public Square, a large building had been erected around the Perry Monument in the shape of a Greek cross to accommodate the Northern Ohio Sanitary Fair that opened on February 22. In the center was Floral Hall; the east wing housed an auditorium seating more than three thousand; the west, Bazaar Hall, where Leland's Band played daily; the north, a dining hall; and the south, an implement hall. Gas lighted the buildings, and stoves and steam pipes furnished the heat. Major General James A. Garfield delivered the principal address at the dedication, and the governor and state officials were present. Exhibits ranged from art treasures to animals and implements, many of them auctioned for the Sanitary Fund. Post offices were established for the sale of Sanitary Fair stamps to swell the fund, and other cities copied the idea, which became the forerunner of the tuberculosis stamp and Christmas seal. The fair continued until March 10, netting more than $78,000 for the Soldiers Aid Society and the United States Sanitary Commission. Pittsburgh purchased the huge fair building for $8,500 to house a sanitary fair of its own.

James Hill, one of the most colorful figures in Fire Department history, returned from the war and again became head of the fire-fighters. The fifth fire engine was purchased this year, and an engine house was provided for each steamer. A fire-alarm telegraph system was installed, with signal boxes placed on posts near the sidewalks throughout the business district. Soon it was being copied by large cities. The sound of the fire alarm in the station of Steamer No. 1 was the signal for Mose, a big, shaggy mongrel, to rush to the stall doors barking frantically. When they were opened, the "volunteer" seized a halter and dashed to a horse's head. At night he frequently carried a lantern, bounding ahead of the swaying steamer, clearing its path.

With the extension of the city water system, there was a gradual elimination of the seventy-five strategically placed cisterns that once were the source of water for fire-fighting. Only two remained, kept in condition for emergency use at Bank and Superior streets and at Water and St. Clair.

A discordant note in the community's fine sense of loyalty to the President's war policy was struck when the first national political-party convention held in Cleveland assembled on May 31 in Chapin's Hall. It founded the Radical Democracy Party, dominated by anti-Lincoln Missouri Republicans, and boomed General John C. Fremont for President. Attendance estimates ranged from two hundred to two thousand, depending upon the political leanings of the estimator. The party left little impression upon the devoted North, and it died from failure to win a place on the ballot.

Captain W. J. Morgan and his younger brother, George W., established W. J. Morgan & Company (later Morgan Lithograph Corporation) on Superior Street near Seneca. A hand press constituted their equipment, and paper was cut by hand. To meet growing demand for their output, they purchased a steam press and moved to the Bratenahl Building at Superior and Water streets, where the first of their famous theatrical lithographs was made.

The country's first "one-sheet" masterpiece in color, featuring John T. Raymond in *Millions in It,* originated here. The nation's stars of the stage were company customers, and the business expanded rapidly despite high prices set on lithography because of the unreliability of the show business. The firm received high honors in international exhibitions, among them the gold medal awarded for artistic poster display in the Exposition Universelle, Paris, the winning entry being Morgan's reproduction of Rosa Bonheur's "Horse Fair," the world's first twenty-four-sheet billboard poster. Offices and warehouses had been established in foreign countries by 1904, when George W. Morgan became head of the company upon his brother's death. He died in 1905, and his son, P. J., became president.

George W. Johnson brought his bride, Maggie Clark Johnson, to Cleveland, and he joined the *Plain Dealer* as associate editor. His wife died before they had been married a year. Grief-stricken, he resigned from the paper early in 1866 and returned to Canada. Later in the year, J. A. Butterfield of Detroit composed music for a poem written by Johnson before his marriage and dedicated to his future wife—*When You and I Were Young, Maggie.*

Dr. Richard Fry retired from a life of public service and settled in Rockport this year on twenty-seven acres of land extending from Detroit Street to the lake (just west of West 117th). He had served as principal of the St. Clair Street Grammar School, where he had taught John D. Rockefeller and Marcus A. Hanna. At the same time, he practiced medicine in Cuyahoga Falls. Dr. Fry was one of the community's most distinguished men. Fry Avenue in Lakewood bears his name.

A sympathetic atmosphere prevailed in Plymouth Congregational Church on September 11 when nineteen earnest Negroes organized the Mount Zion Congregational Church. All the Congregational churches of Cleveland were represented in the council meeting. The Rev. J. H. Muse was the first minister. A brick meeting house was erected on Erie Street opposite Webster in 1866, but the debt was heavy and the property was sold. On Maple Street, just south of Central, a smaller, frame building was built debt free. Membership grew slowly, as newcomers, largely from the South, leaned toward the Baptists and Methodists. Internal dissension born of confusing times threatened the life of the church, and some energetic members were lost. The Rev. Sterling Brown, who became pastor in 1885, was an Oberlin graduate of marked talents and energy. His crusade for members resulted in one hundred and nine accessions in the winter of 1886, launching a new era of advance.

William Halsey Doan, leading citizen of Doan's Corners and grandson of pioneer Nathaniel Doan, organized the firm of W. H. Doan & Company, and began selling crude oil on commission. With Dr. Worthy S. Streator, he brought to Cleveland the first tank cars loaded with crude petroleum. Two years later, the firm of Harkness & Doan was established, and with Stephen V. Harkness, he supplied a large volume of oil to local refineries. He owned the business by 1870, and the I. X. L. Oil & Naphtha Works, which he built near Kingsbury Run, was for many years the largest plant refining petroleum products in the world. Doan sold his holdings to the Standard Oil Company. The Doan family lived in a fine residence at Streator and Euclid streets, and a long row of homes along the east side of Streator belonged to the industrialist.

The city's first pleasure yacht in the luxury class was launched on September 26 from a Cleveland shipyard. T. W. Kennard, who bought the Angier House, had spent money lavishly on his steam craft, the *Octavia,* fitting her handsomely and rigging her as a top-sail schooner for ocean travel. Captain Christopher D. Goulder, father of Harvey D. Goulder, lawyer, commanded on the first voyage abroad, a trip equaling a Twentieth Century world cruise.

The Jones-Potter Company, founded this year, later became Chandler & Abbott. In 1868 William C. Rudd and George H. Chandler formed Chandler & Rudd, operating a small store facing the south side of the Square (May Company site), and specializing in fruits and vegetables. Rudd, his brother, George A., and Chandler built an enviable reputation in the grocery business, selling baked goods, candies, and a complete line of foods and specialties. A larger store was opened in 1888 east of the original location (234 Euclid), as well as an uptown store at the corner of Willson and Euclid.

Fifty thousand political enthusiasts poured into Cleveland on October 5 to attend the big Republican rally boosting the re-election of Abraham Lincoln for President. John Sherman, Benjamin Stanton, and Governor David Tod spoke to the noisy throng on the Square, and a torchlight parade with scores of bands closed the day's events. Followers of George B. McClellan, friend of the copperheads, carried their cause to the citizens on October 8, but election night gave the Republicans the victory with a comfortable majority. Saloons were ordered closed by the mayor. Crowds were tense and silent as many waited in Brainard's Hall; but as a sweeping victory rolled up for Lincoln, cheers and songs filled the air, only to be caught up by thousands in the streets who rejoiced until daybreak.

For eighteen years, Mrs. Sarah Josepha Hale, editor of Godey's *Lady's Book,* had urged that a national Thanksgiving Day be established. While the holiday had been observed in the past, each governor named the day of his choice. This year the presidential proclamation of Abraham Lincoln fixed the fourth or last Thursday in November as the nation's day of thanks. Hearts were heavy and delicacies few, as large quantities of poultry and substantial foods had been sent to the boys in camp.

Wooden awnings were declared old-fashioned in New York City. Consequently, Cleveland's law-makers voted for removal of the unsightly sidewalk shelters. The deadline, December 1, was upon many merchants before they realized that they had not complied with the ordinance; and they hastily turned from counting their profits to hire workmen to perform the face-lifting operation.

Death claimed Leonard Case, Sr., one of Cleveland's greatest benefactors, on December 7, at the age of seventy-eight. Although crippled and frail since boyhood, he was a tower of civic, business, and financial strength. His influence had furthered municipal improvements, encouraged banks and railroads, and advanced religious and cultural movements. From 1827 to

1855, he had been agent for the Connecticut Land Company, buying lands with rare judgment. In the Panic of 1837, he acquired a large amount of real estate from debtors who offered it as security for loans. His sons, William and Leonard, Jr., inherited his estate and his zeal for the upbuilding of their city.

Hamilton Fisk Biggar came to Cleveland this year to enter the Western Homeopathic College. Born in Canada in 1839, he was apprenticed to a merchant when a boy. Saving his money for an education, he was graduated from the University of Victoria and was prepared to practice law when he decided to study medicine. Supplementing his Cleveland training with study in eastern hospitals, he returned to the city to practice. Dr. Biggar served as professor of anatomy and clinical surgery in the Homeopathic Hospital

Superior Avenue in 1865, Cleveland's leading business district. The third building from the right housed the city offices during the forties and fifties.

College, as surgeon-in-chief of the Surgical Institute, and as founder and dean of the Training School for Nurses during his long career that closed with his death in 1913. For many years, he was John D. Rockefeller's close friend and physician.

Wartime Christmas-gift suggestions were practical: bonnets, hoopskirts, breakfast shawls, and dress goods for ladies; moustache cups, photographs, stereoscopic views, wigs, photograph albums, and vulcanite-based teeth for gentlemen.

1865

English-speaking Catholics west of the river organized St. Malachi's congregation and worshiped in the old church on the "Flats." On the brow of the hill overlooking the lake and the valley (Washington Avenue, facing the High Level Bridge) they erected a church in 1869. An oil-burning lamp lighted the cross mounted on its tall spire, serving as a beacon to sailing craft for many years. The historic landmark was destroyed by fire on December 23, 1943. Plans to restore its Gothic grandeur were soon under way.

The City Bank received a national-bank charter on February 12, and opened the next day as The National City Bank of Cleveland in the City Bank quarters. The former officers, Lemuel Wick, president, and John F. Whitelaw, cashier, were retained. Wick, Whitelaw, and P. H. T. Babcock were the leading stockholders. Capital of $100,000 doubled in a few months and had increased to $250,000 in 1887. Assets reached $2,000,000 by 1901. W. P. Southworth, retail grocer, became president in 1873, and Whitelaw was elected in 1889. For most of the time between 1848 and 1912 the bank was located on or near the site of the Perry-Payne Building on Superior Street.

War-weary Cleveland men were in the ranks at Appomattox when Lee surrendered to Grant on April 9. Cuyahoga County furnished 10,000 of its available 15,600 men, and their names are engraved in enduring stone in the Soldiers and Sailors Monument on the Public Square.

Leadership and daring characterized Cleveland's "Boys in Blue." Fourteen men, from a regiment of 610 Cleveland soldiers, escaped after the rain of shot and shell in the Ringgold, Georgia, engagement. Led in a mountain-side charge by two Cleveland officers, Colonel William R. Creighton and Lieutenant Colonel Orrin J. Crane, the famous fighting 7th Ohio Infantry was almost annihilated. Creighton and Crane, "two of the bravest men in the army," went down, and were buried in Erie Street Cemetery with military honors. Colonel Charles Whittlesey, Cleveland scientist and editor, led the 20th Ohio Volunteers through their baptism of fire at the capture of Fort Donelson in Tennessee. Colonel Rutherford B. Hayes commanded the famous "charging regiment," the 23rd Ohio Infantry, in which there were 341 Clevelanders. William McKinley was a member. More than 400 Cleveland men were in the ranks of the 41st Ohio Infantry, part of Brigadier General William B. Hazen's brigade, that won its laurels in the thick of the Tennessee campaigns. Colonel Philip C. Hayes, with 461 Cleveland men of the 103rd Ohio Infantry, made a brilliant charge at Resaca.

Colonel Oliver H. Payne of the 124th Ohio Infantry, in which there were 567 Clevelanders, lost heavily at Chickamauga, and won high honors with General Philip H. Sheridan at Missionary Ridge. The traveling 2nd Ohio Cavalry, under Colonel Charles Doubleday, was the pride of Cleveland. It fought under twenty-three generals, including Custer, Sheridan, and Grant; its horses drank from twenty-five rivers; it campaigned through thirteen states, traveled 27,000 miles and participated in ninety-seven battles. Heroic service of the Cleveland Grays and the 1st Ohio Light Artillery has been mentioned earlier. Three hundred Clevelanders were killed in action in the Union Navy while serving in blockading squadrons on the Atlantic coast and in the river navy of ironclads on the Mississippi. Some of them heard Farragut's famous outburst, "Damn the torpedoes," at Mobile Bay.

News of the end of hostilities reached Cleveland by telegraph early in the morning of April 10 and spread quickly. Crowds gathered in the dismal Public Square, and the old "Secesh" cannon thundered until daybreak. Bonfires were lighted as citizens gathered to read morning headlines. The Union flag and banners were raised over the Old Stone Church and prominent buildings. Business ceased, and the people celebrated wildly until noon, when a nondescript parade formed, joined by bands amplified by a variety of noise-making instruments. Celebration continued and fires blazed far into the night.

A salute of one hundred guns on the Public Square, fired by the Brooklyn Light Artillery at ten o'clock on the morning of April 14, announced a day of thanksgiving in Cleveland as proclaimed by Governor John Brough. A united church service attracted capacity attendance and overflowed outdoors. Parades, speeches, bonfires, and rockets continued until a late hour, celebrating the peace. As the tattered remnants of regiments returned, their colors riddled with shot and shell, the grim total of the cost in lives mounted. Of the 10,000 Cuyahoga County men and boys who served the flag, 1,700 died on the battlefield or in prison, and 2,000 were crippled or disabled for life.

On the morning of April 15, a telegram reached Cleveland stating that the shot fired by John Wilkes Booth in Ford's Theater, Washington, the evening before had claimed the life of President Lincoln. The news traveled swiftly through the city. A day of mourning was proclaimed by Mayor George B. Senter. Flags were lowered; churches and public buildings were draped in black; workmen assembled in Clinton Park to pay tribute. In the afternoon citizens met on the Square to hear appropriate addresses by Governor John Brough, ex-Governor David Tod, and Rufus P. Spalding. Speeches denounced the assassination. There were those, however, who made indiscreet remarks approving the murderous act, and five men narrowly escaped lynching during the day. Although J. J. Husband, architect of the new Court House, hastened to deny that he said Lincoln's death was a "small loss," he was exiled from the city, and his name was chiseled from the corner-stone of the building.

During the period in which the late President's funeral train passed through eastern cities on its way to the last resting place in Springfield, Illinois, Cleveland paid homage to Abraham Lincoln in special church services and made preparation for the day when the body would lie in state in the city.

Artillery salute announced the dawn of April 28. Early in the morning, thousands of mourners began to arrive, and shortly after seven the Lincoln funeral train reached the Euclid Street Station. In the last black-draped car lay the mortal remains of the martyred President. At the foot of the massive coffin stood a smaller one in which lay the body of Lincoln's son, Willie, who died in 1862, and was to be interred beside his father. Governor John Brough, 150 members of the civic guard of honor, committees, and military units had assembled at the station with the honorary pallbearers. Cannon thundered and the Camp Chase Band played a solemn dirge as the coffin was raised to the shoulders of the Reserve Guards and placed in the plumed hearse, drawn by six white horses. A procession of about six thousand—men of influence and lowly citizens—began to move down Euclid Street in slow time, headed by Colonel James Barnett, marshal.

Cleveland had no hall large enough to accommodate the vast throng that was expected to pay homage to Abraham Lincoln, and a canopied pavilion had been erected in a grass plot on the Public Square, east of Perry's Monument. Guards were posted at entrances to the fence-enclosed area. Black-and-white plumes and festoons decorated the pavilion, while evergreens and the national colors relieved the severity. The coffin was placed upon a low catafalque in the center and banked with white flowers, the tribute of Cleveland ladies. The Rt. Rev. Charles P. McIlvaine, bishop of the Diocese of Ohio, read the Episcopal burial service, and heavy rain was falling as the gates were opened to the public. When they closed at ten o'clock that night, a hundred thousand people had looked for the last time upon the face of the Great Emancipator, and thousands waited in line. In the great throng was a small child who stood on tiptoe to look over the edge of the casket. Stepping forward, a distinguished gentleman lifted her up and said reverently, "Little girl, there lies a great and good man. Never forget him." He was Salmon P. Chase, chief justice of the Supreme Court of the United States, who had lost the leader whom he had served devotedly; she became Ella Grant Wilson, well-known Cleveland florist and historian. Rain and wind lashed in fury as the solemn company returned to the railroad station with its sacred burden. At midnight the train bearing the two Lincolns began the slow respectful journey westward.

The *Plain Dealer* presses had stood idle since early in March, failing to record two events of great national importance—Lee's surrender at Appomattox and the assassination of President Abraham Lincoln. Major William W. Armstrong, Tiffin newspaperman and former secretary of state of Ohio, was finally induced to purchase the paper on April 25, and the climb began to restore it to its position as a leading Democratic journal. Armstrong was as much a partisan as his predecessor, and he fought ably to defend his party's principles against stormy Republicanism.

Distinguished military figures were visitors to Cleveland during the year. General Philip H. Sheridan stopped only between trains on May 24, but a dinner was arranged for him at the Weddell House. Shortly afterward, General George A. Custer, of "the flowing hair and brilliant red sash," was toasted in the hotel while en route to Michigan. The top-ranking war hero, General Ulysses S. Grant, and Mrs. Grant were greeted at a grand reception; and, before the year was out, the city honored General William S. Rosecrans.

John R. Wagner set up a sail-making business, and two years later, his brother, Jacob, became a partner. They branched out into awnings and flags in a plant on River Street. In 1883, John R. sold his interest to his brother, who then brought his son, F. A., into the firm. In 1892, they organized the Wagner Awning and Manufacturing Company which grew rapidly. In 1913, the Cleveland-Akron Bag Company purchased the business, retaining the Wagner name. Eleven years later, this firm merged with ten Cleveland awning concerns to form again The Wagner Awning & Manufacturing Company, centering operations at 2658 Scranton Road. C.R. Forward became president of this nationally known company, with branches in Ohio and West Virginia, in 1942, succeeding Fred L. Lohiser, who was made chairman of the board.

A brick chapel, erected south of Trinity Church through the generosity of Mr. and Mrs. Samuel L. Mather, inspired W. J. Boardman and fellow parishioners to provide a rectory on the lot west of the church, purchased for $10,000. The Rev. Charles A. Breck served the parish from 1869-72 and founded the Ladies' Guild, or Woman's Auxiliary. The Rev. William E. McLaren followed, and during his three-year pastorate, a marble memorial altar was placed in the sanctuary by S. O. Griswold, the Children's Home was started, and the Chapel of the Ascension was built on Detroit Road. Rev. McLaren left the parish upon election to the Episcopate of Chicago and was succeeded by the Rev. John Wesley Brown, who served until 1882.

Thomas H. Lamson, Isaac P. Lamson, and Samuel W. Sessions joined forces in a small plant at Mt. Carmel, Connecticut, to make carriage bolts. Cleveland's rapid growth and its availability to raw materials prompted them to move their plant in 1869 to a site near the Cuyahoga River (on Scranton Road), the railroads, and labor supply. They brought with them a number of employees and their families, and the Connecticut colony became an inspiring influence in community, church, and charitable endeavors. Here the partners were the first in the country to roll screw threads on stove and kindred bolts; to forge carriage, machine, and other bolts hot from steel rods; and to introduce in the West newly designed machines to meet increasing demands of implement and machinery makers, construction companies, and other industries. The Lamson & Sessions Company was incorporated in 1883, and its story of the development of bolts, nuts, and fasteners is the story of the metal-fabricating trade, with expanding production that found its way into foreign lands. The Kent, Ohio, plant of the Falls Rivet Company was purchased in 1921. Five years later, Lamson & Sessions merged with the Kirk-Latty Manufacturing Company at 1971 West 85th Street. Gradually, Scranton Road operations were moved to West 85th Street. George S. Case, elected president in 1929, became chairman of the board in 1938. Vice President Roy H. Smith became president.

A system of street cleaning was attempted, and the first sprinkling wagon was put to work on Euclid and parts of St. Clair and Prospect streets during the hot summer months.

Since about 1840, a large white house built by T. P. May, merchant, had stood on Erie Street facing Superior. It was taken down this year to permit extension of residential Superior Street beyond Erie.

A goat walking down exclusive Prospect Street on August 8 suddenly abandoned its idle curiosity when it became conscious of strollers on the thoroughfare. Newspaper headlines were made when it began to clear the street with force, and peace was restored only when the "law" arrived and placed the animal under arrest. As a safety measure, "timid ladies and nervous gentlemen" were warned to proceed with caution at street intersections. Horse-drawn traffic had become a problem.

Increasing numbers of wounded soldiers were returning to Cleveland, and the city faced an urgent need for hospital care. Calling upon Catholics and Protestants alike, Bishop Amadeus Rappe received generous support; and when $10,000 had been subscribed, he purchased land for a hospital site, bounded by Perry, Garden, and Marion streets. St. Vincent Charity Hospital opened this year, managed by the Sisters of Charity of St. Augustine. It was Cleveland's first general hospital that endured, ministering to all faiths and races. St. Vincent's facilities being far superior, the little Cleveland Homeopathic Hospital closed, and Dr. S. R. Beckwith and his associates in homeopathy took their patients to the new institution. In 1917 the new Charity Hospital Annex was dedicated.

Baseball was beginning to take hold in Cleveland, and the first amateur team, called the Forest City Club, was organized. On October 21, the first match game was played in Cleveland, the Penfield Club of Oberlin trouncing the Forest City nine, 67-28. Casualties added to the drama of the opener when Cleveland's Mr. Leffingwell, left field, injured his throwing arm, Mr. Smith lost two teeth in a collision with another player, and Oberlin's Mr. Ryder suffered a blow on the face from a swift ball. Games were played on the Case Commons on Putnam Street between Garden and Scovill. There was no enclosure for a time, and no backstop. The catcher often played "back" through the game, with neither chest protector nor mask. Gloves were considered effeminate. Games ran a long time and scores were large. Woodland Avenue cars operated on a half-hour schedule carrying fans to Case Avenue, where they boarded a dinky horsecar that took them to the ball ground. Most of the young players walked to and from their homes in downtown Cleveland.

Warren Gamaliel Harding, twenty-eighth President of the United States, was born at Corsica, Ohio, on November 2.

Toward the end of the year, William J. Rainey came to Cleveland from Pittsburgh and worked for a coal and coke firm. Investing in coal fields in the Connellsville, Pennsylvania, region, he had amassed a fortune by the nineties, and was recognized as the leading coke operator in the business. Mrs. Grace Rainey Rogers made notable contributions to the Cleveland Museum of Art in memory of her father.

"Several sporting gentlemen of this city had private races on the course on Kinsman Street yesterday," reported a news item on November 15, "each driving his own nag. The races were for a wine supper. The second class horses ran first. Lady Suffolk ran into Insurance, threw his wagon against the fence, and spilled the driver. Judges decided that foul driving was the cause of the accident."

The last necessary State ratified the Thirteenth Amendment to the Constitution, abolishing slavery, on December 6. The *Plain Dealer* stated: "We accept the edict as a part of the great mystery of this eventful period."

Settlement of war problems delayed the observance of Thanksgiving Day until December 7, as proclaimed by President Andrew Johnson. Beginning in 1866, the day was celebrated regularly as set aside by President Lincoln, until 1939.

1866

Henry A. Sherwin, eighteen, had come to Cleveland in 1860 from his birthplace in Vermont upon the advice of his uncle, Nelson Sherwin, local lawyer, who told him that the city was a good place in which to grow up. Young Sherwin joined with Truman Dunham this year, selling paints, oils, and supplies in a small store on Superior Street. In partnership with E. P. Williams and A. T. Osborn, Sherwin-Williams & Company was organized on February 3, 1870, with $2,000 capital. Sereno P. Fenn, early bookkeeper, became a partner in 1880, and later vice president. In 1882, the company disposed of its retail business and moved to a new office and warehouse building on the site of a great future plant, 601 Canal Road, and two years later, incorporation was effected. The business of the Sherwin-Williams Company became so diversified that it was more than Sherwin, Williams, and Fenn could handle, and, in 1898, Walter H. Cottingham was made general manager.

The Cleveland Academy, the second school of that name, opened on January 29 in a two-story brick building on a shady, unpaved road (south side of Huron Road, Osborn Building site) with ninety students. Linda T. Guilford, an educator of rare gifts who had broadened her experience with a trip to Europe, was principal of this popular private school for young ladies. She had a passion for punctuality, discipline and order, English and mental arithmetic, ten-minute daily exercises, and Monday-morning analyses of Sunday's sermons. Her innovations in education became a pattern for schools in other cities. The long career of the famous "Brick Academy" lay, undoubtedly, in the fact that it was incorporated and well supported. The school was discontinued soon after Isaac Bridgman took charge in 1881, when Miss Guilford recognized rising competition in Miss Mittleberger's school. Miss Guilford took an active part in the Young Women's Temperance League, and devoted part-time to writing, her best-known work being *The Story of a Cleveland School*, recounting her experiences.

A distinguished career was ahead for a Clevelander, Dr. John S. Newberry, who was appointed professor of geology and paleontology in the School of Mines of Columbia College, New York City, this year, advancing to professor of Columbia University in 1878 and serving until 1890. Appointed director of the Ohio State Geological Survey in 1869, his reports of natural resources were of permanent importance. In 1884, Dr. Newberry was commissioned paleontologist of the United States Geological Survey, and was awarded the Murchison Medal for distinguished service by the Geological Society of London. One of the great scientists and naturalists of his time, he held high offices in leading scientific societies in America and Europe, and published many valuable reports of his research. In later years, his health declined, and he died in 1890, aged seventy. His son, Spencer B., became acting professor of chemistry at Cornell University. He served until 1892, when he and his brother, Arthur St. John, organized the Sandusky Portland Cement Company, one of the largest companies in its field.

"An Act to Authorize the Incorporation of Boards of Trade and Chambers of Commerce" was passed by the Legislature on April 3. Twenty members of the Cleveland Board met in the Atwater Block, as was their daily custom, and signed incorporation papers, dated April 5, declaring that the purpose of the Board of Trade (later The Cleveland Chamber of Commerce) was "to foster, protect and advance the commercial, mercantile and manufacturing interest of the city." The signers were Philo Chamberlain, R. T. Lyon, J. C. Sage, A. Hughes, C. W. Coe, H. S. Davis, J. E. White, J. H. Clark, S. W. Porter, H. D. Woodward, A. V. Cannon, E. D. Childs, W. F. Otis, M. B. Clark, W. Murray, S. F. Lester, A. Quinn, George W. Gardner, E. C. Hardy, and George Sinclair. The revitalized organization was created, however, to serve particularly its members who dealt "in grain, provisions, etc." Leading business and professional men served as presidents of the board: W. F. Otis, 1867; George W. Gardner, 1868; R. T. Lyon, 1869; A. J. Begges, 1870; Thomas Walton, 1871; Charles Hickox, 1872; B. H. York, 1873; F. H. Morse, 1874; H. Pomerene, 1875; B. A. DeWolf, 1877; Daniel Martin, 1879; William Edwards, 1886; George W. Lewis, 1888; William Edwards, 1889. Theodore Simmons became secretary in 1879; X. X. Crum, 1884; and A. J. Begges, 1887.

The first report of the Board of Trade, for the year 1865, indicated the condition of Cleveland business as the peacetime reconstruction period gained momentum. Coal receipts, 465,550 tons; pig iron and scrap, 23,000 tons sold and used in Cleveland, valued at $1,051,000. Manufactured wrought iron, railroad iron, bar, plate, hoop, sheet, spikes, and nails sold for over $6,000,000. Cleveland and Newburgh were operating two blast furnaces, six rolling mills, two forges, eight foundries, and three spike, nail, rivet, nut, and washer factories, with 3,000 employees and an aggregate capital of about $3,000,000. Hide-and-leather sales reached $1,500,000, and boots and shoes totaled $1,250,000. Petroleum products of thirty crude-oil refineries were valued at $4,500,000, and manufactured-clothing sales at about $2,500,000. Bank capital exceeded $2,250,000, and average deposits, $3,700,000. The long list of commercial and industrial enterprises proved that the city's business was well established in the fifty years of steady growth from a mere village.

The first issue of the *Christian Standard*, one of the leading independent religious periodicals of the Disciples Church, appeared on April 7. James A. Garfield, J. P. Robison, and Dr. Worthy S. Streator had organized the publishing company, with an office on Bank Street. Headquarters were later moved to Cincinnati.

A need for intensified police protection in the larger cities inspired the Metropolitan Police Act, passed on May 1, creating a board of police commissioners. The first Cleveland board consisted of H. M. Chapin, mayor; W. P. Fogg, James Barnett, Philo Chamberlain, and Nelson Purdy, appointed by the governor. Power to levy a tax produced $30,000, which fell short of the first-year's expenses of $51,710. As of May 30, sixty patrolmen constituted the politically dominated department. Three precinct stations were located in downtown Cleveland and one on the West Side. Horse-drawn patrol wagons stood ready for emergency. The policeman on the beat came to know intimately the families in his district, as the shifting of population had not yet become a problem. Neighborliness promoted order in society and helped to retard crime. After two years, the governor abandoned his interest, and the mayor inherited the responsibility, reporting as the "acting board." J. W. Frazee was the first superintendent, or chief, of police.

A "magnificent" luxury train, a "triumph of Cleveland workmanship," went into service on the Cleveland, Columbus & Cincinnati road on May 14. The great attraction was the palace car, a sleeping coach lavishly decorated and paneled in polished, carved woodwork. A saloon in the center provided observation quarters; and glass chandeliers, a water cooler, a new spring window catch, and the "gingerbread" design created excited conversation. On the 18th, the *Herald* announced proudly that "two very handsome, commodious, comfortable and well ventilated sleeping coaches" were introduced on the Cleveland & Toledo road from Cleveland to Chicago, carrying fifty-six passengers each. The dining car made its debut on the rails the next year.

The Cleveland Wire Mill Company, incorporated by H. L. Hoadley, Henry Marble, H. Dunbar, George E. Dunbar, and A. J. Hamilton, erected the first wire mill in Newburgh. In 1868 the Cleveland Rolling Mill Company purchased it as an outlet for steel.

The Angier House was purchased by T. W. Kennard, of the Atlantic & Great Western Railroad. After having been remodeled, it opened on June 14 as the Kennard House, "one of the finest hotels in the nation." Moorish influence was introduced in the design of the lobby, with its colorful fountain, which was copied from a room in the fabulous Alhambra in Spain. Black-walnut woodwork was utilized throughout the building. Statesmen, theatrical artists, and prominent businessmen made the Kennard their headquarters, and Tom L. Johnson held most of his private conferences there. The famous barroom was a favorite meeting place of racing fans and ball players. The hotel changed hands many times. As wholesale houses moved into the district and modern hotels claimed its prestige, traveling men stopped at the Kennard. In the early twenties, however, a large part of the building was taken over for a clothing factory. Permanent rather than transient guests made the historic house, later known as the Lincoln Hotel, their home.

General William T. Sherman's informal visit to Cleveland on July 29 attracted great throngs of admirers who gathered at the Kennard House for a glimpse of him, but without success. Shortly after five o'clock the next morning, however, determined citizens arranged an unusual reception under his Bank Street window. The airs of Leland's Band brought the general to the balcony with Amos Townsend, who introduced him to the early-risers; and, at Sherman's suggestion, he and his friends exchanged greetings on the sidewalk. After breakfast, the great soldier, in a "military vest and an old linen duster," was driven down Euclid Street to the station.

A big, brown gelding named Dexter won a $2,000 racing event in Cleveland on August 25 from George M. Patchen, Jr., and General Butler in

2:32¼—2:32½—2:32½, his record at that time being 2:19 under saddle and 2:21 to sulky. On August 14, 1867, Budd Doble drove him at Buffalo to establish a record of 2:17¼.

A central location near markets and materials induced Thomas H. White, aged thirty, to move his pioneer sewing-machine business from Templeton, Massachusetts, to Canal Street in Cleveland, where a small factory housed The White Manufacturing Company. White was president and treasurer; Rollin C. White, vice president; and Howard W. White, an intimate friend, secretary. Thomas H. White, born in 1836 in Templeton, had invented a small, hand-operated, single-thread machine in 1857, and two of his mechanical wizards, George Baker and D'Arcy Porter, urged him to concentrate on sewing-machine production. Associated with William Grothe, salesman and partner, he launched the business with capital of $500, and began making "The New England Sewing Machine," retailing at $10. In 1876, the White Sewing Machine Corporation was organized to make the famous White machine. By 1881, two thousand units per week were being produced as against twenty-five a month at the start. An extensive organization of branch dealers was established and a London office was opened. The need for small sewing-machine parts required special machinery, leading to the manufacture of kerosene street lamps, automatic lathes, screw machines, roller skates, phonographs, bicycles, and automobiles. Thus the company became the parent of the White Motor Company and the Cleveland Automatic Screw Machine Company. By the mid-1890s, White's bicycle production had reached 10,000 vehicles per year, but sewing machines continued to be the principal product.

Herman Sampliner was the father of the B'nai Jeshurun Congregation (later the Temple on the Heights), organized this year by sixteen devout Jews in his home in California Alley. D. L. Beck was the first president. Services were held in members' homes and in public halls until 1869, when a synagogue was established in Halle's Hall on Superior Avenue (near the Arcade). "Family pews" were introduced in 1873 over the objections of the more Orthodox members, who resigned to form the Oheb Zedek Congregation in 1904.

The first President of the United States to visit Cleveland while in office was Andrew Johnson, accompanied by cabinet members. The party was escorted from the railroad station to the Kennard House; and, after an informal supper, the President was introduced to a waiting crowd from the balcony by Frederick W. Pelton, president of the City Council. A long discussion of his unpopular plans for reconstruction aroused enmity in the audience. J. W. Walton, young eye-witness, reported that the next morning President Johnson was escorted to his train. As his victoria neared the Public Square, he caught sight of a banner stretched between the Forest City House and the Rouse Block reading, "In the work of reconstruction, traitors must be made to take back seats." Angrily, "he jammed his beaver hat down over his eyes and kept his glance on the floor of his carriage until he had passed." The President and his party then continued on their western trip.

W. S. Chamberlain, lawyer, offered a tract of swamp land (Central Avenue and East 67th) near the Cleveland & Pittsburgh railroad to a group of Buffalo iron molders as an industrial site, if they would give him an interest in a proposed foundry. The Cleveland Co-operative Hollow Ware, Stove & Foundry Company was incorporated the following year with Chamberlain as president. For forty years, the company concentrated on making the massive, ornate, coal-burning stoves of the period. In 1909 it brought out a complete line of gas ranges. The entire plant was leveled by storm this year. "Grand" ranges, stoves, air-conditioning equipment, and gray-iron castings produced by The Cleveland Co-Operative Stove Company, found profitable markets. James Mitchell became president in 1934.

In a "wigwam" tent, reportedly seating five thousand, raised on the Public Square, the convention of Union Soldiers and Sailors opened on September 17. Five hundred delegates, many from below the Mason and Dixon line, supported President Andrew Johnson's reconstruction policy as opposed to the attitude of Congress. This resulted in a divided welcome to the guests in Cleveland and provoked intense controversy.

During the Civil War, the Home for the Friendless was organized in the Old Stone Church parlors to care for refugees from the South; and in a rented dwelling on Lake Street, the sick and needy received care. An outgrowth of this charitable Protestant effort was the incorporation this year of the Cleveland City Hospital (later Lakeside Hospital), a private venture, with Joseph Perkins, president. In 1868, the Willson—or Wilson—Street Hospital Association was created, with H. B. Hurlbut, president, supported by both allopathic and homeopathic physicians. On the medical and surgical staffs were Drs. Maynard Brooks, Henry K. Cushing, and D. H. Beckwith. Work was carried on in a small, rented building on Willson Street opposite Clinton Park, but the homeopaths soon withdrew to establish their own hospital.

In his long career at the bar and in public life, Samuel Williamson had lived a full life. Retiring from the legal profession this year, he devoted his time to the Society for Savings, of which he was president until his death in 1884. Samuel Williamson was born in Crawford County, Pennsylvania, in 1808, the eldest son of Samuel Williamson, Sr., a tanner and a public-spirited citizen of Cleveland until his death in 1834 in the family homestead at Euclid and the Public Square. Probably the first young man in the village to enjoy a college education, he was graduated from Jefferson College, Washington, Pennsylvania, in 1829. He read law in the office of Sherlock J. Andrews, was admitted to the bar in 1832, practicing law with Leonard Case for two years, and for most of thirty years with A. G. Riddle. Williamson served as county auditor, councilman, member of the Board of Education and the Legislature, and prosecuting attorney. He had a practical interest in early railroads, and was a director and attorney for the Cleveland, Columbus, Cincinnati & Indianapolis road for many years. Quiet, modest, and retiring, Samuel Williamson gave fully of his energy to his many interests and to the advancement of his city. He was a devoted member of the First Presbyterian Church (Old Stone) for more than two decades, and an incorporator of Case School of Applied Science. His sons, Samuel E., George T., and James D., were worthy descendants of their distinguished father.

In the fall, Eugene R. Grasselli and his assistants, Daniel Bailey and R. H. Andrews, began erecting a plant in Cleveland (Independence Road and East 26th Street, near Broadway) to expand the pioneering chemical business that Grasselli had launched in Cincinnati in 1839. Sulfuric acid, the principal product, had been in growing demand by soap and candle makers; and, during the Civil War, newly developed chloroform was supplied to the medical forces of the Union Army. Cleveland was on the way to leadership in oil refining, and in the industry's need for sulfuric acid lay Grasselli's fortune. Soon processes for making muriatic acid and salt cake,

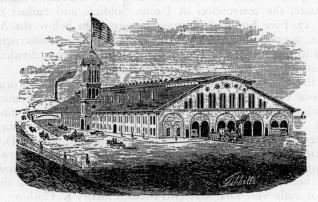

The second Union Depot.

a step in the production of soda ash, were in operation. Nitric acid was added, and shortly the plant was marketing a steady output of chemical products. Young Caesar A. Grasselli, son of the founder, was taken into the new firm organized in 1873, known as Grasselli Chemical Works, E. Grasselli & Son, Manufacturing Chemists. His father died in 1882, and he became company head. Not long afterward, he began a business association with E. I. du Pont de Nemours & Company, furnishing acid for the making of nitroglycerine. This led Grasselli to become the first chemical manufacturer to produce high-strength sulfuric acid, increasing yields, and lowering costs. After patient selling efforts to overcome prejudice, his salt cake won market acceptance over foreign products, and glass makers began to buy from him on a large scale.

The Union Depot, the finest railroad station west of New York City, was dedicated on November 10, replacing the old terminal at the foot of Water and Bank streets which had been declared unsafe. The "massive" 603-foot structure, built of Berea stone by Alex Forbes and costing $475,000, was lighted with gas lamps and lanterns. Flags and bunting decorated the long waiting room on the track level on the memorable evening. A brilliant banquet, held in the station dining hall, presented to three hundred guests an astonishing bill of fare listing more than one hundred items, exclusive of wines, and including bear meat, venison, wild turkey, quail, and squirrel. Amasa Stone, early president of the Cleveland, Columbus & Cincinnati Railroad, presided, and speeches were made by H. B. Payne, former president of the road, and L. M. Hubby, who succeeded him; Colonel J. H. Devereux, general superintendent of the Cleveland & Pittsburgh Railroad; and representatives of the Cleveland, Painesville & Ashtabula line and the Cleveland & Toledo road. These companies had united to build the station, which also housed railroad offices. In a breathless 178-word sentence, the *Herald* editor pointed out the great significance of the event and stressed the growth of railroad travel.

A 96-foot tower with tin-covered dome was mounted on the new Union Depot the next spring, topped by a 50-foot flagstaff. Presidents and world celebrities stepped from their trains and crossed the tracks to the station, where they were met by welcoming delegations and escorted in state up the cobblestone hill. In later years, a large portion of the smoke-stained terminal gave way to expanded tracks, and stairways leading to the trains were installed. After decades of service, the depot became inadequate and unworthy, and it was relieved of much of its great burden when the stately Union Terminal received most of the roads in 1930. The Pennsylvania, however, continued to use the antiquated depot.

West St. Clair Street School, on the north side of the street between Seneca and Bank, had fallen behind the other city schools as business increased in the district and population shifted. The pupils united with Rockwell, and in due time a new sign was mounted above the entrance, "Headquarters of the Fire Department."

The names of three artists stand out among the few in the profession in Cleveland at this time: Caroline L. Ransom, who was allowed $1,000 by Congress this year for her portrait of Joshua R. Giddings, and the princely sum of $15,000 in 1875 for her likeness of General George H. Thomas, both to be hung in the Capitol at Washington; Allen Smith, early-day portrait painter; and Archibald M. Willard, born in Bedford, Ohio, in 1836. Willard sketched the horrors of the Civil War, and as a wagon painter in Wellington, Ohio, in peacetime, exhibited unusual talent and a keen sense of humor as he decorated circus wagons and vehicles.

A new "secret organization," the Cleveland Post of the Grand Army of the Republic, held its first regular meeting on December 11, pledged to defense of the Union. The GAR had been gathering strength through the Middle West, and estimates stated that 600,000 veterans had joined forces.

1867

John N. Stockwell had completed service during the war in the United States Naval Observatory at Washington, and, after three years as statistician for the United States Sanitary Commission, he decided to make his home in Cleveland this year. Born in Massachusetts in 1832, his parents moved to

Portage County, Ohio, the next year. When a small boy, he went to live with an uncle on a farm in Brecksville, Ohio, and attended the common school. An eclipse of the moon in about the mid-forties inspired young Stockwell's interest in astronomy, and he made close friends of the few scientific books that he could find. At the age of twenty-one, his first creative work, the *Western Reserve Almanac for 1853,* came to the attention of scientists. The next year, his acquaintance began with Dr. B. A. Gould, editor of the *Astronomical Journal* and director of the United States Coast Survey, leading to a government position under that eminent man. Stockwell's research and study resulted in astronomical and mathematical calculations of increasing importance, particularly as related to the theory of the moon's motion. Recognizing his achievements, Western Reserve University awarded him the degrees of M.A. and Ph.D.

Fourteen families in the University Heights district formed the United German Evangelical Protestant Church in January, and a church built at the corner of College and Tremont streets was ready for occupancy in the fall. The next year, a day school was organized. A new site was secured in 1872 at the corner of Branch and Jennings streets to which the church building was moved, and this became the traditional church location. Five years later, during the pastorate of the Rev. Otto Schettler, the congregation joined the German Evangelical Synod of North America, and the name Zion was adopted. In 1884 a new structure was erected, and its tall steeple attracted wide attention. To assist church families moving westward, Zion provided funds to launch Bethany Church (on West 43rd Street) in 1890. In 1916 English services were introduced at Zion, at first once a month, then on alternate Sundays until 1923, when services were held every Sunday in both English and German. Zion Church became nationally famous in June, 1934, when it was host to the historic merger ceremony of the Evangelical Synod of North America and the Reformed Church of the United States. In 1939 it witnessed the merger of denominational women's work. The Rev. Oscar E. Wittlinger began his long ministry to the congregation in 1922.

Ralph Waldo Emerson appeared in Cleveland for the last time on January 10, when he lectured in Brainard Hall on *The Man of the World,* under the auspices of the Cleveland Library Association. The *Herald* reporter made a point of mentioning the author's "carefully prepared paper, replete with ideas, pertinent to passing events," and advanced the suggestion that "more spirit in the manner of delivery would have added to the pleasure of the occasion." "People from elite circles" made up the audience, which "toward the close of the gentleman's remarks smiled approvingly upon some well turned and quaint sayings relative to the present state of the country."

Daniel R. Taylor, aged twenty-nine, of Twinsburg, Ohio, made his initial real-estate investment in a piece of residential property fronting 57 feet on Euclid to a depth of about 200 feet (4222 Euclid), paying $50 a foot. Upon his confidence in Cleveland's future greatness he built his career in business and property negotiations. His brother, William G., joined him in 1874, and they opened a real-estate office in the Morison Block.

At a meeting on January 14, addressed by Henry W. Brown, the First Unitarian Society of Cleveland was organized. The Rev. T. B. Forbush, called as minister in 1868, remained until 1876 and impressed large congregations that met in Case Hall. On the first board of trustees were Dr. H. H. Little, S. A. Jewett, Rodney Gale, John Outhwaite, and Frederick C. Goff. Meetings were held in Weisgerber's Hall in the seventies, and in 1880, the first house of worship was dedicated on Bolivar Street

Lake View Park, the first park property purchased by the city.

at Prospect. The Rev. Frederick L. Hosmer, called as pastor in 1878, built a large congregation, and he retired in 1892. An era of great spiritual and intellectual advance began in 1900, when the Rev. Minot Simons began his nineteen-year pastorate.

Although the city had been offered splendid park sites on generous terms, the Council admitted no need for them. In fact, there was little public demand until the late fifties, when there was an awakening of the citizenship. After ten years of reports to a stubborn Council, it recommended on January 22 of this year that the first park property be purchased, bordering on Seneca, Wood, Bond, Ontario, and Erie streets "from the edge of the hill to the railroad property." The district, unsightly and cluttered with squatters' hovels, became Lake View Park.

The Rocky River Railroad Company received a charter on February 20 to operate a dummy line from Bridge Street, just west of Waverly Avenue, the city limits, to the east bank of Rocky River (Lakewood), a recreation spot. Daniel P. Rhodes, Elias Simms, Ezra Nicholson, John H. Sargent, and others promoted the project, and the first through run was made on September 1, 1868. The abbreviated train consisted of a small, brass-trimmed locomotive trailing one car, and it whistled and puffed through orchards and gardens on 5.33 miles of narrow-gauge road at twenty miles an hour, carrying outing parties and serving the West Side communities. In 1869 the Cliff House opened near the river bank, greatly increasing the popularity and revenue of the line. The Nickel Plate purchased the dummy road in 1891 for its right-of-way.

Horace Greeley, fearless reformer and editor of the *New York Tribune,* delivered his famous lecture, *Abraham Lincoln,* in Case Hall in February.

Parts of Brooklyn and Newburgh townships and portions within the big bends of the river on the West Side were annexed to Cleveland on February 28.

Artemus Ward's feeble hand guided a pencil through reminiscences of the *Plain Dealer* and his days with the paper as a "local," before it was stilled forever on March 6 in Southampton, England. Born Charles Farrar Brown in Waterford, Maine, he roved the country as a tramp printer when he was a young man. While employed by J. W. Gray of the *Plain Dealer,* he discovered his talent for humorous, carefree writing, and his pen name, Artemus Ward, carried him to fame as a lecturer. Ward lived for today, believing that all should "be happy and live within our means, even if we have to

The first Society for Savings Building on the Public Square.

borrer the money to do it with." His death of tuberculosis came at the age of thirty-three, and he was buried in the town of his birth. In recognition of his genius, Ward was called the "Father of American Humor." The School of Journalism of Ohio State University enrolled his name in its Hall of Fame in 1931; and, in 1942, Dr. Albert Jay Nock, eminent historian, gave him rank as the "first and greatest critic of American social conditions."

The Society for Savings occupied its new building on Rockwell Street at the northeast corner of the Public Square (Cleveland College site). It was the first fireproof structure in Cleveland, and served until 1873, when it was enlarged by adding twenty feet to the depth. Samuel Williamson was president from 1866 until 1884, when he was succeeded by Samuel H. Mather.

The Cleveland Dorcas Society was organized by fourteen women who met regularly in rooms in the City Hall to sew for the hospitals and the needy.

One hundred German immigrants on the West Side met in the Freie Deutsche Schule on Mechanic Street on March 24 and formed the Socialer Turn-Verein. A constitution was adopted on April 7. Gymnastic classes were held outdoors until September, when the auditorium of a school was rented for $75 per year (3919 Lorain). The next year, the "turners" purchased the building and converted it into a gymnasium. This was the health and cultural center of the German community. On the original site, a $150,000 building with modern gymnasium and recreational equipment was erected in later years, and singing, debating, and a variety of diversional activities were provided for the enjoyment of young and old. When the 75th anniversary was celebrated, membership had reached 1,400, representing many nationalities.

Largely through the efforts of the Rev. Anson Smythe, Cleveland educator, sometimes called "The Father of the Cleveland Public Library," an act was passed by the Legislature on April 3, authorizing boards of education to elect boards of managers of public libraries, and providing for support of public libraries through taxation. On October 2, 1871, a Board of Managers was elected to govern the Public School Library, consisting of A. G. Hopkinson and Dr. Elisha Sterling, one year; J. H. A. Bone and S. H. Mather, two years; Rev. S. Woolcott and A. Thieme, three years. When the board resigned, July 14, 1873, management reverted to the Board of Education.

Young men were attracted to Cleveland from all over the country, and in this wave of newcomers was Charles E. Bolton. Progress of the Young Men's Christian Association in other cities inspired discussion in a bookstore on Superior Avenue and the Square, and Bolton arranged a meeting at which the "Y" was revived on April 22 in the First Presbyterian Church parlors. Prominent members were J. W. Walton, E. B. Holden, H. J. Herrick, J. W. Clarke, J. J. Wilson, Sereno P. Fenn, S. H. Stilson, C. J. Dockstader, and E. C. Pope.

In April, Charles C. Baldwin, distinguished lawyer, called together close friends who were also members of the Cleveland Library Association, to discuss his plans for a new cultural society. Among those present were Colonel Charles Whittlesey, noted scientist; Joseph Perkins, public benefactor; Judge John Barr, author of a short history of Cleveland; and A. T. Goodman, dynamic writer and lawyer. Organization was completed on May 28, and the historical department of the Cleveland Library Association came into being. Its object was "to discover, procure and preserve whatever relates to the history, biography, genealogy, antiquities and statistics connected with the city of Cleveland and the Western Reserve, and generally what relates to the history of Ohio and the great West." On June 5, the name, Western Reserve Historical Society, was adopted, and Colonel Whittlesey was elected president. Quarters were provided on the third floor of the Society for Savings Building on the Public Square, where a few cases easily accommodated the relics, specimens, books, and historic exhibits that had been assembled. Through the influence of Colonel Whittlesey and Judge Baldwin, who succeeded the former as president upon his death in 1886, prominent citizens supported the society generously, making possible the acquisition of increasingly valuable collections.

Mark Twain—Samuel L. Clemens—and his fellow "Innocents Abroad" sailed from New York City on June 8 on their famous excursion to the

Holy Land in the sidewheeler *Quaker City.* Clevelanders who made the voyage were Mr. and Mrs. Solon L. Severance, Mr. and Mrs. T. D. Crocker, S. N. Sanford, T. S. Beckwith, Mrs. A. W. Fairbanks, and W. A. Otis. They returned in November.

War's aftermath was forgotten with the arrival of Dan Rice, famous showman, and his circus on June 24. This was the first circus of importance that had visited the city for several years. For twenty-five cents, children could see a great show, amplified by "the latest and most thrilling equestrian and acrobatic acts." Adults paid double the amount.

Immigration of Czechs had increased steadily. Lumir, a Czech singing society, was founded in Rychlik Hall, on the northeast corner of Croton Avenue and Phelps. Several times a week, the merry members got together "to enjoy things like we did in the old country." The society gave concerts and took part in musical programs. In 1899 it presented the first performance in Cleveland of Smetana's *The Bartered Bride.* The Hlahol chorus, organized in 1896, merged with the Lumir society in 1918; and the Tyl dramatic society, founded in 1881, joined the group in 1940, forming the Lumir-Hlahol-Tyl, the oldest Czech singing society in the United States.

Sunday concerts, presented in Brainard's Hall by Carl Braetz' new Great Western Band, were well attended. Frank Hruby, Czech music teacher and father of the famous Hruby family of musicians, became the director in 1889. The band played at national events throughout the country.

Sammy, the "little old man" with battered hat, long, frock coat, and high, side-laced shoes fashioned of papier-mache, identified E. L. Dodd & Company's shoe store (on Superior, west of Hotel Cleveland) for many years. Dodd newspaper ads featured Sammy's wit and wisdom, and broadcast the fashions. Stylish footwear in the sixties, according to Sammy, featured "French imported fancy slippers for gents' wear; fancy boots for little boys; skating boots for ladies; serge kid-fixed lace boots for ladies; heelless white kid slippers for ladies . . . extra broad congress gaiters, made of old-fashioned prunella, so nice and comfortable for 'old folx.' " Quoting Sammy in 1876: "One of the young men belonging to a choir had his hair cut free by a generous barber on Saturday. Sunday he sang for a solo—*Cover My Defenseless Head.*" Dodd's mascot was presented to the Western Reserve Historical Society, where it was preserved.

A goodly number of the citizens owned livestock that was permitted to graze on vacant lots about the city. Complaints that the "vagrants" were wandering at will in search of greener pastures had been laid at the door of the Council for a long time. Scenting a source of revenue for the city treasury, the councilmen created an animal pound. While this solved the problem at large, people living near the confinement lost many nights' sleep. Some of them evened the score, however, by helping themselves to the supply of fresh milk at their doorsteps.

Since 1852, a fraction of the citizenry had argued that the Public Square park was an obstacle to progress and a commercial nuisance. The *Herald,* waxing poetic, joined the opposition and declared:

A line of Cleveland's famous mounted police.

Police on their beat in 1866, when a metropolitan system was introduced.

Home of the Police Department. Criminal Branch of the Municipal Court in the background.

CLEVELAND'S AMERICAN LEAGUE CHAMPIONS, 1920

*Tris Speaker was manager and center fielder of the 1920 champions. His all-round
ability won for him a place in Baseball's Hall of Fame.*
*Front row: Jack McCallister, coach; J. P. Evans, l.f.; Charles D. Jamieson, c.f.;
W. B. Johnston, 1st b.; James C. Dunn, pres.; Tris Speaker, mgr. and c.f.; Walter
McNichols, sec.; Elmer J. Smith, r.f.; Stanley Coveleskie, p.; Joseph Sewell, s.s.
Middle row: Chester D. Thomas, c.; J. Gladstone Graney, c.f.; Guy Morton, p.;
James C. Bagby, p.; Ray Caldwell, p.; Leslie Nunamaker, c.; George J. Burns, 1st b.;
Robert W. Clark, p.; Steve F. O'Neill, c.; W. L. Gardner, 3rd b.; Odenwald, sub.
Back row: J. Walter Mails, p.; Cykowski, sub.; Hamilton, sub.; George E. Uhle, p.;
Joe Wood, r.f.; William Wambsganss, 2nd b.; Harry Lunte, l.f.; Smallwood, trainer.
Insert: Ray Chapman, s.s.*

THE FOREST CITY CLUB OF 1869, *Cleveland's first professional team.*

*Standing: John Ward, l.f.; Eben Smith, s.s. and captain; Albert G. Pratt, p.; Arthur
Burt, "middle field," and John Reilly, r.f.
Seated: Leonard C. Hanna, 2nd b.; Austin R. "Pikey" Smith, 3rd b.; Arthur Allison,
1st b., and James L. "Deacon" White, c.*

> Let fossils creak their crumbling bones,
> Let dotards shriek in quavering tones;
> They cannot stop the tides that flow,
> The fence about the Square must go!

Property owners and merchants, headed by Leonard Case and H. B. Payne, took the "fence war" into court, where a decree ruled that Superior Avenue had been dedicated to extend continuously from Water to Erie streets. On August 21, the rail-fence obstruction was removed, permitting through traffic. In September, Ontario Street was restored.

While Cleveland was called a beautiful city, its sanitation could not bear inspection. Garbage disposal and street cleaning were in the primitive stages. Waste water was tossed into contaminated mudholes, and refuse was

The home of Colonel Charles Whittlesey on the south side of Euclid, nearly opposite Dunham Street.

often thrown into the streets. The health officer complained that collections of swill for pigs were being made irregularly and carelessly, but his pleas fell on the deaf ear of the Council.

This year marked Charles Whittlesey's crowning achievement as a writer—his volume, the *Early History of Cleveland*. Field notes and data representing twenty years of experience as an archeologist, explorer, and geographer were assembled, presenting an invaluable record of the period dating from the ice age. During his lifetime, Whittlesey wrote many technical books and pamphlets, and his articles appeared in newspapers and scientific journals. When he died in 1886, Cleveland lost a many-sided man of exceptional ability.

Andrew J. Rickoff, former head of the Cincinnati schools, became superintendent of the Cleveland system. After a survey, he set out to unify the schools through more efficient organization. Definite classifications were set up—primary, grammar, and high—and girls' divisions were abolished. The superintendent's wife, Rebecca D. Rickoff, was an authority on educational work, and she compiled and illustrated reading charts for use in the primary department.

The little wooden Ark was shifted again to the east (Public Library site), to permit the Case family to erect Case Hall (easterly portion of Federal Building site). Formal opening was celebrated on September 10 with a grand concert in the public auditorium on the third floor, the finest in the city. Signora Peralta and Signors Steffani and Bellini performed to a capacity house, reserved seats commanding the high price of $2, and general admission, $1.50. The hall seated 1,500 people, featured "patent opera chairs," and decorations by Garibaldi, an Italian artist, on the walls and 36-foot ceiling. Great musicians and performers of the world appeared

Case Hall as it appeared when erected in 1867.
This was the cultural center of Cleveland.

on its stage. It rang with the eloquence of Henry Ward Beecher, Robert G. Ingersoll, and famous lecturers of its day. Portions of the lower floors provided quarters for the Cleveland Library Association. The project failed as a profitable investment, however, and after a score of years, it was converted into offices.

Forces that had violently opposed the Central Market a decade before, hailed the new, gas-lighted market house, built on the same site and ready for occupancy on September 14. As the years went on, the frame building deteriorated and its facilities proved inadequate. The market, although well patronized, became an increasing menace to progress, and civic campaigns tried vainly to secure a new municipal market on a suitable site that would replace the old structure; but the building continued to stand eight decades later, an obstacle to fast-moving traffic.

Brainard's Hall was the scene of the widely publicized billiard match on

September 26 between John Frawley of Cleveland and Fred Ackerman of Cincinnati, played to 1,500 points for $500 a side and possession of the golden cue valued at $250. Admission was $1, and the entire audience remained for the five-and-a-half-hour match in which Ackerman scored 1,239 points, the championship being held in Cleveland.

Several prominent families reorganized the Western Seamen's Friend Society into the Cleveland Bethel Union this year. Property was purchased at Superior and Union Lane, and in 1869 the Bethel Building opened to provide a home for seafaring men. This glorified wayfarers' lodge had the backing of prominent citizens such as Loren Prentiss, Dan P. Eells, H. C. Blossom, General and Mrs. James Barnett, S. L. Severance, John G. Jennings, Edwin Cowles, H. A. Sherwin, E. C. Pope, Mrs. Henry Chisholm, Mrs. Hiram Little, and Mr. and Mrs. Marcus A. Hanna. In its flourishing days, women and girls were given shelter, an employment office was added, and an outdoor relief program was conducted. Missionary services were held in the basement. Men from the boats, the docks, and the shipyards crowded the big dining hall, where Bethel's twenty-five-cent special included ice cream. On the premises was the wood yard, where the able-bodied wanderer could earn a meal by the sweat of his brow. "That Bethel wood-pile," said Police Superintendent J. W. Schmitt, "is worth a platoon of my finest." The Bethel building, one of the most colorful spots in Cleveland, was converted into the Bridge Central Hotel about 1900.

A Masonic Hall was opened in the Case Hall, and on October 2, one-quarter's rent, amounting to fifty dollars, was paid. Membership in the Cleveland City Lodge was now 142. Tyrian Lodge No. 370 and Newburgh Lodge had been organized in 1866, followed by the Forest City Lodge on the West Side in 1867, West Side Lodge in 1874, and Woodward Lodge in 1875. Thatcher Chapter, Royal Arch Masons, was formed in 1867, and Baker Chapter in 1879; Al Koran Temple, Nobles of the Mystic Shrine, 1876, and Holyrood Commandery, Knights Templar, 1878.

Daniel H. and Henry M. Austin acquired the property of The Cleveland Powder Company, located at the Five-Mile Lock of the Ohio Canal (under the Harvard-Denison Bridge) this year. The business dated back to 1833, however, when the brothers, with Alvin and Lorenzo B. Austin, had built a plant and commenced to manufacture black powder in Akron. When the latter two withdrew to form the partnership of Austin & Carlton at Xenia, Ohio, the Akron plant was dismantled. Daniel H. Austin became the first president of the reorganized Austin Powder Company. Disaster leveled the Cleveland plant in 1907 and it was never rebuilt. During the year, properties were acquired in Solon and Twinsburg townships, which became the Glen Willow plant, one of the most modern and efficient blasting-powder plants in the country. In 1930 a high-explosive plant was built at McArthur, Ohio, with a capacity approximating 1,500,000 pounds of explosives a month. Upon the death of Joseph Kendrick in 1940, V. H. Moorehouse became president of the company, with headquarters in the Rockefeller Building, Cleveland.

The Rev. J. B. Allen, Presbyterian pastor of the Congregational Church of Brooklyn since 1856, brought new life to the feeble organization, which united officially with the Congregationalists this year. During his pastorate, a house of worship was provided on Newburgh Street that served until 1879, when a new brick church was erected on Archwood Avenue near Pearl Street. Faithful stewardship strengthened the influence of the congregation, which took the name, Archwood Congregational Church. Perplexing years of economic unrest and problems peculiar to the changing community challenged the life of the church; but Archwood lived and served. In 1923, the Rev. Lawrie J. Sharp succeeded Dr. Robert B. Blyth, pastor since 1917. The church buildings were razed in 1928, and a typical colonial-style edifice was erected on the site, 2794 Archwood Avenue. Under the pastor's dynamic leadership, membership in Cleveland's oldest Congregational church had reached almost eleven hundred in the 1940s.

Novelty in relay racing was introduced at the new Cleveland Driving Park on November 2 when three Indians competed in a three-mile race against three horses running six miles around the track. The braves won the hundred-dollar purse with nearly a quarter mile to spare.

Edward Payson Weston, twenty-eight-year-old champion long-distance pedestrian, stopped in Cleveland on November 19 on his famous walk from Portland, Maine, to Chicago. He was escorted from Willoughby, Ohio, by a police squad, and his public reception was considered one of the largest ever accorded a visitor. He traveled the 1,326-mile journey in 24 days, 22 hours, and 40 minutes. Weston walking clubs were organized in Cleveland, and his influence was felt for a long time. The Weston fad extended to new styles in clothes, hats, and gloves.

The success of the ice-skating rink in other cities inspired Amos Townsend and well-known citizens to erect the first rink in Cleveland on the north side of Lake Street, between Bond and Wood. Completion of the Forest City Skating Rink was celebrated with a grand ball on November 27. Although the 230-by-84-foot shed was "colder than all outdoors," ice-skating under cover to music was a great novelty. Noted skaters gave exhibitions here —Joseph H. Murch, Frank Carleton, John Powers, Emma Elliott, Charlie Cleveland, and others.

Cleveland's first serious labor trouble resulted from an attempt to readjust values inflated by the Civil War. Labor shortage had been relieved by soldiers returning from war duty. When specie payment was resumed, wages were cut and strikes followed.

Increasing numbers of Bohemians were settling on the West Side. Many were Catholics, who organized the St. Wenceslas Parish, the first Czech parish, completing a church on Arch Street, December 22. They later moved to a new building on Broadway, near Forest Avenue. In 1869, St. Mary's Parish was divided, and German Catholics in the western part of the city established St. Stephen's. The first church, located between Courtland and Scott streets, was replaced by a fine stone structure in 1876.

1868

The Cleveland, Columbus & Cincinnati Railroad had a large financial stake in the Bellefontaine Railroad, called the "Bee Line," which was absorbed in January. The Cleveland, Columbus, Cincinnati & Indianapolis Railroad Company emerged, also known as the Bee Line. Soon afterward, the Cincinnati & Springfield Railroad was leased, connecting Cleveland with the Mississippi River.

"Palace Coach" on the "Bee Line."

The East Cleveland Railway Company received a grant on January 14 for lines running on Brownell and Prospect streets to Garden, and on Garden to Willson. They were later extended to the Cleveland & Pittsburgh tracks and to the city limits on Quincy.

Edward Payson Weston, famous long-distance pedestrian, created a sensation with his performance in the Forest City Skating Rink on January 15, when he walked twenty-five miles in five hours, then backward one mile in twenty minutes. Case Hall was packed the next evening when he lectured on *Athletic Sports* for the benefit of the Industrial School.

From employment on the rich agricultural estates of German nobility had come the residents of Aaron Street in Cleveland. They were honest, hardworking people, who conscientiously saved a good part of their twenty-dollar weekly wage, earned in the rolling mills, the shops, and lumber yards—a sum that would have taken a year to accumulate in Germany. A German Sunday School was the origin of the Third Reformed Church. Its founder, the Rev. Herman J. Ruetenik, guided the congregation until 1871, when the Rev. Paul Schuelke became pastor and teacher of the "parochial" school, organized to encourage the study of the German language. In 1882 the little wooden chapel on Aaron Street was replaced by a larger brick structure. Under the leadership of Pastor William Friebolin, the Ninth

Church was formed, and, in the 1940s, it continued to serve at East 74th Street and Lockyear. The fifth pastor of the "Old Church" was the beloved Dr. Henry Schmidt, friend and counselor to German-Hungarian newcomers. Under his guidance, two churches were founded, spreading the influence of the Third Church: Tenth Church, 1897, which became Glenville; and Eleventh Church, which became Grace, both continuing to serve a half century later. Third Church ultimately joined in a merger, forming Faith Evangelical and Reformed Church in 1945.

Western Homeopathic College having suspended the granting of a medical degree to women, The Homeopathic College for Women was organized under the leadership of Dr. Myra K. Merrick. It was short-lived, however, as the Cleveland Homeopathic College, by a one-vote majority, opened its doors to women in 1870. The women's college transferred its property to the established school.

A small West Side store, opened by Charles Fries at 515 Pearl Street on April 13, had a single aisle and sixteen-foot frontage. When Will Kline and Charles Hoover joined the venture, it became Fries, Kline & Hoover, dealing in dry goods, carpets, and curtains. Two of the partners passed on. Christian Schuele acquired an interest, and the partnership of Fries & Schuele resulted. In 1885 the growing store moved one block south to a three-story building adjoining the West Side Market. This was the gaslight era, and stores kept open at night as long as prospective customers were in sight. The Fries & Schuele Company was incorporated in 1909, and a five-story building was erected adjoining the former location (1948 West 25th), extending from Pearl to McLean Street. Descendants of the early merchants continued to carry on the business. O. A. Schuele succeeded Christian Schuele as president in 1926 and was succeeded by K. C. Schuele in 1947.

The horrors of war were revived in *The Drummer Boy,* a pretentious wartime drama staged by members of the Grand Army of the Republic in the Forest City Skating Rink, May 5. The performance continued for three extra nights to meet the demand.

The life of William Augustus Otis, one of Cleveland's most useful citizens, closed on May 11. During his thirty-two years in the city, he had supported many worthy projects—commercial, industrial, financial, religious, and political, and he was a founder of a number of them. While building Cleveland, Otis won fame and fortune.

Upon order of General John A. Logan to the Grand Army of the Republic, May 30 was observed as Decoration—or Memorial—Day this year. Graves of Civil War soldiers were visited in the city's cemeteries. Appropriate decorations honoring the dead were arranged by a committee of fourteen women, and addresses and prayers were offered.

Thirty-two lives were lost when the *Morning Star,* steamer of the Detroit & Cleveland Steam Navigation Company, collided with the barque *Cortland* off Black River (Lorain) on the stormy night of June 20.

The small store opened by E. I. Baldwin and his father, S. I., when they came to Cleveland fifteen years earlier, was moved to a new block erected this year at the southeast corner of Superior and Seneca Street. This was the leading retail dry-goods house for forty years. When the elder partner retired, H. R. Hatch joined the firm, which became H. R. Hatch & Company. It later moved to elegant new quarters in the New England Building.

A move to keep horsecars off the Public Square was defeated when the Council authorized tracks around the south side of the city's center on July 2.

Captain Alva Bradley moved his shipyards from Vermilion, Ohio, to Cleveland this year. Born in Connecticut in 1814, his parents came to Ohio when he was a small boy. He set out early on a seafaring career, and became master of several ships, devoting a number of years to this rugged life. As a young man, he settled for a time in Milan, Ohio, where he secured for a youth of the village his first job. The boy, Thomas Alva Edison, was named for Captain Alva Bradley. Turning to shipbuilding, Bradley and Ahira Cobb began building schooners at Vermilion. They built one of the first propellers on the lakes, the *Indiana,* 350 tons, that sailed between Buffalo and Chicago. Captain Bradley invested much of his wealth in real estate, and took a practical interest in the development of industry and commerce.

One of the most important Jewish charities, the Jewish Orphan Asylum, was founded by the Independent Order of B'nai B'rith and dedicated on July 14. It was located in the Seelye Water Cure Sanitarium that had been purchased for $25,000, and opened with thirty-eight children under the care of Mr. and Mrs. L. Aufrecht. Mrs. Kaufman Hays, daughter of Simson Thorman, pioneer Jewish settler, was a member of the board from 1868 until her death in 1907. Her husband maintained a prominent interest in the institution and in philanthropic movements benefiting their people. A son-in-law became the eminent Rabbi Moses J. Gries. Dr. S. Wolfenstein was appointed superintendent of the asylum in 1878; and under his leadership, it became a model institution in operation, in the development of personnel, and in the molding of character and responsibility of its boys and girls. In 1888 a spacious home was established at Woodland and Sawtell avenues. It served until business and industry closed in, and a new campus of cottages known as Bellefaire was provided in University Heights at Fairmount and Belvoir Road.

In 1867 the Legislature had created a new financial institution by which associations of persons could raise funds to be used by their members "for building homesteads and for other purposes." The Citizens Saving & Loan Association, organized on August 1, 1868, was the first of many organizations in Cleveland, later known as building-and-loan associations. J. H. Wade was the first president, and capital was a million dollars. The Citizens opened on Bank Street; but it soon moved to the Atwater Block, then to Case Hall and later to the south side of Euclid near Erie Street. Subsequent presidents were H. B. Payne, F. W. Pelton, D. Z. Norton, and J. R. Nutt. The Citizens was a unit in the great merger forming the Union Trust Company in 1924.

The Cleveland Malleable Iron Company was incorporated on August 14, and its single furnace (Platt Avenue and East 79th Street) provided strong, shock-resisting metal for the manufactures of the Middle West. Robert Hanna, Orson Spencer, Stiles C. Smith, Frank L. Chamberlin, and Lucius M. Pitkin were the incorporators. The following year Alfred A. Pope was elected president, and he brought experienced men from the East into the business. New companies were organized in Chicago, Indianapolis, and Toledo during the next few years, all with practically the same ownership. In 1891 they were combined into The National Malleable Castings Company (later National Malleable & Steel Castings Company) with Pope as president. Castings for the railroad industry, for wagons and buggies, farm tools and equipment, were produced in ever-increasing quantities, and the line of products broadened to meet demand.

The first iron steamer built in Cleveland was the *J. K. White,* a little pleasure boat that plowed Lake Erie for fourteen years. Rocky River, with its swings, bowling, dance floor, and picnic grounds, was the county's favorite recreation spot. City folk reached it by the luxurious steamer route or by the dinky railroad.

The first Bessemer steel blown in the County, and the fifth produced in America came from the plant of the Cleveland Rolling Mill Company in Newburgh on September 6.

While the International Young Men's Christian Association Convention was in session in Cleveland on October 20, Thane Miller called the ladies of the city together in the "Y" rooms and stressed the importance of a similar association for women. Loss of manpower in the war and subsequent rise in prices made it imperative that many women who had never worked should find employment, and an influx of job-seekers resulted. Mrs. Dan P. Eells presided at the meeting. The ladies listened, but organization as the Women's Christian Association (later Young Women's Christian Association) was not effected until November. Sarah Elizabeth Fitch, enthusiastic worker in the Old Stone Church, was elected the first president, and she served until her death in 1893. The WCA was organized "to serve especially young women of the operative class—to aid them in seeking employment; in finding suitable boarding places; in reading suitable literature; in establishing Bible classes; and in establishing religious exercises." The aid of Protestant pastors was enlisted; hospitals, infirmaries, and jails were visited regularly by the missionary committee, and house-to-house visitation was organized. The Cleveland institution was among the earliest in the chain of societies that eventually spread throughout the world.

The Cleveland & Newburgh Railroad Company began operating a steam dummy line on October 20. It originated at Willson Avenue, and followed Kinsman, crossing Kingsbury Run on a trestle to Broadway near Newburgh, a distance of 3.33 miles. Connection with the Kinsman street-railway line afforded excursions for Clevelanders into the countryside. Stillman Witt, J. H. Wade, Amasa Stone, Hiram Garretson, and others built the road at a cost of more than $68,000. The dummy engine, outwardly resembling a streetcar, was operated from the forward end by the engineer, who managed the car and the boiler, collected the ten-cent fares and kept an eagle eye open for signaling passengers. The steam engine was concealed; thus the car became known as a dummy engine. A trailing car made up the train, and two trains operated on the line. Ten years later, the company went into receivership and ceased operations.

More control over the Cleveland public schools, including power to levy taxes, had been centered in the Board of Education by the Legislature. The City Council now had a voice only in purchasing school sites and erecting buildings, and this interest was severed in 1873. A week before school opened in the fall of 1868, Superintendent Rickoff inaugurated a teacher-training institute that continued for a week. During the school year, the office of supervising principal was created as a step in his organization program. Grammar schools were strengthened by placing capable women in full charge without teaching duties. There were Ellen G. Revely, revered head of Sterling School; Bettie Dutton of Kentucky; Eliza Corlett of North Case; Carrie Lawrence of Rockwell; and Kate Parsons of Brownell.

Hanlon Brothers, in their popular stage extravaganza, introduced the first bicycle to the city, an iron-framed, high-wheeled velocipede, on November 16. It was a heavy, iron-tired contraption, modeled after the French "boneshaker." For many years, the Hanlons appeared in Cleveland with their ever-successful production, *Eight Bells*.

Reporting on the lecture held in Case Hall on December 9, a local paper failed to mention the speaker's name, merely stating he "drew a good crowd. Grumblers were held up to ridicule and were subjected to the severest criticism. The anecdotes were new, witty and apropos and the hearers were convulsed with laughter." It was a foregone conclusion that everyone knew the lecturer on the subject, *Grumbler & Co.,* was the sensational Presbyterian clergyman, Thomas DeWitt Talmage, whose fame soon spread beyond the Atlantic.

1869

Reviewing his shipbuilding production since he had established a partnership in 1847, Thomas Quayle found that he had built seventy-five vessels, thirteen of them in one year. The firm of Quayle & Martin was well known, and upon Quayle's retirement, his son, William E., continued to build ships until wooden vessels were antiquated by steel. The firm built some of the largest wooden ships on the lakes and pioneered in developing the wooden propeller. Shipyards along the Cuyahoga River had turned out nearly five hundred vessels of all classifications between 1849 and 1869, a great number having been produced in Cleveland.

Cleveland Baptists pooled resources of leadership and money and organized The Cleveland Baptist Mission Society on January 19. Merger with The Cleveland Baptist Association came in 1920. Dr. D. R. Sharpe, who became executive secretary in 1925, was not only a denominational leader, but he was prominent in civic and cultural movements.

Upon invitation of Mrs. Solon L. Severance, her friend, Mark Twain, thirty-four-year-old humorist, came to Cleveland to lecture for the benefit of the Cleveland Orphan Asylum. He had gained recognition in 1867 with his first book, *The Celebrated Jumping Frog of Calaveras County*. In his first appearance in the city on January 22 in Case Hall, Twain gave an account of his famous voyage to the Holy Land in 1867, under the title, *American Vandal Abroad*. A tidy net total of $594, turned over to Mrs. Benjamin Rouse, then president of the asylum, stimulated a low treasury. Twain's second volume, *Innocents Abroad,* published this year, added to his fame. In the following November he visited his friend, Mrs. A. W. Fairbanks in Cleveland, for advice as to whether he was worthy of the hand of Olivia Langdon, who also made the Holy Land journey. Inspired by Mrs. Fairbanks' encouragement, he hastened to Elmira, New York, where the lady accepted his proposal, and the marriage took place in February, 1870.

Daniel P. Rhodes and fellow promoters in the Rocky River Railroad Company opened the Cliff House on January 28, overlooking the Rocky River valley (Riverside Drive at Sloan and Edanola avenues, Lakewood). The resort hotel was a large, three-story, frame building, with the most beautiful ballroom in Cleveland on the third floor, a famous dining room, bar, and a captain's walk on the roof, from which the surrounding area could be surveyed. It was a popular choice for parties, outings, and picnics, and guests came by buggy in summer, by sleigh in winter, or rode the dinky railroad. A large addition was built in 1870; and, in 1873, J. H. Murch took it over, naming it the Murch House. Its original name was restored in 1877, and the height of its popularity was reached when James Starkweather was manager. John A. Weber was operating the Cliff House in 1882 when it burned. It was not rebuilt.

A rented room in the Northrup & Harrington Block, on the south side of Superior just west of Seneca, became the home of the Public School Library (later Cleveland Public Library), administered by the Board of Education. Dedication ceremonies on the evening of February 17 also celebrated the appointment of Luther M. Oviatt as the first city librarian. The free circulating library opened the next day with 5,800 volumes, representing books transferred from the school library and those purchased with the proceeds from the tax authorized for library purposes.

Owners of the S. B. Marshall farm (100 acres bounded by West 117th, Madison, West 112th, and the lake) offered it to Charles E. Ferrell, real-estate dealer, at $100 an acre.

Ulysses Simpson Grant was inaugurated the eighteenth President of the United States. He was born at Point Pleasant, Ohio.

One of the first financial institutions on the West Side was the Peoples Saving & Loan Association, organized in March and capitalized at $100,000. Early presidents succeeding Daniel P. Rhodes were John H. Sargent, Hiram Barrett, and R. R. Rhodes.

Webb C. Ball, jeweler and watch expert, opened a shop at Superior and Bank streets on March 19. Business grew steadily in the little store, furnished with two show cases and a work bench.

Continuous struggle marked the early years of John P. Green, born in

North Carolina in 1845. His father had purchased his freedom from slavery, and in 1850 died. Green's widowed mother brought the family of four to Cleveland in 1857. A graduate of Central High School, the young man read law in the office of Judge Jesse P. Bishop and completed the course at Union Law College in 1869. Practicing for a short time in North Carolina, he returned to Cleveland in 1872, where he became the first Negro member of the legal profession. He was elected justice of the peace in 1873, holding office for nine years. In 1881 he won the office of state representative by a strong majority, and was renominated in 1889.

The Michigan Southern & Northern Indiana Railroad Company, connecting Chicago and Detroit, and the Lake Shore Railway Company, operating a continuous line from Erie to Toledo, merged on May 8 as the Lake Shore & Michigan Southern Railroad, bringing Erie-to-Chicago operations under one management. On August 10, the Buffalo & Erie Railway was absorbed, consolidating 1,013 miles of road into one of the country's most important trunk lines (later New York Central), with headquarters in Cleveland.

In May the city fathers placed a price of seventy-five cents on the head of every dog found wandering at large without a muzzle. Newsboys and bootblacks combed the streets for strays that were quickly converted into cash and deposited in a dog pound.

The Civil War had interrupted the activities of the Cleveland Academy of Natural Science. Although its revival had begun two years earlier, reorganization came on May 15, this year, as the Kirtland Society of Natural Science (later Cleveland Museum of Natural History), honoring its president, Dr. Jared P. Kirtland. Its service lay in promoting "the study of the natural sciences and the collection and establishment of a museum of natural history, as a means of popular instruction and amusement." In September, 1870, it became a department of the influential Cleveland Library Association. Leading men of medicine and science were members.

A 200-acre site was selected for Lake View Cemetery (12316 Euclid), and the first president of the cemetery association, organized on May 24, was J. H. Wade. Scores of monuments, magnificent and simple in design, were to mark the resting places of Clevelanders, among them the massive Garfield monument, the towering Rockefeller monolith, and the modest tomb of Theodore E. Burton.

Cincinnati had organized a professional baseball team this year, and Cleveland wasted no time in reorganizing the Forest City Club on this basis. In the local line-up were James L. "Deacon" White, catcher; Albert G. Pratt, pitcher; Arthur Allison, first base—his brother, "Doug," one of the best catchers of his time, played for Cincinnati; Leonard C. Hanna, brother of Mark Hanna, second base; Austin R. "Pikey" Smith, third base; Eben Smith, shortstop and captain; Arthur Burt "middle field"; John Reilly, right field; and John Ward, left field. Peter Rose was the first president of the Forest City Baseball Association, and Captain Frank H. Mason, L. O. Rawson, H. Clay Doolittle, C. B. Pettengill, N. B. Sherwin, and Dr. N. B. Prentice were directors. White started at $75 a month and was later raised to $2,100 a season. In his twenty-odd years, he played on seven pennant-winning teams and was one of the best players of his day. Pratt, Allison, Reilly, and Ward each received $65 a month to start, and the others played for love of the sport. Average age of the team members was twenty-four years. There was no regular season schedule, and games were arranged by mail. During their 1869 inaugural, the Forest Citys played teams in Mansfield, Cincinnati, Portsmouth, and Columbus, Ohio, and met major clubs in New York State and the East in bitter contests. The 1870 season furrowed the directors' brows, the worst encounter being with the New York Athletics, when Cleveland trailed in the dust, 85-11. Home games were played on the Case Commons, with twenty-five-cent admission. The Forest City team entered the National Association of Professional Baseball Players, formed in 1871, and remained until the close of the following season. The last season for the league came in 1875.

At an exhibition of photography presented by the newly organized National Photographers Association in Boston, James F. Ryder of Cleveland took top honors. His entry was a collection of photographs made from retouched negatives, the first exhibited in America by an American photographer. Ryder was honored many times, and his writings were published widely.

Twenty pairs of English sparrows, imported from Europe, were brought to Cleveland, according to the United States Department of Agriculture, in the hope that they would destroy insect pests and save the trees. Despite the wisdom of knowing Englishmen, the City Council purchased fifty additional pairs. During the winter of 1872, bird houses were built on the Public Square by the city for the creature comfort of the feathered newcomers. After quick inspection, they frowned on the architecture and sought shelter elsewhere. Came the eighties and the country regretted the day that the quarrelsome little nuisance was introduced, but it was too late to repair the damage.

The Main Street Bridge, completed this year, was one of the first iron bridges in the city. It was 200 feet long and 31 feet wide, and swung on 24 rollers. The *Herald* reported: "So perfect is the mechanism . . . a boy of 12 years can swing the mighty mass with ease." The bridge was rebuilt in 1885 and operated by steam. In 1915 it was moved a short distance, and longer approaches were built to allow large vessels to pass through.

President Ulysses S. Grant invited the Forest City Baseball Club to the White House in July. "Boys," said the chief executive, "I have never seen a baseball game. I haven't had time, but I know a great deal about this game. Let me prove it to you. I'll call the positions and then let each man step forward as his position is named. Catcher!" "Jim" White stood out. "Pitcher!" Pratt answered. "First base!" The President called eight men into line. "Wait a minute," he said, "there are nine on the team. Hold on, there's the shortstop." Turning to W. R. Rose, five feet six inches tall and acting as cashier for the team, he put his arm around the young-man's shoulders and exclaimed, "This must be the shortstop!" Cleveland's Forest Citys, "the most gentlemanly club in the country," beamed as the President went with them to the door, puffing on his black cigar.

Fire losses mounted as the oil industry grew. Chief James Hill's valiant men found their new steam pumpers a great advantage when they fought a fire on July 15 that consumed forty-three cars of oil on the Atlantic & Great Western tracks. George A. Wallace, a rookie who joined the department on June 1, began his climb to the top as the city's "grand old fire-fighter."

Four Sisters of the Good Shepherd came from Cincinnati in July, upon Bishop Rappe's invitation, to establish the Convent of the Good Shepherd, a training home for delinquent girls. In a small frame house on Lake Street they began their pioneering work in Cleveland. Leading citizens, Catholic and non-Catholic, helped the worthy cause, among them William J. Gordon, Joseph Perkins, John Huntington, and Jeptha H. Wade. For many years, the sisters carried on their good work at East 30th and Carnegie Avenue. In the mid-1940s, plans were under way to build Marycrest, a new million-dollar home, at Bishop Road and Euclid Avenue in Wickliffe.

Great preparations were made for witnessing the eclipse of the sun on August 7, an event that did not recur during the century. Newsboys carried on a big business in smoked glass. Citizens' affairs came to a standstill as the hour approached, and Superior Street was a sea of faces peering skyward through smoked glass, as the moon darkened almost the entire portion of the sun. The great show lasted almost two hours.

Sewage and industrial wastes dumped into the lake contaminated the water close to shore, and a larger water-works tunnel was planned, extending farther into Lake Erie. Work was commenced on the new passageway on August 23, when a shaft was sunk near the pumping station to a depth of sixty-seven feet below the lake's surface, and a five-foot tunnel was started lakeward.

City officials, led by Mayor Stephen Buhrer, had been urging the building of a new City Hall for some time. At a Council meeting on August 25, sentiment directed that the project be undertaken. A competition for the best building plans was launched, and the $600 first prize was awarded to Walter Blythe. Here the record seems to end; and, until early in the next century, Cleveland, a rapidly growing city, was to have the distinction of housing the administration within rented walls. There were fifteen wards in the city at this time. In 1884, Council provided for twenty-five; in 1886, forty; and in 1894, forty-two, the largest number Cleveland ever had.

Jews of Polish origin organized the Anshe Emeth Congregation (later the Cleveland Jewish Center). Their tabernacle was a building near the Central Market that served until 1880, when a church on Erie Street was purchased. As members became Americanized, there developed a movement to abandon Orthodox traditions and follow the lead of German Jews by converting the synagogue into a Reform temple. The issue was settled permanently, however, when the great majority of the members elected to remain loyal to traditional Judaism.

Despite critical attacks of "moralists," pioneering women of the Women's

Christian Association (YWCA) founded the Retreat, "an asylum for fallen ones" on Perry Street. It soon outgrew its quarters; and, in 1873, a new building, largely the gift of Joseph Perkins, was dedicated on land donated by Leonard Case adjoining the Protestant Orphan Asylum on St. Clair Street. The Retreat ministered to the unfortunate for many years, later joining an independent agency.

Homeopathic physicians withdrew from the Willson Street Hospital and opened the Cleveland Protestant Hospital (later Huron Road Hospital) in the Humiston Institute building, where fifty beds had been provided. In 1873 a building on Huron Road was purchased (Telephone Building site) and remodeled. Incorporation as the Cleveland Homeopathic Hospital Society was effected in June, 1874, providing a homeopathic medical, surgical, and lying-in hospital. Drs. David H. Beckwith, H. F. Biggar, John C. Sanders, and H. H. Baxter were prominently identified with the project.

Cleveland felt the effect of "Black Friday," September 24, when New York financial houses suffered disastrously from the gold corner. During the panic, the distressed Lake Shore & Michigan Southern Railroad came under control of shrewd Commodore Cornelius Vanderbilt, New York Central genius. Having acquired substantial interest in the road, he not only became its president in 1873, but bestowed upon it New York Central policies and management.

Grace Episcopal Church, South, was organized in Newburgh with help from St. Paul's in Cleveland. The white meeting house was purchased from the First Presbyterian Church and moved to a site secured at Harvard and Sawyer Street. The Rev. Frederick Brooks of St. Paul's served as the first rector, and was succeeded by the Rev. Royal B. Bascom, who was also rector of St. Mary's. In times of crisis and economic strife, St. Paul's helped to sustain the parish that continued to be of great influence in the life of the industrial community. The Rev. Ralph E. Fall was rector of Grace Church in 1946.

Educators, meeting in the Weddell House in October, formed an organization for the professional improvement of their members, the advancement of education in northeastern Ohio schools, and the dissemination of educational ideas. Thomas W. Harvey of Painesville, Ohio, was the first president. This was the beginning of the Northeastern Ohio Teachers Association, familiarly called NEOTA, that was to become one of the strongest and most progressive institutions of its kind. The first president from Cleveland was J. M. James, elected in 1880. The association made recommendations that resulted in legislation improving conditions relating to schools and teachers. It was largely responsible for the School Foundation Law, providing for an underwriting of pupil education with state-tax monies, and guaranteeing to each pupil a certain minimum education, and to each teacher, certain salary provisions.

A meeting of Presbyterian pastors and elders on November 13 resulted in forming the Cleveland Presbyterian Church Union on January 10, following. All churches in the district were represented—First of Cleveland, First of East Cleveland, Miles Park, Parma, Second, Euclid Street, and Cleveland

Westminster, the object of the union being to promote Presbyterian Church extension in the city. R. F. Smith was the first president. Many prominent laymen gave liberally of time and energy to the Union, T. P. Handy having been president for nineteen years. Dr. C. L. Zorbaugh, the first superintendent, served from 1913-24, the Rev. J. J. Coale until 1927, and Dr. Louis F. Ruf until 1935, when he was succeeded by Dr. Arnold W. Bloomfield.

Out of the historic Seneca Falls, New York, convention of 1848 had come tireless leadership for the cause of women's rights. The banner had been carried the length of the country by the fearless crusaders of the day —Elizabeth Cady Stanton and Susan B. Anthony. Time after time, they faced defeat and derision. The bitter blow came when the Fifteenth Amendment gave the voting franchise to liberated Negro men, but not to the women who had helped to win it through distinctive war service. In May, the National Association for Woman Suffrage, headed by Miss Anthony, was formed in Washington to urge equal suffrage through an amendment. A call, signed by Lucy Stone (Blackwell), Julia Ward Howe, Mrs. Caroline M. Severance, and others, brought women from twenty-nine states to the first national suffrage convention, held in Cleveland, on November 24 in Case Hall. Lucy Stone opened the meeting, and Mrs. H. M. Tracey Cutler of Cleveland was the principal speaker. At the closing session, fiery Miss Anthony urged her followers to go home and work unceasingly for the right to vote. Out of the two-day event came the American Woman Suffrage Association, with Henry Ward Beecher, president, and William Lloyd Garrison, a vice president, its purpose being to work through state legislatures for the cause. The *Herald* gave generous space and a weak endorsement to the movement, observing that some day good might come of it, and warning feminists to proceed with caution. In a four-page pamphlet, eccentric Irad Kelley aired his views, concluding in a vein of ridicule:

> When women gain their honest rights
> We'll have no drunkards, no more fights;
> And then, no doubt, will surely come
> The long desired millennium.

Women went to work in communities where hostile foes predicted that suffrage would shatter the sanctity of the home and destroy reverence for the weaker sex; but they were determined, and in 1920 they attained their goal.

The Knights of Pythias began their work in Cleveland, organizing two lodges this year—Washington on the East Side and Lake Shore on the West Side, leading citizens being identified with the order. In 1871 Herman and Standard lodges began; Owatana and Cleveland Lodge, in a German community, in 1873; South Side, Oak, and Forest City, 1875; Red Cross, 1876; Sections 76 and 89 of the Endowment Rank, and the Cuyahoga Division of the Uniform Rank, 1879. In the early nineties, Edwin Cowles and Western Reserve lodges for Negro members were thriving.

The Brooklyn Street Railroad Company was granted a franchise on December 7 to run a line from Lorain Street on Pearl southward to the city limits. The two-mile road failed to pay, and it was leased the next year to Truscott & Ingram. At about this time, Council ordered that bells be attached to harness or cars, to warn pedestrians, wagons, and sleighs to clear the tracks for the horsecar!

Figures of the "Midshipman" and "Sailor Boy," carved by William Walcutt, had been completed; and on December 8 the work of mounting them on the Perry monument on the Square began. The statue was raised on a high, granite base, and a little later an iron fence was built around it, with four ornamental lamp posts at the corners.

At a meeting of lawyers in the Court House on December 18, the first steps toward forming the Cleveland Law Library Association were made. On January 8, 1870, organization was completed, and S. O. Griswold was elected president, and W. J. Boardman, vice president. Books contributed by the president, R. P. Spalding, Loren Prentiss, W. S. C. Otis, John C. Grannis, Benjamin R. Beavis, E. J. Estep, Samuel Williamson, S. E. Williamson, and I. Buckingham made up the nucleus of a valuable library. J. P. Bishop, G. M. Barber, Franklin T. Backus, and H. V. Willson were among those who made notable gifts of money, books, or service.

The decade of the sixties witnessed the establishment of business firms that were in existence in the 1940s: 1860, Koebler Company Funeral Home; 1862, Lake Shore Saw Mill & Lumber Company, James & Manchester Company; 1863, George M. Edmondson Company, Stone Shoe Company; 1864, Bowler Foundry Company, Neal Storage Company, Taylor & Boggis Foundry Company; 1865, Kirchners Flowers, Inc., Lake Erie Provision Company; 1866, Hugh Huntington Roofing Corporation, H. J. Votteler & Son; 1867, Babcock & Wilcox Company, Thomas H. Geer Company, Haskins Roofing Company, Mount & Company, Norris Bros. Company, E. A. Schwarzenberg Company, Western Newspaper Union; 1868, Cleveland Steam Gauge Company, Erving Dress Funeral Homes, Guenther Art Galleries Company, H. H. Hackman Leather Company, Herman Krebs Pharmacy, Ohio Plating & Manufacturing Company, Tropical Paint & Oil Company; 1869, Cleveland Transfer Company, David Round & Son.

CHAPTER 10

The Industrial Age

1870-1879

THE SMOKE of prosperity mingled with the odor of hemp and canvas, oil, and grease as the decade opened. The air was filled with hoarse blasts from steamship whistles, the clang of ships' bells, and the hoot of tugs and locomotives. Industry was making men rich. Wealth beyond dreams was being attracted to Cleveland as factories expanded to meet increasing demands for their products.

It is hard to tell whether Clevelanders found more pride in magnificent Euclid Avenue or in the remarkable growth of their city, now fifteenth in the nation, according to the census. While Cincinnati stood eighth in the list of cities, with a population of 216,239, its gain in the decade past was about 56,000 as compared with more than 49,000 for Cleveland, which brought the total of the latter to 92,829, more than double that of 1860. In the forward drive, Cleveland passed Detroit, 79,577, and Milwaukee, 71,440; but Chicago, the metropolis of the West, with a long lead of 298,977, and Buffalo, with 117,714, still outdistanced the Forest City, whose area now embraced 12.012 square miles.

Immigrants began to flock to Cleveland after the Civil War, and the census of 1870 showed a native population of 64,018—over four-fifths born in Ohio, 38,815 of foreign birth, and 1,293 Negroes. Represented in the enumeration of the foreign-born were Germany, leading with 15,855, followed by Ireland, 9,964; England, 4,533; Bohemia, 3,252, as of 1869; Switzerland, 704; Scotland, 668; with lesser totals from other nations. From Hungary had come only 97 newcomers; Poland, 77; and Italy, 35. Cuyahoga County had a population of 132,010, of which 50,696 were of foreign birth.

The early seventies saw the launching of big-business enterprises and the beginning of a new industrial age. In order to escape government taxes imposed upon separate processes, steps in manufacture were being combined into large plants equipped with expensive machinery and manned by hundreds of workers under hired "bosses." Unrestricted immigration brought a steady stream of cheap labor, encouraging concentration of special industries in large cities, thus reducing prices. Capital investment per worker in the United States for tools and plant facilities was $2,115; unskilled factory hands drew twenty-seven cents an hour in wages.

The outstanding large-scale consolidation in Cleveland and the Middle West was that of the Standard Oil Company of Ohio in 1870. This was the era of oil. Cleveland investors had a number of small refineries in operation, and it was estimated that more than one-third of the entire production of the oil region was shipped to local plants. The city was flavored and saturated with oil; the river and lake were smeared with it. Oil wagons rumbled through the streets and tanks blocked the railroads. Oil fires kept the city firemen eternally vigilant and filled the valley with painful apprehension. Kerosene lamps were instantly popular, replacing feeble, flickering candles and whale-oil lamps. Rockefeller and his associates envisioned Cleveland as a great refining center; and, buying up their small rivals, they launched the gigantic Standard Oil empire. Three years later, the foundation of the vast Otis Steel operations was being laid, pioneering in the making of acid open-hearth steel.

Rockefeller oil and Newburgh steel were attracting the Czechs. Standard Oil employed many of them, and it was reported in the later seventies that almost every Czech man had spent some time "making barrels for John D. Rockefeller." Although he encouraged them to invest in his oil interests, the thrifty declined, waiting for a safer place for their savings. This employment and encroachment of the city inspired the colony of Czechs to move from Croton Street across Kingsbury Run, where they established a hill district. On farm land around Broadway, then a country road, "a city of Bohemia" took form gradually, with stores, churches, banks, and a national hall centering at Willson Avenue. Other Czechs moved to Quincy (and East 82nd). On the West Side, they sought to escape the city by moving to Kubu—or "Cuba," west of the creek (at West 41st Street).

Beginning in 1870, a small number of Lithuanians found their way to Cleveland, settling in the neighborhood of Oregon, Hamilton, and Lake, between Erie and Sterling avenues. Italians, Slavs, Syrians, and other immigrants were crowding into the Haymarket district in the vicinity of Central and Broadway. Nearby on "Whisky Hill" were the worst tenements in Cleveland. It was an impoverished area, with the largest birth and death rates and the greatest number of saloons.

Traveling through Ohio on their way to Illinois in the early seventies, Susan B. Anthony and Elizabeth Cady Stanton, suffrage champions, were unable to get sleeping space on their train, and they spent the night peering into the darkness between naps. They were astonished at the number of homes in which lights shone during the late hours; and, questioning the conductor, they learned that women were so busy with chores in the daytime that at night by feeble lamplight they patiently provided clothing for the family by hand. Miss Anthony resolved to spread the news about the sewing machine, and the result was a broadcast of handbills bearing suffragist information on one side and a sewing-machine advertisement on the other. Thomas H. White, Cleveland manufacturer, and eastern firms footed the bill and brought a new luxury into many homes. Cleveland had become a center for the making of sewing machines and paint and varnish. In 1874 David and Morris Black launched a new industry in America when they began making ready-to-wear cloaks for women. Carriages, four- and six-seat phaetons, sulkies, basket and pony phaetons, coupe rockaways, and heavy road wagons were made in Cleveland.

Unions were gaining strength, and in 1870 there were thirty-two national labor organizations in the United States, the most powerful being the Knights of Labor, organized in 1869. Rapid industrial advance made Cleveland an important city in the labor movement, and it became the home of the Brotherhood of Locomotive Engineers in 1873. When labor turned to politics after the panic of '73, the first Farmer-Labor representatives met in the lake city in 1876; and two years later, the Miners National Association met in their second convention. Bloodshed and destruction resulted from the great railroad strike of 1877, particularly in Pittsburgh; but through the steadying influence of Mayor William G. Rose, Cleveland experienced only work stoppage.

The first barge for carrying grain, introduced in 1871, practically revolutionized the business. The era of sailing ships was nearing the end; but, until the turn of the century, grain schooners continued in use, a maze of masts pointing skyward in the bends of the Cuyahoga. The West Side had been closely identified with shipbuilding and shipping traffic since early days. Along the river channel that wound its way to the lake (near West 58th Street), shipyards, dry docks, and related establishments had produced a major industry, and some of the largest steamers and propellers were launched here.

Land values were increasing steadily as the decade opened. Climbing commodity prices are indicated by a few items: flour, $5.25 to $7.25 per barrel; potatoes, 45 to 50 cents per bushel; hams, 18 to 18½ cents per pound; dressed hogs, 10½ to 11 cents; best butter, 28 to 30 cents; chickens, 14 to 15 cents; turkeys, 16 to 18 cents; granulated sugar, 15¾ cents; Rio coffee, 21½ to 26 cents; eggs, 26 to 28 cents per dozen; New Orleans molasses, 90 to 95 cents per gallon.

Postwar prosperity and the urge to get rich quick were too great for some of the country's men of power. Reckless overspeculation, unsound banking, wildcat financing of railroads, greed, and graft plunged the nation into a period of financial depression in 1873. While Cleveland business suffered, its diversified structure cushioned the impact. Relief work was extended by charitable agencies. The Bethel Home opened a free soup house, and during the winter one hundred and twenty gallons of soup were sent in large cans by horsecar to the needy of the city. Ladies sewed for the poor. Here organized charity had its beginning in the ward system, which was the basis for greatly expanded effort. The banks weathered the storm, but city development was retarded. Real-estate speculators were dealt a body blow, and long newspaper columns announced delinquent-tax sales. Bankers operated with caution, and by 1877 business advance had been restored.

Commercial expansion and the movement eastward were influencing major changes in Cleveland's complexion. To escape from the smoke of factories and railroads, retail trade followed the residential shift eastward from the business district on lower Superior Street. The banks, however, ignored the trend, and in 1870 the first bank building in Cleveland, six and a half stories high, was erected at Superior and Water streets.

New commercial blocks—or office buildings—were being erected by Cleveland merchants, comparing favorably with other cities. They were usually substantial, narrow, four-story structures, with ornate fronts in which were set deep, arched windows. Large, decorative pillars emphasized the shallow entranceways. Taylor & Kilpatrick's "one-price" store opened in the new Cushing Block on the south side of the Square in 1870.

"Have you been up Euclid Avenue?" was the first question asked of a visitor to Cleveland. "As well go to Rome without seeing St. Peter's, or to London without visiting the tower." No avenue in the world, it was claimed, presented such a "continuous succession of charming residences and such

Euclid Avenue in the 1870s was known as one of the most beautiful streets in America.

uniformly beautiful grounds for so great a distance." The peak of a Clevelander's earthly ambition was to have a mansion on the Avenue beyond Erie Street.

A dignity long overdue was extended to Euclid Street in 1870, when it officially reached the stature of an avenue and joined the "distinguished" company of Case, Cedar, Giddings, Longwood, Payne, Sawtell, Scovill, Sterling, Wade, Willson, Clark, Gordon, Jennings, Madison, Rhodes, Starkweather, and Scranton avenues.

The doom of lower Euclid Avenue as a beautiful residential street was sealed, however, when John Main opened a drug store and Thomas O'Rourke opened his tailoring shop. Time erased most of the early retail-business ventures; but three-quarters of a century later, Burrows, book-and-office-supply firm, pioneer on the avenue in '71, flourished several blocks east of the Public Square.

The entering wedge of commercialism that darkened the horizon of Euclid Avenue was the beginning of a gradual but steady change that continued decade after decade. In 1873 the Standard Block, home office of Standard Oil, was erected on the north side of Euclid. Across the street, on the site of St. Paul's Church, at the southwest corner of Sheriff, a four-story structure of the latest architecture was erected by the leading music publisher and musical-instrument dealer in 1876. The interior featured massive woodwork, a lofty, main-floor ceiling from which hung clusters of gaslight fixtures, and a steam-driven elevator. Over the doorway, the width of the building, was an unmistakable sign in strong, Gothic letters: "343. S. Brainard's Sons. 341." This impressive establishment represented the business founded by Silas Brainard in the basement of the American House in 1836.

The tribulations of an over-worked Fire Department were reflected in mounting fire losses and in the construction of the new $250,000 Court House, one of the first buildings erected almost entirely of fireproof materials. Brick walls and partitions, floors of iron and brick, an iron-and-slate roof, and stairs and landings of iron constituted the latest challenge to the demon, Fire.

On Superior Avenue, east of the Square, the transition from a residential to a commercial street was also evident, private homes having been displaced by the Hoffman Block, the Crocker Block, Case Hall, and the Case Block —or City Hall. Suburban residences and cottages extended as far as the Northern Ohio Fair Grounds, an ambitious project launched in Glenville by local promoters in 1870. Wade Park, an enchanting natural woodland, was being developed with walks and drives by its owner, Jeptha H. Wade. The future of downtown Cleveland's lakefront as a fashionable residential district faded in the mid-decade, when wealthy William J. Gordon moved from his fine Water Street home eastward to his beautiful estate in the valley of Doan Brook (Gordon Park).

The district beyond Willson Avenue was developing steadily, and fine residences began to fill in the open spaces to the east on Euclid. Doan's Corners was a flourishing crossroads town, with stores, churches, hotel, post office, and comfortable homes sheltered under tall trees.

Along the lakeshore, between East Cleveland and Collinwood, lay Glenville. Shady glens, through which tumbled little streams, gave it the picturesque name. Early New England farmers had settled there, followed by immigrants from Scotland, England, and Ireland. Almost surrounding the flourishing village center at St. Clair and Doan Street were truck farms operated by Germans, who hauled their produce to the city and returned with loads of manure from the Central Market horse barns. In time, the St. Clair horsecar line was extended in the form of a horse-drawn truck, which was stored in favor of a canvas-covered sled when deep snow fell. Glenville residents could board the Ashtabula accommodation train at Coit Station to reach Cleveland at a quicker pace. The rustic community attracted wealthy Clevelanders to a summer playground for sportsmen and their families. Fast horses made the Glenville trotting track the most famous in the country. For almost four decades, Glenville was the gayest community in the Cleveland environs—"the garden spot of Cuyahoga County."

Green acres surrounded Cleveland and its suburbs, many of them taking geometric patterns in the form of truck gardens, orchards, and vineyards. Grape culture had begun on the ridges, increasing to hundreds of acres. The Collamer district became the largest shipping point for grapes in the United States, closely followed by Dover, Ohio, the second largest.

Horsecar lines expanded to meet the needs of the city as it grew. Despite uncertain schedules, delays while waiting for an extra horse at the foot of grades, and no heat in winter, the streetcar contributed steadily to urban development. A dummy railroad brought Euclid Village closer to Cleveland and introduced steam heat in the coaches. Young Tom L. Johnson, the new owner of the financially embarrassed Brooklyn line, adopted this innovation, the first of his aggressive moves that irritated local promoters.

The city limits pushed eastward to a short distance beyond Doan Brook when the original Village of East Cleveland, with its western boundary at Willson Avenue, was annexed in 1872, swelling the population by more than five thousand. Newburgh came into the Cleveland fold the next year, increasing the population by over six thousand. Union in both instances had been sharply opposed by voters in the annexed territory.

Lack of city planning became more evident as the city grew and gathered in its neighboring suburbs. An awkward and inefficient street pattern had developed on the map, serving the dictates of convenience and politics rather than experienced engineering and good judgment. There had been perennial discussions of major bridge-building projects for more than a decade, but war and economic factors had delayed practical progress. Small bridges no longer met the needs of the growing industrial city. The seventies, however, saw the launching of viaducts, or high-level bridges, of masonry and iron to unite thriving districts.

The first Board of Park Commissioners adopted the Public Square as its initial improvement project. Prodded by the far-flung reputation established by beautiful Euclid Avenue, extensive face-lifting operations in 1872 raised the city's front yard to a level of respectability. The Square took on a rustic, rest-provoking air, where citizens could enjoy concerts and oratory, or spend leisure time in familiar exchanges with friends and neighbors. On the broad avenues that crossed it, horse-drawn buggies and aristocratic carriages carried men and women on errands of business and society. Horsecars with tinkling bells rumbled on schedules measured by the pace of little, black mules. Celebrating the centennial of the nation's independence in 1876, a flagpole of Bessemer steel, the first of its kind, was shaped in Henry Chisholm's shops and erected on the Public Square on the Fourth of July. Religious and community meetings shifted from the Square with the opening of the Tabernacle, erected by devout William H. Doan.

In 1875 the Case Block opened, and it was distinguished as the rented quarters of the city administration. On the top floor of the City Hall, Archibald M. Willard and his artist friends, the sons of poor, hard-working families, united in an art colony that brought out hidden talent worthy of international fame.

During the decade, water facilities were extended in the city, fire protection was increased, new schools were built, and steps were taken in promoting public health and welfare. While a few civic-minded souls pleaded for preservation of the lakefront as a beautiful breathing spot that would be a credit to Cleveland, the authorities took the path of least resistance, and the lake and the river were sacrificed to the indignities of shipping, industry, and sewage. Haphazard attention had been given to improvement of the Cleveland harbor until the seventies, when construction of the breakwater began.

Adoption of the board plan of municipal government was a constructive move in the direction of better city management. Late in the decade, the Public School Library was considered strong enough to stand on its own feet, and it came under the direction of a library committee elected by the Board of Education.

A few influential men and women were devoting their wealth to the support of cultural projects, but Cleveland's advance in the fine arts ranked far behind the older cities in the East. Young women of well-known families were being taught French and polite manners by Augusta Mittleberger in her famous private school on fashionable Prospect Avenue. As Notre Dame Academy was opening in 1874, a college-preparatory institution for boys, known as Brooks School, was getting under way. Many of Cleveland's leaders studied under its able faculty. In its affiliate, Brooks School for Young Ladies and Misses, Hathaway Brown School had its beginning.

Central High School moved to lovely, tree-arched Willson Avenue, where it educated generations of students. Stately residences, crowned with iron balustrades, and with graceful fountains in front lawns, were secondary to those on showy Euclid Avenue, but trim carriages carrying beautifully dressed ladies told the wealth of the street.

The Cleveland Bar Association and the Union Club were among the professional and social organizations founded in the seventies that included some of the nation's leaders in their memberships.

Jules Verne's fantastic best seller, *Twenty Thousand Leagues under the Sea,* appeared in 1870, and moved quickly from stores to many family bookcases at $3.50 a copy. The Alger stories reached the height of their popularity. Case Hall drew the most popular lecturers of the day—Harriet Beecher Stowe; Alexander Winchell, famed geologist with a poet's soul; Henry M. Stanley, world traveler; Thomas Nast, cartoonist; and others. In the mid-decade, the trek to Lake Chautauqua, New York, inspired the privileged few who attended the summer lectures.

Temperance champions saw victory in sight before the Civil War, when a number of states enacted laws prohibiting the manufacture and sale of alcoholic drinks. The war influence and increased European immigration turned the tide, however, fostered by the influx of Teutons, who loved their beer. Outraged at the alarming number of saloons, courageous women in the Women's Christian Association (YWCA) in Cleveland laid aside their lapboards and needlework and rose in mighty protest, determined to drive out the curse. In opposing the "sumptuary" or Sabbath laws, Germans paraded with beer kegs on their shoulders along Garden Street and Willson Avenue to Haltnorth's Gardens, just beyond the city limits. They claimed that the closing of saloons on Sunday interfered with personal liberty. In the earnest crusade against the liquor traffic was the germ that expanded to world proportions as the Woman's Christian Temperance Union. Missionary effort carried on by the YMCA fathered the world's first Railroad "Y," dedicated in Cleveland in 1872.

Civic-minded ladies of the Woman's Christian Association were taking increasing interest in public affairs. A record of 1875 states: "It has been an arduous but edifying privilege of late to attend some meetings of the City Council." Women were finding varied employment outside the home, and prejudice against admitting them to the professions was being challenged.

The opening of the Euclid Avenue Opera House in 1872 marked a milestone in the history of the theater in Cleveland. To its boards John A. Ellsler brought the greatest names in the show business, and his stock companies were the proving ground for actors who went on to bright careers. Ellsler also operated the Academy of Music and the Pittsburgh Opera House, alternating his stock companies between Cleveland and the Smoky City. For several decades, the Euclid Avenue Opera House was acknowledged as one of the nation's best-known theaters.

Music organizations and choral societies were taking substantial form in the period of slow recovery in cultural life. A great stage name or the coming of the Saengerfest stimulated interest in local endeavors. In the schools of William Heydler and Alfred F. Arthur, the teaching of music not only inspired appreciation, but pointed the way to its future place in the community. Yet genuine interest in cultural movements lagged, and politics and industrial and commercial advancement seemed to be uppermost in the minds of the city's leaders.

Horse racing was increasing in popularity, and a large carriage house and stable was an essential part of the building program of a fine residence. Cleveland had cast off the early custom of hugging the fire at the sign of winter. With the first heavy snow there was the music of sleighbells, and soon the races began on Euclid Avenue from Case to Erie. Bundled in bright afghans and buffalo robes, citizens raced spirited horses in trim cutters until the last snowfall of the season.

There were six daily newspapers in Cleveland in 1876—the *Plain Dealer, Herald, Leader,* and *Evening News,* and the *Anzeiger* and *Waechter am Erie* in the German language. The *Sunday Morning Voice* survived opposition of the clergy and those who defended the Sabbath against worldly influences, but it suffered competition from the short-lived *Post* and *Times.* Weeklies and monthlies came and faded after a while, the Germans alone circulating two tri-weekly, four weekly, and three monthly publications. The rapid development of the city brought many journals representing special trades, labor, business interests, and the multiplied activities of the people. Demand for foreign-language newspapers and periodicals increased with immigration.

In cramped, dusty quarters on Frankfort Street, Edward W. Scripps, a six-foot "radical" from Illinois, founded *The Penny Press.* A passion for the welfare of the "common folks" was expressed in the young editor's introductory statement: "We intend simply to support good men and condemn bad ones, support good measures and condemn bad ones. . . . We shall tell no lies about persons or policies for love, malice or money. . . ." Surviving ridicule and scorn, the penny paper triumphed, and as *The Cleveland Press,* it became an important link in the nationwide Scripps-McRae chain, forerunner of Scripps-Howard Newspapers.

A journal of increasing influence was *The Catholic Universe,* founded by

Bishop Richard Gilmour, successor to Bishop Amadeus Rappe. Two decades of service of this forceful religious leader to the diocese were marked by great progress in church and school.

Alexander Graham Bell's crude telephone stirred the scientific world in 1876, but for some time only a small number of forward-looking people realized its great potential usefulness. A few phones used by commercial firms began to inspire inquiry into the telephone business, but the public regarded the invention as a toy born of inventive fantasy that would benefit and entertain a few until its novelty had worn out. By an historic agreement of November 10, 1879, Western Union withdrew from the telephone field and the Bell company agreed to stay out of the telegraph business, thus paving the way for advance through creation of a unified phone system. Steadily the telephone proved its worth as essential to industry, commerce, and welfare, and the growth of its business came to be regarded as a dependable yardstick upon which to base the city's future expansion and development. Association with the American Telephone & Telegraph Company in later years gave Ohio Bell Telephone subscribers access to the telephones of the world.

A golden era of progress had its beginning in Cleveland on April 29, 1879, when electric street lighting was successfully demonstrated on the Public Square. At the signal of Charles F. Brush, developer of the arc light, "a dazzling glory filled the park, crowds being present to witness the practical demonstration of a scientific victory." Thus Cleveland became the first city to light its streets extensively by electricity. While the arc light was not entirely an original invention, Brush combined it with a dynamo into a practical power station that was quickly adopted in New York. Soon exterior and interior installations had been introduced abroad, and the name "Brush" became known universally. Gaslight, the horsecar, and the sad-iron were doomed. Less than two years later, the *Scientific American,* recognizing the genius of the inventor, declared: "It is difficult to estimate the effect of an invention on existing practices and industries. Occasionally a new invention will appear which will greatly affect a whole range of allied inventions and industries in such a way as to change entirely time-honored customs, inaugurate new practices and establish new arts. The commercial development of electricity is a notable example of this." In the years to follow, Cleveland plants were producing an ever-increasing number of appliances, lamps, and diversified electrical products for home, industry, and farm. Dr. Brush earned renown as "one of the greatest pioneer scientists and inventors in the field of electricity," and his inventions were important contributions to the founding of the General Electric Company.

1870

The Standard Oil Company was incorporated under Ohio laws on January 10, by John D. Rockefeller, Henry M. Flagler, Samuel Andrews, Stephen V. Harkness, and William Rockefeller. Capital was a million dollars, and offices were opened in the Cushing Block on the Public Square. Envisioning a great future in oil, Rockefeller introduced sound business principles and rigid economies into company management. Products were standardized, mass production and distribution were inaugurated, and local refineries were integrated until Cleveland became the oil capital of the world in the eighties, wiping out Pittsburgh's threat. In 1879 stock in Standard Oil and its affiliates was conveyed to three trustees: M. R. Kieth, George H. Vilas, and George F. Chester, thus consolidating ownership of properties. Pitched battles to secure refining facilities, preferential freight rates, pipe lines, wells, and markets marked the years with stirring drama, while Standard expanded production, lighting kerosene lamps all over the world, and multiplying Cleveland wealth.

The Cushing Block had been erected by Dr. Henry K. Cushing, son of Dr. Erastus Cushing of the famous family of physicians. It was a four-story building on the south side of the Public Square (eastern portion of May Company site). Prominent tenants were the Standard Oil Company and the city's water-works department. Its predecessor had been the Cushing office and residence, erected in 1839. Dr. Harvey W. Cushing, son of Dr. Henry K., became professor of surgery at Harvard Medical School and surgeon in chief of the Peter Bent Brigham Hospital in 1912. An eminent brain specialist, he was honored many times for his achievements. In 1925 he received the Pulitzer Prize for Biography for his *Life of Sir William Osler*. Upon retiring from Harvard in 1932, Dr. Cushing engaged in research in medical history at Yale, his alma mater. Death closed his brilliant career on October 8, 1939.

When the State Board of Agriculture refused to select Cleveland as the location of the Ohio State Fair, there were charges of patronage favoring southern Ohio, and the lake city determined to have a fair of its own. On February 26, a $300,000 stock company, the Northern Ohio Fair Association, was incorporated by Amasa Stone, J. H. Wade, J. P. Robison, Dr. Worthy S. Streator, Azariah Everett, and other leading citizens to promote agriculture, horticulture, and the mechanical arts, as well as to encourage trotting races. Eighty-seven acres of land were purchased on St. Clair near Glenville and buildings were erected.

The Theatre Comique, once a fashionable entertainment house, had presented Primrose and West, the famous song-and-dance minstrel team; George Knight, comedian; Denman Thompson, who laid the foundation of "Joshua Whitcomb" on the variety circuit; and other stars of the day. Now its popularity lay in the "Varieties," and it was reputed that "all in all no more wicked place of amusement ever existed in Cleveland." B. C. Hart and others tried unsuccessfully to raise the moral standard, but it flourished in its degradation.

A hardware store was opened this year by George A. Tinnerman at the northeast corner of Lorain and Willett Street. A stove-manufacturing business, started in 1875, became so successful that in 1910 hardware was abandoned. In 1913 stoves and ranges were made exclusively in the factory at 2038 Fulton Road, forerunner of the large plant operated by Tinnerman Products, Inc.

On April 14 the Negro population of Cleveland celebrated ratification of the Fifteenth Amendment, which established the equal right of white and colored citizens to vote. Proud banners inscribed to antislavery heroes were carried in a long procession that marched to the tune of *John Brown's Body*.

Two Scotchmen, William Taylor and Thomas Kilpatrick, opened a one-room dry-goods store, known as Taylor, Kilpatrick & Company, on April 21, on the first floor of the new Cushing Block. Contrary to advice that this would be an unfortunate commercial location, the store, staffed with thirty-six salesmen, prospered. Thus began the retailing trend away from Superior Avenue to Euclid. Ten large chandeliers blazed on certain evenings when Taylor's was open until ten o'clock. "One price for all" was the pioneering principle introduced to the trade by William Taylor. He was a devout Presbyterian, who insisted upon strict Sabbath observance; and, traditionally, no Sunday advertising was used and curtains of show windows were drawn on the Sabbath until 1939. In 1885 John Livingstone Taylor, only son of the founder, was admitted to partnership. Kilpatrick moved to Chicago, and the store assumed the name of William Taylor Son & Company. Floor space was steadily enlarged until the entire building block was occupied.

The first pretentious bank building was erected early in the year at the northeast corner of Superior and Water streets, as the home of the Commercial National and the Second National banks. It was the six-and-a-half-story National Bank Building, the upper floors being given over to offices, and the semi-basement to the Western Union Telegraph Company.

Control of the Cleveland Library Association was placed in the hands of five directors, elected for life, on May 3: Samuel Williamson, James Barnett, H. M. Chapin, William Bingham, and B. A. Stanard. An endowment fund of $25,000 provided by Leonard Case, Jr., relieved financial anxiety, and a perpetual lease of rooms on the second floor of Case Hall solved the library's housing problem.

"Every freshet makes a sand bar," reported the city engineer; and the mayor complained, "the dredging of the river is a source of continued expense." For years wharf owners and the city co-operated reluctantly in dredging the riverbed to keep pace with commerce and the increasing size of vessels. The narrow inner harbor had become congested with boats docked on either side, and trade was being lost. Two decades passed, however, before systematic development was accomplished. In 1874 the channel depth was fourteen feet.

Cleveland had about ten and a half miles of stone pavement and eight and three-quarters miles of Nicholson, or wood block, paving. Manual labor cleaned the streets on an average of four or five times a year.

Racing fans crowded into wagons and fashionable landaus and made their way to Glenville to witness the opening of the new race track on St. Clair Avenue (at East 88th Street). The Cleveland Driving Park Company, the first amateur driving club in America, had built the course in co-operation with the Northern Ohio Fair Association, and a bridge over St. Clair connected the track with the fair grounds. Stockholders in the company were

T/BBITTS Clev

John D., William, and Frank Rockefeller, Sylvester T. Everett, J. V. Painter, Warren H. Corning, Charles A. Brayton, and Howard M. Hanna. Only three presidents served the club until it disbanded in 1908: Tom Axworthy, Colonel William "Billy" Edwards, and H. M. Hanna; its secretaries were Sam Briggs, William B. Fasig, who gained repute as a dealer in race horses, Sidney W. Giles, and George J. Dietrich. In 1872 the Quadrilateral Circuit, consisting of Cleveland, Buffalo, Rochester, and Utica, met at Glenville, considered the "model" of the circuits; and the next year the Grand Circuit was formed as the major league of harness racing. Famous horses made turf history and drew record crowds to Glenville.

Colonel William Edwards was largely responsible for the great success of the driving club. He had many civic and business affiliations, and served as president of the Board of Trade. The Edwards home was one of the most hospitable in the city, and here were entertained international celebrities, such as Sir Henry Irving, Ellen Terry, Edwin Booth, Lawrence Barrett, and Lotta Crabtree. The colonel had lived a full life when he passed on in 1898. Until 1919, the Edwards mansion on Prospect east of East 22nd Street was owned by the family. It was then sold, and during the 1930s, Fenn College used it for classrooms. The historic house was razed in 1940 to provide parking space.

In a one-story building on Woodland Avenue, Francis H. Glidden began mixing paints and varnishes. In 1875 he took over the Forest City Paint & Varnish Company, pioneer in the industry, formed in 1856, and organized the Glidden Varnish Company, forerunner of the vast Glidden operations. It was largely a family concern, making varnish and enamels and marketing them internationally under the name "Jap-a-lac."

The lower grinding stone of the pair used in the old Williams grist-mill, built in 1799, was mounted on the Public Square.

The city Infirmary, or poorhouse, was the only haven for the aged poor until this time, when the Little Sisters of the Poor opened an asylum on Erie Street. It enlarged to meet increased needs; and, in a new location on Perry Street, the Home for the Aged Poor gave shelter to all races and creeds.

Among its benefactors were William J. Gordon, John Huntington, and Joseph Perkins.

Charles Coit, grandson of Daniel L. Coit, original Western Reserve landholder from Connecticut, converted the farmhouse on his lakeshore property (Bratenahl) into a summer hotel called the Coit House, with facilities for swimming, boating, and fishing. When Jacob H. Silverthorn, genial tavern-keeper, took it over soon afterward, he made it a popular resort, competing with similar hotels at Nelson and Thompson ledges, Little Mountain, and Put-in-Bay. The Coit House had no bar, but oyster suppers brought it fame. Ladies correctly attired in the newest, long-sleeved, navy-blue or black bathing suits spent little time on the beach, handicapped as they were with knee bloomers and long skirts, stockings, and slippers. When the hotel closed in about 1878, Silverthorn went back to the cozy, white tavern on the West

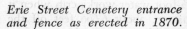
Erie Street Cemetery entrance and fence as erected in 1870.

Side. Here he served chicken dinners with an art that attracted buggy-riding Clevelanders and their best girls from a wide area.

An iron fence with a Gothic gateway was built around Erie Street Cemetery. The arch cost $8,296. Almost all of the lots had been sold as early as 1860.

When the Most Rev. Amadeus Rappe resigned as bishop of the Catholic Diocese of Cleveland in August, there were many evidences of his inspiring activities: an impressive cathedral, 137 churches—many with parochial schools, 4 institutions of higher learning, 5 orphanages, 4 convents, a home for the aged, and Charity Hospital. Petty jealousies on the part of groups that wanted to preserve the languages and customs of lands from whence they came led to charges against him, and he resigned his high office. After a visit to Rome, he became a missionary in Vermont. He was completely vindicated and offered another diocese by the Pope, but declined because of his advanced age. In 1877, he died a missionary at the age of seventy-six. His body was laid to rest in a crypt of St. John's Cathedral, which he built.

The Clarendon Hotel opened at the corner of St. Clair and Ontario Street, with John Barr, attorney, as proprietor. At times it was referred to as the St. Clair Place Hotel. W. J. Troy became proprietor in 1909 and named it Troy Hotel. In the 1940s, it was known by the original name which had been restored in 1915, and it was one of the oldest hotels in downtown Cleveland. Fred J. Woods managed it for the Hawleys, who gave it to him in recognition of his service.

Word that President Ulysses S. Grant was passing through the city brought out crowds and flags on August 16. Jeptha H. Wade entertained the distinguished visitor quietly in his magnificent Euclid Avenue home, presenting him with flowers and choice grapes from his famous garden. The chief executive declined to make a speech at the Kennard House.

A high, wrought-iron fence enclosed the stone mansion of wealthy Jeptha H. Wade on the northwest corner of Euclid and Case avenues, and the adjoining show place of his son, Randall. Ornate gate pillars reputedly cost a thousand dollars each. Widely separated on the spacious grounds, which extended northward to Perkins Avenue, were cottages for the coachman and the gardener. They remained long after the fabulous Wade residences had been razed. To the west was the home of T. S. Beckwith, dry-goods merchant, its tall, iron fence and stone pillars harmonizing with those of its neighbors. Many years later it housed the University Club.

Thousands of tons of stone loaded the 87½-foot water-works crib when it was anchored in 36 feet of water on August 17, about 6,600 feet off the lakeshore. A shaft was then sunk beneath the crib's center to about 90 feet, and a tunnel started shoreward to meet the one being built lakeward. Water meters were introduced this year.

The Cleveland Grays moved into an abandoned fire station on Frankfort Street, using it as an armory.

Byron D. Annewalt moved to Cleveland this year, and for a half century led in the development of the *City Directory* in Cleveland and in other Midwest cities. The local volume was published intermittently, however, until 1899, when Annewalt organized the Cleveland Directory Company.

The teaching of German, introduced in grammar and primary grades, was soon extended to all city schools. School districts were growing rapidly, and the policy of building "relief" structures was instituted. These small, frame buildings, each providing for two hundred and forty pupils, proved to be a temporary measure that was never abandoned.

Since 1859 the First Presbyterian Church (Old Stone) had fostered the Wasonville Sunday School in the vicinity of Charles W. Wason's car shops on St. Clair. From it stemmed North Presbyterian Church, named for the Old North Church of Boston and organized on September 19 of this year, with fifty-one charter members, all of whom came from the mother church. The Rev. Anson Smyth became the first pastor in 1872, when the Sunday School had an enrollment of a thousand. During the pastorate of Dr. William Gaston, North Church was erected at Case Avenue and Superior Avenue by the benevolent First Church, and dedicated in 1887.

The Young Men's Christian Association had been housed in various buildings around the Public Square until this year, when the dwelling of James F. Clarke on the north side of the Square (Society for Savings

Building site) was secured. Emphasis was placed on reform. Religion was carried to jails and the Infirmary, and open-air meetings were held on the Square and the lakefront.

Memorial Presbyterian Church, organized on October 2, originated in a small Sunday School that met in a grocery store under the care of the Euclid Street Presbyterian Church. Thirteen of its thirty-five members came from the mother church. The congregation struggled through the Panic of 1873, and in 1881 dedicated a substantial structure under a new name, Case Avenue Presbyterian Church, at Cedar and Case avenues. In later years the congregation joined with the Eells Memorial Church to form the Phillips Avenue Presbyterian Church.

The first fair held at the Northern Ohio Fair Grounds opened on October 4. Exhibitions ranged from fancy horses to inventions, crafts, and beautiful hair switches. Although the five-day event ran in competition with the state fair at Springfield and the county fair in Ashtabula, eighty-five thousand paid admissions pronounced it a greater success than the state undertaking. Sam Briggs, popular secretary and general manager, added sparkle to the annual affairs, but the project was doomed to financial failure and faded out in the winter of 1880-81. W. J. Gordon bought the buildings to house his cattle. He painted them yellow, and villagers called the colony Yellowtown.

The most severe earthquake shock recorded to date occurred on October 20, causing scores of chimneys to fall, horses to run away, and the fire-alarm system to go out of order.

Three Catholic parishes were organized this year: Annunciation for the French, on Hurd Street; St. Columbkille's, at Superior and Alabama; and Holy Family (later St. Edward's) for English-speaking Catholics, on Woodland Avenue. A little congregation of devout South Brooklyn followers attended services in members' homes in 1873, and later in a cooper shop, until their church was dedicated to the Sacred Heart of Mary (later Our Lady of Good Counsel) in 1875. St. Procop's, the second Catholic parish in a Czech community, was founded on Burton Street in 1875. The Rev. Joseph M. Koudelka, the first pastor, later became the bishop of Wisconsin and the first Czech raised to a bishopric in the United States. A beautiful house of worship was erected in 1907 at West 41st and Trent streets.

The United States Weather Bureau was established in Cleveland on November 1. The government weather table, printed for the first time, was of great value to lake interests.

The *Leader* staff rejoiced when the November 24 issue left the plant, for in it was this announcement: "As this is Thanksgiving, the *Leader* will not appear tomorrow morning."

One of the most extensive fires that the local Fire Department had been called upon to subdue occurred in the "Flats" on December 9, when the works of the Cleveland Iron Company were destroyed with a loss of $200,000.

Coal trade may be taken as a barometer of industrial advance. Coal receipts in Cleveland in 1865 exceeded those of 1860 three-fold; now they were 894,000 tons, nearly double the 1865 figure. Of the 1870 receipts, local industry consumed 411,610 tons. Much of the Massillon coal was still brought to the city by canal. Increased transportation facilities were badly needed, as the coal supply failed to keep pace with the demand. The manufacture of iron and steel had become a flourishing industry.

Oil won the race with iron for supremacy in Cleveland during the preceding decade of industrial transition, at the same time driving the candle and lard-oil business into obscurity. According to the federal census of 1870, 16 reporting companies with 209 employees had produced coal-oil products valued at $4,283,065; while the valuation of pig, forged, and rolled iron manufactured by 10 firms with 664 workers was only $2,688,784. Seventeen machinery firms, however, bore the largest payroll, $550,925 paid to 1,105 workers, whose output was valued at $1,175,515. Cooperage had grown with oil, and 63 firms with 606 employees had built a production total of $1,051,785. Although there were only 13 flour mills, their output had risen to $1,903,155. Meat packing came to the forefront, and 5 firms reported products valued at $1,261,870. Iron castings skyrocketed from $74,170 in 1860 to $1,097,000, with only 12 firms operating. The clothing industry, employing 528 workers, totaled $588,389 in output, of which $77,644 represented a new industry, women's wear. The sewing-machine industry had grown to $290,000, iron stoves to $270,000, and paint and varnish to $267,400. Fifty-five water-wheels were producing 2,179 horsepower, and 274 steam engines, 9,388. The 1,149 firms reporting in 54 industrial classifications represented a capital investment of $13,645,018; materials valued at $16,861,357, and products valued at $27,049,012. Wages totaling $4,539,065 had been paid to 10,063 employees.

1871

The Work House and the House of Correction were removed from the Infirmary on January 1 and centered in a new $250,000 building on Woodland Avenue (at East 79th). The first Board of Directors consisted of Harvey Rice, J. H. Wade, George H. Burt, S. C. Brooks, and William Edwards. The property was abandoned in 1912 when new buildings were provided on the Cooley Farms in Warrensville.

In the pleasant home of James and Meribah Farmer, at Superior and Bond Street (Hotel Hollenden site), the idea of a Friends Church was born. Here a few elderly people worshiped after the manner of the early Friends. As the number grew, the home of Alton Pope became the meeting place, then the YMCA Building on the Square, and, in 1872, the Swedenborgian Church at Prospect and Huntington Street. The aid and guidance of James Farmer, banker and railroad promoter, went into the modest church erected on Cedar Avenue near Blair Street. Traditionally, there was no "hired ministry" and no instrumental music. Friends spoke as they were "moved" and sang when led. Meetings of these peaceful, earnest folk concluded when Elder Farmer shook hands with his neighbor to the left, inspiring general handshaking and adjournment. With the coming of J. Walter Malone in 1880, the Society of Friends grew and services broadened.

RES. OF J.P. KIRTLAND, EAST ROCKPORT, CUYAHOGA CO. OHIO.

Dr. Jared P. Kirtland's home in 1873 from an old lithograph. The house was standing at 14013 Detroit Avenue in the 1940s.

The Public Square in 1873 when Cleveland was known as the "Forest City."

The Spirit of '76, America's greatest patriotic painting.

Archibald M. Willard, the wagon painter, whose impressive picture first inspired Americans when shown at the International Centennial Exposition in Philadelphia in 1876.

Nathan and Esther Frame, his successors, served well for several years. Malone and his wife, Emma B., started the Cleveland Bible Institute in 1892, and then came the founding of missions. South Cleveland built a meeting place in 1918 after nine years of planning, and missions were started on Union Street and Clark Avenue. The Malones returned as pastors, 1908-17, and became pastors emeritus. They were succeeded by others who enlarged the church and increased its influence. Pastor Malone died in 1935. The First Friends Church moved to Superior Avenue at Melbourne Road, East Cleveland, in 1932. The Rev. Amos N. Henry succeeded Dr. Walter R. Williams as pastor in 1944.

J. E. Upson and J. W. Walton formed a partnership on February 1 to carry on the business of ship chandlers and grocers in the Winslow Building on River Street, a stone's throw from Moses Cleaveland's landing place in 1796. In their late twenties, the young men had been clerks in W. Bingham & Company. When Henry Lyman joined the firm in 1878, the name was changed to Upson-Walton & Company, with assets of $14,000. Incorporation as The Upson-Walton Company came in 1893. Upson, the first president, was succeeded by Walton, in turn followed by Oliver Upson, C. H. Mathews, O. C. Kiehne, and Glenn H. Sheldon. The ship-chandlery business grew, expanding into general jobbing in northern Ohio, distributing and selling wire rope, manila rope, tackle blocks, fittings, and related items. During World War I, the Cleveland Block Company, tackle-block makers, was purchased. At about this time, The Upson-Walton Company of New York was formed, making wire rope at the Belleville, New Jersey, plant until 1942, when it moved to Cleveland. In 1926 the Cleveland factory moved to 12500 Elmwood Avenue. Jobbing was gradually eliminated. Upson-Walton, a world-wide distributor, became the only company in the country combining manufacture of wire rope, tackle blocks, and rope fittings, and it operated the only wire-rope mill in Ohio. In the 1940s the marine department still served lake shipping from the original location on the river, 1310 West 11th Street.

According to the famed evangelist, Dwight L. Moody, a shipwreck off the Cleveland harbor inspired P. P. Bliss, author of gospel songs, to write *Let the Lower Lights Be Burning,* with music by Ira D. Sankey. The song, published this year, was prefaced by this extract from a Moody sermon: "On a dark, stormy night, when the waves rolled like mountains and not a star was to be seen, a boat, rocking and plunging, neared the Cleveland harbor. 'Are you sure this is Cleveland?' asked the captain, seeing only one light from the lighthouse. 'Quite sure, sir,' replied the pilot. 'Where are the lower lights?' 'Gone out, sir!' 'Can you make the harbor?' 'We must, or perish, sir!' And with a strong hand and a brave heart, the old pilot turned the wheel. But alas, in the darkness he missed the channel, and with a crash upon the rocks the boat was shivered, and many a life was lost in a watery grave. Brethren, the Master will take care of the great lighthouse; let us keep the lower lights burning!"

S. H. Laman opened the Empire Hotel on Water Street, opposite the lighthouse and near the depot. The four-story, brick house had only sixty rooms, but it was considered one of the leading hotels until the eighties, when its popularity declined with the district. Its day of usefulness ended in 1900.

German citizens opened their Peace Jubilee with a concert in Case Hall on April 8, celebrating the end of the Franco-Prussian War. Streets were gay with decorations, and on the Square an elaborate triumphal arch was erected. An historical pageant, two miles long, concluded the event on the 10th.

In a little, frame building on Quincy Avenue, John N. Fuller started the Fuller Carpet Cleaning Works. The business boasted "pick-up" service, conducted by a driver with a two-horse wagon, and the first-year's sales reached $10,000. In 1905, a new plant was erected (at 7606 Carnegie Avenue), complete with power weaving looms. Two vacuum wagons were added to the equipment that cleaned rugs on the customer's parlor floor. A four-story building went up on the same site in 1918, trebling cleaning facilities and making Fuller's one of the ten largest cleaning plants in the world. In 1945, upon the death of Charles F. Bryan, president of The Fuller Cleaning & Dyeing Company since 1936, R. Arthur Bryan became the head of the half-million-dollar concern.

Henry Chisholm gave a tenth of all he possessed toward construction of a new building for the Erie Street Baptist Church at the southwest corner of Euclid and Huntington Street. It was dedicated this year. The name was changed to The Second Baptist Church of Cleveland, and again in 1877 to Euclid Avenue Baptist Church. John D. Rockefeller became superintendent of the Sunday School in about 1872, serving until 1905, assisted by others. The annual Sunday School picnic was the big event of the year, when teachers and scholars migrated to the Rockefeller home at Case Avenue, and in later years enjoyed chestnut hunts on the Forest Hill estate. The wealthy oil man was a trustee and financial pillar of the church, and for many years matched members' contributions dollar for dollar.

An experiment in laying macadam pavement topped with stone was begun on Superior Avenue at the Square. The process was also tried on other principal streets, and a steam roller was purchased the next year; but Medina sandstone remained the choice of the city engineer.

The office of city auditor was created, and Thomas Jones, Jr., was elected to serve as the watchdog of the municipal treasury.

Samuel Barker opened a small printing business in a room on River Street on June 7, equipped with two small presses, a little steam engine, hand cutter, and stationery stock. The business grew and moved to St. Clair Avenue, where, in 1890, Raymond H. Barker joined his father and began to expand the office-supply-and-equipment department. In 1911 The S. Barker's Sons Company was incorporated, with the son as president-treasurer, and Alice M. Barker, secretary. After several moves, a four-story building was erected at 729 Prospect Avenue in 1922 as headquarters for one of the leading office-equipment firms in northern Ohio.

Horace Greeley, a great national figure, lectured in Case Hall, July 5, on *Texas and the Lower Mississippi*. At this time he was planning for his presidential campaign the next year. Greeley was badly defeated. This misfortune and the death of his wife were more than he could bear, and he died insane, November 29, 1872.

General James Barnett became president of The Geo. Worthington Company, succeeding the founder, who died this year at the age of fifty-eight. The hardware store, erected at St. Clair and Water streets in 1868, burned in 1874 and was rebuilt on the same site. W. D. Taylor became president upon the death of General Barnett in 1911, followed by Hugh E. Hulburd in 1936, who joined the firm in 1889. Founded in 1829, Worthington was Cleveland's oldest company a century later in point of continuous existence under its original name. Floor space had been gradually enlarged to twenty acres, as the business grew to be one of the nation's largest wholesale hardware firms. A. G. Rorabeck, in 1947, succeeded Hulburd as president.

The first Board of Park Commissioners, created on August 22, consisted of Dr. Azariah Everett, president; Oscar A. Childs, and John H. Sargent. Prior to this time, the Council controlled public grounds and granted small sums to committees for specific park improvements.

The Mahoning Valley coal fields had been depleted, and the Valley Railway Company was organized on August 31 to build a railroad from Cleveland to Canton via Akron into the Massillon mining district. Work began in 1873, but depression times halted progress, and the road did not open until February, 1880. The line entered Cleveland by way of the abandoned canal bed, which the State had deeded to the City of Cleveland on November 3, 1879, on condition that a weighlock be built at the new junction between the canal and the river. The Valley road leased the canal bed the next day, the city receiving in payment $265,000 in the railway's first mortgages. Voters repudiated an attempt to make the city part owner, and J. H. Wade, N. P. Payne, S. T. Everett, L. M. Coe, and others raised $500,000 to make the road possible. The passenger station was at the foot of Water Street, and the freight terminal was located on Columbus Street. A branch was built from Willow to Newburgh in 1894, and the next year the Valley was back in receivership. M. R. Dickey, W. F. Carr, James Bartol, C. H. Gale, and F. H. Goff organized the Cleveland Terminal and Valley Railroad and purchased the property in 1895. The Baltimore & Ohio Railroad became financially interested in it, operating the line as a part of its system after 1909. In 1915 it purchased the Valley properties.

William Heydler, son of Gottlieb Heydler, who organized early community choral societies, opened the Cleveland Conservatory of Music in September. Heydler was an accomplished musician who had studied in Europe, and the loosely knit private-teaching arrangement in his institution included John Hart, instructor in violin and harmony, and John Underner, singing. John Nuss, talented violinist, succeeded Hart. He was followed by his pupil, Charles Heydler, who became a leading cellist, and other able musicians, including William Schramm, George Layman, John Marquardt, and Sol Marcosson. Musical soirées were presented through united effort.

The Board of Education operated the Public School Library until October 2, 1871, when it elected a Board of Library Managers to assume management.

Control reverted to the original board two years later, however, when four members of the library board resigned.

Popularity of the ice-skating rink led to construction of the Central Rink about this time. It was a pretentious, 210 by 90-foot brick structure on the site of the Winslow home on the south side of the Public Square, standing well back from the sidewalk. As a rink, it was moderately successful for two seasons; then it served large assemblies until it was razed to make way for the Kresge Company store.

Flames started in Mrs. O'Leary's barn on October 8, causing the great four-day Chicago fire, destroying 18,000 buildings, with an estimated loss of $196,000,000. Within two days, Clevelanders aided sufferers with money and thirteen carloads of clothing and provisions. A number of insurance companies became bankrupt and others were forced to close. In later years, the week containing the fire anniversary was designated as Fire Prevention Week.

When the *Sunday Morning Voice,* founded by W. Scott Robison, appeared on October 15, clergymen denounced it from their pulpits, and blue-law merchants refused to buy advertising space. Harry L. Vail edited the family paper that featured the latest political news, quaint humor and illustrations, helps for the housewife, weather reports headed "probabilities," reports of City Council meetings, book reviews, and scandals. The first church notices were confined to the Universalist Church. Colonel Orlando J. Hodge, who purchased the paper in 1878, relates that in a sermon on spiritual power, the pastor of the Old Stone Church had reached a dramatic climax with the query, "There is one thing more you need. What is it?" He paused as for a reply, when outside a newsboy's voice split the Sunday morning quiet with "The *Sunday Voice!*" Later, Robison issued the *Sunday Sun,* which also fell into the hands of Hodge in 1885, resulting in the *Sun and Voice,* which became the *Sunday Voice.* The paper enjoyed popularity until competition of the dailies' Sunday editions forced it from the field. Among its staff members were George Hoyt, C. C. Ruthrauff, E. C. Hardy, George A. Robertson, W. R. Rose, William E. Sage, H. H. Burgess, and Franklin E. Denton.

Rising to a position of influence had not come easy for Orlando J. Hodge, who worked out his passage on a steamboat when he came to Cleveland from New York State in 1842. In 1847, at the age of eighteen, he enlisted for Mexican War duty. Returning to Cleveland, he became a salesman in a crockery store, the city's first police clerk, and later city editor of the *Plain Dealer.* He was elected to the City Council in 1871, serving three terms, and became its president in 1885. For eight years he was a member of the Ohio Assembly and speaker of the House. Hodge gave freely of his time to humanitarian and civic effort, serving as president of the Early Settlers Association, 1903-11.

In a flourishing West Side community, the Rev. Lewis Burton, rector of St. John's Episcopal Church, began to hold services at "Stone's Addition." A chapel was built on Vega Avenue near Scranton Road, and All Saints Parish was organized this year. The congregation struggled through years of adversity, and laid the cornerstone of a new building in 1886. Many prominent families were identified with the house of worship at Mentor Avenue and Scranton Road. Rev. Burton also founded a mission in 1871 from which grew St. Mark's Parish.

The National Chess Congress, held in the Kennard House, December 6-15, attracted worldwide attention. First prize went to J. H. MacKenzie of New York and second prize to a Mr. Hosmer of Chicago. At this time, the American Chess Association was organized to promote the game and arrange tournaments.

General J. H. Devereux and a party of distinguished citizens went by train to Willoughby to meet a special train carrying the Grand Duke Alexis of Russia and his imperial party to Cleveland for a visit. Thousands waited on the hill, and the Union Depot was crowded as Mayor F. W. Pelton escorted the regal company through an honor guard of Cleveland Grays. The big band never played better, but its music was almost drowned by wild cheers. From the Kennard House balcony, the mayor introduced the royal guest to the crowd below. The towering duke bowed respectfully—but said never a word.

As superintendent of military railroads during the Civil War, General John Henry Devereux made an enviable record that qualified him to become general superintendent and vice president of the Cleveland & Pittsburgh Railroad in 1869, and at the same time, president of the strategic Lake Shore & Michigan Southern. Devereux' stature in railroading increased in 1876 when he became president of the Atlantic & Great Western and the Cleveland, Columbus, Cincinnati & Indianapolis lines. While he took an active interest in public affairs, he twice refused the nomination for Congress. In 1873 he built a homestead of fine architecture in "Millionaires' Row" (3226 Euclid Avenue). Years later, it was converted into the Fine Arts Building, and in the 1940s it was providing quarters for artists, musicians, and writers.

The first Inventors Exhibition opened December 27 in the Central Rink and continued for almost a month and a half. On display were 1,500 entries, including machinery and "curiosities of science and the arts." The central attraction was a "talking machine," the invention of Professor Faber of Vienna. Resembling a piano, it was built on the principle of the human throat, and could utter Hebrew phrases as well as English, after a most peculiar fashion. Six years later, Thomas A. Edison patented his phonograph, the first practical device for recording and reproducing sound.

1872

Captain Thomas Wilson, who came of a seafaring family in Scotland, launched his freight-transportation business with a single ship, the 757-ton *D. M. Wilson,* named for his baby son. It was a wooden vessel built at St. Clair, Michigan, the first in the Wilson Transit Company fleet that became one of the oldest on the lakes. The *Spokane,* the lakes' first steel steamer, was built for Wilson in 1886. The company pioneered in safety developments, introducing electric lights on the *Yakima* in 1887; the gyro compass in 1924, patented hatch covers in 1925, and radio telephone in 1934 on the *William C. Atwater*. In the 1940s the black hulls, white superstructure, and large "W" on the stacks identified twelve ships in the fleet, of which Captain Joseph Sutherland Wood, a leader in the industry, had been president since 1929.

Edward A. Sothern and a brilliant company presented *Our American Cousin* at the Academy of Music, February 12. Lord Dundreary had been played by Sothern more than 3,500 times, and it was a household word. In the early seventies the playhouse was at the height of its fame. James O'Neill, tragedian, whose son, Eugene, became a modern dramatist, played leading roles and went on to fame as Edmond Dantes in *Monte Cristo*. Edwin Forrest appeared in a round of his famous Shakespearean tragedies and produced crowded houses. "Uncle John" Ellsler's interest, however, was turning to the building of his new Euclid Avenue Opera House, which opened in 1875. He transferred to it the stock company, and the Academy played vaudeville until 1878, when he returned it to the "legitimate," hoping to recover losses incurred by the new house. Grand opera and top-flight stars played here, among them Janauschek, Frank Mayo, Frederick Warde, Marie Geistinger, Annie Pixley, and Kate Claxton. Ellsler proved a poor financier, however, and although B. C. Hart tried his hand as manager, the fine old theater continued down-hill. In 1887 "Old Drury," as it was sometimes called, became the Cleveland Variety Theater; later in the year it opened as James Doyle's Winter Garden; early in 1888, Phillips New Casino Theater; in June, the Theater Comique; and in September, 1888, after a series of failures, it again bore the famous name, Academy of Music. On June 30, 1889, it was partially destroyed by fire, but was rebuilt and opened as a vaudeville house.

By act of March 7, control of the Police Department was established in a Board of Police Commissioners, consisting of the mayor and four members elected by the people. The first commission consisted of Charles A. Otis, Dr. J. C. Schenck, John M. Sterling, Dr. J. E. Robinson, and George Saal. Seven precincts were designated, and 318 miles of streets were patrolled with thirty-seven day and sixty-two night beats. Headquarters operated in five station houses, a rented room, and two jails. The three-story, brick building erected in 1864 on Champlain Street continued as the center of operations downtown; and in the rear was the two-story, stone jail with sixty cells. In the seventies, Cleveland merchants doubled their vigilance by employing "merchant police."

An orchestra trained by Alfred F. Arthur gave the first symphony concert in Cleveland on March 7. Mrs. Nellie Glaser was the soloist. Her son, Vaughan, became Cleveland's most popular actor in the Vaughan Glaser Stock Company after the turn of the century. Arthur had come to Cleveland in 1871, with a background of study in Boston conservatories and with teachers abroad. He and William B. Colson, Jr., opened a studio in the Cushing Block. For several months, Arthur was engaged as soloist at Trinity Church; then he became choir master at the Euclid Avenue Baptist Church.

William F. "Buffalo Bill" Cody was the star in Ned Buntline's production, *Buffalo Bill, King of the Border Men,* at the Academy of Music in March. At the first performance, the leading man forgot his lines; and Buntline, realizing that he had stage fright, came to his rescue, but the performance was ruined. The next morning, a newspaper critic observed, "If it really took Ned Buntline six hours to write *Buffalo Bill,* I wonder how he managed to fill in the time." Nevertheless, seven performances were played to capacity audiences.

At a meeting of the Young Men's Christian Association in a "church" corner in the Union Depot, provided by Station Agent George Myers, Henry W. Stager, a blustering train dispatcher on the Lake Shore road, envisioned Christian effort devoted to railroad men. Tirelessly he worked until April 14, this year, when the first Railroad YMCA was dedicated in Cleveland. From this humble beginning developed the worldwide Railroad "Y." G. W. Cobb was the first secretary.

The Rt. Rev. Richard Gilmour was consecrated second bishop of the Diocese of Cleveland in Cincinnati on April 14. Born in Glasgow, Scotland, in 1824, his family had come to America when he was a small boy. After his schooling, he wrote a *Bible History* of short stories for young people that became a text-book in the Catholic schools. When Bishop Gilmour came to Cleveland, he found the jealous factions and anti-Catholic bigotry that had troubled his predecessor still active. Tactfully and forcefully he went to work; and, during his regime, he made such progress that the diocese became one of the most important in the United States. In nineteen years, sixty-six new churches and many parochial schools were built. He founded the Convent of the Poor Clares and the Ursuline Academy at Villa Angela, 1877; St. Alexis Hospital and the Protectory for Girls in charge of the Sisters of Notre Dame, 1884; St. Joseph's Seminary, opened by the Ursulines at Nottingham for the education of boys, 1886. Cleveland was enriched with benefactions that originated in his public-spirited endeavors. Bishop Gilmour died in 1891, and the memorial service attended by people of all religious beliefs was one of the most impressive in the city's history. Gilmour Avenue bears the name of this great man.

The City Council gave to the Park Board a $5,000 budget with which to lay out and beautify the Public Square, and this was amplified by a $30,000 bond issue authorized in August. Soon the "dilapidated open space . . . a sort of public receptacle for dirt" began to show gratifying results of the spending spree. An artificial pond was created in the southwest section, with a waterfall that tumbled into a pool nestled in a rock garden below. Over it a quaint bridge was built. Circling the fountain in the upper pool was the *E. B. Nock,* a three-foot, working model of a steamboat, said to have been constructed by Captain Lorenzo A. Kelsey. It was a Public Square institution until 1905, when it was removed, and later preserved by the Western Reserve Historical Society. Nock, for whom the boat was named, was an Ontario Street photographer. In the northeast section of the Square, under the tall, shady trees, a large rustic pavilion was built of logs and bark-covered branches, over which creeping vines trailed. Flowers bloomed from hanging boxes, and a platform served as the stage for public events for many years.

A circular basin with a lily fountain was moved from Franklin Circle, West Cleveland, to the northwest section of the Public Square this year. Franklin Street was extended through the Circle, a stone pavilion was built, new shrubs and walks were added as well as a speaker's rostrum, and the area was nicknamed "Modoc Park." Tradition says that Mark Hanna first heard young William McKinley speak at a meeting here. Distinguished citizens built fine homes in the vicinity, among them Daniel Warmington, Daniel P. Rhodes, the Dexters, Marcus A. Hanna, James F. Rhodes, and John H. Sargent. The Circle lost much of its charm when Tom Johnson's Forest City street railway was run through it in 1907-8, and its importance as a social center dwindled.

The Lighthouse, as rebuilt in 1872, replacing a much smaller structure.

The German Baptist Publication Society moved to Cleveland, locating on Forest Street, and later on Payne Avenue. During the year, the *Anzeiger,* a German paper, was founded. In 1891 it absorbed two new ventures, the *Germania* and the *Deutsche Presse.*

Ole Bull, famed Norwegian violinist, gave his farewell Cleveland concert in Case Hall on May 3, the last of a dozen or more appearances.

The lighthouse tower, on Water Street north of Lake, was replaced by a more modern structure 83 feet high and towering 157 feet above the level of the lake. Two keepers' houses were erected as a part of the project, the total cost being $55,725. The white light was visible for twenty miles, and 300 gallons of "mineral oil" were required annually to operate it. The Whitakers, Waltons, and Whittleseys lived near the light, and around the corner on Lake Street were the homes of the Crawfords, Ranneys, Yateses, Bradfords, and General James Barnett.

The Jefferson Street Bridge was built, the finest in the city, at a cost of

$39,275. It had a canal span of 117 feet. In 1907, it was replaced by an electric rolling lift bridge.

Central Way opened under the Cleveland & Wheeling tracks, carrying the heavy traffic of refineries and iron mills. The flood of 1883 destroyed the wooden drawbridge in lower Central Way, and a 200-foot iron bridge replaced it the same year. Electricity was installed in 1917 in the thoroughfare which had become known as the Upper West 3rd Street Bridge.

Cleveland was normally Republican, the retiring mayor being Frederick W. Pelton, and the Democrats were determined to win the coming election. Willie Edouin, of the Lydia Thompson troupe, was playing in the city during the vigorous contest between John Huntington, Republican, and Charles A. Otis, Democrat. One night, after a dozen verses of his song, *If Ever I Cease to Love,* Edouin injected a shot at the campaign:

> Which I wish to give notice
> Your next mayor is Otis!

With these lines there was a whoop from the audience, and Otis was on his way to victory.

Memories of Perry's historic rescue of the Great Lakes from the British in 1813 were revived when a priceless relic was placed on the Public Square near Perry's Monument on July 2 with a placard reading, "Thirty-six pounder surrendered by Capt. Robert Barclay to Commodore Perry in the Battle of Lake Erie. Property of the Western Reserve Historical Society." Two days later, it was the feature of the Fourth of July celebration. Across Superior Avenue on the southwest section of the Square, a Civil War field piece with high wheels was mounted. Eventually, the Park Board gave the Perry gun a carriage but never a fixed location, although it always remained on the Public Square.

"The most elegant photograph studio in this country, if not in the world" was opened by James F. Ryder on Superior Avenue, east of Seneca, August 11. The building was gaily painted, and a large display window was set in a handsome, iron front. Pictures of all kinds were exhibited in spacious art galleries, with frescoed walls and ceilings. Up the broad stairs was the photographic studio, and everyone of prominence had his likeness preserved by Ryder. Sitting for a photograph was more or less of an ordeal. The subject was seated before the camera—a huge, mahogany contraption with flowing, black hood, and two adjustable prongs supported by a metal pedestal were adjusted to the back of the head. Thus the subject was held in a steady position at the desired angle, and it was no wonder that a frozen, self-conscious expression generally registered. Near the end of the century, Ryder retired and closed his famous gallery, after having photographed "over a million faces," including those of several Presidents.

Associated with James F. Ryder for a time was his brother, John H., who later opened a photographic studio of his own near by (211 Superior, N.W.). Marking his establishment at the curb was "Smiling Solly," a hitching post fashioned as the replica of a Negro boy's head. Many years later, it was mounted on the beautiful lawn of the Western Reserve Historical Society on East Boulevard.

A Protection Company, consisting of four men and a wagon, was formed by the Fire Department in August. It was equipped with canvas covers and apparatus for protecting property from water damage.

"Live and Let Live" was the slogan by which Tom Larter gained fame for his restaurant on the south side of Superior near Bank Street. George W. Perkins, then operating a school-supply store in Cleveland, was a patron of Larter's. As a partner of J. Pierpont Morgan and one of the world's great financiers, he liked to recall that "no boy with three cents needed to go hungry at Larter's, and I would sit on a high stool there and swing my short legs between young bank clerks of the neighborhood. Some of these young men later became presidents of banks themselves, while all of the others became vice presidents!"

Co-education was prevalent in western colleges, and women had been admitted to Oberlin since its founding. Upon his inauguration as president of Western Reserve College (later Western Reserve University and Western Reserve Academy), Carroll Cutler announced that women would be permitted to enter on an equal status with men. In the autumn, several girls enrolled in the preparatory school, and a young woman was admitted to the freshman class in the college in 1874. The decade of the seventies witnessed a long battle for survival, and the student body averaged only sixty-five; yet some of Reserve's graduates brought honor to their alma mater, particularly John H. Clarke, who became a member of the United States Supreme Court.

The Cleveland Wire Works was established by Washington S. Tyler, a native of Ohio City, born in 1835. His father, Royal W. Tyler, a New Englander, owned considerable property in northeastern Ohio, and, after a brief residence here, the family moved back to Connecticut. However, the son foresaw opportunities in Cleveland and returned, finding a position with E. I. Baldwin & Company, where he later became a partner. His wire-works venture was due to practical vision, and the organization bearing his name grew from a two-story, frame building to a plant that occupied eight acres. In the meantime, he quietly performed acts of philanthropy, taking particular pride in starting young men on successful careers. Tyler served on the boards of charitable and educational institutions and helped them with counsel and financial backing. He died in 1917, but The W. S. Tyler Company that he founded continued to grow, producing woven wire screens, screening machinery, elevator entrances, elevator cars, and other products marketed throughout the world. There were four branch offices in 1946 besides the Cleveland headquarters at 3615 Superior Avenue. The company's president was E. P. Disbro.

The *Empress,* a luxurious sleeping car built in Philadelphia at a cost of $55,000, went into service on the Cleveland, Columbus, Cincinnati & Indianapolis Railroad. Three additional cars were on order.

William Chisholm, Henry Chisholm, Amasa Stone, A. B. Stone, and H. B. Payne, Newburgh mill owners, founded the Union Steel Screw Company with capital of $1,000,000. Their factory, at the southeast corner

of Case and Payne avenues, was the only one in the country making wood
screws from Bessemer steel. Later bolts, rods, nails, tacks, and other fasteners
were produced. The National Screw & Tack Company, forerunner of the
National Screw & Manufacturing Company, acquired the pioneer company
in 1908.

A certain group in the Cleveland Club, organized on January 3 this year
with quarters on Ontario Street, felt that sports and cards should not
predominate. Consequently, "60 or 70 of the most companionable and
cultured gentlemen" organized The Union Club of Cleveland on September
25 for the promotion of "physical training and education." William Bingham

First Union Club building.

was the first president. The beautiful Euclid Avenue home of the late
George B. Senter was purchased for $60,000 for a clubhouse. It was the two-
story, brick mansion built by Truman P. Handy about 1842 "out in the
woods"; but now it nestled deep in its lawn, still dominated by five, massive,
stone pillars (Hippodrome Building site). The Union Club became one of the
most important social organizations in the West, uniting men of influence
and ambition as a social and intellectual force in the community. From the
Union Club stemmed much of Cleveland's future greatness.

Carelessness of workmen while repairing the roof of the Northern Ohio
Hospital for the Insane in Newburgh is said to have started a fire on
September 26 that cost several lives and destroyed the building. Nearly
five hundred patients were rescued with great difficulty, and housed in
charitable institutions. The Dayton hospital cared for them until a substantial

building was erected. The name was changed at intervals as the structure was improved and enlarged, and it was eventually known as the Cleveland State Hospital on Turney Road.

"Epizootic" attacked horses in October, bringing Cleveland transportation practically to a standstill for some weeks.

In a growing Czech settlement, a rural district centering at Broadway and Willson Avenue, the Broadway Methodist Church was founded, originating in a humble, frame "wigwam" at Trumbull Street and Warren Alley. Its influence in interpreting the American way of life to newcomers cannot be estimated. Over the years, the area expanded and became densely settled, semi-industrial and semi-residential, the fourth largest Czech community in the world. In the early 1920s, a large church building was erected at 5246 Broadway to meet growing religious, social, and community needs. In 1946, the Rev. Joseph Kenney, pastor, was still conducting a Sunday-morning service in the Czech language.

Twenty-two Cleveland men formed the Excelsior Club (later the Oakwood Club), a "social and intellectual" organization, at Halle's Hall on Superior Avenue on October 20. Solomon Austrian was the first president. Important contributions were made to civic, charitable, and social undertakings.

Many East Cleveland citizens were content in their village government, and the proposed annexation to Cleveland won by a majority of only seventy votes. By ordinance of October 24, the area outlined roughly by Willson, Quincy, a line east of Doan, and another north of Superior came into the city. East Cleveland High School (Bolton School site) continued with only a change in name as East High School, Cleveland's third secondary school. Dr. Elroy M. Avery, who had been superintendent of the East Cleveland schools, became principal; and Mrs. Avery, formerly the high-school principal, became his assistant. From this time, the district beyond Willson Avenue developed more rapidly.

Case Hall was crowded on December 30 when the West Side Dickens Club presented *Mr. Pickwick and His Friends*. Leading citizens portrayed the characters, among them Marcus A. Hanna as Mr. Pickwick, Clarence Lewis, and Tony Weller.

1873

Charles A. Otis had returned from Europe, where he studied steel-making, and, with W. S. C. Otis and E. B. Thomas, he organized The Otis Iron & Steel Company. Capital was $300,000, and Charles A. Otis was elected president. The first plant was an industrial wonder, built on the lakeshore (at East 33rd Street), the site of the great Lakeside Plant of later years. It consisted of two seven-ton acid open-hearth furnaces, plate, bar, and guide mills, and forging hammers. The Otis company was the first in America, if not in the world, formed solely to make acid open-hearth steel. Samuel T. Wellman, twenty-six-year-old engineer, who was designing and building industrial furnaces in the East, was hired to build the new steel works. The company sent him to Europe to study steel-making, and in 1880, shortly after his return, the first basic open-hearth steel produced in America was turned out at the Otis mill, the process continuing in general use. English interests purchased control in 1889, reorganizing the firm as The Otis Steel Company, Ltd., but leaving the management under George Bartol, who came to Otis in 1879 and became president in 1898. When reorganized as an Ohio corporation in 1912 with $5,000,000 capital, the name was changed to The Otis Steel Company.

Charles A. Otis, founder of the Otis Steel empire, was born at Bloomfield, Ohio, in 1827, the son of William A. Otis, Cleveland's pioneer ironmaster. He grew up with the industry, launching a business of his own in 1852, and heading the Otis works until 1898. Otis served as mayor in 1873-74 and gave an admirable administration. He declined to accept a second nomination and concluded his political career. He became president of the Commercial National Bank in 1894, resigning when he retired from business in 1904, the year before he died. He was a founder of the American Wire Company (later American Steel & Wire Company), and was interested in the Standard Sewing Machine Company, American Steel Screw Company, Cleveland Electric Railway Company, and Society for Savings. Otis was a rare combination of keen business ability and enthusiastic spirit, and Cleveland profited greatly through his progressive leadership. The big, brick residence of the Otis family became the home of John Huntington Polytechnic Institute, 3133 Euclid Avenue. Across the street, at 3146 Euclid, was the plain, three-story residence of George Hall, piano merchant, that in the 1940s bore the name, Cleveland Osteopathic Hospital.

Stillman Witt gave a large sum toward the second boarding home of the Women's Christian Association (YWCA), to house fifty-five girls. Years later, the words, "Stillman Witt Boarding Home," remained in the stone over the 18th Street entrance to the YWCA Central Building.

Professor Gustavus A. Hyde, the city's weather authority, claimed that January 29 was the coldest day of record in Cleveland, 20° below zero. The United States Signal Service reported 15°, and a compromise was finally reached at 17° below zero.

Portions of Brooklyn, industrial Newburgh, and East Cleveland townships were annexed to Cleveland on February 8, expanding the city eastward to a line just beyond Woodland Hills Avenue; on the south, to Union Street and Storer Avenue; and on the west, to Buffalo Street. An additional portion of Newburgh was annexed on December 8.

Although Newburgh became known as the "iron ward" after the annexation, it held fast to its traditional name. There was little of beauty for the homefolks to boast about. Roads were rutted, and modest houses were grimy with smoke from the mills and the railroad that ran through the heart of the village; but to Welsh, Irish, and Scotch families, Newburgh was home. There was a spirit that bound the citizenship together, born, perhaps, of sweat and toil in the hot mills, or of clannish fellowship, as many were newcomers to America.

Out of the Newburgh mills came William R. Hopkins, later city manager of Cleveland, and his famous brothers. Harry L. Davis rose to be governor of Ohio and mayor of Cleveland. Dr. John Toomey, foremost authority on infantile paralysis, grew up in Newburgh and worked in the mills. Tom Jenkins, mill worker and wrestler, became a national figure and later wrestling instructor at West Point. John Boyle, county treasurer, was a water boy. Thomas Coughlin, president of the Bank of Ohio, and William J. Corrigan and Harry B. Howells, attorneys, started in the mills. Al Rumsey, a Newburgh policeman, became shipping master of the Lake Carriers Association. A pictorial record of old Newburgh was preserved by W. R. Dunbar, of the Provident Savings & Loan Association, veteran of the community.

James Gordon Bennett of the *New York Herald* had stirred the world with the dramatic story of how Henry M. Stanley found David Livingstone in the wilds of Central Africa on November 10, 1871. Stanley gave his famous lecture, *How I Found Dr. Livingstone,* in Cleveland on February 17, 1873, and captivated listeners paid seventy-five cents to hear the story of his spectacular journalistic feat that climaxed with the famous words, "Mr. Livingstone, I presume." The explorer returned twice during the winter of 1896-97 to tell of his momentous discoveries in the dark continent.

The literary light of the western mining camps, Bret Harte, thirty-four, lectured to an appreciative audience in Case Hall on the evening of February 28. *The Argonauts of '49* was his subject, and he painted sketches of frontier towns, concluding with his story of the famous card game between Bill Nye, "Ah Sin," and himself, taken from *The Heathen Chinee,* which had carried his fame eastward from 'Frisco.

The Great Royal Japanese Troupe from the Imperial Theater of Yeddo appeared at Brainard's Opera House on February 28. The program announced the attraction as "Two Hundred Years in Advance of Any Performance Ever Seen."

The Brotherhood of Locomotive Engineers, organized in Detroit in 1863 as the Brotherhood of the Footboard, and reorganized in Indianapolis in 1864, moved its headquarters to Cleveland. P. M. Arthur, the first executive head, was succeeded by Warren S. Stone.

Fifty-three Cleveland lawyers met in the library of the Court House on March 22 to organize the Cleveland Bar Association, their purpose being "to maintain the honor and dignity of the profession . . . and to increase the usefulness of the members by aiding in the administration of justice and in the promotion of legal and judicial reforms." Sherlock J. Andrews, the first president, served until his death in 1880.

Although an ordinance had been passed in 1871 to prevent and punish cruelty to dumb animals, little attention was paid to it. On April 4, 1873, final steps were taken to organize the Cleveland Society for the Prevention of Cruelty to Animals, under the leadership of Orlando J. Hodge. General Jabez W. Fitch was elected president. An exhibition of implements of torture used in mistreating animals was displayed in a museum in the City Hall for years. The work of the society broadened to include protection of women and children, and the name was changed to the Cleveland Humane Society. Through Hodge's efforts, a state society was organized in 1874 with General Fitch as president.

Four Striebinger brothers opened the Striebinger House on Michigan Street, April 15. It flourished for two decades and became the stopping place for visiting show people and commercial men. For a time, Mark Lamb, well known in political and sporting circles, was the manager. In 1919 the hotel closed as the Terminal development was progressing.

Management of the Fire Department passed into the hands of a Board of Fire Commissioners, appointed on April 29 for five-year terms. The first board consisted of Charles A. Otis, mayor; A. T. VanTassel, chairman of the Council committee on fire and water; H. D. Coffinberry; W. H. Hayward; and H. W. Leutkemeyer. In 1876 the law was repealed, and four commissioners were elected for four-year terms.

The second Superior Court was created on May 5, with jurisdiction only for civil cases coming from the City of Cleveland, thus easing the burden of the Cuyahoga County Court of Common Pleas. At a special election, Seneca O. Griswold, James M. Jones, and G. M. Barber were elected judges. In 1875 relief was again needed as the tribunals were flooded with panic casualties, and the court was abolished. Its business was transferred to the Court of Common Pleas, and four judges were added to deal with the cumbersome docket.

The Park House was erected at the corner of Seneca and Summit streets, serving as a hotel until 1895. One of its first tenants was Dr. J. Weeks, who advertised, "Cancer cured without plaster or knife."

Late in the spring, Alfred F. Arthur became conductor of the Cleveland Vocal Society, newly organized by W. W. Andrews, president, John Mansfield, J. F. Isham, Hulbert and John Fulkerson, Alfred Darby, and G. A. Walter. The first concert, given at Brainard's Opera House on February 10, 1874, followed by another on May 5 in Case Hall, gave the society a good financial start. Programs of early years were made up entirely of part-songs and madrigals, sung a cappella or with piano. Annual festivals became more and more pretentious, featuring outstanding soloists and drawing large crowds from surrounding towns. Leading citizens headed the association— the Rev. Dr. John Wesley Brown of Trinity Church, T. P. Handy, J. F. Whitelaw, the Rev. Paul F. Sutphen, Charles F. Olney, and L. A. Osborn. Membership far exceeded one hundred, and Charles F. Brush was honorary president when the last concert was given at the Cleveland Chamber of Commerce, assisted by the Cleveland Orchestral Club, in May, 1902. To Alfred F. Arthur, musician and conductor, belongs high praise for excellence attained by the society through these years. Its valuable library became an addition to the Cleveland School of Music.

The grandniece of James Fenimore Cooper, Constance Fenimore Woolson, was born in New York City, but went to school in Cleveland. She came to the city this year, at the age of twenty-five, remaining until 1879; then her travels on two continents began, while she gathered realistic material for novels and poems that brought her international fame. Among them were

East Angels, Anne, Jupiter Lights, and *The Front Yard,* stories of Italy, where she spent much of her time. She died in 1894.

A mission fostered by Zion Evangelical Lutheran Church in the district east of Willson Avenue near Superior was the forerunner of St. Paul's Evangelical Church. Seven years later, a house of worship was dedicated. Membership grew as the community developed, and in 1873 a school was launched, providing education through the eight grades. A larger edifice on Willson Avenue (1486 East 55th), occupied in 1896, was serving the congregation a half century later, when membership had reached 1,400. The Rev. Theodore H. Dorn, pastor, had come to St. Paul's Evangelical Church in 1938.

There was a growing interest in the importance of park improvements, as evidenced by the first tax levy of two-tenths of a mill for the purchase of Lake View Park and improvement of the Public Square and Franklin Circle. The Park Board voted on June 9 to pay their clerk, Theodore Voges, $100 for his first fourteen-months' service, and his salary was placed at $150 per year. Two special park policemen and overseers were hired, subject to Council approval, at $80 per month; and a man was hired at $2 a day to keep Clinton Park in good condition. Drives and walks, fountains, and little lakes made Lake View Park a popular downtown breathing spot in the late seventies and the eighties. Bands entertained, and it was the favorite location in the city for picnics and outings. An iron picket fence separated the park from the railroad at the bottom of the slope to the north. The smoke of industry and commerce eventually shrouded the park, population shifted, and less money was spent on its care each year. Then the shore became a dump, increased by stretches of "made" land without a future.

John Sage, Cleveland newspaperman, a close friend of P. T. Barnum, was troubled because his little boy was ill and could not see the circus. Barnum asked that Johnny be at his window at two o'clock. At the appointed time, a brass band swept around the corner from Euclid north on Dodge Street, followed by a "golden chariot" filled with noise-making musicians. Next came a carriage in which the great showman was seated. As he passed the house, at the northeast corner of Payne and Dodge, he bowed to his audience at the window. Behind the shuffling elephant came the camels, ponies, and the rest of the pageantry of the "Greatest Show on Earth," while the clowns performed in the side yard. "It made me as happy as it did the boy," said Barnum, who gladdened the heart of little John C. Sage, later Episcopal bishop of Iowa.

L. E. Holden, William Halsey Doan, H. C. Ford, and Otis Boise purchased the Wright House at Euclid and Fairmount for $35,000 and closed the hotel bar. The historic tavern was then moved (to 10013 Cedar Avenue) and converted to residential and business use. In 1876, on the original site of the tavern, Holden began to erect the Fairmount Court Hotel, forerunner of the apartment hotel. It was built of brick, trimmed with stone, and fronted on Fairmount Street, overlooking the grove that became Wade Park. Prominent families made it their home. From 1898 to 1932 the hotel had a number of owners, and its valuation mounted until $400,000 was paid for

"The Fairmount Court property." The Holdens sold it to the Hollenden Hotel Company in 1898; but after holding it for eleven years, the company failed to develop a proposed hotel project, and new owners built modern Fenway Hall at the busy corner, continuously devoted to hotel purposes since Nathaniel Doan built his cabin tavern in 1799.

The Broadway & Newburgh Street Railroad Company received its first grant on August 26 to lay double tracks on Broadway from Kinsman Street (Woodland) to the Newburgh city limits. Although the Newburgh mills employed many men, the road failed to pay until Joseph Stanley took it over. Equipment consisted of nineteen cars and eighty-six horses in 1879.

A refuge for foundlings and unmarried mothers was provided this year by the Sisters of Charity of St. Vincent Charity Hospital, when they fitted two rented frame houses on Garden Street with hospital facilities. St. Ann's Maternity Hospital, the city's first lying-in institution, later extended its services to married women; and, early in the century, the L. H. Severance homestead was purchased and a modern building opened at Woodland and East 35th Street. A hospital building was erected in 1910, and the Loretta House, or "Rescue Home," in 1918.

John D. Rockefeller considered the purchase of a large tract of land east of the city (East Cleveland) a "good investment" at a thousand dollars per acre. Four years later, a company purchased the property and erected a sanitarium. The project failed in 1879, and Rockefeller and his friends used the building as a clubhouse for a year or so. The natural beauty of the surroundings captured the oil-man's fancy, and he remodeled the house as a country home for his family. This was the famous Forest Hill estate to which he retired to work and play with his children. Here he developed roads and trails for driving, walking, and bicycling; constructed a lake, planted trees, and built a half-mile track on which he exercised his fast trotters. A private golf course gave Rockefeller his fullest measure of enjoyment with a few old friends.

The Fire Department had made great strides during the decade since it was converted to steam operation and commenced paying its men. In the city were 23,000 dwellings, and the population had mounted rapidly. Cleveland now had 10 engine companies with 20 hose reels, 1 protection company, 4 hook-and-ladder companies, 1 telegraph-line company, 3 fuel wagons, 55 horses, 130 miles of telegraph line, 147 alarm boxes, and 485 hydrants. One hundred and forty-eight men, including officers, were required to maintain and handle this equipment.

Banks commenced to fail in New York City, the New York Stock Exchange closed, and September 19 was to be remembered as "Black Friday" in the nation's history. Inflated currency, over-extended credit, and excessive investments in railroads and industrial ventures caused scores of railroads to default on bonds, and more than five thousand firms failed in the nation during the year. Vast unemployment resulted. On September 30 the Exchange reopened, and the upward climb began. Drought and food shortage added to the hardship. Although there were some failures in business and industry in Cleveland, not a bank was compelled to suspend. To the city's saving credit was her diversification of industry, producing essential products with wide markets. Speculation in Cleveland real estate had sent the prices of suburban farm land as high as a thousand dollars an acre, and some investors were ruined when the bubble burst. Recovery began to be felt in 1878.

The Post Office commenced to stamp on letters the time of arrival this year. On January 11, 1875, Nelson B. Sherwin became postmaster. He was succeeded by Thomas Jones, Jr., on March 3, 1883; William W. Armstrong, February 28, 1887; Alfred T. Anderson, March 3, 1891; and John C. Hutchins, March 30, 1895.

A telegram announced President Ulysses S. Grant's unexpected stop-over between trains on October 17. A reception committee was hastily organized, headed by Mayor Charles A. Otis, and the members sped to Elyria in a special railroad car. Crowds thronged the depot and the Kennard House to greet the President, who was entertained with a drive on famous Euclid Avenue, dinner, and a reception. He departed in the evening for the East.

A familiar figure of the day was the old apple woman who sat with her basket on Superior Street at the ladies' entrance to the Weddell House. She had queer, persuasive powers of speech that varied with the importance of the customer.

Charles W. and Harris B. Burrows, booksellers and stationers, opened their first store at 7 Euclid Avenue (Williamson Building site) on November 8. Friends deplored the risk they were taking in forsaking the fashionable lower Superior shopping center. When the firm incorporated as The Burrows Brothers Company in 1886, it was also a jobbing concern and publishing house. Two years later, Cobb, Andrews & Company, its competitor, was purchased.

A new street, opened this year, was intended to lead through a fine residential district. It was projected between Superior and Euclid avenues, and was first called Superior; but its name was changed to Payne, honoring Henry B. Payne, owner of large acreage in the area and leader in civic and political life. Delay in placing his lots on the market blighted their future, and prospective home owners shunned the open squares, called "Payne's Pastures," that lay close to the smoke belt of "light" industry. Hough Avenue also opened from East Madison to Giddings. It was a street of homes; and at the crossing of Crawford Road, a business section was developing. The major improvement of the year was the paving of Euclid Avenue from the Square to Erie Street with Medina sandstone. By 1875 the street had been surfaced from the Square to Willson Avenue.

A system was adopted by which physicians' certificates and permits for interment became the basis for determining a record of vital statistics. Dr. H. W. Kitchen published the first report, indicating that 2,641 deaths had occurred during the year, with a mortality rate of 19.2 per thousand on a population of 137,000. Smallpox had been prevalent in the city, but this year an epidemic threatened. Health precautions and free vaccination, offered to all, checked the scourge.

1874

A new industry started in America when D. Black & Company, a wholesale notion house on Water Street, conceived the idea of making women's ready-to-wear cloaks for the trade. A few linen dusters and evening coats were their first products. Moritz Printz, who had been a master tailor of women's apparel in Europe, was secured as designer. Soon Jacob Landesman and his family were making dusters and dresses in their home. About 1878, Felix Hirschheimer joined the business, and The Landesman-Hirschheimer Company was organized. Other pioneers in the industry were M. T. Silver, John Anisfield, and A. W. Sampliner.

The Union of American Hebrew Congregations, organized the previous year, held its first "Council" in Cleveland on January 14.

Returning to Cleveland from her New York successes as an emotional actress, Clara Morris was acknowledged by local critics as beyond criticism. Appearing with the Daly Company, she was one of the most dramatic of the Camilles, and had won success in Shakespearean roles. Only an "extra" at the age of fourteen in 1862, when she played "bit" parts at fifty cents a performance in Cleveland, she had reached the top. When the actress died in 1925, her body lay in state in the Little Church Around the Corner in New York City, where the remains of Edwin Booth, Richard Mansfield, and other great players had reposed. In her autobiography, *Life on the Stage,* Clara Morris recalled her excellent training in the Academy of Music, and she paid tribute to Cleveland's early-day library: "So many plays were produced representing so many periods, so many countries, I don't know how I should have satisfied my craving for the books they led me to, had not the Public Library opened just then."

A fire that started on Water Street on January 30 spread rapidly to the buildings of The Geo. Worthington Company, resulting in a loss of almost $500,000.

The Lake View & Collamer Railroad Company, a deluxe, steam dummy line chartered February 3 and promoted by John D. Rockefeller and others, made its initial run with 150 passengers on October 7, 1875. Pittsburgh-made miniature engines, complete from polished dome to cowcatcher, hauled passengers and freight from the Superior Avenue depot, between East Madison Avenue and Becker Street, about seven miles through East Cleveland to Euclid, crossing Doan Brook, Nine Mile Creek, and other streams on long, high trestles. Comfort in steam-heated coaches aroused criticism of the forbidding cold on Cleveland horsecars.

Quicksand and unforeseen difficulties hindered the building of the first crib in the lake, and seven lives were lost in the undertaking. Almost five years elapsed before the big engines at the pumping station forced water through to the Kentucky Street Reservoir for the first time on March 2, and on July 18, 1876, the new engine house began operation, the total cost of construction being $320,351.72.

On March 10, Council authorized the Superior Street Railroad Company to lay a double track on Superior Avenue from the Square to Willson Avenue. After a few months, the line was extended to East Madison. The road connected with the Lake View & Collamer steam dummy line at Becker Street. A movement started this year to give women first rights to car seats, and to permit smoking only on open summer cars.

Six hundred women of the Women's Christian Association (YWCA), fired with religious spirit, organized the Woman's Christian Temperance League (later Woman's Christian Temperance Union) on March 13, to "alleviate the misery entailed by intoxication." Sarah Fitch was elected president, and Mrs. W. A. Ingham, secretary. Four days later, the first public demonstration against the liquor traffic was held when Mrs. Ingham led a solemn prayer meeting in a Public Square saloon. Praying bands held services in billiard rooms and bars. Temperance processions sometimes filled the streets, inspiring many signed pledges at open-air meetings. Clergymen thundered their protests against liquor, and the Dorcas Society joined in the stirring drive. Reading rooms were opened near saloons, and it was hoped that their drawing power would surmount the bar. Welfare and relief centered in a resolute campaign to rout alcohol and its evil influences from Cleveland.

Praying workers of the Woman's Christian Temperance League had created a liquor-conscious community in the short period since organization in March, and the time had come to count the gains. At a "report" meeting in the Old Stone Church on May 1, it was stated that crusaders had visited 3 distilleries, 8 breweries, 30 drug stores, 35 hotels—of which 10 closed their bars, 40 wholesale dealers, and 1,100 saloons; and the pledge had been signed by 75 dealers, 200 property owners, and 10,000 citizens! It is related that a "gentle lady," Mrs. Samuel Williamson, "by her potent influence closed seven of the worst saloons in Union Lane." In 1880, five thousand women in the local movement incorporated as the Woman's Christian Temperance Union, with Mrs. M. E. Rawson, president. From Cleveland the crusade spread, and in 1883, under the leadership of Frances E. Willard, America's foremost temperance enthusiast, the WCTU became a world organization. This represented a noble beginning, but the liquor tide continued to rise, and a long fight was ahead for the champions of temperance.

The South Side Railroad Company received a grant on June 16 to run a line from Seneca Street, between Superior and Frankfort Place, southeast to Scranton, and over Jennings to the city limits. The Fairfield extension was authorized the next year.

Cleveland was host to the Nineteenth Saengerfest, June 22-29. It was an annual event, held in the city for the third time, and attended by 56 of the leading singing societies of the West with 1,600 competing singers. Saengerfest Hall, a large temporary building, 220 by 152 feet, was erected by a stock company on Euclid Avenue, between Case and Sterling, at a cost of more than $30,000. Seating capacity of the auditorium was 9,100, with 500 on the stage. Cleveland streets were gay with evergreens and flags of the United States and Germany. Railroad fares were cut in half, and hotels and spare rooms were crowded. Schools were closed on the day in which the children participated under their conductor, N. Coe Stewart, director of music. Professor William Heydler directed the opening concert. The Philharmonic Orchestra of New York, Carl Bergmann conducting, participated during the entire week, and Mme. Pauline Lucca, prima donna, sang at three concerts. Cleveland strengthened its reputation for music appreciation and hospitality.

During the temperance crusade, fearless women of the Women's Christian Association (YWCA) opened the Central Friendly Inn in a small rented store on Central Place in the Haymarket district, the notorious slum section of Cleveland. Here they provided a reading room and a safe meeting place for idle men and boys. A restaurant and a kindergarten and playground for children were added. Linda T. Guilford established a library for boys and girls. The first community laundry was opened at the Inn. In 1888, a new building was erected at Broadway and Central, with low-rate boarding rooms for derelicts. Activity in the community center included chapel services every night and outdoor temperance meetings. The shifting population influenced the location, and the Friendly Inn gradually moved eastward to 3754 Woodland Avenue.

The Catholic Universe, influential denominational journal, was established by Bishop Gilmour, the first issue appearing on July 4.

Sisters of Notre Dame came from Germany upon invitation of Bishop Gilmour and established an academy for girls this year (at Superior and East 18th). A convent was erected here in 1877, and a branch academy with boarding school was opened on Woodland Hills Avenue. This was the beginning of Notre Dame College, that moved years later to an impressive location at Green and College roads, South Euclid.

With the realization that Chicago must be the ultimate western goal of the Erie Railway, steps were taken to acquire the unprofitable, but valuable, Atlantic & Great Western Railroad by lease, which was, however, soon repudiated. The road went into receivership, and it is to be regretted that it became more closely identified with financial misfortune than with public service. In 1880 it was sold on foreclosure and reorganized as the New York, Pennsylvania & Ohio Railroad, familiarly known as the Nypano. General J. H. Devereux of Cleveland, who had acted as receiver, was elected president, and the offices were moved from Meadville, Pennsylvania, to Cleveland. Erie leased the line in 1883, acquiring the entire capital stock in 1896. Property of the Nypano was conveyed to the parent company in 1941.

The grant of July 28 authorized the Woodland Hills Avenue Railway Company to lay a line on Kinsman to Willson, southeast to the Cleveland & Pittsburgh tracks. In 1882 the road was purchased by the Woodland Avenue Street Railway Company.

Two thousand Clevelanders witnessed the first game of lacrosse played in Cleveland on September 9, between the Onondaga Indians and the Victorias of London, Ontario. The tribe, the best in the sport, won the event. Special trains ran to the Northern Ohio Fair Grounds where the contest was held. The game of lacrosse originated among the North American redskins.

During the pastorate of the Rev. Frederick Brooks, brother of the Rev.

Phillips Brooks, distinguished New England clergyman, business crowded in on St. Paul's Episcopal Church at Sheriff and Euclid Avenue, and the building was razed this year to make room for Brainard's music house. The congregation worshiped in temporary quarters until a new home was completed at Euclid and Case in the residential district at the end of the horsecar line. The tragic loss of the beloved Rev. Brooks by drowning in 1874 was a great blow to Cleveland. On Christmas Eve, 1876, the bells of the new St. Paul's rang out, and the first service was held. It was a superb building, with sandstone walls, carved door-and-window casings, and beautiful windows. Distinguished Clevelanders were members, among them Zenas King, F. W. Hubby, Harvey Rice, C. J. Comstock, A. C. Armstrong, J. H. Devereux,

Brooks School, a college-preparatory school for boys, introduced military training. Many prominent Clevelanders were enrolled as students.

and H. C. Ranney. Seven Cleveland churches stemmed from St. Paul's, including Emmanuel Church, 1876; St. Philip the Apostle, 1894; and Christ Church, 1909.

The Rev. Frederick Brooks, beloved rector of St. Paul's Episcopal Church, met his death while on a trip to Boston. He had long cherished the hope of founding a college-preparatory school for boys, and in his memory, the congregation and prominent Clevelanders fulfilled his desire in Brooks School, or Brooks Academy. It opened this year in Weisgerber's Block, and John S. White of Harvard was the first headmaster. Through the efforts of J. H. Devereux, J. H. Wade, Samuel Andrews, Dan P. Eells, Colonel William H. Harris, C. E. Smith, and William Edwards, the picturesque building was erected near Sibley and Hayward streets and opened in 1875. It was of Anglo-Swiss architecture, beamed on the outside, and painted in chocolate and vermilion upon the projecting portions over a drab groundwork. It provided a drill hall, armory, gymnasium, and chemical laboratory. Military training was introduced, reflecting the general feeling that increased patriotism and preparedness were essential to national security. Major Clarence R. Edwards commanded the uniformed school battalions. Thrilling sports contests were held on a lot adjacent to General Devereux' estate on Euclid Avenue. The school continued until 1891, and the building was destroyed by fire in 1908. Many Brooks graduates gained prominence in business and the professions.

Work had begun on construction of the Superior Viaduct, and a move to extend the Newburgh, Rocky River, and Collamer steam dummy lines into the Public Square over the new bridge gained support, especially from the suburbs. Newspapers reported that steam was supplanting horsepower in large cities, and that "one dummy was equal to nine mules." City officials gave the "fireless locomotives" a trial on the East Cleveland line on September 30. A strong receptacle containing steam, about 125 pounds pressure, was installed under the floor to furnish the power when the car left Willson Avenue for Doan's Corners. Pressure remained at 40 or 50 pounds upon return, and the report was enthusiastic—"no noise, no smoke, no failure, and a warm floor." Powerful horsecar operators took the matter to Council, however, and an ordinance banning steam from the streets stopped the suburban dummies from extending their lines.

A local editor reported sorrowfully on October 19 that "duty compels us to announce that the days of big hoops and bulging crinolines are coming back. The narrow skirts of the past six months, pinned back so that the wearer had to go mincing along with dainty steps, were certain to be followed by excess in the opposite direction. . . . A lady will fill an opera box or a carriage and three will crowd a street car. . . . The big skirt will drive the male population to the reform movement."

"First class accommodations and a good stable" were the prime attractions at the new Euclid Hotel (East 14th and Huron Road). Anthony Carlin and his son operated the house until it was razed in 1900 for the widening of Brownell Street.

Lake traffic at the five eastern ports of Ohio was heavy, there being 8,861 entrances and clearances this year at Cleveland, Lorain, Fairport, Ashtabula, and Conneaut. Of this total, 93 per cent were at Cleveland. Tonnage of vessels amounted to 2,750,000, and 96 per cent came to Cleveland.

The first half of the decade witnessed the establishment of firms that were in existence in the 1940s: 1870, Bingham & Douglas Company, Cleveland Window Glass & Door Company, Henry J. Dress Company Funeral Homes, Thomas W. Easton's Sons, Inc., McGorray Brothers Company, Northern Ohio Lumber & Timber Company, George Rackle & Sons Company, Star Elevator Company; 1871, Herrman-McLean Company, Taylor Brothers Company, Fred P. Thomas Company; 1872, Binz Monumental Works Company, Gustav Buesch & Sons Funeral Home, Saxton Funeral Home, V. C. Taylor & Son, Inc.; 1873, The Barrett Company, Bowler & Burdick Company, Hechler Pharmacy, Martin-Barriss Company, The Teachout Company, Troy Laundry Company; 1874, W. W. Sly Manufacturing Company, Chris B. Wilhelmy.

1875

James F. Ryder, Cleveland art dealer, had been displaying and selling comic chromos produced by Archibald M. Willard, Wellington, Ohio, wagon painter, the first royalties going to his protégé for an art course. Ryder encouraged the artist to create a semi-humorous, patriotic subject for exhibition at the International Centennial Exposition in Philadelphia in 1876, and Willard began painting "Yankee Doodle" this year in a fourth-floor studio room in the Union National Bank Building (308 Euclid), where he and a handful of artist friends started the first life class in Cleveland. The models for his picture were: center figure—his father, the Rev. Samuel R. Willard, a Disciples minister, whose death before the painting was finished influenced the artist to turn to a serious subject; fifer—Hugh Mosher, a lad who attended Brooks School; drummer boy—Harry K. Devereux, also known as Henry, son of General J. H. Devereux; soldier in foreground—Charles A. Spicer. Ryder sold reproductions of the painting at the centennial, and their popularity led to demand for an exhibition there. Crowds stood before the picture, wrapped in silent emotion. Its fame swept the country, and exhibits were arranged in large cities. While in Boston, the "Spirit of '76" was suggested as the title, and adopted. The painting traveled to San Francisco and back to Boston, where it remained in Old South Church for several years. Then it was returned to Ryder's gallery in Cleveland, and upon his death was acquired by the Western Reserve Historical Society.

In his *Cultural Story of an American City—Cleveland,* Elbert J. Benton, director of the Western Reserve Historical Society, traced the painstaking research that is believed to have established the origin of Willard's six successive "original" versions of his famous painting, each bearing certain refinements. After visiting the centennial, the artist painted a large, eight-foot version, presented by James F. Ryder to the Cleveland Grays and said to have been destroyed in a fire. A colorful 8 by 10-foot reproduction was sent to the new Corcoran Gallery of Art in Washington in the late seventies. In 1880 General J. H. Devereux presented to his native town of Marblehead, Massachusetts, a version painted to order by Willard in his City Hall studio and hung in Abbott Hall. When returned for repair in 1892, the artist made a number of changes, and it has been determined that the original was discarded in favor of a new reproduction. On commission of Mayor Newton D. Baker in 1912, Willard, then seventy-six years old, painted the "Spirit of '76" for permanent exhibition in the Cleveland City Hall. Still another version, executed for his friend, the Rev. W. E. Barton, in 1916, went to the Herrick Library, Wellington, Ohio. Two years later the artist died. Through major conflict and in peacetime celebration, the "Spirit of '76" inspired patriotic devotion in the hearts of Americans. It is said to have been "copied more times and in more forms than any other of the world's paintings."

Kalakaua I, king of the Sandwich Islands, arrived at the Union Depot in the evening of January 11, stopping only long enough for a hasty dinner of pork and beans at Wheeler & Russell's dining hall. Then with his retinue he departed for Chicago.

In January, the first piston fire engine was purchased and named the *Charles A. Otis.* John A. Bennett became chief of the Fire Department on February 5, and on the 9th Newburgh had its first engine house.

Despite the foresighted planning of the founder and his men, Cleveland was growing up "like Topsy," expanding along the lines of least resistance.

Beginning this year, state law and municipal ordinance took a hand in regulating the planning of new allotments.

Leonard Case erected the Case Block, Cleveland's newest and finest commercial building, at Superior and Wood streets. Charles W. Heard was the architect of the $800,000 building. On February 18, city officials leased it as the City Hall for twenty-five years at an annual rental of $36,000. The building was so large, however, that the excess space was rented. Artists used the top floor for studios, and several retail stores took over the Superior Street frontage. In 1906 Cleveland purchased the building from the Case estate, and, for the first time, the city administration was housed in a home of its own. The block was evacuated in 1916 when the new City Hall was completed, and it was razed to make room for the main Public Library. The City Hall served during the terms of the following mayors: Nathan P. Payne, 1875-76; William G. Rose, 1877-78; R. R. Herrick, 1879-82; John H. Farley, 1883-84; George W. Gardner, 1885-86; Brenton D. Babcock, 1887-88; George W. Gardner, 1889-90; William G. Rose, 1891-92; Robert Blee, 1893-94; Robert E. McKisson, 1895-98; John H. Farley, 1899-1900; Tom L. Johnson, 1901-09; Herman C. Baehr, 1910-11; and Newton D. Baker, 1912-15.

Building of the Case Block brought about demolition of the famed Ark, parent of science and culture in Cleveland. Chairs, tables, and fixtures were made from its wood for new rooms provided in the Case Library Building. Here the thinning group of "Arkites" met now and then; but, as they grew old, gaps were left in the roster until but three survived—J. J. Tracy, John Coon, and Levi T. Scofield. The door closed and dust gathered, but the gracious memory of wit and good fellowship lived on in boundless civic achievement. When progress demanded the library-building site for a new Federal Building, "damages" were awarded to Ark survivors by the court.

Following the Civil War, in which Mortimer D. Leggett advanced to the rank of major general, he was appointed commissioner of patents by President Grant. Now that his four-year service had come to an end, General Leggett made Cleveland his home. In the late 1840s, he had begun practicing law in Akron, Ohio, where he organized the first system of free graded schools west of the Allegheny Mountains under what was known as the Akron school law. He also practiced for a time in Warren, Ohio, and became a nationally known patent lawyer.

Government improvements on the outer harbor at Cleveland from 1825-75 had amounted to $346,881.61, representing irregular appropriations, sometimes with long lapses. This had provided a wholly inadequate port of make-shift piers, built of timber frames resting on the lake bottom and loaded with stone, constantly in need of repair; and a narrow, artificial channel eternally menaced by shifting sand. After years of agitation, a harbor-improvement project was authorized by Congress on March 3, this year, that resulted in construction of a breakwater as a refuge for vessels in time of severe storm. Work upon the west wing commenced in the fall.

The Rev. Charles Terry Collins, called as pastor of Plymouth Church, had carried on mission work in New York City, before he launched Olivet

Chapel this year at Hill and Commercial streets. From it grew the nation's pioneering missionary work among the Bohemians, established by Dr. Henry A. Schauffler, founder of Schauffler College. A house of worship, seating a thousand persons, was dedicated by Plymouth Church at Prospect and Perry streets in 1882, and the next year, Rev. Collins died. Out of Plymouth's Congregational mission work grew the Mount Zion and Swedish Congregational churches. It also furnished a large number of the original members of the Woodland Avenue Presbyterian Church. Routed by encroaching business and never financially strong, the Plymouth Church organization disbanded in 1913; and in authorizing disposition of the property, the trustees made provision for a foundation fund for a new church somewhere on the "Heights" (later Plymouth Church of Shaker Heights).

The city's finest musicians formed the Cecilian String Quartet—John Nuss, violin; Phillip Grotenrath, second violin; and the Koenigslow brothers, viola and cello. It became the Schubert Quartet when it was reorganized, with John Beck, violin; Julius Deiss, second violin; John Lockhart, viola; and Charles Heydler, cello. In the nineties, it was known as the Philharmonic String Quartet, the pride of Cleveland, with Heydler playing the cello; Sol Marcosson, first violin; James D. Johnston, second violin; and Charles V. Rychlik, viola.

A torrential rain swept the city on April 29, sending the towering wooden flagstaff on the Square crashing to the ground. The tall spire on the Old Stone Church swayed uneasily in the gale, and the pinnacles on the corners of the towers fell to the sidewalk.

Early in the year, the East Cleveland Railway pioneered in the United States in an unsuccessful attempt to use electricity on its Garden Street line by placing trolley wire in a trench in the street. Improper drainage permitted streets to fill with water during heavy rains, thus defeating the experiment.

Martha Canfield's graduation from the Homeopathic Hospital Medical College this year represented a victory over prejudices and barriers that handicapped women in their desire to serve outside closely defined vocations. She was one of the first women in northern Ohio to choose medicine as a profession, and her career continued until her death in 1916 at the age of seventy. Dr. Canfield gave generously of her time to humanitarian interests —the Federated Charities, as president of the Women's Hospital Association, and as a founder and member of the board of managers of the Maternity Hospital.

An old "tabernacle" on Warren Road was used by East Rockport families for a Sunday School and an occasional service with a Cleveland pastor in the pulpit. When the building was moved, worshipers met in a schoolhouse on Detroit Road (near West Clifton Boulevard). A society of Methodists was organized in 1876, and a country church was built on Detroit Road and Summit Street during the ministry of the Rev. Robert McCaskey. It was called the East Rockport Methodist Church until the hamlet of Lakewood was organized, when the name was changed to Lakewood Methodist Church. A modern frame building was erected in front of the old church in 1905, and the Rev. John M. Blackburn became pastor. Both city and church grew rapidly, and a second church building was dedicated in 1913. The building unit for religious education was added in 1914. Membership increased from 150 to 1,300 during Rev. Blackburn's pastorate. Steady growth and broadened influence continued under the ministry of the Rev. W. W. T. Duncan, who came to the church in 1931 and was succeeded by the Rev. Harold F. Carr in 1942. Under the direction of George K. Ogden, four choirs were maintained.

"The most extensive shooting contest ever held in the United States" opened on the Northern Ohio Fair Grounds on June 10. The four-day Grand National Pigeon Shooting Tournament attracted 139 crack shots from all over the country to win cash prizes amounting to $4,100.

A pretentious, four-story Court House was begun this year on land facing Seneca Street, and extending to the old Court House on Rockwell Street. Built in Renaissance style, nearly seventy feet square, the stone-faced building cost $250,000, and was one of the first to be constructed almost entirely of fireproof materials. The probate and criminal courts, the principal county offices, and the jail were located here, and later, other county courts, offices of the Board of Education, Board of Health, Soldiers and Sailors Relief Commission, County Farm Bureau, and the Citizen's League. Mounted on her pedestal was the statuesque goddess of justice that marked the Seneca Street entrance until the sturdy, musty building fell a victim of progress in 1931.

This was an eventful year for the B'nai Jeshurun Congregation (later Temple on the Heights). The Rev. M. Klein was engaged as the first rabbi, cantor, teacher, and collector, and land was purchased for Glenville Cemetery. Care of poor and needy Jews was concentrated in a new charitable organization, the Hebrew Relief Association. It was reorganized in 1904, and a trained superintendent was employed to provide more efficient service to the steadily increasing Jewish population.

A speed demonstration, envisioned by the ingenious James Gordon Bennett, publisher of the *New York Herald,* and Commodore Cornelius Vanderbilt I, aged railroad magnate, was top Fourth-of-July news for the nation. Shortly after midnight, a fast, special, three-car train left New York City carrying a generous supply of the newspaper's latest edition, and raced against time over the New York Central and Lake Shore rails, reaching Chicago in 29½ hours. For nine consecutive Sundays, the "special" shot across country at unprecedented speed, costing Bennett's stunt-advertising department a thousand dollars per trip.

A late-afternoon crowd of thousands packed the Public Square on July 4 to watch the balloon ascent of the *Buffalo,* piloted by "Professor" Samuel King, professional aeronaut from Philadelphia. Three newspaper reporters, Robert S. Pierce, W. E. Chapman, and John C. Covert, climbed into the wicker basket with him. They soared out over the lake, south over Chagrin Falls, and a threatening storm brought them down near Mantua, Ohio. The newsmen returned home, but King continued his voyage to Pennsylvania in the morning. The balloon was wrecked east of Pittsburgh.

Probably in an effort to strengthen its enforcement of sanitary regulations, the Board of Health merged with the Board of Police. During the year, the first annual report of the Health Department was published, reflecting comprehensive advance. The principal causes of death were stated as cholera, diphtheria, scarlet fever, and diarrhea infantum. Health education was initiated with the house-to-house distribution of a "circular of advice." Steps were taken to sample and analyze the milk supply, when it was recognized that milk was a possible purveyor of disease; and, soon after, a full-time milk inspector was employed.

Selah Chamberlain purchased at receiver's sale the property of the Lake Shore & Tuscarawas Valley Railway Company, organized in 1871, consisting of an eight-mile line between Elyria and Charleston (Lorain) and a road from Elyria through Massillon to Uhrichsville, Ohio. A corporation formed by Amasa Stone, R. L. Chamberlain, E. B. Thomas, and others designated as the Cleveland, Tuscarawas Valley & Wheeling Railway Company, bought the property and pushed a line to West Wheeling on the Ohio River in May, 1880. The road was again in receivership when Edwin R. Perkins bought it in 1883. He turned it over to Amasa Stone, Selah Chamberlain, W. S. Streator, R. L. Chamberlain, and A. J. Begges, who incorporated the Cleveland, Lorain & Wheeling Railroad Company, which made extensions in the Wheeling area. Consolidation with the Cleveland & Southwestern Railway Company, organized in 1887 to build a road from Cleveland to Zanesville, resulted in the Cleveland, Lorain & Wheeling Railway Company, which constructed a 28-mile stretch from the Lorain-Wheeling at Lester to Cleveland in October, 1895, terminating at Literary Street on the river. The Baltimore & Ohio Railroad Company became financially interested in the project about 1900, operating the property after 1909, and purchasing the holdings in 1915.

The need of hospital service for soldiers and sailors having passed, the Marine Hospital was leased for twenty years by a private organization under its original name, the Cleveland City Hospital Society, upon condition that care for sailors be provided at sixty-four cents per day. In 1889, when municipal authorities decided to erect a city hospital, the name was changed to Lakeside Hospital. Upon expiration of the lease, plans were made for a new building east of the Marine Hospital (between East 12th and East 14th streets), and it opened on January 14, 1898. Mrs. Mary H. Severance contributed generously to the institution for many years, serving as trustee until her death in 1902 at the age of eighty-six.

The Public School Library (later Cleveland Public Library) had been located in larger quarters in Clark's Block, farther west on Superior Street, and this year rooms were acquired in the new City Hall. On September 1, I. L. Beardsley succeeded Librarian Oviatt, whose health had failed.

When John A. Ellsler opened the new $200,000 Euclid Avenue Opera House on September 6, it was the most brilliant theatrical event in the city's history. A long series of financial obstacles had been surmounted by the incorporators, J. H. Wade, H. P. Weddell, Earl Bill, John A. Ellsler, and A. W. Fairbanks, and Cleveland had one of the finest playhouses in the country. Planned by Charles W. Heard, it was "the most perfect theater in

America or England," declared Edward A. Sothern. The entrance opened on Sheriff Street, with the expectation that the city would widen the roadway. The interior was magnificently decorated and ornamented, with marble foyers, fine paintings, crimson velvet, luxurious carpets, and a massive chandelier of sparkling prisms with 325 gas jets, the largest of its kind. Capacity of the house was about a thousand.

Cleveland society flocked to the opening-night performance in the Euclid Avenue Opera House, featuring *Saratoga* and the first stock company, in which Ellsler, Mrs. Effie Ellsler, his wife, and Effie E., his daughter, had principal roles. After the first week, the brightest stars in the business were engaged as headliners, among them Lawrence Barrett, Maggie Mitchell,

The Euclid Avenue Opera House with its main entrance on Sheriff Street (East 4th). "Too far up town," said the pessimists, but "Uncle" John Ellsler soon made the playhouse popular and famous with the finest stage attractions.

Barry Sullivan, Edward A. Sothern, Frank Weston—later Effie Ellsler's husband, Edwin Booth, Modjeska, and Edward H. Sothern. Within three years, Manager Ellsler was in financial straits, and the theater was sold at auction to Marcus A. Hanna. At the end of the season, on June 30, 1879, Ellsler was given a farewell benefit, in which he appeared as Powhatan in *Pocahontas*. When he left the Sheriff Street stage door that night, the famous stock company ended. Management of the house passed to L. G. Hanna, the owner's cousin, who continued until 1884.

Selling peanuts and candy in the gallery of the Opera House was Abraham Lincoln Erlanger, a Cleveland schoolboy. Under Marcus A. Hanna's ownership, young "A. L." became manager of the theater. His next step was to manage Joseph Jefferson and Effie Ellsler, and he is said to have been the first to purchase page-size newspaper space to advertise his stars. He became president of Klaw & Erlanger in New York City, and their stage productions surpassed any that America had seen. The firm dissolved, and Erlanger joined the Shuberts, later becoming an independent producer with more than fifty theaters in the country. He was associated with Florenz Ziegfeld before his death in 1930.

The Cleveland Grays, under Captain John N. Frazee, were feted in London, Ontario, on September 10. This was considered an unusual meeting with British neighbors to the north, as on this day in 1813, Perry had won the decisive victory on Lake Erie.

Spurred by his father's famous speed exhibition of July 4, William H. Vanderbilt set out to better the record with the inauguration of the *Fast Mail*. The demanding Post Office Department had been urging faster service to the West, and rivalry had developed between the New York Central and the Pennsylvania roads. Early in the morning of September 14, the fast, white, mail train left New York City, the first long-trip train devoted exclusively to mail. Four coaches painted white, striped and lettered in gold and bearing the names of governors of the states en route, were trailed by Vanderbilt's private car. Over the New York Central and Lake Shore lines they sped, crowds lining the tracks for a glimpse of the streaking white monster. Clevelanders enjoyed a fifteen-minute stopover. A weary crew piloted the *Mail* into Chicago twenty-seven hours after leaving New York, beating the best passenger time by nine hours. Not long afterward, the train was discontinued when the Government protested over payment for the service; but white cars continued to identify the mail on the line.

A mission in East Rockport, fostered by Trinity Episcopal Church, became the Church of the Ascension. A frame building was consecrated in 1879. The Rev. Lewis Burton was the first rector. As the trend to the suburbs increased, the parish gained strength, serving a community of homes from its location at 13216 Detroit Avenue, where an impressive house of worship was dedicated in 1918. The Rev. John R. Pattie became rector in 1940.

The Altenheim Association was organized as a charitable effort that narrowed gradually to work for the aged. Its trustees were chosen from the West Side Deutscher Frauen Verein—West Side German Association of Women. On September 19, 1891, the cornerstone of the Altenheim—home for old people—was laid (7719 Detroit), each officer of the Verein striking the stone with a mason's mallet while the singing societies sang "Brueder, Reicht die Hand zum Bunde."

Bond Street was extended from Superior to Euclid, its width being only fifty feet, a shortcoming of serious import as north-and-south traffic mounted. Waldemar Otis, cousin of Charles A. Otis, Sr., owned the property at the northwest corner of Euclid, extending northward to an alley. At the bend of Bond, he built the Otis Block, the first building on the new street. On the ground floor was a cafe, on the second a billiard parlor, and on the third apartments. Otis, lawyer and realtor, continued to develop his Bond Street property. Vincent Street, named for John A. Vincent, whose property lay midway between Superior and Euclid, opened later off Bond to the east.

A small, frame building was dedicated on December 6 at Prospect and Willson Avenue in the name of the Cottage Methodist Episcopal Church;

and for eight years the Revs. Dillon Prosser and J. H. Tagg conducted services for small compensation. In 1883 the Prospect Street Church, which originated in the Erie Street Church in 1850, merged with the Cottage congregation, forming the Central Methodist Episcopal Church. Commemorating the founding of the Epworth League in Central Church in 1889, the new building, dedicated in 1893, bore the name of Epworth Memorial; and pilgrims came year after year to visit the birthplace of the young-people's organization that became worldwide. The Scovill Avenue Methodist Church merged with Epworth in 1895; and in 1920 the pioneer Euclid Avenue Methodist Church joined forces as the Epworth-Euclid Methodist Church.

Following his diplomatic career in Paris, Vienna, and Madrid, John Hay became a member of the editorial staff of the *New York Tribune* under Horace Greeley. Here he wrote his *Pike County Ballads,* which appeared in the paper, and *Castilian Days.* He had been with the *Tribune* five years when he married Clara Stone, daughter of wealthy Amasa Stone of Cleveland, in 1874. He came to Cleveland the next year, and entered Stone's office on the Public Square. The Hays lived in a fashionable residence erected for them next to the Stone mansion on Euclid near Brownell. Economic security permitted John Hay to write, to travel, and to fill prominent political offices. In 1878 he was appointed assistant secretary of state and moved to Washington. Returning to Cleveland, he wrote a social novel, *The Bread Winners,* which appeared anonymously in 1883, the authorship of which he never admitted publicly. Here he also wrote much of the ten-volume masterpiece, *Abraham Lincoln, a History,* published with John G. Nicolay in 1890. For relief from serious writing, he turned to humor; and his poems, "Jim Bludso" and "Little Breeches," were his most popular verses.

1876

January 1 ushered in the National Centennial Year in a carnival of tumult and blazing lights. As midnight struck, a huge cauldron of oil sent up a mighty flare in the Public Square, and pandemonium reigned. The day dawned clear and warm, "and overcoats were left on the walnut hat-rack." A reception in the City Hall marked the beginning of the nation's New Year.

William Halsey Doan, trustee of the Euclid Avenue Congregational Church of East Cleveland, arranged with the Burying Ground Society at Doan's Corners to lease the corner of the tract in front of its abandoned meeting house for one year for a dollar. Entanglements were involved in the title, which was disputed by the society owning a cemetery to the north. Nevertheless, Doan built a large, frame building attached to the front of the church and extending to the Euclid and Doan Street sidewalks. It was dedicated on February 10, this year, as Doan's Armory. The Euclid Light Infantry rented it as a drill hall. The Infantry never reached the importance of the Cleveland Grays; but the armory was a popular meeting place for social and religious events, political rallies, and lectures. In 1899 Doan deeded the property to the church, and the income was a welcome supplement to its treasury. The Doan Street church continued under the ownership of the congregation until it was razed in 1906, while serving as a Grand Army of the Republic hall above, and John Hill's carpenter shop and Wheaton's butcher shop below. The land west of the church was used as a village commons. Clear title of the church to a long tract covering the corner at Euclid and extending north on Doan was established in 1905. The Cleveland Trust Company purchased the property on which was later located its branch office at the corner, and its adjoining neighbor, the Alhambra Theater.

The Women's Christian Association (YWCA) recognized another need, and established the Home for Aged Protestant Gentlewomen on Kennard Street, through a gift of Amasa Stone. Beginning in 1931, it was managed independently as Amasa Stone House, 975 East Boulevard, the property having been given by W. G. Pollock.

Cleveland's most popular caterer was Henry Weisgerber, located at the corner of Prospect and Brownell streets. He served sumptuous repasts at weddings, receptions, and social functions. The upper floor of the Weisgerber Block was well patronized by dances and parties.

Seeing the need for religious services in the new sparsely settled Collinwood community, Horace and Horatio C. Ford, of the Euclid Avenue Congregational Church, sponsored and contributed largely to the erection of Ford Chapel (on East 152nd Street) in 1874. The Ford family was devoted to the cause. The first definite church in the community, it was organized on May 11, 1876, as The First Congregational Church of Collinwood, with about twenty-five charter members. A stone sanctuary was erected in 1895 during the ministry of the Rev. Owen Jenkins. It was enlarged and improved through the years, as religious and social work of the Collinwood Congregational Church expanded to meet community needs. The Rev. Henry C. Stallard came to the pulpit in 1944.

John G. W. Cowles took charge of the real-estate interests of John D. Rockefeller in June, and, a little later, those of Charles F. Brush. He had come to Cleveland in 1871 at the age of thirty-five to become associate editor of the Leader; but real estate became his chosen field, and he succeeded as an agent for others as well as an investor. For many years he was one of the city's distinguished citizens.

When Jacob D. Cox and C. C. Newton organized a business on June 27 for the making of twist drills, only one small eastern company was engaged in their manufacture. Cox was the son of Jacob D. Cox, who became governor of Ohio in 1865, Secretary of the Interior under President Grant, and president of the Wabash Railroad. In 1880 Newton sold his half interest. F. F. Prentiss entered the firm and took charge of sales while Cox ran the factory and designed the machinery. Cox and Prentiss operated until 1905, when The Cleveland Twist Drill Company was incorporated. A plant site was purchased in 1891 (at 1242 East 49th Street), and the first two buildings were erected. Profit-sharing, inaugurated in 1915, was broadened by a par-

A little "Dummy Line Railroad" was operated between Cleveland and Rocky River in 1880. It carried outing parties from Cleveland to the popular Rocky River picnic grounds.

The Ohio Canal continued to transport freight in the 1880s. STANLEY L. M^cMICHAEL COLLECTION, CLEVELAND PUBLIC LIBRARY.

Cutters racing on Euclid Avenue in the 1880s

The Four-in-Hand Club, May 30, 1901, on Euclid Avenue near East 40th Street

ticipating investment plan for employees. Many years of metallurgical research resulted in the discovery of "Mo-Max" in 1934, a new molybdenum, tungsten, high-speed steel, a forward step in metal-cutting.

Emmanuel Church was organized with the help of St. Paul's Episcopal Church. Its first chapel was at Euclid and Case avenues. The Rev. B. C. Noakes was called from Elyria to be the rector. When permission to form a new parish was denied, he and his followers withdrew from the Protestant Episcopal Church in 1889, joined the Reformed Episcopal Church and organized the Parish of the Epiphany, erecting a church across the street from Emmanuel. Hiram Kimball, senior warden, and a few members kept Emmanuel Church alive. The Rev. Albert B. Putnam was called as rector, and through initiative and constructive effort it gained strength. In a location to the east (8614 Euclid), it served a community in which residences were replaced with apartment houses. The Rev. Andrew S. Gill became Minister in 1931, succeeding the Rev. Kirk O'Ferrall.

The observance of Independence Day in the Nation's Centennial Year began on Saturday, July 1, and ended on the Fourth. The Perry Monument was illuminated with gas jets, and buildings were decorated with colored lights. Crowds gathered in the Public Square late in the evening of July 3 to participate in the midnight jubilee ushering in the nation's birthday. As the clock struck, lights blazed and whistles shrieked all over the city. Church bells chimed, and firearms, firecrackers, and cannon boom mingled with the shouts of thousands. At daybreak, a 168-foot flagstaff was erected near the center of the Public Square, marking the centennial observance. The pole, made of Bessemer steel, was said to be the first of its kind ever erected. It was the gift of Henry Chisholm on behalf of the Cleveland Rolling Mill Company. The crowning event was the ascension of a balloon from the Public Square, and spectators were on hand from a great distance. Hacks and hotels did a rushing business. In the dining room of the fashionable Forest City House, the best meal in town was served in elegant style for fifty cents.

Trustees of the Cleveland Library Association were called together on July 6 by Leonard Case. In serious fashion he declared that the ownership of Case Hall, the pride of its founders, was about to change hands. "You are to decide its future," he said. There was silence. "You will find the name of the new owner in this deed," he added, then turned and walked away. The association had received the $300,000 building as a gift, the only reservations being those relating to leases and the rooms of his friends, the "Arkites." In 1880 the name of the library was changed to Case Library. For nineteen years, Dr. John W. Perrin served as librarian and built up its usefulness. The association was famous not only for its many valuable scientific and special book collections, but for the admirable lecture courses offered each winter. The building, which appropriately became the Case Library Building, was razed to make room for the new Federal Building. The library was located in the Caxton Building for twenty years. Known as the Leonard Case Reference Library in 1928, it became affiliated with Western Reserve University.

The Kirtland Society of Natural Science opened a natural-history museum in Case Hall this year, placing on display specimens of birds and mammals assembled by William Case, R. K. Winslow's bird collection, the entomological collection of John Fitzpatrick, casts of fishes arranged by Dr. Elisha Sterling, valuable scientific exhibits of Dr. Jared P. Kirtland, and others. After the death of Dr. Kirtland, the geological, zoological, and botanical exhibits were moved to the Case School of Applied Science. The museum continued to function, however, and its work was in effect continued by the Cleveland Museum of Natural History when it was formed in 1920.

A Normal School was established in the Eagle Street school building in the fall, admission requirements being a Cleveland high-school diploma or the equivalent. Alexander Forbes was principal of the teacher-training project, and only girls attended. At the end of the year, twenty-six pupils were graduated. The institution was the forerunner of the School of Education of Western Reserve University.

In a free-for-all trot to high-wheel sulkies at the Cleveland Driving Park in Glenville on July 27, Smuggler defeated Goldsmith Maid in what has been considered by many experts as one of the greatest races in trotting history. The first heat was timed at 2:15½, and the fifth at 2:17¼. The event captured national interest, as Goldsmith Maid had established a world record of 2:14 in 1874. Oliver Wendell Holmes recorded the famous race in enduring verse, "When Smuggler Beat the Maid."

William J. O. Astrup, a Danish sailmaker, began making sails, awnings, and canvas products on Pearl Street in Cleveland, the center of marine business on the lakes. In the early nineties, tents were added to the line. To meet his own needs, Astrup designed the first awning hardware, and was soon supplying other companies with products that numbered in the thousands a half century later. In 1909 The Astrup Company was incorporated. When the founder died in 1914, the company was taken over by his sons, William E., who died two years later, and Walter C., who became president in 1917. A modern factory was built in 1924 at 2937 West 25th Street. Astrup had become a leading name in awning manufacture, its gaily striped tents and awnings making up a large export business.

The Brooks School for Young Ladies and Misses, a branch of the Brooks School for boys, was established at Euclid and Willson avenues this year. Gertrude Hooker and Fannie Noakes made up the first graduating class. In 1880 Mrs. Mary E. Salisbury took charge, and the school knew several locations and the ownership of Frances Fisher before Anne Hathaway Brown purchased it in 1886. She named it Hathaway Brown School and gave it a new home at 768 Euclid Avenue. Sixty pupils were enrolled when Miss Brown retired and sold it to Mary E. Spencer, who retained the name. Within a few years, a goal of 125 students had been reached. Cora E. Canfield purchased the flourishing institution in 1902, and a great future was ahead.

While a member of Congress, James A. Garfield purchased "Lawnfield," 160 acres in Mentor, Ohio, with a little, white farmhouse, for a hundred dollars an acre. "I have bought this farm," he said, "so my boys can learn to work, and where I can myself have some exercise, where I can touch the earth and get some strength from it." In 1893, James R. Garfield purchased 23 acres adjoining his father's farm.

Flames swept the Otis & York grain elevator on River Street on October 9, spreading to the Michigan Central freight depot and other buildings. Burning embers borne by the wind set fire to the Second Presbyterian Church on the south side of Superior, east of the Square, leaving it in ruins. A new sanctuary seating 1,300 persons was erected and occupied in 1878 at the northwest corner of Prospect and Sterling avenues. Beloved of both church and community was Dr. Charles S. Pomeroy, the fourth pastor, who served from 1873 until his death in 1894. He was succeeded by Dr. Paul F. Sutphen, an eloquent preacher who "wrote a sermon as an artist paints a picture." In 1920 the congregation merged with the Euclid Avenue Church to form the Church of the Covenant.

Riverside Cemetery was opened on November 11 with a centennial memorial service attended by distinguished guests, including Governor Rutherford B. Hayes. It contained 102½ acres that had been the old Brainard farm overlooking the valley near Scranton and Columbus Street, and the association had paid a thousand dollars an acre. Josiah Barber was the first president.

Struggling young artists in Archibald M. Willard's studio formed a nucleus for the Art Club, the first in the city, familiarly known as The Old Bohemians (later Cleveland Society for Artists). There was potential genius in the enthusiastic members that included Willard, president, George Groll, George Grossman, Frederic C. Gottwald, John Semon, Adam Lehr, Louis Loeb, Herman Herkomer, John Herkomer, O. V. Schubert, Daniel Wehrschmidt, Emil Wehrschmidt, Otto Bacher, Arthur Schneider, and Max Bohm. Little by little they acquired studio headquarters on the top floor of the new City Hall, and the club flourished. In a *Sketch Book* published by the club appeared reproductions of pictures painted in Cleveland by Kenyon Cox, then in his twenties. Prophetically, it was noted that he was a painter whose ability and attainments "should give him high rank among the strongest and best of our American artists." Cox went on to New York, Europe, and international fame as a mural and figure painter. Willard was an organizer of the Academy of Fine Arts, encouraged unsuccessfully by a number of citizens in 1876. The Cleveland School of Art, fostered by the Art Club, thrived within the same gaily decorated walls until city authorities needed the space for offices in 1898. After the club relinquished its home, it soon disappeared.

Bridges and railroads were paramount in the life of Amasa Stone. In earlier years in New England, he and his brother-in-law, William Howe, had perfected the Howe truss bridge. They built hundreds of successful wooden structures, and Stone was the first to erect pivot drawbridges of long span. In the late fifties, railroads began to replace wooden bridges with iron or stone. When conversion of the span over the Ashtabula gorge was discussed by Cleveland, Painesville & Ashtabula executives in 1863, President Stone held out for a 150-foot bridge erected on the Howe truss principle, overriding his engineer, who warned that such great length would prove a dangerous experiment. On the evening of December 29, 1876, a westbound train, fighting its way through a snow storm, plunged seventy feet and burst into flames when the main arch of the bridge gave way. Four baggage and express cars and six coaches and sleepers lay a twisted mass of wreckage, and only 8 of the 159 holiday travelers and crew escaped injury. Among the 92 dead were the Rev. A. H. Washburn, rector of Grace Episcopal Church in Cleveland, and P. P. Bliss, singing evangelist. Stone's health failed as a result of the Ashtabula Disaster, it is said, and hastened his untimely death in 1883.

Mahlon Loomis was credited by some with the discovery of wireless telegraphy. He had patented his process in 1872, two years before Marconi was born. He had come to Cleveland in 1848 and studied dentistry in the office of Dr. M. L. Wright, who was located over the famous Handerson & Punderson drug store. As an avocation, Loomis carried on wireless experiments, and it is believed that he conceived the idea of wireless telegraphy during his years in Cleveland.

1877

At a meeting in Weisgerber's Hall, the first Cleveland Troop was formed. There were forty members in this cavalry company, every man owning his own horse. W. H. Harris was the first captain, and E. S. Meyer, first lieutenant. The next year, the troop moved into a fine, brick armory on Euclid near Case Avenue; and in 1884 larger quarters were secured on Willson Avenue. The troop ranked with the leading independent military organizations in the country. Later it became known as the 1st Cleveland Cavalry, and as Troop A, Ohio National Guard, it earned high honors for Cleveland in war and peacetime service. It served as escort for Ohio's Presidents, accompanied President Theodore Roosevelt at President McKinley's funeral, took part in Secretary John Hay's funeral procession and in many national events through the years.

Incorporation of the Plain Dealer Publishing Company was effected on February 13 by W. W. Armstrong, George Hoyt, David P. Foster, George Judson, A. P. Winslow, Charles Gordon, and O. H. Payne. As president, Armstrong's salary was set at $2,100, and Hoyt's as vice president at $1,500.

Suspended harness for fire horses, the invention of Reuben Osborn, early settler of Bay Village, came into use this year. It was standard equipment until automotive apparatus was developed. The first aerial ladder for firefighting was also purchased this year.

Rutherford Birchard Hayes, nineteenth President of the United States, was inaugurated. He was born at Delaware, Ohio.

Henry Chisholm became interested in a new industry, the manufacture of nails, and organized the H. P. Horse Nail Company (later American Steel & Wire Company) to make nails under the Huggett process patents. He built a factory at the foot of Case Avenue, but making cut nails proved impractical, and Chisholm turned to plain wire nails and staples. The economical wire nail produced a business volume greater than that of any other factory in the world, selling to an international market. When Chisholm died in 1881, he was succeeded as president by his son, Stewart Henry. The fine home that the son erected about 1891 was still standing in the 1940s at 3730 Euclid Avenue, one of the few reminders of proud "Millionaires' Row."

After graduation from the University of Michigan as a mining engineer, Charles Francis Brush became an analytical chemist and consultant in the iron-ore industry in Cleveland, 1873-77. During this time, he experimented patiently with electricity in the factory of the Cleveland Telegraph Supply Company and developed a successful arc light and dynamo. On a May evening, a parade was scheduled, and Brush decided to try out his electric light. He fastened the apparatus to the sill of his laboratory window, on the second floor of a little building at the southwest corner of the Square. The carbons were set, and as the cavalry came around the Forest City House, he threw the switch. A purplish light glowed in the crude lamp. The horses pranced in bewilderment. Brush's amazement knew no bounds. He was already counting his fortune, when the door was thrown open by a huge policeman who brandished his club and barked, "Put out that blamed light!" During the year, Brush exhibited his pioneer arc lights at the Franklin Institute in Philadelphia. Two of his newly invented dynamos were built for the lights.

Passage of the National Guard Law this year gave local military units the opportunity of enlisting in the State's service. Militia in Cleveland organized the 15th Regiment of the Ohio National Guard in June, which was soon joined by organizations from Chagrin Falls, Elyria, and Berea under the command of Colonel Allen T. Brinsmade. Almost the entire regiment disbanded in 1881.

John R. Ranney, J. Ford Evans, and Robert S. Pierce composed the charter committee that organized the Cleveland Gatling Gun Battery, the pride of Cleveland. Captain W. F. Goodspeed was its first commander. Businessmen later raised a fund to purchase a lot on Sibley Street, near the Brooks School, where a brick armory was erected. High military and social standards characterized the battery, and many well-known young Clevelanders were members. It ceased to exist in about 1905, but its property was managed for some time afterward by Malcolm G. Vilas, Harry W. Avery, B. W. Housum, George S. Russell, Harry L. Vail, N. S. Bidwell, and W. C. Spalding, trustees.

The Public School Library (later Cleveland Public Library) was at low ebb, as measured by Librarian I. L. Beardsley's annual report: "The library was peremptorily closed on the 30th of June, 1877, and the assistants, all but one, discharged, and the library was left to perform an amount of labor so excessive as to forbid that it would be done with the exactness which would otherwise have characterized it." Two assistants had been provided when the institution reopened on September 10, probably gentlewomen devoted to reading, as was the custom. Despite its handicaps, the library continued to grow in usefulness to the community.

"Brother" J. D. Jones, short, stout, and one-armed, was a popular figure in Cleveland for many years. The chaplain fitted an old scow in grand style, and called it the "Floating Bethel." At the foot of St. Clair Street, he held prayer meetings with such power that river men and dock hands passed saloon doors to hear him preach religion. It is said that he gave tickets in Sunday prayer meetings; and when a designated number had been collected, they could be "cashed" for a pair of shoes or a suit of clothes. This man of God was known from one end of the lakes to the other. In the eighties or nineties, he joined the Bethel Home, where he continued his prayer meetings.

In the depression following the panic, railroads engaged in vicious competition for the greatly reduced traffic volume, often carrying freight at less than cost. Wage cuts of about ten per cent, made by the companies in the spring, precipitated the great railroad strike of '77, marked by riots, bloodshed, and destruction to property in other cities, particularly in Pittsburgh. Five hundred men employed by the Lake Shore left their jobs in Cleveland on July 22. In an amazing resolution they pledged themselves to "abstain from all intoxicating liquors during the trouble," and declared that "all property belonging to the railroad company at this point shall be respected and protected to the utmost of our ability." Paralysis prevailed for two weeks, but not a dollar was lost in property damage nor a blow struck in the city. Poultry and livestock perished by the thousands, however, on halted freight trains in the railroad yards. Wages were gradually restored, beginning in the fall.

That Cleveland did not suffer mob violence in the railroad shut-down and the coopers' strike this year was due largely to the influence of Mayor William Grey Rose, a Republican who held the confidence of all classes. With a background of experience as newspaper publisher and legislator in Pennsylvania, he had come to Cleveland in 1865 to expand his earnings from oil ventures through investments in oil refining and real estate, opening subdivisions east and south of the city. Retiring from business in 1874 after financial successes, he served as mayor in 1877-78, and was known for economy and efficiency. He was a man ahead of his time, for in his address to the Council in 1879 he advocated that a juvenile court and probation system be set up to meet the menacing problems of delinquent youth, but it was not achieved for more than two decades.

It was reported on July 25 that the telephone was operating successfully over short stretches of wire. Many leading businessmen regarded the invention as a scientific toy, and the Council was slow in granting wiring privileges.

One of the most distinguished members of the legal profession was James Humphrey Hoyt, who formed a law partnership this year with Henry S. Sherman under the name of Sherman & Hoyt. Born in Cleveland in 1852, the son of James Madison Hoyt, prominent lawyer, he received his higher education at Western Reserve College, Amherst College, Brown University, and Harvard Law School. The partnership expanded until it became Hoyt, Dustin, Kelley, McKeehan & Andrews. Hoyt was a successful trial lawyer, an authority on civil law and counselor to many corporations and business firms. He was an able advisor to the Republican Party, influencing policies, particularly in Ohio. As Cleveland's most brilliant after-dinner speaker, he enjoyed wide social activities, and became the friend of many of the nation's leaders. Apart from his law practice, Hoyt developed diverse official connections with industry, banking, railroads, shipbuilding, and steamship lines, and his civic and fraternal interests were varied. His son, Elton II, became an executive in Pickands, Mather & Company. The Hoyt family lived in a fine home that withstood the years at 2445 Euclid Avenue.

Sixty-three commanderies and fifty-six bands met in Cleveland on August 27 for the Knights Templar Triennial National Conclave. The Cleveland Grays escorted them on parade, and a reception and ball were held in the Central Rink.

When Sunday editions of the *Leader* and the *Herald* appeared this year, churchmen raised loud protests.

Upon the death of her father, Augusta Mittleberger, daughter of William Mittleberger and niece of James M. Hoyt, decided to support herself by conducting private classes for girls in her home near Erie Street in the fashionable Superior Avenue residential section. This formed the nucleus of Miss Mittleberger's School, opened this year on Prospect Street near Case. Its success attracted students from out-of-town, and a boarding department was established on Sibley near Case that operated until the school expanded in 1881.

Missionary endeavor and the work of the Bethel Union was close to the heart of William H. Doan, son of Job Doan, early settler. When meetings were banned on the Public Square, the devoted churchman made plans to provide a public auditorium for Cleveland. The Tabernacle, or People's Tabernacle, a barn-like, brick structure, was dedicated on October 7 to the cause of "advancing religion, temperance and the improvement of the masses." It occupied an area 120 by 125 feet on the southeast corner of Ontario and St. Clair, and seated 3,500 people. Moody and Sankey drew capacity audiences with their soul-stirring revivals, and reform movements, lectures, concerts, and community gatherings centered in the Tabernacle. The building was destroyed after the Music Hall was built in 1885.

The Crawford Road Christian Church, of the Disciples faith, was organized this year, succeeding the Cedar Avenue Church. In 1945 the Rev. Oscar C. Jenkins, became pastor of the church which was located at 1607 Crawford Road succeeding the Rev. Russel Osgood.

The death of Dr. Jared P. Kirtland on December 10, at the age of eighty-two, closed four decades of distinguished service to the Cleveland community as teacher, physician, and pioneering scientist and naturalist. His research and discoveries attracted the attention of the great scientific men of his day.

The *Herald* is believed to have published on December 18 the first suggestion for putting condemned murderers to death by electricity. Electrocution was legalized in New York State in 1888.

1878

The first Brush dynamo and arc lamp sold by the Cleveland Telegraph Supply Company was shipped to Dr. L. R. Longworth of Cincinnati in about January. He exhibited the light from the balcony of the building in which he lived at 136 West 7th Street, and the four-thousand-candlepower lamp attracted a great crowd. "A man in the assembly explained everything," Charles F. Brush, the Cleveland inventor, said later. He called attention to the solenoid at the top of the lamp, stating, "That is the can that holds the oil." The side rod, according to the "expert," was "the tube that conducts the oil from the can to the burner." Not a word was said about electricity, and the crowd went away satisfied in their newly acquired knowledge of the electric light.

Lured to America by the vast reconstruction of Chicago after the great fire in 1871, young Samuel Austin, carpenter's apprentice, stopped to visit friends in Cleveland. Offered a job, he went to work at his trade on residences then rising along Broadway, Woodland, and Case avenues. This year, Austin was invited to undertake as contractor the remodeling of a doctor's home on Broadway; and from this beginning there developed a contracting firm engaged in residential and commercial building (later The Austin Company). Austin's first out-of-town contract came in 1895, when an early client, the Mineral Wool Company, engaged him to build a factory in Chicago.

The Terrapin Lunch, on Bank Street, provided regular dinners for 25 cents, and defied "competition in either price or quality." Sirloin steak with potatoes, hot bread and tea or coffee was priced at 20 cents; and at the same figure, there was a choice of veal cutlet, pork chops, fried fish, fried pigs' feet, liver and bacon, mutton chops, and salt mackerel. Cold ham, cold roast beef, or cold corned beef, with bread, butter, and tea or coffee, cost 15 cents. Cleveland lived well at small cost.

A Disciples mission on Detroit Street, sponsored by the Franklin Circle Church of Christ, became the Lakewood Christian Church, one of the most influential religious organizations in the community. Located at Detroit and Roycroft Avenue, membership had reached 1,802 in 1946 during the notable pastorate of the Rev. G. R. Goldner. On the East Side, the Collinwood Christian Church was also organized in 1878, at the instigation of E. M. Dille of Collamer, the second church body in the community. The Rev. R. T. Parks was pastor of the church which was located at School and East 154th Street in 1946, when membership was 706.

Fire destroyed the Atwater Building on March 19. It was occupied by the Non-Explosive Lamp Company, and had been the leading business block for many years. The loss was $87,200.

A vessel-building program was initiated by the Detroit & Cleveland Steam Navigation Company when James McMillan, Michigan senator and industrialist, joined the company this year. The first steamer, *City of Detroit,* cost $175,000 and was the finest passenger and freight steamer commissioned to date. It went into service on the Detroit-Cleveland route, followed by the iron-hulled *City of Cleveland.* The iron steamers, *City of Mackinac* and *City of Cleveland II*—later called *City of Alpena,* were built to carry pleasure travelers through the picturesque lake country on the Detroit-St. Ignace route in 1883. McMillan became president in 1889, the year that the new *City of Detroit* replaced the original vessel on its run. The *City of Mackinac II* and *City of Alpena II* took to the Mackinac course in 1893.

On April 8, a law was passed authorizing the Board of Education to elect a library committee, of not less than three or more than seven of its number, to govern the Public School Library, with full authority excepting to fix salaries. The first committee consisted of Sherlock J. Andrews, president, Rev. John Wesley Brown, Wilbur F. Hinman, Dr. William Thayer, John Hay, W. J. Starkweather, and Dr. H. McQuiston.

The first professional baseball club had disbanded in the fall of 1872, and there was little interest in the game until this year, when William Hollinger organized a team. The players were "Doc" Kennedy, catcher; James Mc-Cormick, pitcher; William Phillips, first base; George Strief, second base; Jack Glasscock, third base and later shortstop; Tom Carey, shortstop; Charlie Eden, right field; Fred Warner, center field; William Reiley, left field. The team went into a slump, and Barney Gilligan was signed to catch. Reporting his first big game, the *Leader* stated, "The wiry, agile, little Gilligan caught the swift shots of Big Jim McCormick with an ease that made him a hero with the fans right from the start." At this time, the ball park was at Kennard and Cedar Avenue. Cleveland was a member of the National League of Professional Baseball from 1879 until the end of the 1884 season, when the loss of five of its star players to an outlaw league took the heart out of the team. The ball club then joined the American Association. Frank De-Haas Robison, streetcar operator, was president and principal owner of the team, and a ball park was opened on Douglas Street, south of Payne, on Robison's Payne Avenue car line. Among early-day promoters of the local association were Marcus A. Hanna, Charles H. Bulkley, Azariah Everett, Amos Townsend, and O. A. Childs.

James H. Van Dorn's Akron neighbors admired the iron fence that he had designed to surround his home, and wanted fences like it. This led him to set up a small fence business that he moved to Cleveland this spring nearer major sources of supply and shipping facilities on the site of a great future plant (2685 East 79th Street). While waiting to turn in his bid for fencing a Milwaukee cemetery, someone mentioned jail cells, and he quickly realized that "jail cells are nothing more than fences built indoors." Jails soon became the principal business of the Van Dorn Iron Works Company. Stove manufacturers were having trouble with frame breakage, leading Van Dorn to master the art of metal fabrication. He made ornamental iron work, streetcar vestibules, bicycle parts, and metal office furniture. Van Dorn's structural-steel business developed through the interest of T. B. Van Dorn, son of the founder. The Williamson Building, the five-mile crib providing Cleveland's water supply, and many major undertakings rose on the company's structural work.

The Union Stock Yards were established at about this time, with Isaac Reynolds, freight agent for the Cleveland, Columbus, Cincinnati & Indianapolis railroad, acting as executive head until an experienced manager was found in John B. Foster of Kentucky. It was he who started the long and successful history of livestock marketing in Cleveland. He secured the first four commission merchants for the new market.

In order to increase the efficiency of city management, a serious attempt was made on May 14 by the Legislature to develop the board plan of municipal government. Under the new code, the people elected the mayor, councilmen, treasurer, police judge, and prosecutor; and the Council appointed the auditor, city clerk, and civil engineer. The first Monday in April was declared as election day. The following boards were elected by the people: police commissioners, composed of the mayor and four members; infirmary directors; water-works trustees, three members; fire commissioners, four members and the chairman of the council committee on fire; cemetery trustees, three members. Boards appointed by the Council: health, consisting of the mayor and six members; improvements (optional), comprising the mayor, civil engineer, street commissioner, chairman of the council committee on streets and one member, their duty being to keep the streets clean and in repair; also inspectors of oil, flour and bakery products, meat, fish, and pot and pearl ashes, if expedient. Boards appointed by the mayor: park commissioners, three members, with Council consent; directors of the house of refuge and correction, five members. A superintendent of markets was appointed by the mayor, subject to Council approval. The Board of Revision, made up of the mayor, president of the Council, and the city solicitor, met once a month to review the operations of all municipal departments and boards and report to Council. Nearly all boards served without pay, which in the light of history might be considered an economy that invited excuses for inefficient or indifferent service on the part of some public servants.

The newly organized East End Conversational Club could hardly have chosen a more appropriate name to further women's interests.

A small worsted mill opened by Joseph Turner & Sons this year was the nucleus of Cleveland Worsted Mills, Inc., formed in 1902. Well-known Cleveland men—O. M. Stafford, Kaufman Hays, and Martin A. Marks—guided the concern to a position of national stature, operating a number of completely equipped mills in the nation. In 1946, when L. O. Poss was president, the Cleveland Worsted Mills Company was one of the largest manufacturers of woolen and worsted goods in the field, and the Cleveland plant at 6114 Broadway employed about 2,500 workers.

The Perry Monument, with its granite foundation, was moved to the southeast section of the Square.

Sensitive Clevelanders complained when the newest city institution went into operation in the "Flats." It was an experiment in garbage disposal, housed in a shed, where grocery stores, hotels, and large producers of garbage deposited their collections. Although the refuse was removed daily and the shed was disinfected, the neighborhood hardly recognized the fact. The plan was wholly unsatisfactory, and the city turned to contractors to remove garbage; but they were often neglectful, and the people's health suffered. Housewives were urged to continue to burn as much garbage as possible.

An ornate clock tower without a clock was the crowning feature of the proud new home of Central High School, a $74,000 building erected on Willson Avenue (2200 East 55th). It was designed by Captain Levi T. Scofield upon recommendations of Superintendent Rickoff, and the shortcomings of the former building were remedied in advance construction plans that won approval of experts at home and abroad. High ceilings improved the ventilation. Stairs were built around a central well from the large main hall to the roof. The interior was light, bright, and featured improved heating. Central abandoned the old Euclid Avenue building to the Public School Library and the Board of Education, and moved to Willson Avenue in the fall, where the original East High School was absorbed. A new home-room principle was introduced, and some declared that Central would never more be a "great big family." School spirit emanated from the opening musical program in which the entire school joined under the direction of N. Coe Stewart. Solo parts were sung by Ella Russell, who gained world fame as an opera singer and married an Italian count.

Many of the faculty of Central High School made notable contributions, not only to education, but to character-building and good citizenship. Harriet L. Keeler, early teacher, earned the devotion of thousands of her students and high honors from her city. The service of Principal Edward L. Harris, 1889-1912 and 1917-21, stands out in the history of education in Cleveland. He was a born organizer and beloved of boys and girls. So many of his faculty members were promoted to head other city schools that Central became known as the "mother of school executives." Harris erected a gymnasium, and soon interscholastic athletics claimed equal interest with debates. School clubs and publications were introduced. In 1896 Mrs. John D. Rockefeller provided a clock for the bell tower. The community around Central High gradually became a melting pot of many nationalities, and Principal Harris demonstrated his gifted ability in making devoted and useful citizens of the newcomers. Young men and women went out from Central High School to win distinction in many fields.

Woman doctors, under the leadership of Dr. Myra K. Merrick, organized the Women's and Children's Free Medical and Surgical Dispensary on Webster Street in the Haymarket district, to aid self-supporting women and girls of low income. Women had found difficulty in securing hospital-staff appointments, and this pioneer endeavor provided a center for their practice. Prominent in the profession of early days were Drs. C. A. Seamon, Martha Canfield, Martha Stone, Kate Parsons, and Eliza Johnson Merrick. Among those of a later day were Drs. Alice Butler, Clara K. Clendon, Eva F. Collins, Josephine Danforth, Mary V. Davidson, Viola J. Erlanger, Mabelle S. Gilbert, Mary C. Goodwin, Julia Egbert Hoover, Fannie C. Hutchins, Sarah Marcus, Eliza H. Patton, Margaret Rupert, Minabel Snow, and Mary H.

White. The hospital moved eastward as it grew, and the name ultimately became Woman's Hospital where both men and women were served. A new building was occupied at 1946 East 101st Street in 1918.

On the night of October 21, Engine Company No. 6 rushed down the Columbus Street hill to answer an alarm from the "Flats." The horses plunged through the open drawbridge into the river; the firemen jumped for their lives, and several suffered injury.

Edward W. Scripps had established the *Detroit Evening News* in 1873, and Cleveland looked like a good place in which to launch another afternoon paper. With three-fourths of his $10,000 capital, the twenty-four-year-old, red-bearded six-footer purchased a steam press. He and his cousin, John S. Sweeney, business manager, ran off ten thousand copies of the first edition of *The Penny Press,* dated November 2, in small quarters at 12-14 Frankfort Street. Cleveland ridiculed, but respected, the oddity, calling it *The Frankfort Street Handbill.* It was an abrupt departure from custom—seven eighteen-inch columns to the page, and four pages of news in capsule form, all for one cent! In three years, its circulation exceeded its combined competition, and when Editor Scripps left Cleveland to establish the *Cincinnati Post,* W. H. Little became editor. Shortly after, he was succeeded by Robert F. Paine, who served until 1902 and managed the Scripps-McRae Press Association until 1905. On November 10, 1884, the name in the masthead was reduced to *Press;* and on September 21, 1889, *The Cleveland Press* appeared. A succession of aggressive editors directed the paper, among them Harry N. Rickey and Earl E. Martin. Most of them advanced to executive positions in the nationwide Scripps-Howard system, the United Press, or the publication field.

This year witnessed the first industrial use of Brush electric lights on an extensive scale. The year 1878 also marked Thomas A. Edison's patent of the incandescent lamp. Referring to his achievement years later, Charles F. Brush said, "It was this invention that made arc lighting from central stations commercially possible. I think it may justly be regarded as marking the birth of the electric-lighting industry as it exists today." The first series plant, a six-light Brush outfit, was sold in December to light a Boston clothing store. One of the arc lights was hung over the sidewalk in front of the store, and nightly attracted crowds of people. This was the first electric light used on Boston streets. The largest plant of about twenty lights was bought for Wanamaker's store in Philadelphia, and several lamps were used to light a part of the Mechanics Fair in Boston. By September, 1879, a worsted mill in Providence, Rhode Island, had purchased eighty lights, the largest electric-light plant in the world. Other mills in Providence, Hartford, and Lowell, a hotel in San Francisco, and several New York City dry-goods houses purchased plants in 1879. The new lights were exhibited in London in 1880. English capitalists organized a corporation and started a large plant there.

One of the earliest four-light Brush machines was exhibited to invited guests at the works of a large company in Cleveland. After examining the apparatus carefully for perhaps a half hour, one gentleman pointed to the line wire and asked, "How large is the hole in that little tube that the electricity flows through?" The shop superintendent pondered, then explained, "The electricity is generated by that there revolving affair rubbing the air up against them iron blades (meaning the pole-shoes of the magnets), just as you get sparks when you rub a cat's back." Brush, the inventor, stepped into the breach and suggested that while this was a simple and beautiful theory, it did not fully meet the facts. But the plant authority insisted, "the whole thing is plain. If you run that machine in a vacuum, where there is no air to get rubbed, you couldn't get any electricity." To him, the miracle of electricity was as simple as that.

William Nahum Gates of Elyria, Ohio, envisioned a profitable business in the handling of advertising, and he opened an office on the Public Square (Hotel Cleveland site). Among local and national advertisers served in the early days were the Beeman's Chewing Gum Company, E. R. Hull & Dutton, A. H. McGillin Dry Goods Company, The Sterling & Welch Company, and the Chandler & Rudd Company. A. H. "Bish" Madigan, a founder of The W. N. Gates Company and president from 1927 to 1942, was known nationally for his contributions to the advertising profession. Interests shifted to specialization in financial and insurance accounts, and in the 1940s the agency was reported to be servicing a major number of the life- and casualty-insurance companies requiring legal advertising in Ohio. Service of two of the officers with the agency approached the half-century mark: E. D. Wheeler, president, a nephew of the founder; and A. H. Van Duzer, vice president. The company, located in the Keith Building, was said to be the second oldest advertising agency in the nation, superseded by N. W. Ayer & Son, Inc., of Philadelphia.

Agitation for the first high-level bridge dated back to the sixties, but parties with financial interests involved had blocked this progressive step that would permit direct east-and-west communication. After approval by the General Assembly and the voters of the location for the new Superior Viaduct at the corner of Merwin and Superior Avenue on the east with the intersection of Pearl and Detroit streets on the west, there came the laborious and expensive securing of right-of-way. This included lowering the CCC&I railroad tracks to permit overhead street crossings from Champlain to Spring streets, and moving the locks and vacating about three miles of the canal bed. When it was completed, after four and one-half years of construction, Cleveland's new free bridge was one of the country's remarkable engineering achievements. Its total length was 3,211 feet; the width, exclusive of the draw, was 64 feet. Ten arches of Berea stone supported it, and the total cost was $2,170,000. At daybreak on December 28, the Cleveland Light Artillery fired a salute announcing the day of dedication. The holiday began with a gay parade in the morning. At noon, a mass meeting attended by the governors of Ohio and West Virginia was held in the Tabernacle, and there was much speech-making by the many noted guests and dignitaries. A banquet in the Weddell House closed the memorable event. In 1880 the West Side street railroad was given the right to cross the Viaduct.

This was the wettest year in 150 years of Cleveland's history, according to the Weather Bureau, with rainfall totaling 53.51 inches, of which 28.59 inches fell during the first seven months. There was little intervening dry weather.

1879

Gymnastics and physical fitness ranked with music and drama in Czech life, and the great Sokol of the Old World found roots in Cleveland in the Sokol Czech founded this year (4820 Wendell). Sokol, meaning falcon, aimed to develop "a sound mind in a sound body, inspired by patriotism and the spirit of brotherhood," achieved "through dramatic and musical training, lectures on educational subjects, and the establishment of libraries." The Czech National Union, also established this year, expanded into many states, and became one of Cleveland's oldest Czech fraternal organizations. As Czech communities grew, new societies were established. Sokol athletic exhibitions, characterized by brilliant performance, brought fame time and again to Cleveland. Ceska Narodni Sin—Bohemian National Hall, center of nationality, cultural, and social activity, was erected at 4939 Broadway in 1896. The Bohemian Sokol Hall, 4314 Clark Avenue, was erected in 1910. In the 1940s the Sokol-Czech-Havlicek was the city's oldest Sokol society.

Young Tom L. Johnson came to Cleveland from Indianapolis and rescued the unfortunate Brooklyn Street Railroad from financial straits "for a song." Then commenced a struggle to build a paying line through aggressive management that stirred local traction companies. Equipment consisted of four small cars, thirty mules, and a barn, with two and one-half miles of rusty rails. Johnson ran a double track on Pearl Street to Lorain Avenue, as far as he could go in the direction of the Square. Heated cars were introduced by installing small stoves and piling straw on the floor for added warmth. The straw smelled terribly, but it helped to build business. Fares were five cents each or six for twenty-five cents.

The last official hanging in Cuyahoga County took place on February 13, when Charles R. McGill, twenty-eight, paid the penalty on the Court House scaffold for fatally shooting his sweetheart, Mary Kelley. With the passage of a state law in 1885, executions in Ohio took place in the State Penitentiary at Columbus.

On the top floor of a three-story building at the corner of Superior and Bank streets, W. B. Davis opened a custom shirt factory. Two years later he secured a ground-floor location for a men's-furnishings store on the north side of Superior, between Seneca and the Square. In 1896 The W. B. Davis Company moved to Euclid Avenue, a few doors west of the site of its future home, 325 Euclid, on which the Davis Building was erected in 1917. Presidents Garfield, McKinley, and Harding traded with Davis, as did John D. Rockefeller. Trevor P. Jones served as president of the company from 1927 to 1934, when the founder succeeded him. W. B. Davis, pioneer retail merchant of Cleveland, founded The Davis Laundry & Cleaning Company after the turn of the century, and devoted much of his time to religious endeavor. George Rothen became president of the W. B. Davis Company in 1941.

The Public School Library (later Cleveland Public Library) moved to the second and third floors of the Board of Education Building, the former home of Central High School. Although Cleveland ranked eighth in circulation and fourteenth in the number of volumes among the thirty-three public libraries of the time, a noted Pacific Coast librarian claimed it had "about the worst public library in the world." Libraries were in their infancy, however, and trained librarians were few. In 1880 there were 29,155 volumes in the library, and the circulation had reached 130,443.

By late afternoon of April 29, downtown hitching racks were crowded with mud-splashed conveyances that had brought curious crowds to the Public Square from miles around Cleveland. An experiment with arc-light street illumination had been arranged by the City Council with Charles F. Brush, local inventor, and the Cleveland Telegraph Supply Company for the erection of twelve lamps of two thousand candlepower on high, ornamental poles in the Square. Newspapers had heralded the exhibition widely, and tense thousands, many carrying smoked or colored glass and eye shades with which to protect their sight, awaited the momentous signal that was to produce the "bright as day" wonder. Skeptics were there, too, contending that there could be nothing better than gas lamps. Attention focused on the 150-foot standards, at the top of which large globes of opalescent glass were suspended. At 8:05 in the evening, Brush gave the "go" sign, and a lamp flickered with a purplish light. As other beams joined it to pierce the darkened corners of the park, thundering cheers rose to mingle with a spirited serenade by the Cleveland Grays Band and the boom of artillery from the lakeshore. Thus street lighting by electricity was inaugurated in the world. Council contracted for the lighting of the Public Square and adjacent streets at a cost not to exceed $1,348.95 for the year; and during the next six months, Brush arc lamps appeared on streets in the downtown area.

Continuous growth and diversification of interests followed founding of the Cleveland Faucet Company this year, forerunner of The Bishop & Babcock Manufacturing Company. The heating and ventilating division was brought into existence in 1915, when the Massachusetts Blower Company was acquired. About ten years later, the manufacture of seamless metal bellows began, with many applications to controls and heating specialty devices. The automotive thermostat business started in 1926, when the bellows was incorporated into a control device for the cooling system of an internal-combustion motor. The automobile-hot-water-heater branch of the business was launched in 1935, and a single-motor-type of defroster heater was invented and developed by the company. After several years of developing air conditioning for the passenger compartment of an automobile, Bishop & Babcock introduced the first practical cooling equipment in 1939, selling it to the Packard company. In 1946, when Edward L. Mayo was president, the company was operating plants at 4901 Hamilton Avenue and 1194 East 55th Street.

Gilbert & Sullivan's *Pinafore* had become the most popular stage production in the country. The Bostonians introduced it to America in 1878 at the Boston Museum with Joseph Haworth of Cleveland in the role of "Bill Bobstay." The amateur local presentation in the Opera House, May 19, 1879, with Mrs. Seabury C. Ford and J. E. Herrick in leading roles, and J. T. Wamelink as musical director, was a spectacular success. It was natural that a burlesque of *Pinafore* should be presented a little later at the Theatre Comique. *The Mikado* succeeded *Pinafore* as the nation's favorite light opera.

The Crocker Block opened on Superior Avenue opposite the City Hall. Offices were built around a central well, and each floor was encircled by a walk and a handrail on the arcade plan. Timothy D. Crocker, art patron, who lived in an impressive residence east of Sterling on Euclid, adjacent to Samuel Andrews' extravagant "castle," had his office in the Crocker Block. The structure was later renamed the Superior Building. Some of its rooms were rented as apartments, one of its prominent tenants being distinguished Colonel A. T. Brinsmade, lawyer. The building and site were purchased by the Women's Federal Savings & Loan Association, and in 1946 a modernization program was undertaken.

For seven years, the Catholic Poles had worshiped in the historic St. Mary's Church in the "Flats." This year they built a frame church on Tod Street in South Cleveland, and two years later began the erection of one of the largest and finest churches in the country under the patronage of St. Stanislaus. Several heroic attempts to preserve the venerable St. Mary's as a relic were unsuccessful, and in September, 1888, Bishop Gilmour had the church razed.

Detroit Street had been planked for quite a distance, and it was a popular drive for Clevelanders who did not seem to mind the dust or mud. Suburban residences, wooded groves, and rail-fenced farms bordered it, with the charm of the lake to the north. Since 1850, when Dr. Jared P. Kirtland had introduced the culture of fruit and grapes into Rockport, vineyards and orchards had been planted in increasing numbers, yielding a crop estimated at $50,000 in 1872.

The cornerstone of Immanuel Evangelical Lutheran Church was laid on September 7 (at 2920 Scranton Road). The congregation originated, however, in a school launched in Brooklyn in 1872 by members of Trinity Church. In 1876 the assistant pastor of the mother church, the Rev. Henry Weseloh, was assigned to serve the new district, and three years later, a separate congregation was formed. There were 2,354 church members in 1884 and 494 children in the school, and an offspring known as St. Matthew's resulted from this rapid growth. Immanuel Church suffered serious damage by tornado in 1909; and when renovated after the storm, an auditorium was built to serve the many societies of the growing congregation. After a half century of devoted service, Pastor Weseloh died in 1925. The Rev. A. W. Hinz began his long and notable pastorate in 1926.

A strange instrument called the telephone went into service in Cleveland on September 23 in a room in the Board of Trade Building on Water Street. It was a near relative of the telegraph, and the office was in charge of E. P. Wright, superintendent of the Western Union Telegraph Company. His spare time had produced seventy-six subscribers to the Cleveland Telephone Company service in the central business area. Among them were the Standard Oil Company and Dan R. Taylor, who were willing to give the "new speaking telegraph" a trial at $72 per year. Eight employees handled the operations, and a volume of a hundred calls a day was considered rushing business. Soon the network of wires strung from roof tops expanded, indicating that the contraption really worked. The office moved to the attic of a building on Superior Street, where a tower housed a confusion of wires entering through the roof. Poles began to appear on the principal streets, and in 1881 an exchange opened on the West Side at Pearl Street and Detroit. Seven years later, the company moved to the northwest corner of Seneca and Michigan streets.

The Tabernacle was filled to capacity and there was an overflow in the old Stone Church on the evening of October 5, when Dwight L. Moody and Ira D. Sankey opened their famous revival meetings which continued for five weeks. This was one of the greatest revivals ever held in Cleveland.

Central High School, 1878.

Colonel John Hay invited a few friends to a private reception in his elegant Euclid Avenue home on the evening of October 16 to welcome William Dean Howells, with whom he had studied journalism while a boy in Columbus. Among those who greeted the eminent editor of the *Atlantic Monthly* were President Rutherford B. Hayes, General James A. Garfield, Charles Paine, Amasa Stone, Henry B. Payne, Mr. and Mrs. W. J. Boardman, S. H. Mather, R. C. Parsons, S. L. Mather, and James Mason.

The idea of erecting a monument to commemorate the heroic deeds of the soldiers and sailors of Cuyahoga County, who defended the Union in the Civil War, was first proposed by William J. Gleason at a meeting of the Camp Barnett Soldiers and Sailors Society, held in Cleveland on October 22.

At a meeting of leading citizens, inspired by Hiram M. "Father" Addison, pioneer, the Early Settlers Association of Cuyahoga County was formed on November 19 in the Probate Court room. The first officers were Harvey Rice, president, who served until his death in 1892; Sherlock J. Andrews and John W. Allen, vice presidents; Thomas Jones, Jr., secretary; George C. Dodge, treasurer. The first annual meeting was held on May 20, 1888, in the Euclid Street Presbyterian Church. It was determined that henceforth the annual meeting should be held on September 10, commemorating Perry's victory on Lake Erie.

The *Plain Dealer* devoted 4½ columns on December 31 to a list of hostesses who would be at home to New Year's callers in northern Ohio. Church watch meetings and New Year festivities were also announced.

The last half of the decade witnessed the establishment of firms that were still in existence in the 1940s: 1875, American Agricultural Chemical Company, Bosworth Hardware Company, Brooks Company, Cleveland Paper Company, Connelly Boiler Company, Herringshaw Company, Millard Son & Raper Company, Cleveland Agency of Penn Mutual Life Insurance Company; 1876, Charlesworth & Company, City Stove & Repair Company, Cleveland Laundry Company, Cleveland Agency of Equitable Life Assurance Society of the United States, Collver-Miller Travel Bureau, F. W. Grosse & J. F. Steinmetz Funeral Home, Sheets Elevator Company, Wood & Company, Inc.; 1877, Becker Storage Company, Greif Brothers Cooperage Corporation, Cleveland Agency of Northwestern Mutual Life Insurance Company, Cleveland Agency of State Mutual Life Assurance Company; 1878, William A. Howe Company, H. Miller & Son; 1879, Benes Custom Tailor, The Joseph Carabelli Company, Mullaire Company, Cleveland Agency of National Life Insurance Company of Vermont.

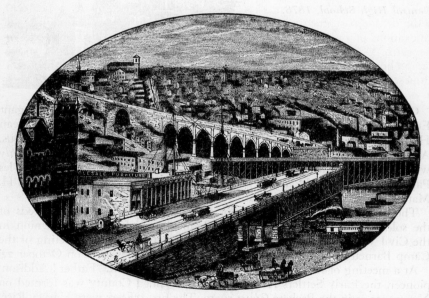

Superior Avenue Viaduct, Cleveland's first high level bridge.

CHAPTER 11

Wheels Turn Faster
1880-1889

CLEVELANDERS held their heads high in the 1880s. The city's
fame lay not only in beautiful Euclid Avenue. In the forest of masts
riding at anchor on the river were many vessels, built in Cleveland shipyards,
that plied the lakes and the seas bearing products of local industry to markets
throughout the world. Jobs were plentiful, as men of vision and wealth
launched new business enterprises and enlarged mills and factories. These
were prosperous times, fostering substantial gains in all phases of endeavor.

Cleveland won the population race with Buffalo, its census figures of 160,146
in 1880 surpassing the total of its rival, which stood at 155,134. This placed
the Forest City twelfth on the list of American cities. Cincinnati held her
rank of eighth with 255,139. Cleveland had grown more than 40 per cent
in the decade past. Its area, 28.164 square miles, had more than doubled, the
annexations of East Cleveland and Newburgh making up the large part of
the gain. A rising tide of immigration was reflected in a total of 59,409
foreign-born. Of the city's population, 2,038 were Negro, and only 23 were
Chinese and Japanese. In Cuyahoga County there were 196,943 inhabitants,
of which 68,753 were of foreign birth.

Nationality distribution had changed very little since 1870, with a marked
exception—the Bohemians, whose representation had increased to 5,627.
There were only about 500 Poles in Cleveland in 1880, employed for the most
part in the Newburgh steel mills. Theirs was a closely knit community,
preserving customs and traditions, and centering their activity in churches,
national societies, and business endeavor. Hungarians displaced the Germans
and Irish in the factory district (Rawlings-East 79th vicinity), where they
entrenched themselves firmly, following their trades. Many of these thrifty
folk walked to downtown Cleveland, where they deposited their earnings
with the Society for Savings, known familiarly to them as "The Bank
Where the Green Gardens Are." In 1889 the West Side people built
Hungarian Hall on Clark Avenue as their social center, and the next year
the Hungarian Home on Holton Street was erected by the East Side colony.

The first Russian Jews arrived in 1881. They settled along Woodland
Avenue, later moving to a district north of Doan's Corners. They were
victims of persecution in Lithuania, Poland, and the Ukraine, and represented
the beginning of a wave of Jewish immigrants that continued to seek
liberty in America until 1929. Yiddish was their common language. They

differed from the German Jews, adhering to the habits, dress, and religion of their fathers.

Industrious Czechs—known in America by the English designation, Bohemian—began to move out Broadway in 1883; and in the neighborhood of Hamm Avenue, named for a German city, they set up a village with carefully tended lawns and gardens. Here Dr. Henry A. Schauffler began his pioneering missionary work from which stemmed religious effort among the Slavic peoples in America. Schauffler College sent workers into many lands. On Sunday afternoons, the Czechs took picnic lunches and walked to the old canal lock. Sometimes a Cleveland pleasure boat came along with a gay party and a band aboard, and Czech spirit joined the voyagers in laughter and song. It is said that an enthusiastic drummer once hit his drum so hard that he fell overboard. In 1888 the influx of Croatians settled along St. Clair, from Minnesota eastward to East Madison.

The industrial lead once claimed by pot and pearl ashes, burr stones, saleratus, and candle and lard oil had been claimed by flourishing enterprises dealing with iron ore, coal, meat packing, petroleum, and clothing. Iron and steel had made the greatest gains during the seventies, producing castings for stoves, sewing machines and the like, tools and machinery, agricultural implements, and railway cars and equipment. The first basic open-hearth steel in America was produced at the Otis plant in 1880. Demand for wire increased, and Otis capital launched the American Wire Company, which became a sturdy link in the American Steel & Wire chain. In the American mills, captains of industry started their careers, some of them as boy apprentices, among them William P. Palmer, who became president of the American Steel & Wire Company, and Henry Barren, its vice president; Bertram D. Quarrie, president of Oliver Iron in Pittsburgh; Fred J. Griffiths, president of the Timken Steel & Tube Company, Canton; and George W. Burrell, president of The Wellman Engineering Company, Cleveland.

Fortunes in ore, coal, and steel were to be made in the Mather and Hanna companies launched in the eighties. As the industrial interests of Marcus A. Hanna broadened, his power and influence increased. The electrical developments of Charles F. Brush opened a new industry with ever-expanding opportunities, and local shops were finding difficulty keeping pace with a flood of orders from at home and abroad. Here the National Carbon Company had its beginning. Success did not come easily to two young toolmakers, Worcester R. Warner and Ambrose Swasey, but hard work and honest purpose saw the founders of a gigantic business through the problems of the early days.

Cleveland was the oil capital of the world! In 1884, eighty-six refineries were operating in the city. Many of them were destined to accept John D. Rockefeller's terms of outright sale or a share in the Standard Oil Company, as the oil magnate gathered in his competitors. Those who chose the latter course reaped unbelievable riches.

The clothing industry began in the home, and diligent housewives probably welcomed the day that garment-making moved into industrial plants. Great worsted mills were operating in 1888, and St. Clair Avenue, west of Ontario, had become a center of suit-and-cloak factories. By 1920 Cleveland had become one of the three leaders in the ready-to-wear industry.

In five short years William J. White, an obscure popcorn salesman who added flavoring to a barrel of "worthless" Mexican chicle, had become known internationally as the Yucatan "Gum King." Dr. E. E. Beeman had a flourishing business in pepsin, an aid to digestion. Combining it with chicle, he offered Beeman's pepsin chewing gum to the public in a little package bearing his bewhiskered portrait, and it developed into a colossal business.

Late in the decade, Francis E. Drury and Henry P. Crowell were experimenting with oil heat as an improvement over wood and coal stoves for cooking purposes. Here the famous Perfection line of oil-burning devices had its beginning. In the fertile Schaaf Road district south of Cleveland, pioneering truck-gardeners had introduced greenhouse culture, which grew into a highly productive industry.

As the trend toward consolidation of shops and factories continued, larger numbers of workers were employed, and they united in organizations for mutual benefit. Rapid industrial and civic advance inspired unrest in labor camps and encouraged agitation for improved working conditions and shorter hours. The Federation of Organized Trades and Labor Unions of the United States and Canada, at its organization meeting in Cleveland in 1882, pointed the way that led to May Day strikes in behalf of the eight-hour day. Clashes between capital and organized labor came in "the great upheaval" of the mid-decade. The city's labor relations suffered as strikes in the nation increased from 485 in 1884 to 1,411 in 1886, in the latter year affecting almost 10,000 establishments with a half-million workers. Radicals admitted in the immigrant tide made matters worse by encouraging violence and social revolution.

History-making industrial and scientific "firsts" marked a short span of years in the eighties. Albert A. Michelson continued his explorations on the velocity of light at Case School of Applied Science, and in collaboration with Edward W. Morley of Western Reserve University conducted the famous experiments on ether drift, "the results of which, as interpreted by Einstein, formed the basis of some of his revolutionary theories concerning relativity." Dr. Charles F. Mabery and Herman Frasch pioneered in petroleum research. Charles Martin Hall developed the electrolytic process for the reduction of aluminum ore. Alfred and Eugene Cowles patented an electric furnace for smelting ores. Albert W. Smith and Herbert H. Dow developed chemical processes leading to the founding of the Dow Chemical Company. Samuel T. Wellman patented the open-hearth charging machine, marking a new era in steel-making.

Between 1841 and 1882, more than six hundred wooden propellers had been built on the lakes at a cost of from $75,000 to $125,000 each, to carry coal, grain, iron, lumber, and freight. As timber costs increased and wood began to grow scarce, builders followed England's lead and turned to iron. Cleveland yards constructed marvels of the freight-transportation industry. Contrary to the belief of old-time shipbuilders that only timber craft would float, Captain Henry D. Coffinberry and Robert Wallace produced the *Onoko,* the first iron ship, that broadened the avenues of trade. It was soon outmoded by the *Spokane,* the first steel bulk freighter on the lakes, built in Cleveland. In 1884 the Board of Trade reported the city's registered tonnage at 84,295. Although the cigar-shaped, steel whaleback was launched with great promise in 1889, its weaknesses soon made it unpopular. Widening of the river channel through the old riverbed facilitated dry-dock operations, and dredging of the Cuyahoga became increasingly necessary as shipping mounted. Construction of the east breakwater provided greater refuge for vessels and helped to protect the lakeshore.

While ships were increasing in size to bring greater cargoes to hungry furnaces and factories, industry was choked by a slow, laborious unloading method at the docks. A horse hoisted a huge bucket of ore from the hold with a tackle, the ore was dumped into wheelbarrows and shoved slowly to the iron-ore stock pile in the marshland along the old riverbed. Sometimes it took a week or more to discharge a thousand-ton cargo. As the decade opened, a young inventor named Alexander E. Brown found an efficient and rapid solution in his hoisting machine that revolutionized the handling of ore and coal on the Great Lakes and extended its influence into other industries.

From Cleveland, railroad lines radiated to connect markets to the east, west, and south, transporting materials essential to ever-expanding industry. As corporations increased their wealth, an epidemic of railroad-building resulted. Using their power to throttle action detrimental to their interests, they gained control of the legislatures of many state governments. This led Congress in 1887 to pass the Interstate Commerce Act, regulating conduct of the great railroad systems. The Nickel Plate, organized in 1881, broke all speed records in building its Buffalo-to-Chicago road, and set up its headquarters in Cleveland.

The Savings & Trust Company, founded in 1883, was one of the first financial institutions organized under the law that created the trust company. One of the nation's first neighborhood banks, known as The Broadway Savings & Trust Company, opened in Cleveland the next year. Banks were being organized in flourishing communities populated by thrifty workers in mills and on farms. Cleveland's financial institutions played a large part in making possible vast industrial expansion. Eight national banks, the Society for Savings, and a number of smaller banking houses were serving industry and commerce in 1885.

Liberty E. Holden and associates rescued the financially distressed *Plain Dealer* and purchased the early-day *Herald,* which lost its identity. The *Leader* then acquired the *Evening Herald,* which became the *News and Herald.* Now that both the *Plain Dealer* and the *Leader* were publishing morning, evening, and Sunday editions, competition heightened in the newspaper field.

The prosperity era was reflected in new undertakings dedicated to the public. The generous interest of William H. Doan made possible the Music Hall, a public auditorium of greater capacity than its predecessor, the

Tabernacle. Several theaters opened; and the Cyclorama, featuring realistic Civil War scenes, attracted a continuous stream of spectators from the city and distant points. The Stillman, the first large apartment hotel east of Erie Street, opened in 1884, followed the next year by the Hollenden, the first major hotel east of the Square.

Cleveland hotels were the center of brilliant social and political functions, and many strategic plans for national, state, and local progress originated within their walls. Keen competition existed, particularly in the operation of their barrooms. Massive mahogany bars grew longer and heavier with gleaming brass. White-aproned bartenders presided with importance before broad expanses of shiny mirrors studded with rows of fancy bottles, shaving the foam from cold beers and producing masterful mixtures for thirsty patrons. The American House, Forest City House, Kennard House, Weddell House, and Hollenden had famous bars; but they found keen competition in popular saloons, such as Richards & McKean on the northwest side of the Square, and the Oyster Ocean on Bond Street. Men transacted "important business" over the crowded rails of Cleveland bars until the coming of prohibition; then the old-time boisterous spirit became history.

Cleveland looked upon James A. Garfield as one of its sons. Earnestly campaigning for him, local enthusiasm paved the way to the White House. When he was assassinated, citizens mourned deeply. The bullet that killed the President stirred the nation to a consciousness of the disgraceful condition of the civil service, and resulted in creation of the Civil Service Commission early in 1883.

Although leading retail business houses were located on Superior Avenue, the trend was eastward on Euclid and not on Superior, as had been envisioned by early planners. Substantial stone or brick stores were going up on the "Avenue" to accommodate new business establishments. The Public Square had been commercialized, and four-story buildings predominated on the south and west sides. On almost every downtown corner was a newsboy and a bootblack. Resting his foot on a small toolbox, the customer could have a shine for five cents.

The smoke nuisance that inevitably accompanied railroad and industrial development was hastening the blight along broad Superior Avenue and the vast Perry-Payne "pastures." As time passed, the two blocks of Superior west of the Square suffered increasing desolation as profitable business deserted them. A half century later, cheap hash houses, quarter-a-night hotels, and employment agencies catering to laborers and construction crews prevailed.

When Lily Langtry, lovely English star of *She Stoops to Conquer,* praised Cleveland for its beauty, the *Plain Dealer* commented on March 17, 1883, that she could hardly have seen Euclid Avenue beyond Erie Street. Directing a sharp thrust at the official housekeepers in the City Hall, the editor declared, "Our streets are hog pens of filth and unsightliness," and Euclid Avenue is "the nastiest and most unkept part of the city." Impatient journalistic outbursts urging city improvements seemed to have little influence upon the Forest City's standing among large municipalities. "I know of no city in this country, always barring New York," wrote a *Cincinnati*

Enquirer correspondent early in 1884, "that makes a more favorable impression upon a stranger than Cleveland."

Stately Euclid Avenue, eastward from Brownell Street, was the show place of America, except for a commercial crossroads at Willson Avenue. Some of its finest homes were built after 1889 between Perry and Case Avenue. Architecture of the Greek Revival period had given way to romantic Victorian design. Elegant houses with mansard roofs, shutters, and arched windows provided an appropriate background for beautifully gowned ladies carrying flirty fans and tiny parasols. Iron fences enclosed spacious lawns, and an iron stag in a prominent setting was a mark of distinction.

Ladies venturing beyond social boundaries sought culture and enlightenment in new organizations: the Nineteenth Century Club, founded in 1880; Western Reserve Club, 1882; Women's Press Club, 1886; and the Cleveland Literary Club, 1889. Never, never called "women" in the eighties, ladies painted china, worked as hired girls, schoolteachers, seamstresses, bookkeepers, or waitresses to earn extra income. Defying the edict that woman's place is "in the home," devoting herself to "children, cooking and church," tempting employment opportunities in offices increased with the advent of the telephone and the typewriter.

The waltz, two-step, and schottische were popular, and *Where Did You Get That Hat?* was the top tune. Fashionable ladies posed under plumed picture hats with lorgnettes, the hems of their sidewalk-sweeping gowns weighted with iron discs. High-top button shoes could be purchased for a dollar. Gay-colored fascinators deserved the name. Silk stockings worn on festive occasions featured bright bars and broad stripes, and carried shocking price tags up to fifteen dollars. Black cotton stockings served for everyday, and lisle in the afternoon.

As Cleveland expanded, the number of streets had multiplied until in 1880 there were 975 streets, 183 avenues, 113 lanes, alleys, and places, and 5 roads. Wood pavements were gradually being replaced with Medina sandstone. This trend prompted a plea for preservation of dirt roads in the city, so that driving could be enjoyed without "shaking our bones over the stones." While it was agreed that street cleaning was a good idea, the taxpayers declared it cost too much. Street lighting, on the other hand, met with less opposition when the first central power station developed by Charles F. Brush went into service to illuminate Cleveland streets. Soon downtown stores were installing Edison's incandescent system, which proved superior for illumination purposes.

An experiment in the management of public health by the Police Department proved unsatisfactory. When the Health Department was returned to a board of physicians, they attacked the city's problems with a vengeance that produced results. Reorganization of the Fire Department promoted more efficient operation. Although new equipment was purchased, frequent disasters overtaxed its ability, and Cleveland's neighbors were called upon for assistance more than once. Industry brought progress that shrouded much of the city in smoke; and although the inspector indicated the worst offenders, abatement was scarcely evident.

The Kentucky Street Reservoir had become inadequate as the city expanded. A high-pressure water-supply system was introduced, and the Fairmount and Kinsman reservoirs, opened in 1885, were expected to keep pace with population growth and expansion for a long time. Three years later the Central Viaduct attracted wide attention as a remarkable engineering achievement.

The problems of the Police Department multiplied as the city grew, and patrol boxes were introduced to speed the exchange of information and instruction. The municipality began sharing with private hospital agencies the burden of caring for the sick when it erected City Hospital in 1889. Wade Park, the first large gift to Cleveland, was the pioneer of the city's modern parks, a monument to the character and humanitarian spirit of a great Clevelander, Jeptha H. Wade.

The eyes of the world focused on Cleveland as the first electric streetcar went into operation in 1884. Many citizens, however, had to be satisfied to ride horsecar lines for another decade. The city was trying to support a confusion of competing street-railway lines. As Tom Johnson's power in the traction business increased, clashes over plans and policies precipitated the famous feud with Mark Hanna that continued for more than two decades.

Transportation had made great strides; but for everyday travel in and out of the city, the horse had no equal. Hitching posts were everywhere. Horses stamped the pavement as long lines of express wagons parked on the Square. Businessmen drove to their offices or rode the horsecar, and ladies used carriages to shop and pay social visits. Every fine residence had its stable and carriage house. Livery stables and blacksmith shops were common. All-day picnics were fast becoming the custom as the city expanded. Buggies and carriages were washed and polished in the morning, and, with family and napkin-covered basket, the trek began to the country for a holiday.

Sportsmen trained fast horses on the Glenville track, hoping for a winner like Maud S. The temptation to race in the streets was thwarted by Glenville, which set a speed limit of six miles an hour. Many church members condemned horse racing as they did playing cards and whisky, claiming that runaways aggravated traffic problems.

Glenville was taking on airs as wealthy Clevelanders erected fine homes at the resort. At Nine Mile Creek, Samuel Mather and his family spent their summers. Across the stream was William Bingham's summer home. Maurice B. Clark, early Standard Oil partner, built a fine house on the lake, and peacocks strolled on the lawn around the residence of C. P. Born, Jr., industrialist. There were many more beautiful homes that fell before the path of progress; but the sturdy, square, brick house built by William Foster, son of pioneer Robert Foster, in about the 1840s (on Foster Avenue) was spared.

Sleigh races on Euclid Avenue had added to the Forest City's fame. With the first snowfall, well-to-do drivers, bundled in buffalo robes, began racing their fastest horses in afternoon contests on the "course" from Case to Erie Street. As many as thirty or forty sleighs waited at the starting line for the take-off. Crowds running into the thousands lined the avenue, cheering the sportsmen. Cleveland's "first" families were represented in the races of the eighties and nineties, among them J. B. Perkins, W. J. Gordon, John D. Rockefeller, Colonel William Edwards, H. K. Devereux, Charles A. Otis, Jr., A. C. Pennock, L. C. and Mark Hanna, W. H. Corning, General B. M. Caldwell, C. A. Brayton, J. E. French, G. A. Garretson, Amos Townsend, Albert A. Lawrence, Joseph Ingersoll, C. E. Grover, Henry Blossom, George A. Baker, I. P. Lamson, F. W. Bell, M. A. Bradley, Harry Chamberlain, Echo Heisley, W. F. Putnam, William Roader, and Frank D. Robertson. At the turn of the century, the sleigh races fell a victim of the automotive age.

Dobbin's burden was eased as the bicycle gained in popularity. Traffic came almost to a standstill as Jeptha H. Wade, Jr., threaded his way down Euclid Avenue toward the Square on a summer day in the early eighties. Raised head and shoulders above astonished pedestrians, he gripped uneasily the handlebars of his new high-wheeled bicycle. Known as the "ordinary," the solid-rubber-tired vehicle had a 58-inch front wheel to which the pedals were attached. On the saddle, mounted on a tube connected to the small, rear wheel, the rider perched precariously, liable to pitch headlong upon sudden impact. Nevertheless, the $150 curiosity gained favor, providing spills and thrills.

Bicycle enthusiasm really began with the arrival of the "safety" about the mid-decade. Two wheels of equal size, the pedals connected by a chain drive with the rear, after modern fashion, were a welcome change after the hazardous high-wheeler. Office workers rode to work, children burned up the road on their way to school, and soon the ladies were riding. Bicycle clubs were organized, and at Athletic Park, "bike" champions competed in exciting inter-city meets. High-wheelers and tricycles, polished to perfection, paraded on special occasions, and exhibitions of trick and fancy riding found spots on theater programs.

Sports activities flourished. Ice-skating rinks found competition in a new pastime, roller skating, and promoters capitalized to the utmost on the craze. Tennis clubs were being organized, and ladies ventured onto the courts under a handicap of wasp waists and long skirts. Football, introduced in Cleveland late in the decade, was primitive indeed. Uniforms consisted of old clothes; there were no goal posts, and rules were determined as the game progressed. Cleveland's big-league baseball club had its ups and downs in the eighties.

Case School of Applied Science, planned by civic-spirited Leonard Case, one of Cleveland's greatest benefactors, was founded in 1880. At this time, there were only three institutions devoted exclusively to higher technical education in America—Rensselaer, Massachusetts Institute, and Stevens, all in the East. Industry had not yet demanded technically trained men, consequently specialized engineering education was subordinated by classical schools. From the founding, Case was outstanding in its field, and faculty members were widely known for pioneering discoveries and developments. Prominent industrialists of the city, appreciating the value of the institution in training young men and in advancing industrial progress, manifested practical interest from the start, endowing it with wise leadership and notable bequests. Out of the Case laboratories over the years came valuable research that contributed greatly to Cleveland's industrial advance.

The financial future of Western Reserve College in Hudson, Ohio, had become unstable in an era of rapid change as the tide moved cityward. For more than a half century it had stood high in the academic world; but now it was caught between the trend of state-supported institutions and those sustained by churches. The suggestion that a university be established in Cleveland had been projected in 1880. A small group of community-minded citizens, convinced that it would be wise to build upon the foundation laid in Western Reserve, influenced the move to Cleveland. Here the institution could collaborate with Case School in common interests and fulfill the city's need for a cultural center.

The Western Reserve University Corporation, chartered in 1884, began with a single school, the Medical Department which was transferred to it by Adelbert College of Western Reserve University, successor to Western Reserve College. The college continued as an independent corporation "affiliated with the University," but in all ways autonomous, common officers being elected. Western Reserve University developed in two different patterns: first, by direct establishment of new units, of which the College for Women in 1888 was the first; and, second, by "affiliation." Faculties of exceptional talents and abilities characterized Western Reserve, which broadened its opportunities to thousands of young people decade after decade.

Bishop Gilmour's desire to found a Catholic institution for the education of young men was fulfilled in 1886 when St. Ignatius opened. The forerunner of John Carroll University, it achieved high standing among institutions of higher learning.

Specialized education gained firm footing in the eighties. Instruction in pharmacy began in 1882. Cleveland women founded the Cleveland School of Art this year, and energetic members of the Art Club imparted strength to the new undertaking that steadily gained in importance. Alfred F. Arthur, well-known singing teacher, gathered about him an able faculty and founded the Cleveland School of Music in 1884, from which developed orchestral and choral endeavors that advanced music appreciation. While a little group of young ladies were learning the fine art of domestic science in a church basement, Newton M. Anderson formed a class in manual training that pioneered the secondary technical school. Under able leadership the public schools had achieved high standing in the nation, yet a large percentage of Cleveland children of school age did not attend.

The word "School" had been deleted from the name of the city's principal book-lending agency. William Howard Brett, appointed librarian of the Public Library in 1884, inaugurated policies and practices during his career that raised the institution to a high place in the nation.

Books and short stories for young girls written by Sarah Chauncey Woolsey of Cleveland under the pen-name of Susan Coolidge, were being widely read. Her series of "Katy" books earned increasing popularity. Lydia Hoyt Farmer's books relating to biography and history enjoyed gratifying acceptance. During the decade, Albert Gallatin Riddle, of the city, completed a series of historical works devoted to the Civil War and American leaders of the time. Adventurous young sprouts buried their noses in Mark Twain's crowning achievement, *The Adventures of Huckleberry Finn*. The author was well known to Clevelanders.

Newspaper headlines in the scrapbooks of the Charity Organization Society revealed the need for increased interest in charitable effort and reform: "Old Man of Three-Score and Ten Deserted by Thankless Children"; "The Wages of Sin—A Young Girl Old in Wicked Practices, in Severe Straits, Throws Herself Upon Charity"; "Mock Marriage—and How a Worthy Woman's Life was Wrecked by One." In a drive against vagrancy, "the boldest and most fertile street beggar in the business" was arrested. Breaking into her rooms, police found trunks bulging with clothing, among which were "One merino dress, much trimmed; one delaine dress; three chinchilla sacques; one breakfast shawl; one lady's cloth dolman; one purple alpaca dress; one elegant wrapper, garnet colored."

An overabundance of welfare societies were conducting campaigns, however, some of them paying exorbitant commissions to agents who solicited finances. An intolerable situation had developed; but in the merger of the leading charities, a forward step was taken toward efficient management in solicitation and administration. Hundreds of squalid and destitute homes were visited, and aid was brought to the despairing. When death came, the right of sepulchre was provided.

Emphasis on character-building rather than upon reform became the new policy of the YMCA. Here young men found opportunities that helped to shape useful and productive careers.

While the growth of church influence cannot be measured in terms of denominational expansion, it is interesting to observe that in Cleveland in 1880 there were 164 churches—Protestant, Catholic, and Jewish. Aristocracy worshiped at St. Paul's Church in "Millionaires' Row," at Trinity Episcopal, and at Old Stone. Fashionable carriages driven by liveried coachmen in long processions deposited elegantly dressed ladies and silk-hatted gentlemen at the curb. Vestrymen in frock coats ushered parishioners to the pews. Crowds at St. Paul's were attracted by the singing of the thirty-voice choir and its soloist, Mrs. Seabury Ford. The church was the scene of many notable weddings, the most spectacular being the marriage of Ruth Hanna, daughter of Marcus A. Hanna, to Joseph Medill McCormick. During the eighties, the church bells were silenced in deference to venerable Jeptha H. Wade, who lived across the street.

Cleveland celebrated its ninety-second birthday by unveiling a bronze statue of the founder, General Moses Cleaveland, on the Public Square. Appropriately, it had been made possible by the Early Settlers Association, formed less than a decade earlier as a link between the pioneers and future generations. Since the summer of 1796, when the general and his men set on paper the plan for the "capital city" of the Western Reserve, new leaders had greatly expanded their blueprint. Here was the Public Square, as the first planners laid it out, and the pattern of neighboring streets that they had envisioned. If, on July 22, 1888, the founder could have visited the city that bore his name, he would have been happily surprised to find that out of the surrounding forests had risen a flourishing city far greater than he had predicted, reaching out along the lake and deep into the valleys. Thousands of chimney tops marked the homes of its citizens. Rail and steamship lines radiated from the city of iron and steel, transporting the products of its many-sided industry far and wide. Institutions contributing to the happiness and well-being of the people had been made possible by a lengthening roll of those who had given generously over the years. General Cleaveland would have been proud of Cleveland—a good place in which to live and to work.

1880

Leonard Case, sole guardian of the Case fortune, fulfilled the dreams of the family when he executed trust deeds setting apart certain lands to establish and endow a scientific school in Cleveland. Upon his death, January 6, his good friend, Henry G. Abbey, made known the well-laid plans based upon Case's intense interest in science. On April 6, articles of incorporation of The Case School of Applied Science were filed by James D. Cleveland, R. P. Ranney, Levi Kerr, Reuben Hitchcock, J. H. Devereux, A. Bradley, Henry G. Abbey, W. S. Streator, Samuel Williamson, T. P. Handy, J. H. Wade, E. B. Hale, H. B. Payne, James J. Tracy, and Joseph Perkins. Case School had thus become the first endowed and independent college of applied sciences west of the Alleghenies.

Alexander Ephraim Brown, twenty-eight, born in Cleveland, the son of Fayette Brown, had a background of engineering training gained at the Brooklyn Polytechnical Institute, the United States Geological Survey, the Massillon Bridge Company, and while working with Charles F. Brush, inventor. His own inventive genius was first evidenced in bridge-building. Later, while watching long lines of laborers slowly moving bulk cargoes of iron ore by wheelbarrow from vessel holds to the Whisky Island docks, he conceived the idea of an automatic hoist that would give the workmen "something better to do." Five years of diligent effort produced the Brown hoisting machine this year. The first mechanical hoisting device for unloading vessels, it soon reduced the cost of handling materials, such as iron ore and coal, influenced the design and construction of vessels, made possible rapid excavation of canals, and facilitated the building of ships.

With capital of $100,000, a company was organized in 1880 to design and manufacture hoisting machinery, with Fayette Brown, president, and the inventor, vice president and general manager. The Brown Hoisting & Conveying Machine Company was incorporated in 1893, with offices in the Perry-Payne Building and the works at Belden and Hamilton streets. The company name was later changed to The Brown Hoisting Machinery Company. Brown's superior inventions had revolutionized unloading of heavy bulk materials, and it was estimated at this time that 75 per cent of Great Lakes ore was handled by his hoisting machinery. The market for Brown equipment expanded over the globe; and the company produced varied material-handling equipment for docks, coal companies, steel plants, railroads, and shipyards. Fayette Brown died in 1910 at the age of eighty-seven, and was succeeded by his son, Alexander E., as president. Ships were carrying ten-thousand-ton cargoes in 1911, the year the inventor died, honored many times for his benefactions. His brother, Harvey H., then became president, and his son, Alexander C., vice president and general manager. Upon the death of Harvey in 1923, Alexander C. was made president. In 1927 a merger of The Brown Hoisting Machinery Company with Industrial Works of Bay City, Michigan, was effected. Alexander C. became president of the merged company, known as Industrial Brownhoist Corporation.

Fayette Brown had begun his steady rise to leadership in the iron industry when he returned from Civil War duty to become general agent and manager of the Jackson Iron Company. He held the presidency of the Union Steel Screw Company, the National Chemical Company, and the G. C. Kuhlman Car Company, as well as chairmanship of the board of the Stewart Iron Company, Ltd. He was a partner with his son, Harvey H., in Harvey H. Brown & Company, representing two of the largest mining concerns in the Lake Superior region. Fayette Brown's career and those of his sons left an indelible impress upon industrial Cleveland.

The last curtain was lowered at the Globe Theater on January 29, with the final performance of *Uncle Tom's Cabin* by the Anthony & Ellis Company, Minnie Foster playing Topsy. Shortly after, demolition of the famous theater began, to permit erection of the Wilshire Block.

New Yorkers were enjoying *Hazel Kirke,* a melodrama, that opened at the Madison Square Theater on February 4 for a record run, featuring Effie Ellsler in the leading role. Its spectacular success is said to have influenced the popularity of "Hazel" as the name for a generation of new babies. The star, who was the daughter of the Cleveland actress, Euphemia Emma "Effie" Ellsler, made her entrance on the stage in infancy, as Little Eva in *Uncle Tom's Cabin*.

The brilliant career of Sherlock J. Andrews closed on February 11, when he died at the age of seventy-nine. A man of magnetic personality, well versed in the law, he was one of the most eloquent trial lawyers in Cleveland. He worked tirelessly for his city and his profession for more than a half century, serving in Congress in 1840 and as a member of the constitutional conventions of 1850 and 1873.

By decree of the Lake County Court of Common Pleas on February 23, the old Mormon Temple at Kirtland, Ohio, was legally acquired by the Reorganized Church of Jesus Christ of Latter-day Saints and was again occupied as a church.

Curious interest in the great Pyramids of Egypt, and objection to the introduction of the metric system inspired Charles Latimer, chief engineer of the Atlantic & Great Western railroad, to promote an organization of local engineers. C. H. Burgess, Hosea Paul, and Walter P. Rice, son of Captain

Percival W. Rice and grandson of Harvey Rice, had little time for the mystic Pyramids, and they favored the metric system. Nevertheless, they joined with their fellows in pooling their professional interests at a meeting in the county-surveyor's office in the Court House on February 28, when the Civil Engineers Club (later The Cleveland Engineering Society) was organized. A. M. Wellington was the first manager, followed by election of the first president, Charles H. Paine. The club's first home was in the Case Library Building.

Lutheran families had met two years earlier in the sparsely populated rural district southeast of Cleveland to plan for a church and school, but it was not until this year that they were able to erect a house of worship for the German congregation of Zion Lutheran Church, in a location later known as Dunham Road and Rockside, Maple Heights. A grade school provided education for Lutheran children. Many members objected to the proposal in 1883 to hold English services regularly; and a compromise was reached on the basis that all singing be in German. The structure built in 1896 (at 5754 Dunham Road) was serving Zion Lutheran Church a half century later. The school closed in 1944, due to a shortage of teachers. The Rev. Arthur C. Keck became pastor this year.

Newburgh was making way for railroad progress, and this year Cleveland sold land to the Connotton Railroad Company that included the old Axtell Street Cemetery—or Eighteenth Ward Cemetery. The eight-acre grounds had been opened about a quarter of a mile north of Broadway as early as 1800, and here pioneer families were laid to rest. In the winter of 1881, the remains from more than three thousand burials were moved to the new Harvard Grove Cemetery.

The City Armory on Long Street opened with a charity ball on March 20. This was the home of the Cleveland Grays until fire destroyed the building in 1892.

Construction of a new building had been started by the Cleveland Homeopathic Hospital Society in 1878, and it opened this year in the name of Huron Road Hospital. It was the last word in architecture and facilities, and served until 1923.

The merger of health and police administration must have proved unsatisfactory, as the Council returned the Health Department to the direction of a board composed of medical men. They improved the milk supply, prosecuted for the first time a charge for adulterating milk, and issued permits for the sale of milk. They attacked problems relating to sewage and garbage collection, and exposed "quacks and illiterate persons" for practicing medicine unlawfully.

James W. Dickinson became chief of the Fire Department. His first general order was the reorganization of the seventeen companies into three battalions, each in command of an assistant chief. His leadership initiated efficient practices on which future expansion was built. George A. Wallace, who served under Chief Dickinson and became a distinguished head of the department, often picked up J. H. Maddy, a *Leader* reporter, when responding to an alarm. Loss in a factory fire one day was trifling. Wallace put the figure at $50, but the *Leader* reported $100. The chief demanded an explanation. "It's like this," Maddy told him, "I didn't get to ride with the department and had to hire a horse and buggy. Under the rule of the office, the loss had to be $100 or more in order to entitle a reporter to hire a rig, so you see I really had to make my estimate the limit to get under the wire."

Clevelanders followed the career of James A. Garfield with pride in his political and intellectual attainments, claiming him virtually as their own. When word came on June 8 that he had been chosen as the Republican candidate for the Presidency, there was great rejoicing. An elaborate reception was arranged to welcome him to the city three days later. Excursion trains brought thousands to join in a brilliant evening celebration. The Public Square was gay with Chinese lanterns, and fireworks closed the festivities. In reality, Cleveland became the campaign headquarters. By unique circumstance, Garfield, a member of the House, was at the same time a senator-elect, and Republican nominee for President. Burke A. Hinsdale, Cleveland educator, wrote the text-book for the Republican campaign of 1880. Garfield inaugurated front-porch campaigning from his Mentor, Ohio, home.

The street-lighting system and the central power station, the first in the world, developed by Charles F. Brush had brought him phenomenal fame. Brush patents and the demand for commercial street illumination were bringing worldwide business to George W. Stockley's plant, the Cleveland Telegraph Supply Company, which Brush and his associates purchased at about this time to form the Brush Electric Company, capitalized at $3,000,000. Before the end of 1881, public-street lighting from a Brush central station was in operation in New York, Boston, Philadelphia, Baltimore, Montreal, Buffalo, San Francisco, and other cities. One of the largest stations was that of the Brush Electric Light Company of New York, located at 133 West 25th Street, which pioneered in generating power to light a two-mile circuit on Broadway from 14th to 26th streets on December 20, 1880. The first central station in the Orient went into operation in Shanghai, China, in 1882. Comprehensive patents were secured by Brush for a storage battery in 1881, but the success of his street-lighting system far overshadowed it. The inventor erected a stone mansion for his family on Euclid Avenue (Arena site) in 1884. An enormous windmill in the rear operated Dr. Brush's laboratory experiments for many years. It was taken down in the early 1930s to make way for Chester Avenue. In 1889, the Brush plant was located on the north side of Mason Street, east of the Pennsylvania railroad tracks.

James H. Rogers, accomplished musician, was engaged as organist at the Scovill Avenue Temple. He served the congregation (later Euclid Avenue Temple) for fifty years, during which he was also music critic for the *Plain Dealer* and organist at the First Unitarian Church.

Valerius D. Anderson, twenty-five, was working in a tin shop in 1855 in Milton, Wisconsin, repairing leaky roofs and making tinware and hoops for hoopskirts, selling his products from door-to-door. An inventor by nature, Anderson developed and patented an improved steam boiler that he sold in the Midwest until this year, when he moved to Cleveland. Here he invented

The Sylvester T. Everett home at the northeast corner of Euclid and Case avenues, built in 1883. Celebrities from many countries were entertained here.

The famous hostess balcony in the Everett home.

The Samuel Andrews home, built in the early 1880s at the northeast corner of Euclid and Sterling avenues. A hundred servants were required, hence it was called "Andrews' folly." It was torn down in 1923. CLEVELAND PICTURE COLLECTION, CLEVELAND PUBLIC LIBRARY.

The Society for Savings Building, the city's first large bank building, was completed in 1890.

The Cleveland Chamber of Commerce Building, dedicated in 1899, became the home of Cleveland College in 1938. STANLEY L. MᶜMICHAEL COLLECTION, CLEVELAND PUBLIC LIBRARY.

a rendering tank for butchers; but packing houses began to replace butchers, his sales dropped, and he turned to making fertilizer dryers. The industry centered in his home, where two older sons, Frank and Charles, and two younger brothers helped their father. In 1893 a tract of land was purchased in West Cleveland, and a small shop was erected, the first unit in the large factory later operated by The V. D. Anderson Company on the original site, 1935 West 96th Street. In 1876 Anderson had conceived the idea of a continuous press for extracting oils from oleaginous seeds and nuts; but it was not until 1900 that the first successful oil expeller was produced. Curiously, packing houses, rather than vegetable-oil mills, were the first to recognize its advantages. The manufacture of certain steam specialties resulted from Anderson's new steam trap that contributed to efficient drying of products before they reached the expeller. In 1946 The V. D. Anderson Company was the world's largest manufacturer of oil and moisture expellers, at work in nearly every civilized country. Carl W. Zies was president, and A. D. Anderson, son of the founder, treasurer, of the oldest manufacturing plant on Cleveland's West Side.

Some of the first tennis games were played on the lawn of the Billings home on the south side of Euclid, where East 88th Street was later designated. Charles and Frank Billings, Henry Wick, Harry Judd, Orlando Hall, and Sterling Beckwith were in the group that played later on George Worthington's lawn. Organized tennis began about this time with the forming of the East End Tennis Club and the Buckeye Club in the Euclid-Willson Avenue neighborhood. The former continued for a longer time, eventually moving to Euclid and Kennard Street. Prominent on Cleveland courts were Elizabeth Dean Sprague, Ida Riddle, Mary Wilkinson, Kate Kendall, and Ina Ingersoll.

F. H. Wallace, an organizer of the Cleveland Gun Club, was called the father of trap-shooting in Cleveland.

On August 2 the *Leader* devoted fourteen inches of space to the obituary of John Malvin, pioneer Negro benefactor of his people and a respected citizen of the city.

Virgin timbers were felled in Cedar Glen (south of University Circle), to make way for Dan O. Caswell's sanitarium, the Blue Rock Spring House. Clevelanders sought invigorating health in treatments and in drinking the repulsive, blue-green water of the famous Blue Rock Spring.

The Connotton Valley Railroad Company opened a line to Canton this year, and the Connotton Northern Railroad Company was incorporated to build from Fairport to Canton; but plans were changed to make Cleveland the lake terminal of the narrow-gauge road. In January, 1882, trains ran through to the miserable little Cleveland depot on Commercial Street. After considerable persuasion, Council permitted the extension of tracks across Commercial and along Canal Street to the corner of Ontario and Huron, where a new passenger depot was opened in August, 1883. Consolidation of the Northern and the Valley, under the latter's name, was followed by receivership; and in 1885, reorganization as the Cleveland & Canton Railroad Company was effected in Cleveland. The road was sold in 1888 to the new Coshocton & Southern Railroad (later Wheeling & Lake Erie), and a line was projected southward through the coal fields to Zanesville.

Machinery and astronomy were the consuming interests of Worcester R. Warner and Ambrose Swasey when they were young apprentices in New England. In April they took their savings and struck out for themselves, starting a machine-tool business in Chicago. Skilled mechanics were scarce and their market lay to the east, prompting them within the year to move to Cleveland. On East Prospect Street, at the Cleveland & Pittsburgh tracks, they built their first shop, a 100 by 45-foot, three-story, brick structure, the site of a vast future plant (5701 Carnegie). At this time machine tools were used largely to make parts of plumber brass, pistols, rifles, and carriage and saddlery hardware. Then came sewing machines, bicycles, and automobiles. Warner's hobby of astronomy inspired the building of the first telescope by the company in 1881, which was followed by substantial orders.

An Irish Catholic parish known as St. Colman's was organized in the west end of the city on Gordon Avenue; and the Germans, east of Willson Avenue, established the Holy Trinity Parish, erecting a church that was replaced by a fine, stone structure in 1907. German families formed St. Michael's Parish in 1882, and built a small, frame church that was soon outgrown. One of the finest churches in the country was erected in its place in 1891. In 1883 Bohemians founded St. Adalbert's Parish on Lincoln Avenue; and Our Lady of Lourdes was organized on Randolph Street, by the Rev. Stephen Furdek, the "Father of American Slovaks." An Italian congregation utilized the old Turner Hall on Central Avenue as its first church home in 1887; and, during the same year, Germans in the East End dedicated a new parish to St. Francis. The Slovaks formed the St. Ladislas Parish on Corwin Avenue in 1888.

The largest rally of the Garfield Presidential campaign took place on the evening of November 4, when President Rutherford B. Hayes reviewed a torchlight parade and spoke from the Kennard House balcony. Hayes was a frequent visitor to Cleveland in the 1880s. He came from his Fremont home to visit friends and study in the rooms of the Western Reserve Historical Society, of which he was vice president in 1892 and a life member.

Clevelanders attracting public attention at this time were Dr. Hiram H. Little, who devoted forty years to banking and the successful development of real estate in addition to his professional practice; Ebenezer H. Bourne, manufacturer, banker, and, for a time, city treasurer; Jonathan C. Forman, who began his printing career as roller boy for the *Western Reserve Chronicle,* and became a partner in Short & Forman, later Forman-Bassett-Hatch Company; and John Meckes, merchant, who was developing one of the leading dry-goods stores on the West Side.

Cleveland ranked fifteenth in manufacturing in the United States, with 1,055 plants having a capital investment of $19,430,989, employing 21,754 wage earners on a payroll of $8,502,935. Cost of materials totaled $31,629,737, and products were valued at $84,860,405. Economic affairs were in good condition. Iron and steel was the leading industry, employing 2,999 workers and producing products valued at $9,435,432, followed by slaughtering and meat packing, $5,427,938; foundry and machine shop, $3,820,685; men's clothing, $2,687,409; paint and varnish, $1,893,905, or one-sixth of the nation's output; malt liquors, $1,249,502; lubricating oil, $1,163,174; flour, $1,105,768; lithographing, printing, and publishing, $889,509. There was a bright future ahead for the bolt-and-nut industry, that showed a production total of only $68,074; hosiery and knit goods, $97,550; wire products, $287,000; drugs and chemicals, $557,500, and railroad cars, streetcars, and repairs, $661,000. Of the 1,908,745 gross tons of iron ore shipped from the Lake Superior mines, 55.4 per cent had been received at ports in the Cleveland district—Cleveland, Ashtabula, Conneaut, Fairport, and Lorain. This was a year of crop failure, yet Cuyahoga County farms produced 184,680 bushels of wheat, 550,108 bushels of oats, and 360,604 bushels of corn.

1881

The first ambulance was brought to Cleveland by B. E. Harris on January 2.

City Hospital and the YMCA benefited in the amount of $4,000 from the Authors Carnival that opened on January 31 in the Tabernacle. Many prominent citizens took part in the eight-day pageant of history, literature, and the stage.

A new trunk-line railroad took definite form on February 3, when a group of businessmen, representing subscribers who were successful builders and operators of railroads, met in the New York office of George I. Seney. Seney was the leading figure in the syndicate identified by his name. Daniel P. Eells, Cleveland banker, who was not present, had a vital interest. The new company, the New York, Chicago and St. Louis Railway Company, organized under the laws of the State of Indiana with authorized capital of $16,000,000, set out to build a main line from Cleveland to Chicago along a route already surveyed, paralleling the Lake Shore & Michigan Southern route. A proposed branch to St. Louis was abandoned, and plans to construct a Cleveland-Buffalo road were forwarded. Early in March of this year, headquarters were established in Cleveland, and work began at many points with giant strides, despite the shortage of engineers and construction men in the highly competitive railroad-building era. Nowhere along the line did the struggle for the road reach the burning heights to which it flared between Norwalk and Bellevue, Ohio, the latter emerging the victor. From this rivalry came the nickname, Nickel Plate, bestowed upon the new road by the fiery editor of the *Norwalk Chronicle*—a familiarity that became permanent and official. Columns of newspaper controversy were provoked by many others who claimed to have inspired it, in this era when the ultimate in elegance was accomplished by nickel-plating. The dramatic history of the road was written in 1946 by Taylor Hampton under the title, *The Nickel Plate Road*.

Judge Stevenson Burke was one of the foremost corporation lawyers of his day. Possessed of brilliant intellect, thorough knowledge of the law, and distinguished bearing, his experience as counsel for leading railroads of the Middle West had developed his great ability. He was instrumental in effecting a number of the important railway mergers of his time, contributing both the legal plan of procedure and the executive direction that converted weak lines into consolidated roads, operating more efficiently and economically. Stevenson Burke was born in 1826 in a modest New York State home. At six, he had mastered the old English readers; and at eight, when his parents moved to Lorain County, Ohio, he had read Pope's *Essay on Man*. His earnings made possible graduation from Ohio Wesleyan University, and in 1848 he was admitted to the bar. Leaving the bench of the Court of Common Pleas of Lorain County, Judge Burke came to Cleveland in 1869. Forming a partnership with Franklin T. Backus and E. J. Estep, he entered upon "a legal career that has had no parallel in the bar of Ohio." Backus died in 1870, and Burke became associated with W. B. Sanders, and later with J. E. Ingersoll. Some of his cases related to the railroads won national recognition. His career closed with his death in 1904.

James Abram Garfield was inaugurated twentieth President of the United States on March 4. The First Cleveland Troop (Troop A) and the Cleveland Grays participated in the ceremonies in Washington.

Wooden sliding poles were introduced in fire houses in March. Firemen protested that they generated great heat on the "slide," and they were replaced with iron. With the new "Darwinian descent," firemen were out of bed and at the horses' heads in four seconds, as compared with sixteen when they used the stairs.

The Brush Electric Light & Power Company, incorporated on March 16, established a central power station near Ontario and St. Clair streets this year. It also began construction of a station on Lime Street, near the river, to light streets and downtown stores. Wires were carried along the streets on high poles. The Union Depot was lighted this year. Lower Woodland Avenue, Garden Street, and Willson Avenue were illuminated. At the southeast corner of the northwest section of the Public Square, a towering steel mast was erected to light the central area. Eight lamps of four thousand candlepower were clustered at the top; near the base was a platform to which they were lowered for frequent inspection and carbon renewal. Similar masts were raised at Lake and Bank Street, Water and Superior, and Erie and St. Clair.

L. A. Bailey opened a dry-goods store, forerunner of The Bailey Company, at Ontario and Prospect, on the northern third of the future store property.

Case School of Applied Science opened in the red-brick dwelling of the Case family on Rockwell Street (opposite Federal Building). Instruction in the preparatory department commenced in April. College classes began on September 3, the first-year's enrollment totaling sixteen students. Nominal head of the faculty of six was Dr. John N. Stockwell, self-educated astronomer and eminent scientist, who had collaborated with Leonard Case in a number of investigations relating to the motion of the moon. Dr. Stockwell became the first professor of mathematics and astronomy. His contributions to the Smithsonian Institution and to American and foreign scientific journals marked him as one of the leading men of his day. His works relating to the heavenly sphere revealed practical and pioneering observations, and research pertaining to ancient eclipses opened new vistas to science. When he died in 1920 at the age of eighty-nine, Dr. Stockwell was regarded as the "dean of American astronomers."

The Charity Organization Society was formed in Cleveland (later Family Service Association) as part of a national movement to "reduce pauperism" and combine "thorough investigation with personal home visits." J. H. Wade was the first president, and prominent citizens were identified with the non-sectarian endeavor. Henry N. Raymond was the first superintendent.

Under the leadership of Joseph B. Meriam, president, the policy of the Young Men's Christian Association was directed toward character development rather than reform. Largely through his vision and generosity, a new home for the "Y" was established, with the purchase of the five-story Windsor and Waverly blocks at the southwest corner of Euclid and Sheriff streets. Modern innovations included a gymnasium, bowling room, chapel, library, and two classrooms. A physical department opened with a hundred gymnasium members. Remodeling had been completed when the International Convention met in Cleveland this spring. A night school was introduced (later Y-Tech and Fenn College), with volunteer teachers, offering classes in bookkeeping, commercial law, drawing, German and Latin, practical electricity, and shop mechanics. Some of the students came from outlying districts. William R. Hopkins, a lad in his teens, came from Newburgh on the horsecar to study bookkeeping. Greek, French, and elocution were added to the curriculum, and the latter attracted young Edmund Vance Cooke, who entertained his listeners with readings from Shakespeare and later earned wide renown as a poet. George A. Rutherford, Carl W. Brand, Stephen G. Rusk, and William J. Semple were among early-day students in the night classes. In March, 1882, the East Cleveland Branch "Y" was organized (at Euclid and East 19th), the West Side Branch in November, and the Newburgh Branch in March, 1883. The Association was incorporated in the spring of the latter year, and in 1887 the first work with boys began. Presidents who succeeded Meriam were Julius King, J. B. Perkins, G. W. Stockley, and J. Livingstone Taylor.

When, on May 9, news came to the men in the Cleveland Rolling Mill that their employer, Henry Chisholm, had died, they laid down their tools and went home sorrowing. For years this simple man, unspoiled by wealth, had been their friend, and his passing was a blow to them and to the entire city. The Newburgh mills had grown steadily, providing capital to launch Illinois subsidiaries. The combined business aggregated $25,000,000 annually and provided employment for eight thousand men. Earnings in turn assisted small railroad companies and struggling business concerns; and in this policy of diverse interests in banking and manufacture lay the secret of the pioneer's great success. It has been said that had Henry Chisholm lived a decade longer, Newburgh's future would have been different, and the name of Chisholm and the Cleveland Rolling Mill Company would have ranked in greatness with that of Andrew Carnegie and the Carnegie Steel Corporation.

When John D. Rockefeller purchased the property at the southwest corner of Euclid and Case in the heart of "Millionaires' Row" in 1868, two houses faced on Euclid. He took for his residence the second. Workmen jacked up the corner brick mansion and inched it to the southeast corner of Prospect and Case, where it became the new home of Miss Mittleberger's school this year. It was the first attempt to move a brick house in Cleveland, and the undertaking created wide interest. The street number was then 1020, and the young ladies adopted "Ten-Twenty" as the school's familiar name. The curriculum covered courses from kindergarten to college, and Augusta Mittleberger's fame was widespread. From 1887 to 1889, Cornelia F. Blakemore—Mrs. Worcester R. Warner—served as associate principal. Many influential women attended the school, among them Belle Sherwin, Elizabeth R. Cutter—Mrs. Dwight W. Morrow, and the daughters of Presidents Hayes and Garfield and of John Hay. Miss Mittleberger's unusual success was attributed to gifted qualities that made her "a teacher, leader, and friend." She closed the doors of her school when she retired in 1908. "Ten-Twenty" then became a hotel, and the building was razed in 1930.

The Rockefeller mansion was a plain brick structure relieved by arched windows, and the interior reflected the modest economies of the Standard Oil king. This was the birthplace of John D., Jr., and his sisters, and it was the Rockefeller home until the family moved to New York City in 1884. The dark, high-ceilinged parlors were the meeting place of the world's celebrated personalities. In the 1930s the house was razed to make way for a gas station and parking lot. The stone stable and coach house remained, however, a sturdy reminder of the shelter it had given to Strong Ned, Gallant Steed, Flash Eye, and famous Rockefeller carriage horses. A night club moved in for a brief stay, then came a restaurant; and the landmark's glamour was lost in the transition.

The Standard Tool Company, incorporated this year, pioneered the development of high-speed, metal-cutting tools, and an electric-welding process for welding carbon steel to high-speed steel. It became one of the principal manufacturers of twist drills, reamers, taps, dies, milling cutters, and special tools used in metal-working plants. In the 1940s when R. R. Higgins was president, the company's products, marketed internationally, were in use in mass-production industries, such as the automotive, aviation, appliance, farm-implement, electrical-manufacturing, and railroad fields.

In early summer, the faculty of the Medical Department of the University of Wooster concluded an agreement to unite with the Medical Department of Western Reserve College, apparently without the knowledge of Wooster authorities. Out of the unfortunate circumstance emerged a Wooster medical department with a reorganized faculty headed by Dr. Leander Firestone, dean. During the eighties, Wooster Medical College held its own with Western Reserve. Prominent on the faculty were Drs. Henry J. Herrick, William A. Knowlton, Marcus Rosenwasser, and Frank J. Weed. In 1896, however, it ceased to function under the Wooster charter, and under a new name, the Cleveland College of Physicians and Surgeons, it became the Medical Department of Ohio Wesleyan University, which promised the new building for which the faculty had been clamoring. Some years later, it merged with Western Reserve.

As President James A. Garfield entered the Baltimore & Potomac railroad station in Washington on July 2, accompanied by Secretary of State James G. Blaine, he was shot by Charles J. Guiteau, a disgruntled office seeker. The assassin's bullet wrung anger and anxiety from Cleveland citizens, and on Sunday, the 3rd, ministers "preached appropriate sermons." The City's Fourth of July celebration gave way to eulogies of Cleveland's President. At a public mass meeting on the Square, four thousand people listened to speeches by prominent men honoring their leader who lay in death's shadow. Banners bore Garfield quotations. Crowds milled around the newspaper offices daily, eager for encouraging reports.

City health authorities protested against the discharge of twenty-five sewers and a growing number of factories and oil refineries into the Cuyahoga, and the mayor referred to the river as "an open sewer through the center of the city." In 1877 it had been estimated that only about one-third of the people were using "city water." The dangers of using a common well or spring as a source of water supply were investigated in 1881, and a plan for placarding scarlet fever and diphtheria cases was introduced.

On August 10 Barnum's Circus was down at Stone's Levee on the river, east of the site later chosen for the eastern approach to the Central Viaduct. The great feature was Chang Woo Gow, the Chinese giant, reportedly several inches over eight feet tall. Exhibited with him was his wife, of ordinary size, "General" and Mrs. Tom Thumb, and a thirty-six-inch dwarf, Chung Mow.

Cleveland's President, James A. Garfield, was dead. The news came in the night of September 19. Bells tolled and cannon boomed their grave tribute until dawn. With heavy heart, the city prepared to honor its fallen leader on the 20th. Business ceased, a mass meeting was arranged in the Tabernacle, and deepest mourning prevailed. Mayor R. R. Herrick joined the trustees of Lake View Cemetery in requesting burial in Cleveland. Captain George A. Wallace and the men of Hook and Ladder No. 1 of the Fire Department, who had draped many of the downtown buildings with mourning emblems, turned to the erection of a catafalque on the Public Square to receive the martyred President's remains.

The funeral train bearing the slain President arrived at the Euclid Avenue Station on Saturday, September 24. With measured step, citizens and soldiers accompanied the hearse to the lofty catafalque on the Public Square, where the Cleveland Grays stood guard. Distinguished men of the nation came to Cleveland for the solemn occasion—ex-Presidents Grant and Hayes, Generals Sherman, Sheridan, and Hancock, the cabinet, and high officials in government. The body lay in state for two days, and 100,000 people came to mourn. On the 26th, public services were conducted on the Square. The Rev. Isaac Errett of Cincinnati, Garfield's devoted friend, preached the funeral sermon, after which the sorrowing procession, five miles long, moved slowly out Euclid to Lake View Cemetery. Here a resting place was provided in a private vault until a great mausoleum could be built. A movement to raise funds for the monument was already under way, J. H. Wade, H. B. Payne, and Joseph Perkins having been appointed to solicit money from the nation. The Garfield family returned to "Lawnfield," their home at Mentor, Ohio. The late President's sons became men of achievement: James R., prominent lawyer and Secretary of the Interior in the Theodore Roosevelt administration; Harry A., president of Williams College; Abram, "dean of Cleveland architects," and Irvin McDowell, lawyer.

Young C. A. Selzer opened a business this year, on lower Euclid Avenue, that was the show place of Cleveland. It was stocked with imported china and glass, silver, furniture, furnishings, and decorative art that made it a veritable museum of the Old World. A great attraction was a white crane in the playing fountain where the lower level of the store began. Selzer later moved his famous galleries to the Hickox Building, then to the Bulkley Building, and they were eventually taken over by the George Bowman Company.

The City Armory on Long's Alley was the scene of a boxing exhibition between Paddy Ryan, champion of America, and Charley McDonald, champion of Canada, on October 22. Ryan was the winner of the bareknuckle contest in the fourth round, and many claimed he would prove a good match for John L. Sullivan in the heavyweight clash in February. So he was, but not good enough to win.

A landslide on November 12 had wiped out the Scranton Road stock yards, which were moved to a new site (West 65th Street) this year. The Cleveland Stock Yards Company was incorporated, with O. B. Skinner, traffic manager for the Cleveland, Columbus, Cincinnati & Indianapolis Railroad, as manager, and John B. Foster, superintendent. Stock pens, an office building, and a hotel were erected. During the next few years the slaughtering business gradually moved to the new location, and a permanent livestock and meat industry was taking form. In 1892 The Cleveland Union Stock Yards Company was organized, with J. F. Whitelaw, president, and E. A. Murphy, secretary-treasurer. The Farmers & Drovers Stock Yards Company was acquired in 1903. The Cleveland company was one of the first to construct all pens under cover. Succeeding presidents were E. A. Murphy, Allen S. Waltz, and A. Z. Baker. The area of the yards in the 1940s was forty-six acres.

Proceeds of the opening night at the Euclid Avenue Roller Rink, November 16, were donated to the Garfield Monument Fund. The rink, entered on Euclid, extended along the rear of the Opera House on Sheriff Street.

Remnants of the old 15th Regiment united as the 5th Regiment, with Captain E. W. Force of Chagrin Falls as the first colonel. Companies from Burton, Berea, Geneva, Wellington, Chagrin Falls, Norwalk, Youngstown, and Painesville also served in this early Ohio National Guard unit.

Mr. and Mrs. Dan P. Eells, staunch members of the Second Presbyterian Church, erected the Idaka Chapel as a memorial to their daughter. Its service as a Sunday School reached church stature, and when it united with the First Baptist Church, the chapel became a part of the beautiful new structure at Prospect and Kennard Street.

Dan Parmelee Eells, wealthy and influential, developed railways and was identified with large industries, local and national. Nevertheless, he devoted money and energy to the encouragement of cultural and welfare institutions. For many years the Eells family lived in a stone mansion on Euclid Avenue that was the scene of brilliant gatherings. It is said that Marcus A. Hanna and William McKinley met with Eells in a conference in the library, leading to McKinley's Presidential nomination. The family later moved to their Rocky River estate (Beach Cliff), and the house was occupied for a while by the Warren Cornings. It was the home of Spencerian College, 3201 Euclid, for several decades. To the east stood the impressive residence of H. B. Hurlbut, banker, art patron, and philanthropist, where massive, bronze dogs decorated the lawn. Anthony Carlin of The Standard-Foundry Manufacturing Company, makers of rivets, purchased the Hurlbut house in 1910, and on the site, 3233 Euclid, built a pillared mansion.

1882

The affairs of the vast Standard Oil Company were brought under a parent management organization through creation of a trust, managed by nine trustees, providing that a "Standard Oil Company" be set up in the separate states. When the holding company came into vogue, however, stock of the thirty-three corporations was transferred to The Standard Oil Company of New Jersey through a gradual process not completed until after 1900. Kerosene for household lamps was the backbone of Standard's business, supplemented by a variety of lubricating oils and greases. Cleveland-made tank wagons were familiar equipment throughout the world; and, at one time, the old Standard Oil cooperage department turned out 10,000 barrels a day and employed 3,000 people. Ambrose M. McGregor of Cleveland had given many years of valuable service to Standard Oil, and in the late 1890s he became president of the Ohio Company. Rockefeller, however, continued to guide the destiny of the business he had founded, retiring in 1911.

Clevelanders agreed that twenty-eight-year-old Oscar Wilde, Irish "Apostle of Estheticism," was both a serious and comic sensation, but they made no effort to lionize him as did other American cities. Wilde's reputation for worshipful adventures in esthetics, his devotion to exotic women, and his passion for the sunflower—called a perfect medium of artistic expression—had preceded him. On February 18, "600 of the most intelligent and refined people of the city" found more interest in his black-velvet knickerbockers and silk stockings than in his lecture, *The English Renaissance*. The young genius left behind him an enthusiastic demand for sunflowers and sunflower seeds.

In February the East Cleveland horsecar line was granted the right to extend service from Prospect on Hayward to Cedar and east to Fairmount.

The Day Nursery and Kindergarten Association was founded by the Women's Christian Association (YWCA), and the first day nurseries were established in many parts of the city. In 1886, free kindergartens were opened, and a decade later they became a part of the public-school system.

A union Sunday School at Payne and Willson avenues had reached an enrollment of more than six hundred in eight years. The Second Presbyterian Church took it under its wing, and on March 21, the Willson Avenue Presbyterian Church was organized with forty-eight members, half from Second, seeking a church home farther from "down town." Through the generosity of Dan P. Eells, a pillar of the Second Church, a new site near the corner of Lexington and Willson and a fully equipped house of worship were presented to the congregation debt-free in the early eighties. After his death in 1903, the church society changed its name to Eells Memorial Presbyterian Church. In 1912 it was established as the Phillips Avenue Presbyterian Church in East Cleveland at 1179 East 125th Street. The Rev. John T. Middaugh succeeded the Rev. Paul W. Hollar as pastor in 1944.

Passengers on the Brooklyn streetcar line were obliged to pay an extra fare from the end of the line on Lorain to the Square, and Tom Johnson sought concessions from the West Side Railway in their behalf. When Mark Hanna, who dominated the road, refused, Johnson installed buses without extra fare. It was not until April 1 that the Brooklyn line succeeded in securing a grant permitting its cars to operate over West Side tracks to the west end of the Superior Viaduct and over city-controlled tracks on the Viaduct to Water Street. As Johnson extended his lines along Scovill to the Woodland Cemetery, on Clark Avenue and on Willson from Scovill to Beyerle Park in Newburgh, Hanna recognized his competitor's ambitions. Opposition increased, and other Cleveland lines joined with Johnson. The famous traction "fight of the centuries" had begun.

With increasing demand for wire, the American Wire Company was organized in Cleveland with Charles A. Otis as president. The next year, a factory at the foot of Marquette Avenue was producing fence wire from purchased rods. A rod mill was installed in 1885, and products eventually included the scope of industrial wires, including wire for welding and for weaving wire cloth. The plant expanded until it covered a city block. It later became the American Works of the American Steel & Wire Company.

An army of men in the Newburgh mills left their jobs in May in the first steel-workers' strike in Cleveland. Agreement was not reached until the following month.

A lecture course was arranged for the benefit of drug clerks and apprentices by a committee of the Cleveland Pharmaceutical Society, consisting of E. A. Schellentrager, Edward Classen, and Hugo Linden. Its success led to incorporation of the Cleveland School of Pharmacy in 1886. In 1908, it became an affiliate of Western Reserve University, and it was incorporated in the university in 1919.

The Home for Aged and Infirm Israelites was dedicated in June. It was housed in a building at the southwest corner of Woodland and Willson avenues that had been purchased for the purpose. In 1884 the name of Sir Moses Montefiore, famed English and Jewish philanthropist, was adopted. Encroachment of business and industry necessitated expansion that was later provided by the Montefiore Home at 3151 Mayfield Road, where there was peace and quiet for the old folks.

A through line was established between Cleveland and St. Louis, via Indianapolis, on June 23, when the aggressive Cleveland, Columbus, Cincinnati & Indianapolis Railroad Company purchased the Indianapolis & St. Louis railroad and the St. Louis, Alton & Terre Haute line.

An ordinance of June 26 required that streets laid out in new developments must conform as nearly as possible to existing streets, and must be graded, numbered, and properly bridged. Haphazard, bottleneck streets were in marked contrast with the wide, straight streets planned in the early days. Repaving of Euclid Avenue with Medina sandstone began this year, and extended to the city limits in 1886.

Since 1868 Captain Alva Bradley and his associates had built eighteen lake vessels in their Cleveland shipyards, and now he was the largest single vessel owner in the city. His son, Morris A., twenty-six, who had entered the business in 1880, took over management when his father died in 1885, one of the foremost figures in Great Lakes shipping history. He enlarged his father's firm, ably handling the extensive real-estate holdings he inherited. Bradley became one of the largest owners of real estate in the city, and erected many important buildings on his downtown properties. Among his varied business interests were the Bradley Transportation Company, United States Coal Company, Cleveland & Buffalo Transit Company, Alva Realty Company, St. Clair Street Realty Company, and Ohio Transportation Company. His sons, Alva and Charles, carried on his many interests.

According to the school census there were 58,926 persons of school age in Cleveland. The enrollment, however, showed only 26,990 students in the public schools, and 1,005 in the high schools. Only 29 of the 472 teachers were men. Receipts on account of the school fund totaled $458,858.50, while expenditures amounted to $462,768.65.

The Cleveland public schools had won a high place in the nation under the superior leadership of Superintendent Andrew J. Rickoff. It was charged, however, that politics had gained control of the administration, and after fifteen years of distinguished service, Rickoff failed to be re-elected, an act that was condemned by educational authorities and his many friends. The community was agreeably surprised to learn of the appointment of Dr. B. A. Hinsdale, president of Hiram College and a profound scholar of high standing, as the new superintendent. Within a short time it was clearly evident that his aim was to strengthen the schools. In October, he reported a serious need of expanded facilities: 30 schools were operating in rented rooms, of which 11 were housed in churches, 9 in saloon buildings, 5 in dwellings, and the remainder in storerooms, former stables, and a society hall. As a result, 14 new buildings were erected at a cost of $645,000 to provide for 8,250 pupils, relieving the pressure of overcrowding, but only for a short time. Dr. Hinsdale stressed the importance of teachers' meetings, and reorganized the normal school. He edited the works of his personal friend, James A. Garfield, and they were published in two volumes. He also wrote *President Garfield and Education, The Old Northwest, How to Study and Teach History,* and *The American Government.*

Features of the canal boat and wooden propeller were combined in the first iron ship, the 302-foot *Onoko,* built in Cleveland by the Globe Shipbuilding Company. The vessel, carrying a 3,000-ton cargo on a 14-foot draft, was constructed for the Wilson Transit Company, and was the forerunner of the giant, bulk-cargo freighter. The Globe Shipbuilding Company, founded in 1880, developed from the Globe Iron Works, established in 1869. It launched the first vessel built entirely within its yards, without dividing the work among specialized contractors. It turned out some of the largest freighters and passenger steamers afloat, among them the twin ships, *Northland* and *Northwest,* that ran between Buffalo and Duluth on the Northern Steamship line.

Clingstone, owned by William J. Gordon, was one of the outstanding trotters of his day. On July 28, he won a $3,000 feature race from Edwin Thorne, J. B. Thomas, and So So in 2:14—2:16¼—2:23½ in Cleveland. Gordon had accumulated great wealth in his wholesale-grocery business and through his pioneering interest in the Cleveland Iron Mining Company. His association with George Fellows in 1856 led to large and successful commercial enterprises. He served as councilman and mayor of Glenville, where he had built a fine home on a 122-acre tract of lakeshore property that he was grooming as the future Gordon Park. Gordon was known nationally for his fast horses, and his stock farm was one of the finest in the West. Refined and cultured, he loved books and traveled extensively.

Officials of the New York, Chicago and St. Louis Railway Company had leased the four-story Hoyt Block at the northwest corner of Bank and St. Clair streets as headquarters in January. In twenty-one months, the Buffalo-to-Chicago railroad had been located, built, and was ready for trains! August 30 marked the entrance into Cleveland of the first passenger train over the Nickel Plate, a "special" carrying an official party; but it was not until October 23 that the line was formally declared open for business. Three days later the railroad was sold to the New York Central; and on January 5, 1883, a new board of directors was elected with William K. Vanderbilt, president. Judge Stevenson Burke of Cleveland was prominently identified with the Vanderbilt negotiations and served as a director of the company. Passenger schedules were so co-ordinated by the new owners at Buffalo as to make possible through traffic to New York over existing lines. In 1887 reorganization as the New York, Chicago & St. Louis Railroad Company was effected.

Samuel E. Williamson resigned as judge of the Court of Common Pleas this year, having served since 1880, and became general counsel for the Nickel Plate Railroad. In 1898 he joined the New York Central Railroad, heading the legal department until his death in 1903. Williamson, the son of Samuel Williamson, was born in the old homestead at Euclid Street and the Public Square in 1844. After graduation from Western Reserve College in 1864, he studied law with his distinguished father, then completed a course in the Harvard Law School. He was an eminent lawyer and jurist, a founder of University School, and a trustee of Western Reserve University, the Society for Savings, and the Old Stone Church. He bore a great Cleveland name with high honor.

The first chemical engine for fire-fighting was purchased and put into service with a new hook-and-ladder company on Pearl Street near Clark. There was public protest, however, as some people believed that chemicals would ruin property.

The Knights of Labor, "a strange confused amalgam of political action, of socialism, of reformism, of straight trade unionism, of crafts, and of industrial unions," represented organized labor, swelling its ranks with the slogan, "An injury to one is the concern of all." Internal dissension resulted in refusal of the New York City Knights to obey instructions from Grand Master Terence V. Powderly, and they staged a surprising demonstration of strength in a parade. Thus Labor Day was born this year. Samuel Gompers and leaders of craft unions deserted the Knights in 1886 and established the American Federation of Labor, devoted to the craft principle and denouncing political action. In the eighties, there had grown up in Cleveland a substantial membership in the Knights of Labor under District Assembly No. 47, and in the American Federation, which maintained both a building-trades council and a trades assembly.

For almost a decade, Jeptha H. Wade had been beautifying his tract of about 75 acres of farm land along Doan Brook at great expense, and generously allowing it to be used as a public park. In June, 1881, he offered to the Council as a gift, with simple restrictions, 1,100 feet fronting on Euclid Avenue, estimated to be worth $500,000. For fifteen months, the councilmen wrangled, opposing further park outlays, especially for "a rich man's luxury, available only for the owners of carriages." After a refinement of conditions, a deed was executed on September 15 of this year; and, on the 26th, it was accepted by the City Council. Under the terms, the tract was to be known "forever by the name of Wade Park." The city agreed to spend at least $75,000 for improvements, including the construction of drives and walks and the centaur pond. An area called the "College Reservation" was excepted from the transaction as the proposed location of an "art gallery."

Olivet Chapel, a mission founded by the Rev. Charles Terry Collins, pastor of Plymouth Congregational Church, at Hill and Commercial streets, was serving a needy neighborhood of various nationalities. On October 12, upon Rev. Collins' invitation, Dr. Henry Albert Schauffler, returned missionary from Bohemia, became its pastor. He soon realized the great need for ministry to 25,000 Bohemians to the east in the Broadway district. Here, under the auspices of the Bohemian Mission Board, of which Horace Ford was a staunch supporter until his death in 1905, Dr. Schauffler began his missionary work among the Slavic peoples; and from this center, all other Slavic religious work in America developed. Bethlehem Church, founded by Dr. Schauffler in 1883, was the first church provided by Americans to be used exclusively for Slavic mission work. Other projects sprang from it, and in the 1940s, at Broadway and Fowler Street, it still served as the chapel of Schauffler College and the activity center of a cosmopolitan community.

The Cleveland School of Art, founded in October by eight Cleveland women, among them Mrs. Sarah M. Kimball, Mrs. Henry B. Payne, and Mrs. L. E. Holden, filled an immediate need, and soon there were more pupils than the Kimball residence could accommodate. Quarters were secured on the top floor of the City Hall, where members of the neighboring Art Club, affiliated with the crafts of lithography, wood carving, and kindred activities, gave the school a powerful impetus. The institution was known as the Western Reserve School of Design for Women from 1888 to 1891, a department of Western Reserve University. Resuming its independence, it moved to the Kelley mansion on Willson Avenue, near the railroad station, in 1892, and Georgia Leighton Norton became the principal and guiding influence in the steady development of the institution.

A report that a university had been proposed for Cleveland inspired Dr. Hiram C. Haydn, trustee and prominent Cleveland clergyman, to suggest to his associates at Western Reserve College in Hudson, Ohio, that they consider moving the school to Cleveland. Earnest debate followed, and then, as a local writer put it, they "hitched their educational wagon to the new star of progress and threw old-fashioned prudence to the wind." Dr. Haydn's careful negotiations resulted in the practical interest of Amasa Stone, wealthy Clevelander, who agreed on September 20, 1880, to give the college $500,000 on condition that the institution be moved to a satisfactory Cleveland site provided by the citizens; and, further, that the name be changed to Adelbert College of Western Reserve University as a memorial to his only son, Adelbert Stone, who drowned while a student at Yale. The terms laid down by Amasa Stone having been fulfilled, a citizens' committee made up of C. C. Baldwin, Moses G. Waterson, and C. H. Bulkley raised the funds to secure a site. A portion of the L. E. Holden homestead was acquired on the south side of Euclid Avenue, opposite Wade Park. Eight trustees resigned from the college board so that Stone could select a number of trustees of his own choice: John Hay, Rutherford B. Hayes, James A. Garfield, W. J. Boardman, Samuel E. Williamson, George H. Ely, William Harris, L. E. Holden, W. H. Doan, Samuel Andrews, and the Rev. Charles T. Collins.

Adelbert College was dedicated on October 26, 1882. Ex-President Rutherford B. Hayes and President D. C. Gilman of Johns Hopkins College delivered the principal addresses before large assemblies that included many visiting dignitaries. Orlando J. Hodge represented the old Burton Academy that many years earlier had cradled the spark of Western Reserve learning. Two buildings were erected on the easterly portion of the L. E. Holden homestead (opposite Wade Park, adjoining Case School of Applied Science). A four-story, gray-stone structure costing $175,000, set back from Euclid Avenue and Adelbert Road, housed the administration and teaching departments and, years later, became the administration building. In the long, brick structure near the south end of the campus, the president lived, and the west wing became the dormitory. The two wings later became Cutler Hall and Pierce Hall.

Western Reserve College had moved to Cleveland, the little college church had closed, and the people of Hudson who had sacrificed for the institution's survival were greatly dismayed. The preparatory department, however, remained as the Western Reserve Academy to serve as a "feeder" for Adelbert College of Western Reserve University in Cleveland; but the number of students failed to justify the expense borne by the college trustees, and support was withdrawn in 1903. More than a decade passed before the academy was revived.

The Hawley House, Cleveland's newest commercial hotel, opened at the southeast corner of St. Clair and Seneca streets in October. The four-story, one-hundred-room hostelry was built by David R. and Davis R. Hawley, brothers, and John Langton, and it was a popular meeting place for civic organizations. In its restaurants famous Sunday dinners were served. Another floor was added to provide expansion, and in 1901, David R. Hawley purchased his partners' interests and remodeled the building. In later years, known as the Hawley Hotel, it catered to permanent guests.

The Benevolent and Protective Order of Elks, founded in New York City in 1868 on the principle of the brotherhood of man, had its beginning in the Forest City in Cleveland Lodge No. 18, organized in November, in the City Hall Building, with thirty-four charter members. Under wise leadership, the order grew steadily in numbers and prestige, manifesting its influence in the founding of new lodges. Many of its members were prominent in the city's political, professional, and business life, and some made practical contributions to state and national associations. A bronze elk marked "Elks Rest," was dedicated by Cleveland Lodge in Lake View Cemetery in 1912, where the remains of twenty brothers were buried. In 1946, when Thomas V. Gilmore was exalted ruler, headquarters were located at 1901 East 13th Street. William F. Bruning was serving his twenty-fifth year as secretary.

When the Blackstone Building opened in November (at 1426 West 3rd), it was occupied almost entirely by lawyers. Jacob B. Perkins built it solidly and well, and named it for the famous English lawyer, Sir William Blackstone, whose bust he placed above the entrance. In 1946 the building was one of the best preserved in Cleveland. Gates Legal Publishing Company was the only remaining tenant related to the courts. The only surviving hydraulic passenger elevator was in the Blackstone.

Jacob B. Perkins built the Perkins Power Block on Frankfort Street simultaneously with the adjoining Blackstone. It was the first building to furnish tenants with steam power, generated by an engine in the basement. He also erected a block on Superior below Seneca, and gave it a family name, Wilshire. It was the home of the J. L. Hudson Company, and for many years a prominent office building. These sturdy buildings continued to serve in the 1940s.

Until the 1930s, Jacob B. Perkins was prominent in Cleveland business. The son of Jacob Perkins, railroad promoter, and nephew of General Simon Perkins, early settler in the Western Reserve, he had acquired valuable real estate in the downtown area and became a wealthy man. Perkins raced his fine horses on Euclid Avenue and at the Glenville track; and the high point of his life came when he rented Pytchley House for a season of hunting and coaching at Pytchley, England.

Confident that Cleveland would become a large manufacturing center, Leonard Case, Jr., had directed in his will that approximately two hundred acres of land within the area bounded by Willson Avenue, St. Clair, Minnesota Street, and the lake, be reserved for industrial plants, and that a right-of-way be designated for a railroad. In November his heirs entered into an agreement with the Pennsylvania Railroad for the location of the Silver Plate Branch, a line which at first consisted of a single track extending on the Case right-of-way (to East 49th), thence north to the American Wire Company yards. Two years later, the Kingsbury Branch was projected from the main track at Bessemer Avenue. In 1887 the Lake Shore, of which William Case was once president, joined in the lease. These lines were steadily lengthened to meet growing industry and trade. For many years industrial plants located wherever a site was available along the seven railroad lines serving the city. Most of the development was on the East Side along the Pennsylvania Railroad from the lakefront to Broadway in Newburgh.

Sportsmen came from Pittsburgh and Detroit to witness the foot race between two of the country's noted short-distance runners, Smith and Kettleman, at the Cleveland Driving Park on December 1. Braving snow, slush, and wind, the athletes, wearing brief track suits, swept up the 125-yard stretch "like a pair of frightened ghosts," Smith winning in the unofficial, but "reliable," time of 12¾ seconds.

When Graham W. Clarke, a young chemist, sought Dr. C. S. Hurd for relief from an aching molar, a great chemical company had its beginning. The dentist was having difficulty getting enough nitrous-oxide gas—commonly called "laughing gas"—for his business, and young Clarke agreed to try to supply the need. Into the venture he put his last forty dollars. His small investment and pioneering efforts paid dividends in 1883, when he developed commercial compressed and liquefied gas for dentists' use throughout the nation. Clarke was the first to liquefy the carbonic-acid gas that made the soft-drink industry possible. Dr. Hurd's faith in the pioneer chemist and his modest financial encouragement led to the founding of the Cleveland Nitrous Oxide Works, followed by expansion and the carbonic-acid-gas invention. Clarke organized the Lennox Chemical Company in 1896 at the foot of Willson Avenue, where commercial production of compressed oxygen gas by chemical reaction was first made. The project was absorbed by the Ohio Chemical Company in 1923, and became affiliated with Air Reduction, Inc.

1883

Pickands, Mather & Company was formed as a partnership by Samuel Mather, Colonel James Pickands, and Jay C. Morse to engage in the sale of iron ore, pig iron, and coal. The business grew until in the 1940s it included operation of iron-ore mines on all the Lake Superior ranges, mining and distribution of coal, distribution of coke, and management of The Interlake Steamship Company fleet—36 freighters transporting iron ore, coal, lime-stone, and grain on the Great Lakes. In addition to mining operations in the Lake Superior district, the company was engaged in developing processes for the beneficiation of low-grade iron formations. This material, called taconite, existed in large quantities in the Lake Superior district, and was looked upon as a major source of future supply of iron-bearing material for the steel industry. Members of the Cleveland firm in the 1940s were Elton Hoyt II, John Sherwin, Alex D. Chisholm of Duluth, Herbert C. Jackson, and George W. Striebing.

Quickening interest in pleasure excursions prompted the Detroit & Cleve-land Steam Navigation Company to build the iron steamer *City of Mackinac,* followed by the *City of Cleveland II*—later called the *City of Alpena.* Cruise service to the scenic lake country began on the Detroit-St. Ignace route.

Heavy rains caused the Cuyahoga River to leave its banks on February 3 almost without warning. Lumber valued at $300,000 was swept away, oil tanks exploded, and industry in the "Flats" suffered from flood and fire. The loss mounted to almost $750,000 in the three-day disaster. Burning oil on the river painted night scenes of fury that were long remembered.

Cleveland had received legislative power "to regulate and compel the consumption of smoke emitted by the burning of coal." The inspector's first attempt at smoke restriction resulted in orders to 140 furnaces to comply with the law. Very little practical progress in smoke abatement was accom-plished, however.

Following the Civil War, Franklin J. Dickman, law partner of Judge Rufus P. Spalding, had added a term as United States district attorney to his public record as Ohio legislator in 1861. He became a member of the Ohio Supreme Court Commission this year; and, in 1886, Governor J. B. Foraker appointed him a judge of the State Supreme Court, completing the unexpired term of Judge W. W. Johnson the following year. He was re-nominated by the Republicans by acclamation in 1889 and elected for a six-year term.

A franchise granted in April permitted the East Cleveland Railway to extend its line from Willson to Fairmount on Euclid, and the following year to Doan Brook. Fare beyond Willson was three cents. The Payne Avenue extension, opened with horsecars this year on the Superior Street line, was built to East Madison and Hough in 1885, and came to be the most-converted line in Cleveland. Cable operation came in 1889, electricity in 1890, gas buses in 1935, and trackless trolleys in 1936.

Assassination of President Garfield by an "unqualified office seeker" aroused public interest in a civil-service reform movement that began shortly after the Civil War. Passage of the famous Pendleton Act, aimed at political scandals of the seventies, compelled many classes of workers to prove through competitive examination their fitness for government positions.

An act of April 18 changed the designation of the Public School Library to Public Library and that of the library committee to Public Library Board. In 1886 the number of members was fixed at seven, to be elected for three-year terms by the Board of Education.

Among the notable performances given by the Cleveland Vocal Society, the Max Bruch concert on April 25 stands as the peak of achievement. The evening was given to compositions of Bruch, and the renowned composer conducted. At the end of the first number, the artist laid down his baton and exclaimed, "Bravo, ladies and gentlemen!" It was a great event in musical circles, and scarcely a season passed without encouragement from kindly Max Bruch.

Eighteen charter members organized St. Peter's Lutheran Church, May 6, with the blessing of Zion Church, which fostered it. On a lot presented to the congregation by Frederick Schoenewald, a two-story, frame sanctuary was dedicated at Craw and Quincy avenues on September 2. The first pastor, the Rev. Max Treff, served four years, teaching the children in the church school and ministering to the congregation. Church and community grew, and 1913 witnessed St. Peter's located in a new structure at East 79th Street and Sherman Avenue. The Rev. Arthur F. Katt began his long and fruitful era of service as pastor in 1925. He helped to establish a Lutheran Negro mission in 1926 that became St. Philip's, one of the most flourishing congregations among Negroes in the northern field.

One of the first institutions organized in Ohio under the law permitting the establishment of trust companies was The Savings & Trust Company, capitalized at $750,000. It opened in the Benedict Building on May 8, with C. G. King, president. Consolidation with the pioneer Citizens Saving & Loan Association and the American Trust Company in 1902 resulted in The Citizens Savings & Trust Company, an important unit in the Union Trust Company merger.

Food prices, generally, continued to climb, as reported on May 25: old potatoes, 75 cents per bushel; new potatoes, 10 cents a quarter peck; beets, 5 cents a quarter peck; asparagus, 5 to 8 cents a bunch; lettuce, 10 cents a pound; rhubarb, two bunches for 5 cents; russet apples, 10 cents a quart; oranges, 25 and 30 cents a dozen; chickens, 18 cents a pound; eggs, 20 cents a dozen; and butter, 15 to 28 cents a pound.

The American Society of Mechanical Engineers—only three years old— met for the first time in Cleveland, June 12-14, in the Vocal Society rooms in the City Hall. J. F. Holloway, president of the Cuyahoga Steam Furnace

Company, who became head of the organization in 1884, called the convention to order. A special train carried seventy-seven of the nation's leading engineers on a tour of industrial Cleveland, the ore docks and the water works. Inspection of the Superior Viaduct closed a "red-letter day" that was devoted to consideration of weighty technical problems.

One of the most distinguished American teachers of chemistry was Edward W. Morley, who joined the faculty of Western Reserve College in 1869, continuing as head of the chemistry department of Western Reserve University until 1906. He became internationally famous for his accurate determination of the atomic weights of oxygen and hydrogen, upon which all chemical measurements are predicated.

Albert A. Michelson, thirty-one, a graduate of the United States Naval Academy, became professor of physics at Case School of Applied Science this year; and an association of six years with Professor Morley of Western Reserve in research in the velocity of light and other physical-science subjects of world import began. According to Dr. William E. Wickenden, subsequent president of Case School, a track walker on the Nickel Plate right-of-way at the rear of the Case campus came upon a man who was fussing with a contrivance of mirrors. The trackman accosted the supposed trespasser gruffly. "What are you doing here?" "Why," was the quiet reply, "I'm trying to measure the velocity of light." "Well, why should anyone want to make a fuss over a thing like that?" the workman grunted. "Because it's such good fun," came the answer. The trespasser was Michelson, the great wizard of optics, and his fun lasted a lifetime. His research became indispensable to industry, which learned decades later that light waves served as the final measuring rod in checking the accuracy of gauges on which modern, precise production depended. Michelson was awarded the Nobel Prize in physics in 1907.

An eminent name was added to the faculty of Case School of Applied Science, that of Dr. Charles F. Mabery, professor of chemistry, who served until 1927. He earned world renown for his pioneer research on the qualities of petroleum; and for fifty years, he contributed to scientific journals on the subject of petroleum chemistry.

John Baldwin, Sr., donated to the Baldwin University (later Baldwin-Wallace College) endowment fund this year 1,000 acres of Berea land valued at $25 per acre. The stone-quarry industry had been the school's principal source of income; but management of operations became burdensome, and quarry excavations came closer and closer to the campus, bringing smoke, gritty dust, and noise of machinery. During the administration of President Joseph E. Stubbs, the campus property was sold to the Cleveland Stone Company in 1887 for $100,000. Trustees, alumni, and citizens joined in opposing the moving of the school from Berea, and 20 acres, constituting North Campus, were finally purchased as a new site. In 1892 the new Recitation Hall—later Wheeler Hall—and the Philura Gould Baldwin Memorial Library were erected, financed by Mr. and Mrs. John Baldwin, Jr., the latter being named for their daughter, the first school librarian. A new Memorial Building, replacing Wallace Hall, was dedicated in 1896. It was re-named Marting Hall for the Rev. John G. Marting, financial leader and benefactor, before his passing in 1941. Dietsch Hall, gift of Mr. and Mrs. Michael Dietsch of Spencerville, Ohio, was erected as a young-ladies' dormitory of German Wallace College in 1899, and later became the Administration Building of Baldwin-Wallace. Ladies' Hall, "an elegant and commodious boarding hall" built in 1883, served until 1902, when it was moved to North Campus for erection as Carnegie Science Hall. John Paul Baldwin, grandson of the founder, saw to it that the stones were marked and set in their original places in the re-building. Funds for reconstruction were the gift of Andrew Carnegie. During the same year, the first women's dormitory on the new campus was built and named Hulet Hall, honoring the original building and its donor.

Albert Bushnell Hart, born in Cleveland in 1854, joined the Harvard faculty this year as a teacher of history and government. He became the nation's foremost authority on American history.

A crowd gathered at the ball park on Kennard Street on September 27 to see Mervine Thompson, six-footer weighing almost two hundred pounds, make good his boast that he was "the strongest man in the world." A ladder had been chained to a tree. Grasping one rung and bracing his feet against another, Thompson, wearing a heavy harness, resisted the strain of a team of draft horses for fully five minutes. He appeared in wrestling matches and sports events around town for a long time.

The state election centered in the proposed Second Amendment to the Ohio Constitution, prohibiting the manufacture and sale of intoxicating liquors. The Woman's Christian Temperance Union of Ohio, with head-quarters in Cleveland, was the guiding factor in the drive, and Mary A. Woodbridge was in charge. In the local union, F. Jennie Duty, an early crusader, directed the vigorous drive. Churches and campaigners expressed themselves long and loudly for the cause, and the *Second Amendment Herald* strengthened the efforts of tireless workers in preaching and prayer meetings. Cleveland's advisory committee consisted of Joseph Perkins, John D. Rockefeller, E. C. Pope, W. H. Doan, J. B. Meriam, Edward S. Meyer, and Alva Bradley. The city's liquor dealers threw out a "wet" warning stating: "If prohibition wins the farmers will be unable to sell surplus grains, and pork and beef will come down to such an extent that farmers will not be able to clothe their children in silks and satins, and to give them pianos. Schoolhouses will disappear, because there will be no money to pay teachers. ... We have raised $75,000 to spend principally in Cincinnati and Cleveland, and we are going to teach prohibitionists to let our business alone." In the contest for lieutenant governor, George Hoadly of Cincinnati, who spent his boyhood in Cleveland, carried the banner successfully for the Democrats in a close race. Governor J. B. Foraker and W. G. Rose of Cleveland headed the Republican ticket, but neither party declared a stand on the hot moral issue. On election day, October 10, more than 721,000 votes were cast, 323,189 favoring the amendment, but falling short of the necessary majority. This surprising total favoring the amendment immediately influenced plans for the regulation and taxation of the liquor traffic.

The west breakwater was completed this year, providing a harbor of refuge with an area of 100 acres for anchorage of vessels in depths of from 17 to 29 feet.

The Park Theater opened on October 22 with a comedy, *The School for Scandal,* an event marked with splendor and social importance. Managed by Augustus F. Hartz, the playhouse was a part of the three-story Wick Block, erected this year on the Public Square (Illuminating Building site) by the Wick family as the home of the private banking house of Henry Wick & Company. "Gus" Hartz was one of the best-known theatrical figures in the city's history. Born in Liverpool, England, in 1843, he was apprenticed to a stage magician at the age of eight and studied with a tutor in the evenings. He followed a stage career until 1880.

Considerable commotion resulted when standard time was adopted in the nation on November 18. Railroads and local business favored the new time, and the City Council fell in line. Farmers and old-timers stood by old-fashioned sun time, but their protests fell on deaf ears. Clocks and watches were set by factory whistles. The city's first chronometer went into service in Webb C. Ball's jewelry-store window, and it was a novelty for a long time. Legislative action governing time for the country as a whole did not come until March 19, 1918, when Congress directed the Interstate Commerce Commission to establish limits for the various time zones.

Fire had taken a heavy toll in Cleveland. With the rapid growth of industry, area, and population, the Fire Department was unable to meet the demand for its service, and at times was obliged to turn to neighboring cities for assistance. As a consequence, five new engines were purchased this year, and an extension-ladder truck was put to work. The new ladder, reaching skyward eighty-five feet, astonished the citizens.

Sylvester T. Everett commissioned Charles F. Schweinfurth, noted architect, to design for his bride, the former Alice Louisa Wade, granddaughter of Jeptha H. Wade, a brown-stone mansion at the northeast corner of Euclid and Case avenues. When completed this year, it was the costliest home erected in Cleveland. Its Romanesque architecture reflected the cosmopolitan personality of Colonel Everett, railroad magnate financier and Republican leader, who entertained distinguished visitors from many foreign nations as well as Presidents Grant, Hayes, McKinley, and Taft, and captains of industry and finance, such as Andrew Carnegie and J. Pierpont Morgan. A grand staircase swept up through the magnificent structure, past exquisite, stained-glass windows and elegant furnishings. On the hostess balcony, dominating the top flight, Mrs. Everett greeted her guests as they entered the elaborate, third-floor ballroom. The Moorish room, lined with sandalwood, featured a beautifully carved wishing well and fountain. Enraged when an apartment hotel called the Del Prado (4213 Euclid) was erected on the line of his front lawn, Everett put up a spite fence in retaliation. In the fall of 1938, the palatial residence, one of the last of Cleveland's million-dollar homes, was torn down.

As a lad of twelve, in 1850, Sylvester T. Everett had come to Cleveland from his father's farm in Trumbull County to live with his brother, Dr. Henry

Everett. His banking career began as messenger boy and collection clerk in 1851 with the house of Brockway, Mason, Everett & Company. In 1864 he became superintendent of a Pennsylvania oil-producing concern, continuing for four years, when he returned to Cleveland as manager of the banking house of Everett, Weddell & Company. Aside from his executive connections with leading Cleveland banks, and as an organizer of the Union National Bank, he had many and varied interests—in the Cleveland Rolling Mill Company and as promoter of street railways and railroads. He financed the first successful electric street railway in the country in Akron, and organized the Erie, Pennsylvania, Electric Motor Company. Everett had mining interests in North Carolina, Wisconsin, and Michigan, and mining and ranch properties in Colorado. From 1869 to 1883, he served as city treasurer, supported by both political parties, yet he was a staunch Republican, and a party leader in state and nation.

Street-cleaning machines were introduced on city streets this year. Although they were a great improvement over the manual method, the year's cost was $8,994, an increase of $8,000 over that of hand labor. "About the only difference under the old method of cleaning, between a dirt street and a paved one," reported Mayor John H. Farley to the Council, "is the depth of the mud." Adequate machines were not available, and the whole matter was considered unsatisfactory, especially by the taxpayer.

1884

Only the walls of the new Wick Block remained, sheathed in icy desolation, after a gas explosion turned it into a flaming furnace on January 5. The Old Stone Church, adjoining, was badly damaged, and faced agitation by those who believed the church should move to a residential section. Others, led by John A. Foote and Colonel John Hay, preserved the historic location, and plans were made for restoration of the interior by Charles W. Schweinfurth. The credit for the fine, open-timber ceiling belonged to him, and the wall decorations were executed by his brother, Jules. Although the lofty steeple survived the disaster, it was later declared unsafe and taken down from the east tower, which was ornamentally finished through a gift of Mrs. Samuel Mather.

Dr. Hiram Collins Haydn returned to the First Presbyterian Church— Old Stone—as pastor this year, succeeding the Rev. Arthur Mitchell. He had come to the Western Reserve in 1866, serving a Painesville church for a short time. In 1872 he was called to Old Stone as associate pastor; and two years later he became the third active pastor upon the death of the Rev. William H. Goodrich. His impelling personality inspired increased membership and influence, and Calvary, Bolton Avenue, and Windermere churches rose as monuments to his initiative and fortitude. After four years as secretary of the Congregational Missionary Society, he returned to Old Stone, as pastor until 1901, and pastor emeritus until he died in 1913.

Long a leader in Presbyterian activities in northern Ohio, he was recognized throughout the nation as a motivating force in the denomination. Parallel with his interests in the church life of the city, was his devotion to Western Reserve University as president of the board of trustees for three years and as university president, 1887-90. During this time he founded the College for Women, and a building honors his name.

Store owners banded together in March, believing that through co-operation the best interests of both business and the public would be served. Most of them were German, English, and Irish. Thus one of Cleveland's oldest trade associations, The Cleveland Retail Grocers Association, had its beginning. W. W. Ford, retail grocer, was the first president; George H. Theuer, treasurer; and A. W. Kilbourne, secretary. Benjamine Madden encouraged interest on the West Side. P. C. O'Brien, elected president in 1885, stimulated membership and activity for five years and eliminated cut-throat practices. Food shows, launched early in the Twentieth Century, proved so popular that they were made a permanent feature. During the 1930s, the association, through its secretary, Walter W. Knight, helped merchants to weather hard times, handled relief, and directed the use of food stamps. In the 1940s John Pressler was president, and Knight, third secretary since 1911, continued in that position.

A well-rounded music education was made possible with the founding of the Cleveland School of Music by Alfred F. Arthur, noted singing teacher, in the Benedict Building. Early members of the able faculty included William B. Colson, Jr., piano, for many years organist at the Old Stone Church; James H. Rogers, piano and organ, later a noted composer and critic; George Brainard and Miss M. S. Wright, piano; Julius Deiss and Margarete Wuertz, violin; Frank Hruby, clarinet; Rocco Rottino, flute; and Mrs. Anna P. Tucker, elocution and expression. The first graduates were Helen Briggs, Belle Benton, and Kate Gerlach. Flora Butler Brinsmade, an early graduate, taught for more than fifty years in the school. In 1893, spacious quarters were occupied in the Arcade. Teachers of exceptional talent, many of them having studied with master musicians, were on the faculty, among them Henry Miller, violin; Wilson G. Smith, piano, voice, and organ, later a composer of note; Johannes Wolfram, Charles E. Clemens of England, Jay R. Hall, Isabelle Beaton, and James Garfield Chapman, who organized an orchestra, increasing interest in recitals and concerts. The Madrigal Club, a chorus of fine singers, developed in the school, and was popular in Cleveland. During these years, Alfred F. Arthur was constantly studying and composing while teaching, his best-known operatic work being *The Water Carrier*. He compiled two hymnals besides producing text-books and many songs.

The final step in transforming Western Reserve College to the status of a university was accomplished when Western Reserve University was incorporated on April 11. The subscribers were Rutherford B. Hayes, Truman P. Handy, Joseph Perkins, Rev. Carroll Cutler, Dr. Gustave C. E. Weber, George H. Ely, and Samuel E. Williamson. In the transition, the last traces of denominational ties were severed. The college transferred to the newly created Western Reserve University Corporation its Department of Medicine, as the first unit of the university. Adelbert College of Western Reserve University, successor corporation to Western Reserve College, continued as an independent institution "affiliated with the University."

The state district courts were abolished, and on April 14 the Circuit Court was created in their place. The sixth judicial circuit consisted of Cuyahoga, Huron, Lorain, Medina, Summit, Sandusky, Lucas, and Ottawa counties, and the judges were Charles C. Baldwin of Cleveland, William H. Upson of Akron, and George R. Haynes of Toledo. In March, 1887, the sixth circuit was subdivided, and Cuyahoga, Summit, Lorain, and Medina counties formed the eighth district, served by three judges elected for six years. Their time was occupied almost entirely with the hearing of appeals.

A merger of the Bethel Relief and the Charity Organization Society combined relief with "efficiency and investigation" in the new Bethel Associated Charities (later Family Service Association of Cleveland). General James Barnett, "Cleveland's Grand Old Man of Charity," was the first president, and his service to local charities covered thirty-six years. Henry N. Raymond continued as superintendent. J. W. Walton, whose active interest in charity extended from 1874 to 1926, was treasurer of the Bethel and of the Associated Charities from 1890 to 1916, when he was succeeded by William T. Higbee, treasurer, who began a long period of devoted service. C. B. Lockwood, a founder of the Associated Charities, was deeply interested in social welfare through his attendance at the Concord School of Philosophy, where he was closely associated with Ralph Waldo Emerson and Amos Bronson Alcott. Among the earlier presidents were Captain Charles C. Bolton, Homer H. Johnson, C. A. Nicola, and Thomas P. Robbins. William J. Akers, a member of the board, became director of charities and corrections in Cleveland in 1896.

The Stillman, the first large apartment hotel east of Erie Street, opened on June 2. It stood well back from the street on a spacious lawn on the site of the Stillman Witt residence (Stillman Theater site, 1111 Euclid). Wealthy families made it their home. Fire destroyed the upper floors in 1885, but they were restored. Business invaded the district at the turn of the century, and the proud structure was torn down.

The Cleveland Electric Light Company, founded on June 21, purchased a generating station on Johnson Street, between Bank and Water, that had been built in 1883. Thomson-Huston machines were installed by the company to operate the Edison incandescent system, providing illumination for certain downtown stores. Lines were routed over building roofs instead of on poles. The company moved its station to the rear of the Brainard Block on the Public Square in 1886.

Under the direction of Bishop Gilmour, the Franciscan Sisters opened St. Alexis Hospital in July, in an eight-room building, formerly a school, at the corner of Broadway and McBride Street. There were financial struggles in the early days, but in 1897 a fine, new building was made possible.

The Cleveland Bicycle Club opened Athletic Park, on East Madison, between Cedar and Garden streets, on July 10, with its first annual races. A crowd of 1,200 packed the stands to see the fastest riders compete on the quarter-mile cinder track, one of the finest in the country. Will H. Wetmore, local racer and spectacular trick rider, won the gold medal for the quarter-mile in 43½ seconds. Asa Dolph of New London, ace cyclist of his day, twirled his black mustache and shot off to establish the fastest Ohio record for the mile in 3:01⅘. The country's racing champions and amateurs met at the park in thrill-packed clashes with Cleveland entries that included Wilbur F. Knapp, George Snyder, Taylor Boggis, J. H. and George Collister, A. M. Cushing, C. E. Vaupel, Will Rainey, C. B. Childs, Ed Douhet, F. W. Palmer, E. E. Stoddard, and John Sherwin. The Forest City Ramblers organized a club in 1887, and two years later came the Cleveland Wheel Club.

July 26 marked a great achievement in the city, when The East Cleveland Railway Company operated "the first electric railroad for public use in America" for one mile on Garden Street, ending in Quincy. "The experiment was so successful," reported the Associated Press, "that the company expects to change its entire system, comprising over twenty miles, into electric roads." Current was carried on underground conductors from a Brush arc-light generator in the Euclid Avenue car barns, a development perfected by E. M. Bentley and Walter H. Knight. As many as five cars could be run at a time on a single circuit from the machine. The power station, perfected by Charles F. Brush, was rapidly adopted, and brought him great fame.

Two stories were added to the Court House at a cost of $100,000 to meet the growing needs of the county administration. When a new building was erected as a part of the Group Plan, criminal trials were held here until the new Criminal Court Building was built. The "Old Court House" was razed in 1935, and the historic landmark was erased by a parking lot.

The Dorcas Society rented a small house to provide a haven for aged women who were ill, and called it the Invalids Home. The Dorcas Society and the Invalids Home were incorporated the next year as the Dorcas Invalids Society. In 1892 the home was moved from Euclid Avenue to East Madison Avenue. John D. Rockefeller and generous Clevelanders made possible extensive expansion, and a new location was provided on Addison Road.

William J. White, a struggling Cleveland salesman, whose humble parents brought him to Cleveland in 1856 at the age of six, put his natural talent to work when he found that a trinket dropped in each bag of popcorn he offered to the children boosted his sales. A local grocer who received a barrel of Mexican chicle instead of nuts, gave it to White. He and his young wife experimented with it, added flavoring, and produced the first flavored gum that was a pleasure to chew. Others had made chewing gum, and in 1869, William F. Semple of Mount Vernon, Ohio, had patented a combination of rubber and other ingredients to form a gum. White's business soon outgrew the kitchen. A small plant was set up on Water Street this year, and he peddled his crude product in baskets. The demand convinced him that his fortune was made. Taking his Yellow Band brand to Washington, he passed it out to the Congressmen, and every day more jaws exercised the delicacy. A large factory went up on Detroit Avenue (Conkey poultry-feed-plant site, 10307 Detroit), with a new name, "Yucatan," in heroic letters on a yellow ground reproducing the yellow band that held five sticks together.

While a salesman in the bookstore of Cobb, Andrews & Company, William Howard Brett had made a host of friends during his ten years of service; and his appointment on September 1 to succeed I. L. Beardsley as the third librarian of the Public Library was indeed wise. Revolutionary changes characterized Brett's administration of thirty-four years. He introduced friendliness and cheerfulness, efficient operation, improved lighting, prudent use of space, comforts for readers and workers, systematic classification and cataloging of books, and higher standards that benefited both personnel and public. Step by step, his vision and resourcefulness laid the foundation of one of the largest and best-equipped libraries. The decimal system of classification was adopted in 1885, and magazines were first circulated. Two years later the first classroom library was sent to a school.

William Howard Brett was born in Braceville, Ohio, in 1846. He fought in the Union Army during the Civil War, studied medicine in the University of Michigan and at Western Reserve College, then came to Cleveland as a bookstore salesman. The personality of gentle, helpful William Howard Brett is revealed in an incident that occurred during his book-vending days. A little girl had just turned away regretfully when told that a book needed in her school work was not available. Having heard the conversation, the little man urged her to wait, and someone would hurry out and buy a copy for her. Perhaps it was this friendly, unexpected interest that helped to influence Linda A. Eastman to choose library work as a career. It remains a fact, however, that she became his assistant, serving the system for forty-six years, twenty of them as successor to her former chief. During his remarkable career as public librarian, Brett founded and was the first president of the Ohio Library Association; and in 1897, he was elected president of the American Library Association. In 1903, he founded the Western Reserve Library School, serving as dean until his death in 1918.

St. Matthew's Evangelical Lutheran Church was the outgrowth of the flourishing Immanuel Evangelical Lutheran Church on Scranton Road. The Rev. Henry Weseloh, assistant pastor of the mother church, had been ministering to families living south of Clark Avenue; and on September 1, this year, the new congregation was organized. A house of worship was erected on Meyer Avenue near Scranton, and the first pastor, the Rev. J. J. Walker, served with great zeal until illness caused his resignation in 1908. The pastorate of the Rev. George Eyler, his successor, was marked by notable expansion of activities. In 1932 the Rev. Edgar M. Luecke came to the church as assistant pastor, and upon the death of Rev. Eyler, he became pastor. Church membership exceeded eight hundred in 1946, and the

Christian day school and Sunday School were institutions in which the church took particular pride.

The great $890,000 fire in the "Flats," said to be of incendiary origin, started in the lumber yards of Woods, Perry & Company in the early evening of September 7. Acres of property were swept into blazing ruin. The docks and a lard refinery across the river were destroyed by racing flames that threatened the Superior Avenue business district. All city fire departments responded, and Youngstown, Columbus, and a score of Ohio cities rushed horses and equipment by rail. Two weeks later, a second fire in the lumber yards taxed the fighting strength of the Fire Department, and neighboring cities were again called upon to help. A loss of $110,000 emphasized the need for a fireboat and improved equipment.

Twenty young ladies opened a "kitchen garden" in the basement of the Unitarian church on Prospect Street in the fall. This pioneer domestic-science effort, one of the first in the country, was so successful that within two years the Cleveland Domestic Training Association had been organized on Superior Avenue, and Rockwell School girls were attending.

Cleveland turned out an estimated 75,000 citizens on September 26 to hear James G. Blaine and John A. Logan, Republican candidates for President and Vice President, speak on the Public Square. A rousing parade, complete with torchlight, drill corps, and bands, added spirit, and a revolving electric light on a telegraph pole near the Forest City House added brilliance to the occasion. The vote in the "plug hat" campaign was close. Cleveland seethed with excitement of rival clubs until November 15, when it became officially certain that the Democrats had gained control with the election of Grover Cleveland.

The roller-skating craze descended upon Cleveland. One of the first of the large rinks opened on Forest Street, between Scovill and Garden. The Casino Roller Rink, 195 by 95 feet, featured a band in the evening, and young Clevelanders flocked to the hall, where admission was a quarter. A year later Cleveland had twenty-four rinks.

Adherents to the Disciples faith organized the Glenville Christian Church this year. Located at East 105th and Helena in 1946, membership exceeded five hundred.

The Broadway Savings & Trust Company opened at the northwest corner of Broadway and Willson Avenue in the midst of the Bohemian and Polish district. It was one of the nation's earliest neighborhood banks. Joseph Turney, president, was succeeded by C. A. Grasselli, who with Oliver M. Stafford had organized the bank. Peter J. Slach, who became secretary-treasurer in the nineties, was a leader in the community and served on the City Plan Commission for many years. In 1886 Grasselli and Stafford organized the Woodland Avenue Savings & Trust Company. Both banks became branches of the Union Trust Company.

The charter of the Merchants National Bank expired in December, and it was reorganized at once, its successor being the Mercantile National Bank with capital of a million dollars. Edwin R. Perkins served as president until expiration of the charter in 1905. Perkins was born in New Hampshire in

1833. He came to Cleveland following graduation from Dartmouth College about 1856 and taught in the public schools. In 1863 he was admitted to the bar; and although he developed many interests, he gave much of his time to education, serving on the Board of Education from 1868 to 1874, part of the time as president. His banking career began with the Commercial National; and with Selah Chamberlain and A. S. Gorham, he organized the private banking house of Chamberlain, Gorham & Perkins. In 1878 he became cashier of the Merchants National Bank. Perkins was an organizer of the Cleveland, Lorain & Wheeling Railroad Company, and its president, 1890-93; president of the Cleveland & Mahoning Valley Railway Company in 1904, serving until his death in 1915; and trustee of Western Reserve University, Cleveland Museum of Art, and John Huntington Art and Polytechnic Trust. For more than a half century, he was actively identified with the Second Presbyterian Church and with denominational affairs nationally.

The Board of Trade report for the year showed the rapid expansion of oil interests in Cleveland. Capital invested in 86 refineries totaled $27,395,746. A payroll of $4,381,572 was paid to 9,869 employees. Raw materials consumed were valued at $34,999,101; 731,533,127 gallons of crude petroleum cost $16,340,581. The aggregate value of crude-petroleum products was $43,705,218, of which $36,839,613 represented illuminating oils. It was estimated that 3,179,263 barrels of crude oil were refined, 75 per cent being converted into refined oil and 15 per cent into gasoline, naphtha, and allied products.

The Cleveland Training School of Nurses was founded by the trustees of the Huron Road Hospital. Students found the course so difficult that many failed to graduate. Huron Road Hospital School of Nursing, the oldest nursing school west of the Alleghenies, became the official name in 1948.

The first five years of the eighties witnessed the establishment of business concerns that were in existence in the 1940s: 1880—American Stove Company, Cleveland Desk Company, Eberhard Manufacturing Company, D. E. Evans & Son, Inc., Flynn-Froelk Company, R. E. Greene & Son Company, Paine, Webber, Jackson & Curtis, Rudolph & Son Company, Saunders Manufacturing & Novelty Company, Schaefer Body, Inc., Theurer-Norton Provision Company. 1881—Arco Company, Cleveland Hardware & Forging Company, DeKlyn's, Eclipse Electrotype & Engraving Company, Koblitz-Kohn Company, John I. Nunn Company. 1882—Albright Coal Company, Ames & Son, Dickey-Grabler Company, J. H. Libby Company, National Refining Company. 1883—Billings-Chapin Company, Cleveland Agency of Equitable Life Insurance Company of Iowa, Fridrich Bicycle & Auto Supply Company, General Plating Company, Haserot Company, Kohn & Sons Company, Ohio Legal Blank Company. 1884—Beattie & Sons Jewelry, Inc., A. Claus Manufacturing Company, Cleveland Frog & Crossing Company, O. A. Dean Dairy Company, Dunbar Company, Goff-Kirby Company, Johnston & Jennings Company, Kelly Company, R. B. Biscuit Company, John F. Schulte Sons, Inc., Simonds Worden White Company, James A. Webb.

1885

Wealthy James Ford Rhodes retired this year to devote his time to the writing of history inspired by the Civil War and confused, postwar political and business conditions. He was born in Cleveland in 1848, the son of Daniel P. Rhodes, a power in industry and politics, who bred fast horses on his stock farms near the city. The Rhodes home on fashionable Franklin Circle (later Lutheran Hospital nurses' home) represented the height of luxury. Young Rhodes enrolled in the University of the City of New York and attended the University of Chicago for a year. The next three years were spent in Europe, studying and visiting iron-and-steel works in Germany and Great Britain. He joined his father in the iron business in Cleveland in 1870, and later became a partner in Rhodes & Company. His monumental seven-volume work, the *History of the United States from the Compromise of 1850*, written 1893-1906, won national attention and admitted him to inner literary circles. *Historical Essays*, 1909, and other writings were widely accepted. The historian moved to Cambridge, Massachusetts, in 1891, and spent the remainder of his life in New England, frequently visiting the Forest City. The James Ford Rhodes High School in Cleveland was erected as a fitting memorial to the city's eminent historian. He died in 1927 and was buried in Cleveland.

Collars and Cuffs, a farce comedy featuring Charles Gilday and Fannie Beane, opened the People's Theater in January. This was a short-lived play-house, originally the Euclid Avenue Roller Rink on Euclid opposite Bond Street. Managed by B. C. Hart, it offered good talent—Daniel Bandman, well-known tragedian; Maude Granger, Joe Proctor, Newton Beers, Frank Aiken, Frank I. Frayne, and others. Its career as a theater ended in 1887, except for occasional circus stunts, and it became a business block. Fire destroyed the building in 1892.

In the office of the Postal Telegraph Company on Merwin Street, the new long-distance telephone was tried out on January 26. To the amazement of those present, H. P. McIntosh, of the Citizens Telegraph & Telephone Company which staged the demonstration, W. B. Hale, Joseph E. Ingersoll, and George J. Johnson conducted conversation with persons in New York City easily and rapidly. The extraordinary event was considered "the most wonderful thing in telephoning the world has seen."

Increasing interest in athletic prowess led to organization of the Cleveland Athletic Club on February 6 in Benes' tailor shop in the Quinby Building. The first officers were C. A. Billings, president; W. P. Wightman, vice president; G. D. Benes, secretary; W. B. Castle, treasurer; and William Upson, Samuel Alden, Charles Potter, and George Collister, directors. The enthusiasts found quarters under the same roof with the Cleveland Bicycle Club at Euclid and Case avenues, and they practiced on the quarter-mile cinder course of Athletic Park. Local bike riders burned up the track with their high-wheelers, and there could be found the Collisters, George

Snyder, Wilbur Knapp, Charley Potter, Taylor Boggis, and others pedaling against the second hand. In 1886 the athletic club moved to a new gymnasium and clubhouse on Frankfort Street.

The M. A. Hanna Company was the outgrowth of the Rhodes & Card partnership in pig iron and iron ore, initiated by Daniel P. Rhodes, and which Marcus Alonzo Hanna entered in the sixties. In 1885 Hanna, Leonard C. Hanna, and Arnold C. Saunders took over the business, forming M. A. Hanna & Company, a partnership that continued until 1922, when The M. A. Hanna Company was incorporated with Matthew Andrews, chairman of the board, and Howard M. Hanna, Jr., president. Interests in iron ore, coal mines, and blast furnaces were acquired.

Marcus Alonzo Hanna had found his place in industry. His powerful personality, keen vision, and vigorous manner led him into many fields, and in each he found good fortune. He became a leading coal-and-iron executive, banker, builder of a steamship line, owner of the city's opera house, newspaper publisher, street-railway magnate, and a constructive force in numerous organizations. A dominant power in the Republican Party, his efforts put William McKinley in the White House. Hanna was elected United States senator in 1897, serving until his death in 1904, and he was chairman of the National Republican Committee, 1896-1903. The company he founded grew in importance, reminding the nation of the great man for whom it was named, a builder of Cleveland and an eminent statesman.

In February, twelve Central High School boys, directed by Newton M. Anderson, physics teacher, set up a carpenter shop in a barn on Kennard Street as a training school. In the class were Harvey W. Cushing, who became a famous brain specialist; C. Avery Adams, later a Harvard professor; Herbert McBride, Horace Hutchins, Perry W. Harvey, George Collins, Edward Childs, and George Olmstead. The school's popularity inspired prominent citizens to organize the Cleveland Manual Training Company in June, with Judge Samuel E. Williamson, president. In the following February, they erected a building on East Prospect Street, with Anderson as principal. Although this pioneer school was private, public-school pupils were admitted free. The use of tools and materials was taught, and instructions were given in mechanics, physics, chemistry, and mechanical drawing. In 1887 a cooking school was opened as a branch.

The City Council authorized in February the consolidation of the Woodland Avenue Street Railway, owned by Stillman Witt, Dan P. Eells, and others, and formerly the Kinsman Road, with the West Side company into the Woodland & West Side Railway Company. Riders traveled the entire length of the line for one fare, and did not change at the Square. During the year the Superior Street Railway extended its line along Payne Avenue from the Superior Street intersection to Russell Avenue, through Willson and Lexington. The company was allowed to use the tracks on Superior to Water Street in 1888.

Grover Cleveland, twenty-second President of the United States, was inaugurated. He was of the same ancestry as Moses Cleaveland, founder of the City of Cleveland.

In making a success of the *Plain Dealer,* Major W. W. Armstrong had become financially embarrassed to the point that it was common knowledge. Liberty E. Holden, long-time friend who had acquired wealth through real-estate and mining interests, rescued the evening paper, and with Charles H. Bulkley, a brother-in-law, and Roman R. Holden, his brother, became the new owners on December 15, 1884. The desire to publish morning, evening, and Sunday editions led to their purchase of the *Herald,* the city's oldest paper, including the building and plant on Bank Street. Here the *Plain Dealer* was established, and the first morning edition of the Democratic newspaper appeared on March 16, 1885, with the aid of almost all of the *Herald* editorial staff—a Whig-Republican aggregation. A valuable inheritance was that of J. H. A. Bone, a veritable encyclopedia of knowledge and a writer of ability, who served the *Herald* for three decades, and wrote for the *Plain Dealer* until his death in 1906. His quaint observations, signed "Spectacles," were an institution in Cleveland. Benjamin F. Taylor, Cleveland poet and humorist of rare talent, contributed to the *Plain Dealer* and other local papers. He left enduring word pictures of the Civil War, and his nature sketches and *Poetical Works* contributed to his success as a traveling lecturer. He died in Cleveland in 1887. Edwin Cowles of the *Leader* took over the *Evening Herald* in 1885. It became the *News and Herald,* and intense rivalry developed between the *Leader* and the *Plain Dealer* as they competed day after day with morning, evening, and Sunday editions.

The linotype was patented by Ottmar Mergenthaler, an amazing machine that did the work of many typesetters. Its practical use was not in evidence in Cleveland, however, until six years later, and some considered it a threat to employment.

Spring made her appearance on March 21, bundled in a frigid four below zero.

William H. Doan gave land on the north side of Vincent Street, between Bond and Erie, plus $10,000 toward construction of the Music Hall, a public auditorium to be used for religious, educational, and musical advancement. The cost exceeded $50,000, and, as the city's largest meeting place, it seated 4,300 persons. Entrance was gained through Doan's Block on Erie Street. Title was vested in five trustees, three chosen by Doan and two by the Cleveland Vocal Society. Thousands of Clevelanders climbed the steep stairs to the uncomfortable galleries to hear the world's greatest musical stars and witness commencement exercises and public functions. After damage by fire, the hall was rebuilt, facing on Vincent Street; and fire brought its untimely end in 1898. Its builder, known for his philanthropies, died in 1890.

Mary P. Spargo of Cleveland—Mrs. W. D. Fraser—was admitted to the practice of law by the Ohio Supreme Court. She was the first woman lawyer in the city, and she prepared for her career by studying in the office of Morrow & Morrow.

The partnership of E. Grasselli & Son was dissolved this year, and the Grasselli Chemical Company was incorporated, capitalized at $600,000.

Caesar A. Grasselli was chosen president; Eugene Grasselli, his brother, vice president; Daniel K. Bailey, secretary; and Kenneth B. Bailey, treasurer, all related to the Grasselli family, makers of chemicals for generations in Europe. By acquisition and consolidation, the firm increased in size and prosperity, establishing plants in New Jersey, Indiana, West Virginia, Alabama, New York, Pennsylvania, Ohio, and Canada. Capital was increased to $20,000,000 in 1913. During World War I, the company entered the explosives field, producing dynamite and black powder for blasting after the war. Dye intermediates were added to the output in 1919.

A law governing the registration of voters, passed on May 4, was the foundation of future voting procedure. The city was divided into wards by the Council, and the wards into precincts. A "register" of each political party was appointed in each precinct. On stated days, the voters appeared at the voting places where their names were recorded. Prior to this time, elections had been held in public buildings, such as engine houses and police stations. Under the precinct system, there were not enough public locations, and headquarters were rented until the advent of the voting booth.

A proud banner bearing two words, "The Hollenden," flew from the tower of Cleveland's newest hotel on June 7, signifying its opening. Liberty E. Holden recognized the great need of high-grade, apartment-house facilities; and in the Hollenden, the city had the first large hotel for transients east of the Square as well as accommodations for permanent residents. Holden had purchased the Philo Chamberlain property, fronting on Superior, Bond, and Vincent streets; and a corporation, in which W. J. Gordon and Charles H. Bulkley were interested, carried out his plans. Electric lights, one hundred private baths and fireproof construction added to the Hollenden's fame. Its high, paneled walls, massive redwood and mahogany fittings, exclusively designed furniture, and "crystal" dining room marked it as sumptuous. George F. Hammond, architect, designed much of the interior. Holden consented reluctantly to provide a dining room. Politicians claimed it and made it famous as a meeting place. "Hanna hash," Mark Hanna's favorite dish, originated here. The Superior Avenue hostelry, which took its name from an early English form of the name "Holden," was "a small-talk center for precinct workers," the *Plain Dealer* reported. In the gay nineties, it was the scene of colorful balls and festivities. Its bar was the longest in town. George Meyer, who had a shop in the Hollenden, was the best barber in the United States, according to Elbert Hubbard. Five Presidents—McKinley, Theodore Roosevelt, Taft, Wilson, and Harding, heads of foreign governments, celebrities of stage and lecture platform, political enthusiasts, industrial giants, and champions in sports were its house guests.

According to the will of T. S. Beckwith, for many years an elder of the Second Presbyterian Church, when the income from certain stocks reached $10,000, the session of his church was empowered to invest it in founding a church with free pews to be known by the Beckwith name. When it became entirely or partially self-supporting, another was to be created, and

Windsor T. White, with his younger brothers, Rollin H. and Walter C., built White steam cars in 1900.

Alexander Winton made his first practical Winton car in 1897.

Early Baker Electric. CLEVELAND PICTURE COLLECTION, CLEVELAND PUBLIC LIBRARY.

Walter C. Baker built electric cars in the 1890s and was the first advocate of streamlining.

The Union Trust Building, later the Union Commerce Building, was opened in 1924 at Euclid Avenue and East 9th Street—one of the largest office buildings in the world.

The Lennox Building formerly occupied the site.

so on. The stipulated sum had accumulated in the Beckwith Fund, and on June 17, 1885, the Beckwith Presbyterian Church was organized with twenty-three members in the Doan's Corners community. Mrs. Beckwith offered to contribute $5,000 toward the purchase of a lot at Fairmount and Deering Street, near the new cultural center in which Case and Reserve had located. The Rev. Mattoon M. Curtis, later professor of philosophy at Adelbert College, was the first pastor. He was succeeded in 1888 by Dr. James DeLong Williamson, son of Samuel Williamson, pioneer. Family responsibilities compelled him to retire from the active ministry in 1901. Dr. Williamson was a leader in denominational, civic, and cultural activities, and he gave invaluable counsel when, during the pastorate of Dr. Albert J. Alexander, the Beckwith Memorial Church united with the Euclid Avenue Presbyterian Church in 1906 (later Church of the Covenant). In 1914 the Beckwith Church was purchased for use as a gymnasium for Case School of Applied Science.

Basic refining processes developed by Herman Frasch, a Cleveland chemist who sold his patents to Standard Oil, included methods for removal of paraffin and sulphur from petroleum, and for acidizing oil wells to increase production.

Haltnorth's Garden was in its glory. It took its name from the owner, who operated the popular beer garden at Rock's Corners, at the northeast corner of Willson and Woodland, just outside the Cleveland city limits. A wooded lot, nearly half a block square, contained a pond crossed by a rustic bridge, and a garden that was a favored picnic spot. Light opera was presented by a stock company on summer evenings in the large, open-air theater. The Holman Opera Company, the Wilbur Opera Company, and the Murray-Lane Opera Company were favorites for many years. After the turn of the century, it became the Coliseum, featuring Yiddish drama under I. R. Copperman, manager.

Tom Johnson bought the South Side Railway Company, modernized its equipment and service, and increased his power in local traction business. In 1887 came the Abbey Street extension on his Brooklyn line. The Scranton line was built by the company in 1889, a narrow-gauge road extending from Superior through Seneca, Scranton, and Clark avenues; and in the same year, the two roads merged under one ownership, although operated separately. Horsecar drivers worked from twelve to eighteen hours and received $1.40 a day, paid in tickets which they sold for cash. Rear platforms for smokers were introduced about this time.

Safety of the great mills in Newburgh was endangered during a strike of workers in July.

Racing history was made at the Glenville track on July 30 when Maud S., owned by William H. Vanderbilt and driven by W. W. Bair, trotted to high-wheel sulky in 2:08¾, establishing a world record. In the great throng of fans was a lad named Charlie Otis, who had ridden his pony from his home on Euclid Avenue near Sterling to follow the races. His heart was with the harness horses, and in many a contest during the golden era of racing in Cleveland, he drove fast-stepping trotters and pacers at Glenville. In 1889 Edward "Pop" Geers, "the silent man from Tennessee," made his debut at the Grand Circuit meeting at Glenville, and began a career of fame as king of the reinsmen. His reputation for honesty and unchallenged judgment was as well known as were his record-breaking horses.

Mass production of printing presses was the goal of W. H. Price, who believed that with jigs and special machinery he could cut costs and increase output. H. T. Chandler, who had broad experience in business and banking, joined him this year in a partnership to manufacture Gordon-type presses in a small factory on East Prospect Street near the Pennsylvania tracks. Equipment was secured, enabling them to machine a thousand or more parts at one setting, and assemble one hundred printing presses of a size and kind on one floor. In 1895 the partnership grew into Chandler & Price Company, manufacturers of presses and paper-cutting machines. Before long, its products were at work the world over. Battleships and pleasure boats, hotels and banks, business offices, and even missionary headquarters in remote lands were using these labor savers. It is said that there is no printed language that has not been printed on Chandler & Price presses. Eight additions were built to the first factory, forming a great plant on the original site, 6000 Carnegie Avenue. D. W. Frackelton, elected vice president in 1913, succeeded his brother, R. J., as president in 1940.

Schaaf Road was planked across the valley from Cleveland when Gustave Ruetenik and his sons introduced vegetable forcing under glass this year. Their first greenhouse, developed from Peter Henderson's horticulture book, was 50 by 11 feet, built of sashwood and glass at a cost of $100. Martin L., who succeeded his father as head of the business, was a master farmer. He was one of those who developed the great truck-gardening industry in Cuyahoga County, and pioneered in establishing co-operative farm ownership. In 1946, three and one-half acres of the seventeen in the Ruetenik Gardens on Schaaf Road were covered with greenhouses.

A four-story commercial building bearing the Williamson family name was erected at the corner of Euclid and the Public Square, on the site of the Chapin Block and the Williamson homestead to the east. Fire severely damaged the structure in 1895, and plans were then made by H. Clark Ford and G. E. Herrick to erect a skyscraper on the site as soon as certain leases expired.

The Liberty E. Holden homestead (opposite Wade Park) had been purchased by Cleveland citizens as a site for Case School of Applied Science and Adelbert College of Western Reserve University, and the westerly section became the permanent location of Case. A new building had been partially completed when classes opened in September this year. Five students were graduated at the first commencement.

Cleveland's expansion toward the "Heights" made necessary a high-pressure water system of greater capacity. Two reservoirs were built, far from the city's industrial area, on a new principle. At the old Kentucky Street plant, the water was pumped directly into the reservoir, then distributed to consumers. With the opening of the Fairmount and Kinsman reservoirs this year, water was pumped directly into the city mains. The old reservoir was abandoned, and eventually converted into a park (Fairview Park).

Charles H. Bulkley built the Cleveland Theater on the north side of St. Clair, west of Ontario, opening it on October 19 under the management of Frank M. Drew, and featuring the Charles L. Andrews Company in *Michael Strogoff*. Stars of the day were presented in popular melodrama. H. R. Jacobs, "King of Diamonds," who won attention by traveling in a private car and opening low-priced theaters, took over the house. He changed the name to H. R. Jacobs' Theater, and opened it in September, 1886, with *The Lights o' London*. A mixture of melodrama, comedy, and comic opera brought a line of patrons down the alley from the Square. Drew, a cousin of the younger John Drew, had served an apprenticeship with Dan Rice, pioneer showman and circus clown, and he had spent ten years with P. T. Barnum. Before he became manager of the Cleveland, he had operated a dime museum and variety show on Superior Avenue.

A "thin dime" had admitted many curious Clevelanders to Drew's Dime Museum on the north side of Superior Avenue east of Bank. Up the steep steps on the third floor was Drew's continuous performance of grisly, nightmarish freaks and curiosities—a Borneo wild man and bearded women, "Siamese twins" and animal monsters, fat men and "living skeletons," dwarfs and giants. Famous talent appeared in his music hall—Weber and Fields, Billy Van, the blackface minstrel and his namesake, Billy B. Van, and others. It is said that an African native died from pneumonia in the museum, his covering consisting only of a plug hat and a breech-clout. Plastering the corpse with mud in native fashion, members of the troupe were preparing to conduct a ceremonial tree burial by hanging it from a telegraph pole when Drew rescued it. For years, the mummy was exhibited in a downtown ambulance station, then it disappeared, and periodic searches by historians to retrieve it were in vain.

C. O. Bartlett rented a small back room in downtown Cleveland and started to manufacture machinery with which to make oatmeal. Soon he began jobbing boilers and other lines. K. F. Snow, a brother-in-law, joined the Columbus Street business, which became C. O. Bartlett & Company, and in 1902, The C. O. Bartlett & Snow Company. Oatmeal machinery was installed in all parts of the nation as well as in Italy, Russia, and Scotland, "home" of oatmeal. Corn shellers were added to the company line in 1904; mechanical-handling equipment was adapted and sold to a wide variety of industries, and paint-making machinery was developed.

Among Cleveland leaders at this time were Charles G. Taplin, Standard Oil executive, and Frank Rockefeller, investor in the company; D. Edward Dangler, founder of the Dangler Stove Company, pioneer manufacturer of gasoline stoves; Caleb Gowan, leader in the builder's-supply business, and William Greif, producer of kegs and barrels.

Cleveland's importance industrially can well be measured by its yearly manufacture of 2,000,000 pounds of tobacco products and 4,500,000 barrels, machinery totaling $42,000,000, railway equipment amounting to $12,000,000, a total of 200,000,000 feet of lumber handled, and a yield from its lake fisheries of 600 tons.

1886

To meet the need for "native helpers" in his missionary work among the Bohemians, Dr. Henry Albert Schauffler founded the Cleveland Bible Readers School in January, under the auspices of the Bohemian Mission Board. It was later known as The Schauffler Missionary Training School. The school opened with a single pupil and a single instructor in the home of Donley Hobart on Broadway. Pioneering in America in the training of young women for Christian work, Schauffler was also unique in its purpose to train Bohemian and other Slavic women for work among their own people. A rented house became inadequate, and a new home was provided on Fowler Avenue, from which Schauffler College of Religious and Social Work developed. A dormitory was dedicated in 1890. Dr. Schauffler died in 1905.

Associated with Charles F. Brush in the Brush Electric Company were W. H. Lawrence, superintendent, and W. H. Boulton, foreman. In 1881 Boulton and Willis U. Masters formed a partnership to make electric-lighting carbons. Lawrence purchased an interest in the Boulton Carbon Company five years later, and organized the National Carbon Company, taking over the Boulton plant on Willson Avenue. The carbon department of the Brush company was purchased in 1891. Associated with Lawrence were Myron T. Herrick, James Parmelee, and Webb C. Hayes, son of ex-President Rutherford B. Hayes. More than a score of carbon-and-battery companies were purchased and consolidated in National Carbon operations in about two decades. In 1917 the company became a unit of the Union Carbide & Carbon Corporation. National Carbon was America's largest corporate authority on carbon in the 1940s, with two plants in Cleveland —at West 73rd and the New York Central railroad, and West 117th and Madison, as well as in other cities. Notable among its many products were electrodes, brushes, high-illumination carbons, and "Karbate"; Eveready batteries for flashlights, radios, hearing aids, and industrial, laboratory, and other uses; flashlight cases; Prestone, Anti-Freeze, and Krene plastic products.

Charles Martin Hall of Thompson, Ohio, had been graduated from Oberlin College in 1885. Here his research in aluminum began. In 1886, at the age of twenty-two, he developed the electrolytic process for the reduction of aluminum ore, making it possible to market the cheap product. Hall was an early officer of the Aluminum Company of America; and when he died in 1914, he left much of his great fortune to his alma mater and to Harvard University.

The Educational and Industrial Union was established by the Women's Christian Association (YWCA) to provide expert teaching for girls of "operative class" in "sewing, millinery, cooking and stenography." The Wedge, a lunchroom for business girls, was opened on Euclid at Erie Street, where everything on the menu was priced at five cents or under!

Although corporal punishment had been discouraged for some time in the public schools, it was not abolished until this year.

William G. Mather, charter member and early president of the Brotherhood of St. Andrew, the basic organization of the Episcopal Church, founded in Chicago in 1882, was instrumental in establishing the Trinity Cathedral Chapter this year. A simple requirement of members was to encourage men to go to church and to further the spreading of Christ's kingdom. Recreation and reading rooms were provided for young men, and many were inspired to join the church and the ministry. Parishes and missions in the diocese bearing the name St. Andrew represent the chapter's efforts.

The Board of Elections was organized on June 5, with authority over city and county elections. The first members were General James Barnett, president; William W. Armstrong, J. H. Schneider, Herman Weber, and William J. Gleason, secretary.

The B'nai Jeshurun Congregation (later Temple on the Heights) purchased the Eagle Street Temple for $15,000, and Rabbi Sigmund Drechsler was engaged as spiritual head. Beloved of his people, he served until his death in 1908.

The Euclid Avenue National Bank was organized this year, with capital of $500,000. Located a short distance east of the Square, it was the first bank to shun the Superior Avenue business district and stake its future on Euclid. The first officers were John L. Woods, president; Charles F. Brush, vice president; and Solon L. Severance, cashier. Succeeding presidents were Brush and Severance, who was the executive head when a merger was effected with the Park National Bank in 1903, to form the Euclid-Park National Bank. Solon L. Severance was one of Cleveland's ablest bankers, and he continued his official connection in the institution which ultimately became the First National Bank of Cleveland, the largest bank in Ohio, serving as a director until his death in 1915. Born in Cleveland in 1834, the son of Solomon Lewis and Mary H. Severance, he began his financial career in local banking houses and became a power in business. He gave liberally of time and money to the Presbyterian Church and to worthy charitable projects, and his travels carried him into many nations.

The Cleveland Stone Company was incorporated in July, succeeding companies in the Berea and Amherst fields. The first officers were William McDermott, president; James M. Worthington, vice president; George H. Worthington, secretary-treasurer. Other members of the board of directors were Andrew Squire, James Nicholl, Frank M. Stearns, and Michael Mc-Dermott. In 1922 the company extended its operations into the field of artificial abrasives. Through a merger with The Ohio Quarries Company, founded in 1903, The Cleveland Quarries Company was organized in 1929, with H. W. Caldwell, president. Berea and Amherst sandstone went into bridges, paved streets, and roads. It was standard building material in the construction of many major building operations, among them the Michigan State Capitol, the Milwaukee City Hall, the St. Louis City Hall, and the Parliament Buildings at Ottawa, Canada. E. T. Ripley succeeded to the presidency in 1943.

In July, the Kingsbury Run Viaduct (later East 34th Street Bridge) opened, connecting Davis and Humboldt streets. The wooden trestle, 490 feet long with a 36-foot roadway and two footways, was designed to be filled in later with soil.

The East Cleveland Railway franchise was extended eastward on Euclid to the city limits (near East 115th), and in July, extensions were granted on Water, Lake, and Bank streets.

Dr. Cady Staley had brought with him from Union College, Schenectady, an enviable record as an educator, when he became the first president of Case School of Applied Science in July. He was one of the country's leading civil and sanitary engineers, and he had helped to build the Central Pacific Railroad. The faith of the trustees and faculty, however, were put to the test on October 27, when the fine, new, three-story building and most of the apparatus were destroyed by fire at a loss of about $150,000. Generous trustees of Western Reserve University offered the facilities of Adelbert College until September, 1888, when the building was again occupied. High standards of scholarship and management characterized Case School from the beginning. Upon the death of Henry G. Abbey, Eckstein Case, cousin of the founder, became secretary-treasurer and served for more than fifty years. Distinguished men of science were members of the faculty, among them Edward W. Morley, Charles Frederic Mabery, Albert A. Michelson, Dayton C. Miller, and Jason J. Nassau. Generations of students cherished years of study with Frank M. Comstock and Frank H. Neff, a graduate, under whom Theodore M. Focke studied, later to become dean and friend to thousands of Case men who went out to build bridges, shape industrial progress, and explore uncharted avenues of the universe.

The Cleveland Athletic Club held its first summer meet on July 31 at Athletic Park. Official sportdom and Cleveland society packed the stands, cheering as athletes from the Midwest competed in a variety of contests. H. M. Johnson, well-known professional, made a record-breaking 100-yard dash in 9⅘ seconds from a standing start for a $20 prize. A four-lap bicycle race swelled the chests of Clevelanders, as Will Sargent, John Huntington, and Lucien Davis of the local club won by six feet in 2:55⅗. Winding up the historic meet, E. S. Heydorn of Cleveland defeated T. Moffat of Canada by covering the quarter-mile in 52 seconds, just short of a record. In the same year W. A. Rowe, a shoemaker of Lynn, Massachusetts, established a world record on a Cleveland track, riding his high-wheel bicycle in 2:29⅘, a mark that stood for three years.

After four turbulent but highly productive years, Superintendent Hinsdale resigned as head of the public schools to join the faculty of the University of Michigan, where he served until his death. Summarizing a "beneficent" administration in his final report, Dr. Hinsdale stated, "I soon discovered that what the schools most needed was not revolution in external organization and system, but more fruitful instruction, a more elastic regimen, and a freer spirit. . . . In this path, I have steadfastly sought to tread." He was succeeded by Lewis W. Day, who had risen from the rank of teacher.

The foundation of electric smelting was laid by Alfred and Eugene Cowles, sons of Edwin Cowles, Cleveland newspaper editor. They were the first to smelt many refractory ores in their electric furnace, patented this year. They pioneered in making carborundum, artificial graphite, and a number of new alloys, and made early progress in the manufacture of aluminum.

Vault doors trembled, the seven-story Mercantile Bank Building rocked, and people were panic-stricken as the Charleston earthquake tremors shook Cleveland on August 31. When reports came through, it was learned that the three-minute shock had destroyed three-fourths of Charleston and hundreds had perished.

The 2,257-ton *Spokane,* the first steel bulk freighter on the lakes, was built in the Globe Iron Works yards for the Wilson Transit Company of Cleveland. Steel rapidly displaced iron in the construction of lake ships.

St. Ignatius College opened on September 6 with seventy-six students. A few Jesuit fathers, under the leadership of Father John C. B. Neustich, had erected a small building at Jersey and Carroll streets in a district predominantly German; but it was soon inadequate, and in 1888, a new, five-story, brick structure was provided. Under the second president, Father Henry Knappmeyer, S.J., a wing was added that was later occupied by St. Ignatius High School. The college, forerunner of John Carroll University, was incorporated in 1890. Meteorological and seismological departments were added, and here Father Frederick L. Odenbach, S.J., renowned man of science, made notable contributions to the world from his small laboratory.

The Park Theater reopened on September 6, but during the restoration period after the fire in 1884, Manager Augustus F. Hartz joined the Euclid Avenue Opera House. His successor was the veteran showman, "Uncle John" Ellsler, with his son, John J., as treasurer. The first season featured the best opera companies and first-class talent—Rosina Vokes, Lilian Olcott, J. K. Emmett, Janauschek, and Robert Mantell. The premier of *Captain Cupid,* a comic opera by Ferdinand Puehringer, William E. Sage, and W. R. Rose of Cleveland, was presented on May 16, 1887. Ellsler failed again as manager; and he was a poor man when he appeared on the stage for the last time on June 13, 1887, as Kazrac, the dumb slave, in *Aladdin,* one of his feature productions. On September 2, 1889, the house opened after renovations as the Lyceum Theater, featuring great artists, such as E. H. Sothern, the Kendals, Sarah Bernhardt, Lillian Russell, and Mrs. John Drew. It changed managers several times until leased by the E. D. Stair syndicate.

Thirteen dentists met in the office of Dr. D. R. Jennings on the evening of October 6 to form the Cleveland Dental Society, with Dr. Jennings, president; Dr. John Stephan, vice president; Dr. P. H. Keese, secretary; and Dr. S. B. Dewey, treasurer. Significant progress in dental education and generous clinical aid to the needy originated in the constructive programs of the society. Dr. John Ralph Owens, who was secretary pro tem when the society was organized, was the oldest living charter member six decades later at the age of ninety-three. One of Ohio's leading dentists, he had served as president of the Northern Ohio Dental Association and as a member of the Ohio Board of Dental Examiners. Membership in the Cleveland Dental Society had reached 1,050 in 1946, when Dr. Harold H. Sell was president.

The Masonic Temple, a five-story, brick structure costing $175,000, was dedicated on October 19 at the northeast corner of Superior and Bond Street (Federal Reserve Bank Building site). The keystone from the doorway arch of the first lodge rooms in 1826 had been found by workmen while razing the foundation of a barn, and the relic was cemented in the arch over the entrance to the chapter room. Cleveland City Lodge now had a membership of 246. In the early eighties, Irish Lodge had taken the lead in Ohio, with more than 300 members; and Webb Chapter, Royal Arch Masons, exceeded 350 members. In 1889 Lake Erie Consistory, Scottish Rite Masons, was organized with 428 charter members. Until this time, Cleveland Masons were under the jurisdiction of the Ohio Consistory, meeting in Cincinnati. Freemasonry was well established, and from these early lodges stemmed a vast fraternal organization as the city grew.

Thirteen men, meeting in Goldschmidt's Hall on Woodland Avenue on October 20, under the leadership of the Rev. John Heiniger, held the first service of the Immanuel Evangelical Church. The first house of worship was erected at what became Colfax Avenue and Minnie Street, later moving to Kinsman Road and East 72nd Street. In 1927 the church followed its congregation eastward, meeting for services at Sussex School in Shaker Heights until a new home at 20120 Lomond Boulevard, dedicated in 1938, was ready for occupancy. At this time, the name Immanuel Church of Shaker Heights was adopted, the congregation being identified with the Evangelical and Reformed denomination. All church indebtedness was liquidated when the Rev. Robert J. Baldauf became pastor in 1946.

The ravaging fire in the "Flats" in 1884 had resulted in a $25,000 appropriation for new equipment for the Fire Department. On November 1, river fire-fighting was inaugurated when the first fireboat was launched. Named the *J. L. Weatherly,* honoring an able chief of the volunteer department, it served until May 18, 1894.

On November 6, the Otis grain elevator on River Street burned with a loss of $45,000 and the new fireboat was initiated into service.

Civil War memories were revived when the Cyclorama opened on November 6, featuring heroism and horror in a spectacular indoor exhibition of vivid battle scenes. The large, circular structure had been erected in the rear of the Lennox Building, an apartment house with store space under construction at Euclid and Erie Street (Union Commerce Building site). Visitors climbed stairs to a central balcony to view vast expanses of highly colored canvas portraying fierce encounters, galloping artillery, and brave men driving headlong into conflict, the sky charged with smoke and fire. "The Battle of Shiloh" was a powerful and moving drama, but without shot or shell, for all was silence and nothing moved. Only the light from the glass roof overhead warmed the scene. "The Battle of Gettysburg," "Lookout Mountain," and other decisive engagements moved into the Cyclorama in turn; but interest waned after about six years; and in 1896, a bicycle-riding school took over the building.

At the junction of Willson Avenue and the Erie Railroad, George R. Canfield, twenty-eight, located the plant of The Canfield Oil Company, incorporated December 23, to manufacture lubricating oils and greases, and to prepare signal oils for lanterns and petroleum jelly for ointments. The Penn Petrolatum Company was incorporated in 1897 to operate a refinery at Coraopolis, near Pittsburgh, Pennsylvania, providing adequate facilities for making petroleum jelly, and the company merged with Canfield in 1901. With the approach of the automobile age, the Coraopolis plant was converted to the manufacture of high-quality lubricants, and thus continued through the years.

The Kelley Island Lime & Transport Company was incorporated on December 28 with a broad purpose: "to quarry stone, burn lime, harvest ice, cultivate the soil for cereal and other crops, and to buy and sell the same, to buy and sell goods and merchandise of every kind," to engage in transportation "by land or water, or both, and to supply all necessary means therefor." Moses C. Younglove was the first president; Caleb E. Gowan, first vice president; and E. B. Merriam, secretary. The Cleveland company became the world's largest producer of lime and limestone products, serving agriculture and the steel, building, chemical, and processing industries. Plants and docks were maintained in Ohio, Michigan, New York, and Pennsylvania, as well as a lake sand fleet and subsidiary companies. Ralph L. Dickey, elected president in 1940, succeeded George J. Whelan, who became chairman after having served since 1924.

1887

The pioneering Cuyahoga Steam Furnace Company was purchased on January 1 by the Cleveland Shipbuilding Company, forerunner of the American Shipbuilding Company, organized by Robert Wallace, William Chisholm, J. H. Wade, Captain Phillip Minch, and others, with Henry D. Coffinberry, president. In 1897 they commenced to build the largest dry docks on the lakes at Lorain, Ohio. Coffinberry became president of the Minch Transportation Company and the Nicholas Transit Company, as well as a director of banks and industrial companies.

Burglars entered a Cleveland store in January, stealing a large quantity of valuable furs. Although the loot was never recovered, one of the thieves was arrested at Allegheny City, Pennsylvania. While returning with their prisoner, Captain Henry Hoehn and Detective William H. Hulligan, Cleveland police, were attacked in the early morning, as the train stood at the Ravenna station, by three armed men who freed the prisoner and escaped. Hoehn recovered, but Hulligan died. In a gun encounter with the law in

Michigan in June, three men were arrested and identified by Captain Hoehn as his assailants. Their trial in Ravenna attracted wide attention, and Charles "Blinky" Morgan, the bandit who had a hideout in Cleveland, was convicted and executed. His companions were found guilty, but upon a new trial were set free.

On February 1, the·Cleveland Press Club was organized. Officers were John C. Covert, editor of the *Leader,* president; Gilbert W. Henderson, associate editor of the *Plain Dealer,* vice president; John B. Foster of the *Leader,* secretary; and W. R. Rose of the Sunday *Voice,* treasurer. Club rooms at 8 Euclid Avenue were found to be too small, and quarters were secured in the former residence of Henry Chisholm. Great mirrors in gilded frames rose above carved Italian-marble fireplaces, the walls were hung with paintings, and the Cleveland-club headquarters was pronounced one of the finest in the country. In 1888, seventy-two members and sixty-seven honorary members were on the roster.

General Erastus N. Bates, one of the earliest Christian Science workers in the nation, came to Cleveland with his family in March. In the two years following, seven students of Christian Science received instructions in Boston from Mrs. Mary Baker Eddy, founder of The Mother Church.

In the shelter of their farm home, Mayor Carlos Jones of Brooklyn Village and his wife started an orphanage that came to bear their name—Jones Home, 3518 West 25th Street. Forty acres of land and more than $150,000 were dedicated by Mayor Jones for the "care, support and education of destitute children." To this was added from time to time the gifts of friends and the support of Cleveland institutions that made possible facilities to meet the ever-growing demands for expanded child care.

One of the most notable gifts to medical education in America was made by John Lund Woods, banker and retired lumberman, who gave a fund of $175,000 to provide a new building for the School of Medicine of Western Reserve University. A five-story, brown-stone structure, erected on the old site at St. Clair and Erie Street, was dedicated on March 8. At this time, attendance at three full sessions of instruction before graduation had become obligatory for medical students. A dispensary was established, as well as laboratory work in chemistry and histology, and demonstrations in pathology. The next year, graded courses of three full years were established, requiring also individual laboratory work in physiology, the first in the West and probably the first in the nation. In 1892 Woods further endowed the school with a gift of $125,000 for laboratory subjects, also permitting employment of the first full-time teachers. Requirements were raised to four years in 1896; and in 1898, a chemical laboratory was erected adjacent to the old medical building.

Industrial and building arts had been stimulated by the International Centennial Exposition at Philadelphia in 1876. Its influence inspired architects to study abroad, to launch publications, and to seek closer association within the profession. Eight members had banded together early in the decade as the Cleveland Architectural Club, and, on April 7, this year, the society was reorganized as the Cleveland Chapter of The American Institute of Architects, dedicated to architectural improvement of the city.

More than 125 guests attended the Cleveland Press Club banquet at the Hotel Hollenden on April 23, honoring the three-hundred-and-twenty-third anniversary of Shakespeare's birth. A brilliant assembly of ladies and gentlemen heard a scholarly discourse on English literature before the days of the bard, presented by J. H. A. Bone of the *Plain Dealer*. F. L. Purdy of the *Press* picked up the theme of literature after Shakespeare, and Henry A. Griffin of the *Leader* brought women of the Sixteenth Century to life. W. R. Rose of the *Voice* closed the speaking program in a light-hearted vein by exposing Shakespeare, the humorist. "It is not probable," a newspaper report stated, "that so many active laborers on the daily and weekly press have ever come together before in this city." The high-caloried banquet menu ran the gamut of the day's delicacies.

Thomas A. Edison conceived the idea for his kinetoscope, a peep-show machine that enlivened penny arcades and was the forerunner of motion pictures. In later years, when asked for a word of advice to young people, the great American, who patented more than a thousand inventions, said, "Find something that interests you and work at it." Work was the soul of Edison's success, and one of his favorite inspirations was, "You can work your way through things you cannot see your way through."

The northeast corner of Euclid and Erie streets (Union Commerce Building site), a frontage of 145 feet on Euclid and 158.5 feet on Erie, was leased for ninety-nine years to the Panorama Company for $6,000 per year. In 1912, the same property was leased for $40,000; and five years later for $83,560 annually.

Council was asked to prohibit parking of express wagons and moving vans on the northeast side of the Square.

Cleveland citizens of English birth or descent celebrated the Golden Jubilee of the reign of Queen Victoria on June 21, with a dinner, concert, and literary exercises in Case Hall. John Walker was the general chairman, and five speakers followed W. S. Kerruish, paying happy tributes to the good queen.

On July 2, the first number of *Church Life* appeared, a publication of the Episcopal Diocese of Ohio. The weekly, edited by W. W. Williams, soon became a monthly. The columns of this Cleveland journal contain a priceless account of the years of struggle and sacrifice and of progress and promise that portray the history of the diocese down through the years.

More than twenty acres of land, fronting on Mayfield Road, were acquired by Jewish leaders on July 31 for cemetery purposes. Three years later, the Anshe Chesed and Tifereth Israel congregations entered into an agreement for joint control and maintenance of the United Jewish Cemeteries in Cleveland. On May 30, 1893, the chapel in the new Mayfield Cemetery was dedicated.

The Disciples Union of Cleveland was organized at a meeting in the Franklin Circle Church of Christ on August 21, inspired by A. J. Marvin,

W. S. Streator, H. E. McMillan, A. R. Teachout, and Lloyd Darsie. Through its mission work, new congregations were formed, and denominational effort was furthered.

As the city expanded and transportation increased in speed, officers of the law encountered greater difficulty in combating crime. The Police Department introduced the patrol-and-exchange system, equipment consisting of 50 patrol boxes, 2 patrol wagons, 21 signal instruments, and 21 miles of wire. The clumsy boxes, erected at street corners, resembled phone booths; but the new telephonic communication carried the high-hatted bluecoat's message to headquarters faster than shoe leather or horsepower.

Although the Eagle Street Temple had been enlarged in 1860, the Anshe Chesed Congregation (later Euclid Avenue Temple) had outgrown it. A building committee, including Simon Newmark, Simon Skall, S. Fishel, Moses Halle, M. Wyman, Abraham Strauss, E. J. Weil, and Ferdinand Strauss, selected a site at Scovill and Henry streets for a new $85,000 temple seating 1,500 persons. Farewell services were held at the Eagle Street Synagogue on September 2, at which Rabbi Isaac Mayer Wise of Cincinnati was the principal speaker. After the service, the assembly marched to the new Scovill Avenue Temple, the officers carrying the scrolls of the law.

As evidence that management and labor were on friendly terms, employees of the H. P. Nail Works saluted Michael Baackes, general manager, when he resigned. On September 5, they formed a torchlight parade, headed by a brass band, and marched to his home on Willson Avenue, where they presented him with a diamond stud and his wife with pearl opera glasses.

T. W. James built a small greenhouse on Schaaf Road this year; and, in 1892, Fred Witthuhn opened another at Pearl and Dover streets, later moving to Schaaf Road, where under family management the business grew to be one of the largest in the district. Progressive developments in the greenhouse industry originated with Cleveland's pioneer gardeners.

September 12 was the opening night of the Columbia Theater, and playgoers climbed into shays and drove from as far as Doan's Corners to attend the premiere of Hanlon's *Fantasma*. Waldemar Otis had erected the house (Embassy Theater site, 709 Euclid) and engaged B. C. Hart as manager. Favorite stars of the show world were featured on its stage, among them James A. Herne, Minnie Maddern, Maude Banks, Marguerite St. John, Kate Castleton, Dan Sully, and Lizzie Evans.

A church "good enough for the rich man and not too good for the poor man" voiced the sentiments of the builders of the new and larger Euclid Avenue Congregational Church, dedicated debt-free on the site of the old building, September 25. The bell tower, retained from the former church, was veneered with stone and housed the historic bell. Memorial windows to Captain Alva Bradley, trustee, and his daughter, featured glass folded as representing drapery, the first of the kind in the city. The Rev. Henry M. Ladd, African missionary and explorer, had become pastor in 1883; and during his long service, membership grew and the church took a leading part in denominational affairs. It mothered and aided a number of Congregational churches, among them East Madison Avenue Church, founded as a mission in 1875, and continuing until 1917; Park, 1886, which became Calvary, and evolved into the Mayflower Church in 1920; Hough Avenue, organized in 1890, returned to the parent in 1934; and Lake View, 1890, serving an Italian community.

High on the roll of Cleveland's distinguished citizens is the name of John W. Allen, who died on October 5, aged eighty-five. Refined, courteous, and friendly, and a lawyer of rare talent and ability, he had helped to guide young Cleveland through its early years. He was elected to the Ohio Senate in 1835, sent to Congress in 1836 and re-elected in 1838. In 1841 he became mayor of Cleveland. Identified with the Whig Party, he was a close friend of Henry Clay; later he became an influential Republican. Allen was one of the first bank commissioners of Ohio. He furthered the interests of sound banking and became the first president of the Society for Savings. He lent persuasive and constructive support to railroad-building, and served two terms as postmaster.

Case School's first football opponent was Central High School. At the Kennard Street ball park, the freshman tide was hurled back by Central, 12-0. This historic clash both started and wound up the season.

A Cleveland woman started something when she took off her hat at a performance in the Opera House. Men applauded and the newspapers opened a booster campaign.

Prominent physicians organized the Society of the Medical Sciences of Cleveland in December. Dr. H. K. Cushing, the first president, continued in office until 1895, when he declined further service. Dr. Isaac N. Himes, his successor, died in office, and Dr. John H. Lowman was at the helm when the organization was abandoned in 1896.

1888

Indigestion was an accepted, every-day affliction until Dr. E. E. Beeman discovered in the seventies that pure pepsin brought relief to his patients. Beeman was born in Lorain County in 1840, graduated from the Cincinnati Medical College in 1861, served in the war with the Cleveland Grays for a short period, and operated a drug business in Cleveland on Ontario Street for several years. He then practiced in northern Ohio, including six years at Wakeman, returning to Cleveland in 1870. Beeman's pepsin, advertised as an aid to digestion, grew into a thriving business, bolstered by financial aid from Albert Johnson, brother of Tom L., and William Cain. The suggestion of Nellie M. Horton, a bookkeeper, that the doctor add pepsin to chicle was a ten-strike, and when the Beeman Chemical Company was reorganized, she was remembered generously. Beeman's pepsin chewing gum was first sold in boxes at fifteen cents each. The package was later reduced in size, and the little five-cent item, bearing the founder's portrait, had developed into a half-million-dollar business in 1892. Beeman had become an esteemed man of wealth and a power in Democratic politics, and he served four terms in the City Council. He eventually sold his chewing-gum business to the American Chicle Company, organized by William J. White of Cleveland, who developed Yucatan gum.

The *Cleveland Town Topics,* a weekly review of society, art, and literature, was launched in January, with Colonel Felix Rosenberg, manager, and William R. Rose, editor. Helen DeKay Townsend's society notes had a notable following. The publication continued to be popular for a number of years.

Julia Marlowe, eighteen, made her Cleveland debut in the Lyceum Theater as Parthenia in *Ingomar* on March 5.

The West Boulevard Christian Church, first known as the West Madison Avenue Church, of the Disciples denomination, had its beginning in the missionary efforts of the Franklin Circle Church of Christ. Located at West Boulevard and West 101st Street, membership approached six hundred in 1946, when the Rev. Arthur J. Russell was pastor.

In the Harrison-Cleveland Presidential campaign, the old Tippecanoe Club was revived by six staunch Republicans in the Case Block, who took the name Young Men's Tippecanoe Club. At a banquet in the Forest City House on March 31, at which William McKinley was guest of honor, the silk-hatted party leaders pooled their strength. On Saturday night before the election, the first industrial parade in the city was held. Benjamin Harrison led the county and the nation. McKinley had made his first appearance in Cleveland in 1876, during the Hayes-Tilden Presidential contest, when he spoke on the Public Square. His political career was to be closely identified with the city, through his association with Marcus A. Hanna and Myron T. Herrick, his confidential advisers.

While classmates at Case School of Applied Science, Albert W. Smith and Herbert H. Dow worked out the fundamentals of processes for the recovery of bromine from natural brines, which led to the founding of the Dow Chemical Company. Dow graduated from Case this year, and, backed by Cleveland capital, established the company in 1890. Smith developed a process for the manufacture of chloroform, which was the first organic product of the Dow company. He succeeded Dr. Charles F. Mabery as head of the chemistry department at Case.

In the early days, Lewis Dibble, cook on a lake vessel, bought a lot fronting 49 feet on Euclid near Sheriff Street for $300, despite the advice of friends who said it was worth only half the amount. His heirs leased it this year for fifty years at $2,500 per year. When a ninety-nine-year lease was effected in 1919, the figure was set at $11,250 annually for the first twenty years and $30,000 thereafter.

Francis E. Drury and H. P. Crowell organized the Buckeye Foundry Company (later Perfection Stove Company) to manufacture cast-iron frames for school desks, hot-air registers, and sad-irons. Thirty men were employed as molders and coremakers in a little factory erected in 1887 on Platt Avenue at the Pennsylvania railroad. In 1894 the first oil-burning heater for homes was produced, little more than a glorified oil lamp. Oil stoves were put on the market at the turn of the century, when the name "Perfection" was first used to designate the new, advanced oil stove of the day. In 1906 came the "long chimney" oil stove that became known to more than five million homemakers. Water heaters followed in 1912—always new products to keep pace with progress.

Building permits were granted haphazardly until this time, and the Fire Department enforced the few existing restrictions. A joint committee of the Cleveland Chapter of The American Institute of Architects and the Builders Exchange introduced a bill in the Legislature this year by which a department of building was created similar to that established in Cincinnati. Building in Cleveland was governed by this law until 1905, when a comprehensive code was adopted.

Despite the new west seawall, storms from the east continued to invade the harbor, threatening the safety of vessels seeking refuge. An act of Congress in 1886 authorized construction of an east breakwater, begun this year and eventually extended to Gordon Park. At the same time, development of the inner harbor was systematized. The channel was widened from 50 to 75 feet, the old riverbed was enlarged for dry-dock purposes, a 16-foot channel was maintained as far as the upper blast furnace, and the city signed a five-year contract for dredging.

Work was started this year on a new building for Cathedral School, east of St. John's Cathedral on Superior Avenue. It provided for a thousand pupils, and was erected at a cost of $55,000, a large expenditure. Graduates of Cathedral represent a "who's who" of the Cleveland Diocese. The outward shift of population cut deeply into the enrollment as the school approached the end of its first century, and in 1943 it closed and classes were moved to St. Peter's School at Superior and East 17th Street.

In the presence of five hundred "early settlers" and a large assembly, the statue of Moses Cleaveland, the city's founder, was unveiled in the southwest sector of the Public Square, on Monday, July 23, the city's birthday having fallen on Sunday. The Early Settlers Association, through their committee consisting of R. P. Spalding, Dudley Baldwin, and Bolivar Butts, had made the bronze likeness possible. They were escorted from their annual meeting in the Music Hall to the Square by the Cleveland Grays, the guard of honor. Illness kept President Harvey Rice away from the ceremony, and A. J. Williams presided. Mayor B. D. Babcock accepted the monument for the city. A brief program followed in the Music Hall, where Samuel E. Adams made the principal address. A circular pedestal of granite costing $4,378 supported the life-size figure of the pioneer surveyor, which had been designed in miniature by J. C. Hamilton.

The first brick pavement was laid in Cleveland on Bolton Avenue and Carroll Street.

Walworth Run Viaduct was built to span Walworth Run and the Cleveland-to-Cincinnati railroad tracks at a cost approximating $42,150. It was remodeled in 1911 in connection with the grade crossing of the Nickel Plate Road.

The Christian Science Church organization was formed in August as a Cleveland branch of The Mother Church, the First Church of Christ,

Scientist, in Boston, Massachusetts. The Rev. George A. Robertson, local newspaperman, was named pastor. This was the fifth Christian Science branch church in the world.

Samuel T. Wellman, Otis Steel engineer, patented the open-hearth charging machine that put an end to the slow, man-killing, hand-charging method. The invention contributed to the rapid development and success of the open-hearth process, and marked a new era in steel-making. Wellman patented about eighty designs, one of the most important being the Wellman hydraulic crane, of inestimable value to industry.

Higher education for women was not fully accepted, and an experiment in co-education at Western Reserve University produced a serious conflict that spread from the classrooms to the newspapers. President Carroll Cutler resigned from office in 1886, and the next year Dr. Hiram C. Haydn was elected. To solve the difficulties, it was decided to restrict Adelbert College to men, and establish a co-ordinate women's college. In September this year, the College for Women (later Flora Stone Mather College) opened in the Ford homestead (Allen Memorial Medical Library site) with thirty-eight students. The Adelbert faculty pledged themselves to provide instruction for three years, and John Hay and Mrs. Amasa Stone gave substantial financial aid. At the end of the three-year period, a separate faculty was engaged, but classes continued to use Adelbert laboratories. Gifts of land and money made possible the removal of the women's college to a new home on Bellflower Road, where two buildings were dedicated in October, 1892: Clark Hall, named for the donor, Mrs. Elizabeth Ann Clark; and Guilford Cottage, honoring Linda Thayer Guilford, a great Cleveland teacher, the gift of Mrs. Samuel Mather, her devoted pupil. Alice Freeman Palmer, president of Wellesley College, delivered the dedication address. Miss Guilford later became a member of the advisory council of the College for Women, and president of the Alumnae Association of the Mt. Holyoke College.

The *Hebrew Observer,* the first Jewish newspaper, began publication this year.

A handbill of the Cleveland & Canton Railroad stated: "Theater train will leave Cleveland at 10:35 P.M. and run through Bedford daily except Sunday. This train will wait, if necessary, until theaters are out."

Not being within reach of Trinity Lutheran Church, West Side families organized the Christ Evangelical Lutheran Church, building a combination church and school at what later became 3271 West 43rd Street. The Rev. H. P. Eckhardt, the first pastor, was succeeded in 1898 by the Rev. Frederick Keller, who served for forty-six years. A. C. Schumm, who came as a teacher in 1897, taught in the same classroom for forty-two years without missing a day. The Rev. E. M. Malkow came to the pulpit in 1944.

Mary Love's years of unselfish devotion to an invalid sister had left her in poverty, and afflicted with an incurable nervous condition. Reluctantly, she sought refuge in the City Infirmary. The Rev. Lewis Burton, rector of St. Mark's Episcopal Church, took an interest in his parishioner's plight; and when his wife's sister, Mrs. Eliza Jennings, came to Cleveland for a visit, she was inspired to give seven and a half acres of land (10603 Detroit) as the nucleus of a fund to provide a home for twenty-five needy Cleveland women with incurable ailments. Clevelanders lent their support, and, in October this year, the Eliza Jennings Home opened, under the direction of the Women's Christian Association (YWCA). The endowment fund was amplified for many years by popular interest in the annual flower sale on "Rose Day." Women worked diligently making quilts that won fame as coveted works of art. Auctioneer Charles A. Otis once pushed the price of a masterpiece to a thousand dollars. In 1925 the home became an independent corporation, and spacious buildings were erected.

The minstrels were at the height of popularity, and the city was known for its good talent. Clever burlesque was presented by the Clover Club Minstrels, and their engagement at the Lyceum Theater this year featured a concert extraordinary in which the Arions apeared—Isham, Duckett, Jaster, and Lang, with Harry W. Judd, S. H. Chisholm, and Al Johnson, supported by a strong chorus. John Faust was capellmeister and W. R. Rose, maestro.

Architect Daniel H. Burnham designed a brick-and-sandstone, commercial building for Samuel Mather, of Pickands, Mather & Company, that was completed this year on the northwest corner of Superior and Water streets. Known as the Western Reserve Building, it was a towering, eight-story, fireproof structure near the heart of the business district (1468 West 9th) boasting plate-glass windows and imported Italian marble, mosaics, and tile.

The Central Viaduct, the longest bridge in the city, was completed at a cost of $885,000, after almost ten years of agitation and more than two and a half years of construction. Extending for a distance of 3,931 feet and rising 101 feet above the water, the bridge had a river span of 2,839 feet and a Walworth Run span (Abbey Avenue Branch) of 1,092 feet. This great expanse classed the structure as a remarkable engineering feat, accomplished by the King Bridge Company of Cleveland. The bridge, connecting Ohio and Hill streets with Jennings Avenue on the South Side, opened on December 11 with formal ceremonies, concluding with a banquet at the Hollenden. The shifting hillside on the west river bank raised the question of safety continuously. In 1912 the viaduct was converted into a high-level structure by removing the central pier and replacing the swing draw with permanent steelwork.

Mrs. Julia D. Tuttle, who lived on Fairmount Street, offered S. J. Kelly and his young friends ten acres of Florida land in her large, undeveloped tract on Biscayne Bay if they would settle on it and take with them her cow. They agreed, but declined to take the cow. Shipwreck off the coast and a tour of the virgin Seminole country dampened their spirits, and they returned to Cleveland. In 1891 Mrs. Tuttle settled on her isolated territory, salvaged a dwelling from the ruins of Fort Dallas and began to improve her property, but she was unable to attract settlers. Henry M. Flagler, wealthy Cleveland oil man, had begun to build elaborate hotels and an east-coast railroad in northern Florida. After much persuasion, Mrs. Tuttle convinced him of the superior natural advantages to the south, and he agreed to extend his line. One hundred acres of Tuttle land became the site of the railroad terminal and a hotel. Reserving thirteen acres for her home, Mrs. Tuttle designated that the remainder be laid out in lots and streets by Flagler. In April, 1896, the railroad reached Miami; in July, Miami was incorporated; and early the next year, the Royal Palm Hotel opened. Mrs. Tuttle died in 1898, as the resort city was taking form, a decade after she and her young friends had begun planning.

1889

A small band of men and women in uniform went out from their new headquarters on Hill Street, south of the Haymarket district, under their banner, "Save to Serve," and started the first Salvation Army work in Cleveland. Under the leadership of Captains William Brandt and William Walker, street meetings and preaching services were conducted. A little more than a half century later, their ministry and social service had broadened to include operation of the Booth Memorial Home and Hospital, and the Mary B. Talbert Home and Hospital for mothers and babies, the Fresh Air Camp, the Men's Social Service Center, Citadel Home for men, the Evangeline Residence for young business women, and eight neighborhood centers.

The Young Men's Hebrew Association, which had its origin in the membership of the Cleveland Literary Union, was formed on January 21 with 34 charter members and Albert Straus as president. This was a spirited organization that was soon making its mark in the community. By July there were 350 members, and the third floor above Fix's meat market on Scovill Avenue, just east of Perry Street, had been outgrown. The YMHA moved from one building to another, as it devoted its efforts to cultural advance under such able leadership as that of Hiram Halle, Michael Moses, and Nathan Loeser. Interest waned, however, and it disappeared about 1899.

Taxpayers called it an extravagance when inter-office speaking tubes were installed in the City Hall. Keeping pace with progress, the county commissioners set up a dynamo in the basement of the gaslighted Court House and converted it as well as the jail to electricity.

The Star Theater, formerly the Columbia, opened February 17, managed by Drew & Campbell. Vaudeville, melodrama, and comic opera predominated until the nineties, when burlesque was introduced. Big names in the business were brought to the boards, among them Al G. Field's Minstrels, Ted Healy, Weber & Fields, Lottie Gilson, Lew Kelly, Watson's Beef Trust, Clark and McCullough, and Snuffy the Cab Man.

The *Plain Dealer* moved into larger quarters at the southeast corner of Bank and Frankfort streets. Electric light was produced by the company in its own plant. In 1896 the paper moved to Superior and Bond streets. The old *Herald* Building was converted into a hotel, a cafe, and a restaurant, and then it was torn down.

The Cleveland Grays marched in the procession when Benjamin Harrison was inaugurated the twenty-third President of the United States. He was born at North Bend, Ohio.

John Huntington invited a few close friends to his home on March 8, where he announced that he had placed in their hands $200,000, most of it in Standard Oil stocks, to be known as the John Huntington Benevolent Trust. His practical planning resulted in the founding of John Huntington Polytechnic Institute, providing free educational opportunities for Cleveland people, and a generous contribution to the Cleveland Museum of Art. Over the years more than forty educational and charitable institutions benefited from the fund.

England was the birthplace in 1832 of John Huntington, son of a mathematics professor. He was well educated, and when he brought his bride to Cleveland in 1852, he started a roofing business. He joined Clark, Payne & Company, investing in oil, where his knowledge of mechanics enabled him to improve methods in the business that soon merged with Standard Oil. Huntington expanded his interests and became the owner of a large fleet of vessels. He also became vice president of the Cleveland Stone Company. While a member of the City Council, 1862-75, he introduced the resolution for construction of the Superior Viaduct, and was a member of the committee that supervised the erection. In the eighties, Huntington returned to England, where he observed the foundation of the first polytechnical schools. He died in his native land in 1893, leaving to Cleveland a great heritage of business and cultural achievement.

During a Shakespearean engagement at the Euclid Avenue Opera House in April, an incident occurred that gives an insight into the character of two great actors. *Julius Caesar* was being presented on the evening of the 17th. After the dramatic oration of Marc Antony, Edwin Booth gave the cue for Caesar's ghost to appear in the tent of Brutus; but Frederick Vroom, who played the part of Caesar and the ghost, failed to respond. Lawrence Barrett explained the incident in next morning's *Plain Dealer:*

> It was a most awkward blunder and if it had been anyone but Vroom, who is a sensitive, good, tender-hearted German, I should have scolded him severely. We looked all over the stage for him, upstairs and down, and finally when I found him he admitted it was absent-mindedness, that he had begun dressing for the street after Marc Antony's oration. When the truth dawned on him that his ghost scene had passed, he locked himself in his dressing room and was ashamed to see anyone. The poor fellow has a great deal of worry and trouble and sickness in his family and one thing and another and he is despondent and melancholy in consequence, so I hope you won't be hard on him.

Representatives of the life-insurance companies in Cleveland formed an association on April 20 with Captain Frederick A. Kendall, president. Kendall had seen Civil War service, and was professor of military science in Brooks School, 1876-80. He entered the life-insurance field in 1885 and was a founder of the National Association of Life Underwriters. Later the name of the local body changed to Cleveland Life Underwriters Association, which encouraged co-operation, furthered insurance education, and helped to make Cleveland one of the nation's leading cities in life insurance. John N. Lenhart, C.L.U., was president in 1946, and Thelma Louise Rudgers, executive secretary.

Within the plain walls of Central Methodist Episcopal Church (later Epworth-Euclid), various young-people's societies merged under the name Epworth League on May 14, with twenty-eight charter members. It became an organization extending a world-wide influence, with more than two million members. In 1939 it was renamed the Methodist Youth Fellowship.

In the business district of downtown Cleveland (740 Superior, N.W.), Henry B. Payne built the million-dollar Perry-Payne Building, perpetuating his name and the maiden name of his wife, the daughter of Nathan Perry, Jr. The eight-story brick commercial block was "an architectural mecca which attracted visitors to Cleveland as one of the 'sights' to remember." For many years it was occupied by lake-shipping and iron-ore interests, and prominent firms were tenants through the years.

Henry B. Payne had come to Cleveland in 1832, and he soon gained prominence as a lawyer in partnership with Hiram V. Willson, formerly of Painesville. He also managed the landed estate inherited by his wife. His service to his city and to the State Senate attracted the attention of northern Ohio; and in his race with Benjamin F. Wade for election to the United States Senate in 1851 on the Democratic ticket, he was defeated by one vote. In the gubernatorial contest of 1857, Payne lost to Salmon P. Chase, Republican, by only a few hundred votes. He was elected to Congress in 1874 and 1884, and was a member of the commission that settled the disputed Hayes-Tilden election of 1876. Payne became identified with railroads and a variety of interests. Death came in 1896.

A German Sunday School mission, organized by the Rev. Herman J. Ruetenik in 1886, was sheltered in the basement of the Archwood Congregational Church and in the Brooklyn Memorial Methodist Church until a chapel was provided on Terrace Street, dedicated in 1888. The congregation organized the Eighth Reformed Church on May 17, 1889, with twenty members, representing the Wagner, Ruetenik, Coppelt, Keller, Mueller, Land, Hinke, Buehrer, Reimer, Bernhardi, and Schopfer families. Pastor Ruetenik's early salary of fifty dollars was supplemented by earnings as theological professor and other interests. He was devoted to his congregation and was distinguished in the denomination. He served as vice president of the General Synod of the Reformed Church, member of the faculty of Heidelberg College, organizer of the Central Publishing Company, and was the author of many religious papers. The venerable minister was succeeded in 1908 by the Rev. Frank W. Goetsch. A new church was dedicated at 2409 Willowdale Avenue in 1910. Beginning with the pastorate of the Rev. J. H. String in 1911, services were held in English, and accessions began to multiply. The Rev. Harry W. Baumer became pastor in 1938 of the Eighth

Evangelical and Reformed Church, as it was now known, one of the leading churches in the denomination.

At Bond and Rockwell streets, pupils and teachers were obliged to cross two muddy unpaved streets to get to Rockwell School. When the city proposed that Bond be paved, some members of the school board were indignant when told that the board must share the expense. Considering it a waste of money, one member declared, "It would be cheaper to buy rubber boots for the children."

The Cleveland baseball club, admitted to the National League this year, was dubbed the "Spiders" because of its lean players. Champions in the making were on the team: "Cub" Stricker, second base; "Jim" McAleer, center field; "Ed" McKean, shortstop; Larry Twitchell, left field; Faatz, first base; Paul Radford, right field; Pat Tebeau, third base; "Chief" Zimmer, catcher; Darby O'Brien, pitcher. In July the club was in second place, only a few games behind Boston, but it failed to take top honors.

The National Screw & Tack Company, predecessor of the National Screw & Manufacturing Company, entered the fastener field on May 22. In a frame building on Willson Avenue (southwest corner of Carnegie), tacks were made for upholstery and household use, and horseshoe nails for blacksmiths. Within four months, National moved to a new location (Stanton and East 75th), and in 1891, a second plant was erected. Products increased in the next year to include woodscrews, machine screws, stove and tire bolts, and square nuts. Prior to World War I, the company was making electric motors, industrial lamp shades, and motorcycles. The latter led to the manufacture of fasteners for the automotive industry, and for the aircraft industry in World War II. National Screw was one of the world's largest fastener manufacturers in the 1940s, producing more than fifty thousand items. H. P. Ladds became president in 1939.

More than 2,200 lives were claimed by the Johnstown, Pennsylvania, flood of May 31, out of a population of 30,000. Cleveland raised more than $44,400 in cash for the sufferers, and sent carloads of clothing and supplies to the stricken city. Relatives and some Clevelanders were among the missing.

The Vanderbilts had gained control of the Cleveland, Columbus, Cincinnati & Indianapolis railroad—the Bee Line, and had a substantial interest in the Cincinnati, Indianapolis, St. Louis & Chicago line. The latter, incorporated in 1880, was the original Big Four. On June 7, 1889, the Bee Line and the Big Four were merged as the Cleveland, Cincinnati, Chicago & St. Louis Railroad Company (later New York Central), carrying on the Big Four tradition and operating a network of strategic north-south and east-west lines connecting the great cities of the Middle West. Controlling interest was gradually acquired by New York Central executives, and the familiar Big Four orange and Bee Line red trains gave way to the drab green of the Vanderbilts; yet Central did not lease the road until 1930.

In the spring, Hiram M. "Father" Addison founded the Children's Fresh Air Camp in Woodland Hills, that needy children might enjoy summer outings. Elroy M. Avery, Cleveland educator, who became president upon incorporation in 1895, gave many years to the project, and was known as the "builder." With a gift of $100,000 from J. H. Wade in 1902, twenty acres were bought on Buckeye Road, where model buildings, including a hospital, were erected. Other prominent benefactors were General James Barnett, R. R. Rhodes, and John D. Rockefeller. In 1917 a year-round program was introduced.

The Cleveland-to-Canton railroad had been operating on standard-gauge tracks since November, 1888, and a line had been pushed on the extension from Coshocton through the coal fields to Zanesville. On June 12 the first through train arrived in Cleveland over the Cleveland & Canton road, bearing a jubilant Zanesville delegation of one hundred and fifty Commercial Travelers on a rocky run "made in five hours, excellent time, considering the fact that the extension had been completed but two or three days." The road opened with formality on the 17th, and a through coach to Youngstown was expected to be arranged in a week or so. The *Plain Dealer* reported the company's service as first-class, and "with the completion of their Wheeling line will add much to their revenue." In May, 1892, the Cleveland & Canton, Waynesburg & Canton, and Chagrin Falls & Northern roads were consolidated into the Cleveland, Canton & Southern Railroad (later Wheeling & Lake Erie Railway Company).

The Fourth Annual Meeting of the National Christian Scientist Association was held in the Music Hall, June 22.

In five short years William J. White had achieved phenomenal success with Yucatan chewing gum, and luxurious living had made him an international figure. This year he built "Thornwood," a fifty-two-room mansion on the lakeshore (Edgewater Drive at West 110th), the showplace of "the Chewing Gum King." Mrs. White was presented to the King of England while her husband sailed the Great Lakes in his new steam yacht. He developed a huge stock farm, "Two Minute Villa," where he bred harness horses. George A. Schneider's advice that he buy Star Pointer proved the name was not a misnomer—the horse made a history-making mile in 1:59¼. White went to Congress in 1893-94. He built the New Amsterdam Hotel, where he lived in later years. World headlines announced his gift of a $120,000 necklace to Anna Held, stage beauty.

For more than a year, the East Cleveland Railway had experimented with the overhead trolley on its Euclid line, and on June 30, service was extended downtown. The first car, carrying officers of the road, attracted much attention, and three breakdowns on the round trip were easily repaired. For a long time the public was wary of falling lines and electric shock from contact with trolley poles. Expense of change-over to electric power was tremendous, as heavier, more expensive rails were required and old rolling stock was rendered useless. The Brooklyn and Broadway & Newburgh roads soon adopted the new system. The East Cleveland company opened its Wade Park line in 1889, extending from Euclid and Case to Wade Park Avenue and the city limits, and consolidated it with the Central Avenue—formerly Garden Street—and Cedar roads.

Cleveland now had 440 miles of streets and alleys. Paving had moved at only "an average of less than two miles a year," and attention was called to "piecemeal" improvements that left the city lagging behind other municipalities. A one-mill levy, allowed for street purposes, was a progressive step.

Western Union began providing the nation with Naval Observatory time through self-winding, synchronized clocks.

Michael Baackes, C. B. Lockwood, and R. D. Noble organized the Baackes Wire Nail Company. Its factory (foot of East 67th) produced wire rod which was converted into nails, fence, and barbed wire. In 1895 the plant was purchased by the Consolidated Steel & Wire Company, organized in 1892, and later absorbed by the American Steel & Wire Company as its Consolidated Works.

Anxiety for safety of lake mariners prompted citizens to petition the Federal Government for a fog-horn to replace the harbor bell. A $5,200 signal was finally installed on the breakwater this year after many demands. Although it was the pride of Cleveland, citizens protested that it was a public nuisance on shore, and a reflector behind the siren brought some relief. For many years, it was a topic of keen interest, and time was divided into two periods—before and after the fog-horn.

The Cleveland Philharmonic Orchestra was giving summer "pop" concerts at Haltnorth's Garden under the direction of Emil Ring. Seated at outdoor tables, the audience enjoyed presentations by the city's finest talent while drinking beer. From this early organization developed music appreciation upon which was founded the great Cleveland Symphony Orchestra.

Two hundred West Siders, led by Marcus A. Hanna, John Meckes, and other leading citizens, met in Rhodes Hall, at Pearl and Franklin streets, in August and framed the West Side Citizens League to spearhead civic progress and incite action at the City Hall. Resolutions demanded such public improvements as a public library, passenger depots on railroad lines, a first-class hotel, and better streetcar service.

"Two black bears, two catamounts—or wild cats, a family of crows, a pair of foxes and a colony of prairie dogs" were given homes in the new Zoo in Wade Park. When the octagon house was finished, it housed birds and tropical animals. The alligator was moved from the pool in the Public Square to a more peaceful habitat, and a herd of American deer was the gift of Jeptha H. Wade in 1890, the year he died. Popularity of the recreation spot increased as band concerts were presented from the new music pavilion, and boating facilities on the lagoon were provided. Sleek horses paced the drives, drawing fashionable carriages silently on new rubber-tired wheels, the liveried coachmen perched high on the driver's seat. Skating in winter was a major attraction.

Whether to ride "side" or astride was being debated in social circles. Riders of fashion were learning to trot their horses, with reports that the single-foot was out of date. Cleveland's pace was set by forty leading ladies and gentlemen of the Bit and Bridle Club, prominent members being Mr. and

Mrs. Homer Wade, Mr. and Mrs. J. B. Perkins, and Colonel and Mrs. George A. Garretson.

This year marked a number of unfortunate journalistic ventures. On August 29 the first issue of the *Daily World* appeared, whose parent was the *Sunday World*. The *Evening Star,* the *Sunday Sun and Voice, Evening Sun,* and *Morning Times* were launched bravely; but through merger and elimination, only the *World* survived. After several ownerships and a receivership, it was amalgamated in 1907 with other papers as the *News*.

To quiet complaining housewives, Council passed an ordinance on August 31 forbidding the ringing of a doorbell or "agitating a door knocker" for the purpose of "distributing advertising matter," under penalty of a ten-dollar fine.

The Shaker colony had dwindled until only twenty-seven members were left in North Union Village (Shaker Heights), affectionately called the "Valley of God's Pleasure." The society was dissolved this year, and the faithful few moved to Shaker colonies at Watervliet, New York, Union Village near Lebanon, Ohio, and a community near Dayton, Ohio.

One of the fashion centers of Cleveland was Park Row, a block of three-story brick apartments erected at Bond and Rockwell streets by Clinton D. French, retail dry-goods merchant. It was the first building of terrace construction in the city. A miniature park with fountains and flower beds made it the show place of the downtown district. French lived at the Rockwell end; and the tower and several floors were devoted to his private museum, in which he exhibited his fine collection of antiques, jewels, porcelains, uniforms and costumes, musical instruments, and a powerful microscope operated on a revolving table. His prize piece was the coach, brought by Lafayette from France, in which he toured America in 1825. Park Row deteriorated upon the owner's death; and as the city grew, wealthy Clevelanders sought homes in the suburbs. It was razed in 1914 to permit erection of the East Ohio Gas Company building.

A wedding at St. George's, Hanover Square, London, on September 14, was a great social event, with the entire royal family of England in attendance. Jennie Chamberlain of Cleveland, the oldest daughter of William S. Chamberlain, known abroad as "The American Beauty," became the bride of Lieutenant Herbert S. Naylor-Leyland, later knighted. Wedding presents included a large diamond-and-pearl, horseshoe brooch, the gift of the Prince of Wales—Edward VII, and a check for $10,000 from the bride's uncle, Selah Chamberlain.

Who owned the lakefront—the city or the railroads? When the Federal Government established a dock line in Lake Erie, a thousand feet from the shore line, the railroads immediately claimed ownership to submerged lands. The city contended, however, that the roads had been trespassing for years on the old riverbed at Whisky Island. Here was a knotty subject to occupy legal minds decade after decade.

An event of theatrical significance was the combined performance of Edwin Booth and Mme. Modjeska, the nation's greatest Shakespearean exponents, at the Euclid Avenue Opera House for a week's engagement late in September. Otis Skinner played minor parts. Pittsburgh and Cleveland were the only cities outside of New York in which appearances were made.

This was the year of the baseball war. A number of players rebelled at "being sold and traded like so much cattle," and they formed the Brotherhood of Professional Baseball Players. When the National League would not meet their demands, the brotherhood warned that it would invade its territory with a new league. Albert "Al" Johnson became president of the Cleveland Brotherhood. He built Diamond Park on Willson Avenue south of Kinsman, and persuaded his older brother, Tom L., to run "special" streetcars from the Square. Passengers were so few that the losing venture brought many complaints. The demise of the brotherhood came the next year, and baseball, generally, suffered from the unfortunate experience.

Parallel street-railway lines on St. Clair, Superior, and Payne avenues, owned by the Superior and St. Clair companies, were consolidated on October 11 by the Cleveland City Cable Company. Cable power was introduced at enormous expense on the Superior and Payne roads, previously equipped with horsepower. Cars operated from an underground cable driven from the power house on Superior Avenue, and a "grip" controlled by the motorman's lever propelled them as fast as twelve miles per hour. An auxiliary cable, operated from an underground terminal on the Square, ran on Superior to the Union Depot. After two years, the noisy, cumbersome machinery was abandoned as too slow and inefficient to operate, and electricity was introduced. An extension of the electrically operated St. Clair railway from Bank to Water Street was granted in 1890.

Delegates to the Congress of the Three Americas arrived on October 15. An able committee representing municipal, business, and civic interests had carefully planned two days of entertainment for the distinguished Pan-American guests. The program included a tour of the city, with special emphasis on manufacturing resources, a public reception, and a banquet. Henry B. Payne presided at the banquet, and a sparkling, oratorical program followed.

City Hospital was erected on the Scranton Road grounds of the Infirmary, the first hospital in Cleveland under municipal operation since 1837. It served from 175 to 200 persons. The first staff, organized in 1892, consisted of 28 physicians and surgeons, including representatives of the various medical schools. The original building was used for the out-patient department, as the institution expanded to meet increased demands and opportunities.

Dressed in flowing white robes, several hundred members of the two Second Adventist churches in Cleveland were prepared for the second coming of the Messiah, October 26. There was grave disappointment when the trumpet failed to sound.

A strange new disease attacked Cleveland. It was called Russian influenza, as it was known to have swept Russia. As a precaution, the influenza mask was introduced, and hundreds of people wore the white covering downtown.

A "stylishly dressed" audience attended the concert given by the Theodore

Thomas Orchestra in the Music Hall in early winter. "Thoroughly absorbed" by the orchestra's playing and the piano number of Rafael Joseffy, famous virtuoso, the listeners had only "ample applause" for the performance of the head of the cello section—Victor Herbert, modest artist with a brilliant future ahead.

The "world's tallest man" had retired from Barnum's circus and was living in his home town, Seville, Ohio, in Medina County. He was Captain M. V. Bates, nearly eight feet tall, and he visited Cleveland often, stopping at the Weddell House. On one occasion, a new bellboy was slow, in the giant's opinion, in delivering ice water to his room. Finally, hearing the clink in the pitcher, Bates stretched to his full height, stuck his head out of the transom and roared for speed. The frightened boy turned on his heel and raced down the hall, unmindful of the big-fellow's bellow.

Women's organizations demanded that the horse-drawn patrol wagon be covered, hiding the sight of drunks and law-breakers from children's eyes. The Police Department, however, believed in horrible examples and refused. A count showed 1,418 saloons in the city of about 200,000 people in 1885, and law-and-order forces were clamoring for reform and a general shutdown of business of every kind on the Sabbath.

The National Bank Building, Superior and Water streets, the most imposing business block of its day.

The Public Library began to publish the *Dictionary Catalog,* a printed author, subject, and title guide to circulating books that was a great help to readers.

A wealthy brewer, Leonard Schlather, purchased forty-three feet fronting on the south side of Superior, east of the Square, for $60,000. The building he erected became Weber's Cafe, famous restaurant and meeting place, still popular in the 1940s.

Christmas Day was the warmest that Cleveland had ever known—66°, with dandelions in bloom, and relaxation in the form of outings, fishing, and lawn tennis. The traditional turkey that graced the holiday board cost nine cents a pound, live weight.

The last five years of the eighties witnessed the establishment of business concerns that were in existence in the 1940s: 1885, Cowles Detergent Company; J. L. Goodman Furniture Company; Housum-Kline Company;

Judson Printing Company; B. Lackamp & Sons; Trebing Manufacturing Company; Zipp Manufacturing Company. 1886—Dancyger Manufacturing Company; Fieg Electra Sewer Cleaning Company; Hodell Chain Company; Cleveland Agency of Massachusetts Mutual Life Insurance Company; Cleveland Agency of Provident Mutual Life Insurance Company; H. J. Sherwood Company; West Side Savings & Loan Association. 1887—American Savings Bank Company; Central Ohio Paper Company; Consolidated Fruit Exchange, Inc.; Cuyahoga Lumber Company; Evarts Tremaine Flicker Company; D. O. Summers Company. 1888—Fred R. Bill Studio; Brooks Oil Company; Cleveland Towel Supply Company; Forest City Book Binding Company; John Heiniger & Company; Kaynee Company; Kilby Manufacturing Company; Nicola Stone & Myers Company; Norton Brothers Company; Muehlhauser Brothers Piano Company; Spang Baking Company; Universal Cleansing & Dyeing Company. 1889—Benner & Company; Cleveland Crane & Engineering Company; J. D. Deutsch Funeral Home & Crematory, Inc.; Godfrey Holmes Printing Company; Greeley General Warehouse Company; Jacob Laub Baking Company; The Ohio Savings & Loan Company; Opper Cap Company; F. Ziehm Company.

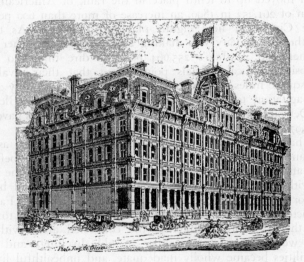

The Case Block housed the offices of the City of Cleveland beginning in 1875.

CHAPTER 12

The Great Nineties
1890–1899

THE GAY NINETIES brought Cleveland's hundredth birthday and a happy spirit with which to celebrate the notable event. They brought much more than the Centennial—they carried on a march of Cleveland's industry and commerce, and witnessed developments far beyond the dreams of the pioneers in the nineties of the century past. It was a decade of transition, quick-stepped to the accompaniment of *Ta-ra-ra-boom-de-ay, After the Ball,* and *Comrades,* sung in the musical revues, on the vaudeville stage, and in burlesque shows during the "good old days" of entertainment.

Cleveland moved up to tenth place in the rank of American cities with a population of 261,353 in 1890, an increase of more than 600 per cent over 1860, while Cincinnati held eighth place with 296,908. As the margin narrowed, the Queen City was making annexation bids to her suburbs to safeguard her lead. Buffalo's 255,664 posed a dire threat to Cleveland's superior position. Local officials pointed out that their rival embraced forty-three square miles in its count, while Cleveland had only 28.318. This stirred up agitation to annex Brooklyn, West Cleveland, Glenville, and Collamer. Detroit had climbed steadily to 205,876. The census gave Cuyahoga County 309,970, an increase of almost 60 per cent since 1880.

Industry had centralized near railroads and steam power, as it needed both for manufacturing and distribution in these early days before the era of highway and air transportation. Into the industrial districts the immigrants swarmed with their large families, eager to work for small but alluring wages. Labor laws and factory protective devices were few. Factories and still more factories rose around downtown Cleveland, southeast to Newburgh and along the lakeshore, blanketing the congested areas with soot and smoke. As workers crowded together in old dwellings and tenements, housing facilities became wholly inadequate, and unhealthful living conditions developed. The more fortunate families escaped to the suburbs and the country, but the poor hurried into their places in the blighted sections. Here they struggled to keep body and soul together in communities where even the trees had died. Disease and crime were mounting, and decentralization had raised its ugly head. Thus the city, a pulsing, groping thing, fanned out toward the ravines and gullies in order to contain its inhabitants who shunned living in the shadow of mill and factory.

The census disclosed that of the 261,353 people in Cleveland, 164,258 were native-born, and only about one-fourth of these were of native parentage.

Nationality influences had almost obliterated the mark of the New England pioneers. Diverse races made up the foreign-born total of 97,095, indicating the cosmopolitan character of the city. The Negro population had reached 3,035. There was a noticeable increase in the number of Slavs. Immigration from Great Britain and Ireland was on the downgrade, however, with only 2,831; and the Germanic peoples continued to hold a lead of 5,770, of which 4,735 were from Germany. It is interesting to note that in 1880 five persons made up the average family, while in 1890 there were 4.9 persons, showing the trend toward the small-family group. Urban population was steadily increasing, and 35 per cent of the people lived in cities and towns.

Large numbers of Jews continued to seek liberty and opportunity in Cleveland, where they found employment in the garment industry, building trades, and manufacturing plants. Some of them became leading merchandisers, and many opened small stores. They rose to influential positions in business and civic development. A number achieved prominence in the professions. Dr. Marcus Rosenwasser and Dr. A. Peskind were well-known physicians. Louis Loeb and George Peixotto became artists of international fame.

Wong Kee and his brother, Wong Sing, reigned over the thirty-eight Chinese in Chinatown in 1890—a bit of the Far East crowded close to the Old Stone Church and extending northward on Ontario Street. Here was the On Leong Association, headquarters of Chinese merchants. From its balcony long strings of firecrackers were touched off in a colorful ceremony each Chinese New Year. Younger Chinese had adopted modern dress; but Lee Foo, who lived in a plain room that he called Lily Garden of the Seven Butterflies, wore a queue, and shuffled along with a few elders in traditional cotton shoes and trailing shirt tails. Chinese children attended Sunday School at the Old Stone Church. In quarters above his Chinese restaurant, the first in Cleveland (1253 Ontario), Wong Kee entertained visiting countrymen. He also owned the Gold Dragon, a restaurant on the west side of the Square. Here Dr. Sun Yat-sen counseled his followers and encouraged fund-raising to oppose the Manchu dynasty.

In the Orange Street neighborhood of needy foreign folk, George A. Bellamy established Hiram House, Ohio's first social settlement. It was soon followed by Goodrich House in the St. Clair section. Dividends of inestimable value in terms of good citizenship, community welfare, and human happiness stemmed from these pioneering efforts, which became patterns for the nation.

From its early days America was identified as a nation of investors. Much of capitalists' money found its way back into industry, expanding established business and paving the way for new enterprise. There were, however, unsound investments made with a reckless hope that they might be secure. Storm clouds of financial crisis were gathering in President Cleveland's administration as the World's Columbian Exposition opened in Chicago in 1893. Panic and depression prevailed in the United States, aggravated by famine and drought. Its severity was felt in Ohio, but banks were cautious, and business expansion suffered a short-lived interruption. Depression in

'96 and '97 brought hard times for many; but William McKinley's administration saw continuous improvement, with the exception of a small recession in 1900. However, Cleveland was not seriously affected by the downward trends because of its diversity of industry, and it capitalized upon the upward trends. The decade was a period of sound advance for the City on the Lake.

Cleveland's industrial wealth was put to work in new banking institutions, a few of them being established in populous neighborhoods away from the city's center. The directory of 1897, listing twelve national banks and thirty-nine other banking and savings companies, would seem to testify that banking as a business was on a fairly firm footing. Early in the decade, several of Cleveland's important banks were founded: Central National Bank, The Cleveland Trust Company, and The Guardian Savings and Trust Company.

Commercial sailing ships were rapidly disappearing from the lakes as steam displaced the forests of masts. Scores of Great Lakes shipyards were launching ships to meet the demand of growing trades and to replace the heavy toll of disaster. Mariners were amazed at the success of the few steel ships that had been built, multiplying earnings with increased cargo capacity and speed. With the enlargement of the Soo Canal locks and the discovery of ore on the fabulous Mesabi Range, bulk lake vessels increased in size. Iron ore from the northern mining fields, pioneered by Clevelanders, had edged its way past coal to the top of lake commerce in 1888, and it was destined to mold the course of shipping despite the rise in coal trade. There was no corresponding increase in Cleveland's dockage facilities, however, and large shipments of ore were being diverted to lower-lake ports. To remedy this alarming shortcoming, more attention was devoted to efficiency of handling cargoes and the erection of docks and wharves.

Cleveland was riding the prosperity wave. It led the lakes in shipbuilding, and its shipyards were launching more vessels than any other center in the country, fresh-water or salt. Lake shipping, steel, and the fabrication industries were booming, and the city stood high in the nation in manufacturing, shipping, transportation, and distribution. It was first in the manufacture of heavy forgings, nuts, bolts, wire nails, wagon and carriage hardware, vapor stoves, sewing machines, and heavy street-railway machinery. During the eighties, the value and number of products of its business doubled, employees multiplied two and a half times, and capital invested by manufacturers and wages paid to workers trebled. There were 2,300 manufacturing concerns—10 in the chemical industry and 8 shipbuilding and dry-dock companies employing 2,083 workers, with a payroll of $1,188,662, and producing products valued at $3,091,300. Cleveland's industrial frontiers now lay at Doan Street on the East Side and Gordon Street on the West Side. Eleven railroads carried 37,829,711 tons of freight and grossed $56,087,349, connecting with a vast network that crossed Ohio. These lines and the huge tonnage of Lake Erie promoted commerce and manufacture, and fostered the growth of inland cities. The canals passed out of use, and navigation ceased on the few rivers, except on the Ohio, which still retained some of its trade.

Revolutionary inventions were being developed by Cleveland men who were willing to risk their time and money in creating new products that would influence the lives of people the world over, establishing giant industrial companies, and generating wealth and employment to swell the growing city.

The Duryeas built the first gasoline motor vehicle in the country in 1892. Then came Charles B. King, who drove his four-cylinder motor car in Detroit, the first automobile to appear on its streets, and Henry Ford followed shortly. Citizens stared and unsuspecting horses reared in fright when a visiting gas buggy made its noisy debut in Cleveland in 1894. Alexander Winton startled citizens in 1896 with a chugging four-wheeled departure from his pedaling Winton bicycle that brought greater fame to the Clevelander's name. Baker and Winton, and a little later, Stearns, made early cars; but their great contribution to Cleveland was in the encouragement they gave to others to enter the field, until the city became, first, one of the leading producers of cars, and later, the greatest manufacturer of automotive parts.

The future of bicycles, victorias, buggies, and surreys began to totter as the strange contrivance introduced the automobile age, transforming habits and customs and broadening the lanes of human progress. The romantic era dominated by horses, carriages, wagons, and saddles, once as essential to everyday living as the ring of the smithy's anvil, was fading.

Clevelanders were still awed at the wonders of the telephone when the practical use of electricity for light and power was proved. Brush and Edison developments were in worldwide demand, and local plants were working feverishly to supply requirements for conversion from gas.

Pedestrians crossed downtown streets in a maze of bicycles and horse-drawn conveyances, with an occasional runaway to heighten the adventure. The bicycling craze reached its peak about the mid-decade, and it was estimated that fifty thousand Clevelanders pedaled during the nineties. Racing competitions brought the best riders to the city's tracks. "Century bars," awarded by local clubs and the League of American Wheelmen for completing a hundred-mile circuit, were coveted by bicycle enthusiasts.

Kathleen Norris pictured realistically the nineteenth-century lady of fashion who had become captivated with the "safety" bicycle: "She wore a wide-brimmed hat that caught the breezes, a high choking collar of satin or linen, and a flaring gored skirt that swept the street on all sides. Her full-sleeved shirtwaist had cuffs that were eternally getting dirty, her stock was always crushed and rumpled at the end of the day, and her skirt was a bitter trial. Its heavy binding had to be replaced every few weeks, for constant contact with the pavement reduced it to dirty fringe in no time at all. In wet weather the full skirt got soaked and icy. Even in fair weather its wearer had to bunch it in great folds and devote one hand to nothing but the carrying of it."

Style dominated enjoyment in cycling at first; but gradually jaunty skirts replaced "bell" skirts and bustles, not only on the bicycle but on the tennis court, the ballroom floor, at work, and on parade. The Spanish-American War influence was reflected in tailored military lines featuring broad shoulders, and in the use of broadcloth and braid. Release from the bondage of clumsy dress had its repercussions in the business of the dressmaker, the petticoat manufacturer, and the maker of dress goods.

Theater audiences were thrilled by William Gillette's performance in *Sherlock Holmes*, and they wept over James A. Herne's play, *Shore Acres*. They applauded Minnie Maddern Fiske as *Becky Sharp*, Julia Marlowe as Rosalind in *As You Like It*, Joseph Jefferson in *Rip Van Winkle*, and Maude Adams in *The Little Minister*. Blanche Bates in *Naughty Anthony* was a favorite, as were Leslie Carter in *The Heart of Maryland* and James O'Neill in a creaky drama, *The Count of Monte Cristo*. George Bernard Shaw's satirical plays brought smiles, and big crowds went to see Denman Thompson in *The Old Homestead*, John Drew in *The Liars*, Ethel Barrymore in *Captain Jinks*, and J. H. Stoddard in *Beside the Bonnie Briarbush*. Two before-the-curtain features will never be forgotten—DeWolf Hopper's famous recitations and Frank Daniels' speech in words of a half-dozen-or-more syllables. *Cyrano de Bergerac*, with Richard Mansfield, was considered the most artistic production ever seen in the Euclid Avenue Opera House. Farewell appearances of the divine Sarah Bernhardt began in the nineties.

Society shook disapproving fingers as burlesque moved into local theaters. Choruses tripped lightly down the runways, showing trim ankles and winking coquettishly at the bald-headed-man's row. Stage exits punctuated with a flair of ruffled skirts tossed merrily over the heads of flirtatious soubrettes were a menace to morality, declared the reformers. Burlesque thrived, however, and fledglings had their start in Cleveland, only to go on to fame in the "legitimate" and motion pictures.

Edison's kinetoscope was collecting pennies from the curious who viewed the "movies" through a peephole in a slot machine. Listeners enjoyed the phonograph by holding tubes to their ears. Movie photographs, consisting of a pack of cards that produced movement when thumbed quickly, sold for a dime in a magazine shop near the Public Square. The action was increased as the cards were cranked in a machine called the mutoscope. These forerunners of the motion picture were instantly successful in providing cheap entertainment for the masses, and they continued to furnish amusement in penny arcades and parks.

The first movies were shown in storeroom nickelodeons for five cents admission. They were jittery "shorts," thrown on a sheet to the tune of improvised piano accompaniment while the audience munched peanuts and threw the shells on the floor. Fans dodged fearfully as speeding trains rushed precariously toward the audience, or breaking surf threatened to engulf them.

Managers used novel methods to build traffic lines to their storeroom-theaters. One small space represented the interior of a railroad car with the floor so constructed as to suggest motion of the train. A uniformed attendant at the door represented the conductor, and the movie consisted of scenery as viewed from the back platform. There were several of these downtown theaters in Cleveland.

Cleveland's art life became well-rounded in the nineties as enthusiasts

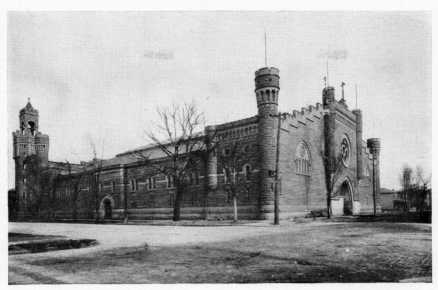

Central Armory, erected in 1893 to house military units, eased the urgent demand for space required by public events.

Grays Armory, built in 1893 by the Cleveland Grays, was also a center of civic and cultural activities. CLEVELAND PICTURE COLLECTION, CLEVELAND PUBLIC LIBRARY.

The little boat of Nock the Photographer ran around the pond in the southwest corner of the Square soon after the turn of the century.

Fire destroyed the two upper floors of the first Williamson Building in 1895, reducing it to two stories. The Soldiers and Sailors Monument was dedicated in 1894 in the southeast section of the Public Square. The W. P. Southworth Company, grocers, and William Taylor Son & Company, dry goods, were prominent merchants in the area.

found expression in new organizations, exhibitions, and galleries. In the carefree Old Bohemians was the spark that inspired art appreciation in Cleveland. Young artists were laying the foundations for fame in light-hearted fellowship over heavy Dutch pipes and white-capped steins. They struggled for survival, but when exhibition time came, they managed to secure dress suits in keeping with the honor.

Many of the Art Club members went out from the City Hall colony to achieve fame at home and abroad. Herman N. Matzen came to Cleveland from Denmark as a young man, returning to Europe for study. His execution of the "War and Peace" groupings for the Indianapolis Soldiers and Sailors Monument won wide acclaim; and his statues of "Moses" and "Gregory IX," the law-givers, in the County Court House represent a rare portrayal of strength and character.

Hubert Herkomer became the soul of an art center at Bushey near London; his uncle John was a woodcarver of note; his cousin Herman became a portrait painter of rich Americans. The skill of the Herkomers remained in splendid wood carvings and decorations in old Euclid Avenue mansions. John Semon's success lay in landscapes. Daniel and Emil Wehrschmidt taught and painted at Bushey. Max Bohm won French honors in painting and excelled in murals. Frederic C. Gottwald, a painter of remarkable versatility and charm, began his career decorating the figureheads and salon walls of early lake boats. Arthur Schneider became court painter to His Highness the Sultan of Morocco. George Grossman and Otto Bacher, landscape painters, joined the New York art colony. Louis Loeb became a portrait and mural painter of importance, and an illustrator for *Harper's Magazine*. Archibald M. Willard is best known for his "Spirit of '76." Charles Francis DeKlyn's forte was landscape and marine painting. Joseph Thormann won distinction as a painter of animals. Carl Niehaus—Charles Henry Niehaus—became internationally famous as a sculptor. Henry G. Keller's earnings as a painter of circus posters enabled him to study abroad, where he was honored as a landscape painter.

Stephen Foster's songs, particularly *Oh, Susanna* and *Old Folks at Home,* were being sung on the Cleveland stage and by barber-shop quartets; but even more popular for a time were *The Banks of the Wabash, Little Annie Rooney, The Bowery, I Don't Want to Play in Your Yard, Sidewalks of New York, After the Ball,* and *Sweet Marie.* At home, the family gathered around the parlor organ and joined in the melodies.

Boys enjoyed stolen moments with Nick Carter, Old Sleuth, and Dead-wood Dick in forbidden dime novels. Young blood was stirred by *Peck's Bad Boy.* The works of Whittier, Lowell, Longfellow, Holmes, and Emerson were popular. At the mid-decade, the era of the comics began with the Richard F. Outcault cartoons. The Katzenjammer Kids made their debut in 1899.

"Gentleman Jim" Corbett had proved that a bank clerk could become a world-champion prizefighter, only to lose his heavyweight title to Robert "Bob" Fitzsimmons, who went on to take the light-heavyweight crown. John L. Sullivan, heavyweight champion who turned to temperance, found little pleasure in public appearances. These fighters visited Cleveland as "actors" from time to time and received admiration not entirely deserved for histrionic performance.

Whist, progressive euchre, and crokinole were popular indoor games, and guests were entertained with phonograph concerts, magic-lantern shows, and the stereoscope. Charades, guessing games, and anagrams were played at socials. On hot summer evenings, crowds cooled off on the Ferris wheel and the haunted swing at Wade Park, or danced and rode the roller coaster at Beyerle's Park. While "society" arranged gay tallyho parties with two pairs of horses, ordinary folk were content with trolley outings or short drives in canopied surreys with fringe on top. Ladies were fascinated with the new outdoor game of golf. Other diversions included grace hoops, battledore and shuttlecock, and archery. Sportsmen were planning to introduce to Cleveland a new Canadian winter sport called ice hockey.

Cy Young, Chief Zimmer, and some of the biggest names in baseball were earning fame on Cleveland's major-league team that won the Temple Cup Series in 1895, a contest comparable to the World Series of a later day. Horse racing made headlines across the nation as the greatest trotters and pacers of the day thundered down the famous Glenville track. Scions of Cleveland's first families, who had raced their best horseflesh behind fast cutters on Euclid Avenue in the wintertime, found new thrills in widely heralded competitions under the banner of the Gentlemen's Driving Club.

Two new armories, the Central and the Grays, erected for military purposes in 1893, were pressed into immediate service to house public events. They were substantial improvements over the barn-like Tabernacle and Music Hall. The first annual horse show was held this year, and in '96 came the first Cuyahoga County Fair.

The spirit of the light-hearted nineties was reflected in the home, tempered by the sublime motto, "God Bless Our Home." Gay chenille tasseled fringe was used generously along with artificial flowers, heavy hangings, ornate furniture, and gaslight fixtures. Fancy mohair plush couches, silk-plush trimmed and fringed, could be had for $7.50 to add class to the dignified Sunday parlor, on whose walls hung chromos and family portraits in massive frames. Shades were drawn and the room kept dark, except when "company" came. Steel and iron bathtubs were replacing those of tin enclosed in wood; and pitchers and washbowls could be had in a range of colors. A hall tree and umbrella stand stood at the front doorway. Gentlemen drank from tall, decorated mustache cups, and the condiment caster occupied the center of the dinner table. Yet with all the glamor of the gaslight decade, there was still drudgery in home-making. The wooden washtub had a contemporary in the sad-iron. Hungry coal grates, base-burners, and the kitchen range were always empty and in need of polish, and they heated as well as they could.

Women of all ages fashioned their dress, their hair-dos, and their manners after the style idealized by Charles Dana Gibson in his gorgeous creations of the Gibson Girl. His drawings brightened the walls of many homes and started a revolution in fashions that continued for more than a decade.

A stylish lady could hardly be expected to dress in a hurry. As if to heighten the struggle, whalebone, lacings, and hooks-and-eyes were used with abandon by dressmakers. Black-patent shoes with white-kid uppers and needle-point toes came with the longest laces, and one forward-looking store offered a chiropodist's services with each pair. Seven-hook kid gloves were reasonable at sixty-nine cents a pair, but such a bother. Dainty parasols were of little practical use in the era of monstrous plumed hats, but flirtatious fans had their good points.

Wading was usually the extent of a lady's activity in a bathing suit. By the time a complicated collection of street clothes had been exchanged for a heavy-woolen, three-piece suit with long, black stockings and slippers, and long hair had been tucked under a shapeless cap, there was little incentive left for sport. Besides, there was hardly any pleasure in enduring the sopping, clinging costume after the dip. Then the Gibson Girl took some of the comedy out of women's bathing attire, and soon skirts ended above the knee, as chorus girls adopted the style. The bathing beauty had been given a start.

Prince Albert coats, plug hats, skin-tight breeches, and walking canes identified men of distinction. Handle-bar mustaches were quite the mode. Derby hats came satin-lined and bound with silk, and Hull & Dutton offered suits at from five to ten dollars. Stiff-bosomed dress shirts could be had for fifty cents each, and extra-long nightshirts with fancy collars and embroidered fronts for forty-nine cents. Red flannel underwear was a match for the toughest winter. Up-to-date businessmen wore diamond stickpins, pointed shoes, and carried the new open-face watch, three-eighths of an inch thick and an inch and a half in diameter, and leaned back luxuriously before roll-top desks full of mysterious pigeonholes and drawers. Wooden Indians stood grimly before shops where men purchased cigars and pipe tobacco. The cigarette was the mark of a "hot sport" who rolled his own. Ladies had not yet cultivated the habit. School authorities waged war on stores that sold smokes to boys and operated penny slot machines. Children studied frightening anatomical charts at school, exposing the effects of "deadly poisons of tobacco and alcohol." Small boys wore Little Lord Fauntleroy suits, despising the wide white collars, frilly waists and cuffs, and the wide-brimmed hat and curls. A peace offering of licorice "shoe-string" candy, however, made everything all right.

The cost of living in 1895 can be measured by a few commodity prices: ham, 13 cents a pound; tub butter, 18½; chickens, 8; strictly fresh eggs, 16 cents a dozen. Chandler & Rudd were selling roses in their grocery at 50 cents a dozen and carnations at 25 cents. Yucatan and Beeman's pepsin gum, products of Cleveland ingenuity, were bringing chewing pleasure to people around the world. Soda water sold at 5 cents a glass and ice cream at 10 cents a dish. Licorice root, sweet flag root, slippery elm, and spruce gum were penny treats. February was the time to prepare for a spring pick-up by taking sassafras tea or sulphur and molasses. Patent medicines for any ailment crowded store shelves, among them Garfield Tea, Hood's and Ayers' Sarsaparilla, Radway's Ready Relief, and Warner's Safe Cure.

Under the superior leadership of William Howard Brett, Cleveland's

Public Library was no longer a retreat enjoyed largely by scholars and bookworms. Its days of usefulness as a vital community institution had begun. Now that open shelves permitted the people to browse in the alcoves and handle the books, the library became a necessary part of their lives, and circulation figures proved its success to skeptical librarian experts. Here the immigrant could find carefully selected titles that helped him to master English and the fundamentals of citizenship, and children found enjoyment in a friendly department of their own. The policy of taking books to the readers through the branch library increased influence and opened boundless opportunities for service.

Cleveland had approximately 275 churches in 1895, including missions and a variety of religious organizations. Many of them were faced with crisis, as congregations moved outward and neighborhoods deteriorated. Gradually some merged and gained strength, continuing on the move; and in new suburban locations they grew in numbers and in influence as communities became more densely populated. Others found new opportunities in adjusting their services to changing needs in fields that had now become semi-industrial with shifting populations. There were some that fell by the wayside, too weak to endure. A few downtown churches remained in their early locations. Chief among them was pioneering Old Stone, which held fast to its uninterrupted career of usefulness that had helped to mold the cultural, business, and civic life of Cleveland for three-quarters of a century.

As the decade opened, a building boom was sweeping Cleveland to keep pace with the era of industrial expansion. The Hickox Building and the Cuyahoga Building, office skyscrapers of eight stories, were surpassed by the Arcade, the marvel of the age, with nine stories, the Society for Savings Building and the Garfield Building with ten, and the towering New England Building—later the Guardian—that dwarfed them all with fourteen stories. Banks, merchants, industry, churches, and home owners went on a building spree. Two landmarks characterize architectural achievement: the Garfield Monument in Lake View Cemetery, which brought President Harrison and a host of the nation's dignitaries to Cleveland for the Decoration Day dedication in 1890; and the Soldiers and Sailors Monument that had risen four years later on the Public Square on the site relinquished by Perry's Monument.

Enduring business, professional, and civic organizations found sturdy roots in the nineties, among them the Builders Exchange, the Cleveland Real Estate Board, and the Lake Carriers Association. The revitalized Board of Trade emerged as The Cleveland Chamber of Commerce, and the Cleveland Architectural Club, the Cleveland Medical Society, and the Cleveland Medical Library Association were formed.

The Federal Plan of municipal government, introduced in 1891, was long overdue, and its far-reaching effects made for efficiency in the management of city affairs. Nevertheless, citizens protested the mounting cost of local administration, and organized a vigilance association, the forerunner of the Citizens League, to keep close watch on public officials. Practical progress was made toward providing adequate water supply and solving the garbage problem. Sound planning was manifested in the development of a comprehensive system of parks and parkways by public-spirited business men, preserving natural beauty spots for enjoyment of the people. The Zoo had a substantial start in the nineties.

The public schools were overcrowded, and there was a desperate need for expanded facilities and broadened avenues of the new trends in education. Development of the city and its conveniences had eliminated many of the chores that once kept boys out of mischief; and organized athletics, manual training, and practical teaching served to combat street-corner gatherings and the gang influence. Newton M. Anderson launched University School in 1890, the forerunner of the country day school.

Industrial and civic growth had taken their toll of the magnificent elms, hickories, oaks, and maples that had characterized Cleveland as the Forest City. Towering trees eventually disappeared, particularly in the central area, as increased paving diverted essential water, and public-utility and sanitary mains tunneled through their roots. Smoke and gas from industry conquered even the sturdiest; and early settlers protested as the last of what had once been stately elms were removed from the Public Square.

Clevelanders boasted of Euclid Avenue, comparing it with Unter den Linden of Berlin and the Champs Élysées of Paris. The grandeur that was Euclid began to fade, however, with the passing of the horse and buggy and the coming of the automobile. Cleveland's bid for size and importance left its mark as commerce and industry began to push eastward to the doorsteps of the great and the near-great. Then one by one there appeared in the city directory the names of the "first" families, located in fine new suburban homes in the peaceful countryside.

Magnificent residences lined Franklin Avenue west of the Circle, with landscaped grounds, owned by leaders in iron and steel, coal and shipping. Here was the Euclid Avenue of the West Side; and under the great elms society drove spirited horses to glistening landaus, broughams, and phaetons. Not far away, however, in what became the flourishing Lorain-West 117th Street crosstown district, gypsies camped in the fields, and stumps were still standing on the farm land.

Buggy-riding on a plank road on Saturday night, to the rhythm of the horse's clop-clop, was pleasant diversion that was likely to be interrupted upon meeting a rig coming in the opposite direction. Disputes frequently arose as to who had the right-of-way on the planks, and who should take to the dirt strip. There were many plank roads in and around Cleveland. Detroit Road was planked from the city limits west. A toll gate operated at Warren Road, and tolls were still being collected on some of the leading highways.

Streetcar lines were reaching out into the rapidly growing city, and on Euclid, the Erie Street frontier fell when a right-of-way was granted for extension of tracks to Perry Street in 1890. As city planners catered to the easterly trend, they gravely neglected to open north and south streets to provide for downtown metropolitan expansion. The gradual spread of the electric-trolley system on car lines spelled doom to the horsecar. A grand consolidation of the city's street-railway traffic in 1893 resulted in two competing companies, the "Big Con" and the "Little Con," operating a hundred miles of double tracks within twenty-three separate lines, of which the "Big" Cleveland Electric controlled seventeen. Tom L. Johnson was planning his explosive three-cent-fare campaign, and was laying the foundation for his political regime.

With the opening of Ohio's first interurban electric railway in 1895, connecting Cleveland with Akron, the lake city became the hub of an extensive network of lines, providing cheap transportation of passengers and freight. Many of the roads were financed by the Pomeroy-Mandelbaum Syndicate, and the names of Henry A. Everett and E. W. Moore headed the list of Clevelanders who were prominent in electric railroading. Their luxurious private car, the *Josephine,* was the palace car of its day.

Cable car with trailer.

Open streetcar.

Streetcars in the 1890s.

The World's Fair in Chicago was the great attraction of the nineties, and it had particular significance for Cleveland. The magnificent grouping of white buildings, unmatched in any fair, here or abroad, was to influence the development of a central mall in the Cleveland of a quarter-million people. The suggestion of a group plan of public buildings had inspired far-sighted Clevelanders to urge the project, and the Columbian Exposition showed what might be achieved with sound planning, artistic arrangement of structures, equal cornice heights, and good architectural design. Daniel H. Burnham was the inspiring guide of architecture at the Fair, and so was the ideal leader to foster Cleveland's Group Plan, with the aid of Arnold W. Brunner and John M. Carrere, famed for artistic skills. So it was in the Gay Nineties that the vision of a great Group Plan for downtown Cleveland started its way from blueprint toward achievement.

Gaiety was largely forgotten in the period of the short-lived Spanish-American War; Cleveland patriotism promptly responded to the Government calls for service; the "Remember-the-Maine" cry woke the nation to the reality of war; the quick and decisive victory stirred America and impressed the world. The United States was growing stronger; its fleet inspired admiration at home and commanded respect abroad.

Cleveland's greatest celebration came in 1896, when the world marveled at the strides that the wilderness village had taken in its first hundred years. Candlelight had been traded for electricity. Stage coaches and canal boats had been exchanged for express trains and automobiles. Log cabins had been superseded by mansions and skyscrapers. A great arch on the Square was the central feature of the city's decorations, and Cleveland's new city flag flew proudly on all centennial occasions.

For ten days, parades, meetings, and entertainments emphasized the justified pride of the citizenship. While his home town was celebrating, Marcus A. Hanna, Cleveland iron-ore magnate and the strongest political figure in the nation, was steering Ohio's Governor William McKinley into the White House.

The close of the century was a time for looking backward, for recalling the early struggles of the sturdy pioneers who followed Moses Cleaveland to "New Connecticut" to make a home in the western wilderness. It was a time for giving thanks that those men and women had faith and courage to meet and overcome obstacles that seemed insurmountable. It was a time to realize that Cleveland's advancement had not been due alone to the advantages with which Nature had endowed it, but to leaders, stout-hearted men characterized by vision, strategy, and determination.

This was a time for looking forward. A philosopher had observed that "the first hundred years are the hardest," but practical Clevelanders knew that all would not be easy sailing in the new century. Wars have a way of recurring; business valleys of depression always come between hills of prosperity. Some local governments are weaker than others; some periods lack for leadership; some eras find a sluggish civic spirit. It was a time for envisioning ways of capitalizing upon the past, for keeping the wheels of industry spinning, for increasing cultural advantages, for keeping Cleveland happy as well as busy.

1890

The partnership of Squire, Sanders & Dempsey, established on January 1, brought together three of Cleveland's leading lawyers. Andrew Squire, born at Mantua, Ohio, in 1850, had been practicing law since 1873. While he became one of the ablest corporation lawyers in Cleveland, he had a variety of financial and business interests, and served as president and director of the Cleveland & Pittsburgh Railroad Company. William B. Sanders, born in Cleveland in 1854, became a junior partner with Judge Stevenson Burke in the seventies. He was appointed judge of the Court of Common Pleas in 1888, resigning to join the new law partnership in 1890. Judge Sanders opposed Tom L. Johnson's political battle for control of the street railways and was largely responsible for the Tayler Grant. His business interests included the Society for Savings, of which he was vice president, the Cleveland Stone Company, and the Kelley Island Stone Company. He was instrumental in establishing the John Huntington Polytechnic Institute and the Cleveland Museum of Art, and contributed to the success of the Western Reserve Historical Society. James H. Dempsey, born in Shelby, Ohio, in 1859, was admitted to the bar in 1884. He became associated with a number of large business concerns, and maintained a practical interest in schools and community institutions. The partners' outstanding legal abilities and their wide range of activity attracted large corporations, and the firm became one of the largest and best known in Ohio.

An epidemic of "la grippe" attacked the city, and an estimated five thousand persons were on the sick list in early January.

A flourishing clothing and furnishing store known as E. R. Hull & Company, located on the west side of Ontario Street at Champlain (Higbee Company site), was being operated by E. R. Hull and his associates, J. C. McWaters and Samuel E. Graves. The firm was reorganized this year, when William F. Dutton of Baltimore joined Hull in establishing the E. R. Hull & Dutton Company. In expanding, the store moved across the street into its new six-story building, where it was known as "headquarters for the family's needs." Hitching posts were at a premium in the neighborhood. A one-story building on Euclid at the southeast corner of a narrow street (East 1st Street) served as an annex and was the modest beginning of The May Company's future Public Square frontage. The Ontario store had as neighbors to the north the Cleveland Dry Goods Company and the W. P. Southworth Company; while east of the annex on the Square were William Taylor Son & Company, Crow & Whitmarsh, and Sterling & Welch. Hull & Dutton was famous for its advertising stunts, offering prizes ranging from baseballs and bats to ponies and carts as premiums. It was the forerunner of The May Company, which took over the stores in 1899, and soon announced the slogan, "Watch Us Grow."

Despite forceful protests from manufacturers in the "Flats," Council refused to change the ordinance forbidding the blowing of whistles except as an emergency. Screaming whistles started at five o'clock in the morning to call the workers from their slumbers; but no more—the anti-whistlers won, and there was an immediate demand for watches and clocks.

When James Whitcomb Riley and Bill Nye, humorist, appeared at Case Hall on January 10, Cleveland applauded with greater enthusiasm than the entertainers had received anywhere. The crowning feature was Riley's famous recitation, "Little Orphant Annie."

Shipmasters met in VanTassel's Hall on Detroit Street late in January to organize Cleveland Lodge No. 4 of the International Ship Masters Association, and elect Captain Edward Kelley the first president. This mutual-improvement organization grew to first place in the twelve units on the lakes. From December until sailing time, weekly meetings were held in the picturesque headquarters in the Perry-Payne Building, opened in the 1920s. Captain Robert Thompson, who had sailed wooden and steel ships, and Captain Dana T. Whitlock were prominent in local- and grand-lodge affairs, Thompson's service as secretary of the local association starting in 1924.

Ladies invaded the privacy of the Union Club on January 17, when a new suite devoted to their use was opened with a gay celebration.

Nellie Bly, born Elizabeth Cochrane in Springfield, Ohio, completed her famous trip around the world, arriving in Jersey City on January 25, her time being 72 days, 6 hours, and 11 minutes. She set out on order of the *New York World* to beat the record of Phineas Fogg, the hero of Jules Verne's fantastic best-seller, *Around the World in Eighty Days,* and she did it without automobile or airplane! Clevelanders followed her over land and sea through the newspaper columns, and betting was high as her trip reached the final stages.

Central and West high schools held joint commencement exercises in the Music Hall on January 31. Diplomas were presented to forty pupils from Central and twenty-two from West.

In January, marriage licenses averaged four a day, and divorce petitions, two and a half a week.

Although there had been attempts to establish a builders' exchange within the past decade, it was not until this year that a successful organization was formed, known as the Builders Exchange of Cleveland, with E. H. Towson, president. In 1892 the Exchange was incorporated. In their headquarters in the Arcade, representatives of the flourishing building-construction industry developed and expanded their common interests. The Exchange moved to the Chamber of Commerce Building in 1899. E. A. "Teddy" Roberts, its first permanent secretary, served for thirty-six years.

Trinity Parish had purchased the Lawson Carter property at the southeast corner of Euclid and Perry Street, and for a time the house was used for the Church Home. Early this year, Trinity Church, on Superior near Bond, was offered to the new bishop of the Episcopal Diocese of Ohio, the Rt. Rev. William A. Leonard, for his cathedral. The offer was accepted, and the Rev. Yelverton Peyton Morgan, rector, was instituted as dean, with Dr. James A. Bolles as senior canon. In 1893 the Rev. Charles D. Williams became dean and rector, serving until 1906. Plans were launched for the building of a cathedral that would be "rich and beautiful in architecture and adornments, and solid and honest in construction, so that it might be an offering to God of the best that skill and taste could devise and money procure." William G. Mather was chairman of the building committee, and Charles F. Schweinfurth, nationally known Cleveland architect, was commissioned to design the structure. The vestrymen were delighted with the magnificent plans, but the project appeared hopeless when it was learned that the cost exceeded by a million dollars the funds available. The meeting adjourned, but the designer, Samuel Mather and two others remained. Pondering the matter, Mather announced, "I'll give the million dollars." So it was that the undertaking was saved, and Cleveland was to have one of America's most beautiful cathedrals on Euclid Avenue at East 22nd Street.

Librarian Brett's faith in people convinced him that his plan to allow the public free access to books in the Public Library would be a success, despite the warning of experts that his books would be taken out and never returned. The open-shelf system was put into practice for the first time this year, and all books, excepting fiction, were made available. Soon large libraries adopted the method. The plan was also introduced by which books were grouped in alcoves, special attention being devoted to children's books. This was the nucleus of the divisional system and of the children's room. There were now

62,380 books in the library, and the circulation had reached 234,228. The first station was opened during the year in a manufacturing plant.

Homer B. Hatch and Carroll B. Ellinwood decided to form a club of men who could sing songs "better than those of the barber-shop and corner-saloon variety," and by this time an organization had been developed. It was known merely as the YMCA Choir, and weekly concerts were given at the "Y" in return for the use of rehearsal rooms. Ellinwood was the first director. In 1893 twenty-nine men signed the charter of The Singers Club of Cleveland, and high membership standards were adopted, requiring candidates to take a musical examination. After rehearsals, spirits and song rose over good food and tall steins of beer as concerts were planned at the Bismarck Restaurant on Huron Road, where the father of Adolphe Menjou, film celebrity, was the host. The first outside concert was given at Idaka Hall of the First Baptist Church at Prospect and Kennard streets. Guest soloists were Sarah Layton Walker, Edwin H. Douglass, and Fred T. Sholes. The urge to do big things inspired the club to introduce to Cleveland great artists, among them David Bispham, Reinald Werrenrath, Fritz Kreisler, Anna Case, Sophie Braslau, Tito Schipa, Mme. Louise Homer, Nelson Eddy, Ezio Pinza, and John Charles Thomas. Ellinwood directed for seven years, and was succeeded by Charles E. Clemens, Albert Rees Davis, Harvey B. Gaul, Edwin Arthur Kraft, James H. Rogers, J. VanDyke Miller, Beryl Rubinstein, Boris Goldovsky, George F. Strickling, and Maurice Goldman. The club's first home was the Chamber of Commerce Building; then it migrated as new auditoriums opened, finally moving to Severance Hall. Homer B. Hatch, a prolific composer, continued for more than a half century to be the inspiration of the democratic club, whose membership of about a hundred included millionaires, mechanics, and professional men, and ranked with the finest male choruses in the country.

The winter had been mild, and the steamer *City of Cleveland* arrived on March 2, reporting no ice on the lake between Cleveland and Detroit. It was the earliest opening of navigation in the history of the port.

On the evening of March 17, George J. Bailey, stamp collector and agent for the Harkness estate, invited a few young friends to his office in the Harkness Block, erected by Stephen V. Harkness, oil magnate, at the southwest corner of Euclid and Willson avenues in 1876. This was the first step toward forming a local chapter of the American Philatelic Association. W. H. Schneider, Charles Kress, W. Wallace MacLaren, C. A. Brobst, Frank G. Putz, and ten others signed the charter. The name, Garfield-Perry Stamp Club, adopted later, originated in the fact that the portraits of James A. Garfield and Oliver Hazard Perry, closely identified with Cleveland, appeared on five- and ninety-cent postage stamps. Expensive collections built by the members brought Cleveland to top rank in philately. Alvin Good became George H. Worthington's philatelic assistant, directing the accumulation of his million-dollar stamp collection, the second largest in the world. Charles Lathrop Pack, W. Wallace MacLaren, and John V. Painter also had extensive collections. The club, one of the oldest in the country, had a membership of more than two hundred and fifty in the 1940s.

The Central Market on Ontario Street was declared inefficient and out-grown, and the Council was considering a resolution in March to appropriate $500,000 to build a new building. City commission merchants and the Board of Trade opposed the move, declaring the market was good enough.

Claims of Euclid Avenue and Prospect Street property owners that trolley wires were dangerous, and that electric motors were so noisy as to make sleep impossible, resulted in a suit early in the year to compel the East Cleveland Street Railroad to discontinue operation of cars. In a deposition made at Menlo Park, New Jersey, Thomas A. Edison, inventor and electrical expert, defended the system, declaring that life was not endangered if equipment was properly installed. Professor Edward W. Morley of Western Reserve University testified that he directed an experiment in which a full current from a trolley wire was run through a horse with no ill effects. An ordinance, passed in June, provided that electric wires, except trolley wires, in the downtown section between Water and Erie streets, must be buried within the next two years.

The "outrageous charges" made by hackmen resulted in an ordinance in April regulating hack and bus fares. A passenger could now travel from a depot or boat landing to a point west of Erie Street for fifty cents; after 11 P.M., the tariff went up 50 per cent.

The Society for Savings Building, the highest weight-bearing-type structure in the world, depending upon its walls for support, was nearing completion. Two years earlier, the sturdy Crittenden Block on the northeast corner of Ontario and Rockwell, erected in the thirties by N. E. Crittenden as a residence, was razed; and Andrew Dall and Arthur McAllister began construction of the first of Cleveland's great bank buildings, as designed by Burnham & Root of Chicago. Ten stories high, the red-sandstone giant towered over the Public Square, a blending of Gothic and Renaissance architecture with arched windows set in thick masonry, and heavy, granite columns. It was equipped with electricity and gas and was fireproof. The banking room, which was opened in June, said to be the finest in the world, was enriched with glistening marble, classic columns, mosaic flooring, and polished redwood, and counters were enclosed with glass in wrought-iron frames. William Prettyman of Chicago decorated the interior; and Walter Crane, the English artist, created the whimsical murals depicting the goose that laid the golden egg. S. H. Mather was president at this time, and the Society was serving 41,498 depositors, their deposits totaling $19,279,000. Myron T. Herrick became president in 1894, Albert L. Withington in 1905, Herrick was re-elected in 1908, and John H. Dexter succeeded him in 1921.

At the Rockwell-Ontario corner of the new Society for Savings Building, a beacon light was erected in the form of a hand-forged, mast-like fixture entwined with iron vines. During the observance of Cleveland's 150th Year, the historic landmark, the city's oldest outdoor incandescent lamp, attracted wide attention with its cheery welcome glow.

One of the busiest places in Cleveland in the nineties was the south side of the Public Square at Ontario Street. On the southwest corner stood a drug store, that took the name May's when it came under the control of wealthy Arthur F. May. D. S. Humphrey leased the corner of the store and opened a peanut, popcorn, and taffy stand that was as popular with the grownups as with the children. South of the Public Square, in the vicinity of Michigan, Champlain, Diebolt's Alley, and adjacent streets (cleared for the Union Terminal), were the popular restaurants and dining rooms of the nineties. Joe Keiferle's Black Whale, with the leaping mammal in the stained-glass sign, attracted stock actors who presented plays in German. Victor Herbert visited the Hof-Brau every night that one of his operas played in town. Paul Schmidt's wine shop and sausage emporium next door opened into his famous, old-world, wine room. Fifteen-cent lunches in neighborhood saloons included a stein of beer, soup, potato, and a cut of roast. The Wright House advertised a free bear-meat lunch.

Gleaming marble walls and mosaic floors were introduced in the Hickox Building, which was well on the way to completion when Charles Hickox, industrialist and civic leader who built it, died on April 17. The eight-story office building was erected on the northwest corner of Euclid and Erie, the limit of the business district. When the First Baptist Church was razed on the site, its members asked that the historic clock be mounted in the new 156-foot tower. Early steel-and-ore men had their offices here, and in it was Mrs. Ethel Standiford's famed photographic studio. C. A. Selzer's renowned china and glassware store occupied the first floor until 1919. The landmark was razed in 1946 to make way for the three-story, streamlined, sales center of Bond Clothes.

As a member of the Ohio Legislature, John P. Green of Cleveland introduced the bill that declared Labor Day a legal holiday in Ohio, April 28. Four years later, Labor Day was established nationally by Congress. The first Negro senator in the State, Green was highly regarded in the profession and was a staunch supporter of William McKinley. He served as United States postage-stamp agent and acting superintendent of finance in the Post Office Department in Washington, 1897-1906, and then returned to his law practice. On the night before Labor Day, 1940, the ninety-five-year-old veteran of the Cleveland bar was killed when he stumbled and fell under an automobile.

Originating in a Cleveland ore-handling agency founded in the early fifties, Oglebay, Norton & Company was incorporated this year by Earl W. Oglebay and David Z. Norton, Oglebay's partners in Tuttle, Oglebay & Company both having died. In addition to its properties, the company managed mines for John D. Rockefeller, Sr., during the nineties. Leonard B. Miller of Cleveland, who had been associated with the Tuttle company in the mining and sales departments, was admitted into the firm in 1891 and became manager. Henry K. Bourne, an officer for a number of years, became associated with the company in 1917. Interests broadened as a fleet of lake freighters was acquired that became known as The Columbia Transportation Company in 1921. Oglebay, Norton branched into the mining and sale of coal in the 1920s, the management of docks at Toledo, Lorain, and Fairport in the late 1930s, the sale of fluorspar and ferro alloys, and became affiliated with The Ferro Engineering Company. Offices were moved from the Wade Building, West 9th and Superior, to the Hanna Building in 1921. Crispin Oglebay succeeded his uncle as president in 1924.

David Z. Norton, one of the founders of Oglebay, Norton & Company, was born in Cleveland in 1851, the son of Washington Adams Norton, who came to the Western Reserve in 1845 and built a blast furnace in Clyde, Ohio. Young Norton was educated in Cleveland schools. He started his business career in 1868 with the Commercial National Bank, resigning as cashier in 1890 to join in founding the company that bore his name. Norton maintained his interest in banking, however, and became president of the Citizens Saving & Loan Association; and, upon consolidation with other institutions to form the Citizens Savings & Trust Company in 1903, he became vice president and later president. He gave generously of time and wealth to the cultural and educational life of the city. Norton Hall was a gift to Kenyon College; and he served as trustee of Western Reserve University, University School, Cleveland School of Art, Cleveland Museum of Art, and the Western Reserve Historical Society. He loved art and litera- ture, and owned fine collections of paintings, books, and Napoleonic treasures. He married Mary Castle, daughter of William B. Castle, in 1876 and died in 1928, twelve hours after her funeral. Two sons, Laurence H. and Robert C., and a daughter, Miriam (Mrs. Fred R. White), continued to play important parts in civic and cultural advance.

George Francis Train stopped at the Union Depot for ten minutes on his record-breaking trip around the world. Sixty-three days earlier he had set out from Tacoma, Washington, sponsor of the stunt, to beat Nellie Bly's record. Wearing a Turkish fez, an old suit, and a gingham shirt, he left Cleveland and reached his goal on the 24th, having circled the globe in 67 days, 13 hours, 3 minutes, and 3 seconds, more than four days under the Bly elapsed time.

Now that Newton M. Anderson's manual-training experiment, launched in 1885, was to become an essential part of the public-school system, leading businessmen showed practical interest in his revolutionary plan for the com- bined training of boys in mental, manual, and physical education. On May 20, University School was incorporated as a non-profit, private institution that would train hands as well as minds, and prepare young men for advanced education or a business career. The officers and executive commit- tee were Samuel E. Williamson, president; Samuel Mather, vice president; W. E. Cushing, secretary; David Z. Norton, treasurer; J. H. McBride, Henry S. Sherman, C. W. Bingham, E. P. Williams, and F. P. Whitman. In Sep- tember classes assembled in A. A. Pope's large dwelling at East Madison and Hough, out in the country, where they met until the new building was ready for occupancy. Ex-President Rutherford B. Hayes made the principal address at the formal opening on April 12 of the three-story building at Hough and Giddings. Striking in its Gothic simplicity, it was considered one of the most beautiful school buildings in the world, and one of the largest single-unit schools in the country. In it was the first swimming pool in a Cleveland school. In June, seven boys were graduated in the first class, and enrollment had reached 143. Under the leadership of Headmaster Anderson and his associate, Charles A. Mitchell, University School served as a vital supplement to the public-education system, and was the forerunner of the country day school. From the start, healthful exercise and athletics had a large place in the school program. George D. Pettee served as headmaster, 1900-08, when he was succeeded by Harry A. Peters, who had been a faculty member for six years. During his administration, approaching four decades, University School molded the lives of thousands of boys who became prominent in the business and civic world.

Jeremiah J. Sullivan, national-bank examiner in his early forties, interested ten prominent citizens in organizing the Central National Bank that opened in the Perry-Payne Building on May 26. Capital was $800,000. The first officers were George H. Ely, president; Thomas Wilson, vice president; and Sullivan, cashier and an executive officer. Wilson succeeded to the presidency in 1894, serving until 1900, when Sullivan, familiarly known as "Colonel," a military honor of the 5th Regiment, Ohio National Guard, became president. He held office until 1920, when ill health forced him to retire as chairman of the board. His son, Corliss E., succeeded him. When the Rockefeller Building opened, the bank moved into new quarters. A merger with a near neighbor, The Superior Savings & Trust Company, organized by Sullivan in 1905, created Central National Bank, Savings & Trust Company in 1921.

Seldom has Cleveland entertained more distinguished guests than on the occasion of the dedication of the Garfield Monument in Lake View Cemetery, erected to the memory of President James A. Garfield. On May 29, the day before the historic event, the guest of honor, President Benjamin Harrison and his cabinet were met by a Cleveland reception committee at Alliance, Ohio, Major William McKinley making the introductions. Boarding the special car were Dan P. Eells, Mayor George W. Gardner, L. E. Holden, D. A. Dangler, ex-Alderman Lee McBride, Marcus A. Hanna, R. C. Parsons, ex-Governor Charles B. Foster, Senator George H. Ely, John Tod, S. T. Everett, and ex-Congressman Amos Townsend. There were brief stops en route to Cleveland, and upon arrival at the Union Depot, a vast crowd awaited the party. A public reception was held in the evening at the Stillman Hotel, and ten thousand persons greeted the President, while thirty thousand tried vainly to enter.

The lofty Garfield Monument was dedicated in Lake View Cemetery on Decoration Day. It is said to be "the first real mausoleum ever erected to the honor and memory of an American statesman, and the fourth like structure in history." Veterans of the 42nd Regiment of the Ohio Volunteer Infantry, Garfield's old command, led one of the city's largest and most impressive processions, with General James Barnett, marshal. General William "Uncle Billy" Tecumseh Sherman drew tremendous applause. Mrs. James A. Garfield had arrived earlier with her children and intimate friends, and placed a basket of red roses at the foot of her husband's statue. Ex-President Rutherford B. Hayes, chairman of the Garfield National Monument Association, presided. Among those on the platform with President Benjamin Harrison and the cabinet were Chief Justice Melville W. Fuller, Major William McKinley, and Colonel William Edwards. General Jacob D. Cox of Cincinnati, former Ohio governor, was the principal orator. The project dated from June, 1882, when the association was incorporated to raise funds for the monument, its members including Charles B. Foster, ex-President Hayes, Senator Henry B. Payne, Jeptha H. Wade, Joseph Perkins, T. P. Handy, D. P. Eells, W. S. Streator, J. H. Devereux, Selah Chamberlain, John D. Rockefeller, John Hay, and J. H. Rhodes. In a national competition, the design of George Keller of Hartford, Connecticut, representing the results of his visits to many ancient and modern memorials in Europe, was chosen. Construction began in 1885. The 180-foot, gray-stone mausoleum, surmounted by a tower 50 feet in diameter, cost $225,000, and contributions came from all over the world. In the center of the memorial chapel, rich with rare mosaics and colored marble, was placed the famous Garfield statue created by Alexander Doyle of New York. Fourteen beautiful stained-glass windows memorialized the thirteen original States and Ohio. In a crypt at the base of the monument, the remains of not only President Garfield, but also of his wife, Lucretia R., and his mother came to rest. In 1923 the great shaft was turned over to cemetery authorities by the association trustees, and free admission was declared.

Cleveland's "crystal palace," the Arcade, the second public building in the city of that name, opened on Decoration Day. An architectural marvel, it was erected at a cost of $867,000 by the Cleveland Arcade Company, of which Stephen V. Harkness was president and Charles F. Brush, vice president. Large stockholders were John D. Rockefeller, J. M. Curtiss, the Severance family, and others. The sandy bed of a prehistoric lake was the site of the Arcade, its southern shore being Euclid Avenue, opposite Sheriff Street; and the wide stairway descended, on what was once a natural grade, to the esplanade that formed the Superior level. Railed balconies on upper floors surrounded a central well, 400 feet at its greatest length, connecting Euclid with Superior Avenue. Over all, at a height of 100 feet, was a sheltering roof of glass. John Eisenmann and George H. Smith were the architects of the structure, the world's finest arcade with but a single rival, in Milan, Italy. Professional men and real-estate firms occupied the first two floors of the nine-story building, sometimes called the Superior Arcade. This space was later converted into 112 bazaar-like stores, with offices on the upper levels. Brush and John L. Severance had their offices in the Arcade for years, and Nichols Flower Shop was a tenant from 1897. William E. Malm was building manager for many years. In 1940 the Euclid Avenue entrance was modernized, featuring medallion portraits of the founders, Harkness and Brush. The Arcade was purchased by Albert A. List and James B. Wolfe in 1945. Although commonly called the Old Arcade, it continued to be a thriving shopping center and office building, and a popular step-saver between the avenues.

Detroit Street was the only highway to Rocky River until this year, when the county commissioners authorized Lakewood to open Lake and Madison avenues to the river at the expense of the property owners. Garden Street was renamed Central Avenue. Many of the lovely front-yard gardens had disappeared.

The rugged Chagrin Valley attracted F. B. Squire, vice president of Standard Oil, at about this time, and he gradually acquired approximately 525 acres. Squire, who was English-born, planned River Farm, a country estate, and a New York landscape architect designed two buildings after the style of English or German baronial halls. Only the smaller was built, early in the nineties, with stone quarried on the property. Eight miles of gravel roadway, groves of trees, bridges and walls, a trout stream, and a large pond improved the estate. Squire disposed of the property to a syndicate in 1922, and in 1925 it was purchased by the Metropolitan Park Board as the nucleus of the North Chagrin Reservation. The builder of "Squire's Castle" died in 1932, but a portion of his beautiful country home remained as a picturesque shelter house in the park.

The Kentucky Street Reservoir was abandoned for water-works purposes, and on June 16 the grounds became known as Reservoir Park. After the question of reversionary interest was debated, the Tyler heirs deeded their claim to the city for $7,500 in 1896, and the next year the park's name was changed to Fairview.

Demand for a new wage scale precipitated a general strike of switchmen on June 16, and railroad traffic entering the city came to a halt. Acceding to labor's demands, the companies involved restored operations by the 22nd and the strike ended without violence.

Bicycles were the style, and Cleveland wheelmen were well organized. The Cleveland Wheel Club, with headquarters in Case Hall, was the largest in the city. The Forest City Ramblers were going places, too, one member having ridden 6,666 miles in nine months. Pneumatic tires and air pumps were introduced, and the "social wheel," forerunner of the tandem, appeared.

Four Poles asked Joseph Hoffman for land on which to build a church in the German-Irish neighborhood of East Madison and Superior Avenue. He gave them a block from his farm as the site for St. Casimir's Catholic Church and parish school (East 82nd and Pulaski). Polish countrymen had built the church with their own hands by 1892, and families from Lake Street, Hamilton Avenue, and Newburgh, who worked in industrial plants, were moving into the area. Community gatherings centered in Joseph Hoffman's hall, East Madison and Hoffman Avenue. During World War I, the name of the hall was changed to Kosciuszko. Orchard Grove, owned by Charles A. Bramley, was the favorite picnic ground (Donald Avenue between East 71st and East 74th) of the community. In 1918 the old church was converted to a school, and a new church was erected next door. A few old German and Irish residents continued to live in the district, now identified as Polish. As industry expanded, transitions took place after this fashion in the city's inner belt, populated largely by nationality groups who were the soul of mills and factories.

J. L. Johnson, a "'49er", erected the Johnson House (at Broadview and Pearl Road), the overnight stopping place for farmers from the rich agricultural district to the south. At the Johnson House, news was exchanged from miles around, and the hotel flourished until the automobile reduced its popularity.

Vast salt beds, deposited when a salty sea covered northern Ohio millions of years earlier, lay untouched under Cleveland until this year, when the United Salt Company penetrated the caverns 1,800 feet below the surface near the lakeshore (at East 65th Street). Fresh water pumped into the subterranean area returned as brine and was converted into salt for home and industry. Frank J. Venning served as president from 1920 until his death in 1944. The Morton Salt Company acquired the properties this year, operating them as the Union Salt Company.

Salt was discovered with the drilling of a 2,000-foot gas well in Newburgh. Near Willson and Cedar, the Cleveland Salt Company was also extracting salt from the thick underground layer, with waste heat from the power plant in the vicinity that operated streetcars. When the railway company began to purchase power about 1910, these operations were abandoned. Some of the leading citizens of the West Side had their own gas wells in the nineties— William J. White, Marcus A. Hanna, Hannes Tiedemann, and J. M. Gasser.

America's leading rabbis assembled in Cleveland, July 13-15, to attend the first regular meeting of the Central Conference of American Rabbis, founded by Dr. Isaac M. Wise of Cincinnati in 1889.

A stock company was organized on August 2 to erect a new market house between Huron and Bolivar, to be known as the Sheriff Street Market. It was one of the largest in the city, complete with an electric-power plant. Prudent housewives who patronized it found fresh supplies of meat each morning, as facilities did not provide safe protection for perishable foods. Prevailing prices for pork chops were 8 to 10 cents per pound; pork roast, 7 to 9 cents; fresh ham and round steak, 10; sirloin, 12; and porterhouse, 15.

August 5 was a red-letter day in Cleveland baseball. With only one pitcher to meet Chicago in a double-header the next day, the management purchased Denton T. "Cy" Young from the Canton, Ohio, club for two hundred dollars. He was a huge fellow, dressed in a nondescript uniform that was quickly assembled, but his odd appearance failed to influence his game. He gave his heavy-hitting opponents only three singles, not one pass, and walked from the box with a winning 3-1 score. Reporting the next morning, the *Leader* commented, "Can Cy Young pitch? Say, can a fifer fife?" And it was right, for Young's unequaled record—511 games won and 315 lost, 1890-1911—was perpetuated in baseball's Hall of Fame.

Cy Young's catching partner was Charles L. "Chief" Zimmer of Cleveland. He excelled in catching, throwing, and batting, and his mark of having caught 126 complete, consecutive games established a record. Famous players were being developed in Cleveland at this time: Pat Tebeau, "Cupid" Childs, Eddie McKean, Jesse Burkett, George Cuppy, and James McAleer.

Cleveland's first tennis tournament was launched on August 20 at the East End Tennis Club under the direction of George Worthington, C. A. Post, and T. Sterling Beckwith.

Sawtell Avenue was widened to sixty-six feet, paved and lighted with electricity. Gas and water mains served the community of homes which not many years earlier had been rural. On the fashionable avenue lived T. G. Pomerene; Felix Guenther, art-store owner; the Asa Farnsworths, and Andrew Freese; Frank M. Chandler, commission merchant; Dr. Robert G. Hutchins, grandfather of college presidents; Dr. Paul Sutphen, pastor of the Woodland Avenue Presbyterian Church, Fire Chief Joseph Speddy, and others. On adjacent Holyoke Place lived Archibald M. Willard, famous artist.

Forty-two public schools opened for the fall term. In the upper floor of West High School, a manual-training school enrolled its first students, and it was soon followed by a blacksmith shop in the basement. Manual training should be a part of the high-school curriculum, declared Superintendent Day, and from this small beginning the technical school developed. The high schools were offering a two-year business course.

The Rev. August Juranyi arrived in Cleveland from Hungary on October 1. He visited Hungarian families and soon held the first religious service in the Hungarian language at the First German Reformed Church on the West Side. A decade and a half had to pass, however, before systematic work west of the river was possible; and the pastor moved to the East Side, where he began his work as missionary of the Reformed Church of Hungary.

Varied interests of the Cleveland Iron Mining Company, organized in 1850, and the Iron Cliffs Mining Company, which originated about the same time, were merged to form The Cleveland-Cliffs Iron Company. William G. Mather succeeded to the presidency upon the death of his father, one of the founders, in October. Mather started as a company clerk in 1878. In 1900 the Jackson Mining Company, dating from 1845, was acquired, increasing operations of Cleveland's pioneer iron-ore company, a leader in the industry.

The Trinity chimes were stilled and a bell tolled a single, solemn note on October 8, the day that Samuel Livingston Mather died. Born in 1817 at Middletown, Connecticut, he was eighth in descent from the Rev. Richard Mather. He had come to Cleveland in 1843 in the interest of Western Reserve lands belonging to his father, Samuel Mather, Jr. Soon after, he was admitted to the bar. The discovery of iron ore in the Lake Superior district fascinated him, and he was instrumental in developing properties with local capital through organization of the Cleveland Iron Mining Company in the early fifties. Mather directed mining and shipping activities, and became president in 1869, creating wealth and power for Cleveland and honor and prestige for his name. The company was the parent of subsequent industrial concerns that had vast operations in the great Marquette ranges of the Iron Mountain district. Mather's position in the iron-ore field led to executive offices in the Marquette Iron Company, the Cleveland Boiler Plate Company, and the American Iron Mining Company. He was a director of the New York, Pennsylvania & Ohio Railroad Company, and one of the original directors of the Merchants National Bank. The courage to venture into unexplored opportunities characterized the life of this pioneer industrialist who gave liberally of his friendship, wisely of his wealth, and generously of his spirit to many endeavors. He was devoted to Trinity Church, of which he was vestryman and warden for thirty-eight years; and he had at one time or another held almost every office in the Episcopal Diocese of Ohio, contributing generously to its work. Samuel L. Mather was remembered as "'a man known and revered of all men' and as thoroughly respected as he was widely known." His sons, Samuel and William Gwinn, inherited his civic and humanitarian spirit, and continued his loyal interest in their church.

Theodore E. Burton and Tom L. Johnson held the first of their famous debates in the Red Cross Skating Rink on October 21, in their campaign for election to the Congress. The protective tariff was the issue, and for nearly three hours four thousand people enjoyed the contest. Johnson won election to the House, unseating Burton.

In the early nineties, Tom L. Johnson purchased the beautiful George W. Stockley residence on the northwest corner of Euclid and Oliver Street. To the west he built a white-stone addition, washing it with a soot solution so that it would harmonize with the original structure. There were five bathrooms in the mansion, which was one of the show places on Euclid Avenue. After Johnson's death the property changed hands; by 1913 it was being used as a rooming house, and in 1926, after having served as a hotel and studio building, it was razed to permit a business block to be erected.

On October 25, the first high-school football game took place on the University School gridiron, when the US team defeated Central High School, 26-0. Charles A. Otis, Jr., was the referee. The University lads sported the latest uniforms, while Central's gridders appeared in a variety of home-made outfits that may or may not have influenced the score. In the spring, Central retaliated and defeated the "preps" 11-0 on the baseball diamond.

Protesting the award of a franchise to the Woodland Electric Company to supply electricity for Woodland Avenue streetcars, Dr. L. B. Tuckerman, in a speech on November 5 before the city board of improvement, urged that the city government start a municipal electric plant in the two waterworks buildings, which he declared could accommodate the largest dynamos.

The Emmanuel Church Chapter of the Brotherhood of St. Andrew started a Sunday School near the Nickel Plate tracks and Euclid Avenue, and a chapel was soon built at the corner of Murray Hill Road and Fairview Avenue. In 1892, the Rev. A. B. Putnam began to hold services in the mission known as St. Andrews-in-the-East (later St. Alban's Episcopal Parish).

A portion of Brooklyn Village north of Big Creek Valley (Brookside Park) was annexed to Cleveland on November 10. Plans were made to pave Pearl Street to Denison.

Improved water supply and higher pressure were made possible by a second tunnel, 9,177 feet long and 7 feet in diameter. It was completed on November 17 and connected the crib in the lake with the pumping station on the shore. Typhoid fever continued to be a menace, and 182 deaths resulted during the year. On streets where city water was available, 1,483 wells were in use in 1889. Thousands of wells were supplying water where city facilities were not available. Health authorities attributed the disease to contaminated well water.

The will of Horace Kelley, who died on December 4, revealed that he had left valuable real estate to be used in founding an art gallery and art school in Cleveland, his birthplace in 1819. His father, Joseph Reynolds Kelley, had come to Cleveland in 1812; and Alfred Kelley, his uncle, was the first mayor. Horace Kelley managed extensive properties in the city and on the Isle of St. George, later called North Bass Island, northwest of Sandusky in Lake Erie. He traveled much of the time, and spent a number of years abroad. The fact that Kelley and John Huntington each had provided unknowingly for the foundation of an art museum, created legal difficulties that had to be reconciled before the Cleveland Museum of Art became a reality in the city they both loved.

Among those advancing the city's interests at this time were Mary C. Quintrell, educator, welfare worker, and leader in women's activities; Ezra Nicholson, inventor of the Nicholson log used by the United States Navy, manufacturer, and realtor; Lord M. Coe, leader in the iron trade; John K. Hord, lawyer; Fred M. Nicholas, interested in oil refining, shipping, and the promotion of theatrical and social projects; and Samuel M. Southern, active in real estate.

Cleveland's relation to the iron-and-steel industry serves as an index to its business prosperity and that of the country generally. In 1890 the nation consumed 17,500,000 gross tons of iron ore, of which only 1,246,830 were imported. Lake Superior mines shipped 9,012,379 gross tons, according to the Board of Trade, or more than half the raw-material needs of the nation, then leading the world in the production of pig iron, Bessemer steel, and steel rails. The ports of the Cleveland district—Cleveland, Ashtabula, Conneaut, Fairport, and Lorain—received 61.02 per cent of the total, or 5,499,080 gross tons. Cleveland companies conducted the sale and movement of Lake Superior ore and owned the large part of the mines, controlling the docks at Lake Erie ports, excepting Buffalo and Erie, and owning fully 80 per cent of the vessels engaged in lake commerce. Cleveland had become the largest shipbuilding factor in the United States, with a lead of 71,322 gross tons over Philadelphia with 53,811, and Bath, Maine, reporting 49,830.

Highlighting industrial leadership, according to the Board of Trade, was Cleveland's claim to the greatest shoddy mills in America, a plant unequaled in the world for the making of sewing-machine woodwork, a steel-bridge works erecting massive structures over the entire continent, and an electric-light carbon works with an annual capacity of ten million carbons and a worldwide market for its product. City growth is reflected in combined figures representing national and savings banks, as compiled by the Board for 1890: Capital, $10,019,460; deposits, $51,950,960; clearings, $264,-470,453. The assessed valuation of Cleveland property had climbed to $99,614,055, and a number of investors in real estate were amassing fortunes.

The year 1890 marked the establishment of business firms that were in existence in the 1940s: J. Berger Wall Paper & Paint Company, A. C. Blair Company, Brown Fence & Wire Company, Cleveland Automatic Machine Company, Cleveland Trinidad Paving Company, Albert Rees Davis Company, Eickhoff Florists, Forest City Foundries Company, Hill Acme Company, Cleveland Agency of John Hancock Mutual Life Insurance Company, Marquard Sash & Door Manufacturing Company, Maxson, Perdue & Ketchum, Mustee Heater Company, Cleveland Agency of New England Mutual Life Insurance Company, A. Nosek & Sons, Inc., Patterson-Sargent Company, Cleveland Agency of Phoenix Mutual Life Insurance Company, West Side Carpet Cleaning Company.

1891

The rapid growth of the YMCA night school (later Y-Tech and Fenn College) contributed to the need for larger association quarters. Generous assistance from Sereno P. Fenn, John D. Rockefeller, and others made possible the erection of the first building designed for YMCA use, at the southeast corner of Prospect and Erie Street. The model home opened this year, attracting nationwide attention with its fine auditorium, gymnasium, marble swimming pool, and the first electric elevator in Cleveland. Fenn became president of the "Y" in 1892, serving for twenty-five years. In 1893 Glen K. Shurtleff was appointed general secretary, and broadened policies characterized his efficient service until his untimely death in 1909.

Increasing interest in gymnasium and field athletics had resulted in the organization of large clubs in New York, Chicago, and the major cities, and handsome buildings were erected. In Cleveland, a move to increase the membership of the Cleveland Athletic Club and provide for it a new uptown clubhouse was launched. Frank DeHaas Robison was elected president; R. W. Wright, secretary; L. Dean Holden, treasurer; and incorporators included Myron T. Herrick, George H. Gardner, George W. Howe, Charles W. Burrows, Sheldon Q. Kerruish, and C. A. Billings. The H. H. Dodge residence on Euclid (Bulkley Building site) was purchased and converted into club quarters with a gymnasium in the rear. Almost five hundred members were on the roll. Crowds packed the club arena to witness fierce encounters featuring Kid McCoy, Johnny Wittaker, Pat Ready, Johnny Lavack, "Mouse" Siddons, and well-known fighters of the day. Wrestling nosed out all other sports when Cleveland's Tom Jenkins, "Strangler" Lewis, and others struggled and grunted for long periods, unhampered by time limits. The club promoted baseball, football, fencing, and whist teams, billiard and pool competitions, and even featured an operatic group. It thrived for a time, then faded out.

On February 7 Salmon P. and Samuel H. Halle, brothers, opened a shop in a one-story building, 25 by 220 feet, on Superior Avenue west of the Square, the stock being limited to hats, caps, and furs. Their specialty was "railroad" and "society" caps made to order, and twenty clerks and "hands" were employed. In 1893 Halle Brothers moved to the Nottingham Building at Euclid and Sheriff Street. Women's ready-to-wear garments appeared in the store in 1896, and it was reported that Mrs. William McKinley wore to Washington a blue-serge dress and sealskin coat purchased at Halle's, one of Cleveland's foremost fur shops. In 1902 the name was changed to The Halle Bros. Co.

Henry M. Stanley, journalist-explorer, told a Music Hall audience on the evening of February 7 the story of his four history-making expeditions into *Darkest Africa,* and how the assignment of his editor, James Gordon Bennett of the *New York Herald,* led to his finding David Livingstone, the missionary, in 1871.

A small group of women organized the Cleveland Sorosis Club to "bring together women engaged in literary, artistic, scientific and philanthropic pursuits." Mrs. William G. Rose was the first president, and the City Hall was their meeting place. In November, 1916, the club moved to a permanent home at 2040 East 100th Street. The auditorium, a reproduction of the Old State House in Chester, Pennsylvania, was built in 1925, William Dunbar, architect, donating his services. Sorosis, sometimes called the maker of club presidents, became the oldest departmental woman's club in Cleveland. Among the able presidents was Mrs. S. C. Selover, who was one of the leading parliamentarians and clubwomen of the country. Membership had reached 230 in 1946, at which time Mrs. William C. Davis was president.

The Brush Electric Company was combined with the Thomson-Huston Company of Lynn, Massachusetts, manufacturers of dynamos and arc lamps. Equipment and lease were taken over by The Brush Electric Light & Power Company. The combined organizations consolidated with the Edison General Electric Company of Harrison, New Jersey, generators and distributors of power, to form the General Electric Company. Works of the Brush company were moved from Cleveland to Schenectady, New York.

Reform of municipal government had been demanded by public sentiment for several years; and, upon the suggestion of Colonel John M. Wilcox, a plan was patterned after that of the national government. The Hodge bill was introduced to the Legislature, but it was amended to monstrous proportions and rejected. Colonel Orlando J. Hodge persisted, however, and on March 16 the Federal Plan was enacted into law. Power that had formerly been spread among officials, commissions, and boards, was now concentrated in the legislative body, or City Council, and the executive body, or Board of Control. The mayor approved or disapproved all ordinances, resolutions or orders, but a two-thirds vote could pass the measure over his veto. Executive power rested in the mayor and the directors of six departments of public works, police, fire, accounts, law, and charities and correction, each appointed by the mayor for two years with Council confirmation. The mayor and department heads made up the Board of Control. Council consisted of twenty members, two from each of the ten districts representing the forty wards, and each received $5 for attendance upon a regular weekly meeting. The city treasurer, police judge, prosecuting attorney, and police-court clerk were elected by the people. A salary schedule provided $6,000 annually for the mayor, $5,000 for the law director, and $4,000 for remaining directors. At the April election, William G. Rose was the people's choice for mayor under the new plan.

William Grey Rose had maintained an intense interest in municipal affairs since his retirement from the office of mayor in 1879, and a tour of Europe, where he studied city governments, enriched his experience. Rose accepted the unanimous nomination for lieutenant governor in 1883, receiving the heaviest vote of any candidate on the Republican ticket. During his administration as mayor, 1891-92, the price of gas to the consumer was reduced, the city debt was cut, and a general program of needed city improvements was undertaken. His wife, Martha Parmelee Rose, was energetic and public-spirited. She was deeply concerned with the problems of the working woman, and gave ardent support to public welfare and city betterment. Mrs. Rose was a member of a committee of five who drafted the constitution for the Ohio Federation of Women's Clubs. Among her literary efforts were a pictorial Centennial album, *The Western Reserve—Some of Its People, Places and Woman's Clubs,* and contributions to the daily papers. William G. Rose died in 1899, at the age of seventy. Mrs. Rose passed on in 1923, aged eighty-nine.

The Broadway Christian Church was organized on March 22, the offspring of the Miles Avenue Church of the Disciples denomination. Located at Broadway and Engle Avenue in 1946, the Rev. H. M. Knowles was pastor.

Louis S. Bing, Sr., founded the Bing Furniture Company on Seneca Street on March 25 with ten employees. In 1907 a new store was opened on Prospect Avenue; and in 1916 Jay M. Halle, his son-in-law, joined the firm. An eleven-story building opened in 1929 at 514 Prospect Avenue to house the store. Louis S. Bing, Jr., who entered the business in 1918, succeeded his father as president of The Bing Company. He was elected president of the National Retail Furniture Association in 1942; and in 1944 won the Cavalier Cup, awarded annually to "the outstanding furniture merchant in the United States who has best served his Industry, his Country and his Community." Three branch stores were opened by the company, commencing in April, 1945, in Shelby, Mansfield, and Tiffin, Ohio. Three more were scheduled to open in 1947 in Sandusky, Warren, and Coshocton.

The Cleveland Belt & Terminal Railroad was incorporated to operate a six-and-a-half-mile road from Newburgh to the Nickel Plate tracks at Willson Avenue, thus speeding the movement of freight.

The Australian, or secret, ballot was voted into law this year. Loitering was prohibited at polling places. At the first election employing the new ballot, metal voting booths were set up. Urged by Major William W. Armstrong, editor of the *Plain Dealer* and city treasurer, the state convention bestowed its official blessing on the proud symbol of the rooster at the head of the Democratic Party column on the new ballot. In the Seventeenth Ward, young Maurice Maschke, Harvard student, was working as a clerk and gaining his first experience in Republican politics that was to lead to a colorful career in Cleveland.

League Park, home of Cleveland's major-league baseball club, opened on

Dunham Street (at Lexington), May 1. The field was later enlarged, and steel stands were erected, so that the park eventually had a capacity of 27,000. During the presidency of James C. "Sunny Jim" Dunn, 1914-22, the grounds were known as Dunn Field. President Dunn died in 1922 and was succeeded by E. S. Barnard. Big-league games were played here until the Stadium was erected, when the schedule gradually shifted to the downtown bowl.

The Cleveland Athletic Club baseball team prepared for its first season on the Payne Avenue grounds at Kelley Street. Players of exceptional ability were in the lineup, and the club soon ranked with the best amateur clubs in the country. Harvey W. Cushing, center fielder, became a famous surgeon; Charles Sturtevant was later a mine owner in Mexico; Wilbur Parker had been a star player at Yale in the 1870s; John H. Kilfoyle, manager, was at one time part owner of the Cleveland American League team; Warren Bicknell became a well-known contractor; Emil and Albert Baehr were brothers of Mayor Herman C. Baehr; Eddie McFarland gained fame as catcher for the Chicago White Sox; Herbert McBride, one of Yale's greatest football players, was an officer of the Root & McBride Company; Nathan Kendall was the son of Major F. A. Kendall; Charles Black became a director of the Standard Oil Company of New Jersey; Albert B. Coates became a mine owner; and Fred K. Gatch joined the Grasselli Chemical Company. Gatch, catcher for the team, began his career with the Cleveland Malleables in 1886, before baseball gloves were invented. Unpadded mittens without fingers cushioned the impact of the heavy ball, and catchers played close to the back-stop. Charles Klumph, pitcher for the Malleables, was one of the first to develop a "drop ball."

With the aid of the Reformed Men's Sick Benefit Association, the Rev. August Juranyi officially established the First Hungarian Reformed Church, May 3, with between fifty and sixty charter members, at the German Reformed Church, East Madison and Rawlings. This missionary enterprise of the Reformed Church of Hungary was the first congregation of the Reformed faith among Hungarians in America. The Rev. Alexander Harsanyi was pastor at the dedication of the first sanctuary late in 1894. The Rev. Alex Csutoros began his thirteen-year ministry in the fall; and, in the spring of 1904, a new stone church was dedicated that was the largest Hungarian Reformed Church in America. His successor, the Rev. Alexander Toth, was unable to hold his flock together, and some of the members went over to the newly organized Hungarian Presbyterian organization. The changing of pastors was a source of much concern in the parish that struggled through years of hardship and economic crisis.

Charles W. "Billy" Stage, of the class of '92 at Adelbert College, ran one hundred yards in ten seconds, setting a Western Reserve University record. Then he broke the standing-high-jump, the standing-broad-jump, and the standing-hop-step-and-jump records.

When Hungarian Hall opened, May 19, on Clark Avenue near Burton Street, it was the finest meeting place west of the river. Theodor Kundtz, president of the largest society, was the principal speaker. Merry-makers danced the czardas in the "summer gardens" to music of the Cleveland Grays Band and gypsy orchestras. Wedding receptions lasted three days. Kundtz, a penniless Hungarian immigrant of twenty-one years, had come to Cleveland in 1873 as a cabinet maker. Within a few years he had started the business that became known as the Theodor Kundtz Company, and was making sewing-machine cabinets for Thomas White. Craftsmen followed him from the old country, and found practical and friendly helpfulness in his factory and in the social center that he made possible. Decades later, Kundtz died a millionaire in his baronial Lakewood home at 13826 Lake Avenue.

Through good weather and bad, two boys, twelve and ten, picked up their papers at a Fairmont Street store, north of Euclid, and trudged up the hill to make delivery to scattered farmers on the country roads (Shaker Heights area). Sometimes housewives gave them cookies and cakes as good-service awards. On Saturday afternoons, the older boy worked in a grocery store on Cedar (at East 107th). At this early age, Orris P. and Mantis J. Van Sweringen learned the value of money. Later they worked for the American Agricultural Chemical Company, and with careful saving they were able to buy a lot in the Shaker country on the hill. Selling it, they had enough money to make down payments on two lots, and so they found themselves in the real-estate business. Buffalo investors had taken over a tract in the district, but sales moved slowly. They contracted with O. P. to sell a number of lots each year, and soon learned that he was a go-getter, always ahead of his program. As time went on, the "Vans" dreamed of a town founded upon rare idealism. Step by step they met obstacles that often taxed their ingenuity and demanded more than their small capital. When an investor purchased land on Warrensville Center Road near South Woodland, and erected seven stores despite pleas of the young operators, they borrowed money, bought the property, and tore down the stores before a tenant could move in, thus preserving the standards they had set for the new residential community. That the brothers built with vision and purpose is reflected in the words of Lord Rothmeer of England, famous traveler and brother of Lord Northcliffe, when he visited Shaker Heights in later years: "You have developed the finest residential district in the world."

In the success achieved by fighting fires with the fireboat, Chief Dickinson conceived the idea of a high-pressure system. By laying a series of high-pressure water mains in the business district, connected with headers at the river, a fireboat hitched to these headers could furnish added pressure for fire-fighting in the area. From this system the high-pressure pumping station was developed, and other cities copied.

The Rainbow Circle of King's Daughters, organized by a group of young ladies in 1887, rented a house and a fourteen-acre tract of land on the lakeshore in Glenville at the foot of Doan Street this summer, and in Rainbow Cottage (later Rainbow Hospital for Crippled and Convalescent Children), they brought fresh air and sunshine to thirty-two convalescent children from the city. Money was raised by donations, through a benefit ball, and by the sale of "fancy articles."

Charter members of First Church of Christ, Scientist, organized this year, were General Erastus N. Bates, Daisette D. Stocking, Mrs. Lida S. Stone, Edward A. Merritt, Mrs. Matilda H. Merritt, Mrs. Lida Fitzpatrick, Mrs. Mary E. Crawford, and Mrs. Mary S. Allen. Services were held in various locations with increasing attendance, and rooms were obtained in the Pythian Temple. Four years after the cornerstone was laid in 1900, a house of worship was dedicated at Cedar Avenue and Kennard Street, debt-free. A Methodist church building on Euclid Avenue (at East 93rd Street) was purchased, and the congregation moved eastward in 1921. Ten years later, a million-dollar structure at 2200 Overlook Road in Cleveland Heights was occupied, a beautiful Georgian building of limestone with a graceful dome, dedicated free of debt in 1946. From the influential First Church stemmed sturdy branches in Greater Cleveland, founded upon the principles of The Mother Church.

Progressive unionists had formed the Central Labor Union, which sought co-operation with the Knights of Labor. This year, two young members of the Cleveland Typographical Union, Henry C. Long and Max S. Hayes, began publishing a vigorous weekly, the *Citizen,* which became the official organ of the Ohio Federation of Labor in 1893. Cleveland, leader in lake shipping, was the birthplace of the Lake Seamen's Union in 1893. Many unions were formed when the Central Labor Union and the *Citizen* began an aggressive campaign of organization and education, and women relatives of union members later formed an auxiliary. When Robert Bandlow, manager of the *Citizen,* died in 1912, David Jones became his successor. He was followed by Isaac Cowan, the first paid business representative.

The local Weather Bureau began publishing a daily weather map on August 21.

Principals appointed in the public schools, as announced on September 9, are remembered by thousands of pupils: Edward L. Harris, Central High; Theodore H. Johnston, West High; N. Oda Beers, Bolton; Jennie B. Johnson, Brownell; Eliza E. Corlett, Case; Mary A. Morrow, Giddings; Ella Hills, Hough; Harriet E. Corlett, Mayflower; Carrie Lawrence, Rockwell; and Clara Tagg—Mrs. A. T. Brewer—South Case.

Homesick Hungarian newcomers had a new tie that brought the homeland closer to Cleveland, when the *Szabadsag*—Liberty—appeared on September 12. Soon Tihamer Kohanyi's newspaper inspired publications in other cities, but the local daily continued to lead the country. It was instrumental in the erection of the statue of Louis Kossuth in Cleveland, the statue of George Washington in Budapest, and a bronze tablet of American Hungarians on the destroyer *Ingraham.* The paper became the largest Hungarian daily in the country. In 1946 vast relief programs were successfully carried out by the *Szabadsag* under the direction of Zoltan Gombos, publisher and editor.

The business launched by Webb C. Ball in 1869 was incorporated as The Webb C. Ball Company. An engineer's watch running four minutes slow is said to have caused the tragic Kipton, Ohio, train wreck this year; and as a result of the disaster, Ball developed a standard watch and initiated plans for rigid watch inspection and synchronized railroad timing. In the nineties, he was associated with the Hamilton Watch Company. As treasurer and manager, and later president of his company, Ball gave a lifetime to the improvement of watch mechanism, inventing many appliances used in the construction of railroad-watch movements. "Ball's time" became synonymous with accuracy in the standardized construction of railroad watches, and an elaborate watch-inspection system had headquarters in Cleveland. The firm became one of the largest jewelers in the Midwest.

A field meet organized by the Cleveland Athletic Club officially opened Athletic Park, at Payne and Oliver Street, on October 14. Captain George Collister had arranged an elaborate program of bicycle races and track contests, and amateurs came from Pittsburgh, Akron, and neighboring towns to participate.

Marcus A. Hanna, industrialist, was the controlling power in the Ohio Republican machine, and his support this year centered in the campaign of William McKinley for governor. On October 23, one of the greatest political rallies in the city's history was held when McKinley visited Cleveland. Republican clubs from Pittsburgh and Buffalo joined local organizations in cheering their candidate in an afternoon parade, and thousands packed the Music Hall with its greatest crowd to hear McKinley declare the benefits of the protective tariff. The "infant" metal industry, created in this country by the McKinley tariff law, was symbolized by all manner of emblems of American-made tin, borne aloft by enthusiasts. In the gubernatorial contest of 1891, McKinley was easily the winner.

Andrew Squire presided over a meeting of prominent citizens at the Hollenden on November 10, at which the Park and Boulevard Association was proposed. Contributions of five dollars per person, it was agreed, were to be solicited toward a movement to establish a boulevard and park system that would be "everybody's joy." Bishop William A. Leonard made a plea "for the benefit of people who have no recreation." Myron T. Herrick presided on November 19 at a meeting called to plan a connected park-and-shore-drive system for the city. This was one of the first evidences of modern city planning in Cleveland.

Dunham Christian Church was organized in November with ninety-three members, the outgrowth of a Christian Endeavor Society formed by the Euclid Avenue Christian Church. Located at East 66th and Quimby in 1946, the Rev. G. A. Johnstone was pastor.

Mayor William G. Rose received the building-inspector's report of December 3, and there was no doubt that this was the horse-and-buggy era. Cleveland had 6,311 barns—one to each six dwellings, of which there were 38,463, valued at $42,746,807; 3,034 stores valued at $15,912,175; 1,291 mills and shops, with an estimated value of $5,238,565. In three and a half years, 9,425 new buildings had been erected and there had been 4,748 building improvements at a cost of $18,141,932. Cleveland was at the peak of a building boom.

Case School freshmen organized a self-coached football team and challenged the Adelbert frosh of Western Reserve, defeating them 12-4 in their first clash on the gridiron, December 5. Four hundred spectators paid twenty-five cents admission to see the game at YMCA Park, East Madison near Cedar. O. R. Rieley, Case halfback, scored two of the three touchdowns. Three days later, Rieley kicked the first field goal scored in Cleveland football when the Scientists defeated Adelbert Academy (Western Reserve Academy) at Hudson, 31-0.

During the week of December 7, H. R. Jacobs' Theater was badly damaged by fire, but it reopened on March 21, 1892. A feature in the house was the Corinne sofa, named for a popular young actress who starred in the playhouse. Each sofa accommodated two and proved a special attraction for young Cleveland couples. A year or two later the house changed hands, and the original name, Cleveland Theater, was restored by the Stair syndicate. A career of sensational blood-and-thunder murders, train robberies, tormented heroines, and hairbreadth escapades continued until March 5, 1910, when the gory, melodramatic span ended with a dramatization of the Elsie Siegel Chinese-trunk mystery case. Two days later the theater opened as a cheap vaudeville and moving-picture house, returning in a few weeks to low-grade stock. Some years later it was remodeled as a commercial building housing the Union Paper & Twine Company.

The National Association absorbed the American Association and became the National League, comprised of twelve baseball clubs: Cleveland, New York, Chicago, Brooklyn, Boston, Philadelphia, Pittsburgh, St. Louis, Louisville, Cincinnati, Baltimore, and Washington.

The Western Reserve Chapter of the Daughters of the American Revolution was organized on December 19. Mrs. Elroy M. Avery was the first president.

There had been some enthusiasm in football played by class teams in 1890. Reserve's first schedule of three games, two with the Clevelands, a local club, and the third with Wooster, resulted in three defeats. This year, however, the university had a powerful varsity team, captained by Charles W. "Billy" Stage and managed by W. E. N. Hemperly, and consisting of Stockwell, Sawyer, Lynch, Eisenhard, Kneen, Stewart, Nesbit, Breckenridge, Taylor, Matthias, Clisby, Wilson, and Smith. Crushing their opponents, including Ohio State University by 56-4, they won the state championship. The first game of the traditional Case-Reserve varsity contests was played on December 20 at Athletic Park before a shivering but enthusiastic crowd of five hundred spectators, Reserve winning, 22-0. On the Case team were Towson, Stone, Smith, Andrews, Kurz, Gleason, captain, Freeman, Rieley, Neff, Updegraff, Richards, Greene, Repp, and Marshall. In 1893 Case captured the state title, trouncing Reserve, 34-0, Buchtel, Cleveland Athletic Club, and Oberlin, 22-8, the latter having beaten the University of Chicago and the University of Illinois, so that Case claimed a championship including more than Ohio. Action in early games centered in the flying wedge and power plays, with occasional sweeping end runs and long field goals. The annual Case-Reserve contest became one of the oldest continuous rivalries in the nation.

Yachtsmen of four cities met at the Forest City House and organized the

Lake Erie Yacht Racing Association with Commodore George Beals of Toledo, president, and ex-Mayor George W. Gardner of Cleveland, secretary.

The year 1891 marked the establishment of business firms that were in existence in the 1940s: Bardons & Oliver, Brown Brothers Furniture, Cleveland Insurance Agency, Inc., Dodd Company, K-B Company, Nieding Sign Company, The Union Savings & Loan Company.

1892

Alexander Winton, twenty-five, had come to Cleveland in 1885 from his native Scotland. In the Clyde shipyards he had trained as a marine engineer, and he found employment in the Phoenix Iron Works as superintendent. With Thomas Henderson and George H. Brown, he organized the Winton Bicycle Company. Their plant, located at Perkins Avenue and the Pennsylvania tracks, increased production of Winton bicycles to fifty per month, and although the price was high, riding was the fashion and the demand was great.

Leading merchant tailors of the country, meeting in Cleveland early in January, declared that men would wear more bowler hats, squarer sack coats with high lapels and narrower trousers—without cuffs.

The Cleveland Commercial Company, capitalized at $10,000, was founded by William A. Harshaw to deal in oils, pigments, dry colors, and other chemical commodities. In 1897 he established the C. H. Price Company in Elyria, chemical manufacturers; the companies merged the next year as The Harshaw, Fuller & Goodwin Company, later known as The Harshaw Chemical Company. Greater capacity was needed, and plans for construction of a glycerine refinery in Philadelphia began in 1914, providing seacoast facilities and expansion to meet the constantly changing chemical needs of industry.

The first Marshall drug store was opened in the Rouse Block at the northwest corner of Superior Avenue and the Public Square. Founded by Wentworth G. Marshall, who built the Marshall Building in 1913, a chain of forty-six stores, including a number in northern Ohio cities, comprised the Marshall Drug Company in 1946, when Wentworth J. Marshall, son of the founder, was president. Headquarters were located at West 9th and Lakeside.

Adelina Patti ran out of encores at the Music Hall, yet 4,500 music lovers clamored for more on a memorable evening, February 2.

Fairmount School opened on Fairmount Street (1950 East 107th), February 5. It served elementary grades until 1916, when it became a junior high school, one of the first in the country. Famous athletes trained by Coach Charles Riley brought world fame to Fairmount—Jesse Owens, track star, and Bennie Friedman, all-American quarterback at the University of Michigan, heading the list. Comedian Bob Hope is an alumnus.

Book lovers and collectors organized the Rowfant Club in February. John C. Covert was its first president, and the critics met in rented quarters in the

Case Block until 1895, when the brick house built by George B. Merwin on Prospect Street (3028 Prospect) in 1836 was purchased. In terms of 1946, when Edgar A. Hahn was president and Gordon W. Thayer, librarian, the building was one of the oldest in Cleveland in active, daily use. The club had published one hundred privately printed books.

Purchase of land for St. John's Hospital by Bishop Gilmour in 1890 had been made possible by a gift of W. J. Gordon. The institution, whose parent was St. Alexis Hospital, was organized this year to serve the West Side community from its central location (7911 Detroit). It was in charge of the Franciscan Sisters.

The Rt. Rev. Ignatius Frederick Horstmann was consecrated third bishop of the Diocese of Cleveland on February 25 at Philadelphia, his birthplace in 1840. He succeeded Bishop Gilmour, who passed on in 1891. Prosperous German parents gave him a comprehensive education, and in 1860 he was chosen as one of the first Americans to attend the American College in Rome. There he won medals for outstanding scholarship; and, upon his return to America, he became, first, a successful teacher and author, later a pastor, and finally, bishop at Cleveland. During the years of his administration, 1892-1908, the Catholic population of the city increased rapidly. Many new parishes were formed, particularly among the Slovaks, Poles, and Bohemians, who were newcomers to Cleveland. New churches were replacing the old, ranking in size and beauty with the finest in the country. Bishop Horstmann was distinguished for his democratic relations with the public; and businessmen, politicians, and churchmen of all faiths were his friends. When he died suddenly in 1908, the church, public officials, and the citizenship paid a remarkable tribute to the third bishop of Cleveland, whom they remembered as "The Beloved."

The Western Reserve Historical Society was incorporated on March 7 by Henry C. Ranney, D. W. Manchester, Amos Townsend, William Bingham, Charles C. Baldwin, David C. Baldwin, Percy W. Rice, James D. Cleveland, and A. T. Brewer. Its activities were broadened, and it was to maintain a museum and a library, and employ literary meetings, publications, and "other proper means" to carry on its educational work. Maps, manuscripts, books, records, and relics dating from prehistoric periods had been assembled, many of them small but priceless gifts. In April, the old Society for Savings Building on the Public Square was purchased for $40,000 with money raised by subscription, John D. Rockefeller heading the list of 116 contributors with $10,000.

Reorganization of the public schools was effected by the Federal Plan of municipal government enacted by the legislature in March. Under the new law, the Board of Education consisted of a school director, chosen by the people, in whom was vested executive authority and broad powers; and a school council of seven members elected at large, in which rested all legislative power. In April, H. Q. Sargent was elected director, and Andrew S. Draper, former commissioner of education in New York State, succeeded Superintendent Day. Precedents fell as Superintendent Draper began to decentralize the school system, increasing the authority of principals, and encouraging teachers through meetings, clubs, and self-improvement means. The promotion of students no longer depended upon examination, and strict orders against corporal punishment were issued.

A School of Dentistry was established by Western Reserve University School of Medicine in March, in the Medical Building. Rented quarters were provided in 1896 in the Bangor Building, and although the institution was turned over to an independent organization in 1906, affiliation with the university continued. In 1918 a modern building was erected at the southeastern extremity of Adelbert Road; it also housed the dental clinic. The school was conveyed to the university in 1919.

Sarah Bernhardt thrilled a capacity audience at the Lyceum Theater on March 31 in *Cleopatra.*

When Franklin G. Smith took over management of the Osborn Manufacturing Company this year, it employed eight workers to make by hand wire brushes for foundries, butchers, sweeping and street-cleaning, also fine-wire horse brushes. Smith became president the next year. The company progressed steadily, pioneering in the development of power-driven wire brushes, until it became one of the world's largest producers of industrial brushes, making more than four thousand types in its plant at 5401 Hamilton Avenue. Osborn molding machines and kindred foundry equipment were being used in all countries having large foundries. Smith also became the president of the Ohio Rubber Company in Willoughby, Ohio, incorporated in 1893, which he took over at the request of the stockholders at about the middle of the depression of the 1930s. The company was a large producer of bicycle handlebar grips, automobile floor mats, hard-rubber tires, and other rubber products.

The Lake Carriers Association was founded on April 28 in Cleveland. It originated in an organization of the same name established in 1885 by Buffalo vessel owners, and in the Cleveland Vessel Owners Association, dating from 1880, headed by Captain Alva Bradley. M. A. Bradley was the first president of the new alliance of steamship companies, incorporated in 1903. Its purpose was to reduce lake-navigation hazards, provide adequate facilities and suggest needed improvements in harbors, channels, and lighthouses. Recommended improvements include the Sault Ste. Marie locks and the deepening and widening of the St. Marys, St. Clair, and Detroit rivers. In its early years, the organization maintained at its own expense certain lights and other aids to navigation, and financed important channel developments. The Livingstone Channel in the Lower Detroit River was named for William Livingstone, association president, 1902-25; and the Livingstone Memorial Lighthouse, at the head of Belle Isle, was erected jointly by the Lake Carriers and the City of Detroit. Captain Joseph S. Wood, a leader in lake shipping, served as president, 1931-38.

The Western Reserve Society of the Sons of the American Revolution was chartered on May 5, with jurisdiction over Cuyahoga, Ashtabula, Lake, Geauga, Trumbull, Portage, Summit, Medina, Lorain, Ashland, Huron, and Erie counties. Elroy M. Avery was the first president. Membership had reached five hundred in 1946 when Edward M. Hall was president; he was succeeded by Wayne G. Smith. At this time, Donald F. Lybarger, past president, was historian-general of the National Society of Sons of the American Revolution; and Charles Henry Fisher, also a local past president, was president of the Ohio Society.

A house on residential Lake Street, with eight rooms and gas lighting, was offered for rent at $18 per month. Selected lump coal retailed at $2.75 per ton.

In a little abandoned chapel, moved to Euclid and East Madison Street, a Sunday School was organized with the help of Dr. Hiram C. Haydn of Old Stone Church. He conducted the first preaching service in 1880. An impressive sanctuary was occupied in 1892; but it was not until May 22 of this year that Calvary Presbyterian Church was organized with 311 charter members, 308 of them from Old Stone. The Rev. David O. Mears was the first pastor. The church grew in numbers and influence, increasing its usefulness during the pastorate of Dr. T. S. McWilliams, which commenced in 1902, by broadening its efforts and adapting its program to the needs of a changing community. Dr. McWilliams was chairman of the committee that formed the Association of Federated Churches of Cleveland. Dr. John Bruere became pastor in 1944 succeeding Dr. Adelbert Higley.

In the spring the first branch in Cleveland's Public Library system opened on the second floor of a Pearl Street building (nearly opposite the West Side Market) with five thousand volumes that increased to over seventy-two thousand before the year-end. On the staff of the West Side Branch was Linda A. Eastman, who was just entering library work. The Library later moved to Fulton Road and Bridge Avenue. A new building, erected with the help of Andrew Carnegie, became known as the Carnegie West Branch.

Demand for store space and success of the new Arcade inspired John F. Rust to erect the Euclid Arcade (510 Euclid). It was followed by the Colonial and Taylor arcades, popular indoor avenues of shops.

Unscrupulous competition in the real-estate business prompted local realtors to organize the Cleveland Real Estate Board on June 21. The founders were Daniel R. Taylor, Henry P. McIntosh, W. H. VanTine, Jr., J. W. Simpson, J. G. W. Cowles, J. A. Selover, William G. Taylor, E. Worthington, C. H. Kidder, W. W. Lottridge, Charles E. Ferrell, V. C. Taylor, J. M. Odell, and M. S. Hogan. Daniel R. Taylor, the first president, was honored by re-election in 1893. The board's many public-service achievements include pioneering in establishing modes of procedure and standardizing methods that set the pace for organizations throughout the country, establishing tax values, and maintaining the ethics of the profession. Stanley L. McMichael was appointed the first regular secretary in 1911, and he became known for his intense, constructive interest in the city's development.

Daniel R. Taylor, realtor, was one of the first men in Cleveland to envision the vital importance of preserving the welfare of the community through practical city planning. Dealing in real estate on a large scale, he and his brother, William G., moved to the Williamson Building after the turn of the century. Upon the death of "Uncle Dan" in 1924, the firm, then the

Stately banking room of the Union Bank of Commerce, formerly home of the Union Trust Company.

The Arcade, scene of the Convention of Republican Clubs in 1895. CLEVELAND PICTURE COLLECTION, CLEVELAND PUBLIC LIBRARY.

The Cleveland Golf Club, organized in 1895, located its first home on Coit Road, and in 1902 it was consolidated with the Country Club. CLEVELAND PICTURE COLLECTION, CLEVELAND PUBLIC LIBRARY.

The Cleveland Yacht Club opened its home in Rocky River in 1918. CLEVELAND PICTURE COLLECTION, CLEVELAND PUBLIC LIBRARY.

oldest real-estate organization, moved to the National City Bank Building.

The city operated a ferry at Front Street, and another at the foot of Superior hill. Five cents would take a passenger across the river from the fireboat dock.

A modern lighthouse at the end of the breakwater had replaced the historic Water Street tower, whose feeble light had been outdistanced by beams from the new arc-light masts in downtown Cleveland. In 1897 the old lighthouse was torn down; but the remaining buildings stood until the neighborhood was cleared for the gigantic Main Avenue high-level bridge.

Frank A. Scott was appointed head of the new United States Purchasing Board on August 3. His experience gained in civic work and at the Warner & Swasey Company, where he was to serve as president, 1920-28, fitted him admirably for the position.

The low "safety" bicycle was the style, and the first meet of the Cleveland Wheel Club attracted the fastest riders in the country to Athletic Park for the two-day event, starting August 26. In the evening before the classic, a spectacular parade of riders bearing lanterns on their elaborately decorated "bikes" and tandems made its way from the Square eastward and back again. A crowd of two thousand filled the stands the next day—many of them ladies, and it rained as the first race was to start. "Ernie" Johnson of Cleveland won the quarter-mile in 35.3 seconds; the mile novice race went to curly-headed Arthur I. "Doc" Brown, local dentist, in three minutes flat. R. O. Baumann of Dayton took both heats of the half-mile, with 1:20⅘ in the first and 1:16 in the second. Nineteen riders entered the mile handicap, with Arthur A. Zimmerman, world champion of Freehold, New Jersey, the favorite; but the 250-yard lead of F. C. Chandler of Cleveland at the start proved more than he could overtake. Zimmerman managed to win every other race that he entered, and he took home with him a piano, several bicycles, and silver dinner sets among his trophies. To add to the excitement, three hundred spectators were hurled to the ground as the bleachers gave way on the second day, with no serious casualties. J. T. Huntington was chairman of the racing committee, assisted by George Collister, Will F. Sayle, R. T. Deacon, Fred Brandt, and W. A. Skinkle.

About half of the 150 students enrolled in Case School of Applied Science studied chemistry. The department expanded with the erection of the Chemical Engineering Building, which also housed the mechanical-engineering department.

In August, the Committee on Promotion of Industry of the Board of Trade (later The Cleveland Chamber of Commerce) was appointed, headed by Wilson M. Day, and began a far-reaching, business-building movement. New industries were encouraged to locate in Cleveland, improved freight facilities were sought, practical interest was taken in legislation affecting the city's advance, valuable business information was disseminated, and there was an awakening to the need for civic co-operation.

Within three years, the building on Bank Street that had once housed the proud Academy of Music had served as a vaudeville house, a Friends church, and a variety theater. After a fire on September 8 that left the interior in ruins, it was rebuilt as a dance hall of the western type. Then the historic walls provided a meeting place for labor, and later for the making of caps and neckties. In the 1940s no traces of the famous theater could be found in the obscure commercial building, once the center of drama and fashion in Cleveland.

As general agent of the Detroit & Cleveland Navigation Company, T. F. Newman envisioned a new passenger-freight steamship line connecting Cleveland and Buffalo. M. A. Bradley of Cleveland showed interest, and on September 13, the Cleveland & Buffalo Transit Company was incorporated, with Bradley, president; George W. Gardner, vice president; R. C. Moody, treasurer; Harvey D. Goulder, counsel; and Newman, secretary-general manager. The most "commodious wharves on the Great Lakes" were constructed on the east side of the river at the foot of St. Clair Street. The steamers *City of Alpena,* 225 feet, and *City of Mackinac,* 203 feet, were secured from the Detroit & Cleveland line; and when reconditioned and equipped with electric lights, they took new names—*State of Ohio* and *State of New York.* Service began on April 26, 1893, when both steamers set out for Buffalo, carrying many prominent people. Popularity of lake travel at low rates soon exceeded carrying capacity; and in April, 1896, the new *City of Buffalo,* 298 feet, the largest sidewheeler on the lakes, replaced the *State of New York.*

When Dr. Charles F. Thwing came to Western Reserve University as president in 1890, he quickly realized the need for a school of law. He discussed his plans with members of the profession, and on September 25, the university established a law school in the Ford homestead at Euclid Avenue and Adelbert Road. An endowment fund of $50,000 was provided by Mrs. Lucy Mygatt Backus, honoring her husband, a prominent jurist, and the name was changed to the Franklin Thomas Backus School of Law. In 1896 the new limestone building designed by Charles F. Schweinfurth was completed on the east side of Adelbert Road, and a brick addition was built in 1914. The Graduate School was also established in 1892, and instruction was given by the faculties of Adelbert College and the College for Women.

A portion of East Cleveland Township, roughly bounded by University Circle, Cedar, Lakeview, and a line north of Superior, was annexed on September 28.

An organization that was to market its products in ninety foreign countries was incorporated as the Sandusky Portland Cement Company with Dan P. Eells as president. A number of the most prominent leaders in Cleveland were associated with the venture, including the Newberry brothers, Arthur St. John, Dr. Spencer B., and William B., sons of the famous scientist Professor John S. Newberry; Charles F. Brush, J. H. Wade, and Frank Billings. In 1929 the trade name "Medusa" was adopted as the corporate name, and as the Medusa Portland Cement Company vast expansions were made. Seven plants, employing about 1,300 workers, were operated: including two in Ohio—Bay Bridge at Sandusky and Silica at Toledo; three in Pennsylvania; and one each in Wisconsin and Illinois. Besides gray and white Portland cement many allied products were developed. J. B. John, who became president in 1922, continued in that office in the 1940s.

The Cleveland Electric Illuminating Company was organized on September 29 to provide Cleveland with adequate, dependable electric service. At this time, The Brush Electric Light & Power Company was lighting parts of several main thoroughfares in the city with Brush arc lamps, and the Cleveland Electric Light Company was lighting various stores, the first being Steinfeld's on lower Superior. The new company, consolidating the Brush Electric and Cleveland Electric Light companies, began immediately to install superior illumination facilities developed by Thomas A. Edison; and, at the end of 1893, its investment for lighting service amounted to $1,280,000. The Brush electric-light masts had been declared inadequate for street illumination and were soon removed.

"Ernie" and L. C. Johnson and Dr. Arthur I. Brown, representing the Lakeside Cycling Club, broke the world's triplet bicycle record at the Glenville Track, covering the mile in 2:10. "Doc" Brown's greatest claim to bicycle glory was in setting the world's standing-start, quarter-mile record of 28⅖ seconds in 1894, a feat, it is believed, never equaled.

Cleveland school children and committees of the Grand Army of the Republic joined in celebrating the four-hundredth anniversary of the discovery of America by Christopher Columbus in flag raising and special assemblies in the schools. In the afternoon, the pupils participated in inspiring patriotic meetings in seven of the public halls and churches, where they were addressed by prominent citizens. President Charles F. Thwing, of Western Reserve University, spoke to a large audience at the Music Hall on Vincent Street. A colorful parade of students carrying flags concluded the event, and their marching was "so soldierly as to win the enthusiastic applause of such a multitude as Cleveland never saw on her streets before."

Marie Dressler was a member of the theatrical company at the Euclid Avenue Opera House when fire destroyed the theater on October 24. It was rebuilt with greater elegance by Marcus A. Hanna, and reopened on September 11, 1893, with Richard Mansfield in *Beau Brummell*. Seats for the sensational event sold at auction. It was during this engagement that Mansfield refused to proceed with the play in competition with hissing steam radiators. A. F. Hartz continued to manage the house, presenting the best stars for many years. Playhouse patrons remember Louis Rich, leader of one of the theater's orchestras, one of the youngest directors in the country, and Otto Moser's bar opposite the stage door, on Sheriff Street, where Moser displayed his famous collection of stage photographs. Everyone knew genial Fred Coan, treasurer of the theater, and his conscientious brother, Al, head usher, who were identified with the opera house for many years. "Be good, Jake Mintz is in the house" was a slogan that warned pickpockets to shun the theater. In the eighties, Mintz began his career that covered six decades as private detective, and he became the best-known sleuth in Cleveland's history. The Opera House reigned until it was displaced by the Hanna Theater, the new "legitimate" favorite. The last curtain fell in 1922, but a portion of the historic building remained and was utilized by the Kresge five-and-ten-cent store.

From 1816 to 1892 the pioneer meeting house of the First Presbyterian Society of Euclid stood on the hill (16200 Euclid), surrounded by vineyards and open fields, in a district of cultural improvement and rapid industrial development. A new sanctuary was dedicated on the site, November 3, 1895. In 1896 the society changed its name to conform with that of the community—First Presbyterian Church of East Cleveland. The Rev. Dormer L. Hickok, a man of imposing figure and keen intellect, served as pastor from 1882 to 1902, and as emeritus until 1911, his helpful sermons and sympathetic understanding endearing him to his people.

A rendezvous for the gay blades of Cleveland's "first" families was the select Tavern Club, organized this winter by top-flight sportsmen and socialites: Harry K. Devereux, H. R. Edwards, Addison H. Hough, William C. Rhodes, E. V. Hale, P. W. Harvey, Charles A. Otis, Jr., and S. L. Smith. A residence on the northeast corner of Case Avenue and Prospect Street served as their clubhouse until 1898, when The Tavern Company was incorporated, and a lease was taken at 968 Prospect Street. On January 1, 1905, a new home was opened on the southwest corner of East 36th Street and Prospect Avenue.

The first shipment of iron ore produced from the fabulous Mesabi Range in Minnesota was made on November 11 from Duluth. It consisted of 2,073 gross tons consigned to Oglebay, Norton & Company, Cleveland, tapping rich reserves that were the lifeblood of the city's industry.

Conflict between the Soldiers and Sailors Monument Committee and the City Council centered on Perry's Monument in the summer, when the Supreme Court of Ohio handed down a decision legalizing the building of the veterans' monument on the southeast section of the Square. After stormy sessions, Perry's statue was taken from its pedestal on December 3 and placed in storage.

Fire destroyed the City Armory on Long Street, headquarters of the Cleveland Grays and the 5th Regiment, Ohio National Guard, on December 8. Equipment, uniforms, and guns were lost, but Major Otto Schade and his men saved the Grays' costly bearskin shakos and the charred remnants of the colors. Before the day was out, generous contributions were pledged toward a new armory. Until it was ready in 1893, the men drilled in the Gatling Gun Battery Armory on Sibley Street.

On Christmas Day, it was announced that Jeptha H. Wade had made a gift to the city of the "College Reservation" tract in Wade Park to be used as the site for an art gallery (Cleveland Museum of Art), with the restriction that the property should never be fenced. Christmas was observed by church attendance and the traditional family reunion. Songs were sung around candle-lighted trees, gaily decorated with cornucopias filled with sugar-coated caraway seeds, colored-popcorn strings, gilded walnuts, and cookies. Sometimes there was a cardboard miniature village nestled in cotton underneath. An orange in a stocking was a special treat.

The year 1892 marked the establishment of business firms that were in existence in the 1940s: Cleveland Agency of Aetna Casualty & Surety Company, F. Z. Cikra, Inc., Cleveland Punch & Shear Works Company, Cleveland Wire Spring Company, Economy Savings & Loan Company, Fred Epple Company, Foote-Burt Company, Otto Konigslow Manufacturing Company, J. V. O'Brien Company, Osborn Engineering Company, F. W. Roberts Company, and the South Side Federal Savings & Loan Association.

1893

The Hoffman Block had been leveled, and in its place rose the eight-story Cuyahoga Building at the southeast corner of the Square and Superior Avenue. The brick-and-granite office building, designed by Burnham & Root, was erected by Myron T. Herrick and James Parmelee in a strategic location near courts and public buildings. Here were the offices of conspicuous Cleveland figures, among them Tom L. Johnson, John H. Farley, and Myron T. Herrick, who was often visited by his friend, William McKinley; Horace Andrews, Henry A. Everett, and Frank DeHaas Robison, who directed the city's street-railway affairs, and Charles A. Otis' brokerage firm. The Cleveland Electric Illuminating Company was a tenant until its new building was completed on the Square. The Cuyahoga was headquarters of the Cleveland baseball club; and a ball raised on the flagpole was a reminder that the team was playing at home. The Hamilton Restaurant in the basement was a popular meeting place. Meyer & Gleim occupied the traditional drug-store corner, which, in the transition, became Selzer's, and later Schroeder's, with a popular book-and-magazine section. The city's best-known detective, Jake Mintz, one of the first tenants, was one of the last to relinquish space in 1945, when the Veterans Administration and the United States Civil Service Commission made the remodeled Cuyahoga Building their headquarters. In 1944 the Cuyahoga and Williamson buildings united under joint ownership in The Williamson Company, of which A. A. McCaslin was president. Stanley M. Buckingham was managing agent.

A Sunday School had its origin in the kitchen of the home of Mr. and Mrs. Benjamin Coutant on Detroit Street in West Cleveland (at Coutant Street, Lakewood). Under the guidance of the First Congregational Church it grew and became known as the Detroit Street or West Cleveland Mission. On November 9, this year, the Lakewood Congregational Church was organized with twenty-six members. A church building was erected on the southeast corner of Detroit Street and Highland Avenue, and the congregation took the name of the Highland Congregational Church. The Rev. E. A. Fredenhagen, pastor since 1892, was succeeded by the Rev. Howard A. N. Richards, a kindly man and much beloved by the members. The pastorate of the Rev. Will Arthur Dietrick, 1902-6, was remembered particularly for his intense interest in young people, in music and drama. A new institutional-church building was dedicated on the original site in 1915, the year that the Rev. Dwight J. Bradley became pastor. The son of the Rev. Dan F. Bradley, he inherited the keen mind and gentle spirit of his famous father. He served until 1917, when he went on to broader fields in Christian service. The church program broadened under a succession of able leaders. The Rev. J. Edward Lair came to the pulpit in 1946, succeeding the Rev. Paul B. Van Horn, who served from 1936 to 1945.

Enrolled in Marion Elementary School were Angela and Vivian Ogden, sisters, who were to become well-known actresses. Pretty Nonnie May Stewart was in the same school, and one day she was to become Princess Anastasia of Greece.

On young Grover Cleveland's way to the West in 1855, his uncle in Buffalo persuaded him to make that city his home, and it is claimed that only once during his lifetime did he visit the city that bears his family name. In the evening of January 20, 1893, while returning from the funeral of ex-President Rutherford B. Hayes at Fremont, Ohio, President-elect Grover Cleveland enjoyed a twenty-five-minute stop-over in the city. He was met by his nephew, Charles M. Cleveland, who resided in the city, and together they walked up and down in the Union Depot. The distinguished visitor was quickly recognized by people in the waiting room, and he greeted them with hand-shaking. He is said to have remarked, "At last I have come to Cleveland."

Julia Marlowe closed a highly successful engagement at the Lyceum Theater on January 21, and it was observed that women attending the performance had begun to surrender their hats. In fact, a faithful admirer of Miss Marlowe wore no hat at all! only a pretty scarf that she discarded as she entered the foyer.

Organized medicine was revived in Cleveland on February 3, when medical men united under the old name, Cleveland Medical Society. Dr. W. J. Scott was the first president.

An enlarged and progressive program developed by the Committee on Promotion of Industry aroused businessmen to the need for a revitalized Board of Trade. On February 6, a complete reorganization was effected under a new name, The Cleveland Chamber of Commerce, with bylaws permitting broader activity and service. The Chamber was unique in that it was the first successful attempt to foster the interests of a great city through concerted action emanating from a single organization, and it became a model for Detroit, Pittsburgh, Boston, Rochester, and other cities. The first president, Henry R. Groff, was succeeded in turn by Luther Allen, 1894; Wilson M. Day, 1895; J. G. W. Cowles, 1896; Worcester R. Warner, 1897; Harry A. Garfield, 1898; and M. S. Greenough, 1899. Ryerson Ritchie became secretary in 1893.

Electric light and power were being produced on a small scale by a steam engine of the Williams Publishing Company for its immediate neighborhood. The Cleveland Light & Power Company, organized this year, took over the business, operating at the northwest corner of St. Clair and Ontario. Dudley J. Hard joined the firm in 1894, and was its head when The Cleveland Electric Illuminating Company purchased the interests in September, 1946. Hard, for many years Cleveland's leader in military affairs, earned the title of major general in military service, his first experience being in the Spanish-American campaigns.

A four-room house on Scranton Avenue was rented this year by the Society for the Christian Care of the Sick and Needy, organized by the Reformed churches of Cleveland. Here the German Hospital was located until it moved the next year to Franklin Circle. Two years later, a permanent home was established adjoining Fairview Park (3305 Franklin). Trustees changed the name to Fairview Park Hospital in 1918, and voted to place facilities at the disposal of the Government for the war's duration.

Henry Trenkamp, Sr., Paul Schneider, and associates established the Ohio Foundry Company on March 4, and the first plant soon opened (at 2469 East 71st Street). Schneider and Trenkamp were the owners of the Schneider & Trenkamp Company, manufacturers of "Reliable" ranges. Trenkamp, elected president of the Ohio Foundry Company in 1895, bought Schneider's interest in the foundry in 1902, and from this time the control was in the Trenkamp family. John A. Trenkamp succeeded his father as president in 1917, serving until 1925. William H. Smith, the third president, son-in-law of Henry Trenkamp, was succeeded in 1944 by Henry J. Trenkamp, son of Herman J. The company's business became nationwide, the principal products of the modern plant at 9812 Quincy Avenue being castings for washing machines, water heaters, electrical equipment, and the stove industry; automotive parts, and machine tools.

A Music Hall audience was thrilled on March 15 as it enjoyed a concert by Ignace Jan Paderewski, playing selections from the classics of the greatest composers. For more than four decades, the famed Polish pianist, composer, and patriot drew large assemblies of music lovers to his Cleveland concerts.

Cleveland's fire loss of $1,482,000 in 1892 resulted in the largest increase of equipment to date. Six engines, three trucks, a water tower to be erected on Engine House No. 1, on St. Clair Street, a fireboat, and three new engine houses were authorized.

Azariah Everett, Jeptha H. Wade, and J. M. Curtiss, park commissioners, had envisioned for ten years the unimproved Doan Brook Valley as the backbone of a park development, but their hands were tied by lack of support from public and City Council. Parks developed haphazardly until April 5, this year, when the Park Act was passed after much agitation. It provided for a Board of Park Commissioners, with the right of appropriation and of issuing bonds. The first board consisted of Robert Blee, mayor; A. J. Michael, president of Council, soon succeeded by Charles A. Davidson; Charles H. Bulkley, Amos Townsend, John F. Pankhurst, and F. C. Bangs, secretary. A comprehensive plan was finally adopted that included provision for "a large park on the outskirts of the city in each of the seven main sections, the same to be so located . . . that such outlying parks could be readily united and connected by a broad, smoothly paved boulevard, enclosing the city." E. W. Bowditch, Boston landscape architect, was engaged to begin perfecting the Cleveland Park Plan. Bonds totaling $800,000 were issued, and steps were taken to acquire Doan Brook Valley and sites for Edgewater, Brooklyn (Brookside), and Newburgh (Garfield) parks, and Ambler Parkway. Plans were made to connect Gordon and Wade parks with an upper drive, and bridges were built at Wade Park, Superior, and St. Clair avenues. New names were given to many of the parks in 1897.

A franchise for long-distance telephone service was approved by Council in April. The Midland Company was the first firm in the field. Local business responded quickly to this new but expensive development. The list of Cleveland telephone subscribers had reached 2,979 in 1890; a half century later, the Greater Cleveland total showed 199,400, with 296,400 telephones.

Plodding horses with their tinkling bells were disappearing from streetcar lines as electricity displaced them. A sale was held in April at the Woodland Avenue car barns, and three hundred horses were sold to New York City to pull cars. Single-truck, open cars were being readied for the summer season. Smokers took over the seats and platform at the rear, where they frequently entertained themselves by rocking the car to the disgust of peace-loving passengers. Crowds hung precariously on the running board along the side in rush hours.

At noon on April 27, the historic Liberty Bell reached Cleveland on its way to the World's Columbian Exposition in Chicago. In four hours, an estimated sixty thousand persons viewed it in the railroad yard and from old Lake View Park, amid cannon salute, band music, and cheering. The priceless relic was carried on a flat car, in an enclosure of thirteen nickel-plated posts representing the original States. The other states were identified by thirty-one railings fastened to the posts by links symbolizing unity. Silk flags decorated the beams. C. C. Burnet and L. E. Holden of The Cleveland Chamber of Commerce and D. O. Caswell of the City Council joined the mayor of Philadelphia and his official party at Pittsburgh. The Cleveland Grays served as military guard.

The concert of the Cleveland Vocal Society, presented on April 27, consisted of music to be sung at the Chicago Exposition. The society won first prize in the World Choral Competition.

A merger of the East Cleveland, Broadway & Newburgh, Brooklyn, and South Side traction companies was authorized by ordinance of May 15, creating the Cleveland Electric Railway Company, commonly called the "Big Consolidated," and headed by Henry A. Everett, president. At this time, the East Cleveland company operated four lines: Euclid, Central—or Garden, Cedar, and Wade Park.

Three days of rain caused the river to leave its banks, sweeping two million dollars worth of lumber and property from the "Flats" into the lake. Seven lives were lost in the flood.

A mile a minute was the breath-taking speed attained by the new *Exposition Flyer,* crack special running from Chicago to New York on the New York Central-Lake Shore railroad. Clevelanders made a quick inspection when the train stopped to change the "mammoth" locomotive on its initial run to the Chicago Exposition, May 28. Luxurious interior innovations were a barber shop, bathroom and library, two leather-upholstered sections for card-playing, gaslight chandeliers, mahogany woodwork, and silk hangings. When the fair closed, the flyer was withdrawn, as it was believed that ordinary traffic would not justify operating so fast and splendid a train.

A second great consolidation of railway lines was authorized on May 29, when the Cleveland City Cable Company and the Woodland & West Side road merged in the Cleveland City Railway Company, familiarly known as the "Little Consolidated," of which Marcus A. Hanna was president.

The cornerstone of Grays Armory, erected by the Cleveland Grays (1234 Bolivar), was laid on Decoration Day. Besides serving military purposes, it was used as a public auditorium, seating five thousand, where concerts, and civic and cultural events took place. Following World War II, the armory became the headquarters of the 7th Infantry Battalion of the United States Marine Corps Reserve.

Decoration Day was long remembered by the people of northern Ohio, for it marked the great railroad disaster involving the Walter H. Main Circus near Tyrone, Pennsylvania. When the engineer lost control, the train jumped the tracks on a mountain grade, crushing men and animals. Menacing wild beasts that escaped were hunted down by farmers and killed, and loss to the circus exceeded $150,000. Main and his father had organized one of the largest circuses in the world, featuring a forty-horse wagon, and great crowds filled the "big top" when the show came to Cleveland. The owner retired from circus business to his home in Geneva, Ohio, in 1939.

The Cleveland Chamber of Commerce opened its new quarters in the Arcade on the evening of June 20, as the center of business and community interest and a meeting place for associated organizations. During the first year, achievements of lasting benefit were initiated through Chamber leadership, according to the secretary's report of April 9, 1894: locating the Central Armory on Bond Street; advancing the city's interests at the Chicago Exposition; launching a movement that brought a United States hydrographic office and the Federal Building to Cleveland; securing improved freight conditions and favorable taxation; promoting interests of wholesalers and manufacturers in neighboring territory; raising relief funds for the needy; furthering the street-railway system and harbor development; laying the groundwork for Cleveland's centennial observance in 1896; adopting a system to promote efficient recording of freight receipts and shipments and other business statistics. The crowning achievement, however, was realized when the Ohio State Board of Commerce was organized on November 15, after the pioneering efforts of the Cleveland Chamber. This year of fruitful activity was indicative of the scope of early-day interest that was continuously broadened and intensified in order to protect and develop the business, civic, and cultural interests of Cleveland.

A mission fostered in flourishing Glenville by the North Presbyterian Church held its first meeting on June 25 in a schoolhouse on St. Clair Avenue (near Lakeview). From it emerged the Glenville Presbyterian Church, organized on June 10, 1894, with thirty-two charter members. The Rev. C. L. Zorbaugh served both the Glenville and Windermere congregations. Through the untiring efforts of Dr. Hiram C. Haydn of Old Stone Church, and the generous gifts of friends, such as Mr. and Mrs. Samuel Mather, Mr. and Mrs. Edward P. Williams, Judge and Mrs. Samuel E. Williamson, Mrs. C. W. Bingham, Mrs. Samuel A. Raymond, Mrs. Amasa Stone, and Mrs. D. B. Chambers, a building site was purchased at Doan Street and Helena Avenue. Services had been held in the Glenville town hall until the spring of 1895, when a new chapel was dedicated, which was enlarged in 1912. The Rev. Theodore Y. Gardner was called as the first pastor in 1895. As families moved eastward, the neighborhood became almost entirely Jewish; but many of Glenville's members who moved away remained loyal to their church home. Under the inspiring leadership of the Rev. Arnold W. Bloomfield, pastor from 1925 to 1935, steady progress was made. Broadened activity continued during the ministry of the Rev. Benjamin V. Andrews, who was succeeded in 1941 by the Rev. Clifton E. Moore.

The Cleveland Art Club invited the City Council to attend a brilliant reception at the Hollenden on July 3, honoring Mlle. Rita Elandi, operatic celebrity who was appearing in Cleveland, her birthplace. Upon entering opera in her girlhood days, Amelia Groll created her stage name by Italianizing "Cleveland" into "Elandi." She enjoyed many European successes, and in Berlin she sang before Emperor Wilhelm.

The *Viking,* graceful, old-world vessel of the Norsemen, was the central feature of the Fourth of July celebration. Throngs gathered at the waterfront which was gaily decorated for the holiday. Next morning, the "canoe with its ends turned up" departed for the Chicago Exposition.

While searching for a source of electric motors with which to drive his ore-and-coal-handling machinery, Alexander E. Brown was attracted to the Elwell-Parker line, produced in England. This resulted in the incorporation of The Elwell-Parker Electric Company of America on July 6, this year, to make motors for hoisting machinery. Capital was furnished by Brown, Fayette Brown, and Henry D. Coffinberry of the Brown Hoisting company, and Stewart H. Chisholm. Caught in the Panic of 1893 at the start, progress was slow, and the small output went to Brown Hoist, which sheltered the company as a department. Development of a varied line of motors and generators broadened the market, and in the late nineties, the plant was large enough to justify its own quarters on the north side of Hamilton Avenue.

Governor William McKinley addressed the great audience at the opening of the Twenty-seventh Saengerfest on July 11, in a spacious, temporary concert hall at Scovill and Willson avenues (East Technical High School site). Rita Elandi, famous opera star, had come home for the occasion, and she won a great ovation. The Philharmonic Orchestra, directed by Emil Ring, played during the event, and Sousa's Band attracted capacity audiences. A feature selection from *The Creation* was sung by a chorus of almost 4,000 school children under the direction of N. Coe Stewart. Eighty-five singing societies of 2,200 voices came to Cleveland to compete for musical honors. An effort to create practical interest in building a large Cleveland public auditorium was inspired by the four-day event, but enthusiasm soon subsided. Reorganization of the North American Saengerbund was planned at this time under the direction of J. Hanno Deiler; and the next year, at Pittsburgh, plans were launched for a larger and stronger Saengerfest.

Whether excursions were pleasant experiences was a matter of opinion, according to Henry Weidenthal. "A Sunday at Brady's Lake was a treat," he recounted. "You boarded the Pennsy train at the old Union Depot where the soot and gloom were about in even proportions. The plush seats of the day coaches were hot and dusty. As the car filled with excursionists, the odor of bananas from the lunch boxes piled on the baggage racks predominated. The train pulled onto a siding at the park and remained there until time for the return home in the evening. Tired, dusty, but happy after a day at the lake and park, the crowd piled onto the train in response to impatient tootings. The odor of coal oil or of Pintsch (acetylene) gas from the coach lamps made you long for the bananas. Approaching Cleveland, one could pick out amid the maze of light, the tall mast lights down town. The climb up South Water Street hill from the station to the street cars was a chore, especially for those carrying children and luggage."

At a meeting of the Early Settlers Association held on July 22, John C. Covert proposed that a committee be appointed to confer with the City Council, the Chamber of Commerce, and local bodies to plan a celebration of Cleveland's Centennial, July 22, 1896. The committee included Richard C. Parsons, chairman; Covert, A. J. Williams, Bolivar Butts, General James Barnett, George F. Marshall, Wilson S. Dodge, Solon Burgess, and Hiram M. "Father" Addison.

Harry A. and James R. Garfield, sons of the late President Garfield, Amos D. McNairy, and Charles L. Pack had razed the three-story brick office and residence of Dr. Benjamin Strickland, pioneer dentist, at the northeast corner of Euclid and Bond Street; and on the site rose the Garfield Building. The modern, ten-story structure was the first steel-framed commercial office building on Euclid Avenue. Basement quarters and an elaborate steel vault were provided for the branch of an eastern bank that failed to materialize; but the space was put to use when the new Cleveland Trust Company opened in the fall of 1895. Cowell & Hubbard, jewelers, occupied the first floor. A number of attorneys secured space in the building, which became the National City Bank Building in 1921.

Opposite the fire station on lower St. Clair Avenue was a loft with a window that afforded a fine view of the big, gray horses galloping to answer an alarm. It was here that the Printz-Biederman Company, women's-wear manufacturer, had its beginning this year. Moritz Printz, his sons, Michael and Alexander, and his son-in-law, Joseph Biederman, founded the business. Expansion was steady, and in 1934, a modern building was erected at East 61st Street, where the famous "Printzess" trade-mark was adopted. A second plant was opened in Lorain, Ohio. Alexander Printz became president of the company in 1910, and the Printzess line reached into all parts of the country through more than twelve hundred retail stores.

Wearing the Cleveland Athletic Club colors, Charles W. "Billy" Stage entered a track meet in Chicago and established the 220-yard-dash record of 21⅗ seconds. For a time, he held the national-amateur, 100-yard-dash record of 9⅖ seconds. Stage was one of the greatest all-round athletes in the history of Western Reserve University. He became closely associated with Tom L. Johnson and Newton D. Baker, and was vice president of the Cleveland Union Terminals Company.

The "writing machine," invented by Christopher L. Sholes in 1867, did not come to Cleveland until this year, when the *Press* is said to have put it to use. Before the advent of the typewriter, writing was done laboriously in longhand.

Appearing at the Star Theater in late September was the first Negro troupe of entertainers to visit Cleveland.

The Cleveland Day School for Deaf Children opened in the Rockwell School in the fall with twenty pupils, despite much agitation by a few parents who wished to educate their handicapped children at home. The Board of Education employed a faculty of two teachers. Manual training was introduced in the elementary schools, and kindergarten training was begun in the Normal School. Science work and brief courses in conduct, civics, physiology, and physical culture were added in the lower grades.

On October 2 the *Waechter am Erie* and the *Anzeiger* united under the name *Waechter und Anzeiger,* which was published on Seneca Street. The Consolidated Press & Printing Company took over the paper in 1927. Dr. A. Cherna was president. The company, once controlled by a group headed by William R. Hopkins, changed hands several times. An organization of employees eventually acquired the daily as the Press & Plate Company, located at 1243 Rockwell Avenue. *Waechter und Anzeiger* was the only German daily newspaper in Ohio and western Pennsylvania in the 1940s. F. W. Oberacker became president and general manager in 1927, and Walter Eckstein was made editor in 1941.

The first issue of the *Evening Post,* a penny paper, appeared on October 2. Formerly the *Evening Plain Dealer,* it was believed that the new masthead would identify it as independent of the parent publication. It continued through 1896, when the name *Plain Dealer* was restored to the afternoon field.

Thick masonry walls and stone towers, of the fortress type of architecture of the day, characterized the Central Armory, erected by the County at the southeast corner of Lake and Bond streets. It opened in the fall, and housed National Guard units and the 112th Engineers.

Since 1865, William J. Gordon, wholesale grocer, had been purchasing tracts fronting on the lake and bordering Doan Brook in Glenville, converting them into a beautiful estate. Upon his death in 1892, his will directed that the 122-acre area become a public park. Title passed to the City of Cleveland on October 23, 1893, upon condition that the name be known as Gordon Park, that the lakefront be protected, that drives and ponds be maintained, that no fence obstruct the lake view, and that the city preserve the Gordon burial lot. In 1894 the 30-acre picnic grounds adjoining the park were purchased from the Gordons.

Mrs. Dan P. Eells began twenty years of service as president of the Women's Christian Association in November, succeeding Sarah Elizabeth Fitch, who died in April. Mrs. Eells accompanied her husband to Berlin, where she addressed the International YMCA Convention, representing the women of America. The name Women's Christian Association was changed to Young Women's Christian Association this year, in order to lay greater emphasis on work among young people. The "Y" moved to Euclid Avenue from its Walnut Street rooms, its home for some years.

Society and art enthusiasts previewed the beautiful Olney Art Gallery on Jennings Avenue as Professor Charles F. Olney was about to open it to the public. The long, narrow, brick-and-stone building housed more than two hundred oil and water-color paintings, statuary, porcelains, and other art objects. Upon the owner's death in 1907, the gallery was closed, and its treasures were bequeathed to Oberlin College.

This was a year of world financial disaster, when silver agitation, industrial depression, farm mortgages, rash railroad financing, and unsound banking brought the collapse of eight thousand business ventures in six months and receivership to one hundred and fifty banks in the nation. Cleveland's ability to weather the Panic of 1893 may be credited to the sturdy roots of its diversified industry and its guarded banking policies.

One of William McKinley's close friends, whose notes he had endorsed for a large sum, lost his business in the panic. This crisis was more than McKinley's resources and his wife's fortune could meet, but rescue from financial and political ruin was arranged by Marcus A. Hanna of Cleveland. The McKinley property was deeded to trustees, headed by Myron T. Herrick, and the deficit was met by contributions of many Republican followers; Mrs. McKinley's estate was saved. The governor of Ohio was re-elected.

A committee was appointed by The Cleveland Chamber of Commerce on November 21 to make further plans "for an appropriate celebration of the city's Centennial, to the end that various important public improvements now in progress or in contemplation, may, by unity and harmony of action, be brought to a culmination in that year, and the occasion be thus distinguished by tangible evidences of the city's growth and glory." The committee, consisting of Wilson M. Day, chairman, William J. Akers, Harry A. Garfield, S. F. Haserot, Webb C. Hayes, George W. Kinney, and O. M. Stafford, made its report, providing for a commission representing the city, the citizenship, and the state.

Artists in the City Hall colony formed the Brush and Palette Club, with Archibald M. Willard, president. In May, 1894, the first exhibition was held, displaying the talents of painters who were on the way to fame. Annual shows attracted both the public and society, and were an inspiration to local art. The Camera Club and the Water Color Society, organized about this time, contributed to artistic improvement.

A Catholic burial ground known as Calvary Cemetery, containing 105 acres of land, was opened in Newburgh (4255 East 99th) on November 26.

To relieve the suffering of the poor in the bad times, art lovers arranged the first Art Loan Exhibition, held in the Garfield Building. Professor Charles F. Olney, Charles F. Brush, William J. White, and local collectors generously loaned their art treasures, and paintings from other cities were displayed. A large sum was realized for the benefit of the poor fund. The event was repeated the following year with equal success, arousing enthusiasm for the art movement which was taking substantial form.

The year 1893 marked the establishment of business firms that were in existence in the 1940s: Bailey Wall Paper Company, Sol Bergman Company, P. J. Breuer & Son Company, Cleveland Builders Supply Company, Cuyahoga Savings & Loan Company, Dyke School of Commerce (later Dyke & Spencerian College), A. S. Gilman, Inc., Oster Manufacturing Company, Provident Savings & Loan Association, Star Bakery, Strong-Carlisle & Hammond Company, The Union Paper & Twine Company, Watt Printing Company, The H. N. White Company.

1894

The Willard Electric & Battery Company was formed this year by Theodore A. Willard, who had set up a small shop and laboratory at Norwalk, Ohio, two years earlier. Edison phonographs, dentists, and physicians provided a ready market for batteries, and, in 1896, Willard moved to Cleveland and established a factory on Sheriff Street with ten employees. In 1902 he organized the Willard Storage Battery Company. He made his first batteries for automobile-ignition purposes in 1908. Willard collaborated with Charles F. Kettering in developing a satisfactory generator for use on automobiles. He also assisted in developing a practical tungsten-filament automobile lamp, and contributed to the development of the electric starter.

The second branch in Cleveland's Public Library system, and the first east of the river, opened in Miles Park. The *Open Shelf,* official publication of the library, made its initial appearance.

Clevelanders were wrestling with questionnaires required by the Federal Government, as evidenced by an entertaining circumstance revealed in the records of the Home for Aged Women: "The secretary has had an amusing experience with the Census Department . . . repeated cards, circulars, and letters were received, soliciting information regarding our institution or school; prompt letters were sent in reply, explaining the character of our institution; further letters came, almost demanding the number of pupils in our care and their age. As promptly as before, ignoring all past correspondence, the secretary wrote: 'There are 25 pupils in our institution, ranging in age from 60 to 80 years.' " By return mail came an acknowledgment of thanks from the superintendent of the department.

West Cleveland, incorporated in 1871, was annexed to Cleveland on March 5. The village contained 6,000 inhabitants and about 1,500 acres extending north of Lorain Street to the lake, between Gordon and Highland avenues.

About one hundred dissatisfied members of Bolton Chapel, of the Old Stone Church, met at the home of J. G. James on Bolton Avenue on March

19 and organized Trinity Congregational Church. On Easter Sunday following, the congregation assembled in a new, temporary house of worship erected in two days by volunteers. The Rev. R. A. George was the first minister. Organization was completed on April 22, when 163 members signed the charter. The cornerstone of a new church was laid (at Cedar and East 80th Street) in 1895. With the influx of Negroes into the community, the church property was sold to the St. James Methodist Church. Trinity worshiped in a theater and in Taylor School for a time, and an alarming loss in membership resulted as the congregation moved eastward. A beautiful stone building was dedicated in 1928 at Washington Boulevard and Thayne Road, Cleveland Heights. Although for several decades Trinity barely survived prevailing economic conditions, the faithful remained steadfast, and the church slowly gathered strength and membership. In 1946 plans were being made for a $280,000 building at Brainard Circle in Pepper Pike Village. The Rev. Theodore E. Frank was pastor.

In 1872 Claus Greve, eighteen, left his Danish homeland, then dominated by a ruthless Bismarck, to seek freedom in America. He acquired an interest, in 1894, in the Union Electric Company, makers of electrical equipment. The firm name was changed to The Cleveland Pneumatic Tool Company in 1899, and Greve was elected president. In a ten-man shop in the Perkins Power Block, the pioneering manufacture of air-operated tools began. A son, Louis, went to work in the company in 1902, and he was soon patenting new improvements. The riveter was introduced early in the next decade, and Bowes couplings and hose fittings were swelling production. The Cleveland Rock Drill Company, formed in 1908, launched the rock drill and other revolutionary mining and drilling devices; a Canadian plant opened; and the Champion Machine & Forging Company, owned and managed by Greve interests, was set up to supply drop forgings for "Cleco" tools. After fifteen years on East 65th Street at Hawthorne Avenue, the company moved into a new and enlarged plant on East 78th Street near Broadway, the first building in a grouping that steadily expanded.

On Easter Sunday, March 25, Jacob S. Coxey and his army of unemployed left Massillon, Ohio, on their march to Washington to demand legislation that would provide jobs. A bulletin issued before the start read, "We want no thieves or anarchists—boodlers and bankers—to join us. We want patriots, not bummers. No firearms, but manhood . . ." In the ranks were some enthusiastic Cleveland followers.

Policemen were training city-shy horses at the riding academy on Willson Avenue in April, according to rules laid down for the new mounted-police squad. Upon making an arrest, the officer was required to dismount and conduct his prisoner on foot to the nearest station house or patrol box. Buggies in which police captains could inspect their precincts had been ordered earlier in the year.

In Cleveland there were ten thousand horses, it was estimated, and to pick up a horseshoe on the street was a common occurrence. A set of shoes cost from $1.80 to $10. Newest conveyances included phaetons and traps for four or six persons. For the less privileged, buckboards and road wagons were plentiful.

The Permanent Savings & Loan Company, organized in 1889, moved from the Arcade to the new, eight-story Permanent Building on Euclid at Oak Place.

Brooklyn Village joined with Cleveland on April 30, adding 1,700 acres and 5,000 inhabitants to the city, as well as 4 schools and 1,781 pupils.

Construction of the first large wharves, equipped with coal-loading machinery with a capacity of twenty cars per hour, was begun on the lakefront east of the river. A scheme was proposed to build a dock suitable for loading the cars on a car ferry for shipment to Detroit, but it was abandoned.

In the afternoon of May 17, a devastating hail storm descended unannounced on Cleveland. Many reports stated that hailstones measured more than three inches in diameter and exceeded a half pound in weight. Great damage was suffered by greenhouses.

A worthy location for the wandering Perry Monument was provided in Wade Park overlooking the lagoon.

The new fireboat, *Clevelander,* went into service on June 15, stationed at the Seneca Street dock. It served until May, 1916.

A campaign conducted by the *Herald* to rid streets of wandering cows and hogs resulted in revival of the animal pound.

The Guardian Trust Company was incorporated on June 28 with a capital of $500,000 that was doubled on October 1, when the name changed to The Guardian Savings & Trust Company. It began business on December 10 in the Wade Building on lower Superior Avenue. John H. Whitelaw was the first president, and William G. Dietz, secretary. An "uptown" office opened in the Arcade in 1902. Business grew rapidly, and a twelve-story building was erected at 322 Euclid Avenue and occupied in 1906, absorbing the Arcade Branch. In 1912 the original office united with the others. Combined capital and surplus had reached $4,000,000 in 1913.

W. B. Fasig was providing the papers with interesting copy as he drove the great pacer, Flying Jib, in Gordon Park and on Euclid Avenue. This harness performer was the first to better the two-minute mile, pacing in 1:58¼ with a running mate over the Chillicothe track this year. Fasig was one of the most amusing writers in the racing world, and he enjoyed great popularity as a citizen of Cleveland. He inaugurated the greatest standard-bred and thoroughbred sales organization of all time, The Fasig-Tipton Company.

The service of valiant Union defenders in the Civil War was commemorated on Independence Day with the dedication of the Cuyahoga County Soldiers and Sailors Monument, located on the southeast section of the Public Square. The holiday was proclaimed with cannon, bells, and whistles. A yacht race, a band concert on the Square directed by Professor Frank H. Hruby, and dedicatory exercises in a drizzling rain marked the event. Governor William McKinley and Senator Joseph B. Foraker served as orators of the day. N. Coe Stewart directed a chorus of school children, and the mammoth parade was "one of the greatest and most comprehensive processions ever seen in Cleveland." A commission was appointed in 1888 to plan and construct the monument, consisting of William J. Gleason, president; Levi F. Bauder, secretary; J. B. Molyneaux, Edward H. Bohm, Levi T. Scofield, Emory W. Force, James Barnett, J. J. Elwell, Charles C. Dewstoe, James Hayr, Dr. R. W. Walters, and M. D. Leggett. Captain Scofield designed the memorial. A statue of "Liberty" surmounted the central granite shaft 125 feet above the Square. Life-size battle groups in bronze represented the Infantry, Artillery, Cavalry, and Navy, modeled in the studio of J. Q. A. Ward of New York City. The names of officers and men from Cuyahoga County were cut in marble, and bronze panels portrayed life-size figures of men and women who gave outstanding service. Trophies and exhibits perpetuated heroic deeds. Decorative flower beds on the lawn represented corps badges of the Grand Army of the Republic, Women's Relief Corps, Loyal Legion, Sons of Veterans, Ladies of the Grand Army, Daughters of Veterans, and the American flag. The cost of about $280,000 was secured through a county tax that was levied and collected "without authority of the law but was not resisted by any tax payer."

At the end of the school year, Superintendent Draper resigned to accept the presidency of the University of Illinois. Louis H. Jones, formerly superintendent of the Indianapolis schools, succeeded him and announced that no radical changes in the system would be made. The public schools had suffered greatly from overcrowding, and a tax levy of one mill on the dollar was authorized for building purposes. Methodist ministers waged an attack on dancing in high schools, and it was pointed out that boys and girls danced separately under strict regulation.

One of Cleveland's most spectacular outdoor shows, *The Storming of Vicksburg,* was presented for the first time, July 12, at Cedar and Madison avenues. The Cleveland City Guards provided the military, and a ballet and fireworks were features that drew large audiences.

Great crowds came to Cleveland to attend the Thirteenth International Convention of Christian Endeavor on July 12. Saengerfest Hall being filled to capacity, an enormous tent was erected at Willson and Cedar avenues; three thousand Endeavorers organized a third meeting in Epworth Memorial Methodist Church, while a fourth formed in the Woodland Avenue Presbyterian Church at Woodland and Kennard. Governor William McKinley gave the principal address, and speakers hurried from one meeting to another on an improvised schedule. The total attendance of thirty thousand set a new high for Christian Endeavor events and emphasized the imperative need for enlarged convention accommodations in Cleveland.

General James Barnett and John C. Covert presided at a meeting of sixty citizens to form the Law and Order Association of Cleveland. Law enforcement as relating to the operation of saloons, and dissatisfaction with the way police were handling the "tenderloin" problem were at the top of the list of issues for discussion.

During the campaign of General Benjamin Harrison in 1888, Republicans had formed the Young Men's Tippecanoe Club, a revival of the early-day organization. On July 26, this year, club rooms were opened in the Masonic Temple. William McKinley was guest of honor on the occasion. W. E. Cubben, David Brown, and A. E. Aikens were among those who served as president of the standard-bearers.

Eighty-nine acres of lakefront land west of the river were acquired by the city for Edgewater Park at a cost of $205,958.07. The park on the lake was first proposed by Jacob B. Perkins at a meeting of the West and South Side Citizens' League on August 21, 1889. Park grounds embraced Wenham's Grove and Perkins' large estate at the foot of Waverly Avenue. In 1896 work commenced on the highway skirting the lake, connecting the park with Detroit Street near the Superior Viaduct. It became known as Bulkley Boulevard, perpetuating the name of Charles H. Bulkley, early park champion who worked tirelessly to make the park system a reality. Portions of the Barker, Poe, and Quirk farms, totaling almost 150 acres, were also purchased at a cost of about $58,000 as the beginning of Brooklyn Park, called Brookside in 1897.

Through the generosity of Mrs. Martha B. Ambler and the influence of Dan O. Caswell, a relative and leading citizen, the city received twenty-five acres of land lying between Cedar Avenue and Ambler Heights; and fifty-five acres were purchased the next year for completion of Ambler Parkway, connecting Rockefeller Park, south, with Shaker Heights Park. In the deep ravine were preserved some of the finest trees in the Forest City.

A two-story brick-and-steel building was erected this year (712 Lakeside, N. E.) to house the Morgue and the offices of the county coroner.

Chaplain J. D. Jones introduced the spectacular into his missionary efforts when he began to recruit converts on August 16 with a revival of his Floating Bethel Gospel Boat, horse-drawn and mounted on wheels. A driver maneuvered the open craft from his perch in the bow, and "Brother" Jones and two singers managed the organ and the preaching. Services were held on downtown streets, and many souls were reborn.

A group of Clevelanders purchased ten acres of land in the Puritas Springs area southwest of Cleveland, and erected a bottling plant. Although unpleasant to taste, there was a great demand for the mineral-laden water. Many preferred it to city water supplied from the lake, which was considered unsafe. A park and amusement development later became a popular West Side pleasure resort.

Doan Street was unpaved, and it was bordered with fields along much of its distance. Cyclists riding the popular "Century Run" on Euclid Avenue to Geneva, Ohio, stopped at Doan's Corners for rest and refreshment and a cool drink from the ornate, red fountain erected by church groups and the Young Women's Christian Temperance Union. It bore an inscription in gold letters, "With Compliments of East Side Temperance Societies," and was ice-refrigerated.

Increased traffic in the Public Square demanded that the center of streets be cleared of moving vans and express wagons that parked while waiting for business. Drivers provided their horses with feed bags and water, and many left teams standing all night, even in bad weather, in order to be first in line for business in the morning. Humane interests were asked to intercede for the animals.

The Cleveland Trust Company was founded with capital of $500,000 on September 20, the original trustees being Luther Allen, F. L. Alcott, Edmund Clarke, J. D. Cox, H. Clark Ford, H. A. Garfield, M. S. Greenough, R. A. Harman, J. M. Henderson, A. B. McNairy, Charles L. Pack, and H. A. Sherwin. J. G. W. Cowles was the first president; Sherwin, Garfield, and McNairy, vice presidents, and E. G. Tillotson, secretary-treasurer. The company opened its doors on September 10, 1895, in the Garfield Building, four employees transacting the business in an office 12 by 26 feet. Deposits passed the million mark before the close of 1896, and enlarged quarters were secured in the new Williamson Building in 1903.

Rabbi Moses J. Gries had come to fill the pulpit of the Tifereth Israel Congregation (later the Temple) in 1892, when plans were under way for the building of a new house of worship at Willson and Central avenues. Dedicatory services in the new Temple continued from September 21 to 24, the distinguishing feature being a fellowship evening in which ministers of other denominations participated. The new sanctuary was recognized as the first "open temple" or institutional church established by Jewish people in the world, where all those interested in religious, educational, and cultural activities were welcomed. Through lectures, a library, and many liberal forms of endeavor for young and old, the Temple became a vital influence in the community. Rabbi Gries' liberal social services attracted nationwide attention. He became president of the Central Conference of American Rabbis, a member of the board of governors of the Hebrew Union College, and exerted a strong influence in numerous Cleveland organizations. He helped to found the Cleveland Council of Jewish Women, the Federation of Jewish Charities, and the Council Educational Alliance. When he died in 1918, his loss was felt keenly, for he had inspired higher religious thought and deeper civic interest.

Public demand for a new Union Depot was growing rapidly, and sentiment seemed to favor the east end of the Superior Viaduct as the site. The station at the foot of Water Street was a poor advertisement for a city that was becoming one of the nation's great centers, but several decades passed before plans for the Union Terminal on the Square had taken form.

The Tower automatic railroad-car coupler, designed by Clinton A. Tower in the Cleveland Works of The National Malleable Castings Company, was introduced, meeting the requirements of the Safety Appliance Act of 1893.

Friends of Louis Gimm, bicyclist, who raced for the Cleveland Wheel Club, were boasting of his world record established on the Newburgh Driving Track—383¾ miles in 24 hours.

A joint committee composed of Drs. Henry E. Handerson, Marcus Rosenwasser, and Henry W. Rogers of the Cuyahoga County Medical Society; Drs. Isaac N. Himes, B. L. Millikin, and Dudley P. Allen of the Society of the Medical Sciences of Cleveland; and Drs. W. H. Humiston, Joseph E. Cook, and P. Maxwell Foshay of the Cleveland Medical Society were appointed to consider the best means of organizing a medical library. On

November 7, The Cleveland Medical Library Association took form, and Dr. Cook became the first president. The county society donated its books and journals and the balance in its treasury amounting to $419.35; the Society of the Medical Sciences gave $2,000, and the Cleveland society offered books and $100 in cash. Case Library set aside a corner of its main room for the library collection.

The second president of the Cleveland Medical Library Association was Dr. Henry E. Handerson, distinguished physician, who served from 1895 to 1904. In 1895 he was also elected president of the Cleveland Academy of Medicine. He was born in Orange, Ohio, in 1837. Graduating from Columbia College of Physicians and Surgeons, Dr. Handerson came to Cleveland, serving as professor of hygiene and sanitary science in the Cleveland College of Physicians and Surgeons, 1893-1903, and as professor emeritus. His contributions to medical literature were numerous and important.

The Woman's Christian Temperance Union came home to Cleveland, its birthplace, to hold its national convention which opened in the Music Hall on November 17. Mrs. S. M. Perkins welcomed the delegates. Convention speakers discussed methods by which scientific temperance instruction could be given in the schools. "Living pictures," a popular feature of stage shows, and military toys were condemned. A vote to support the Prohibition Party ended in a split and the formation of the Non-Partisan Women's Christian Temperance Union, headed by Mrs. E. J. Phinney, whose members frowned on political ties. At the final session on the 24th, Mrs. Frances E. Willard was re-elected president.

A merger of the benevolent interests of Jewish women was consummated, and on November 20, the first regular meeting of the Cleveland Council of Jewish Women was held at the Temple. Rabbi Moses J. Gries was the first president, and there was a membership of 271. In 1896 Mrs. M. B. Schwab succeeded him, serving for ten years. The Council's contribution to the well-being of women, girls, and children, not only in the Jewish community, but in Cleveland and in the nation, is indicative of enthusiastic spirit and able leadership.

November 23 marked the dedication of Pilgrim Congregational Church at Jennings Avenue and Howard Street on the South Side. A massive, stone structure, costing $150,000, it was the first large institutional church in Cleveland. Heralded as the best-equipped church in America, it had a seating capacity of three thousand. Distinguished visitors came to see the building as its fame spread. An exhibit sent to the Paris Exposition in 1899 upon request received high praise. Building plans were designed to carry out a broad and revolutionary community-service program launched by the Pilgrim Church Institute on November 9, 1894. Educational, social, and recreational services centered in the church, where non-denominational classes and clubs were maintained for young and old by able instructors and leaders, among them Professor Henry C. King of Oberlin, Bible study, and Professor Charles F. Olney, fine arts. Under the leadership of the Rev. Charles S. Mills, pastor from 1891 to 1905, and the Rev. Irving W. Metcalf, who came in 1894 as associate pastor, church membership reached 537 in 1894, and there were

1,252 in the Sunday School. At one time the Sunday School was the largest in the denomination in Ohio. The Jennings Avenue church property was purchased by St. Augustine's Catholic Parish in 1896.

The first "Union" Thanksgiving service was held on November 29, when the Anshe Chesed Congregation and the Unitarian Church joined in worship in the Jewish temple.

A meeting at the home of Mrs. Curtis Webster, attended by Mrs. Alice Cole, Mrs. William Crowell, Mrs. W. E. Cushing, Myrta Jones, and Sarah Walker resulted in a club "to further the interests of music in Cleveland." The first executive board of The Fortnightly Musical Club of Cleveland consisted of Mrs. Cushing, Mrs. Warren Corning, Miss Jones, Mrs. Webster, and Lillian Hanna, with Mrs. Edward W. Morley, president. Music lovers quickly filled the membership quota of five hundred, and there was a long waiting list. Sol Marcosson, eminent violinist, was engaged, and with Charles Heydler, James D. Johnston, and Carl Dueringer, whose place was later taken by Charles V. Rychlik, the Cleveland Philharmonic Quartet was formed. Chamber music formed an integral part of club programs. Seasonal concerts were presented until 1901, when the Symphony Orchestra concerts were established, and members were privileged to enjoy them as well as concerts of visiting orchestras.

The year 1894 marked the establishment of business firms that were in existence in the 1940s: Ajax Manufacturing Company, Bonfoey Company, Byerlyte Corporation, City Ice & Fuel Company, Fanner Manufacturing Company, F. G. Nickels & Son Funeral Homes.

1895

Mrs. John Drew—Louisa Lane Drew, seventy-five, "the grand old lady" of the stage, was playing Widow Warren in *The Road to Ruin,* a comedy at the Lyceum Theater on January 2-3. She was the mother of John, Louisa, and Georgiana Drew, and the grandmother of Lionel, Ethel, and John Barrymore, who became famous stars.

Equipment and parts of the fireboat *J. L. Weatherly* were transferred to the *John H. Farley,* named for the former mayor. It went into service on January 5 and was relieved in 1932.

Crosstown streetcar service began on Willson Avenue, January 11, connecting St. Clair Street with Newburgh, and there was a disturbance about issuing transfers. Streetcar operators were about to have protection from the weather in wooden vestibules with windows and a door. This was a great improvement over flimsy canvas makeshifts.

Two hundred Cleveland women pooled their talents, and, with some professional assistance, issued a woman's edition of the *Plain Dealer* in January. Mrs. Howard M. Ingham was editor-in-chief of the weekday, morning, journalistic venture; F. Jennie Duty, managing editor; Mrs. George A. Robertson, exchange editor—her son, Carl T., was later associate editor of the *Plain Dealer;* and Helen DeK. Townsend, society editor. The success of the undertaking eased the financial burden of the Friendly Inn social settlement for whose benefit it was created.

Norton T. Horr and E. M. Tillinghast were among Cleveland Athletic Club members who organized a duplicate-whist section in February. In 1898 the Ohio Whist Association was organized in Bucyrus, and Cleveland teams began bringing home state championships, Horr, Tillinghast, Will McClintock, and A. R. Horr proving tough competition. Others in the local team were A. W. Ellenberger, James C. Beardsley, Thomas White, James Storer, Judge Martin A. Foran, Judge Arnold Green, Howard Prescott, Arthur Halle, and Carl T. Robertson. Whist was the forerunner of auction and contract bridge.

Charles A. Otis and his schoolmate, Addison Hough, established the house of Otis, Hough & Company, an iron-and-steel commission and agency business. Beginning December 9, 1899, they dealt in stocks and bonds as Otis & Hough, purchasing the first Ohio-owned seat on the New York Stock Exchange. In 1912 the name Otis & Company was adopted. The company disposed of its brokerage business in 1931, and all of the partners except Cyrus Eaton retired from the firm. Upon reorganization, William R. Daley became president of the investment-banking concern. Otis & Company played a large part in the upbuilding of the Middle West through financing in the automotive, steel, rubber, paint, iron-ore, and other giant industries. It carried through the negotiations that resulted in acquisition of the local transit system by the City of Cleveland in 1942. It pioneered in urging the development of independent financial centers throughout the country, and greatly expanded its business through branch offices in New York, Chicago, Denver, Cincinnati, Toledo, Columbus, and Buffalo. Otis & Company's sales volume was over $200,000,000 in 1929, and its total underwritings were reported to be consistently larger than those of any other investment house outside of New York City, with the exception of one Chicago house. Cyrus Eaton became known for his manifold business activities in the fields of steel, coal, railroads, and utilities.

In the dining room of the Forest City House, Marcus A. Hanna announced the Presidential candidacy of William McKinley on March 19.

Radio was unknown, but 1,500 persons in Columbus, Ohio, enjoyed the nation's first long-distance "broadcast" on March 19, when the University School string quartet presented a unique concert as a part of the school's homecoming celebration in Cleveland. Charles Heydler, Dudley S. Blossom, Mason Hatch, and George A. Schryver played into a large trumpet attached to a transmitter in the telephone-company offices on East Superior Avenue and the event was a "pronounced and complete success."

Adelbert College Library, the gift of Mr. and Mrs. Henry Reynolds Hatch to Western Reserve University, was erected at Euclid Avenue and Adelbert Road. Its capacity of 118,000 volumes was soon inadequate, and in 1898 wings were added.

An effort was made to change the name of the Public Square and three suggestions were considered—Monument Park, Monumental Square, and Perry Square; but the public would have none of them. A commentator of the time paid tribute to the center of Cleveland in this fashion:

> Oasis in the city's heart,
> An islet in the tide;
> While men and decades both depart,
> It stays—a people's pride.

The Cleveland Architectural Club, an organization of junior architects, draftsmen, and artists in the Arcade, was now a year old. Proposed public buildings for Cleveland had created much comment, the federal, county, and city governments each planning to erect monumental structures to meet their separate needs. Inspired by the fine groups of buildings displayed at the Chicago Exposition, the club arranged a competition in March in which members competed to produce a "grouping of Cleveland's Public Buildings." Professor Charles F. Olney, one of the judges, became an enthusiastic supporter of the Group Plan idea. He was a leading member of The Cleveland Chamber of Commerce, and introduced to that body in January, 1899, a resolution providing for a Committee on Grouping Plan of Public Buildings. Prominent speakers were brought to Cleveland, and a vigorous program was launched by the club to interest the citizenship in the Group Plan advantages.

The Canal Road power plant of The Cleveland Electric Illuminating Company, completed this year, was the most modern in the world. Engineers from all parts of the nation and foreign countries came to inspect this model plant. Until construction of the Lake Shore power plant in 1911, Canal Road was the company's only electrical generating plant. In 1903 the service supplied from Canal Road was expanded to provide steam heat for near-by buildings; and, in 1906, the first distribution lines of a downtown heating system were installed. This system was extended until by 1946 it was providing steam for 660 customers in downtown Cleveland. In the early 1940s, the Canal Road plant was converted entirely to supplying steam service; in 1946, a $4,500,000 modernization program was started, giving Cleveland one of the best central steam-heating systems in the world.

Lillian Russell, one of America's most beautiful women, was featured in *The Grand Duchess* and *La Perichole* on April 20 at the Lyceum Theater.

David J. Champion, son of Irish parents who came to Cleveland in 1842, decided that better and cheaper rivets could be made from steel than from wrought iron, and the Champion Rivet Company was founded this year at what later became East 108th and Harvard Avenue. Savings of a few hundred dollars and the meager help of Champion's school-teacher wife made the company possible. Welding the understanding teamwork of the old generation with the efficiency of the new, he took to the road and sold his idea to boilermakers from coast-to-coast. A son, T. Pierre, who learned to make rivets in his father's shop, became vice president in 1930, and later president.

The young executive contended that welding would some day take its place in a fabricating machine beside riveting. Thus a flourishing business in the making of rivets and electrodes resulted.

In May, Mayor Robert E. McKisson and Wilson M. Day, president of The Cleveland Chamber of Commerce, representatives of the Early Settlers Association and civic interests, appointed a commission to direct the city's centennial celebration in 1896. Officers of the Centennial Commission were Asa S. Bushnell, honorary president; Samuel G. McClure, honorary secretary; Robert E. McKisson, president; L. E. Holden, first vice president; A. J. Williams, second vice president; Edward A. Roberts, secretary; Charles W. Chase, treasurer; Wilson M. Day, director-general. In the Women's Department were the following officers: Mrs. Mary B. Ingham, president; Mrs. Mary Scranton Bradford, Mrs. Sarah E. Bierce, Mrs. George Presley, Jr., and Mrs. Joseph Turney, vice presidents; Mrs. Ella Sturtevant Webb, recording secretary; Mrs. S. P. Churchill, corresponding secretary; Elizabeth Blair, treasurer; Elizabeth Stanton, assistant treasurer; Mrs. Gertrude V. R. Wickham, historian. Many important committees gave devoted service that contributed to the great success of the Centennial.

For years Mrs. Mary B. Ingham, head of women's activities of the Centennial, had been one of Cleveland's most useful citizens, teaching in the city schools, devoting her time to the Methodist Church, and crusading for temperance. She was a founder and trustee of the Cleveland School of Art, and took an active interest in the Daughters of the American Revolution, the Press Club, and the Northern Ohio Columbian Association, of which she was president. A flag festival and a four hundredth anniversary program relating to the discovery of America were developed by Mrs. Ingham, and were given throughout the United States. In 1893 she wrote the story of the *Women of Cleveland* and their work.

Case School of Applied Science now had an enrollment of 229 students. To keep pace with the new electrical age, the Electrical Engineering Building was erected to provide new educational opportunities. In May, Mrs. Laura Kerr Axtell of Painesville deeded to the school a one-half interest in lands that she and her late brother, Levi Kerr, had inherited from their uncle, Leonard Case, Sr. The bequest, valued at over $100,000, established a professorship of mathematics. She also made a subsequent gift of $50,000.

South Brooklyn and Cleveland were united by the Brooklyn Viaduct, built over Big Creek.

In 1890 the *Duluth* and the *Superior,* two 98-foot ferry steamers, had been built in Cleveland for service on Lake Superior. They operated until May 25, this year, when they were introduced on the Cleveland-Euclid Beach route under Cleveland ownership. The pair were affectionately called the "Euclid Beach tubs." From the Superior Avenue dock, the white boats with bright red letters appeared to be rounded like tubs as they made their way toward the resort. They carried pleasure seekers until 1901, when they were acquired by outside interests which moved them away from Cleveland waters.

A commission on public improvements, consisting of J. G. W. Cowles, Samuel Mather, Dr. W. H. Humiston, Kaufman Hays, Henry W. S. Ward, and H. M. Case, went to work on the long-neglected garbage problem; and, in 1896, the Legislature authorized the city to erect a garbage-reduction plant, to be operated by a contractor. It opened in 1898, and two years later it was remodeled, operating capacity being a hundred tons per day. Garbage-collection and disposal came under city management in 1905, when a net profit of $5,685 resulted. Cleveland was "the first . . . city in the United States, and probably in the world, to own and operate a garbage and reduction plant."

At a meeting of thirty newspapermen in the Tippecanoe Club rooms, May 31, E. W. Doty of the *World* presided, Munson Havens of the *Plain Dealer* served as secretary, and Edward B. Lilley, also of the *Plain Dealer,* offered a resolution providing for organization of a press club. Edward A. Roberts of the *Leader,* Lilley and Ralph Williams of the *Plain Dealer,* John F. McCauley and Jake Waldeck of the *Press,* and C. N. Frier of the *World* were appointed to draw up a constitution and by-laws. Among those present were Elmer Bates of the *World,* who became known as the "Little Old Man" of the *Press* sport page; Robert K. Beach, Will B. "Skippy" Colver, Tommy Hinley—chalk-plate artist, Will S. Lloyd, Eugene Walter—later a famous author and playwright, and Charles S. Shanks of the *Plain Dealer;* Russell Thompson of the *Leader;* Walter C. Kelly—sports writer and prizefight referee, Norman McLoud—dapper man-about-town, R. B. Larkin, W. L. Bloomer, and R. L. Christian of the *Press.* The Press Club of the nineties produced not only men who won journalistic fame, but others who were successful in more prosaic fields.

Horsemen passing the time on the Roadside Club veranda near the Glenville-track entrance agreed that racing their horses to four-wheeled wagons would be great sport. Thus the Gentlemen's Driving Club became a reality on June 1. Officers were H. M. Hanna, honorary president; H. K. Devereux, president; Dan R. Hanna, vice president; and F. L. Chamberlin, secretary-treasurer. On the executive committee were Devereux, M. A. Bradley, Hanna, Chamberlin, John Sherwin, Charles A. Otis, Jr., L. Dean Holden, and C. G. Barkwill. Society filled the boxes, and northern Ohio sportsmen were attracted to the track, where matinee harness racing provided many of the most brilliant events in amateur turf history. Steel tires were soon traded for bicycle wheels and greater speed, as the millionaire drivers raced their horses "for the fun of it." Soon the club became the leading association of its kind in America. Competitions with Chicago, Pittsburgh, Syracuse, Toledo, Boston, and New York brought to Cleveland the finest horseflesh in the country, and Lou Dillon, Angus Pointer, Major Delmar, Morning Star, and others hung up new records at the track. The champion trotter in 1895 was Incense, time 2:16½, owned and driven by O. G. Kent. Doc Sperry, owned by W. F. Dutton and driven by C. F. Emery, set the pacing record of 2:17½.

Cleveland voters had elected to build a new City Hall on the Public Square, and ground was broken on June 4. Mayor McKisson's workmen enclosed the two north sections with a board fence preparatory to digging the foundation. Stern opposition developed, however, demanding that another site be selected, and formal protest questioning the right of the city to use the land put a stop to the project. There was rejoicing on June 11 at news that the fence must come down. Civic-minded citizens were not interested in saving the cost of the land at the expense of trespassing upon Cleveland's historic front yard. The city administration continued to use leased quarters in the Case Block.

Sunday School children paraded to the Madison Avenue exhibition grounds where a great pageant was held in June. Twenty thousand children assembled in the amphitheater.

Methodist ministers started a campaign against "living pictures" and suggestive posters. Crusaders continued their attack on the saloon evil, and pulpits denounced the "rum power," with the slogan "The dram shop must go!" leading the campaign.

Henry P. McIntosh presided at the organization of the Colonial Club, for many years the center of society on the East Side. Intoxicating liquors were prohibited, and the club was closed on Sunday.

Forty of the city's finest musicians formed the Cleveland Orchestra on June 14, with Max Droge as director and Charles Sonntam as concertmaster. Large audiences gathered to enjoy summer afternoon concerts, and winter programs on Sunday afternoons filled Grays Armory to capacity. Praiseworthy were the foundations laid earlier by Emil Ring and Johann Beck, conductors of the Cleveland Philharmonic Orchestra, and it was hoped that one day the Cleveland Orchestra would become as well known as those of Cincinnati and Pittsburgh.

The Superior Street level, the Euclid Avenue level, and the balcony of the Arcade were transformed into a great banquet hall, and two thousand delegates of the National Convention of Republican Clubs and their friends sat down to dine on the evening of June 22. It was an exciting night, with the party favorite, Governor William McKinley of Ohio, Senator Marcus A. Hanna, and many notables in attendance. "Free silver" coined at the ratio of "Sixteen to One" was the Democratic battle-cry that stirred the blood of the Republicans, and their straightforward answer was the "full dinner pail and the gold standard." Thousands viewed the brilliant scene from the upper galleries of the Arcade.

Increasing numbers of young girls were leaving the countryside to make their way in the big city. At about this time, the YWCA established the Travelers Aid, patterned after the service that originated earlier in London. A secretary met the trains to guide girls to the "Y" boarding home for shelter. The agency joined the National Travelers Aid Society in 1919.

"The largest single source of light in the world," a huge searchlight known as a cloud projector, was being installed on the roof of the E. R. Hull & Dutton store (later May Company) on the Public Square, July 4. Carbon arcs one-half inch in diameter were mounted in the center of a 60-inch iron drum, 5½ feet long. Backed by a 30-inch reflector, a 1,500,000-candlepower beam pierced the sky and was said to be "visible for 140 miles." "The searchlight is 'primarily the invention of a Cleveland man, Lewis A. Rogers, formerly assistant manager of the Brush Electric Company and now manager of Adams-Bagnall Company,'" reported the *Plain Dealer* on the 5th. "It is the result of years of experiment and study, receiving trials from the top of Mount Washington in 1892. There it attracted considerable attention, sending Morse code messages to Portland, 70 miles away; relaying weather reports, etc. The War Department became interested in it as a message conveyor and expedited Mr. Rogers' patents." This advertising attraction focused national attention on Cleveland.

Steps were taken by the Park Commission on July 6 to acquire Cable Park from the Cleveland City Railway and add it to the park system. At the eastern end of Hough Avenue and Doan, the brook had been dammed to form a pond; and under the bluff on which the cable-car power house was located, an amphitheater had been built. Frank DeHaas Robison, head of the railway company, had built Cable Park, and colorful spectacles, such as *The Last Days of Pompeii,* were presented from its stage. The power house at Ansel Road and Hough Avenue later became a brewery.

The Cleveland & Southwestern Traction Company grew out of the dormant Cleveland & Berea Street Railway Company, chartered in 1876. It received a new charter in 1891, and opened a suburban electric line to Berea in July, 1895. A. E. Akins, A. H. Pomeroy, O. D. Pomeroy, and F. T. Pomeroy were its directors. Horsecars were rapidly giving way to observation cars and luxurious parlor cars, costing as much as $25,000.

While visiting in the East, Samuel Mather was invited to play golf on the St. Andrews Club course at Mount Hope, New York. Enthusiasm for the game led to organization of the Cleveland Golf Club, of which he became president, and R. H. Clarke, secretary. On July 14, this year, the club formally opened in Glenville, and T. S. Beckwith and J. D. Maclennin gave demonstrations on the crude links near the Country Club site. The interest of a group of young women is told by Alice D. Seagrave in *Golf Retold,* published by the Cleveland Women's Golf Association. It is believed, however, that "pasture pool" had been attempted at Dover Bay Park prior to the time that Mather introduced it to Cleveland. In 1902, the Cleveland Golf Club was consolidated with the Country Club, and enjoyed its home on the lakeshore, adjacent to the enlarged golf course. In 1930, members opened a new Country Club on Lander Road. The former clubhouse, built in 1908, became the Lake Shore Country Club restaurant.

An immense audience greeted Mark Twain in the Music Hall on the evening of July 15, when he delivered one of his famous lectures, *The Regeneration of the Race.* It was a benefit performance for the Newsboys Home, and the stage was crowded with restless youngsters. In his whimsical manner, the great humorist convulsed his listeners when he admitted that "he had passed through two-thirds of the crimes of which the race is capable, and that he hoped in a few more years to complete the list and reach the stage of perfect moral manhood." That Twain was not happy about the speaking experience is indicated in a letter written the next day to his friend, H. H. Rogers of Standard Oil: ". . . last night I suffered defeat. There were a couple of hundred little boys behind me on the stage . . . And there was nobody to watch them or keep them quiet . . . Besides, a concert of amateurs had been smuggled into the program . . . so it was 20 minutes of 9 before I got on the platform . . . I got started magnificently, but inside of half an hour the scuffling boys had the audience's maddened attention, and I saw it was a gone case. So I skipped a third of my program and quit. The newspapers are kind, but . . . there ain't going to be any more concerts at my lectures." A carbuncle added to Twain's suffering. Time most certainly deepened appreciation of the master of American humor, as young hearts grew older.

On July 22, Cleveland's ninety-ninth birthday, the City Council authorized a committee of artistic and patriotic citizens, headed by Archibald M. Willard, famous artist, to select a design for a city emblem. The idea developed when inquiring Julian Ralph, representing *Harper's Monthly,* brought up the subject of a municipal flag while visiting with his friend, Will S. Lloyd, *Plain Dealer* star reporter. Sensing a centennial-promotion feature, Lloyd approached the mayor, and soon the project was in the legislative mill.

Frank S. Barnum was appointed school architect as an era of modern school construction began. The new buildings were fireproof, with flat roofs. Space was used efficiently, and electric light and steam heat were installed. An assembly hall, gymnasium, shower baths, and adjustable seats were standard features.

A Chamber of Commerce inquiry to determine why Cleveland manufacturers were not securing more trade in the East revealed that the Erie Canal gave Buffalo an advantage in freight rates. Upon Charles E. Wheeler's proposal, steel canal boats were built to carry a cargo of streetcar rails direct to New York City, a steamer and five consorts—or barges—making the first trip in August.

Walter C. Baker had helped to build the world-famous "Electrobat" for the Chicago Exposition in 1893. It was an electric road wagon, built of tubular steel, with pneumatic-tired wheels like those of a bicycle. Its weight with batteries was 1,180 pounds, the lightest electric car ever built, and it could attain a speed of twenty miles an hour. It was the first machine equipped with anti-friction bearings. Foreseeing industrial possibilities, Baker, Rollin C. White, John J. Grant, and F. Philip Dorn organized the American Ball-Bearing Company in 1895 to make ball bearings for bicycles and the axles of automobiles and horse-drawn vehicles. The breaking of race-track speed records—trotting and pacing—was credited to the new feature on racing sulkies. In 1917 the company joined with thirteen others to form the Standard Parts Company.

Rest Cottage, located on the Rocky River estate of Mrs. Dan P. Eells (Beach Cliff), was given to the YWCA for the use of working girls. This was the pioneer girls' camp in Cleveland. Mrs. Charles Long Cutter—mother of Mrs. Dwight W. Morrow and grandmother of Mrs. Charles A. Lindbergh —was chairman of the first "camp" committee. The first gymnasium for girls opened in the "Y" this year.

Salvaged parts and determined effort under incredible difficulties resulted in invention of the first multiple-spindle, automatic screw machine this year by Edwin C. Henn and Reinhold Hakewessell in Hartford, Connecticut.

In 1896 The Acme Machine Screw Company was founded to build machines for the making of screw products. It has been said that these machines accelerated American mass-production methods, producing, automatically, identical parts in large quantities. On a journey to Cleveland, Henn had inspired his brother, Albert W., a bookkeeper, to put his savings into the project. The business had struggled for several years, when A. W. finally secured an order for twenty Acme machines from W. D. B. Alexander, president of the National Screw & Tack Company of Cleveland. Organized as the National Manufacturing Company, the machines went to work, the Hartford company taking part payment in National stock. In 1901 the Hartford plant moved to Cleveland (7500 Stanton Avenue), and The National Acme Manufacturing Company (later The National Acme Company) was formed, with Alexander, president; E. C. Henn, vice president and general superintendent; A. W. Henn, secretary; and O. S. Werntz, treasurer.

Henry Chisholm's mansion, the last of the fine residences in the block that stretched eastward from Bond to Erie Street, was razed to make way for the New England Building (later Guardian Building) that opened this year. The fourteen-story, sandstone office building, towering above its neighbor, the new Garfield Building, was designed by Charles F. Schweinfurth. E. I. Baldwin, Hatch & Company moved their stock of fine merchandise into the western store, and Burrows Brothers leased the eastern space in 1897. Professional men and leading architects became tenants— Schweinfurth, the firm of Coburn, Barnum, Benes & Hubbell, Fenimore C. Bates, F. S. Barnum & Company, Steffins & Searles, and others in the Cleveland Architectural Club.

While appearing at the Lyceum Theater in September, Keller, the great magician, told a newspaperman how his career started in Cleveland. He was a poor boy who worked in the printing plant of a local newspaper, and the huge rolls of paper were often his bed at night. One day he read an advertisement of a magician who wanted to employ a boy. At the wizard's boarding house a huge dog approached the lad, wagging a friendly tail. When the door opened, a precise greeting settled the matter, "Boy, you're hired!" Young Keller learned later that many boys had applied, but the dog barked at each of them. "I like animals," said the magician, "and I like the people that animals like."

The Cleveland Yacht Club was established in its new three-story clubhouse, built on piles at the shoreline just east of the Erie Street pier.

The second convention of the International Deep Waterways Association assembled in Cleveland on September 24 in Army and Navy Hall. Organizer Thomas H. Canfield, of Burlington, Vermont, builder of railroads, portrayed in a forceful address the increasing need for improved transportation facilities, and pleaded for a Great-Lakes-to-the-Sea waterway. Cleveland participants in the three-day assembly were Luther Allen of the Maritime Board, William Livingstone of the Lake Carriers Association, Harvey D. Goulder, and Charles E. Wheeler. Delegates departed with high hopes for early success of the project, which over a half century later had not materialized.

Cleveland won first place in the pennant race and was awarded the Temple Cup, having defeated the Baltimore Orioles, who held second place in the National League. Cy Young, masterful pitcher, was on the mound for Cleveland. In the decisive inning, on October 12, with Tebeau on third, Chief Zimmer drove a home run that won the game. It was reported that the Cleveland players collected $500 each as their share of the proceeds. Zimmer, a remarkable catcher, was the fans' hero. In a game with Washington on July 11, 1894, he made six hits in six times at bat, including three doubles. On Bunker Hill Day, June 17, 1895, Zimmer stunned the Bostonians with four hits in four times at bat, including two home runs, the last with the bases loaded! When a close game needed breaking up, the "chief" generally produced the thriller. Cy Young finished the season with thirty-five victories and ten defeats for a percentage of .778. Cleveland took second-place honors at the close of the 1896 season, its quartet of pitchers, Young, Cuppy, Wilson, and Wallace, each chalking up victories of .600 per cent or more.

The Cleveland Chamber of Commerce was a center of activity, with more than eleven hundred members, and badly in need of a home of its own. A building fund had been started in 1894 by President Luther Allen, banker, manufacturer, and railroad executive, one of the most useful citizens of his time. On October 22, 1895, the Chamber purchased as a building site the Public Square property of the Western Reserve Historical Society for $55,000 and a lot at Euclid and Fairmount Street, and acquired from the Society for Savings the land on which the Historical Society building stood (eastward to East 2nd Street).

Mayor McKisson's street department completed the "locating" of Bank and Water street extensions to the lake north of the railroad tracks, paving the way for further controversy with the railroads over disputed title to the ground.

The Akron, Bedford & Cleveland Railway Company, chartered in November, 1894, ran its first car on October 26, 1895, on the 27½-mile road from Akron through Cuyahoga Falls to Newburgh, where it connected with the Cleveland Electric Railway. This was Ohio's pioneer interurban traction line. Fare was a dollar for the round trip. Officers of the road were Henry A. Everett, president; F. S. Borton, secretary; and E. W. Moore, treasurer. Conservatives bought heavily of traction stocks, and were content with small but "certain dividends." A consolidation with the Akron Traction & Electric Company, which operated the Akron street-railway and light plant, resulted in a new company in 1899, headed by Everett, operating 60 miles of track. Reorganization as the Northern Ohio Traction & Light Company came in 1902, when several Akron and Canton lines were acquired, expanding trackage to a 214-mile interurban system connecting Cleveland with Canton, Kent, Ravenna, and Barberton.

On October 31 it was announced by the City Council flag committee that eighteen-year-old Susie Hepburn, graduate of the Cleveland School of Art, had submitted the best-suited design for a Cleveland flag, thereby winning the fifty-dollar prize awarded by the *Plain Dealer*. Curiously, she was a descendant of Seth Pease of Moses Cleaveland's pioneer surveying party, and her great-grandfather, Morris Hepburn, was a member of Cleveland's first City Council. The new flag featured the word "Cleveland" by dividing a shield mounted on a wide, white, perpendicular panel separating the red from the blue. In the upper left-hand corner of the shield were a hammer, anvil, and wheel, representing manufacturing; opposite were an anchor, windlass, and oars, typifying marine interests. In the lower portion was a laurel wreath with the founding date, 1796. A young *Plain Dealer* reporter named Robert K. Beach delivered the prize to the winner at her home in Columbus, Ohio. This chance meeting touched off romance, and the name of Cleveland's Betsy Ross was eventually changed to Beach.

The Mohawk Building was erected on the northwest side of the Public Square, replacing the Lemen and Perkins blocks that had occupied the site since 1881. In 1900 the American Trust Company purchased the brick building and called it the American Trust Building. Twenty years later, the Ulmer interests acquired it, naming it the Ulmer Building. Early in the 1930s, it took a new name, Public Square Building, capitalizing upon its central location.

A streetcar on the Cedar-Jennings line of the "Big Consolidated" system plunged through the open draw of the Central Viaduct into the river, one hundred feet below, on November 16, and seventeen persons perished.

Prominent in the life of the city were Charles P. Gilchrist, vessel owner and shipping agent; Joseph Carabelli, monument manufacturer; John W. Walton, founder of The Upson-Walton Company, student of sociology and donor of educational books to the Public Library; John H. Webster, lawyer and industrialist; General Jared A. Smith, who improved rivers and harbors of Cleveland and other lake cities, introducing new and advanced construction methods; George C. Groll, artist and businessman; Willis B. Hale, banker and realtor; John C. Hutchins, lawyer and jurist; Albert R. Teachout, dealer in building materials; and George W. Benedict, wholesale merchant who became senior partner of Benedict & Rudy, furriers.

The Cleveland & Elyria Electric Railway, chartered in 1894, opened a seventeen-mile road in December. In 1897 a consolidation of lines into the Cleveland, Berea, Elyria & Oberlin Railway Company was effected, with A. H. Pomeroy, president. Subsequent mergers resulted in extended interurban lines.

Milk was selling for six cents a quart at the consumer's doorstep, dipped fresh from the farmer's big ten-gallon cans. With the introduction of bottled milk, young William E. Telling needed more capital than his small one-man route afforded to meet competition. With his brother, Charles, he opened a confectionery store opposite Lake View Cemetery, making ice cream in the basement. On December 12, 1895, the Telling Brothers Company was incorporated with William E. as president. A brother, John, took charge of the store, and in 1897 the Tellings established Cleveland's first commercial ice-cream plant, on Willson Avenue near Euclid. With three ten-gallon freezers and a gasoline engine they could produce a thousand gallons daily. In the meantime, the Belle Vernon Dairy Farms Company, founded in 1897 with J. A. Beidler, president, had acquired a number of city dairy firms, moving to 5812 Euclid after the turn of the century. The two companies were closely related, occupying small adjoining storerooms and sharing conveniences on Willson Avenue, and were destined to merge as The Telling-Belle Vernon Company.

Woman, her right to independence and her behavior in society, had been censured from the pulpit and the lecture platform, and social circles were indignant. Tempers were soothed, however, on December 18 when the Rev. Thomas DeWitt Talmage, famous preacher, lectured in Music Hall. He was asked to comment on "the new woman," then emerging from "her place in the home" and casting off style traditions. Said the good clergyman, "The new woman will be the same as the old woman, only younger . . . Woman is a poem, whether clad in the poesy of lace or in the blank verse of bloomers."

Centennial spirit may have prompted a meeting on December 21 of Cleveland's New Englanders at Plymouth Congregational Church. At any rate, speeches by Dr. Charles F. Thwing, H. Q. Sargent, Nelson B. Sherwin, M. M. Hobart, F. J. Dickman, and R. C. Parsons; reminiscences by old-timers; and songs by "Grandfather" Snow and "Grandma" Hawley resulted in cementing the move to revive the New England Society of Cleveland and the Western Reserve. Albert G. Colwell had been elected president of the revitalized society in 1894, and Nelson B. Sherwin succeeded him in 1896. Lucius F. Mellen served as secretary, 1894-1910. He was succeeded by Leon B. Bacon, William T. Higbee, and Karl O. Thompson. A half century later, when Frank M. Baker was president, the society continued to carry reverently the torch brought to the wilderness by New England pioneers.

Lands of the Shaker Society, totaling 1,366 acres, had been purchased by a realty company for $316,000 in 1892. A vast level stretch of 278 acres, including the Shaker lakes, was donated to the city this year by the Shaker Heights Land Company for Shaker Heights Park, another link in the Greater Cleveland park chain.

The year 1895 marked the establishment of business firms that were in existence in the 1940s: City Blue Printing Company, Garland Company, Harris-Seybold Company, Mouat Vapor Heating Company, Ohio Provision Company, Vlchek Tool Company.

1896

Samuel T. Wellman, his brother, Charles H., and John W. Seaver organized The Wellman-Seaver Engineering Company this year. The founders were well-known engineers, and Wellman was the inventor of the revolutionary open-hearth charging machine. A large business developed in the designing and building of industrial plants in the United States and foreign countries, amplified by the manufacturing of steel-mill equipment. The Hulett unloader, a mechanical giant invented by George H. Hulett, early vice president, was an exclusive Wellman development that revolutionized

John D. Rockefeller's Forest Hills home.

Home of Henry B. Payne, Euclid Avenue at East 21st Street.

The famous Perry house, 2157 Euclid Avenue, built in 1824.

Home of William G. Mather, 12407 Lake Shore Boulevard.

Group of American Press Humorists at Rockefeller's Forest Hills home. Rockefeller in white coat is in the center of the picture; fifth from left wearing cap is Mayor Tom L. Johnson and next to the right is Dr. Hamilton F. Biggar, the Rockefeller family physician.

Right:
John Davison
Rockefeller.
GEORGE M. ED-
MONDSON.

Left:
Charles Francis
Brush. FRANK
MOORE STUDIO.

Dr. Brush, center, with fellow scientists, Dr. Elihu Thomson, Dr. Frank J. Sprague, Dr. Elmer A. Sperry, and Dr. Edwin W. Rice, Jr.

the transportation end of the ore industry on the lakes. In 1901 construction of a plant on Central Avenue (at East 71st Street) began, to which the large downtown offices were moved. Thomas R. Morgan, Jr., joined the firm, and The Wellman-Seaver-Morgan Company was incorporated in 1903, with Wellman, president. The Webster, Camp & Lane Company of Akron, founded in 1848, was acquired this year. Willard N. Sawyer became president in 1906 when Wellman retired, and he was succeeded in 1917 by Edwin S. Church. George W. Burrell, who rose from the ranks, became president in 1928. The Wellman Engineering Company became the corporate name in 1930; and the next year, the G. H. Williams Company of Erie was acquired, adding "Williams" excavating buckets to the Wellman line. Burrell became chairman of the board in 1937, and Alfred E. Gibson was elected president. In the 1940s the company was building furnaces and charging machines, gas producers, and steel-plant and ore-handling equipment. Inventions of Wellman engineers were widely used in the steel, glass, ceramic, chemical, mining, and aviation industries, as well as in power plants and railway terminals.

A mission, started in 1894 at Euclid and Windermere Street in the thriving Collamer community (East Cleveland), grew in stature; and on January 5, this year, the Windermere Presbyterian Church was organized with thirty members. The first elders were Charles H. Fuller, William C. McEwen, and Henry A. Taylor. The Rev. C. L. Zorbaugh, the first pastor, also served the Glenville congregation. In 1906 a building was dedicated debt-free. The Rev. Tracy R. Spencer became pastor of the Windermere Church in 1944, succeeding the Rev. Thomas D. Ewing, and served one of the most important communities in the Cleveland Presbytery.

The City Council passed a resolution to extend Erie Street northward to the dock line of deep water in Lake Erie, and authorized the director of public works to prepare plans accordingly. Negotiations for lakefront development were kept alive by the steamship companies until 1913, when practical progress was made.

On a bitter-cold Saturday night, January 25, the steamer from No. 2 fire house slid out on the icy street to answer an alarm. Two horses pulled the engine and the four-man crew. The Seneca Street drawbridge had been opened to permit the fireboat to reach the scene, and into the black waters plunged the horses and two firemen who were unable to leap to safety. The men were rescued, but the horses perished.

The first high-school branch of the Public Library opened in Central High School.

Anna Perkins, pioneer woman newsboy, shouted each edition of the *Press* from the southeast corner of the Public Square and Ontario Street. Dressed in a white cotton coat, white stockings, and knee trousers, she announced the news in a cracked, high-pitched voice. Besides writing poetry, she gave occasional talks; yet mystery shrouded her, and she lived alone in a dingy room on Detroit Street. "Popcorn Charley" Lewis strolled around the Square, selling his wares from a basket.

An ordinance adopting the city flag was passed by the City Council on

February 24 after more than two months of controversy. Veterans' organizations protested the need of a municipal flag, one body contending "such action to be un-American and calculated to detract from the one and only flag which we, as citizens, soldiers and true Americans, delight to honor." It mattered little that New York City had recently adopted a flag, and Buffalo and Cincinnati were discussing the question. As an appeasement measure, the word "flag" was changed to "banner" in the ordinance, and a clause was added prohibiting use of the emblem for commercial purposes under heavy penalty. While the controversy seethed, a good-will delegation of The Chamber of Commerce unfurled the Cleveland flag for the first time at the Atlanta Exposition on November 11, 1895.

The New Idea Dairy Lunch on Bond Street was the original restaurant of the Clark chain, opened by J. B. L. Clark this year. The founder's sons joined in the enterprise. One by one new locations were added, and in 1919 quarters were established for a bakery and meat department. In the late 1920s table service was provided with more luxurious settings, as women were dining out in increasing numbers. Modern improvements met the trend of the times; and by 1946, more than ten million guests had been served at Clark's in Cleveland, Akron, and Erie. The three sons of the founder, S. A., R. D., and A. Y., were proprietors of the chain.

As early as 1887 there had been agitation for reduced streetcar fares, Alderman R. J. Cooney having introduced an ordinance advocating six tickets for twenty-five cents. Henry A. Everett's effort in the winter of 1896 to secure a franchise to build three-cent lines was followed by an ordinance fathered by Councilman William R. Hopkins the next fall to reduce Woodland Avenue fares from five to four cents at stated hours, and to three cents during other hours of the day. Under Mayor Tom L. Johnson's regime, the controversy reached a climax.

A new six-hundred-foot dock had been erected on the lakefront east of the river, ready for the navigation season. On it was mounted a car dumper designed and built by the McMyler Manufacturing Company for the Cuddy-Mullen Coal Company. The dumper elevated a railroad car and turned it over sidewise, dumping the coal into an apron from which it ran into the ship. The machine continued in use for many years. Three coal companies on the Pennsylvania railroad also erected a car dumper, designed by Alexander E. Brown, on Whisky Island this year. A railroad car was run into a cylinder, and its contents emptied into six buckets that were picked up and lowered into the vessel hold. Upon formation of the Pittsburgh Coal Company, the machine was shipped to Toledo.

Harbor improvements estimated at $1,354,000 were authorized by Congress, including extending and completing the east breakwater, rebuilding the west seawall and the old piers, and widening the river mouth. A hundred-foot channel was opened from the old riverbed to the lake by the Lake Shore & Michigan Southern Railroad.

Newburgh citizens wanted a public park, but could not agree on a site. Finally, the commissioners selected a location a half mile from the city limits. Here they purchased the Dunham, Rittberger, and Carter farms, totaling about 156 acres, for $32,229.64. In addition, 19 acres of pasture land were purchased from the Cleveland State Hospital for Newburgh Park, called Garfield Park in 1897.

Under the auspices of the Cleveland Wheel Club, the Civic League of Cleveland Wheelmen was formed, which promoted races and meets. The Van Sweringen boys had a bicycle shop on Bond Street, and Leonard P. Ayres was riding in the national matches.

A $4,000 legacy, designated to found a Lutheran charity, gave Lutheran Hospital its start, when organization was effected by the Evangelical Lutheran churches of Cleveland in May. For two years, it operated in a dwelling on Franklin Circle. It was then moved to the former residence of Marcus A. Hanna (2609 Franklin Boulevard). A new building was dedicated on the site in 1922. The adjoining former home of R. R. Rhodes was purchased in 1928 as a nurses' home, and later converted into an Episcopal orphanage. A new building was erected in 1937 for the nurses' home. The School of Nursing was founded in 1902.

Popularity of Cleveland parks was measured on May 10 along the upper drive of Doan parkway. A count showed that 5,918 carriages contained 14,873 occupants; 14,690 people rode bicycles, and 14,152 were enjoying themselves on foot—a total of 43,715.

Alexander Winton's Euclid Avenue neighbors were relieved when night after night of noisy experimentation in his back yard produced a snorting, horseless carriage that really ran. Those who prized life and limb declined Winton's invitation to share a ride in the first Cleveland-built automobile, a gasoline-powered, single-cylinder model with bicycle-style wheels. It accommodated six passengers—three facing forward and three backward.

For several years, The Ball Bearing Car Wheel & Manufacturing Company on Wason Street had been producing a small volume of industrial cars, but capital was limited and progress was slow. Bolts, screws, and related products were in more general demand, and when the company turned to this line in 1896, its name was changed to The Atlas Bolt & Screw Company. The manufacture of cars continued under the trade name, The Atlas Car & Manufacturing Company, owned by the older firm. A plant erected on Marquette Road, north of St. Clair, soon proved inadequate, and the car shop was moved to property purchased on Lakeside near Marquette. The company grew rapidly, and, in 1912, the car department was established in new buildings on a six-acre tract at 1100 Ivanhoe Road. Plant capacity was increased, and the bolt business was moved in 1917. Electric locomotives, cars, storage-battery locomotives, storage-battery trucks, tractors, and special cars and equipment were being produced in the 1940s; output of the bolt company included a wide range of bolt and screw products. J. Edward Weit became president in 1940, succeeding S. D. Wright.

Coffee and doughnuts for a nickel, a glass of beer with every pool game, and the latest songs ground out on the tinny piano typified "Dutch" Henry's on Bank Street. The genial, bearded host was a favorite with newspapermen.

The Cleveland Society of the Archaeological Institute of America was organized this year. Dan P. Eells was president for many years, and prominent members included James J. Tracy, Dr. Henry K. Cushing, Samuel Mather, Dr. Charles F. Thwing, F. F. Prentiss, and Charles F. Brush. On the Cleveland society's golden jubilee, Dr. Sterling Dow of Harvard University, president of the national institute, described the local organization as "one of the half-dozen learned societies in the country."

Andrew Squire, eminent lawyer, built a pillared, colonial mansion on "Millionaires' Row" (3443 Euclid) to which he brought his bride. It was designed for luxurious living, with a large library to house Squire's many books, a recreation room where he played billiards with his friends, a wine cellar, and a gymnasium for his wife. The Squire home was a center of culture and hospitality, and William Howard Taft visited here. When the Squire estate was settled, the twenty-seven-room mansion was made available to the local Red Cross in 1938 by Western Reserve University, a major beneficiary under the wills of Mr. and Mrs. Squire.

Conrad Mizer, a custom tailor who loved music, started a movement this year to present band concerts in the parks on Sunday afternoons. A monument to his memory was erected in Edgewater Park.

Violence and disorder resulted during a strike in the summer at the plant of The Brown Hoisting and Conveying Machine Company. It lasted for several months, and troops were required to preserve order.

July 4 marked the opening of the Cleveland, Painesville & Eastern Railway, incorporated in 1895, operating nineteen miles of track from East Cleveland to Painesville. In 1898 the Willoughby-Cleveland "Shore Line" was inaugurated. The Cleveland, Painesville & Ashtabula Railway Company opened a line in 1903 connecting with the former road, and in 1909 the interurban lines consolidated.

An investigation of social conditions in Cleveland was made as a practical application of Bible-class discussion in Hiram College, Hiram, Ohio. A crying need for social service was reported, and George A. Bellamy and fellow students volunteered, without financial aid, to try to establish Hiram House. Bellamy headed the project, and in July, this year, Cleveland's first social settlement opened temporarily in a house at Hanover and Washington streets (Lake View Terrace site). Eight settlements were operating in the nation, and this was the first in Ohio. In October, 141 Orange Street was selected as a central location. Here Bellamy began his activity with foreign groups, "people of hardy natures, possessed of self-reliance, cultural yearnings and love of freedom." A community center was established for young and old, and the end of the first year saw him $500 in arrears of his small earnings from other pursuits. Missionary help came from the Ohio Disciples Church, Judge Henry C. White, and interested Clevelanders that enabled Bellamy to advance his plans.

On Sunday morning, July 19, Cleveland's One Hundredth Anniversary celebration opened officially with the Trinity Cathedral chimes. Morning and evening centennial services were held in the churches. J. G. W. Cowles opened a great mass meeting in the Central Armory in the afternoon, where prayer was offered by the Rt. Rev. William A. Leonard, followed by addresses by the Rev. Levi Gilbert for the Protestant churches, Msgr. T. P. Thorpe for the Catholic church, and Rabbi Moses J. Gries for the Jewish faith. The Cleveland Vocal Society sang the chorus from *Elijah*. German Lutherans gathered in the Music Hall, where the Rev. Paul Schwan presided over the program conducted almost entirely in German. In the evening, German Protestants held a mass meeting in the Central Armory.

Encampment of the Ohio National Guard and the United States troops was opened on the Jacob B. Perkins farm, west of the city, and dedication of Camp Moses Cleaveland took place on July 20 in a drizzling rain that swelled to a downpour. Liberty E. Holden, of the Centennial Commission, introduced Mayor McKisson, who presented the encampment to Governor Asa S. Bushnell of Ohio in the presence of his staff and distinguished citizens. The opening of the centennial exhibition of the Cleveland School of Art also marked the day.

A log cabin, fashioned after pioneer architecture, built under the direction of Bolivar Butts and "Father" Addison on the northeast section of the Public Square, was dedicated at a centennial celebration on the afternoon of July 21. Richard C. Parsons was chairman of the day, and tributes were paid to the generations that had laid the city's foundations. Women of the Early Settlers Association held a reception at the cabin. The evening feature was a concert in Central Armory, and a historical musical spectacle, "Battles of Our Nation," depicting a hundred years of military history.

At midnight, one hundred guns fired by the Cleveland Light Artillery (Battery A) thundered the close of Cleveland's first century and announced Founder's Day, July 22. The principal event was a mass meeting in the Central Armory in the morning, in which Old Connecticut and New Connecticut joined in celebrating the Centennial. James H. Hoyt, chairman, prefaced his remarks by reading a message from the President of the United States. Prayer was offered by Rev. Charles S. Mills. James R. Hawley, Connecticut senator, delivered the principal address, which was followed by the reading of the centennial ode, written by John J. Piatt, the poet. Governor O. Vincent Coffin brought greetings from Connecticut. Here the program was interrupted to permit J. G. W. Cowles, president of The Cleveland Chamber of Commerce, to announce a generous gift of $300,000 in cash by John D. Rockefeller that would make possible completion of the boulevard between Wade Park and the Shaker Heights Park. In addition, Rockefeller had deeded to Cleveland 276 acres of Doan Brook land, valued at $270,000, that became Rockefeller Park, thus completing a seven-mile chain of picturesque lands for public enjoyment.

Resuming the Founder's Day centennial program, Governor Bushnell of Ohio extended a welcome. Prolonged applause greeted Major William McKinley, who praised the pioneers and Cleveland's great achievement. John Sherman, Ohio senator, was introduced amid cheers. The exercises closed with a benediction pronounced by the Rev. Samuel P. Sprecher. Criticism that the committee did not invite William Jennings Bryan, Democratic nominee for President, brought a quick reply from Director Day to the effect that the celebration was not a political side-show. McKinley, he declared, was the city's guest as former governor of Ohio and not as a

Presidential candidate. Rain fell in the morning, but the sun came through as the grand parade formed in the afternoon, Colonel J. J. Sullivan, chief marshal, leading the procession. At 8:15 P.M., President Grover Cleveland, in his home at Buzzard's Bay, Massachusetts, touched the button that illuminated the monumental Centennial Arch on the Public Square amid the cheers of thousands. Then followed a great historical float-parade, "The Passing of the Century." Founder's Day reached a brilliant conclusion with a reception and ball in the Grays Armory.

July 23 was New England Day. Five hundred guests enjoyed a typical New England dinner, given under the auspices of the New England Society of Cleveland and the Western Reserve, in large tents on the Adelbert College campus. N. B. Sherwin, president, presided over the meeting that followed, and there were brief addresses relating to New England and its prodigious offspring. After an early meeting at the Hollenden Hotel, Ohio editors were entertained with a lake trip on the *City of Buffalo,* a trolley ride around the city, dinner on the Adelbert campus, a tally-ho ride through Wade and Gordon parks, and a reception at the Artemus Ward Club. The centennial opera, *From Moses to McKisson,* written by W. R. Rose, was presented by the Gatling Gun Battery in the Euclid Avenue Opera House to a large audience in the evening.

Cleveland on wheels—that was Wheelmen's Day, July 27. Nine divisions of bicycle riders turned out on the eight-mile parade route from Wade Park to the Public Square and back to Willson Avenue. Gay decorations, flying colors, and grotesque, imaginative creatures never before seen on bicycles characterized the centennial event, of which Carlos M. Stone was grand marshal, and J. E. Cheesman, chief of staff. In the evening, the German, Bohemian, and Swiss societies united in spectacular gymnastic and athletic exhibitions in Central Armory.

The centennial celebration of Women's Day, July 28, was marked by educational and cultural features. Mrs. Mary B. Ingham, president of the Women's Department of the Centennial Commission, presided at a morning gathering in the Central Armory, where papers and discussions emphasized philanthropy and themes relating to the home. In the afternoon, attention centered on women's clubs, with Mrs. Elroy M. Avery presiding. An inspiring centennial ode was read by Hanna Foster, the author, and the venerable Truman P. Handy offered a few words of wisdom. Following a reception at Grays Armory, an elaborate banquet was served in the drill room.

Early Settlers Day, a centennial event held on July 29, was devoted to the annual meeting of the Early Settlers Association. Richard C. Parsons, president, traced the history of Ohio and the Western Reserve, and leading citizens praised the founders. "Father" Addison entertained with his violin at the log cabin on the Public Square in the afternoon.

Western Reserve Day, July 30, dedicated to the pioneers, brought participants from the entire Reserve. This centennial event centered in a colorful parade of the military, floats depicting a century of progress, and exhibitions of early-day life. Max Faetkenheuer's Centennial Band entertained with an evening concert in the Public Square.

On August 5 it was announced that Patrick Calhoun had given a strip of Euclid Avenue land to the city for park purposes. Case School of Applied Science and Jeptha H. Wade had also given portions of property, making possible the development of the new boulevard through Rockefeller Park near its junction with Euclid Avenue. University Circle thus came into being as the beautiful entrance to the park system, and it was planted with traditional college elms.

The Centennial Yacht Regatta, sponsored by the Centennial Commission and the Cleveland Yacht Club, continued August 10-13. The lakeshore was crowded with observers who enjoyed the thrilling demonstrations.

The Council passed an ordinance on August 12 prohibiting factories, mills, and railways from filling the air with dense smoke.

A beautiful Centennial Floral Exhibition opened on August 18 for a three-day showing in the Central Armory. It was held under the auspices of the Centennial Commission, the Cleveland Florists Club, and the Society of American Florists.

A city of tents had been set up in "Payne's Pastures" along Payne Avenue, east of Hazard Street, as temporary shelter for eight thousand members of the Uniform Rank, Knights of Pythias. Known as Camp Perry-Payne, it continued from August 22 to 29. Knights came from all parts of the nation to participate in a wide variety of events, highlighted on the 25th by the most imposing parade in the history of the order.

In an intense Presidential campaign, Ohio's William McKinley, backed and counseled by Marcus A. Hanna of Cleveland, opposed William Jennings Bryan, Democrat, the principal issues being protective tariffs and free coinage of silver. Bryan's famous declaration, "You shall not crucify mankind on a cross of gold!", brought a "tremendous crush of people to see the daring orator" when he spoke from the Hollenden balcony and in the Central Armory on August 31. Touring Union generals, industrial torchlight parades, journeys to Canton, Ohio, and oratorical exhibitions on the Public Square marked the Cleveland campaign. From his home in Canton, McKinley conducted his political operations, giving "front-porch" addresses to visiting delegations.

The extent of service in the Public Library is shown in the annual report dated August 31. On the shelves were 96,921 books; 595,169 volumes had been borrowed from the main library and its three branches, Pearl Street, Miles Avenue, and Woodland Avenue, and thirty-seven workers were employed.

The Cleveland Home for Aged Colored People was incorporated on September 1.

A series of historical conferences devoted to discussions of education, religion, and philanthropy opened on September 7 as a feature of the centennial program. Two days were devoted to education at meetings over which Dr. Charles F. Thwing, president of Western Reserve University, presided. Notable contributions on this theme were made by Linda T. Guilford, L. H. Jones, superintendent of schools, and Professor B. A. Hinsdale of the University of Michigan and former head of the Cleveland schools.

Msgr. T. P. Thorpe reviewed the work of the parochial schools, and the Rev. Levi Gilbert, pastor of the First Methodist Episcopal Church, stirred his audience with an eloquent address on character building. Dr. Thwing discussed the development of higher education, and Dr. Jeremiah Smith of the Harvard University Law School closed the two-day educational section with a discussion of the special requirements for the profession of law. The several denominations were represented in the sections of religion and philanthropy on the third and last day. L. F. Mellen traced the history of Cleveland charities, Dr. C. F. Dutton spoke on the relationship between riches and poverty, and the remarks of Rabbi Moses J. Gries related to organized philanthropy.

At daybreak on September 10, a national salute brought return fire from the guns of the *U. S. S. Michigan,* anchored in the Cleveland harbor. This was Perry's Victory Day, commemorating the historic battle of Lake Erie, and the crowning event in Cleveland's Centennial celebration. Great crowds poured into the city. Governor Asa S. Bushnell presided over a mass meeting in the Central Armory at which descendants of Perry's men were guests. The principal address was made by Governor Charles Warren Lippitt of Rhode Island, Perry's native state. A resolution was then adopted petitioning Congress and the Ohio Legislature to erect a suitable memorial "over the long-neglected graves of the patriotic American soldiers and sailors" who died in battle. This ultimately came to pass at Put-in-Bay, Ohio. A great industrial and military parade in the afternoon continued until nightfall. Spectators hurried to the lakeshore to see the Battle of Lake Erie fought in mimic warfare in the evening, and a confusing and disappointing situation developed when the eastern fireworks managers, who operated on eastern time, touched off the sky show almost an hour early. A banquet, arranged by the Centennial Commission at the Hollenden in the evening, honored the city's distinguished guests. Mayor McKisson's remarks concluded an evening of sparkling oratory; and rapping on the table with a gavel, the city's chief executive declared Cleveland's Centennial Celebration officially at an end.

Western Reserve University and Baldwin University (later Baldwin-Wallace College) clashed in the first of their traditional meetings between the Red Cats and the Yellow Jackets on the gridiron, October 3, at Berea. Reserve had been playing Michigan and Cornell, and the local game was rated as practice. There was no grandstand, and several thousand fans strained on the ropes as Reserve was held to one touchdown in the first half. This was the day of the forward-passless game, when a touchdown counted four points, and kick after touchdown, two; so the big-town team's winning score of 16-0 wrested from Baldwin, in its first game of the season, was not impressive. On Coach C. O. Jenkins' Reserve team were Dick Gaylord, captain, Francis Collins, Theodore Egbert—who scored the winning touchdowns in the contest, Allan E. Goodhue, Allan H. MacDonald, Allen Carpenter, Harry Ammon, Edward Lane, John D. Gilchrist, George H. Sampson, John Kramer, Walter McMahon, Frederick Becker, George Clisby, George Thompson, and Arthur H. Bill. On the Baldwin varsity were W. R.

Reed, captain, John Jones, A. C. Hoak, Jerry LeDuke, J. D. Watson, C. D. Castle, Frank Smith, F. Lowe, J. L. Bowen, Joe Akins, Frank Bohn, David Jones, Ora Shoop, Glenn Watson, Charles Akins, and George Underhill. This season also witnessed the first football game between Case and Baldwin University, the Scientists losing, 4-0.

Bottled waters were in demand, as water from the crib in the lake was spurned by many as unsafe and not palatable. Sanitation and improved water facilities received expert attention, however, when a special committee consisting of Samuel Mather, Charles F. Brush, L. E. Holden, and Wilson M. Day, urged prompt action in the construction of a modern water-supply system that would be adequate to meet Cleveland's rapid growth and expansion. On October 8, work was begun on the Kirtland tunnel, one of the largest water-intake tubes in the world.

Free kindergartens were opened in the Cleveland schools during the year 1896-97, and within a year eleven were operating in the system. A new state law permitted the election of women to the Cleveland school council, and Catherine H. T. Avery—Mrs. Elroy M. Avery—became the first woman to hold an elective office in Ohio.

The champion trotter of the Gentlemen's Driving Club for the season was Eloise, 2:16¼, owned by W. B. Fasig and driven by Harry K. Devereux. William J. White owned the champion pacer, Prussia Girl, 2:16½, driven by W. B. White. Devereux lived in an impressive residence that had been erected by Julius E. French. It ultimately became the home of the Family Health Association, 2525 Euclid Avenue.

While the people understood little of the weighty monetary discussions in the Presidential campaign, McKinley's slogans, "A full dinner pail" and "Cash on the barrelhead," helped to produce a victory of 271 to 176 electoral votes, the first popular majority since 1872. When it became certain that Bryan had failed to run up a victorious total, the local Tippecanoe Club chartered a train and journeyed to Canton, where it became the first delegation to congratulate their standard-bearer. While Marcus A. Hanna could have had a cabinet post for the asking, he chose to succeed Senator John Sherman, who became Secretary of State.

A bridge-building record was established late in the year, when City Hall planning and strategy erected a bridge in a night! A dispute had arisen between city officials and representatives of the Lake Shore and Pennsylvania railroads as to the right of the city to fill in the lakefront and make land opposite old Lake View Park. The project was stymied, and the Council and Mayor McKisson decided to take matters into their own hands. Step by step they maneuvered, to have timbers, engineers, and workmen from the street department on the spot at the right time, awaiting the signal for action. At ten o'clock at night they went to work; and at dawn the next morning a new bridge spanned the tracks at the foot of Bank Street, permitting access to the "new" land north of the railroad right-of-way.

Having gained his electrical-engineering experience in the pioneering Brush shops, J. C. Lincoln organized the Lincoln Electric Company this year. In one room of a building at Frankfort and Seneca streets, a boy helped him to manufacture electric motors. The company outgrew its quarters and, in 1908, moved to a new building at the corner of East 38th Street and Kelley Avenue. A younger brother, James F., joined the concern in 1907. Lincoln Electric pioneered in the arc-welding industry. The variable-voltage, single-operator-type generator, introduced in 1915, radically changed the existing equipment. The "Fleetweld" electrode, which gave to the world shielded arc welding in 1929, opened unlimited fields for the use of welding. The unusual production record of the Lincoln Electric Company was attributed largely to the philosophy of James F. Lincoln, president and general manager, who succeeded his brother. An advisory board formed in 1914, comprised of workers, foremen, and management, was created to develop employee abilities, unify company effort, and act as the board of directors. Production increased steadily through more efficient operation, inspired by the suggestion system and the incentive wage, thus reducing prices, increasing markets, and benefiting Lincoln workers by raising their standard of living. In 1923 the Lincoln Electric Company moved to 12818 Coit Road, where it expanded continuously as a leader in the manufacture of arc-welding equipment. Factories were opened in England, Australia, and Canada.

"Hundreds of incandescent lamps" added to the splendor of the Colonial Club's new $50,000 home (9104 Euclid), dedicated on November 24. In the absence of President Henry P. McIntosh, William F. Carr, vice president, formally presented the clubhouse to the members, Judge Henry C. White responding. The club was the center of many gay social affairs; but it disbanded during World War I and sold its property in 1918.

Goodrich House, planned by Mrs. Flora Stone Mather—Mrs. Samuel Mather—to supplement the parish activities of Old Stone Church, of which she was a member, was launched in December and named for Dr. William H. Goodrich, beloved pastor for many years. Her new project rapidly evolved into a social settlement, and within a few weeks after the building was completed at Bond and St. Clair, a four-year plan had been initiated under Starr Cadwallader, the first headworker. It began with a drive for cleaner streets and neighborhood pride from which grew outstanding "firsts" in many phases of urban life. Volunteer aid in neighborhood legal problems led the first year to the founding of the Legal Aid Society, sheltered in the settlement. The next year Goodrich set out to separate youthful offenders against the law from real criminals; and from its effort the Cleveland Boys' Farm at Hudson, Ohio, developed, one of the first of its kind in the nation. The Home Gardening Association started with a ten-cent membership fee; within two years, fifty thousand packages of seeds were being distributed, pioneering city beautification that became widespread. The Goodrich downtown vacation school became a summer camp in 1898. Sunbeam School for Crippled Children originated in the settlement. Following a summer of experimentation at Goodrich House, the Society for the Blind opened its offices and workshop there. The Book and Thimble Club fathered a consumers' league based on a New York league that became statewide. The growing city crowded in, and the settlement moved eastward to a new center at 1420 East 31st Street in 1914. Alice P. Gannett, a leader of national reputation, came to Goodrich in 1916. Pioneering continued in intercultural relations, nursery schools, pre-school health, the unique nursery mothers' co-operative camping project south of Northfield, Ohio, the Golden Age Club which became nationwide, and in extension work designed to meet the complex problems of modern city life. The Goodrich Social Settlement represented a living monument to Mr. and Mrs. Samuel Mather and loyal associates devoted to the cause of community betterment.

Shortcomings of public servants and the mounting cost of city government stirred fifty leading Clevelanders to answer the meeting call of Harry A. Garfield, law professor at Western Reserve University, on December 5. This was the beginning of the Municipal Association of Cleveland, later known as the Civic League, organized to inspire citizens and taxpayers to take a more active and earnest part in municipal affairs, to choose competent officials, and to encourage prudent and efficient government. Garfield was chosen president; and the executive committee included Samuel Mather, D. Z. Norton, John Sherwin, and Samuel Williamson. Constant vigilance was maintained against graft, corruption, and fraud, and increasing interest was taken in metropolitan improvements as the organization grew in influence and importance. Mayo Fesler, brought from St. Louis in 1910, served as secretary until his retirement in 1945. Reorganization as the Citizens League in 1925 resulted in a membership of four thousand at that time. Robert W. Chamberlin, director in 1946, was succeeded by Guy C. Larcom, Jr.

Jennie Warren Prentiss—Mrs. Ward—opened a school for girls in her residence on Streator Avenue, known as the Wade Park Home School for Girls. It was incorporated as Laurel Institute in 1899, and the next year moved to larger quarters (10001 Euclid) where the first commencement was celebrated with three graduates. When Miss Prentiss resigned in 1902, Florence Waterman became principal. Mrs. Arthur E. Lyman, prominent Cleveland educator, acquired the institution in 1904 and reorganized it as Laurel School. A stock company was formed in 1908 to secure part of the beautiful Streator estate on Logan Street as a home.

A large audience gathered in the assembly room of the Public Library on December 18 to witness an impressive ceremony arranged by the Women's Department of the Cleveland Centennial Commission. Mrs. W. A. Ingham, president, presided. Historical records, mementoes, and newspapers relating to the city's first centennial were placed in an aluminum casket with an American flag and a message, "To Women Unborn—1896 sends greeting to 1996." The lid of the box carried a directive that it be opened "by a lineal daughter of a member of the executive board in 1996." Then followed the official roster: Mrs. W. A. Ingham, Mrs. Mary S. Bradford, Mrs. S. P. Churchill, Mrs. T. K. Dissette, Mrs. H. A. Griffin, Mrs. O. J. Hodge, Mrs. L. A. Russell, Mrs. M. B. Schwab, Mrs. W. G. Rose, Mrs. Elroy M. Avery, Mrs. Ella S. Webb, Elizabeth Blair, Mrs. W. B. Neff, Mrs. G. V. R. Wickham, Mrs. Charles W. Chase, Mrs. A. J. Williams, and Mrs. Sarah E. Bierce. The sealed box was deposited with the Western Reserve Historical Society for a century of safe-keeping.

Cleveland was bursting its municipal seams as it settled into a second-century groove. The assessed valuation of city property now stood at $138,473,385. The banking business had expanded phenomenally to keep step with the booming city, and national and savings banks represented a total capital of $15,385,300; deposits, $73,716,081; and clearings, $299,397,076. Chamber of Commerce reports showed that of the 9,934,828 gross tons of iron ore shipped from the Lake Superior mines, 6,166,236 gross tons, or 62.07 per cent, were received in the Cleveland district. Receipts of coal and coke in Cleveland totaled 3,476,312 tons, and 1,935,136 were shipped from the city by rail. Freight received by lake and rail amounted to 9,360,468 net tons, and 5,440,589 net tons were forwarded. Grain trade was falling behind as the westward trend developed. Receipts at Cleveland totaled 9,016,973 bushels, and 3,788,264 bushels were shipped.

The year 1896 witnessed the establishment of business firms that were in existence a half century later: D. Asadorian, Bartunek Brothers, Buckeye Ribbon & Carbon Company, H. B. McGrath, Maresh Piano Company, Republic Structural Iron Works, Geo. A. Rutherford Company, West End Lumber Company.

1897

Walter C. Baker was building passenger electrical automobiles in Cleveland, having the co-operation of Thomas A. Edison with regard to batteries. The Baker Motor Vehicle Company was organized and soon began making cars equipped with bevel gears, supplanting the chain drive. The first car of this character and other inventions of Baker were placed permanently on exhibition at the Ford Museum at Dearborn, Michigan. Baker is said to have been the first advocate of streamlining to meet air resistance and secure greater speed. His streamlined electric Torpedo racing car attracted world attention. Baker and Elmer A. Sperry, inventor of the gyroscope, worked together on projects in the basement of the Universal Power Block, located at Central Avenue and the Pennsylvania Railroad. Mrs. Baker, who was Frances "Fannie" White, daughter of Rollin C. White, gained prominence as the "first woman automobile driver."

Women bicyclists in a six-day race starting January 17 were attracting the attention of northern Ohio. The track in the Central Armory was continuously surrounded by great crowds who came to see Dottie Farnsworth, Jennie Brown, Helen Brown, Tillie Anderson, and others in their racing thrills and spills.

Gus Heege, well-known Swedish actor whose most famous role was Yon Yonson, died on February 3. Central High School was the scene of his first display of dramatic talent.

Cleveland's best-known swindler was engaging in a career of financial crookedness that drew the attention of the world. Born in Canada, she had succeeded as a fortune-teller under assumed names. She was an artist whose goal was the accumulation of money, no matter how unscrupulous the methods. She married Dr. LeRoy S. Chadwick of Cleveland, who apparently never knew of her activities until they were publicly disclosed. Bankers listened to her plausible stories and seemed hypnotized. Claiming confidentially that she was the illegitimate daughter of Andrew Carnegie, she borrowed substantial sums secured by her notes. For several years, Cassie Chadwick succeeded in avoiding the law, and during this time it is said that two of her victims committed suicide. A large part of her money went into extravagant furnishings for her home and a wardrobe of bewildering quality and quantity. When the crisis came, Andrew Carnegie stated he had never known the woman who deposited a $5,000,000 certificate forged with his name as security for loans. Her trial in 1905 is another story.

John Hay became ambassador to Great Britain; but after a year's service, President McKinley called him home and made him Secretary of State. He will long be remembered for his successful negotiation of the Hay-Pauncefote Treaty under which the Panama Canal was begun; his "Open Door" policy in China which stressed freedom and commercial enterprise for American merchants; and his aid in preventing dissolution of China following the Boxer Rebellion. President Theodore Roosevelt continued Hay's service as Secretary of State.

William McKinley became the twenty-fourth President of the United States on March 4; he was an Ohioan well known and well liked in Cleveland. Troop A returned to Cleveland on March 8, after having acted as personal escort to the President at the inaugural ceremonies in Washington.

The official story of Cleveland's one-hundredth birthday program, *The Centennial Celebration,* compiled by Edward A. Roberts, was issued March 21. Roberts was the efficient secretary of the celebration, and later the executive who made the Cleveland Builders Exchange the nation's leading institution in its field.

The *Plain Dealer* on April 18 included not only an Easter Sunday section, but also a full section devoted to bicycling, on the front page of which was the legend, "The Bicycle is All the Rage." In proof thereof, an artist's conception of Easter Sunday on the boulevards portrayed men and women in their finery pedaling along in utter joy. Bicycles "built for two" were advertised. Various Cleveland ministers debated in several columns the moral question of "wheeling" on Sunday. The majority believed it was not wrong if the recreation did not interfere with church attendance.

The Cleveland baseball team was getting ready for a big season. Its manager was scrappy Patsy Tebeau, who played first base and inspired such enthusiasm that every player gave his best until the last man was out. At second base was "Cupid" Childs, a roly-poly infielder who covered his territory with alacrity despite his avoirdupois. At third base was "Chippy" McGarr, one of the most earnest players that ever guarded the difficult corner. At shortstop was Ed McKean, barrel-chested and broad-shouldered, who drove home runs over the fence with ease. In the field were three of the most famous "gardeners" of their time: James "Jimmy" McAleer in center, one of the fastest men in the history of the game; in left field, Jesse Burkett, who led the league several years in batting; while in right field was Sock-alexis, an Indian of remarkable natural ability who would not adhere to training rules. Behind the plate were O'Conner, McAllister, and Criger, O'Conner being one of the most popular players Cleveland ever knew. Cuppy, Powell, Gear, and McDermott were among the pitchers to start the season, Cuppy being a mainstay for several years.

John H. Clarke came to Cleveland this year to join the law firm of Williamson & Cushing. He had been educated at Western Reserve College at Hudson and had practiced law in Youngstown. Later he was appointed general counsel for the New York Central Railroad, and also served other railroad corporations. Clarke was prominent in state and national democratic issues. He served as United States district judge for the northern district of Ohio in 1914-16, and from this position went to the United States Supreme Court. Cleveland remembered him as an eminent lawyer and a devoted citizen.

Eight workmen were victims of a deadly gas explosion in the new water-works tunnel on May 12. They were 6,300 feet from shore when the explosion occurred.

The Dow Chemical Company was incorporated on May 18 to manufacture commercial chlorine. Before long it became the largest producer in the United States and one of the greatest chemical companies in the world, its products including the startling light metal, magnesium. Cleveland and Case School of Applied Science were important to the founding. Herbert Henry Dow, a student at Case, conceived the ideas, and J. H. Osborn of the National Carbon Company provided financial support. Discouragements were met, and James T. Pardee of Cleveland, Dr. Cady Staley, president of Case, Albert E. Convers, S. T. Wellman, G. E. Collings, and Charles A. Post joined with Dow and Osborn to extract chlorine and other products out of the salt wells of Midland, Michigan, where they located their headquarters. The Dow ideas expanded and were realized, one after another, first, under Dow's direction, and later under the leadership of his son, Willard H. Gross sales in one year reached approximately $130,000,000. So it was that ideas born in Case School and encouraged by Cleveland capital built a great chemical institution serving people all over the world.

The first Sunday concert in Gordon Park was played on May 30 by the Great Western Band. From that time, Cleveland's parks grew in popularity.

An earthquake was felt in Cleveland on May 31, and those who did not feel it were doubters until it was confirmed by Professor Morley's seismograph at Adelbert College. Windows rattled, pictures on walls played pendulum, and tall buildings swayed gently.

The Denison Avenue Congregational Church originated in a Sunday School that began in 1893 in an old building at Richard Street and Lorain Avenue. Membership increased, and a farmhouse was purchased and moved to Richard Street and Denison Avenue to serve as a house of worship. The Rev. Claude M. Severance was called as pastor shortly before the church was organized on July 7, this year, with fifty-four charter members. A new sanctuary, dedicated in 1898, served until 1915, when a modern building was completed on the site, West 99th at Denison Avenue. The Rev. Ernest E. Morrill brought capable leadership and new spirit to the church when he became pastor in 1943, and membership neared the five hundred mark in the mid-forties.

An aerial torpedo, designed to revolutionize the methods of war, was invented by Archie C. Walker of Cleveland. The young inventor claimed that his missile could be sent to a high altitude, and then, controlled by electricity, could be propelled in any direction for a distance of nine miles. Dynamite could be discharged at will into an enemy camp.

The first Americanization classes in Cleveland were started by George A. Bellamy at Hiram House. He also opened Hiram House Camp near Chagrin Falls, a summer-camp experiment with crude furnishings, the first of its kind for "well" children. In 1903 its success was assured when Samuel Mather gave an extensive wooded tract for the project.

The entire city was equipped with new street signs on July 9, "signs of progress," according to a local wag.

It cost two dollars a month to lay the dust in front of a Euclid Avenue home. The driver of a horse-drawn sprinkling wagon shut off the water in front of a house if the owner did not pay. A two-foot strip was preserved along the curb and kept dry for wheelmen, according to law.

Star Pointer, the first horse to break the two-minute-mile record, having paced in 1:59¼, was purchased by W. J. White, the chewing-gum king, for $20,000. White's "Two Minute Villa" in Rocky River was the home of many famous horses, including the magnificent Russia.

The Burrows Brothers, booksellers, stationers, and publishers, had made several moves since their courageous launching on Euclid Avenue in 1873, and this year a spacious home was found in the New England Building (later Guardian Building). In 1912 the Burrows brothers, Charles W. and Harris B., and their associates sold the business, and the company retired from publishing to operate a retail store. The first of a chain of local branch stores opened in Playhouse Square in 1922. Burrows changed hands several times until 1944, when control centered with a group of Clevelanders headed by Howard B. Klein. "You'll *feel* our Welcome" was the well-known slogan of Burrows, one of the largest book and office-supply firms in the country.

Interest in golf grew rapidly when Cleveland sent its best players to Buffalo for inter-city matches, July 24. Cleveland won, with Will Boardman as the hero of the occasion. Women took up the game at the Country Club, and, in October, Mrs. Kenyon V. Painter became Cleveland's champion, Benedict Crowell winning the championship among the men.

The Baldwin University Law School was established at Berea under the leadership of Judge Willis Vickery. At about the same time, the Cleveland Law School was incorporated, F. J. Wing being one of the founders. Two years later, the institutions joined to become the Cleveland Law School of Baldwin University, Judge Vickery serving as dean. The affiliation with Baldwin-Wallace College continued until 1926, and graduating classes went to Berea to receive their diplomas. That year the Cleveland Law School separated from Baldwin-Wallace and continued its activities in Cleveland until June 24, 1946, when it merged with the John Marshall Law School, then in its thirtieth year. Judge Lee E. Skeel was president of the new institution, Cleveland-Marshall Law School at 1240 Ontario Street; Judge David C. Meck, Jr., director of education, and Wilson G. Stapleton, dean.

Kites were seen flying at great heights on July 29. The Rev. Fr. Odenbach of St. Ignatius College was sending his scientific kites eight thousand feet into the air as the first of a series of experiments to measure temperature and wind velocity.

Howard Parmelee Eells, manufacturer who devoted much time to philanthropy, art, and education, became president, and later chairman of the board, of the Bucyrus Steam Shovel Company. This concern manufactured dredges and steam shovels for use throughout the world. Eells held executive positions in other manufacturing concerns, was a leader in the National Metal Trades Association, and a director of banks. Among the numerous welfare and educational institutions he helped in his home city were the Cleveland Humane Society, the Cleveland Protestant Orphan Asylum, Western Reserve University, the Cleveland School of Art, and the Children's Aid Society. His sons similarly distinguished themselves in important activities.

"Buffalo Bill's" Wild West Show entertained Clevelanders, and the stagecoach fight between the Indians and the scouts, headed by Colonel William F. Cody himself, thrilled and chilled parents and the youngsters who clung to them. Annie Oakley, the most famous of all rifle shots, was a star performer, and in her most picturesque act cantered around the ring, shooting glass balls which a man on horseback ahead of her tossed into the air. The show was called the "Greatest Congress of Rough Riders in the World," and, besides the Indians, there were cowboys, Bedouin Arabs, Russian Cossacks, and a detachment of the United States Cavalry. Cleveland's interest was particularly great because members of the Cody family lived in the city.

The second Brooklyn-Brighton Bridge, built at an estimated cost of $160,-000, was 1,575 feet long with an all-steel frame, a marvel of the day.

Charles H. Wellman of The Wellman-Seaver Engineering Company arranged with A. C. Dinkey, chief electrical engineer at the Homestead Plant of the Carnegie Steel Company in Pittsburgh, to build a controller which Dinkey had designed. This resulted in the founding of The Electric Controller & Manufacturing Company, which occupied space on Merwin Avenue, later moving to Champlain Street and Central Avenue. The first controller was sold to The Brown Hoisting and Conveying Machinery Company. The organization grew substantially, and many forms of electrical equipment were made, including automatic controllers and compensators, lifting magnets, switches, motor starters, and weld timers. The company was the first to make commercial electrical lifting magnets for lifting and handling steel, and in 1909 it produced the first dynamic lowering crane hoist control. In 1943 F. R. Fishback, who had served as president, became board chairman and R. G. Widdows was elected to the presidency. High-voltage motor starters with unique features were the newest products of the plant located at 2700 East 79th Street.

A Department of Forestry and Nurseries was established, with M. H. Horvath as the first city forester. Cleveland's claim as the Forest City was waning, and a new effort to save trees was launched.

The champion harness horses of the Gentlemen's Driving Club for 1897 were: trotter, Elloree, time 2:10, owned and driven by Calvary Morris; pacer, Pine Wood, 2:13½, owned and driven by William B. White.

The Perkins Power Block and surrounding buildings were severely damaged by fire and water on December 23. The disaster was caused by an explosion of benzine, and the loss was estimated at a million dollars.

Since 1892, the Homeopathic Hospital College had been established in a new home on Huron Road. A split in the organization had healed, and this year the institution emerged as The Cleveland University of Medicine and Surgery. Early in the Twentieth Century, when the country's medical schools were standardized, all Cleveland medical-training institutions, with the exception of the School of Medicine of Western Reserve University, lost their identity. The Cleveland College of Physicians and Surgeons, descendant of the medical departments of Wooster and Ohio Wesleyan universities, joined Reserve, thus uniting the medical schools of the past with the pioneer Medical Department of Western Reserve College which originated in 1843. Noted instructors served medical science through positions on the staff, including Drs. George C. Ashmun, William T. Corlett, John P. Sawyer, Carl A. Hamann, Charles F. Hoover, Frederick C. Waite, Roger G. Perkins, Howard T. Karsner, Carl J. Wiggers, William H. Humiston, Arthur H. Bill, Frank E. Bunts, George W. Crile, Torald Sollmann, George N. Stewart, Thomas Wingate Todd, Henry J. Gerstenberger, and William E. Bruner.

1898

One of the first shops to make an internal-combustion motor car was operated by Alexander Winton on Perkins Avenue. The firm was the year-old Winton Motor Carriage Company, later the Winton Motor Car Company. The Winton was a one-lunger, "Very elegant in appearance, fashioned after the pattern of an equine runabout and lacking little but the shafts and whipsocket." The motor was under the car, and intermittently so was Winton. The vehicle carried two passengers, and made a speed of ten miles an hour. The engine was cooled with ice, and infinite patience was required to start it. Erratic motion of the single cylinder was unmusical to the ears of its builder, who gradually increased the number to six cylinders.

Hiram M. "Father" Addison died on January 14 at the age of eighty. His bent figure, quaint utterances, and simple habits of life were known to hosts of Clevelanders; and while there was no monument of bronze or granite carrying his name down the valley of the years, his works and his memory endured in the hearts of those who best appreciated the seed he sowed and tended. He was the pioneer in the children's-camp movement, having laid the foundation of the Children's Fresh Air Camp in 1889. His helpfulness to humanity was remembered in a verse published the week of his passing:

> Dead is the kindly man whom all men knew
> As father. With Time's trouble he is through.
> Upon life's lengthened thread he strung like beads
> The precious jewelry of gentle deeds.

The College Club, organized on January 15 "to promote social, philanthropic and literary interests in Cleveland," made its first home in the "Wedge," near Erie Street and Euclid Avenue. The two women mainly responsible for the founding of the club were Louise Pope, Mrs. Homer H. Johnson, who served as first president, and Carolyn Shipman, secretary. The club was incorporated February 19, 1908, and the new plan of uniting college women to achieve cultural purposes flourished. In 1913 the ever-growing group purchased an attractive clubhouse on East 93rd Street near Euclid Avenue, through the co-operation and generosity of Mr. and Mrs. Charles W. Wason. In addition to the regular Monday meetings, there were many associated groups which carried on special studies and activities related to scholarship funds and cultural interests. The membership in 1946 included five hundred women, representing ninety colleges. Mrs. Frank H. Birnbaum was president; Mrs. Frederick C. Loweth, corresponding secretary; and Mrs. J. C. Carpenter, recording secretary.

The first issue of the *University School News*, Ohio's oldest school paper, appeared on January 18. Young Robert J. Bulkley was editor-in-chief.

The Cleveland Medical Library Association received the residence at 2318 Prospect Avenue in January for the housing of medical books. Previous to this time, books and papers had been cared for by Case Library. This was the library's first home.

The Baker's Dozen, a group of young society women, became interested in the pioneer public-health work being done by Antoinette Higley, parish visitor of the Old Stone Church. They furnished her with supplies and contributed to her pioneering visitation effort.

During the winter, Cleveland suffered from an epidemic of influenza, then called "the grippe." Many deaths resulted.

The Detroit & Cleveland Navigation Company was incorporated, the word "Steam" having been dropped from the name. Upon the death of James McMillan in 1902, his son, W. C. McMillan, became company head. He died in 1907, and during the administration of his successor, Phillip H. McMillan, the steamers *City of Detroit III* and *City of Cleveland III* were built for the Buffalo run.

Charles and Kate B. Babcock acquired a portion of the Judge Thomas Bolton farm, selling it to Mary H. Severance for $50,000. The Severance home was built on the site of the famous Spring Pond House (northwest corner of Euclid and East 89th Street). In 1906 it was inherited by Emily A. Severance. With the adjoining property of Mrs. Elisabeth S. Prentiss, it became the temporary home of Huron Road Hospital in 1923, and was later occupied by the Cleveland Health Museum. The Bolton homestead, built in 1850 on Euclid at Giddings, was eventually taken down and rebuilt at Mentor, Ohio.

The Knights of Columbus granted the first Cleveland charter to Gilmour Council on February 6. There were sixty-seven charter members of whom nine were in the city in the mid-forties. The first grand knight in Cleveland was P. J. Brady, prominent attorney. Dr. Thomas A. Burke, Sr., father of Mayor Thomas A. Burke, served as grand knight in 1905-6. Ten councils in the county sprang from Gilmour Council, and the first headquarters were at the Pythian Temple at Erie and Prospect streets. In 1939 Tudor Arms Hotel, 10660 Carnegie, became the headquarters, and inspirational meetings and social gatherings continued to be important features of the annual program. R. J. Mylott was grand knight in 1946.

The battleship *Maine* was blown up in Havana harbor, February 15, by the Spanish. Diplomatic relations were broken April 21. The conflict between the countries over disorders in Cuba under Spanish rule was soon settled. Admiral George Dewey took Manila on May 1; American troops captured the heights of El Caney and San Juan on July 1-3; and Admiral William T. Sampson destroyed Cervera's fleet and blocked Santiago harbor on July 3. Under the Treaty of Paris, signed on December 10, Spain agreed to withdraw from Cuba and ceded Puerto Rico and Guam to the United States, and the United States paid $20,000,000 for the Philippines. Cleveland's volunteers numbered approximately a thousand under such able leaders as General George A. Garretson, Majors Charles F. Cramer and Arthur K. A. Liebich, Adjutant Fred B. Dodge, and Captains Joseph C. Beardsley, Daniel H. Pond, Charles X. Zimmerman, Edwin G. Lane, Edward A. Noll, and Walter S. Bauder, of the 5th Ohio Volunteer Infantry; Captain John C. Fulton, Company D, 9th Battalion, O. N. G.; Major Otto M. Schade, Quartermaster H. W. Morganthaler, and Captains John R. McQuigg, Edward N. Ogram, Henry Frazee, Clifford W. Fuller, and Edward D. Shurmer, 10th Ohio Infantry; Captain George T. McConnell, 1st Battalion, Ohio Light Artillery; Major Webb C. Hayes, Adjutants Arthur C. Rogers and Paul Howland, Surgeon Frank E. Bunts and Captains Russell E. Burdick, Carlyle L. Burridge, Henry W. Corning, and William M. Scofield, 1st Ohio Volunteer Cavalry.

The Delsarte System, emphasizing the movements of the body that should accompany different emotions, was being employed in local elocution classes. Exaggerated gestures portraying fear, joy, anger, and sorrow characterized the recitations and orations until ridicule branded them as humorous. Enunciation was also being taught in many schools, and Cleveland pupils were chanting:

> Peter Piper picked a peck of pickled peppers;
> Did Peter Piper pick a peck of pickled peppers?

If Peter Piper picked a peck of pickled peppers,
Where's the peck of pickled peppers Peter Piper picked?

The American Steel & Wire Company of Illinois was organized, taking over the mills of the Consolidated Steel & Wire Company, the H. P. Nail Company, and the American Wire Company. In 1899 the American Steel & Wire Company of New Jersey was formed, absorbing the Illinois company and others, including the Cleveland Rolling Mill Company, thus bringing the city's wire mills into one organization. In 1901 the United States Steel Corporation was formed, and the American Steel & Wire Company became its subsidiary, the largest producer of wire in the world, with five enormous plants in the Cleveland district: the American Works, Central Furnaces, Coke Works, Cuyahoga Works, and Newburgh Works. Clifford F. Hood was elected president in 1938, succeeding C. F. Blackmer.

Robert Allison, a mechanical engineer of Port Carbon, Pennsylvania, had no priorities to worry him when he purchased from Alexander Winton his first practical automobile. But when the cash-in-advance deal, at a price of a thousand dollars, was consummated in Cleveland, March 24, Allison did have some gasoline worries which were not the result of war. He had to make sure that the nearest hardware store was supplied with enough fuel to keep the one-lung Winton running, or he had to carry a reserve tank of a gallon or two if he contemplated a trip. Allison had answered Winton's small advertisement in the *Scientific American*. Delivery of the car was to be made on April 1. The inventor had achieved fame the preceding year with the "horseless carriage" he had driven from Cleveland to New York. In less than a year, twenty-two Wintons were destined for sale, only one of them being purchased by a Clevelander, George L. Weiss. Winton bought back the first car he sold and donated it to the Smithsonian Institution in Washington.

Hardly in gear with the winter's horseless-carriage progress was the half-hour wagonette service between Wade and Gordon parks, announced on March 25 by J. H. McBride, chairman of a park-board committee. The fare contemplated was ten cents one way. Lighter wagonettes for hire by the hour also were being provided.

Stores in Cleveland's arcades were in great demand, and the Colonial Arcade, erected by Charles G. King at 600 Euclid, quickly attracted tenants. King's son, Ralph T., art patron, became one of the largest Euclid Avenue property owners, owning the Colonial and Euclid arcades and the Nottingham Building, and heading the Realty Investment Company.

In a hall over a grocery store at Detroit and Winchester avenues, the Detroit Avenue Methodist Church was organized on April 10, with the Rev. Howard K. Hillberry as pastor. Later a small building was erected across the street, but it was soon outgrown, and an addition was constructed. In 1921, on January 23, a fine new church was dedicated, and the older frame structure was moved to the rear of the lot. Dr. Melvin C. Hunt came to the Lakewood church in 1935 and, under his leadership, the membership grew to nine hundred, while activities were expanded.

Since 1893 the Rauch & Lang Carriage Company had been making electric vehicles. The Rauch & Lang Electric car, introduced in 1905, was the first American car commercially equipped with a closed body, and was developed primarily to furnish a market for bodies. At this time C. L. F. Wieber became an executive of the firm. The carriage company and the Baker Motor Vehicle Company, one of the earliest in the field, founded by Walter C. Baker and Fred R. White in 1898, combined in The Baker-Raulang Company in 1915. Four years later, quantity manufacture of closed bodies was begun, followed by a line of industrial machines for the handling of war material. Baker-Raulang, located at 2168 West 25th Street, was one of the oldest manufacturers of electric vehicles, making industrial trucks, tractors, cranes, and mobile handling equipment in the 1940s. E. J. Bartlett was elected president in 1926, succeeding F. W. Treadway.

Kite-flying in Cleveland was practiced by William B. Schlomer on April 14, not for fun alone. He was a special agent of the Weather Bureau, making upper-air experiments with kites carrying small registering thermometers and barometers. Schlomer kept his work-play a secret until the bureau made it known. Clevelanders complained there was no improvement in either predictions or weather.

The annual meeting of the Western Reserve Historical Society was held in its new home at University Circle on May 3. The mosaic floor on the ground level of the three-story, terra-cotta, brick building was the gift of Jeptha Homer Wade II. The library occupied the second floor and proved of great value as a medium of research. Henry C. Ranney served as president from 1895 to 1900, when he was succeeded by Liberty E. Holden, who served until 1907.

A pioneer enterprise was developing in the gas industry. Businesslike control of natural gas, with compression and meters, had begun in Pennsylvania in 1890. Long-distance transmission under high pressure was started when the incorporation of the East Ohio Gas Company, a subsidiary of Standard Oil, took place. A trunk line was planned to bring gas from new fields in Wetzel County, West Virginia. There was, however, a natural-gas field in Cleveland, and the shallow wells of the "Lakewood Field" were the source of private light, heat, and cooking fuel for many homes in the western and southwestern part of Cuyahoga County until 1932. The deeper wells often furnished gas in commercial quantities.

A committee of three gave first impetus to the organization of the University Club of Cleveland: Charles Harris, Samuel Ball Platner, and Abraham Lincoln Fuller. The club was incorporated on June 8, and at the first meeting, 40 institutions of learning were represented by 140 members. The Tod house on Prospect Street was chosen as the first home. In 1913 residence was changed to 3813 Euclid Avenue, the former home of T. Sterling Beckwith. The following were officers in 1946: William Edward Baldwin, president; Frank L. McFarlane, vice president; Carlton L. Small, treasurer; and Julius M. Kovachy, secretary.

The *City of Erie,* 324 feet, and the fastest inland steamer, set out on her maiden voyage from Cleveland to Buffalo on June 19. Built for the Cleveland & Buffalo Transit Company, the ship replaced the *State of Ohio,* which went into night service between Cleveland and Toledo with the *City of the Straits,* a vessel of the Detroit & Cleveland line, in a joint operation. The latter ran a daytime schedule between Cleveland and Put-in-Bay in 1899, and sailed in night service between Cleveland and Toledo until 1914, when the joint arrangement ended. The C & B then continued service to Put-in-Bay and added Cedar Point as a port of call.

Librarian William Howard Brett introduced the first special accommodations for children at the Public Library.

For a long time the historic First Baptist Church building at Seneca and Champlain streets had been serving commercial purposes. This year the Cleveland Telephone Company erected its headquarters on the site, and set up a central system that continued until the towering new downtown building was ready in 1927. The familiar crank on the side of the phone box began to disappear along with the mussy batteries, and the modern telephone was definitely on its way.

The first Ohio law providing for state aid to boards of education for the purpose of maintaining schools for the deaf was passed; and, with funds made available by this law, the Willson Avenue School was leased and opened as the Alexander Graham Bell School. The Cleveland Board of Education, at the suggestion of the Cleveland Society for the Blind, provided for the instruction of blind children in the public schools. For educational purposes these children were enrolled in classes of two distinct types: Braille classes for the totally blind, and sight-saving classes for those who could use their eyes if the work was suitably presented.

Countless lights for the world's highways, airways, industry, and commerce, and air-conditioning equipment for homes and buildings were to come from the Cleveland Works of the Westinghouse Electric & Manufacturing Company. This year the local concern was established in buildings of the old Walker Manufacturing Company; but it soon outgrew them, and additions followed in rapid succession until operations included eighteen inter-connected buildings. Westinghouse played an important part in Cleveland, the lighting center of the world, the Cleveland Works being the sales center for a large area. Frederick G. Hickling became manager of district sales in 1931. The name of the company was changed in 1945 to Westinghouse Electric Corporation.

The permanent water-works intake crib was placed in position on July 1, but the shaft was not completed until July 8, 1901. While men were working in the tunnel the next month, the crib superstructure caught fire, and five workers were suffocated while five others were drowned. The work of rebuilding was started immediately, but on August 20 the shaft broke at the bottom of the lake and five more men died as a result of the accident. Operations were carried on from both ends of the line until the tunnels met on December 11, 1902. Again calamity came, this time in the form of an explosion of gas, and four lives were claimed. The work proceeded through 1903, and the first water was pumped from the tunnel by the Kirtland Street station in February, 1904. When completed, the tunnel was one of the largest in the world—26,000 feet long, 9 feet in diameter, with a daily capacity of 170,000,000 gallons. W. M. Kingsley, superintendent of the water works, was chief engineer, and C. F. Schultz was chief assistant.

The churches of Cleveland held Thanksgiving services on July 10 for "glorious American victories" in the War with Spain. In his sermon at the Old Stone Church, Dr. Hiram C. Haydn stated that wars seemed "necessary now and then to bring out the qualities of courage and bravery" among the people. Then he added that peace offered "daily opportunity for heroism."

Mlle. Rita Elandi, prima donna of the opera, was honored on July 23 upon her return from a successful tour abroad. The former Amelia Groll of Cleveland had sung in England, Scotland, Ireland, and Germany before enthusiastic audiences. She had been presented to Frau Richard Wagner, who entertained her as a guest in the household, and she sang Wagnerian parts in the room in which the great composer had originated them.

The widening of the Cuyahoga River was at last begun August 11. The first shovel of earth to widen the harbor entrance was removed by Mayor McKisson, while enthusiastic crowds cheered.

The first meeting of the Board of City Hall Commissioners was held on August 23. Members of the board, appointed by Mayor McKisson to recommend a city-hall site, were Thomas W. Hill, Stephen C. Gladwin, Matthew F. Bramley, Nathan I. Dryfoos, and Frederick W. Gehring. They gave particular attention in their investigation to the civic-center idea, and eventually recommended the lakefront site as part of the envisioned Group Plan. J. Milton Dyer was authorized to prepare plans for a new city hall to cost $2,600,000, and work was begun with the purchase of the site under the administration of Mayor Herman C. Baehr.

Lake Erie Female Seminary at Painesville had developed rapidly, and this year a charter was granted to the Lake Erie College and Seminary, the name being changed to Lake Erie College a decade later. Vivian Blanche Small became fourth president in 1909, and during thirty-two years inspired important advances. The fifth president in an unbroken succession of Mt. Holyoke alumnae was Dr. Helen Dalton Bragdon. The small residence college provided an environment well adapted to the stimulation of intellectual development so essential in an era of rapid change. Many alumnae brought honor to their alma mater, among them Dr. Louise Baird Wallace, faculty member of the Women's College, Constantinople, and of the Mt. Holyoke College faculty for years; Dr. Georgia L. White, dean at Cornell, and home-economics director for the Michigan Food Administration during World War I; Mrs. J. J. McKay, director of safety education, Ohio Automobile Association, and originator of important safety plans; Mrs. John Edward Brown, philanthropist; and Henrietta Roelofs, president, National Peace Council in 1941, national board member of YWCA, writer, and lecturer.

Frank DeHaas Robison transferred the Cleveland National League Baseball Club to St. Louis and gave the city a team unworthy of organized baseball. The Cleveland Spiders finished in last place in 1899 and the team dropped from the National League. Happily, the American League had come to the front with Charles W. Somers as president and owner of the Cleveland Club; and baseball interest, weakened by the Robison fiasco, became stronger than ever. Somers was a friend of B. U. Rannells, the first principal of East High School; and, as the result of the latter's recommendation, he gave Roger Peckinpaugh, East High star athlete, his first chance to break into professional baseball.

Adella Rouse Prentiss—Mrs. Adella Prentiss Hughes—appeared on Cleveland's horizon as a concert manager. She managed the Fortnightly Evening Concerts and brought distinguished artists and, later, visiting orchestras, to Cleveland.

Clifton Boulevard was completed in 1898, bringing Lakewood nearer to Cleveland.

Liberty E. Holden, owner of the *Plain Dealer,* reached the conclusion that "newspaper sense" was an invaluable asset to success. At this time he had the morning, evening, and Sunday *Plain Dealer* on his hands. He entered into an unprecedented contract with Elbert H. Baker and Charles E. Kennedy, trained newspapermen, providing for a profit-sharing arrangement, whereby Baker took over the business and Kennedy the editorial management. This was one of Holden's far-seeing ventures.

The Cleveland Retail Credit Men's Company was organized in November during a luncheon discussion in the Chamber of Commerce Building. It was the first merchant-owned co-operative and non-profit credit bureau in the United States and possibly in the world. As credit accounts grew in number, it was decided that a pooling of credit experiences would enable a merchant to profit by consulting the Central Credit Exchange. Started by a few retailers and merchants, two thousand business, financial, and professional men and institutions were to share these benefits later on. William H. Gray was serving in his thirtieth year as secretary, and C. Glenn Evans of the Halle Bros. Company was president in 1946.

Fire almost completely destroyed the popular Cleveland Theater, November 8, during a serious conflagration in the heart of Cleveland's business section. Not one of the fifteen hundred people in the theater was injured in the realistic melodrama.

The Gatling gun, a rapid-fire weapon made in Cleveland, promised to revolutionize gun-making. The new process by which it was being manufactured was a triumph for the inventor, Richard Jordan Gatling, and for the Otis Steel Works, the manufacturer. The slang word for revolver, "gat," originated with the Gatling gun.

The Wade Memorial Chapel was in the process of construction in Lake View Cemetery, erected in memory of Jeptha H. Wade by his grandson, Jeptha H. Wade III. The architects were Hubbell & Benes, and plans called for one of the world's most impressive memorials. Built of granite, the interior of the classic structure was a blending of bronze, marble, and glass, the decorations being designed by Louis C. Tiffany of New York City. Beautiful glass mosaic panels were executed from designs of Frederick Wilson. "The Voyage of Life" was the theme of wall decorations.

1899

New Year fun included skating, watch parties, balls, and a parade of horseless carriages.

Robert G. Ingersoll appeared at the Opera House on January 9. The theater was filled to overflowing, and his lecture on *Superstition* created controversy. Dr. Louis A. Banks, pastor of the First Methodist Church, likened the event to a circus. Replied Ingersoll, "Everybody enjoys a circus."

Frozen masses of water were piled many feet high as a huge ice gorge formed in the river, January 15. Heavy rains caused the dam at Herron's Pond to give way, and the escaping flood broke the Willson Avenue culvert. Street traffic was stopped for several hours. Four days later, bridge piers collapsed, and the Willson Avenue high-level bridge fell in a heap of scrap iron. The Kingsbury Run flood caused great damage.

The Arion Quartet, composed of H. Warren Whitney, Vincent B. Woboril, James A. McMahon, and B. W. Willard, was winning popularity. An earlier Arion Quartet, born in the seventies, and consisting of Frank Ishman, Charles J. Jaster, John B. Lang, and George Duckett, had been Cleveland's favorite for many years.

A small group of women was the nucleus of the Rubinstein Club, organized in February, and there were sixteen members when the club presented its first musical at Plymouth Congregational Church in May. Under the guiding influence of Mrs. R. B. Fry and Mrs. Seabury C. Ford, the organization grew in numbers and importance, giving concerts to large audiences, assisted by noted artists. The Rubinstein Club was prominent in the musical life of the city, participating in the dedication of the Public Auditorium.

The Gem Pharmacy at Erie Street and Superior Avenue was opened by C. E. Roseman. Its success led to the opening of other stores and the establishment of the Standard Drug Company, of which Roseman was president. The business expanded into northeastern Ohio, and in 1946 there were fifty-two stores in the chain.

Clevelanders experienced Arctic weather when the thermometer on the Society for Savings Building recorded 17.1 degrees below zero at 8 A.M. on February 10, establishing an all-time low.

The close of the Chinese New Year was observed with lavish festivities, February 20. About 600,000 firecrackers were exploded on Seneca Street at the Chinese headquarters, and a good report was heard by downtown Cleveland.

The American Ship Building Company was incorporated, March 16, merging properties of the Cleveland Shipbuilding Company, the Globe Iron Works Company, and the Ship Owners Dry Dock Company of Cleveland. Shipyards were maintained at Buffalo, Detroit, Milwaukee, West Superior, West Bay City, and Chicago. Sixteen vessels were under construction, and five years later, the phenomenal total of 181 had left the yards. William L. Brown of Chicago was the first president, and James C. Wallace, general manager, succeeded him in 1904. A proud record was made during the war years. President Wallace had retired, and Merton E. Farr was president when ships for immediate ocean duty were demanded by Washington. Within record time, 40 large vessels were ready for service in World War I. This intense production schedule was followed by readjustments, and large lake freighters and luxurious passenger liners were built. Farr resigned in 1924, and Alfred G. Smith became president. During his term, two of the largest ships to sail the Great Lakes were built, the *Harry Coulby,* a freighter, and the *Carl D. Bradley,* famed for its self-unloading conveyor belts. These vessels discharged two thousand tons of bulk cargo an hour, were well-adapted to the coal and limestone industry, and displaced dock equipment for coal unloading. Following the death of Smith in 1928, William H. Gerhauser became president. Ship-building activity in the early 1940s was determined by the ever-increasing demands of the Army, Navy, and United States Marine Commission. The company responded by building many submarine tenders, trawlers, minesweepers, frigates, Liberty ships, ore carriers, and oil tankers, and by converting passenger liners to training ships. In the 1940s operations included dry docks in Chicago, Toledo, Lorain, and Buffalo, with general offices and a complete engineering department in Cleveland.

A group of financial leaders met in March upon the recommendation of Herbert Wright, W. H. Lamprecht, and R. H. York to establish the Cleveland Stock Exchange. The membership fee was set at $100. After several meetings, James Parmelee was elected president; Addison H. Hough, vice president; John Sherwin, treasurer; and Frank B. Sanders, secretary. The Exchange commenced operations on April 16, 1900, in the Williamson Building. Growth of business was steady, and the local organization soon won national recognition for its good management and the conservatism of its members. Cleveland became the center of stock-market activity in Ohio, although able exchanges were established in Cincinnati and Columbus. Early presidents were William G. Mather, Charles A. Otis, Jr., Addison H. Hough, and Edward M. Baker. Active membership of Eugene S. Halle began in 1901.

A Spanish cannon, trophy of the War with Spain, was mounted on the Public Square.

The Browning Engineering Company was organized to build coal and ore-handling machinery. Incorporated in 1900, it became known as The Browning Crane & Shovel Company, with B. F. Miles, president; Victor R. Browning, vice president; and Earl H. Browning, secretary. The company's steam locomotive cranes were in great demand, and beginning in the early 1920s, rubber-tired truck and wagon cranes were built for world-wide usage. In 1914 Sheldon Cary became president; and under his leadership extensive expansions were made at 16226 Waterloo Road, until the plant covered twelve acres. Cranes were built for industrial use in many countries and for the United States Government. Browning machinery played an important part in such projects as the Panama Canal, the Alaskan Railway, and the navy yards at Brooklyn, Norfolk, and Honolulu.

The United Spanish War Veterans formed a permanent organization in

Cleveland and soon built up a substantial membership. The first camp was named for General George A. Garretson, who had been one of the city's leading civic and military leaders. Major O. M. Schade was the first commander, and under his direction activities grew rapidly. In 1946 Frank H. Sherman was county council commander and Charles G. Pitcock, county council adjutant. There were seven camps in Cleveland and Lakewood, and membership was seven hundred.

An inventive Cleveland mind found that the gutta-percha golf ball, universally used, admitted of great improvement. So it was that Coburn Haskell patented on April 11 a ball with a rubber-wound core. Joe Mitchell, professional at the Country Club, put the first rubber winding on the first rubber core, and Bertram Work, of The B. F. Goodrich Company, handled the mechanical winding. Greater distances and lower scores followed, and the game became more popular.

The highly successful season of Metropolitan Opera in Cleveland attracted large audiences to the Opera House. The firm but artistic director, Maurice Grau, presented *The Barber of Seville, Carmen, La Traviata,* and *Faust.* The stars included Calvé as Carmen, Mme. Sembrich as Violetta and Marguerite, and Edouard De Reske in leading roles. The appearance in Cleveland was described by the newspapers as a notable occasion. Two years later, the company returned to Cleveland and had another successful four-night stay at the Opera House. In 1910 and 1911 the Metropolitan Opera Company came to the Hippodrome and was greeted by large audiences. The outstanding production was *Madame Butterfly.*

Prominent businessmen met on April 19 to form a Convention League, the purpose of which was to bring conventions to Cleveland. This was the forerunner of organized effort to make the city one of the leading convention and exposition centers of the nation.

The Council Educational Alliance, incorporated in April, was conducted along settlement lines. On April 27 Moritz and Yetta Joseph gave the deed to their home at 2104 Woodland Avenue to the Alliance as a headquarters. Mrs. A. Wiener was the first president; and, when she resigned a month later, B. Mahler was given the office. He was succeeded in 1904 by Rabbi Moses J. Gries. In 1909 the Alliance moved into its new home on the south side of Woodland Avenue between East 37th and East 38th streets. The Alliance provided recreation centers and informal education primarily for Jewish children.

The Elwell-Parker Electric Company of America made its first motors for battery-driven automobiles this year. In 1903 it developed both the motors and chassis for street trucks. Four years later, the factory site on St. Clair between East 40th and 45th streets was acquired. Purchase of a controlling interest in the company was consummated by the Anderson Carriage Company of Detroit in 1909. Through the influence of Morris S. Towson, vice president and consulting engineer, the plant remained in Cleveland to be known as Elwell-Parker. With the passing of the electric car, the Detroit firm was segregated, and a new company, The Elwell-Parker Electric Company, was formed in 1920 with Towson as president. Stemming from the old electric car was the storage-battery street truck, a product of Towson's ingenuity. From it he developed the first power industrial truck, to speed the handling of materials safely and economically. The company became producer of the greater share of the electric trucks in the United States, building industrial trucks and mobile cranes in a wide range of capacities. Upon the death of his father in 1942, S. K. Towson became president.

Hiram House, founded in 1896, was incorporated on May 1, this year. Bishop Charles D. Williams, dean of Trinity Cathedral, was the first president of the board, on which served Dr. Paul F. Sutphen, Frank Billings, Samuel Mather, Charles A. Nicola, and W. H. Canniff. Mr. and Mrs. Mather made possible the first night-lighted playground in America, opened in 1900 with trained workers. Soon the city and the school board established public playgrounds. A survey showed only one bathtub in the six hundred homes of the neighborhood; and through the generosity of Mrs. Mather, the first public bath-house in Cleveland was erected on Orange Street. The city's first trained visiting nurse was engaged by Bellamy in 1901 to care for the sick in the district. Manual training, arts and crafts introduced at Hiram House paved the way to classes in the public schools. Prominent Clevelanders gave their time and money to help the pioneer Ohio settlement, and on the early boards were men of the caliber of F. F. Prentiss, William G. Mather, William H. Hunt, and F. H. Goff. George A. Bellamy, who pioneered character-building, family conservation, and community planning, made Hiram House a pattern for the nation, as he continued to expand facilities to meet changing conditions.

The Brotherhood of Railroad Trainmen chose Cleveland as its home, moving from Peoria, Illinois, where the headquarters had been located since 1896. The trainmen organized on September 23, 1883, enrolling 1,780 during the first year. Alexander F. Whitney, elected president July 1, 1928, soon became a national figure, representing his organization in many important conferences with the Government and industry. Under his direction the membership grew to 215,000 in the 1940s.

The Cleveland Chamber of Commerce Building on the Public Square was dedicated, May 2. Many important functions took place in its auditorium. The body of John Hay lay in state there in 1905; Marshal Ferdinand Foch was welcomed in 1921, and David Lloyd George in 1923; and here world-famous leaders spoke while the building was occupied by the Chamber.

Failing to influence the founder of the famous Glidden Tours to undertake a trek to Cleveland, the *Plain Dealer* sponsored Alexander Winton, who agreed to drive to Boston with Charles B. Shanks, sports reporter. The journey in the "hydro-carbon motor carriage" was accomplished in forty-seven and a half hours running time at 14.5 miles per hour, establishing a record.

The Cleveland Directory Company was incorporated by Byron D. Annewalt, Edwin Potter, David W. Wilson, and W. E. Annewalt. A. E. Perlin joined the organization in 1910; and, in 1921, when the company merged with R. L. Polk & Company, he undertook the direction of the indispensable Cleveland guidebook. The publication grew with the city, and the 1946 edition was a two-thousand-page volume, listing about 650,000 names, used throughout the United States and Canada as a key to Cleveland. In 1898 the Association of North American Directory Publishers was organized in the city.

John H. Farley, who had been mayor in 1883-84, succeeded spectacular Mayor McKisson in the City Hall in 1899. His administration was characterized by economy and by furthering the city's interests through careful attention to needed public improvements. "Honest John" Farley's two years seemed particularly tame by comparison with his predecessor's, and yet sound progress was made.

A strike was declared against the Big Consolidated street-railway company, June 10, and the entire street-railway system was involved. Scenes of wild confusion marked the opening days of the strike, the principles involved including pay, working conditions, and union recognition. Rioting and lawlessness marked the next five weeks, and the Naval Reserves were assembled, July 22, to protect workers and public. The situation growing constantly more serious, the militia was called out. An attempt was made to blow up a car at Willson and Kinsman Street on July 23, and the next day ten people were injured when a Euclid Avenue car was destroyed by nitro-glycerine. State troops patrolled city streets, July 26, and violence subsided. However, it was fall before order prevailed and the car lines operated according to schedule.

Professor Leo Stevens announced he would perform a wonderful stunt in balloon and parachute navigation on July 4 at Scenic Park in Rocky River (opposite Sloan Avenue). It was planned that he and his assistant would make an ascension and then cut loose for a parachute race. The balloon rose ahead of time, and the two men went with it, tangled in the ropes. The large bag drifted over Lake Erie; but the aeronauts were saved by John Christoferson and Edward Christersen who reached them in a launch and towed the balloon to shore. There were legal proceedings involving pay for the rescuers.

A "Riding School" was established, August 6, where lessons were given in operation of the horseless carriage. Driving a car was considered an engineering feat, and getting the car home, a miracle.

The Health Department ruled on August 10 that all manufacturing plants must be provided with smoke consumers. However, industry grew, smoke persisted, regulations were abused, and, in spite of all, Cleveland remained one of the most healthful cities, according to the records.

The Bailey Company was first known as the L. A. Bailey store, founded in 1881. Colonel Louis Black, son of Morris Black, the first Hungarian to make his home in Cleveland, was joined by C. K. Sunshine, well-known business man, and together they assumed management of The Bailey Company, located at Ontario and Prospect Avenue. Under their capable leadership the company was incorporated in 1899. As the city expanded, the Bailey organization created a revolutionary precedent among local department stores by establishing East Side and West Side branches: at Euclid Avenue and East 101st Street, and at Detroit and Warren Road in Lakewood.

L. G. Oppenheim became president in 1927. In 1941 a modernization program was completed at Bailey's main store. Howard L. Boynton was the store superintendent.

After serving with the Ohio Volunteer Infantry during the Civil War, Colonel Louis Black became interested in manufacturing, banking, and realty. He was the first director of fire service under the Federal Plan of government during the administration of Mayor Rose. Besides being treasurer of The Bailey Company, he was a leader in civic enterprises.

Elizabeth Sprague was woman city tennis champion for three years in succession, 1899 to 1901, and she and Helen Smith became doubles champions at this time. In 1902 Elizabeth VanDuzer and Rachael Studley won the women's doubles championship. T. Sterling Beckwith was the outstanding player in Cleveland prior to 1900. He not only held the city and state championships, but dominated the Florida courts as well. With George Worthington, he won the doubles championship of Ohio.

A funeral streetcar was seen for the first time on the streets of Cleveland, September 15, an innovation of the Big Consolidated. Cleveland funeral directors were given a ride to certain cemeteries, but the public was not carried away with the idea.

Mr. and Mrs. Elroy M. Avery visited the grave of Moses Cleaveland near Canterbury Green, Connecticut, on October 15. Leaving the road, they crossed a cornfield to reach the old burial ground, surrounded by a rough stone wall which they climbed. A path through weeds led to graves bearing markers almost obliterated by mud and slime. When scraped, one stone slab revealed the inscription, "Gen. Moses Cleaveland. Died Nov. 16, 1806. Aged 52." Another marked the grave of "Esther, Relict of Moses Cleaveland, Esq. Died Jan. 17, 1840, aged 74." Nearby were graves of the General's parents. The *Plain Dealer* put this question to the public: "What are you going to do about it?" The answer was forthcoming when the Cleveland Chamber of Commerce appointed a committee to take suitable action.

The Gentlemen's Driving Club of Cleveland announced Temper as the trotter of the year, time 2:09½, owned and driven by W. M. Cummer; and the champion pacer, Sunland Belle, time 2:07½, owned and driven by H. K. Devereux.

The Park Board bought twenty-six acres of land between Brookside and Garfield parks in 1899, known as Washington Park. The following year, forty additional acres were purchased, and twenty more at a later date.

A special train bearing representatives of fifteen nations arrived in Cleveland on October 15. They had concluded their International Congress of All the Americas in Washington and were on a tour of leading American cities. A committee of Clevelanders met the train with Jacob B. Perkins, Amos Townsend, Dan P. Eells, S. A. Fuller, and John C. Covert as prominent members. The guests were shown the greatest oil-refining plant in the Americas, the leading factory for the production of astronomical instruments, and the foremost of light-producing plants. The fifty-three members of the Pan-American party were royally entertained. At a banquet, Henry B. Payne was toastmaster. One speaker sounded the keynote: "America should be what it ought to be, a light to the world, where sixteen nations dwell in peace and harmony without armies and without fear."

Charles F. Brush, one of Cleveland's greatest sons, received the Rumford Medal from the American Academy of Arts and Sciences. The President of France once said of him, "I know not which to admire the more, the physique of the man or the genius of the inventor." As his fellow townsman, John D. Rockefeller, had lighted the world with oil and gas, this scientific genius proceeded to light it with something better.

The May Company of Cleveland, destined to become "Ohio's Largest Store," was founded this year when David May and his associates purchased the well-known store of the E. R. Hull & Dutton Company. The May Company of Cleveland was the third unit of the nationwide organization known as the May Department Stores Company, founded in Denver in 1888. It grew to include other large stores and a number of branches, each operating independently under its own management. In 1901 the Cleveland company acquired property on Euclid Avenue on the south side of Public Square, increasing its floor space from 73,000 to 131,000 square feet. Rapid and consistent growth resulted under the leadership of Nathan L. Dauby, vice president of the May Stores, his merchandising ability having been proved in his own shoe store on Ontario Street. The store expanded ten times after its beginning until it occupied more than a million square feet, and plans for further remodeling were under way in the later 1940s.

Mail was collected by automobile for the first time on December 15. In 2 hours and 27 minutes, the horseless carriage traversed a route usually covered in 6 hours by horse and wagon. Colonel Charles C. Dewstoe had been appointed postmaster on June 28.

A popular question attracted nationwide attention: "When does the new century begin?" Many thought January 1, 1900, was the time; but analysts proved that the hundredth year of the old century would conclude December 31, 1900, and that the new century would begin January 1, 1901. However, there were some unprejudiced people who celebrated both dates.

CHAPTER 13

New Century—New Advance
1900-1909

THE UNITED STATES was now regarded as a great world power. It had assumed an important position in international trade, and had become the leading creditor nation. It had acquired colonies and protectorates, and was growing rapidly in population, wealth, and naval strength. The national income rose from $10,000,000,000 in President Harrison's time (1890) to $22,000,000,000 at the beginning of President Theodore Roosevelt's second term (1905). During Roosevelt's two terms, prosperity was the rule; and the federal debt declined from $1,263,000,000 in 1900 to $1,132,000,000 in 1905, when a gradual rise began. A short-lived panic brought a national scare in 1907-8. However, a recovery was made as the decade ended with the incoming of President William Howard Taft.

Cleveland concluded the Nineteenth Century as one of America's most promising industrial and commercial centers. Its highly successful centennial celebration had inspired civic leaders to take stock of the rapidly growing municipality. They studied its problems and capitalized upon its possibilities.

The population of the Forest City at the turn of the century, when John H. Farley was giving an economical administration as mayor, was 381,768, making Cleveland the seventh of American cities; the Cuyahoga County total showed 439,120. The striking comparisons, however, had to do with industry. Only New York and Chicago led Cleveland in the manufacture of women's and children's garments. The city had assumed a strong lead in the production of wire and wire nails, malleable iron, twist drills, and highly refined gasoline. It was well to the front in the manufacture of hardware, paints and varnishes, electrical apparatus, bridges, printing presses, druggists' preparations, car wheels, chemicals, sewing machines, bolts and nuts, washers, rivets, and astronomical instruments. In the production of merchant vessels, in number as well as in tonnage, Cleveland held a high place.

Cleveland's industrial growth in the early years of the century was reflected in the founding of thirty-two banks and other financial institutions from 1900 to 1903. More than half were neighborhood banks, and many of them later lost their identity through mergers.

New industries, like the well-established ones, were prospering. The automobile business was getting a substantial start, and Cleveland-made cars

Alva Bradley   William Grey Rose   John Huntington

Gen. James Barnett   William Edwards   Stevenson Burke

Liberty E. Holden   Worcester R. Warner   Ambrose Swasey

John A. McKerron, driven by Harry K. Devereux (left), defeating The Monk (center) and Lord Derby in the world famous Boston Challenge Cup Race, at the Gentlemen's Driving Club, Glenville Track.

Uhlan, great trotter, was a favorite in Cleveland. Right: Lou Dillon, trotter, C. K. G. Billings driving, was crowned "Queen of the Turf" at the Glenville Track.

Dutch Mowrey of the "hairless tail" driven by Charles A. Otis, Jr., defeating Nicol B. (left), driven by Banker John Sherwin, and Tiger, driven by Actor Johnny Ray.

were known nationally. Steam cars were built by the White brothers, Baker was making his electrics, and Winton and Stearns were trying to keep pace with the increasing demand for their gasoline cars. Cleveland was the hub of the automobile industry, and new manufacturers were considering the establishment of plants in the city.

The electrical industry was developing rapidly, and the making of lamps was begun by the National Electric Lamp Association, forerunner of the gigantic Nela Park development. Impetus was given to the industry late in the decade by the newly formed Electrical League of Cleveland. Natural gas was piped to the city in 1903, and it contributed to the comfort of homes and the efficiency of factories.

New construction features were being introduced by the American Ship Building Company, and ships began to appear with deep side tanks and transverse arches. Because of the growth of the steel industry, receipts of Lake Superior iron ore at lower lake ports increased 100 per cent in six years—21,000,000 tons were carried in 1904, and 42,620,201 tons in 1910. Many new ore carriers were built to meet this increased demand, and luxurious passenger ships were being constructed as well. At the end of the decade, ships were larger, steel deckhouses were used, and wood was gradually disappearing. With the advent of new industries and a shift of importance from ore to oil, tankers took the place of bulk freighters, and barges replaced carriers.

Loading and unloading iron ore, which required several days for a single cargo, was the great bottleneck retarding industry until George H. Hulett designed a car dumper and invented the stiff-leg unloader, revolutionizing shipping and the transportation end of the iron-and-steel business. Bulk freighters were redesigned to carry greater cargoes. Wheel house and crew quarters were built far forward, and power plant and operations area far aft; and into the many hatches was poured in a short time ore tonnage that could be removed in less than a half day by mechanical unloading giants in seventeen-ton bites. Ships of increased size plied the lake lanes from the mines, speedily feeding furnaces of the lower lakes with enormous tonnage.

Local industrial companies were learning of their inter-dependence. They realized that better understanding and closer co-operation were essential to future progress. Chemicals were necessary to oil refining; machinery depended upon tools. If parts made in Cleveland by one company could be used by another, transportation costs and time would be saved. An era began that was to witness scientific research, specialized products, and volume production.

Business leaders became aware early in the new century that a shortage of well-located industrial sites was developing. Happily, the Belt Line encircling Cleveland from Collinwood to West Park, touching various railroad lines, was projected by W. R. and Ben F. Hopkins, who also laid out factory districts in the vicinity of the road that were to become valuable locations for new plants.

Sound progress was being made in retail trade, and the stores realized that their best interests could be served by co-operative efforts. The Retail Merchants Board was formed as a part of the Chamber of Commerce, seventeen merchants banding together to launch the project.

Advertising of a modest character was helping to sell Cleveland goods; and, in the belief that co-operation and competition could flourish among members of one organization, twenty-nine advertising men founded the Cleveland Advertising Club. It was the first association of its kind in the world, and it maintained its leadership in activities and membership from the pioneer days.

The political giants, Marcus A. Hanna and Tom L. Johnson, were attracting far more than local attention in their verbal clashes. Hanna was proposed as candidate for the Presidency on the Republican ticket, but he denied having ambitions in this direction. Johnson, winning popularity by cheap carfare, greater use of parks, and socialistic tendencies, was lauded by his followers as the embittered fight over traction matters continued.

The newspaper field witnessed important changes in 1905, when Charles A. Otis, firm believer in his city's future, purchased the *World,* the *News and Herald,* and the *Evening Plain Dealer.* Out of the merger came the *News.* It vigorously opposed Johnson's policies, and the long and bitter contest between Johnson and the railway property owners finally resulted in receivership. Reorganization came under a franchise drawn by Federal Judge R. W. Tayler and led to the formation of the Cleveland Railway Company.

Industrial progress was reflected in building construction of all kinds. Larger office buildings were erected, higher, more spacious, and with the newest appointments, including the Williamson Building, Rose Building, Schofield Building, Citizens Building, Park Building, Rockefeller Building, and Hippodrome Building, the latter famed for its beautiful theater. Impressive banking headquarters were built by The Cleveland Trust Company and the First National Bank. Merchants were moving eastward on Euclid Avenue; and adjacent to its new store, the William Taylor Son & Company built an arcade connecting Euclid and Prospect avenues. The Federal Building, the first unit in the Group Plan was under construction. Citizens benefited from new bridges, harbor developments, expanded water-works and sewage systems, and enlarged health institutions. Theaters, colleges, and churches shared in the building era. Renowned Trinity Cathedral was consecrated. The Cleveland Museum of Art was assured and building plans were under way. New residential suburbs were taking form.

The National Educational Association held a highly successful convention in 1908, and attention was drawn to the excellence of the Cleveland public schools, a reputation that was to grow in future years. Two new schools of outstanding importance were opened in this decade: the Cleveland School of Art, soon to become a national leader in its field, and East Technical High School, considered a model institution of technical training.

Women were making a stronger appeal for the right to vote. Only four states had gone on official record for woman suffrage: Wyoming, in 1869; and Colorado, Utah, and Idaho in the nineties. Prohibition was widely discussed, but only four states had become completely dry: Maine, Vermont, North Dakota, and Kansas. However, there were many states partially dry, and there was no doubt that the movement against liquor was becoming stronger.

Entertainment flourished in the era of prosperity. The Glenville races had become social affairs as well as popular sport features, and the Gentlemen's Driving Club had helped to make Cleveland the leading trotting-race city of the country. Baseball was attracting increasing attention. Trainloads of Clevelanders went to the Pan-American Exposition in Buffalo in 1901. Euclid Beach Park was opened by the Humphreys, and was to become the most successful free-gate amusement park in America.

Theaters were playing to large houses when the Empire, Prospect, and Hippodrome opened. The Euclid Avenue Opera House and the Colonial presented the leading attractions of what was called the "legitimate" stage. The Lyceum belonged to the Stair Circuit, and presented a variety of attractions of a popular character at somewhat lower prices than were charged at the Opera House. The Cleveland was the city's melodrama theater with "blood and thunder" thrills; vaudeville was presented by the Empire, Prospect, and Lyric; and the Star and later the Empire produced burlesque. When the Hippodrome opened, it was the finest playhouse in the city, and particularly suited to large spectacles. Haltnorth's Gardens offered summer stock and usually drew well with better-than-average talent.

In the summer of 1904, the Empire offered Shakespeare with William Farnum, one of the most promising dramatic actors of his time, and Percy Haswell, who read her lines superbly. Later Farnum's company experimented with *Damon and Pythias* and other good old-timers of dramatic strength, with such success that the line of ticket buyers often extended to Erie Street.

The Colonial kept busy in the summertime with stock; and when Vaughan Glaser and Laura Nelson Hall played the leads, generally every seat in the house was filled. The Lyceum, too, offered summer-stock productions, in which Eugenia Blair was a popular favorite in such old-time plays as *East Lynne*.

The Euclid Avenue Garden Theater was operating on the north side of Euclid opposite Kennard Street, under the management of Max Faetkenheuer. Huge umbrellas sheltered tables in the garden, and at the south end was a complete stage and outdoor auditorium. A series of light operas made the undertaking popular. It was unable to withstand the competition of downtown theaters and summer amusements, and made way for commercial improvements.

Older theater-goers regret that motion pictures took the place of the attractions that delighted them in the first decade of the century. They recall Sarah Bernhardt, "the divine"; Henry Irving, whose *Louis, the 11th* and *The Bells* will never be forgotten; Richard Mansfield in *Old Heidelberg;* Minnie Maddern Fiske, finest of all "four wall" actresses, and John Drew with his sparkling comedy dramas.

Of the many others, special mention should be made of Nat Goodwin, delightful comedian; Margaret Anglin, finest reader of her time; Julia Marlowe, lovely in many roles; Olga Nethersole, powerful in dramatic parts; Blanche Bates, with her *Darling of the Gods* and *Under Two Flags;* Isabelle Irving, E. M. Willard, Sol Smith Russell, Joseph Jefferson, E. H. Sothern, William Faversham, Leslie Carter, Eleanor Robson, Henrietta Crosman, Maxine Elliott, and Maude Adams—all players who glorified the stage in this particular decade. Theater-goers who enjoyed the lighter touch would protest if mention were not made of DeWolf Hopper, Dan Daly, Anna Held, Lew Dockstader, Willie Collier, Lillian Russell, Weber and Fields, the Four Cohans, Johnny and Emma Ray, Ward and Vokes, Montgomery and Stone, all of whom bring nostalgic recollections of the theater in "the good old days." Cleveland was represented on the stage by Joseph S. Haworth, who appeared in leading Shakespearean and romantic roles. Charlie Hopper of Cleveland was a favorite both on and off the stage, and his humorous impersonation of *Chimmie Fadden* won popularity for him throughout the nation.

Motion-picture theaters were growing in number, and films were improving in quality. *The Great Train Robbery* was the first plot-thriller to come to Cleveland, and, a few years later, local theater-goers were applauding Mary Pickford, Charlie Chaplin, Theda Bara, and Marguerite Clark.

Entertainment and excitement were halted for a time by the assassination at the Pan-American Exposition of President McKinley, who enjoyed a legion of personal friends in Cleveland. The Grand Army of the Republic Encampment proved the largest convention that the city had known, and President McKinley was to have been the guest of honor. His assassination brought grief to the mighty assembly of soldiers and to the whole nation.

Fashions inspired by the Gibson girl were in strange contrast to the old-fashioned garments of a decade earlier. The phrase "modern woman" was used to distinguish those who wore the graceful light dresses that came into vogue, and Charles Dana Gibson's artistic pen showed women as men liked to see them. Women were now dressing to suit the occasion, and American influence was supplanting the dominant Paris creation. As the well-dressed woman suited herself to the latest styles, she took on a new freedom of poise, action, and independence.

A substantial costume for the lady of fashion in this horse-and-buggy era was made from heavy material and secured with horse-blanket hooks. The "bloomer girl" wore a bulky, pleated sports outfit. The blouse had leg-o'-mutton sleeves, and this "fetching ensemble" was completed by side-buttoned gaiters.

Bailey's department store in 1905 offered a number of specials for men. Derby hats were sold at 95 cents, and caps and hats were priced at from 15 cents to $1.90. All-wool suits and overcoats in the latest fabrics, usually $10 and $12, were offered for $6.80; stiff- or soft-bosom shirts were sold for 39 cents, and kid gloves for 49 cents. Overalls were priced at 35 cents, corduroy pants at 29 cents for children, and ordinary school pants at 15 cents.

This was the time when Jesse Wilcox Smith, Howard Pyle, and Maxfield Parrish attracted attention with their distinctive art; when the most popular books were *Janice Meredith* by Paul Leicester Ford, *Richard Carvel* by Winston Churchill—the American author, *When Knighthood Was in Flower* by Charles Major, *David Harum* by Edward Noyes Westcott, and *Mr. Dooley* by Finley Peter Dunne. William Dean Howells, whose home was in Jefferson, Ohio, for some years, was taking his place among the better writers of the world. Everybody was singing *I've Got Rings on My Fingers, Put on Your Old Gray Bonnet,* and *Casey Jones,* with Blanche Ring teaching the rhythm.

A new municipal code went into effect in 1903 providing for a mayor; a vice mayor who acted as president of the Council, which consisted of thirty-two members; a board of public service of three members, a city solicitor, a treasurer, and an auditor. All of these officials were to serve for terms of two years. The municipal government of Cleveland had undergone several changes since 1836 when the administration consisted of a council of nine members, and also a board of aldermen, of three members. In 1852, came the era of administrative boards, and it was not until 1891 that a centralized form of government was established—the Federal Plan, administered under an elected mayor. In June, 1902, during Johnson's administration, the Supreme Court of Ohio ruled that Cleveland's Federal form of government and all municipal charters in the state were unconstitutional. It was necessary to adopt a new plan of government under which the mayor named the members of the board of public safety, while the city solicitor, the city auditor, and the city treasurer were elected. In 1910 the Paine law permitted the mayor to name a director of public service, who, with the mayor and the director of safety, made up the board of control. This law also established a civil-service commission. Home-rule agitation finally lead to a constitutional convention in 1912, enabling Ohio cities to adopt their own charters and to assume all powers of local self-government.

Throughout the decade, immigrants were coming to Cleveland because it had won a reputation as a prosperous city. Newcomers from Europe in recent years represented many nationalities. However, those from Great Britain and Germany in about equal number made up more than one-half of the total. Swedes, Russians, Austrians, Italians, and Hungarians were next in order.

Increasing immigration brought manifold welfare problems. Clevelanders had been generous in giving to charitable enterprises, but they felt that the philanthropic institutions of the city should operate on a more businesslike plan. Consequently, the Chamber of Commerce organized a Committee on Benevolent Associations from which local organizations sought endorsement. From that early beginning, Cleveland set an example of sound management in its charitable endeavors.

When the Group Plan was first projected in 1900, thousands of Clevelanders visited the district, envisioning the improvements. Engineers, architects, and financiers were soon at work making plans for the development, and the State Legislature passed a bill permitting the county commissioners to lease to the City of Cleveland their half of the space between the City Hall and the Court House at a nominal rental fee for an indefinite number of years. The Chamber of Commerce helped with the early financing, and Frederick Law Olmsted, city planner from Brookline, Massachusetts, was brought to Cleveland to give his counsel. Daniel H. Burnham, famous architect and planner of the White City of the World's Columbian Exposition, Chicago, made a statement that exemplified the aims of the architects and engineers when he said, "Make no little plans; they have no magic to stir men's blood and probably themselves will not be realized. Make big plans; aim high in hope and work, remembering that a noble, logical plan once recorded will never die, but long after we are gone will be a living thing asserting itself with growing insistence." The spirit of Burnham's stirring words continuously influenced those who envisioned the great projects of the city. The planners wished to make Cleveland as beautiful a place in which to live as it was a profitable place in which to work.

A local controversy that lasted for a period of months concerned the substitution of numbers for names for the streets of Cleveland. Many people felt that a system that had worked for more than a century should not be abandoned. Stores disliked the idea of changing their mailing and billing lists, and many citizens opposed discarding such fine historic names as Case, Willson, Sterling, and Erie for simple numbers. But the majority of citizens were in favor of the new plan, and in a short time Clevelanders realized that the innovation meant efficiency.

"Payne's Pastures," near the downtown district, east of East 21st Street between Chester and Superior, were still awaiting home-building customers, the owners believing that their valuation would be enhanced a little later. However, continuously better transit service upset this calculation. Those who lived two miles from the Square and had spent a half hour riding to work on horsecars, could now live four miles from the Square and reach work in the same time as formerly. As transit facilities improved, residential sections were developed further and further from the Square. In the meantime, property around the city's center had begun to deteriorate, a process characteristic of large cities.

When the Chamber of Commerce, in the fall of 1908, planned an industrial exposition, it regarded the undertaking as an investment in civic pride that might earn dividends of business value. The undertaking was an outstanding success: retail business thrived, the real-estate market improved, a new industrial plant was brought to Cleveland, and several foreign nations were represented among the large number of visitors. Manufacturers learned of the products made in their own city, and discovered new ways to further Cleveland business. City pride was said to have reached its highest point, and the exposition proved a fitting conclusion to the most important decade of advance Cleveland had yet known.

Rapid business development was manifesting itself in many ways. The retail shopping district had been moving steadily eastward from lower Superior, west of the Square, to lower Euclid; residential neighborhoods were spreading out to the east and west; new bridges were being built across the valley to accommodate the growing railroad lines and to meet the demands of increasing automobile traffic. New areas for manufacturing were being developed in this city of diversified industry. Noise and smoke and rumbling trucks were advertising that here was a flourishing manufacturing center. With its spirit of enterprise, its leaders with inventive minds, and its central location, Cleveland felt sure that the industry and commerce so rapidly developed in the past half century would experience greater growth in the era to come.

The canals, accelerators of Cleveland's growth in the early days when the mule-drawn boats brought coal to the city's busy little factories, were regarded as historical landmarks. Several old reservoirs were preserved—Grand Lake, Indian Lake, and Buckeye Lake—and the surrounding property was converted into state parks. Picturesque sections in the Cuyahoga Valley became sentimental reminders of tow-path days, when counterfeiters and "bad men" haunted hills and taverns, and Cleveland gained its commercial start.

The turn of the century witnessed many changes in the physical appearance as well as in the general character of the city, and the Public Square showed these changes more than any other section. Ever since village days it had been the principal meeting place, made inviting by big trees, a fountain, bandstand, benches, and other evidences of the small town. But now Cleveland had become sophisticated. Horseless carriages were chugging through Superior and Ontario streets, and horse-drawn vehicles were becoming old-fashioned. Only a few years before, people hitched their horses to posts along the curbs, did their shopping, visited with the clerks, then philosophized with friends at the curbstone while unfastening their hitching straps. Under the big shade trees, they settled national affairs, found fault with the party in power, and swapped stories about their troubles. But now nearly everyone seemed in a hurry. Cleveland was growing, and clerks knew few of their customers personally. Business was the topic of conversation. Smoke was damaging the trees. The picturesqueness and poetry of the village had given way to the confusion of complex city life. Some people objected to the change, and there was an increasing number who moved to the suburbs to escape the hustle-bustle of the rapidly growing industrial and commercial center. Although the Public Square had changed with the growth of the city, it remained the center of a great metropolitan district, the people's commons, trade-mark of Cleveland and the proud inheritance from far-seeing early-day engineers.

1900

The New Year's Subscription Ball, held in the Chamber of Commerce Auditorium, was a "brilliant success." Favors were brought from New York for the two hundred guests who joined in the grand cotillion after supper. A "pretty effect" was obtained by the array of electric lamps and frosted electric globes. In spite of wind and snow flurries, several hundred onlookers witnessed the New Year's Day automobile parade which started from Public

Square and covered the main thoroughfares. Stanhopes, electric road wagons, and light electric phaetons fell into line at six miles per hour, while a "one-horse ice wagon" brought up the rear.

The population of Cleveland was 381,768. Of this number 87,740 were native-born of native parents; 163,570 were native-born of foreign parents, and 124,354 were foreign-born. The ethnic groups, besides the whites, included 5,988 Negroes, 103 Chinese, 11 Japanese, and 2 Indians. Cleveland's population was naturally an industrial population. In manufacturing and mechanical work there were 55,879 males and 10,602 females; in trade and

"Sorry, kind lady, but I can't wait." (*Donahey in the* Plain Dealer.)

transportation, 34,927 males and 6,248 females; in domestic and personal service, 17,415 males and 14,246 females; in professional service, 5,401 males and 2,496 females. In the population race, Cincinnati reported 325,902.

The Cleveland Automobile Club chugged into motion on January 8, its founders all being owners of "self-propelled pleasure vehicles." The first board of trustees was made up of Walter C. Baker, George L. Weiss, Alexander Winton, E. L. Strong, Fred R. White, Windsor T. White, L. H. Rogers, F. B. Stearns, and R. A. Rainey. Strong was the first president. The organization set up modest headquarters in a rented room in the Chamber of Commerce Building on the Public Square. The original purpose was to maintain a social club devoted to the sport of motoring throughout the country and to secure national legislation for the protection of motorists and their vehicles.

The partnership of Worcester R. Warner and Ambrose Swasey continued until this year, when The Warner & Swasey Company was incorporated, its history closely paralleling the development of metal-working in America. Demand for turret lathes and other machines began to come from abroad, wherever men used metal-working machinery, and the company grew. Warner's hobby of astronomy grew into a business that established an international reputation for building scientific instruments, including the telescope for Lick Observatory; the refractor of the Yerkes Observatory, the largest refracting or lens-type telescope in the world; the 82-inch reflector of the McDonald Observatory, the second largest telescope in the world; and the giant telescope of the Warner & Swasey Observatory at Case School of Applied Science. The company's major business, however, continued to be the designing and building of turret lathes to supply a worldwide market. The apprentice-training plan became a model for the industry. Phillip E. Bliss, who had joined the firm as accounting clerk in 1910, became president in 1929, after the retirement of Frank A. Scott. Ten years later, Charles J. Stilwell succeeded the deceased president, and his brother, Clifford S., was elected executive vice president. Both began their careers as machine operators in the Warner & Swasey plant. Warner Seely, who entered the plant in 1913, became secretary of the company in 1924.

Alta House grew out of a day nursery and kindergarten established in "Little Italy," an Italian community, in 1895. John D. Rockefeller took a practical interest in the project, and paid for the construction of a settlement house (12515 Mayfield) erected this year. It was named for his daughter, Mrs. Alta Rockefeller Prentice, and was dedicated on February 20. At Rockefeller's request, Alta House was made an independent social settlement with its own governing board. Joseph Carabelli, who lived in the neighborhood, was also interested and helpful.

Ban Johnson, president, reorganized the Western League, which became the American League. A Cleveland club, the Bluebirds, was formed, by Davis R. Hawley and M. E. Gaul, who named John Kilfoyle and Charles W. Somers as president and vice president. League Park was secured, and James "Jim" McAleer, famous retired outfielder of the Cleveland National League Club, was made manager. The team finished the 1900 season in sixth place, Chicago winning the pennant. In 1901, the American League was strengthened in member cities and in players, and the Cleveland team finished seventh.

A gift of a hundred thousand dollars for an arch over the lower boulevard at Superior Avenue in Rockefeller Park was made to the city by John D. Rockefeller on condition that Cleveland raise twenty thousand dollars more to complete it. The financier's partnership gifts meant much to the city's development. Charles F. Schweinfurth designed the bridges erected over St. Clair, Superior, and Wade Park avenues to connect Gordon, Rockefeller, and Wade parks.

The American Federation of Labor began a decade of membership expansion. National prosperity and the success of the typographical union, the building-trades unions, and the coal miners helped to build the membership from 548,000 in 1900 to 1,676,000 four years later. Strikes were called in the steel industries and in the railroads, but they were unsuccessful. It was not until World War I that the unions again made highly important gains.

The Cleveland Graduate Nurses Association was founded, and soon investigated district-nursing organizations in New York, Boston, Chicago, and Philadelphia, giving the city the benefit of its research.

A petition was granted on March 7, forming the township of West Park out of a portion of Rockport Township.

The Council of Jewish Women, a world organization, met in Cleveland on March 9.

"Peerless" was an important name in the automobile world at the turn of the century. Fifteen years before, Simpson & Goff were making machine tools in Cincinnati, and in 1889 their plant was moved to Cleveland where bicycles became the leading product. The next step was automobiles, and the Peerless "White Streak" attracted attention at the nation's first automobile show in New York. The Cleveland company was the only show exhibitor still in business in 1931. J. B. Crouse, J. Robert Crouse, A. J. Tremaine, B. G. Tremaine, and F. S. Terry, who had laid the foundations of Nela Park, bought a controlling interest in Peerless in 1917, built a model factory at Quincy and East 93rd Street and made E. J. Kulas the sales manager. Cars of the luxury class produced in Cleveland became famous; but James A. Bohannon, president in 1929, seeing that the market for the highest-grade cars was not promising, effected the transition of the motor-car company to the Brewing Corporation of America.

A great increase in ocean travel was forecast on March 14, with five thousand Cleveland people going abroad during the year.

The death of Maude S. on March 18, within one week of her twenty-sixth birthday, recalled to Cleveland her record mile of 2:08¾ made at the Glenville track, July 30, 1885. The famous race horse was owned by Robert Bonner, who had paid forty thousand dollars to William H. Vanderbilt for the "Queen of the Turf."

At the corner of Euclid and the Public Square, the second Williamson Building opened on April 1. The massive, eighteen-story office building, rich in historic background and tradition, was erected on the site of the earlier Williamson Building and the Williamson family homestead. It was named for one of Cleveland's best-known families, fathered by Samuel Williamson, pioneer judge. George B. Post & Sons designed the skyscraper for the Williamson Company, organized in 1897, with H. Clark Ford, president; Charles W. Wason, vice president; and S. P. Baldwin, secretary. The building housed the Cleveland Trust Company, the Federal Reserve Bank, the Midland Bank, and many leading business firms. The Williamson Building and the adjoining Cuyahoga Building were united in 1944 under one ownership, Stanley M. Buckingham continuing as manager of both. Major alterations were undertaken, resulting in a modern and impressive structure dignified by beautiful new façades. A. A. McCaslin was president of the Williamson Company.

Membership in The Union Club of Cleveland had increased to 500, with a list of 125 applicants who could expect to wait as long as ten years for admission. The Mary Castle property, at the northeast corner of Euclid and Muirson Street, was acquired in 1901, and a new clubhouse was formally opened on December 6, 1905. The original home (Hippodrome Building site) was sold in 1902 for four hundred thousand dollars. Cleveland wealth and leadership characterized the Union Club from the start in 1872. Many of its members attained great prominence in Cleveland and in the nation, among them Henry B. Payne, Samuel L. Mather, and Waldemar Otis, who were founders; Marcus A. Hanna, Charles F. Brush, Samuel Mather, James A. Garfield, Ambrose Swasey, Liberty E. Holden, Theodore E. Burton, Myron T. Herrick, and Charles F. Thwing. William G. Mather, who joined the club in 1880 and was awarded the distinction of honorary life member, and Charles A. Otis, who joined in 1890, held the two longest membership records, it was reported in 1946. In the city's Sesquicentennial Year the president was Robert C. Norton.

The Bethel Associated Charities was the predecessor of the Cleveland Associated Charities (later Family Service Association), incorporated in May, and the Bethel Union Building became its headquarters. Leading men and women of the city supported the work of the association. In 1904 James F. Jackson became general secretary, guiding the welfare program for most of twenty-two years. He changed relief work from alms-giving to wise administration as a part of family rehabilitation, stressing more and more the need for personal and preventive work with families not yet in need of relief. The strengthening of family life became the organization's objective. Jackson died in 1927, and was succeeded by Edward D. Lynde, who served until 1933, when he resigned to become associate director of administration of the Family Welfare Association of America.

James Harrison "Hal" Donahey came to the *Plain Dealer* from the *World* in May, at the invitation of E. H. Baker and Charles E. Kennedy, who wished to popularize the paper. Donahey soon became the nation's best-known cartoonist.

The Retail Merchants Board was formed on June 8 as a division of the Chamber of Commerce, with time-honored names like Hower & Higbee, Strauss Bros. & Company, W. B. Davis & Company, and W. H. Quinby among the seventeen original members. H. R. Hatch was the first president. The board acted as a medium of exchange or clearance point for information or assistance alike to store and customer. W. H. Gray, elected president and secretary in 1939, served through the years, becoming one of the nation's leaders in his field. The board participated in civic and educational events, working actively throughout World Wars I and II as a unit in advertising and assisting War Bond, recruiting, and Red Cross drives.

The Cleveland Chamber of Commerce, anxious to centralize appeals for charitable purposes, set up a Committee on Benevolent Associations which endorsed local welfare organizations.

Ryerson Ritchie was elected president of the Cleveland Chamber of Commerce. In the decade, he was succeeded in turn by Charles L. Pack, 1901; Harvey D. Goulder, 1902; J. J. Sullivan, 1903; Amos B. McNairy, 1904; Ambrose Swasey, 1905; Francis F. Prentiss, 1906; Lyman H. Treadway, 1907; Charles S. Howe, 1908; and Charles F. Brush, 1909.

The Cleveland Electric Railway joined the city in erecting shelter stations on the Public Square. They were more serviceable than attractive.

There were 106,453 children of school age in Cleveland; but only 58,105 pupils were registered, and the average attendance was 45,700. The teaching staff totaled 1,250. The value of school buildings was $4,619,676, and there was need for expanded facilities.

Through purchase and gift, the city acquired Woodland Hills Park on Kinsman and Woodland Hills avenues, consisting of fifteen acres of splendid forest trees.

Due to an increase in typhoid fever, the water-works tunnels were extended further into the lake in order to obtain purer water.

The Euclid Club, Greater Cleveland's second golf club, opened on July 4 in Cleveland Heights with one of the finest clubhouses in the country. Its first president was William B. Chisholm. W.H. "Bertie" Way of Detroit was secured to lay out the eighteen-hole course and serve as professional. The upper nine holes were on the property of John D. Rockefeller, honorary member, and the lower nine on Patrick Calhoun's property. When the Mayfield Country Club opened in 1910, it drew so heavily on the Euclid Club membership that the latter was abandoned, the course giving way to real-estate development.

The Ferro Machine & Foundry Company had its beginning this year in the Hoffman Hinge & Foundry Company, manufacturers of metallic hinges and car couplers. The first location remained the company's home in the 1940s, 3155 East 66th Street. The Ferro name was adopted in 1905, and substantial expansion developed under the leadership of Crispin Oglebay, president and treasurer. He envisioned the future of the automobile business and began the production of cylinder blocks for the Ford Manufacturing Company. Gasoline marine engines were made for a time, but later the organization centered its efforts in the manufacture of automotive products. During World War II, Ferro produced more than 100,000 tons of castings for armored vehicles, trucks, landing craft, battleships, and motor equipment for the Army and Navy, a vast number of end-connectors for tanks, and millions of shells. In December, 1946, the officers-and-management group purchased the company from the Oglebay interests, forming a new company known as Ferro Machine & Foundry, Inc. John M. Price who joined Ferro in 1935 became president in 1940.

Harry Vardon, greatest golfer of his time, gave a thirty-six-hole exhibition at the Cleveland Golf Club on July 28, with only about fifty people present. Golf in Cleveland was in its infancy.

Eldred Hall, designed by Abram Garfield, was erected on the Adelbert campus of Western Reserve University, south of the main building. One of the best-known buildings of the university, it served student purposes, was the YMCA headquarters, and later housed the department of drama and theater.

The Cleveland Whist Club first entered a team in the Hamilton Trophy contest at the Eighth Congress of the American Whist League at Boston in

July. This trophy, which represented the championship of the United States for teams of four, was sought by the Cleveland team of E. M. Tillinghast, William E. Talcott, A. R. Horr, and Carl R. Apthorp. The loss of but one trick gave the Forest City team second place. In 1902 the Cleveland team defeated Boston, winning the coveted Hamilton award at Manhattan Beach, Long Island, the players being Talcott, Apthorp, Horr, and Carl T. Robertson. The following year Cleveland once more gained justifiable praise by defeating the famous Knickerbocker Club of New York, to win the trophy twice in succession. Talcott, Robertson, Horr, and Prescott made this consecutive record which was never equaled.

The firm of Vinson & Korner began a business on August 1 in a niche on Euclid Avenue, 6 by 25 feet, next to the Vincent-Barstow Building. Merritt Vinson had developed a small circulating library and suggested to Harry Korner that they start a bookstore. John J. Wood, formerly manager of Burrows Brothers, came into the firm in 1905, Vinson having left, and the store became known as Korner & Wood in 1906. The original sign read, "Books, Stationery, Pictures and Some Other Things," which gave the partners a certain leeway in their stock. The store, located at 1512 Euclid, became known throughout Ohio for its books and decorative art. The founder, Harry Korner, continued to direct the business in the 1940s.

In the early 1900s, the books of Charles W. Chesnutt, Cleveland's distinguished colored novelist, were widely read. His works elevated the plane of Negro authorship. Chesnutt's life was devoted to the cause of the colored people, for whom he sought equal opportunity along every line of advancement. He was born in 1858 in Cleveland, the son of parents who came from North Carolina by wagon train. His father, Andrew Jackson Chesnutt, served four years as teamster in the Union Army, and Charles, who had attended the Cleveland schools and the Howard School in Fayetteville, North Carolina, became a teacher at the age of sixteen. His experience was broadened by employment in New York when he wrote a column of "Wall Street Gossip" for the *Mail and Express*. Coming back to Cleveland in 1883, he served for a time in the auditing department of the Nickel Plate Railroad, and then as a stenographer in the office of Judge Samuel Williamson, where he found time to study law. He was admitted to the Ohio Bar in 1887, standing at the head of his class. At this time he was also writing for the McClure Syndicate, and he attracted wide attention when the *Atlantic Monthly* published his first "conjure" story, *The Goophered Grapevine*. More stories were written for the *Atlantic Monthly* which were collected and published in 1899 by Houghton, Mifflin & Company under the title of the *Conjure Woman*. After valuable experience with Henderson, Kline & Tolles, he set up in business as a court reporter, but continued to write stories and articles for leading magazines and newspapers. Among his books are *The Life of Frederick Douglass* in the *Beacon Biographies, The Wife of His Youth, The House Behind the Cedars,* and *The Colonel's Dream.*

Probate Judge Henry C. White on August 29 appointed a County Bicycle Path Commission, which included George Collister, W. A. Skinkel, E. W. Doty, and C. W. Heaton. The purpose was to construct and maintain bicycle paths in the county outside of cities, because there was so much horse-and-buggy traffic that the roads were not safe for wheelmen. Bicycle riders were to pay a dollar a year to the county in license fees to finance the paths.

The YMCA established one of the first equipped and supervised playgrounds in Cleveland.

Property fronting 104 feet on Euclid Avenue (Statler Hotel site) was purchased by Charles L. Pack for $150,000. In 1911 it was leased to The Statler Hotels Company at a maximum rental of $34,000 a year on a valuation of $750,000. This land sold for $100 an acre 65 years earlier.

The first Stearns automobile developed by F. B. Stearns had a single-cylinder engine carried on a spring-supported frame. Within a year, a four-cycle engine had been introduced. The Stearns was a popular car for a long period, eventually becoming the Stearns-Knight.

The Hebrew Observer merged with the *Jewish Review* to form *The Jewish Review and Observer,* published by Dan S. Wertheimer. In the 1940s the Wertheimer family continued to manage the paper under Ralph M., president; James D., vice president; and Howard M., editor.

The Rose Building was completed (at 2060 East 9th Street). Rated as the largest building in Ohio at the time, its ten stories covered nearly an acre of ground. *The Plain Dealer* of September 16 advertised: "No gloomy halls; all convenience in shape of electric lights, hot and cold water, quick elevator service, drinking fountains on every floor, and a smoke consuming device attached to the engine building." Thousands of invitations were sent out for the Rose Building's gigantic housewarming. Benjamin Rose, the owner, well-known philanthropist, was head of the Cleveland Provision Company, one of the largest packing houses in the country. An asset of his estate, the building's earnings, contributed to the welfare of the community by providing care and support for old people and crippled children, under the terms of the Benjamin Rose Institute, organized in 1909. Rose died at the age of eighty in 1908.

Cleveland celebrated "Home Week," beginning October 7, and visitors and former residents came by the thousands. Attractions included street carnivals, red fire, concerts, a floral festival, fire-department exhibitions in the gaily decorated streets, speech-making, and conducted tours of the city. An immense American flag was sent skyward from the American Trust Building on the Public Square to be anchored a half-mile in the air by means of box kites. Incandescent lamps threw a merry blaze over the streets where thousands of people were gathered, while the Great Western Band gave a concert.

William Jennings Bryan closed his extensive Presidential campaign tour of Ohio with a speech in Cleveland, October 15. Such a crowd met him at the Erie Station that it took him ten minutes to reach his carriage for the procession, which was made up of clubs and bands with red fire and much din. Some ten thousand persons squeezed into Central Armory while thousands more were unable to enter. The eloquent Democratic candidate pleaded for reduced tariffs, blasted at Mark Hanna, and, as a peace lover, shuddered at the proposal that the United States maintain a standing army of ten thousand men.

The Hunkin-Conkey Construction Company, incorporated this year, succeeded a partnership founded by Samuel and William J. Hunkin. Having built many of Cleveland's larger industrial plants, the Detroit-Superior High Level Bridge, and Akron rubber plants, in addition to hotels, banks, power plants, and office buildings, the War Department engaged the company, prior to World War II, to construct the seventy-million-dollar Ravenna Ordnance Plant. In 1946 the company was engaged in the largest railroad construction

Uncle Mark: "Just step down a moment, Teddy, I want to talk to you."
Hanna and McKinley were not pleased by Theodore Roosevelt's aggressiveness and personal publicity. (Donahey in the Plain Dealer.*)*

and relocation job in the country for the Pennsylvania Railroad east of Pittsburgh. Officers in 1946 included: G. E. Conkey, president; S. E. Hunkin, vice president; and C. A. Lohmiller, vice president.

Twenty thousand men marched in the McKinley-Roosevelt parade on Euclid Avenue, November 3. Rough-rider hats and white-duck suits were prominent. "Full dinner pails" were carried on floats and on marchers' shoulders. An elephant ambled along in a procession that included thirty-eight bands. Two old-time horsecars were reclaimed to operate along the avenue where men carried canes with red-white-and-blue streamers. In the election, the voters overwhelmingly supported William McKinley for President and Theodore Roosevelt for Vice President.

A Cleveland paper made this reference to the coming national holiday:

> These are degenerate days, when the Thanksgiving dinner of our fathers is not Thanksgiving dinner enough for us. Around the festive boards we gather with hearts full of cheer and minds full of memories, but with appetites dull. Turkey, which was once very acceptable, if well browned and stuffed with any old thing, must now be set forth with chestnuts inside, with oyster dressing, perhaps, or with an interior redolent with celery.

In the preceding five years the population of Lakewood increased from 400 to 3,355, making it Ohio's fastest growing community.

When F. S. Terry, B. G. Tremaine, J. B. Crouse, and J. Robert Crouse met in Cleveland this year, Terry had already embarked on his career in the lamp business. His experience in the retail field convinced him that success was not coming at the time to small independent dealers, and this conviction led to ultimate association with the General Electric Company. The growth of the Terry-Tremaine-Crouse National Electric Lamp Association (NELA) had become so rapid by 1910 that the East 45th Street headquarters were no longer adequate. Terry was convinced of the advantages of a suburban location, and ground was broken for Nela Park in East Cleveland in 1912. The expanding young business was established in a group of Georgian structures in a beautiful eighty-five-acre park, called "The University of Light." The tower building became the Institute in 1933, and here modern displays and an auditorium were popular features. Lighting development advanced rapidly with the increased demand for illumination, directly traceable to the Nela research and training programs. Nearly two thousand "professors" and their assistants made experiments in the Nela training school and conference center for the industry. The famous annual Christmas display of outdoor lighting, which transformed the park into a fairyland of color, attracted as many as 250,000 visitors in one Christmas season. M. I. Sloan was vice president and general manager of the Lamp Department of the General Electric Company at Nela Park in the 1940s; other executives were F. F. Harroff, M. S. Hamner, R. H. Humbert, K. G. Reider, N. H. Boynton, and Ward Harrison, director of engineering, who was succeeded by Willard C. Brown.

Labor-saving machinery throughout the world is the heritage left by George H. Hulett, one of Cleveland's great inventors, who patented the Hulett unloader this year, and whose ore-handling devices revolutionized the transportation end of the ore industry. Born at Conneaut, Ohio, in 1846, he was the son of pioneer settlers who came from Vermont in 1831. The family left their farm and moved to Cleveland in 1860. Hulett had been a merchant and operated a produce-and-commission business prior to 1890, when he began developing coal- and ore-handling machinery. He invented a car dumper and the stiff-leg unloader while employed as engineer with the McMyler Manufacturing Company. He joined the Wellman-Seaver-Morgan Company and became vice president; and conveyor bridges, unloading and handling devices of greater efficiency and capacity which embodied

Hulett inventions, were produced, influencing the growth of industry and transportation in many fields.

During the year, several commercial buildings were erected: Caxton Building, 800 Huron Road, home of the Caxton Company; and Electric Building, 700 Prospect Avenue.

At the turn of the century, Clevelanders attracting attention for their civic and business activities included William J. Akers, owner of the Forest City House and organizer of the Cleveland Hotel Men's Association, who was identified with local politics for forty years; Frank A. Arter, whose oil operations and other business associations covered a wide field, and who was a leading benefactor of religious and educational institutions; and William H. Canniff, general manager of the Lake Shore & Michigan Southern Railroad and later president of the New York, Chicago and St. Louis road. Samuel D. Dodge, United States district attorney in 1895, was a lawyer with civic and business affiliations; Judge John C. Hutchins, a prominent jurist and public-spirited citizen; Charles T. Richmond, an executive of the National Carbon Company; George P. Comey, president of the Comey & Johnson Company, pioneer in the manufacture of women's hats; William H. Lamprecht, banker and investor. Dr. Samuel W. Kelley was a national authority on children's diseases; Drs. James C. Wood, A. B. Schneider, and John B. McGee were outstanding in their profession. Leaders in education were Mattoon M. Curtis, professor of psychology; Lemuel S. Potwin and Oliver F. Emerson, English; Samuel Ball Platner, Latin; Henry E. Bourne, history, and Abraham L. Fuller, Greek.

Iron and steel maintained a strong lead in Cleveland industry, as reported by the census of manufactures as of 1899. Fifteen iron-and-steel producers reported $24,276,197 as the value of their products, 6,915 wage earners employed on an average, with a payroll of $4,014,589; 127 concerns operating foundry and machine shops, product value of $15,428,053—8,658 wage earners, with a payroll of $4,487,398; 10 slaughtering and meat-packing firms, products valued at $7,514,470; 77 women's clothing firms, $4,213,248; 10 malt-liquor firms, $4,033,915. Printing and publishing, book and job, products were valued at $1,787,106; 38 publishers of newspapers and periodicals valued their products at $2,073,324. There were 118 producers of men's clothing, their products valued at $3,410,299; electrical apparatus and supplies, $3,357,923; petroleum refining, $2,963,169; paint and varnish, $2,902,471; bridges, $2,416,595; bolts and nuts, $2,405,856; stoves, $1,905,391; forgings, $1,874,029; sewing machines, $1,759,320; chemicals, $1,729,313; confectionery, $1,705,311; hardware, $1,653,374; oil, $1,421,089; railroad cars and repairs, $1,209,947; wirework and cables, $1,137,416; tools, $890,342; bicycles, $862,024; carriages and wagons, $729,292. There were 2,927 manufacturing establishments in Cleveland, employing 58,810 wage earners, the payroll totaling $27,892,689, and value of products, $139,849,806. The construction industry was enjoying the prosperity era, and 2,692 building permits issued in 1900 represented operations valued at $3,845,833. Cleveland's boundaries now embraced 34.34 square miles.

1901

The Cleveland Chamber of Commerce greeted the Twentieth Century with a banquet and a toast to Cleveland and its future. A year of unparalleled prosperity was predicted. The *Plain Dealer* stated that it would be "a year of big things, a record-breaker in all lines of manufacturing." Money was easy and stocks firm. The New York market was strong, despite a temporary business recession during which fortunes were swept away.

President McKinley, at the height of his career, entered his second term with Theodore Roosevelt as Vice President, a running mate whom neither McKinley nor Marcus A. Hanna wanted. Prosperity was running high during McKinley's regime, and many boy babies were given "McKinley" for a middle name.

A daring page of bloomer girls doing Delsarte exercises at the YWCA appeared in a local daily and shocked some readers.

The Cleveland Cap Screw Company on January 2 began modest operations with twenty-nine employees in a small structure, the nucleus of a great future plant at 2196 Clarkwood Road. Charles E. Thompson was a welder in the company, and he believed that the principle of making electrically welded heads and screws could be applied to valves. In 1904 he began to make valves for the "horseless carriage." Alexander Winton, pioneer manufacturer, placed an order that diverted operations into the automotive-parts industry, and the company became the first independent maker of engine valves for cars and trucks. In 1908, its name changed to Electric Welding Products Company; in 1915, to Steel Products Company; in 1926, to Thompson Products, Inc. The "poor man's car" was born with mass production of Henry Ford's Model T; and as the auto industry grew, the Cleveland company expanded, thriving on the policy that "We must make our parts so good and at such low cost that the car manufacturers won't want to make their own."

The Cleveland Trust Company purchased the property of the First Methodist Church at the southeast corner of Euclid Avenue and Erie Street early in the year at a cost of $500,000 as the site of its future home. The church had acquired the parcel in 1865 for $9,150; in 1827, one and four-fifths acres of land, embracing this and adjoining sites on the same corner, had sold for $64. Many warned that the bank had made a fatal step, as upper Euclid had not been invaded by business.

The Empire Theater opened on Huron Road as a vaudeville theater, with L. M. Eirick, president; Charles L. LaMarche, vice president and treasurer; and Max Faetkenheuer, musical director. The talent presented included so many stars that the shows were called "the headliners of America." For weeks the theater, featuring "high class fashionable vaudeville," was packed at every performance. Later on, the local management was superseded by out-of-town promoters, the Columbia Amusement Company finally converting the house into a burlesque theater. Standing out in the Empire's burlesque career was the appearance of John L. Sullivan, world-famous prizefighter, bulging in a dress suit. He delivered a monologue dealing with his spectacular adventures. The Telephone Building was erected on the theater site.

Ideals regarding the operation of a properly planned amusement park inspired the Humphrey family to lease the Euclid Beach Park property in 1901. Dubious attractions that had hitherto constituted the entertainment policy were discarded, and the Humphreys enlisted the advertising support of church and newspapers. Arrangements were made for the streetcar company to carry people to the park for one fare. Shortly afterward, the family bought the property and installed on the ninety acres modern developments in the amusement field, and, in addition, camp grounds. The family's popcorn business, which provided money for the venture, continued to thrive, the popcorn being raised on the 150-acre Humphrey farm. D. S. Humphrey's ideals were proved practical, when wholesome entertainment and attractive surroundings drew hundreds of thousands to the "fairyland with the free gate." The entire family helped to establish and operate the park, and on the death in 1932 of the civic and business leader who founded it, his son, Harvey, was made president, and later, Dudley S. Humphrey III, son of Harvey, became his associate.

Cleveland lake carriers started for Detroit at noon, January 15. A big season began early.

Although the Euclid Avenue Baptist Church saw its members move to new residential districts, it remained a downtown Baptist stronghold, establishing missions and working aggressively under outstanding pastoral leadership. Dr. Charles Aubrey Eaton began his notable ministry this year at the "Rockefeller Church," as it had become widely known. Passion Week services drew vast audiences and were held in the Star Theater. Dr. William W. Bustard, energetic and eloquent crusader, served the church from 1909-25, and during this time plans were made for a million-dollar edifice. In 1927 a new sanctuary was dedicated on leased property at the northwest corner of Euclid and East 18th Street.

Cleveland's dirty streets were being criticized by the citizenship. City Engineer Walter P. Rice urged that the white-wings system used in New York be copied in Cleveland. His ideas finally prevailed, and in 1902 the effort was made to clean principal streets twice a week. However, it was not until 1906 that flushing machines were used and the city adopted a system of collecting ashes and refuse.

The United States Steel Corporation acquired Standard Oil's ore and transportation holdings. How John D. Rockefeller wandered from his chosen field is a story all its own, as Rockefeller told it to Elbert H. Baker, publisher of the *Plain Dealer*. Desiring to put some of his wealth to work in varied investments outside of oil, Rockefeller settled on steel. He realized that the industry would soon have to be organized and stabilized to avoid over-production and suicidal competition, and that ore and ships and railroads would be essential. As opportunity offered, he began picking up stocks, and J. Pierpont Morgan and his friends were surprised at what he had to offer. The odds and ends that he turned in amounted to more than $200,000,000 and gave him a place on the United States Steel board.

An explosion and fire at the five-mile water-works crib in February attracted the populace. It was marked by dramatic incidents and heroic sacrifices.

George A. Wallace, who had joined the Fire Department in 1869, was made chief on March 4. He became known as "America's grand old fire-fighter."

The Cleveland Branch of the Fraternal Order of Eagles was organized, March 31, three years after the national organization was founded. Two of the prominent organizers were John Cline and Hyman D. Davis. The fraternity grew rapidly, and in 1946 there were twenty thousand members in Greater Cleveland, with P. J. Daley, president.

In the interest of health, Cleveland began the construction of an intercepting sewer system. Small sewers were connected with the lake or streams in the early days. The rapid growth of population made it clear that higher standards of sanitation would have to be observed. City Engineer Walter P. Rice in 1888 had made a survey and recommended a comprehensive study of conditions relating to the sewage system and the purifying of the Cuyahoga River. An intercepting system was recommended, but the matter lay dormant until 1895, when City Engineer M. E. Rawson secured a board of national experts who confirmed Rice's recommendation. A main sewer was laid from the river to East 140th Street, and a scientific procedure resulted in dividing the city into major sewer districts with main sewers to which the other sewers were attached. Sewage was then carried to modern and efficient treatment plants east, west, and south. The disposal plants in the 1940s had cost about twenty million dollars and their operation and maintenance involved an expenditure of a million dollars per year.

The White Motor Company pioneered in the field that made Cleveland a national bus-transportation center. The first successful steam car appeared in 1900, made by the White Sewing Machine Company. Rollin H. White, son of Thomas, pioneer in Cleveland's motor industry, had invented a new flash boiler; and, with the assistance of his brothers, began production of the Stanhope. Not only did the Whites think in terms of the horseless carriage, but also horseless wagons for transporting goods. Thus one of their first successes was a car with a truck chassis. Windsor T., the eldest brother, assumed administration of the new business, while Rollin, joined later by Walter C., operated the plant. In 1902, when motorized trucks were generally regarded as impractical, five White trucks made a perfect record run from New York to Boston and return. In 1904, the White car won the grand prize at the World's Fair in St. Louis, and by 1906 White had attained an output of 1,500 steam cars a year. The White Motor Company now considered itself a full-fledged industry, no longer a branch of White Sewing Machine, and moved to St. Clair and East 79th Street, where it occupied the first buildings of what later became a huge plant. Windsor T. White was president, and Walter C. White, vice president. For some years, White Motor was Cleveland's largest independent manufacturer in any field, and it continued to be one of the country's foremost automotive concerns, selling trucks and buses in every civilized country. The merger of the White company and the Studebaker Corporation was effected in 1932, the White company maintaining its identity. Later Studebaker reorganized, releasing White from the connection. Robert F. Black became president in 1935.

The Episcopal mission called St. Andrews-in-the-East was moved to Cleveland Heights where it was reorganized as St. Alban's Parish. Its house of worship, erected at Euclid Heights Boulevard and Edgehill Road, is said to be the oldest church in the suburb. From 1912-17, Dr. Walter R. Breed, rector of St. Paul's, gave strength to the weak parish, and it grew steadily in influence and membership. The Rev. Frank L. Shaffer became rector of St. Alban's in 1945, succeeding the Rev. Harold G. Holt.

The first large bath-house and pavilion was erected in Gordon Park. "Keep off the Grass" signs were prominent in city parks. It was George A. Bellamy of Hiram House who won his contention that parks should be playspots for public enjoyment. Most of the signs came down.

The successful 1899 tour to New York by Winton and Shanks inspired another *Plain Dealer*-sponsored venture, this time a cross-continental trek. The pair left San Francisco amid cheering crowds, but were forced to abandon the tour on the sands of Nevada after nine days. The newspaper had organized a contest with cash prizes for the best estimate of time required on the trip.

Newton D. Baker, city solicitor, read a paper before the Social Service Club, revealing unfortunate conditions in local jails. It led to the establishment of a juvenile court. Out of the club, formed in the YMCA, also came Cleveland's first free, public bath-houses, the Legal Aid Society, the City Club, and the reorganized Associated Charities.

Mrs. Carry Nation was called the "Modern Samson" by the Cleveland WCTU. Saloon-keepers said they could cope with her should she come to Cleveland. Later she arrived unheralded and without applause. Her only weapon was her sharp tongue.

A bacteriological laboratory was located in the Medical Building of Western Reserve University with Dr. Roger Perkins in charge. It provided physicians with equipment for testing diphtheria culture, typhoid blood, and sputum of suspected tuberculosis. Distribution was also made through police stations, drug stores, and the health office.

Everybody off to Buffalo for the Pan-American Exposition! The Buckeye Building at the Fair was well situated, and served as a pleasant headquarters for Cleveland visitors.

A big boom in real estate started in May, investors buying land instead of stocks, and Cleveland property was considered a good investment.

Tom L. Johnson became mayor of Cleveland in May 1901, succeeding John H. Farley, and throughout his eight years in office there were few dull months. Disputes over transit control, agitations on many municipal questions and difficulties with labor, marked the administration of the mayor, who followed the teachings of Henry George. Cleveland was kept in the national limelight, and the mayor's name became known throughout the land. Shortly after he took office, Council passed an ordinance to establish three-cent fare on the West Side. Opposing interests obtained an injunction in court, and a long legal battle followed.

Rainbow Cottage was now ten years old, and Mr. and Mrs. William L. Harkness provided a larger home on Richmond Road near Mayfield, where a year-round program of care for convalescent city children started. After a fire in 1904, a site on Green Road was purchased and a new retreat provided. Young women who were caring for children at the Kinderheim joined with Rainbow in 1905; and in 1913 a new name was adopted, Rainbow Hospital for Crippled and Convalescent Children. A school was built and given to the hospital by Mrs. Dudley S. Blossom in 1923, and a hospital building with a hundred beds opened in 1928. Rainbow was one of the first institutions in the United States to install a pool or underwater gymnasium for the correction of defects following infantile paralysis, and it had one of the first nursery schools. In 1924 it was affiliated with Western Reserve University for teaching purposes, and in 1926 it became a member of the University Hospitals.

The Cleveland Automobile Club estimated on June 27 that there were not less than 150 automobiles in use, and reported that the city had six automobile factories. The May Company had introduced "special delivery service by the 'White Flyer' truck." The advent of the motor car was hardly appreciated by the local editor who wrote on July 1, "For all except people with generous incomes, the cost of a horseless carriage is really prohibitive. As long as an auto costs as much as a team of horses with the carriage attached, it cannot be expected that the craze will grow with any marked degree of rapidity."

The New Amsterdam Hotel was built by W. J. White, the "chewing-gum king," on Euclid Avenue (and East 22nd) as a business venture. It was one of the most fashionable apartment hotels in the Middle West.

The dust was settling, June 30, over a hundred-mile route from Cleveland to Medina, Lodi, Wellington, Elyria, Lorain, and Cleveland, after the first "century run" of the season arranged by the Cleveland Automobile Club. Walter C. White, in a steamer, was the first to complete the circuit. Others participating were Mr. and Mrs. E. L. Strong, William M. Wright, F. L. Rankin of Hartford, Connecticut, and H. F. Henderson and son in gasoline cars; Otis Southworth and Benjamin P. Bole, Windsor T. White, and Guerdon S. Holden in steamers.

In a spectacular race, reported for the *Press* by carrier pigeons, special dispatch boats, wires, buoys, and box-kite signals, the sidewheeler *City of Erie* won the hundred-mile race against the steamer *Tashmoo* of the White Star Line between Cleveland and Erie, Pennsylvania. Thousands watched the contest from watercraft and from the banks along the race course. Only a length separated the two fast passenger steamers.

Mission work among German immigrants, sponsored by the Cleveland Disciples Union, led to the founding of the Cleveland Christian Home for Children. Thirty needy children found shelter in a large house acquired for the purpose this year; and two years later, the project came under the care of the national board of the Disciples. The work expanded with the growing city, and through a substantial bequest from A. R. Teachout, gifts from the Knights Templars, and board assistance, a $300,000 modern home was erected at 11401 Lorain Avenue. In the mid-1940s, it was home to about 120 children.

John A. Penton moved to Cleveland with his *Machinery Molders Journal,* conceived while president of the Brotherhood of Machinery Molders, 1886-92, in Detroit. Experience with this modest publication convinced Penton of the importance of commercial technical organs to the growing foundry industry. He affiliated his publication with the *Iron Trade Review,* and it became part of the newly organized Iron and Steel Press Company. The company also acquired an interest in the Whitworth Brothers commercial printing business, and, on January 29, 1904, the Penton Publishing Company was incorporated. In 1921 it built the nine-story Penton Building at 1213 West 3rd Street. The British subsidiary, the Penton Publishing Company, Ltd., was established in London shortly after the close of World War I. Numerous Penton publications printed since 1904 were sold or discontinued. The *Iron Trade Review* was changed to *Steel* and vastly improved. In 1938 the *New Equipment Digest* was purchased, and in 1943 the company established *Revista Industrial* in the United States, and *Service Station* in England. Besides these three trade papers and *Steel,* Penton published in 1946 *The Foundry* and *Machine Design.* Officers included E. L. Shaner, president and treasurer; G. O. Hays, vice president and general manager; and F. G. Steinebach, vice president and secretary.

Thousands were turned away from "Buffalo Bill" Cody's Show in July. Ruth Hanna was forced to crawl under the tent to reach her party.

Society was in gala dress at box parties at the Glenville races on July 24. Cresceus broke the world's record, trotting a mile in 2:02¾, and became undisputed king of the trotting turf.

First Church of Christ, Scientist, was instrumental in launching Second Church in August. The new church was later to make its home in Engineers Hall, St. Clair Avenue at Ontario Street. Third Church of Christ, Scientist, was established in October, 1903, its home being located on West 25th Street at Mapledale Avenue; seven years later, First Church, Lakewood, was founded. Fourth Church, 1931 East 105th Street, was established in August, 1914, and, the following spring, Fifth Church, Lake Avenue at West 117th Street, was given a substantial start. Sixth Church, George Washington School, was founded in 1922; First Church, Cleveland Heights, Fairmount Boulevard at Lee Road, in 1924; Seventh Church, 14713 Lake Shore Boulevard, and Christian Science Society, Fairview High School Building, in 1929. In 1945 Christian Science Society, South Euclid, was formed, and plans were laid for this organization in John Hubbard Memorial Hall, East 84th Street and Cedar Avenue, and Christian Science Society in Rocky River. Christian Science grew rapidly in Cleveland under able leadership, and the *Christian Science Monitor,* an international daily newspaper, was widely read throughout the Cleveland district.

The Baker Electric Torpedo, built by the Baker Motor Vehicle Company of Cleveland, established the world's kilometer record at Sheepshead Bay, New York, attaining a speed of 104 miles per hour.

A downpour of rain starting shortly after midnight, September 1, continued for eight hours and was pronounced the most severe in the thirty years of the Weather Bureau. Streets were flooded in an area eight miles long and about a mile and a half wide. The foundations of many homes were undermined. The area south of Euclid in the vicinity of Fairmount was a miniature lake, and residents took refuge in the upper stories of their homes. Rescue parties of police went through this area in boats, removing frightened families. The property damage was estimated at a million dollars.

President William McKinley paid his last visit to Cleveland on September 5 while on his way from Canton to the Pan-American Exposition at Buffalo. He reached the Union Depot shortly after noon and addressed the small group that had assembled to greet him; then he visited for twenty minutes with Senator Mark Hanna, shook hands with W. J. Akers, and waved farewell to the little assembly. The next day he was assassinated by Leon Czolgosz. The murderer signed a confession identifying himself as an anarchist, and stated he was influenced by a lecture given in Cleveland by Emma Goldman. Elaborate preparations had been made to receive the President in Cleveland as the most distinguished visitor to the Thirty-fifth Encampment of the Grand Army of the Republic. The white columns in the Public Square, erected in honor of the GAR visitors, were entwined with streamers of black as a symbol of the city's grief. The GAR parade, in which 15,600 Civil War veterans marched, proved one of the most impressive processions Cleveland had known, inspiring strong patriotic sentiment. It was said that more than 200,000 people were attracted to the city. Taking the wounded President's place in the reviewing stand was Senator Mark Hanna, and when "the Ohio boys in blue" marched by, he fell into line with them. Reviewing stands lined both sides of Bond Street, from Euclid to Lake; and in the Court of Honor on Bond Street, a great assembly of school children in costume formed a living flag. When the Encampment adjourned, the many thousand members little dreamed that forty-six years later Cleveland would be the scene of the Eighty-first Encampment with only five veterans to participate in the traditional parade. A tribute to the GAR was written for the occasion by W. R. Rose:

> Slowly they come with throb of drum,
>   The flag with its stars above;
> In memory's name the loyal flame
>   They feed from the cruse of love.
> Shoulder to shoulder they come in view,
>   Side by side in the dear old blue;
> Halting and bent, and with faltering feet,
> Onward they plod through the cheering street;
> Burdens of age under blouses of blue—
> Many the dead, and the living so few!

Loyalty's army, remnant of yore,
Drifts toward the mists of the silent shore.

The Pittsburgh Steamship Company, organized in October, soon had the largest fleet on the lakes. It was a combination of the Carnegie, Rockefeller, M. A. Hanna, Pickands-Mather, Lake Superior Iron, Menominee, Mutual, and Minnesota fleets.

Henry P. Edwards, who had been sports writer for the *Cleveland Recorder* and editor of *The American Sportsman,* was made sports editor of the *Plain Dealer.* He soon became a national authority on baseball matters, and his recommendations of local amateurs influenced their placement in the major leagues. In 1927 E. S. Barnard became president of the American League, and he made Edwards head of the organization's service bureau. With Ed Bang, sports editor of the *News,* Edwards started the Baseball Writers Association of America in 1908, and for fifteen years served as an official. He earned the title, "dean of baseball writers."

A Committee on Library Extension was added this year to the Public Library Board, an addition justified by the first Andrew Carnegie gift of seven branch libraries. These branches were offered and accepted with the condition that the city should provide the sites and expend twenty-five thousand dollars annually for their support. The headquarters of the Cleveland Public Library having been sold to make room for the Citizens Building, a lot was secured at the corner of Rockwell and Wood, and a temporary Main Library Building was opened for public use in October.

The Everett-Moore Syndicate was formed to own and operate interurban trolleys over the Lake Shore Electric Company lines from Cleveland to Toledo. Within a year, the company was placed in the hands of a receiver, and the proceeds went to the Huron Road Hospital.

When the first biennial festival of the National Federation of Music Clubs was held in Cleveland, the hostesses were the Fortnightly Club, the Rubinstein Club—a chorus of fifty voices directed by James H. Rogers, and the Friday Morning Music Club. Adella Prentiss (Hughes) was chairman of the public concerts, and through her efforts in planning the three orchestral concerts, with Schumann-Heink as soloist, the foundation of the Cleveland Orchestra was laid. An outstanding feature of the festival was the appearance of the Pittsburgh Symphony Orchestra, Victor Herbert conducting.

The Cleveland Advertising Club was the first organization of its kind in the world, having been established November 27 by twenty-nine men in the profession. They met in the old Forest City House on the Public Square and organized for business and social purposes. Elected were Seth Brown, president, and Will Gilbert, secretary. The membership grew, and the club headquarters grew with it, first in the Williamson Building, then in the Hollenden, and finally in the Statler. In 1909 the clubs of Cleveland, Detroit, and Buffalo organized the Advertising Affiliation, the first meeting being held in Cleveland on October 23. The club drew its members together through their interest in advertising, sales distribution, and social activities. Its broad purpose was to foster useful citizenship; its special purpose, the practice and ethics of advertising. The nation's distinguished speakers appeared before the club through the years. The organization played a part in many of Cleveland's greatest civic projects, helping to promote the Public Auditorium and the Stadium, giving assistance to expositions, and, through the Come-to-Cleveland Committee, advertising Cleveland throughout the nation and helping to bring organizations to the city. During World War II, the War Efforts Committee, with Sterling Graham, chairman, attracted wide attention through many successful campaigns. With a membership of 1,200, the Cleveland Advertising Club maintained a high national position in 1946, when the officers were Clay Reely, president; Chester W. Ruth and Grant Stone, vice presidents; Lester S. Auerbach, treasurer; and Horace C. Treharne, secretary-manager. Ruth, Stone, and Auerbach succeeded to the presidency. Among the earliest advertising agencies were The W. N. Gates Company, the Griswold-Eshleman Company, and the Fuller & Smith Company (later Fuller & Smith & Ross, Inc.). Many agencies followed through the years, including Bayless Kerr Company, Campbell-Sanford Advertising Company, The Carpenter Advertising Company, Foster & Davies, Inc., Hubbell Advertising Agency, Inc., Lang, Fisher & Stashower, Inc., Carr Liggett Advertising, Inc., McCann-Erickson, Inc., Meerman's, Inc., Meldrum & Fewsmith, White Advertising Company, and Will, Inc.

The Metropolitan Opera Company played a brief engagement in Grays Armory, resulting in a small financial loss because there was no theater large enough to meet the seating demand. The management stated it would not bring the company to Cleveland again until there were adequate accommodations. Later, the city was to become the company's favorite host.

1902

The first experiments with gas cooking appliances were made by gasoline-stove manufacturers. The early methods of cooking with wood, coal, and kerosene were gradually abandoned in favor of the gas stove, constructed mainly of cast iron with the bake oven below the cooking top. Nine of the nation's pioneer companies in the manufacture of gasoline stoves merged into one on January 7, under the name of American Stove Company, with Charles A. Stockstrom, president. Three Cleveland concerns joined this merger: Dangler Stove & Manufacturing Company, Schneider & Trenkamp, and Standard Lighting Company. Natural-gas development boomed the gas-stove business markedly. In December, 1914, the American Stove Company introduced a new development, the Lorain oven regulator. A new type of range called the "Magic Chef," which was radical in design, was developed in 1929. The company operated in nine cities in the 1940s. Henry Moecker was general manager of the Cleveland offices.

A bill to legalize Sunday baseball elicited newspaper comment on March

11. Consternation was expressed that Cleveland might experience the "wide-open" Sunday of Chicago and St. Louis.

The Florence Harkness Memorial Chapel at Western Reserve University was dedicated on Easter Sunday, March 30; and in November, Haydn Hall was opened. Named for Hiram C. Haydn, former president, it was donated by Mrs. Flora Stone Mather and used for recreational purposes.

The Schofield Building, an impressive structure at the southwest corner of Euclid and Erie, was completed in March. Built on the site of the former residence of the Scofield family, it was fourteen stories high. Many Cleve-landers regretted to see several popular stores, including Mayell's Drug Store, taken down to make way for the new building. Captain Levi Tucker Scofield, who spelled his name without the "h," planned the office building. He had followed an army career and had also become a leading architect and sculptor. Until his death in 1917, he maintained offices on the fourteenth floor. His best-known work was the Soldiers and Sailors Monument in the Square.

The original New York Floradora Company came to the Opera House on April 28. The famous sextette, made up of American beauties, received twelve curtain calls. Cleveland fashions were influenced only for a time, but *Tell Me, Pretty Maiden* lived through the years.

The Cleveland Congress of Mothers was organized in April at the Old Stone Church, with not enough present to fill the offices. The institution grew rapidly in numbers and influence. Mrs. Martin Striebinger was elected the first president, and she served until 1904, when Mrs. James A. Logan was elected for a term of two years. The third president was Mrs. W. E. Lindin, whose five-year term concluded in 1911. The early committees dealt with education, the home, the church, and the school. Mothers' conferences were organized throughout the county, and, by 1910, there were seventeen clubs affiliated with the congress. Under the leadership of Mrs. Austin Estabrook, who was president in 1911-12, the twenty-three clubs in the congress gave financial aid to the maternity dispensary of St. Luke's Hospital, and thus laid the foundation of the Maternity Hospital. The members then successfully campaigned against long hat pins, and interest was taken in juvenile de-linquency, the Lancaster Boys School, teachers' pensions, and plans for educating the deaf and mute. Each year witnessed greater activities. In 1927 the Congress became the Cleveland Council of Parent-Teacher Associations.

Cleveland "white wings" on April 28 voiced their "offended dignity" to Parks Director Charles P. Salen. They complained that drays and automobiles frequently ignored the street-cleaning army and jeopardized the members' safety. They also requested that, in addition to their remuneration of $1.50 a day, they be allowed twenty-five cents a day to pay for keeping their uniforms immaculate.

The Independent Building Trades Council and some unattached local unions were merged into the Cleveland Central Labor Union, and the name of the consolidated central body was changed to United Trades and Labor Council.

A group of young men in their early twenties, who belonged to an active social-service club of the YMCA, laid the foundation for the first Juvenile Court. This they furthered at their own expense in co-operation with an Associated Charities committee. Among the founders were Newton D. Baker, W. H. Kinnicutt, Glenn K. Shurtleff, William A. Greenlund, Starr Cadwallader, William A. Stinchcomb, Frederick C. Howe, and Robert M. Calfee. They successfully urged the passage of a bill in the State Legislature; and in May, 1902, the Juvenile Court, attached to the Court of Insolvency created in 1902, assumed authority over delinquent and dependent children under the age of sixteen years. The Cuyahoga County court was the first juvenile court established in Ohio and the second created by a legislative act in the nation. The first probation officers were volunteers, but paid officials were provided by an amendment to the act in 1904. A further amendment in 1906 gave to the court the power to deal with adults responsible for the neglect of children. Physical and mental examinations were later required of all persons coming before the court. Appreciating the importance of the institution, the county commissioners planned separate buildings for the expanding services on East 22nd Street in 1930.

Mrs. Charles E. Porter, president of the U and I Literary Club, issued a call to presidents of leading women's clubs of Cleveland to meet for the purpose of federation. The bylaws and constitution of the Cleveland Federation of Women's Clubs were adopted, May 6, by eighteen founding clubs, comprising seven hundred women. Eight of the original clubs continued to be in existence in the 1940s, the Colonial Study Circle, Cleveland Literary Guild, Cleveland Sorosis, Melvin Reading Club, Research Club, Thursday Fortnightly Club, Utilian Fortnightly Club, and U and I Literary Club. These forward-looking clubs realized that through united strength they could channel their efforts and activities to greater advantage to themselves and the community. Initial programs were developed along cultural lines, but interests broadened into civic problems of welfare and kindred activities. The first officers were Mrs. Charles E. Porter, president; Mattie C. Smith, secretary; Mrs. Lottie L. Saunders, treasurer.

"The craze for ping-pong" was described May 12, in a sermon reported in the local press as "striking evidence of absolute degeneracy."

The Academy of Medicine of Cleveland was organized on May 28, at a joint meeting of the Cuyahoga County Medical Society and the Cleveland Medical Society, attended by forty-one members. Dr. F. E. Bunts was elected president. During its early years, the Academy met in hotels, but later found headquarters on Prospect Avenue just east of East 22nd Street.

Announcement was made on May 30 that Napoleon Lajoie, the greatest baseball player of his time, had signed a contract with Cleveland. Never had the baseball spirit been so depressed as at the beginning of 1920. Cleveland had dropped into last place, and there were rumors that the franchise might go to Cincinnati or Pittsburgh. The spirit changed with the coming of Lajoie. The mighty second baseman made his first appearance June 4, and before 10,000 rooting fans Cleveland beat Boston 4-3. Three days later, the city's largest weekday baseball crowd of nearly 13,000 was on hand, and, before the season was over, Cleveland climbed from last place to fifth, Lajoie batting .369. In 1903, the team took the name Naps, honoring the star player.

Memorial Day was marked by the dedication of Brookside Park, with more than 20,000 observers in attendance. The holiday brought the debut of the Four-in-Hand and Tandem Driving Club, recently organized. Seven teams of four- and two-tandem turnouts began the day's drive at the Euclid Avenue residence of E. A. Merritt. President Dan R. Hanna held the ribbons which guided his quartet. Other four-in-hands were driven by C. A. Otis, Jr., W. L. Rice with Mayor and Mrs. Tom L. Johnson aboard, L. Dean Holden, H. M. Hanna, Jr., and James H. Hoyt. Tandems were driven by Belden Seymour and R. H. York. "Each had invited guests," the *Plain Dealer* related, "and the socially distinguished party dashed out the avenues to the Euclid Club, as the first objective; then through the parks and down the boulevard and back to the home of C. A. Otis, Jr., where tea was served."

The development of the harbor proceeded under the authorization of Congress through an act passed on June 13. The breakwater eastward to Gordon Park, for a distance totaling 16,000 feet, was being constructed at a cost of $4,500,000. The enlargement of the main entrance to the harbor was completed in 1908. In the meantime plans were made to build a government dock at the foot of Erie Street at a cost of $100,000. As planned by the basic acts of 1875, 1896, 1899, 1902, and 1907, passed after hard-fought appeals, harbor improvements involving expenditures of more than $5,000,000 had been completed.

A severe epidemic of smallpox occurred in the summer. There were 1,248 cases and 224 victims died. This was directly traceable to the suspension of vaccination the previous year. Vaccination was then reinstated, and the City Council made a special appropriation of four thousand dollars for smallpox research in the city laboratory.

The New York Central train "which made New York a suburb of Chicago," had its first run on June 15. The *Twentieth Century Limited* amazed citizens all over the world by traveling this distance in twenty hours. Forty-four years later, the total time for this run had been reduced to fifteen and a half hours. One Pullman car in 1946 cost as much as the whole train in 1902; one five-car train was sufficient in 1902, but in 1946 eighty or ninety cars were needed to fill the demand, and the Diesel locomotive had supplanted the old steamers.

One of the leading athletic events of the decade was the initial meet of the Ohio Collegiate Athletic Association—the Big Six—at the Glenville track, June 19. Participating were Western Reserve University, Case School of Applied Science, Ohio State University, Oberlin College, Ohio Wesleyan University, and Kenyon College.

The Group Plan Commission was created on June 20 by Governor George K. Nash, as a result of bills prepared by the American Institute of Architects and the Cleveland Chamber of Commerce, and passed by the Ohio Legislature. Members of the commission appointed by Mayor Johnson were Daniel H. Burnham, who had been director of public works for the Chicago Exposition of 1893; John M. Carrere and Arnold W. Brunner, experts in the erection of public buildings. In 1903 the commission made its first report to the mayor, providing for a grouping of public buildings surrounding a central mall, located northeast of the Public Square and extending from Rockwell northward beyond Lake Avenue. Not only did this plan erase a blighted area in the heart of the city, but it also inaugurated a project of far-visioned civic and artistic achievement. Not since the City of Washington had been planned, had such an elaborate remodeling project been put on paper. The undertaking was at first under the direction of a committee including Frank B. Meade, chairman, Abram Garfield, A. D. Taylor, Charlotte Rumbold, and Frank R. Walker. In 1911 Meade and Frederick Law Olmsted succeeded Burnham and Carrere. The Federal Building was the first Mall building to be completed.

GROUP PLAN INVESTMENT AS OF 1946

	LAND	BUILDINGS	TOTAL
Federal Building	$ 556,000	$3,319,000	$ 3,875,000
County Court House	1,095,675	4,500,000	5,595,675
The Mall (including landscaping)	4,999,100		4,999,100
Public Library	1,000,000	4,500,000	5,500,000
City Hall	676,000	2,600,000	3,276,000
Public Auditorium	848,000	9,652,000 ⎫	12,970,300
Underground Expo. Hall		2,470,300 ⎭	
Board of Education	845,000	1,800,000	2,645,000
Stadium		2,500,000	2,500,000
			$41,361,075

At the turn of the century, Ernest E. Merville and Caroline T. Arnold became principals of Spencerian Business College. After several moves, a pillared building was erected this year on the northwest corner of Euclid and Huntington Street. Merville became president in 1904, and served for almost four decades. The Daniel P. Eells mansion, 3201 Euclid, became the school's home in 1922. John D. Rockefeller, who had been graduated in 1855, maintained a keen interest in the institution for many years. In 1942 Spencerian, one of the nation's oldest private commercial schools, merged with Dyke School of Commerce, dating from 1893, the new name being Dyke & Spencerian College.

"Wire pictures," the first practical experiment in sending photos from one city to another by means of a telegraph wire and current of electricity, were recorded in the *Plain Dealer* of July 2. Pictures of Harvey D. Goulder, Tom L. Johnson, and John D. Rockefeller were printed on the front page to show results.

A colored prophet predicted Cleveland would be wiped out by water in August. Some folk left the city to get away from the "deluge."

The Visiting Nurse Association was formed, and Matilda Jones was appointed as superintendent. Prior to this time, Hiram House had on its staff a trained nurse whose salary was paid by Mrs. S. H. Morse. Prominent citizens gave practical assistance, among them Mrs. Arthur D. Baldwin, Mrs. James R. Garfield, Mrs. Perry W. Harvey, Mrs. John Lowman, Mr. and Mrs. Samuel Mather, Mr. and Mrs. Jay C. Morse, Belle Sherwin, Newton D. Baker, Frederick C. Howe, and John D. Rockefeller. The Visiting Nurse Association and the Milk Fund Association started the first Infant Clinic, which became later the Babies and Childrens Hospital.

Records were shattered by the Winton Bullet at the Glenville track, and Rollin H. White broke the world's track record for steam carriages. Over ten thousand persons witnessed the greatest automobile races held in America up to this time.

Henry C. Osborn developed the multigraph, invented by Harry C. Gammeter, a Cleveland typewriter salesman, and organized The American Multigraph Company in Cleveland this year. The addressograph had been invented by Joseph S. Duncan, a founder of the Addressograph Company, organized in Chicago in 1893. After several acquisitions, the Chicago company emerged in 1929 as the Addressograph International Corporation. It consolidated with The American Multigraph Company on May 5, 1931, forming the Addressograph-Multigraph Corporation. Joseph E. Rogers, formerly executive vice president of the International Business Machines Corporation, had been the active head of the Addressograph Company. He guided the merger move, and continued as president of the new corporation. Headquarters were located in Cleveland, and at 1200 Babbitt Road, Euclid, the largest industrial plant constructed in the United States during 1931-32 was erected. Here were manufactured ingenious and highly efficient addressing and duplicating machines that revolutionized the office-equipment industry. Before World War II, the corporation was doing business in sixty-four countries; the postwar era witnessed a return to active status in foreign markets. Rogers retired in 1945, retaining an interest as director; and on January 2, 1946, George C. Brainard succeeded to the presidency.

Loftin E. Johnson, son of Mayor Tom L. Johnson, described a trip he had just taken in an automobile. The drive started from New York City, August 17; he reached Cleveland in eleven days. On August 21 a cold, drizzling rain forced Johnson to stop east of Buffalo and sleep in the car. When Buffalo was reached, parts had to be sent from Cleveland to make the car run. Two friends gave up the trip after hardship and went home. Near Cleveland, the steering apparatus broke, and Johnson telephoned home for help. "A handsome carriage drawn by horses in silver-studded harnesses driven by a coachman in whipcord went to his rescue." The next day, Loftin returned to the car, again repaired it, and drove triumphantly home. Motoring was serious business in 1902.

Planned to manufacture farm implements, The American Fork & Hoe Company was incorporated in New Jersey, with Cleveland as the main office and William H. Withington as first president. Two important mergers were effected in 1930, The Skelton Shovel Company of Dunkirk, New York, and The Kelly Axe and Tool Company of Charleston, West Virginia, adding to the original line of products hand shovels, axes, hammers, sledges, and edge tools. In 1926 the company began the production of golf shafts and fishing rods, making world-famous these "True Temper" products. G. B. Durell served as president from 1924 to 1933, when he was succeeded by A. F. Fifield. The company operates plants in Geneva, Ashtabula, and Conneaut, Ohio, and in sixteen other states.

One of the most exciting harness races Cleveland ever witnessed was the Boston Challenge Cup Race for trotters to wagon, September 5. It took place at the Glenville track under the auspices of the Gentlemen's Driving Club of Cleveland. John A. McKerron, representing Cleveland and driven by H. K. Devereux, won both heats, the first mile in 2:07¼ and the second in 2:08. Lord Derby, driven by E. E. Smathers of New York, was third in the first heat and second in the second heat; while The Monk, driven by C. K. G. Billings of New York, was second in the first heat and third in the second. In the pacing cup race a Cleveland horse was also victorious. Ananias, owned by C. F. Emery and driven by H. K. Devereux, won both heats in 2:08½.

The Western Open Golf Championship was played at the Euclid Club in September, Willie Anderson winning first place; W. H. Way, second; and Willie Smith, third. The Dover Bay Club and the Oakwood Golf Club became popular in this decade. The district amateur championships were played in Cleveland, beginning in 1906; C. H. Stanley won that year, J. D. Climo in 1907, and Stanley in 1908-9. The first annual tournament for the women's championship, played July 27, 1909, was won by Mrs. J. E. Young, with Ruth Chisholm runner-up. Women's driving was handicapped by the confining apparel of the Gay Nineties.

Upon the departure of Superintendent Louis H. Jones to become president of a Michigan normal school, Edward F. Moulton was appointed superintendent of schools. He had enjoyed years of experience as a supervisor, and diligently fulfilled his new duties until 1906, when William H. Elson succeeded him. The latter was an executive of unusual ability who developed greater efficiency in the system. His career was characterized by far-sighted policies, particularly those related to technical and commercial high schools.

Sixty thousand Clevelanders witnessed the unveiling in University Circle of the statue of the Hungarian patriot, Louis Kossuth, September 27. The ceremonies were of international interest and inspired one of the most picturesque pageants ever seen in the city. Natives of Hungary contributed liberally to the building of the monument. The wreath placed on the Kossuth statue by Mayor Tom L. Johnson was sent to Cleveland by the mayor of Budapest. It contained a hundred branches of palm, one for each year since the birth of the Magyar patriot. Joseph Zseni, president of the Hungarian National League, represented that organization in the ceremonies. In the parade from Public Square to University Circle were eight thousand marchers under the banners of several countries.

An auction sale of bachelors took place at a Methodist Church fair in October. A dozen handsome, unmarried men were disposed of to the highest bidders. They were the young ladies' property for the evening.

On Thanksgiving Day, November 27, Case added Reserve to its football

Marcus A. Hanna   Prof. Edward W. Morley   Alexander E. Brown

Tom L. Johnson   John N. Stockwell   John P. Green

Rev. Hiram C. Haydn   Rabbi Moses J. Gries   S. T. Wellman

Ella Russell

Amelia Louise Groll (Rita Elandi). LEO WEIDENTHAL COLLECTION

Harry Lacy in The Still Alarm. LEO WEIDENTHAL COLLECTION

Augustus F. Hartz. LEO WEIDENTHAL COLLECTION

Gus Heege as "Yon Yonson"

Johnny Ray in Down the Pike

victims for the season, 20-0, and claimed the state championship. Such teams as Ohio State and Ohio Wesleyan had fallen before the Scientists, captained by Dick Muter.

A few Clevelanders journeyed to the Grosse Point track in Detroit on December 1 to see Henry Ford drive his seventy-horsepower automobile a mile in 1:01⅕.

Anna Held was presented by Ziegfeld at the Opera House, December 4, in *The Little Duchess*. The French girl had little dramatic talent, but no one denied that she was decorative and fascinating. The *Plain Dealer* critic versified: "Anna Held the audience, Anna held its gaze; Anna held it breathless with her Frenchy ways; Anna held a train up in manner unexcelled. Countless eyes did Anna hold with those of Anna Held."

A small section between Doan Street and Hallwood Avenue, and Armor Street and the city limits, known as Glenville Village was annexed to Cleveland, December 20; but the remainder of Glenville vigorously opposed annexation.

At the close of the year, there were 185,000 volumes in Cleveland's Public Library, which then consisted of the Main Library, four branches, five sub-branches and twenty-one stations. Cleveland was becoming known as a city of readers with unusual library advantages.

1903

Cleveland celebrated the New Year and its release from the tea shortage which had been caused by a ten-cents-a-pound duty imposed by the Government as a tax to help defray the cost of the Spanish-American War.

The Cleveland Trust Company system of branch banking had its inception, January 17, when stockholders ratified a merger with the Western Reserve Trust Company, organized in 1900. By the end of 1906, the company had fifteen branch offices, representing, with two exceptions, the acquisition of successful banks in their respective localities. Calvary Morris was elected president this year, succeeding J. G. W. Cowles, who became chairman of the board. While conservative in policy and management, the bank was among the first in America to use modern advertising aggressively. It was a leader in stimulating home building, extending services advantageous to home owners and builders.

The city's first automobile show opened in Grays Armory, February 1. The *Leader,* in a special edition, hailed Cleveland as "the leading automobile manufacturing city in the universe" and stated that "more automobiles are owned by individuals in Cleveland, in proportion to population, than in any other city in the world and most of these are Cleveland-made." Almost a full page was given to the list of 476 cars, their owners, license numbers, and types. The total estimated value was $714,000, an average of $1,500, with prices ranging from $550 to $5,000. The first ten license numbers were issued to the Winton Motor Carriage Company. D. Z. Norton had No. 13, electric;

H. M. Hanna, Jr., 26, steam; George H. Worthington, 29, electric; Loftin
E. Johnson, 36, gasoline.

More than thirteen hundred immigrants arrived during the past year, and
Cleveland was becoming a greater cosmopolitan center. Macedonians were
among those coming to work in the steel mills. They lived on Berg Street
and Broadway. Most of them belonged to the Russian Orthodox Church.

The entrance of natural gas into Cleveland was made the occasion of a
civic celebration on February 9. The project of piping natural gas by long-
distance transmission from West Virginia to Cleveland and other eastern
Ohio cities was conceived by Standard Oil and operated by that company
for many years. In 1902, after long experience in the natural-gas business,
Martin B. Daly had secured from the City of Cleveland, for the East Ohio
Gas Company, a franchise to supply the city with natural gas, despite the
fact that Mayor Tom L. Johnson opposed the granting of any franchise to a
private corporation. Daly served as president of the gas company until his
death in 1926. He was succeeded by Ralph W. Gallagher, who left the company after several years of successful administration to become vice president and later president of the Standard Oil Company of New Jersey. His
brother, Charles E., became head of the gas company in 1933, and later chairman of the board, retiring in 1940 after forty-eight continuous years in the
industry. J. French Robinson was his successor as president. The oil-gas
relationship was broken in 1943, when the Standard Oil Company divested
itself of its public-utility holdings. At that time, the Consolidated Natural
Gas Company was formed, with the East Ohio Gas Company as a subsidiary. At the time of its inception, long-distance transmission of natural
gas was regarded as a highly uncertain financial and engineering idea, but
later the East Ohio brought gas from the distant states of Texas, Kansas,
and Oklahoma. The major part of Cleveland's supply in the 1940s came from
eastern or Appalachian fields. Gas contributed materially to comfort,
and to smokeless and effortless heating of homes; and for industry it provided the even, clean, automatic precision controls of temperature which,
in a diversified industrial-production area, were not only important but
essential.

Western Reserve University received a gift of $100,000 from Howard M.
Hanna to endow the Henry Wilson Payne chair of anatomy in the School
of Medicine. Hanna and Oliver H. Payne gave an additional $200,000 three
years later for building and endowment of experimental medicine; and in
1909 Hanna gave $250,000 as the first part of a million-dollar general endow-
ment fund for the school.

The Colonial Theater was opened on Superior Avenue (NBC Building
site), March 16. Max Faetkenheuer directed the orchestra and Nora Bayes
was the vaudeville headliner. Drew & Campbell, proprietors of the Star
Theater, leased the Colonial. At first they presented vaudeville and then
turned the playhouse over to the Vaughan Glaser Stock Company, which
enjoyed several highly successful seasons. Later, Ray Comstock leased the
theater and presented Shubert's productions.

A successful Sportsman's Show was given in the Central Armory, opening

March 23. The building looked like "a bit of the north woods." This show set the precedent for a series of popular annual exhibits.

Police, disguised with glasses and cutaways, entered saloons on Sunday, March 30, and arrested sixteen liquor dealers.

Both candidates for governor were citizens of Cleveland—Myron T. Herrick, Republican, and Tom L. Johnson, Democrat. Herrick carried the city by forty-six hundred majority and the State by more than a hundred thousand. Two Clevelanders were also candidates for United States senator, Mark A. Hanna running for re-election, opposed John H. Clarke, Democrat. Senator Hanna was returned to office.

Blanche Bates scored a triumph in the *Darling of the Gods,* a magnificent production in the Opera House, with George Arliss in an important part.

A library for the blind was organized this year by the Public Library, which eventually established a department for the blind and featured "Talking Books." These were recordings of many books, both fiction and non-fiction, made by skilled readers, and were designed to educate and entertain.

"Cleveland had gone baseball mad—actually raving mad," said the *Plain Dealer* on April 29. "Last year, when over 11,000 witnessed the opening game at League Park, the public hurrahed that Cleveland was far from being a dead baseball town. Then came a few Saturdays with crowds from 9,000 to 12,000 . . . and a throng numbering 17,286 on Labor Day. Yesterday was no holiday, yet nearly 20,000 wedged their way into the park . . . 3,000 were turned away. A temporary bleacher section collapsed, but only two men were injured."

The "corner policeman" became a Cleveland institution. Chief Fred Kohler ordered seventeen policemen taken off their beats, May 3, and stationed at the busiest corners in the downtown section and on the West Side. There had been complaints that no one could ever find a policeman when he was needed. Citing this practice in other cities, Kohler decreed that there should be "walking information bureaus" in uniform on duty at designated intersections.

The Citizens Building was built (at 850 Euclid Avenue) west of the Schofield Building. One of the city's most imposing structures, it served as the home of the Citizens Savings & Trust Company, with a dignified and beautiful banking room. In 1924, it was remodeled for retail stores.

The cornerstone of Trinity Cathedral, on the southeast corner of Euclid Avenue and Perry Street, was laid on May 12, with appropriate ceremonies witnessed by church dignitaries and city leaders. The great stone was set in place, and Bishop William Andrew Leonard spoke the dedicatory words. The Rev. Charles D. Williams, who had become dean and rector in 1893, participated in the ceremonial.

Upon the recommendation of Mayor Johnson, a bond issue for $200,000 was passed by the Council, the funds to be used for the construction of a light plant. However, the legality of the bonds was questioned and they were not sold. Two years later, upon the annexation of South Brooklyn Village, Cleveland acquired its small plant which was used to furnish light and power. Another plant was added when Collinwood was annexed in 1910. Mayor Johnson then proposed a $2,000,000 bond issue, which carried, and in 1914 a new plant was opened, the largest municipally owned central station in the country. From time to time the capacity of the plant was increased until, in 1938, the Public Works Administration joined the city in providing an enlarged institution. The city claimed that its municipal undertaking was useful as a "yardstick" in protecting the public as to rates charged by the privately owned competition. By 1940 the municipal plant, located on the lakefront at East 53rd Street, represented an investment of more than $23,000,000 in its manufacturing and distribution system.

One of the most notable weddings in Cleveland history was that of Ruth Hanna, daughter of Marcus A. Hanna, and Joseph Medill McCormick on June 11. President Theodore Roosevelt and his daughter, Alice, attended. The service took place in St. Paul's Church, Euclid and Case avenues. The guests passed through an arch of peonies and ferns, and the church was filled at twelve noon with distinguished social leaders of the Cleveland area. Ruth Hanna McCormick soon became a champion of women's rights, and she was given much of the credit for the election of her husband as senator from Illinois. McCormick died in 1925, and some time later his widow became the wife of Congressman Albert G. Simms of New Mexico.

Three Bulgarians came to Cleveland this year, and the next year a group of Bulgarian molders arrived, the nucleus of a little settlement near Herman and Stone avenues.

Expansion of the firm of Ernst & Ernst, certified public accountants, kept pace with industry and banking until in 1946 its practice was conducted through fifty offices. Founded on June 24 by A. C. Ernst, who continued through the years as managing partner and director of all activities, an association was perfected in 1922 with a firm in London, England, to handle foreign accounting requirements of clients. Later, an office was established in Toronto, Canada. Services of Ernst & Ernst included auditing, banking, and management-control procedures. The firm assisted the Federal Government during World Wars I and II in numerous important undertakings having to do with the establishment of cost and accounting procedures used in connection with government contracts. The organization was identified with outstanding community projects in its home city.

The Middle Seneca Street Bridge was completed, June 25. It was a lift bridge costing $160,000.

A world record was broken, June 30, when Lou Dillon drew a wagon at a Glenville matinee, finishing a mile in 2:04¾.

John D. Rockefeller realized that walking around his Forest Hills golf course was tiring, and so he planned to enjoy his favorite pastime without unnecessary physical labor. He employed two boys at twelve and a half cents an hour to journey the links with him, one pushing him on a bicycle, while the other held a parasol over his head. The boys were Clifford and Charles J. Stilwell, whose father, Dr. H. F. Stilwell, the inspiring minister of the First Baptist Church, was the industrialist's good friend. The Stilwells afterward served their apprenticeship in the Warner & Swasey Company and advanced to high executive positions, the boy who carried the parasol becoming president of the great machine-tool business. Rockefeller's golf cronies at this time were Dr. Hamilton F. Biggar, Dr. Charles A. Eaton, W. C. Rudd, Dr. E. B. Rhodes, Captain Levi T. Scofield, and Andrew Squire. Mrs. Rockefeller had learned the game from Joe Mitchell, one of the first golf professionals at the Cleveland Golf Club (later the Country Club), and she had been the first to interest her husband in the game.

The Cleveland Electric Railway Company—the "Big Con"—and the Cleveland City Railway Company—the "Little Con"—merged into the Cleveland Electric Railway Company, familiarly known as "Con-Con." This company opposed Tom L. Johnson's three-cent fare and municipal ownership. Prevailing carfare was five cents. There was no city-wide blanket franchise. As "Con-Con" franchises on various streets expired, each expiration and each renewal aggravated the big issue. Johnson opposed renewals except on the three-cent basis. When the company balked, his plan was to let franchises on various streets to a competing company, encouraging, even with personal backing and financing, organization of three-cent companies.

The Collinwood Railroad Terminal was rebuilt. At this time, it was the largest gravity switching yard in the country. When it was rebuilt in 1929, it included 120 miles of track and could handle two thousand cars a day.

John D. Rockefeller had come into possession of the original section of the Weddell House property on Superior Avenue, and he ordered that portion of the famous hotel closed as a step in the construction program of the new million-dollar Rockefeller Building. There were protests from the citizenship who had seen the historic house play a leading part in the city's development, but it was sacrificed to progress. The Bank Street section continued in business as an unpretentious, but time-honored, hotel. When completed in 1905, the building became the headquarters of lake interests. It is said that Rockefeller never set foot inside the building; but his son, John D., Jr., who became owner upon payment of one dollar to his father, was a frequent visitor. The first tenant was George M. Steinbrenner, president of the Kinsman Transit Company.

A large crowd gathered at the Glenville race track to witness the spectacular automobile races, September 3-5. The Gray Wolf, a Packard car driven by Charles Schmidt, went out of control, hit the fence, and injured both car and driver. Doctors and mechanics went to work, and Schmidt and the Gray Wolf participated in events the next day. Barney Oldfield was the hero of the occasion and drove his Winton Bullet No. 2 a mile in 1:00½. As he finished, a front left tire exploded, but the skillful driver held his car on the track. M. C. Shroeder and F. B. Stearns, in Stearns cars made by the latter, won several racing events. Dan Chisholm of Cleveland drove a Baker Electric five miles in less than 6½ minutes. In the last two races, the audience of nine thousand saw Chisholm lose control of the Baker Electric Torpedo Kid. He was able to stop the car, but several spectators were injured. The exciting races concluded with a banquet at the Cleveland Automobile Club.

The Richman Brothers Company opened its first Cleveland store in the historic Mechanics Block at the southeast corner of Prospect and Ontario, where the system of making and selling moderately priced men's clothing direct to the wearer at a single profit was inaugurated. Frank C. Lewman joined the company in 1913, and steadily brought the Richman manufacturing operations under one roof, installing the mail-order plan, and maintaining modern retail stores.

Great crowds assembled at the lakefront on September 10 to see the *Niagara,* Commodore Oliver Hazard Perry's restored flagship, the main attraction of Cleveland's observance of Perry's Victory Week. During the program, relics of the *U.S.S. Maine* were unveiled in Washington Park, lake drill exhibitions were given by naval ships, and there was a mock destruction at night of the old barge, *Eliza Gerlach,* by the navy ships, *Dorothea, Essex,* and *Hawk.* A military parade, boat races, concerts, church services, an exhibition of the *DeWitt Clinton* train, and fireworks made the celebration a gala affair.

One hundred and sixty-two acres were purchased in Hudson, Ohio, for the Boys' Farm, the first institution of its kind in the United States. Dr. Harris R. Cooley was instrumental in its establishment, believing delinquent city boys would benefit through this contact with Nature.

A Winton runabout, made in Cleveland, was the first motor car to cross the United States. The trip took sixty-three days. The Winton was among the first cars with the engine installed in front, under a hood. Winton's experiments with two-cylinder cars led to the development of more powerful engines with a greater number of cylinders. His success with a gasoline-powered vehicle was largely responsible for overcoming competition of steam cars and electric automobiles, and establishing gasoline engines as the most practical.

The first "plot" movie, the Edison company's *Great Train Robbery,* was seen in Cleveland at Saengerfest Hall. *The Kiss,* with John C. Rice and May Irwin, was the silent "short" preceding the feature.

Organized on November 14, under the leadership of L. W. Greve, J. F. Conley, and Claus Greve, for the purpose of manufacturing, designing, and selling machine tools, the Champion Machine & Forging Company began with a capitalization of $15,000. Patents were obtained on various types of forging and upsetting equipment that found markets in the automotive and trucking industries. Champion, located at 3685 East 78th Street, produced 85 per cent of all the forgings used in aircraft landing gears prior to 1942, and its years of skill, knowledge, and experience contributed greatly to the war effort. H. W. Foster became president in 1940 succeeding L. W. Greve.

The leading Jewish welfare institutions and societies on November 17 affiliated with the Cleveland Federation of Jewish Charities, which became the budgeting and disbursing agency for Jewish organizations. Over a period of years, it assumed responsibility for the Cleveland Council of Jewish Women, Council Educational Alliance, Hebrew Relief Association, Infant Orphans Mothers Home, Jewish Orphan Asylum, Mt. Sinai Hospital, National Jewish Hospital for Consumptives, and the Sir Moses Montefiore Kosher Home for "aged and infirm Israelites." The first officers were Charles Eisenman, president; Julius Feiss, vice president; Meyer Weil, treasurer; and E. M. Baker, secretary. In 1926 the name was changed to Jewish Welfare Federation, to indicate that the organization was concerned with the welfare of the entire Jewish community and not restricted to charities.

On Thanksgiving Day, November 26, Case won a football victory over Reserve, 56-0, on snow-covered Van Horn field. The Scientists were state champions, with Harry H. Canfield, captain. Canfield later became city manager of Cleveland Heights.

Adelina Patti came to Cleveland, December 4, on her farewell tour. This was not her first "farewell tour," but it was the first as Baroness Cederstrom. "The divine Patti" thrilled the audience with Mozart's aria from *Figaro*, Gounod's aria from *Faust, Comin' Through the Rye,* and *Home Sweet Home.*

The Wright brothers accomplished their first successful flight at Kitty Hawk, North Carolina, on December 17, remaining in the air twelve seconds in a heavier-than-air biplane. Cleveland manufacturers closely watched the developments in aeronautics that followed and helped the progress of flying by the manufacture of parts. Thus the city's factories, before long, held the leadership for parts in both the automotive and aeronautical fields.

Mrs. Leslie Carter played *DuBarry* at the Opera House in December. Fifty-five men and twenty-two trucks were required to handle the scenery for the massive Belasco production. Clevelanders recalled that the actress had once attended Rockwell School. Several years before, she played in *Zaza*. One night police censorship stopped the performance. However, she returned to Cleveland at a later date, and produced the play without interference, proving the fickleness of moral standards.

An advertisement published in December by the Cleveland Motor Company asked this question: "Why throw away your horse-drawn vehicle, when it can be converted in a few minutes into an automobile?" The advertisement went on to say that a gasoline attachment could be installed in front between the wheels of an ordinary phaeton. "We guarantee a saving of 50 percent over horse and delivery trade and freight wagons." The appeal concluded, "Can you afford to lose 50 percent by using your horse?"

1904

A survey of the city's health revealed that 10 per cent of all deaths were due to tuberculosis, and the Anti-Tuberculosis League was formed to develop a preventive program. The total number of typhoid-fever cases had risen to 7,332 as against 5,650 the previous year. An educational program in typhoid control was initiated, and people were instructed to boil drinking water. With the introduction of water from a new crib in March, the epidemic subsided.

An overflow of the Cuyahoga on January 23, caused by two days of rain, resulted in an immense loss of property. Barges were torn from moorings and hurled downstream. The Nickel Plate Railroad bridge was swept away, and ships were carried into the lake. Losses totaled half a million dollars.

Frank B. Meade, an architect whose hobby was music, invited a group of his cronies to dinner and suggested that Cleveland develop a club where its members could eat, sing, dance, and enjoy good fellowship. So enthusiastic was the response that the Hermit Club was launched, money was raised, and plans were drawn for an ideal home. Land was secured on Hickox Alley, ground was broken in June, and in record time the clubhouse was ready for occupancy on November 5. In the membership roster of a hundred were many good voices, and a chorus was formed. There was also the nucleus of an orchestra, which quickly grew through the addition of the best professional and amateur talent in the city, and Meade was the inspiring leader. With writing and acting talent to call upon, a show was planned even before the clubhouse was finished; and in the spring of 1905, members Charles A. Otis and Roger Enwright auctioned off the tickets for a musical mélange to be presented at the Opera House. In the meantime, the Hermits' charming home was occupied, and many passersby would halt before it to enjoy the delightful music of the singing and playing groups composed of Cleveland's leading professional and business men. What the Lamb's Club was to New York, the Hermit Club was to Cleveland.

Marcus Alonzo Hanna died on February 15. He had been one of the nation's strongest leaders and one of Cleveland's ablest citizens. Remains were brought to Cleveland from Washington after ceremonies in the Senate chamber. Thousands passed before the body, which lay in state in the Chamber of Commerce Building. President Theodore Roosevelt, members of his cabinet, J. Pierpont Morgan, and other leading figures paid their respects at Cleveland's St. Paul's Episcopal Church, where the funeral was held. Said Edward Everett Hale, "Here is one who loved his country and his fellow men."

This year marked the first appearance of the automobile as an implement of war, when General Corbin used three White "steamers" in the Virginia maneuvers. White steam cars later became regular army-staff cars, and White gasoline cars eventually succeeded the steamers.

For two years prior to the completion of the First Unitarian Church (at Euclid and East 82nd Street) this year, services were held in the Western Reserve Historical Society Building. The former edifice on Bolivar Street at Prospect was sold to Grace Episcopal Church. Dr. Minot Simons resigned to take charge of church-extension work for the American Unitarian Association and was succeeded by the Rev. Dilworth Lupton, who served until 1941. Membership tripled, and Dr. Lupton became one of the best-known ministers in the nation. He retired to devote his efforts to newspaper writing, and in 1942, Dr. Everett Moore Baker was called to succeed his friend of many years.

The School of Library Science was established by Western Reserve University with a gift from Andrew Carnegie. William Howard Brett was its first active dean. He had gained national recognition as librarian of the Public Library.

Local or township boards of education, in charge of three directors, were created by the State in 1853; they were abolished in 1904, and rural schools were placed under the township board of education composed of five members.

It was decided to locate the Infirmary at Warrensville, and 850 acres were purchased. The service building of the Infirmary was soon completed, and another structure was erected for aged couples. Other buildings were to follow, making the city farm one of the leading institutions of its kind in America. Construction of the Tuberculosis Sanatorium was completed in 1906, the institution being equipped to care for eighty-nine tuberculosis cases.

Under the guidance of Frank B. Many, the Energine Refining & Manufacturing Company was organized to make cleaning compounds. From this small beginning, Energine, the product of the Cummer Company, became a popular item on the world's store counters.

An early move for transportation from Lakes to tidewater began when an appeal for a ship canal across New York State or through the St. Lawrence River was made in Washington to the Congressional Rivers and Harbors Committee. Harvey D. Goulder of Cleveland was a leading spokesman. This movement, it was said, would assure Cleveland of tidewater advantages as well as a gain in inland benefits. Following this move, spasmodic and unsuccessful efforts were made to secure the St. Lawrence River project.

The Pennsylvania Railroad purchased the pioneer Williams grist-mill in Newburgh, built in 1799, and tore down the building to make room for relocated tracks.

The Prospect Theater opened on April 4, on Prospect Avenue, just east of the Colonial Arcade, as the home of the Baldwin-Melville Stock Company. A year later B. F. Keith bought the playhouse and changed its name to Keith's Prospect. The first headliner was *Rice and Old Shoes* presented by Ralph C. Hertz & Company. When Keith centered his interest in the Hippodrome and gave up the smaller theater, the name Prospect Theater was again used for several years; however, the playhouse degenerated into a 10-20-30-cent vaudeville house and after failure was made over into retail stores.

Linndale became part of Cleveland on April 11. This area, south of Lorain Street along the Big Four tracks between the city limits and Highland Avenue, had been incorporated as the Village of Linndale in 1902.

Samuel Austin, contractor, had never enjoyed a technical education. His son, Wilbert J., however, was graduated from Case School of Applied Science in 1899, and joined his father's twenty-six-year-old millwork business, incorporated this year as Samuel Austin & Son Company. The firm could now offer the combined services of contractor and engineer to expanding industry for scientific plant development. Cleveland concerns, national in scope, employed the local company, which won prestige and recognition at home and abroad. The Austin company had built the Buckeye Electric

Company factory in 1895 and the National Electric Lamp works; therefore, the General Electric Company, of which they had become a part, turned to the firm, forerunner of The Austin Company, to build plants and laboratories.

The Rumanians had begun to displace the Irish in the neighborhood of Gordon and Detroit streets on the West Side, and this year forty families organized St. Mary's Rumanian Orthodox Church, 6201 Detroit. The oldest and largest Rumanian Orthodox parish in America in the 1940s, it had become widely known under the leadership of the Rev. Fr. John Trutza, pastor since 1928 and revered by his countrymen for his religious and cultural guidance.

The Park Building, at the southeast corner of Ontario and the Public Square, was completed this year by the Park Investment Company. Designed by F. S. Barnum, the nine-story structure was one of the first buildings in Cleveland to utilize floor slabs of reinforced concrete. The original investors were Truman Monroe Swetland, Raymond H. Swetland, J. G. W. Cowles, and J. M. Henderson. F. L. Swetland, Sr., was manager in the 1940s. The traffic line passing the building was one of the greatest in the city.

The A. M. McGregor Home for the Aged was organized this year.

Two automobiles raced on Clifton Boulevard, May 5, for the deliberate purpose of getting a ticket—to the Bennett Automobile Cup Race that was to be held in Germany the following month. The speeders were Barney Oldfield and a rival driver named Mooers. Oldfield in a Winton Bullet, and Mooers in a Peerless, were making test runs over a three-mile stretch of asphalt and were clocked by a visiting committee of the Automobile Club of America, which was to select the American representatives for the international race. Oldfield drove the Bullet 66 miles before the breaking of a part forced him to stop. His time was not impressive because of the necessity to turn at each end of the course, but at one time he reached a speed of 75 miles an hour. The Peerless covered a distance of 51 miles before mechanical failure brought an end to the trial. Barney Oldfield, with his big black cigar, soon achieved international fame on the track.

Alexander Winton ran his first local advertisement in the *Plain Dealer*. Charles W. Mears, Winton's advertising man, became president of the Cleveland Advertising Club and first dean of the club's Advertising School.

The bicycle "old timer's run" on Euclid Avenue, on May 22, was described by the *Plain Dealer* as "an apparently never ending line of wheelmen" who made it "look as if bicycles have become a fad again." With "Pop" Skinkle as the pacemaker, more than two thousand cyclists formed the procession from the Public Square through Superior Street to Erie, to Euclid, and then eastward, with Gordon Park as the destination. Some two hundred men wore medals won as wheelmen two decades before. There were gray-haired, bearded riders wearing derbies, and younger men with caps. Some of the mustaches might have served as handle-bars. There were long-skirted, shirt-waisted, and pompadoured women, and boys in overalls. Numerous spills occurred when cyclists sprinted to reach the front row. High-wheelers were ridden by Art Neal and Elmer Kermode. The marshals were George

Collister, Paul Goucher, Harry S. Moore, John Peterson, James Josephi, James Crawford, and George Huberty.

A motor cavalcade of a hundred tourists in twenty-five automobiles arrived in Cleveland on their New York-St. Louis journey to the Louisiana Purchase Exposition. In the tour were Mr. and Mrs. Charles J. Glidden of Boston, former Clevelanders. Glidden was president of the Cleveland Telephone Company for seventeen years. The Gliddens were to exhibit their twenty-four-horsepower Napier car at the St. Louis exposition, then continue their globe-circling travels that eventually took them a distance of forty thousand miles through thirty-two countries.

A group of Lakewood people interested in forming a Baptist church met on July 4, and one year later began to hold meetings in the United Presbyterian Chapel at the corner of Lakewood and Detroit avenues under the leadership of the Rev. T. J. Edwards of West Cleveland Baptist Church. On October 1, 1905, the Lakewood Baptist Church was organized with twenty-three charter members, and the next month the Rev. Cyrus S. Eaton became the pastor. In 1923 a new church building at Lincoln and Detroit avenues costing $107,500 was dedicated, and six years later the mortgage was burned. Rev. Robert N. Zearfoss came to the church as associate pastor in 1939, and became pastor two years later. The church had a membership of more than eight hundred in the 1940s, including sixteen organizations offering varied community services. Plans were made for a large addition including educational and recreational facilities.

At the turn of the century the Jewish population was moving eastward, new settlements being established in the Woodland-Willson district. This fact influenced the Anshe Emeth Congregation to sell the Erie Street Synagogue this year and erect a new and finer place of worship near Woodland Avenue (and East 37th), dedicated in July this year. At this time, the Anshe Emeth was recognized as the leading Orthodox congregation of Cleveland, and the distinguished Rabbi Samuel Margolis was called from New York. He remained its rabbi until 1917, when he met with accidental death after a brilliant career. Following the eastward trend, church leaders secured the land upon which the million-dollar Center Building was to be located.

The Oheb Zedek Congregation was formed and occupied a synagogue on Scovill Avenue (at East 38th Street) under the leadership of Rabbi Teitelman. As the Orthodox congregation grew, larger homes were required, and in 1922 a new building was occupied at Parkwood Drive and Morrison Avenue, dedicated August 20. In 1939 Rabbi Louis Engelberg came to the synagogue, which was the largest of the twenty-five Orthodox congregations in the city. A daily Hebrew School and a Sunday religious school were conducted. In 1946 plans were being made for a new synagogue at 1940 Taylor Road, adjoining Cain Park. The land had been purchased some time before, and a branch of the synagogue had been established in a large home. The president of the Oheb Zedek Congregation in 1946 was William Bokor.

Twenty divisions with fifteen thousand of the city's workers marched in the Labor Day Parade, September 6.

An editorial of October 25 announced, "Cleveland women have shown once more what a power for good they can be. The new YWCA building will be a monument to their pluck." The deadline for raising the building fund, set by John D. Rockefeller, having been met, he gave $50,000 for the building that opened in 1908 at Prospect and East 18th Street.

The Woodland Public Library, the first Carnegie branch of the Public Library, was opened on the south side of Woodland east of Willson Avenue.

The Cleveland High School Athletic Senate was established, November 28, and its rules were approved by the Board of Education on December 5. This was the first organization of its kind, and the pattern was followed by many other school systems. The rules efficiently governed athletic events in a businesslike manner, fostering that great influence—good sportsmanship.

The *Voce del Popolo Italiano,* influential Italian newspaper, appeared in November. Established by Olindo G. Melaragno and his cousin, Fernando, it served as an invaluable aid to Italian immigrants in their adjustment to the new world, and as a source of native flavor and atmosphere.

The first burials in Highland Park Cemetery on Kinsman Road, Warrensville Township, took place on December 13.

Robert L. Ireland, who had descended from early New England stock, came to Cleveland after his graduation from Yale and entered the employ of the Cleveland Hardware Company. Within a decade, he showed his business enterprise by organizing a bicycle company, becoming associated with the Globe Iron Works Company, giving general direction to the Ship Owners Dry Dock Company, and helping to create the American Ship Building Company. He entered the firm of M. A. Hanna & Company as a partner in 1904 and was also identified with many important business corporations in the mining, shipping, and banking fields. He died in 1928 at the age of sixty-one.

Lakewood villagers formed a church congregation this year that became the Lakewood Branch of the Old Stone Church in 1905. In October, 1907, the first building was erected, and Dr. A. B. Meldrum preached the dedicatory sermon on January 5, 1908. In 1912 Lakewood Presbyterian Church was organized with 342 members, and the Rev. A. J. Wright was called as pastor. The cornerstone of a new building was laid at 14500 Detroit Avenue in 1916, and two years later the edifice was completed. Upon Dr. Wright's resignation, Dr. LeRoy Lawther became minister in 1927. On the fortieth anniversary observance in 1945, the congregation numbered 2,363 members, the twenty-seventh largest Presbyterian church in the United States.

William Bingham, founder of the sixty-three-year-old W. Bingham Company, died this year at the age of eighty-eight. He had not only built one of the largest hardware concerns in the Middle West, but he had been prominent in Cleveland finance, serving as director of the Merchants National Bank, its successor, the Mercantile National Bank, and the Society for Savings. He was active in the early development of the municipal waterworks system, served on the City Council and in the State Senate, and is remembered as a patron of the arts and sciences. J. E. Green served as president of the hardware company until 1912, when he was succeeded in turn by C. W. Bingham, H. L. Thompson in 1914, and H. D. Cram in 1931. In 1915 Bingham built one of the finest and most serviceable wholesale warehouses in the nation at 1278 West 9th Street. In the Bingham Company and The Geo. Worthington Company, Cleveland had two of the largest wholesale hardware institutions in the country.

1905

One of Cleveland's leading educators and historians, Samuel P. Orth, president of the Board of Education, appointed an Educational Commission on January 1 to investigate all departments of the public schools. This commission was challenged to discover the causes of the great loss of pupils between the sixth grade and the high school. J. G. W. Cowles was appointed chairman. The commission report was presented to the board on July 24, 1906, recommending a pedagogical program designed to make education a more vital force in the life of the city. The recommendations involved increased efficiency and "a readjustment of the schools to the problems of the bread-winners." In 1910 Orth indicated that the commission's suggestions had been carried out by Superintendent Elson: the establishment of the Technical High School and the Commercial High School; reorganization of the Normal School; revision of the course of study in the elementary schools; and establishment of a vocational school, known as the Elementary Industrial School, for boys under the high-school age.

The forerunner of the Eagle Street Ramp was the old "rolling road" which brought traffic from Canal Street in the "Flats" to the Ontario level. It served as an escalator, and illustrations indicate that wagons and livestock were safely carried up the steep hill in bad weather.

The Legal Aid Society was organized and incorporated. Its purpose was described as "rendering legal assistance gratuitously or for a moderate charge to deserving persons not otherwise able to obtain the service of a competent attorney."

The American Red Cross came into existence as a national organization in the form of a quasi-governmental agency on January 5. The Greater Cleveland Chapter dates from that time. It was created when a group of organizers, headed by Samuel Mather, met at the Cleveland Chamber of Commerce for the purpose of establishing the Cleveland unit which became a chapter in 1910. The purpose of the chapter was to furnish volunteer aid to the Army and Navy, to act as a channel of communication between families and members of the armed forces, to carry on a system of disaster relief, and to help prevent emergencies.

Albert Einstein announced his theory of relativity, and Dr. Dayton C. Miller of Case School of Applied Science questioned one of his premises. Only six Americans were said to understand the theory, and debate was limited.

Hathaway Brown School was incorporated, preserving the name of Anne

Hathaway Brown, who purchased the school in 1886, ten years after it was organized as a branch of the Brooks Military Academy. In 1907 it moved into a beautiful building on East 97th Street, remaining there for twenty years, with Mary E. Raymond as principal from February, 1911.

Liberal friends made possible a permanent home for the Cleveland School of Art at 11441 Juniper Road this year. Substantial support came from Mrs. Mary Scranton Bradford, Mrs. Stevenson Burke, Mrs. Ben P. Bole, Ralph M. Coe, and George Gund. Georgia Leighton Norton, principal, was succeeded on retirement by Henry Turner Bailey, whose wise policies and capable selection of personnel expanded the school's usefulness as a civic institution. Dr. Bailey resigned in 1930 to devote his time to writing and lecturing. Alfred Mewitt served as acting dean until September, 1931, when Henry Hunt Clark was appointed to the office. He widened the general artistic viewpoint, attracting students from greater distances, even from abroad. Distinguished artists and teachers, among them Archibald M. Willard, Louis Loeb, the Herkomers, Herman N. Matzen, Frederic C. Gottwald, Henry G. Keller, Louis Rorimer, May Ames, Horace Potter, Nina Waldeck, Grace V. Kelley, and James H. Donahey, characterized the faculty that over the years inspired talent that excelled in the world of art. In 1946, when the institution was recognized as one of the three leading art schools of America, Dr. Laurence E. Schmeckebier was director, and George Gund, president of the board of trustees. Cleveland Institute of Art was later adopted as a name emphasizing "the increased stature of the institution."

The unveiling of the statue of George Washington in Budapest, Hungary, took place, February 13, in the presence of a large Hungarian delegation from America. The idea was originated by Tihamer Kohanyi, editor of the *Szabadsag,* Cleveland Hungarian newspaper. The inscription on the monument reads, "Not a king among men but a man among kings."

This year marked the sale of the Eagle Street Temple of the B'nai Jeshurun Congregation and the purchase of the corner of Scovill and Willson avenues. A new temple was dedicated, September 16, 1906, and three years later Rabbi Samuel Schwartz was called to the pulpit. Upon his resignation, Rabbi Jacob Klein was brought to Cleveland, and was succeeded in 1919 by Rabbi Solomon Goldman, who before long achieved national fame. He left to lead the new Jewish Center on East 105th Street in 1922. A year later, a building site on Mayfield Road near Lee Road was secured. Henry Spira and Morris Amster headed the movement, and Rabbi Abraham Nowak was elected spiritual head. The new million-dollar building, the Temple on the Heights, in Cleveland Heights, was designed by Charles Greco.

The Rev. Dan F. Bradley, a dynamic personality, was called to the pulpit of the Pilgrim Congregational Church this year. Constant population shifts brought increasing problems to the church at West 14th and Starkweather Avenue, as it endeavored to adapt its service to the needs of the South Side community, largely made up of Poles, Slovaks, and Lithuanians working in the steel mills. A firm believer in good citizenship and government, Dr. Bradley became a leader in civic life; and his labors, continuing until March 28, 1937, earned for him wide renown and the increasing devotion of his congregation. He died on November 12, 1939. The Rev. Walter H. Stark, assistant pastor for thirteen years, became pastor upon Dr. Bradley's retirement, serving for six years, when he entered naval service and was succeeded by the Rev. E. Milton Grant. Church membership in the mid-1940s approached one thousand.

While the modern history of the *News* dates from 1905, it originated in the *Herald,* founded in 1819 to serve the principal settlement of the Western Reserve. Charles Augustus Otis, Jr., formed the *News,* an evening paper, as a merger of the *World,* the *Evening Plain Dealer,* and the *News and Herald.* At the same time, Otis and Medill McCormick bought the morning *Leader.* In 1912 Dan R. Hanna, Sr., son of Marcus A. Hanna, purchased the *News* from Otis. Dan Hanna had entered the newspaper field two years earlier by acquiring the morning *Leader* from McCormick, his brother-in-law and at that time editor and publisher of the *Chicago Tribune.* Under Hanna's ownership, the *News* and *Leader* were published in the *Leader* Building at Superior Avenue and East 6th Street until 1917, when the *Leader* was sold to the *Plain Dealer.* The Sunday edition of the *Leader,* however, remained with the *News* and was published as the *Sunday News-Leader.* It was called the *Sunday News* when the publication was suspended, January 8, 1933. At Hanna's death, the property passed to the Dan R. Hanna Trust and Dan R. Hanna, Jr. The *News* moved to Superior Avenue and East 18th Street in 1926, where one of the most modern and efficient newspaper publishing plants in the country had been erected. In 1932 the Forest City Publishing Company, a holding company, acquired the stock of The Cleveland Company, publisher of the *News,* and of the Plain Dealer Publishing Company, publisher of the *Plain Dealer.* Under all its ownerships the *News* was a Republican paper. Top *News* officials in 1946 were Nathaniel R. Howard; editor; Hugh Kane, managing editor; Charles F. McCahill, general manager, and Leo P. Doyle, business manager. I. F. Freiberger was president of the Forest City Publishing Company, and Dan R. Hanna, Jr., was vice president and director.

Sensation seekers were disappointed, March 11, when the trial of Cassie L. Chadwick in Federal Court became a lawyers' battle without the calling of Mrs. Chadwick to the witness stand. On the following night, the world-famous figure of frenzied finance, who had duped conservative bankers out of hundreds of thousands of dollars, put on a show in court worthy of a tragedienne when the jury found her guilty. Through the six-day trial, thousands seeking admittance had been turned away. The crowds that were admitted heard a few witnesses and mostly documentary evidence of her machinations. Almost by whispering the magic name of Andrew Carnegie, whom she claimed to be her father, she had convinced bankers that he had provided her with great wealth. Carnegie, who was present through the trial, denied her story in public before Judge Robert W. Tayler. District Attorney John J. Sullivan and Jay P. Dawley, defense counsel, starred in the battle of legal arguments. After five hours' deliberation, the jury convicted Mrs. Chadwick on all seven counts of conspiracy against the government. She plunged into hysterical antics, shrieking, "I'm not guilty. Oh, how can

District Attorney Sullivan.

Mrs. Chadwick.

Judge Wing.

Attorney Dawley.

Andrew Carnegie.

Srivester Everett.

Sketches made at the famous Chadwick trial. (Donahey in the Plain Dealer.)

they say I am." Her son, Emil Hoover, faithfully at her side through all her ordeal, joined in trying to quiet her. She collapsed in his arms as she was sentenced to ten years in prison, where she died, October 10, 1907. It is interesting to note that when her belongings were attached, O. P. Van Sweringen, then a poor young man, was employed to guard the property.

John J. Sullivan was one of Cleveland's most distinguished lawyers during the first three decades of the century. He came to Cleveland from Trumbull County where he had served as school teacher, reporter, city editor, and prosecuting attorney. President McKinley appointed him United States district attorney for northern Ohio in 1900, and he was reappointed in 1904. His success in convicting the notorious Cassie Chadwick added to his laurels as an able trial lawyer. He served as chief justice of the Appellate Court in 1928.

Realizing the important part metal-cutting tools made of alloy would play in industrial development, Edward A. Noll established the National Tool Company in a rented barn on Madison Avenue. World War I created a tremendous demand for its products, and by 1917 the plant and facilities were doubled. The factory, between West 112th and 114th streets on Madison Avenue, was again enlarged to meet World War II demands. Samuel J. Kornhauser became chairman of the board, and H. W. Barkley was made president in 1946. The company was the nation's largest manufacturer devoting substantially all of its facilities to the making of special metal-cutting tools.

The First Methodist Episcopal Church, organized in 1827, held its last service on March 19 in the church at the southeast corner of Euclid and Erie Street, the site having been sold to The Cleveland Trust Company in 1901. A week later, a beautiful house of worship costing $250,000, ornamented with Gothic spires and gargoyles, was dedicated at Euclid and Sterling, during the pastorate of Dr. Charles Bayard Mitchell, later a bishop to the Philippines. Dr. Harold Lancaster came to the church in 1945 to guide the congregation in its important activities.

Construction of the Belt Line Railroad was begun by the Cleveland Short Line Railroad in April, promoted by W. R. and Ben F. Hopkins. Built for a distance of nineteen miles, the Belt Line intersected every railway at a point near the yards of each road, without crossing at grade any of the principal thoroughfares, street-railway lines, or county roads—a remarkable engineering and legislative achievement. This line left the New York Central main line at Collinwood on the east, encompassed the city on the south, and at Lakewood it joined the main line. Constructed to handle heavy traffic, it was a double-track road that solved many industrial problems.

The Chamber of Commerce instituted housing investigations out of which developed a building-code commission and the compilation of a code.

On May 14 a prophetic article appeared in a local paper with this subhead: "Powerful Faction in the Fatherland, Headed by Kaiser Himself, Bent on Worldwide Expansion of the German Empire at All Costs." The author wrote of German plans for an aggressive campaign and a Danish invasion.

Holland was to suffer the same fate and give the Germans full sweep of the North Sea.

On the site of the future May Company store, located just south of Euclid Avenue on the east side of Ontario, the first S. S. Kresge store in Cleveland opened its doors to the public in May. In 1912 the company was incorporated, growing with the city until in 1946 there were eleven stores in Cleveland and thirteen in Cuyahoga County.

The Fifth District Club and the Fourteenth Ward Republican Club merged this year to form the Western Reserve Club—a group of earnest young men who sought to create and maintain civic ideals for the benefit of Cleveland. E. H. Towson was the first president. It was largely due to the efforts of W. J. Crawford that this amalgamation was effected. At his death in 1909, plans were under way for a clubhouse, which later materialized as the Crawford Memorial of the Western Reserve Club, 2164 East 55th Street.

The cornerstone of the Federal Building was laid in the northeast corner of Superior and the Public Square, May 20. While the building was under construction, the Post Office and other federal-government activities were housed in the Wilshire Building.

"Certified milk" came to Cleveland as a novelty from a Novelty, Ohio, farm on May 24. Rules were formulated by the Cleveland Milk Commission to provide a product "absolutely pure and free from all injurious germs, especially for babies and invalids."

Eight aged men, the youngest seventy-seven and the oldest ninety-two, engaged in a foot race, June 3, from Doan's Corners down Euclid Avenue to Public Square. Henry D. Humiston, eighty-one, won in a walk, his time, 59:32½ minutes.

The Cleveland Museum of Art was to be a reality, as the city was assured of a magnificent structure to cost from $1,000,000 to $1,500,000. Trustees of the John Huntington estate were to spend $500,000 at once, and the Horace Kelley bequest was ready. Liberty Emery Holden, influential in bringing the museum into existence, was president this year of the building commission responsible for the structure. Mrs. Holden made gifts of art objects. In his will, Holden provided for financing outdoor art and care of paintings.

The City of Glenville was annexed to Cleveland, June 19; part of Newburgh Heights was annexed, September 25; and the Village of South Brooklyn joined Cleveland on December 11.

Funds from a gift of John D. Rockefeller to Case School of Applied Science made possible the erection of the Physics Building and the Laboratory of Metallurgical Engineering, at a combined cost of $181,000.

When Alfred Cahen started a single-room bindery with a capital of five hundred dollars, he was laying the foundation of a business that was to have world-wide relations. The little enterprise grew and in two years occupied substantial space in the Caxton Building. Here Cahen developed ideas for line production and installed machinery that increased output. A new plant was erected on West 110th Street to accommodate the rapidly growing business, but disaster struck in 1920 and fire wiped out the plant and its equipment. Knowing that the insurance was barely sufficient to cover indebtedness, the creditors paid tribute to the character of Cahen, insisting that the insurance money be used for re-building purposes. The new plant soon doubled the size of the old one, and in 1928 The World Syndicate Publishing Company of New York was acquired.

The second phase of World's development began when Ben D. Zevin was made advertising manager. His idea that good books could be sold in vast quantities if prices were put within the reach of millions of people was proved. The *Tower Books* were first published in 1939, and the public soon found them in drug stores, chain stores, and department stores as well as book stores throughout the nation. An additional plant was erected, giving the company an area of 278,000 square feet so that it might issue ten million books each year. Zevin was made president of The World Publishing Company in 1945, and under his direction the organization became the largest publisher of *Bibles* in the United States and one of the largest reprint publishers, its Cleveland-made books being shipped all over the world.

Ohio was now the fourth state of the nation in the value of its products. The industrial growth in a half century had been fabulous. The newspapers pointed out that capital invested in industrial establishments in 1850 had been $29,000,000, while in 1905 the total was $857,000,000. The average number of wage earners grew from 51,491 in 1850 to 364,298 in the 1905 census.

The Pennsylvania Railroad bought the site of the historic Cataract House, near 8820 Broadway, for right-of-way. The building was converted into an automobile sales room and service station in 1917, and was razed in 1931.

Activity of the Northern Ohio Dental Association lagged until this year, when, through the efforts of Dr. W. G. Ebersole, corresponding secretary, a new era of progress began. Dr. Ebersole attracted wide attention by recording his free service to underprivileged children, achieving remarkable results as reflected in behavior and scholarship. Through the efforts of association members who were leaders in the science of dentistry, highly developed scientific methods were advanced. Among the Clevelanders who had served as presidents were Dr. J. F. Stephan, Dr. J. R. Owens, Dr. F. M. Casto, Dr. W. A. Price, Dr. E. H. Shannon, Dr. J. A. Loughry, Dr. J. V. Gentilly, Dr. E. S. Braithwaite, Dr. Edwin D. Phillips, Dr. C. T. Story, and Dr. James C. McConkey. Believing that the Northern Ohio association overlapped the work of the national organization and its components, it was disbanded on November 8, 1943. Dr. McConkey, president since 1934, authorized that records be deposited with the Western Reserve Historical Society. The treasury balance of $3,057.16 was turned over to the Callahan Award Commission of the Ohio State Dental Society. In the darkened ballroom of Hotel Statler, in the city of its birth eighty-six years earlier, taps sounded for the Northern Ohio Dental Association that had served nobly and well.

The depot on the lakefront was the scene of anxiety and grief on June 21. At 9:20 P.M. the *Twentieth Century Limited* had been wrecked at Mentor at a cost of twenty-one lives and serious injury to nineteen persons. A crowd at the station met the train bringing the victims to Cleveland. The *Century,* then an eighteen-hour train between New York and Chicago, was speeding eastward when it ran into an open switch.

John Hay died on July 1, and his body lay in state July 3-5 in the Chamber of Commerce Building on the Public Square. President Theodore Roosevelt, Vice President Fairbanks, cabinet members, and diplomats attended the statesman's funeral in Cleveland. Save for a chief executive, no such tribute was ever paid an American citizen. Hay was buried in Lake View Cemetery.

The Glidden Tours were formally launched with an 870-mile run from New York City through New Hampshire and back to the starting point. Percy P. Pierce in his Pierce car was awarded the trophy, but four other cars finished with clean scores: a White, Maxwell, Darracq, and Cadillac. Walter C. White in a fifteen-horsepower car, representing the White Sewing Machine Company, was presented with a certificate stating that he had completed the run. The tours were inspired by Charles J. Glidden, a wealthy motoring enthusiast who offered a handsome trophy to the winning car. The award was made on the basis of performance, price, equipment, and appearance in runs governed by the American Automobile Association.

The first social organization to pass through the guarded gates of Forest Hill, John D. Rockefeller's great estate, was the American Press Humorists. While touring the grounds in one of the Rockefeller surreys, Mayor Johnson turned to his host and said, "Wouldn't this make a beautiful park for Cleveland?" The keen financier replied quickly, "Wouldn't it?" Strickland Gillilan, famous member of the Humorists, discovered that by electing Rockefeller a member the small organization would "average too much wealth." Rockefeller's honorary membership resulted in many articles that portrayed the human and humorous sides of this famed international personality.

The Reliance Electric & Engineering Company was founded on September 19, by Peter M. Hitchcock, who was interested in electrical experiments of the day and directed his attention primarily toward the design of improved electric motors. Upon his death in 1906, the business was incorporated as the Lincoln Motor Works, and in 1907 Clarence L. Collens became president. The company took the name Reliance on May 21, 1909, and two of Hitchcock's sons, Charles and H. Morley, continued in the 1940s as members of the board of directors. In 1910 a factory was built on Ivanhoe Road, and operations were moved from downtown Cleveland. J. W. Corey became president in 1944, at which time Collens assumed chairmanship of the board. The company was a leading manufacturer of especially designed power equipment for use in heavy industries, operating a plant twelve times its original size.

A committee headed by Worcester R. Warner, appointed to investigate the desirability of building a subway, reported on September 19 that surface transportation was satisfactory and conditions did not call for a subway.

The Gentlemen's Driving Club announced a tie between H. K. Devereux' Orrin C. and Charles A. Otis' picturesque Dutch Mowrey, for the honor of winning the greatest number of races for an owner. The latter horse was famous for its almost hairless tail and its ability to come through with victory in the last few strides.

The six-hundred-foot lake vessel became a reality. The Pittsburgh Steamship Company on September 19 closed a contract for two of these monster freighters costing $900,000.

The Anti-Tuberculosis League, with the help of the Associated Charities and the Visiting Nurse Association, induced the city government to care for and control tuberculosis by employing nurses. A free tuberculosis dispensary was opened in the Medical School of Western Reserve University.

A former district engineer for American Steel & Wire Company, Arthur G. McKee, established himself as a consulting engineer on November 1, and shortly thereafter formed a partnership with two other engineers, Robert E. Baker and Donald D. Herr. The firm of Arthur G. McKee & Company built blast furnaces and steel works. The Widdell Engineering Company was absorbed in 1926, and the oil department under H. E. Widdell became an important part of the business. The company designed plants from Asia to Africa, from Europe to South America, and during World War II built seven of the seventeen new blast furnaces installed in the United States and all of the new Canadian blast furnaces. Widdell succeeded McKee in 1946 as president of the company, with offices at 2300 Chester Avenue.

Emma Calvé gave her first concert in Cleveland on December 2, and an audience that filled Grays Armory cheered her. Before the concert, "the capricious but irresistible songbird" refused to use her dressing room until electric lights were installed in place of gas. Wires were strung to the room, the concert went on, and the greatest Carmen of the time won another triumph.

Families of the Pilgrim and First Congregational churches had been holding prayer meetings in their homes in the vicinity of Detroit Avenue and West Clifton Boulevard, Lakewood. Their objective, the organization of the First Congregational Church of Lakewood, was realized on December 8 at the home of Charles E. Newell, with twenty-seven charter members. On the 21st, the church received official recognition. During the pastorate of the Rev. Benjamin A. Williams, 1906-8, a portable chapel was erected on a rented lot on West Clifton Boulevard north of Detroit Avenue. A period of retarding influences was weathered with the help of Dr. Dan F. Bradley, F. C. Case, John G. Jennings, and George S. Case of Pilgrim Church; and on January 6, 1913, the First Congregational Church Society of Lakewood, Ohio, was incorporated, with Cleaveland R. Cross, president. The generosity of Mrs. S. S. Southern made possible the purchase of an expanded building site extending southward to the street intersection. In November, 1916, a beautiful Colonial house of worship was dedicated, the total property value being $150,000. Envisioning community needs, it was designed as an institutional church with facilities for social and recreational activities. The Rev. George LeGrand Smith, pastor from 1912 to 1917, was known especially for his devotion to children. He resigned to become secretary of the Congregational Union, and the Rev. Roy E. Bowers became pastor in 1918. Under his energetic leadership, spiritual emphasis was kept uppermost, and membership increased from 364 in 1917 to 1,086 in 1939. Dr. Bowers, beloved of his congregation, was succeeded by the Rev. Everett W. MacNair. Youth activities had gained impetus under the direction of able pastor's assistants, and particularly under the Rev. Merrell M. Brammer, who became associate minister in 1937. In 1946 Lakewood Congregational Church was conducting the largest youth program in Ohio. Church membership exceeded 1,200.

Clevelanders who were prominent in the early years of the new century included John G. White, corporation lawyer, student of Oriental literature, and donor of several thousand rare volumes to the Cleveland Public Library; Stiles Curtis Smith, known for his industrial, financial, and charitable undertakings; Virgil P. Kline, lawyer of outstanding attainments; William Finley Carr, corporation lawyer associated with business enterprises; Frank R. Gilchrist, whose interests were transportation and lumber; Thomas H. Hogsett, corporation lawyer; Herbert Mathews, lawyer and real-estate broker; and Henry W. Corning, capitalist and manufacturer of sewing machines. Allyn F. Harvey was a leader in lake transportation; John M. Henderson, lawyer, president of the board of directors of Case School of Applied Science; Horace Carr, master printer; William E. Sage, dramatic editor of the *Leader,* and Archie Bell, of the *News;* and John Anisfield, clothing manufacturer and leader in the city's charitable and philanthropic circles.

1906

The St. Luke's Hospital Association of Cleveland became successor to the Cleveland General Hospital organized in 1894, and planned a hospital to be erected through the united efforts of physicians and the Methodist Episcopal Church. Francis F. Prentiss was made president of the Association, a position he held until his death in 1937. The small hospital on East Prospect Street, dedicated in July, 1908, was soon outgrown, and plans were made for a great new institution in a suburban location.

A vigorous controversy developed over the plan of numbering streets instead of naming them. Leading stores of the city protested against the idea, claiming it would be confusing and costly. The new plan was adopted, March 6, becoming effective, December 1. Before long, the idea was considered an improvement over the old system, making it far easier for people to find their way about the fan-shaped city. For years, however, many citizens expressed regret that fine historic names had to give way to mere numerals. (See street index in back of book.)

The *Jewish Independent* was first issued on March 9, and Maurice Weidenthal, one of Cleveland's ablest and best-known newspapermen, became editor on May 25. His brother, Henry, was sports editor of the *Plain Dealer,* managing editor of the *Press,* staff writer of the *News,* and was particularly known for his historical features, "Those Days." A third brother, Leo, served on the *World,* predecessor of the *News,* and as political reporter for the *Plain*

Dealer, prior to succeeding Maurice as editor of the *Jewish Independent.* A son of Maurice, William R., was for a number of years an official of this publication.

A council committee approved buying for the proposed Mall the Case estate and other property from Wood to Bond streets for $1,900,000.

A great earthquake shook the City of San Francisco on April 18. Buildings crumbled, water mains broke, and, within three days, fire had destroyed 514 city blocks. Known dead numbered 452, and property loss amounted to $350,000,000. Several Clevelanders were in the stricken city. Relief was sent quickly and generously from Cleveland.

A benefit performance was given, April 27, in the Opera House by Mrs. Nicola Cerri and William Ganson Rose for the victims of the San Francisco earthquake and the Vesuvius disaster. A net profit of more than two thousand dollars was realized at the one performance. Stage managers of all the Cleveland theaters were the ushers, and every playhouse contributed its most important act, while other talent was brought from a distance. Among the participants were Laura Burt, Henry Irving's leading lady; Joseph Sheehan, star of the Savage Opera Company; Cressy and Dayne, popular vaudeville performers; the Braatz Brothers, greatest of ground tumblers; R. C. Hertz, outstanding character actor; Lulu Glaser, light-opera comedian and her company; and Vaughan Glaser and Laura Nelson Hall, Cleveland stock-company favorites. There were fourteen acts, each delighting the great audience that packed the house.

White City, an amusement park on the lake at East 140th Street, burned on May 26. Here Bostock presented his famous animal shows for several summers, with Bonavita, lion trainer, and Madame Morelli, leopard trainer, as leading stars.

An airship took a flight into Luna Park on June 1; then it rose and maneuvered at will. Lincoln Beechey had given Cleveland a new thrill. The summer amusement park was privately operated at the intersection of Woodland Avenue and Woodhill Road. For a generation it was one of Cleveland's gayest outdoor entertainment centers, with an over-the-water chute as a spectacular feature. Eventually it deteriorated, and two fires leveled it. The site was later built up with the Woodhill Homes improvement.

An Infants Clinic was opened by Dr. John Lowman in the Central Friendly Inn.

Rival streetcar lines submitted their franchise proposals to Council on July 24. The Cleveland Electric Railway asked a five-cent fare and agreed to provide subways or elevated roads at some future time when a rate of fare could be agreed upon. The Forest City Railway was more liberal in its offer, promising three-cent fare, subways, and elevated roads when Council directed. The Low Fare company was formed for the purpose of operating cars on certain streets on the West Side. A year later, the Forest City Railway bought the franchise of the Low Fare company and operated cars on Denison Avenue and on Fulton Road, with a car station at about 6700 Denison Avenue. This small line charged a three-cent fare and became known as the "Threefer."

Mayor Tom L. Johnson was hailed to court on July 26 on contempt charges. The ripping up of tracks on Fulton Road to embarrass a competing streetcar line brought Johnson and Director W. J. Springborn to Common Pleas Court.

The farmers of northern Ohio were organizing to seek legislation that would slow down the speed of automobiles touring the country roads. They complained that some cars were going forty miles an hour and frightening the farm horses.

"Ride anywhere for a three-cent fare!"
(*Donahey in the* Plain Dealer.)

Morning Star, driven by C. K. G. Billings to wagon, broke the world's record for the half-mile at the Glenville track, July 31, the time being 59½ seconds. He also drove Major Delmar to wagon on the same day, one-half mile in one minute flat. The champion trotting gelding was paced by a horse driven by "Doc" Tanner and just missed a collision with a billy goat that strayed onto the track.

A mirage afforded a rare spectacle on August 13. Clevelanders saw the City of Rondeau, Canada, reflected in an atmospheric phenomenon.

Mayor Johnson proposed on August 23 that a holding company be formed by the Cleveland Electric Railway Company, and that the Forest City Railway be included. He favored three-cent fare with a penny transfer. Johnson also recommended that the property be tax-free insofar as the law permitted, and that the City of Cleveland ultimately become the owner of the properties, "if the state laws can be revised and if the earnings of the company can retire the stock and bonds." He recommended that subways and elevated roads be built by increasing the capital of the company doing the work, the stockholders to have nothing to say about these improvements. "The earnings of the company would go to extensions and improvements of the property and to the retirement of stocks and bonds to a certain extent before fares are lowered. The franchise granted by the city would be the only guarantee to the stockholders of the Cleveland Electric that the terms of the lease would be carried out. The property of the Cleveland Electric would revert to the stockholders in the event the holding company fails to pay the interest on the bonds and the dividend on the stock." The mayor's declaration of plans naturally led to vigorous opposition.

North of Detroit on Gordon Street was St. Helena's Rumanian Greek Catholic Church founded this year. The Rev. Fr. George Babutiu came to the parish in 1934. The congregation worshiped in the oldest Rumanian church building in the country in the 1940s.

A war against straphanging in street cars was waged by the Health Department, which lost the fight.

The production of White steam cars had attained an output of fifteen hundred a year, which represented twice as many large touring cars as were made by any other manufacturer in the world. By this time, the Whites' automobile business was considered a mature endeavor, having previously been a stepchild of the sewing-machine business.

The Euclid Avenue Presbyterian Church considered the Wade Park community for its future home, and this proposed move inspired a union with the Beckwith Memorial Presbyterian Church on September 24. Three years later, the cornerstone of a new church was laid at 11205 Euclid Avenue in Cleveland's growing cultural center. The architect, Ralph Adams Cram, planned the structure to express "the nature of the Presbyterian church in beautiful and historical forms." The great arched front, flanked by turrets, the rose window above the entrance, and an impressive tower were distinguishing features of the building which was set back from the street in a lovely lawn. The high nave, the auditorium with unbroken columns, and the transepts with deep galleries were other features of the beautiful church. Dr. Albert J. Alexander, pastor, had been succeeded in 1908 by Dr. Alexander McGaffin. In 1920 the Euclid Avenue and Second Presbyterian churches joined in this home under a new name, Church of the Covenant. Dr. Paul F. Sutphen, who had exerted a strong influence over the community near Prospect and Sterling where the Second Presbyterian Church had been located, and Dr. McGaffin served as associate pastors until 1926, when Dr. Sutphen retired due to ill health. He continued as pastor emeritus until his death in 1929. Dr. McGaffin's pastorate ended in 1927, and his death came as he was on his way to conduct the funeral service of his associate. Dr. Philip Smead Bird became pastor in 1928. Christ Chapel, the gift of Mr. and Mrs. Willard M. Clapp, and the Williamson Chancel were dedicated in 1931. The manse was presented in 1940 by Mrs. Worcester R. Warner and her daughter, Helen Blackmore Warner, in memory of Worcester R.

Warner, long-time member of the church. Dr. Bird was soon regarded not only as an inspiring spiritual leader of his congregation and the affiliated Western Reserve University, but also as a constructive and dynamic force in the civic life of Cleveland.

The First National Bank was building one of the finest banking structures in the Middle West at 247 Euclid Avenue. Its capital at this time was $2,500,000, and its deposits, $23,000,000. John Sherwin was president. The bank grew rapidly, and in 1913 organized the First Trust & Savings Company. These affiliated institutions advanced together until the merger that brought about the Union Trust Company.

The first three-cent streetcar was operated from Denison Avenue to Detroit Avenue on November 1. Tom L. Johnson was the motorman over the decorated route, and he was showered with flowers and cheered by crowds that lined the streets. Thus the three-cent fare was introduced after a little less than five years of legal and verbal disputes. The public seemed interested only in the low fare, not the economics of the undertaking. This was the "Threefer" line.

The Chamber of Commerce sent a delegation of members to Canterbury, Connecticut, to erect a memorial in front of the cemetery where Moses Cleaveland, founder of Cleveland, was buried. F. F. Prentiss, Munson Havens, Ambrose Swasey, Hubert B. Fuller, and Elroy M. Avery constituted the party, with Liberty E. Holden representing the Western Reserve Historical Society. Land between the burying-ground and the highway was bought and given to the town. A monument was erected, and the ceremonies in connection with its dedication were conducted in the church. Text of the bronze memorial reads, "In this cemetery rest the remains of Moses Cleaveland founder of the City of Cleveland. He was born in Canterbury January 29, 1754, and died there November 16, 1806. He was a lawyer, a soldier, a legislator and a leader of men. In grateful recognition of his services, this memorial is erected by The Cleveland Chamber of Commerce on November 16, 1906, the one hundredth anniversary of his death."

Mayor Johnson's administration was attacked, November 25, because of the annual increase in the city's bonded indebtedness since he became mayor. This indebtedness was approximately $14,503,000 in 1900, climbing to approximately $27,688,000 in 1906.

The Infants Clinic and Hospital of Cleveland was incorporated in December, and on February 6, 1907, it became the Babies Dispensary and Hospital. Charles A. Otis was instrumental in establishing this charity, and secured many gifts and bequests. To Dr. H. J. Gerstenberger and Dr. E. F. Cushing went much of the credit for planning this important work. During 1909 the trustees voted to build a dispensary on East 25th Street, and in 1925 the name was changed to the Babies and Childrens Hospital of Cleveland. In that year, the new hospital opened on Adelbert Road with a bed capacity of 147.

Several important institutions that were to contribute to the city's well-being were organized. These included the St. Anthony's Home for Boys, the Baptist Home of Northern Ohio, the Miles Park and Broadway branches of the Public Library, and the Orthodox Old Home for aged and friendless Jewish men and women.

A permit to begin the construction of the most expensive house ever built in Cleveland was issued, December 18. Designed by Charles F. Schweinfurth, architect of the impressive Trinity Cathedral, the imposing residence of Samuel Mather at 2605 Euclid Avenue rivaled the finest homes in New York. R. K. Winslow's stone residence stood at the northeast corner of East 24th Street; next was G. E. Herrick's brick mansion, and west of the Mather home, the stone house of Harry K. Devereux. To the east was the white-columned home of Leonard Hanna, the Charles Hickox house, and the Chisholm stone mansion. The William Bingham and Lucy Backus homes were standing at the corner of East 30th Street. Rare woods, exquisite sculpture, and finest workmanship went into the Mather house, which for more than thirty years was the home of one of Cleveland's most distinguished families. In 1940 the residence was purchased by the Cleveland Automobile Club for its headquarters.

An injunction forbade the use of "free-territory" tracks from the Superior Avenue Viaduct to the Public Square by Johnson's Forest City Railway Company. On December 26 the company started laying tracks on top of the Superior Avenue pavement, with makeshift poles supported by barrels and crude trolley wiring. Another injunction halted the effort.

1907

The city had closed a twelve-month of unequaled prosperity. Building increased 32 per cent, ore business experienced a banner year, and ship-builders enjoyed unusual activity. The amount of merchandise handled showed vast gains, and factories were running to capacity.

To settle the traction dispute, Mayor Johnson had suggested a holding company to operate all lines. Elbert H. Baker proposed that a single spokes-man represent the City Council and another the street railway. Mayor John-son and Frederick H. Goff were named, and mediation was begun.

City officials voted to move the Zoo from Wade Park to Brookside Park. After the opening, buildings for deer and elk were constructed and a bird-house was subsequently built. The demand was growing for a much larger Zoo.

This was to be a year of civic improvements. Plans for a West Side market house were approved, smoke-prevention study was revived, and fifty-five thousand dollars was raised to complete the Central Armory.

The Cleveland Chamber of Industry was incorporated on January 28 to foster and promote the general interests of the West Side. It was particularly active in advancing bridge and building projects. Alonzo E. Hyre was its first secretary, serving until his death in 1922. This group merged with the Cleveland Chamber of Commerce in October, 1930. At the time of the union, Harvey Spellman was president of the West Side organization.

On February 2 the city solicitor gave his opinion that the city might move the Erie Street Cemetery and use the land for public purposes. Sentiment, however, was stronger than law.

Manning F. Fisher established a grocery store at 4623 Lorain Avenue, the first unit in the Fisher Brothers chain. It was a radical departure from long-established marketing precedent, inaugurating the cash-and-carry system. By 1916 there were 48 stores in operation and in 1928 the company entered the retail meat field. Fisher Brothers Company became the largest retail food distributor in the Greater Cleveland area, and at the end of 1946 there were 213 stores in operation. The president was Ellwood H. Fisher; Patrick Grady, chairman of the board; and Timothy J. Conway, executive vice president.

The property of Western Reserve Academy had lain idle until this year, when James W. Ellsworth, a former student, returned to his boyhood home in Hudson, Ohio, and launched a one-man campaign to provide major public improvements in the town. He eventually restored the old school plant, aptly termed a "Hardscrabble Hellas," into a useful institution, erecting Seymour Hall in 1912 on the site of the Middle and South buildings. In 1916 Western Reserve Academy reopened under control of the Presbyterian Church as a co-educational school, serving also as the high school. Title reverted to an independent board in 1923. By 1925 girls were no longer admitted, and the school became strictly a boys' college-preparatory academy, richly endowed with the benefits of The James W. Ellsworth Foundation, which favored "aristocracy of character" among the selected students. The influence of Dr. Joel B. Hayden, headmaster 1931-46, in religious, educational, and social movements, broadened the scope of the school, extending its fame far and wide. When ill health forced him to retire, John W. Hallowell succeeded him. The Hudson academy shaped the character of many Cleveland boys whose names stand high on the city's roster of leaders.

A refinery was erected by The Canfield Oil Company at the foot of East 52nd Street at the Wheeling & Lake Erie tracks for the processing of petroleum spirits to be used in thinning paint and varnish and for the making of asphalt from petroleum residue. Both techniques, new in the industry, developed into large-scale processes. This refinery was eventually used for bulk storage and as a distribution center for Canzol products. To supply the growing export trade, a lubricating-oil plant was purchased and equipped in Jersey City, New Jersey, in 1921, to produce lubricants for industrial and automotive use. In 1945, The Canfield Oil Company became a subsidiary of The Standard Oil Company of Ohio, operating under the Canfield name. In 1946, when A. L. Bailey was president, Canfield was furnishing the nation's wholesalers with lubricating oils and greases, its retail trade being confined to northern Ohio. The original plant at the foot of East 55th Street, dating back to 1886, was still in operation.

Edwin Arthur Kraft gave his first organ recital in Trinity Cathedral on March 1. He had studied in Berlin and Paris as well as at Yale University, and was to become not only one of the nation's best organists, but also the inspiring choirmaster of the church. In 1926 he married Marie Simmelink of

Cleveland, a mezzo soprano whose artistic concert work made her an outstanding favorite.

Barton Haggard of Cleveland established the world's indoor pole-vault record, 11′ 8″, and in the same year was runner-up in the outdoor American championship.

The interurban had become a flourishing transportation medium, and on March 4 a number of lines were merged in the incorporation of the Cleveland, Southwestern & Columbus Railway. A 208-mile network of interurban roads operated from Cleveland to Berea, Elyria, Oberlin, Norwalk, Medina, Bucyrus, and Mansfield, carrying passengers and freight.

Lakewood Hospital was incorporated by Dr. C. Lee Graber and a few other far-sighted physicans who believed their city was to grow rapidly. A frame structure was erected at the corner of Detroit and Belle avenues, and the first superintendent was Alice M. Brooks, who served for twelve years. The demand for larger quarters led to a financial campaign in 1914, and, as a result, a four-story hospital was erected. The original hospital was moved to the rear and used as a nurses' home. Enlargements were necessitated in 1933 and again in 1935. It was in 1931 that the hospital became the property of the city. The phenomenal growth of Lakewood led to enlargements through a building program in 1940. Five years later a bond issue of $1,500,000 was passed, and in 1946 the voters approved another bond issue of $850,000. Lakewood envisioned a great new hospital to meet the growing needs of the community, and plans were being developed.

The Alhambra Theater, 10403 Euclid, was heralded as one of the most comfortable and attractive theaters in Cleveland. For a time it was under Keith management and played vaudeville. Later, however, public interest in vaudeville waned, and the house was transferred to Loew management with motion pictures as the attraction.

The Van Dorn Iron Works Company not only erected the first group of buildings for the White Motor Company this year, but it was soon producing White truck frames and pressed-steel items, pioneering in developing the first mechanical dump-truck hoist used on motor trucks, and continuing to supply White cabs. From combat tanks in World War I, Van Dorn turned to special railroad equipment in 1921. A container-type system of handling less-than-carload freight, the forerunner of systems later widely used, was developed by the company in 1921 in collaboration with Benjamin Fitch. T. B. Van Dorn succeeded his father, who founded the business in 1878, as president in 1913, serving until 1923 when he became chairman, and H. A. Rock assumed leadership. He was in turn followed by A. J. Croenke, F. G. Smith, and N. T. Jones, the latter elected in 1938. The Van Dorn Iron Works Company became builders of special machinery for companies in almost every major field. Familiar park benches and mail boxes on street corners bore the Van Dorn name, and prison equipment continued to be a major part of the business. The Van Dorn & Dutton Company, which became the Ohio Forge & Machine Corporation, makers of high-grade gears, originated in the iron-works company, as well as the Van Dorn Electric Tool Company, which came under the Black & Decker Company banner.

Van Dorn, located at 2685 East 79th Street, entered the plastics field in 1945, organizing a plastics-machine division to produce injection-molding presses and molds that promised to be one of the most important of the company's operations.

The Society for Crippled Children was established as the result of a tragic interurban accident in Elyria, Ohio, when a car crowded with Memorial Day excursionists collided with another car. Edgar F. Allen, wealthy industrialist of Elyria whose son was among the victims, devoted his life to work with crippled children, first building a hospital in Elyria. The Rotary Clubs of Cleveland, Elyria, and Toledo continued the work. Until 1945 headquarters were maintained in Elyria; then they were moved to Chicago. The annual sale of Easter seals made possible the society's important work.

A survey showed the Ukrainians in Cleveland's southwest section, around the steel plants, had twenty-five organizations, two churches, two choirs, two banks, a dancing club, and a gymnastic society.

The half year ending July 1 set a new prosperity record. Wages were the highest in the history of the city. Business never before reached such totals. Night shifts at the factories were more than common, and the transportation agencies, both rail and lake, had never been called upon to move such quantities of raw and manufactured materials. Late in the year, a panic crippled the nation, but Cleveland was not seriously affected. In 1908 the economic upset came to an end, and business was generally good as the decade closed.

The first National Amateur Golf Championship held in Cleveland was played over the Euclid course on Cedar Hill in July. Jerome D. "Jerry" Travers was the winner, and the gallery included the world's most-talked-of man, John D. Rockefeller. Cleveland qualified two players, Charles H. Stanley and Joe K. Bole. Charles "Chick" Evans, Jr., sixteen years old, was in the field. Rockefeller was a center of interest, and when asked by a group of newspapermen how to get rich, he responded, "Save a little money, not next week, but this week; have you tried it?" and the unanimous answer was that they had not.

On July 10 eighty-two automobiles started the third Glidden Tour from Cleveland to New York via Chicago and Indianapolis. The Cleveland Club was represented by ten motor cars. The race was won by the Buffalo entry, traveling 1,591 miles in fifteen days. Harvey S. Firestone initiated a move to improve tire quality, thus ensuring safer travel and reducing trip mileage. The historic tour was abandoned with the 1913 competition, but was revived in August, 1946, by the Veteran Motor Club of America and participating clubs.

The Last Days of Pompeii was staged July 24 at White City Amusement Park on the lakeshore, but not for long. A terrific wind and rainstorm really made Pompeii fall, volcano and all. White City roofs were blown off, and serious damage was done to the popular amusement place.

The Gabriel Company was organized with Claude H. Foster as president and J. F. Gibler, manager, its product being a musical horn that operated from the exhaust of the motor. Later hydraulic and aerotype shock absorbers were made for automotive vehicles and distributed throughout the world. The company's name was changed to Gabriel-Snubber Manufacturing Company in 1925, and later to the Gabriel Company, located at 10709 Quincy Avenue. John H. Briggs was president in the 1940s. Ward Products was bought out on January 1, 1947, and the plant was moved to 14500 Darley Avenue.

Voters blocked bridge bonds on July 26 by decisively defeating the plan to rebuild Central Viaduct.

The Cleveland Life Insurance Company was organized on August 27 with William H. Hunt, well-known business and civic leader, as president. Among those who served as directors were William H. Hunt, Charles E. Adams, Frank A. Arter, Elbert H. Baker, Dr. H. C. Brainerd, N. P. Goodhue, George F. Gund, Munson Havens, Henry W. Heedy, H. A. Higgins, M. P. Mooney, E. W. Moore, J. T. Murphy, M. J. O'Donnell, Charles A. Otis, F. F. Prentiss, L. Q. Rawson, W. D. Sayle, D. R. Warmington, J. H. Webster, H. C. Wick. The offices were located in the Engineers Building. With a strong board of directors, the company grew and prospered until June 15, 1926, when it was purchased by the Sun Life Assurance Company of Canada.

Trinity Cathedral at Euclid Avenue and East 22nd Street, one of the finest examples of English Gothic architecture in America, was consecrated on September 24. The auditorium was filled, and a vast throng of Clevelanders were unable to gain admission. The assembled crowd watched the procession of church dignitaries and laymen of the Episcopal Church, led by Bishop William A. Leonard, go up the high steps, through the heavy oak doors, and down the aisle. Samuel Mather, representing the wardens, read the articles that transferred the cathedral from the committee to the church. Consecration was pronounced by Dean Frank DuMoulin, and psalms and prayers were read by visiting bishops. This magnificent million-dollar structure, breathless in beauty and exquisite in grandeur, had been built by gifts and offerings large and small. In the chapel on East 22nd Street, and throughout the great cathedral, memorials were placed by families and individual members. The cathedral, which was designed in perpendicular Gothic style, was adapted from fifteenth-century English models. The plan of the main building was in the form of a cross, permitting convenient communication with the parish house, the choir room, Cathedral Hall, and the church home. The bell tower rose over the edifice at the crossing of the nave and transepts and was supported from the interior by four cruciform pillars with ornately carved capitals. The Euclid Avenue entrance was formed by three deeply recessed, molded, and carved arched openings, and there were other entrances on east, west, and south sides of the cathedral. The wood furnishings were of English paneled oak, and the seating capacity of approximately eight hundred could be augmented by adding eight hundred chairs to the auditorium. The following day the *Leader* said editorially: "Cleveland and Ohio can take unalloyed pride in the noble temple of faith which was consecrated yesterday with the stately ceremonies of the Protestant Episcopal Church. Trinity is a Cathedral in all that the word implies.

It is also a civic glory, a new object of pride and interest for all Ohio. . . . In exterior form and interior finish, in appeal to the eye and the imagination, in utility as well as beauty, the great pile . . . is one of the finest buildings in the country."

William Taylor Son & Company erected a five-story building at 630 Euclid, and, six years later, four stories were added. The adjoining Clarence Building was acquired and became the annex to the west. Upon the death of John L. Taylor in 1892, his wife, Sophia Strong Taylor, succeeded him as president and controlling owner.

The Rev. Henry Seymour Brown, who succeeded Dr. Dormer L. Hickok as pastor of the First Presbyterian Church of East Cleveland, commemorated the centennial celebration of "Old First" by purchasing the Tiffany baptismal font with money given by a prominent member, Charles F. Brush. Dr. Brown this year assisted in the organization of the Noble Heights Bible Chapel which became Noble Road Presbyterian Church in 1921. Dr. Howard M. Wells became pastor of First Church in 1926. Inspiring leadership developed religious-education programs, stimulating youth activities and community functions that enriched East Cleveland, and adding to the goodly heritage handed down by the pioneers. In the 1940s the First Church stood proudly on its original site, 16200 Euclid, a record unequaled in Greater Cleveland.

The political campaign began in October, with Tom L. Johnson running for re-election, his slogan being "The People's Choice," while Theodore E. Burton, with the blessing of President Theodore Roosevelt, was the Republican opposition. There was much bitterness because Johnson was a hero to many and a mountebank to others. Burton's great campaign speech was made before a vast audience of Republicans. In true political fashion, and with dignified and scholarly manner, he started by stating that he had spoken in the great Crystal Palace in London, in the halls of Congress, and in the auditoriums of many cities, but never had he been so gratified as now in facing such an audience of his fellow-citizens. He declared that he did not seek the office of mayor, that it had been urged upon him. Then he concluded by saying, "I have decided to yield to the wishes of many Clevelanders and campaign for the office of mayor. Jacta est alea—the die is cast!" The next night Johnson replied to Burton. He told his audience that his opponent had selected a platform in a foreign language so that no one could understand it. "He calls it," boomed Johnson, "jacta est alea! And what does it mean? In your language and mine it means, 'Let 'er go Gallagher!'" The audience roared, and if Burton had any chance of election up to this time, ridicule seemed to have killed it. Homer Davenport, famous New York cartoonist, celebrated for his portrayal of the late Senator Mark Hanna in a suit marked with dollar signs, and for stimulating hatred of monopolies by his cartoon figure of "Trust," was loaned to the *Leader* to campaign by caricature against the re-election of Johnson. J. H. Donahey, *Plain Dealer* cartoonist, was credited with outdoing the famous Davenport. The vote for Johnson was 48,342 and 39,016 for Burton.

Women skated in flowing dresses in the new Elysium, one of the three

The Cuyahoga County Court House opened on January 1, 1912.

The Constitutional Convention — a mural by Violet Oakley.

Entranceway.

The spirited horses of Engine Company No. 2 on the way to a fire in 1913.

Fighting a stubborn fire with the aid of an extension ladder. Lower left: George A. Wallace, the city's most famous chief.

largest indoor ice rinks in the country. Dudley S. Humphrey, "popcorn king," laughed at skeptics and built it at a cost of $150,000 at Euclid and East 107th Street. Here were held international figure-skating contests and school, college and professional hockey games. War restrictions and uncertainties brought the closing of the building in 1942, and the land was turned back to the original owner, Case School of Applied Science.

The Park Drop Forge Company was established to make forgings for various industrial uses. George C. Gordon became president in 1913 succeeding Dwight Goddard, the first president. The company then specialized in products for the railroad and automotive industries. Its crankshafts and heavy drop forgings manufactured in the plant at 777 East 79th Street found markets throughout the country. Crankshafts made in dies were the largest of their kind produced in the United States.

Many of Cleveland's newcomers from European lands found friendliness and fun at the East End Neighborhood House, 2749 Woodhill Road. Organized in November by the Rev. Wilson R. Stearly of the Emmanuel Episcopal Church to help make the adjustment to new ways of life easier for countless immigrants, the first meetings were held in a storeroom at 244 East 89th Street. In 1910 the Emmanuel Club, as it was first known, was reorganized as the East End Neighborhood House Association. Six years later it moved to 2749 Woodhill, the site being donated by the Van Sweringens. Hedwig Kosbab, founder and head resident, served as a volunteer during the early years, and directed the important program. In 1943 Dorothy Smith took over the direction of the settlement house, which was helping people of all ages and nationalities to become happier socially. Its encompassing program of education and entertainment was enjoyed by 17,047 persons in 1946.

The city closed up tight on Sunday, December 23, as Cleveland observed Chief Fred Kohler's rigid crusade to enforce recognition of the Blue Sabbath.

Glenville Hospital, 701 Parkwood Drive, was organized this year. Operated by the Parkwood Hospital Association, it included a nurse's-training program from its inception. In 1934 the hospital was enlarged, and an expansion program was planned for the future.

1908

Valentine Christ, an aged millionaire who owned many parcels of real estate, died, January 20, in a hovel on Theresa Court. One of Cleveland's largest land owners, despite his wealth, had been nursed by charity.

A group of progressive business and professional men organized the Cleveland Athletic Club, the second of that name. William P. Murray was the first president, and directors were Elbert H. Baker, Walter C. Baker, A. H. Bedell, George H. Eichelberger, Cliff W. Fuller, Arthur J. Huston, Homer H. McKeehan, William B. Maxson, Edward W. Moore, Sam T. Nash, Charles A. Otis, Proctor Patterson, George L. Schryver, William E.

Wall, and Lindsay H. Wallace. George A. Schneider was the secretary and manager. The club took over the Century Club quarters in the New England Building.

The *Americke Delnicke Listy,* Bohemian weekly newspaper, was established, with headquarters at 4032 Broadway.

The *Plain Dealer* suffered severe loss in the destruction of its building at Superior and East 6th Street by fire on February 2. Plans were immediately made for a new building to be erected on the site.

A committee of twenty from the Chamber of Commerce investigated complaints made by charitable organizations and their supporters regarding incessant appeals to the public for money. The burden of charitable support was being borne by only a few hundred people. Out of this dissatisfaction, the plan for a Community Chest was born.

One of Cleveland's greatest disasters was the Collinwood School fire on March 4, when 174 persons, mostly children, were lost. Two teachers died in an effort to save their charges. It was said at the time that the exit doors in the Collinwood School opened inward, causing the children and teachers to be trapped. Safer construction of school buildings and more rigid fire inspection of schools, theaters, and public buildings resulted throughout the nation.

Cleveland invited the schools of the country to compete in a spelling contest in April, as a feature of the National Educational Association Convention to be held in June. Cleveland, Pittsburgh, Erie, and New Orleans promptly entered, each city agreeing to send fifteen contestants and fifteen alternates. Cleveland won, with Pittsburgh second, New Orleans third, and Erie fourth. It was said that the publicity developed by this contest served to improve spelling in the nation's schools, and Cleveland was advertised widely.

Under the leadership of the Rev. Jacob H. Goldner, the sixty-five-year-old Euclid Avenue Christian Church had made great gains; and to provide for expansion, the new "greenstone" edifice at 9990 Euclid Avenue was dedicated free of debt on April 12. Howard G. Spangler, called as pastor's assistant in 1912, became associate pastor in 1919, and the two clergymen enjoyed the longest pastor-assistant relationship in Cleveland history. The Rev. A. Dale Fiers succeeded Dr. Goldner, and in the mid-1940s membership reached 1,800.

Receivership seemed inevitable for the Erie Railroad in 1908, but E. H. Harriman procured a $5,500,000 loan, thus averting catastrophe for the Erie and enhancing his own reputation as an outstanding constructive railroader. Frederick Underwood was president of the road until 1927.

The Lindner Company started in business in April on East 9th Street, in part of the premises later occupied by The Cleveland Trust Company. It moved to 1331 Euclid Avenue in September, 1915. From that time, its growth was rapid, and it became the largest specialty shop in Cleveland, selling women's apparel. Executives of the company in the 1940s were Mack Gordon, president, and Simon Olson, vice president.

Mayor Johnson and his friends celebrated their victory, April 27, whereby the Forest City Railway Company, chartered in 1903; the Municipal Traction Company, 1906; the Low Fare Railway Company, 1906; and the Neutral Street Railway Company, 1908, sold their franchises and other property to The Cleveland Railway Company. April 28 was Streetcar Day, when anybody and everybody could ride the streetcars free, because Tom L. Johnson thought he had won his three-cent-fare fight; but additional difficulties were yet to be overcome in the question of three-cent traction fares. President A. B. duPont of the street-railway company announced that strict economy must be adopted to make the new fares pay; Johnson suggested dropping unprofitable lines; East Cleveland claimed unfair treatment; the car men's union protested discrimination. Then several developments followed that still further upset transit conditions in Cleveland. When a number of employees of the old company were discharged, a strike was called on May 16, beginning one of the most serious labor struggles the city had known. Shortly afterward, a depression and the strike by streetcar union men cut revenues and affected service.

The Jewish Religious Education Association of Ohio, composed of rabbis, teachers, and superintendents of religious schools, was formed, May 16, with Rabbi Gries as president. The Ohio Rabbinical Association was also formed under the same leadership.

Membership was nearing the thousand mark this year, when St. John's African Methodist Episcopal Church congregation moved into its new home at 2261 East 40th Street. In 1946, during the pastorate of Dr. Charles S. Spivey, the total had reached 3,200; there were 2,000 on the Sunday School roll, and the church was one of the most influential in the denomination. St. John's was the parent or grandparent of eight colored congregations, including St. James, 1882; Bethel, 1917; Avery, 1918; West Park, 1919; Quinn Chapel, 1923; and St. Luke's 1924.

The Civil Engineers Club had flourished, and this year, during the presidency of Willard Beahan, it was reorganized as The Cleveland Engineering Society, including all branches of the profession. Engineers, architects, and scientists, pre-eminent in their achievements, made the roster a veritable "architectural Who's Who." *Cleveland Engineering,* the official bulletin, appeared in 1917, and the society's library of some fourteen thousand volumes on technical subjects was placed in the Public Library. In 1922, the organization of the Associated Technical Societies of Cleveland co-ordinated the city's engineering activities, but was abandoned after four years.

Statesmen sounded the praise of the late Senator Mark A. Hanna on May 24, as his daughters unveiled the memorial in University Circle.

George A. Bellamy, head of Hiram House, started the first citizenship school in the country with an enrollment of fifty. Thousands of immigrants had been coming to Cleveland and little was done for their welfare. Many were being exploited; politicians railroaded them through naturalization, seeking their votes. With Manuel Levine, once an immigrant, a product of Hiram House, and later a prominent jurist, Bellamy started the movement that was copied in other cities. Americanization as a community task was born.

F. H. Goff was named president of The Cleveland Trust Company in June, succeeding Calvary Morris, who retired. Goff's pioneering policies in bank management were adopted by many other institutions, one of them, "No loans to officers or directors," being enacted into law. In 1909 the monumental banking house was opened at the southeast corner of Euclid and East 9th Street, as the home of the main office. Typical of the bank's sound and steady development was the series of thirteen colorful mural paintings surrounding the lofty rotunda, a tribute to hardy pioneers who pushed back the wilderness and established new frontiers founded on faith and high ideals. With three assistants, Francis Davis Millet, famous mural painter, worked more than a year to execute the series depicting the development of civilization in the Middle West. Millet lost his life on the ill-fated *Titanic* in 1912. In 1924 the company extended its main-office properties to Huron Road, acquiring the Anisfield Building for needed expansion. It was the eighth largest financial institution in the nation in point of savings deposits in 1927, with 443,000 deposit accounts.

Keith's Theater suffered a small fire, June 2, and the crowd filed out to safety. The cool-headed leader of the orchestra, Herman Biringer, averted threatened panic. A soubrette, Carolyn Deimore, no less brave, sang until she was exhausted. Actor Eugene Jepson died of heart failure as the theater burned.

The National Education Association met in Cleveland on June 29. Meetings were outstanding educational gatherings, and the outdoor reception at University Circle, with fireworks in Wade Park, attracted an audience estimated at 150,000. Cleveland profited through the resulting good advertising and good will. The executive committee appointed to undertake local responsibilities for the convention included: F. F. Prentiss, chairman, F. H. Haserot, J. J. Sullivan, N. D. Chapin, S. M. Bond, Thomas P. Robbins, George W. Kinney, W. H. Hunt, W. H. Elson, E. H. Baker, Dr. Dan F. Bradley, and William Ganson Rose, executive secretary.

The National Bronze & Aluminum Foundry Company had its origin this year in the Comstock Brass Foundry. Three years later the principals were joined by new business associates in expanding the institution and giving it the name it bore henceforth. A spacious plant housed the business at East 79th Street and Woodland Avenue, and in 1919 new buildings were constructed at East 88th Street and Laisy Avenue, comprising 160,000 square feet of factory space, making National Bronze one of the largest plants in America. Fire destroyed much of the property in 1940; but new buildings, comprising 225,000 square feet of foundry space, were quickly erected at East 45th Street and Hamilton Avenue, so that during the war the completely mechanized foundry could be of the greatest service. Under the direction of William I. Neimeyer and his associates, new methods were developed for producing precision castings by using frozen mercury patterns. National Bronze was a pioneer production-run supplier of precision castings in all types of metals and special alloys.

At the turn of the century, A. L. MacLaren, a druggist on Cedar Avenue, interested his friend, George H. Miller, and others in developing and selling a remedy called Musterole, designed to replace the mustard plaster. The business outgrew its basement quarters, and in 1915 a factory was erected on East 27th Street near Payne Avenue. In the 1940s Miller was president of the Musterole Company, which marketed its products throughout the world.

At a fireworks counter in a five-and-ten-cent store at 2025 Ontario Street, a sparkler in a child's hand ignited a fluttering flag, touching off a disaster that cost seven lives. From this tragedy the safe-and-sane Fourth of July developed in Cleveland and then in the nation.

The Collinwood Village council voted "No" to annexation on July 14.

The Cleveland Whist Club team of Maurice Maschke, Carl T. Robertson, Arthur Halle, and Henry P. Jaeger finished second in the national championship. Robertson with Ralph Reed Richards of Detroit won the pair trophy. Bridge had supplanted whist, and a controversy arose in Cleveland as to the merits of the two games. The interest of the best whist players had subsided as they did not readily respond to the new game, and it was not until 1927 that the Cleveland Whist Club again entered a national contest.

At the invitation of Charles A. Otis, a number of well-known Clevelanders met at his Tannenbaum farm in Waite Hill, followed his beagles, and laid plans for a riding association. Some years before, the Cleveland Hunt Club had been organized, but its life was short. The new organization was named the Chagrin Valley Hunt Club. A. D. Baldwin was the first secretary, and those instrumental in developing the organization were Windsor T. White, J. B. Perkins, Otis, and Baldwin. Women soon became active in the organization, among them Olive Corning, Mrs. Otto Miller, Katherine Hoyt, Helen Murray, Pansy Ireland, Katherine Holden, Caroline Pickands, Katherine Haskell, Delia White, Kathleen York, and Eloise McLaughlin. In addition to hunting activities, the club sponsored horse shows, the first being held in June, 1909. Polo was taken up, and soon an excellent team was developed. The first inter-city match was won by Chagrin Valley over Cincinnati, the home team being made up of Corliss Sullivan, E. S. Burke, Jr., Lawrence Hitchcock, and A. D. Baldwin. In 1921 the Kirtland Country Club was organized, many of its sponsors belonging to the Chagrin Valley club. Dan R. Hanna, Cyrus C. Ford, Quay Findley, Robert C. Norton, John Sherwin, Jr., and Francis Sherwin were polo leaders in the new club. The Chagrin Valley club won the National Inter-Circuit Tournament and the Central Circuit Cup in 1927; and, four years later, won a second inter-circuit championship. International polo came to Cleveland when Courtney Burton arranged a contest with the Mexican Army team, the visitors winning two out of three games in 1939. The local team included Tom White, captain, Otto Knutsen, Jr., Burton, and William Kuykendall of Texas. In *The Horse, The Valley and the Chagrin Valley Hunt* by J. Blan Van Urk, the many activities of the club were recorded.

Nelson Moses, leader in the real-estate business and senior member of Nelson Moses & Brothers, died July 21. He was one of the founders of Collinwood, a bank director, and a dealer in railroad ties and ship timber as well as real estate. With him were associated two brothers, Charles W. and Augustus L., both prominently identified with Cleveland's progress. A son of the latter, Louis A., succeeded his father in the real-estate business, holding high offices in the Cleveland Real Estate Board, the Ohio Association of Real Estate Boards, and the National Association of Real Estate Boards. As president of the Cleveland Metropolitan Park Board and as a leader in other constructive activities, he kept prominent the name of the pioneer family that had settled in Euclid, Ohio.

An ordinance introduced by Councilman Daniel S. Pfahl became effective, August 1, prohibiting possession, sale, or use of fireworks in Cleveland. This was believed to have been the first measure barring the sale of fireworks in an American municipality.

Pay-enter cars were introduced in Cleveland on August 5. Men were placed in the cars to call out instructions to the passengers with the admonition, "Smoking on the three rear seats only."

At about this time, H. L. McKinnon, E. J. Neville, and H. H. Bighouse brought valuable experience to The C. O. Bartlett & Snow Company, relating to the design and manufacture of mechanical-handling and heat-processing equipment, coal tipples, and incinerators. They later became members of the board of directors. McKinnon's idea of applying mechanical-handling principles to foundries, conceived about 1911, became standard practice, substantially increasing production, reducing costs, increasing workers' wages, and improving working conditions. The company's mechanized foundry systems and designs were put to work in plants throughout the world. In 1924 a new plant was occupied at 6200 Harvard Avenue. H. S. Hersey became president and general manager of the company in 1942.

One of downtown Cleveland's unique structures was the Hippodrome Building, completed this year. It embraced a theater and many offices. A magnificent stage was located between the two towering portions of the structure, the eleven-story section facing Euclid Avenue, and the seven-story part facing Prospect. Construction of the building was representative of the finest engineering skills. The theater's spacious auditorium and its grandiose appearance attracted artists of distinction and audiences of magnitude. Max Faetkenheuer, who had planned the theater, directed its activities. He was a familiar figure in Cleveland's entertainment life for a number of years. He had led the orchestra in the Lyceum Theater, directed summer opera at Haltnorth's Gardens, brought the Bostonians to Cleveland several times for delightful productions of light opera, and developed a company that gave popular musical entertainments at the Euclid Avenue Garden Theater, east of Case Avenue. The opening attraction at the Hippodrome was *Coaching Days,* with music by John S. Zamecnek and book and lyrics by William J. Wilson. The great feature was the diving of horses into a large water-tank built into the front part of the stage. Subsequently the Hippodrome was used for grand opera, popular musical shows, vaudeville, and motion pictures. People came from long distances to see the immense playhouse which took rank among the world's greatest.

Pitcher "Dusty" Rhoades of Cleveland on September 18 pitched a no-hit game against the Boston Red Sox, although the latter scored one run, due to a base on balls, a sacrifice, and an error. The score was 2-1. Addie Joss pitched one of the great games of big-league history on October 2, not permitting a man to reach first base. The Chicago team was the victim. In desperation, Manager Jones of the White Sox called upon three pinch hitters in the ninth inning, but they met the fate of their predecessors.

"The grandest battle in the history of the American League," was the appraisal by Henry P. Edwards of the *Plain Dealer* of the baseball race that saw the Cleveland Naps eliminated from pennant contention. Detroit's final percentage was .588, Cleveland was second with .584 and Chicago third with .579.

Cleveland was one of the early cities to plan a technical high school, a forward step that developed out of the manual-training principle. East Technical High School opened on October 12 at East 55th and Scovill Avenue to about seven hundred students. Its steady increase in enrollment and the constant demand for its graduates proved the success of this experiment in education.

Fred H. Goff, new Glenville mayor, declared that betting was illegal, and the famous Glenville race track was abandoned, October 15. Maude S.'s famous golden horseshoe at the entrance was taken down, and many devotees of harness racing in Cleveland and the nation expressed sentimental regret. Sportsmen moved into a village organized as North Randall on May 2, 1908. B. O. Shank was the first mayor, and H. K. Devereux, gentleman amateur horseman, was treasurer. Although several industries located in the village, horse racing, both running and trotting, continued as the principal attraction over the years. At the North Randall and Thistledown tracks, thousands of fans congregated each season to witness the races.

Clevelanders, in a referendum on October 23, voted to restore the streetcar system to private ownership. Mayor Johnson attributed the outcome to confusion, but apparently the voters had tired of the confusion of the past few years. The bitter contest between Johnson and the railway-property owners on November 12 resulted in receivership of the properties.

The Northern Ohio Chapter of the American Guild of Organists was organized on November 10 at Trinity Cathedral, Edwin Arthur Kraft presiding. Sixteen Cleveland organists became members at the first meeting.

The Fortnightly Club consistently presented choral works of distinction and great beauty. Long-remembered was the outstanding performance of Rossini's *Stabat Mater* in Trinity Cathedral. Mrs. Seabury C. Ford, a Cleveland singer of national fame and a club member, Lila Robeson, Warren Whitney, and Francis Sadlier were soloists; and Edwin Arthur Kraft played the organ for this concert. Later in the same season, in the Chamber of Commerce Hall, Mrs. Ford, Mrs. F. A. Seiberling, Harry E. Cole, and Felix Hughes were soloists in a brilliant rendition of the song cycle by Liza Lehmann, *In a Persian Garden.*

Through his tar still, young James W. Corrigan began an association with the Standard Oil Company that made him a millionaire. Then he turned to ore, forming the Corrigan-Ives Company, and in 1907 his secretary, Price McKinney, became a partner. Corrigan died in 1908, and his fortune helped to provide the funds that created The Corrigan-McKinney Steel Company in 1910, one of the nation's largest independent steel producers (later acquired by the Republic Steel Corporation). In 1919 James "Jimmie" Corrigan, son of the founder, secured control. McKinney was ousted, and the blow brought his suicide. The McKinneys had lived for some time in a beautiful mansion on East Boulevard (later home of the Western Reserve Historical Society) built by Mrs. John Hay, but never occupied by her as she had decided to make her home in Washington. Although Mrs. James W. Corrigan spent most of her time in France and England, as society leader and practical philanthropic friend of the people, she was a contributor to worthy Cleveland undertakings.

As a member of the sanitation committee of the Chamber of Commerce, Dr. Lyman W. Childs opened the first school dispensary in the United States at the Murray Hill School to compile health data for the committee.

1909

Death and distress were brought by a raging storm on February 16, that left wires and gas mains in wreckage. Cities and towns in Ohio were completely cut off, as telegraph and telephone service halted. Fruit trees were damaged and trains were stalled.

William Howard Taft was inaugurated the twenty-sixth President of the United States. This genial and scholarly statesman was born in Cincinnati, Ohio, and had a host of friends in Cleveland.

Women's skirts dragged on the sidewalks, for that was the fashion. Hence, a councilman urged passage of a measure on March 9 to make "society's street gowns short enough to keep out of the dirt."

"Billy" Whitla, kidnaped Sharon, Pennsylvania, boy, was returned to his waiting father in the lobby of the Hollenden Hotel on March 23. The ransom of ten thousand dollars was paid. Two days later, the kidnapers, Mr. and Mrs. James Boyle of Sharon, were apprehended in Cleveland and confessed.

The slogan for the coming Cleveland Industrial Exposition selected in March was "Onward, Cleveland, Onward." A city-wide debate over the merits of the slogan gave far more publicity to the project than any perfect war-cry could have given. One minister denounced it as a parody on *Onward, Christian Soldiers,* and Willoughby, through the wit of Sidney S. Wilson, capitalized upon the slogan by adopting it in this fashion: "Onward, Cleveland, Onward to Willoughby!"

Walter H. Cottingham was elected president of the Sherwin-Williams Company, succeeding Henry A. Sherwin, who became chairman of the board and died in 1916. Sherwin was known for his practical support of the YMCA over many years, and his interest in banks and philanthropic enterprises. Plants and properties were purchased and expanded in other cities, followed by establishments in Canada, England, Australia, and New Zealand. George A. Martin, employed in 1890, became president in 1922; Cottingham became chairman and passed on in 1930. Several large American companies were acquired in 1929, and plants were eventually established in Cuba, Argentina, and Brazil. The business trebled during Martin's administration; and when he retired in 1940, Arthur W. Steudel, who entered the company in 1908, succeeded him. Under Steudel's direction, many new products, developed after intensive research in company laboratories, were reaching the consumer through more than 150,000 retail outlets. Since the founding in 1866, Cleveland was the home of Sherwin-Williams, the world's largest manufacturer of paints, varnishes, lacquers, insecticides, and associated products bearing the familiar trademark "Cover the earth."

Cleveland was the second city in the United States to organize sight-saving classes for public-school children with serious eye defects.

The State Primary Law went into effect, the purpose being to insure free elections not influenced by party bosses, and to compel civic interest among indifferent citizens.

City Council passed an ordinance in March permitting the Cleveland Underground Rapid Transit Company "to construct and operate electric underground railroads, defining the routes and fixing the rate of fare," but nothing further happened.

Cleveland's pioneer carpet and interior-decoration house, The Sterling & Welch Company, as it was now known, ventured on upper Euclid Avenue to a permanent location, 1225 Euclid, site of the James J. Tracy home. The store was one of the largest and finest home-furnishing stores in the world, with a great commercial gallery of decorative art. Arthur V. Hook, official for thirty-four years, became president in 1944, when F. A. Sterling died.

Dr. Charles A. Eaton, who had been the inspirational minister of the Euclid Avenue Baptist Church from 1901 to 1909, left to become minister of the Madison Avenue Church in New York City. A particularly able writer and speaker, he served as correspondent and special writer for publications in the United States and Canada. For a short period of time he turned to industrial relations, serving the National Lamp Works of the General Electric Company in Cleveland. Taking up his residence in New Jersey, he was elected to the Congress in 1925, and became one of its leading members, giving particular attention to world affairs.

Robert E. Peary made a dash to the North Pole on April 6. Upon announcing that he had reached his goal, he learned of Dr. Frederick Cook's prior claim. Years of debate followed, but Peary, well known in Cleveland, really reached the Pole, according to scientists.

Seven were killed and scores injured on April 22 in a windstorm that destroyed property valued at two million dollars. It was the most violent wind in the history of Cleveland, leaving many half-demolished homes and tangled live wires. Twelve churches and seventeen schools lay in ruin.

With the defeat of the Schmidt Grant, which would have authorized the building of a street railroad on Payne Avenue, Mayor Johnson lost his last chance to give the city a three-cent fare. The three-cent structure collapsed, and Johnson's Depositors Savings & Trust Company went down with his fortune, including his Euclid Avenue mansion. The lines were thrown into receivership temporarily, Warren Bicknell operating them until March 1, 1910.

Spring had come to southeast Cleveland, but not to Gates Avenue, a block long and miserably poor. A pathetic little Gates Avenue girl had attended Miles Park Elementary School all winter in a soiled, ragged middy and skirt. Responding to the sympathetic interest of her teacher, she appeared one morning in the classroom scrubbed and combed, but in the same soiled clothes. A suggestion that her clothes be washed went unheeded; but the teacher's present of a bright-blue pinafore produced results. Within a week, this small investment in cleanliness inspired a clean-up campaign in the humble home in the form of scrubbed floors, repairs to the backyard fence, rubbish removal, a spaded garden, and house-painting next door. The Rev. T. Alfred Fleming encouraged the betterment project by persuading landlords to improve property while the city brought in paving, water, and street light. Within six months, citizens had transformed their homes in the Gates Avenue Cleanup. The young pastor spread the story. It reached Cincinnati, where Captain J. J. Conway of the Salvage Corps incorporated fire-prevention with features of the Cleveland achievement to launch in 1913 the first city-wide clean-up campaign in the nation. Rev. Fleming turned to welfare work, and as a member of the National Board of Fire Underwriters, advanced the clean-up cause.

The Cleveland operations of the Aluminum Company of America began in May of this year in a sand foundry at 6205 Carnegie Avenue, established to supply parts to the growing Cleveland and Detroit automotive industries. Seven years later, farm land south of Harvard Avenue at East 22nd Street was selected for a mold plant, and here in July, 1917, the first metal was poured, destined principally for the production of automotive and aircraft pistons for the Allied forces of World War I. Then came the manufacture of crankcases for the "Liberty" aircraft engine in the early twenties. Alcoa's Cleveland Works pioneered the forging of aluminum and later produced ingots of aluminum alloy. In World War II, the Works was a principal producer of forged aluminum for propeller blades and numerous other aircraft parts, $15,000,000 being expended for plant expansion. Employment grew to 10,300 in 1943-44, and the Cleveland Works units expanded to include an aluminum sand foundry, aluminum permanent mold foundry, aluminum forging plant, aluminum ingot plant, magnesium permanent mold foundry, and aluminum-research laboratories. Harold C. Erskine became Works manager in 1943, succeeding Allen B. Norton, who was made manager of Alcoa's Casting Division.

On May 12 Cleveland Elks opened a $125,000 clubhouse on Huron Road.

The human voice was proved visible to the eye on May 26, when Professor Dayton C. Miller showed an audience every word he spoke, by throwing an instantaneous record on a screen by means of a new electric machine.

Tell Berna won the intercollegiate cross-country championship this year, and captured the outdoor two-mile championship in 1910 and 1911. His two-mile mark of 9:17.8 stood until 1929, when Paavo Nurmi eclipsed it.

At the Stockholm Olympics in 1912, Berna won the three-thousand-meter race in 9:01.

Unique in the history of home-product expositions was the Cleveland Industrial Exposition which opened under the auspices of the Cleveland Chamber of Commerce on June 7. A temporary building was constructed (City Hall site), larger than the Coliseum in Chicago or the Madison Square Garden arena in New York. It was a novel structure with side walls of staff and a roof of canvas supported by huge masts mounted on structural-iron supports. An elaborate street-decorating scheme attracted wide attention. All records for expositions of the kind were broken, 215,000 people having paid admission in twelve days, while thousands were necessarily turned away. The Central Armory was utilized, and the two buildings were connected by a bridge concealed by an ornamental façade spanning the street. The halls provided the greatest amount of space ever devoted to an exhibition of manufacturers of one city, and displays told the story of Cleveland's leadership in industry. The purposes of the project were ably carried out—"to teach Cleveland to know itself, and to teach the world to become better acquainted with Cleveland." A substantial profit was expended to secure conventions. The executive committee included F. F. Prentiss, chairman; C. E. Farnsworth, treasurer; William Ganson Rose, secretary-manager; and Charles E. Adams, W. D. B. Alexander, S. P. Fenn, Munson A. Havens, William H. Hunt, H. A. Higgins, John G. Jennings, L. H. Kittredge, M. A. Marks, Harry New, Robert W. Ney, Charles A. Paine, S. L. Pierce, Willard N. Sawyer, W. D. Sayle, F. R. Scofield, Ambrose Swasey, and Lyman H. Treadway.

Bishop John P. Farrelly, the first of Cleveland's bishops to be consecrated abroad, was installed in St. John's Cathedral on June 13 after he had returned from an extensive term of service as spiritual director of the American College at Rome. As the fourth bishop of the Cleveland Diocese, he was particularly influential in improving the parochial-school system and in organizing the Catholic Charities. Under his supervision, which lasted twelve years, forty-seven churches and schools were built, including Cathedral Latin High School. A soft-spoken southerner, he proved to be an efficient organizer and capable executive equal to the varied tasks and myriad of duties placed upon him. He succeeded the eminent Bishop Horstmann, who died May 13, 1908.

Cleveland was treated to a "double astronomical phenomenon," the newspapers reported on June 17. At sundown, the city, storm-swept a few hours before, gazed upon what Father F. L. Odenbach of St. Ignatius College described as "one of the finest solar eclipses ever seen in this part of the world." With about four-tenths of its surface obscured by the moon's shadow, the sun, when it dropped into Lake Erie, took the form of a "great flaming Indian canoe." As its center slipped below the horizon, the two ends of the canoe "stood up like great icebergs until haze blotted them from sight." About 11 P.M., watchers beheld in the southwestern sky the tail of the Brooks Comet, discovered on the preceding May 23.

The nation's first safe-and-sane Fourth of July was celebrated in Cleveland. The welcoming of new citizens, inspired by welfare pioneering at Hiram House, was a feature of the day. Newspapers throughout the nation praised the city for making Independence Day one of patriotism unmarred by needless accidents. The next year Cleveland's example was followed by other cities, and in the course of a few years the sale of fireworks and pyrotechnic exhibitions were controlled by law. Countless eyes, fingers, and lives were saved by Cleveland's practical precedent.

The grand-circuit meeting was held, August 10-13, at the new North Randall track, just completed at a cost of $250,000. Despite the fact that the location seemed a long way from the Public Square, the attendance was large. The sensational event that attracted the greatest attention was the 2:07 trot, won by the mighty Uhlan in two straight heats, 2:06¼ and 2:03¾, the latter being North Randall's first world record for five-year-old geldings. Harry K. Devereux, president of the Grand Circuit, asked Secretary George J. Dietrich to arrange a match race between the most sensational horses of the day, Hamburg Belle and Uhlan. The race was held August 25 on the Randall Track. Hamburg Belle won in the fastest consecutive heats on record, 2:01¼ and 2:01¾. H. M. Hanna bought the winner for $50,000 and C. K. G. Billings, the loser for $35,000. Someone observed that the history of harness racing in America is a Cleveland story.

The Chamber of Commerce entertained the Commercial Commissioners that Japan sent to the United States, arranging dinners and sight-seeing tours of the business and industry of the Cleveland area for several days in October. The visitors showed the efficiency and research that characterized their island kingdom.

Plans for a permanent electrical organization were made by representatives of Cleveland industries on October 16, at a meeting held at the Hotel Hollenden. They materialized rapidly, and on October 30 the first meeting of the Electrical League of Cleveland was held. G. E. Miller was elected president, and so successful was the organization that it became the model for the nation. J. E. North became president in 1922; and, after a quarter of a century of leadership, remained as the league's head. In 1924 the Electrical League promoted the world's first Electrical Maintenance Engineers' Association, and in 1927 the *Electrical Production* magazine was founded. A non-profit institution, the league was financed in 1946 by 338 member companies, represented by 628 members.

The Cleveland Fire Department consisted of thirty engine companies, eleven hook-and-ladder and two hose companies, manned by 515 men.

The winners of the Challenge Cups for the fastest time to wagon in the Gentlemen's Driving Club of Cleveland for the first decade of the Twentieth Century were: John A. McKerron, H. K. Devereux's champion trotter for three successive years, 1900, 1901, and 1902, with times of 2:09, 2:06¾, 2:06½; 1900, pacer, Ananias, 2:06¼, C. F. Emery; 1901, pacer, Nicol B., 2:11¼, John Sherwin; 1902, pacer, Tiger, 2:07¾, John Ray; 1903, trotter, Lou Dillon, 2:04½, C. K. G. Billings; pacer, Babe Allerton, 2:09¼, C. K. G. Billings; 1904, Lou Dillon, 2:04¾, C. K. G. Billings; pacer, Greenline, 2:07½, C. K.

G. Billings; 1905, trotter, Major Delmar, 2:04, C. K. G. Billings; pacer, Morning Star, 2:03, C. K. G. Billings; 1906, trotter, George G., 2:05, A. N. Brady; pacer, Blacklock, 2:03¼, C. K. G. Billings; 1907, trotter, Dewitt, 2:09½, E. S. Burke, Jr.; pacer, Morning Star, 2:04½, E. S. Burke, Jr.; 1908, trotter, Alexander, 2:09, Miss K. L. Wilkes; pacer, Morning Star, 2:07, E. S. Burke, Jr.; 1909, trotter, Dewitt, 2:09¼, E. S. Burke, Jr.; pacer, Morning Star, 2:06¼, E. S. Burke, Jr.

Yugoslavian groups in Cleveland became better integrated citizens and happier individuals as they read the *Clevelandiska Amerika*. The pioneer Slovenian tri-weekly in America, it was edited by Louis J. Pirc, recognized leader and accepted advisor of many nationality groups in Cleveland.

The late J. H. McBride bequeathed to Western Reserve University a fund amounting to $7,300 in memory of his son, Herbert. In 1913 his sons and daughters increased the amount to $50,000 and dedicated it to the memory of their father, mother, and brother. They prescribed that the income from this sum bring authoritative lecturers to Cleveland. Contributors to the foundation were Mrs. Herbert McBride, Malcolm L. McBride, Donald McBride, Mrs. Henry S. Sherman, Jr., and Mrs. George W. Crile. Lectures were given by such personalities as war correspondents, literary critics, theatrical producers, and military observers. Compared with the world-famous Lowell Foundation of Boston, the McBride Lecture Foundation offered year by year the freshest outlook on the newest ideas. Amasa Stone Chapel became outgrown by capacity crowds that attended the free lectures, which were later held in Severance Hall. Dr. Webster G. Simon, who had served as chairman of the course for nine years, resigned in 1932 and was succeeded by Dr. Arthur Cole.

One of the first brick country roads in the United States was laid from Cleveland to East Liverpool.

The new Ball Building, 1114 Euclid Avenue, was occupied by The Webb C. Ball Company, jewelers and watch experts since 1869. A massive bronze street clock measured Cleveland time at the curb until 1946, when a truck ripped it from its base. In 1913 the Norris-Alister Company, a Chicago wholesale jewelry house, was purchased and united with the Cleveland wholesale watch business as the Norris-Alister-Ball Company, and Webb C. Ball's son, Sidney Y., was made president. The company became the largest wholesale distributing house of railroad standard watches in the country, and a leading jewelry concern. The founder of the Cleveland company died in 1922. The store had been enlarged in 1914; and in 1930 the art galleries opened on the second floor. M. V. Shane became president in 1932, succeeding H. R. Avery in this widely known jewelry store.

The Tayler Grant, the traction plan of Cleveland, became a law, December 18. It was devised by Federal Judge Robert W. Tayler, and provided for a sliding-fare scale limiting trolley profits to 6 per cent, with control over railway operations by City Council. Peace had come, following a traction war that cost the city and the railway interests millions of dollars, and the public years of poor service. The Tayler Plan went into effect, March 1, 1910, and John J. Stanley became president of the Cleveland Railway Company, serving until 1926. Stanley was born in Cleveland in 1863. He became connected with local traction companies in the eighties, built several street-railway systems for other cities, and was one of the best-known street-railway executives in the nation. Joseph H. Alexander, who succeeded Stanley as president of the company, was followed in turn by George D. McGwinn in 1931; Paul E. Wilson, May to September, 1937, and Frank R. Hanrahan, who began a five-year term of office which concluded when the City of Cleveland purchased the lines.

While his parents performed in a Jewish theater at the southeast corner of Woodland Avenue and East 22nd Street, a lad busied himself about the house and understudied character parts. His great opportunity came this year, when in an emergency he was allowed to play a prominent role. Muni Weisenfreund went on to fame as Paul Muni, winner of the Academy Award for the best motion-picture performance in 1936.

CHAPTER 14

War—Peace—Progress

1910-1919

THE EXCITING DECADE beginning with the year 1910 was marked by the influences of wartime confusion and peacetime progress. Census figures showing a population of 560,663 were gratifying to the Forest City, as they proclaimed Cleveland the sixth city in the United States, with a growth of 46.9 per cent from 1900 to 1910. Cuyahoga County had increased to 637,425. Statisticians presented interesting figures concerning the growth of American cities. It was learned that in 1850, the year of the first official comparison, Cleveland was the nation's thirty-seventh city as the following table shows:

New York	515,507	Williamsburg	30,780
Philadelphia	408,815	Chicago	29,963
Baltimore	189,048	Troy (N. Y.)	28,785
Boston	136,871	Richmond	27,482
New Orleans	116,348	San Francisco	25,000
Cincinnati	115,435	Syracuse	22,271
Brooklyn	97,838	Allegheny (Pa.)	21,262
St. Louis	64,252	Detroit	21,019
Albany	50,763	Portland	20,815
Pittsburgh	50,519	Mobile	20,513
Louisville	43,196	New Haven	20,345
Charleston (S. C.)	42,985	Salem	20,264
Buffalo	42,261	Milwaukee	20,061
Providence	41,512	Roxbury	18,384
Washington	40,001	Columbus	18,183
Newark (N. J.)	38,894	Utica	17,565
Rochester	36,403	Worcester	17,367
Lowell	33,383	Charleston (Mass.)	17,216
		Cleveland	17,034

By 1910 many interesting changes were made. Cincinnati, the sixth city of 1850, had dropped to thirteenth place, and Cleveland, the thirty-seventh city, had climbed to sixth place. It was seen that in the six decades from 1850 to 1910, Cleveland cleared the widest hurdle of the leading thirty-seven cities, and, as a local humorist observed, it "still holds the long-jump population record."

679

Civic pride, which was accelerated during the Industrial Exposition of 1909, was again stimulated. The manufacturers' census also brought good news, showing Cleveland to be the fifth industrial city in the United States and one of the outstanding manufacturing centers of the world.

As the decade opened, the nation was rapidly developing new industries. Tools and machinery were at work upon products designed for comfort and convenience. The electric starter—when it worked—was a distinct addition to the automobile. Standard equipment included a tow-rope, tire patches, dusters, and a bulb horn that frightened horses and bicycle riders. The one-man top was a new feature. Noisy and powerful Winton and Stearns gasoline cars were favorites with Cleveland men drivers, but most women preferred the quiet and refined Baker and Rauch & Lang electrics, which would run fifty to a hundred miles without recharging, and frequently carried their owners home. Automobiles were raising so much dust that the paving of more streets became a necessity.

Even the Haymarket was beginning to feel the influence of the automobile. As machines gradually displaced horses, there was less demand for hay, and many spaces set aside for hay wagons at the south end of Ontario Street were vacated. Horse liniment was giving way to metal polish.

Cleveland was making nine automobiles of national reputation, and during the decade it became foremost among cities in the production of automobile parts. It had every advantage to offer prospective manufacturers of motor cars; but for the first time in its history, Cleveland, with seeming indifference, let a major industrial opportunity go by. Across the lake, Detroit showed greater initiative in securing new plants and encouraging the enlargement of pioneer factories. So it was that before Cleveland fully realized the force of its competition, the damage had been done, and Detroit, "the dynamic," became the largest motor-car center in the world, taking with it a decided population lead. The realization of its severe setback woke Cleveland to action in time to preserve its automotive-parts business. By 1914 the federal-census figures indicated that thirty cents of each dollar invested in automobiles in the United States came to Cleveland. The business had become third among the city's industries, exceeded only in value of output by the iron-and-steel and foundry-and-machine-shop industries. For years afterward, regret was intermittently expressed that the motor-car business had been lost; but on the other hand, some leaders felt that, had Cleveland retained the car-manufacturing industry along with that of automotive parts, it undoubtedly would have become predominantly a one-industry center instead of continuing to be a well-balanced city of diversified interests.

Glenn H. Curtiss flew his fragile biplane from Euclid Beach Park to Cedar Point and back in 1910, and this longest flight over water attracted world attention and helped to make Cleveland aviation-minded.

Railroad orders started a steel boom early in the decade, and calls for equipment from big trunk lines led to business that lighted up the midnight sky. Repairs that had been needed for several years inspired the rush. A railroad empire was in the making, with Cleveland as the capital and the phenomenal Van Sweringens as the builders. War and economic uncertainties were unsurmountable barriers that prevented the dreams of these modest men of genius from coming true. However, marks of their achievement will remain as a noble inheritance for Greater Cleveland.

Electricity was becoming the illuminant in homes and on the streets, and natural gas was supplanting artificial gas for cooking and heating. Power-driven appliances were taking drudgery out of housework, and the public became better acquainted with them at the colorful Cleveland Electrical Exposition.

A City Plan Commission was created in 1913 under the charter of the City of Cleveland. Up to this time, most people regarded city planning as an engineering necessity related to opening a street, constructing a bridge, or providing a park. The building of a community that would serve the health, wealth, and happiness of the citizenship was not generally understood.

A great new artery, linking the East and West sides, was the Detroit-Superior High Level Bridge, designed to carry highway and streetcar traffic. The city had learned that modern bridges not only promoted business, but helped to unify a municipality divided by great valleys. Other bridges were in the making, and still others were planned to save time and money for a busy city.

The contest for mayor in 1915 was particularly interesting, with two contestants who had known poverty, Harry L. Davis opposing Peter Witt. The former had gained his early experience in the Newburgh rolling mills, and the latter gave up school in the fifth grade to make baskets and later to work as a molder in an iron factory. Both had some political experience. Davis had served as city treasurer in 1910-11, and had been defeated by Newton D. Baker in the mayoralty campaign of 1913. Witt had been city clerk under Mayor Tom L. Johnson, and traction commissioner under Baker. Davis had a pleasing personality, an infectious smile and the knack of making friends. Witt was keen, sarcastic, and vitriolic. At the time of the campaign Germany was on the march, and war was the universal subject of conversation. Yet the two candidates held their own in competing for public interest. Davis, supported by Maurice Maschke, won by a plurality of 2,831 on combined first, second, and other choices on the preferential ballot, although Witt polled 3,017 more first-choice votes than Davis. The successful candidate became the fourth Republican mayor elected in the city in twenty years. Henceforth, Davis was to become one of the city's political leaders, winning four elections out of six for mayor and one out of two for governor. He was elected mayor in 1917 and 1919, and then retired from office to run for governor.

The old problems of purifying the Cuyahoga and straightening it were revived again in this decade. In defense, historians called attention to the fact that the river was really Cleveland's foster mother, an extremely troublesome parent that had meandered at its own sweet will since the glaciers slid back to their ice-locked confines. In the early days it was shallow and sluggish, but its current was clean and clear. Then came the sixties when practical use was made of the river. Abetted by the incoming iron and coal, the refuse of furnaces, factories, and tanneries ran into the stream and mixed with the oil that trickled over the banks. From that time the river remained a contaminated current with a malodorous influence.

The much-discussed Tayler Grant went into effect early in the decade, and all of the street-railway lines were consolidated into the Cleveland Railway Company, after the long-drawn-out streetcar war. This plan united public and private interests and assured transportation at "the cost of service." The cost included interest on the company's floating and bonded debt, with a 6 per cent rate on its stock which was taken over at an agreed valuation. The plan made the company literally an agent of the city, with its rights guaranteed. According to this system, the city had the authority to control service, equipment, and expenses, only limited by the company's ability to finance, and was at liberty to purchase the company's stock at any time on six months' notice, paying capital value plus 10 per cent interest. The Tayler Grant attracted nationwide attention, and other cities discussed the idea of adopting the new system.

The Home Rule form of government was approved by the voters in 1913. The charter was drawn under the leadership of Newton D. Baker, and was considered one of the most practical ever adopted by a large city. The self-government plan was temporarily interrupted by an unsuccessful experiment with the City Manager Plan.

Interurban electric railroads enjoyed their greatest financial success in the mid-decade. Cars bearing the names of Ohio towns were seen regularly on the Public Square, many of them built at the G. C. Kuhlman car works in Collinwood. Cheap, convenient, and efficient transportation characterized the electric lines, which contributed to suburban growth and inter-city trade. Cleveland was an important center of operations for roads that reached deep into the State. After World War I dividends became less frequent. It was revealed that the promoters, a few executives, and property owners along the routes had made money, but that bondholders and stockholders were nearly all losers. As the decade closed, the automobile, bus, and truck were cutting into interurban business. Taxes played a destructive part in the history of the electrics, and in the thirties, most of the lines had been discontinued. Rails were rusting, weeds covered rights-of-way, and a romantic system of transportation passed out of the northern Ohio picture.

Beneath the surface of the nation's industrial advance was an unhealthy economic condition sadly in need of reform. Banks were finding greater difficulty in meeting increased seasonal and emergency needs for currency on the part of manufacturers, merchants, and farmers. Although the national-bank system was sound, it was not elastic. There was no central control over national-bank policies, and surplus money could not be shifted from one section of the country to meet the needs of another. This unfortunate situation, which came to a head in the Panic of 1907, was remedied by the Federal Reserve Act of 1913, establishing the Federal Reserve System which ensured greater reserves for member banks and elasticity of currency through the issue of Federal Reserve notes.

Cleveland's banking prestige grew materially, and its economic importance was accentuated when the announcement was made that the city was chosen as headquarters for the Fourth Federal Reserve District. With the establishment of the Federal Reserve Bank of Cleveland, the city became the financial center of one of the most important industrial, commercial, and agricultural areas of the country, in which were located more than seven hundred national banks.

Cleveland's Welfare Federation had its origin in 1913, and charity and philanthropy were placed upon a sound, efficient footing. The next step was the development of the Community Chest which had its precedent of procedure in the highly successful Victory Fund Campaign. So it was that the city's pioneering developments in the field of welfare not only benefited the citizenship but served as an example for the cities of the country. The forerunner of the Welfare Federation was the Federation for Charity and Philanthropy.

The Cleveland Foundation was established in 1914, and one of the greatest influences for good in the fields of education and charity was steadily and rapidly developed. Its first public service was the educational survey undertaken in 1916. As a result of its recommendations, important benefits accrued to the Cleveland public-school system. The initial recreation survey followed three years later, and its comprehensive study led to community improvements. The nation soon recognized the fact that the Foundation was a practical plan to meet the changing needs of a changing world.

This was the era in which Cleveland was undergoing physical changes to the detriment of the city's beauty. The trees that had advertised it as the Forest City were disappearing. The automobile, with its fumes and noise, was a disturbing element, and the fine horses for which Cleveland was famous were less in evidence each year. Euclid Avenue, still rated as one of the nation's beautiful streets, was being threatened by inroads of commercialism. The fine old homes of the East Side and the West Side were being abandoned by families that were seeking the beauties of the suburbs. However, as the attractiveness of the city suffered, the charm of the outlying communities grew. Decentralization was quickening, and incomes earned in the city were building attractive homes and boulevards beyond the city limits.

Although the Heights area was being built up, there were few churches, and the Euclid Avenue churches drew a number of people from this district. After the war, however, the situation changed. Beautiful new religious centers were being built in the Heights, and downtown churches were forced to meet the challenge of a changing community with new and interesting programs developed under wise leadership.

The monumental Federal Building on the Public Square had special significance, as it held a key position in the Group Plan. Other units in the group, erected during the decade, were the Cuyahoga County Court House and Cleveland's first made-to-order City Hall, the earlier municipal headquarters having been rented or purchased.

This was a decade of cultural advance.

With the formal dedication of the Cleveland Museum of Art in 1916, the dreams of three men were realized. John Huntington left money for a museum in 1889, Horace Kelley in 1890, and Hinman B. Hurlbut in 1884. The accumulated funds were freed of legal entanglements, and the Cleveland Museum of Art was built, seven-tenths by the John Huntington Art and Polytechnic Trust and three-tenths by the Horace Kelley Art Foundation, on ground in Wade Park given by Jeptha H. Wade. The Hinman B. Hurlbut Trust became an endowment fund for the newly created museum. The Cleveland Museum of Art was considered the most beautiful building of its kind in the world, with the most attractive setting. Fine treasures acquired before the opening formed an important nucleus to which were added each year valuable contributions of art and money, ensuring the growing prestige of the institution.

Appreciation of good music was given new inspiration with the founding of The Musical Arts Association, which fostered the best in entertainment and planned the Cleveland Orchestra.

The Shakespeare Garden in Rockefeller Park was opened, and trees and shrubs planted by distinguished authors and actors added beauty and sentiment to the setting. The garden inspired the Cleveland Cultural Gardens of worldwide fame.

Motion pictures, despite their static flashes and intermittent breaks, were coming into their own, with Gloria Swanson and Rudolph Valentino as popular favorites, while resourceful Max Sennett, jolly John Bunny, rotund Fatty Arbuckle, impish Mabel Normand, quaint Charlie Chaplin, and cross-eyed Ben Turpin were making the nation laugh with their boisterous comedy. Thrills were provided by daring Pearl White and virile William Farnum. As the screen action changed, the house pianist pounded out *Cheyenne, The Bird on Nellie's Hat, San Antonio, Hearts and Flowers,* and *Love Me and the World is Mine.* Illustrated songs were still in favor in neighborhood theaters, and audiences continued to weep as slides and music combined in *My Mother was a Lady, Two Little Girls in Blue,* and *The Bird in a Gilded Cage.* The tango was going out, dancing teachers said, and the hesitation waltz and maxixe would steal the spotlight. Paul Whiteman headed the most popular dance band. Ragtime was the rage in dance halls, and the newest airs were whistled up and down the avenue. It was a great time to live!

Baseball gained favor with the advent of several star players who helped Cleveland to reach second place. Amateur baseball was put on a sound foundation in this period. Ice-boating was popular inside the harbor break-water, and moonlight cruises on the *City of Erie* attracted summertime crowds. Golf was coming into its own, and seven courses were developed during the decade.

Croquet mallets and balls were coming out of storage, following a newspaper warning that whether "you like to play croquet or not, it is going to be the social fad; for croquet is always revived with Chantilly and chignons." The ladies were advised: "you must wear your hat . . . if you would win your game in proper style. You must provide your costume especially for the game. Doubtless it will be of old-fashioned muslin, white and frilly, and you will wear a broad-brimmed, drooping, flower-laden picture hat. For grace and elegance your gown will trail over the 'sward, but the girl who really enjoys her croquet will cut off her skirt four inches from the ground, and, as a compensation, will wear French heels and hosiery of lacy lisle."

The hobble skirt was in fashion, and its tightness handicapped milady when she went through the gyrations of the "bunny hug." The style parade of shoppers inspired wonderment when the slit skirt appeared on the avenue. High-top, laced shoes were plentiful, selling at from $3.90 to $5.90 a pair.

Easter styles for men featured high-waisted, pinched-back coats, and narrow trousers. Summer was officially marked by the opening of the straw-hat season. Straws with buzz-saw brims and colored bands were in demand, and the "dandy" favored a silk cord anchoring hat to buttonhole as a safety measure in gusty winds. Linen-like paper collars were worn a day or two and thrown away, thus saving laundry bills.

This was the decade when Colonel George W. Goethals was successfully digging the Panama Canal after others had failed, and the period in which Captain Robert F. Scott reached the South Pole. In America, as in other countries, there was some uneasiness caused by the rapid expansion of Germany's army, navy, and commerce, and by suspicions of Japan's ambitious trade program. The *Titanic* sank in 1912, and the world shuddered at the greatest of sea disasters.

Many of the nation's outstanding leaders, including Ex-President Taft, came to Cleveland to attend the World Court Congress with its constructive program designed to promote peace. Few of the delegates appreciated how soon the war conflagration would envelop their country.

Politics were in the limelight. Judge William Howard Taft was the candidate of the Republican Party for re-election in 1912; Governor Woodrow Wilson of New Jersey was the Democratic candidate; and Eugene V. Debs was the choice of the Socialists. Colonel Theodore Roosevelt broke with the Republican Party to head the new and short-lived Bull Moose Party. Many Clevelanders who had always been friendly to Roosevelt criticized his attitude, believing he had made a mistake in deserting his personal friend, Taft, and splitting the Republican vote; but others admired the most vigorous statesman of his time and followed the Bull Moosers to defeat. At any rate, Wilson was elected and soon was confronted by world problems of the greatest importance. His two terms were marked, first, by a prewar depression in 1914, followed by strong war prosperity that continued until the end of his regime.

The European war started in 1914 and soon became a world war—the most frightful in history. In February, 1917, the United States broke off diplomatic relations with Germany. Then came participation in the vicious struggle, Cleveland sending her youth to camps and overseas.

The greatest troop movement in all history began June 14, 1917, when the transportation of soldiers across the Atlantic proved the most important influence upon final victory. The continuous arrival of Americans upon the shore of France slowly but surely broke the morale of Germany. Secretary of War Newton D. Baker was criticized for incurring unnecessary expenses in transporting troops; but he declared that his first duty was to move men to Europe as rapidly as possible, no matter what the cost, in order to shorten the war and save lives and property.

German raids on London awakened the Allies to the fact that "a vast superiority in aircraft means the complete blinding of the enemy." The people became "air conscious." The airplane would develop a race of super-men, endowed with mysterious power, liberating "new forces in the aviator's brain" when air pressure was removed by ascent, according to a writer in a local paper. "The psychological changes produced in an aviator in the upper strata of the ether tend to develop a hitherto unknown variety of mental activity," he observed. "The face of one who has been in the air for any period of time appears to be absolutely different from its original appearance. There is a faraway spiritual aspect to it which no words will describe. . . . The greatest idea of perfection was symbolized by the power of the flight of angels. And man's attainment of this new capacity ought to have, as it now appears in reality to have, a purifying and uplifting influence upon him mentally and spiritually." Late in 1917 the call went out for greater produc-tion of planes, Liberty motors for ships, trucks, and tractors to win the "food war."

The war brought to Cleveland a problem well described by State Senator Harry E. Davis in his writings: "War industries . . . induced a mass move-ment of colored workers into Cleveland which almost completely submerged the older elements of the colored population. Industry sent agents into the South to recruit labor, and they were brought to Cleveland in carloads. Many of them came with only the clothing they were wearing, with no preparation for housing, and with little idea of the problems they must inevitably encounter." The limited social agencies were wholly inadequate to meet the serious situation. As factories piled up war orders, the influx of workers mounted, creating a shortage of 5,000 houses.

Cleveland responded to every war call with outstanding patriotism. The first American flag to fly in Europe was carried by the Crile unit. Men called to the colors went willingly, and homefolks and school children gave volunteer service unsurpassed in the nation. Measures were introduced to conserve light, power, gasoline, and products essential to war production. War-bond drives were all carried over the top, and the city stood first in the sale of war-saving stamps, the campaign having been greatly stimulated by the gigantic War Exposition, which thrilled hundreds of thousands of visitors with battles and exhibits on the lakefront. The Victory Chest Cam-paign amazed the world when, in a few days, the goal of $6,000,000 to support the city's various war services was quickly passed, a total of $10,616,032 being reached. In the plants, from the beginning of war preparations, Cleveland broke all production records.

The Cleveland Army Ordnance District was created in 1917, and it secured a vast amount of material throughout World War I. It was then discontinued until February, 1923, when it was re-activated under the National Defense Act of 1922, Cleveland being one of the thirteen ordnance districts. The purpose was to obtain supplies for the Army within the Cleveland area, which covered northeastern Ohio and three western counties in Pennsylvania.

Vessels on the Great Lakes in 1917 constituted approximately 25 per cent of the total shipping owned in the United States. More than three hundred Great Lakes ships were put into war service on the Atlantic Ocean—a proud record. There were more than three thousand ships on the inland seas, with an aggregate of three million tons. Nearly half the total was owned or managed in Cleveland.

War came home to the dinner tables of the nation as rationing programs were launched. Housewives were required to take a specified amount of corn meal or other cereal when purchasing white flour. Some who baked their own bread found that adding ground-crushed oats made a tastier wartime loaf, for the use of mixed flour, urged by Uncle Sam, produced bread that tasted and looked like "gray, woolen mufflers." Meatless Tuesdays were enforced.

The United States Food Administration in 1917 fixed war prices: granulated sugar, $9\frac{1}{2}$ to $10\frac{1}{2}$ cents per pound; corn meal, 7 to 8 cents; rice, 12 to 14 cents; butter, 56 cents; white flour, $3.35 to $3.50 per quarter barrel; potatoes, 45 to 50 cents per peck. The nation's conservation slogan was "Eat all you can't can." Real-estate salesmen boomed "city farms" in the suburbs to help relieve the food shortage. Eggs had soared to $1.05 per dozen in 1919, butter retailed at 78 cents a pound; dressed chickens, 50 cents; pork chops, 48 cents; but there was plenty of sauerkraut at 4 cents a pound. Many complained of the high cost of living.

The "war to end wars" came to an end on November 11, 1918—Armistice Day—with victory for the Allies and losses for everybody. Clevelanders solemnly affirmed with the rest of the nation, "Never again." The city's loss in men and in wealth could not be measured, nor could the grief experienced in Cleveland homes. Nearly 41,000 men had joined the services of the country, and many fought under Allied flags. Those who never came back numbered 1,023, and many of those who returned were seriously wounded. Cleveland's reputation for patriotic responsiveness grew mightily in the first world war.

After the Armistice, thoughts turned to reconstruction and the change-over to peacetime economy. City leaders predicted plenty of jobs for returned veterans and all workers, plenty of orders for industries, resumption of normal production of so-called non-essentials, public-improvement programs calling for expenditures of twenty million dollars, and need for twelve thousand homes.

War had created demand for many products, and the Government became the great purchaser. An army of workers, many of them women, were in the ranks at home, and production reached new highs, interrupted at intervals by strikes and labor unrest. New processes naturally developed, and factories, farms, and mines shared in the prosperity wave. History repeated itself, and the impression grew that the wartime boom could be depended upon to continue in peacetime. Victory was followed by a continuation of the advance, with Cleveland in the forefront of the cities, its business institutions contributing to the forward march. Wages rose, prices rose, hopes rose. The value of the city's manufactured products advanced from $350,000,000 in 1914 to more than a billion in 1919. Manufacturers put more men to work, bought new machinery, and enlarged plants. Expansion knew no bounds; spending was fabulous; the national debt was $1,191,000,000 in 1915 and $25,482,000,000 in 1919, or $246.09 per person. The transition from war to peace seemed comparatively easy in the first months after the conflict, but new difficulties were to be faced as time went on.

Cleveland followed with interest the many meetings that led to the signing of the Treaty of Versailles on June 28, 1919. The treaty embodied the covenant of the League of Nations and aimed at idealism; but its planned punishment of Germany, its unfortunate territorial rearrangements of European nations, and its involved system of reparations, not only failed to establish peace, but actually contributed to a new world war. The plans and their enforcement failed because of racial hatreds, national antagonisms, and other causes, the importance of which were underestimated by the makers of the treaty. Despite Newton D. Baker's strong advocacy of the League of Nations, a vast number of his fellow citizens believed that the plan was doomed to failure and that the threatened foreign entanglements should be avoided. Furthermore, many believed that the treaty meant an unjust peace which the United States should not be called upon to enforce. The treaty failed to secure the necessary two-thirds vote in the Senate and became the issue of the political campaign of 1920.

The most momentous decade in the city's history concluded with every reason to be proud of Cleveland's war record, and with firm conviction that sound progress would be made in the transition to a period of peace.

1910

Newspapers were selling for one cent on New Year's Day. Herman C. Baehr of the West Side became mayor. Retiring, Mayor Johnson spoke of his triumphs and sorrows of the past years, announcing that he would study mathematics as part of a rest cure.

The use of leather by automobiles was held responsible for the 10 per cent increase in the price of shoes, as reported January 3. With motor cars, however, shoes were not worn out so quickly.

James J. Tracy, civic leader and retired capitalist, an incorporator of Case School, was injured by a fall and died on January 5.

The Rocky River Bridge was completed this year. Built of reinforced concrete, it had a central span of 280 feet in the clear, the longest masonry arch in existence. The total length of this graceful structure was 708 feet, spanning the deep Rocky River gorge. In 1865 there had been a toll bridge over Rocky River, several hundred feet to the south of Silverthorne's Tavern. This was replaced in 1889 by a steel span costing $60,000. Horses and wagons on their way to the Cleveland market crowded this narrow bridge across the valley.

The Harvard-Denison Bridge, 3,232 feet long, was built this year at a cost of $527,440.

The Halle Bros. Company ventured into the residential district at Euclid and East 12th Street this year, where Henry Bacon, later the architect of the Lincoln Memorial in Washington, had designed an imposing new building. Space was doubled in 1914, and Halle's became a department store. Salmon P. Halle resigned to devote himself to philanthropies and private interests in 1921, and his brother, Samuel H., succeeded him as president. Many important expansions were made during his regime. Purchase of the Elks Club Building on Huron Road to the west provided expansion in 1922 as the Halle Annex.

The South Cleveland Banking Company, on Broadway near Harvard, closed its doors on January 7, forced to suspend business because of large loans made to the embarrassed Werner Publishing Company of Akron. Founded in 1879 with capital of $150,000, it was the oldest suburban bank in Cleveland.

The Bell Telephone and Cuyahoga Telephone companies began to exchange services to gain greater efficiency and economy.

Cleveland was dark during mid-day on January 13, the city being enshrouded by a pall of fog, snow, and hovering smoke. Lack of wind to clear the atmosphere was held responsible for the ominous condition.

A survey praised the section bounded by Euclid Avenue, East 55th, Quincy, and East 105th as the healthiest in Cleveland, with the best-behaved citizens.

Collinwood, after a court battle and a contest at the polls, was annexed to Cleveland on January 21. At this time, the city's area had expanded to include approximately 45.9 square miles.

The Wade Allotment was developed by Jeptha H. Wade III, who carried out the plans of his famous grandfather. The allotment extended from East 105th to East 115th Street, and from Euclid Avenue through Wade Park and its nearby residential area. It became a district of attractive homes near Cleveland's great cultural center.

Ezra Kendall, monologue-comedian, who made his home in Cleveland for a number of years, died January 23. His first stage success was made as a quaint character in the comedy *We, Us & Company;* and, after playing the leading part in *A Pair of Kids,* he went into vaudeville. Here his amusing monologues, written by himself, were so popular that he put them in book form, and the J. B. Savage Company of Cleveland ran editions of several hundred thousand each. On the stage, Kendall wore a stovepipe hat and grotesque clothes, and his patter, delivered with a drawl, kept the audience in continuous laughter during his twenty-minute act.

The Rotary Club of Cleveland was organized as the eighteenth club in the national chain, starting with twenty-five members. Major Charles R. Miller was the first president, and William Downie was secretary. The club's slogan was "Service," and its first activity was in behalf of crippled children.

Plans were made in Cleveland for a National One-Cent Postage Association, designed to persuade the Government to reduce the two-cent rate to one cent. Charles W. Burrows was the leader of the futile movement.

The American Civic Reform Union was established "to promote civic reforms, suppress vice, and safeguard girls."

A national Bohemian daily newspaper, to be called *Svet,* was planned in February, and the publication soon justified the hopes of its owners. It absorbed the *Dennice Novoveku* in 1915 and bought the *American* in 1939. Its name was changed to *Svet Bohemian Daily,* and the publication office in the 1940s was at 4514 Broadway.

Cleveland established a branch of the National Association for the Advancement of Colored People. There were 8,448 Negroes in Cleveland when Thomas W. Fleming was elected councilman-at-large, the first colored elective official in the municipal government.

Mother Machree, which became the most popular "mother" song written by an American, was copyrighted by Ernest R. Ball of Cleveland. It was inspired by devotion to his mother, and was written in collaboration with Chauncey Olcott. Other world-famous songs by the local composer were *Love Me and the World Is Mine, Little Bit of Heaven, Dear Little Boy of Mine, When Irish Eyes Are Smiling,* and *'Til the Sands of the Desert Grow Cold.* Composer Ball was born July 21, 1878, and died May 3, 1927. His mother, who lived in Cleveland, was laid to rest beside him in Lake View Cemetery. Ball received his musical education in the Cleveland Conservatory of Music.

Trustees of the YMCA voted unanimously on March 28 to pay $135,000 for the Childs property on the southeast corner of Prospect Avenue and East 22nd Street as a site for a new "Y" building of at least 250 rooms.

The Andrews School for Girls opened in Willoughby on April 4, the faculty consisting of a superintendent and four teachers. The institution was made possible by the wills of Mr. and Mrs. Wallace Corydon Andrews, providing an endowment of more than $4,000,000. In 1879, they had foreseen the advent of young women into vocational activities. Andrews moved to New York City in that year and promoted the New York Steam Company, of which he was president and moving spirit. He also owned coal lands and oil properties. Mr. and Mrs. Andrews drew their wills providing for the establishment of a school where girls would learn to be self-supporting. Their tragic deaths, April 7, 1899, in a fire which destroyed their home and most of its occupants, were followed by ten years of litigation through court after court until finally the Supreme Court of the United States gave its decision in favor of the proposed Andrews School for Girls in Willoughby. The institution grew rapidly; more than three hundred acres of land were acquired, sixty thousand trees were set out in a nursery, and buildings were constructed as needed. The school proved Mrs. Andrews' statement of many years earlier: "She who hath a vocation, hath an estate." Ralph Otis Hibschman became director in 1929.

George W. Kinney was elected president of the Cleveland Chamber of Commerce. In this decade, he was succeeded by Charles E. Adams, 1911; Homer H. Johnson, 1912; Warren S. Hayden, 1913; Morris A. Black, 1914;

Bascom Little, 1915; Ralph L. Fuller, 1916; Charles A. Otis, 1917; Myron T. Herrick, 1918; and Paul L. Feiss, 1919.

There was one streetcar at this time that never stopped for passengers. The *Leader* described it on April 10: "Of immense aid in gathering and distributing the mail is the street-railway mail car in use here for the last few months. This car is fitted up much the same as the postal car on a steam railway. It carries a crew of five clerks and makes nine trips between

The death of Samuel L. Clemens, Mark Twain, April 21, was the subject of a Donahey picture in the Cleveland Plain Dealer. *The great American humorist had endeared himself to Clevelanders through his lectures as well as his books. Later a bust of the writer was to be placed in the American Garden.*

post office and sub-stations every 24 hours." Ray G. Floyd was named postmaster on May 1. Michael F. O'Donnell became head of the letter carriers.

Geraldine Farrar triumphed in *Madame Butterfly* at the Hippodrome on April 13, climaxing the Cleveland season of the Metropolitan Opera Company.

Lives were imperiled, April 13, by a $200,000 fire at the Eagle Storage & Moving Company. The Salvation Army Citadel was saved, but many houses were burned.

Two thousand boys competed in Cleveland's first Boys Exposition, April 17.

They swarmed to Grays Armory to view an exhibition of their own handiwork. The undertaking was sponsored by the boys of the West Side Branch of the YMCA, where a similar project was successfully conducted under the resourceful leadership of Secretary M. D. Crackel.

Addie Joss became the first Cleveland pitcher in the American League to toss two no-hit games, when he triumphed over the White Sox on April 20 at Comiskey Park, Chicago.

Cleveland began to ride in its first taxicabs. They were livery cars without meters operating in the center of the city. The following year Andrew F. Waite entered the business and brought system into the operation of a fleet of cars consisting of the open touring type in summer and cabs with limousine bodies in winter. In 1916 his fleet was called the Black and White, the cablike vehicles being equipped with meters. His Yellow cabs followed in 1918. Two years later the Yellow Cab Manufacturing Company, which produced Waite's cabs, protested when he purchased a number of Cleveland-made Templar cars and painted them yellow to conform with his fleet. As a result of the disagreement, Waite launched the Green Cab Company in 1921 and introduced his popular Checker cabs, trimmed with a checkered border. Waite sold out in 1929 when the Yellow Cab Company of Cleveland, Inc., was organized. He re-entered the field in 1935 with the Waite Cab Company for a period of two years, then retired from the business.

The Sunbeam School for Crippled Children was opened, and it soon became the model in its field.

Smoking was banned on streetcars on May 3. Conductors favored this new ruling, but found trouble in enforcing it.

The Physical Culture Society protested vaccination on May 12 and asked a halt in inoculation against smallpox.

The Brotherhood of Locomotive Engineers moved from the Society for Savings Building to its new home, the thirteen-story Engineers Building on the southeast corner of Ontario and St. Clair. Dedication of the $1,400,000 building designed by Knox & Elliott, Cleveland architects, was held on May 14. Governor Judson Harmon addressed five thousand engineers and friends and called it the finest labor temple in the world and the first of its kind built in its entirety by any branch of organized labor. Engineers Hall, an auditorium, seating twelve hundred people, helped to relieve the urgent need of space for public events. William B. Prenter, financial officer of the Engineers, was elected president following the death of Warren S. Stone in 1925.

Cleveland was the second city in the United States to make an inventory of all city-owned property, May 15. Canaries to elephants were listed.

Halley's Comet swept by Cleveland on May 16. Feared for ages, the comet had been robbed of its terrors by scientists. A falling meteor heralded its coming and frightened West Siders when it struck the earth at West 73rd Street and Grace Avenue.

May 18 had been proclaimed by Mayor Baehr as Mother's Day. On this Sunday, the Rev. Duston Kemble, pastor of the Detroit Avenue Methodist Church, saw success in his crusade encouraging women to remove their hats before sermons. His hints had been in vain until the Ladies Aid Society took up the matter and voted to yield. As the pastor began preaching, millinery of the chanticleer and tall, rangy, peach-basket vogue began dropping into feminine laps.

Demand for the revolutionary White rotary sewing machine was so great that the White Sewing Machine Company, founded in 1866, moved to St. Clair Avenue and East 79th Street this year, where metal operations were carried on. Thomas H. White, the founder, died in 1914, and W. W. Chase became president. Shortly after World War I, the company took a substantial financial interest in and an option on the Theodor Kundtz Company, started in the sixties by Theodor Kundtz, Sr., to supply White with sewing-machine woodwork. A few years later, the option was exercised, although both the White and Kundtz companies continued to operate independently. Windsor White, eldest son of the founder, became president in 1921, serving until 1923, when A. S. Rodgers was elected president and general manager. Rodgers was formerly with the Standard Sewing Machine Company on Cedar Avenue, and had joined White in 1914. About 1924, the White Motor Company acquired the St. Clair-East 79th properties. The White Sewing Machine Company moved to the Kundtz plant, 1231 Main Street, and purchased the King Sewing Machine Company of Buffalo, excepting land and buildings. Robert E. Wagner purchased the Theodor Kundtz Company name and some equipment about 1932 and continued to operate the church-furniture and seating business, discontinued by White, at the Kundtz site leased to him. In 1946 White sewing machines were used in the homes of the world, and the Cleveland company was exceeded only by Singer in sales volume and production capacity.

The Ohio State Golf Tournament was played at the Euclid Club on June 25, J. K. Bole being the winner. In this decade, the Willowick Golf Club, Mayfield Country Club, Keswick Country Club, Westwood Country Club, Shaker Heights Country Club, Woodland Hills Park (later Highland Park) municipal course, and Sleepy Hollow club were established. In July, 1915, the Western Amateur Golf Championship was played at the Mayfield Country Club, "Chick" Evans defeating Ned Sawyer to become the champion. On August 10, 1917, the Cleveland District Golf Association was formed. The following year, the first championship inter-club matches were played, Mayfield winning in 1918. The first two tournaments under the Cleveland District Golf Association were won by Ellsworth Augustus in 1918-19. The women's championships, leading to the formation of the Cleveland Women's Golf Association, were won by Ruth Chisholm in 1910; Mrs. A. R. Davis, 1911; Ruth Chisholm, 1912-13; Mrs. Ward B. Jackson, 1914; Jennette Kinney, 1915; Mrs. R. S. Leonard, 1916-17; Mrs. Ward B. Jackson, 1918; and Mrs. Alexander Printz, 1919.

Atlee Pomerene, eminent statesman who brought renown to Ohio by his illustrious public career, served as chairman of the Democratic state convention in 1910. That year he became lieutenant governor of Ohio, and the following year was elected United States senator. Pomerene discharged his duties in this office with such a high degree of intelligence that he was re-elected in 1917 for an additional six years, defeating a most worthy opponent, the former ambassador to France, Myron T. Herrick. As senator he served on the foreign-relations committee. He was active in the ratification of peace treaties, in passing the resolution declaring a state of war with Germany and Austria, and in the ratification of the Colombian treaty settling claims resulting from the Isthmus of Panama revolution. His service on the interstate-commerce committee resulted in the establishment of the Federal Trade Commission. He was a member of the banking-and-currency committee which framed the Federal Reserve Act.

The Cleveland College of Physicians and Surgeons was consolidated with the School of Medicine of Western Reserve University. During the year, a gift of $250,000 from John D. Rockefeller and another of $100,000 from Samuel Mather were received as initial contributions toward general endowment. In 1911 the total was brought to $1,000,000 by additional subscriptions. A further gift from Oliver H. Payne was added to the fund in 1912, and the next year Liberty E. Holden established the Albert Holden Foundation for medical research in memory of his son.

Aviation experienced its first heavier-than-air flight in Cleveland on June 28. Captain William Mattery circled the Country Club grounds twice at a height of from five to ten feet.

Buckeye trees were fast disappearing, according to Forester M. H. Horvath, who announced on June 29 a plan to plant these trees in honor of the Buckeye State. He became nationally known for his scientific development of new plant species at his Mentor nurseries.

This year marked the golden anniversary of The Higbee Company, and erection of the new Higbee Building at Euclid and East 13th Street to house the flourishing department store. It was constructed under the supervision of Will T. Higbee, son of the founder and president of the company until 1913, when Asa Shiverick succeeded him. On the site of the monumental building had stood the impressive Amasa Stone house. When Stone built a fine home to the east for his daughter and son-in-law, John Hay, he declared "he was building a barn for his Hay."

The Cleveland Health Department on July 1 closed three tattooing establishments and put a ban on the decorations that sailors love.

The big event of the Fourth of July was a parade of ten thousand children and adults. Minnie, the Zoo's famous elephant, bought by pennies of the city's youngsters, led the procession, a flag in her trunk. "Blazing fireworks" concluded the celebration.

Drilling was done for John D. Rockefeller on his seventy-first birthday, July 8, but the purpose was not to locate oil. Dr. John F. Stephan did the drilling for the oil magnate, the dental appointment accidentally coming on the birthday.

The Gentlemen's Driving Club held its harness races at the new Randall track but public interest waned because of the lack of transportation facilities. For several years H. K. Devereux, "greatest driver of them all"; C. K. G. Billings, M. A. Bradley, David Shaw, and others drove their fast trotters and pacers before small audiences. Then the foremost club of its kind passed out of existence. In the meantime leaders who had contributed most to the Cleveland Grand Circuit races were also retiring from the sport. Roland Harriman of Goshen, New York, succeeded Harry K. Devereux as president of the Grand Circuit and George J. Dietrich, who had inspired success in harness horse racing since 1902 retired from the secretaryship. Running races were now dividing interest with harness racing.

The West Side Market, under construction at West 25th and Lorain, was to become America's finest. This market, like the older Central and Broadway markets, was city-owned.

William J. Akers was writing a *History of the Cleveland Public Schools* and was assisting charitable and educational projects. He was one of Cleveland's leading hotel men, and for many years was identified with local politics.

A motor-driven balloon, flown over Cleveland on July 24, was piloted by Harry Ginter of Luna Park.

Cleveland soldiers of Troop A were sent to Columbus to quell strike riots on July 29. They camped on the broad lawn of the State House.

Traffic became confused at Euclid Avenue and East 9th Street on August 14. Pedestrians, motorists, and those in horse-drawn vehicles stopped to watch a girl wearing "the first real hobble skirt seen in Cleveland."

Ex-President Theodore Roosevelt inspired twelve thousand listeners during an hour's stop at the Union Depot on August 22. He praised local women, pure water, and babies.

Glenn H. Curtiss, pioneer flyer, predicted that he might break his existing record of fifty-two miles per hour on his flight from Euclid Beach Park to Cedar Point and return. Just a year before, Orville Wright had passed the official government test. Curtiss stated: "My biplane is capable of doing a mile-a-minute provided I am flying with the wind." More than 150,000 persons assembled along the shore to see the famous pilot undertake the historic trip over water in the frail, bicycle-tired, Hudson aeroplane on August 31. Curtiss reached Cedar Point, but unfavorable flying weather prevented his return until the next day, when a crowd welcomed him at Euclid Beach Park. The flier received $5,000 for the event from the *Press,* his sponsor; and with this amount and $10,000 received from the *New York World* for a successful flight in May from Albany to New York, he established himself in the aviation field as a builder, the forerunner of the great Curtiss-Wright aviation company.

The first Boy Scout troops in Cleveland were organized at the West Side Branch of the YMCA. By 1913 the membership had grown to 1,785 boys in 53 troops, which were mostly affiliated with churches. The purpose of this organization was to promote the ability of boys to do things for themselves and for others; and to teach them patriotism, courage, and self-reliance by placing emphasis on character development, citizenship training, and physical fitness. The program included training and experience out-of-doors, in camp, and on the trail, in association with suitable adult leadership. It aimed to develop skills contributing to physical fitness and resourcefulness. Under the leadership of Scout Executive George E. Green, whose service began in 1928, the Greater Cleveland Council, Boy Scouts of America, boasted a membership of 20,400 with 6,500 leaders in 1946.

A Cleveland man, Captain Klaus Larsen, was victorious over the raging waters of Niagara on September 18, when he ran the rapids below the falls in a small motor boat, emerging unhurt.

Five thousand fans jeered as police stopped a ball game on October 3. A state law barred Sunday games at which admission fees were charged.

Ty Cobb led the American League in batting, Lajoie being the runner-up, and the next year Lajoie won with Cobb just behind him. The Cleveland Naps, managed by Napoleon Lajoie, 1905 through 1909, finished in sixth place in 1910. In 1911 the team was third in the league, George Stovall replacing Jim McGuire as manager. "Shoeless" Joe Jackson, who had come to Cleveland in 1910, proved a power both at bat and in the field. Harry Davis soon replaced Stovall. "Doc" Johnston, first baseman, and Ray Chapman, shortstop, were added to the team in 1912. Joe Birmingham became manager, and Cleveland finished fifth despite the hard hitting of Jackson and Lajoie. In 1913 Charles W. Somers became president of the club upon the death of Jack Kilfoyle, and Ernest S. Barnard was made vice president and business manager. The team finished in third place. In 1914 Cleveland was last, and Manager Birmingham was replaced by Lee Fohl. President Somers being unable to finance the team, James C. "Sunny Jim" Dunn was induced to head a syndicate to take over the ball club. In 1915 Cleveland finished seventh.

The Amasa Stone Memorial Chapel was erected on Euclid Avenue at University Circle, the gift to Adelbert College of Mrs. Samuel Mather and Mrs. John Hay in memory of their father, Amasa Stone. It was one of the finest examples of Gothic architecture in the country. The Morley Chemical Laboratory, named in honor of Edward W. Morley, world-famous chemist and teacher at the college, was completed the same year.

Cleveland celebrated the County Centennial on October 10 with yells of Chippewas, flag raising by pioneer citizens, daring aerial features, and salutes from lake craft. The week's program included a military and historical pageant, a night carnival, the dedication of the Harvard-Denison and Rocky River bridges, and a ceremony at the site of the new Cuyahoga County Court House.

The Ohio Legislature made a holiday of Columbus Day, and, in the city's first official celebration, two thousand Clevelanders of Italian extraction marched in a parade. Four white horses drew a model of the *Santa Maria* in the procession, part of the Cuyahoga County Centennial celebration.

Lathrop Cooley, friend of the needy, died at the age of eighty-nine. A minister of the Disciples faith, he served many Cleveland churches and preached words of hope and encouragement to inmates of the Work House, city jail, sailors' mission, and the Aged Women's Home. Wealth came to him through shrewd investments in Cleveland real estate, and his will directed that a major portion of his estate serve a local hospital. When the Huron Road Hospital was built it received a legacy, the donor's only recognition, as he directed, being a plaque bearing the words "I was sick and

Dr. Frank E. Bunts   Dr. George W. Crile   Dr. William E. Lower   Dr. John Phillips
Founders of The Cleveland Clinic

The Lakeside Unit, organized by Dr. George W. Crile, Sr., carried the first American flag overseas in World War I, and was received by King George V and Queen Mary.

The Cleveland Clinic

Southwest corner of Ontario and the Square, 1920. May's Drug Store was at the corner, and in front of it the Humphreys, who established Euclid Beach Park and the Elysium, sold popcorn and white taffy. Kendel's Seed Store occupied a building next to the corner on Ontario, and "credit to all" was the slogan of surrounding stores.

The same corner is shown in the 1940s with Higbee's modern department store in the Terminal Group replacing the shabby structures of twenty years before.

ye visited me." Cooley quietly financed a chain of Disciple missions around
the world. His son, Harris R., was pastor of the Cedar Avenue Church of
Christ, attended by Tom Johnson. One of Johnson's first acts when he took
office as mayor was to appoint Cooley charities director. Cooley's progressive
social planning made him a national figure; and his purchase of the Warrensville farms, a forward step from the work-house era, was a successful social
and financial investment for the city.

Ex-President Theodore Roosevelt was honored in Cleveland, November 5,
when he concluded a state-wide tour in behalf of the gubernatorial candidacy
of Warren G. Harding. In Chief Kohler's escort was Patrolman C. L. Marsh,
first precinct, who rode beside Roosevelt's car and chatted with him. Marsh
had been in a regiment that carried Teddy's Rough Riders by transport
to Cuba.

The Chandler & Rudd Company moved its uptown store from Euclid and
East 55th Street to 6000 Euclid this year. A system providing for delivery of
telephone orders was inaugurated here, attracting national attention. The
company was also probably the first grocery concern to adopt newspaper
advertising. Expansion into nine shopping centers, undertaken in 1932, was
eventually abandoned. In 1940 the main store moved from 6000 Euclid, and
business was centralized at 1252 Euclid. Harry D. Sims, president, at one
time secretary to John D. Rockefeller, was the son-in-law of George A.
Rudd, partner in the firm who died in 1933. Frank H. Rudd, vice president,
was the son of William C. Rudd, founder, who passed away in 1916.

To the surprise of *Plain Dealer* subscribers, a new column appeared on
November 29, "The Philosopher of Folly" by Edwin Meade "Ted" Robinson,
who had been identified with the *Leader* since 1905. Philosophy, criticism,
exchanges, and sentimental verse characterized his work until his death in
1946. His column was widely read and frequently copied, and it was one
of the newspaper's most valuable institutions. Robinson's devotion to his city
is expressed in his poetic lines:

> I see a City that is not content
>   To follow counsels ignorant or blind,
> Or leave its future to a chance event—
>   A City with a Mind.
>
> I see a City looking forward, free
>   To open all its doors to joy and art;
> Eager for all men's wonderment. I see
>   A City with a Heart.
>
> A City whose devotion shall not fail,
>   That keeps its eyes upon the lofty goal,
> Against whose light no shadow shall prevail—
>   A City with a Soul!

The airplane skirt was approved, December 5, at a national convention of
stylists who warned possessors of hobble skirts that they should send them

to the Smithsonian Institution. According to a local newspaper, "the similarity of the skirt to the airplane is strikingly evident." The skirt had simple lines with innumerable accordion pleats.

After experimenting with a horseless police ambulance, the City Council approved its purchase on December 7. The Peerless Motor Car Company of Cleveland had put ambulances on trial for the city's consideration.

In this era of civic pride, many Clevelanders were contributing to the city's welfare while furthering their own business and professional interests. Among them were Edmund H. Leutkemeyer, hardware merchant; Frank Billings, industrialist and philanthropist; Will P. Blair, leader in the paving-brick business; Frederick W. Bruch, prominent in industry; Horace A. Fuller, iron-and-steel manufacturer; George C. Haskell, paint manufacturer; Dewitt C. Moon, railroad executive; Fred A. Pease, engineer for a number of villages in the county; James J. Roby, coal operator; and Truman M. Swetland, real-estate dealer and promoter of building enterprises.

Other well-known leaders were Edwin G. Tillotson, banker; Francis W. Treadway, lawyer, with business and philanthropic interests; Elmer B. Wight, civil engineer, responsible for many public-works improvements; Alexander S. Taylor, realtor; Francis H. Haserot, wholesale grocer; Louis H. Hays, clothing manufacturer; Frederick A. Henry, lawyer and jurist; Edward P. Hyde, physicist; William G. Lee, president of the Brotherhood of Railroad Trainmen; Robert E. Lewis, general secretary of the YMCA; Homer H. McKeehan, outstanding lawyer; Dr. William E. Bruner, oculist, nationally known for his research; William E. Cushing, attorney; Charles H., W. H., and O. W. Prescott, brothers, leaders in the lumber business; and Frederick L. Taft, distinguished attorney.

Also in the public eye were Charles P. Salen, newspaperman and leader in municipal affairs; William Campbell Boyle, one of Cleveland's leading trial lawyers; William Parmelee Murray, who gave up banking to enter the iron-ore and coal business; Matthew F. Bramley, paving contractor and Republican leader; William H. Hunt, executive in the building-brick and insurance business, devoted to philanthropy; and Paul Howland, lawyer, who served as a member of Congress, 1907-13.

Dr. William T. Corlett, one of the foremost physicians, purchased the William Chisholm home at 3618 Euclid Avenue this year, and built to the west a stone office, joined with the house by a glass-covered passageway which was heated to grow Brazilian orchids. The Chisholm brownstone residence had been built in the nineties at a cost of $125,000, and among its features was an antique chandelier from India. Dr. Corlett had begun his practice in an office on the Public Square during the 1840s. He won international fame for his research in skin diseases, and took a prominent part in medical enterprises in the United States and abroad. The Corlett residence was serving as a studio apartment house in the 1940s, a reminder of Euclid Avenue in its heyday.

In less than a decade, the production of automobiles, bodies, and parts had risen to third place in the manufacturers census, reported as of 1909, increasing in volume more than 360 per cent since 1904. There were 32 establishments in the Cleveland industry, employing 6,408 wage earners, with a payroll of $4,023,000, producing products valued at $21,403,926. Iron and steel, steel works, and rolling mills showed a sharp increase of more than 60 per cent during the decade, 14 producers reporting products valued at $38,463,316. Foundry and machine-shop production more than doubled, 231 concerns reporting products valued at $37,443,039, and 17,915 wage earners with a payroll of $10,485,000. The value of slaughtering and meat-packing products, $17,192,048, had more than doubled; women's clothing, $12,788,-775, had trebled. Printing and publishing, $9,634,683; paint and varnish, $6,138,466; and stoves and furnaces, $4,977,096, had more than doubled in volume during the decade. Manufacturers of men's clothing reported products valued at $5,953,321; malt liquors, $5,124,478; bread and bakery products, $4,730,649; electrical machinery, apparatus, and supplies, $4,035,-808; lumber and timber products, $4,021,326; copper, tin, and sheet-iron products, $2,966,476; hosiery and knit goods, $2,957,248; confectionery, $2,851,927; tobacco, cigars, $2,769,129; bronze and bronze products, $2,567,-768; tools, $2,395,000; cars and general shop construction and repairs by steam-railroad companies, $2,055,672; chemicals, $1,865,957. Carriages and wagons had dwindled to $462,000.

Consolidation and reorganization of industrial companies is reflected in a marked decline in the total number of manufacturing establishments to 2,148, employing 84,728 wage earners, with a payroll of $48,052,971, products valued at $271,960,833, and value added to manufacture, $117,045,810. With abundant facilities for commerce by lake and land, Cleveland showed an increase of 58.2 per cent in the value of manufactured products from 1904 to 1909. Growing importance as a manufacturing city is indicated by the fact that when ranked by value of products, Cleveland was fifth among cities of the United States in 1909, seventh in 1904, and eighth in 1899. For the majority of wage earners employed in manufacturing industries, the prevailing hours of labor ranged from 54 to 60 a week.

Capital invested in industrial operations had increased from $98,303,682 in 1900 to $227,397,484 in 1909. Banks continued to consolidate and gain strength to meet the growing demands of industry. Thirty-one banks in Greater Cleveland reported total resources of $299,950,000 in 1910; and 20 building-and-loan associations, $11,310,000. The construction industry was booming; 7,460 building permits issued in Cleveland in 1910 represented operations valued at $13,948,413, more than 3.5 times the volume of 1900.

1911

Two women of worldwide renown visited Cleveland on January 16. Sylvia Pankhurst, English woman suffragist, inspected the jail, and Emma Goldman, anarchist, made a speech assailing the government.

The Workmen's Compensation Law was enacted this year, to go into effect in 1912.

The rush to sink wells in search of gas in northern Ohio recalled the gold rush of '49. On February 25, four Cuyahoga townships were thronged with eager land-seekers. Rumors of rich ore and gas strikes were being circulated.

The Sam W. Emerson Company was organized as a general-contracting company in the building field. The company constructed many important factory and commercial buildings in the Cleveland area, including huge plants created for war purposes. It also served as an auxiliary maintenance department for many of the industrial and commercial companies of the city. The president in the 1940s was the founder, Sam W. Emerson.

The Federal Building on the northeast corner of Superior and the Square, a feature of the Group Plan, was dedicated in March. Built at a cost of approximately $3,300,000, it was designed by Architect Arnold W. Brunner. Visitors were impressed by the dignified granite exterior, the beautiful corridors and offices of gleaming imported marble, polychrome ceilings and superb mural decorations by Blashfield, Low, Millet, Cox, Zogbaum, and Crowninshield. On the south façade were two impressive statuary groups, "American Commerce" and "American Industry," by Daniel Chester French. The monumental structure served as the United States Post Office, Custom House, and Court House. Ray G. Floyd was postmaster at this time. He was succeeded in turn by William J. Murphy in May, 1914; and Henry A. Taylor in March, 1923. Postal receipts for the year 1911 amounted to $2,522,000.

Plans for the Miles Theater, to be located at 2071 East 9th Street, were being developed. The theater was built for vaudeville. When burlesque was presented in 1920, the name of the house was changed to Columbia; a decade later, when motion pictures were shown, it became the Great Lakes Theater, and eventually the Carter.

Judge William L. Day, of Cleveland, became the youngest member of the United States judiciary, when he assumed office as federal district attorney on April 7. His father was William R. Day of Canton, Ohio, associate justice of the United States Supreme Court.

Tom L. Johnson, former mayor, died on April 11 and was mourned by thousands. In 1879 Johnson came to Cleveland, and from that time until his death, he dramatically influenced the political and business life of the community. His first move to secure a street-railway grant was opposed by his competitor, Marcus A. Hanna. For thirty years, Johnson was identified with the slogan, "home rule, three-cent fare and single tax." He engaged in politics successfully, serving as mayor four terms, 1901-9. He served two terms in Congress, and each of his campaigns was colorful and sensational. On his promise to secure a three-cent fare by municipal operation, Johnson made a strong appeal to the public. The war for control of Cleveland's traction system continued for years and involved serious strikes and bitter disagreements. Johnson capitalized upon his claims by winning the support of the voters, but eventually lost his battle, and the railway properties were reorganized under the Tayler franchise. Johnson was finally defeated for mayor by Herman C. Baehr. In his political struggles, he enlisted the vigorous support of Newton D. Baker, Peter Witt, Burr Gongwer, and other well-known Clevelanders. Mayor Johnson established playgrounds and public bath-houses and popularized the city's parks. During his administration, the idea for the Mall and Group Plan became a reality, and he inaugurated the fight for the Municipal Light Plant. He acquired wealth through the invention of street-railway devices and his association with traction companies, but lost his fortune in the streetcar war. During his colorful service as mayor, he inspired new interest in municipal government. A monument was erected on the Public Square to the memory of Tom L. Johnson, considered by many the "champion of the common man."

The Diocese of Toledo was created from sixteen counties on the western end of the Cleveland Diocese. Auxiliary Bishop Joseph Schrembs of Grand Rapids became its first head. In 1922 Erie, Huron, and Richland counties were taken from the Cleveland Diocese and added to the Toledo area. In 1943 the Youngstown Diocese was created from six counties along the eastern border of the Cleveland district and Bishop James A. McFadden, then auxiliary bishop of the Cleveland Diocese, was made its head.

The Greeves measure, legalizing Sunday baseball, became a law on May 7.

Council declared on May 23 that ladies' long hatpins must go, a fifty-dollar fine to be imposed if the pin projected more than one-half inch from the hat crown.

An act, passed by the State Legislature on June 5 and inspired by interested Cleveland groups, authorized the establishment of parks, boulevards, and public grounds outside of city limits for recreation purposes. Six years earlier, William A. Stinchcomb, a young engineer, had urged this public-park program, indicating how Nature had provided in Cuyahoga County opportunities of exceptional character. In 1912 the first Board of Park Commissioners was appointed by the county judge, but no funds were provided to finance the project. Three years later the General Assembly permitted the county commissioners to allot funds to the Park Board, so that Frederick Law Olmsted and Stinchcomb might study the undertaking and recommend a long-range program. Three commissioners appointed by the probate judge constituted the board. In 1917 Commissioners Harry M. Farnsworth, Louis A. Moses, and William Diehl urged the purchase of outlying woodland spots, and tax levies and bond issues provided the money for expansion and development of the Metropolitan Park System. From the beginning Stinchcomb was the director, and Cleveland's forward planning set a pattern for the nation.

The organization of Federated Churches of Greater Cleveland was officially effected on June 11 at the Old Stone Church. The spark that led to this union was lighted in December at Trinity Cathedral in the study of Dean Frank DuMoulin, who was conferring with Dr. Thomas S. McWilliams and the Rev. Worth M. Tippy. Sixty-seven churches sought to present a unified front on common problems without conflicting with creeds of the several denominations. The Very Rev. Frank DuMoulin was elected president; Rev. Tippy, vice president; Charles E. Adams, treasurer; and the Rev. N. M. Pratt, secretary. Many committees were formed to safeguard all phases of church work—secular, religious, educational, social welfare, and civic betterment, touching upon marriage and the home, industry, motion pictures, and social hygiene; phases of women's work, temperance, world friendship, drama, and music. Later known as the Cleveland Church Federation, it encouraged Christian fellowship through four auxiliary organizations: the Ministerial Association of Greater Cleveland, the Cleveland Council of Federated Church Women, the Cuyahoga County Youth Council, and the Churchmen's League. The federation provided practical channels of Christian unity and interchurch co-operation in Greater Cleveland. In 1945 the Rev. Raymond L. Spoerri succeeded the Rev. O. M. Walton as executive secretary. Judge Julius M. Kovachy was elected president in 1946, and was succeeded by Bishop Beverley D. Tucker, 1947, and Frank P. Celeste, in 1948.

On June 16 a Lake Erie wireless call brought one ship to another's aid. A flash through the air summoned the *City of Cleveland* to the side of the *Western States,* disabled in mid-lake at night. Two hundred and five passengers, all Michigan bankers on a vacation trip, were taken off the stricken vessel. With the blowing out of the chartered craft's cylinder-head, an S.O.S. was sent for the first time on the lake.

James E. Granger of the Fire Department was appointed battalion chief of the newly organized 10th Battalion at East 105th Street and St. Clair Avenue. He had been made a lieutenant in May, 1898, and captain in 1903.

With Henry Ford's Model T came mass production of automobiles, and colossal markets were created for the oil companies. Gasoline, once a waste product, became fuel for the internal-combustion engine. Standard Oil's holding company, forced to dissolve, was split into thirty-four companies, and The Standard Oil Company of Ohio again became a separate corporation. Competition among refiners, new and old, grew keen, and crude-oil production increased rapidly. W. T. Holliday, Standard Oil's attorney since 1917, became president, and a new construction program increased capacities of producing plants. Sohio service stations, evolved out of corner stores and garages, were staffed by uniformed attendants. Sales-training programs were introduced; oil fields were acquired; and Standard, founded in Cleveland, expanded through mass-marketing.

Cleveland, on June 21, was the third city in the country to establish a department of neurology in the public schools. Assistance was offered to pupils handicapped either mentally or physically.

John Paul Jones of Cleveland established a collegiate mile record of 4:15⅗, which stood for two decades, and made the half-mile in 1:55⅘. In 1912 he bettered his half-mile record to 1:54.4, and, in 1913, he ran the mile in 4:14⅖. He also held the intercollegiate cross-country championship for three successive years, 1910-12. In the latter year he ran in the Olympic games held at Stockholm.

On July 7 Sterling E. Graham received the Samuels Medal at DeWitt Clinton High School, New York City, for the best combined record in scholarship and athletics. Later he entered Columbia University where he won three letters in track. He also won the National AAU title in the hop-step-jump event.

The Phillis Wheatley Association, an organization designed to provide a home for Negro girls, was founded in August by Jane Edna Hunter, a nurse of idealism, energy, and vision. Named in honor of America's first Negro poetess, the association acquired a nine-story building at 4450 Cedar Avenue in 1927 after a money-raising campaign in which many Cleveland leaders co-operated. Although clubs and hobby classes, discussion groups, and inspirational programs constituted the major activities, the association also became a leading placement center of great value to the colored working girls of Cleveland. Heading the staff of professional social workers, Miss Hunter had been the executive secretary since the launching. Though a member of the Welfare Federation, Phillis Wheatley strove to become as nearly self-sustaining as possible. It was interesting to compare the 1946 budget of $153,000 with the $1,500 spent in the year of founding.

When the public first viewed the sport of polo in Cleveland, the game was pronounced "a short-cut to suicide." The leading team included Corliss E. Sullivan, E. S. Burke, Jr., Lawrence Hitchcock, and A. D. Baldwin. "Croquet on horseback" soon became one of the fastest of games, with a large following of fans. Edmund Stevenson Burke, "the father of local polo," not only provided the field, but also bought a carload of wiry little Texas ponies and hired expert Earl Hopping to teach the game.

John D. Rockefeller counted the congregation at the Euclid Avenue Baptist Church on August 28 to learn if a new building was justified. He walked methodically up and down the aisles as ushers took up the collection, and scanned those in attendance to determine whether or not to delve down into his pockets for $500,000 to build a new edifice in the heart of the city. His decision was favorable, and the church was built at 1926 East 18th Street.

The first turbogenerators at the Lake Shore power plant of The Cleveland Electric Illuminating Company were put into operation on August 29, an event which transformed the company from a one-plant operation to a multiple-plant system. By this time, the company's service area had been expanded to include Bratenahl, East Cleveland, Euclid, Cleveland Heights, Lakewood, Rocky River, and nearly all of Cleveland. A total of 31,000 customers in 1910 had grown to 167,000 a decade later.

Chlorination of the Cleveland water supply began on September 11, as recommended by Drs. Howard Haskins and R. G. Perkins. Chlorine was applied in the form of bleaching powder as a purification measure.

Ore docks, said to be the largest on the lakes, were being erected on the lake front. The Pennsylvania Railroad rushed work on an enormous plant on the West Side basin of the harbor, and $3,000,000 bins were constructed to hold the cargoes of nearly one hundred vessels.

The first of her sex in the city to act in the capacity of police officer, Mrs. Rose Constant, widow of a city employee, became sanitary inspector on September 23.

The first statue in America of the composer Richard Wagner was designed by Herman N. Matzen and unveiled at Edgewater Park on October 15. It was the gift of German-Americans of the Goethe-Schiller Society, and an impressive ceremony was held.

J. O. Eaton founded The Torbensen Gear & Axle Company in Bloomfield, New Jersey, October 25, for the purpose of manufacturing an internal gear drive for commercial vehicles. Operations were moved to Cleveland in 1915. In 1916 the name was changed to The Torbensen Axle Company, and a plant started on East 152nd Street. A pioneer in the field of automotive parts and equipment, the company's history is one of research and invention. An important series of acquisitions took place through the years, among them the Perfection Spring Company and the Easy-on-Cap Company of Cleveland, the Reliance Manufacturing Company of Massillon, and plants in Albany, Detroit, and Kenosha, Wisconsin. The corporate name became the Eaton Manufacturing Company in 1932. The company's success was due largely to the vision and executive ability of the founder, J. O. Eaton. When he became chairman of the board in 1925, he was succeeded as president by his associate, C. I. Ochs. In the 1940s the company's Cleveland activities were divided among four factories and a laboratory. The general offices were located at 739 East 140th Street.

A group of Cleveland business and professional men, impressed by the purposes and achievements of the newly organized Exchange Club of Detroit, formed the Exchange Club of Cleveland. Present at the permanent organization meeting of the National Exchange Clubs in Toledo in 1917 were Robert G. Pate, president of the Cleveland club, and E. B. Berkeley, secretary, who were elected national officers. Activities broadened, contributing to civic and educational advancement, and clubs were founded in East Cleveland, Brooklyn, Fairview Village, and Cleveland Heights.

Newton D. Baker was elected mayor of Cleveland by more than twelve thousand majority, and he carried the Democratic ticket with him.

A brilliant celebration marked the opening of the Cleveland Athletic Club's new quarters in the fourteen-story CAC Building, 1118 Euclid, November 18. The club had built ten floors above the original five-story business structure, the arrangement having unique legal features that attracted wide attention. The new quarters included beautiful reception rooms, special meeting rooms for women, dining rooms, complete gymnasium, a spacious swimming tank, and artistic furnishings—the many features combining to make the home one of the most beautiful and useful of the nation's athletic clubs. Track and field championships, in fact all kinds of sporting honors were won by club teams in the early days after the founding in 1908. James A. "Jimmy" Lee began his long career as director of athletics in 1919. With the motto, "Make exercise good fun," he inspired the membership to use the club's many facilities in the promotion of health. Furthermore, he represented the Amateur Athletic Union and the Olympic games in this important sports area. The CAC took an active part in World War I by sending an ambulance to France and sponsoring a boxing show that raised a fund of $27,453 for athletic equipment for Ohio servicemen in both Ohio camps and overseas. In World War II, the club again was a leader in raising money; and, in co-operation with the Chamber of Commerce, sponsored war-bond auctions that brought a $515,000,000 sale of bonds. Through both wars the club was guided by the able leadership of George A. Schneider, enthusiastic manager during most of the life of the organization. In the mid-1940s the CAC membership had reached 2,200.

1912

Newton D. Baker, who had been city solicitor under Tom L. Johnson, took office as mayor. Through his careful planning and persuasive public speaking, Baker advanced civic spirit and gave the city able administration. He worked diligently for home-rule, and rejoiced with the citizenship when a new charter was approved and the home-rule form of government became a reality.

When the great bronze doors of the stately Cuyahoga County Court House opened, January 1, Clevelanders climbed the marble stairway to the rotunda to view the magnificent stained-glass window representing Law and Justice, the central figure. The $4,500,000 granite building on Lakeside Avenue was recognized as one of the country's finest public structures erected for county purposes. Designed by Lehman & Schmidt, the Court House was an integral part of the Group Plan. The marble interior, with spacious corridors and paneled walls, was designed by Charles F. Schweinfurth of Cleveland. Historical paintings by well-known artists decorated the walls, among them the mural by Frank Brangwyn, "Signing of the Magna Charta," Violet Oakley's "The Constitutional Convention," and C. Y. Turner's "The Conclave between Pontiac and Rogers' Rangers." On either side of the south entranceway were the imposing statues of Thomas Jefferson and Alexander Hamilton, executed by Karl Bitters. At the north entrance were the statues of John Marshall and Rufus P. Ranney by Herbert Adams. The county commissioners at the time of the opening were John G. Fischer, William F. Eirick, and Harry L. Vail.

The Municipal Court was established in Cleveland, and the need of justice courts, in what had been the Township of Cleveland, no longer existed. The new court became the trial court for both city and state misdemeanors, with the municipal prosecutor, a member of the city law department, representing the city. The defendant was given the privilege to demand a jury or to waive a jury trial. All cases before the Municipal Court not criminal in nature were to be termed civil suits, and unless twelve jurors should be demanded by the defendant, six persons were to make up the jury. A conciliation branch of the court was established to adjust minor difficulties without the necessity of going into court. Experience quickly showed the great superiority of the Municipal Court over the old-fashioned justice court of an earlier day.

On the corner of East 30th Street and Scovill Avenue, Adolph Weinberger opened his first drug store. In 1928 Weinberger Drug Stores, Inc., was formed with seven Cleveland stores. The company expanded through purchase of chains and stores in other cities, until in 1946 there were seventy-eight stores in a vast chain known as Gray's Drug Stores, Inc. of which Weinberger was president.

The term of William H. Elson, superintendent of schools, expired January 7, and Harriet L. Keeler was appointed to fill the vacancy—the only woman to hold this important position. She remained in office until the conclusion of the school year, when J. M. H. Frederick, former head of the Lakewood schools, became superintendent. During the previous decade, several Cleveland women were prominently identified with the school system. Mrs. Sarah E. Hyre was elected member of the school board in 1905, and a little later became clerk of the board. May C. Whitaker, clubwoman and settlement worker; Mrs. B. F. Taylor, Mrs. Elroy M. Avery, and Mrs. Virginia D. Green gave efficient service on the board.

A fire, aggravated by a zero gale, swept the north side of lower Euclid Avenue stores on January 16. Browning & King and nearby shops suffered a loss of $250,000. A number of firemen were injured, and a hundred men and women were driven into the bitter cold after a narrow escape.

To relieve the overtaxed Lakeside Plant of The Otis Steel Company, 325 acres of scrubby wilderness in the river bottom, south of Clark Avenue between the river and Jennings Road, were secured for the Riverside Plant this year. Business depression retarded construction, and it was not until 1916 that the mammoth mills were in full wartime production. Postwar depression caused the British owners to sell their holdings to an American syndicate headed by John Sherwin, Sr., of Cleveland. Shortly after, the Cleveland Furnace Company, adjacent to the Riverside Plant, was acquired, and additional mills and furnaces commenced to operate in December, 1923. E. J. Kulas became president in 1925. In 1932 rolling began on the gigantic new seventy-two-inch continuous hot strip mill, the widest in existence. The Otis Company merged with the Jones & Laughlin Steel Corporation of Pittsburgh in 1942, and America's two oldest steel companies were thus united. In 1946 the historic Lakeside Plant was being dismantled, and plans were under way to construct an immense furnace at the Riverside Plant. From its founding the company was identified with transportation progress, making plate castings and heavy steel products for locomotives and steamships and later for the automotive industry and great industrial projects. Under far-seeing management, Otis grew steadily until it was practically a self-contained business, from ore to finished product, with interests in coal, stone, and ore properties.

Moving from Huron and East 9th Street out of the path of expanding business, Grace Episcopal Church found a new home in the Unitarian church on Bolivar at Prospect during the pastorate of the Rev. Charles C. Bubb. One by one its evangelistic neighbors followed their congregations into residential districts; but Grace remained, ministering until December 31, 1941, when it closed its doors and merged with Trinity. The Church of God occupied the building until 1946, when it was sold to a business concern, and its long career of religious service ended.

Theodore A. Willard originated the service-station idea, and this year he established his first battery service station. Three years later, the Willard Storage Battery Company moved into its fifteen-acre plant on East 131st Street. Willard built WTAM, Cleveland's first high-power radio station, in 1922. R. C. Norberg succeeded the founder as president of the company in 1928, the year in which the Cleveland Electric Illuminating Company purchased the station. S. W. Rolph was president in 1946, having been elected in 1941; and C. E. Murray was executive vice president, directing management of the company. Willard products were contributing to transportation and communication all over the world.

The Van Sweringens and the New York Central Railroad, foreseeing the growth of the Heights area, planned a rapid-transit route from downtown Cleveland, the Vans to have two tracks for passenger cars, and the New York Central one for freight; the latter plans never materialized. In 1913 the Van Sweringens, by arrangement with Cleveland Heights, laid tracks on Coventry Road and Shaker Heights Boulevard, and provided short-line service under the name of Shaker Heights Line. The war interrupted further development for several years. The Cleveland Heights service was discontinued and the rapid-transit lines along the Nickel Plate right-of-way were completed to the Terminal, utilizing the Shaker Heights Boulevard tracks as part of the system. Service began in 1920.

Johnny Kilbane defeated Abe Attell in a twenty-round fight at the Vernon Arena, Los Angeles, California, on February 22, winning the featherweight championship of the world. For nine years, Kilbane held the title. He had been a clerk in a Pennsylvania law office before being attracted to the prize ring. James Dunn of Cleveland became his manager and trained him in the gymnasium in which Kilbane and Dunn, who was also an excellent boxer, became world famous. Johnny was considered one of the cleanest of fighters, but, more than that, a ring general whose strategy was too much for his opponents. He defeated Herman Zahniser, Jack White, Frankie Burns, Joe Goldberg, Wilbur Saylor, Johnny Whitacre, Tommy O'Toole, Patsy Brannigan, Oliver Kirk, Patsy Kline, Joe Rivers, Benny Chavez, and many others. Kilbane was given a reception by 100,000 enthusiasts when he returned triumphantly, March 18, from his championship fight with Attell. Mayor Newton D. Baker reviewed the mammoth parade of the fighter's followers.

The Public Library had outgrown its quarters and had moved eastward to the Kinney & Levan Building, 1375 Euclid Avenue. A bond issue of two million dollars was approved for a new building on Superior Avenue, the site of the old City Hall. Increased building costs and the necessity for more space than was originally planned called for an additional two-million-dollar bond issue.

The Cleveland Bar Association attempted to improve the administration of justice in the courts by advising the public of judicial candidates' qualifications. For nine years, this was accomplished by means of a poll of lawyers' opinions. In 1922 the method was improved by the circulation of a questionnaire and ballot to obtain opinions, particularly with reference to a candidate's legal experience and judgment. However, it was agreed that adequate emphasis was not being given to the most important qualification

—integrity, and in 1946 a new system was evolved whereby greater stress was placed on this character quality. The new program was directed at two essential points: maintaining good judges on the bench, and advising the public to remove incapable judges.

The efforts of Henry Wood Elliott were instrumental in effecting the Hay-Elliott fur-seal protection treaty. For forty-five years, Elliott strove to keep Alaskan seals from becoming extinct. Born in Cleveland in 1846, and, at sixteen, private secretary to an official of the Smithsonian Institution, he was called "Savior of the Seals."

The four-story plant of the Union Paper & Twine Company was destroyed by fire, March 11, with a loss of approximately $250,000. Guests fled from two near-by hotels, the Hawley House and King's Hotel.

Cleveland held its first National Sales Review in March under the auspices of the Women's Wear Manufacturers, concluding the Chautauqua with an impressive banquet. Buyers were brought to the city from all parts of the United States, and pronounced the undertaking the most successful of its kind the nation had known. It was decided to continue this merchandising plan.

Dr. Luther Halsey Gulick during a visit to Cleveland told of the beginning of the Camp Fire Girls, an organization he and his wife started for his daughters and their friends. A number of Cleveland women, including Mrs. I. Walter Sharp, Mrs. Ralph Bing, and Mrs. Erwin C. Arndts, became interested, organizing informal groups of girls under Dr. Gulick's plan. Thus Cleveland was one of the pioneer cities to undertake the work that was to become widespread. In 1912 the Gulick organization for girls was chartered and was said to be the first association of its kind to be formed nationally. The Cleveland groups were united into a local organization that joined the national in 1922. "Wohelo," the watchword, was made up of the first two letters of three words—"work, health, love." Camp Fire programs symbolized the beauty and ritual of Indian lore and folklore of other lands.

The three-day dedication exercises of the Euclid Avenue Temple at East 82nd Street and Euclid Avenue were begun on March 21, with ten rabbis participating. The new building, designed by Lehman & Schmidt, was a dignified and impressive structure, with its semi-circular auditorium under a great mosque-like dome. Large though the Temple was, an annex was necessarily constructed in 1923 for the growing religious school. In the spacious auditorium there were 1,400 seats, and adjoining were offices, a library, and kitchen facilities. Rabbi Louis Wolsey had been called to the pulpit of the Scovill Avenue Temple in 1907 by the Anshe Chesed congregation. His eighteen years of leadership witnessed remarkable progress.

The City Council on April 7 approved a lot-garden plan. Citizens took up lot-gardening to reduce the cost of living and beautify the city.

The shipbuilding and automotive industries afforded growing markets for products of The National Malleable Castings Company, and this year the company established a research laboratory, the first in the malleable-iron industry. Steel castings had become an important part of the business by

1923, when the National Malleable & Steel Castings Company was organized, a world leader in the field. Alfred A. Pope was succeeded by his nephew Henry A., as president in 1913, in turn followed by Carl C. Gibbs in 1934, Charles H. McCrea in 1942, and Cleve H. Pomeroy in 1946. The company, with headquarters at the Cleveland Works, 10600 Quincy Avenue, had become the world's largest producer of anchor chain and heavy-duty castings for the aviation industry, operating plants in Chicago; Indianapolis; Sharon, Pennsylvania; and Melrose Park, Illinois.

During the past three years, a long labor fight had been waged by the lake seamen. In 1916 the Central Labor Union was supplanted by the Cleveland Federation of Labor, and from thirty-two affiliated unions the number grew to more than a hundred. The federation embodied principles determined by an annual convention, and a vote expressed the will of the membership. Industrial and craft unions comprised the organization. One principle contended that labor fosters mutual interdependence. The old Knights of Labor had disappeared from the picture, and the alternative to craft unionism became the IWW—Industrial Workers of the World, a revolutionary industrial union organized in 1905. It had set out to unite all skilled and unskilled workers into one body for the purpose of overthrowing capitalism and rebuilding society on a socialistic basis.

The Woman's Club was an active social force in the community and, in 1914, signed a long-term contract for the James Jared Tracy mansion at 3535 Euclid Avenue. Here it enjoyed beautiful headquarters until 1926, when it turned over the property to the Masonic Order and met at the Allerton Hotel. Many well-known Cleveland women were associated with the organization, and among the past presidents were Mrs. E. H. Baker, Mrs. Clarence J. Neal, Mrs. Charles Tozier, and Mrs. J. R. Hinchliffe. Mrs. George Lang was president in 1946.

The dynamic personality of an accomplished blind musician, Almeda C. Adams, who felt that music education should be available to all persons, was the inspiration for the establishment of the Cleveland Music School Settlement. Miss Adams with Adella Prentiss Hughes presented the idea to the Fortnightly Club, which contributed a thousand dollars to start the project at Goodrich House. Under their guidance the school was founded in April, and its growth in faculty members and student enrollment led to securing in 1938 the beautiful mansion at 11125 Magnolia Drive, former home of Mr. and Mrs. E. S. Burke, Jr. Ranging in age from four to sixty-five, more than five hundred students received free individual instruction in instrumental music, voice, theory, composition, and accompaniment, while eight hundred were members of various groups. Through the efforts of a well-trained staff, excellent facilities, and financial support from the Welfare Federation, the school developed untold musical talent. At this time Walter Logan was dean and head of the violin department, Nathan Fryer, the piano department, and Mrs. Harvey D. Goulder, the vocal department. Louise W. Dasher became director in 1933.

The city received a gift to help Clevelanders "Remember the Maine," when on April 29 the Government presented part of the conning tower of the ship. The 6,700-pound souvenir was later mounted in Washington Park.

Three young men—Paul Schwan, Clarence H. Handerson, and Edmund L. Kagy—desiring to perpetuate their college association, organized on June 24. The name, Gyro Club of Cleveland, was inspired by the gyroscope, symbol of power, poise, and purpose. Its influence spread until Gyro International, organized in 1917, consisted of almost a hundred clubs, uniting a membership of about five thousand in a fellowship bond and promoting interest in movements for the common good.

The YWCA West Side Branch was formed in June, and the eighty-acre Mary Eells Camp at Madison-on-the-Lake was purchased. Mrs. Dan P. Eells retired as president of the YWCA in November, 1913. She was succeeded in turn by Mrs. Levi T. Scofield, Mrs. William P. Champney, Mrs. Francis F. Prentiss, Mrs. Walter H. Merriam, Mrs. Frank L. Sessions, Mrs. David W. Frackelton, Mrs. Robert S. Wensley, Mrs. J. H. Griswold, Mrs. E. G. Gilbert, Mrs. Richard S. Douglas, Mrs. Judson L. Stewart, and Mrs. Earle W. Brailey.

The big fire horses were about to become history, as the Fire Department installed the first motor apparatus on June 28. The citizens liked efficiency, but they regretted that the beautiful, spirited horses were to be replaced.

Newburgh held a celebration at Luna Park on July 10, with the historic slogan, "Cleveland is six miles from Newburgh." Games and dances of the early days were revived.

The Women's Art Club was organized, August 1, in Belle Kaufmann's studio in the Gage Gallery, 2258 Euclid Avenue. Mrs. Caroline Harter Williams was the first president.

To provide a home for the *Leader* and the *News,* which he had purchased from Charles A. Otis, Dan R. Hanna, president of the *Leader* Building Company, erected the *Leader-News* Building (later *Leader* Building) at the southwest corner of East 6th and Superior, on the site of the earlier building. Charles A. Platt, New York architect, designed the fifteen-story building, known for its interior of choice black walnut and imported marble, and its sturdy exterior of Indiana limestone and granite. In the sub-basement were tanks containing 2,500 gallons of ink which was forced through the presses by compressed air. This arrangement was designed for the printing of the *Leader* and *News.* The *Leader* Building continued to be one of Ohio's finest office homes.

On August 3 several prominent Cleveland women gathered in the garden of "Gwinn," home of Katherine L. Mather, to sign the charter of the Garden Club of Cleveland, organized "to cultivate the spirit of gardening in its fullest sense, together with appreciation of civic beauty and betterment in and about Cleveland." At this time, the garden movement was relatively new, but the charter members of the Cleveland club determined to achieve success for their home city. Mrs. Andrew Squire was made president; Mrs. John E. Newell and Katherine L. Mather, vice presidents; Mrs. L. Dean Holden, treasurer; Mrs. T. P. Howell and Clara Sherwin, secretaries; Mrs. C. E. Ricks, curator, Mrs. Charles A. Otis, Mrs. A. S. Chisholm, and

Mrs. E. T. C. Miller were other leaders. A year after it was organized, the club became affiliated with the Garden Clubs of America, and meetings were held in members' homes and gardens. Through illustrated talks and lectures portraying native and foreign landscapes, gay and successful street fairs, and festive flower shows, the club gained prominence in the city's life as an important asset to its beautification. Two of its most important activities were the development of the Fine Arts Garden, surrounding the Cleveland Museum of Art, and the Garden Center of Cleveland. In 1946, under the leadership of Mrs. Frank C. Newcomer, the Garden Club of Cleveland was actively participating in the city's progress.

Mary K. Browne, having won the singles, was pronounced woman tennis champion of America on August 10, and she participated victoriously in the doubles and the mixed doubles. She repeated her success in 1913 and 1914, and was a winner in the doubles championships in 1921 and 1925, her partner in 1921 having been Mrs. L. R. Williams, and in 1925, Helen Wills.

Under the authority of a new state constitution, Cleveland voters on September 3 determined to assume all powers of local self-government, and elected fifteen commissioners to frame a home-rule charter for the city. All of the large municipalities of the State had been agitating for home-rule, and Mayor Newton D. Baker was a leader in the movement. Under the new legislation, approved by the voters in July, 1913, the mayor, elected for a two-year term, was given power to name the seven city department heads, the mayor and these executives constituting the Board of Control. The new city charter eliminated primary elections and provided for the nomination of candidates by petition only. Members of the City Council, now reduced to twenty-six, were to be elected each two years and limited in power to legislative matters only. Both the mayor and council members were subject to recall. The new charter became effective January 1, 1914, and Baker, seeking re-election, was the first mayor elected under the Home Rule form of government.

Suffrage was denied women when Ohio adopted a new constitution on September 4; but women of Cleveland and the Buckeye State kept up their courageous efforts.

The Junior League was founded on September 6 with a membership of sixty-seven young women. Its first president was Mrs. John Cross (Katherine Hoyt). The league became a member of the Association of Junior Leagues of America, and its purpose was "to foster interest in the social, economic, educational, cultural and civic aspects of the community and to make efficient its voluntary service." Membership had passed seven hundred in 1946, when Mrs. Edwin C. Higbee was president.

Records were broken in the automobile meet at the North Randall Track on September 15. Louis Disbro traveled ten miles in 8:17. Barney Oldfield, with his inevitable big black cigar, made two miles in 1:35, lowering the record by two seconds.

A night fire on September 20 caused a $500,000 loss to the H. C. Christy Block on Huron Road in less than half an hour.

The City Club of Cleveland was incorporated on October 12. There were

111 men present who listened to speeches by Newton D. Baker, John H. Clarke, Judge Frederick A. Henry, and Professor A. R. Hatton. Noon-day luncheons and Saturday meetings, with a distinguished speaker, attracted wide attention to the organization, which grew rapidly. It was guided by this credo:

> I hail and harbor and hear men of every belief and party; for within my portals prejudice grows less and bias dwindles. I have a forum as wholly uncensored as it is rigidly impartial. 'Freedom of Speech' is graven about my rostrum; and beside it, 'Fairness of Speech.' . . . I am accessible to men of all sides—literally and figuratively—for I am located in the heart of a city. Spiritually and geographically, I am the city's club—the City Club.

Daniel E. Morgan was the first president; E. M. Baker, vice president; Amasa Stone Mather, treasurer; and Mayo Fesler, secretary. The early meetings were held in the Chamber of Commerce Building on the Public Square.

The formal opening of Hotel Statler at the northwest corner of Euclid and East 12th Street made October 19 a memorable date. There were two great banquets on the mezzanine floor, one of which was given in honor of E. M. Statler by eastern hotel executives, and the other given by Charles L. Pack for many of his business associates. An elaborate entertainment was planned for the public opening, and fine orchestras played for the assembled crowds. The thousand-room building was modern and complete, one of the nation's finest hostelries. Its beautiful ballroom became the meeting place of business and social organizations and the scene of many brilliant events. The first manager was James P. A. O'Connor, who was succeeded by T. P. Cagwin.

Registration of voters set a new high record on October 23, reaching 93,686.

A new idea developed in the Cleveland automobile industry when Walter C. Baker, president of the American Ball-Bearing Company, coupled a gasoline motor and an electric motor in one car, with the foot controlling the speed. The ingenious principle was discarded as cumbersome.

Woodrow Wilson was elected the twenty-seventh President. He was the first Democratic Presidential candidate to carry Ohio since the Republican Party was organized in 1854.

The great five-hundred-foot *Seeandbee,* largest and most costly inland steamer, was launched by the Cleveland & Buffalo Transit Company on November 6. Queen of the sidewheelers, 6,381 gross tons, of all-steel construction, 1,500 passengers could be accommodated on the four-deck vessel. On her maiden trip to Buffalo, the ship carried members of the Cleveland Chamber of Commerce. The luxurious steamer operated on the Buffalo route and on special C & B cruises, calling at Cleveland, Buffalo, Detroit, and Chicago for almost three decades.

The parcel-post system was established, November 11. Clevelanders quickly took advantage of this new and inexpensive means of transporting goods.

Carl D. Salisbury drew the first pay-check issued November 13 in Alexander Winton's marine-engine plant. Here were laid the foundations for the great Diesel industry of Cleveland. After investigating various types of marine gasoline engines for use in his motor yacht, *LaBelle,* Winton had decided in 1911 to design and build his own power plant. In 1912 the Winton Gas Engine & Manufacturing Company was organized. Having devoted considerable attention to the possibilities of the Diesel-type engine, then coming rapidly to the front in Europe, in 1913 the company completed the first all-American Winton Diesel engine. From 1917 to 1930 the company powered numerous commercial and government vessels and led in the powering of fine Diesel yachts. In 1930 General Motors Corporation, at the recommendation of Charles F. Kettering, acquired the Winton Engine Company, which became the Cleveland Diesel Engine Division, 2160 West 106th Street. George W. Codrington joined the organization in 1917, advancing to president in 1928. He was largely responsible for the company's outstanding progress in the marine and railroad fields.

The first complete research laboratory in the malleable-iron industry was established, November 17, by the National Malleable Castings Company of Cleveland.

Successful experiments by Drs. Carl H. Lenhart and David Marine indicated that goiter could be prevented by adding a minute amount of iodine to the diet of children.

Earl E. Martin was editor of the *Press* when it occupied its new home at East 9th and Rockwell Avenue on December 2. Louis B. Seltzer, a young reporter who had worked on the *Leader* and the *News,* came to the *Press* in 1917. Eleven years later, he succeeded Ted Thackrey as editor of the paper. In 1937 Seltzer's service as editor-in-chief of the Scripps-Howard Newspapers of Ohio began, continuing simultaneously with his position as editor of the Cleveland daily. John G. Meilink joined the *Press* in 1921 and became business manager in 1927.

There was jubilation at the dedication of the new YMCA building, December 29, at the corner of East 22nd Street and Prospect Avenue, because a fund-raising campaign had left the structure, costing $759,767, debt-free. Speakers included Bishop William A. Leonard, Dr. Henry Churchill King, President Sereno P. Fenn, Charles E. Adams, chairman of the building committee, and Secretary Robert E. Lewis. New buildings for the Central, East End, and West Side branches of the YMCA were constructed from funds secured from Cleveland's first short-term, money-raising campaign, resulting in $540,000.

1913

The first superintendent of schools of the Catholic Diocese of Cleveland was the Rev. William A. Kane, appointed this year.

The Lakewood Gas Company was organized on January 24. By the following year there were thirty-four wells, twenty-three of which were producing.

Cleveland had become grand-opera conscious. Max Faetkenheuer, popularly known as "the Oscar Hammerstein of Cleveland," opened the Metropolitan Theater on Euclid Avenue west of East 55th Street on March 2, with a production of *Aïda*. Prices ranged from a dollar to fifty cents. Adelaide Norwood was the star.

Frightened by the activity of the Baptist Brotherhood, the saloon-keepers' association on March 2 ordered every bar closed on Sunday, and, for a time, enforced the order to the letter.

While engaged as a draftsman at the Swartwout Manufacturing Company, makers of sheet-metal products, Carl M. Yoder conceived the idea of utilizing strip steel, formed edgewise to required shape and bent around suitable forms. This method eliminated scrap and effected a considerable saving of time. In 1913 The Yoder Company went into production near East 55th Street and Euclid Avenue. Organized by Carl M. and Harvey Yoder, it made substantial contributions to the industry with its metal-working machinery. In 1922 the plant on Walworth Avenue burned, but was rebuilt and in production again in twelve days, a reconstruction record. Carl M. Yoder died in 1944, and John Lucas became president the following year.

The Cleveland Advertising Club, during the presidency of William R. Creer, formed a division known as the Vigilance Committee to encourage truth in advertising and good business ethics. Newspapers joined the movement and voluntarily refused advertising of questionable character. This led to the establishment of the Fair Practices Committee, which soon took the name of the Better Business Bureau, one of the first in the nation. S. A. Weissenburger was employed as secretary. The Bureau's slogan, "Before you invest, investigate," was used nationally, particularly by financial institutions. Other cities were starting similar projects, and in 1919 the Better Business Bureau of the Cleveland Advertising Club joined with other bureaus throughout the country to form a national organization, thus improving ethics in business and maintaining files on enterprises and individuals. Cleveland's influence in the continuous better-business campaign benefited trade and protected the community's interests.

Loss of life and property followed the big Ohio floods in March. At Columbus and Dayton, where the greatest damage occurred, conservation and flood-control projects were soon started to promote future safety. Clevelanders contributed to the relief of sufferers.

The Apex Electrical Manufacturing Company was organized, April 1, by Clarence G. and Walter Frantz, with William V. Orr, to make Orr's new electric vacuum cleaner for home use. It started in two-room quarters in the Whitney Power Block, 1011 Power Avenue. When the Cuyahoga Stamping Company's plant at 1070 East 152nd Street finished making war materials in 1918, Apex purchased it and began making a washer. An electric ironer was added to the line in 1922, and business expanded into worldwide distribution of the company's products.

Ed Hermann of Cleveland became the all-events champion of the American Bowling Congress, rolling 1,972.

The Perry Statue was again moved, this time to the bank of the lake in Gordon Park.

Believing that building products should be sold on an "erected-complete" basis, Earl F. Hauserman organized The E. F. Hauserman Company in April, with headquarters in the Society for Savings Building. The firm sold steel sash, agreeing to erect it completed, glazed, and painted anywhere in the United States. The manufacture of steel partitions for industry led to the development of "Masterwalls." In 1918 the factory was located at 6800 Grant Avenue, Cuyahoga Heights, where a model plant was later built. Prefabricated steel houses and aircraft parts were built for the Government during World War II. When steel was available after the war, the company continued its manufacture of movable, steel interior walls. Fred M. Hauserman succeeded to the presidency in 1943 upon the death of the founder.

The Cleveland Federation for Charity and Philanthropy was organized on May 1. It determined the financial needs of the Cleveland welfare agencies and budgeted available funds. This plan later led to the development of the first Community Fund in the world. The idea of the Federation began in 1900 when the Chamber of Commerce appointed a committee on benevolent associations from which local organizations sought endorsement. This year, these organizations, including the Jewish Welfare Federation, the Bureau of Catholic Charities, and the Associated Charities, united to become the central money-raising body for all constituent members. A year later, the Welfare Council was organized to promote co-operation between public and private social agencies—religious, educational, and civic. The federation and the Welfare Council united in 1917 under the name of the Welfare Federation of Cleveland.

The National City Bank was reorganized in May. It had been located in the Hirsch Building, next to the Rockefeller Building, only a year, when progress forced another move to new and enlarged quarters in the *Leader-News* Building in May. The assets had risen to $4,500,000. Charles A. Paine was president.

"Sight Seeing Autos—The Easy Riding Cars" was the promise painted on the sides of vehicles introduced to Cleveland on May 10. The *Plain Dealer* report of the innovation began, " 'Well I do declare,' exclaimed Mose Cleaveland as he shifted his position on his pedestal on Public Square. 'Do my eyes deceive me?' Mose stared hard as a brilliant-hued rubberneck auto paused to the shrill blast of a traffic policeman's whistle . . . 'The Cleveland Railway Company sight-seeing cars are going to have some competition now.' "

The *Jewish World,* established by Samuel Rocker, first appeared as a weekly, then as a daily, and subsequently became a weekly.

Baldwin University and German Wallace College in Berea merged this year as Baldwin-Wallace College, continuing under the jurisdiction of the Methodist Church. The Music Building, completed on a site donated by Berea citizens, was dedicated the next year, marking the fiftieth anniversary of the founding of German Wallace College. The finest pipe organ in the State was installed in the Fanny Nast Gamble Auditorium, named for the first woman graduate of the college, the daughter of Dr. William Nast, first president. Through the generosity of Mr. and Mrs. E. J. Kulas of

Cleveland an addition was provided, and the enlarged building was dedicated in 1939 as the Kulas Musical Arts Building. A modern organ, built by W. Holtcamp of Cleveland, was installed in 1942. The first Bach Festival, held in 1921, became an annual event, attracting music lovers from many parts of the country. The Rev. Arthur L. Breslich became president of Baldwin-Wallace in 1914, and in 1918 he was succeeded by Dr. Albert B. Storms, who served until 1933. Dr. Louis C. Wright was president, 1935-48, and Dr. Albert Riemenschneider, head of the Conservatory of Music for many years, was made acting president in 1948.

Commercial cracking of petroleum was discovered by William M. Burton, chemist of the Standard Oil Company of Indiana, later its president. Gasoline production doubled, and the oil-refining industry was revolutionized. While a student in Western Reserve University, Burton was encouraged to study chemistry by world-renowned Professor Edward W. Morley.

Homegrown strawberries glutted the market, and the best grades were selling for a dime a quart on June 10. There were shortcakes on many tables.

The Garden Club of Cleveland held its first annual flower show on June 17 and inspired the planting of many gardens. The activities of the Garden Club led to the formation of other clubs throughout the county.

A five-million-foot gas well was "shot" on the grounds of the National Carbon Company in Lakewood on June 20, and there was an all-night struggle before it could be capped.

Humanity lost a noble benefactor on June 25, when death claimed Louis H. Severance, financier and business leader. He was born in Cleveland in 1838, the son of Solomon L. and Mary H. Severance, just after the death of his father. After serving in the Union Army, Severance went to Titusville, Pennsylvania, and became interested in oil. This led to association with The Standard Oil Company of Ohio, as treasurer, 1876-95, and a large stockholder. Through financial interests in banks, railroads, and industrial companies, he accumulated great wealth, which he put to work furthering religious education and public welfare in Wooster College, Oberlin College, Western Reserve University, the YMCA and YWCA, and many worthy institutions in the nation and beyond the seas. Severance Hospital and Severance Medical College in Seoul, Korea, were created as living monuments to a man who was a friend to all men. Severance was a devoted member of the Woodland Avenue Presbyterian Church for many years. His children, John L. and Elizabeth S., who married Dr. Dudley P. Allen and, after his death, became the wife of F. F. Prentiss, inherited their father's generous spirit, giving liberally for the common good.

The Housemaids Union was growing in strength under the leadership of Rose Charvat, its organizer. The union was preparing on June 27 to present a wage scale and a demand for a ten-hour work day, with a threat to blacklist housewives who hired non-union girls.

From 75,000 to 100,000 persons knelt on the greensward of Rockefeller Park on June 29 for the first military field mass held in Cleveland. On a hill behind the throng a cannon boomed six times in lieu of a church bell. On the opposite slope faced by the kneeling multitude stood a white-canopied outdoor altar of the Catholic Church. Forming its background was an American flag. Before it were the officiating priests, in the midst of whom was the Rt. Rev. John P. Farrelly, bishop of Cleveland, celebrant of solemn pontifical mass.

Councilman James "Jimmy" McGinty insisted that Christian Timmner play ragtime in the park concerts. The director of the city's symphony orchestra had been playing nothing but classics. However, he agreed that the *Hungarian Rag* would be included in his next concert at Edgewater Park. That seemed to satisfy the councilman until it developed that the *Hungarian Rag* was one of Brahms' Hungarian dances.

The City Council authorized the director of public service to lease to the Cleveland & Buffalo Transit Company and the Detroit & Cleveland Navigation Company the real estate belonging to the city at the foot of East 9th Street as the site of a pier. The lease extended from July 1, 1913, to July 1, 1953, with the provision that the steamboat companies pay the city $55,000, with which the city agreed to erect a bridge over the railroad tracks at East 9th Street. The city also provided a street railway to the pier.

The city tennis championship was won by Charles E. "Chick" Benton, who defeated the veteran Sam Nash on July 5.

Rose Pastor Stokes made a speech in behalf of Socialism at Acme Hall on East 9th Street, July 11. As a girl, Rose Pastor, daughter of immigrants, worked in a Cleveland cigar factory. Later she married J. G. Stokes, New York millionaire, but even then her socialistic activities continued.

The Easiest Way, written by Eugene Walter, Cleveland playwright, was presented at the Colonial Theater, starring May Buckley. The play had been seriously criticized as "too rough," but it proved highly successful from a financial standpoint, as did several of Walter's other dramas.

D. A. Upson of the Cleveland Gun Club won the city clay-target championship on July 14. He added many victories to his credit during a decade.

Alfred Henry Lewis, a native Clevelander, returned to the city for a visit, July 18. He had become nationally famous as the author of *The Wolfville Stories* and other successful books. He liked Cleveland, but humorously said he stayed in New York so that he could keep an eye on his publishers.

The theatrical season opened at the Colonial Theater with a minstrel show led by George Primrose and Lew Dockstader, who had reunited. Primrose continued to be one of the best soft-shoe dancers on the stage, and Dockstader's humor and topical verses made him the leading minstrel of the day.

Manager Frank M. Drew of the Star Theater, burlesque house, announced that no more peanuts, pop, and candy would be peddled in the playhouse because "it lowers the tone of the theater."

John Philip Sousa and his band gave concerts at the Hippodrome on August 12. The march king for many years was popular with Cleveland audiences, and school children often packed the auditorium at matinees. During World War I, Sousa's band thrilled tens of thousands of Clevelanders in a parade when it came down Euclid Avenue three hundred strong. The band provided the music at the concluding meeting of the Victory Chest campaign when more than ten million dollars was raised. The *Washington Post, El Capitan, Stars and Stripes Forever,* and other stirring Sousa marches held their popularity over the years.

Marie Dressler was the headliner of a vaudeville bill at the Hippodrome on August 26. A member of the Baker Opera Company, she played several seasons in Cleveland, and was known as "the best clown of the clan of stage women." She was also successful in serious roles. Later she was to become a world favorite in motion pictures in such popular parts as Tugboat Annie.

From September 14 to 17, Clevelanders celebrated the centennial of Perry's victory on Lake Erie. Mayor Baker, chairman ex officio of the Cleveland Perry Centennial Celebration, declared, "Our aspiration for a finer and higher city civilization in Cleveland will be stimulated by the recollection that it rests upon foundations of so heroic and patriotic a character." The celebration included special commemorative services, a naval parade to display Perry's rebuilt flagship, the *Niagara,* and other demonstrations and exhibitions of historic and patriotic interest.

E. M. Holland, sixty-seven, who was appearing in *Years of Discretion* at the Opera House, died in his hotel room on September 16. Holland was one of the finest character actors the American stage had known and was particularly popular in Cleveland.

The Jewish Hospital Association of Cleveland opened the East Side Free Dispensary at 2443 East 55th Street, the project being staffed and financed by members of the Jewish medical profession. Paul L. Feiss was president of the board; S. P. Halle, first vice president; John Anisfield, second vice president; N. L. Dauby, treasurer; and Max Myers, secretary.

In the fall, the first all-American Diesel engine was completed in Alexander Winton's plant.

Friendship Clubs and Girl Reserves had their beginnings in a *Bible* discussion group at Lakewood High School, led by a YWCA worker.

Two events turned many people away on September 28: Paderewski gave a recital at Grays Armory, and the Rev. Dan F. Bradley preached to women on "how to choose a husband."

The Cleveland-made Chandler automobile created a sensation at the Chicago Automobile Show in September, as the price for the six-cylinder car was only $1,785. The car was named for F. C. Chandler, head of the company, who had been president of Lozier Motor Car Company.

The first Hi-Y Club west of the Alleghenies was founded at West High School.

Wallace H. Cathcart, who had served as president of the Western Reserve Historical Society since 1907, became the first director of the institution. William P. Palmer was elected president and served until 1928. Otto Miller, investment banker, served from 1928 to 1934, when Laurence H. Norton became president.

Probate Judge Alexander Hadden reduced the fee for a marriage license from a dollar to eighty cents on October 14, because the license department was taking in more money than it needed.

An outgrowth of the Art Club, organized in 1876, the Cleveland Society of Artists was formed by George Adomeit and Charles Shackelton. At first the group met in members' homes, and later in the Hollenden Hotel. As the membership grew, it moved to the Gage Galleries, to Edmondson's Studio, and finally to its own quarters on Prospect Avenue. A building fund was started in 1920; and seven years later, the residence at 2022 East 88th Street was purchased, and a two-story brick gallery designed by John Kelly, authority on early American architecture, was constructed. One of the features of the society program was the auction held annually for the purpose of establishing a Cleveland School of Art scholarship. The membership roll included such outstanding names as Henry G. Keller, Sandor Vago, Carl Gaertner, William Edmondson, Hans Busch, Walter Sinz, Viktor Schreckengost, Paul Travis, Wray Manning, Rolf Stoll, Lawrence E. Blazey, Glenn Shaw, Frank Wilcox, Ernest Whitworth, Joseph Jicha, Frank Jirouch, Kenneth Bates, Paul Gebhart, Willard Combes, Howard Cramer, and Joseph Motto. In 1946 Blazey was president of this social organization which was making an important contribution to the city's encouragement of art talent.

The Illuminating Building, fifteen-story home of The Cleveland Electric Illuminating Company, was designed by Hubbell & Benes and erected on the north side of the Public Square, adjacent to the Old Stone Church.

Elbert H. Baker, *Plain Dealer* manager and publisher, was instrumental in breaking a deadlock between the city and the East Ohio Gas Company on the expiration of a franchise this year. He had also devised the formula which brought the ten-year traction war to an end, and was instrumental in planning the street-numbering system.

The Rev. Frank DuMoulin, dean of Trinity Cathedral, was consecrated as coadjutor bishop of Ohio on October 21. Trinity was crowded when Bishop Leonard acted as chief consecrator. Dean DuMoulin had come to the Cathedral as third dean and rector in 1907. Under his leadership the parochial work was enlarged, the cathedral type of service was developed, and greater attention was paid to participation in civic activities. He resigned to accept election as bishop coadjutor of the Diocese of Ohio and was consecrated January 8, 1914. Dean DuMoulin was succeeded by the Rev. H. P. Almon Abbott, who served for five years, during which time the Cathedral took its place as a center of important sociological work in the life of the community. In 1929 Dean Abbott was elected to the Episcopate in the Diocese of Lexington, and the Rev. Francis S. White became fifth dean. During his twelve years of leadership, the endowment of the Cathedral was increased, and parochial units were established in the outlying districts of the city.

Mrs. Emmeline Pankhurst, leader of the militant woman-suffrage movement in England, received reporters on October 24 and told them, "Women are going to get the vote." The fragile, well-dressed, graceful, graying woman appeared at Grays Armory, and to an audience that packed the house answered the question, "Why when you break the laws, don't you take your punishment?" Her reply was, "When I am tried by a jury of men, before a judge in whose election I had no voice, under laws with the making of which I had nothing to say, and am convicted, don't you think I have the right to refuse to take punishment?"

A four-day blizzard, beginning on November 7, raged in the city and was the worst in history. Almost without warning, a summery afternoon was turned into a frenzy of wind, sleet, and snow, with a velocity of 79 miles per hour and a snowfall of 18.02 inches, which almost doubled anything on record. The city was completely paralyzed. Hotels were filled with people unable to get to their homes. Light-and-power lines were down, and communication was suspended. Schools were closed. Transportation was hazardous and almost at a standstill. A food famine threatened. The lakes took a toll of 32 steamships and tugs with 277 lives, and the total money loss ran into millions.

Walter Camp, foremost football expert, selected Robert Hogsett, captain of the Dartmouth College team, for his all-American 1913 eleven. Five Cleveland players had previously won the great honor: William Rhodes, Yale, 1890; Malcolm L. McBride, Yale, 1899; Ralph Kinney, Yale, 1904; Frank Alcott, Yale, 1907; Earl Sprackling, Brown, 1910-1911.

The bandstand in the northeast section of the Public Square had become an eyesore and a storage house for tools, and the Chamber of Commerce asked the city to remove it. The bandstand had supplanted the ornate pavilion of earlier years which had been a proud ornament in its day but was later regarded as an obstruction to pedestrian traffic. A geyser, succeeding the landmark, had little attractiveness when turned low, and had the habit of sprinkling the passers-by when given enough pressure to be effective.

The Cleveland Art Loan Exposition opened, November 25, under the auspices of the Cleveland School of Art, in the Kinney & Levan Building. The undertaking, planned as a fitting observance of the thirtieth anniversary of the school, continued until December 17, stimulating local interest in art and attracting nationwide attention. Directors were Worcester R. Warner, chairman; F. F. Prentiss, vice chairman; Charles F. Brush, E. S. Burke, Jr., H. P. Eells, H. H. Johnson, and Ralph King. The directors of art were F. Allen Whiting, who had been chosen director of the Cleveland Museum of Art, and H. W. Kent, secretary of the Metropolitan Museum of Art, New York, with William Ganson Rose, manager. Representative art works from the homes of Clevelanders, art treasurers lent by collectors throughout the country, and displays by the Cleveland Public Schools were arranged in temporary galleries effectively lighted. So enthusiastic was the interest that a new public demand gave impetus to the building of the famous Cleveland Museum of Art.

The little house organ, *The Silent Partner,* published in Cleveland by the Globe Machine & Stamping Company (later Globe Stamping Division of Hupp Corporation) under the direction of A. F. Schroeder, was winning national attention because of its wit and philosophy. Among the early editors were David Gibson and Leonard W. Smith. After several years of success, the magazine was purchased by a New York firm.

Twenty-eight downtown property owners met on December 29 and planned an organization "to look after the interests of said property owners." On June 20, 1914, the Cleveland Association of Building Owners and Managers was incorporated, the articles having been signed by Alonzo M. Snyder, A. A. McCaslin, Ben B. Wickham, N. I. Young, and George D. McGwinn. The organization soon became a leading civic and business influence in the community. In 1946 eighty office buildings, stores, and single-purpose buildings were members. The president was George D. McGwinn, and the executive secretary was Henry Eccles, who had been elected in 1944 to succeed Roy G. Engstrom.

1914

Newton D. Baker began his second term as the mayor of Cleveland on January 1 under the new home-rule charter, and again his administration was characterized by good government and resourceful leadership. The mayor was attracting national attention because of his ideals of government and his quiet yet forceful ability on the platform.

Under the state laws, the automobile speed limit in congested districts was eight miles an hour, and in residential districts fifteen miles an hour.

The City Immigration Bureau was organized to aid, advise, and protect immigrants arriving in Cleveland, and to help them to become citizens. There was a continuous influx from European countries.

Cleveland wage earners in the manufacturing industry in 1914 averaged hourly $.291 for skilled labor and $.203 for unskilled. In the construction industry, however, skilled workers received $.57 per hour, and $.177 was being paid for common labor.

The Welfare Council was created for purposes of mutual counsel and co-operation among welfare agencies.

Cupid had been busy in 1913, according to an announcement made on February 9. Marriage licenses issued numbered 9,001, breaking all previous records.

When Pennsylvania Railroad trains reached the station at Harvard Avenue, the conductors shouted, "Newburgh!" in conformance with the sign on the station. South End people complained, the sign was changed on February 13, and conductors began to announce, "Harvard Avenue!"

President Henry C. King of Oberlin College revealed on February 17 that the man who had anonymously given $75,000 to the college for the erection of a new administration building was Jacob D. Cox of Cleveland.

Fire started, March 1, in the Fisher & Wilson lumber yards on the "Flats." It raged for twelve hours, wrecked twenty acres of lumber yards and buildings, and damaged the Central Viaduct. The bridge was out of commission for a year, and the total loss was more than a million dollars.

A city ordinance requiring all vehicles to carry tail lights went into effect March 3. City Hall ruled that even baby buggies were not exempt if they were used after dark, but there is no record that a baby ever received a ticket.

The Hippodrome on March 19 was the scene of the largest and most impressive Style Show the nation had seen. The audience included buyers from every part of the country. Mammoth settings introduced new methods of displaying garments, and the Association of Women's Wear Manufacturers of Cleveland added to the city's prestige as the third largest women's-wear center in the country. Only New York and Chicago led it. Harry New of the Landesman-Hirschheimer Company and Morris A. Black of the H. Black Company were the moving spirits. The project concluded the next evening with a banquet.

In the spring of 1914, Florence E. Allen passed the state bar examination and was admitted to practice. The years brought her honors. She was a member of the Ohio Supreme Court from 1922 to 1928 and became judge of the United States Circuit Court of Appeals. Interviewed on the day she became a lawyer, Miss Allen said, "If more women entered into competition for jobs now held exclusively by men, women would show their capability of running the government, and a woman would be nearer the White House."

George Lomnitz, a Cleveland banker whose hobby was unique, died in April. His avocation was studying the Fire Department and the problems of fire-fighting. Over a long period of years, few were the important fires in Cuyahoga County that he did not witness, alarm systems installed in his home and office directing him to the scene. He knew personally most of Cleveland's firemen, who mourned his passing. He died rescuing another, while responding to a fire call from the Alma Hotel, Superior and East 12th Street.

The new Edgewater bath-house was opened, May 1, and the near-by park increased in popularity.

The Tom L. Johnson Monument in Library Park on Fulton Road was unveiled May 3. Charles P. Salen, who had served under Johnson in the City Hall, presented the statue, and a song written for the occasion by Charlotte Salen was sung by two hundred school children.

The Cleveland Foundation was organized under the leadership of Frederick H. Goff, president of The Cleveland Trust Company. Its purpose was to provide a means of distributing funds "for assisting charitable and educational institutions whether supported by private donations or public taxation; for promoting education and scientific research; for the care of the sick, aged or helpless; to improve living conditions and to provide recreation for all classes; and for such other charitable purposes as will best make for the mental, moral and physical improvement of the inhabitants of the City of Cleveland, regardless of race, color or creed." This pioneering "community trust" plan was to become the model for organizations established in many American cities.

Cleveland's first boxing commission was organized, May 12, with A. A. Benesch, J. J. McGinty, Charles A. Otis, Mike Lavin, and Arthur Day as its members.

The Cleveland Yacht Club house at the foot of East 9th Street was put on three scows and towed to Rocky River, where it was combined with the Lakewood Yacht Club house on May 15.

Harry Lauder, Scotch comedian, came to town to appear at the Hippodrome May 15. He was a Rotarian in Glasgow, and two hundred members of Cleveland Rotary met him at the depot and escorted him to the Hollenden where they banqueted him.

To educate the community as to the advantages of electricity for illumination, industrial power, and household use, the Cleveland Electrical Exposition was held May 20-30. Thomas Alva Edison touched the button that started the machinery. Impressive displays in the Coliseum (later Euclid Square Garage) on East 13th Street won for Cleveland national acclaim as the "first city" in the electrical industry. The exposition committee was headed by J. Robert Crouse, with George S. Milner, chairman of the executive committee, and William Ganson Rose, manager. Visitors from many cities learned the scope and importance of Cleveland's electrical output.

The City Council passed an ordinance requiring the use of safety belts by window washers. Pedestrians were greatly relieved—so were the window-washers' families.

Cleveland was paying ten cents a hundred for flies on June 8, but they had to be fresh-caught. This was part of the "swat-the-fly" campaign.

Father Odenbach, St. Ignatius College scientist, interested people everywhere when he announced on June 9 that his computations showed that Lake Erie weighed 1,378,980,000 tons more in winter than in summer. No one disproved his deductions.

The Guardian Trust Company purchased the New England Building, 619 Euclid Avenue, remodeling and enlarging it from 250 to 800 rooms. The sixteen-story Guardian Building, as it was renamed, extended from Euclid through to Vincent Avenue. At this time the bank's officers were H. P. McIntosh, president; J. A. House, H. C. Robinson, George F. Hart, J. A. Mathews, and H. P. McIntosh, Jr., vice presidents; W. R. Green, secretary; and W. D. Purdon, treasurer. Later House succeeded McIntosh. The Guardian Saving & Trust Company had acquired the assets of the National Commercial Bank, and a few days later took over the State Banking & Trust Company, organized in 1899, and the Columbia Saving & Loan Company, organized in 1891. At the time of the financial crash in the early 1930s, the Guardian was one of the city's principal banks. However, unwise business policies and untrustworthy management led to its closing, and resulted in involved legal entanglements, the forcing of stockholders to pay liability assessments, the imprisonment of two officers, and liquidation under the able direction of Conservator Sidney B. Congdon.

The law creating the Cuyahoga County Board of Education was passed, the members to be chosen by presidents of the township and village school districts. The first meeting was held in the Old Court House on June 13, and the following members were chosen: E. S. Loomis, Berea; A. R. Ritchey, Solon; K. K. Hastings, Rocky River; E. J. Riedel, Mayfield Township; and C. G. Howe, Strongsville. On June 27 Howe was chosen president;

on July 18 A. G. Yawberg was elected county superintendent and secretary of the board, and he served until 1929, when Earl J. Bryan came into office.

The Pennsylvania Railroad proudly advertised on June 16 that it operated on its main line nothing but steel coaches, electrically lighted. Wooden cars and gas illumination were becoming old-fashioned.

On June 19 Horace Perry Weddell, son of Peter M. Weddell, owner of the once-famous Weddell House, died in his ninety-first year. He was born in the most pretentious brick structure of its day, at the corner of West 6th Street and Superior, and during his lifetime Weddell witnessed the trading post of the 1820s become the nation's sixth city in population.

Notice was served on the public that nickelodeon admissions would be raised to ten cents. The war in Europe had stopped the importation of chemicals used in making the films.

"Jitney" buses invaded Euclid, Prospect, Payne, and Superior avenues from East 55th Street to the Square. The nickel fare did not seem to appeal to many people, and the privately owned jitneys soon disappeared.

The city on June 28 abolished the old-fashioned horse-watering troughs, scattered throughout the city, as a menace to the steeds that drank from them. Sanitary troughs with running water replaced the old ones. The automobile still had competition.

Senator Theodore E. Burton on July 6 returned to Cleveland as a private citizen for the first time in twenty-two years. He had served in the Senate and the House under five Presidents: Cleveland, McKinley, Theodore Roosevelt, Taft, and Wilson. The City Club welcomed him at a banquet in the Hollenden on July 6.

The Cleveland baseball team was defeated by the Boston Red Sox on July 11, and the victorious pitcher in his first major-league game was George Herman "Babe" Ruth. The raw-boned hurler, who had come from a Baltimore industrial school where he had been placed as an orphan, was to become the greatest home-run hitter and the foremost drawing card in the national game. The center fielder of the Red Sox was Tris Speaker, the "Gray Eagle" of baseball's immortals.

On August 8 an audience was thrilled at the North Randall Track when Barney Oldfield raced against Lincoln Beechey in an airplane. The plane at times seemed only inches above the head of the auto driver. Oldfield won by making his mile in fifty-one seconds.

Signor Bernard Landino was singing at the Miles Theater, August 16. Clevelanders recalled him when he sold newspapers on the streets as Barney Landesman. He saved his money and went to Italy to study music.

School Director F. G. Hogen gave orders on August 18 that every school building in Cleveland must fly the American flag every day.

The celluloid-collar factory of Parsons & Parsons was destroyed by fire on August 23. For several years collars with a glossy finish that could be cleaned with a damp cloth sold widely. However, the humorist and the cartoonist soon put them out of business, and linen came back.

The Metropolitan Theater, 5010 Euclid Avenue, opened its season, August 30, a stock company presenting *The Man Who Owns Broadway*. It was an admirable playhouse, but its location was unfortunate. In it were presented opera and drama. Motion pictures moved in, and the theater deteriorated, presenting boxing matches and special events.

The Mall Theater, 303 Euclid, with an entrance on Superior, was built to capitalize on two good traffic lines. It became a successful motion-picture house.

On Early Settlers Day, September 10, Robert Carran, who had been identified with Cleveland for more than eighty years of his century span, celebrated the occasion by dressing in a Prince Albert coat and a silk hat, as was his custom; and with his own hands he raised the flag at the Public Square. Upon his death, November 16, 1914, flags were lowered to half mast in tribute to a useful and devoted citizen.

The Pioneers Memorial Association was organized to preserve the Erie Street Cemetery which had fallen into a deplorable condition. Buried there were the pioneers: Lorenzo Carter, the early "law and the spirit"; Levi Johnson, early builder; Samuel Dodge, business leader; the Rev. Stephen J. Bradstreet, pastor of the Old Stone Church; John W. Willey, first mayor; Joseph L. Weatherly, founder of the parent of the Chamber of Commerce; and Leonard Case, "source of all wisdom" on Ohio land laws. In the cemetery also were the graves of soldiers of the Civil War and the Mexican War; six soldiers of the War of 1812; one soldier of the Revolutionary War, Gamaliel Fenton; soldiers of the Spanish-American War, one soldier of World War I; and the famous Indian, Joc-O-Sot.

To the great surprise of Clevelanders, a census of horses on September 13 showed that there were still 21,808 in the county. A humorist observed that Cleveland was far from being a "one-horse town."

School children on September 14 sang *The Star Spangled Banner* to celebrate the hundredth anniversary of the writing of the national anthem by Francis Scott Key.

The city closed its municipal dance halls in Edgewater and Woodland Hills parks on September 15. The total number of dancers for the season was 1,254,480, and the price per dance was three cents. An old-timer recalled that Artemus Ward, Cleveland's father of American humor, had expressed positive views on the subject of dancing in the late 1850s: "Dancing is a great evil, and destroys more people than War, Pestilence and Famine. Yet how many thoughtless people whirl in the mazy dance as often as two times a week . . . their minds continually upon the sinful dance . . . Frown indignantly upon the first attempt that is made to induce you to dance. Studiously avoid the ballroom; but if you Must go there, and you Do dance, I intrigue you to shake a lively foot."

Mr. and Mrs. Vernon Castle were appearing at the Hippodrome in September in their celebrated dancing act featuring the foxtrot. Castle announced in an advertisement that he would accept private dancing pupils at his suite in the Hotel Statler at thirty dollars an hour. Time was money.

Cleveland women were holding suffrage-peace rallies. On September 21 great crowds assembled when Carrie Chapman Catt spoke on *War and Women*. She was introduced by Mrs. Harriet Taylor Upton.

Ex-President Theodore Roosevelt came to Cleveland, September 27, and spent two days with James R. Garfield at his Mentor home. Garfield had been his Secretary of the Interior. On the 28th Roosevelt addressed the City Club.

The old St. John's Hospital was torn down to make room for a modern structure at 7911 Detroit Avenue. On September 27 Bishop Farrelly laid the cornerstone, and a parade of ten thousand marchers preceded the ceremony.

The Ellen Garretson Wade Women's Work Fund was established in connection with the Associated Charities. Later, a home-economics department and a sewing center were added. In 1926 psychiatric counseling on mental and emotional problems of families was made available to the staff.

The lily fountain in the northwest section of the Public Square was torn down to make room for the Tom L. Johnson Statue. The Square became an open-air meeting-place for those who wished to tell their religious, political, or economic stories.

An informal gathering held in the home of Charles S. Brooks, where a half-dozen theater-goers watched a miniature performance upon a four-foot stage, was the first step in the formation of Cleveland's Play House. A new freedom in dramatic art was being attempted, and these enthusiastic pioneers were eager to accept the offer of Mr. and Mrs. Francis E. Drury to use an empty residence known as the "Ammon house," on Euclid Avenue near East 86th Street, for their theater. A puppet performance, *The Death of Tintagiles* by Maeterlinck, was their first production. The large third floor of the house was used for the first stage presentation, *Motherlove,* the cast including Marjory Sigler, Claire Eames, Margaret Parkhurst, and Olive Russell. The success of this beginning led to the forming of a Play House Company in 1916 "for the purpose of establishing an art theater." Brooks was made president and Raymond O'Neil, music critic of the *News-Leader,* was appointed art director. The Drurys, through a gift, made possible the purchase of a church at East 73rd Street and Cedar Avenue which served as a theater for ten years. In 1921 Frederick McConnell became director. He had enjoyed wide experience in important theaters, and brought with him K. Elmo Lowe as assistant director, and Max Eisenstat as technical director. The fame of the productions spread far beyond the city's borders. Greater space was needed, and again the Drurys came to the rescue and gave land on the west side of East 86th Street, midway between Euclid and Carnegie. Ground was broken on June 11, 1926, for the new playhouse built to order.

The Cleveland Advertising Club dedicated its new home in Hotel Statler on October 7. It was the largest club of its kind in the world with the finest quarters. William Ganson Rose was president and Thomas W. Garvin, secretary.

The new jay-walking ordinance, providing punishment up to thirty days in the Work House, went into effect on October 18; but Safety Director Benesch told the policemen not to enforce it until the citizens had become accustomed to using the crosswalks.

Mme. Namara-Toye gave her first recital in Cleveland, October 24, in the Hotel Statler ballroom, after a successful tour of Europe. She was Marguerite

Banks, daughter of Mrs. Margaret Banks of Cleveland. The Forest City nightingale was a pupil of Melba.

The first "Get Out and Vote" campaign was conducted in October by the Boy Scouts with a house-to-house drive.

It was expected on October 25 that the new East 9th Street Pier would be ready for the Detroit and Buffalo boats by the spring of 1915, and the city decided to spend $30,000 to pave the East 9th Street approach. Up to that time, the boats took on passengers at the smelly Cuyahoga docks.

Peter Witt, traction commissioner, packed the Hippodrome for his Sunday-night town meeting on November 3. The audience liked the way Witt ridiculed wets and drys and public personages. His annual meetings brought reverberations, constructive and antagonistic.

Bankers and industrialists attended the opening of the Federal Reserve Bank of Cleveland in the Williamson Building on November 16. As a result of the persuasive powers of a Chamber of Commerce committee, which included Newton D. Baker, mayor of Cleveland; J. J. Sullivan, president of the Cleveland Clearing House Association; Warren S. Hayden, president of the Chamber of Commerce; Elbert H. Baker, president of the Plain Dealer Publishing Company; and F. H. Goff, president of the Cleveland Trust Company, the city had been chosen as the logical site for the Fourth Federal Reserve District headquarters. Lyman H. Treadway represented Cleveland on the first board of directors. David C. Wills, a Pittsburgh banker, came to the city to serve as chairman of the board of governors, a position he held until his death in 1925. E. R. Fancher, president of the Union National Bank of Cleveland, was elected governor of the Cleveland institution, and Edwin C. Baxter was appointed secretary. Guided by the principles encompassed in the Federal Reserve Act which President Wilson signed in 1913, Cleveland's bank played a vital part in the rapidly expanding economy of the area, and successfully kept abreast of the financial needs of the rich industrial and agricultural Fourth Federal Reserve District. The bank's territory included the 88 counties of Ohio, 19 counties in western Pennsylvania, 56 in eastern Kentucky, and 6 in the panhandle section of West Virginia. Indicative of the bank's steady growth and development were statements showing that its resources in 1946 had multiplied sixteen times; that its capital had almost tripled, and its deposit total was seventy-six times larger than in 1915.

William R. Hopkins, who advocated a subway for Cleveland, announced on November 20 that, if built, the running time for cars in the Euclid Avenue tunnel would be a mere twelve minutes from the Square to East 105th Street, including a stop at East 55th Street. The plan failed to awaken practical public interest.

Klaw & Erlanger's colossal *Ben Hur* was the Thanksgiving-week attraction at the Opera House. Horses in the chariot-race scene galloped on a treadmill.

Leopold Stokowski brought the Philadelphia Symphony Orchestra to Cleveland, December 5, for a concert in Grays Armory. Olga Samaroff was soloist. Cleveland was looking forward to the day when it might have its own symphony orchestra.

Two Sapphos competed for the attention of northern Ohio at two play-houses in Cleveland on December 7. At the Cleveland Theater, the Holden Players presented Margaret Neville in the title role in *Sappho;* and at the Grand Theater, East 9th and Bolivar, Eliza Day was the heroine. Olga Nethersole would have been amused if she could have attended either performance in the Daudet play she had made famous.

The Union Building, 1836 Euclid Avenue, and Prospect-Fourth Building were built during the year; and the Regent Hotel at 10539 Euclid Avenue and Fern Hall at 3250 Euclid Avenue were erected.

The New York Central & Hudson River Railroad, the Lake Shore & Michigan Southern Railroad Company and subsidiaries, covering about five thousand miles of line and fourteen thousand miles of single track, became part of the New York Central System. The New York Central served eleven states and two provinces of Canada. Cleveland proved to be one of its many strategically located terminals from which emanated the rails called "the life line of national welfare."

1915

The Chamber of Commerce endorsed a new movement on January 5, a "Buy Made-in-Cleveland Products to Keep Workmen Busy" campaign, which was an extension of the "Give-a-Job" campaign inaugurated by the Cleveland Foundation.

Dr. Dudley P. Allen, one of Cleveland's foremost surgeons, died January 6 after outstanding service to his city, to Lakeside Hospital, and to the School of Medicine of Western Reserve University. Born in Kinsman, Ohio, the son and grandson of able doctors, he entered the medical profession after graduating from Oberlin College and the Harvard Medical School. He and Mrs. Allen (Elisabeth S. Severance) were cultural leaders who contributed to the advance of Cleveland in many ways. He served as president of the American Surgical Association in 1906-7, and of the Ohio State Medical Society. In his honor, the Dudley P. Allen Memorial Library was erected by his wife in the University Hospitals group.

At the annual Cleveland Automobile Show held in the Wigmore Coliseum, 1901 East 13th Street (later Euclid Square Garage) in January, the following cars exhibited were not on the market twenty-five years later: Imperial, Haynes, Pullman Junior, Briscoe, Mercer, Pioneer, King, Oakland, Empire, National, Chalmers, Maxwell, Winton, Saxon, Sphinx, Apperson, Princess, Argo, Chandler, Interstate, Cartercar, Grant, Allen, Jackson, Enger, and Mitchell. There were twenty-nine makes in all. Spectators crowded around the Ford car to inspect a curiosity called the self-starter. A crank for the Ford could be had without extra cost, but the starter cost seventy-five dollars additional.

"An heroic figure of white marble, a giant of stone whose head beneath a Grecian helmet is bent in meditation, whose hands are folded above a

Caesar A. Grasselli   Frederick H. Goff   Theodore E. Burton

Charles F. Thwing   Myron T. Herrick   Newton D. Baker

Charles W. Chesnutt   Elbert H. Baker   John H. Clarke

The Main Public Library, center of the renowned Cleveland library system

William Howard Brett
Librarian 1884-1918

Brett Memorial Hall

Linda A. Eastman
Librarian 1918-1938

A portion of Eastman Park, east of the library

sword that rests upon a pedestal, has taken a place in Lake View Cemetery, near the Garfield and Rockefeller monuments," said the *Plain Dealer* of January 18. "It is the monument to perpetuate the achievements in peace of the late John Hay." Three noted American sculptors joined in the work. Augustus Saint-Gaudens, one of the three, did not live to see it finished. He had collaborated with James E. Fraser of New York in the design for the heroic figure. The base and the pedestal were the work of Henry Bacon of New York. The monument bore the inscription from James 3:18: "The fruit of righteousness is sown in peace of them that make peace."

In the mid-winter graduation exercises of January, 370 students received their diplomas from the city's nine high schools: West, Central, South, East, Glenville, Lincoln, West Technical, East Technical, and the High School of Commerce. In 1890 Cleveland had only two high schools, and 62 pupils were graduated.

A small group of energetic businessmen, led by S. H. Mansfield, H. E. V. Harmer, and H. J. Richards, organized the Mid-West Purchasing Agents. In 1927 the magazine *The Mid-West Purchaser* was established, and in 1930 the organization was incorporated. The following year, the first of the annual "Inform-a-Shows" was initiated. The magazine became *The Mid-West Purchasing Agent* with R. R. Ricker, editor. F. J. DeCrane was elected president for 1948-49, succeeding Clarence L. Lesmer, 1947-48.

The French Terrace and several neighboring buildings were condemned on January 25 to clear the way for the East Ohio Gas Company Building, thus making a change in the physical appearance of downtown Cleveland. The French Terrace, named for its owner, Clinton D. French, was a land-mark—a row of attached brick residences extending from Rockwell Street along East 6th to Theresa Court. For many years the suites were occupied by the first families of Cleveland.

A kiosk was located in the northwest section of the Public Square on January 29. It was a little ornamental booth with a glass front through which the curious could peer at an official government thermometer. During extremely cold days or hot spells there was always a crowd around the kiosk discussing the weather.

The Cleveland Cosmopolitan Congress gave a banquet at the Hollenden, January 29, honoring Myron T. Herrick, former ambassador to France. Seventeen nationalities were represented, and seventeen short speeches were made, praising Herrick for what he had done in Paris to help Americans stranded in Europe after the war broke out. The congress had been organized to further mutual understanding among the nationality groups.

The relief committee, appointed to help the city's unemployed, sponsored a plan to raise $100,000 for the needy. Thursday, February 4, was set aside as a day on which every employed person in the city was to turn over voluntarily to the committee his salary or wages for that day.

The Rev. Ferdinand Q. Blanchard was called as pastor of the Euclid Avenue Congregational Church, Euclid Avenue and East 96th Street, this year. War influences and the accelerated shifting of population presented increasing problems to church and community. Dr. Blanchard's ministry was to be characterized by remarkable service to Congregationalism, to his church, and to his city. At the twenty-fifth anniversary dinner in his honor, the degree of Doctor of Brotherhood, created for him, was presented by his congregation as a token of devotion. In 1942 he was named moderator of the general council of the Congregational Christian Church in the United States. A feature of the centennial service of the Euclid Avenue Church in 1943 was the dedication of a memorial window to the late Dr. Charles Franklin Thwing. The centennial anthem was composed by Vincent H. Percy, organist and choir leader since 1919.

Man turned to the flying machine, and in 1915 France became the first aviation customer of the Electric Welding Products Company, contracting for engine valves for military aircraft. This year the company name was changed to Steel Products Company. In 1924 it entered the market for automotive replacement parts throughout the United States and Canada. As a tribute to the founder and president, Thompson Products, Inc., became the company name in 1926. Eighteen Thompson valves in Lindbergh's historic *Spirit of St. Louis,* which conquered the Atlantic in 1927, brought fame to their maker. In 1928 fifty-four Thompson valves were used in Sir Charles Kingsford-Smith's epochal journey from California to Australia, the first crossing of the Pacific. Planes used by Commander Richard E. Byrd in his trans-polar flights in 1926, 1929, and 1933 likewise were Thompson-equipped. The company gave a trophy for an international free-for-all race for land planes in 1929. A year later it established the Thompson Trophy Race, an annual feature of the National Air Races in peacetime.

Dirva, Lithuanian weekly newspaper, was established.

The chlorinated, unfiltered water that Cleveland had to drink was so unpalatable that thousands of people patronized the park springs daily. They filled bottles and casks and carried the water home. The congestion at the springs in Wade and Rockefeller parks became so great it was found necessary to post policemen at the water sources to preserve order.

Rollin H. White developed the first crawler-type tractor for general farm use. Farmers welcomed it, and the Cleveland Motor Plow Company was organized. In 1917 the name was changed to the Cleveland Tractor Company. "Cletracs" helped pull the world through the critical years of war and reconstruction. The company, at Euclid and East 193rd Street in Euclid, later became part of The Oliver Corporation.

Representatives of many musical organizations held a meeting and formulated a plan to abandon the Municipal Symphony Orchestra that had such rough financial sledding under the leadership of Christian Timmner. The hope was to raise $30,000 as a guarantors' fund and maintain a new orchestra under independent direction. Mayor Baker thought the idea a good one, but said the city ought to keep control. Thus, lack of harmony delayed progress of the Symphony.

The Cleveland Union Terminal project was authorized—made legally possible—by an act passed in the Ohio Legislature in 1915, permitting electric and steam railroads to combine in erecting a subway station. Mayor Baker submitted terms to The Cleveland Union Terminals Company, agent for the railroads. The conditions were approved, and later the arrangement was ratified by City Council. The Terminals Company began to acquire the land between Ontario Street, Prospect Avenue, West 3rd, and Canal Road. While the Interstate Commerce Commission reported adversely on the project in 1921, the matter was re-opened and the plans approved. In the early 1920s, the wrecking of buildings was under way; steam shovels were rattling in the mighty excavations, and thousands of sidewalk super-intendents watched the gigantic foundations grow. The railroads had urged the advantages of locating the great Terminal on the Square. They empha-sized the importance of through-ways for passenger traffic, the freeing of industrial areas of the interruption of passenger trains, easing lakefront traffic and transportation problems, and taking the interurban lines from the surface in the downtown section of the city.

A disaster that shocked the American people into action was the sinking of the *Lusitania* on May 7. Loss of the great liner, sunk by a German sub-marine, stirred the nation to consider war on Germany.

An inter-relationship had developed in the official families of the Telling Brothers Company and the Belle Vernon Dairy Farms Company, and they merged this year as The Telling-Belle Vernon Company. A modern plant was built on Cedar Avenue. The company was the first in Cleveland to pasteurize milk, to set up its own staff of farm inspectors, to deliver milk in glass bottles, to inaugurate its own bacteriological laboratory, and to transport milk from farm to plant by thermos-truck. In the early 1920s, the baby food known as S.M.A. was developed, and the S.M.A. Corpora-tion was a Telling subsidiary for several years. The company became a division of National Dairy Products Corporation in 1928. F. J. Andre suc-ceeded the founder as president in 1929. The Sealtest symbol appeared on Telling products in 1935, as headquarters were established in a new three-story building at 3740 Carnegie Avenue on property extending through to Cedar Avenue, the earlier location. Frank W. Edwards, who had worked up through the ranks, became president in 1941. Telling was the largest distributor of dairy products in the Cleveland area in 1946, and the largest company in the industry in Ohio. It was operating ice-cream plants in a number of Ohio and West Virginia cities, as well as the Windsor Evaporated Milk Company, also a division of National Dairy, which made Formulac, a complete baby food.

On May 12-14 the World Court Congress was held in Cleveland, proving one of the greatest inspirational gatherings in the city's history. Ex-President William Howard Taft, distinguished statesmen, and national leaders repre-senting many interests assembled to plan a world tribunal that would further universal peace. The most important public event was a luncheon given by the Cleveland Advertising Club on May 13 to the 250 nationally famous delegates in the ballroom of Hotel Statler, with more than a thousand in attendance. At the speakers' table were: John Hays Hammond, Mayor Newton D. Baker, Henry Clews, Judge Alton B. Parker, Rabbi Joseph Silverman, Professor Jeremiah W. Jenks, Dr. John Wesley Hill, Bainbridge Colby, W. W. Wilson, E. A. Filene, Judge D. D. Woodmansee, Samuel

Mather, Theodore Marburg, Senator Atlee Pomerene, Emerson McMillin, George W. Kinney, James Brown Scott, Dr. Washington Gladden, Herbert S. Houston, and William Ganson Rose, who presided. The enthusiasm of the meeting was remarkable, the great audience rising more than twenty times to cheer the eloquence and patriotism of the eminent speakers. This great forward step was interrupted by World War I.

Russell and Rowena Jelliffe of the Chicago School of Civics, invited to Cleveland by Dr. Paul F. Sutphen and Dr. Dudley P. Allen, conceived the idea of establishing a center that would overcome racial conflict through the medium of the cultural arts. The Playhouse Settlement was the result. Clubs and classes were established, and the aid of the Board of Education was enlisted. The settlement later was accepted for membership in the Welfare Federation. Soon after its founding, a theater group, the Gilpin Players, was formed. On East 38th Street and Central Avenue an old wooden building was remodeled into Karamu Theater. "Karamu" means "house of feasting or entertainment." The Gilpins were rated as one of the best amateur theatrical groups in the United States. The bringing of the Jelliffes and the successful development of the project were due in large measure to the characteristic initiative and fine judgment of Dr. Sutphen, for many years an inspirational leader.

The first landing at the East 9th Street Pier, the new lake terminal erected by the Cleveland & Buffalo and Detroit & Cleveland lines, was made on June 6 by the *City of Buffalo,* C & B sidewheeler. The Cuyahoga River wharf property was sold to the Upson-Walton Company in 1917.

Mayor Newton D. Baker on June 15 appointed the following committee members to the first City Plan Commission which received its charter in 1913: Francis F. Prentiss, chairman, Alfred A. Benesch, Morris A. Black, Harris R. Cooley, Thomas Coughlin, H. M. Farnsworth, William G. Mather, Thomas L. Sidlo, Charles W. Stage, John N. Stockwell, and O. P. Van Sweringen. William Ganson Rose was appointed executive secretary on January 3, 1917, and a study was made of city-planning progress in other cities. The early activities of the commission related to the development of the Mall, the improvement of the street plan, and the set-back of buildings. Rose resigned to undertake war work for the Government and the American Red Cross. F. R. Walker of Cleveland and R. H. Whitten of New York were appointed technical advisors early in 1918, and Charles E. Conley served as plan engineer from 1918 to 1934, and again from 1938 to 1942.

The National Acme Manufacturing Company had become one of Cleveland's largest industrial concerns, and this year the Windsor Machine Company, makers of Gridley automatic screw machines at Windsor, Vermont, was purchased. From this time, Acme-Gridley identified the machines. War in Europe brought heavy demands on the company. Re-incorporation as The National Acme Company was effected in 1916, with A. W. Henn, president. To meet expansion needs, a fifteen-acre tract was purchased at Coit Road and East 131st Street as a new plant site. The Stanton Avenue property was abandoned in 1923; and ten years later the Windsor operation consolidated with the Cleveland plant. The inventive genius of Edwin C. Henn, the founder, served the company until his accidental death in 1924. His brother retired in 1925, continuing as a director. In association with J. L. Free, Albert W. Henn developed real estate on Prospect Avenue east of East 9th Street, was a leader in philanthropic and civic endeavors, and developed on his Mentor farm one of the largest collections of gladioli in the country. Fred H. Chapin, elected president of National Acme in 1926 and chairman of the board in 1933, instituted new developments in the engineering of automatic machines to serve a broader market, as well as a policy of utilizing engineering and mechanical facilities for a diversified line of products to offset the depressional cycles common to the machine-tool industry. National Acme, the world's largest builder of automatic multiple-spindle bar and chucking machines, utilized twelve and a half acres of floor space in the 1940s. Major products born of National develop-ment were opening dies and collapsing taps, chronologs, limit switches, solenoids and centrifuges, and the production of complete units for the automotive, aviation, marine, and other industries.

Among the drivers at an automobile race meet held at North Randall Track on June 17 was Eddie Rickenbacker who drove a Maxwell Special. This was the man who was destined to become America's ace in the first World War.

Riders who used the so-called penny car line to the East 9th Street Pier discovered a joker in the one-cent fare. Conductors were ordered to make no change. The real rate of fare was the smallest coin possessed by the passenger, whether a penny, a nickel, or even a dime.

Junior high schools were established in the city, thus developing a new step in the educational system for pupils of the seventh, eighth, and ninth grades. Under the direction of Superintendent of Schools J. M. H. Frederick, junior high schools were established in September in the Detroit School Building, the Empire School Building, and the Observation School Building.

The East Cleveland Hospital was organized this year at 13240 Euclid Avenue.

The city's swan-boat that plied Shaker Lake at a nickel a ride was equipped with a motor on June 27, because it was hard to find an operator with sufficient leg power to propel it.

The Cleveland Federated Churches conducted a whirlwind evangelistic campaign in various parts of the city. Each Wednesday night the gospel was spread from fifteen downtown corners, and in outlying districts. Pastors of local churches conducted services, and the Rev. E. R. Wright, secretary of the federation, managed the campaign.

Cleveland's pioneering efforts in helping the foreign-born to become good citizens were recognized when National Americanization Day, July 4, was inaugurated.

The Panama Canal was formally opened by proclamation of the President of the United States. The total cost was $366,650,000. Cleveland machinery helped to build it and Cleveland trade was to profit.

Two playgrounds were dedicated on Cleveland's birthday, one at Kingsbury Park and the other on East 62nd Street. Pageantry, folk dances, and games marked the celebrations. In the evening, Mayor Baker and Public Service Director Thomas L. Sidlo led in the dedication of the new East 9th Street Pier.

At a meeting of the Chamber of Commerce on August 1, members were provided with head-telephone connections so that they might listen to a cross-country conversation between Mayor James Rolph, Jr., of San Francisco and Mayor Baker of Cleveland. The Californian used the opportunity to discuss the International Panama-Pacific Exposition.

At midnight, August 9, the famous bar on the Public Square side of the historic Forest City House closed. The days of public service of this famous hotel had come to an end, and upon the site of Mowrey's Tavern, built a century earlier, the new Hotel Cleveland was to rise. The last man to register at the old Forest City House was A. E. Castles of Oberlin. At 6 P.M., September 16, the hotel concluded its business and the sign "Closed" went on the front door. Shortly afterward, wrecking crews tore down the landmark.

The city, the Pennsylvania Railroad, and the New York Central Railroad entered into an agreement on August 12, by which the city was to release its rights in the so-called Bath Street tract between West 9th Street and the river; and in exchange, the two railroads were to deed to the city an equivalent amount of acreage of submerged and filled land in front of their upland east of East 9th Street, the merged part of which the railroads agreed to fill out to a point about seven hundred feet from the right-of-way of the New York Central. The railroads were to buy a site for the depot on the lakefront, paying to the city about a million dollars. Such exchange, with a settlement for various other disputed street rights, constituted the main provisions of the so-called 1915 Union Depot Ordinance which, however, was never carried out, although the railroads years later were claiming rights along the lakefront because of it.

Automobile racing under lights was introduced, August 27. A canvas-rimmed bowl was built at North Randall and was brilliantly lighted. At the opening races, Art Klein drove a Maxwell for a track record of 25 miles in 21:20⅖. Prominent racers were Louis Disbro and William Endicott.

Mayo Fesler of the Civic League asked both Republicans and Democrats to support an independent school-board ticket. He proposed Mrs. Virginia D. Green, J. Wayne Hart, and Frank W. Steffens as candidates. Fesler was proving annoying to unscrupulous politicians and was inspiring the citizenship to take a keener interest in local government. For years he was to be a strong influence for good in City Hall affairs.

A combined meeting of the Inter-city Matinee Amateur Driving Clubs was held in September at the historic track at Goshen, New York, where ten members provided the money to insure the public a free gate. The great event was a race for the league's gold cup which would have to be won by a club three times for permanent possession. George H. Tipling of Cleveland had won two legs with his famous Dago F. Binville, his entry in the

Goshen event, was matched against a field of the best trotters that eastern millionaires could muster. Binville brought the gold cup home, whereupon Robert Goelet offered $30,000 for the horse, but Tipling, president of the North Randall Trotting Club, refused to sell at any price. He subsequently won more than fifty races with Binville.

The political career of Theodore E. Burton ended this year, when he declined the candidacy for re-election to the United States Senate. Born in Jefferson, Ohio, in 1851, he studied law with Lyman Trumbull of Chicago, a personal friend of Abraham Lincoln. Borrowing $150, Burton began his law practice in Cleveland, where his first public office was as a member of the City Council. He helped to frame the McKinley Tariff Act in 1890, and from 1895-1909 served as a member of the House of Representatives. His fight against wasteful appropriations for doubtful improvements gained for him untold friends. As chairman of the committee on rivers and harbors for ten years, he was recognized as a leading authority on waterways and harbor development. He was also identified with monetary and banking legislation, and helped to frame the Aldrich-Vreeland Currency Act. As a member of the National Monetary Commission, he wrote many findings on world financial legislation and conditions. He was one of the strongest influences in promoting the Federal Reserve Act, and was largely responsible for selection of the Panama Canal route. He took his seat in the Senate in 1909. Millions of dollars were saved through his outstanding work involving waterways and improvements.

Young James A. Hawken had the backing of leading Cleveland families in the founding of Hawken School. It opened in October of this year in a small house on Ansel Road, enrolling eighteen students of grade-school age the first year. A pioneer in promoting closer relationship between teachers and students in small classes, the school grew rapidly, and in 1922 a beautiful Georgian building was provided by Mr. and Mrs. Chester C. Bolton on Clubside Road in South Euclid. Carl N. Holmes became the second headmaster after the retirement of the founder in 1925.

Before a hundred thousand people in the Brookside Stadium on October 10, the White Autos defeated an Omaha team for the National Amateur Baseball Championship by the score of 11-6, with Louie Crowley pitching for the winning team. The crowd was said to have been the largest ever to witness an amateur game in America.

Huge slates in front of the National Refining Company service stations carried amusing epigrams by Charles L. Archbold. The nation's foremost collection of valentines—two thousand of them—was the property of Frank H. Baer, who became transportation commissioner of the Chamber of Commerce. Names well known to Clevelanders included John S. McCarrens, store-advertising manager, who joined the *Plain Dealer,* became its general manager, president of the Forest City Publishing Company, and president of the American Newspaper Publishers Association.

Other leading Clevelanders were Edward M. Baker, broker; Drs. John J. Thomas, Jacob E. Tuckerman, and J. Richey Horner, prominent in medicine; William V. Backus, attorney and inventor; Emil Joseph, lawyer, who served on the Library Board and in philanthropic work; William McKinley Duncan and Harry J. Crawford, widely known members of the firm of Squire, Sanders & Dempsey; Lyman H. Treadway, president of the Peck, Stowe & Wilcox Company; George A. Rutherford, leader in the building industry; Arthur A. Stearns, attorney; H. W. Beattie, for many years a leading diamond merchant, whose artistic window displays of precious jewels were watched with interest; and Sidney S. Wilson, merchant and executive in Western Reserve University.

J. Robert Crouse, leader in the electrical and dairy industries, was Elbert Hubbard's ideal for the Presidency of the United States. Robert Crosser, lawyer, served in the Congress, 1913-19 and 1923—; Emma M. Perkins was a scholar, teacher in the College for Women, and an accomplished public speaker; and John "Jack" Raper, *Press* columnist, was a witty and satirical critic of Cleveland people and institutions.

The continuous reverberations of war abroad led to the slogan of "preparedness" at home. Newspaper editorials, speakers on a thousand platforms, and sidewalk conversations were turning to the theme of strengthening national defense should the war cross the Atlantic. The Ohio National Guard Training School for Civilians was organized under the leadership of military officers, and more than seven hundred Clevelanders enrolled for the school opening. This was the nation's first institution of the kind, and the attendance at lectures and drills was gratifying. Governor F. B. Willis and Adjutant General B. W. Hough showed personal interest, and soon other schools were launched throughout Ohio. Then followed organization of the Women's Auxiliary of the school. Women were trained for various war responsibilities in this first school of its kind in the nation.

Music lovers, eager to encourage good music in Cleveland, organized The Musical Arts Association this year. Led by Adella Prentiss Hughes, it sponsored orchestra concerts, visiting artists, choruses, and operas, and made plans for the organization of the Cleveland Orchestra. David Z. Norton was the first president, serving until 1920 when he was succeeded by John L. Severance. In 1918 the association made a musical survey of the schools and named Nikolai Sokoloff leader of the city-wide development. Under his guidance and direction, the nucleus of the Cleveland Orchestra was formed. In 1930 The Musical Arts Association, through funds provided by President Severance, built a home for the Cleveland Orchestra known as Severance Hall, at Euclid Avenue and Wade Park. Through the years the association substantially supported the orchestra, and helped to launch new projects, such as the summer "Pop" concerts. In 1945 Mrs. Hughes retired as an officer of The Musical Arts Association and the Cleveland Orchestra. Her devotion to the furtherance of music appreciation in Cleveland was a far-reaching influence. Thomas L. Sidlo became president of the association in 1939, and successfully directed its activities.

1916

Harry L. Davis followed Newton D. Baker as mayor of Cleveland, and, like his predecessor, was a leader with many personal friends. Both believed in the philosophy that "the way to have a friend is to be one." Davis, of Welsh descent, had lived in Newburgh and worked in the rolling mills. He had been elected city treasurer in 1910 before the home-rule charter, and had run for mayor against Baker in 1913 but was defeated. His busy and successful first term continued into the difficult period of World War I. Baker had resumed the practice of law in preference to seeking political office and Peter Witt was his choice for mayor in 1915.

Woman suffrage was a major issue, and the administration of Mayor Baker encouraged women's civic activities. The desire of feminine leaders to keep the gains for which they had struggled so long led to the organization of the Women's City Club. The need for such an organization inspired three Cleveland women—Mrs. Edward S. Bassett, Mrs. Morris A. Black, and Mildred Chadsey—to suggest that the scope of the already functioning Downtown Club of Cleveland be enlarged to include homemakers, as well as business and professional women. On January 18 Belle Sherwin presided over an organization meeting at the Hotel Statler, and many loyal supporters of the idea attended, including members of the men's City Club. The Downtown Club agreed to merge with the newly organized group under the name of the Women's City Club; and on March 23 Mrs. Charles F. Thwing was elected president; Mrs. Amy S. Hobart, formerly head of the Downtown Club, vice president; Louise Prouty, secretary; and Mrs. Louise Dewald, treasurer. The first board of directors also included Linda A. Eastman, Hester Getz, Professor Mary B. Gilson, Judge Mary B. Grossman, Mrs. Mary Coit Sanford, and Belle Sherwin. The first home was in the Stillman Building. Organized during World War I, the club devoted itself to war projects, and its Patriotic Shop at 1115 Euclid Avenue made Cleveland conscious of the need for food conservation. So successful was this project that it became one of the club's leading activities with particular reference to adequate nutrition for school children. When the Suffrage Amendment was ratified in 1920, the emphasis of the club's activities turned to civic responsibilities.

The third Brooklyn-Brighton Bridge was completed. Crossing the Big Creek Valley, it connected West 25th Street with Pearl Road. Of reinforced-concrete construction, it was 1,726 feet long. In 1922 a new bridge was built at a cost of $220,000; it was 42 feet wide and 1,700 feet long with six arches.

An ordinance was passed requiring the pasteurization of milk, and a Bureau of Health Education was developed, financed by private funds.

One hundred leading civic boosters left Cleveland for an extended visit to the Southwest. These members of the trade-extension excursion of the Manufacturers and Wholesale Merchants Board of the Cleveland Chamber of Commerce visited St. Louis, Oklahoma City, Dallas, Fort Worth, San

Antonio, Houston, and New Orleans. The object of the visit was to make the acquaintance of the businessmen of the Southwest, "not only to have a good time, but to meet old customers and to make new friends that may some day become customers." One of the unique features of the trip was the publication of miniature editions of the *Press* and the *Plain Dealer* in Texas papers to keep the visitors informed of events in their home town.

The Cleveland Grays became part of the Ohio National Guard as F Company, 3rd Regiment, and served with General John J. Pershing in the campaign against Villa in Mexico.

The Van Sweringens on February 17 offered $2,000,000 cash and $6,500,000 in notes for the New York Central's controlling stock in the Nickel Plate Railroad. The offer was accepted on April 13, and the transaction was concluded on July 5. The history of this deal is unique and interesting. In 1915 the Attorney General of the United States notified the New York Central that control of the Nickel Plate constituted a violation of the Clayton Anti-Trust Act. At this time, the Van Sweringens were developing Shaker Heights and needed transportation facilities from downtown Cleveland to their promising residential district. Meetings were held, and the sale of the Nickel Plate to the real-estate operators offered a solution of problems on both sides. So it was that the Van Sweringens, seeking 5 miles of right-of-way for a rapid-transit line, bought a railroad of 513 miles. J. J. Bernet, experienced railroad executive, was placed in charge of the newly acquired Nickel Plate.

Seeking to establish a community church in Shaker Heights in which doctrinal and ecclesiastical differences would be minimized, a group of citizens learned that the old Plymouth Church, now disbanded, would make the Heights church a beneficiary if it would perpetuate its name and traditional spirit. At a meeting of nine men and women on March 1 in the home of F. E. Bruce, the new Plymouth Church was organized. A portable chapel was moved from Lakewood to Coventry and Weymouth roads, the site given by the Van Sweringen Company. City pastors served until the Rev. John Evans Stuchell was called to the pulpit. Plymouth Church of Shaker Heights was officially recognized on October 15, 1916. When the Rev. Charles Haven Myers became pastor in 1919, both church and suburb showed growth and promise. On Palm Sunday, March 25, 1923, 105 members were received into church fellowship, and a beautiful Colonial meeting house, with 150-foot spire, was dedicated. The Rev. Dr. Miles F. Krumbine, who came to the pulpit in 1929, was widely known as a preacher and author of inspirational books and magazine articles. Plymouth had 2,000 members in 1946. While Congregational in government, it was distinctly a community church, filling a large and important place in the lives of the people it reached.

The E. W. Rose Company was manufacturing its Zemo products in St. Louis when an affiliation was made with the Musterole Company, and the organization was moved to Cleveland. Rose, a graduate in pharmacy of the University of Illinois, had developed ointments and soaps for scalp-and-skin irritations since 1905; and, under the name of Zemo, they were marketed in all countries. E. W. Rose, the founder, was president in the 1940s; the factory was located at 1750 East 27th Street.

The Morris Plan Bank of Cleveland was organized on March 8 with Thomas Coughlin as president. Six years before, the first Morris Plan Bank in the United States had been founded in Norfolk, Virginia, on the principles devised by Arthur J. Morris. In 1919 Coughlin was made first president of the National Morris Plan Bankers' Association. The Cleveland bank of the chain grew soundly and opened a new home on Huron Road near East 9th Street in 1922. In 1946 the institution became the Bank of Ohio Company, a commercial bank offering, in addition to personal loans, complete credit facilities and checking-account services. Coughlin remained president of the organization.

Due to deplorable living conditions in city jails, Sabina Marshall organized the Women's Protective Association, later known as the Girls Bureau. Newton D. Baker played a vital part in this establishment, designed to "protect and safeguard girls and women against social and moral dangers." The agency became a member of the Welfare Federation. Sterling House was established in 1918 as a temporary home for girls, and in 1920 Prospect House was organized as a boarding home. The Big Sister Council became part of the system in 1922, and, as a direct outgrowth of the agency work, the Women's Police Bureau was established. In 1943 the Girls Bureau, as it had become known in 1930, became the Youth Bureau, having expanded its services to take care of boys. The agency, located at 1001 Huron Road, served boys and girls, fourteen to twenty-one, and their parents, through the counseling of trained case workers.

President Wilson announced on March 10 the appointment of Newton D. Baker as Secretary of War. Baker was trying a case before Common Pleas Judge Martin A. Foran when the news of the appointment arrived. The judge stopped the trial to give those in the court room the opportunity of congratulating the man who had served as mayor of Cleveland and who, within a few hours, would become Secretary of War in the world's greatest struggle.

The Hruby brothers, Frank J., Alois H., John J., Fred H., Charles J., and William, members of one of Cleveland's best-known musical families, launched a music school. At one time, five brothers played in the Cleveland Orchestra and accompanied such artists as Caruso, Spalding, Kreisler, and Paderewski. The Hruby Conservatory of Music had an enrollment of 750 students in the mid-1940s.

The twentieth-century edition of the hoopskirt and its companion, the pantalet, "came dancing into Cleveland to the tempo of the two-step, the foxtrot, and the hesitation." The hoops—synthetic by comparison with those of the Nineteenth Century—were so constructed as to enable the wearer to sit comfortably and gracefully. "They poked out filmy folds of chiffon and wiggled about quaintly under flowered taffetas. With the ultra full skirt came the old-time tight basque, the point pulled primly down into the skirt. From under the hem at the ankle emerged the demure, lacy pantalet with bow."

The Cleveland Hospital Council was organized, the first of its kind in the country, and was incorporated in 1918. Its purposes were to promote efficiency and co-operation between interested hospitals, and to improve their service to the community. Arthur D. Baldwin was the first president. Eighteen hospitals joined the Council, and the initial program was expanded to meet demands. Later the Council was appointed as agent of the county commissioners, and was given authority to certify what service could be charged to the County and paid for from tax funds, and what service should rightly be assumed out of funds from private sources available to the member hospitals. Minimum standards for the practice of major surgery were determined, and various principles relating to the hospitals and patients were developed after long and careful study. An important function of the Council was the discussion of the hospitals' common problems and the finding of practical solutions. Furthermore, the Council inspired co-operation among the hospitals and materially helped to improve service for patients. Ray G. Bodwell became president in 1944 and Guy J. Clark, who had joined the Council in 1918, served as executive secretary.

Samuel Austin & Son Company had moved to 16112 Euclid Avenue, East Cleveland, near the site of the Nela Park development, when it was retained by the General Electric Company to create the plans and construct the buildings. This became the national headquarters of The Austin Company, incorporated in 1916. During World War I, a large number of structures were erected by this company for the Army in France; and after the conflict, Austin rebuilt a huge glass plant at Mauberg, the first industrial rehabilitation project in Belgium. The company led the way in airport development in the United States, and erected the great Curtiss aviation plant at Buffalo. Wilbert J. Austin succeeded his father as president of The Austin Company and its subsidiaries. Upon his death in an airplane crash in 1940, George A. Bryant, executive vice president and general manager since 1930, became president. Bryant negotiated for design and construction of the sixty-million-dollar Soviet Industrial Center in 1930, said to be one of the largest contract projects ever undertaken. From 1904 to 1946, Austin methods had been used in nearly a billion dollars' worth of industrial construction.

Medal awards for the best apartment, factory, and commercial buildings were made by the Chamber of Commerce for the purpose of recognizing good architecture and structural excellence. Each year, after careful study by a committee, plaques were awarded, and it was believed that the custom stimulated higher standards.

The one-room rural school was the accepted educational institution until shortly after the turn of the century, when a number of consolidated and centralized schools began to spring up in the State. The first consolidated building in the county was erected at Olmsted Falls this year, followed by Strongsville in 1918. Under the Cuyahoga County Board of Education, created in 1914, consolidation developed rapidly because of able leadership and accelerated population of the rural areas. The board reported in 1917 that since September, 1915, twenty-nine of the system's ninety one-room schools had been abandoned; and in four years all would be replaced by modern, efficient school buildings.

Tris Speaker, Boston's star outfielder, was purchased by President James C. Dunn of the local ball club. The reputed price was $55,000 and players Sam Jones and Fred Thomas. Speaker was leading the American League in batting, and he soon established himself as one of the greatest batters, fielders, and leaders in the history of the diamond. When the season closed, Cleveland stood sixth. However, the Indians finished third in 1917. The team took the name Indians in 1915 when Lajoie left the club.

Traction Commissioner Fielder Sanders endorsed a plan to put Cleveland street-railway tracks in a subway under Public Square. Little did he realize that the same idea would be revived every decade.

The tercentenary of Shakespeare's death was commemorated on April 14 with the inaugural planting of the Shakespeare Garden on the hillside east of Doan Brook Valley in Rockefeller Park. Laid out under the direction of John Boddy, city forester, closely planted arbor-vitae hedges marked the borders of a setting reminiscent of Birnam Wood. Here were planted maple seedlings from Scotland, "Juliet" roses grown from cuttings sent by the mayor of Verona, and a cutting of the mulberry said to have been planted by the bard himself. Two American elms were set at the gateway by the celebrated Shakespearean artists, Julia Marlowe and E. H. Sothern. On October 21 a bust of Shakespeare, the work of Joseph C. Motto and Stephen A. Rebeck, was dedicated in the garden. Judge Willis Vickery and William J. Raddatz, collectors of Shakespearean books, were speakers. A lovely sun-dial, gift of Robert B. Mantell, later graced the southern wing. The Shakespeare Society gave a garden bench in 1926, and the Federation of Women's Clubs directed the birthday observance. The garden grew in importance as famous theatrical and literary folk planted memorial trees and filled urns, among them William Faversham, Edwin Markham, Otis Skinner, Stephen B. Leacock, David Belasco, Effie Ellsler, Jane Cowl, Edmund Vance Cooke, Mme. Sarah Bernhardt, Ethel Barrymore, and Chayim Nachman Bialik, Hebrew poet. In 1925 an English gateway was dedicated as a tribute to Marie Leah Bruot, beloved teacher of English speech at Central High School for more than thirty years. The Shakespeare Garden, later sponsored by the Daughters of the British Empire, was renamed the English Garden.

This was the day of real-estate development and easy investors. New allotments included Tuxedo Heights at Pearl and Ridge roads, Coventry-Mayfield and Meadowbrook in Cleveland Heights, and Richland Heights and Waterbury in Lakewood.

The Rev. John Timothy Stone of Chicago and John R. Mott, general secretary of the YMCA, opened an international convention in Grays Armory on May 12. The war-service program was the conference topic.

A Clevelander attracted international attention on May 13 for his double tenotomy—"tendon dissection." The specialist was Dr. C. A. Hamann, chief surgeon at Charity Hospital, and the patient, Walter Jacobs, victim of infantile paralysis. Dr. Hamann, dean of Western Reserve medical school and chief surgeon at City Hospital, possessed rare skill.

The first Kiwanis national convention was held in Cleveland, May 18, with six states represented.

Construction was started on the Coke Works of the American Steel & Wire Company, but disturbed economic conditions hindered progress. The first coke was pushed on April 25, 1918; gas was first pumped to the Newburgh and Cuyahoga works the next month; the first light oil was recovered on July 3 followed by pure benzol products, September 20.

The magnificent Cleveland Museum of Art opened in Wade Park on June 6. The white Georgian marble structure, costing about $1,250,000, the gift of generous Clevelanders, was designed by Hubbell & Benes of Cleveland. Inaugural visitors to the museum saw the beginnings of the Hinman B. Hurlbut and John Huntington art collections, the J. H. Wade collection of textiles and jewelry, the Worcester R. Warner collection of far-eastern art, the Ralph T. King collection of Chinese art, David Z. Norton's Japanese collection, the armor collection given by Mr. and Mrs. John L. Severance, Italian tapestries, the gift of Mrs. Dudley P. Allen, and a collection of Italian paintings presented by Mrs. Liberty E. Holden. Participating in the opening ceremonies were Judge William B. Sanders, head of the trustees; Henry W. Kent of the Metropolitan Museum of Art; Charles L. Hutchinson, president of the Chicago Art Institute; and Director Frederic Allen Whiting. Administrative and educational departments, a tea room, library, lecture rooms, and auditorium increased the usefulness of the museum, which was privately endowed and said to be one of the finest in the world. Later a lovely garden court and fountain provided an exquisite setting for the stately building, dedicated to the people of Cleveland. Art treasures of wide renown were later displayed in the spacious galleries, including the William J. Rainey memorial, the Elisabeth Severance Prentiss collection, the Charles Walker Hanna bequest, the Harkness collection of lace, and works of famous American artists provided by the Charles W. Harkness memorial fund. Many objects were bought with funds especially entrusted to the museum. From the opening day the museum, made possible by the Huntington, Wade, and Hurlbut bequests, became a popular as well as a cultural influence upon the citizenship and art lovers from beyond the city's borders. Under the management of William M. Milliken, who became director in 1930, the attendance showed rapid growth, until in 1946 the grand total had exceeded 9,500,000. Officers in 1946 were William G. Mather, president; Leonard C. Hanna, Jr., Edward B. Greene, Lewis B. Williams, vice presidents; and John Huntington Hord, treasurer.

Adella Prentiss Hughes presented Wagner's *Siegfried,* featuring Mme. Schumann-Heink, on June 19 before fifteen thousand people at Dunn Field.

The historic Franklin Circle Church of Christ added a community building to the sanctuary at 1688 Fulton Road to meet the needs of a large social-service program in a changing community. The Rev. F. H. Groom became minister in 1921, and his long and fruitful pastorate was to witness peak membership and greatly expanded service to a needy neighborhood. He was succeeded by the Rev. H. S. Dickinson. This early church was the mother of the Lakewood church, 1878; West Boulevard, 1888; and Highland, 1897.

The Cleveland Advertising Club, represented by more than a hundred delegates at the Fourteenth Annual Convention of the Associated Advertising Clubs of the World in Philadelphia, June 25, carried off honors on the platform and in the parade. Membership in the local club approximated eight hundred, and attendance at its weekly inspirational meetings averaged the highest in Cleveland. The organization, the largest and strongest in the Advertising Affiliation, was made up of clubs in the Great Lakes area.

The national clay-courts tennis tournament was held at the Lakewood Tennis Club on July 3, with nearly two thousand in attendance. Willis Johnson defeated Conrad Doyle in the singles championship, and Molla Bjurstedt and George M. Church won the national mixed-doubles trophy.

Cleveland's stately City Hall in the Group Plan was impressively dedicated on July 4, Honorable Myron T. Herrick serving as chairman. Speakers included Arch C. Klumph, president of the Builders Exchange; Ralph Fuller, president of the Chamber of Commerce; J. Wayne Hart, president of the Cleveland Federation of Labor; W. F. Thompson, president of the City Council, and Mayor Harry L. Davis. J. Milton Dyer, architect, presented the key of the new City Hall to Mayor Davis. Five stories high with a basement and sub-basement, the architecture was an adaptation of the early Roman school to modern ideas of dignified simplicity. Chief executives who served in this City Hall were Harry L. Davis, 1916-20; William S. FitzGerald, mayor, Republican, 1920-21; Fred Kohler, mayor, Republican, 1922-23; William R. Hopkins, city manager, 1924-29; Daniel E. Morgan, city manager, 1930-31. Serving as mayor during the regimes of Hopkins and Morgan were Clayton C. Townes, 1924-25, and John D. Marshall, 1925-31. Succeeding mayors were Ray T. Miller, Democrat, 1932-33; Harry L. Davis, Republican, 1934-35; Harold H. Burton, Republican, 1935-40; Edward Blythin, Republican, 1940-41; Frank J. Lausche, Democrat, 1942-45; and Thomas A. Burke, Democrat, 1945—.

More than four hundred thousand people lined the curbs, July 14, to see the Shriners' illuminated parade. Police officer George J. Matowitz described the crowd as "the biggest I have seen in Cleveland streets."

Cleveland's fireboats underwent changes in July when the equipment of the *Clevelander* was transferred to the *George A. Wallace*. This fire-fighter, named in honor of the chief under whom the department had made great forward strides, served until 1935. Eleven years later, a new boat, *Engine Company No. 21*, went into action.

An explosion on July 24 in the water-works tunnel, which was extended to crib No. 5, killed eleven trapped workmen and ten others who tried to save them. Garrett Morgan, a colored man who hastened to the scene, rescued two victims and recovered four bodies.

Howard P. Eells became active in the management of the Holran Stone

Company, and expanded the facilities to include a processed dolomite refractory. In this small quarry operation at Maple Grove, Seneca County, Ohio, Basic Refractories, Inc., had its origin. By 1918 regular shipments of dead burned dolomite were being made to the American steel industry as a substitute for Austrian magnesite, shipments of which were suspended during World War I. Upon the death of Eells in 1919, his sons, Howard P., Jr., and Samuel, guided the company through years of expansion as a producer of dead burned dolomite for commercial, metallurgical, and agricultural liming uses. In 1936 the company extended its line to include magnesia refractories, raw materials being produced from extensive deposits of brucite and magnesite uncovered in northern Nevada. Basic Refractories, Inc., through a subsidiary known as Basic Magnesium, Inc., designed and erected a $100,000,000 magnesium metal plant in Nevada in 1941 as a defense measure of the Government. Control of the vast operation passed to the Anaconda Copper Company. A dead burned dolomite plant designed, built, and operated at Maple Grove by Basic Refractories for the Defense Plant Corporation was later purchased and expanded by the corporation. Howard P. Eells, Jr., was president in 1946, Dan P. Eells was chairman of the board, and Samuel Eells, vice president in charge of sales. Headquarters were located in Cleveland.

"Stan" Covaleski was pitching against Boston at Dunn Field on July 28. A large Polish delegation was in the stands to honor him. The young men's band of St. Stanislaus Church provided so much music that the umpire could not hear his own decisions. He ordered the drummer to desist, but the drummer, Joe Cetkoski, sixteen, could not hear the umpire, "Silk" O'Laughlin. Intermittently, the drummer rested, but at every exciting play he boomed forth. Only the outcome was sad—Cleveland lost 7-6.

The beautiful Shaker Heights allotment was thrown open to public sale on July 31 by the Green-Cadwallader-Long Company, agents for the Van Sweringen Company.

Mayor Harry L. Davis led a procession of six hundred automobiles full of orphans to Euclid Beach Park for an outing. The Cleveland Automobile Club brought sunshine to the lives of many children year after year with its annual orphans' day.

County Auditor John A. Zangerle and trustees of the John Huntington estate, after three years of argument, agreed that the Huntington properties should be valued at $8,600,000. Much of this huge sum was spent to help establish the Cleveland Museum of Art and the John Huntington Polytechnic Institute.

May Buckley and Thurston Hall were heading a summer stock company at the Colonial Theater in July. Appropriately, they played to "standing room only" when they produced *A Full House*.

A major undertaking of the Cleveland Foundation was the Education Survey, completed in July. The study, under highly competent direction, covered all phases of the organization and activities of the Cleveland public-school system, and resulted in approximately a hundred recommendations for improved conditions. Fundamental and far-reaching changes in the system resulted, 74 per cent of the recommendations being completely adopted and 18 per cent being adopted in part. There soon grew a gratifying public interest in education and a better public understanding of educational aims and processes. This pioneer survey of the Cleveland Foundation heralded a new era in the Cleveland public-school system and made its mark in the educational world generally.

The "slates" of both the Republican and Democratic parties were broken at the county primaries of August 7. Fred Kohler for commissioner, George A. Meyers for treasurer, and William B. Woods for prosecutor, all known as "anti-Maschke," were winners. Congressmen Robert Crosser and William Gordon, opposed by the Baker-Gongwer organization, won. Myron T. Herrick decisively defeated Harry M. Daugherty for the Republican nomination for the Senate.

Deliveries of the Jordan motor car started in August, Edward S. Jordan, the founder of the company, having introduced colorful features of appeal to women. He capitalized upon them in flowery, sentimental advertisements that won national attention and kept the manufacturing author in constant demand as a speaker.

The Stillman Theater opened at 1115 Euclid Avenue as one of the most elaborate motion-picture houses in the nation. Its seating capacity was 1,800, and the leading pictures of the time were immediately booked. From this beginning, Playhouse Square was developed over the next few years, giving Cleveland an unusual grouping of fine theaters between East 9th Street and East 17th Street. Joseph Laronge, leader in realty developments, envisioned the opportunity for making Euclid Avenue, in this district, a street of theaters and fine shops. He presented his plans to leaders in the theatrical business and offered strategic locations, with the result that in five years several beautiful playhouses were either completed or under construction.

Snow White, the Grimm fairy tale, produced by Clevelanders and acted by Cleveland children, was proving a distinct success on the screen. The principal scenes were enacted on the estate of H. A. Tremaine, Fairmount Boulevard, at the home of C. E. Warner in North Randall, and in the picturesque grounds surrounding the home of P. L. Miller, Cedar Road. Eleanor T. Flynn and Mrs. Norma Harrison Thrower assisted Charles Weston with the directing, and, among those playing leading parts were Aimee Ehrlich, Eleanor Assmus, Ruth Richey, June Harrison, and Pansy Lichtenberg. This Cleveland picture of the silent days, shown locally at the Stillman Theater, was presented in this and several foreign countries and proved a particular hit in London.

Representatives of civic and business organizations met in August with Mayor Davis to discuss ways and means of making possible a great exposition and convention building. A committee appointed to direct the undertaking consisted of William Ganson Rose, chairman; Stanley L. McMichael, secretary; Myron T. Herrick, treasurer; E. H. Baker, Scott Cannell, F. H. Caley, Judge John H. Clarke, William G. Davies, Mayor Harry L. Davis, Samuel H. Halle, J. W. Hart, Arch C. Klumph, William P. Leach, Bascom Little, William G. Mather, Victor Morgan, F. F. Prentiss, L. Q. Rawson, and John J. Wood. In the campaign that followed, 116 associations with 200,000 members, known as the Committee of One Hundred Organizations, generated the enthusiasm that carried the $2,500,000 bond issue by a vote of about four-to-one. More votes were cast for and against the project than were cast for all the Presidential candidates in the primary.

The School of Applied Social Sciences was organized in September by Western Reserve University, the plans having been completed in 1913. In making the announcement, President Charles F. Thwing said, "Cleveland with its great and varied business activities, its cosmopolitan population, and its rapid growth, is a fitting place to teach the sociologic sciences."

Prices were rising, wages were following the uptrend, and union membership was naturally gaining. The American Federation of Labor had more than 2,000,000 members in 1916; 2,726,000 in 1918; and 4,078,000 in 1920. Cleveland's greatest Labor Day celebration was held this year and witnessed by a crowd of 50,000 at Luna Park, where members were enthusiastic over the gains they had made.

Johnny Kilbane defended his featherweight championship of the world on September 3 against George Channey, winning in the third round at Cedar Point, Ohio.

"Let us consider our patients as our honored guests," said Paul L. Feiss, first president of Mount Sinai Hospital, when the buildings were dedicated at 1800 East 105th Street on September 17. The institution had originated in the charitable efforts of the Young Ladies Hebrew Association, organized in 1892 by Herman Sampliner. Known in 1900 as the Jewish Women's Hospital Society, the membership had grown to 1,500. Welfare interests centered in a former residence called Mount Sinai Hospital, with capacity for twenty-nine patients, dedicated under the leadership of President Nathan Loeser at 2373 East 37th Street in 1903. Urgent need for expansion was reported to the Jewish Charities in 1912, leading to formation of the Jewish Hospital Service Association and opening of the East Side Free Dispensary at 2443 East 55th Street in 1913. A drive was launched by the Jewish Welfare Federation for the new hospital at 1800 East 105th Street, under the direction of Salmon P. Halle, first vice president of the hospital board; John Anisfield, second vice president; N. L. Dauby, treasurer; and Max Myers, secretary. Dr. Harry L. Rockwood was the first director of Mount Sinai, which soon won an enviable record of service to people of every creed, class, and color. Under the leadership of Harry F. Affelder, president in 1946, and William B. Seltzer, director since July, 1945, it continued to expand its broad facilities for medical care and nurses' training. An affiliation with Western Reserve University was being planned for teaching and co-operative purposes.

A luncheon was given on September 23 by one hundred lawyers honoring John H. Clarke, who was to leave Cleveland for Washington to become associate justice of the United States Supreme Court. He resigned in 1922 to devote his time to encouraging public opinion favorable to world peace.

Charles Evans Hughes talked to an audience that packed Central Armory on September 24 in his campaign for the Presidency. He attacked President Wilson's international policies, after an introduction by Mayor Davis. Hughes impressed Clevelanders as a man of great personal ability and fine judgment, but he was not a success as a political campaigner.

The first unit of the Richman Brothers factory at 1600 East 55th Street opened. After the war, in 1919, Richman became one of the first companies in America to give its employees vacations with pay. An employee-stockholder policy was adopted in 1920, the year that the Richman Brothers Company was incorporated. Interest of Richman officials in the welfare of their workers resulted in a unique and harmonious "family" relationship that attracted national attention. Henry C., one of the three famous Richman brothers, died in 1934; and two years later, upon the death of Charles L., Frank C. Lewman became president.

Fairmount Presbyterian Church, at Fairmount Boulevard and Coventry Road, Cleveland Heights, was organized on October 23, and the first service was held the following Sunday. Of the eighty-five charter members, twenty-eight were active in 1946. While in use as Red Cross headquarters in 1917, the original structure burned; it was replaced by a second frame edifice, in use until 1924 when a parish house costing $265,000 was ready for occupancy. In June, 1941, the cornerstone of the sanctuary was laid, and the first service was held on Palm Sunday, March 29, 1942. Outstanding features of the beautiful structure, built in traditional English village church style, were the thirty-six exquisite stained-glass windows created by J. Nicholas, a Hollander, considered the foremost stained-glass designer of Europe. The Rev. Elwood Erickson was minister from 1917 to 1922, and Dr. Joel B. Hayden guided the congregation from 1923 to 1931, when Dr. Frank Halliday Ferris became minister.

The Union National Bank opened its towering seventeen-story building at 308 Euclid Avenue on November 17. The bank had occupied a small building on the site for many years, purchasing the property from the Citizens Savings & Trust Company. Title passed to the Union Commerce National Bank in 1918 for a million dollars. The property was sold to the Brotherhood of Locomotive Engineers in 1922, providing headquarters for a banking experiment known as the Co-operative National Bank; and the Central United National Bank purchased it from the Brotherhood in 1926. Looking back on the history of this site, the city's oldest continuous banking location, the names of leading citizens appear in some of the early real-estate transactions. Lorenzo Carter purchased a two-acre lot, including the building site, in 1807 for $25 at delinquent-tax sale, selling it to Abram Hickox without profit in 1810. Peter M. Weddell paid $2,000 for it about 1838; and, upon liquidation, the Commercial Bank had an equity in this institution. Horace P. Weddell, Samuel L. Mather, and Selah Chamberlain, bankers, then became the owners. In 1883 the Benjamin Harrington heirs sold it for $51,000 to the Savings & Trust Company, later the Citizens Savings & Trust Company.

War demand for threaded fasteners inspired J. W. Fribley and C. M. Prell to combine efforts in the production of cap screws late in the year. With second-hand machines and crude equipment, the founders began operations in an old horse barn on East 77th Street near Central Avenue as the

F-P Screw Company. Incorporated as the Cleveland Cap Screw Company in 1920, the organization secured Charles Kaufman as engineer, and he introduced new manufacturing developments known as "boltmakers." Able direction made the company a leading producer of cap and set screws, bolts, nuts, special headed and threaded products. Fribley continued as president in the 1940s, and the factory was located at 2917 East 79th Street.

The Plymouth Building was constructed this year at 2036 East 22nd Street, and the Hotel Olmsted was built at East 9th and Superior.

A Committee of Fifteen was appointed to investigate the advisability of the City Manager Plan of government for Cleveland. Those naming the committee were Probate Judge Alexander Hadden, Thomas G. Fitzsimons, and Dr. Charles S. Howe, president of Case School of Applied Science, representing fifty civic organizations. The committee included Benjamin S. Hubbell, chairman, Thomas J. Dolan, Sam W. Emerson, Walter L. Flory, A. R. Hatton, A. T. Hills, D. S. Humphrey, C. A. Laubscher, Bascom Little, Dr. J. D. McAfee, Robert McDermott, Walter P. Rice, William Ganson Rose, Dr. J. E. Tuckerman, and G. W. Luetkemeyer, who died before the report was made in 1919.

The Ziegfeld Follies played to large audiences at the Opera House with Will Rogers, Fanny Brice, Ina Claire, Ann Pennington, and Bert Williams as featured stars. Will Rogers used his lasso and gave a monologue dealing with events of the day. His homely philosophy and quiet humor delighted the large audiences. A Clevelander recalled that his entertainment was quite different from that of twelve years before when he appeared at the Lyric Theater on East 9th Street, south of Prospect, an old church made into a playhouse. At that time Rogers used two horses in his act and lassoed them as they galloped across the stage. The Clevelander, knowing Rogers' ability to tell a story, suggested to him that he would enjoy the act more himself if there were less lasso, with half the time given to patter. Rogers agreed to try the plan, and it worked so well that the great comedian and "ambassador of good will" was soon using the rope only as an accompaniment to his fun and philosophy.

Despite a blizzard that halted trains and streetcars on December 22, two thousand children assembled on Public Square to sing Christmas carols, led by the Hiram House Boys Band.

1917

Dr. Frank E. Spaulding, former Minneapolis superintendent of schools, was chosen superintendent of the Cleveland schools on January 9 at $12,000 a year. He succeeded J. M. H. Frederick, who had served since 1912.

Florence E. Allen, attorney for the Ohio Suffrage Party, complimented East Cleveland supporters on January 13 on capturing the municipal ballot in their new city charter, thus making them the only enfranchised women east of Chicago.

Munson Havens, secretary of the Cleveland Chapter of the American Red Cross, received instructions from Washington on February 6 to mobilize forces. Police guards were stationed at public buildings, water works, and utility plants because of the war crisis.

At a meeting at Cleveland Heights High School, four charter members founded the Heights Women's Club: Mrs. C. M. Finfrock, Mrs. J. H. Owen, Mrs. Fred R. Bill, and Mrs. H. F. Staples. Activities related to community betterment were soon under way.

The Clark Avenue Viaduct, 6,687 feet, spanning the Cuyahoga Valley, was finished at a cost of $1,398,000.

Cleveland was recovering from a "bomb scare" on March 12, and public feeling was tense over U-boat attacks on Atlantic shipping. The city was the first to declare formally that preparation for war was necessary. Grays Armory was packed in the evening of March 12, with three thousand citizens who represented civic organizations, and the crowd roared approval of Chairman James R. Garfield's declaration, "We must prepare for war!" Four days later, the School Board adopted a resolution urging, in view of Germany's attacks on United States ships, that children should be taught to combat injustice and oppression.

The Cleveland Cinema Club was organized through the efforts of Bertelle M. Lyttle on April 3. This was one of the first organizations of its kind in the United States, and it became widely known for its successful meetings dealing with the motion-picture industry, its educational activities to raise the standard of screen plays, and its intensive program of work through schools and junior cinema clubs. Its three-decade record of achievement was reviewed in 1946 when Mrs. William Roger Thomas was president.

Mayor Harry L. Davis appointed an Advisory War Board on April 4, to plan war activities for Cleveland. Myron T. Herrick was chairman; Harry L. Vail, executive secretary; and Fred H. Goff, treasurer. The executive committee also included Mayor Davis, Charles A. Otis, Charles E. Adams, Paul L. Feiss, F. W. Treadway, M. P. Mooney, Warren S. Hayden, Otto Miller, W. A. Greenlund, Richard F. Grant, and Andrew Squire. Many assisting committees watched over the city's food supply, guarded the citizens and their property, provided relief for women and children, and guided other war efforts. The service of the board attracted nationwide attention.

The United States declared war upon Germany on April 6. It was a day memorable in the annals of world history, and patriotism ran high in Cleveland. The newspapers carried grim headlines. Stores selling flags were swamped with customers. Harry Coulby gave a stirring patriotic speech at the annual banquet of the Pittsburgh Steamship Company, and many other inspirational meetings were held. On the day following the declaration of war, the crew of the *Dorothea,* two hundred strong, under Captain E. J. Kelley, left the armory at 3433 Carnegie Avenue and marched to the Union Depot to entrain for combat. Cleveland was turning its thoughts to the essentials of modern warfare: to the cannon, the laboratory, the ship, and the garden.

"City Warned to Save Food Supply" was the grim headline in the *Plain*

Dealer on April 10. Food stores claimed prominent space during the war, reporting on food supply, war-garden production, food speculation, the sugar shortage, the merits of horse meat as suitable for human consumption, meatless and wheatless days, soaring grain prices, and the high cost of living. Patriotic fervor ran high in well-organized giant parades, flag-waving rallies, and meetings on the Public Square, where home-front problems were submerged in enthusiasm to aid the boys "over there."

The audience that filled Grays Armory on April 10 to hear Galli-Curci on the occasion of the prima donna's first public appearance in Cleveland, joined with her at the close of the concert in singing *The Star Spangled Banner* with patriotic fervor.

The Cleveland Trust Company was the first state bank or trust company in the city to enter the Federal Reserve System, being admitted to membership on April 11. It was the second such bank in the district, and the first institution with resources of fifty million dollars or over to volunteer affiliation with the Federal Reserve Bank of Cleveland. The company then added commercial banking to its original functions of savings bank and trust company.

Federal agents and police were checking on April 12 to learn whether the three hundred registered wireless-telegraph stations in Cleveland and those that were not registered had obeyed wartime orders to "dismantle for the duration."

The Brotherhood of Locomotive Firemen and Enginemen established headquarters in Cleveland in April. The organization had been founded in 1873 at Port Jervis, New York, with eleven members. David B. Robertson, an engine wiper on the Pennsylvania Railroad in 1895, had risen to the vice presidency of the Brotherhood in 1913, and was elected president in 1922, succeeding William S. Carter. Membership grew until it exceeded 112,000 in the mid-1940s. Activities had expanded greatly. Main offices were in the Keith Building.

The building fund of $125,000 raised by the Women's Home Missionary Federation made possible the administration building of The Schauffler Missionary Training School, dedicated this year. Many nationalities were represented in the student body through the years. Dr. Raymond G. Clapp served as president from 1924 until 1941, when he retired because of ill health. He developed the institution from a three-year training school to a four-year college which gave a degree. Dr. Clapp was succeeded by Dr. Earl Vinie. Hundreds of young women went out to serve as pastors' assistants in large institutional churches, where shifting populations of many tongues multiplied problems, or as missionaries and social workers in cities, villages, and remote places. In 1946 Dr. George P. Michaelides succeeded Dr. Vinie as president of the Schauffler College of Religious and Social Work, as it was now known, at 5115 Fowler Avenue. A faculty member for six years, Dr. Michaelides was widely known, having served in church-related educational capacities in the Near East and in leading colleges.

The Legislature attempted to settle disputes of many years over the rights to the lakefront. It passed the Fleming Act, a declaratory act claiming for the State a full title in trust for the area of the lake, recognizing in the shore owners *only* a right to make reasonable use of the water in front of their land for consumption purposes and the right to gain by natural accretion. No right to fill in or wharf out was recognized, but some rights in existing fills were conceded. The act granted to municipalities with lake frontage the power to administer in some respects the public rights in the lake area. This legislation was from the first claimed to be unconstitutional, but after thirty years it had not been finally tested.

Cleveland planted its first "official" war garden on May 4, despite a cold, sleety rain. Soon backyards and vacant lots were dedicated to food production. Society ladies attracted attention as they went about their gardens in white bloomers, while some women stimulated home-front effort in overalls. A fine Euclid Avenue lawn was plowed for potatoes.

Cleveland's first official contribution to the Allied forces was made, May 6, when the Lakeside Unit, Base Hospital No. 4, entrained for an Atlantic port, sailing for France on May 8. There were flowers, tears, and cheers in the leave-taking of 250 men and women at Union Depot, but there was no organized civic farewell. Grace Allison carried a large silk flag and the unit's white streamer. Major H. L. Gilchrist commanded, Major George W. Crile was medical director, and Major Charles F. Hoover, assistant director. Officers wore for the first time their military uniforms and khaki greatcoats. Amy F. Rowland, assistant registrar, and her aides, Dorothy Barney and Ida F. Preston, were conspicuous in the service uniforms of olive-green skirts, khaki blouses, Norfolk jackets, tan shoes, and green velour hats. The Lakeside Unit arrived on European soil at Rouen, France, May 25, with the first American flag carried by American forces in World War I.

Prohibition found a powerful ally in food conservation. Women rebelled at saving in the kitchen so brewers could have grain for beer. At the Northern Baptist Convention, meeting at the Hippodrome on May 17, three thousand delegates voted unanimously for prohibition, upbraided "vampires" hanging around army camps, and congratulated the Russian people, who "under the leadership of Almighty God, have thrown off the yoke of autocracy."

Rabbi Abba Hillel Silver succeeded Rabbi Moses J. Gries as leader of the Tifereth Israel Congregation, East 55th Street and Central Avenue. Rabbi Gries had been recognized throughout the city for his loyal adherence to the principles of religious freedom. His successor, who came from Wheeling, was to become a distinguished spiritual head, writer, and lecturer. A leader in the world Zionist movement, he became active in charitable and civic programs, a moving spirit in the Jewish Welfare Federation, and a dynamic worker for refugees of his faith.

The Winton Hotel, completed at 1012 Prospect Avenue, was promoted and later managed by J. L. Free. It was named for Alexander Winton, head of the Winton Motor Car Company. In 1931 the hotel was taken over by the Metropolitan Life Insurance Company and named The Carter in honor of Lorenzo Carter, early pioneer, who built the first tavern in the village of Cleveland. Under its new name, the hotel and its famous Rainbow Room were formally dedicated, December 16, 1932, with a program including Governor George White, Mayor Ray T. Miller, Dr. Joel B. Hayden, and Orchestra Leader Rudy Vallee with his Connecticut Yankees. Later the Carter became a unit in the Albert Pick hotel system with Allen Lowe as manager of the six-hundred-room establishment.

The Ohio branch of the Council of National Defense was created, June 1, by Governor James M. Cox, the purpose being to place the State on a war-time basis. The Cleveland members were A. A. Augustus, Paul L. Feiss, James L. Fieser, Joseph R. Nutt, and Warren S. Stone. On the women's committee were Belle Sherwin, Mrs. Malcolm L. McBride, Mrs. Frank Muhlhauser, Mrs. F. W. Striebinger, Eleanor Walker, and Mrs. Charles W. Wason. More than 3,250,000 people were canvassed to produce $37,000,000 for the State's war chests. The Cuyahoga County chest held $10,000,000. The great tasks of the State Council were achieved through the self-sacrific-ing labor of many hundreds of patriotic workers. Funds were to be ap-portioned for the use of certain home-front organizations serving emergency needs.

The first Liberty Bond issue went far beyond expectations, and there was great jubilation on June 15. Cleveland could well be proud of its record, for the quota was $45,000,000, and the final count indicated that 75,000 citizens bought $68,711,350 worth of bonds, an excess of 50 per cent over the assignment.

Theresa Sheerer applied for entrance to the Western Reserve University Law School on June 15, and was the first woman to be admitted.

Cleveland was the leader in the total amount raised per capita in the Red Cross drive, and a carnival spirit justly reigned on the Public Square on the night of June 25, when it was announced that Clevelanders had pledged $5,000,000. The American Red Cross headquarters sent this message: "The showing made by Cleveland is regarded by the War Council as the best in the country." Samuel Mather was named head of the Ohio Red Cross.

The main feature of the Fourth of July celebration was an Americanization mass meeting at the Hippodrome. Patriotism ran high as Senator Atlee Pomerene announced to the audience, "This is the greatest Fourth of July the world has ever witnessed." Three thousand newly naturalized citizens were in the audience.

A number of Clevelanders were giving talks at the picture theaters in support of Americanism and the fighting forces. Included among the home sentinels were Mrs. Emma E. Gross, Mrs. Chester Pitcock, Lillian Westropp, Mrs. Edwin S. Connor, Bertelle M. Lyttle, Mrs. W. E. Fowler, and Mrs. L. J. Wolf.

Pat Lynch, gate keeper at Forest Hill, welcomed John D. Rockefeller on July 8, after he had spent some time away from the city. Lynch was a familiar figure often seen near the little house at the entrance way. He provided surreys for distinguished visitors, as automobiles were prohibited from the grounds for a number of years.

A heat wave brought a temperature of 104 degrees to Cleveland and caused fourteen deaths in the county.

An impressive service marked Cleveland Day, July 22, when representatives of the city's military units, headed by the 5th Ohio Regiment Band, took part in memorial services. The Rev. F. B. Avery paid tribute to the memory of Thomas Winch Barrett of Cleveland, the first member of the American Aviation Corps to lose his life in Europe, July 6.

The first church service in the United States in memory of the first American soldier killed in World War I was held July 26, in St. John's Episcopal Church. Soldiers representing seven military organizations took part in the service.

The national campaign of the "drys" attracted a number of Clevelanders who went with J. A. White, prohibition leader, to Columbus on August 12, to file 175,000 names with the secretary of state.

The Cleveland Federation for Charity and Philanthropy, which had been organized in 1913, and the Welfare Council, which was established in 1914, were united to form the Welfare Federation of Cleveland. Money planning and social planning were thus joined in one organization under able leadership. The first president was Martin A. Marks, and the first executive secretary was Whiting Williams. When it became necessary to raise large sums for war relief, Cleveland applied the Federation idea to its money-raising, and amounts required for local agencies were included in the Victory Chest. This procedure led naturally to the Community Chest of 1919, the first in the United States. The Welfare Federation, while giving up its function of money-raising, retained and developed budgeting, and the distribution of about 80 per cent of the Fund money. Before long, the Federation was guiding the spending of approximately ten million dollars a year, including agency earnings, endowment, and public subsidies. The functions of the Federation were described as follows: "linking together the social agencies of Greater Cleveland, public and private, providing a medium for constant interchange of information between these agencies, and furthering education both for agencies and community." The main divisions of the Welfare Federation were the Health Council, the Hospital Council, the Children's Council, the Group Work Council, the Case Work Council, and Homes for the Aged. Harry F. Affelder, president 1946-7, was succeeded by Louis B. Seltzer; and Edward D. Lynde, who had served since 1935, was executive secretary.

The 145th United States Infantry, which before the war was the 5th Ohio Infantry, left by train for Camp Sheridan, Montgomery, Alabama. Of the fourteen hundred soldiers, more than seven hundred were Clevelanders. Colonel Albert W. Davis commanded the troops which were escorted to the station by three thousand veterans of the Spanish-American War who were holding their encampment in Cleveland.

The Americanization Board was organized and gave valuable aid to draft officials in their work with the foreign-born. It helped in naturalization cases and gave legal advice. Naturalization classes were inaugurated, and Dr. Raymond Moley took charge. When the board dissolved, the Citizens Bureau, with George Green as a tireless and efficient director, assisted aliens in naturalization, immigration, and legal matters. Later, fifty classes were centered in libraries, settlements, and public schools, with a membership of five thousand, the most comprehensive system maintained in any city.

The Lake Division of the American Red Cross was organized, September 1, with headquarters in Cleveland; the division included Ohio, Indiana, and the western half of Kentucky, with 353 chapters, each representing a county. James R. Garfield headed this important district.

The Junior Red Cross, founded September 15, became the largest youth organization in the world. The Cuyahoga County Chapter was organized in April, 1918, with James A. Hawken as chairman and Mrs. Bartlett C. Shepherd as executive secretary. In 1947 there were nearly 400 schools enrolled with 200,000 boys and girls working tirelessly in many service projects, where heart and hand contributed to human welfare and understanding.

To tell the community how each citizen could constructively aid the war effort was the purpose of Uncle Sam's Salesmen, organized September 8. Representatives of manufacturers and merchants to the number of 2,800 enrolled and made their first goal the sale of war-savings stamps. So successful were the initial efforts that the national war-savings headquarters planned to organize chapters throughout the country; however, the war came to a conclusion before the larger organization could be formed.

Adrian D. Joyce and associates acquired the Glidden Varnish Company, dating from 1870, and incorporated The Glidden Company. Two years later, eleven manufacturers and distributors in the paint-and-varnish industry came under the Glidden name in a reorganization program. The food division started in 1920; and the business expanded until in 1946 the company was operating thirty-four factories throughout the United States and Canada, and twenty-six research laboratories were searching out new products and processes. Multifold expansion, directed from the main office in Cleveland, Berea Road and Madison Avenue, by President Dwight P. Joyce, son of Adrian D., and R. H. Horsburgh, executive vice president, resulted in the manufacture of highly diversified products, including paint, varnish and related coatings, chemicals and pigments, metals refining, naval stores, vegetable oils, Durkee famous foods, soybean processing, and livestock and poultry feeds. The paint division was one of the largest in the country.

A crowd of spectators gathered on East 6th Street near St. Clair Avenue on September 10 to watch the beginning of the excavation on the Public Auditorium site. However, the big steam shovel did not arrive, and the event was postponed. Some of the bystanders disappointedly left the advertised free show and went to the Hippodrome to see vaudeville. Again they were disappointed, a strike of union musicians having just been called. Others, however, sought free entertainment and were repaid by an impressive address by Colonel Myron T. Herrick on the Public Square to the Early Settlers Association.

Leo Weidenthal was given an unusual honor by the City Council on September 24, when a resolution was passed praising his "splendid service to the city during ten years as city-hall reporter for the *Plain Dealer*." Weidenthal had resigned to become editor of the *Jewish Independent*. He was one of the organizers of the Cultural Gardens, a quiet, constructive contributor to civic advance, whose collections relating to literature and the stage were of great value.

The war demanded organized helpfulness on the part of the citizenship, and the American Red Cross launched a campaign to increase its membership to ten million, in order to secure the practical co-operation of a loyal legion of Americans. The need for bandages, clothing, food, and supplies for the army and navy was great, and an organized effort was required at home to relieve the families of the armed forces. The Lake division, including Ohio, Indiana, and the western half of Kentucky, was asked for 1,600,000 members, and a spirited campaign was waged until more than 2,500,000 were enrolled, leading all other divisions per capita.

Henry Turner Bailey came from Massachusetts to become dean of the Cleveland School of Art. Under his leadership, the enrollment was to grow from 500 to 1,500. Bailey's genial personality, his love of nature, homely philosophy, and unusual speaking ability made him a particularly valuable leader in the community. He resigned in 1930 to devote his time to writing and lecturing, and he died the next year.

A crowd in Public Square saw Tris Speaker buy the first bond in Cleveland's Second Liberty Loan drive on October 1. Cleveland's quota was 250,000 subscribers for $60,000,000. The national goal was $3,000,000,000. The total reached $101,724,100 on November 1, or more than $40,000,000 above the quota, while the Fourth Federal Reserve District reached $490,639,000.

The John G. White collection of Orientalia and folklore, at Cleveland's Public Library, numbered in October more than 30,000 items and represented more than 140 languages. It was known to scholars all over the country, and the contents were made available for public use.

A young Methodist minister came to the city from Buffalo, October 14, and founded the Cleveland Goodwill Industries. The Rev. Frank M. Baker brought a slogan with him: "Not charity but a chance," and with that philosophy he salvaged street-corner rowdies. He opened workshops in which aged and crippled men and women found the chance they wanted in paid work. Dr. Baker had been called to Cleveland by an inter-denominational committee, and his salary during the first year was paid by the Cleveland Deaconess Board. From the garage headquarters used at first, he moved into Acme Hall, at one time a center for left-wingers, and transformed it into workshops and gymnasium where "a chance" was given those who needed it. Many of the activities centered around the mending and remaking of unwanted articles which had been secured in-continuous collections from Cleveland homes. Through Dr. Baker's untiring efforts, good will was being expressed in many ways from the headquarters at 2416 East 9th Street.

Daykin Brothers, plumbers, used unique advertisements. One said on October 16, "Not one drop of Anarchistic, Communistic, Nihilistic, Law-breaking, Trust-busting, Traitorous Blood in Our Breed. We have 116 Daykins fighting with the English, and 74 of our kind with the USA."

Lord Northcliffe, guest of the Cleveland Advertising Club, spoke at Grays Armory on October 22 on the war situation, and thousands were turned away. His simple, straightforward war message was addressed to what proved to be one of the great inspirational gatherings associated with World War I.

The local branch of the American Protective League was organized by the Department of Justice, but had no official standing. It supplanted the police authority and proved effective in locating "slackers," investigating food hoarding and profiteering, and in keeping down the number of alien disturbances.

Cleveland won a new distinction in war activities when Major Benedict Crowell was appointed assistant secretary of war in November, 1917, Newton D. Baker being Secretary. Major Crowell had entered the Ordnance Department in December, 1916, when he became commanding major. His service in the War Department concluded in July, 1921.

Streetcar conductors around town wore smiles on November 6. For the first time, little swinging stools called seats were provided for them.

Sarah Bernhardt "the divine," in her seventy-fourth year, appeared on November 19 at the Opera House in bits from *Cleopatra, L'Aiglon,* and other plays. As the Nile queen, the aged actress was able to walk but a few steps, but she had all of her artistry and dramatic fire at her command.

The service flag used throughout the nation was designed by a civic and business leader of Cleveland, Robert L. Queisser. He was prominently identified with the builders'-supply business and with fraternal and trade associations. The flag had a rectangular white field with a red border. Blue stars were placed on the white field, each to represent an individual from the home, the church, the business or the factory, serving under the colors in a uniform of the armed forces.

A local newspaper had this reference to Thanksgiving: "Once again eatables were being sent to soldiers, and the army cooks in France took pride in preparing a home-cooked turkey dinner for the dough-boys. At home, the homemakers made the cranberry sauce without sugar, did without butter, and for dessert served '1917 pudding' which was concocted from graham flour, bread crumbs, sour milk and unsweetened applesauce."

Cleveland, on November 26, feted a party of Japanese railroad officials, headed by Dr. Yasujiro Shima of the Japanese Imperial Railway. The visitors inspected Cleveland's coal-and-ore docks and made a study of transportation conditions.

News reached Cleveland on December 2 of the death of Sculptor Auguste Rodin in Paris. Clevelanders took interest in the great artist because of his statue of the "Thinker" which was attracting attention in front of the Cleveland Museum of Art. A local traveler humorously reported, after the signing of the Versailles Treaty, that he saw five copies of the "Thinker" being made ready at Rodin's home for shipment from Paris to various parts of the world. He observed that this was the largest group of thinkers he saw at any one time in one place in Europe.

East Cleveland had demanded taxes from John D. Rockefeller on a valuation of five million dollars placed on his Cleveland property. Before this, the oil magnate had become legally a resident of New York City, and the court so ruled.

Cleveland learned that two of her sons were killed in action, at sea, in the first World War. George Dolezal, thirty-one, and Terrel R. Wood, thirty-one, were reported drowned when the destroyer *Jacob Jones* was torpedoed and sunk by a U-boat in the war zone on December 6.

It was eight degrees below zero in Cleveland on December 10. There was a scarcity of coal, and gas pressure was low. Many schools and manufacturing plants closed, and Governor James M. Cox seized the coal within the borders of the State and shipped it where it was most needed, thus averting a more serious situation.

Clevelanders had been paying three cents carfare, but the rate was raised to four cents on December 15. The increase was charged to higher federal taxes, increased labor costs, and more expensive materials. From that time on, the rate of fare continued to rise.

Superintendent Spaulding of the public schools provided a topic of conversation when he announced on December 17 that teachers who married would not lose their jobs.

The Forest Hill home of John D. Rockefeller burned to the ground on December 17. The famous financier never returned to Cleveland after his visit in July prior to the destruction of the old home. However, great new developments were to take place on the famous Forest Hill estate, benefiting the Greater Cleveland area substantially. A public park and model community were to be developed where the "greatest giver of all time" had resided with his family and where twenty-two miles of beautiful drives were enjoyed by the owner and his frequent guests. Adjacent to the park, streets were to be laid out; and homes of English and Colonial types were to be built. Forest Hills Park of East Cleveland and Cleveland Heights was ready to serve the 100,000 residents of these communities in 1942, the land having been deeded to the two cities by John D. Rockefeller, Jr., in memory of his father. The value of the property was estimated at a million dollars, and about two million dollars more was expended up to 1942 by the communities, the Rockefellers, and the Work Projects Administration. What of the famous nine-hole golf course where the "oil king" played with his cronies? It became the Great Meadow where picnic parties replaced the famous foursomes of earlier years. The lake was enlarged for wading, boating, and skating, and other improvements were made for public enjoyment. Forest Hills was another of the many reasons why the people of Greater Cleveland were indebted to Rockefeller.

The Negro Welfare Association was established on December 17 in the neighborhood of East 40th and Cedar Avenue. William Connors served as the first executive secretary of this agency, which had as its program interracial planning for industrial relations, vocational services, public education, community organization, and social work. In 1930, it became affiliated with the national organization, the Urban League, which had been established eight years before the Cleveland group was formed. Serving as consultants were ten workers, all professionally trained in the particular field in which they were interested. In 1941 Sidney R. Williams became executive secretary as successor to Connors, Edward L. Worthington was president of the board, and W. O. Walker, chairman of the executive committee. The League was completely supported by the Community Fund, and had its headquarters at 8311 Quincy Avenue.

The first streetcar to cross the Detroit-Superior High Level Bridge, December 24, carried city and county officials. A local paper reported that a stop was made in the middle of the bridge so passengers could leave the car and look around. The newspaper commented, "It's getting more and more like New York in Cleveland." The bridge, 3,112 feet long, was built at a cost of $5,407,000. A double-deck type, it had 12 concrete arches and one 591-foot steel arch spanning the river 196 feet above water. The bridge was not dedicated, as it was opened to traffic during World War I. The span was designed by county engineers A. B. Lea and Frank R. Lander, and completed under the term of William A. Stinchcomb. The county commissioners serving when the bridge was designed and constructed were W. F. Eirick, H. L. Vail, J. G. Fischer, F. T. Andrews, Joseph Menning, P. D. Metzger, and J. T. Kelly. The Superior Avenue Viaduct, built in the seventies and the pride of the horse-and-buggy era, had become inadequate, and older citizens watched its gradual dismantling with mingled feelings of regret. They remembered the injunctions and objections that caused repeated changing of building plans; they recalled that the bridge when completed was regarded as one of the finest in its day; but they realized that Cleveland had grown tremendously during the past forty years, requiring the greatly improved service of the new High Level Bridge, the largest double-deck, reinforced, concrete bridge in the world.

1918

Edna K. Wooley, women's editor of the *News,* revealed on January 11 that many women around town were suffering from "knitters' nerves" induced by continued work on clothing for the soldiers.

Clevelanders were practically snowbound by a blizzard and ten-below-zero temperature which tied up the railroads on January 13. The weather set one of the lowest records since the Weather Bureau started its reports forty-eight years before.

The coal shortage dealt the city a hard blow on January 29. Many persons were out of work because factories and shops were forced to shut down. The street railway, short of coal, ran fewer cars, and thousands of persons were forced to walk to work.

When the World War broke out, the French Government promptly ordered 600 White trucks, and many orders from the Allies followed. The United States Army adopted the two-ton White truck as standard, and the French Government awarded the Croix de Guerre to the White-truck fleet for its service. There were 18,000 of these trucks in the armies of the United States and allied powers, and, in 1918, the United States Government took the entire production.

Heatless days found stores dark and cold in February. Uncle Sam's calendar called for one meatless day, two porkless days, and two wheatless days, besides five wheatless-and-meatless meals in every week. A two-ounce bread ration was ordered in restaurants on February 8.

Having been impressed by the "polytechnic movement" in England, John Huntington provided in his will for the founding of a tuition-free institution in Cleveland. With a nucleus of a few student architects, the John Huntington Polytechnic Institute was organized on March 1, occupying a small upstairs room at 2032 Euclid Avenue until 1920. After several moves, through arrangement with the estate of the late Judge William B. Sanders, the Otis-Sanders mansion at 3133 Euclid Avenue was leased and remodeled. Members of the board of control in 1947 were John Huntington Hord, grandson of the founder as chairman, Harold T. Clark, and Lewis B. Williams. Alfred Mewett was dean and treasurer, and capacity enrollment testified to the popularity of the institute. Courses were offered in art and engineering subjects, industrial technic, languages, drawing, design, and the graphic arts.

The Association for the Crippled and Disabled was established upon the recommendation of a survey conducted by the Welfare Federation aided by funds from the Sunbeam Association. In 1915, Alpha Robbins (Mrs. Ray S. Gehr), active in welfare and social-service work since her graduation from Vassar College, recognized the need for a citywide organization to help the crippled and disabled. She secured the co-operation of the Sunbeam Circle, which had helped bedridden children in Lakeside Hospital in 1889 and had expanded to become the Sunbeam Association with broadened services in 1916. After having suggested the survey of 1917, Alpha Robbins became executive secretary of the Association for the Crippled and Disabled and served until 1923. The purpose of the association was "to make possible for every physically handicapped person in Cleveland and vicinity the best physical condition he is able to attain, the most useful education he is capable of grasping, and the most suitable employment he is competent to undertake." An orthopedic center was established in 1922 at 2233 East 55th Street, where the outstanding service achieved wide interest and commendation. The association was a member of the Cleveland Welfare Federation.

With the arrival of spring, many householders were purchasing ornamental iron fences to be placed about lawns. They were light and easily installed, with swinging gates held closed by a spring handle that fitted in a notch.

Samuel Scovil was appointed ordnance production chief for the Cleveland district, and he secured Andrew F. "Andy" Kelley as labor-relations man for this highly important area employing 377,000 workers in war industries. Their responsibility was so well handled that not one hour was lost through labor trouble in the district during the first World War. Kelley had owned and managed a shoe store in Cleveland, but his ability to tell stories took him to the vaudeville stage, and later, as the "Horse Sense Philosopher," he talked for a long period over national radio chains. John F. Royal pronounced him "the greatest story-teller of them all," and Owen D. Young, Alfred P. Sloan, Elihu Root, and a legion of others sang his praises for his sound philosophy.

The seriously needed new Division Avenue Filtration Plant near Edgewater Park was put into operation, the earlier plant having been dismantled. The old tunnel was carried to a submerged intake about twenty thousand feet farther from the shore. The valuation of the water department in January of this year was $30,000,000. The growth of the city necessitated further improvements, and the Baldwin Reservoir, upon which work started in 1914, was placed in service in 1925, when the Fairmount Pumping Station was completed.

The Cleveland Federation of Women's Clubs moved into beautiful and efficient headquarters especially prepared for them in the Hotel Statler. It was recalled at the first meeting in the new home that Mrs. Charles Edwin Porter had founded the organization in 1902, and had become its first president. The early meetings had been held in Pythian Temple, and later gatherings were held in various auditoriums and churches. In 1929 the name of the organization was changed to the Federation of Women's Clubs of Greater Cleveland. A review of activities proved that women all over the city could benefit from differing points of view, and that contacts with leaders of active groups throughout Greater Cleveland would deepen their understanding of mutual community problems. The Federation was cooperating with movements for community service and civic affairs particularly relating to the city's health and happiness.

Cleveland's Third Liberty Bond campaign, with a goal of $55,000,000, went over the top by $475,000 on May 3. Samuel Gompers, labor leader, and Douglas Fairbanks, motion-picture star, had been the featured speakers. The final total was raised to $112,106,550 with 252,000 contributors.

The First National Bank, 247 Euclid, carried on a spectacular Liberty Loan campaign. When the institution opened in the morning, a choir of fifty voices with Lila Robeson sang patriotic songs; and during the noon hour, celebrities, including James J. Corbett, gave short talks. Mammoth blackboards recorded every sale with the name of the buyer. Each day the blackboard records were transferred to large cards, which were displayed about the banking room, enclosing it with a wall of names. In the third loan campaign, 28,354 names of bond buyers were thus recorded. John Sherwin was president of the bank at this time.

Study of the German language was to continue in Cleveland high schools, it was decided on May 6 by a six-to-one vote of the Board of Education on recommendation of Superintendent Spaulding. His report contended that high-school boys who might be called to the colors to fight Germany should know the language as a "military necessity." This study had been dropped from the grade schools on patriotic grounds.

Clevelanders united to raise a great war fund in the Victory Chest

Rocky River

Hinckley Lake

Bird walk

Bridle path

Golf course

METROPOLITAN PARK SYSTEM

The Cleveland Museum of Art mirrored in a lake as seen from Euclid Avenue.

"La Danse Dans un Pavillon" by Watteau.

The Garden Court

*Portrait of Sir Thomas
Hanmer, Bart., by
Van Dyck.*

*Portrait of a Lady
by Rembrandt*

*Portrait of Isabella Brant
by Rubens.*

Fountain of the Waters

*The Ohio Bell
Telephone Com-
pany Building*

*Standard Build-
ing* (BELOW).

*Brotherhood of
Locomotive En-
gineers Build-
ing* (BELOW).

Drive, sponsored by the Cleveland War Council. The $6,000,000 goal was submerged by pledges reaching $10,616,032. Sousa's Band participated in the final victory meeting, May 19, which was unparalleled in Cleveland history. Crowds gathered on Euclid Avenue to hear Sousa and his three hundred sailor musicians. When the band stopped at East 9th Street, a woman stood in an automobile and sang patriotic songs while the band and the crowd accompanied. The singer was Lila Robeson, Clevelander in the Metropolitan Grand Opera Company. The nation called the drive "incredible" and "amazing," and from it grew the pioneer Community Chest. Thus a co-operative solicitation of public support of worthy agencies devoted to welfare and the common good was launched, fostering systematic and efficient management, and pointing the way to adoption nationally.

Charles A. Otis, treasurer of the Cleveland War Works Industries Commission and representing the War Industries Board under the chairmanship of Bernard Baruch, was appointed to make a survey of industrial war resources in the United States.

Six hundred people attended the opening of the Cleveland Yacht Club at Rocky River on May 28. Commodore Josiah Kirby's flagship, the *Suzanne,* was launched as a program feature.

The Boy Scouts were asked to take a census of all the black-walnut trees in Greater Cleveland, as the wood was needed in making firearms.

The Hippodrome, on June 10, offered summer vaudeville. Matinee prices were ten and twenty cents; evenings, twenty to thirty-five cents.

A. M. Willard personally directed the tableau, *The Spirit of '76,* a real-life representation of the famous painting from his brush, when a Flag Day pageant drew an estimated 150,000 to Wade Park on June 14. Parts in the tableau were played by George H. Bender, G. F. Shillats, and Bion Boggs. The spectacle, in which there were 1,500 picturesquely costumed performers and a chorus of 2,000 voices, was entitled, *Freedom for All, Forever.* Walter Logan was the conductor of the Young People's Symphony Orchestra, and a four-million-candlepower searchlight played from the platform.

Lieutenant Flachaire on June 25 made an exhibition flight that thrilled thousands at Gordon Park. There were shudders when the ace, who had downed fifteen German planes "over there," sent his Hispano-Suiza into a roaring dive to within a hundred feet of the crowd before he shot upward to disappear in the clouds. It was a good publicity stunt for the lectures he was giving at Grays Armory where he exhibited battle paintings by Lieutenant Henri Farri.

Ever-increasing demands of commercial advertisers for posters, displays, calendars, streetcar cards, and the like had greatly expanded the business of W. J. Morgan & Company, lithographers since 1864, and the plant erected at Wood and St. Clair streets in 1898 had become inadequate. A modern building was designed this year to accommodate the firm at East 17th Street and Payne Avenue. Three New York companies were absorbed in 1925; and in 1926 the Otis Lithograph Company of Cleveland was taken over by the Morgan Lithograph Corporation. P. J. Morgan passed away in 1941, and his son, George W. II, fourth in the Morgan line of presidents, came into control of one of the country's outstanding lithographic concerns, with offices in metropolitan cities.

The First Church of the Brethren was founded in June, and its house of worship was erected at 14284 Superior Road. The congregation included a substantial representation of the Dunkards living in Cleveland. Home missionary work was the principal activity. The Rev. Otis Landis became pastor in 1947, succeeding the Rev. Jesse Reber.

Eugene V. Debs, four times Socialist candidate for President, was arrested in Cleveland, June 30, charged with violation of the Espionage Act. He had previously been indicted by the Federal Grand Jury on charges growing out of an address given in Canton, Ohio. He was sentenced to prison and subsequently released by President Harding.

Nettie Eisenhard, Cleveland nurse and member of the original Lakeside Unit, was awarded a war cross for bravery under fire and was decorated by King George V.

Secretary of War Baker announced that all baseball players must get essential jobs or go to war after September 1. When the American League season closed on September 2, Labor Day, Cleveland was in second place, Boston winning the pennant by two and a half games. The season over, a local philosopher said, "the baseball player went to bat for democracy." Theaters and golf clubs were closed for a time during the emergency.

Justice of the Peace William Zoul fined automobile speeders thrift stamps instead of money, thus promoting safety and patriotism at the same time.

The streetcars of the city on August 6 suddenly stopped at 6 P.M. Members of the Electrical Workers Union had pulled the switches at the power stations as practical evidence of their strike. It was estimated that there were 100,000 passengers in the cars that were tied up for forty minutes. The temperature was 100 degrees and there were many prostrations among the passengers. Nearly 50,000 people were waiting on the Public Square and near-by streets for their cars. John J. Stanley, president of the Cleveland Railway Company, hired new electrical workers, and Fred Telschow, president of the Car Men's Union, condemned the cutting off of current.

When troop trains stopped at the Glenville station, soldiers were permitted to march to "Spring Bank," the Walter H. Cottingham estate on the lakeshore, west of East 105th Street. Here the railroad canteen operated by Cottingham and his neighbors provided accommodations, so that the boys who had been riding in hot, stuffy trains for hours could take a dip in Lake Erie.

Thomas J. Herbert, a young Clevelander who was a first lieutenant in the United States Air Service, had been wounded when his plane, one of six, was brought down in an encounter with eighteen German planes. He was awarded the British Distinguished Flying Cross, the American Distinguished Service Cross, and the Purple Heart. Later he was made president of the National Aeronautic Association and, in 1946, was elected governor of Ohio.

Worcester Reed Warner and Ambrose Swasey gave to Case School of Applied Science a nine-inch refracting telescope, which they had built and remodeled for observatory use after it won first prize at the Panama-Pacific

Exposition in 1915. Joint gifts of the benefactors now made possible the Warner and Swasey Astronomical Observatory to house the telescope. Further gifts included a zenith telescope, astronomical transits, chronographs, and other instruments. The observatory was located on an elevated site on Taylor Road in East Cleveland, and completed in 1920. In 1939, friends of the college, interested in astronomy, gave a total of $237,000 for the enlargement of facilities. A twenty-four-inch Schmidt-type telescope, a model auditorium for lectures, and an exhibit hall were added features. The committee in charge of raising funds and creating new interest was headed by Dr. Wilbert J. Austin. So popular were the lectures by Dr. J. J. Nassau, whose fame as an astronomist became worldwide, that reservations for seats had to be made well in advance for the public meetings.

The Fortnightly Musical Club of Cleveland now had 1,529 members, and it was said to be the largest musical club of its kind in the country. It had migrated from church auditoriums to ballrooms, theaters, and hotels, and in Halle's Steinway Hall it found a convenient home. A chorus formed under Sarah Walker (Mme. Charles Cahier of Vienna) was discontinued after a time, but was revived in the 1930s under Mrs. Zoe Long Fouts. Lecture courses featured leading authorities in the music world. Philanthropic concerts brought cheer to shut-ins and music appreciation to young people. Local composers were inspired through sympathetic interest. In 1933 two club scholarships were established—one named for Mrs. David Z. Norton, whose term as president had been of the longest duration, and one for Adella Prentiss Hughes, whose service to Cleveland was of inestimable value. Great artists were presented in concert and recital by the club over the years, the name of Dr. Richard Strauss standing out in the symphony series, when he conducted the Pittsburgh Orchestra in a performance of *Till Eulenspiegel* and *Tod und Verklaerung*. Mrs. Norman W. Goldsword was president of the Fortnightly in 1946.

The eyes of Clevelanders turned skyward on August 18, when American and British aviators gave an exhibition over the city. Daily reports were being received of the influence of aviation over the European battlefronts, and the local demonstration was watched with awe and thrills.

William Howard Brett, librarian of Cleveland's Public Library, died on August 24 from injuries received in an automobile accident. Under his direction the library had grown remarkably, and its extension work had surpassed that of any institution in its field. Brett's finest monument was the great library he fostered through his long period of stewardship. Largely through his efforts, it was brought near and made dear to a great cosmopolitan community. Linda A. Eastman, vice librarian, was made acting librarian.

The first gasless Sunday of the World War period came on September 1. Munson Havens, secretary of the County Fuel Administration, secured the co-operation of police in carrying out orders issued from Washington. The Federal Fuel Administration had decreed that cars using gasoline should cease in order to conserve fuel for the fighting forces. Doctors' automobiles and trucks delivering essentials were exceptions. It was estimated that

300,000 gallons of fuel would be saved in Cleveland each Sunday. Streetcars were crowded, and livery stables provided all the horses and buggies they had. Churches and theaters reported an increase in attendance of from 10 to 15 per cent. Bicycles were seen all over the city, and sales were brisk. A few of those who abused the voluntary sacrifice were showered with tomatoes, and in some cases tires were slashed. Gasless Sundays proved a practical success.

Gertrude Nader was announced as the city's first conductorette. She was assigned to a Cedar-Fairmount car, and Conductor A. W. Peck was appointed her instructor.

A Cleveland-made battle plane, produced by Glenn L. Martin at his St. Clair Avenue factory, stood its tests September 3 and was accepted by the Government. It was the first airplane built in the city, and it was flown from Cleveland to Dayton in two hours. Martin, a master of research and an able engineer, developed the Great Lakes Airport this year, and rose to one of the world's highest positions as a builder of planes. In 1929 he moved his plants to Baltimore, and the Great Lakes Aircraft Corporation took over the airport for the production of mail planes, dissolving in 1935.

The newly named Shubert-Colonial Theater opened, September 9, with *Look Who's Here,* a musical comedy starring Nora Bayes. Many leading theatrical attractions were presented during regular seasons, with stock-company productions in summer. The earlier name of the playhouse was The Colonial.

Men from eighteen to forty-five years, inclusive, numbering 111,687 had registered for selective service in Cuyahoga County by September 12. It was reported that few of the registered could state correctly the color of their eyes, and one man protested when his hair was recorded red instead of auburn. In September the American Army was marching toward Metz and was giving excellent account of itself on a thirty-seven-mile front.

The Centenary of Methodism was celebrated on September 15, with a parade of many thousands and two large memorial meetings, one at the Euclid Avenue Opera House and the other at the Hippodrome.

Lakewood High School was built on an eighteen-acre site at Bunts Road and Franklin Avenue at a cost of a million dollars.

War gardens of Greater Cleveland were said to be yielding sufficient vegetables to sustain a country such as Belgium on prevailing rations for several weeks. Furthermore, Cleveland was making a fine record saving white flour and meat by using substitutes.

The National Chemical Society on September 16 praised the efforts of Colonel F. M. Dorsey of the National Lamp Company and H. D. Bachelor and Dr. D. K. Chaney of the National Carbon Company for their development of the gas mask.

The conductorettes of the Cleveland Railway Company held a rally at the Windermere car barns to protest against the federal order barring them from their jobs after November 1. Rose Moriarty of the Champion Stove Company, a champion of women's rights, denounced the order and won a strong following by her arguments.

The Board of Rapid Transit Commissioners, appointed on September 19 to study rapid-transit possibilities in Cleveland, employed Barclay Parsons & Klapp as consulting engineers, and instructed them to submit a rapid-transit plan. The board included Charles A. Otis, president; Charles E. Adams, vice president; Morris A. Bradley, Clarence J. Neal, and Fielder Sanders, with William T. Redmond, secretary. It was the belief of the citizenship that rapid transit could benefit Cleveland in many practical ways, and the commissioners lost no time in having studies made.

First Lieutenant Deming Bronson, Company H, 364th Infantry, 91st Division, distinguished himself for service near Eclisfontaine, France. Although wounded by an enemy grenade and rifle bullet on the first day of the Battle of the Argonne, he remained with his men; and, disregarding orders to retire for hospitalization, he joined another company in taking a village. In the course of the attack he killed an enemy machine gunner and retired from action only after receiving disabling wounds from a high-explosive shell. He was later awarded the Congressional Medal of Honor.

Paderewski addressed a meeting in Cleveland on behalf of the Allies, and helped to enlist Poles for the depleted Polish army.

At a Liberty Bond rally, October 17, in front of the Cleveland Trust Company, a citizen bought bonds to secure kindling wood to burn the Kaiser. One liberal fellow paid for a rope to hang the Crown Prince. A philanthropic hater donated a submarine to sink von Tirpitz. A rich optimist purchased the wherewithal to make von Hindenburg surrender. All the while, four cartoonists put the money to work. Donahey and Temple of the *Plain Dealer,* and Clisbee and Scott of the *News,* following suggestions from the crowd, burned the Kaiser, hanged the Crown Prince, sank von Tirpitz, and captured von Hindenburg—on giant posters. Each addition to the pictures was purchased by subscriptions which finally totaled $35,000. Attorney Charles K. Arter sold the privileges.

No public eating house was allowed to sell more than one kind of meat to a customer at a meal. Bread, toast, and bacon were barred as garnitures. All menus were ordered written in English. Eggs reached 90 cents a dozen by October, and an ordinary flat rented for ninety dollars. Everybody made big money except the white-collar class.

Ohio had 200,000 cases of influenza on October 25. During the summer and fall, 400,000 persons died from "flu" in the nation, and 20,000,000 had been victims of the epidemic.

Cleveland's quota of $113,000,000 in the Fourth Liberty Loan drive was announced on October 26 as over-subscribed by $12,000,000. An inspiring feature of the campaign was the visit to Cleveland of fifty-three grizzled veterans of the French Foreign Legion.

The Board of Education on November 4 decided to adopt "Lafayette" as the name of the new school building being completed on East 126th Street to honor France, the nation's ally, and to honor "Lafayette who helped America in time of great need."

The city was recovering on November 8 from an "armistice" celebration without an armistice. Newspaper extras, declaring the war at an end, started citywide demonstrations that continued despite definite assurances from Washington officials that fighting was continuing excepting on that part of the front where German and Allied armistice delegates were to meet.

Admiral William S. Sims, United States Navy commander, cited the deeds of Lieutenant David S. Ingalls. The Clevelander was the Navy's number one ace in World War I and was decorated with the British Flying Cross and the United States Distinguished Service Medal. A British officer, after describing several of his aerial exploits, concluded: "His keenness, courage and utter disregard of danger are exceptional and an example to all. He is one of the finest men this squadron ever had."

Word that the Armistice had been signed came to Cleveland early in the morning of November 11. Blowing of factory whistles, and ringing of bells in fire-engine houses and churches brought thousands of people to downtown Cleveland for a big celebration. Stores closed, factory hands quit work, and all joined in rejoicing. Mayor Davis proclaimed a holiday. A huge night demonstration included fireworks and a seemingly endless parade. Jubilant excesses were frequent, and joy was not the only intoxicant. Police gave up hope of restraining the merry-makers, and scores found sympathetic haven in police stations.

The Allied War Exposition was brought to Cleveland, November 16, for nine days, and, despite rain and snow, drew a record attendance of 650,000 people. Three miles of trenches had been dug on the lakefront as part of the battlefield, extending from East 9th to West 9th streets. Soldiers, sailors, and marines helped in enacting a typical world-war battle, with tanks, barrages, observation balloons, and bombers contributing to the thrills. An army camp, an auxiliary cruiser, and a great exhibit of captured trophies and exposition features so inspired the visitors that Cleveland became the leading city of the country in per-capita sales of war-savings stamps which were promoted by the mammoth show. J. Robert Crouse, head of the local War Savings Committee, was the Cleveland chairman, and William Ganson Rose directed the project for the United States Government. So great was the success that, despite the fact the Armistice had been signed, the Government moved the exhibits to other cities to build morale and inspire interest in future financing.

Happy Thanksgiving Day! Fighting had ceased in World War I. Some sons had already returned, and soon most of the boys "over there" would be back on American soil. Elation and gratitude were paramount everywhere, and at the Canteen Club 150 service men were served Thanksgiving dinners.

Lester M. Sears designed a straight gasoline-powered industrial tractor in November; and with his son, Lester M., founded the Towmotor Corporation in 1919. The versatile Towmotor, produced in the first plant on Bliss Road, Euclid Village, found ready demand on loading docks in the lake region and at ocean ports. The demand for the rough-and-ready fork-lift truck made necessary a larger plant at 1226 East 152nd Street. Towmotor's success paralleled progress made in the field of materials handling. Upon the death of the father in 1934, the son became president.

A streetcar strike was seriously interfering with local business on December 3. Car crews stopped work as a protest against the hiring of women conductors. Trolley lines in Lakewood were cut, but otherwise there was no violence. Drivers of passenger cars, trucks, and delivery wagons helped to move the public to and from work. The strike was settled on March 1, and the women were to be replaced.

On December 11 the Cleveland Orchestra presented its first concert in Grays Armory, under the direction of Nikolai Sokoloff. Founded by The Musical Arts Association through the inspirational leadership of Adella Prentiss Hughes, the Orchestra, under her management, soon became known for brilliant performance and variety of repertoire. There were fifty-seven players in the first orchestra. Sol Marcosson was concertmeister, and among the members were Charles V. Rychlik, teacher, composer, and violinist; Carmella Cafarelli, harpist; the Hruby brothers; Maurice Spitalny and Walter Logan, violinists; Philip Kirchner, oboe; and Victor De Gomez, cellist. Annual concert tours through the Middle West, as well as Canada and Cuba, brought increased fame to Cleveland. Children's concerts and memory contests, arranged in co-operation with the public schools, inspired music appreciation. Under the able direction of Rudolph Ringwall, who became associate conductor in 1926, their popularity grew until, in 1946, thirty children's concerts were given to sixty-one thousand children. In 1928 the first complete symphonic radio program was presented with tremendous success, and popularity of orchestra programs on the airways led to world-wide symphony broadcasts and demand for recordings. Sunday Twilight Concerts and the summer "Pops," directed by Dr. Rudolph Ringwall, lectures, and lecture recitals were high spots in Cleveland's cultural life. In 1931 the orchestra moved from the Masonic Hall, where many concerts had been given, to magnificent Severance Hall, its permanent home at University Circle, made possible through the gift of John Long Severance and the concerted campaign effort led by Dudley S. Blossom. The Cleveland Orchestra enjoyed dynamic leadership that kept it at the forefront in the music field. Artur Rodzinski, distinguished Polish conductor, who came to the orchestra in 1933, was succeeded in 1943 by Erich Leinsdorf, who served until 1946, when he was succeeded by George Szell. Carl J. Vosburgh became its able manager in 1933.

The Hotel Cleveland, on which work was begun in 1916, was completed and opened, December 16. The hotel site on the southwest corner of Superior Street and Public Square had been historically prominent since 1815. Operating under thirteen different names through the years, the property which had been sold to the Terminal Hotels Company on July 14, 1916, by John H. and Mary E. Buggie, became the site of the beautiful thousand-room hotel. It cost $4,500,000 or 1,000 times the outlay for the first Cleveland Hotel that stood on the same site in 1820. L. E. Pierce, the cordial first manager, continued in charge in the 1940s.

Leon D. Smith, an able air pilot, set out from Belmont Park, Long Island, on December 19, with four hundred pounds of mail for Cleveland and

Chicago. His was one of the early attempts to transport mail over a considerable distance. He was scheduled to land at Bellefonte, Pennsylvania, and turn the mail over to E. A. Johnson, who was to continue the journey. However, Smith lost his way and landed in a field near Pennsylvania State College. Johnson waited for some time, and then, without the mail, he proceeded to Cleveland. Here he could not find Woodland Hills Park, where he was scheduled to land, and instead came down on Richmond Road. The early days of air mail were not particularly promising.

The war over, Cleveland proudly reviewed the fine records made by its representatives at the battlefronts, in the camps, and at home—men and women who demonstrated their patriotism by practical service. Major General Clarence R. Edwards, in command of the 26th Division of New England troops, was famous for his leadership in France. Brigadier General Charles X. Zimerman commanded the 73rd Infantry Brigade including the old 5th Regiment of Cleveland; and Colonel John R. McQuigg gave able service in different capacities, among them as colonel of the 112th U.S. Engineers. The Cleveland Grays, Company F., 148th U.S. Infantry, under Colonel George Wood, made an excellent record. Among Cleveland's officers who won distinction were Lieut. Colonels Bascom Little, M. A. Fanning, Chester C. Bolton, F. B. Richards, and L. W. Blyth; Captain J. F. Devereux, Lieutenant Daniel Willard, and Captain H. P. Shupe. Among civilian leaders were J. Robert Crouse, director of the War Savings campaign; F. H. Goff, of the Capital Issues Committee; Christian Girl, aid in developing the Liberty Motor truck; Malcolm L. McBride, promoter of recreational activities in camps; B. W. Housum, of the Food Administration; and hundreds of others. The problems of housing, fuel, and food were made easier by a legion of earnest women working under the leadership of Belle Sherwin, chairman of the Cleveland branch of the Women's Committee of the Council of National Defense; Mrs. Henry L. Sanford, who succeeded Miss Sherwin when she undertook national duties; Ruth F. Stone, secretary of the committee; Mrs. E. S. Burke, Jr., leader in the Red Cross; Mrs. J. N. Fleming, president of the Federation of Women's Clubs; and others of the YWCA, and the various women's organizations who did many unwomanly tasks with a womanly graciousness.

1919

The southeast corner of Ontario Street and the Public Square, the land on which the Park Building and adjacent structures stood, was the most valuable acre in Cleveland, being assessed at $2,178,000. The Cleveland area had cost the Connecticut Land Company $14,502.40 in 1796; the land value in 1919, according to the county auditor, was $400,735,100, which did not include $393,729,220 for buildings, exclusive of exempted property. The district that became Cuyahoga County, totaling 463 square miles, had been purchased by the company originally for $118,528; the current land value was placed at $533,816,330, with improvements at $494,331,380, not including exempted property.

Through the generosity of Mrs. Dudley S. Blossom and Mrs. Chester C. Bolton, League House on Prospect Avenue was started as a low-cost, non-profit residence for young businesswomen.

Merrick House, a social settlement, was organized by the National Catholic War Council, but settlement activities and the day nursery were available to people of all religions. Situated at 2531 West 11th Street among many foreign-born, it provided recreational and cultural activities for young people.

Advertisements of department stores indicated that men's suits ranged from $18.50 to $25. Shirts were advertised at $1.20 each and junior-size dresses at from $3.45 to $4.65. An East Cleveland home with four bedrooms was offered for $5,400, and a smaller property could be had for $3,400, with $200 down. The advertised wage for unskilled labor was $15 a week, and 60 cents an hour was the minimum scale paid.

The Board of Education decided on January 10 to continue military training in the high schools as a health measure.

The Union Terminal plan was approved at the polls, January 10, by a vote of 30,758 to 19,916. This settled a long-disputed question concerning the proposed development on the Public Square. The Van Sweringens announced that trains entering the station would be electrified.

An extension of Chester Avenue, connecting East 17th Street with East 21st Street, was under way. Citizens recalled that Chester was originally Chestnut Street, running eastward from Erie to the easterly line of the J. M. Woolsey allotment, a line within what became East 13th Street. The thoroughfare was extended in 1863 to Dodge Street; and in 1889, it was carried from North Perry Street to Sterling Avenue. The section from East 30th to East 40th Street was opened in 1926. It was carelessly predicted in 1919 that the proposed entire length of Chester Avenue would be opened soon. A quarter century later, the effort was still being made to complete the avenue from East 55th to East 93rd Street, as the final link was needed desperately to ease the traffic problem.

The first night session in the history of the Police Court was held, January 27, to help dispose of more than three hundred crime-wave prisoners caught in the police dragnet.

The first concrete ship built on the Great Lakes was launched by the Liberty Shipbuilding & Transportation Company on February 3. It was a railroad barge 265 feet long, weighing 1,600 tons.

The first non-stop airplane flight between Cleveland and Washington was made in 2 hours and 58 minutes, an average of 117.5 miles per hour. The plane was built at the Glenn L. Martin plant in Cleveland and delivered to the Government.

The Cleveland Safety Council, organized this year, was preceded by only two similar organizations, in St. Louis and Pittsburgh. The council was self-financed and independent, using every dollar received from contributions and memberships for accident prevention. A budget of $15,000 was raised, offices were opened, and a safety program was instituted.

The Cleveland Aviation Club was formed for the promotion and protection of aviation interests; to conduct and encourage exhibitions and contests between all forms of flying machines; to foster the growth of aviation throughout the United States and particularly in Cleveland, and to co-operate in securing national, state, and local legislation for the advancement of aviation. At the twenty-seventh anniversary celebration in 1946, General Dwight D. Eisenhower was the guest of honor. The organization was at that time the largest of aviation clubs, its membership consisting of men who had flown in the army or had a civilian-pilot's license. The club's president was Miles C. McKearney.

A Food Show under the auspices of the Retail Grocers Association was held, February 7, at Central Armory and featured baking contests and free samples. This show and its successors proved highly successful annual events.

Attorney General John G. Price conferred with Federal Judge William L. Day, February 8, and Wilbur D. Wilkin was appointed to conduct a special grand-jury investigation into crime conditions. The Chamber of Commerce furnished funds to finance it.

By will of Andrew Squire, drawn February 12 and modified by seven codicils, the last dated July 3, 1933, his Valleevue farm of 250 acres, located in Orange Township, was left to Western Reserve University for the benefit of teachers and students of the College for Women (Flora Stone Mather College), for women students of other divisions of the university, and for the use of the university in the promotion of scientific, experimental studies in botany and pharmacy. The will expressed the desire that the farm be cultivated and preserved for educational and recreational purposes, and be kept as a place where the practical duties of life might be taught in close contact with the soil. In the wills of Mr. and Mrs. Squire, the university was constituted the residuary legatee of their estates for the benefit of the farm and for the institution. Provisions were made for maintaining and developing the farm, looking forward to the time when the principal provided for these purposes would equal three million dollars.

When the Fortnightly Club celebrated its Silver Jubilee in February by presenting a series of concerts, receptions, and luncheons, it was said to be the largest musical club in the United States. During this celebration, the Ohio Federation of Music Clubs was formed, and Mrs. Alice Bradley of Cleveland was elected president.

Robinson G. Jones became superintendent of Cleveland's public schools. Since the turn of the century, many new schools had been built, reflecting the changes that had come in methods. The old idea of teaching pupils to memorize their text-books had given way to providing a solid groundwork upon which to build a successful life. Teaching by radio was introduced during the administration of Dr. Jones. He stated that the purposes of the high schools should be to train young people to be healthy, to teach them social co-operation, to inspire them to do something that the world wants done, and to encourage them to make good use of leisure time. In this year, Edward M. Williams, a leader in philanthropic effort, became president of the Board of Education, his service as member having started in 1914. His efficient administration continued until 1932, when he resigned and was succeeded by Alfred A. Benesch.

Greater Cleveland welcomed home its "only army ace" on February 24. He was Lieutenant Frederick E. Luff, 3046 Lincoln Boulevard, Cleveland Heights.

An imaginary midwestern town in the United States became famous when Sherwood Anderson published the book *Winesburg, Ohio*. The author realistically described small-town people and their frustrated lives, and Winesburg to many was a classic symbol of a small American community. Cleveland took special interest in the book because many readers thought the location was Clyde, Ohio, where Anderson had spent his boyhood. Although the author died in 1941, the fame of his book lived on; and, more than a quarter of a century after publication, *Life* magazine featured it in a story because one of its artists announced that Clyde was the place he would most like to visit upon his return from the war. He found the people, the industries, and the environment much the same as they were pictured by the author in 1919.

Among the Clevelanders given exceptional honors for service in World War I was Milton C. "Muff" Portmann. He was major of the 353rd Infantry, 89th Division, and was at the front from August, 1918, until the end of the war, being in all offensives excepting that of Chateau-Thierry. He was wounded three times, and was awarded the Purple Heart, the Order of the Silver Star, the Order of Leopold I, and the Distinguished Service Citation—General Pershing's personal citation.

The Women's Advertising Club was organized to promote and encourage the work of women in the advertising field, and to assist in civic enterprises where a knowledge of advertising would be of value. The club became affiliated with the Advertising Federation of America. It joined in many civic campaigns, and in 1934 sponsored the first Intercity Conference of Women's Advertising Clubs. In 1946 it co-operated with Flora Stone Mather College in arranging an Advertising Conference, with a series of meetings addressed by leaders in the profession. The committee assisting Eleanor Frances Dolan, dean of the college, included Mrs. Cora Geiger Newald, chairman; Margaret Coe, Elizabeth Pratt, Hope Johnson, Elizabeth Kardos, Olive P. Gately, Eleanor Hanson, Catherine Dietz, Helen Gordon, and Mrs. Emerich Sabo. Erma Oehler was president.

There were only twenty employees on the payroll of the Cleveland Graphite Bronze Company when it was opened, March 22, to make new types of bearings and bushings against keen competition. Ben F. Hopkins was elected president; J. J. McIntyre, vice president; and James L. Myers, secretary-treasurer. The plant was located on East 152nd Street south of St. Clair Avenue. The rapidly growing business outgrew a succession of factories until 1939, when the old Great Lakes Airport was acquired to meet the needs of the world's largest producer of bearings and bushings. Developments were made that revolutionized the lined-bearing industry, improving the quality and performance of automobiles and trucks, and saving the public many millions of dollars. The history of this company, under the leadership of Hopkins, McIntyre, and Myers, became a romance of industry.

The Catholic Charities Corporation was organized with forty-five officers and trustees under the leadership of William F. Lyon. The organization had as its purpose advancing the work and objects of Roman Catholic charitable and benevolent institutions in the Diocese of Cleveland. It raised money to meet the costs of new institutions for child-care and for the aged, maintained homes for the aged, and provided funds to open Catholic agencies outside of Cleveland proper.

Secretary of the Treasury Carter Glass opened the Fifth War Loan drive, and was the guest of D. C. Wills, chairman of the Federal Reserve Bank of Cleveland. The city's goal in the campaign was $80,658,900 and the subscription and cash sales amounted to $84,380,950. The number of subscribers was 186,751. Again Cleveland went over the top and concluded the campaign with one of the most impressive successes in the nation.

Closer relationship, born of World War I, resulted in the merger, April 22, of The Cleveland Association of Congregational Ministers and Churches with The Congregational Union of Cleveland. The purposes of the Union were to plan new churches, aid existing churches, and help to develop in each church in the county a deep concern for community needs and world-wide tasks. The Rev. Robert Stemme, who had successfully rescued the East View Church, 15615 Kinsman, from foreclosure, was appointed executive secretary of the Union in 1937. The decade to follow was marked by a gain in church membership from 13,000 to 16,500, notable debt reductions, large building improvements, and an enlarged Christian-education program, much of the advance being credited by churchmen to his leadership.

Scores of May Day rioters faced the judge in Police Court following a clash between police and soldiers on one side and paraders carrying red flags.

The H. K. Ferguson Company, named for the founder, was organized to conduct a general engineering and building business in Ohio. So successful was the enterprise from the start that five years later its activities expanded to the Eastern and Central states, and, during the 1930s, to Canada, Mexico, and the Far East. In World War II the company was called upon by the Government to perform engineering and building services, including a large shell-loading plant and the construction of a portion of the atomic plant at Oak Ridge, Tennessee. In 1945 a group headed by the Oman family of Tennessee purchased the business and expanded its activities. A. K. Ferguson, who had been president, was succeeded by John Oman III.

Colonel Cecil B. Whitcomb received for exceptional services in World War I the Distinguished Service Cross, the Silver Star, and the Purple Heart before being discharged in May, 1919. He had served two years, having enlisted in the 5th Ohio Regiment, later known as the 145th Infantry, in the spring of 1917. He served in France and participated in the major offensives. In 1921 he re-enlisted in the 145th Infantry of the Ohio National Guard, was commissioned and served in all company and all staff grades.

The ancient art of enameling was revived commercially when Harry D. Cushman and Ray L. Williams of Cleveland organized the Ferro-Enameling

Company this year. In 1920 Robert A. Weaver founded the Ferro Enamel Supply Company. In 1930 the companies merged under the name Ferro Enamel Corporation, and the "Ferro check" became a familiar symbol. The industry's leading supplier of porcelain-enamel frits also produced porcelain for the finishing of ranges, bathtubs, sinks, and similar household appliances as well as signs, building parts, and store fronts. A period of development and expansion followed the merger in a wide variety of industries, with numerous acquisitions. Branches and subsidiaries of this international organization were managed from 4150 East 56th Street, Cleveland. Officers in 1947 included Robert A. Weaver, chairman of board; J. D. Henry, vice chairman of board; and C. D. Clawson, president.

During the past decade, a number of Clevelanders distinguished themselves in literary endeavors. Munson Havens wrote his delightful story, "Old Valentines," Fred C. Kelly kept his versatile pen busy with magazine articles and characteristic books of whimsical humor and practical philosophy; Charles W. Mears, dean of Cleveland advertising men, discussed the art of speaking, and Millicent Olmsted wrote popular books for children.

The amount of money dispersed by the Cleveland Foundation for charitable and educational purposes within the past year was $25,757.93. Clevelanders were coming to appreciate that the Foundation offered them the opportunity to serve their community through the years to come. National attention was being drawn to this pioneer community trust, and many cities were already considering the idea of profiting through Cleveland's plan. On the distribution committee at this time were Thomas G. Fitzsimons, Malcolm L. McBride, Belle Sherwin, Ambrose Swasey, and James D. Williamson.

Mrs. Harry L. Vail, president of the Cleveland Art Association, invited the Cleveland Museum of Art to co-operate in an annual exhibition of the work of Cleveland artists. Mrs. Grace Harman Mather was chairman, and all branches of art were represented. Thus the May Show was born. Among the many artists who exhibited their work were F. C. Gottwald, Gerrit A. Beneker, Gordon Barrick, Frank N. Wilcox, William J. Eastman, and Merle Boyer, prize winners. The May Shows were soon to become popular events of wide interest, attracting about seventy-five thousand visitors annually.

A corporate charter was issued to Ohio Legionnaires by the State of Ohio on May 15. During the summer months of 1919 there were 193 post charters granted throughout the State, and these early posts met in schools, churches, and lodge halls. Ohio's first County Council of the American Legion was formed in Cuyahoga County, a temporary organization being effected in Cleveland at the Hotel Hollenden on July 2, with Colonel Dudley J. Hard as acting chairman; Frank E. Sweeney, vice chairman, and Al N. Jappe, secretary. At the time of the formation of the Council, three posts in Cleveland held charters: the Arthur S. Houts Post No. 2, the Henry P. Shupe Post No. 22, and the Deckert-Watterson Post No. 26, with a combined membership totaling less than 150. An infant in 1919, Ohio's Legion grew rapidly, and within a year Cuyahoga County Council's membership was to be nearly 7,500 with 30 councils, 464 posts, and a state membership of more than

48,000. The Council participated in many civic and patriotic activities, and gave support to worthy local and national celebrations. In 1946 the officials were: commander, Edward J. Sklenica; vice commander, Walter E. Broge; treasurer, Alden H. Woodley; chaplain, C. Lester Henderson; and executive secretary, William McCourt. The membership was approximately 12,500 in 1946, and headquarters were at 3715 Euclid Avenue.

The announcement was made on May 15 that air-mail service would be attempted on a regular schedule between New York and Chicago, with Cleveland as the important intermediate point. One mail delivery a day was to be made, the planes landing at Woodland Hills Park, Cleveland's "post-age-stamp" airport. The first day's flights were successful and enthusiasts predicted trans-continental air-mail service.

Effie Ellsler, famous Cleveland actress, received a warm welcome as she appeared in *Old Lady 31* at the Shubert-Colonial Theater on May 29.

Dedication of the Liberty Row trees marked the Memorial Day observance. The trees, planted along the boulevards from Gordon Park up to the Heights, were described by W. R. Rose in the *Plain Dealer*:

> The little trees that line the way
> Are trembling in the chilly air;
> Beneath the Autumn winds they sway—
> God give them life and tender care.
>
> Each whispers of the nation's dead,
> Of ghostly hosts, of battles won,
> Of ravaged fields, of poppies red—
> Each wails the requiem of a son.
>
> A wreath has fallen from a limb—
> A mother came and hung it there,
> Then turned away with eyes grown dim
> And softly breathed an anguished prayer.
>
> The little trees that line the way,
> Sad symbols of a nation's pride,
> Are etched against the wintry grey—
> Oh, let them live for those who died!

The auditorium of the Masonic Temple was completed in June, and the remainder of the building at 3615 Euclid Avenue was finished in 1921. Al Koran Temple of the Mystic Shrine had purchased in 1914 the property on the north side of Euclid near East 35th Street, adjoining the site of the Henry Wick mansion, and across the street from the William J. Boardman residence, which was later converted into Temple Court. The opening of the auditorium was celebrated with a huge parade consisting of Shrine uniformed units of Cleveland and neighboring cities. The large building valued at two and a half million was the home of the Al Koran Shrine and

Scottish Rite bodies. The auditorium, seating 2,238 people, was to become the scene of many productions from boxing shows to grand opera. The stage was called one of the most completely equipped in the nation.

The Cleveland Advertising Club organized its Advertising School with Charles W. Mears, dean. Five years before, the club conducted a school for its members, known as the Analad Division, with Robert E. Fowler, director. The new school was opened to the public, and success was enjoyed from the time of the first enrollment. In 1943 the Advertising Club joined forces with Cleveland College in the continuance of the school which became known nationally.

Barclay Parsons & Klapp, consulting engineers, made their formal report to the Board of Rapid Transit Commissioners—C. A. Otis, president, on June 6, proposing a comprehensive transit plan for Cleveland. It contemplated a large subway station under the Public Square, with short subway branches east on Superior Avenue to East 10th Street, west on Superior Avenue to the High Level Bridge, east on Euclid Avenue to East 22nd Street and south on Ontario Street to the Central Market, the cars coming to level after leaving the congested central area. The total cost of this plan was estimated at fifteen million dollars. The citizenship, unfortunately for Cleveland, voted the project down and continued an old-fashioned transit system that added to congested traffic conditions and continuous parking problems. In its Sesquicentennial Year, Cleveland was still considering rapid-transit plans.

A branch of the Murray Body Company of Detroit was established in Cleveland to supply local automobile companies with automobile parts and stampings. Five years later when the parent company was reorganized, C. W. Hannon bought the Cleveland branch, which he had managed, and established the Murray Ohio Manufacturing Company. Until 1930, the character of the business remained unchanged, but with local automobile manufacturers going out of business, the company turned to the manufacture of wheel goods and became the largest producer in the world of "toys on wheels." In 1937 bicycles were added to the line, and so great was the demand for Murray Ohio products that 1500 workers were employed. The company's wheel goods were not only marketed throughout the United States but in many foreign countries. Hannon remained president when the company was completing its third decade.

Cathedral Latin School was dedicated, June 8. The first graduating class totaled seven. In ten years, there was a capacity enrollment of eight hundred boys, and the school soon won a high rating in scholarship and athletics.

A nationwide drive to jail radicals and Red agitators was started, June 12, as a result of the bombing of Mayor Davis' home.

Shaker Players, second of Greater Cleveland's senior dramatic groups, was organized under the direction of Mrs. William Cochran.

Jack Dempsey took the world's heavyweight title by defeating Jess Willard in Toledo, Ohio, on July 4, and carloads of Clevelanders journeyed to the neighboring city. Willard had held the title three years, and Dempsey was to be champion for seven years.

In response to an urgent call made by Newton D. Baker, Secretary of War, to co-ordinate woman power throughout the nation, a group of business and professional women from states east of the Rocky Mountains met in conference in July with the result that the National Business and Professional Women's Club came into existence. Leota Kelly of Cleveland signed the original articles of incorporation. Shortly thereafter, in November, the Cleveland club formed its unit. The purpose of the club was to elevate standards for women in business and professions, to stimulate interest in state and local groups, to bring about co-operation among women in these groups, and to promote educational opportunities for women in industrial, scientific, and vocational fields. K. Lucille Provo was president in 1946 when the membership was 220.

Lieutenant Commander Albert C. Reed and the crew of the *NC-4* that made a historic international flight were given an enthusiastic reception in Cleveland on July 13.

With two men out in the ninth inning, Babe Ruth came to bat at Dunn Field, July 18, and drove a four-run "homer" over the right-field fence, defeating the Indians, 8-7. Lee Fohl, Cleveland's manager, who had been the subject of mounting criticism, handed in his resignation to President James C. Dunn the next day. Tris Speaker took the reins, and the Indians held second place when the season closed.

Daniel Kaber, a well-known printer and publisher, was found murdered in his Lakewood home, July 18. The crime excited attention throughout the nation. Finally, the widow was found guilty of administering poison and hiring assassins. She was sent to Marysville prison to serve a life term.

Andrew Carnegie, iron founder and philanthropist, died August 11. Carnegie libraries in Cleveland and throughout the nation are among the heritages of this useful man who contributed to the cultural progress of humanity. Carnegie's only visit to Cleveland was as a witness in the Cassie Chadwick case, but he numbered many friends among the city's leading manufacturers.

On his return from Europe this year, A. J. Weatherhead, Jr., invested $1,000 of war-salary savings in a tool shop. His engineering education and experience were the background for his inventions, and during the twenties his little company expanded into a flourishing automotive-parts establishment. The original rented space on Frankfort Avenue had long since been outgrown, and the company which later occupied seven large shops in that neighborhood, moved in 1937 to 300 East 131st Street. In that year, plants were built in St. Thomas, Ontario, and Columbia City, Indiana, and later in Glendale, California. The industry was intensified in the late thirties, and particular progress was made in the hydraulics field. Products were made for use in automobiles, trucks, airplanes, mechanical refrigeration, industrial machinery, and numerous other fields. Albert J. Weatherhead, Jr., founder, was president of the Weatherhead Company in the 1940s.

Northeast Cleveland was chosen by the Third Reformed Church for its new home; and, on October 26, the cornerstone of a new house of worship was laid at 862 Eddy Road, during the ministry of the revered Dr. Henry

Schmidt, pastor. His long and fruitful service to the influential Third Evangelical and Reformed Church, as it was later called, came to an end in 1941, and, as pastor emeritus, he was succeeded by the Rev. Arnold W. Meckstroth. Olivet Evangelical and Reformed Church, the result of mergers of small churches, joined with the Third congregation to form Faith Church in 1945. Rev. Meckstroth became pastor of the united church on Eddy Road.

King Albert of Belgium with his royal party passed through the city during the night of October 8.

Cardinal Mercier visited Cleveland on October 17 and deeply impressed a great audience in the Hippodrome. A tribute to him appeared in a local paper:

> Fragile in figure, but great of soul—
> Lift high his name on the deathless roll.
> Braving the foemen whose cruel tide
> Swept o'er the land of his birth and pride;
> Shielding his people from death and blight,
> Fearless he stood for his God and right.
> There through the ages saintly he stands,
> Blessing his people with outstretched hands.
> Fragile in figure, but great of soul—
> Mercier shines on the deathless roll.

The initial Recreation Survey of the Cleveland Foundation proved a comprehensive community study covering recreation, as provided by public, private, and commercial agencies.

The work of the Committee of Fifteen to consider the City Manager Plan had been discontinued during World War I, and was resumed in the spring and summer months this year. Many meetings were held, and distinguished students of the manager plan appeared before the committee. In October two reports were submitted to the sponsoring group. The majority report, signed by seven members, called for "a straight manager form," embodying a municipal government headed by a business manager elected by the City Council, which would be chosen by proportional representation. The minority report, signed by five members, urged the continuation of the existing form of government, with an amended charter permitting the appointment of a business manager by the mayor in the interest of efficiency. The majority plan was later tried and then abandoned.

The nation's first Community Fund campaign, successor to the Victory Chest, was set in motion, November 18, with the following creed: "I will work and give without stint to raise the Community Fund and I will do my part to see that every man, woman or child who helps in raising the fund or for whom the fund is raised, is a better and more self-respecting resident of Cleveland." The goal of $3,425,000 was oversubscribed by 17.5 per cent, the amount raised being $4,026,600.72, contributed by 148,234 people. This was considered a daring step, and no other city followed Cleveland's plan for some time. Among those who led this campaign were Alva

Bradley, chairman, Charles A. Otis, Fred W. Ramsey, Paul L. Feiss, J. S. Crider, and William G. Mather.

City and state bowling championships were won and records were broken by the Ideal Greyhound women's team composed of Mrs. Clara Tomasch, Mrs. Goldie Greenwald, Mrs. Rose Gehring, Mrs. Martha Scott, and Mrs. Grace Garwood.

Clevelanders took keen interest in the announcement on December 27 that John D. Rockefeller, Jr., born in Cleveland, had made a gift of a hundred million dollars to be divided between the Rockefeller Foundation and the General Education Board. Thus he continued his father's generous spirit of giving.

The Seeandbee, *the largest and most costly sidewheel passenger steamer in the world, began her regular trips between Cleveland and Buffalo in 1913.*

CHAPTER 15

Turbulent Twenties

1920-1929

THE DECADE of the "turbulent twenties," the years following the Treaty of Versailles, was marked in the United States by industrial expansion and nationwide prosperity, after the primary postwar depression in the Harding "normalcy" era of 1921. England was suffering from unemployment and the dole, while Germany was agonized by inflation and humiliation that led eventually to the Nazi regime.

A great many Americans were accumulating money, speculating with some of it, riding in automobiles, attending movies, playing mah-jong, working crossword puzzles, and listening to that marvelous new contraption, the radio. It was the prohibition era, the racket period, the jazz age. Materialism was dominating idealism. This was a decade of new inventions and new developments. Many factories changed their products, and others held to the same lines but made remarkable improvements in their machinery. Technological progress had reached its highest point, and new capital awaited new opportunities.

A survey showed the results of the intensive development of our country. In 1920 the nation had nearly half of the railroad mileage of the world and 70 per cent of the telegraph and telephone lines. It was producing nearly 80 per cent of the copper of the world, 70 per cent of the petroleum, 90 per cent of the corn, 60 per cent of the wood, 60 per cent of the iron and steel, and 80 per cent of all of the automobiles. The world had come to recognize the United States as a nation of rapid growth and extraordinary wealth. It was also coming to know Cleveland as a pacemaker among American cities.

In this decade, many ideas that were developed in wartime were being turned to peacetime advantage. The telephone was an example. Bell's "toy" had become a business necessity, with long-distance and transatlantic service speeding up the nation's business. The airplane was making similar advance, and in May, 1927, a great throng in Paris witnessed the conclusion of the first Atlantic flight by one person, when a young man shook hands with Ambassador Herrick of Cleveland and said, "I am Charles Lindbergh."

Farmers were enjoying many improvements with the introduction of new tractors and other advanced machinery. Better lighting was developed, and electric refrigerators and time- and labor-saving appliances were adding comfort to the American home. Chain stores grew in popularity, and filling stations became business institutions wherever there were highways. War had impressed upon the American people the advantages of banks and the desirability of buying bonds. Savings were growing rapidly, and the services of trust companies were used more than ever before.

Tens of thousands became investors and boosted the stock market, some making fantastic fortunes; the Florida boom was attracting millions, the bank clearings in Miami totaling more than a billion dollars in 1925.

Mayor Harry L. Davis resigned as mayor of Cleveland in the spring of 1920 to run for governor. His opponent, A. Vic Donahey, had a strong following, but again, genial, likable Davis proved his ability as a campaigner, and the boy of the rolling mills became governor of one of the greatest states. In 1924 in the gubernatorial campaign, "Honest Vic" Donahey defeated Davis, although the latter carried Cleveland and Cuyahoga County by a large majority.

In 1921 seven candidates entered the mayoralty race, including William S. FitzGerald, who as law director filled out the term of Davis after the latter resigned to run for governor. One of the candidates was Fred Kohler, who had been police chief in Johnson's time and had also served as county commissioner. He was vigorous and independent, and his platform was "to make life and property safe, and live within his income." Never had Cleveland witnessed such a campaign. Kohler "gum-shoed" from house to house, rang doorbells, talked to people in homes, at corner shops, any place but on the platform. He apparently had no organized backing, and yet his system worked, partly because Cleveland wanted a change. He was elected mayor, defeating FitzGerald by 4,500 votes. Kohler drove the police chief out of office, fought the City Council, showed strong prejudices, economized at the expense of service, and led to the conclusion that "the City Hall was a circus with Kohler as ringmaster."

Cleveland naturally became ambitious to lead the way in city government as well as in business and cultural advance. The first experiment with the City Manager Plan by a large municipality was watched with keen interest by the nation. Cleveland's first city manager, efficient and enthusiastic William R. Hopkins, served from 1924 to 1929. However, the politicians were bitterly opposed to the new form of government which deprived them of power. While the city administration was dominated by efficiency, it did not necessarily reflect the voters' wishes; the public lost interest in the plan and joined political leaders in repudiating it. Harry L. Davis and his followers persuaded the people to restore the old Federal Plan. The fact that capable men filled the office and directed constructive achievements did not prevent abandonment of the City Manager Plan along with proportional representation in the early thirties.

Cleveland had been a strategic political center since the early days, and it was natural that the Republican Party should choose the city for its national convention in 1924. An important factor was the Public Auditorium and its many advantages. It was a foregone conclusion that President Coolidge would be renominated; and while there was little excitement, Cleveland was gratified to play host to a great throng of distinguished visitors. Women were enjoying their new privilege, woman suffrage, and the League of Women Voters was beginning to wield an influence.

Clevelanders discussed the cost of living more than any other subject. Clothing and food had soared early in the decade, but within a year both approached normal levels, where they remained until the stock-market crash of 1929 when all major items in the family budget dipped low.

The first World War was followed by three waves of business activity. The postwar-inflation cycle continued through the stimulated prosperity of 1919 and 1920 and ended during the severe depression of 1921. The recovery cycle began in the summer of 1921 and continued through the brief prosperity period of 1923, concluding in the mild depression of 1924; and then followed what was called the Coolidge prosperity cycle, lasting until the financial crash at the close of 1929.

As usual, Americans swung the pendulum too far in the twenties. Installment buying gained a firm foothold in Cleveland and the nation. Loans measured by billions were freely made to foreign countries in the name of postwar reconstruction with the hope that dividends would come in the form of foreign trade. It was the old story of easy-come-easy-go, with the taxpayer footing the bills.

A city's advance depends in large measure upon the faith, resourcefulness, and hard work of its citizenship, but another important influence is the growth and progress of the nation in which it is located. Enterprising and diligent Clevelanders had advanced the industrial, commercial, and cultural standing of their city in the decade 1910-1919. The city had become fourth in the nation in the percentage of homes owned. Citizens knew their municipality was more than keeping pace with the advance of the nation, but they knew also that the general progress of America was contributing to the forward march of the place they called home.

This was an era of metropolitan expansion, made easier through an improved transit system and new bridges crossing the valley. A number of self-contained communities on the outskirts of the city were growing at a more rapid pace than Cleveland. The Van Sweringens purchased a railroad system to make possible rapid transit connecting their beautiful Shaker Heights development with downtown Cleveland. Expansion of their transit plans along railroad rights-of-way to east and west was halted by times and conditions they could not control.

The *Clevelander* pointed out that from 1910 to 1927, airplane speed increased from 40 miles to 278 miles per hour, payloads from 200 pounds to more than 6 tons, and altitude from one to 7$\frac{7}{10}$ miles. At this time, Cleveland was making fine progress in aviation, the Glenn L. Martin Company being an outstanding producer of airplanes, and many industrial companies were making parts. As the city had fumbled the automotive business, so it lost its pioneer aviation industry. Baltimore offered Martin superior advantages late in the decade, and Cleveland's failure to meet the competition cost the city another major industry. However, the lake city continued to develop leadership in aviation-parts production.

The Cleveland Municipal Airport opened in 1925 and was growing in area, equipment, and traffic. The hope of City Manager William R. Hopkins and Commissioner John "Jack" Berry that Cleveland would have the largest municipal airport was being realized. A great stimulant to air activity came late in the twenties in the form of the National Air Races which centered the attention of all nations upon Cleveland.

Automotive improvements had outmoded the Model T. Automobiles were being turned out in ever greater numbers, leading to improved concrete highways throughout the nation. Many Cleveland automotive concerns were profiting, and the transition from the making of cars to the production of bodies and parts was under way in the city. The motor car was changing the habits of the people as more families drove to the country, played golf, tennis, or baseball, or enjoyed picnics. Outlying locations were being brought closer to the Public Square through the automobile and extended streetcar lines. Buses were being introduced on Cleveland streets, proving their worth on feeder lines. Railroads expanded their services, and this was a period of travel when hotels prospered.

A survey of labor organizations showed that Cleveland was a center of union activities. Largest of the labor organizations was the Brotherhood of Locomotive Engineers with six lodges in the city and the Engineers Building as the main headquarters. There were 85,000 members in the United States, and Warren S. Stone was grand chief. Other strong railroad organizations were the Brotherhood of Railroad Trainmen and the Brotherhood of Locomotive Firemen and Enginemen. There were about 150 labor unions in the city, most of them belonging to the American Federation of Labor under the able direction of Samuel Gompers. The goals of the unions continued to be better hours, better working conditions, and better wages. Strikes were being reduced in number through conferences of employers and employees.

In 1924 there were 226 fraternal units in the city, 268 clubs of various kinds, and numerous organizations devoting their efforts to philanthropic causes. The number of civic and business associations was growing, and Cleveland was adding to its national reputation as a center of organized effort for the protection and progress of its citizens.

A large number of small banks had sprung up in the prosperity period of the past twenty years, and bank consolidations were the order of the day. Financial leaders felt that efficiency would be served by consolidating institutions into banks with larger capital and surplus. Furthermore, in great industrial centers, stronger banks were required to provide ample services for greatly expanding mass-production industries, and to advance public improvements. For some time, a merger of several of Cleveland's principal banks and many of its smaller institutions was considered; and shortly after the decade opened, the city became the home of America's fifth largest trust company, the Union Trust, a combination of twenty-nine establishments.

The population of Cuyahoga County was 943,495 in 1920, a gain of almost 50 per cent during the decade ending in 1919. The city, however, showed an advance of about 42 per cent, its total of 796,841 including twenty-nine nationalities, the largest being Polish-speaking people of whom there were more than 130,000. Nearly 45 per cent of Polish families owned their homes. Other large groups were the Hungarians, Germans, Czechs, Russians, Italians, Jugoslavs, and Austrians. These newcomers found a common bond in the expanding Cultural Gardens and gained encouragement in the increasing activities of the Public Library, which was circulating more books per capita than the library of any other large city—3,477,645 in 1919.

The 1920 census revealed that Cleveland led the ten largest cities in the percentage of those from seven to thirteen years of age who attended school. Only Los Angeles surpassed Cleveland in the fourteen-to-fifteen-year group. The public-school system was broadening to keep pace with community growth and technical needs. Cleveland College, a downtown experiment in adult education, found immediate acceptance and support. Originating in the YMCA, Fenn College filled an educational need, particularly in scientific fields.

Playhouse Square was being developed from East 9th Street to East 17th. Keith's Palace opened as America's most beautiful playhouse, and the Stillman, Allen, State, Ohio, and Lake made a remarkable line of fine theaters on Euclid Avenue. The Hanna on East 14th Street became the successor to the famous Euclid Avenue Opera House and presented the leading road shows. Sound was introduced into motion pictures, and there was some doubt as to whether the "talkies" would succeed. With the development of Playhouse Square came the establishment of numerous fine shops to make the upper-downtown district one of Ohio's leading shopping centers. Interest in the little-theater movement was quickened by the opening of the new Play House on the East Side and the Lakewood Little Theater on the West Side.

The twenties proved Cleveland a city of music lovers and of musical talent. The Metropolitan Grand Opera Company set new world's records of attendance and receipts in the Public Auditorium. Then came the thirty-sixth annual Saengerfest, attracting four thousand musical enthusiasts to the city. The Orpheus Male Chorus won international attention when it received the highest choral honor in Wales. The newly founded Cleveland Institute of Music, Singers Club, Fortnightly Chorus, Lutheran Chorus, and others were also playing their parts in making Cleveland a City of Song. As for popular music, the best-selling recordings were *Old Folks at Home,* sung by Schumann-Heink; *Blue Diamonds,* sung by Henry Burr; and *I Love the Land of Old Black Joe.*

Despite static and unreliable reception, the crystal set brought to Cleveland homes the pioneering programs of WHK and WTAM early in the twenties. These stations took their places as broadcasting leaders in the great new field of entertainment. Capitalizing upon the success of radio, industrial companies were producing a volume of equipment in the mid-decade that entitled the city to the rating of third largest radio center. Heading entertainment programs around town were a number of popular band and orchestra leaders whose names were soon to appear in lights across the nation.

Booksellers were featuring *The Four Horsemen of the Apocalypse* by Ibanez, *Man of the Forest* by Zane Grey, *Now It Can Be Told* by Philip Gibbs, *The Outline of History* by H. G. Wells, *The Age of Innocence* by Edith Wharton, *Main Street* by Sinclair Lewis, *If Winter Comes* by A. S. M. Hutchinson, *So Big* by Edna Ferber, and *All Quiet on the Western Front* by Erich M. Remarque. Other popular authors were Booth Tarkington, James Branch Cabell, Gertrude Atherton, and Thornton Wilder.

Bobbed hair was the fashion, and smoking in public by women was becoming an accepted practice. The evolution in bathing costumes was shocking as the bare-knee trend won approval. Skirts grew shorter and shorter in the daytime and longer in the evening. Waistlines approached the knees. Attired in narrow, short-skirted suits and flaring, belted coats, fashionable ladies adopted a "slinky walk, a sort of hand-on-hips glide," and they were lacking in chic unless they wore needle-pointed slippers. Women dressed for the occasion "to preserve femininity and to demonstrate independence."

A marathon terpsichorean expert danced eighty-six hours and claimed a record, and prosaic critics asked, "So what?" Cleveland witnessed several of the ridiculous and degrading competitions. Flag-pole sitting became popular to the entertainment of some and the disgust of others. Eskimo pie, a new frozen confection made locally, was the favorite hot-weather treat.

The Cleveland Indians won the American League pennant and the World Series in 1920! Baseball enthusiasm reached its peak in the historic game that witnessed a triple play unassisted and a home run with the bases filled at the expense of Brooklyn. The amateurs, too, were having their day, with the organization of the Cleveland Baseball Federation, which gave practical support to the game on the sandlots. The city's interest in the amateurs was evidenced when thousands of rooters cheered the teams that were striving for local and national championships. The biggest crowds gathered in the Brookside Park bowl. Cleveland was setting an example for the nation by promoting good sportsmanship.

The development of the Metropolitan Park System proceeded rapidly. The announcement was made that, under the direction of the Metropolitan Park Board, Cleveland had begun the construction of a belt of parks and parkways around the city, surpassing any similar venture in the country. Helping to popularize and make valuable this vast project was the Cleveland Museum of Natural History, which had its origin in the 1840s. Through its extensive programs and exhibits, the public was inspired to take a keener interest in the development of plant and animal life from prehistoric days to the present, and to find fuller enjoyment in the city's parks. Museum collections were enriched by the important South American explorations of the schooner *Blossom*.

The most beautiful art museum in the nation deserved surroundings in keeping with the white marble structure. When the Olmsted brothers' recommendations required substantial donations, the women of the Garden Club, imbued with Cleveland's co-operative spirit, raised more than two hundred thousand dollars, the city furnishing nearly an equal amount to provide approaches and surroundings.

The Cleveland Group Plan made substantial progress with the building of two impressive structures: the monumental Public Library and the Public Auditorium, the main hall of which was opened in 1922 and the music and north halls in 1929. The Public Auditorium far surpassed any convention and exposition hall in size and beauty. Plans were under way for the Board of Education Building, which would fill in the area between the Public Library and the Auditorium on the east side of the Mall.

To the average Clevelander, conventions were interpreted by throngs of visitors wearing badges, and bands playing spirited accompaniments for marching delegations on decorated downtown streets. The public could hardly be expected to appreciate the far-reaching importance of the business brought to Cleveland by the Convention Board of the Cleveland Chamber of Commerce under the management of A. J. Kennedy. The Public Auditorium had fulfilled every expectation in attracting the country's largest gatherings. In 1922, there were 162 conventions held in the city, attended by 72,450 delegates and visitors whose estimated expenditures in the community amounted to $2,535,750. Year by year, new high records were established. The Convention Board reported in 1927 that $147 was spent in Cleveland for every dollar invested in obtaining conventions; and, in 1930, $7,251,735 of outside money was spent by 143,628 delegates and visitors attending 237 conventions.

Industrial growth was marked by the erection of giant commercial buildings of surpassing character. The home of the Federal Reserve Bank truly represented the importance of the vast district it served; the towering Engineers Bank Building was a great credit to union labor; the Union Trust Building, with its mammoth banking quarters, was among the outstanding office buildings of the nation; the Ohio Bell Telephone Building was a marvel of engineering and architectural achievement; the Hanna Building was a majestic addition to upper downtown; and the Cleveland Discount (later NBC) Building was an impressive improvement on Superior Avenue.

A great medical center, known as the University Hospitals Group, with the Medical School of Western Reserve University as its nucleus, envisioned by Samuel Mather and his associates, was to become one of Cleveland's most valuable assets. The plans called for a grouping of health institutions that would soon rank in importance with similar projects in New York and Baltimore.

The expectation of life had advanced materially since the turn of the century. The Bureau of Public Health stated that the average expectation of life in the nation in 1900 was 49.24 years, while in 1920 it was 54.09 years. Better health was fostered by better medical care and by health education in the schools. In 1922 the death rates caused by typhoid, diphtheria, influenza, and tuberculosis went down rapidly; but many more people were dying from cancer, diabetes, and heart diseases. The automobile death rate was climbing steadily in keeping with the increase of automobile production.

The new Cleveland Clinic suffered one of the city's greatest disasters late in the decade. Within two years, the institution had experienced adversities so great that many believed it could not survive. Drs. George W. Crile and William E. Lower continued the work, their confidence in the future of the Clinic unshaken. Beneficent Clevelanders came forward with encouragement, and a new and greater institution rose from the ruins.

For several years speculation founded upon a get-rich-quick philosophy had been gathering momentum. Toward the end of the decade economists warned gently that business was entering upon a period of temporary readjustment. Students of the market knew that stock prices had reached dangerously high levels, but nobody seemed to know what to do about it. Wealthy speculators had been buying in great volume, apparently believing that business would come out of its recent slump. One day in the spring of 1929, Radio jumped eighteen points while General Motors was rising five. New records for total volume of trading were broken again and again. Playing the stock market became a national game, and hundreds of thousands were counting prospective profits when they read the fascinating market reports in their newspapers.

Then came the crash. The stock-market bubble burst, the Florida boom collapsed, Great Britain went off the gold standard, and confusion reigned. Many who thought themselves rich found that not only their estimated fortunes but also their savings had disappeared, and suicides were numerous.

The Turbulent Twenties closed with a foreboding outlook for the future. Economic instability had thrown a pall of anxiety over Cleveland and the nation. The threat of collapse and dark days ahead dampened the spirits of thousands of families who had been enjoying high incomes and light-hearted living. Some found comfort in the city's unusual ability to weather panics in the past; but even as they sought reassurance, the relentless figure of the Great Depression was stalking across the land, sparing no man.

1920

The population of Cleveland was 796,841, an increase of 42.12 per cent over 1910. There were 762,390 whites in the city and 34,451 Negroes; 236,000 newcomers had arrived in the decade; 239,538 foreign-born residents were reported, making the city one of the leading cosmopolitan centers.

Statisticians brought out interesting facts about Cleveland to indicate its growth and standing. There were 410 churches in the city; 17 child-welfare agencies; 80 charity societies with 50 branches; 680 agencies of the Public Library; 23 banks; 43 miles of boulevards; 2,673 acres of park land; 14 daily newspapers, 4 of them published in foreign languages; and 55 weekly publications, 16 in foreign languages. Conventions and tourists found ample accommodations in the city's 76 hotels; more than 5,000 rooms were available in downtown hostelries. The strain on Cleveland's 14 auditoriums would be relieved by the new Public Auditorium, under construction. There were about 125,000 buildings in Cleveland; 2,830 grocery and meat stores were counted. Eighty bridges, totaling seven miles, spanned the valleys, some of them structures of outstanding engineering achievement. Cleveland had 2,204 streets extending 886 miles, of which 601 were paved; 791 miles of sewers, 384 miles of street railways, and 985 miles of water mains. These and many other advantages made Cleveland a good place in which to live and earn a living.

On January 5 Canadian officials thanked John D. Rockefeller for his gift of five million dollars to promote medical education in Canada.

The Brooklyn Branch of the YWCA was formed. A gymnasium and swimming pool were added at the Central Building through a gift of Mrs. F. F. Prentiss, and the Lakewood, East Side, and Northeast branches were opened.

The Cleveland chapter of the Veterans of Foreign Wars of the United States was organized, and posts were established throughout the county. The first post, No. 84, was commanded by George Collyer. In the mid-1940s there were sixty posts in Greater Cleveland with a membership of fifteen thousand. Andrew Vidra served as commander during the first half of 1946 and was succeeded by Robert R. Hill.

On January 13 the first steps were taken to organize the institution which became the American Plan Association. A group of Cleveland industrialists created this organization to provide a means whereby employers could meet to consider methods of solving various industrial problems of common interest to themselves, their employees, and the community in general. In 1930 the name was changed to The Associated Industries of Cleveland. Officers in 1946 were Clarence L. Collens, president; Charles J. Stilwell, vice president; George S. Case, treasurer; William Frew Long, chairman of the advisory committee; and Chester Nikodym, secretary and manager. Collens was succeeded by W. R. Burwell.

The Secretary of State proclaimed the Liquor Prohibition Amendment to be in effect, January 16. In Cleveland, the fight to abolish the liquor traffic had been waged since the early days, women having maintained militant leadership. Before the amendment was passed, there were nearly three thousand saloons in the City of Cleveland. Enforcement of the prohibition laws met with opposition and evasion; and disorder, gang wars, and crime waves in the nation were charged to the dry amendment. Strong antagonism brought repeal on December 5, 1933.

The Rockefeller Building became the Kirby Building when Josiah Kirby, president of the Cleveland Discount Company, became owner after a lawsuit forced John D. Rockefeller, Jr., to fulfill an agreement to sell to Kirby. John D., Sr., objected to the change in name and bought the building back in 1923 at a reported price of $2,972,000, restoring the name Rockefeller.

The Euclid Avenue Association was organized, April 7, to aid in the maintenance and improvement of Euclid Avenue and adjacent streets from the Public Square to Lakeview Road, and to promote civic improvements and transportation facilities. H. P. McIntosh, Jr., was the first president, and his successors were W. A. Greenlund, Mark L. Thomsen, Morris A. Black,

Walter L. Flory, and Robert H. Jamison. J. M. Berne was the first secretary in 1920 and he has continued in an executive capacity since that time. Guy M. Mahon served as director, 1934-1947, and was succeeded by Leonard S. York.

Service on the Moreland rapid-transit line to Shaker Heights was launched on April 11, and on the Shaker line on August 16. The Cleveland Railway Company, by request, operated these lines until 1930, when the Van Sweringens assumed control and operation with their Cleveland Interurban Railroad Company. This organization became so financially involved that Cleveland banks took control in 1937, managing the lines until they were sold to the City of Shaker Heights in 1944.

John D. Rockefeller, Jr., declaring the "brotherhood of man" idea the only remedy for world unrest, opened a world drive in Cleveland on April 12 for a $336,000,000 interchurch world movement. Although it was a business-like plan with many constructive features, the undertaking failed to achieve its goal.

William Butler Yeats, the Irish poet, was a guest in Cleveland in April. He planted a tree in the Shakespeare Garden in Rockefeller Park, and was entertained by the Drama League and the Federation of Women's Clubs, under whose auspices he spoke at Hotel Statler.

Following the eastward trend, Cowell & Hubbard moved into their new building at East 13th and Euclid in the spring, and President Addison T. Hubbard's little grandson unlocked the front door. A portion of the property on which the W. J. Boardman home had stood served as the location. Preserving the family tradition, Sterling B. Hubbard succeeded his father as head of Cleveland's oldest jewelry firm in 1930.

Alva Bradley was elected president of the Cleveland Chamber of Commerce. During the decade, he was succeeded by Alexander C. Brown, 1921; Newton D. Baker, 1922; Richard F. Grant, 1923; Edward B. Greene, 1924; Andrew Squire, 1925; William B. Stewart, 1926; I. F. Freiberger, 1927; and Allard Smith, 1928-29.

Whiting Williams, author, lecturer, and educator, who had directed the Cleveland Federation for Charity and Philanthropy in 1912, went to Great Britain to study industrial conditions. He worked in the coal pits of Wales and Scotland, and later took industrial jobs in France and Germany to become acquainted with the workers and learn their viewpoint on industrial problems. His investigations became nationally known.

The Cleveland League of Women Voters was organized on April 22 to encourage citizens to participate in government activities, to acquire political education, to promote growth of the citizen, and to achieve eventual success for democracy. The league's first president was Belle Sherwin. After the close of World War I, a committee of the league, considering problems of peace, proved to be the forerunner of the Foreign Affairs Council in Cleveland. In 1933 Mrs. Malcolm L. McBride was elected president of the league, serving again in 1943. She had been active in state and national organizations. Acting as president of the organization in 1946 was Mrs. Edward J. Kenealy.

When Mayor Davis resigned on May 1 to conduct his successful campaign for governor of the State, William S. FitzGerald, by virtue of his position as director of law, became mayor. He had been a member of the Cleveland Bar since 1904, served two terms as councilman from the Eleventh Ward, was minority leader of the Council, and was widely known as a public speaker. He was defeated at the polls in 1921 by Fred Kohler.

The orange-and-black color scheme, by which the municipal administration designated park property, was the subject for numerous jokes. Practical pranksters painted the turtles in the Public Square pool the municipal colors to the delight of Clevelanders.

The Cleveland Institute of Music was founded by prominent citizens, led by Mrs. Franklyn B. Sanders. The first president of the board of trustees was Willard M. Clapp, and well-known Clevelanders on the executive committee included Mrs. D. Z. Norton, Mrs. Worcester R. Warner, Victor W. Sincere, Mrs. Frank Muhlhauser, Dr. Charles E. Briggs, Mrs. Albert S. Ingalls, Mrs. Otis Southworth, and Mrs. James E. Ferris. Seven students enrolled in the first institute at 3146 Euclid Avenue, formerly the Hall home; an average enrollment of a thousand was reached in the early 1940s. The institution was moved successively to the Chisholm home, 2827 Euclid; the Samuel Mather home, 2605 Euclid; and thence to the Jacob D. Cox home at 3411 Euclid Avenue, where Willard Clapp Hall, a fine auditorium seating four hundred, was added. Its directors were Ernest Bloch, internationally known composer; Mrs. Sanders, who became director emeritus; and Beryl Rubinstein, distinguished concert pianist and composer.

A Chicago company purchased control of the famous Hotel Hollenden from the Hollenden Corporation this year, but management eventually returned to Cleveland. As expansion in the early years became necessary, properties of the Sterling and Farmer families were acquired—the residence of James and Meribah Farmer was the birthplace of the Friends Church in Cleveland. In March, 1926, a $5,250,000 building program was begun, carrying out the ideas of the founder, Liberty E. Holden. An annex was added to the east, and the rear section of the main building was modernized. Ben Tobin purchased the historic house in 1945, and Alexander P. Spare of the board of trustees began operating it. In November, 1946, the Hollenden, one of the country's leading commercial hotels, had its face washed for the first time, and the rejuvenating measure disclosed a complexion of white and beautiful terra-cotta.

Under agreements with the Cleveland School of Education, Western Reserve University and the Board of Education through a joint committee offered courses for teachers in service who wished to qualify for salary advance in the public schools and for a bachelor's degree. In 1928 the university organized its own School of Education into which were merged the Cleveland Kindergarten-Primary Training School—a private school founded in 1894 to train teachers—and the Senior Teachers College under which name the joint committee of the School Board and Western Reserve University administered the courses for teachers in service. The Normal School, later known as the Cleveland School of Education, had been conducted by the Cleveland Board of Education since 1876. Western Reserve University for years offered some preparation for secondary teaching in The College for Women (later Flora Stone Mather) and in Adelbert College, later organizing a department of education in Mather College in which both Mather and Adelbert students could take technical courses for certification while completing the undergraduate courses. In 1928 the university's School of Education was conducted by a board consisting of representatives of the Board of Education and of the university. It was decided in 1945 to liquidate the School of Education, transfer its full-time women students to Mather College and its full-time men students to Adelbert College. It was agreed that the courses of teachers in service should be transferred to Cleveland College. The university Division of Education became responsible on the campus and in Cleveland College for the technical courses required by state law.

Interest in tennis began to grow when the East End Tennis Club built new courts on Carnegie Avenue west of East 77th Street early in the century. Inter-city tournaments were played here. Women were slow in joining in the game, but each year showed an increasing number who endeavored to develop their skill despite long, cumbersome skirts. The leading tennis players in Cleveland during the past decade included Kirk M. Reid, Charles A. Carran, Harold Bartel, Ralph Oster, Paul Westenhaver, Walter Westerbrook, Sam Nash, Willis Fulton, Vinton Vernon, Andrew Ingraham, Joseph C. Royan, W. H. Prescott, Orville W. Prescott, Franklyn B. Sanders, Harold T. Clark, Kenneth B. Wick, Carl R. Apthorp, Edith and Mabel Boardman, Alice Cobb, Helen Miller, Jennette Kinney, Florence Brown, and Marjorie Bain.

Cleveland's first outdoor air show opened at Dunhamton Field, southeast of Garfield Park on July 2, with Rex L. Uden, secretary of the Cleveland Aviation Club, as manager. Three planes were shown.

The first half of the American League season closed on July 11 with Cleveland in first place with a percentage of .662, while the Yankees were just behind with .658. Tris Speaker had set a new record of eleven consecutive hits.

The Brotherhood of Locomotive Engineers Co-operative National Bank, the first bank of its kind in the United States, opened in a corner restaurant room and employed ten people. The purpose was primarily to loan funds of the Brotherhood and to encourage members to build homes. In five years, resources of the institution exceeded twenty-eight million dollars. It was organized under the direction of Warren S. Stone, head of the Brotherhood, who served as president until his death in 1925. During this year, the bank moved into its magnificent new home at Ontario and St. Clair, with William B. Prenter as president. Banking quarters were also maintained in the Brotherhood Building at 308 Euclid Avenue. C. Sterling Smith succeeded Prenter in 1930 when the bank was reorganized as the Standard Trust Bank. The institution was not a member of the Cleveland Clearing House nor of the Federal Reserve Bank, and Cleveland depositors were relatively few. On December 21, 1931, the State Banking Department took over the Standard for liquidation at the request of the bank's directors. It was found that large loans were being made to friends of the president with inadequate security.

President Smith was tried for misapplication of funds, was found guilty and sentenced to the penitentiary. The closing of the institution brought to an end the union banking experiment.

The National Dancing Masters held their annual convention in Cleveland on August 8 and condemned the "shimmy" and "jazz" dances.

The funeral of Harry Bernstein, popularly called "Czar" because of his dominant political position, was attended by many hundreds of friends on August 9. He had founded the Perry Bank, was a leader in Jewish dramatic circles, and had befriended the poor.

Streetcar officials declared on August 14 that a six-cent fare and a penny transfer would necessarily be the rule after September 1. The days of three-cent fare gave no promise of return. Summertime rides in street cars averaged roughly thirty-eight million miles a month. Many complained about the "roughly."

In a book of the stage by Clayton Hamilton, two Clevelanders were prominently mentioned: Abraham Lincoln Erlanger and Arthur Hopkins. Erlanger, whose first acquaintance with the theater was gained by selling peanuts and running a check-room in local playhouses, had become one of the world's great producers. Of Hopkins the writer said, "His stage direction is admirable, not so much because of what he does, as because of what he refuses to do."

The Tennessee Legislature was the thirty-sixth and binding assembly to enfranchise the women of America, and the colorful fight for woman suffrage came to an end on August 19. Cleveland women had been leaders in the movement since the 1870s.

Johnny Kilbane, world featherweight champion, defended his title successfully against Arty Root before fourteen thousand people at Dunn Field. Johnny was a master of footwork and fast boxing, and was also one of the ring's cleverest strategists.

Thousands assembled at St. John's Cathedral on August 20 for the funeral of Ray Chapman who was killed by a pitched ball at the New York Polo Grounds on August 16. Chapman was called the best shortstop in the American League, and he had been one of the most popular players of his time. Rev. William A. Scullen, chancellor of the diocese, eulogized Chapman as typifying the spirit of youth. Baseball leaders from other cities came to Cleveland to pay their respects. The morale of the Indians received a severe blow, but the team rallied with the spirit of "do it for Ray," and the world championship was won. Chapman's death brought a public demand for rules governing pitching.

Prince Carol of Rumania visited Cleveland, August 21, and, as a guest of Cleveland Rumanians and the Chamber of Commerce, he toured the city and was given luncheon and dinner parties. The crown prince had only one regret—that the Indians were not playing at home.

Labor leaders were seriously surveying the union situation on Labor Day. There was no parade and no demonstration in Cleveland. The World War over, a new battle developed between industry and labor which involved wage-cutting and strikes, and most of the strikes were lost by the unions.

Between 1920 and 1923, the American Federation of Labor lost more than a million members. Employment was falling off, and labor's standard of living declined.

The first scientific study of atmospheric pollution—the smoke nuisance—was made by the J. H. Herron Company for the Community Betterment Council; but through lack of law enforcement, smoke continued its economic waste.

Mrs. Frances Payne Bolton and her sister, Mrs. Dudley S. Blossom, turned over the historic Perry house, 2157 Euclid Avenue, to the nursing groups of the city, and it became known as the Cleveland Nursing Center. These civic-minded women were quietly and continuously giving money and encouragement to worthy undertakings.

Transcontinental air-mail service was started, September 20, two planes leaving Mineola Field, New York, one at 6:30 A.M., the other an hour later. Both planes landed at Martin Field on the east side of Cleveland. Both flights were completed in San Francisco, the time being four hours better than train schedules, and cross-country air-mail service was heralded as a success.

The American Legion opened its second national convention, September 27, in Cleveland. Twenty thousand soldiers marched in the parade on the second day of the three-day reunion. The war was fresh in the minds of the veterans, and the spirit of fun-making did not dominate the gathering as in later years.

Tris Speaker's Indians won the American League pennant on October 2. Henry P. Edwards wrote in the *Plain Dealer* that the fans failed to "go hysterical" because they were so dazed, having seen home teams come close to a league pennant many times, only to fail in the final weeks. Cleveland had been in first place nearly all of the year, and finally won 98 games, while losing 56. Manager Speaker had a batting average of .388, and Jim Bagby won 31 games.

The name of the Cleveland Telephone Company was changed to The Ohio Bell Telephone Company in October. On December 31 the Ohio property of the Central Union Telephone Company was purchased for $28,000,000.

The Cleveland Lions Club of the Lions International Association was chartered in October by 75 business and professional men who were interested in giving aid to the sightless and in fostering the prevention of blindness. The club grew to a membership of 130 and extended its interests to include other welfare activities. The president in 1946 was Dr. E. L. Higgins, and the secretary was Edwin C. Reminger.

What many believe was the baseball game with more thrills than the diamond had ever known was played at Dunn Field, October 10, in the World Series between Brooklyn and Cleveland. The Dodgers had won two of the first three games at Brooklyn before the series moved to Cleveland. Nearly twenty-seven thousand fans crowded into the park, and thousands were on the housetops outside. In the first inning, with the bases full, Elmer Smith, right fielder for Cleveland, came to bat, with the crowd imploring him to "hit 'er over the fence." With two strikes and one ball, he swung,

The Board of Education Building, 1385 East 3rd Street.

Miles Standish Elementary School.

Lincoln statue, by Max Kalish, on the Mall side of the Board of Education Building.

The south side of the Terminal group of buildings. PERRY CRAGG, CLEVELAND NEWS.

The downtown district from the air at East 14th Street.

Operating machine tools

Refining oil

Operating open-hearth furnace

Stamping metal products

Manipulating an aluminum forging

Making women's garments

CITY OF DIVERSIFIED INDUSTRIES

Garfield Park Swimming Pool

A park baseball diamond

Brookside Park lake area

SPACIOUS PARKS, THE PRIDE OF CLEVELANDERS

and the ball went over the right-field screen, hitting a store across Lexington Avenue; but this was not the climax. In the fifth inning came the crowning sensation. Brooklyn was at bat. Kilduff singled to left; Miller singled to center, Kilduff taking second; Mitchell sent a liner in the direction of second base that the crowd thought would hit the wall. "Bill" Wambsganss, Cleveland second baseman, stepped back and leaped into the air, his left hand extended. The ball was caught. Wambsganss stepped on second, doubling Kilduff, who had started for third, and then touched Miller who was running for second and so accomplished a brilliant triple play unassisted in a world-series game. For a full second the stunned crowd was silent, not realizing what had happened. Then began a cheer, greater in volume than any the park had known. The final score was 8-1. The next game was won by Cleveland, with Walter Mails allowing three hits; and then came the concluding game with Covaleski winning his third victory in seven games with a score of 3-0. Cleveland was champion!

The cornerstone of the Public Auditorium was laid on October 20, the speakers being Mayor W. S. FitzGerald; Floyd E. Waite, director of public property; Mrs. W. S. Judson, representative of women's clubs; and William Ganson Rose, chairman of the committee that sponsored the building. The invocation was pronounced by the Rev. A. B. Meldrum, pastor of the Old Stone Church, and Lila Robeson, soprano soloist, sang the *Battle Hymn of the Republic.*

In October the Women's National Open Golf Championship was played at Mayfield, Alexis Sterling being the winner before an enthusiastic gallery. The Women's Ohio State Championship had been played in June, Louise Fordyce winning after a brilliant match with Martha Kinsey. The Western Open was held at Oakwood in 1921, Walter Hagen winning with 287, and "Jock" Hutchinson following five strokes behind. The Canterbury Club, formed by members of the University Club and named for the town in which Moses Cleaveland was born, planned its golf course on South Woodland Road, Shaker Heights. The National Open Golf Tournament was played on the course in 1940 and 1946. The Acacia Country Club opened in 1923 with Grange Alves as professional. In that year the Cleveland Women's Golf Association was formed. The Chagrin Valley club, the Aurora Country Club, and the Pepper Pike Country Club opened in 1925. The Hawthorne Valley Country Club opened in 1927, and the Columbia Hills Course in 1928, while Manikiki opened in 1929. District golf championships in this decade were won by Mike Wilson, 1920; Ellsworth Augustus, 1921; Eddie Hassman, 1922; Ellsworth Augustus, 1923; Fred Lamprecht, 1924; Ellsworth Augustus, 1925; Dave Ogilvie, Jr., 1926; Ellsworth Augustus, 1927; Dave Ogilvie, Jr., 1928; and Harry Sweitzer, 1929. Women's championships were won by Jennette Kinney, 1920-21; Mrs. K. B. Wick, 1922; Mrs. Alexander Printz, 1923; Mrs. K. B. Wick, 1924; Mrs. J. W. Tyler, 1925; Mrs. Chester Crobaugh, 1926; and Mrs. J. W. Tyler, 1927-28-29.

Universal suffrage was introduced to Cleveland on November 2 by women with market baskets and babies in arms. Some husbands tended babies while mothers voted, and election officials also served as nursemaids. The new voters helped Cuyahoga County give Warren G. Harding 75,000 plurality over James M. Cox for President; joined in giving A. Vic Donahey a lead of 7,000 votes over Harry L. Davis in the county for governor, although Davis carried the state by 120,000; and contributed to the lead of Florence E. Allen on the Common Pleas judicial ticket.

Republican and Democratic leaders were elated on November 2 by the performance of the wireless-telephone at a party arranged by the *News* in its editorial rooms. The guests did the broadcasting. This was the first such radio operation in Cleveland and one of the earliest in the country.

The second Community Fund campaign began, November 13, with this keynote: "The whole nation is watching Cleveland, the city of good will, and the miracle it performs in making whole and well the broken members of the community family." The goal was $4,500,000, representing the city's mutual helpfulness budget. The amount raised was $4,333,770.52 with 233,968 pledges.

The first home of The Ohio Crankshaft Company was in a garage on East 152nd Street near St. Clair Avenue, established this year by two young automotive engineers, W. C. Dunn and F. S. Denneen. At this time there were many small independent engine builders with little equipment or knowledge necessary to the manufacture of crankshafts, and the new venture was prompted by a realization of this vital need. In 1922 Ohio Crankshaft moved to 6600 Clement Avenue, which became Plant No. 1; Plant No. 2 at 6600 Park Avenue was purchased in 1934. In the early 1930s the company developed the use of high-frequency heating, an improved hardening method. Plant No. 3, 4000 Harvard Avenue, was built in 1937, and it became apparent that the TOCCO process was adaptable to a myriad of parts. In 1939 a self-contained unit for surface-hardening was developed. These operations were applied to a variety of forging and forming operations, and by 1941, sales were greater than the company could have foreseen. Plant No. 4 at 3800 Harvard Avenue was the first emergency war plant completed in Ohio. The laboratory at 4200 Harvard Avenue was the largest in the world devoted to induction heating problems.

The Cleveland Recreation Council was organized, the outgrowth of the work of the Recreation Committee of the Welfare Federation, which undertook to carry out the program of spare-time activities. It had been recommended by the Cleveland Foundation's Recreation Survey of 1919.

John Nelson Stockwell, distinguished Cleveland scientist in his eighty-ninth year, was given a tribute in the December number of *Popular Astronomy*. The article said of him, "The City of Cleveland may well take pride in the memory of Stockwell's life and discoveries. It will be a long time before we again meet with so humble and so noble an investigator in the pure science of astronomy. The stars in their courses, by the new problems perpetually arising, will preserve his memory." He died in 1920.

The Deaconess Evangelical Hospital in South Brooklyn was organized on December 5, and a modern building was dedicated in 1928 at 4233 Pearl Road.

The murder of two well-known Cleveland businessmen, Wilfred C. Sly and George K. Fanner, shocked Cleveland. The hunt for the four slayers continued for fifteen years, and detectives followed trails in this country, Mexico, and Italy. Finally the four were caught and three were executed, one being sentenced to life imprisonment.

The Cleveland Museum of Natural History, 2717 Euclid Avenue, was incorporated on December 13, having been founded by a civic-minded group devoted to Nature in its scientific, artistic, and popular aspects. The first president was Lewis B. Williams. The purpose was to acquire collections, render scientific and educational service, sponsor exhibits, and promote field expeditions. An outgrowth of the Kirtland Society of Natural Science, organized in 1869, and the Cleveland Academy of Natural Science, organized in 1845, the museum developed into an inspirational and educational institution. Prominent Cleveland naturalists stimulated development—Dr. Francis H. Herrick, Professor Henry Platt Cushing, and Henry Turner Bailey. Noteworthy exhibits, many of them the result of extensive scientific expeditions, included the Windsor T. and W. Holden White collections of African mammals, the Hanna Star Dome, the A. C. Ernst Florida fish room, and displays of birds, animals, and prehistoric life. A comprehensive library was assembled. Popular activities were developed, including free Sunday lectures, special classes for children, radio broadcasts, and scientific publications. Thousands of Clevelanders later enjoyed the beautiful nature trails and trailside museums maintained in the Metropolitan Park reservations. One of the many important acquisitions was the A. F. Holden Arboretum in Kirtland Township, the gift of Mr. and Mrs. Benjamin P. Bole in 1930. Completed approximately fifteen years later, the 228-acre area made possible valuable research and nature experiments, and provided sanctuary for wild life. The museum assumed operation of the Zoo in 1940. In 1939, Harold I. Madison, who had been associated with the museum for eighteen years, resigned as director; and a managerial board was later established, consisting of Dr. Arthur B. Williams, Benjamin P. Bole, Jr., Arthur B. Fuller, and John W. Aldrich. Thomas H. White, president of the board, and Harold T. Clark, president of the museum, guided its activities and policies for many years. Kenneth B. Disher of New York was chosen director in 1946. The former Leonard C. Hanna home and that of Fayette Brown to the east on Euclid Avenue housed the museum, the property at 2727 Euclid being used for offices and laboratories.

The *Cleveland Call,* Negro weekly newspaper, and the *Enakopravnost,* Slovenian newspaper, were established.

The Union Trust Company opened on December 31 in the Citizens Building, the fifth largest trust company in the United States. It was a merger of the First National Bank, the Citizens Savings & Trust Company, and the Union Commerce National Bank with their tributaries, and also the First Trust & Savings Company, the Broadway Savings & Trust Company, and the Woodland Avenue Savings & Trust Company, twenty-nine financial institutions in all. Resources at the launching were $322,500,000, which were more than 40 per cent of the resources of both the national and state banks of the city. Of this large sum, the First National brought to the merger $97,500,000; Union Commerce, $86,600,000; Citizens, $77,500,000; First Trust, $29,200,000; Broadway, $15,300,000; and Woodland, $16,400,000. John Sherwin, who had been president of the First National, became chairman of the board; J. R. Nutt, head of the Citizens, was made president; and in 1924, headquarters in the mammoth Union Trust Building (later Union Commerce Building) were occupied, the bank having the most impressive banking lobby in the world. The State Banking & Trust Company was absorbed in 1926. When Sherwin resigned early in 1929, Nutt served as both chairman and president for a year, when Wilbur M. Baldwin was made president. Upon Nutt's resignation in 1932, J. R. Kraus, who had been vice chairman of the board, became chairman, with George A. Coulton as vice chairman, and Allard Smith as executive vice president. At this time the Union Trust had twenty-two offices in Greater Cleveland. The bank attracted national attention through its spectacular organization and its far-reaching influence. However, when closed by the banking holiday in 1933, it never reopened. Management was criticized for liberality in lending. Later depositors were paid off in full, with the assurance of still another payment, and those stockholders who paid their liability assessments received substantial returns. The seemingly unnecessary closing of the comparatively new bank with vast resources was a blow to Cleveland which hurt the city immeasurably.

Carmi A. Thompson, a leader in Republican politics, both state and national, served as Treasurer of the United States and as Secretary of the Interior under President Taft. Charles K. Arter, prominent corporation and banking attorney, was engaged in business and philanthropic activities; John P. Dempsey was a lawyer and soldier; Ludwig S. Conelly, real-estate dealer, was identified with military affairs; Mrs. Nettie M. Clapp was the first woman to serve in the General Assembly of Ohio, as representative from Cuyahoga County; Virginia D. Green and Sarah E. Hyre were leaders in education; Clara Tagg Brewer was giving able service on the Board of Education; Bernice S. Pyke was active in public affairs and politics, and Maude C. Waitt was the first woman to serve in the State Senate from Cuyahoga County.

Robert J. Bulkley, attorney, had served as Congressman and was elected to the United States Senate, 1930-39; Frank H. Ginn, Maurice Bernon, Edgar A. Hahn, and Gardner Abbott were able lawyers with business affiliations; Irving C. and Newell C. Bolton were well known in business and military fields; Paul Jones began his long career as judge of the United States District Court in 1923; Fred S. and Thomas E. Borton were leading brokers; and Chief Thunderwater, picturesque Indian, was a member of the Early Settlers Association and an earnest spokesman for the valuable part played by tribesmen in the pioneer days of Cleveland.

In the race for industrial supremacy, the automobile was bidding strongly for the lead, as reported in the census of manufacturers of 1919. Eighty-five producers of automobiles, bodies, and parts reported products valued at $154,567,000, 18,873 wage earners employed, and a payroll of $28,047,000. Cleveland ranked in manufacturing importance with any other automobile center, the cars rolling out of its plants including the Baker, Chandler, Cleveland Six, Grant, Jordan, Owen Magnetic, Peerless, Rauch and Lang, Templar, White, and Winton.

Foundry and machine-shop production claimed first place, its total having increased more than 4 times during the decade. Products reported by 421 firms were valued at $157,024,000, 33,324 wage earners were employed, and wages totaled $45,029,000. In third place was the production of iron and steel, steel works, and rolling mills, 16 firms reporting products valued at $84,425,000, 9,719 wage earners with a payroll of $15,847,000; product value of iron-and-steel forgings was $13,373,000.

Industry, generally, had shown great gains during the decade. The value of slaughtering and meat-packing products, $75,728,000, more than quadrupled; electrical machinery, apparatus, and supplies, $52,324,000; printing and publishing, $33,336,000; women's clothing, $35,308,000; paint and varnish, $26,487,000; stoves and hot-air furnaces, $21,907,000; men's clothing, $19,433,496; bread and bakery products, $19,413,000; tools, $17,603,000; bolts, nuts, washers, and rivets, $17,264,000; railroad cars and general shop construction, $11,571,000; confectionery and ice cream, $11,375,000; knit goods, $10,003,000; lumber and timber products, $7,908,000; chemicals, $7,593,000; wirework, $7,071,000; brass and bronze products, $6,622,000; patent medicines and compounds, $6,167,000; copper, tin, and sheet-iron products, $6,164,000; malt liquors, $5,774,000; food preparations, $4,098,830; tobacco and cigars, $3,753,000; paper and other boxes, $3,135,000; carriages and wagons, $891,000, representing a continued demand.

An increase in the number of Cleveland manufacturing establishments was evident, according to the census, 2,946 companies employing 157,730 wage earners, with a payroll of $211,206,276. Their products, valued at $1,091,577,490, entitled Cleveland to fifth place among American cities. Cleveland led in the manufacture of paints and varnishes, nuts and bolts, wire goods, gray iron castings, heavy machinery, electric batteries, twist drills, steel forgings, plumbing fixtures, hardware, vacuum sweepers, steel ships, job-printers' presses, and astronomical appliances. The city ranked second in the manufacture of women's ready-to-wear clothing, and was an American fashion center. More than 80 per cent of the nation's electric carbons were produced here. World War I tested Cleveland's ability to produce industrially. Not a war necessity was manufactured of which local plants could not make a part, from the smallest screw to giant ships built and loaded at Cleveland and bound for European ports. Variety of manufacture gave the city unusual industrial and financial stability. Cleveland's importance as a wholesale and jobbing center attracted many merchants who purchased their season's stocks of goods and merchandise here.

Cleveland, the great iron-ore market of the world, was called the "Sheffield of America." Twelve huge blast furnaces converted into pig-iron one-third of the 8,957,000 net tons of iron ore received from the Lake Superior district at the Cleveland docks in 1920. More than one-half of the pig-iron production was turned into finished products by hundreds of steel-working plants. Of the 58,000,000 tons of iron ore shipped from the upper-lakes region, the

Cleveland District, including Ashtabula, Conneaut, Fairport, Lorain, and Huron, received a total of nearly 24,000,000 tons. Coal, grain, lumber, and building materials moved in vast tonnage.

Six hundred bulk freighters plied Great Lakes waters; 440 of them were American vessels, two-thirds owned or managed in Cleveland. Forty-five steamship lines connected Cleveland with ports on these inland seas. Seven trunk lines—New York Central, Erie, Baltimore & Ohio, Big Four, Pennsylvania, Nickel Plate, and Wheeling & Lake Erie, joined by the Belt Line—gave the city one of the best transportation systems in the country. More than eighty passenger trains and hundreds of freights arrived daily.

For more than six decades Cleveland had been the center of the oil industry. With the discovery of new fields, however, the city lost its leadership; but a half dozen large refineries continued to operate, producing 100,000,000 gallons of petroleum products annually.

Capital invested in industrial operations had increased from $227,397,484 in 1909 to $762,585,305 in 1919. Of the latter figure, $105,637,305 represented the automotive industry. Increases in salaries and wages, cost of materials, and value of products were largely due to changes in industrial conditions brought about by World War I. In the manufacturing industry skilled labor was paid $.687 per hour on an average in 1920, and unskilled labor $.529. In the construction industry, however, skilled workers received $1.05 per hour, and $.579 was being paid for common labor.

While the population of Cleveland doubled in the twenty years from 1900 to 1920, the city's business grew at a greater rate. Bank clearings of $565,963,282 in 1900 increased to $1,000,857,953 in 1910, and to $6,877,387,037 in 1920. Small banks continued to merge with larger institutions. Resources of 23 banks in Greater Cleveland totaled $768,870,000 in 1920. Eighty building-and-loan associations reported resources of $71,130,000 in 1920, an increase of more than six times since 1910. The assessed value of Cleveland property in 1910 was $274,970,605. In 1920 it had grown to $1,753,246,190, of which real estate accounted for $1,073,842,860, and land, $644,045,620. The construction industry gained remarkably, 11,531 building permits issued in Cleveland in 1920 representing operations valued at $65,625,050, more than 4.5 times the 1910 figure. The traffic problem mounted with the registration of 92,600 passenger cars and trucks in Cuyahoga County.

1921

A survey of the field of criminal justice in Cleveland was commenced by the Cleveland Foundation, on request of the Cleveland Bar Association, the Chamber of Commerce, the Welfare Federation, and other organizations. The survey was directed by Dean Roscoe Pound of the Law School of Harvard University and Amos Burt Thompson, chairman. This was an important undertaking, dealing comprehensively with all agencies of law enforcement. The program inspired a major effort to bring about more efficient administration of criminal justice, and its success was gratifying.

The Children's Bureau was organized, an outgrowth of the Children's Survey conducted by the Welfare Federation in 1920, to promote the interests of child care and welfare.

St. Augustine's Academy was organized, and classes were conducted in Hanna Cottage. The school, located at 14808 Lake Avenue, Lakewood, became known for its efficient buildings and attractive surroundings.

The National City Bank of Cleveland, early in January, moved into its own building at the corner of East 6th Street and Euclid Avenue. Formerly the Garfield Building, it had been renovated at a cost of $500,000 and renamed National City Bank Building. In July, 1933, Sidney B. Congdon became president, succeeding H. V. Shulters, who had served since 1918. The bank began a rapid period of expansion, and a branch was established in the Terminal Building. The following year, Lewis B. Williams was made chairman of the board. In 1946 the banking quarters of the adjoining Guardian Building were secured, and the bank's assets had increased to $475,000,000. Edgar A. Hahn, elected a director in 1915, J. S. Crider in 1916, and Charles H. Strong in 1917, had served continuously.

The East End Baptist Church and the Willson Avenue Baptist Church joined in January to form The Church of the Master. The site of the new church was that of the East End Baptist Church at Euclid and East 97th Street. Several outstanding ministers occupied the pulpit, including Dr. Frank Jennings who had been executive secretary of the Massachusetts Council of Churches. In 1946 the Rev. Robert C. Newell, who had been assistant minister, was made pastor, and the active membership had reached six hundred.

The Park Theater was opened as one of the largest motion-picture houses in Cleveland. Joseph Laronge selected the site at 10211 Euclid Avenue, and Thomas W. Lamb built the theater for the Loew interests. The first audiences were deeply impressed by the golden silk-velour walls, the ivory-and-gold decorations, the murals, and the majestic proscenium arch. The spacious promenade and lobby also contributed to make the theater one of Loew's three most important playhouses in the nation at the time of the opening. An excellent orchestra contributed to the programs. Before long, the Euclid-East 105th district was attracting thousands of visitors continuously to its theaters: Keith's East 105th, the Circle, the University, the Alhambra, and the Park. Bailey's branch department store and restaurants of the area west of University Circle were also building up this important neighborhood, known as Doan's Corners in the early days.

Charles D. Dawe enlisted sixteen carefully chosen singers to form the original Orpheus Male Chorus. The group won first honors in each of five Eisteddfods, in both national and international competition. The chorus appeared with the Cleveland Symphony, the Cincinnati Symphony, on the radio, and in foreign countries. Orpheus annual spring concerts became highlights of the Cleveland musical season.

The W. J. Schoenberger Company, founded this year to manufacture valves for gas appliances, was incorporated in 1923. The output of its plant at 8810 Harvard Avenue was sold nationally. The founder, whose name identified the company, had served continuously as president from the time of organization.

Loew's State Theater was opened at 1515 Euclid Avenue to a capacity audience that admired the million-dollar playhouse designed by Architect Thomas W. Lamb and constructed during the past seventeen months. The lobby was called the largest in the world and proved a show in itself, with its Vermont marble, artistic wainscotings, red carpets, and draperies. It was of the Italian Renaissance style, and murals, antiques, and luxurious furnishings contributed to the great promenade. The opening feature was *Polly with a Past* starring Ina Claire, who was supported by Ralph Graves of Cleveland. In the orchestra pit was Hyman L. Spitalny, oldest of the Spitalny brothers, whose orchestra was made up of talented Cleveland musicians.

A career that influenced the educational and social life of Cleveland and inspired nature study throughout the nation closed on February 12 with the death of Harriet L. Keeler. Graduated from Oberlin College in 1870, she taught at old Central High School, served as superintendent of the primary grades of the Cleveland public-school system and as principal of the new Central High School for a short period. She retired in 1909, endeared to the hearts of thousands. So valuable had been her services that the Board of Education recalled her for a short period as superintendent of schools in 1912, the only woman so honored. Through the years, she carried on nature studies, made botanical expeditions, and published such authoritative books as *Our Nation's Trees, Our Northern Shrubs,* and *Our Garden Flowers.* She found time for organization activities, as a founder of the College Club, a charter member of the Fortnightly, and a member of the Woman's Club, Women's City Club, Garden Club, and the Advisory Council of the Western Reserve University College for Women. Oberlin College made her a trustee, and the Cuyahoga County Suffrage Association elected her president. In the Metropolitan Park System at Brecksville, the three-hundred-acre Harriet L. Keeler memorial woods was dedicated in her honor, its wild plants and lofty trees reminding visitors of an eminent educator who loved Nature.

The Interstate Commerce Commission declared that "public convenience and necessity require the construction and operation of the station on the Square." The New York Central Railroad had decided in favor of this location, but the Pennsylvania Railroad continued to use the old Union Depot at West 9th Street on the lakefront.

Cleveland was asked to furnish complete information about the Warrensville group of city institutions as a guide for a similar project in Czechoslovakia. Many features of the local welfare development were later embodied in the Prague Asylum.

The Most Rev. John Patrick Farrelly, eminent Catholic bishop and beloved religious leader, died on February 12, and his body was placed in the Cathedral with those of his three predecessors.

The Domestic Relations Division of the Civil Branch of the Cuyahoga

County Court was established to investigate matters pertaining to divorce, alimony, and custody of minor children.

The Ohio Theater was opened at 1513 Euclid Avenue on February 14 by Ohio Theaters, Inc., which operated the Ohio and the Euclid Avenue Opera House under the management of Robert McLaughlin. The lobby was second in size only to that of Loew's State. An Italian motif was followed throughout, and green and ivory dominated the decorations. This was the first of the upper Euclid Avenue houses devoted to drama. The opening performance was *The Return of Peter Grimm* with David Warfield as the star. The early productions were those of a syndicate headed by A. L. Erlanger.

The Cleveland Clinic, 2020 East 93rd Street at Euclid Avenue, was established on February 26. Founded by Drs. George W. Crile, William E. Lower, Frank E. Bunts, and John Phillips, it was dedicated to better care of the sick, investigation of their problems through research, and furtherance of medical education. Health authorities, specialists, and thousands of Cleveland and out-of-town patients soon proved the value and importance of the undertaking. It was started as a surgical institution and featured surgery through the years.

Director Sokoloff arranged a Sunday "Pop" concert by the Cleveland Orchestra on February 28, with a view to offsetting the influence of jazz and ragtime on the city's young people.

Warren G. Harding, twenty-eighth President, was inaugurated on March 4. He was born in Corsica, Ohio. The genial and easy-going President had many friends in Cleveland who were critical of his close associates and his unbusinesslike regime. Harding died in office on August 2, 1923.

The first music memory contest for children held by the Cleveland Orchestra took place in Masonic Hall on March 12. Led by Nikolai Sokoloff, the orchestra played for teams of thirty students each, from thirty-three public, private, and parochial schools in Cleveland and its suburbs. Concerts for young people were made possible by the alliance between the Cleveland Orchestra and the boards of education of Greater Cleveland. For a time, the orchestra went to school auditoriums; but beginning in 1921, the children were brought to Masonic Hall, and the programs were given during school hours. The work developed under Lillian Baldwin, representing the schools, and Mrs. Adella Prentiss Hughes, representing the orchestra. An outgrowth of the plan was the formation of independent adult groups who received instruction in the music-education room of Severance Hall, the home of the orchestra since 1930. The children's concerts became famous and set a precedent for other cities to follow throughout the world. When Leonard H. Robbins, the distinguished roving writer of the *New York Times,* stopped a passerby near Severance Hall and asked its purpose, the man proudly told him and emphasized the educational features for pupils. In telling the story in his paper, Robbins commented, "You believe you'd like to be a school child in Cleveland."

The million-dollar Allen Theater opened on April 1 at 1407 Euclid Avenue in Playhouse Square with a twin bill of motion-picture entertainment: *The*

Greatest Love, starring Vera Gordon and the Hallroom Boys in a characteristic comedy. Interest of the great audiences was divided between the screen and admiration of the architecture, decorative schemes, and beautiful furnishings in the playhouse. A striking feature was the rotunda surrounded by an open colonnade. At either side of the house were triple groups of great windows illuminated by artificial lighting, lending charm to the luxurious appointments. The motion-picture theater was built by Jules and Jay J. Allen, of Bradford, Pennsylvania, who achieved theatrical success in Canada; C. Howard Crane was the architect.

The Midland Bank opened in April in the *Leader-News* Building, with S. H. Robbins, chairman of the board; D. D. Kimmel, president; Carl R. Lee and Harold C. Avery, vice presidents; and J. Brenner Root, cashier. Larger quarters were occupied in 1923 in the Williamson Building. In 1928, Charles L. Bradley, president of the Cleveland Union Terminals Company, proposed to the directors the formation of a nine-million-dollar banking institution to be known as The Midland Bank and Midland Corporation. The idea was approved. The Midland Bank Company was formed, and spacious and beautiful quarters were opened in the Midland Building of the Terminal Group in 1930. On the board of directors were John Sherwin, Sr., John Sherwin, Jr., Edward E. Barker, Charles L. Bradley, Alva Bradley, Elton Hoyt II, and George A. Tomlinson. John Sherwin, Jr., had been elected president in 1929, a position he held until the institution was merged with The Cleveland Trust Company, of which he was vice president. The merger added twenty-eight million dollars to the deposits of the trust company. While short-lived, the Midland had been important in its functions.

The Cleveland Discount Building, 815 Superior Avenue, was designed by Walker & Weeks for the Cleveland Discount Company, headed by Josiah Kirby. The height of the fourteen-story structure, on a quicksand base, necessitated the construction of a steel raft embedded a hundred feet in the ground. Lobbies and corridors of the beautiful office building were marbled to the ceiling. The name was changed to NBC Building in 1938, when it became the home of The National Broadcasting Company and of radio station WTAM.

Enrollment in the public schools during the 1920-21 school year numbered 130,000 children and 13,479 adults, while 4,056 teachers were employed in day schools and 384 in evening classes. In use were 97 elementary, 16 junior-high and 10 senior-high schools. Increased attention was paid to vocational guidance, a teacher and counselor being installed in every high school.

John D. Rockefeller's deep interest in Cleveland over the years is reflected in a letter, dated May 19, to William Ganson Rose, president of the Diamond Jubilee Committee that arranged the seventy-fifth anniversary of the founding of Central High School:

> I recall our delightful meeting 25 years ago on the occasion of the Fiftieth Anniversary, when we met—at our home—many of the original scholars of the high school in its earliest years. I fear there are very few now left . . .

(There was) E. P. Hunt, so long and prominently identified with the business interests of Cleveland. He was my seatmate in the old Brownell Street School. The graduating class of '55 included Mrs. Rockefeller, then Laura Celestia Spelman, and her sister Lucy; also Julia O'Brien . . . all of whom have passed away. I am proud of my connection with the school, and most appreciative of the many fine characters among the boys and girls of that early period, so many of whom have made their mark and rendered valuable service in the world. I recall with great pleasure and satisfaction the old teachers—among them Mr. Freese and Mr. White—and there were other teachers whom we highly prized and to whom we were devotedly attached. Those were good old days—in the beginning of Cleveland's development . . . I send hearty congratulations and best wishes to all associated with the high school work of today, and the days that are past, and who may be associated in the days to come; and I want to feel, so long as life lasts, that you will count me as one of you, tho it is now 66 years since that summer day in '55 when I bade farewell to the dear old school to take up the burden of life's duties.

The celebration opened May 24 and proved the outstanding high-school event of the city's history. Arthur Spencer, a student in the 1850s, and five hundred alumni came to Cleveland to participate. When the event concluded, the committee presented Principal Edward L. Harris with five thousand dollars in gold, and established a trust fund in the Cleveland Foundation to help worthy pupils.

The Cleveland Inter-Museum Council, an organization composed of the president and director of each of the four leading museums in the city, was formed to co-ordinate and extend museum service and eliminate duplication of effort.

The convention of the Zionist Organization of America, known as the ZOA, opened in Cleveland on June 5. It attracted world attention as the future of Palestine was to be discussed. Professor Albert Einstein was a distinguished speaker. Certain delegates, particularly those of Europe, favored enlisting the masses in a campaign to buy land and finance the upbuilding of Palestine as a people's project. Some American Zionists, enjoying the leadership of Supreme Court Justice Louis D. Brandeis and Judge Julian W. Mack, president of the ZOA, favored private economic development by individual Jews and firms rather than by mass movements. As a result of debates, the Mack administration ended, and a committee of eight, with Louis Lipsky as chairman, undertook ZOA leadership. In 1930 the annual convention was again held in Cleveland, the two groups joining, and an executive committee of eighteen was appointed to take over the administration. Differences were forgotten, and able leaders were chosen in succeeding years. After World War II, Zionist activities centered in the United States, and an American Zionist Emergency Council was formed under the joint chairmanship of Rabbi Abba Hillel Silver of Cleveland and Rabbi Stephen S. Wise of New York. At the annual convention of 1945, Rabbi Silver was made president of the ZOA, and the spirit of militancy against British policy and in favor of securing Palestine developed despite obstacles. The following year, the militant delegation of ZOA had its way in the Congress in Basel, and appeals were made to the United Nations to carry out plans for making Palestine secure for the Jews.

A department of nursing education was organized in the College for Women (Flora Stone Mather College) of Western Reserve University. Two years later it became known as the Frances Payne Bolton School of Nursing, honoring its benefactor.

Ellis C. VanderPyl was a member of the Yale two-mile relay team which set a record of 7:48.4, and the next year he became intercollegiate two-mile champion. He accumulated seven letters in football, track, and cross-country events. Later he devoted his time to radio and relations work in Cleveland.

The Cleveland Foundation published a valuable survey concerning teacher training, which increased efficiency in the public schools.

The Bulkley Building, constructed by a company of which Robert J. Bulkley was president, opened at 1501 Euclid Avenue. The eight-story office-and-store structure had a front of sandstone, and one impressive feature was the Allen Theater. The property included the Selzer Building which had housed the famous Selzer Store with its many treasures and the Cleveland Athletic Club Building, famous for sporting events at the turn of the century. Parking was provided in the Bulkley Building and in the large Bulkley Garage immediately to the north. The architect was C. Howard Crane and the contractor John Gill & Son.

The Cleveland Museum of Natural History and the Educational Museum of the Cleveland public schools gave a six-weeks' course in visual instruction at the summer school of the Cleveland School of Education. It was the first course of its kind known to have been offered in the United States.

The Fantasy of the Flag, an elaborate pageant, was staged in Edgewater Park on Independence Day.

Business slowed down because of the most severe depression in the history of the iron-and-steel industry. Steel production fell to less than 20 per cent of plant capacity, and more than 125,000 workers were unemployed before the year-end.

Mayor W. S. FitzGerald proclaimed July 22 to be the opening date of the 125th anniversary of the founding of Cleveland, the celebration to be held July 22-30. As a special feature of Cleveland Day, a group of well-known citizens re-enacted the landing of the pioneers at the foot of St. Clair Street where the original landing was made. Charles A. Otis impersonated Moses Cleaveland, and Dudley S. Blossom, F. L. Smith, L. M. Williams, C. A. Lohman, H. H. Brown, Jr., and R. C. Norton in pioneer costume represented other members of the landing party. Band concerts, parades, athletic events, a rodeo, and a historical pageant, *The Spirit of a City* by Harper Garcia Smythe, provided entertainment. The undertaking threatened to conclude in debt; but rain insurance saved the day when a great downpour came during the closing hours of the celebration. The officials were Mayor W. S. FitzGerald, honorary chairman; Thomas P. Cagwin, chairman; Henry Turner Bailey, Charles L. Bradley, Robert J. Bulkley, Paul L. Feiss, Fred H.

Goff, Alexander Hadden, Myron T. Herrick, J. R. Nutt, William P. Palmer, Monte F. Bourjaily, secretary, and Thomas V. Hendricks, executive director. A condensed history of Cleveland by Leo Weidenthal was printed as a souvenir of the occasion.

Warren Cox set up a fifty-watt transmitter in his factory at 3138 Payne Avenue where he made automobile specialties, and this served as a make-shift radio studio. On July 26 he began operation under an amateur license. The call letters were 8 ACS. This effort pioneered station WHK.

The Cuyahoga County Public Health Association was created on recommendation of the Hospital and Health Survey to effect co-ordination of private agencies dealing with various phases of public-health work. Dr. E. A. Peterson, former director of health service of the American Red Cross, was appointed director.

The committee on mental hygiene, composed of representatives of all interested organizations, was formed by the Welfare Federation, as recommended by the Hospital and Health Survey. Affiliated with the Cuyahoga County Public Health Association and the state and national committee on mental hygiene, its purpose was to develop more adequate clinical facilities for care of the mentally diseased.

Rum-running was being practiced on the Great Lakes, and Coast Guardsmen were busy on August 2 preventing boats from contacting the *Tranquillo,* a source of supply anchored near Cleveland.

Avery Hopwood's plays were winning the favor of New York audiences. Hopwood, a Clevelander, was soon to become one of the most successful playwrights of his time.

Robert Lindsay was elected president of The Cleveland Electric Illuminating Company in August, and immediately inaugurated one of the periods of greatest expansion in company history. Born and raised only a few miles from Thomas Alva Edison's home and laboratories at Menlo Park, New Jersey, he had begun work at the age of sixteen as an assistant in Edison's lamp factory. Lindsay came to Cleveland in 1893 as consulting engineer on the design of the company's Canal Road plant. For nearly forty years he devoted himself wholly to the service of company and community, and to the development of the art and science of electricity. He served as president from 1921 until his death in 1933, when he was succeeded by Eben G. Crawford. During the period from 1921 to 1926, the company built ten new substations, added capacity at the Lake Shore power plant until it became the "largest steam-electric generating plant under one roof in the country," constructed the East 20th Street steam-heating plant, and built the Avon power plant. The company attracted wide attention during this period, not only by its broad construction program but by its pioneering installations and development of new methods.

After long investigation, Judge Landis ruled out of baseball seven players accused of crookedness in the World Series of 1919. His decision of August 5 attracted so much attention that dishonesty was eliminated from the national game.

A gift of $250,000 was presented by Mrs. Bertha Aiken McMyler and daughters in memory of P. J. McMyler for development of a department of musical art at the Cleveland Museum of Art.

A great procession welcomed the Rt. Rev. Joseph Schrembs to Cleveland on September 8. At the impressive service, attended by high officials of the church and thousands of parishioners, he was installed fifth bishop of Cleveland. The bishopric at this time numbered 443,112 Catholics, 404 priests of the diocese and religious orders, 204 churches, 34 missions with churches, 3,182 high-school and academy pupils, and a parochial-school enrollment of 57,511. Many beautiful churches, such as St. James in Lakewood, and St. Ignatius and St. Aloysius in Cleveland, were erected under his guidance.

The number of playgrounds increased 50 per cent over 1920, and attendance figures had grown from 828,724 for 1920 to 1,414,646 for 1921, or 70 per cent.

Fundamental beryllium research was being conducted in the Brush Laboratories, 3714 Chester Avenue, under the direction of Dr. C. Baldwin Sawyer. Secrets yielded by the "mystery metal" to Cleveland scientists were to result in industrial progress of great significance.

The two telephone systems in Cleveland were merged on September 20. The Ohio State Telephone Company and the Ohio Bell Telephone Company were joined under the name of the latter, the value of the combined properties being a hundred million dollars. The state offices were moved from Columbus to Cleveland, and the first president was Eugene A. Reed. The Ohio Bell Telephone Company was handling a volume of 500,000 local calls a day and 6,000 long-distance calls.

The monumental Hanna Buildings, among the largest and most impressive in Cleveland, were erected this year by Dan R. Hanna, Sr., in memory of his father, Marcus A. Hanna. Covering 1.56 acres, the buildings were constructed in two sections, one fronting on Euclid Avenue and East 14th Street, the other on Prospect Avenue and East 14th Street. The buildings, designed by Charles A. Platt, were located on the site of the old Euclid Avenue Presbyterian Church. In the annex was the famous Hanna Theater, which offered leading stage productions. Seating 1,535 persons, it became one of the best-known amusement houses in the country. The theater interior was of Italian Renaissance style, with artistic design and ornamentation. The side-paneled walls were Travertinstone of buff tints, and the fittings were of harmonious colorings finished with a gold cornice. Marble corridors, bronze trimmings, and unusual lighting fixtures were other features. Monaco's Continental Restaurant on the Euclid Avenue front was a favorite dining and meeting place in Playhouse Square. The management of the Hanna Building was assumed in 1932 by the T. W. Grogan Company. A memorial tablet was placed in the lobby by Daniel R., Jr., Marcus A., and Carl H. Hanna in honor of their father, Dan R. Hanna, who erected the buildings.

Sergeant Edward Younger of Cleveland on October 24 was chosen as the American soldier to designate one of the four bodies of unidentified American dead to typify a member of the American Expeditionary Forces as the "Unknown Soldier." He placed a small spray of roses on one of the four caskets that rested in the City Hall at Chalons-sur-Marne, France. The body was brought to the United States on the U.S.S. Olympia, and, after lying in state at Washington, was interred in Arlington National Cemetery on Armistice Day with solemn ceremonies.

A twelve-page newspaper for free distribution came into being this year, with advertisements occupying most of the space. Four people constituted the staff of the *Shopping News*. The appreciation of the public was so enthusiastic that the paper grew under the able management of Sam B. Anson, an executive with valuable newspaper experience. So steady was the growth that on the twenty-fifth anniversary in 1946 more than twelve hundred were on the payroll, two editions were issued each week, the institution owned its own printing plant and distributed its product by its own carrier staff. More than 270,000 homes in Greater Cleveland received the *Shopping News,* which helped women to do their buying with ease and economy. The publication became the model for many similar papers throughout the country. In 1946 the officers included Charles H. Strong, president; Nathan L. Dauby, a founder of the paper, first vice president; Walter M. Halle, second vice president; Joseph S. Newman, secretary; John E. Crew, treasurer; Sam B. Anson, general manager.

Dr. Charles Franklin Thwing retired from the presidency of Western Reserve University after thirty-one years of service, and became president emeritus. He was hailed as a great educator and a valuable civic leader. Dr. J. D. Williamson was appointed acting president, serving until Dr. Robert Ernest Vinson was elected to office on October 5, 1924. The School of Architecture, organized as a course in the Cleveland School of Art by the Cleveland Chapter of the American Institute of Architects in 1921, was incorporated and affiliated with Western Reserve University in 1929. Under the leadership of Dean Francis R. Bacon, the school established a wide reputation for its technical and comprehensive training.

Fred Kohler, dismissed as police chief in 1913, made good his threat to run for mayor of Cleveland, and conducted his campaign in a famous "gumshoe," door-to-door canvas. Without backing, he made no pledges, promising only to make life and property safe, clean up the town, and live within his income. Kohler won with a lead of 4,500 votes over his nearest opponent. His victory was not the result of his popularity so much as the desire of Cleveland voters for a change of administration. He took office on January 1, 1922, a man of strong prejudices. His was the most bizarre administration in the city's history. In 1924 he became sheriff, but was defeated for the 1928 Republican nomination for governor. He died in 1934 at the age of sixty-nine.

A memorable high-school football game was played on November 5 when East Technical High School defeated Scott High School of Toledo, 14-7. The triumph led the Cleveland school to send its team to Everett, Washington, where it was defeated on New Year's Day, 1922, in a close game.

A bond issue of two million dollars was authorized, November 8, for the erection of a central building for Cleveland's Public Library, this amount to be added to two million dollars provided through a bond issue voted in 1912, when the old city-hall site was offered by the city as a location for the building. Architects were chosen by competition in 1916; but by the time the site was made available, prices had increased so that the amount available was not sufficient.

Marshal Foch was acclaimed by crowds on November 8 as he went to the Gates Mills home of Ambassador Myron T. Herrick. Stirring scenes of his reception were graphically described by E. Arthur Roberts in the *Plain Dealer:*

> Marshal Ferdinand Foch, freeman of the city of Cleveland, doctor of laws, Western Reserve University, to add two distinctions to a bewildering array of honors symbolic of universal gratitude and good will, was overwhelmed by Cleveland's tribute. He made several brief speeches, but nothing he said was quite so impressive as the simple ejaculations of surprise and appreciation frequently muttered in tones so soft and low that only those close to him could catch the words: "C'est magnifique! C'est étonnant!"

Three times the Marshal was taken through cheering lines of citizens on Euclid Avenue from University Circle to Public Square. Former Secretary of War Newton D. Baker, at a great gathering in Keith's Hippodrome on November 9, gave Marshal Foch yet another title: "Immortal Citizen of the United States, as immortal as the citizens of America resting beneath the soil of France." A great roar of acquiescence greeted this designation. Virginia Garbison presented the Marshal with a basket of a thousand roses, each bought by an employee of William Taylor Son & Company. The Marshal, silenced for a moment by the magnitude of the offering, muttered, "Merci, bien," and taking Miss Garbison by the shoulders, he kissed her on each cheek.

The campaign goal set for the Community Fund was $3,763,545. The amount raised, November 12, was $3,819,617.88, by 310,271 subscribers. The campaign chairman was Fred W. Ramsey. Kenneth Sturges, who became director on August 1, helped to make the "chest" the model of the nation.

Cleveland gave a rousing reception on November 17 to General Armando Vittorio Diaz, commander of Italy's army in the World War. The general received two military medals from Judge John P. Dempsey, ex-captain in the 332nd Infantry which served in Italy. Mayor W. S. FitzGerald presented honorary citizenship.

Although a few Chandler and Cleveland car bodies, built in Detroit, had been revamped in the big new Fisher Body assembly plant on Coit Road and East 140th Street early in the fall, the first unit of a Chevrolet order for bodies was completed the night before Thanksgiving, November 23. The glittering body signaled the beginning of production at Cleveland No. 1, a 39-acre site, the first Fisher unit of General Motors Corporation to mass-produce closed bodies for Chevrolet, and the first big body plant to operate in the city. Edward F. Fisher, plant manager, was one of the six famous Fisher brothers, born in Norwalk, Ohio, who found fame and fortune in Detroit by building closed-car bodies. By 1922, 150 coach bodies were being turned out daily. Two years later, output reached 600 finished bodies a day, and seven thousand workers were filling Chevrolet orders, shipping bodies to Chandler and Cleveland plants in Cleveland, to Chrysler in Detroit, and to Oakland in Pontiac. The plant initiated the knockdown system of shipping in 1923, and pioneered the use of lacquer for body finish, thus reducing cost and making color styles possible. It was the first to install safety devices on presses, and to build bodies on a moving line in 1925. In 1936 Cleveland No. 1 became almost exclusively a fabricating plant. When World War II came, much of the floor space was cleared for production of engine nacelles for huge B-29 Superfortresses, tank and gun parts, and materials of war. Reconverted to peacetime operation, the Fisher Body Division resumed the fabricating of body parts, principally Chevrolet, and served as a stock-distribution center. Normal employment in 1946 exceeded four thousand, with an annual payroll of more than ten million dollars, and capacity production of more than five thousand body sets daily.

The Zonta Club of Cleveland was organized on November 30 with fifteen members. Mrs. Anna Moncure P. Tucker, president of the Tucker School of Expression, was the first president. Originally planned in Buffalo in 1919 as a club for professional and executive women, within four months similar clubs were organized in eight leading cities. Zonta is a Sioux Indian name meaning "trustworthy and honest." The club's object was "to work for the advancement of understanding, good-will and peace through a world of fellowship of executive women in business and professions." The Cleveland Zonta Club designated as its permanent project Blossom Hill School for Girls, and established a scholarship fund in the School of Applied Social Sciences at Western Reserve University. The president in 1946 was Caroline A. Benner, who was succeeded by Helen Robertson and Florence L. F. Donley.

1922

A merger of Western Reserve University and Case School of Applied Science was proposed by alumni committees of both institutions, but the suggested University of Cleveland failed to materialize.

The West Side Community House, formerly the West Side Cottage at 3000 Bridge Avenue, was dedicated and ready for occupancy. It was the outgrowth of the Deaconess Home, a project founded in 1890 under a board representing the Methodist churches of Cleveland. It served a neighborhood that was predominantly Hungarian.

Station WHK, the first station in Ohio and the fourth in the nation, was established. The covered wagon was adopted as its insignia to show that it was the pioneer broadcasting station of Cleveland, and one of the original half dozen licensed stations in the United States. Warren Cox, who had started WHK as the short-wave station 8 ACS, moved to 5105 Euclid Avenue, where he operated on a regular daily schedule. Ultimately, Cox obtained a commercial license to operate on a frequency of 1,500 k.c. and changed his call letters to WHK. In 1928 the station moved to its new quarters on the top floor of the Engineers Bank Building. Walter Logan was selected as musical director by the Howlett brothers—Arnold, Harry, and Eric, managers.

The congregation of the Shiloh Baptist Church purchased the temple at East 55th Street and Scovill Avenue from the B'nai Jeshurun Jewish congregation. Great gains in membership continued under the leadership of the Rev. Alexander L. Boone, who became pastor in 1927; in the 1940s, there were 2,450 names on the church rolls and 1,200 in the Sunday School.

O. P. and M. J. Van Sweringen acquired control of the Chesapeake & Ohio Railway Company. O. P. became chairman of the board of directors, and from that time all board meetings were held in Cleveland.

The Academy of Medicine set up an executive office with H. Van Y. Caldwell as full-time secretary. The headquarters were in the Cleveland Medical Library on Prospect Avenue, east of the YMCA. Two years later, the organization moved into the Allen Memorial Library building on Adelbert Road at Euclid Avenue where an auditorium and other facilities were available. At this time, the Academy was incorporated and Dr. J. E. Tuckerman was made president. In 1929 the Academy added the phrase "and Cuyahoga County Medical Society" to its name and expanded its activities.

A morning newspaper was born on March 2, under the name of the *Commercial*. O. K. Shimansky was president and editor-in-chief, and Samuel Scovil was treasurer. The paper sold for three cents, and effort was made to give the Cleveland area an easy-to-read, unbiased publication. In 1923 the name was changed to *Times,* and the paper was sold at two cents a copy, but the circulation grew slowly. In 1926 there was a reorganization for the purpose of introducing new ideas and developing a more popular appeal. Earl E. Martin, former editor of the *Press,* became editor and relations man. He carried out the ideals of the founders to give the public a clean newspaper, minimizing crime details and combating bureaucratic government. For a time there was encouragement, and the circulation grew to nearly seventy-five thousand; but there was not enough money to continue the experiment, and the project ended in 1927.

The Women's City Club activities were expanding; its membership was growing, and this year it moved from its first home in the Stillman Building to elaborate headquarters on East 13th Street. It aided in the establishment of a Women's Bureau in the Police Department, campaigned for the Juvenile Court Buildings, and opened the first nature trail in the Brecksville reservation in memory of Harriet L. Keeler. The club was achieving, through its many civic committees, constructive results in the cultural, educational, and welfare aspects of civic life.

Cleveland's Public Auditorium, East 6th and Lakeside, was formally dedicated on April 15 as the finest convention and exposition hall in the world. Its exterior walls bore the inscription: "A monument conceived as a tribute to the ideals of Cleveland, builded by her citizens and dedicated to social progress, industrial achievements and civic interests." The building was designed in the Italian Renaissance style by City Architect J. H. MacDowell and Consulting Architect F. R. Walker. The exterior was faced with Indiana limestone, and the base was of pink granite. The main entrance was on Lakeside Avenue, and within the great lobby the walls were marble, enriched with ornamental bronze grills. The auditorium proper was more than 300 feet long, 215 feet wide, and 80 feet from the floor to the glass ceiling. Not a single column was used in the main arena, which was pronounced the most impressive large hall in the nation. Spacious corridors encircled the entire balcony. The stage was 104 by 60 feet, and the proscenium arch, 72 by 42 feet. The steel-and-asbestos curtain weighed more than forty tons. Dressing rooms and all stage facilities were provided for the largest productions. Later, the Music Hall and the underground exhibition halls were added, permitting fourteen events to be held in different parts of the building simultaneously. The main auditorium seated 12,000; the Music Hall, 2,800; the ballroom, 1,500; the north exhibition hall, 1,500; the Little Theater, 700; and there were other halls with seating capacities ranging from 60 to 500. The pipe organ was the second largest in America, with 10,010 pipes and 150 direct speaking tubes. Approximately 750,000 people visited the building during its first year. Conventions, expositions, opera, and entertainments of various kinds educated and entertained vast audiences, and gave international publicity to Cleveland as a city of enterprise and culture.

Vincent Percy was the official organist of the Public Auditorium at the time of its opening and continued in this position in the 1940s. He was also widely known as organist for the Euclid Avenue Congregational Church and for the Valley of Cleveland, Scottish Rite. His fame became international when he composed *Light of the World,* based on Tennyson's *Locksley Hall,* the composition being played first before the United Nations organization for which it was written.

The American Building Exposition was the first exhibit in Cleveland's new auditorium, six full-sized houses and three miniature homes having been installed.

The Cleveland Diocesan Council of Catholic Women was founded as a branch of the National Catholic Welfare Conference, a lay organization. The founders were Bishop Joseph Schrembs, Mrs. John J. Bernet, Mrs. M. B. Daly, and Mrs. Samuel McNally. Organizations in Lorain, Elyria, Wooster, Painesville, Akron, and surrounding territory were soon included in the council. The chief function was to co-ordinate and promote the activities of Catholic lay organizations, under the direction of the bishop. The membership grew until it reached sixty thousand in 1946, when Mrs. Michael Geraci succeeded Mrs. Joy Seth Hurd as president. The Catholic Federation of Women's Clubs was also founded in 1922 to co-operate with civic activities in Cleveland. This organization was a unit of the Diocesan Council, and Cleveland soon profited through its encouragement of educational, charitable, and civic enterprises. In 1946 Mrs. Frank J. McMahon succeeded Mrs. Michael Geraci as president. The membership had grown until twenty thousand were enrolled.

The Thirteenth Ward, centering at Clark Avenue and Broadway, continued to be the largest Czechoslovak district in Cleveland. Population of the area, two-and-a-half square miles, was 24,302, of which four-fifths was Slavic. Of the total, less than 5,000 were native-born of native parentage, and more than 19,000 were foreign-born or of foreign parentage. While the Czechs were decreasing, the Slovaks were increasing.

The First Hungarian Reformed Church, founded in 1891, was America's pioneer Hungarian congregation. Its organization followed the "Conference of Tiffin" between representatives of the Reformed Church of Hungary and the Hungarian Reformed Church of the United States, who reached an agreement in Tiffin, Ohio, that the American Hungarian churches should join the Reformed churches of the United States. While educators had come from Hungary to preserve the language and traditions of the old country in the American-born generation, they could not compete with the public schools, for the spirit of young Hungarians was already heart and soul in America. Young and old, however, found enjoyment in traditional folk music in the native tongue. Church members followed the population trend eastward, and a small chapel of the Congregationalists in a new Hungarian section at Buckeye Road and East 123rd Street was purchased and used by the First Church until Bethlen Hall was erected. This beautiful cultural center at East Boulevard and Buckeye Road was dedicated in 1932 during the pastorate of Dr. Joseph Herczegh, who came to the church in 1923. In the mid-1940s the courageous, pioneering congregation, now of the Evangelical and Reformed faith, was planning to erect "the most beautiful Calvinist church in America," under the leadership of Dr. Stephen Szabo.

Bishop Joseph Schrembs attended the sessions of the International Eucharistic Congress in Rome in April, at which time he had four private audiences with the Pope and was presented the Peter's Pence of the Diocese amounting to $120,000.

The enrollment in evening high schools reached 9,255, at a cost of $63,657. On account of the shortage of funds, the Board of Education deemed it necessary to eliminate appropriations, and high schools were reorganized on a self-supporting basis.

A school board consisting of the Revs. Dr. Francis T. Moran, Gilbert P. Jennings, Wenceslas Krzycki, John W. Becka, and John Schaffeld was appointed by Bishop Schrembs to take charge of the diocesan school system. According to the seventh annual report, 58,500 children attended Catholic schools. The Rev. John R. Hagan began his service as superintendent of diocesan schools on January 1, 1923.

The assessed valuation of Lakewood was $77,165,600. "The City of Beautiful Homes" voted against annexation to Cleveland by a substantial margin.

The Federation of Jewish Women's Organizations, founded this year, co-ordinated activities of member groups.

The Rose-Mary Home for Crippled Children, 19350 Euclid Avenue, was organized, Caesar A. Grasselli having given this home to the Cleveland Catholic Diocese in memory of his wife, Johanna. It was designed to serve physically handicapped children of all denominations, assisting convalescent boys and girls in their efforts to get well. It was also planned to give them an opportunity to learn crafts and trades, and to aid them in their school work, thus promoting recovery and adjustment to outside living and working conditions.

Ursuline College, under the auspices of the Ursuline Sisters, moved to a new home at 2234 Overlook Road on September 24. Notre Dame College was established at 1325 Ansel Road under the auspices of the Notre Dame Sisters.

Developing from an Old Arcade dairy-stand, where they specialized in Dutch apple pie and toasted sandwiches, to the modern elegance of the Shaker Square "showplace," was the noteworthy accomplishment of Stouffer's. A. E. Stouffer began his modest undertaking in 1922 with the assistance of his wife. Vernon and Gordon Stouffer joined their father and later became president and vice president. In the 1940s, The Stouffer Corporation, employing 2,500 people, had restaurants in Cleveland, Detroit, Pittsburgh, Philadelphia, New York, Chicago, and Minneapolis. The Stouffer experimental kitchen with its college-trained dietitians was an important feature.

The Astor House, the oldest house in the city, had been moved out of the path of progress to the eastern end of Edgewater Park. Although sentimental interests favored preserving the old log trading post as a museum piece, officials ordered the historic building destroyed on October 14.

The National Aeronautic Association succeeded in welding the scattered aviation meets and races into a single group, operated under rigid rules, which later became the National Air Races with Cleveland as their home.

The Northeastern Ohio Teachers Association held its meetings in Public Auditorium, October 27-28. This was the beginning of a continuous series. Prior to 1922, the Cleveland meetings had been held in the Masonic Temple, Grays Armory, and the Hippodrome. In 1946 the membership of seventeen thousand was united in "a professional organization second to none in point of size and greater than that of the teaching population in any one of more than half the states of the Union." Believing that education is the most important single factor in determining the future of any nation, NEOTA developed programs with nationally known speakers, bringing inspiring and practical messages.

Rabbi Samuel Benjamin having resigned from the Jewish Center, a call was extended by the Anshe Emeth Congregation to Solomon Goldman, spiritual leader of the B'nai Jeshurun Congregation of Cleveland. His installation on October 27 was a noteworthy feature of the dedication of the million-dollar Cleveland Jewish Center at East 105th Street and Grantwood Avenue, with six rabbis participating. Membership increased, and religious and educational programs expanded. The congregation joined the conservative movement and affiliated with the United Synagogue of America. In 1929, when Rabbi Goldman resigned to accept a call in Chicago, he was succeeded by Dr. Harry Davidowitz, whose leadership won the devotion of the congregation for five years, at which time he resigned to live in the Holy Land. It was then that the congregation called Armond E. Cohen, a confirmant of the Center taught by Rabbi Goldman. He led the Center to even greater heights, founded the Center Hebrew Academy in 1936, and later established the Heights Branch of the congregation. In 1942 the Park School in Cleveland Heights was acquired, and later the Park Religious School was established and the Park Hebrew Academy opened. From its small beginning in 1869, the Cleveland Jewish Center grew to become an important religious and educational institution of national reputation. The officers of the congregation when the Park project was completed were: Henry A. Rocker, president; M. E. Glass, vice president; Myron Guren, recording secretary; Herman Stein, financial secretary; and Louis Miller, treasurer. Rocker continued as president in the mid-1940s.

Celebrities, on November 6, passed through the lobby of the seven-million-dollar Keith's Palace Theater into the grand hall surrounded by white pillars that glistened from the brilliance of mammoth crystal chandeliers. Against a background of raspberry-hued brocade hung notable art treasures. A blending of marble, crystal, and brocade characterized the theater proper, with a seating capacity of 3,680. On this colorful opening occasion, Newton D. Baker, president of the Chamber of Commerce, received the theater at the request of E. F. Albee, and presented it to Mayor Fred Kohler for the people of Cleveland. John F. Royal was manager of the magnificent playhouse, heralded as the finest in the world. Headliner of the opening bill was Elsie Janis, for years America's popular mimic. Backstage were forty-eight dressing rooms, each named for a state. In vaudeville days, this arrangement was often the deciding factor in settling disputes over dressing-room preferences. Over the years, performances of popular character attracted large audiences to the peerless theater, and among the leading entertainers were Olsen and Johnson, Van and Schenck, Jack Benny, Johanna Gadski, Eugene and Willie Howard, Mrs. Leslie Carter, Bill Robinson, Harry Houdini, Sophie Tucker, Ina Claire, Belle Baker, and Ethel Barrymore. The theater site had been the Samuel Dodge homestead. The house had been constructed by George Dodge, father of Samuel D. Dodge, in the 1850s, the owner having cut old Dodge Street from Euclid Avenue to the lake a short time before. The B. F. Keith Building, a twenty-one-story office building erected by the B. F. Keith Corporation at 1621 Euclid Avenue and housing the theater, featured daylight illumination from all sides.

The Van Sweringens opened negotiations with the administrators of the Searles and Hawley estates for the purchase of the stock of the Toledo, St. Louis & Western Railroad, known as the Clover Leaf. The Nickel Plate and the Lake Erie & Western were consolidated in 1922. This merger in December, resulting in the New York, Chicago & St. Louis Railroad, fulfilled the founders' dream of establishing a through route from New York to St. Louis. The consolidation caused much comment, being the most important since the passage of the Transportation Act. From this time forward the Nickel Plate was improved, and a complicated history of financing, control, and related projects followed during the Van Sweringen regime, the depression period, and into the war era. John W. Davin became president of the Nickel Plate in 1942, working in close co-operation with Robert R. Young, chairman of the board of the Chesapeake & Ohio, these railroads constituting a "family group."

In the celestial system, about 270,000,000 miles from the sun and 190,000,000 miles from the earth when nearest our sphere, there is a tiny planet revolving in the pathway of asteroids between Mars and Jupiter. Dr. Otto Struve of the Yerkes Observatory discovered the heavenly body, twenty miles in diameter, on November 14, and called it Swaseya in honor of his friend, Ambrose Swasey of Cleveland.

The Community Fund raised $4,250,427.63 with 386,667 pledges. The goal set for the fund had been $4,500,000. The chairman was Fred W. Ramsey.

By 1922 the *Plain Dealer* Building at East 6th and Superior Avenue was practically a part of the Group Plan, the new addition having doubled the size of the building. The design harmonized architecturally with the neighboring monumental structures.

Isadora Duncan danced in the Public Auditorium on December 10 and excited her audience more by her famous red dress and her chatter than by her dancing. James H. Rogers reported, "all things considered, the orchestra did very well."

The mortality rate was 10.67 per thousand population for the year, the rate for Cleveland residents being 9.92, a low rate for a large city.

1923

By virtue of annexation, West Park became Ward 33 of the City of Cleveland, adding 3,560 people and an area of twelve and a half square miles, with assessed property valuation of $25,975,520.

The Illuminating Company and the Northern Ohio Light Company agreed to the interchange of current on January 5. In this way the customers of both were protected.

Opinions varied about the effectiveness of the health creed of Emile Coué when he held clinics in Cleveland, January 19-20. Those who came to know him believed in his unusual ability to help many people suffering from imaginary ills. "Every day in every way, I am growing better and better" was psychology with a purpose.

The first big sports event in the Public Auditorium was the basketball game between the famous world-champion Celtics and the Rosenblums of Cleveland on January 30. Ten thousand people saw the Celtics win the fiercely contested game by the score of 28-24.

It was charged on February 14 that 30,000 people peddled liquor in the city. Officials said that 10,000 stills supplied the trade and 100,000 residents violated the law in homes.

William J. White, one of the nation's most colorful figures, died on February 17 at the age of seventy-two. Through the amazing success of Yucatan chewing gum, he had amassed vast wealth in the eighties and startled the world with his extravagant living. Early in the century, White organized the ten-million-dollar American Chicle Company in New York and became president, and George H. Worthington, Dr. E. E. Beeman of chewing-gum fame, Jonathan P. Primley, and Thomas Adams, Jr., were associates. Business difficulties arose in 1915, and White was forced out, penniless; but five years later, he was back again as the "gum king," with the flourishing William J. White Chicle Company at Niagara Falls. Litigation with the American company led to his second downfall; but he returned to Cleveland, built a factory at Madison and West 112th Street, and was making a brave effort to create a third fortune when he died.

Receivers took over the Cleveland Discount Company on February 23, the court naming T. H. Hogsett and W. L. David. The company, under Josiah Kirby's direction, had enjoyed a gay but speculative career. An audit in 1923 revealed a huge loss. Common stock was declared worthless, and assets were sold to an organization of stock-and-bond holders.

John Adams High School, 3817 East 116th Street, was dedicated as a junior high school. It later became a senior high school with an enrollment of 3,400 students.

Twelve thousand members of the department of superintendents, National Educational Association, opened their convention in the Public Auditorium on February 26. Their meetings were of constructive significance in a confused civilization.

Organized by E. J. Kulas in March, the Midland Steel Products Company was a merger of the Parish & Bingham Company of Cleveland, Detroit Pressed Steel Company, and the Parish Manufacturing Company of Detroit. In its plant at Madison Avenue and West 106th Street, steel frames and axle housings were turned out with great speed and extreme accuracy into many assembly lines that supplied makers of passenger cars, trucks, and buses. The plant became the largest producer of automotive frames. In addition, automotive brakes and heavy metal stampings were manufactured.

Fred H. Goff, president of The Cleveland Trust Company and one of Cleveland's foremost citizens, died March 14. He was born in Blackberry, Illinois, of New England stock, in 1858. The family came to Cleveland in 1864, and after graduation from the University of Michigan, Goff was admitted to the bar in 1883. He began a brilliant legal career as partner in the law firm of Kline, Carr, Tolles & Goff. His services in the settlement of the long-drawn-out street-railway dispute brought wide recognition; but they were overshadowed by his remarkable record of achievement as president of The Cleveland Trust Company, beginning in 1908. He originated the Cleveland Foundation, launched in 1914, which became the model community trust of the nation and was dedicated to the task of carrying forward civic progress and human welfare in Cleveland. His contributions to the city's advancement as lawyer, banker, and public-spirited citizen were notable. Harris Creech, who had been president of the Garfield Savings Bank Company which merged with The Cleveland Trust Company in 1922, became president of the trust company. Under his administration, the bank's deposits more than doubled.

The trustees of the boards of Western Reserve University and the University Hospitals had acquired a tract of land on Euclid Avenue at the east side of Adelbert Road in 1916 as building sites for the two institutions.

On April 18, 1923, the cornerstone was laid for the School of Medicine of the university near the southerly end of the tract. The building, the gift of Samuel Mather, cost $2,500,000, and the first classes were held on September 25, 1924. In 1925 Mather made an additional gift to the university of $3,000,000 for the promotion of medical education and for general purposes. One of the show spots of the campus, the building housed the school and the Hamann Museum of Comparative Anthropology which contained the best collection of mammalian skulls in the world.

The Music Supervisors National Conference was held, with more than 1,500 music educators in attendance. Among the speakers were Dr. Walter Damrosch, conductor of the New York Symphony, and Dr. Charles H. Farnsworth of Columbia University. The Annual Music Memory Contest for school children, conducted by the Cleveland Orchestra, was a feature of the convention.

Automotive vehicles were riding on Cleco-Gruss shock absorbers, produced by The Cleveland Pneumatic Tool Company, which led to the development of aerols for smoother, safer landing of airplanes. L. W. Greve was elected president in 1931. His father, Claus Greve, the founder, became chairman of the board and was active until his death in 1936. Major improvements for the aviation industry played a large part in World War II. A subsidiary, Cleveland Pneumatic Aerol, Inc., a vast wartime plant in Euclid, was organized in 1942 for the production of landing-gear aerols and rocket shells. Upon the president's death this year, John DeMooy served for a brief period, followed by Daniel C. Green, and in 1944 by George P. Torrence. Cleveland Pneumatic was purchased in 1945 by Walter E. Schott and associates of Cincinnati. In June, 1946, the shock-absorber business was sold to private interests; and in December, the rock-drill division was acquired by the LeRoi Company of Milwaukee. Cleveland Pneumatic continued as one of the largest aircraft landing-gear manufacturers, also making a complete line of pneumatic tools and appliances.

Overcrowding in both the college and high school of St. Ignatius College led to a plan initiated by Father Thomas J. Smith, S.J., president, to separate the institutions. The name was changed to Cleveland University in May of this year but it was short-lived; and in September the school became officially known as John Carroll University, honoring Bishop John Carroll, the first Roman Catholic bishop of America. Father Benedict J. Rodman, S.J., succeeded to the presidency, and carried out Father Smith's development plans. A huge fund-raising campaign, launched in late 1928, resulted in pledges of $2,541,382 for the new university. Building operations began; but they were halted by the depression until 1935, and classes opened in the new institution in University Heights at North Park and Miramar Drive on October 7. Enrollment for the year 1936-37 was 604; in the spring of 1945, war influences had brought it to a low of 270; but in 1946, more than 2,000 students were receiving their education at John Carroll, more than 1,600 of them veterans. The Rev. Frederick E. Welfle, S.J., became president in 1946, succeeding the Rev. Thomas I. Donnelly, S.J., who had served since 1942.

John Leonard Whitfield, murderer of a Cleveland policeman who had captured him, was caught after reports of his escape had shocked the public. Later, in attempting to slip out of the Ohio State Penitentiary, he was fatally shot.

The City Health Commissioner asserted there was enough room in Cleveland cemeteries for three hundred years. There was little excitement over the assertion.

The Orpheus Male Chorus, under the direction of Charles D. Dawe, won first place for small choruses in the Welsh Eisteddfod in Mold, Wales. The prize had never before been awarded to a chorus outside of the British Isles.

The Mount Zion Congregational Church purchased the former temple of the Tifereth Israel Congregation at East 55th and Central Avenue. The late 1930s found the membership of about a hundred colored folk struggling under an impossible financial burden; but, with aid from the Congregational Union, a church home was provided at 9014 Cedar Avenue in 1938. Gathering strength, Mount Zion went forward with faith reborn. Membership in the mid-1940s reached 431, when the Rev. John C. Mickle, Jr., was serving his fifth year as pastor.

The Cleveland Bird Club, first known as the S. Louise Patterson Memorial Association, was founded by Mrs. Stella M. Antisdale and several of her friends. C. M. Shipman was chosen as the first president. Five years later the name was changed to the Cleveland Bird Club, and Dr. C. M. Finfrock was made president. The purpose of the organization was to increase the knowledge of birds, to help promote the conservation of diminishing wild life and to foster its protection. The activities included bird walks, screen tours, field trips, and educational lectures by members. Furthermore, the club sponsored scholarships for advanced training of people interested in the field of conservation. Two bird sanctuaries were owned by the club, one consisting of 161 acres in Aurora, and the other, the Hach Sanctuary, consisting of 35 acres of primitive forest along the Chagrin River near Willoughby. An additional tract of 50 acres, adjacent to the Hach Sanctuary, was acquired and named the Harrison Otis Woodland. In 1946 the membership numbered more than a thousand and the officers included Harry E. Duer, president; Warner Seely, E. A. Schuemann, and H. C. Dobbins, vice presidents; I. R. Watts, secretary; Gerry Deuchlander, corresponding secretary; Mrs. Esther H. Ketch, treasurer; and Mrs. Antisdale, trustee at large.

The name of The Public Library of the School District of the City of Cleveland was changed to the Cleveland Public Library. At the same time, the name of The Board of Trustees of the Public Library of the School District of the City of Cleveland was changed to the Board of Trustees of the Cleveland Public Library. On October 17, 1902, the law had been amended so that each of the seven members was to serve seven years, with the years so arranged that one member would retire each year. The Board of Education continued to select members of the library board.

The Cleveland Tennis and Racquet Club was established at Fairhill and

Kemper roads. An outgrowth of the East End Tennis and Racquet Club of Bolton Square fame, the fans' new home in Shaker Heights incorporated a large scope of activities in its program. Of dominant interest were the three championship tournaments held each year from 1923 until 1937 when the Cleveland Skating Club took over. The Cleveland championships were limited to residents of Cleveland, and some of the winners were Charles A. Carran, Kirk M. Reid, Harold Bartel, Leroy Weir, and Johnny Doerr. The state open championship included among its famous winners Bill Tilden, Frank Parker, Bill Talbert, and Frank L. Kovacs.

Huron Road Hospital had outgrown its quarters, and, as a temporary measure, moved to 8811 Euclid Avenue. About four acres of the Forest Hills property of John D. Rockefeller in East Cleveland had been purchased, and in 1931 ground was broken for a modern hospital plant. The Huron Road property was sold to the Ohio Bell Telephone Company as a site for its central building.

The decision to tear down the Andrews home on Euclid at East 30th Street revived memories of the days when "Andrews' folly" was the best-known residence in northern Ohio. Built in the early eighties, it was occupied in 1885 by Samuel Andrews, who made a fortune in Standard Oil. Three years were required to erect the mansion and install the panel woodwork and the lavish decorations and furnishings that characterized many of the rooms. Shortly after its completion, the owner found that it was too large for practical use and too costly to maintain, hence the name "Andrews' folly." It was closed for the greater part of a quarter century; then the furniture was sold and the fabulous landmark was turned over to the wreckers.

A. H. Tinnerman, who carried on the stove-and-range business begun by his father in 1870, originated the first all-porcelain-enameled gas range with concealed fastenings this year. His spring-tension fastening device—the "speed nut," patented in 1924—revolutionized the assembly of the industry. During depression years, George A., grandson of the founder, explored the application of the speed-nut fastener to other industries. Fasteners soon became a rapidly growing business of the expanding plant at 2038 Fulton Road, as they were adopted in the assembly of leading products of mass production. Stove-making had been discontinued in 1940, when Tinnerman Products, Inc., was formed.

The Council for the Prevention of War was formed, twenty-one women's organizations being represented at the founding, with Mrs. E. S. Bassett and Mrs. Siegmund Herzog as officers and Judge Florence E. Allen as honorary chairman. Later reorganization was effected resulting in forming the Council for the Promotion of Peace, with Mrs. Charles H. Prescott as president. After a merger arranged in 1934 with the Adult Education Council, the organization was known as the International Affairs Committee of the association. Because of financial conditions, the committee severed its connection in 1933 and became a separate organization, co-operating with Cleveland College as the Foreign Affairs Council. For four years, men of the community had become active in it. The officers of the new council were

Newton D. Baker, honorary president; Harrison B. McGraw, president; Mrs. James H. Griswold, vice president; Mrs. W. J. Bushea, executive secretary; and Herman L. Vail, treasurer. In 1934, Dr. Brooks Emeny became director of the council, whose motto was "Foreign affairs are your affairs."

The city was host to 2,500 bankers on July 16, as the American Institute of Banking Convention began proceedings. On July 20 the visitors inspected the Union Trust home, then under construction, 250 automobiles driving through the huge lobby.

The new Federal Reserve Bank Building opened on August 27, and sight-seers at the rate of thirty-five per minute passed through the East 6th Street entrance to see one of the nation's finest banking homes. The building fronted 200 feet on East 6th Street, 216 feet on Superior, and was 200 feet high from the street level to the roof, excluding the penthouse. The architecture was a modern adaptation of Italian Renaissance, and the material of the exterior was of Etowah Georgia marble with a base of granite. Flanking the main entrance were heroic figures carved in stone symbolizing Security and Integrity; while on the Superior side was the colossal bronze figure of Energy. The sculptor of the statues was Henry Hering of New York. The lobby walls were of Sienna marble. Above the center door of the central lobby was a mural of the steel industry painted by Cora Holden, Cleveland artist, from actual observation in Cleveland steel mills. In the reception room were portraits of Alexander Hamilton and Robert Morris painted by Alonzo Kimball of Cleveland, and throughout the building were decorative illustrations of historical character. The world's largest vault was one of the practical features. The engineering agencies included a power plant where electricity was generated to supply the demand of the entire building, steam and air-conditioning equipment. The Federal Reserve Bank Building, costing $8,250,000, was pronounced worthy of the vast Fourth Federal Reserve District it served. David C. Wills, chairman of the Board of Governors, died in 1925 and was succeeded by George DeCamp of Cleveland, who served until 1933. Lewis B. Williams, who became chairman of the board of the National City Bank, held the office until 1934 and was succeeded by Edmund S. Burke, Jr., who was chairman until 1938, when George C. Brainard, subsequently president of the Addressograph-Multigraph Corporation, was designated. E. R. Fancher served as governor until his death in 1935, when Matthew J. Fleming, formerly deputy governor, succeeded him. Fleming's title became president through a legal change in name in 1936, and he retired in 1944, when Ray M. Gidney, formerly vice president of the Federal Reserve Bank of New York, succeeded him.

The Cleveland Baseball Federation, under the leadership of William T. "Bill" Duggan, started a medical fund for injured players and a fund for baseball equipment. Cleveland is said to have been the first city to sponsor baseball for youth of from eight to fourteen years of age, and to equip youngsters with complete outfits. This encouragement to boys in school led to the development of more than a hundred players in organized baseball. Duggan's unselfish activity attracted the co-operation of five hundred businessmen who inspired a new interest in sandlot baseball, fostering good sportsmanship and combating juvenile delinquency.

Cleveland announced, September 1, it had $100,000 ready to aid earthquake stricken Japan. The Community Fund offered money from its reserve.

On September 4, the Cleveland Clearing House Association moved to the Federal Reserve Bank Building, and thereby centralized many of Cleveland's important banking activities. Efficiency of the Cleveland system attracted attention in banking circles of other cities. The association gained an enviable record by meeting Cleveland's banking emergencies thoroughly and promptly. It supported the Liberty Loan drives during World War I, and was the local financing vehicle during the desperate national financial crises of 1931 and 1933. Its purpose was to protect and safeguard Cleveland's financial organizations, fostering sound methods of banking and encouraging co-operation among member banks.

One of the nation's most powerful stations at this time, WTAM started broadcasting with a 1,500-watt rating. It was an outgrowth of the experiment of S. E. "Eddie" Leonard, a young radio engineer, who had worked closely with T. A. Willard, president of the Willard Storage Battery Company, in developing a commercial station operated by storage batteries. After three years of experimental broadcasting, largely directed toward the use and sale of storage batteries for transmitters and receivers, the Willard Storage Battery Company bought the Goodyear Station WEAR, and combining it with their own operation, established WTAM as a clear-channel station in September. This year, WTAM pioneered in broadcasting a three-way conversation from a dirigible airship. This was accomplished by dropping a microphone lead from the suspended dirigible to the roof of the Hotel Allerton. The three conversation points were the dirigible, the WTAM studio, and the Goodyear plant in Akron. Louis W. Zimmerman was the first manager and program director of WTAM. On his evening program in 1924 was a little Cleveland band called Guy Lombardo and His Royal Canadians, reaching out for fame. With Alice Keith, formerly supervisor of music appreciation in the Cleveland schools, Zimmerman presented classical-music programs that Dr. Walter Damrosch used as models in New York City.

Rising rents, as usual, were particularly serious for the white-collar man. A survey showed the middle class could not find homes at middle-range prices.

A touch of Spain was brought to the corner of Surrey and Derbyshire Road, Cleveland Heights, with the erection of the Alcazar Hotel, formally dedicated on October 1. The decorative vestibule of colorful limestone featured imported Spanish tiles, duplicates of those in the Alcazar of Seville, Spain. The distinctive, five-story apartment hotel was constructed for George W. Hale, Edna Florence Steffens, Harry E. Steffens, and Kent Hale Smith.

The city was paid new honor on October 23 by a visit from David Lloyd George. The former British Premier addressed the Chamber of Commerce at noon. His discussion of international affairs awakened Clevelanders to a new appreciation of the problem of an involved Europe. A large group assembled later for the cornerstone ceremony at the Public Library site. Arthur A. Stearns, vice president of the library board and chairman of the building committee; John Griswold White, president of the board; and Linda A. Eastman, librarian, officiated. A large copper box containing documents, pamphlets, and pictures relating to the history of library work in Cleveland was placed inside the stone. The speaker of the day was introduced by Newton D. Baker, and the white-haired war Premier of Great Britain, in his dynamic and incisive manner, fascinated the crowd at the dedication.

The campaign goal set for the Community Fund was $4,200,000. The amount raised was $4,175,186.19, with 395,985 subscribers.

General Joseph Haller, "The Savior of Warsaw," was honored in Cleveland when he joined seven thousand citizens of Polish origin at the Public Auditorium, November 19, in a salute to *The Star Spangled Banner*. He told the audience, "Your ideals of liberty, law, order, freedom and peace, are the old ideals of Poland."

Several important apartment hotels were built during 1923: Fenway Hall, 1986 East 107th Street; Wade Park Manor, East 107th and Park Lane; and Bolton Square Hotel, 8907 Carnegie Avenue.

1924

"Dry" Cleveland hailed young 1924. Squadrons of prohibition agents declared the welcome the "most arid" in history.

Mayor Fred Kohler on January 1 ended his two-year stewardship and prepared to turn over his desk to Cleveland's first city manager, William R. Hopkins. At this time it was natural that the citizenship should review the remarkable achievements of Hopkins and his brothers. They came from an old Welsh family that had developed iron mills in the home country and later in America. The father, David J., established his home in Newburgh, where he labored in the rolling mills so that each of his boys could have a good education, and the mother's sound and kindly philosophy gave them strength and encouragement. Jefferey John Hopkins was the oldest, and after providing himself with a theological education, became an influential pastor in Norwood, Cincinnati. Thomas L. was an expert accountant who was sent by the Government to the Philippines as auditor, later continuing his successful work in Cleveland. Evan H. secured a legal education and became the able dean of the Law School of Western Reserve University. George W., an outstanding physician, established a widely known clinic in Newburgh for working men of the district. William R. was the next oldest, and then followed Martin L., who became an executive in the Cleveland Rolling Mill Company and also in the Upson Nut Company. Ben F., manufacturer, railroad builder, and civic leader, was the seventh son, and Arthur H. became one of America's leading theatrical producers. Cleveland owes much to these eight resourceful Hopkins brothers.

Clayton C. Townes, president of the Cleveland City Council, who had been a leader in city affairs and Republican politics, became mayor when William R. Hopkins was made city manager. He served two years and was succeeded by John D. Marshall in 1926.

The Passion Players from Oberammergau, Germany, came to the city as envoys of peace. Anton Lang, interviewed on his arrival in Cleveland, January 4, said the greatest need was world amity. The players exhibited wood carving in the Public Auditorium.

A war on gambling opened, and slot machines were seized on January 9. Few people realized the slot machine was to become a menace involving crime, gang wars, and murder.

The Public Auditorium was the scene of Cleveland's spectacular Annual Automobile Show on January 19, fifty-eight manufacturers exhibiting 240 models in the "million dollar motor spectacle."

Peter Witt opened a fight against smoky engines on January 23, with the idea of compelling all railroads to electrify within the city limits.

An opera audience of 8,689 set a new record, February 13, when *Salome* was presented in the Public Auditorium by the Chicago Opera Company. In four performances, 26,430 paid $72,952, said to be a record up to this time.

A Lincoln meeting held by the Cleveland Advertising Club on February 14 attracted national attention. A number of people who had known Abraham Lincoln personally were introduced: Dr. George C. Ashmun, the last of Lincoln's famous bodyguard; John G. Whitby, who, as a boy of fourteen, ran away from home to carry water at the Battle of Gettysburg; Mrs. Mary V. Thompson, who had been taken into the White House while her parents' home was being repaired after a fire; Mrs. W. W. McGill, who as a little girl was held in her teacher's arms at the railroad station so that the President might place his hand upon her head; George Seaman, who baked a seventy-five-pound cake, four feet high, for Lincoln's inauguration party; O. P. McIlrath, whose father measured stature with Lincoln in the old Weddell House; and Captain Joseph B. Molyneaux, who stood on dress parade when Lincoln reviewed the "Fighting 6th" of the Ohio Volunteer Infantry. Ida Tarbell, Lincoln authority, trying to suppress tears of emotion, told of the Emancipator's genuine love for mankind.

Newton D. Baker, who had led the Democratic Party in Cuyahoga County since the death of Tom L. Johnson, relinquished control in favor of W. Burr Gongwer, his chief lieutenant. Baker became central committee chairman, an honorary position, while his successor was made chairman of the executive committee. Gongwer was a young political writer for the *Plain Dealer* when Johnson, who became mayor in 1901, made him his secretary. Although a Republican, Gongwer was so inspired by Johnson's leadership that he turned Democrat, and for many years was the party leader. He served as collector of customs from 1915 until 1921, succeeding Maurice Maschke who was boss of the Republicans. Gongwer is given credit for securing the position of customs collector for Mrs. Bernice S. Pyke, a party leader, who became national committeewoman and member of the Election Board. Among the close associates of the political boss were James J. McGinty, able minority leader of Council; W. J. Murphy, postmaster at the time Gongwer was collector; Fred Kohler, who won the mayoralty contest in 1921; and Pierce D. Metzger, associate in the insurance business that Gongwer launched in the early 1920s. The *Plain Dealer* in the 1940s called Gongwer "one of the last links between the present generation of politicians and the Tom L. Johnson era."

Visitors walked in summer gardens in the Public Auditorium on March 30. Officials opened the Sixth National Flower Show and christened a rose with the name of Mrs. Calvin Coolidge. It was called the "most lavish and costliest flower show ever seen in America."

The Cuyahoga County Library opened its doors on April 1, on the third floor of the Kinney & Levan Building. Eight branches and fifteen stations were organized the first year, extending to rural districts where people were scattered and unable to reach a library. Mrs. Margaret E. Thayer was appointed county-library head.

Herb's Indians of Cleveland won the American Bowling Congress five-man team championship with a score of 3,044.

St. Luke's Hospital Association, through its board of trustees, announced plans for beautiful new buildings to be erected at Shaker Boulevard and East 116th Street. The building, dedicated in 1908 on Carnegie Avenue, had been outgrown years before, and funds for the new structures had been quietly raised during the past ten years. Francis F. Prentiss had given two million dollars anonymously, but the fact became public in spite of his protestation. Since 1906, and up to the time of his death in 1937, he had been president of the association. Upon his twenty-fifth year of service in 1931, he was honored in Prentiss Auditorium when Newton D. Baker gave an inspiring tribute to his leadership. The new buildings on the Heights were completed in 1927, the center structure being a memorial to Dr. Dudley P. Allen, given by Mrs. Francis F. Prentiss, formerly Mrs. Allen.

The first Cleveland Medal for Public Service was awarded, April 15, by The Cleveland Chamber of Commerce to Samuel Mather, who "has lifted the public imagination to the highest level of usefulness by his own inspiring and unselfish example."

Metropolitan Opera came to Cleveland's Public Auditorium for the first time on April 28 and succeeded in thrilling Cleveland audiences with seven performances. The brilliant season included such favorites as *Aïda, Carmen, Rigoletto, Faust, Il Trovatore, Romeo and Juliet,* and *Boris Goudonoff.* Hailed as "more than a musical event," it was described as "a civic enterprise of great magnitude." Outstanding stars such as Ponselle, Bori, and Tibbett were greeted with great enthusiasm, and it was hoped that this season would be the forerunner of subsequent opera performances in Cleveland. This hope was soon fulfilled, for the Metropolitan returned to the city in 1925 and 1926 under private sponsorship. Some of the citizens who gave characteristic support to this pioneering project included Charles E. Adams, Charles C. Bolton, Alexander C. Brown, F. E. Drury, A. C. Ernst, Michael Gallagher, Kermode F. Gill, H. M. Hanna, Myron T. Herrick, and Edwin S. Griffiths. An unusual and gratifying feature of the 1925 season was the gala concert held on the Sunday afternoon of "Opera Week," when many of the stars

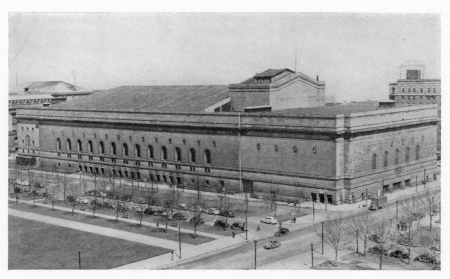

Public Auditorium, foremost in its field.

Severance Hall, magnificent home of the Cleveland Orchestra. PERRY CRAGG, CLEVE-
LAND NEWS.

The Greater Cleveland Home and Flower Show, a typical exhibit.

An audience of twelve thousand and not a pillar to obstruct the view.

IN THE PUBLIC AUDITORIUM

appeared. Sharing in the success of these early endeavors were Philip Miner and Everett L. Jones, under whose management the first local performances were given. In 1926 ten outstanding programs were presented. The following year saw the origin of the Northern Ohio Opera Association, assuring many more seasons of star-studded, beautifully staged, musical extravaganzas.

Four thousand children's voices, the public-schools' finest, were heard in the Public Auditorium on May 9 at a May Festival.

A memorial ceremony was held at Rouen, France, in May, to commemorate the landing of Cleveland's Lakeside Hospital Unit, the first United States Army detachment to arrive in France in 1917, and to honor the French citizens who had opened their homes to the Americans. A tablet was erected on the stone quay where the detachment landed, and those participating in the ceremony were Ambassador Myron T. Herrick, Dr. George W. Crile, Dr. William E. Lower, and Dr. Henry L. Sanford.

A twenty-story skyscraper, the Union Trust Building (later Union Commerce Building) was opened formally on May 19. The opening marked the dedication of the largest and finest bank building ever conceived, and the completion of the second largest office building in the world. The sixteen-million-dollar structure rose like a mountain of steel and stone in the heart of the city. The development covered a frontage of 146 feet on Euclid Avenue, 258 feet on East 9th, and 513 feet on Chester. The building contained more than 30 acres of floor space. The Union Trust Company occupied practically all of the first five stories in addition to the ground floor and basement. The huge lobby spread 50 feet in width between giant marble pillars brought from Italy. Magnificent murals by Jules Guerin added beauty and color to the entranceways and the rotunda. There were three entrances to the building, and four to the bank. The architects were Graham, Anderson, Probst & White.

A peace army of women braved rain and critics on May 19. Age and youth of many lands trudged the streets in a war protest, as silent thousands looked on.

Black Gold won the first running of the Ohio State Derby on May 24, at Maple Heights. The week before, he had won the Kentucky Derby. Running races were becoming more popular.

Fire destroyed the *State of Ohio,* steamer of the Cleveland & Buffalo line, at the Cleveland dock. The *City of Detroit II,* purchased from the Detroit & Cleveland line, was rebuilt as the *Goodtime,* operating on the Cleveland-Cedar Point-Put-in-Bay route until 1938. Automotive transportation began to make inroads on lake shipping in 1926; and in 1930, C & B began offering winter motor-truck service.

Cleveland was the scene of the Republican National Convention, the Public Auditorium proving an ideal building for the large assemblage of delegates and for committee meetings. Chicago had tried to secure the convention, but withdrew its bid after hearing Calvin Coolidge ask that the conclave be held in Cleveland. Senator Theodore E. Burton, temporary chairman, eloquently sounded the keynote, but the outstanding feature was the nomination of Coolidge by Marion Leroy Burton, president of the

University of Michigan and former president of Smith College. For twenty minutes the audience sat spellbound, then burst into continued applause. Many delegates pronounced the speech the most scholarly and impressive nomination effort that the Republican Party had known. Coolidge and General Charles G. Dawes constituted the winning ticket. Radio station WTAM, serving a network of sixteen stations, sent out the report of the convention, the most important broadcasting achievement of its kind up to this time. Later in the summer, the Socialist Party came to the city and placed in nomination for the Presidency Robert M. LaFollette. The meetings failed to inspire much attention in the nation. James L. E. Jappe was in charge of arranging facilities for the participants, the spectators, and those reporting the Republican convention. He served in a similar capacity during succeeding Republican conventions, and became the nation's expert in this field.

The Lorain hurricane disaster, June 28, shocked the nation. Three hundred were reported dead as the storm swept Lorain, Ohio, and other shore cities. Hundreds of homes were demolished, and many buildings were blown down. Autos lay crushed in streets where bricks were piled several feet deep. Bodies were found by the score in the ruins of a wrecked theater. The injured in Lorain alone were estimated at 1,500. Gathering its wasted strength, Lorain started the building of a greater city. The Cleveland Trust Company's Lorain branch set up temporary quarters after the storm, realizing that the first need of the stricken would be their funds on deposit. Branch banks collected relief funds. A little later, President Creech originated a plan by which five hundred Ohio banks joined in furnishing a million dollars in low-interest loans to rebuild homes in the damaged area.

The Friendly Inn moved into the former home of the Council Educational Alliance at 3754 Woodland Avenue. Negroes, newly come from the South, populated the neighborhood.

Kenyon College at Gambier, Ohio, celebrated the centennial of its founding. Leonard Hall, a dormitory, had been given by Samuel Mather in honor of Bishop William A. Leonard of the Episcopal Diocese, and the Samuel Mather Science Hall had been given by H. G. Dalton.

In Wade Park, northwest of the Cleveland Museum of Art, a monument was dedicated in July to the memory of General Milan R. Stefanik, a Slovakian national hero killed in World War I.

Rabbi Abba Hillel Silver and a distinguished group of civic and religious leaders dedicated the new Temple at East 105th and Ansel Road to faith and peace. He commended the achievement of Israel's followers in building the $1,350,000 edifice to the purposes of God. The Temple, built for the Tifereth Israel Congregation, was one of the largest and most impressive synagogues in the country. Expressing the deep religious spirit and essential unity of the Jewish faith, the building accommodated various educational, social, and religious activities, and its three sections were joined by a spacious lobby which ran from Ansel Road to East 105th Street. Confronted by the problem of an unusual ground site, the pattern of a seven-sided building was accepted as the best architectural plan for the Temple. The exterior, of Indiana limestone, had a banded effect which resembled the temple at Santa Sophia. The domes were of yellow-buff tile which provided a striking contrast to the inlays of colored marble over the entrance arches and flanking towers. The focal point of the interior was the Ark, elaborately carved and inlaid. Throughout, gold and color were used in carvings of the symbols and arabesques. The architect was Charles R. Greco.

DeHart Hubbard, who later made Cleveland his home, was the first Negro to capture an Olympic championship. Representing the United States at Paris this year, he won the running broad jump with 24 feet, 5⅛ inches. At Stagg Field, Chicago, June 13, 1925, he established the broad-jump record of 25 feet, 10⅝ inches, in the amateur-athletic meet. He represented the University of Michigan track team, and his record stood until broken by Ed Hamm of Georgia in the 1928 Olympics.

Thomas Alva Edison, on October 17, participated in a motion picture entitled *The Magic Chest,* which was used in the theaters of Cleveland to stimulate interest in the Community Fund campaign. This was the only time that the great inventor assumed the role of actor. So successful was the picture that other cities used it in their campaigns. When Edison concluded his part of the picture in the yard of the famous laboratory at Menlo Park, he signed the following statement:

> I am glad to have this opportunity to show an interest in the metropolis of my home state. I was born at Milan, Ohio, and I have always watched with pride the advance of your city, which stands so high in civic, industrial and philanthropic endeavor . . . Your idea of combining your philanthropic money-raising efforts in the one campaign is practical and I am not surprised that cities throughout the country are adopting Cleveland's plan and benefiting themselves thereby. . . . It is a pleasure for me to participate in your campaign.

John W. Davis, Democratic nominee for the Presidency, visited the city on October 24. He thrilled thousands in Public Auditorium with a plea to end religious hatred.

Ev Jones and Cartwright "Pinky" Hunter were giving Cleveland listeners their first local commercials on the radio. They were appearing on Station WTAM, and Ev played the piano while "Pinky" strummed the banjo. A little later, Ev Jones' band was sponsored by the Willard Storage Battery Company, the broadcast emanating from the factory on Taft Avenue near East 131st Street. These broadcasts made the band nationally famous, and for nine years it was a favorite over WTAM, WHK, and WGAR. "Pinky" Hunter had started his entertainment career as vocalist with Emerson Gill's Band at the Bamboo Gardens on Euclid Avenue west of East 101st Street in 1923. Later he formed his own orchestra and entertained at the Lotus Gardens and other restaurants until 1937 when he became assistant musical director at WHK, working with Louis Rich. The next year he joined Jack Graney in baseball announcing, and in 1942 was made program director of WHK. The era from 1923 to 1935 was one in which bands and orchestras were organized in Cleveland, later to become big names. Austin J. Wylie led his popular dance band at the Golden Pheasant on Prospect Avenue where Artie Shaw, Vaughn Monroe, Claude Thornhill, and Eddie Peabody were among the musicians working for him. Guy Lombardo was playing at the Claremont, the Music Box, and the Lake Road Inn; Kay Kyser started his career at the Bird Cage in Geneva, Ohio, occasionally substituting for Emerson Gill at the Bamboo Gardens; Dick Fidler was leading at the Golden Pheasant, and the Spitalny Brothers were directing their theater orchestras. On their tours, these dance bands and orchestras were making Cleveland well known as the source of popular music.

Superior Avenue's white way opened, and fifteen thousand jammed the street to see the dedication of the new and improved street-lighting system. "The City of Light" was advertising itself.

The Parker Appliance Company was founded on October 31 by Arthur LaRue Parker, inventor of a coupling for joining seamless-tubing lines. Operations were begun at 10320 Berea Road, and these quarters were occupied until 1935 when the building at 17325 Euclid Avenue was purchased. The company became interested in the problems of hydraulic systems in airplanes, and was closely identified with the aircraft industry. The founder died in 1945, and S. B. Taylor was elected president. Besides its principal manufactures, the company produced molded-rubber and plastic products.

The Van Sweringens offered a large site in Shaker Heights as the home of Western Reserve University, but the board did not wish to leave University Circle.

The Community Fund sped past its goal, collecting $4,399,000 as the effort ended, November 26.

The Rev. William H. Leach, of the Walden Presbyterian Church of Buffalo, and Edward E. Buckow of Cleveland organized a religious publication to fill a need not met by others in the field, a professional monthly for ministers. The result was *Church Management,* a journal with broad policies edited by Leach.

A fine reproduction of Leonardo da Vinci's "Last Supper" was unveiled at the Broadway Methodist Church on December 18. Mrs. Oliver M. Stafford had seen the painting in the Louvre and purchased it for the church. The reproduction, more than twenty-five feet wide, was called the only true copy in America. Mrs. Stafford made the presentation in honor of Mrs. Marriett Leek Huntington, widow of John Huntington.

The Miracle, Max Reinhardt's pantomime, was presented in the Public Auditorium for three weeks commencing December 22, and proved the greatest stage production in magnitude Cleveland had seen. It was more imposing than that in New York because of the size of the auditorium, which was transformed into a cathedral. Attendance was 136,994, breaking the record of any seven weeks of the New York run. Gross receipts exceeded $400,000, people coming from long distances to see the stupendous spectacle. The leading role of the Madonna was played by Lady Diana Manners, Rosamond Pinchot appearing in her place in several presentations.

The North American Coal Corporation was launched by Frank E. Taplin, long associated with the coal business and sales manager of the Youghiogheny & Ohio Coal Company for years. He had founded the forerunner of the corporation in 1913 when he organized the Cleveland & Western Coal Company "with an office and a pencil." Taplin continued to direct corporation activities until his death in 1938. Henry G. Schmidt became president in 1942, and the organization continued its expansion until the business mounted to thirty million dollars a year. The corporation owned mines and stores in Ohio and West Virginia; and sold and distributed coal through three subsidiary companies: The Inland Coal & Dock Company, Duluth; The United Coal & Dock Company, Milwaukee; and Canada Coal, Ltd., Toronto.

1925

City Manager William R. Hopkins presented to the City Council recommendations for a great municipal airfield. The city had envisioned an airport for some time, but it was the threatened loss of the United States air mail that inspired final action. Cleveland could have a position on the coast-to-coast route if it could satisfy the Government that it would make the necessary investment in a worthy field. Glenn L. Martin, representing the aviation industry, Major General Mason M. Patrick of the United States Army Air Service, and Captain E. V. Rickenbacker, World War ace, met to confer with real-estate experts and others. Hopkins presented options on one thousand acres of land at Brookpark Road and Riverside Drive. At his request, the site was approved, the options were exercised, and $1,125,000 in bonds for the purpose were issued. Clearing and grading followed at record speed so that the air mail could inaugurate night flying, July 1.

The Lincoln Memorial Association of Ohio was organized; and, annually, on Abraham Lincoln's birthday, a memorial meeting was held in the room at the Weddell House in which the President slept in 1861. In 1931 the room was donated by the owners to the association as a shrine open to the public. It contained valuable relics and was preserved in the original style. Among the many guests who paid tribute to the memory of Lincoln by visiting the room were fifteen Presidents of the United States. Anthony L. Maresh, president of the association for many years, had one of the largest private collections of Lincoln relics.

The survey commission of the Cleveland Foundation urged the establishment of a downtown college offering both day and evening courses to further adult education. Cleveland College was founded this year as an independent corporation in close affiliation with Western Reserve University. Newton D. Baker helped President Robert E. Vinson and Dr. Winfred G. Leutner, university dean, in the founding. Dr. Leutner was the first acting director. Cleveland College was formally affiliated with Western Reserve University in 1926. Three years later it moved from 1935 Euclid Avenue to the Chamber of Commerce Building, which was purchased at a cost of $210,000 and renamed the Newton D. Baker Memorial Building. At the outset, Cleveland College offered only evening courses in the arts and sciences, business administration, and engineering. Upon insistent requests, a few morning classes were scheduled, and then popularity led to complete curricula developed in the succeeding years. The college that opened with one full-time instructor and 31 part-time teachers, numbered 275 teachers in 1946. A work-study program of co-operative education was introduced in 1936 combining college study with practical working experience under supervision. According to this plan, students were placed by the college in positions with business and professional organizations. Engineering, science, and management courses were given to more than sixty thousand factory workers and office personnel engaged in war work. Dr. Alexander Caswell Ellis, who came as director in 1926, retired in 1941, and Herbert C. Hunsaker became dean of Cleveland College. In 1946, the enrollment approximated nine thousand.

An earthquake rocked the city and frightened thousands on March 1. Buildings were shaken and fixtures smashed, and all Ohio felt the quiver. The earth's crust tilted, according to Father Odenbach, astronomer at John Carroll University.

The Finnish world-champion mile runner, Paavo Nurmi, appeared at the Public Auditorium on March 10, and easily won the international 1½-mile race. The most exciting event of the program was the three-mile walk, won by Ugo Frigerio of Italy, for years an Olympic champion.

The Police Women's Bureau was established, and a women's section of the Municipal Court probation department was arranged. The Women's Protective Association hired a psychiatrist and helped unfortunate girls with medical care and vocational assistance.

Grace Garwood of Cleveland won the "All Events" championship of the Women's International Bowling Congress in 1925 with 1,703 pins, and again in 1927 with 1,644 pins.

A tall traffic-signal tower with lights was put into service, April 1, in the middle of the junction of Euclid and East 9th Street. For some time, automobile drivers were so fascinated by the tower that they failed to watch the pedestrians; and the pedestrians, having to watch the automobiles, failed to appreciate the significance of the tower. After an exciting experience, the contraption was taken down.

The forgotten tribe of cigar-store Indians stood again on city sidewalks on April 1. Competing in a prize pow-pow arranged by the *Plain Dealer,* three braves tucked cash in their belts. The squaws smiled charmingly, but judges gave the prizes to Hi-Mucha-Too-La, Tiffany Tecumseh, and a nameless hard-used chief.

A Skinner organ was the gift of Mrs. Dudley S. Blossom to the Old Stone Church, a memorial to her mother, Elizabeth Beardsley Bingham. It was first used in the Easter Service on April 12. Dr. William Hiram Foulkes, pastor from 1924 to 1927, had succeeded Dr. Andrew B. Meldrum, who served from 1902 to 1924 and was pastor emeritus until 1928. The pastorate of the Rev. Robert Wilson Mark continued from 1927 to 1933. The pulpit was vacant until 1935, when Dr. Robert B. Whyte began his notable career as minister. Vibrant and alive to the needs of the cosmopolitan community, the influence of Old Stone was reflected in religious and civic endeavors inspired under his able leadership.

The Cleveland Medal for Public Service was given by the Chamber of Commerce to George Alexander Wallace "in recognition of more than fifty years continuous service in the Cleveland Fire Department, during twenty-four years of which he was chief." The medal was also awarded to Charles Franklin Thwing, "notable contributor to the intellectual life of our city, and for thirty-one years its pre-eminent leader in higher education."

The new Baldwin Filtration Plant, 11216 Fairhill Road, was a masterpiece of architectural skill, according to visitors on May 1. Two hundred club women, thirty-five feet below the earth's crust, discovered they were in a veritable cathedral. The water-works plant began operation in October, with a capacity of 135,800,000 gallons. In 1927 the new Kirtland station was finished at a cost of $3,195,000, and for the first time all Cleveland had pure, filtered water. It was noted that the typhoid death rate declined, and years later no deaths were traced to water supply. In the 1940s the city was served by two cribs, four lake tunnels, two filtration plants, three major pumping stations, and 2,700 miles of water mains. The value of the system had risen to $67,575,000.

The new $4,600,000 home of the Cleveland Public Library, 325 Superior, was inspected on May 5 by 3,363 guests. In the receiving line were Linda A. Eastman, librarian, and Louise Prouty, vice librarian, while eight hundred library workers served as escorts to the public. Eva Cary Thompson withdrew the first book the next morning, *Youth Wins* by Muriel Hine. The book title was significant of the library's great service to the boys and girls of Greater Cleveland.

The Cleveland Public Library was opened to the public on May 6. The marble building, a prominent feature of the Group Plan, was praised as one of Ohio's most imposing monumental structures. Walker & Weeks were the architects. An oil portrait of John G. White by Sandor Vago was unveiled, this being the only formal ceremony in connection with the opening. Only two library buildings in the country were said to be larger, and none surpassed the Cleveland structure from the standpoint of equipment. Six floors, including basement, made up the building which was constructed without wood to minimize the fire hazard. More than forty-seven miles of shelving were available with an ultimate capacity of two million books. The library contained material on nearly all subjects, and included a newspaper room, a library in Braille, business bureau, technology divisions, and a wealth of information on the social sciences. Of special interest were the rooms devoted to students and young people. The library was administered by a board of seven members appointed by the Cleveland Board of Education.

Three hundred engineers and civic leaders toured the Cuyahoga and the projected lakefront on May 17. The trip led to a successful demand for widening and straightening the crooked stream.

When the word "rayon" was coming into use at this time as the official name for synthetic yarn, the newly organized Industrial Rayon Corporation took over the Cleveland plant formerly occupied by the Industrial Fiber Company on West 98th Street. Hiram S. Rivitz became president in 1926, and the same year a plant was built at Covington, Virginia. A continuous-process research program was inaugurated in 1932 to obtain better-quality control in yarn production. A plant was built in Painesville in 1937 under the direction of Hayden B. Kline, research chemist and later executive vice president. The company established Cleveland as a world leader in the growing rayon business. By its new method, viscose was spun into rayon a thousand times faster than before; and to meet wartime needs and demands, the Painesville equipment was adapted to the production of yarns for military fabrics. Patents for this miracle of Industrial Rayon enabled the company to sell its products to the world.

The twenty-three-story Engineers Bank Building erected by the Brotherhood of Locomotive Engineers, southwest corner of Ontario and St. Clair, provided quarters for the Brotherhood of Locomotive Engineers Co-operative National Bank. The seven-million-dollar terra-cotta-faced structure was designed by Knox & Elliott and towered above its neighbors in downtown Cleveland. The name was changed to Standard Bank Building to accommodate the Brotherhood's Standard Trust Bank; and when that institution's fateful career had ended, the abbreviated Standard Building was adopted.

Warren S. Stone, famous chief of the Brotherhood of Locomotive Engineers, died on June 12 at sixty-five years of age. He was the founder of the $145,000,000 business structure of the union and the leader of railroad negotiators. Stone was succeeded by Alvanley Johnston, once a call boy and wiper on the Great Northern Railroad. He became a locomotive engineer on that road, 1897-1909; general chairman of the Brotherhood of the Great Northern, 1909-18, and was elected grand chief engineer of the Brotherhood of Locomotive Engineers in 1925.

Rotarians from thirty countries met in Cleveland on June 14, and the ten thousand visitors filled the city. They advocated the application of the Golden Rule. For a stunt, Rotary brought "snow in June" to Cleveland in refrigerator cars shipped from the Rocky Mountains.

The *William G. Mather,* a 617-foot cargo vessel of 11,400 gross tons, was built for the Cleveland-Cliffs Steamship Company. This lake ship, named for a leading industrialist and philanthropist, was one of the largest vessels on the Great Lakes.

When the Cleveland Municipal Airport, under the direction of Major John Berry, commissioner, was opened July 1, only 100 of the 1,014 acres were available. The airport was eight and a half miles southwest of Cleveland's Public Square, at the junction of Riverside Drive and Brookpark Road, and could be reached in about thirty "long" minutes by motor car. With the removal of some thirty thousand trees, Cleveland boasted that it had the "biggest airport in the world." Approximately 100,000 citizens thronged the airport on the day of dedication. No airlines were in existence at that time. Air traffic consisted of four mail trips east and four west, for which the United States Air Mail Service had erected three small block hangars costing about $200,000. The Ford Motor Company had inaugurated freight service between Detroit and Cleveland. Ship movements for the year approximated 3,600, with no passengers. The appropriation of $1,125,000 made by City Council proved a profitable investment because this pioneer institution became one of the busiest of airports.

The foundations for the new Telephone Building, 750 Huron Road, were laid in what was called "the biggest continuous job of concrete pouring ever undertaken in the country." Quicksand had presented problems. The work started July 1, and the building base was laid five stories underground.

The Adult Education Association, a development of the Open Forum Speakers Bureau, was formed. Each year the appreciation of adult education grew through advantages offered by such institutions as the Cleveland Public Library, Cleveland College, Fenn College, Cleveland School of Art, Cleveland School of Music, John Huntington Polytechnic Institute, and various other institutions that provided day and evening courses for ambitious Clevelanders.

Two hundred thousand people cheered the arrival of night mail planes on July 2. Flyers swept in from dark skies and hopped off on the first night-mail routes, heavily laden with bank clearings, love notes, and business letters at ten cents an ounce.

The program for the Fourth of July was strenuous but safe and sane, 2,800 new Americans receiving citizenship diplomas, and 100,000 seeing *Romance of the Flag* at Brookside Park.

The Woodland Avenue Presbyterian Church joined with the Kinsman Union Congregational Church in July to form the Woodland Hills Union Church. In 1915 the Woodland Avenue Church had started a community center that grew in importance each year. In 1918 the pastor of the church and director of the settlement was Dr. Frank T. Barry, who continued in both positions until 1945, after which he gave his whole time to Woodland Center. When the merger of 1925 took place, the church, realizing the importance of the Center to the neighborhood, gave the property at 7100 Kinsman Road to the settlement, and the Presbytery of Cleveland maintained the project. Woodland Center expressed the church's approach to social problems, conducted community programs, and fostered recreational activities.

Liquor was being smuggled across Lake Erie, and customs officers made charges on August 4 against several leaders in the movement. The Coast Guard was kept busy in a vigilant search for smugglers' boats. United States officers seized twenty-seven thousand gallons of alcohol in a raid on a distillery and warehouse on the West Side on August 12. Nearly every day the newspapers were carrying stories of the abuses of the prohibition law—a law that was proving to be a costly failure.

Proportional representation displeased many voters, particularly party leaders. Consequently, the first attack on the city's new charter was submitted for vote on August 12. Only 41,280 went to the polls, and proportional representation won by a meager 804 majority. Cleveland was beginning to realize that a system is not good if it is not understood.

The Navy rigid dirigible airship *Shenandoah* was destroyed in a thunder squall over Ada, Ohio, September 3. Many Clevelanders saw the great ship as it passed over the city on the fatal trip. The *Shenandoah* split during the storm, and fourteen men plunged to their death.

An ocean-going ship, the *Nico,* slid keel-deep into mud in the Cuyahoga River but docked safely. Officers deplored the lack of harbor facilities, and dredges became busier.

Lake Erie's level was dropping steadily, experts reported, September 5, and each inch meant a hundred tons less cargo in a modern freighter. The situation was causing vessel men concern, and Chicago's growing demand for water was blamed.

John D. Marshall became mayor of Cleveland under the City Manager Plan on September 15, succeeding Clayton C. Townes who resigned.

Since 1853, St. Vincent's Orphanage had provided asylum for poor and needy children of Cleveland. On September 27, this year, a modern institution was dedicated by Cardinal Hayes of New York, known as the Parmadale Children's Village of St. Vincent dePaul. Located at State and Ridgewood roads in Parma, it was the nation's largest and most imposing group of buildings devoted to Catholic charity. The funds were subscribed by the Catholic Charities Corporation of Cleveland, and this orphan city provided for 360 boys and covered 180 acres. Among the activities was the development of large bands which attracted citywide attention in parades and concerts. Half of the boys at the school studied music for recreation and education.

The National Safety Council brought thousands of visitors to Cleveland on September 26. Delegates assembled from factories, railroads, traffic, and automobile organizations. No Accident Week made the city an experimental station.

The Clark Controller Company was established this year by Primus P. C. Clark and associates. Soon the factory located at 1146 East 152nd Street was producing auxiliary electrical control apparatus for heavy-duty applications, such as steel and non-ferrous mills, cranes, rubber calenders, machinery, and power presses. The business grew steadily as industries in different parts of the world recognized the value of the control machinery. In 1947 Robert H. Hoge succeeded W. H. Williams as president.

The Cleveland Art Club was founded in September by a group of artists under the leadership of George S. Novotny, with headquarters in the Buckeye Building at East 4th and Prospect. Its purpose was to give ambitious artists and illustrators a chance to improve their technique, to assist photographers, and to teach beginners fundamental photography.

After eighteen years of successful service, Rabbi Wolsey left the Euclid Avenue Temple to accept a call from Philadelphia. Dr. Barnett Robert Brickner, with a fine background of education and a rich experience in the pulpit, was called to the temple by the Anshe Chesed Congregation. His ministry was marked by achievements and innovations that won national attention. The board of directors of the Euclid Avenue Temple in 1945-46 included Maurice Bernon, president; David Geller and Otto J. Zinner, vice presidents; I. J. Kabb, treasurer; and J. W. Grodin, secretary.

Will Rogers gave Cleveland a laugh at his own expense when he arrived on October 3 for a lecture at Masonic Temple. He gave his reception committee the runaround by failing to leave his Nickel Plate train at the Euclid Avenue Station. When the committee caught up with him at the Broadway Station, he was leaning against a post chewing a straw and watching a freight train roll by. He poked fun at the station and the old Union Depot, and, during the lecture, at the delay in the building of the Union Terminal. In his whimsical evening talk, after nearly an hour of entertainment, he said he was tired and sat down on the stage, his feet dangling in the orchestra pit. In this informal manner he concluded his amusing observations on events of the day.

Maternity Hospital (later MacDonald House) of the University Hospitals group on Adelbert Road was dedicated in October, and the Babies and Childrens Hospital was opened this year. In 1936 the name MacDonald House was given to the Maternity Hospital in honor of Calvina MacDonald who had been director for many years.

The Westlake Hotel was built this year on Blount Street in Rocky River, site of an early-day tavern; and Quad Hall was erected at 7500 Euclid Avenue.

The noted geographer, Dr. J. Paul Goode of the University of Chicago, predicted a great future for the city and said that eventually Cleveland would become one of the three great centers of the world.

The Willys Company of Toledo absorbed the F. B. Stearns Company, and Cleveland lost one of its pioneer automobile plants.

The Community Fund goal was $4,500,000, and the amount raised was $4,430,665.75, with 458,947 subscribers. Sharing the benefits were 111 welfare agencies.

The American House, one of Cleveland's earliest and most revered taverns, passed into history on December 16, when its furnishings were removed to secondhand stores, and the old building was moved out of the way of the Terminal improvements.

The Perfection Stove Company, organized this year, originated in the Cleveland Metal Products Company. The latter represented a consolidation in 1917 of the Cleveland Foundry Company, whose predecessor was the Buckeye Foundry Company, dating back to 1888, Cleveland Metal Products Company, and Cleveland Factory Company. L. S. Chadwick, well known to the stove industry for his many inventions, had become president in 1922. Operations centered at 7609 Platt Avenue, site of the first factory erected in 1887. Complete oil-burning heating stoves were introduced to the trade in 1930, and warm-air furnaces with air-conditioning equipment and automatic controls a year later. The output of two large Cleveland plants was supplying international trade with oil-burning heating devices, stoves, refrigerators, air-conditioning equipment, and allied products in the 1940s.

The Chinese population reached a peak of six hundred this year. Progress had wiped out the old buildings on Ontario Street, the center of the Chinese community. Many of the Chinese left the city, and the remainder of the colony followed the eastward trend to East 55th and Cedar, later moving northward on East 55th to Euclid, and subsequently settling in the vicinity of Rockwell and East 21st Street. In 1927, the On Leong Tong group—or merchants association—occupied their new $400,000 tong-owned headquarters at 2150 Rockwell Avenue. The temple in the building resembled a Chinese Joss House. Colorfully decorated after the tradition of modern China, it served as a community hall and meeting place, and was open to visitors.

Protestant ministers of the Federated Churches held a communion service in the First Methodist Church, December 31. A local paper stated that it was believed to be "the first time ministers of different denominations in the United States or the world have held a union celebration of the most sacred rite of the Christian faith."

1926

The Episcopalians in Gates Mills had increased in number, and this year the diocese took over the Gates Mills Methodist Episcopal Church, now seventy-three years old, remodeling it but retaining the original charm and calling it St. Christopher's. Motorists paused to enjoy the quiet pastoral setting and the chimes that replaced the old bell, which found rest near the river's edge. The chimes became a tradition in the community, sounding the Angelus in the evening, playing hymns, heralding another wedding, or announcing the birth of a new baby. Aside from the many unique features of this quaint sanctuary, there was the annual ceremony of the Blessing of the Hounds, according to ancient English tradition. The Rev. J. Keeney McDowell, who had come to St. Christopher's as pastor in 1933, was serving in the 1940s.

The Cleveland Stunt Club, made up of local speakers and musicians, was attracting wide attention to its weekly programs over Station WTAM. Among the leaders were Thomas V. Hendricks, Charles M. Newcomb, Sid Landon, Joe Williams, Phil Barker, George Zahn, and Ed Vietz, with Charles A. Leedy of Youngstown a frequent guest.

It was largely through the efforts of the Women's City Club that the city government set up a well-financed division of smoke inspection. Colonel Elliott H. Whitlock was appointed commissioner. Smoke was costing the city twelve million dollars annually, according to the new smoke-commissioner's report of January 23.

Colonel Joseph H. Alexander, president of the Cleveland Railway Company, was elected president of the Cleveland Safety Council. He revitalized the council, which was in serious need of funds. The field organizer for the National Safety Council, Carl L. Smith, was brought to Cleveland for three months in order to raise twenty-five thousand dollars. This campaign was so successful that Smith was asked to remain in charge of the council. Work was immediately focused upon accident prevention through education, law enforcement, and engineering, and the council became one of the nation's leaders in the safety movement.

Loyal alumni and friends of University School created a fund of nearly a million dollars for a new school in Shaker Heights, off Warrensville Center Road. Henry S. Pickands, an alumnus, was head of the building campaign, and a dormitory, erected in his honor, was named Pickands Hall. The former Hough Avenue location became the Thomas A. Edison School. University School maintained high educational standards, and was known for the excellent record its students attained in College Entrance Board examinations. School enrollment in 1945 was being held at a capacity of 425, 50 being boarding students. Harry A. Peters, headmaster, had served since 1908.

The office building at 308 Euclid Avenue was purchased by Central National Bank, Savings & Trust Company from the Brotherhood of Locomotive Engineers, providing branch banking quarters until December, when it became the main office, and the Rockefeller office was retained as a branch. The United Banking & Trust Company, founded in 1886 at Lorain Avenue and Pearl Street, in the center of a thrifty community of Germans and Hungarians, consolidated with Central on November 18, 1929. Corliss E. Sullivan became chairman of the board; and Arthur H. Seibig, who had risen from messenger boy to head the United bank, was elected president of the new Central United National Bank, with six outlets, called in 1936 Central National Bank of Cleveland. General Benedict Crowell, prominent in business and governmental agencies, became president in 1938. The next year Sullivan died and was succeeded as chairman by John C. McHannan, "dean of Cleveland bankers." His service with the Central dated from 1892, and for many years he held the ranking position of vice president. General Crowell's experience as assistant secretary of war in World War I was revived during the second world conflict, when he became an expert consultant to the Secretary of War in Washington.

The Cleveland Cultural Garden League, a federation of patriotic, educational, and nationality groups dedicated to cultural enlightenment and mutual understanding, was established upon the recommendation of Leo Weidenthal, who became honorary president, and through the tireless efforts of Charles J. Wolfram, president, and Jennie K. Zwick, executive secretary. Small and large contributions, with the aid of the Work Projects Administration, made the garden chain possible. Land was donated by the City of Cleveland, which also provided design studies and maintained the garden.

The Rosenblum basketball team won the championship of the American Basketball League, defeating the Brooklyn team in the final game. For years, the teams backed by Max Rosenblum and managed by I. S. Rose were among the nation's best.

Graduate instruction in the arts and sciences was for many years incidental to advanced undergraduate instruction in Western Reserve University; but this year all instruction and training in research for higher degrees in the arts and sciences was consolidated in the Graduate School.

Billy Sunday, the evangelist, spoke in the Public Auditorium in behalf of the City Mission on February 23. It was estimated that fifteen thousand people were packed into the great hall and on its stage, while nearly an equal number were turned away. The famous preacher thrilled his audience, particularly with his baseball reminiscences, and he told of the great catch he had made in right field the day after he joined the Salvation Army in Chicago. John Clarkson, who later pitched for Cleveland, was on the mound for the White Sox and "King" Kelley was catching. The score was 3-2 in favor of Chicago when Detroit came to bat in the ninth inning. There were two out and Detroit had men on second and third. Charlie Bennett, Detroit's famous catcher, was at bat; and with three balls and two strikes, Charlie swung with all his might, the ball rising into the air and sailing far into right field. Billy Sunday turned his back to the ball and ran. Deep in the outfield was a crowd. "Stand back!" yelled Billy, as he sprinted as fast as the day he broke the world's record for running the bases. Here is the remainder of the story as he told it. "I ran on, and as I ran I prayed. I said, 'God if you ever helped mortal man, help me get that ball!' I thought it must be near, looked back and saw it going over my head. I jumped, shoved my left hand up and the ball hit it and stuck. The momentum carried me on and I fell into a team of horses out near the fence. I jumped up and held the ball high over my head. As I walked in, a man ran up and handed me a bill. 'That catch won me $1,500,' he said. 'Buy yourself the best suit of clothes you can find in Chicago. My name's Al Johnson, and I'm from Cleveland." Johnson was the brother of Cleveland's Mayor Tom L. Johnson.

The Battle of Gettysburg, the largest production created for radio, was broadcast to the nation by WTAM from the Public Auditorium on March 28. Horses, artillery, sound effects, fifty bass drums, many "stooges" beating leather upholstery with rattan sticks to simulate rifle fire in Pickett's charge, three companies of the 145th Infantry, bands, buglers, and hundreds of assistants participated. Sidney Landon, Charles Milton Newcomb, C. Franklin Morse, and Rosalind Ruby assumed leading parts; Ray Finger and Peg Willin were stage directors; John Fitzgerald was property-man; and William Ganson Rose wrote the script and directed production.

A beautiful $1,250,000 edifice was erected at East 107th Street and Chester Avenue by the Epworth-Euclid Methodist Church congregation. Among the largest and finest of the city's churches in appointments, it embodied features of practical design and architectural beauty, a unique spire towering above the trees bordering Wade Park lagoon. The church, dating from 1831, was fortunate in having enjoyed outstanding pastoral leadership, one of the most revered ministers being Dr. Louis Clinton Wright, who served for fourteen years and became president of Baldwin-Wallace College. His successor, Dr. Oscar Thomas Olson, was a leader in his denomination and in his community.

The Cuyahoga County Parent-Teacher Associations were organized in March at Hotel Cleveland and Mrs. Mary Eggleston of Fairview Village was elected president. The purpose was to develop a Council which would serve the cause of education in the county as the Cleveland PTA was serving the city. Its many activities included crusading for better child-labor laws, juvenile protection in the courts, better motion pictures and radio programs, health legislation, higher salaries for teachers, and more State aid for the schools of the county. The membership grew steadily until in 1946 it totaled 7,800, representing 22 units. Mrs. A. G. Thomas was president; Mrs. R. W. Conway, secretary; and Mrs. Robert Dial, historian.

Station WJW was founded at Mansfield, Ohio, with a power of fifty watts, and moved to Akron six years later. Ownership of the station was aequired in June, 1940, by William M. O'Neil, who became president and general manager. In 1943, power was increased to five thousand watts on a frequency of 850 K.C. and moved to Cleveland. WJW went on the air on November 13 and became the outlet for the American Broadcasting Company network, then NBC, blue.

The Chamber of Commerce Transportation Committee, meeting with Pennsylvania Railroad officials on March 31, learned that the company planned to provide an adequate station of its own "at the proper time." Twenty years later, Clevelanders were asking, "What is the proper time?"

The Cleveland Medal for Public Service was awarded on April 20 by the Cleveland Chamber of Commerce to the late Jeptha H. Wade I, "philanthropist and patron of the arts and constructive leader in city building"; to O. P. Van Sweringen and M. J. Van Sweringen, "masters of business, builders of great enterprises, eager participants in every movement for a better Cleveland"; to Robert Hoffman, city engineer, "who for thirty-three years has served Cleveland in the Department of Engineering, uninfluenced by partisan considerations or changes of administration."

Eight hours from the time a new style appeared on the boulevards of Paris, the William Taylor Son & Company had a photograph of it in its Euclid Avenue store. Taylor's was said to be the first commercial user of radio photography across the Atlantic.

Charles A. Otis and Peter Witt on April 26 debated the merits of the proposed fifteen-million-dollar subway project as a feature of the City Club Forum. The debate was still waging in the 1940s with a patient jury of citizens involved.

The new police headquarters building at 2001 Payne Avenue was opened on April 26. Here were located the bureaus of arms, communications, labor relations, statistics, criminal identification, and investigation. There were headquarters for police officers, the detective bureau, and the probation department. George J. Matowitz became chief of police in 1931, succeeding Jacob Graul. To the north, the modern Municipal Court Building was opened a little later, housing the criminal branch and probation department.

Following the trend to the suburbs, the vestry had elected to move St. Paul's Church from Euclid and East 40th Street to Cleveland Heights, where it joined with St. Martin's Episcopal congregation. On April 29, this year, the first services were held in the impressive white-limestone parish hall, dominated by a monumental tower, at Fairmount Boulevard and Coventry Road. The structure was the beginning of an extensive building plan to cost about $1,200,000. The Euclid Avenue property was acquired by the Catholic Church for St. Paul's Shrine. In 1946, two-thirds of the parish buildings had been erected; and a centennial campaign, headed by Alexander C.

Brown, was organized to complete the group, including the church proper, providing critically needed facilities for the growing parish. Eleven rectors had served St. Paul's since its founding in 1846. One of the most revered was Dr. Walter R. Breed, 1907-39, who was succeeded upon his death by Dr. Theodore Hubbard Evans.

The Clevelander, the official monthly journal of The Cleveland Chamber of Commerce, appeared for the first time in May. It was soon recognized as one of the leading business publications in its field, covering the activities of the Chamber and featuring articles relating to the city, by qualified authorities.

The Cleveland Pneumatic Tool Company was the first Cleveland company to own and operate a commercial airplane. The ship was a Waco, built in Troy, Ohio, and E. W. "Pop" Cleveland was the pilot.

The Sales Executives Club of Cleveland was formed by A. H. Seyler, president of the Cleveland Paper Company, and a group of thirty-five men, each representing a different business classification.

The schooner *Blossom* docked at Charleston, South Carolina, June 4, bringing to a close the historic cruise of more than two years and seven months among the islands of the South Atlantic. Sponsored by the Cleveland Museum of Natural History, the vessel was laden with bird-and-animal specimens, photographs, thousands of feet of movie film, scientific data, and voyagers who were positive that "there is no place like home." It was estimated that specimens numbered twelve thousand, and many had been shipped to Cleveland in advance of the return of the old-fashioned windjammer, skippered by Captain George Finlay Simmons. Before the cruise, this craft, the former *Lucy R.,* had been christened *Blossom* as a compliment to Cleveland's Mrs. Dudley S. Blossom, a trustee of the museum, who financed the expedition launched October 29, 1923.

The Ohio Supreme Court on June 8 upheld the right of the Board of Education to discontinue military training in the public schools. "There couldn't be another world war"—or could there?

Five thousand Canadians, mostly from Ontario, celebrated Cleveland-Canada Day in Cleveland on June 11.

A Midsummer Night's Dream was presented by the Sock and Buskin Club and the Curtain Players of Western Reserve University at the dedication of the Shakespeare Garden Theater in Rockefeller Park, June 15. This outdoor stage, between the upper and lower boulevards, was modeled after the sylvan theater at the Washington Monument in the Capital.

The United Banking & Trust Company (later branch of Central National Bank) erected a nine-story bank and office building at the corner of Lorain Avenue and West 25th Street, the largest structure of its kind on the West Side. The spacious banking room was one of the most attractive in Ohio, and a mural by Glenn Shaw was a colorful feature.

The million-dollar Hilliard Road Bridge, spanning the Rocky River Valley from the intersection of Hilliard Road and Riverside Drive in Lakewood, was dedicated on June 23.

Fenn College stands as a tribute to the memory of Sereno Pack Fenn, who devoted a good part of his life to the organization and education of young men. On the board of the YMCA for twenty-five years, from 1892 to 1917, he had been one of the first to suggest a program of night-school classes. Attendance increased in these popular courses, which began in 1881, and the enrollment in 1911 had reached a thousand. This substantial increase led to the development and planning of a day-school program in 1923. A co-operative plan of education on the college level was introduced, and so rapid was Fenn's growth that facilities soon became inadequate. In 1926 Sereno P. Fenn gave $100,000 for a new building and expansion program. Two years later, the Fenn Building next to the "Y" was erected, and this Prospect Avenue site served until 1937, when its expanded program demanded additional space.

The headquarters of the National Builders Supply Association were moved from Detroit to Cleveland.

Natural gas equal to about one-tenth of Cleveland's consumption was produced in Cuyahoga County. The North Olmsted wells were delivering approximately six million cubic feet each day.

The Inter-Lake Regatta, the first national regatta held in Cleveland, opened September 10. For four days the lakefront was a busy scene with sailboats within and beyond the breakwater. There were 230 Cleveland owners of pleasure yachts who were actively interested.

A civic welcome was accorded the Orpheus Male Chorus on September 20, upon its return from Wales where it won first prize in the International Eisteddfod. More than eight thousand music lovers gathered in the Public Auditorium and enjoyed the program arranged by the Cleveland Advertising Club. The Chorus, under the direction of Dr. Charles D. Dawe, responded to the enthusiastic greeting by singing several favorite numbers.

Gertrude Ederle, who swam the English Channel in 14 hours and 31 minutes, visited Cleveland and received the applause of many thousands as she motored downtown to be congratulated by City Manager William R. Hopkins.

Cleveland was recognized as the third largest radio center, being exceeded only by the New York and Chicago districts. There were about twenty manufacturers whose output was entirely confined to radio, and there were other companies whose radio output was large. Among the leaders were the Willard Storage Battery Company, National Electric Lamp Association, National Carbon Company, Sterling Manufacturing Company, Workrite Manufacturing Company, General Dry Battery Company, Mazda Radio Company, Glenn L. Martin Company, Champion Radio Company, Electric Parts Corporation, Carter Manufacturing Company, Hickok Electrical Instrument Company, and Victoreen Instrument Company. Not only was Cleveland a leader in manufacturing but it was a broadcasting center as well. Two of the finest stations in the country were located in the city, Station WHK and Station WTAM.

Edward Payson Weston, greatest of all pedestrians, came to Cleveland in his eighty-eighth year to address the Cleveland Advertising Club in a momentous meeting on October 20. He marched down Euclid Avenue from East 30th to the Hotel Statler behind a band, with a crowd of cheering admirers. There was one handicap. Weston swung along so rapidly that in no time at all he was leading the parade, just as he had distanced Cleveland's crack walkers of the Post Office, years before. The veteran reminisced with the crowd that packed the Statler ballroom, telling them of his 150,000 miles on foot; his shopping tours in New York, when Lincoln sent him as guard for Mrs. Lincoln; and the championships he had won in different countries. Out of this special appearance grew friendships that led to giving the grand old pedestrian care and comfort during his remaining years.

Cleveland was treated to its most exciting professional tennis matches when Suzanne Lenglen of France defeated Mary K. Browne of America in the Public Auditorium on October 28. The acrobatic Lenglen demonstrated the technique, agility, and power that made her peerless.

Earl William Oglebay died this year, after achievements in varied fields. He had come to Cleveland in 1884 and entered the iron-ore business. Before long, he and David Z. Norton joined to develop Oglebay, Norton & Company, but he never lost his interest in Wheeling, West Virginia, whence he came. Near that city he carried out experiments in scientific farming, leaving the famous "Waddington" farms to Wheeling for a park. He also gave the Oglebay Science Hall to West Virginia University. However, his business activities centered in Cleveland, and his home for many years was on Euclid Avenue next to the residence of T. P. Handy, who was credited with persuading Oglebay to settle in the city.

George Burns of the Cleveland Indians was voted the most valuable player in the American League. Despite broken ribs and a fractured finger, he batted .358, fielded well and helped to inspire the Indians to take second place, three games behind the Yankees.

Called "Cleveland's friendly skyscraper," the Hotel Allerton was opened for inspection on November 10. A part of the famous Allerton chain, the new hotel featured extensive sports rooms, including a swimming pool, squash courts, handball courts, and tennis courts. A spacious sun parlor, a roof garden, and other rooms designed for rest and relaxation were among the newly planned features. Conveniently located near the heart of downtown Cleveland, this sixteen-story hotel was particularly well equipped for convention groups, banquets, and dances. During World War II, the Allerton made a pleasant home for WAVES stationed in Cleveland.

The Dudley P. Allen Medical Library was dedicated on November 13 to the memory of a founder, officer, and benefactor of the Cleveland Medical Library Association. The cost was approximately $650,000, and Mrs. F. F. Prentiss, formerly Mrs. Allen, was the principal donor. Dr. Harvey W. Cushing, famous brain specialist who grew up in Cleveland, delivered the opening address. Within the architectural masterpiece of stone, writings and achievements of able men of medical science were preserved in the valuable library and museum. Dr. L. A. Pomeroy was president of the association in 1946.

Prince Nicholas of Rumania visited Cleveland on November 21. The twenty-three-year-old prince spent ten hours in Cleveland as the proxy for his mother, Queen Marie, who had to cancel the remainder of her American tour to return hurriedly to the bedside of her husband, King Ferdinand, who was fatally ill. Prince Nicholas visited with Rumanian groups, attended church services, and was honored at a dinner for six hundred at Hotel Hollenden.

The first broadcasts of the Cleveland Orchestra children's concerts began in the fall; and, in addition to twenty symphony concerts, twelve children's matinee concerts were scheduled. Five were broadcast so that the schools of all northern Ohio received them, and the music, whether heard by radio or in concert, was part of the regular public-school work in music appreciation. Cleveland was leading the nation in this regard, and the work undertaken in the schools was to make the city one of the great musical centers.

The Community Fund drive resulted in $4,445,506, pledged by 467,918 subscribers, the largest local philanthropic total ever raised in a campaign.

Cleveland's total expenditure for social-welfare services, which vitally affected the life, health, and happiness of the whole community, was approximately twelve million dollars a year. This total included contributions, endowment income, earnings, and such tax funds as were applied to social-welfare purposes, and embraced the services rendered by the Community Fund agencies and parallel agencies under city, county, and school control.

The *News* Toyshop was inaugurated as a plan to provide clothing, food, and toys for the needy at Christmas-time, the funds being raised through the medium of boxing matches. Ed Bang, sporting editor of the paper, originated the idea and was matchmaker and manager, while the Welfare Federation handled the proceeds. So remarkably successful were the events that in twenty-one years more than $400,000 was raised for the Toyshop's worthy purposes.

The Metropolitan Park Board was developing a gigantic belt of parks and parkways to encircle the city. The plan was to follow the Chagrin River on the eastern side of the metropolitan area, Tinker's and Chippewa creeks to the south, and Rocky River to the west. Several important areas had already been acquired. On the left bank of the Chagrin River, near the Mayfield-Willoughby line, a reserve of 1,200 acres was obtained. Ten miles farther south, near the Chagrin River, 700 acres were secured. Near Bedford, in the glen of Tinker's Creek, 1,000 acres constituted another reserve; 1,600 acres more were acquired in the Brecksville area along Chippewa Creek; in Rocky River Valley, 2,000 acres were obtained; the Hinckley reserve, just over the line in Medina County, added 500 acres; and the Huntington tract, site of the John Huntington country place, was a lakeshore property of 100 acres in Bay Village, west of the Rocky River. The Metropolitan Park District consisted of nine separate reservations in 1940, varying in size from 300 to 2,500 acres. With well-developed plans for parkway connections, a park-drive system of about 150 miles over an area of 12,000 acres was half completed. When finished, the nine reservations, together with a chain of parkways, unique in park development and natural beauty, were to surround the city on the east, south, and west.

1927

The Chamber of Commerce reviewed Cleveland's industrial development during the century from the establishment of the Cuyahoga Steam Furnace in 1827 until the city boasted of approximately 2,250 plants in 1926. Leonard Case had laid out the city's first comprehensive industrial district in the 1870s, covering the area between St. Clair and Lake Erie (from East 26th to East 55th streets). Before this time, industries located wherever a site was available along the railroad lines. In 1890, the streets that became East 105th Street and East 93rd Street on the East Side and West 65th Street on the West Side were the "frontiers of industrial Cleveland." In 1899, Daniel R. Taylor, a far-sighted real-estate operator, purchased about a hundred acres bounded by Woodland, Woodhill, and Quincy avenues, paying approximately a thousand dollars per acre. Industries grew rapidly in this district. At the turn of the century, there was a serious shortage of industrial sites, and W. R. and Ben F. Hopkins laid out factory districts along the new Belt Line at East 131st Street, north of St. Clair, Woodhill Road, and East 71st Street, and on the West Side at Grant Avenue. The Cuyahoga Valley above Jefferson Avenue had been swamp land until the steel mills prepared nearly four hundred acres for their uses, and a cement mill acquired a site in the same area.

Hotel Hollenden was filled with celebrities on the evening of January 1, when radio station WJAY first went on the air. At eight o'clock, Manager Charles Burns stepped to the microphone to make the opening announcement but the generator failed, plunging the studio into darkness. Burns ran out into the street, where he appropriated twenty-two batteries from perplexed taxicab drivers, and at 9:30, WJAY made its debut. Outstanding in its public service were nationality programs presented by the city's foreign groups.

Cleveland College was one of the first institutions in the country to offer a course in airplane design. Heraclio Alfaro, a pioneer in the study of air dynamics, conducted the class under the direction of Professor H. B. Dates of Case School.

The Chamber of Commerce Convention Board co-operated with P. E. Bliss of the Warner & Swasey Company to bring about the first exhibition of the National Machine Tool Builders Association in the Public Auditorium in 1927. The undertaking was so successful that it became an annual event, with Cleveland the headquarters of the association.

Drs. J. M. Rogoff and G. N. Stewart of Western Reserve University School of Medicine were doing pioneer work upon the adrenal glands. Dr. Rogoff was successful in isolating the hormone of the cortex and developing its use in the treatment of Addison's disease. Until this time, the disease had been fatal. Dr. Rogoff named this hormone "interrenalin."

A meeting of sixty-five railway officials and industrial traffic representatives on January 25 was inspired by W. V. Bishop, traffic manager of the

Upson Nut Company. The Traffic Club of Cleveland was formed, membership at first being limited to railway-freight-traffic and shipper-traffic representatives. W. F. Hurd, traffic commissioner of the Chamber of Commerce, was elected president. Resident membership in 1946 totaled 734, and Henry Boyer was president.

Charles "Charlie" Gibson, a well-known Clevelander who was credited with spreading joy and sunshine throughout the dismal Union Depot, died on January 28. Known as "Carnation Charlie," he had won many friends among travelers and associates alike, wearing his familiar red carnation and pleasant smile. Starting his service with the New York Central Railroad as a ticket seller, he became passenger agent in charge of the office. The carnations were worn in memory of his mother.

William Russell Rose, who died in Cleveland on February 16, was for years known as the dean of Cleveland newspapermen. He had come to the *Plain Dealer* in 1896 after years of experience on the *Sunday Voice* and the *Press*. As an editor, he helped preserve the annals of the Western Reserve in his column, "All in the Day's Work," and he had been present at the making of much Cleveland history. He was the author of approximately 1,600 short stories that were widely read.

The cornerstone of the new building of Hathaway Brown School, at 19600 North Park Boulevard, Shaker Heights, was laid on March 10, and in September the structure was occupied. The land had been a gift of the Van Sweringen brothers, and the edifice cost approximately a million dollars. In 1938 Mary E. Raymond, who had been principal since 1911, became principal emerita, and Anne Cutter Coburn became headmistress. In 1946, the school opened for its seventy-first year, the enrollment limited to 350, with 46 resident students and 51 faculty members.

The Bingham Laboratory of Mechanical Engineering, one of the finest in the Middle West, was completed on the campus of Case School of Applied Science at a cost of $478,500. It was a memorial to Charles William Bingham, and the gift was doubly enhanced through a subsequent endowment of $500,000 by William Bingham II. Construction of the Worcester Reed Warner Laboratory of Mechanics and Hydraulics commenced this year. Frank A. Quail, lawyer, had been president of the board of trustees since 1924. His vision and practical planning led to new endowments and the valuable expansion of the building program.

The Auditorium Hotel, 1315 East 6th Street, was built by George Ebeling. Of concrete construction, the three-hundred-room hotel cost $1,500,000. Because of its convenient location, it was particularly popular as headquarters for stage celebrities and public figures appearing in the Public Auditorium.

Dedication services celebrating the building of the new temple and sanctuary erected by the Euclid Avenue Baptist Church at Euclid and East 18th Street continued from April 3 to 8. The project originated in 1920 when the trustees leased extensive property at the northwest corner of the avenue and set out to raise a million-dollar fund to provide a gigantic house of worship and a commercial building to be built later at the corner. Half the amount was realized through sale of the old property across the street to John D. Rockefeller, Jr., and the church was razed in 1926. Dr. John Snape succeeded Dr. William W. Bustard as pastor in January, 1926, and the first services were held in the chapel on May 23. Gifts of $250,000 from John D. Rockefeller, Sr., and his son John D., Jr., were made toward completion of the building. An outlay of about $1,500,000 had provided a pretentious church-school unit to which two stories were to be added later. The auditorium seated 2,280 persons, and a banquet hall in the basement had a capacity of 1,000. Club rooms and a gymnasium were to be added, and the 175-foot tower, then half finished, was to be crowned with a carillon. Financial troubles mounted as the business property failed to produce needed revenue; and although the leases on church and business sites were separated, obligations faced the trustees, threatening them with loss of the building. Heroic efforts were made during the pastorate of Dr. Ralph Walker; and in 1936, the Rockefellers came to the rescue with gifts totaling $255,000 to the Cleveland Baptist Association, which redeemed the building, and safeguarded it for the use of the congregation. Through Dr. D. R. Sharpe, executive secretary of the association, a broadened interdenominational social and religious program was developed, directed toward unchurched Protestant homes in the community to the north and east. Dr. Bernard C. Clausen, widely known clergyman, became pastor in 1944.

A private performance and a reception opened the Play House at 2040 East 86th Street, April 9. The reception was for those who had contributed to the building fund. President Charles S. Brooks accepted the theater from the donors and presented it to the public. Then the curtain went up, and *The Jest*, Sem Benelli's romantic tragedy, made its bow to Cleveland. In the cast were Russell Collins, Carl Benton Reid, Paul Foley, Jennette Gage, James Church, Elmer Lehr, and other favorites, the production being under the direction of Frederick McConnell. In the house were two attractive auditoriums, each with a stage, the Drury Theater seating 522, and the Brooks Theater, 160. Later on, the Play House developed numerous civic activities: it conducted a children's theater with an enrollment of more than five hundred young people; maintained an affiliation with Western Reserve University, conducting classes for graduate students in drama; and its School of the Theater gave young men and women tuition-free training in exchange for service in work connected with the theater.

The Thompson Aeronautical Corporation was organized as a subsidiary of Thompson Products, Inc. The company offered flying instruction, engine-and-plane repairs and storage service, distributed Stinson planes, gave Cleveland its first air-taxi service "anywhere in the United States, day or night," carried Government air mail with terminals at Chicago and Detroit, and inaugurated regular passenger service across the lake between Cleveland and Detroit. A large air syndicate purchased the subsidiary in 1932.

The St. James Forum was organized, an outgrowth of the East End Literary Society for colored people and an extension of St. James Mission, founded in 1892. This forum was known for variety of program.

The Cleveland Advertising Club opened beautiful new quarters in the Allerton Hotel on April 13, when a debate on "Debt Cancellation" between

Congressman Theodore E. Burton and Sir George Paisch, famous British economist, was featured.

The spring festivals of Metropolitan Grand Opera, under the direction of the Northern Ohio Opera Association, began this year when "a partnership in grand opera" was established by the city government, the opera committee, and more than five hundred guarantors who underwrote the project. Under the leadership of Robert J. Bulkley, the association was formed, the first of its kind in the nation, with Lincoln G. Dickey secretary of the executive committee. Although the Metropolitan did not continue consecutive appearances in Cleveland during the 1930s because of economic influences, it launched a new series in 1937 when it set an attendance record for a week of indoor opera. In 1939 Bulkley retired from the leadership of the association, and Thomas L. Sidlo was general chairman and executive head. In 1942, with a membership of more than four hundred guarantors, the association proclaimed its faith and confidence in Cleveland audiences, by entering into a five-year contract with the Metropolitan Opera Association. The 1927 season included brilliant productions of *Aïda, La Traviata, Mignon, Lohengrin, La Boheme, Il Trovatore, Turandot,* and *La Forza del Destino.* Among the famous singers in the talented casts were Lawrence Tibbett, Ezio Pinza, Rosa Ponselle, Marion Talley, Beniamino Gigli, Giovanni Martinelli, Giuseppe De Luca, Amelita Galli-Curci, and Lucrezia Bori. The spring festivals continued each year through 1932 when there was a lapse of four years.

The Cleveland Medal for Public Service was awarded April 19 by The Cleveland Chamber of Commerce to Newton Diehl Baker "for the service he has rendered to the people of Cleveland by the inspiration of his voice and pen in behalf of a high-minded attitude toward life, civic loyalty and civic service, patriotism, and devotion to high ideals"; and to Charles Sumner Howe, "scholar, teacher, administrator, citizen, who has illustrated and embodied the highest qualities of noble character and of public service." Dr. Howe served as president of Case School of Applied Science from 1902 to 1929, when he was succeeded by Dr. William E. Wickenden.

Sam M. Gross was elected president of the Retail Merchants Board succeeding Asa Shiverick, president of The Higbee Company. Gross had been connected with The May Company in Cleveland from the time of its organization and was known nationally for his merchandising ability. He was re-elected in 1928.

Keeping pace with the eastward march of its congregation, the First Baptist Church moved to Shaker Heights, where it merged with the Heights Baptist congregation. A magnificent church home was dedicated in 1929 at Fairmount Boulevard and Eaton Road. The Rev. Harold Cooke Phillips had begun his pastorate in 1928, and his broad and influential leadership enriched Cleveland and the Christian cause nationally.

The two-mile, interscholastic relay championship in Philadelphia was won by the Lakewood High School relay team including Captain Dick Womer, Bud Pervo, Harvey Smith, Gordon Reilinger, and Len Ammerman. The new record established by the team was 7:48⅘ minutes.

Uninterrupted daily transmission of photographs by telegraph between New York and Cleveland was being provided by the American Telephone & Telegraph Company.

Charles A. Lindbergh on May 20 made his pioneering solo transatlantic flight in the *Spirit of St. Louis* from New York, reaching Paris the next day, 3,610 miles in 33 hours and 30 minutes. The news of Lindbergh's arrival was marked in Cleveland by factory whistles and cheering at the ball park. Lindbergh's airplane was equipped with Cleveland-made Thompson valves, propeller blades by the Aluminum Company, tubing by Parker Appliance, motor forgings by Park Drop Forge, Sherwin-Williams paint, and he was met by Ambassador Myron T. Herrick, a Clevelander.

The *Leif Ericson* from Bergen, Norway, with a square sail and a crew of four, docked at the Cleveland Boat Club in the East 9th Street lagoon, May 29. It was a queer craft, modeled after the great Viking explorer's vessel which, it is claimed by Norwegians, touched the soil of the Western Hemisphere before Columbus.

The Halle Bros. Company opened its new five-million-dollar, six-story, Huron-Prospect Building on May 31, doubling the store's selling space. At this time, Huron Road was a district of old but imposing residences, and the Halle store influenced improvement of the area. A branch store was opened in Erie, Pennsylvania, in 1929, and in Canton the next year.

The "Heart of the Ohio Bell Telephone," at 750 Huron Road, has been called a "Temple to Telephony." Erected on the site of the old Cleveland Homeopathic Hospital and its next-door neighbor, the Empire Theater, the towering building was officially occupied May 31. Built with artistic simplicity of design, twenty-two stories rose to a height of 365 feet, and the perpendicular style of architecture gave an imposing silhouette. Hubbell & Benes were the architects. *Nation's Business* magazine, of the United States Chamber of Commerce, published an early survey, rating the structure as one of the fifteen finest office buildings in the country. The building alone cost five million dollars, and six million dollars worth of telephone equipment was installed. On December 4, dial telephones started to function in the Main and Cherry offices, covering most of Cleveland's business section. The building, equipped, weighed 500,000,000 pounds and had 325,000 square feet of floor space. The presidents of Ohio Bell were Eugene A. Reed, 1921-23; Charles P. Cooper, 1923-26; Edward F. Carter, 1926-30; Randolph Eide, 1930 —.

Clevelanders and Torontoans celebrated Cleveland-Ontario Day, June 3, in Toronto. The day began with a kiltie band playing *Yankee Doodle* on the dock, and ended, late at night, with a general agreement that there was no better town than Toronto, unless it was Cleveland.

Howard Whipple Green started a two-year survey of atmospheric pollution for the Cleveland Health Council, correlating all meteorological data available. For nearly four years, the educational program of the City's Division of Smoke Inspection produced gratifying results in decreasing sootfall; but with the depression and the shutting down of factories, there was less attention to abatement.

Two of the largest bulk-cargo freighters on the lakes were constructed this year: the *Carl D. Bradley,* 638 feet long, for the Bradley Transportation Company, and the *Harry Coulby,* 630 feet long, for the Interlake Steamship Company.

The Hebrew Garden, second in the chain of Cultural Gardens in Rockefeller Park, was dedicated to "Israel's singers, sages and dreamers of dreams." Oriental in character, it was a sunken circular garden, flanked on one side by a rock garden with plantings from Palestine, and on the other by a plot based on the pattern of a harp. Walks radiated from the central marble fountain to six points forming the Shield of David. At four of the points on the star were memorials to Hebrew philosophers. A bronze bas relief by Max Kalish was a decorative feature, and a section of the garden was dedicated to Rebecca Gratz, the original of Scott's Rebecca in *Ivanhoe.* A ceremony marked completion of the undertaking, June 13, 1937, when Leo Weidenthal was introduced as having made the dedication possible.

Cleveland welcomed the thirty-sixth Saengerfest, June 22-24, this being the fifth time the city was chosen for the great national meeting of the North American Saengerbund. Choruses from all parts of America assembled for the mass ensemble of four thousand trained voices. Elsa Alsen, Julia Claussen, and Lawrence Tibbett were among the famous soloists, and Bruno Walter came from Germany to direct the special festival orchestra of a hundred pieces. The Orpheus Male Chorus, Singers Club, Glenville High School Choral Club, and a school-children's chorus of two thousand voices represented the city. The concerts were held in the Cleveland Public Auditorium.

The American Whist League met at Dartmouth College in June, and, for the first time in the history of the association, auction bridge was recognized. Cleveland took honors by defeating all other teams, and Maurice Maschke, Carl T. Robertson, Carl R. Apthorp, and Henry P. Jaeger proved Cleveland's leadership in the newly accepted game.

The Dobeckmun Company, the title combining the first syllables of the founder's names, Dolan, Becker, and Munson, was incorporated this year, after the development of moisture-proof cellophane by the du Pont Company. The first products were the cellophane bag and the cellophane cigar pouch. The Dobeckmun laminating process was the first of its kind in the country. War years brought about production of thousands of urgently needed items and improved testing methods. A postwar laminated plastic glazing, known as Lurex, was used in dress fabrics, shoes, and other articles. Eventually, there was a $1,500,000 expenditure for the purpose of expansion which involved a new plant in Berkeley, California, and a substantial Cleveland addition at 3301 Monroe Street. Branch offices covered the United States, and export facilities reached every country in the world. T. F. Dolan was president from the time of organization.

The airplane *City of Cleveland,* entered by the Chamber of Commerce in honor of Glenn L. Martin at the International Peace Aviation Jubilee at Santa Ana, California, was christened at Martin Field in Cleveland on June 26 by Mrs. I. F. Freiberger, wife of the Chamber of Commerce president. The plane won two trophies—one for distance and one for performance.

Decorating the beautiful Fine Arts Garden, in which the Cleveland Museum of Art was situated, many impressive sculptures were set in place in 1927-28. Placed at the north end of the garden was the "Fountain of the Waters" by Chester Beach; and on either side, sculptures by the same artist, one representing "Earth," the other, "Sun." These were presented to the museum by Mrs. Leonard C. Hanna. The decorative sculpture, "City Fettering Nature" by Alexander Blazys, was presented in 1927 by Leonard Hanna, Jr., Mrs. Benjamin P. Bole, John L. Severance, and Mrs. Francis F. Prentiss, and was placed north of the museum; while at the Euclid Avenue entrance to the garden there was another impressive statue, "Night Passing Earth to Day," given by Mrs. Benjamin P. Bole in 1928. Other features decorating the garden included the "Mermaids," the gift of Francis E. Drury, and the twelve signs of the Zodiac, presented by a group of art lovers in Cleveland.

For more than four decades, Caesar Augustin Grasselli had been an industrial leader of Cleveland; and when death came on July 28 this year, he was remembered for his great humanitarian acts. Born in Cincinnati in 1850, he was a lad of sixteen when his father expanded his chemical business by building a plant in Cleveland. Young Grasselli grew with the enterprise, and upon the death of his father in 1882, he became head of the firm, directing its destiny until 1916, when he became chairman of the board of the vast Grasselli operations, and his son, Thomas S., succeeded him as president. Grasselli's business interests were primarily in chemicals; but in 1886 he became the first president of the Woodland Avenue Savings & Trust Company; and, in 1893, president of the Broadway Savings & Trust Company. He gave the old family home on East 55th Street to the Cleveland Society for the Blind, and he founded Rose-Mary Home for Crippled Children in memory of his wife, Johanna Ireland Grasselli. Pope Pius XI rewarded him with high honors, and Victor Emmanuel III decorated him with the Knight Order of the Golden Crown of Italy, honoring his assistance to war victims.

Charles A. Lindbergh was given an enthusiastic reception at a banquet in Hotel Cleveland on August 1. He stated that "it will be no more than three or four years before planes will be built for regular ocean service. They will mean faster communication between the nations. They will make for peace."

City Manager Hopkins announced plans on August 7 for a downtown airport on the lakefront, east of the East 9th Street Pier. Twenty years later his idea was taking form.

The American flag flew at the peak of the Terminal Tower, August 18, the structural-steel work on the tallest building outside of New York City being completed. H. D. Jouett, builder of the Grand Central Station, New York, headed the staff of engineers that developed the gigantic project.

Cleveland produced a great polo team this year, with J. A. Wigmore, David S. Ingalls, Captain Wesley White, and Tom White not only winning the Midwest Championship, but going to Narragansett Pier to make Cleveland champion of the twelve-goal teams of the United States.

The Cleveland Industrial Exposition held in the Public Auditorium, closed after twenty-three successful days. The attendance had been nearly 650,000. Praise was given to Colonel Joseph H. Alexander, president of the exposition company; to Allard Smith, chairman of the Chamber of Commerce Industrial Development Committee, which sponsored the exposition; and to Manager Lincoln Dickey and his staff. As a result of the project, a new office of industrial commissioner was established by the Chamber.

A build-a-home-first campaign was launched on September 4 by several civic organizations, to demonstrate that good homes could be built at reasonable prices. Harry Gillett, president of the Builders Exchange, said that "people were turning from the jazz age and, what was much more essential, were buying and building homes."

A large number of evictions due to the demolition of dwellings in preparation for the Union Terminal caused a serious housing shortage. City Manager Hopkins and expert advisers studied methods for securing better living quarters and lower rentals for wage earners.

Business encroached upon the East 96th Street home of Laurel School; and on September 27, the cornerstone was laid for a new building in Shaker Heights near Fairmount Boulevard and Green Road. Mrs. Arthur E. Lyman retired in 1930, and Edna F. Lake was appointed headmistress.

Rapid transit from East Cleveland to Rocky River through the new Terminal Station, using the Nickel Plate right-of-way, was predicted by George D. McGwinn, vice president of the Cleveland Union Terminals Company. The announcement was made at an Optimist Club luncheon, September 29, but the optimists became pessimists as one unnecessary delay after another held up the proposed improvement.

During the past decade, several Clevelanders won distinction for their literary endeavors. Dr. Ferdinand Q. Blanchard added to his list of religious books; Charles A. Post, authority on Doan's Corners, penned picturesque stories of Cleveland; Albert D. Taylor wrote illuminating books on landscape architecture; Wilbur J. Watson compiled authoritative books on bridge building and the world's great bridges; Leo Weidenthal, editor and collector, wrote a book and articles furthering interest in the Cultural Gardens.

The ninth Community Fund drive for $4,600,000 started on November 13 with seven thousand workers. The total raised was $4,524,488.

Cleveland's baseball ownership on November 15 passed into the hands of four Clevelanders who announced their intention of making the Indians a winning team: Alva Bradley, C. L. Bradley, John Sherwin, Sr., and Percy Morgan. The popular umpire and baseball writer, "Billy" Evans, was announced as business manager, and Jack McAllister became manager. The latter was succeeded by able Roger Peckinpaugh who served 1928-33 and again in 1941.

The Citizens League, Automobile Club, Real Estate Board, Women's City Club, Builders Exchange, League of Women Voters, Advertising Club, and Chamber of Commerce joined, November 17, in requesting Mayor John D. Marshall to form a committee that would work for a combination of city and suburbs in larger governmental affairs. The mayor appointed a citizens committee of 250, but no plan of government was acceptable to suburbs and city.

During the year, the Public Library circulated 7,725,742 volumes in Cleveland alone. The county increased the figure by 560,267, making a combined city and county circulation of 8,286,009, a number greater than the total circulation of the first thirty years of the Cleveland library. Cleveland stood at the top of the list of the nation's large cities with a per capita circulation of 7.20, followed by Milwaukee, 6.65, Minneapolis, 5.80, and Seattle, 5.76. The library had 1,181 distributing agencies: 28 library branches including the main library; 36 school branches; 118 stations in factories, stores, fire-engine houses, hospitals, etc., and 999 classroom stations.

1928

Health Commissioner H. L. Rockwood stated that the city's death rate for 1927 was 9.65 per thousand, the lowest among the largest cities of the country.

The Cleveland Medal for Public Service was awarded, January 3, by The Cleveland Chamber of Commerce to Myron T. Herrick "for statesmanship in diplomacy distinguished by high courage, great intellectual capacity and broad human sympathy, reflecting luster on the name of the city in which he lives."

Peter Witt, former traction commissioner and councilman, proposed new designs for streetcars on February 5. His ideas were later embodied in new cars used nationally.

James Arthur House, Jr., captain of the Yale swimming team, broke the intercollegiate back-stroke record, holding the honor for three successive years.

The Illuminating Company on March 7 announced a $1,800,000 high-power transmission line, 59 miles long, to serve a large area of northeastern Ohio— a sign of growth and of faith in more industries to come.

Johnny Risko, heavyweight, came marching home, March 15, victor over Jack Sharkey and hoping for a title bout with champion Gene Tunney. The "baker boy," so-called because he worked in a Cleveland bakery, had become one of the most popular prize fighters in America. Born in Austria in 1902 he had come to Cleveland as a small boy. He liked boxing and at the age of twenty he came under the management and tutelage of Danny Dunn of Cleveland, well-known trainer and fighter, and helped to build the success of Charlie Marotta's Athletic Club. The "baker boy" lost his first important bout to Mike Wallace in 1923, but he learned from that experience and scored thirty-nine knockouts in his next fifty-nine bouts. His victories over Jack Sharkey, George Godfrey, and Max Schmeling made him one of the outstanding heavyweights of his time. Other important victories were recorded over Ernie Schaaf, Mickey Walker, Tom Heeney, and "King" Levinsky. Risko left the ring temporarily in 1936 but returned a year later and won eight out of his next thirteen bouts before retiring in 1940.

Erie C. Hopwood, courageous and just editor of the *Plain Dealer* since 1920, died suddenly, March 19. Paul Bellamy, managing editor, was named editor in 1933. Bellamy became a director of the Plain Dealer Publishing Company, The Associated Press, and vice president and director of the United Broadcasting Company. In 1933-34, he served as president of the American Society of Newspaper Editors.

The Cinema Theater opened as a motion picture house in Playhouse Square, 1630 Euclid Avenue. Within a short time it came under the management of Warner Brothers who changed the name to Lake Theater.

The Chamber of Commerce Medal was also awarded on April 17 to Mrs. Francis F. Prentiss, "whose influence has been far-reaching and who has materially helped to raise Cleveland in the estimation of those interested in the finer and nobler things of life"; to Dr. Dayton C. Miller, "zealous and tireless worker in the realm of physics . . . who has brought honor and distinction to the city in which he has lived for many years"; and to Charles Francis Brush, "who made fundamental contributions to the development of the storage battery; built the first high tension dynamo which would work on a commercial scale; invented an automatic arc lamp which would give continuous light, and gave to Cleveland and to the world the first successful electric street lighting system."

Six shafts of light, visible sixty miles, flashed out from the forty-ninth story of the Terminal Tower, April 28, a beacon to navigators of lake and air.

The American Peace Society celebrated its centennial in Cleveland, May 7-11. Theodore E. Burton was president, and the honorary chairman of the centennial celebration was President Calvin Coolidge.

A "tiny Irishman with a wide grin" trotted through Greater Cleveland on May 13 in the lead of C. C. Pyle's transcontinental foot race from Los Angeles to New York, as cheering, generous folk tossed dollar bills in his path. He was Cleveland's "Mike" Joyce. All the little Joyces and Mamma Joyce were out to see papa in his glory, escorted by motorcycle police. Roads were lined with cars, and sidewalks were crowded. Boys raced beside Mike, more interested in him than in the great "Red" Grange, an official of the race. At intervals, the several dozen competitors of Mike plodded along. The "bunion derby" was not won by Joyce, but he took fourth place and $2,500 when Madison Square Garden saw the finish on May 26. Andrew Payne of Claremore, Oklahoma, was first, his time being 573 hours and 4 minutes for the 3,422 miles. Joyce's time was 636 hours and 43 minutes.

The recent annexation to Cleveland of part of Brooklyn Heights and other small areas increased the total area of the city to 70.67 square miles.

The American Library Association chose Cleveland Librarian Linda A. Eastman for its president, May 23, and a legion of friends rejoiced at this high honor paid one of America's most efficient directors of library work.

Dr. Henry J. John, nationally known specialist in the treatment of diabetes, established Camp Ho Mita Koda in Newbury Center, between Chardon and Burton for diabetic children. With the aid of his wife, the camp became an outstanding institution dealing with the control and treatment of the disease. The undertaking inspired the launching in the 1940s of The Greater Cleveland Diabetes League of which Judge Lewis Drucker was president.

Newton D. Baker on June 3 was named by President Coolidge as one of four American members of The Court of International Justice at the Hague, a signal honor.

A survey by the National Industrial Conference Board of New York showed that living costs for the average industrial worker's family of four were lower in Cleveland than in New York, Philadelphia, Boston, Reading, Springfield, Syracuse, and Lockport. Cleveland's advantage over the other cities, according to the report, was its low cost of fuel and light.

Genevieve R. Cline, who was nominated by President Coolidge as judge of the United States Customs Court of New York City, took her oath of office in the Federal Building, Cleveland, on June 5. She was one of Cleveland's first women to hold a high federal position.

Consolidation of the Grasselli and du Pont interests came this year. In 1927, Caesar A. Grasselli, who relinquished the presidency in 1916, passed on. His son, Thomas S., became president, serving until the merger, when he became vice president of E. I. du Pont de Nemours & Company, continuing until his death in 1942. The Grasselli Chemical Company was dissolved in 1936, and the Grasselli Chemicals Department was formed to take over this phase of the du Pont business. The consolidation thus made du Pont a factor in zinc smelting, and provided facilities for producing such plating materials as cadmium salts, metallic cadmium, and zinc salts. In the 1940s the Grasselli department operated the enormous Cleveland division and fifteen strategically located plants producing an ever-expanding line of industrial products—acids and chemicals, insecticide and fungicide chemicals, wood-preserving salts, fire retardants, and the like. In the Cleveland research laboratory, new products and processes were constantly being developed to benefit industry and mankind.

The opening day in the new Chamber of Commerce home in the Terminal Tower, June 11, brought more than four thousand visitors to the beautiful and spacious quarters.

So weatherbeaten was Perry's Monument, that the Early Settlers Association, raised ten thousand dollars and ordered a bronze replica that was unveiled on June 14, 1929. A second bronze statue was purchased by the State of Rhode Island to be erected in front of the State House in Providence.

Charles Waddell Chesnutt, on July 3, was presented with the Spingarn medal. The presentation was made in Los Angeles at the annual conference of the National Association for the Advancement of Colored People. Chesnutt received the medal "for his pioneer work as a literary artist depicting the life and struggles of Americans of Negro descent and for his long and useful career as scholar, worker and freeman of one of America's greatest cities."

A feature of the Cleveland Orchestra's open-air concerts at Edgewater and Gordon parks in July was broadcasting by WTAM. This meant that besides the audience on the benches and in parked cars, there was an unseen audience of music lovers with which the Cleveland Orchestra made friends.

Six hundred and eighty-one Cleveland restaurants were feeding an average of 300,000 persons daily in July.

Henry A. Schwab, chief clerk at the Probate Court, who was completing fifty-one years of service in the Court House, was decoyed, August 3, into Hotel Cleveland where judges, attorneys, fellow employees, and many friends honored him. He responded with his first public speech, "I thank you!" He died March, 1936, after fifty-nine years of Probate Court work.

The Chamber of Commerce was host on August 3 to an important trade delegation representing the National Chamber of Trade of Great Britain. The party included thirty prominent merchants headed by Sir William Perring, Member of Parliament.

The Cleveland Electric Illuminating Company became interested in WTAM's contribution to the civic and cultural welfare of the city, and purchased the station for the purpose of maintaining it as a community service. The following year, John F. Royal was appointed manager. The station grew in importance and later was purchased by the National Broadcasting Company. Royal joined the NBC executive staff in New York as vice president in charge of programs. In 1929, under the direction of S. E. Leonard, engineer, a fifty-thousand-watt transmitter was constructed at Brecksville, making the station one of the most powerful in the world. Vernon H. Pribble became manager in 1934, and, under his direction, considerable time was devoted to public-service projects. Walter Logan, who had been associated with the station since 1924, became music director in 1929 and soon won for his orchestra a national reputation. Logan, known as Cleveland's dean of music, died in 1940, and was succeeded by Walberg Brown. Tom Manning joined the station as sports announcer in 1927, and in the 1940s had become one of the best-known experts in his field. The programs for years were under the management of versatile Hal W. Metzger. John McCormick succeeded Pribble as manager in 1948.

Several Clevelanders were achieving fame in athletics: Kirk Reid was the state tennis champion, Joseph Goudreau as the state AAU handball champion, the Favorite Knits team won the women's world championship at basketball with Nellie Kyr as captain, Herman Perleberg qualified for the 1928 Olympic skating races, and Barbara Duffy was the women's city tennis champion.

Notre Dame College moved to South Euclid in September and Bishop Schrembs spoke at the dedication of the new fifty-five-acre educational center located on Green Road. The college had been founded by Mother Mary Cecilia, superior-general of the Sisters of Notre Dame, in 1922, and a year later was chartered by the Ohio State Department of Education. At first the college used the buildings belonging to Notre Dame Academy, 1325 Ansel Road, and its early years were under the guidance and leadership of Mother Mary Evarista, first president; Sister Mary Agnes, dean; and Sister

Mary Odila, treasurer. In 1946, more than three hundred students were enrolled in the college which offered an extensive liberal-arts curriculum including teacher training. The attractive new building of English Tudor Gothic architecture housed all the classrooms, laboratories, little theater, gymnasium, library, and chapel. Aiding in the plans for a large expansion program which included the erection of several new buildings was the president, Mother Mary Vera.

Cleveland took its place in world commerce as an "ocean port" when the first cargo of Cleveland-manufactured products to move in a self-propelled vessel departed for Europe in a steel motor ship, September 4.

Westbrook Pegler, sports writer on the *Chicago Tribune,* played golf on the Beechmont course, September 24. He had made several holes in par when a monoplane, taking off from the landing field of the Van Sweringen estate on South Woodland Road, flew low over the players' heads, causing Pegler to miss a shot. He did not complain when he learned that the pilot was Charles A. Lindbergh, Chicago-bound after a visit with Ambassador Myron T. Herrick.

Charles Francis Brush, scientist and philanthropist, endowed the Brush Foundation which he established in honor of his son, who had died the previous year. It was his belief that the most urgent problem confronting the world was the "rapid increase of population which threatens to over-crowd the earth . . . with resultant shortage of food and lower standards of living, which must certainly lead to grave economic disturbances, famines and wars, and threaten civilization itself . . ." The first president and director of the Foundation was Dr. T. Wingate Todd, eminent pediatrician and anatomist, who had gained prominence at the Medical School of Western Reserve University. Under his direction studies were begun "contributing toward the betterment of human stock, and toward the regulation of the increase of population, to the end that children shall be begotten only under conditions which make possible a heritage of mental and physical health, and a favorable environment." Following Dr. Todd's death in 1938, Mrs. William H. Weir became president of the Foundation. Under her adminis-tration a grant of a library of 4,000 X-ray case histories of the growth and development of well children was made to Western Reserve University; a fertility and sterility clinic was established at the Maternal Health Associa-tion; and a grant toward a 10-year study of virus infections in selected families was made to the Department of Preventive Medicine, Western Re-serve University School of Medicine. Publications included more than forty monographs and a Hand Atlas showing skeletal maturing in the hand and wrist of children.

Princess Anastasia of Greece died in September, and many Clevelanders recalled Nonnie May Stewart who spent her youth in this city. She had lived on East Prospect Street near Euclid Place and had attracted attention for her beauty and vivacity. The daughter of a Cleveland banker, W. E. Stewart, she married George W. Worthington when she was eighteen years old, but in a short time obtained a divorce. She then married William B. Leeds, multi-millionaire, head of the "tin-plate trust." Leeds died at the

John Sherwin

Samuel Mather

Archbishop J. Schrembs

Francis F. Prentiss

Mrs. Francis F. Prentiss

James H. Rogers

O. P. Van Sweringen

M. J. Van Sweringen

Dayton C. Miller

A plucky little tug tows a huge freighter around the bends of the Cuyahoga "Crooked" River. PERRY CRAGG, CLEVELAND NEWS.

Giant unloaders remove cargo from the Harry Coulby. CARL McDOW.

age of forty-six, and Mrs. Leeds, a leader of New York society, became known as the "golden widow." She moved to England and leased the estate formerly owned by the Grand Duke Michael of Russia. Prince Christopher of Greece was her third husband, and the little girl from Cleveland became Princess Anastasia of Greece.

A group of men who wanted to paint as a hobby organized the Business Men's Art Club. Headquarters were located in the Hippodrome Building, and Hans Busch was instructor. Men in the club were recognized not so much for pictorial accomplishments as for "creative recreation." L. E. Lattin was president in 1946, with C. V. Lent, secretary. Early leaders were William T. Higbee, E. R. Hodges, Charles E. Doty, and Wilbur J. Watson.

Officials of the Cleveland Tractor Company announced the delivery of two Cletracs to Commander Richard E. Byrd for his Antarctic expedition. These Cleveland-made tractors were to be used largely for work formerly done by dog teams.

Noel Leslie, new member of the regular Play House staff, made his first appearance in *The Man with a Load of Mischief*, September 28.

The Hermit Club moved into its new home on Dodge Court between East 13th and 17th streets. It was of impressive Tudor architecture with murals depicting the productions of earlier days. Nearly a quarter century earlier, Frank B. Meade, architect and musician, had brought together young Clevelanders to form a club where music, art, and poetry could find an outlet for their talents. Theater-goers applauded the *Hermits in Mexico, The Hermits in Sardinia,* and *The Hermits on Main Street,* each year witnessing a different territorial setting. Meade, the founder and perennial president until his death, led the orchestra and helped in directing the successful series with the aid of such talented co-workers as Charles Hopper, Albert R. Davis, Fred Nicholas, Frank Stair, and George Pettingill. The membership in 1946 was 375, with George W. Teare, president.

Airplane service between Detroit and Cleveland was established by the Stout Air Lines.

Post Office officials were emphasizing the advantages offered by air mail. Air routes connected Cleveland with virtually all of the nation's principal cities. San Francisco was approximately 26 flying hours from Cleveland; Miami, Florida, 23 hours; and Montreal, 9 hours. An air-mail letter mailed in Cleveland traveled approximately 6 hours before arriving in New York.

A new Cleveland *City Directory* appeared, containing 518,088 listings, an increase of 69 per cent over the 1918 directory.

Five hundred of the nation's leading bridge players came to Cleveland in November for four days of competition. This was the second annual congress of the American Auction Bridge League, "an organization of serious men and women who take their bridge games without conversation or any other social diversion." It was agreed that the four essentials of successful bridge playing are mathematics, logic, psychology, and character study. First honors for American men's teams went to the Excelsior Club of Cleveland, composed of E. M. Baker, captain, Maurice Kastriner, Phil E. Leon, and S. L. Guggenheim. Another Cleveland team was the runner-up, representing the Cleveland Athletic Club. The duplicate auction men's pair championship for the Richards trophy was also won by Cleveland, Leon and Guggenheim, representing the Excelsior Club, winning first place. In the mixed-pair championship, Maurice Maschke and Mrs. Ann Rosenfeld were the winners.

The campaign goal for the Community Fund was $4,600,000. The amount raised was $4,569,889.75, with 484,467 subscribers.

Charles Francis Brush, who made the arc lamp practical in April, 1879, pulled the lever that let the current flow for the first time into eighty-five modern lights around the Square on November 29, this year. The small group in attendance included William R. Hopkins, city manager; Howell Wright, public-utilities director; and Superintendent L. D. Bale of the power division of the Cleveland Railway Company. Hopkins said to Brush on this occasion, "Nearly fifty years ago on this very Square, you gave to the world its first practical street lighting, and everything of this nature we have had since has developed from your invention. So it will be a great honor to the city of Cleveland if you will turn on our new lights for the first time." Brush demurred, "No, I'd better not do it; something might go wrong." Hopkins laughed, "They went on all right fifty years ago, didn't they?" "Yes, I guess they did," replied the inventor. The chimes in the Old Stone Church began to ring. Brush pulled the switch, and a brilliant installation of 415,000-candlepower street lights lit up the Public Square. "Quite a lot lighter than the twelve arcs we turned on in April of '79," commented Brush.

The long-awaited White House-crossing bridge which carried Broadway over the Pennsylvania Railroad tracks, was completed by the county at a cost of $486,600. Many serious accidents at the site had led to a public demand for a new span.

Benjamin Karr, veteran editorial writer of the *Leader,* died December 5. His droll humor in describing the trip of Henry Ford's Peace Ship had delighted many audiences.

The flagship *Carl D. Bradley* of the Cleveland-owned Bradley fleet, one of the largest Great Lakes ships, established a record for unloading limestone with its own equipment, at 2,922 tons an hour.

High earning power of workers was one of the strongest factors contributing to the twelve-fold increase in general business volume since 1900, as evidenced by bank clearings. Wages paid by Cleveland manufacturing plants rose from $27,892,689 in 1899 to more than $200,000,000 in 1928. According to the *Central National Bank Review,* the average worker—skilled and unskilled—in a local industrial plant earned $1,516 in 1928, his wage topping $1,444 paid in Pittsburgh, $1,348 in Philadelphia, and $1,342 in Boston. The average industrial worker's pay envelope contained more than three times as much as that of his father in 1900, when $480 represented the average year's wages. The number of positions regularly available for men and women had increased steadily from 154,000 in 1900 to 347,000 in 1920, and approximately 440,000 in 1928. Women employed in Cleveland business totaled about 84,000 in 1928, clerical occupations drawing the largest number, 26,000; factories, 24,000; stores, 10,500; professional, 9,000; communications, 3,500; miscellaneous, 11,000.

Tracing the purchasing power of the dollar in Cleveland, according to the United States Department of Labor, the rent dollar of 1920 was worth but 91 cents in 1928. The food dollar, however, fluctuated during the period, and was worth $1.45. In the lead was the clothing dollar, which had gained 72 cents in purchasing power. Consequently, there was more money in the family purse for comforts and luxuries and to increase the standard of living.

1929

Harry Coulby, outstanding industrialist, died in England on January 18, closing a remarkable career. Born in England, he came to the United States at the age of eighteen with the idea of locating in Cleveland where he was told he would have an opportunity to make his way because of the shipping on the Great Lakes. He asked a New York policeman how to get to Cleveland, and the latter smilingly directed, "You're on Broadway, boy. Keep walking west for five hundred miles and you'll come to the city you want." Coulby was practically penniless, so he followed the policeman's advice, working for his food along the way. It was too late in the season to get a job as sailor, so he became a stenographer and later secretary to the president of the Lake Shore & Michigan Southern Railroad, earning forty dollars a month. He improved his position when he became secretary to Colonel John Hay, who was writing a comprehensive biography of Lincoln. When this work was completed, Samuel Mather, brother-in-law of Hay, gave Coulby a position as clerk at fifty dollars a month in the newly formed organization of Pickands, Mather & Company. The young man soon mastered every phase of the shipping business and was admitted to the firm. Before long, he rose to a position of dominance in iron and shipping. Most of his fortune went to charity, three million dollars to the Cleveland Foundation with the stipulation that half the amount was to be used for crippled and needy children and half for Lakeside Hospital. With the same constructive vision that he employed in planning his business activities, Harry Coulby, "Master of the Lakes," planned the welfare of Cleveland children for generations to come.

When the Catholic Parent-Teachers Association was founded, January 25, by the Rt. Rev. John R. Hagan, superintendent, there were eight units in the parochial-school system. Its purpose was to promote the welfare of children and youth in home, school, church, and community, to co-ordinate spiritual and educational welfare of home and school, and to secure adequate laws for the protection of children and youth. Mrs. Catherine Beebe was the first president. Membership in the association had grown to 7,500 in thirty-three organizations in 1946, when Mrs. John J. Cassidy was president.

Herbert Hoover became the thirtieth President, former President William Howard Taft, chief justice, administering the oath of office while the retiring President, Calvin Coolidge, looked on. General conditions seemed favorable, and there was little indication that a grave economic crisis was on the way.

Another Van Sweringen vision took form with the completion of Shaker Square at the junction of Shaker and South Moreland boulevards, Shaker Heights, pronounced one of America's most attractive shopping centers. A model commercial village of Georgian architecture with twelve buildings in the group, it was designed by Philip L. Small and Charles Bacon Rowley. Moreland Courts near by, the nucleus of a fine apartment-house center, had been erected, with Alfred Harris and Philip L. Small and Associates, architects. Other apartments followed in rapid succession in the area around the beautiful Square.

The Cleveland Child Health Association was organized by the Cleveland Health Council to inspire, guide, and assist in the building of adequate facilities for the physical, mental, social, and moral health of mothers and children. Dr. Richard A. Bolt, the first director, served for many years, and gained international reputation for his studies and achievements in maternal and child health. Classes had been conducted for expectant mothers in the University Public Health Nursing District as early as 1922. Lectures had been given on pre-natal and child-care subjects, and the program was expanded to include the pre-natal clinics of several Cleveland hospitals. In 1932, the Cleveland Child Health Association program had the co-operation of the Cleveland Academy of Medicine, and an experimental class was opened at the academy headquarters. Similar classes were developed over the United States, resulting in an increased number of healthy babies born to enlightened mothers. Mrs. Ervin C. Pope, who had headed the organization for several years, was succeeded as president by Wirth Howell in 1945. Shortly afterward, Howell was made director. Following his resignation in 1946, it was decided to discontinue the Child Health Association, turning over to the Visiting Nurse Association the pre-natal responsibilities, and to the Day Nursery Association the activities related to nursery schools. While the Child Health Association went out of existence on December 31, 1946, it had blazed a trail, and its valuable work was assured of continuance.

David Sinton Ingalls, young state representative from Cleveland and one of Ohio's foremost airplane enthusiasts, was appointed by President Hoover on March 9 as assistant secretary of the navy in charge of aviation, serving until 1932.

The first *Plain Dealer* Golden Gloves carnival opened, March 13, with eighty-six preliminary bouts, while four thousand cheered. These boxing matches proved so successful that the project was made permanent. The early shows were held in the Public Auditorium, but, in 1941, the scene changed to the Arena. Besides being one of the leading sports events of the year, the Golden Gloves earned a substantial sum which was spent for needy veterans and families of both world wars. Many Cleveland boxers in these events won fame of a national character, and a few became known internationally by competing in the Los Angeles and Berlin Olympic games.

Myron T. Herrick, "citizen of the world," died on March 31. He was born in a log house on a little farm in Lorain County and earned his first money by driving cattle. At the age of fourteen, he sold dinner bells to farmers in order to earn money to provide a college education. After he had won international distinction, he was journeying through northern Ohio one day with Senator Marcus A. Hanna, his close friend for many years. Suddenly, he pointed out of the window. "Mark," he asked, "do you see the dinner bell on the white post near the kitchen door? I sold that bell to the farmer while I was trying to finance my college education. When I come down here after quail in the autumn, I can hear my bells ringing in all directions." He taught school and worked on a newspaper before entering Oberlin College. When his money would not take him through the next year, he found work that enabled him to complete his education at Ohio Wesleyan University. He practiced law for eight years before becoming a banker. Then followed a relationship with the Society for Savings where he served as secretary-treasurer, as president from 1894 to 1905, and again from 1908 to 1921. He also found time to enter into the business and civic life of the city. He was one of the organizers of The Cleveland Electric Illuminating Company and for a time was president. He was elected president of the American Bankers Association. Herrick's political career began in 1885 when he was elected to the City Council. His experience as Mark Hanna's lieutenant in grooming McKinley for the Presidency in '96 strengthened his position, and he advanced through the ranks of the Republican Party. He was elected governor of Ohio by the largest plurality in the history of the State, taking office in 1904 and serving one term. By 1912, he had refused five ambassadorships, but he finally accepted President Taft's appointment as ambassador to France, to which post he was reappointed by President Harding and President Coolidge. He was serving in this capacity under President Hoover when he died at the age of seventy-four in Paris in the Embassy Building bought for the American Government with his own funds. Herrick found his greatest enjoyment in helping people, in serving the Society for Savings, and in advancing Cleveland, his home town.

The Cleveland Medal for Public Service was awarded by the Chamber of Commerce, April 16, to Theodore E. Burton, lawyer, scholar, and statesman, "in recognition of long and distinguished service to the City of Cleveland in the promotion of its civic, industrial and business interests, and in the development of the Great Lakes waterways." The medal was also given to Linda Anne Eastman, "who for thirty-three years has used her personal knowledge of library science for the benefit of the people of Cleveland."

Cleveland College moved into the former Chamber of Commerce Building on the Public Square, the Chamber having moved to the Terminal Tower. Enrollment at this time was approaching seven thousand. Dr. A. Caswell Ellis had come from Texas in 1926, and as director inspired rapid expansion of activities until there were more than five hundred semester courses. He retired in 1941, returning to the University of Texas as adult-education consultant.

The Cleveland Clinic disaster on May 15 was one of the city's greatest tragedies. Fire, explosion, and chemical fumes from X-ray films brought death to 124 persons, and the damage to buildings and equipment was serious. Among the victims were Dr. John Phillips, a founder, four leaders on the Clinic staff, two Fellows, and thirty-six trained, non-professional personnel. In addition, the institution had lost Dr. Frank E. Bunts, a founder, by death in 1928. However, the courageous spirit of the remaining founders and their associates did not fail, and a far greater institution was to serve humanity. Dr. George W. Crile's ideals were to live on.

The Builders Exchange was making plans for a comprehensive building exhibit on the eighteenth floor of the Builders Exchange Building in the Terminal Group. "A Home in the Sky" was the main feature of the display, and the show house included everything entering into the construction and furnishing of modern residences and buildings. For a number of years it attracted wide attention, and then its popularity waned.

John J. Bernet resigned as president of the Erie Railroad on May 27, a position he had held for two years, to become head of the Van Sweringens' newest and largest road, the Chesapeake & Ohio, a position he retained until his death in 1935. Bernet had long been a railroad man with important associations. He had served as president of the Nickel Plate, president of the Erie, and vice president of the New York Central. When he resigned from the presidency of the Erie, he was succeeded by Charles E. Denny, who was followed in 1941 by Robert E. Woodruff.

While enjoying one of his frequent European trips, death came to Worcester Reed Warner in Germany in June. With his partner, Ambrose Swasey, he had launched the business of the Warner & Swasey Company almost a half century earlier, bringing to the founders fame and fortune as builders of machine tools and astronomical instruments. Warner, born on a Massachusetts farm in 1846, learned the machinists' trade and became a foreman in the Pratt & Whitney shop in Hartford in 1869, where his life-long acquaintance with Swasey began. Somehow he found time to study astronomy and tinker with telescopes. Recognizing his unusual ability, the firm sent him to the Centennial Exposition in Philadelphia in 1876 to take charge of their exhibit. Combining their skills in the Warner & Swasey firm, the partners became recognized among the leading engineers of America, making contributions to scientific progress. So intense was their study of the stars, that they built and housed a telescope in a small observatory between their adjoining residences in Cleveland. Later they gave this telescope to Case School of Applied Science. Warner served as president of the American Society of Mechanical Engineers, the Civil Engineers Club, and The Cleveland Chamber of Commerce. He was a member of the world's leading scientific societies, and was rewarded with high honors. He served as a director of two Cleveland banks, trustee of Western Reserve University, and Case School, and was one of the city's most distinguished and useful citizens.

The Lake Shore Hotel opened at 12506 Edgewater Drive in Lakewood, located on a high bluff overlooking the lake. A 450-room residential hotel of attractive architecture, it became the home of many executives associated with the industries of the Great Lakes region.

The Women's City Club nature trail was established at Brecksville in memory of Harriet L. Keeler, Cleveland teacher and author of note.

Charles Francis Brush, one of the world's foremost scientists, died June 15. Born in Euclid Township on March 17, 1849, he was educated in the public schools of Cleveland and at the University of Michigan from which he was graduated in 1869 with the degree of mining engineer. Subsequently, he was granted honorary degrees by several other universities. He began the study of electricity from a practical standpoint in 1873, invented a dynamo, and then devoted his time to the development of electric lighting. In 1878 he made the arc lamp practical, the first public demonstration being given on April 29, 1879, over Cleveland's Public Square. Even more important than his inventions relating to the arc lamp, the dynamo, and the storage battery, was his development of the central power station. His early experiments and original principles made possible the distribution of light and power and the advance of civilization. For his outstanding work in science, France made him a Chevalier of the Legion of Honor; the American Academy of Arts and Sciences awarded him the Rumford Medal; and the Franklin Institute awarded him the Franklin Medal. World fame, international honors, honorary degrees as doctor of science, all came to Charles Francis Brush, who had lived and breathed science from boyhood. As a memorial to his son, Charles, Brush established a foundation for race betterment to study the effect of eugenics, environment, and science on the human race. Among the many offices held by the great inventor were trustee of Western Reserve University, Adelbert College, University School, and Cleveland School of Art; corporator of Case School of Applied Science; and president of the Cleveland Arcade Company and of the Linde Air Products Company. He was also a devout supporter of Trinity Episcopal Church. Brush improved the living habits of the people of the world through his inventions and discoveries.

"Cleveland's food center" was the title given the Northern Ohio Food Terminal which opened in June. The new project brought the city into the highest rank among fruit and vegetable markets. It was financed by the produce trade and the Nickel Plate Railroad; and the investment became ten million dollars when four unit buildings, each 485 by 100 feet, were completed. The Terminal covered an area of 34 acres, from East 37th to East 40th streets between Woodland and Orange avenues. Adjoining the district, The Federal Cold Storage Company constructed a huge, modern cold-storage plant. Another feature was an Auction Building with a capacity of 110 cars, while close by was a Growers Market with accommodations for 375 growers. Russell Swiler served as general manager since 1929 and president of the board of directors since 1942.

Phil E. Leon and S. L. Guggenheim won the American Whist League pair trophy for auction pairs at the American Whist League Congress held in Atlantic City in June. The Excelsior Club of Cleveland tied for third place in the team-of-four events.

Tenants moved into the new Medical Arts Building at Ontario Street and Prospect Avenue in the Terminal area on scheduled time, July 1. The building's name was later changed to Republic, with the Republic Steel Company as tenant.

General Henri Gouraud, famous war hero and military governor of Paris, visited Cleveland on July 19 to pay tribute to the memory of Ambassador Myron T. Herrick in the name of the City of Paris.

The German Cultural Garden in Rockefeller Park was dedicated, July 30, in commemoration of the Lessing-Mendelssohn bicentennial. A heroic statue of Goethe and Schiller—a replica of the original in Weimar, and monuments of Lessing, champion of human freedom and equality; Heine, the poet; and Jahn, originator of a system of physical education known as Turnerism, were principal features. The rare Untersberg marble fountain was erected to the memory of Froebel, founder of the kindergarten educational system. It once stood in the garden of the Archbishop of Salzburg in Austria. More than one hundred varieties of shrubs, hedges, and trees imported from Germany decorated the garden. The Charles Eisenman Award for 1929 helped to establish the poets' corners. Charles J. Wolfram, local president of the von Steuben Societies, was a founder.

Henry S. Pickands, partner in Pickands, Mather & Company, the mining and shipping business founded by his father, died on August 10. He was born in Marquette, Michigan, and was educated in the Cleveland public schools, University School, and Sheffield Scientific School of Yale University. He was a director of the Union Trust Company, Empire Steel Corporation, Interlake Steamship Company, and Perry Iron Company; a trustee of University School; and, from 1903 to 1908, mayor of the Village of Euclid.

Through movement of Cleveland products to European ports was provided when the *S. S. Dewstone* cleared for Antwerp on August 17. The operator of this service, the Central West-European Transport Company, announced definite sailings from Cleveland every other week, beginning August 29.

Two retail stores, branches of Sears, Roebuck & Company of Chicago, opened in Cleveland on the same day in August, at 10900 Lorain Avenue and 8501 Carnegie Avenue. The first "Community Store" was situated at 5927 Broadway. Charles H. Kellstadt, Cleveland manager, was a leader in civic activities.

The National Air Races, which began in 1920 at Mitchel Field, Long Island, and moved each year to another city, became a Cleveland feature in 1929. The Cleveland Chapter of the National Aeronautic Association, under the guidance of L. W. Greve, played a prominent part in the venture. In 1929, Thompson Products, Inc., offered a silver cup as first-place award for a fifty-mile, free-for-all, pylon speed contest. Doug Davis of Atlanta, Georgia, outdistanced contestants, winning with an average speed of 194.90 m.p.h.— remarkable for that day. Not only did this record-beating classic foretell the doom of the biplane in the race for speed, but it also was the first time a civilian plane had beaten military ships in competition. This race was the inspiration of the famous Thompson Trophy, inaugurated in 1930, when the races were held in Chicago. Cleveland entertained the races in 1931 and 1932, and with the exception of two years in Los Angeles, 1933 and 1936, the big events were held in the lake city. The races proved to be one of the world's leading entertainment spectacles, contributing to the progress of the aircraft industry.

"Learn what a man's hobbies are, and you will uncover the man himself," according to a philosopher. The zest and youthful enthusiasm characteristic of L. W. Greve was best expressed by his hobby, that of flying. His first flight in an old-vintage plane in 1918 kindled an adventuresome spark in his nature which never diminished in intensity. His engineers at the Cleveland Pneumatic Tool Company shared his enthusiasm, and, in 1926, co-operating with Glenn L. Martin, then in Cleveland, designed the first oleo-pneumatic shock-absorbing strut for airplanes, later called "Aerol" struts and in wide use. This type of strut proved so successful that part of the automotive company was turned over to its production. Greve was named president of the sponsoring organization for the National Air Races in 1929. In addition to his activities as president of the Cleveland Chapter of the National Aeronautic Association, and chairman of the aviation committee of the Chamber of Commerce, Greve was president of the Cleveland Pneumatic Tool Company, the Cleveland Rock Drill Company, and the Champion Machine & Forging Company, and vice president of the Carey Machine Company.

A group of Lakewood theater-goers met and decided that their community should develop a little theater. A company was formed, and a modest start was made by playing in high-school auditoriums and halls. Interest grew rapidly, and Lakewood, the fastest-growing city in the state, claimed it had the nation's fastest-growing little theater. In the 1940s the theater group owned an entire business block in which the auditorium, seating 466, was located, besides a large work shop and rehearsal hall. While one attraction was being presented, the scenery for the next show was being constructed. Eight productions were offered in a season, each running twenty nights, and the attendance approached fifty thousand. The Lakewood Little Theater opened its doors to all who aspired to the stage, whether as performers or technicians, and it offered training without charge. Gordon D. Klein, having years of experience in the professional theater, was dramatic director, while Fred Keiffer was full-time technical director. Actors, actresses, and technical people, as well as management executives, were volunteers. Officers in 1946 included Frederick W. Dorn, president; Wilbur J. Wright, Frank Chesney, Betty Klein, and Carl E. Stahley.

The bull market was attaining frightening proportions, and the national unemployment situation had become acute. The Coolidge prosperity was rapidly fading out, and yet stocks rose to their highest peaks in September. The *New York Times* average for fifty leading stocks had reached a high of 311.90, and investors little dreamed that by the middle of November the average would drop to a low of 164.43.

The building at 11111 Euclid Avenue, formerly the Excelsior Club, was purchased by Western Reserve University for a University Library. It was known as Thwing Hall in memory of Dr. Charles F. Thwing, for thirty-one years university president. The School of Library Science was established on the second floor. In 1946 the university libraries were well-known for their comprehensive character, with nearly 600,000 volumes.

The Cleveland Police Department installed a radio transmitter. Communication was maintained with cities as far distant as New York by radio-telegraph. Cleveland was the first city to have its own station. The new system was a great forward step in meeting the multiplied problems related to law enforcement.

Following the death of Matthew Andrews, chairman of the board of The M. A. Hanna Company, this year, Howard M. Hanna, Jr., became chairman and George M. Humphrey, president. During the year, Hanna interests in Lake Superior iron-ore properties, vessels, and lakefront blast furnaces were transferred to the newly formed National Steel Corporation in exchange for National Steel stock; and the forty-four-year-old Hanna Company enlarged its business to include steel, bituminous coal, rayon, oil, plastics, copper, and banks.

The Heights Christian Church, offspring of the Euclid Avenue Christian Church, was organized on September 27 to serve followers of the Disciples faith in Shaker Heights and Cleveland Heights. The first pastor was Dr. Arthur J. Culler, former dean of Hiram College, who came to the church in 1930. Four years later, the beautiful colonial edifice at South Moreland and Avalon Road was erected. "A tower of strength" in the community, Dr. Culler was a leader in national and international social-relief and interdenominational effort. A humanitarian of many interests, he became Red Cross commissioner to Palestine in 1919, and in 1920 organized the Near East Relief in central Turkey. He retired from his pastorate in 1945 and died a year later. The Rev. Waymon Parsons succeeded him as minister.

New citizens for Cleveland: Croatians, Serbs, Slovenians, Czechoslovakians, Italians, Poles, English, Rumanians, Germans, Hungarians, Russians, 466 in all, took the oath of allegiance and became Americans on October 5.

With a gift of $750,000 from the General Education Board the modern and completely equipped Pathological Institute of the School of Medicine of Western Reserve University had been erected on Adelbert Road. It was dedicated on October 7 as part of the University Hospitals Group.

Light's Golden Jubilee honoring Thomas Alva Edison and his invention of the incandescent light was celebrated by Cleveland, the lighting center of the world. The great inventor, eighty-two years of age, was Henry Ford's guest in Greenfield Village, Michigan, where Edison's modest lighting laboratory of Menlo Park had been reconstructed. The nation recalled that Charles F. Brush of Cleveland had developed the arc lamp some months prior to Edison's incandescent, and had developed a pioneer power station in his city's downtown area. Nela Park took a natural leadership in the celebration, and Clevelanders looked with pride upon the best-lighted downtown streets in the nation. Incandescent illumination had been made possible by the inventor, born fifty-five miles away at Milan, Ohio. The most important day of the nation-wide celebration was October 21, the date of the invention of the incandescent.

The dedication of John Hay High School was celebrated, October 23. Mrs. James W. Wadsworth, daughter of John Hay, for whom it was named, said, "Tonight, more than ever, I am proud to have been born in Cleveland." Located at 2075 East 107th Street, the three-million-dollar senior commerce high school was a model of efficiency and practical planning, housing four thousand pupils.

The first passenger train entered the new Union Terminal, October 23, a locomotive and two coaches carrying the Van Sweringens and Erie Railroad officials.

Theodore E. Burton died, October 28, after outstanding service to the nation and his home city. He was considered for years the best-informed man in the United States Senate. Burton had returned to Congress in 1921, serving until his second election to the Senate in 1928. The world knew him as a great scholar and a constructive statesman.

Crash! The stock-market boom broke on October 29, and Clevelanders were shocked by the screaming headlines announcing untold losses. Day after day the gloomy news was reported, and, by the end of the year, the decline in stock values was approximately fifteen billion dollars. Many thousands of Clevelanders were directly affected. Fortunes and savings of all classes, from industrialists to clerks, had been swept away in the feverish speculation. People mortgaged their homes and turned their Liberty Bonds into securities that produced fancy profits in a few days. When the bubble burst, they lost everything. Believing that poverty would come to an end through enduring prosperity, they had gambled heavily and lost in the worst depression in the nation's history. Unemployment mounted as factories closed their doors, banks and business houses failed, and mortgages were foreclosed, paralyzing buying power and lengthening the bread lines of the needy. President Hoover courageously tried to combat the results of the stock-market crash and the effects of the depression. He called meetings of leaders, took measures to inspire confidence in the banking situation, furthered construction work to give employment, and fostered co-operation between employers and workers to avoid strikes. It was clearly evident that the road to recovery would be long and hard, and that the price of greedy speculation must be paid in work and worry.

Thirty prominent Clevelanders met, November 7, at the invitation of Andrew Squire and Samuel Mather, to raise thirty thousand dollars for a memorial reception room to the late Ambassador Myron T. Herrick. The Paris salon was to be a part of the memorial building to American participants in World War I.

The campaign goal set for the Community Fund was $4,650,000. The total raised was $4,652,239.17, with 504,947 subscribers.

The City Club of Cleveland dedicated its clubhouse at 712 Vincent Avenue on November 12. The club's main feature and principal function was a forum, wherein important civic and world questions were discussed. The yearly presentation of the *Anvil Review* was the pretentious outgrowth of the original "stunt nite," written, staged, and acted by members. Public officials formed the audience, along with members, and enjoyed the satire and good-natured raillery directed at themselves. Judge Carl D. Friebolin and Joseph S. Newman were famous for perennial scripts. Edward W. Doty was president at the time of entering the new quarters. Wendell A. Falsgraf was president in 1946, when the membership had reached 1,650.

A Connecticut plant known as "Hitchcock's" was founded in 1837 and later became the United States Button Company. In 1873 the Chase interests purchased control of this organization, and it was incorporated in 1876 as the Waterbury Manufacturing Company. The first brass mill, the Chase Rolling Mill Company, was built in 1900. The Chase Metal Works, one of the largest brass and copper mills in the country, was started in 1910, and in addition to other acquisitions, the third Chase mill was constructed in Cleveland on Babbitt Road, Euclid, in 1929 to make brass and copper sheets, rods, and tubes. This year, the Chase Brass & Copper Company became a subsidiary of the Kennecott Copper Corporation, the largest domestic producer of copper. Vast quantities of the products of the Cleveland mill were made into cartridge cases during World War II. The government-financed plant became known as the Upson Road Plant. This was bought by the company in 1946. Charles E. Hart became president in 1942.

The gift of George C. Lang, of the board of trustees, relieved the housing problem at Baldwin-Wallace College and put into action the plans for Emma Lang Hall, the women's dormitory named for the donor's wife. Susie Wilson of Cleveland and other friends made notable contributions to the $200,000 building erected this year.

Dr. Roy W. Scott, professor of clinical medicine in the Western Reserve University School of Medicine, Dr. Harold Feil, and Dr. Louis N. Katz made an outstanding contribution to the diagnosis of heart disease. The reputation of these specialists was becoming worldwide.

The new Cleveland Terminal was put into use on December 1 by three Cleveland railroads in advance of the formal opening. The Big Four started four trains, the New York Central, six, and the Nickel Plate, two.

The Yellow Cab Company of Cleveland, Inc., established in December, immediately became the foremost taxicab company in the local field. Jesse T. Smith, its president, gained prominence as a civic leader, identified with a number of Cleveland organizations. In 1934 the large fleet of the Zone Cab Corporation, owned by Arthur McBride and Daniel Sherby, joined with the Yellow Cab Company in operation. Licenses were controlled by city ordinance, and these companies held 556, the total number issued. The Yellow and Zone cabs of Cleveland were the first in the United States to hold a two-way radio Federal license.

With the December 14 issue, the leading weekly news magazine, *Cleveland Town Topics,* which had described the city's social and cultural life since 1888, joined with the *Bystander* as a combined journal under the name of the latter. The *Bystander,* founded in 1921, ceased publication in 1934. Charles T. Henderson was editor. For years, Clevelanders had followed the society columns of Helen DeKay Townsend and the interesting feature stories.

Cleveland's importance in the fire-brick industry was developed when companies in Ohio, Pennsylvania, Kentucky, Missouri, and Maryland merged to form the North American Refractories Company. Economies were effected and broader distribution was achieved. J. D. Ramsay was made president, an office he held until 1947 when he was made chairman of the board and was succeeded as president by E. M. Weinfurtner. The main products were silica and clay bricks used principally in steel plants.

A specialized service to Cleveland business men and women began on December 16 when the Business Information Bureau at the Cleveland Public Library was opened. The bureau was organized and developed under the capable direction of Rose L. Vormelker, business-research librarian, and it became a businessmen's laboratory for facts, maintaining a vast and varied amount of source material on industrial and market information. One of the busiest departments of the main library, it gave valuable assistance to five hundred daily visitors. The national reputation won by this important department was further increased in 1940 when the *Christian Science Monitor* and *The American Magazine* paid tribute to its outstanding service and able organizer, and when the American Trade Association executives selected it for additional honors.

Identity of The Harshaw, Fuller & Goodwin. Company was changed to The Harshaw Chemical Company, and central offices and research laboratories were located at 1945 East 97th Street, Cleveland. William J. Harshaw succeeded his father as president in 1936. A series of acquisitions greatly enlarged the business from time to time, and, in 1940, plant facilities were acquired near Los Angeles, California. Occupying an important position in the chemical industry in the 1940s, the twenty-five-million-dollar firm was producing well over a thousand different chemical products. Operating from Cleveland, nationwide sales offices were serving industry and laboratory research, and the company was the exclusive sales agent for four associate firms. The founder's basic philosophy stressing research, well-equipped plants, and diversified products had enabled the company to keep pace with rapid change and the development of new products, materials, and processes, and to occupy an important position in the chemical industry.

CHAPTER 16

Reverses and Reserves

1930-1939

F EW DECADES in American history have started with as discouraging a picture as the 1930s. The bull market concluded with a crash that brought worldwide repercussions. Then came a new realization. This country was not alone in the postwar depression; conditions were serious, economically and politically, in other nations. As hard times developed, each failure tended to produce other failures, and the confident psychology of the prosperous Coolidge days was suffering a severe reaction. Clevelanders, with the rest of the nation, were counting their losses and murmuring, "What next?"

President Herbert Hoover was attempting to answer that question as optimistically as possible. He favored a reduction in taxes and recommended the building of public works to keep up employment; but the trend of trade, with the spirit of the country, went down and down.

When 1930 concluded, business was nearly 30 per cent below normal; questionable investment companies of the twenties were going to smash; real estate and securities were marked to continuously lower values; drought intensified the food problems, and the national wealth showed a drop of more than forty billion dollars from 1929 to 1932. The number of jobless approximated ten million and the great American question, still unanswered, was "What next?"

Never had a great country toppled economically with the swiftness experienced in the United States. Never did a nation take its punishment in a more practical manner. Down in their hearts the American people knew that their suffering was small compared with that of other countries; they realized the nation had been on a postwar spree of financial celebration; they were willing to settle down, sober up, and meet the situation. Paraphrasing, in their hearts, the Salvation Army's slogan, they rolled up their sleeves and declared, "This country may be down, but it's never out!"

This was an era of loan-making—foreign and domestic; loans for great public improvements, such as highways, monumental buildings, and skyscrapers; loans to individuals for installment buying, purchasing stocks on margins, and acquiring real estate. The economic program of the day seemed to be one of lending to encourage business and expand markets. The situation was one of maladjustments, naturally following World War I, and the American bubble that burst in 1929 touched off a period of deflation and unemployment.

President Hoover, able organizer that he was, failed to overcome the economic collapse which had been heaped on his broad shoulders. Yet, even as the Democrats shouted for a change in the White House, encouraging signs were appearing on the horizon in the form of quieted capital-labor relations and the ability of the Federal Reserve System to combat money crises. Nevertheless, the care-free prosperity of the twenties was gone, and with it many economic evils. Americans had paid dearly for the piper's tune.

Franklin Delano Roosevelt rode into unprecedented power on a Democratic landslide in 1932. The banking situation had reached a crisis, and in his first fireside radio talk to the nation, he began to unfold his New Deal policies. The bank holiday of early 1933 was followed by a vast experimental spending program to relieve unemployment, promote public works, and restore prosperity.

The American Federation of Labor surveyed the national situation with alarm. Unemployment had risen steadily for several years, and Federation membership had dropped to 2,100,000. The election of Roosevelt, however, brought new hope, and labor again adopted an enthusiastic program with the slogan, a "forty-hour week." With the introduction of the NRA, workers flocked into unions expecting the New Deal government agency to protect their newly established right to collective bargaining. William Green, who had succeeded Samuel Gompers in 1924, when the "grand old man" of labor passed away, sent organizers into the mass-production industries. Difficulty was experienced in the automobile, steel, and rubber industries, and a new organization was formed to meet this situation. John L. Lewis, Sidney Hillman, Philip Murray, and others initiated the Committee for Industrial Organization which was to make its particular appeal to mass-production workers on industrial union lines. Four million members were claimed by the CIO by the time it held its first convention in 1938. Cleveland labor leaders watched the new split in the labor movement that came in 1939, when Lewis opposed President Roosevelt's foreign policies, joined those against the President in 1940, and later lost his leadership of the CIO to Murray.

After much discussion of currency reforms, President Roosevelt devaluated the dollar. He had been given authority, through an emergency measure in 1933, to reduce the amount of gold in the dollar. On January 31, the President announced that the maximum gold content of the new dollar would be 59.06 per cent of its former (1900) value. This meant that the Government would buy the gold offered to it, but would pay more for it in paper dollars than it had before. The currency had been inflated nearly 41 per cent, yet after three months, it was discovered that prices had risen only 22 per cent. Economists pointed out that 90 per cent of business operations were carried on by credit and that prices did not necessarily follow closely either inflation or deflation of the currency. "Managed currency" was the name given to Roosevelt's attempts to influence prices by manipulating the value of currency. It was an effort to control both prices and currency at the same time, as the Government was controlling other phases of America's economic life. Before the consequences of the new monetary system could be evaluated, the international situation became confused, and export business incident to the war in Europe relieved the tension.

In the middle thirties, government controls and restrictions were shaking the confidence of business and delaying recovery throughout the nation. Uncle Sam regulated transportation, carried the mail, insured bank deposits to a certain maximum, provided social security, stepped into labor disputes, maintained the greatest national police agency, contributed vast sums to the building of highways, inspected food supplies, and influenced the price of food through the New Deal AAA. Emergency alphabetical agencies were identified by a myriad of letter combinations—PWA, WPA, NRA, and a host of others—of such vast proportions that they threatened to become permanent.

Private enterprise felt that the Government had taken from it the opportunity to make reasonable profits, and the public was gradually learning that without profits employment was endangered. Taxes were preventing business institutions from accumulating earnings and planning for the future. Dependence upon pump-priming had continued too long. As Colonel Leonard P. Ayres described the situation: "The greatest nation in the world is still waiting for freedom from regulations and restraint, so that it can journey forward in a sound and steady manner characteristic of American enterprise."

The City Manager Plan and proportional representation came to an abrupt end in Cleveland in 1931 after an eight-year trial under two capable administrators, William R. Hopkins and Daniel E. Morgan. When the Federal Plan was resumed, Ray T. Miller, Democratic leader, was elected mayor, serving one term in a period of serious bank closings and depression. However, under his administration Cleveland met its grave problems with a resolute spirit. Despite Miller's earnest efforts to bring the city out of its severe slump, an insurgent arose in the Democratic ranks in the person of Representative Martin L. Sweeney. While the latter was eliminated in the primary, many of his friends were said to have opposed Miller and supported Harry L. Davis, who made a spectacular comeback. The genial Davis was elected by a majority of 14,446. Again his administration was criticized for failure to suppress lawlessness in the city. It was a serious period because of the continuous depression, but Davis made a strong effort to revive business and overcome the nationwide criticisms of the city's condition. When election time came around again in 1935, Harold H. Burton loomed on the scene, strongly supported by Maurice Maschke and his organization. Burton had been director of law, 1924-32, and temporarily mayor for the months between the regime of City Manager Morgan and Mayor Ray T. Miller's election. Davis lost the nomination by a narrow margin. Ray T. Miller was the Democratic choice, but Burton won the election and was destined to climb the political ladder with sensational success.

As the decade opened, Cleveland's financial strength centered in seven large banks, the city having gone through a period of consolidations: three national banks—National City, Central United National, and Engineers

National; three trust companies—Cleveland Trust, Guardian, and Union Trust; and the mutual savings bank, the Society for Savings.

Two of the largest Cleveland banks, the Union Trust and the Guardian, were ordered in liquidation at the close of the bank holiday. Their unsatisfactory financial condition was traced to over-leniency in making loans without sound security; and in the case of the Guardian, to mismanagement that led to the punishment of officials. Drastic treatment of the Union Trust, however, was probably not justified, according to students of finance. The Engineers National, which had recently changed its name to Standard Trust, was closed with the charge of lax methods and unscrupulous management on the part of its chief executive. The National City, Central United National, Cleveland Trust, Society for Savings, and the new Union Bank of Commerce proved their ability to meet the new conditions, carrying on the vast responsibilities demanded by the district's growing business.

Like other large industrial, commercial, and financial centers, Cleveland was severely affected by the national crisis. Never before had the city experienced so many business failures or such widespread unemployment. However, the depression, with all of its evils, demonstrated the fact that Cleveland had a vast store of invaluable basic assets, far greater than had been commonly appreciated. These assets were not only economic and civic, but spiritual as well. For the first half of the decade Cleveland's community leaders in government, business, and labor, health, education, and religion, concentrated on working their way through the depression toward recovery.

The center of population of Cuyahoga County, totaling 1,201,455, according to the 1930 census, was just west of East 55th Street and south of Woodland Avenue; while the center of Cleveland's population, totaling 900,429, was within a few hundred feet of this location, but north of Woodland. The county figure had almost doubled since 1910, but the city's population increased only about two-thirds, emphasizing suburban growth.

Cleveland's cosmopolitan character had been strengthened by an increase of 114,000 newcomers during the twenties. This was in decided contrast to the City of St. Louis, whose population of 821,960 included an increase of 49,000 immigrants, and that of Cincinnati with 40,000 new arrivals boosting its total to 451,160. It was the large representation of nationality groups that gave to Cleveland the varied cultures for which it was becoming famous.

Interesting population trends were reported by Howard Whipple Green, director of the 1930 federal census in the Sixth Ohio District. The foreign-born population represented 25.5 per cent of the city's total at the end of 1930, and another 40 per cent of the population was of foreign or mixed parentage. Poland contributed the largest nationality group, followed closely by Czechoslovakia. There were 71,899 Negroes in the complex city. Families were growing smaller, now averaging 4.1 persons. Approximately 15 per cent of low-income families owned radios, and nearly 90 per cent in the highest economic scale. There were more radios in Cleveland than telephones, more automobiles than radios. In the low-income group, 25 per cent of families owned their homes, while more than 75 per cent were home owners in the high-income bracket. Infant mortality was more than 100 per 1,000 births in low-income families, and less than 30 per 1,000 in the highest group. In the lowest economic group, population density was 90 persons per acre, while it was less than 8 per acre in the high-income scale. Only 17 per cent of births in low-income families were in hospitals; the high-income figure showed 94 per cent.

The thirties witnessed several of the greatest undertakings in the city's history, which would influence the prestige, health, and culture of Cleveland for generations. The Terminal buildings were completed and were immediately rated as the second most important group of commercial buildings in any nation. A city within a city, the group embodied a tremendous railroad station, towering office buildings, Higbee's modern department store, Harvey's restaurants and shops, the famous Hotel Cleveland, a monumental Post Office, and offices of major banks. The Terminal Tower, the central feature on the Public Square, rose majestically more than seven hundred feet, the tallest building outside of New York City. At the same time, the University Hospitals group was developing rapidly, giving the city an outstanding position as a medical center. This project was magnificent proof of the generosity of Clevelanders, who gave millions, inspired by humanitarian impulses and civic pride. In beautiful Wade Park, which was rapidly becoming a surpassing center of culture, John L. Severance, patron of music and art, made possible lovely Severance Hall, home of the Cleveland Orchestra, providing a spacious auditorium where utility and attractiveness combined to serve Cleveland's musical and educational interests. On the lakefront, the enormous Stadium was built to provide for major civic, sporting, and entertainment events. With the mammoth Public Auditorium, Cleveland could offer the most complete facilities to national gatherings, and the city had become the number-one meeting place of the nation. The huge exhibitions of the National Machine Tool Builders, American Road Builders, and many other industrial and trade organizations influenced buying in all parts of the nation and beyond its borders. The Arena, opened in 1937, was the home of champion hockey teams. Large audiences were attracted to major sporting events, brilliant ice carnivals, circuses, and public features.

Cleveland was becoming a continuously greater center for sports, and its sons and daughters were achieving leadership in several fields; but it remained for a Negro boy, trained at Fairmount Junior High School, to become the greatest sprinter and jumper of all time. Jesse Owens, outstanding hero of the Olympic Games of 1935 in Berlin, brought home trophies symbolic of international victories together with world records of track and field.

During this decade, the development of the Mall witnessed practical improvements with the completion of the Board of Education Building and the Stadium. The hope of completing the west side of the Mall was dulled as money was not in sight for monumental public buildings. However, landscaping made the area attractive on the upper Mall while the lower Mall area was used only for parking.

Many physical improvements were made in the decade within the county borders. The Metropolitan Park System was greatly expanded; the Lorain-Carnegie Bridge and the Main Avenue Bridge, colossal engineering feats, served to unite more closely the East and West sides, and the Lakeland Freeway was being projected as a convenient highway along the lake to the east. The Fulton Road, Brecksville, and Bedford bridges shortened distances over the valleys. Federal funds for public works stimulated river-and-harbor development and vast improvements relating to highways, housing, and health. While complaints were registered against pump priming to relieve unemployment, many gigantic projects in Cuyahoga County that had long been delayed because of lack of funds were advanced through the emergency-relief program, inefficient as it was.

The Cleveland Metropolitan Housing Authority developed a program that would provide dwellings for many low-income families and improve their standard of living. The first three projects afforded homes for 1,849 families, and these improvements necessitated the clearing away of deteriorated districts.

Cleveland had become a production center of aviation parts and accessories, and the Municipal Airport had expanded to follow the upward curve of aviation development. L. W. Greve and associates believed that the city was destined to become one of the world's great aviation capitals, and they secured a sanction to make it the home of the National Air Races. The races had already established their worth to the industry as a proving ground for innovations, and local sponsors were quick to recognize their value to the city in terms of prestige and revenue. Record-breaking crowds journeyed to Cleveland from far and near to enjoy the annual Labor Day classic, where they witnessed thrill-packed flying exhibitions, breathtaking stunts, and military might representing the nation's air defense. The Gordon Bennett International Balloon Race drew the city's greatest crowd to the Airport.

Cleveland, the center of a vast industrial empire, had become the headquarters for several important organizations directly related to the commerce of the Great Lakes. Foremost was the Lake Carriers Association, founded in 1892, which concerned itself with water, channel, loading level, dock and harbor facilities, and the policies of fleet operation. The Ore and Coal Exchange, founded during World War I, dealt with exchange of cargoes from vessels to railroad cars and the reverse; and, to its credit, was the fastest handling of bulk freight in the world. The United States Coast Guard, among its many services, policed the lakes and the five-thousand-mile shore line. The future of the merchant marine was the chief concern of the Cleveland Propeller Club, a non-political organization promoting the best interests of the lakes.

It was a far cry from 1855, when 1,499 tons of ore were moved down the lakes, to 1934, when 826 freighters—521 American and 305 Canadian vessels—represented an investment of a half-billion dollars. Cleveland organizations, including the Cleveland-Cliffs Iron Company, Oglebay, Norton & Company, M. A. Hanna Company, Corrigan-McKinney Company, and United States

Steel Corporation, together owned about 85 per cent of the iron-ore deposits in the Minnesota, Michigan, and Wisconsin ranges. Cleveland's position in the iron-and-steel industry was strengthened immeasurably when a number of companies were merged in 1930 into the Republic Steel Corporation.

Cleveland's reverses had met their master by 1936, and new progress was being built upon the city's strong reserves. One of the most constructive enterprises undertaken by the people of Cleveland, as a reconstruction medium to restore prosperity, was the Great Lakes Exposition, held in 1936 and 1937. This exposition did more than advertise Cleveland and stimulate business and employment during these critical years; it fostered enthusiasm and pointed the way to district recovery.

The year 1936 seemed propitious for the event, as it marked the centennial of the incorporation of Cleveland as a city. Following informal discussions among various groups in 1935, Frank J. Ryan invited Lincoln G. Dickey and William Ganson Rose to collaborate with him in making comprehensive plans for an exposition representative of the commerce and industry, arts and science, and culture of the Great Lakes States and the bordering provinces of Canada. The more important purposes as listed in the prospectus were:

"To advance the industrial and civic interests of Cleveland through an undertaking in which the entire citizenship would find inspiration;

"To advance the business interests by attracting hundreds of thousands of visitors who would patronize commercial institutions, become better acquainted with local products and see first-hand the advantages of the city as a place in which to live and have a business . . .

"To further the efforts of civic and business organizations through stimulating pride, faith and community patriotism;

"To lay the foundation for the work of securing future conventions and expositions through demonstrating Cleveland's ability to take care of important events;

"To imbue in every man, woman and child in Cleveland a newborn confidence in the power of the community to go forward under the concerted leadership that will achieve its due recognition through this enterprise."

The officers of the exposition for 1936 were: honorary chairman, Harold H. Burton, mayor of Cleveland; general chairman, Dudley S. Blossom; president, Eben G. Crawford; vice presidents, A. C. Ernst, H. G. Dalton, I. F. Freiberger, L. B. Williams; treasurer, J. C. McHannan; secretary, H. J. Raymond; general manager, Lincoln G. Dickey.

An executive committee of eighteen members was elected, and this body delegated to an administrative committee, including Ryan, Dickey, and Raymond, the direction of the exposition. The co-operation of the Federal Government was obtained through Congressional action; and the interest of the State of Ohio, the other Great Lakes States, and the Canadian Government was secured. Serving with Dickey as associate directors were Almon R. Shaffer and Peg Willin Humphrey.

The central theme of the exposition was built around the iron-and-steel industry of Cleveland and the Great Lakes region, but there were hundreds of exhibits fully representative of the other industries and activities of this rich and populous area. The project inspired new and comprehensive research into the resources of the region. It was found that while these inland seas were called "Great" because they constituted the largest area of fresh water in the world, their true greatness had a far broader significance. More than any other influence, they furthered the industrial and commercial development of the nation. Their contribution to America's higher standard of living was incalculable. Their value to the states bordering on them had made this district the most important trade empire in the world.

It was found that the eight Great Lakes States—New York, Pennsylvania, Ohio, Indiana, Illinois, Michigan, Wisconsin, and Minnesota—were producing 85 per cent of the nation's iron ore. While the annual production of coal in the United States was a little more than 400,000,000 tons, that of the Great Lakes States exceeded 175,000,000. The survey showed that transportation on the lakes was probably cheaper than any transportation elsewhere. With one-eighth the area of the nation, the eight states touching on the lakes had more than one-third of the people of the country, a greater population than that of Great Britain, France, or Italy. They were producing 70 per cent of the metal-working tools, nearly half of the nation's cement, more than 60 per cent of the nation's rubber, more than 60 per cent of the printing, nearly 60 per cent of the construction, and about 50 per cent of the electricity. Commerce of the lakes exceeded the foreign commerce along the Atlantic, the Pacific, and the Gulf ports. Exports of the Great Lakes region totaled nearly one-half of the nation's exports and two-thirds of the imports.

To summarize, the best available statistics prior to the exposition indicated that the Great Lakes States, when considered as a trade empire, ranked second to Russia in the production of food, and produced more electric power than Germany, Great Britain, France, Russia, Italy, or Japan; more iron ore, steel, and machinery than any of these nations; more chemicals and coal than any excepting Germany and Great Britain; more pig iron than any of the great foreign powers; and more petroleum than any save Russia. But while these states were contributing so much to the prosperity of the nation, they had but 175 of the 432 members in the House of Representatives and only 16 of the 96 in the Senate. With this meager 40 per cent representation in the House and 16 per cent in the Senate, the Great Lakes States were paying 60 per cent of the corporation income taxes and approximately the same proportion of individual taxes.

The Great Lakes Exposition occupied the Mall from St. Clair Avenue north, the Public Auditorium, and the lakefront from West 3rd Street to East 20th Street, an area of more than two square miles. When the project was launched, much of this area was a public dump, and construction of the Lakeland Freeway was just being started. The lakefront was filled in, the western section of the shoreway was rushed to completion, partly at the exposition's expense, transforming the entire area into a place of beauty. Many large buildings of modern design were erected for exhibitions and amusements, and the illumination for brilliance and artistry surpassed that of any other exposition. The Streets of the World, occupying a seven-acre area, built in honor of the many nationality groups of Cleveland, attracted worldwide attention.

Near the close of the 1936 exposition, Eben G. Crawford, president, made a report to the trustees in which he said in part:

> Not only the dollars which the visitors to the exposition have spent here, but the good impression of Cleveland and of the exposition they have carried far and wide, have contributed to the present and future enhancement of this community. Among these visitors have been many men and women of great influence . . .
>
> One of the purposes of the exposition, it should be emphasized, was to spread the fame of Cleveland throughout the nation, and to upbuild the reputation the city deserves. Hundreds of programs emanating from the exposition have been broadcast by the radio chains and by local stations. Thousands upon thousands of columns of the most desirable news and comment, also emanating from the exposition, have been published in newspapers, trade journals, magazines, and other publications in the United States, in Canada, and in many countries throughout the world . . .
>
> The Executive Committee, in large measure, attributed the results obtained to the splendid co-operation given by Cleveland civic and business institutions—schools, colleges, churches, manufacturers, merchants, the railroads, and many more. Finally, acknowledgment must be made of the notable contribution of the Cleveland Museum of Art, through its board of trustees, officers, and staff, in organizing the Twentieth Anniversary Exhibition of the Museum as the official art exhibition of the Great Lakes Exposition.

The trustees enthusiastically approved the report and unanimously voted to repeat the exposition, with additional features, in 1937. For the second year, W. Trevor Holliday served as president, and Clyde T. Foster as chairman of the administrative committee. The total attendance for both years exceeded seven million.

In the great period of industrial expansion from 1900 to 1930, new jobs to the number of twenty million were created by industry in the nation. In 1938, one workman out of every four was making products never heard of by his grandfather. Largely because of the machine, the average work week had been reduced from 72 hours to about 40 hours for the masses. A consolidated report of the country's manufacturing corporations showed that for the seven-year period from 1929 to 1935, 80.6 per cent of available income went to employees, 8.9 per cent to management, and 10.5 per cent to stockholders.

The mid-1930s witnessed greater labor unrest than the country had known since 1921. Following the sit-down strike of 7,000 workers at the local Fisher Body plant in 1936, strikes in automobile plants in other cities were launched in rapid succession. At the same time, the CIO was endeavoring to organize the steel industry, and resulting strikes in Cleveland and other Ohio cities were marked by violence. Finally an agreement was reached between the CIO and the steel companies, and Republic Steel proceeded with its greatest program of expansion. Other serious strikes in the decade included those at the Industrial Rayon Corporation, the National Screw & Manufacturing Company, baking plants, and moving companies. Labor appointed a peace board to eliminate wildcat strikes of young unions.

Radio had become a powerful medium for swaying the public mind. Proof of its efficacy was the persuasive voice of Roosevelt in his fireside chats, with political implications, on "the state of the nation." Millions laughed with Will Rogers, Cleveland's Bob Hope, Eddie Cantor, Fibber McGee and Molly, and Jack Benny; millions followed the soap operas and the adventures of *One Man's Family,* whose star, Mrs. Minetta Ames Ellen, as Mother Barbour, had gone to the old Walnut School in Newburgh; millions hummed with Bing Crosby, James Melton, and Kate Smith; millions caught the swing fever from the jazz maestros—Artie Shaw, Harry James, Tommy Dorsey, Glenn Miller, Duke Ellington, and Paul Whiteman, who pleased the majority and irritated the few. Jitterbugs took time out to enjoy the musical hits, *Three Little Pigs, Stormy Weather,* and *Begin the Beguine. Winter Wonderland* and *Wagon Wheels* were played over and over along with *Thanks for the Memory,* and their popularity never waned. Cleveland stations not only brought into the city's homes the best programs on the air waves, but proved their resourcefulness by local presentations encouraging Cleveland talent. Radio carried the news swiftly, and through international coverage, minimized distance in peace and war. The Cleveland public schools pioneered in developing radio as a medium of education.

The thirties were not a time for light-hearted living, and places of entertainment suffered in consequence. In 1938, it was said that one of every three Clevelanders had been on relief during the depression; those who had wealth held fast to it. Miniature golf courses with small admissions caught the popular fancy out-of-doors; and indoors, bridge and monopoly were the rage. Families sought free recreation in parks created by relief labor.

Early in the decade, skirt hems had come down with prices despite defenders of the knee-length fashion. Evening dresses touched the ground. Wardrobes were altered over and over to give longer service, but enterprising stylists bolstered their business by bringing back frills and flounces along with long, white gloves and corsets. Bobbed hair was losing favor. Subtle grace and glamour characterized a marked departure from the flapper of the flighty twenties. Morality plays and sex discussions had worn thin.

Journey's End and *What Price Glory* emphasized the sobering revolutionary trend in public thinking. Cleveland audiences found pleasant relief in *You Can't Take It With You* by Kaufman and Hart. They flocked to see Charlie Chaplin in *City Lights;* Claudette Colbert and Clark Gable in their movie hit *It Happened One Night;* and paid high prices to see the film version of Margaret Mitchell's *Gone With the Wind.* As Vice President Throttlebottom in *Of Thee I Sing,* Victor Moore brought a rejuvenated spirit to the legitimate stage; and Richard B. Harrison as "de Lawd" in Marc Connelly's *Green Pastures,* and Greer Garson in James Hilton's delightful *Goodbye, Mr. Chips* left a deep impress. *Sherlock Holmes* and *Sweet Adeline* came to the front, reviving the Victorian decade of the nineties. Agnostics and exponents of new scientific theories were finding fewer opponents who had the time to argue, and bold psychologists were at a loss for audiences.

Economic extravagance of the twenties caught the churches in its wake. When the crash came, lavish spending and over-expansion reduced them to the lowest point of finances and morale in their history. Congregations dwindled; many felt they could not afford to support the church. Food and clothing were distributed to the needy. With faith and courage, denominational leaders set out to restore spiritual advance after the mid-decade when the tide had turned to broad programs leading into avenues of service and sacrifice. An event of world significance was the merger in Cleveland of the Evangelical and Reformed churches in 1934. Protestant churches within the Cleveland Church Federation had increased from 67 in 1911 to 325 in 1932.

Cleveland suffered the loss of many leaders in this era, men who had made substantial contributions to the city's growth and well-being. Among them were John D. Rockefeller, who gave wisely and generously to many Cleveland institutions; Newton D. Baker, who had loyally served his city, his nation, and the world; Francis F. Prentiss, outstanding civic worker and philanthropist; John L. Severance, patron of art and music; Dr. Charles F. Thwing, educator whose character-building influence lives on; Samuel Mather, leader in iron and shipping who shared his wealth freely; Ambrose Swasey, engineering genius who furthered industrial progress and education; John Sherwin, a leading banker of his time; Charles E. Adams, industrialist and champion of the Community Fund; Dudley S. Blossom, leader of civic events and benefactor of many institutions; Henry G. Dalton, industrialist and humanitarian; and O. P. and M. J. Van Sweringen, who rose from humble beginnings to become internationally famous for their railroad ventures, the Cleveland Terminal group of buildings, and the City of Shaker Heights.

Transit problems, long the subject of controversy and exasperation, were studied by Mayor Harold H. Burton and Traction Commissioner Edward J. Schweid, for the purpose of finding a solution that would mean adequate, low-cost transportation for Cleveland. After a serious impasse between the city and the Cleveland Railway Company, a plan for municipal ownership was worked out.

One hundred and fifty trains connected Cleveland with the outside world. More powerful locomotives, larger cars, stronger roadways, heavier and better-equipped rails and bridges, and more efficient shops and terminals characterized railroad facilities. Builders, engineers, and executives had worked together to maintain Cleveland's dominant position as a strategic rail center handling increased tonnage demands. Eighty motor-truck lines and six motor-bus lines operated through the city.

This decade witnessed evidences that Cleveland was attracting national attention along other lines. It was host to the Republican National Convention, the American Legion Convention, and major gatherings that drew the greatest number of visitors the city had known. These were due, in large measure, to the success of the Great Lakes Exposition. The most impressive assembly of the decade was the Eucharistic Congress which brought to Cleveland in September of 1935 several hundred thousand Catholics to honor the Sacrament. Ceremonies continued for a week in the Public Auditorium and Stadium, and the crowning event came when 125,000 met in the amphitheater for midnight mass, the greatest gathering in the history of the Stadium, which was aglow with candlelight. The Seventh World Poultry Congress brought delegates from forty-five nations, attracted fifty thousand out-of-town visitors and widely advertised Cleveland as host to this important international event. Rotarians, speaking more than thirty languages, met in Cleveland to further unselfish purposes. Many local companies participated in the New York World's Fair, advancing the industrial fame of Cleveland.

War clouds were throwing black shadows over the world, and the feeling was growing in the nation and abroad that the United States would be drawn into the terrifying European conflict. Since World War I, conditions had been chaotic in many nations. Before the conclusion of that war, Russia in 1917 was the scene of a revolt that overthrew the Czarist rule and substituted a new form of totalitarian government—a communistic police state that made slaves of a mighty people. After World War I, came revolutions in other countries, and the threat of a second great war was born. There was a general feeling that the Treaty of Versailles was not economically sound, was unjust to some nations, and was a cause of discontent regarding boundary lines. Republics were set up in Germany, Austria, and Turkey, and dictatorships in Spain and Italy. Then Mussolini and Hitler demonstrated their growing strength and insatiable lust for power. Italy seized Ethiopia in 1936, despite the little country's protest to the League of Nations. This episode and subsequent aggressive moves inspired the feeling that the League was not strong enough to settle affairs in which large powers were selfishly involved. Austria was annexed to Germany in 1938; Hitler marched across the Czechoslovak frontier, persecuted the Jews within reach, and began his manipulation of territories in Europe, invading Poland in the fall of 1939. The United States watched the changing scene with alarm while clinging to a policy of isolation. While war brought uneasiness to Cleveland, it also brought business orders that stimulated industrial recovery, already well on the way. Patriotic fervor was inspired by the first Festival of Freedom, the most pretentious Fourth-of-July celebration in the nation, stirring young and old to new heights of loyalty and devotion to country.

After a period of hard times, Cleveland's civic spirit, depressed for nearly a decade, had reasserted itself. Citizens were awakened to new opportunities with the realization that

Stone walls do not a city make,
Nor brick and wood a town,
But men and women all awake

Who scoff at Fortune's frown,
Who love the right and hate the wrong,
Who rush when Duty calls,
They are the pillars firm and strong,
They are the city walls.

1930

Prior to 1930, a series of mergers brought several small steel companies into the existing Republic Iron & Steel Company, assembled in 1899 from thirty-eight iron companies. The Republic Steel Corporation was formed in 1930 by a merger including the early-day Bourne-Fuller Company of Cleveland, which owned and operated the Upson Nut Company. Located in the "Flats" on Carter Road (just south of the Detroit-Superior High Level Bridge), this plant was a completely integrated operation incorporating ore boats, a blast furnace, and steel plant. The acquisition in 1935 of The Corrigan-McKinney Steel Company, dating back to 1893, greatly improved Republic's industrial position, as extensive iron-ore and coal reserves were obtained through the purchase. The building of a mammoth ninety-eight-inch strip mill in 1936-37 received international attention. Thousands of tons of ship-plate were turned out during World War II; and to supply wartime steel, Republic, co-operating with the Defense Plant Corporation, built its No. 5 blast furnace and coke plant in record time. Enlargement and improvement of docks made Cleveland a more efficient receiving port for incoming ore moving to Republic plants downstate. The Truscon Steel Company, whose principal plant was in Youngstown, also became a subsidiary in 1935. The Cleveland division of Truscon originated in the Hydraulic Pressed Steel Company, and as Republic's pressed-steel division, it produced items for the automotive trade. In Republic's Cleveland district, covering approximately 540 acres, were the country's finest and most modern steel plants in the 1940s. The corporation was nation-wide in scope, but by far the largest portion of its facilities were concentrated in northeastern Ohio at Cleveland, Massillon, Canton, Youngstown, and Warren. Republic operated a large steel plant and three manufacturing plants in Cleveland. It was one of the largest single employers in the city, with more than nine thousand persons on the 1945 payroll, which totaled $28,950,000. Central offices of the Republic Steel Corporation were moved from Youngstown to Cleveland in 1936, occupying a large part of the Republic Building in the Terminal Group. Besides being one of the country's three leading steel-producing companies, it was the largest producer of alloy and stainless steels. T. M. Girdler, elected president in 1930, became chairman of the board in 1937, when R. S. Wysor became president. Wysor was succeeded by C. M. White in 1945, Girdler continuing as chairman of the board.

A wave of modernization attacked the Public Square, wiping out rustic settings reminiscent of horsecar days. The quaint bridge, pools, and waterfall were erased from the southwest sector, and the Moses Cleaveland Monument was moved to the center of the area, a proud position before the stately Terminal. To the north, near Superior, a new 122-foot steel flagstaff was erected. Completing a survey of the Square, a geyser fountain gave life to the northeast section, the massive Soldiers and Sailors Monument dominated the southeast section, and the Tom Johnson Monument, the northwest. Young trees were struggling for existence, and several unattractive shelter stations offered refuge to streetcar travelers.

There were 12,609 Cleveland retail stores in 1929 with an annual business of $534,240,787, a yearly payroll of $68,657,292 and full-time employment for 46,347 men and women. There were 323 furniture stores employing 2,997 full-time people, and doing a business of $33,608,878; and 1,073 restaurants, employing 5,959 full-time people and doing a business of $27,084,127. The volume of business transacted by 1,774 wholesale establishments was $974,-474,391; 21,746 workers were employed with a payroll of $45,546,307.

The Theater of the Nations was inaugurated on January 12 in the Little Theater of the Public Auditorium with the presentation by Cleveland Syrians of Schiller's poetical drama, *The Robbers*. It was the first of a number of plays given on successive Sundays by the various nationalities in the city. The drama series was sponsored by the *Plain Dealer* for three seasons.

A survey of public-school needs indicated annual requirements of approximately seventeen million dollars for operating purposes and three million dollars for the sinking fund. At this time there were 156 school buildings in the system, including 13 senior high schools and 15 junior high schools. The enrollment was 144,689. At this time, Cleveland was known for the modern policy of its school authorities in giving each child educational experiences to fit his needs. The schools were praised for their non-partisan, non-political control through a capable Board of Education, and for the loyal support of the Parent-Teachers Association.

James T. McMillan, who had served from crew to pilot house, became president of the Detroit & Cleveland Navigation Company this year, serving until his death in 1946. During this time, the *Greater Buffalo* and *Greater Detroit*, the largest and most luxurious fresh-water passenger steamers in the world, were built and commissioned. In 1942 the *Greater Buffalo* was taken over by the United States Navy. The company fleet in 1946 consisted of the passenger steamers *Greater Detroit, City of Detroit III, City of Cleveland III, Eastern States,* and *Western States,* and the automobile carrier *J. P. Wells,* operating daily between Detroit and Cleveland, and Detroit and Buffalo.

Daniel E. Morgan, who was elected by the Republicans in City Council to succeed William R. Hopkins, became Cleveland's second city manager on January 27. Politics were not new to Morgan, as he had been elected to Council in 1909. He retired from the Council two years later to practice law and became an Ohio senator in 1928. A prominent figure in Cleveland's civic circles, Morgan impressed the citizenship with his sound judgment, analytical mind, and calming sense of balance. During his twenty-month administration, he settled gas-and-water disputes and contributed to the development of Cleveland's Mall.

The Motor Transit Management Company, transferred to Cleveland from Chicago in the late 1920s, was titled The Greyhound Management Company early in 1930. The first president of the management company was Orville S. Caesar. Other key figures in Cleveland Greyhound operations included George M. Davidson, vice president of Pennsylvania Greyhound Lines, and George L. Horst, comptroller of Central Greyhound Lines. These major affiliates, sharing headquarters with the company in the Greyhound Terminal Building at East 9th Street and Superior Avenue, were among the largest of the thirteen operating companies in the Greyhound family. The two Cleveland companies, together with Ohio Greyhound Lines of Youngstown, were planning construction of a million-dollar Cleveland terminal on Chester Avenue to be opened in 1948. An estimated average of 9,180 persons passed through the East 9th Street Terminal daily. President R. W. Budd, who developed the Cleveland operations, was succeeded by F. W. Benefiel.

The Brush Development Company was formed this year to commercialize certain research work previously done by the Brush Laboratories relative to the growth and application of Rochelle salt piezoelectric crystal elements for use in microphones, phonographs, pickups, and similar applications. Brush Development, named for the Cleveland inventor, became the principal manufacturer of such elements, and the sole producer of the piezoelectric hearing-aid receiver. The Soundmirror, introduced in 1938 for voice-training purposes, was the first commercial product in the field of magnetic recording. The Brush company, located at 3311 Perkins Avenue, owned many patents under the heading of electronics. Officers in 1946 included W. R. Burwell, chairman of the board; A. L. Williams, president; and C. B. Sawyer, vice president and treasurer.

Cleveland kept the world basketball championship when the Rosenblum team defeated the Centrals of Rochester, 21-15, on March 25. For the third time in the history of the American League, the Cleveland quintet took the title, having won it in 1926 and 1929.

The first Scout-O-Rama, or Boy Scout Exhibition, was held by the Boy Scouts of America, Greater Cleveland Council, in Public Auditorium. More than a hundred thousand homes were visited on one day in June by Boy Scouts of Cleveland in a citywide canvass organized by them for the Goodwill Industries. Their slogan was "one hundred thousand good turns for Goodwill."

The Cleveland Medal for Public Service was awarded on April 15 by The Cleveland Chamber of Commerce to Ambrose Swasey, "authority on instruments of precision, holder of the highest scientific honors, and generous supporter of charitable, educational, civic and scientific institutions of Cleveland and of the nation." The medal was also given to Frederic Allen Whiting, director of the Cleveland Museum of Art for seventeen years, "who has stimulated an appreciation of the social and cultural value of artistic expression"; and to Carl A. Hamann, "beloved physician, exemplar and friend whose fellow citizens in all walks and stations of life have profited by his skill, regardless of financial reward."

R. B. Robinette was elected president of The Cleveland Chamber of Commerce. In the decade, he was succeeded by Randolph Eide, 1931; L. W. Greve, 1932; A. R. Horr, 1933; Herman R. Neff, 1934; Charles K. Arter, 1935; George W. Burrell, 1936; A. C. Ernst, 1937-38; and Frederick C. Crawford, 1939.

A three-alarm fire started on May 9 in downtown Cleveland, destroying the Sheriff Street Market at Huron Road and East 4th Street. It took sixteen fire companies to control the blaze, with eighty-three-year-old Chief Wallace leading the battle. Damage to the familiar landmark was estimated at $140,000. At the time of the fire, the building was being converted to a bus terminal. It was owned by the Realty Corporation of Cleveland, of which John D. Fackler, prominent Cleveland attorney, was president.

The first Braille reading contest in the country was held in Cleveland. Two former pupils of day-school classes won prizes.

At the fortieth annual congress of the American Whist League in Niagara Falls, Canada, the Excelsior Club auction-bridge team, consisting of S. L. Guggenheim, Maurice Kastriner, Phil E. Leon, and E. C. Wolfe, won the all-American auction-bridge championship. The all-American pair championship was won by the Cleveland team of W. E. J. Babin and A. L. Siegel.

Fourteen hundred buildings had been razed to make way for construction of the new Cleveland Union Terminal, which was officially opened on June 28, at a luncheon attended by 2,500 guests. The station area covered approximately 3.5 acres, fronting on the southeast corner of the Public Square. Above and surrounding it were the stately fifty-two-story Terminal Tower, the Hotel Cleveland, the eighteen-story Medical Arts Building (later Republic Building), Builders Exchange (later Guildhall), and the Midland Building, constituting a city within a city. The Higbee store was under construction, and plans for the new Post Office were being prepared. Many legal and political obstacles had to be overcome before work on the station project was definitely started in 1923. The New York Central Railroad, its subsidiary, the Big Four, and the Nickel Plate Road were joint owners of the Cleveland Union Terminals Company, the corporation owning the terminal. The buildings above and around the station were erected by the Cleveland Terminals Building Company. C. L. Bradley was president of both companies. The cost of the project, including passenger terminal, electrification and approach lines, passenger and freight facilities and engine terminals, rapid-transit lines, and buildings in the Terminal Group, totaled $179,000,000. The dominant feature of the buildings, designed by Graham, Anderson, Probst & White, was the Terminal Tower, 708 feet high, the tallest building tower in the world outside of New York City. On the forty-sixth floor a Government airway beacon was maintained, and the observation porch on the forty-second floor was open to the public. The Terminal-opening celebration was arranged by a Cleveland Chamber of Commerce committee, with William Ganson Rose as chairman. Newton D. Baker served as toastmaster, and speakers were Mayor John D. Marshall, President Patrick E. Crowley of the New York Central Railroad, and President W. L. Ross of the New York, Chicago & St. Louis Railroad. At the speakers' table were the presidents of many railroads, and there were hundreds of distinguished guests; but the two men responsible for the great achievement—O. P. and M. J. Van Sweringen—did not attend because of their innate modesty. When the luncheon concluded, the guests were divided into two groups and taken over the electrified-railway sections, east and west. During the summer thousands of visitors came to Cleveland to see the new Terminal Group, one of the most impressive of commercial centers. Interest was focused in the Terminal Tower where lofty arches led into the monumental portico. A series of murals represented the art of Jules Guerin, New York painter, illustrating the four elements: Water, Air, Earth, and Fire, with the central panel portraying Industry and Commerce. The Terminal was used by the New York Central and Nickel Plate roads until 1934, when it was joined by the Baltimore & Ohio. The Pennsylvania continued to operate from the old lakefront station; and the Erie served its passengers from the station in the "Flats," at the east end of the Detroit-Superior High Level Bridge, erected in 1881 on land owned by the Big Four. The Erie planned to move into the Terminal in the late 1940s.

When plans were made for the new Terminal station, it was agreed that the shops and restaurants should be operated under the management of the Fred Harvey System, founded in 1876. Originating in a second-story eating room in the Santa Fe Station in Topeka, Kansas, it had grown into a large organization famous for its hotels, restaurants, shops, and dining cars. In the Chicago, St. Louis, and Kansas City union stations, Fred Harvey was operating with great success, and Cleveland was to be the first city east of Chicago to welcome Harvey restaurants and stores. The total space allotted was 175,000 square feet. The Oak Room was called Cleveland's most beautiful dining room, and other restaurants immediately enjoyed popularity. One of the finest drug stores, a haberdashery, women's shop, gift shop, bookstore, food store, pastry shop, newsstands, toy shop, barber shop, and several specialty businesses formed a modern and complete chain under the new management. Byron S. Harvey was president of Harvey, Inc., and C. D. Brown was made director of the many retail-merchandising activities. The restaurants were in charge of George Maslin. The more than forty shops of Harvey, Inc., were in operation in the Union Terminal Station in August, and dining facilities for nine thousand people were provided during the luncheon period. This was the world's largest unified merchandising service operated in conjunction with a union-passenger station.

Zone fares were introduced on streetcars in downtown Cleveland on July 4.

Industry had encroached upon the community centering around East 40th Street and St. Clair, and the identity of the population had changed. On the membership rolls of North Presbyterian Church, there appeared the names of more and more Slovaks, Croatians, Slovenians, and Rumanians, employed in mills and factories. North Church, to which the Rev. Arthur R. Kinsler, Jr., came as minister in 1930, occupied a strategic place in cosmopolitan life. Westminster Church, at Addison Road and Wade Park, stemmed from North Church, organized in 1870.

"Cleveland has been extremely fortunate over the years in having men of the Bolton type; men who have grown up with the city, accumulated fortunes here and employed them for the upbuilding of the community." This was the tribute which appeared in the August 2 editorial columns of the *Plain Dealer*. Charles Chester Bolton was truly a man of this community. Born on Euclid Street at Giddings, in 1855, he devoted himself to the industry, philanthropy, and public affairs of this city, yet never sought political office nor selfish gain. Two years after graduation from Harvard, his first business venture was with Rhodes & Company, coal operators. He remained with this firm until the business was sold to M. A. Hanna & Company, where his ability earned him a partnership until his retirement in 1904. His financial genius was sought by the Bourne-Fuller Company, and he became associated with them as a director. Later, he was also a director of the National Refining Company and Guardian Trust Company, in addition to being a trustee of the Society for Savings. Troop A, in which Bolton served from private to captain, felt the touch of his organizing genius. His interests were not only in the fields of business, philanthropy, education, and civics, but religion as well, and he was vestryman and treasurer of St. Paul's Episcopal Church for twenty-one years up to the time of his death in 1930. His sons, Chester C., Kenyon C., Irving C., Newell C., and Julian C. became well-known Clevelanders.

To promote knowledge and love of gardening with a view to creating a more beautiful community, the Garden Center of Greater Cleveland was founded by a committee of the Garden Club of Cleveland. Among the founders were Mrs. William G. Mather, Mrs. Windsor T. White, Mrs. Charles A. Otis, Mrs. Thomas P. Howell, Mrs. John Sherwin, Mrs. Walter White, and Mrs. Andrew Squire. An outgrowth of the Fine Arts Garden, which was created by the Garden Club in 1927, the Center was called a unique adventure in the field of progressive education, and it promoted interest in horticulture, conservation, landscaping, and city beautification. The first home was a boathouse of architectural charm and structural strength on the east side of the Wade Park lake. It was renovized, redecorated, and dedicated free to the people of the city. In 1938 two wings were added to the original building, doubling its size, and more than fifty thousand visitors marveled at the fascinating exhibition rooms, the attractive offices, and the distinctive library. Recognized as one of the finest horticultural libraries in the Midwest, it represented one of the many valuable services which the Center offered to the citizens. An expanded program proposed by Mrs. Mather, head of the Center, included co-operation with other civic organizations for the improvement of the community.

The stately Board of Education Administration Building was erected this year, facing the Mall and completing the east side of Cleveland's Group Plan. Walker & Weeks designed the beautiful and practical sandstone structure. The site extended from Rockwell Avenue to St. Clair Avenue, and from the Mall to East 6th Street, the cost of the land being $845,000, and the building approximated $1,800,000. On the same site, the first Rockwell Street School was constructed in 1840, a little building that cost $3,500.

Captain Dieudonne Costes and Maurice Bellonte, brave French aviators, crossed the Atlantic in an uninterrupted westward flight from Paris to New York in 37 hours, 18 minutes, and 30 seconds. They visited Cleveland and laid a wreath on Ambassador Herrick's grave.

The Gordon Bennett International Balloon Race was held, September 1, with a crowd in and near the Airport estimated at 200,000. The project, under the sponsorship of National Air Races of Cleveland, was sanctioned by the National Aeronautic Association, and conducted under rules of Federation Aeronautique Internationale. The entries included balloons from Belgium, France, Germany, and three from the United States. Captain Ernest Demuyter, who had won four previous Gordon Bennett Cup races, was pilot for Belgium; Ward T. Van Orman, pilot of the *Goodyear VIII;* Edward J. Hill of the *City of Detroit;* and R. J. Blair, pilot, with F. J. Trotter, co-pilot, of the *City of Cleveland.* Winds carried the balloons in a northeasterly direction, and Van Orman brought the *Goodyear VIII* down approximately 850 miles from Cleveland, winning the cup.

New quarters for the Cleveland Stock Exchange were dedicated in the Union Trust Building in September, and a four-day program of ceremonies attracted wide attention. Edward M. Baker, who had served as president for sixteen years, turned over the original gavel used in 1900 to President M. C. Harvey, who served from 1925 to 1931. It was pointed out that while seats on the Exchange at the turn of the century were priced at $100, a single seat was sold in 1929 for $15,000. Former homes of the Exchange had been in the Williamson Building and the Hippodrome Building. Cecil B. Whitcomb was given credit for the modern ideas that characterized the impressive new trading quarters. Succeeding presidents included J. P. Drach, 1932-34; Gordon S. Macklin, 1935-37; Joseph H. Millar, part of 1938; Percy W. Brown, part of 1938; Russell L. Cunningham, 1939, 1940, 1941, 1944; David G. Skall, 1942; S. Prescott Ely, part of 1942, 1943; Guy W. Prosser, 1945-46, followed by Richard A. Gottron. William J. Perry, connected with the Exchange since 1933, became assistant secretary in 1940, and succeeded General Cecil B. Whitcomb as secretary in 1946. Among the many well-known stock-and-bond brokerage firms having important offices in Cleveland in the 1940s were Bache & Company; Ball, Burge & Kraus; Cunningham & Company; Curtiss, House & Company; H. L. Emerson & Company, Inc.; Fahey, Clark & Company; Finley & Company; First Cleveland Corporation; Gordon Macklin & Company; Gottron, Russell & Company; Gunn-Carey & Company; Will S. Halle & Company; Hayden, Miller & Company; H. C. Hopkins & Company; Hornblower & Weeks; Ledogar-Horner Company; McDonald & Company; William J. Mericka & Company, Inc.; Merrill, Lynch, Pierce, Fenner & Beane; Merrill, Turben & Company; Morrow & Company; Maynard H. Murch & Company; Otis & Company; Paine, Webber, Jackson & Curtis; Prescott & Company; Quigley & Company, Inc.; Saunders, Stiver & Company; L. J. Schultz & Company; Ullman & Company, Inc.; John P. Witt & Company; and W. H. Zink & Company.

In the Shakespeare Garden

In the German Garden

In the Hungarian Garden

CULTURAL GARDENS IN ROCKEFELLER PARK

Post Office in the Terminal Group.

"Commerce," one of the beautiful sculptural pieces by Daniel Chester French on the Federal Building, Public Square.

Main entrance to the Federal Reserve Bank of Cleveland, East 6th Street at Superior. The statues by Henry Hering represent Integrity and Security. CLEVELAND PICTURE COLLECTION, CLEVELAND PUBLIC LIBRARY.

Fifteen thousand persons heard President Herbert Hoover address the convention of the American Bankers Association at Public Auditorium on October 2. Answering John W. Barton, he defended the American tariff wall and immigration policy, declaring that "any retreat from our American philosophy of constantly increasing standards of living becomes a retreat into perpetual unemployment and acceptance of a cesspool of poverty for a large part of our people."

The Italian Cultural Garden in Rockefeller Park was dedicated on October 12, the two thousandth anniversary of Virgil's birth. A bronze bust of the poet, sent by the Italian government, rested on a pedestal which was part of a column from the ancient Roman Forum. A sunken garden with a four-basin marble fountain, busts, plaques, and tablets were features of this lovely garden, which was of the Italian Renaissance type.

The Ohio Women's State Golf Championship, played at Westwood, was won by Mary K. Browne, known nationally as both golf and tennis expert. In the Western Open in 1932 at Canterbury, Walter Hagen defeated Olin Dutra in a spectacular finish. The Women's Western was played in 1935 at Westwood Country Club, Marian Miley defeating Mrs. Philip Atwood in the finals. The National Amateur Championship was played at the Country Club, 1935, with Lawson Little, Jr., winning by brilliant play and completing his "little slam." The 1937 Western Open Golf Championship was played in September at Canterbury, Ralph Guldahl defeating Horton Smith by a four-stroke margin in the playoff. They had tied at 288 at the end of 72 holes. District golf championships during this decade were won by Ellsworth Augustus, 1930; Jack Cummins, 1931; Dr. T. E. Cannon, 1932; John Racey, 1933; John Schneider, 1934; Eddie Meister, 1935-36; Oliver Transue, 1937-38; and John Schneider, 1939. The Women's City Golf Championships were won by Mrs. Edward F. Lenihan, 1930; Mary K. Browne, 1931-32; Edith Begg, 1933; Mary K. Browne, 1934-35; Edith Begg, 1936; Mrs. Edith Begg Goddard, 1937; and Mrs. John E. Pennington, 1938-39.

The American auction-bridge championship team in the new American Bridge League formed in Cleveland was composed of Vincent F. Boland, John Law, Maurice Maschke, and Carl T. Robertson of Cleveland.

The Cleveland Electric Illuminating Company began generation of electricity at its new Ashtabula plant on November 17. It was the eastern anchor of the Illuminating system, which extended over a 1,700-square-mile, five-county area from Avon Lake on the west to Conneaut on the east.

The campaign goal set for the Community Fund was $5,400,000. The amount raised was $5,425,838.33 with 486,647 subscribers. The campaign chairman was Randolph Eide.

WGAR, five-hundred-watt radio station, opened in the Hotel Statler, December 15, under the direction of John F. Patt, vice president and general manager. It had nineteen employees, and was affiliated with the National Broadcasting Company, blue network. Two years later the station was using a thousand watts in the daytime and five hundred watts at night; and before its first decade was concluded, a new antenna tower was constructed, a mobile unit was equipped, and complete offices were opened. In 1937

WGAR became a unit in the Columbia Broadcasting chain. It adopted the slogan, "Cleveland's Friendly Station," and proved its friendliness by many programs advancing the interests of the city.

L. W. Greve, president of National Air Races, Inc., together with a small group of civic-minded citizens, on December 23 secured a five-year sanction for the races to be held in Cleveland. The contract between National Air Races, Inc., and the National Aeronautic Association had the backing of The Cleveland Chamber of Commerce. Inspired by a fifty-mile race in 1929, Thompson Products established a permanent trophy, "dedicated to the development of higher air speeds, combined with practical maneuverability and safety." The Thompson Trophy was to be awarded annually to the winner of a free-for-all, closed-course race for planes unlimited as to number, horsepower, or types of engines used. The race brought into sharp focus innovations of wing and engine which contributed to aeronautical progress. The coveted award embodied a bronze figure of the Greek hero Icarus, the work of the Cleveland sculptor Walter A. Sinz. Chicago in 1930 was the scene of the first Thompson air-speed contest, won by Charles W. Holman; flying his Laird plane at a speed of 201.91 m.p.h., he captured the first-place purse totaling $16,000.

The American Library Association compiled statistics indicating the activities of public libraries serving more than 200,000 population. In per capita circulation, Cleveland easily led all other cities with 10.95 books. The total circulation was 9,861,888, with 6,048,974 going to adults and the remainder to juveniles. At this time there were sixty-nine branches in the library system.

Iron and steel was the backbone of industry in the Cleveland Industrial Area, consisting of Cuyahoga and Lorain counties. According to the census of manufactures of 1929, 21 steel works and rolling mills reported products valued at $187,509,491, 19,191 wage earners employed, and wages of $35,650,619; products of blast furnaces were valued at $53,468,164; and processed products produced in the Cleveland district, $582,587. Stoves and ranges—other than electric—and warm-air furnaces produced in the Cleveland industrial area were valued at $20,617,854.

The automobile no longer threatened the dominant position held by iron and steel in Cleveland industry. Output of finished vehicles, bodies, parts, and accessories was valued at $125,197,505, 12,572 wage earners were employed by 40 reporting establishments, and wages totaled $22,566,931. Foundry and machine-shop products valued at $95,649,619 were reported by 185 firms employing 16,730 wage earners whose earnings totaled $27,591,689. The manufacture of electrical machinery, apparatus, and supplies was a major industry with an output valued at $60,346,165. Likewise, printing and publishing had reached the upper brackets of production: book and job, 234 establishments, product value of $20,295,670; newspapers and periodicals, 76 concerns, $29,759,316; lithographing, 15 firms, $5,719,637; total value of products in the industry, $55,774,623.

Meat-packing products, wholesale, were valued at $49,345,714; paints and varnishes, $36,187,709; men's and boys' clothing, $30,591,518; bolts, nuts, washers, and rivets, $28,291,206; women's clothing, $28,012,767; bread and bakery products, $26,060,762; machine tools, $23,204,289; structural and ornamental iron-and-steel work, $19,643,222; screw machine products and wood-screws, $17,302,727; machine-tool accessories and small metal-working tools, $15,012,847; iron-and-steel forgings, $14,909,811; knit goods, $12,863,889; non-ferrous metal alloys and products, $12,460,680; wirework, $7,692,889; sausage and meat products, $7,587,112; furniture, including store and office fixtures, $7,486,149; confectionery, $7,221,956; steam fittings and steam hot-water heating apparatus, $7,138,756; plumbers' supplies, $6,446,704; hardware, not elsewhere classified, $4,680,750; ice cream, $4,177,027.

Although disturbing economic conditions in the 1920s were reflected in lowered production totals for some of the major industries, Cleveland held its position as fifth among American cities in the value of manufactured products. Peak production was reported in 1929, 2,573 establishments reporting products valued at $1,245,433,855; and 146,881 wage earners received peak earnings of $229,159,652. Outside of Cleveland's boundaries, 208 establishments in Cuyahoga County boosted industrial output with products valued at $113,888,694. Plants of increasing importance, some of them young industries of great promise, were springing up in greater numbers in suburban communities. Cleveland wage earners in the manufacturing industry averaged $.663 hourly for skilled labor and $.478 for unskilled in 1930. In the construction industry, skilled workers received $1.38 per hour, and $.561 was paid for unskilled labor. More goods were being produced per wage earner in Cleveland factories than in Pittsburgh, Philadelphia, Boston, and other competing centers.

Cleveland was the second largest foundry center in the country. Of the twenty-five companies operating in 1880, seven were in business fifty years later, classified as manufacturers of cast-iron, malleable iron, casting steel, and nonferrous metals. National associations representing the industry—the Gray-Iron Institute, the Malleable Iron Research Institute, and the Foundry Equipment Manufacturers Association—established headquarters in Cleveland.

The largest producer of paints, oils, and varnishes was located in Cleveland, the home of the world's largest paint-and-varnish interests. Here were the headquarters, general offices, and vast laboratories of the world's leading producers of electric lamps. Electrically driven machinery of every kind and a wide variety of products in great demand were manufactured in increasing volume. With one of the largest lumber yards in the nation, and the sandstone center of the world near at hand, Cleveland was an important trading center in both rough and finished products.

Greater Cleveland, the leading lake port in iron-ore receipts, received 12,263,000 net tons in 1929; outbound rail shipments totaled 8,762,000 net tons. Coal-and-coke receipts by rail amounted to 10,199,000 net tons; shipments by lake, 2,170,000. The ore-unloading docks in the Cleveland harbor were the largest in the world. Outbound car loadings were reported at

14,467,000 net tons for the year; inbound, 19,837,000. Exports of Cleveland-made goods to the markets of the world, amounting to more than $150,000,000, were balanced by import business.

The Municipal Airport had become a great factor in industrial growth. Eleven air lines radiating from the port provided daily mail service. Four lines offered daily passenger, freight, and express service; and four companies maintained aerial taxis, sightseeing, and instruction service. The airport was the headquarters of the 112th Observation Squadron, Ohio National Guard, and a station of the Government Weather Bureau had been established at the field. Reports for the year 1930 showed that 21,211 ships cleared at the Cleveland Airport, and passenger traffic totaled 36,461.

There was substantial interest in aviation in other parts of the city. To the east on Richmond Road was the 140-acre airport of the Curtiss Flying Service, Inc. The 92-acre field of the Great Lakes Aircraft Corporation on St. Clair Avenue provided service and landing facilities. The Thompson Aeronautical Corporation was operating hydroplanes on daily passenger schedules from a small lakefront airport at the foot of East 9th Street.

Greater Cleveland was the financial center of northern Ohio. Resources reported by seventeen banks, with a network of neighborhood branches, totaled $1,240,870,000, and bank clearings, $6,638,000,000, representing steady advance. A decline was apparent, however, in the number of building-and-loan associations. Ninety-one associations with resources of $185,190,000 in 1928 had been reduced to eighty-one in 1930, with resources of $161,240,000. A slump in building construction to about half the 1920 value was reported in 1930. As a result of economic influences, building permits fell to 7,635 for the year, with operations valued at $32,440,000. Tax-duplicate valuation of Cuyahoga County property had grown from $316,467,575 in 1910 to $2,914,824,100 in 1930.

Cleveland's prosperity was reflected in enlarged mills and factories providing greater employment. The city's central merchandising center grew in size and importance, larger office buildings were erected, suburban residential districts expanded, and needed public improvements were made possible. While manufacturing plants had brought a number of residents into the millionaire class, according to income-tax returns, economists doubted "that this increased wealth has added as many comforts to the home of the wealthy resident as to the wage earner." Economic wealth was thus regarded as a community asset rather than an individual one. Substantial community prosperity was indicated by the fact that Clevelanders owned 270,000 passenger cars and 29,000 trucks in 1930—more automobiles in proportion to population than Chicago and New York. Cleveland families were buying life insurance at a faster rate of increase than those of Chicago, Detroit, Boston, and New York. The claim was made that more people out of every hundred had savings accounts in Cleveland than in any other large city in the nation. As business and industry grew, the city grew, and the people prospered.

1931

For three weeks, from January 10 to February 1, the spectacular Guelph Treasure attracted 96,751 visitors to the Cleveland Museum of Art, the largest number to attend any single exhibit. This collection of decorative and medieval art objects, dating back to the Tenth Century, was from the estates of the Dukes of Brunswick. The museum purchased nine leading objects, the most important being the Gertrudis Altar and the two accompanying gold crosses. These cherished possessions were given prominent display in the Treasure Room of the Museum.

The Star Theater became the Cameo on February 1. During the 1890s, burlesque was introduced in the Star and continued to be featured in the Cameo. In 1938 the Embassy Theater evolved from the oldtime playhouse, and became Cleveland's newest motion-picture theater.

Music lovers thronged to the University Circle cultural center, February 5, to attend a brilliant symphony concert by the Cleveland Orchestra, Nikolai Sokoloff conducting. It marked the opening of magnificent Severance Hall. Charles Martin Loeffler's *Evocation,* composed for the occasion, was the featured production. The imposing permanent home of the orchestra was made possible by John Long Severance and the combined efforts of The Musical Arts Association and the Women's Committee of the Cleveland Orchestra. Erected on property given by Western Reserve University, the building cost $2,500,000 and was designed by Walker & Weeks. Constructed of Indiana limestone and Ohio sandstone after the Georgian style, it harmonized with the classic Cleveland Museum of Art. The interior of Cleveland's temple of music was a blending of bronze and aluminum and of blue and silver, achieving rare beauty. The hall was completely equipped, with an auditorium seating 1,840 persons, a smaller chamber-music hall, broadcasting studio, library, and lounges. Now opera could be added to regular symphony concerts, bringing to the stage of Severance Hall the world's great artists.

William E. Potter, who served ten years as councilman and was known as "Rarin' Bill" because of his pugnacity in politics and business, was murdered on February 8. Then followed sensational investigations and two trials, a suspect being convicted in the first and acquitted in the second. The question "Who killed Potter?" was unanswered years later.

Lakeside Hospital, which had originated in the Cleveland City Hospital of 1866, opened in February on the campus of Western Reserve University. It was a unit in the University Hospitals Group, incorporated on September 30, 1925, and occupying a city block from Euclid Avenue south to the New York Central Railroad tracks and from Adelbert Road to Abington Road. Dr. Robert H. Bishop, Jr., succeeded K. H. Van Norman as director in 1931, serving until 1947. The group included the Nurses Dormitory, Leonard C. Hanna House, Lakeside Hospital, Institute of Pathology, Babies and Childrens Hospital, Maternity Hospital, School of Medicine, and service buildings. The dormitory housed 410 student nurses; Hanna House, a six-story pavilion, accommodated 66 private patients; and Lakeside facilities served 313 medical and surgical patients. The Institute of Pathology housed a central laboratory for complicated testing, dealing with biochemistry, immunology, and bacteriology. The Medical School included all facilities for medical education. As a medical center and a teaching and research institution, University Hospitals ranked with the finest in the country. Dr. W. B. Seymour succeeded Dr. Bishop as director in 1947.

Ten thousand admirers crowded into the Public Auditorium on Wallace Day, March 1, when Chief George A. Wallace resigned from the Fire Department. After serving the city sixty-two years as a fire-fighter and thirty years as its chief, the beloved and dramatic figure withdrew from public life. He had served in practically every capacity since 1869, and was probably the best-known chief and fire-fighter in the United States. His motto, "Come on in, boys," instead of "Go on in, boys," brought such loyalty and performance from his men that Cleveland's annual fire loss was surprisingly low compared with cities of similar size. The worst fire in his memory was the "Flats" lumber fire in 1914, when he was on duty seventy-two hours without rest. His orders were staccato barks. Men jumped at his commands which were outspoken, curt, profane. He never gave an order that he himself would have hesitated to follow. James E. Granger was appointed chief of the Fire Department on March 17, the thirty-seventh anniversary of his entering the service.

The Troop A Riding Academy started a series of annual horse shows. Cleveland had long been the leading harness-horse city of the country, and it was natural that the events attracted many entries and large audiences. Particular attention was drawn to children's features, to fine harness horses, three-gaited horses, troopers' mounts, and polo ponies.

The Cleveland Medal for Public Service was awarded in April by the Chamber of Commerce to George W. Crile, "surgeon of superlative skill and eminent scientific investigator, whose humanitarian service and stimulating investigations have made him known and honored throughout the world." The medal was also given to Charles E. Adams, "whose service as general chairman of the Community Fund has contributed immeasurably to its outstanding success."

The name of the College for Women of Western Reserve University was changed to Flora Stone Mather College, honoring the late Mrs. Samuel Mather. Four of the seven buildings on the campus, including the administration building—the Flora Stone Mather Memorial of Gothic architecture, designed by Abram Garfield and completed in 1913—were erected either through her gifts or in her memory.

An independent Juvenile Court was provided for Cuyahoga County by legislation which called for a judge appointed to serve a six-year term. Judge George S. Addams was widely known for his long service in the court, from 1905 to 1925. He was succeeded in 1926 by Harry L. Eastman, another able jurist, who served on the bench in the 1940s. A fine grouping of Juvenile Court buildings opened at 2157 East 22nd Street in 1932, including a court building and three structures for a detention home, forming a quadrangle with a playground in the center. The court made significant improvements in its relationships with various civic and welfare groups and agencies, particularly in the field of child welfare. Psychological and psychiatric services, a court clinic, and a girls' referee were added to the court's program. In November, 1946, a second judge, William J. McDermott, was appointed to assist Judge Eastman in his important work.

In a game between Cleveland and St. Louis on April 29, Wesley Ferrell pitched a no-hit victory, the score 9-0.

The birth of the Ohio Poetry Society occurred in May in the home of Rachel Mack Wilson, founder, who at that time was state president of the National League of American Pen Women. Members included Edmund Vance Cooke, Dean Albert C. Fox, Harriet Gleason, Beulah A. Bell, Alice H. Patterson, Pearl R. Mountain, May Winkler Goodman, Rachel M. Wilson, Dr. Frederick H. Adler, Alice C. Redhead, and Ella Deike of Cleveland. Membership quickly spread throughout Ohio with headquarters remaining in Cleveland.

From automobiles to ale is a far cry, but the dramatic history of the Brewing Corporation of America bridged the gap. The home of the huge brewery at Cleveland, one of the largest in the United States, was once famous as the factory making Peerless automobiles. In July, 1931, James A. Bohannon, president of Peerless, told his stockholders that they did not stand a chance of selling cars of the three- to five-thousand-dollar class in the face of a worldwide business collapse, and proposed that the factory be converted into a brewery. The repeal of Prohibition was practically certain, and Peerless executives, engineers, and 2,500 stockholders readily agreed. Financial backing thus assured, the Peerless plant was ready for conversion. Carling's had built up an excellent reputation in Canada, dating from 1840 when its Red Cap Ale was first introduced. Americans who had enjoyed it north of the border would surely welcome it here. Bohannon, realizing this fact, gained Carling's permission to use formulas, name, and technical assistance. In 1933 construction began, two stories were added to the three-story plant, and a new building was erected with capacity for aging a million barrels yearly. Two other breweries were acquired, and distribution covered twenty-three states. In 1946 a million-dollar advertising campaign described Carling's, the world's largest air-conditioned brewery, its products made in Cleveland. James A. Bohannon, president of Peerless, continued as president of the Brewing Corporation of America.

The Cleveland Stadium was completed on July 1, and the following night witnessed an elaborate opening celebration. The building cost $2,500,000 and was so constructed as to accommodate every type of athletic contest and outdoor spectacle. Stationary seats were provided for 78,189 persons, and seating capacity could be expanded to more than 100,000 by placing seats in the field. An elaborate lighting system made the Stadium an ideal location for night events.

Max Schmeling, champion heavyweight, scored a technical knock-out over W. L. Stribling in the fifteenth and last round in the newly completed

Stadium on July 3, before an audience of 36,936. The gate receipts were $350,000.

The Shrine Convention made Cleveland a center of merrymaking, July 14-18. Downtown streets were gaily decorated, and thousands of uniformed nobles made the convention one of the most colorful in the city's history. Spectacular parades and pageants drew twenty-five thousand visitors from all over this country and from other nations. Business institutions entered into the celebration, and the period of the convention was known as "Hospitality Week." The general chairman of the convention was Lawrence A. Slatmyer, prominent in Cleveland's building industry.

Cleveland's 135th birthday was celebrated with a week of interesting events. July 18 to 25 was known as Made-in-Cleveland Week, and hotels, banks, theaters, stores, and other establishments co-operated in the program. Stores featured window displays of Cleveland-made merchandise. The downtown area took on the aspect of an exposition, and many out-of-town people came to the city for the occasion.

A gathering of international importance was the twentieth Conference of the World's Alliance of Young Men's Christian Associations, August 4-9. This convention, with the meetings of the International Association of Men's Clubs and the National Council of the Young Men's Christian Associations brought 4,500 YMCA men and boys to the city.

The Labor Day week-end was celebrated in Cleveland with the return of the National Air Races. The first Bendix Trophy Race, known to the aviation-minded as the "road test race," was flown from Los Angeles to Cleveland as the opening feature. Sponsored by the Bendix Aviation Corporation, the race was founded to stimulate research in aeronautics. Jimmie Doolittle won the first Bendix race in a Laird biplane, flying the Los Angeles-Cleveland course with an average speed of 223.06 m.p.h. From Cleveland he flew to New York to set a new transcontinental record of 11 hours and 16 minutes. The climax of the National Air Races came when Lowell Bayless in his GeeBee rounded the pylons ten times at an average speed of 236.24 m.p.h. to win the Thompson Trophy.

The Higbee Company moved back to the Public Square on September 8, where its new store had been completed as a link in the vast Terminal development. Fronting on Ontario, Prospect, and the Public Square, an unbroken line of sixty-five display windows bordered the street frontages and the Terminal concourse. The store was pronounced one of the finest in America, and large auditoriums on the tenth floor provided a center where the interests of the community and the store merged in friendly comradeship. The Higbee Company, directed and owned by Clevelanders, remained a home-town institution. Charles L. Bradley, who succeeded Asa Shiverick as president in 1937, ably directed its affairs until his death in 1943. John P. Murphy was then elected to the presidency with Will T. Higbee, son of the founder, remaining as one of the vice presidents, the other chief executives being George E. Merrifield, vice president and treasurer, and Paul C. Fleer and C. E. Eerkes, vice presidents.

After having moved from the Standard Bank Building, Station WHK

The Great Lakes Exposition, 1936, one of the nation's most impressive territorial fairs, marked the centennial of Cleveland's incorporation as a city. CLEVELAND PICTURE COLLECTION, CLEVELAND PUBLIC LIBRARY.

The Mall, a refreshing garden spot, and its environs. To the north are Lake Erie, the entrance to the harbor, and the industrial docks. In the foreground is Superior Avenue, with Hotel Olmsted at the corner of East 9th Street and the NBC Building next door. At the northeast corner of East 6th Street is the Federal Reserve Bank Building; at the northwest corner stands the Plain Dealer Building, separated from the Public Library by Eastman Park. Bordering the Mall on the right are the Board of Education Building and the Public Auditorium. Fronting on Lakeside Avenue is the Court House, and beyond the Main Avenue Bridge is the Stadium. PERRY CRAGG, CLEVELAND NEWS.

opened its new studios on the thirteenth floor of the Terminal Tower. One of the finest transmitting plants in the nation had been built at Seven Hills, Ohio, two years earlier. In an educational experiment in co-operation with the Cleveland Board of Education, six thousand school children of thirty-six grade schools were given instruction from the studios each week. So successful was the project that the Board established its own radio station, WBOE. Another pioneering experiment dealt with the Cleveland Police Department, when WHK engineers established a police broadcasting station and operated it for the city. Later, the equipment was purchased by the Police Department. In 1934 the station was bought by the *Plain Dealer* and was operated by the United Broadcasting Company. Three years later, WHK became a basic NBC blue-network station, but in 1939 it transferred to Mutual Network. To foster Cleveland's growth and progress by broadcasting events of local character was the continuous effort of the station. H. K. Carpenter, an executive in Cleveland stations since 1925, became executive vice president of the United Broadcasting Company in 1944, with supervision of its stations in Cleveland, Akron, and Columbus. Kenneth K. Hackathorn became manager of WHK in 1944, and was also vice president of the United Broadcasting Company.

The Cleveland Club, Inc., at Carnegie Avenue and East 107th Street, (Tudor Arms Hotel) near University Circle, opened on September 12 with appropriate ceremonies. The first officers were Douglas S. Campbell, president; George W. Smith, Jr., vice president; Robb O. Bartholomew, secretary; and John D. Fackler, treasurer. Architecture and interior decorations were English in character, and the two-story dining room was patterned after the Tudor banquet hall. Massive bronze chandeliers hung from the ceiling, and at one end of the hall was an attractive stage. A library, card rooms, and two swimming pools were features of the clubhouse, and guest rooms could accommodate two hundred. This private club included in its membership many faculty members of Case, Reserve, and other institutions of the University Circle community. It was the scene of alumni and civic functions.

The United States Navy dirigible *Akron* left the great hangar in the Rubber City, September 23, on its maiden flight. It carried 113 navy officials, crew, and civilians, the largest number that had ridden in a dirigible. The airship passed over the Public Square, soared over Lake Erie, and returned to Akron after a four-hour flight. On April 4, 1933, the *Akron,* unable to weather a storm, plunged into the Atlantic Ocean off Barnegat, New Jersey, carrying 73 persons to their deaths.

Cleveland lost one of its most beneficent citizens on October 18, when death came to Samuel Mather. Born in Cleveland in 1851, the son of Samuel L. Mather, he was educated in the public schools and in St. Mark's School of Southborough. He entered industry, continuing the leadership in the iron-ore and coal-mining businesses established by his father, and became the senior member of Pickands, Mather & Company. He was a prominent figure nationally, and served as a director of the United States Steel Corporation, the Cleveland-Cliffs Iron Company of West Virginia, Interlake Steamship Company, American Ship Building Company, the Union Commerce

National Bank, and a number of other corporations. Appreciating that wealth presented an opportunity for practical sharing in Cleveland's social cultural, and civic welfare, Mather contributed generously and quietly to worthy projects. He served as president of Lakeside Hospital for many years, president of the Children's Aid Society, vice president of University School, director of the Cleveland Museum of Art, and trustee of Western Reserve University. Samuel Mather, "Cleveland's first citizen," was a pillar of the University Hospitals, Western Reserve University, the Community Fund, and other humanitarian enterprises. He was senior warden of Trinity Episcopal Parish, and gave liberally of time and money to the work of the diocese. Dr. Charles F. Thwing said of him, "Samuel Mather was a great man; great in ancestry, great in intellect, great in heart, great in religious conviction, great in service for the community and the whole world, great in his friendships, great in manifold beneficence, great in character."

Eleanor Painter, a star of the opera and theater, became the wife of Major Charles H. Strong, president of William Taylor Son & Company. She took an active interest in the Musical Arts Association and participated in Cleveland's important musical activities. Eleanor Painter Strong appeared with the Cleveland Orchestra on several occasions in artistic readings, and devoted some time to writing about music. She had sung in Covent Garden, London, and had won international fame as a prima donna.

Cleveland voters, on November 3, discarded city-management rule and proportional representation in favor of an elected mayor and ward councilmen. The Manager Plan, losing by a margin of nine thousand votes, had been tried for more than seven years. The plan had not been popular with political leaders, whose powers were usurped. Many people believed it did not reflect the wishes of the citizenship, and the majority of voters felt that the Federal Plan, under which Cleveland had formerly been operating, was more satisfactory. On the other hand, vast improvements had been made under the able direction of City Managers Hopkins and Morgan, and students of the situation regretted that the better features of the experiment could not have been retained. As for proportional representation, it was generally agreed that the system was theoretically sound, but was not understood, and hence impractical. Discontinuance of the Manager Plan discouraged adoption of the principle nationally, as Cleveland was the first large city to have tried it. The decision retired Manager Daniel E. Morgan and made Law Director Harold H. Burton acting mayor pending a mayoralty election.

A merger of the East and Mayflower Congregational churches, effected on November 18, resulted in the East Cleveland Congregational Church. East Church had its beginning in 1900, and its house of worship at Euclid and Page avenues became the home of the united congregation. The Mayflower Church represented the consolidation in 1920 of Park Congregational Church, organized in 1890, and Lake View Congregational Church, 1894, later known as Calvary. The Rev. Howard L. Torbet was called as pastor of the East Cleveland Church, serving until 1937, when he was succeeded by the Rev. Paul S. Kershner.

The Charity football game, sponsored by the *Plain Dealer* and designed to determine a champion team annually in the city schools, was inaugurated this year. The victor was Cathedral Latin over Central High School. There were 19,300 spectators at the game, and $8,200 was dispersed by the *Plain Dealer* in its Give-a-Christmas Fund. John A. Crawford, of the newspaper, initiated the series and managed the undertaking for fifteen consecutive years, when Joseph A. Zucker succeeded him. In this decade, Cathedral Latin defeated Collinwood in 1932; South won over Shaker Heights in 1933; Shaker Heights and West tied in a 0-0 game in 1934; Collinwood defeated Holy Name in 1935; Collinwood tied Cleveland Heights in 1936; John Adams won from West Tech in 1937; Cathedral Latin defeated West Tech in 1938; and John Adams conquered South in 1939. Beginning in 1937, the Schools' Medical Injury Fund was an added beneficiary of the game.

The campaign goal set for the Community Fund was $5,650,000, and the amount raised was $5,692,934.64, with 471,319 subscribers. The chairman was Randolph Eide.

In December, the Harry Coulby Fund of three million dollars was given to the Cleveland Foundation to administer. It provided that one-half of the net income be made available to Lakeside Hospital for its support and maintenance and one-half for the benefit of sick, crippled, and needy children. With this fund, many lives were inspired with renewed hope and enduring faith.

1932

The *Cleveland News* inaugurated its series of annual automobile luncheons on January 30, in the north exhibition hall of the Public Auditorium with 1,500 in attendance. The speakers included Richard H. Grant, sales manager of General Motors; Arthur "Bugs" Baer, newspaper columnist; Charles F. McCahill, vice president and general manager of the *News;* and William Ganson Rose, toastmaster of the luncheon series. Colonel David S. Ingalls represented the Federal Government; Governor George S. White, the State; and Acting Mayor Harold H. Burton, the city. In a modernistic setting, 130 motor cars were displayed.

A Lincoln monument, the work of Max Kalish, was erected on the Mall, February 12, on the west side of the Board of Education Building. A gift of the school children of Greater Cleveland, the statue is best known for the animation given the Emancipator.

Ray T. Miller, Democratic party leader, became mayor on February 20. The City Manager Plan had been abandoned, and he was the first elected mayor under the restored Federal Plan. Miller had served as an assistant law director, 1922-23, and county prosecutor, 1928-32. Later he became chairman of the Cuyahoga County Democratic executive and central committees.

The Cleveland Medal for Public Service was awarded in April by the Chamber of Commerce to John L. Severance "in recognition of a lifetime of distinguished citizenship, marked by generous service to industry, science, and health, and culminating in the gift of Severance Hall as a permanent home of a great orchestra." The medal was also given to Warren S. Hayden "for invaluable contributions to Cleveland's civic life throughout a quarter of a century." Hayden was an investment banker, a member of Hayden, Miller & Company, with many business interests, who had served as president of the Chamber of Commerce in 1913 and had given valuable counsel to Cleveland civic and business institutions.

A Cleveland bowler, Otto Nitschke, won the American Bowling Congress championship, his score being 731.

Although the Metropolitan Opera season in April was reduced to four performances, it provided a lavish representation of stars and sets. Lily Pons, Gladys Swarthout, Ezio Pinza, Lucrezia Bori, Beniamino Gigli, Lawrence Tibbett, Rosa Ponselle, and Giovanni Martinelli were included in the roster for the Cleveland programs. Lily Pons, who had thrilled local audiences many times, commented, "all the singers of the Metropolitan love to sing in Cleveland, and look forward each year to the visit to the West."

The Citizens School Committee, headed by Harold T. Clark, presented its report to the school board on May 27. The report was considered an admirable one because it dealt with the problems of efficiency and recommended centralizing control. On July 14, McRae Parker was chosen director of schools in charge of business management.

Aviation history was made on May 21 when Amelia Earhart Putnam completed her famous flight across the Atlantic. The first woman to solo on a transatlantic flight, she established a world's record, going from Newfoundland to Ireland—a distance of 2,026 miles in 13 hours and 30 minutes. On June 24, Cleveland greeted her. She had just been awarded the Distinguished Flying Cross and the emblem of the French Legion of Honor.

The American Federation of Labor, because of hard times and unemployment, broke away from the principle of Samuel Gompers that labor should stand on its own feet and not ask the assistance of government. It was natural under the severe economic conditions that the Federation should endorse unemployment insurance, and this move paved the way for government intervention in the affairs of industry and labor relations.

Cleveland's two fire tugs, the *George A. Wallace* and the *John H. Farley,* were abandoned when the city decided it was unable to afford maintenance. The *Wallace* was repaired later and served from time to time until 1935.

The first porcelain-enameled house in the world, built by the Ferro Enamel Corporation in Cleveland, attracted wide attention.

A treaty was signed between Canada and the United States, July 18, for the proposed development of the St. Lawrence waterway as a connecting link between the Great Lakes and the sea. Cleveland was naturally interested, but divided sentiment, locally and nationally, halted practical progress.

The Cleveland Indians played the inaugural game of baseball in the Stadium with the Philadelphia Athletics on July 31. The largest crowd of paid customers in Cleveland's sports history, a total of 80,184, poured into the stands, the largest major-league baseball crowd on record. Celebrities from all parts of the country witnessed Governor George S. White pitch the first baseball to Mayor Ray T. Miller. The game was worthy of the crowd, with a pitching duel between Robert Grove of Philadelphia and Mel Harder of Cleveland, the former winning 1-0.

Carmen Barth of Cleveland won the middleweight boxing championship at the Olympic games in Los Angeles.

The Swetland Building, Carnegie Hall, and the Union Trust Building were at intervals the home of the forty-year-old Cleveland Real Estate Board until this year, when quarters were opened in the Williamson Building. Breadth of the board's influence is shown by the fact that enactment of the real-estate-license law, in effect in most states, was accomplished through its efforts. The Federation of Realty Interests, a unified group of realty organizations, originated in Cleveland and had its counterpart in other cities. Real-estate education was promoted through courses, clinics, and lectures; and in 1945, the board began to conduct courses jointly with Cleveland College—the nation's largest real-estate school. O. W. L. Coffin, who succeeded Stanley L. McMichael as secretary in 1931, served almost continuously until 1942, when he resigned to become assistant director in charge of civilian mobilization for the Office of Civilian Defense. Offices were moved to the Arcade in 1942. Charles E. Norlin, former president of the board, became executive secretary in 1944. George E. Forbes in 1946 was president of the Cleveland Real Estate Board, one of the foremost organizations in its field. He was succeeded by Charles A. Braman and Warner Eggleston.

The opening of the Fulton Road Bridge across Brookside Park was attended by sixty thousand citizens on August 9. The bridge, 1,200 feet long, 100 feet high, and approximately 60 feet wide, connected Fulton Road and Denison Avenue on one side with Memphis Avenue on the other.

Theodore Andrica, nationalities editor of the *Press,* made the first of a series of trips to Europe as a "reportorial ambassador of good will." He took messages from people of different nationality groups to their relatives and friends in Europe and brought back reports that were welcomed by many Clevelanders. Andrica produced motion-picture stories of European life, and the films were shown to hundreds of thousands of Greater Cleveland citizens.

The Municipal Airport had expanded until it covered nearly 1,000 acres. In addition to paved runways, 5,400 feet and 4,000 feet long, the field had a paved area of nearly 2,000 square feet which permitted simultaneous landings of a number of planes. Traffic frequently exceeded 100 ships a day. Ship movements for 1932 totaled 26,522, and passenger traffic, 81,023.

Aviation's most colorful sports classic, the National Air Races, drew great crowds to Cleveland over the Labor Day weekend, and displayed a swift-moving pageant of speed and thrills. Known as industry's proving ground, the races attracted the nation's leading pilots. Jimmy Haislip won the Bendix Trophy Race, spanning the continent in 10:19:00 hours, a new transcontinental record which stood until 1937. A spectacular race was won by James H. "Jimmie" Doolittle, when he flew the fifty-mile, closed-course

Thompson Trophy Race in his GeeBee plane with a speed of 252.69 m.p.h. This record was not broken until 1936. Doolittle also returned the world's straightway land plane record to the United States, flying in record time —296.2 m.p.h.

The Stadium Yacht Basin, Inc., started shipbuilding operations on the lakefront west of the Stadium. It repaired yachts and pleasure craft, later extending work to include coast-guard craft and navy contracts.

The Rt. Rev. James A. McFadden was consecrated titular bishop of the Diocese of Cleveland on September 8. He contributed generously of his time and effort to important civic undertakings. Later, he was made the first head of the newly created Catholic Diocese of Youngstown.

The Brecksville Bridge, 1,132 feet long and 145 feet high, was constructed over the Cuyahoga River and the B & O Railroad. The Bedford Bridge, 1,666 feet long and 80 feet high, was built over Tinker's Creek and Broadway in Bedford.

The Real Property Inventory was created in Cleveland in October, and became the basis for parallel institutions throughout the country. During the depression, the National Conference on Construction, sponsored by the Chamber of Commerce of the United States and the United States Department of Commerce, sought ways of solving the problems of the construction industry. Raymond T. Cragin became chairman of the Cleveland committee related to the national plan, and Howard Whipple Green. became the director of a local survey that proved the beginning of the permanent Real Property Inventory. The Bureau of Foreign and Domestic Commerce obtained a special federal grant of $2,500,000 for inventories in sixty-four cities and metropolitan districts. Green was attached to the Bureau as consultant, and he also directed the work in Cleveland, collecting a vast amount of data. This material, representing an inventory of real property, carefully analyzed and interpreted, was important to every concern doing business in the city. It also became significant to every person living in the Cleveland metropolitan district and to outside business concerns with headquarters in the city. The RPI provided answers to such questions as: what is the market for mechanical refrigeration, for gas and electric ranges, for paint, automobiles, gasoline, and shrubs? It furnished data that indicated where stores, factories, and industrial plants should locate, picturing the future of the various sites. Important facts were given about each family unit, dwelling, store, and plant. In 1934, one hundred and forty cities followed Cleveland's example. The value of the inventory was immediately appreciated, and the Real Property Inventory, under Green's direction, was incorporated as a non-profit organization, publishing basic data year after year relating to Metropolitan Cleveland.

Miles Heights Village was annexed to the City of Cleveland after two years of preliminary proceedings.

The Forest City Publishing Company was formed, October 4, acquiring the capital stock of The Cleveland Company, publisher of the *News,* and the stock of the *Plain Dealer*. B. P. Bole was elected president, with the other directors: George M. Rogers, John S. McCarrens, Dan R. Hanna, Jr., John A. Hadden, Guerdon S. Holden, and I. F. Freiberger.

The campaign goal set for the Community Fund was $4,250,000. The amount raised was $3,774,243.70 with 409,139 subscribers.

James H. Rogers, organist, teacher, composer, and music critic of the *Plain Dealer,* retired, and five hundred Cleveland musicians gave him a remarkable farewell dinner. Rogers died in 1940. In 1946 the Cleveland Orchestra dedicated a program to him; and his portrait, painted by Mary Seymour Brooks for a group of admirers, was presented to the Western Reserve Historical Society.

Edmund Vance Cooke, one of Cleveland's best-known poets, died on December 18. His verses were nationally popular as were his lectures. He served as president of the International Lyceum Association and of the Cleveland Single Tax Club, besides being a charter member of the American Press Humorists. Possibly his best-known poem was "How Did You Die?", two verses being reprinted here:

> Did you tackle that trouble that came your way
>   With a resolute heart and cheerful?
> Or hide your face from the light of day
>   With a craven soul and fearful?
> Oh, a trouble's a ton, or a trouble's an ounce,
>   Or a trouble is what you make it,
> And it isn't the fact that you're hurt that counts,
>   But only how did you take it?
>
> And though you be done to the death, what then?
>   If you battled the best you could,
> If you played your part in the world of men,
>   Why, the Critic will call it good.
> Death comes with a crawl, or comes with a pounce,
>   And whether he's slow or spry,
> It isn't the fact that you're dead that counts,
>   But only how did you die?

Described by engineers and architects as one of the most beautiful bridges in the United States, the Lorain-Carnegie span was opened in December. An $8,000,000 bond issue was approved on November 9, 1927, thus ending a fifteen-year struggle to obtain funds for the bridge from Carnegie Avenue to Lorain Avenue. Of steel-and-concrete construction, the structure was 4,558 feet long and 83 feet wide between curbs, providing for two decks—a broad upper roadway and a lower deck reserved for future use. Two unique pylons stood majestically at each end. The cost was $6,148,206, well within the bond issue, but the east and west approaches were not completed. The county surveyors were Frank Lander, succeeded by F. R. Williams; consulting engineer, Wilbur J. Watson; consulting architect, F. R. Walker;

and county commissioners, J. H. Harris, Jerry R. Zmunt, and Walter E. Cook. In 1936 the bridge was recognized by an award of the American Institute of Steel Construction as an outstanding architectural triumph.

Cleveland was proud of the Philharmonic String Quartet and the Cleveland String Quartet. The latter included the names of artists known for years to lovers of fine music: Josef Fuchs, first violin; Rudolph Ringwall, second violin; Carlton Cooley, viola; and Victor D. Gomez, cello. For years, the Musical Arts Association had given assistance to these admirable quartets.

1933

Their operating budget cut the first of the year by more than two million dollars, the schools struggled through the most difficult twelve months in their history. Teachers and employees of the system loyally bore their share of the financial burden. The PTAs decried the over-crowded classrooms and urged greater pay for teachers. In May, Charles H. Lake was elected superintendent of schools, his term to begin September 1, and R. G. Jones was elected director of public relations. The teachers' union, under the direction of the American Federation of Labor, was formed to advance the teachers' interests.

Cleveland's first six-day bicycle race held for men proved such a success that twelve contests followed in the next nine years. After the race of 1942, won by Charles Bergna and Angelo De Bacco, the series was discontinued because of the war. Among the favorite riders were "Torchy" Peden, Alfie LeTourneur, Jules Audy, and Cecil Yates.

Carl Victor Weygandt became chief justice of the Supreme Court of Ohio. He was born in Wayne County, Ohio, in 1888, and was graduated from the College of Wooster in 1912, later studying law at Western Reserve University. He began the practice of law in Cleveland in 1918 and served as judge of the Court of Common Pleas, Cuyahoga County, 1924-30; and judge of the Court of Appeals of Ohio, 8th Appellate District, 1930-33, when he was made chief justice of the Ohio Supreme Court. His professional and social affiliations were many.

Cleveland's annual salute to the automotive industry was given, January 14, in the ballroom of Hotel Statler under the auspices of the *News* and and forty civic and business organizations. Speakers included Colonel Frank Knox, publisher of the *Chicago Daily News,* and A. R. Erskine, president of the Studebaker Corporation, with Charles H. Kellstadt, president of the Cleveland Advertising Club, opening the meeting. The Automobile Show, held in the former Higbee store building, displayed nearly a hundred of the newest-model cars, while Rudy Vallee and his Connecticut Yankees played an accompaniment.

The *Plain Dealer* bought the *Sunday News* and became Cleveland's only morning and Sunday paper.

As modernization of the old Chisholm steel mills of the American Steel &

Wire Company in Newburgh was considered impractical and costly, active units were moved to Lorain, Ohio, and the historic plant closed. The old H. P. Nail Works had been dismantled in 1931. Likewise, in 1944, the buildings of the Consolidated Works were being abandoned. However, expansions went on continuously in the vast Cleveland operations, and the city continued to be known as the wire center of the world. Good leadership had characterized the organization. William P. Palmer was president from 1900 to 1927; J. S. Keefe, from 1927 to 1932; C. F. Blackmer, from 1932 to 1937, when Clifford F. Hood became president and directed expanding activities during the 1940s.

Rabbi Rudolph M. Rosenthal was installed as spiritual leader of the B'nai Jeshurun Congregation in the Temple on the Heights, February 23, by Rabbi Stephen S. Wise of New York. A native Clevelander, Rabbi Rosenthal came to the pulpit with a wealth of education. In 1941, the year in which the Heights Temple celebrated its diamond jubilee, the congregation included more than 900 families, 750 children in the Sunday School, and nearly 200 in the daily Hebrew classes. Among the officers of the congregation at this time were Ben Labowitch, president; Henry Greenberger and Sam Schulist, vice presidents; Seymour Amster, treasurer; and Alfred Savitt, secretary.

To meet strained financial conditions resulting from the depression, the governor of Michigan on February 14 restricted operations in all banks in his state for an eight-day period, limiting withdrawals to 5 per cent. This led to unrest in other cities, and the governor of Maryland on February 24 declared a three-day moratorium. Several Cleveland banks announced on February 27 that withdrawals would be limited to 5 per cent, the rule applying to all forms of deposits. No restrictions were made on new deposits, however. Governor Fancher of the Federal Reserve Bank of Cleveland praised the move. Withdrawals were light, mostly for living expenses. Critical financial conditions became general, and during the next eight days the banks in all states excepting Delaware were closed or restricted.

Clevelanders felt such confidence in the local banking situation that on March 1 deposits were on the rise. Big companies built up wage funds, reassured by the segregated-deposits rule as provided in the new Ohio bank laws. Many new accounts were opened in Cleveland banks, buttressing the city's ability to carry on its normal business. Withdrawals from local banks fell off to a surprising extent. However, a special committee of the Cleveland Clearing House Association on March 2 considered the issuance of scrip during the crisis; but before the plan was completed, Washington vetoed it. Local mortgage holders agreed to delay foreclosures on deserving people as long as possible. Cleveland on March 4 ended its most eventful business week.

Constructive steps had been taken, but many felt that there would be little relief until Washington acted, and it was believed that a recommendation for banking legislation would come among the official actions of the new administration. The Federal Reserve Bank of Cleveland was the only Federal Reserve Bank that did not close on March 4 or prior to that date. Among those Clevelanders taking leading roles in attempting to bring relief were R. G. Roth, president of the Retail Merchants Board; Harris Creech, president of the Clearing House Association; E. R. Fancher, governor of the Federal Reserve Bank of Cleveland; J. A. Schafer, president of the Cleveland Retail Credit Men's Company; and Colonel Leonard P. Ayres, vice president of the Cleveland Trust Company and statistician of the group.

Franklin Delano Roosevelt, inaugurated President of the United States on March 4, ordered a four-day bank holiday two days later. The same day, Secretary of the Treasury Woodin freed Ohio's new deposits, his ruling releasing funds acutely needed in the city to meet payrolls and replace food stocks. On March 8, Woodin called in gold from banks and authorized an advance of currency to members if metal was turned over. At this time, it was announced that the purchasing and resale of passbooks in Cleveland was to be investigated by the grand jury. Hoarded gold came out of hiding in March and succeeding months; on June 5 the president signed an Act of Congress outlawing the gold-payment clause in all moneys and in public and private contracts. Governor Fancher of the Federal Reserve Bank invited people to turn in hoarded gold.

Member banks of the Fourth Federal Reserve District applied on March 10 for license to reopen, and four Cleveland banks with deposits of nearly a half-billion dollars resumed normal operations, March 13, after two weeks of restrictions. The Cleveland Trust Company, Central United National Bank, and the National City Bank opened under newly granted federal licenses, and the Society for Savings opened under permission of the State. The Union Trust Company and The Guardian Trust Company were not permitted to open. The opening freed funds for payrolls. Stocks and bonds made a record rise at the end of the bank holiday, March 16, and business in general was resumed after deposits flowed back to the banks, which were rapidly being reopened under Federal or State licenses. Expansion of bank credit for business improvements was urged on March 19, and renewed factory activity was seen as a definite sign of progress.

The life of Balto, heroic Alaskan husky, came to a peaceful end on March 14, six years after his arrival in Cleveland to spend his old age at the Cleveland Zoo. An engraved stone slab about three feet high marked the grave of the sturdy lead dog of the team that delivered diphtheria anti-toxin from Fairbanks to Nome, Alaska, in 1925, thus checking an epidemic.

The Rev. Frederick L. Odenbach, S. J., meteorologist and seismologist of John Carroll University since 1892, died March 15. He was born in Rochester, New York, in 1857, and received his college education at Canisius College, Buffalo. He went to Europe for his graduate studies in philosophy and the sciences, and after several years of teaching and further study abroad, returned to America and took up a position as member of the faculty of John Carroll University, then St. Ignatius College. He developed a meteorological observatory, and the first observations were made in 1896. In 1899, he devised and built the first ceraunograph, and four years later his first seismograph, the accuracy of which attracted international attention. This distinguished scientist led a particularly useful life.

President Roosevelt signed the legislation legalizing 3.2 beer on March 22, to be effective on April 7.

The Cleveland Advertising Club organized its Come-to-Cleveland Committee, an inspiration for civic improvement and rehabilitation. It sought tourists and events, and gave widespread publicity to Cleveland. George F. Buehler served continuously as president.

The Hankins Container Company was established at 3044 West 106th Street to manufacture corrugated paper boxes. Besides the Cleveland organization, it maintained plants in Elizabeth, New Jersey; Miamisburg, Ohio; and Chicago. Officers in the 1940s included E. R. Hankins, president, and K. A. Bennett, executive vice president in charge of plants.

Depositors in three closed banks organized a Protective Association, March 27, and those in restricted banks demanded the collection of double liability from stockholders.

Upon the death of Charles E. Thompson, founder of Thompson Products, Inc., management passed to a group of younger executives. Frederick C. Crawford, millwright's helper in 1916, became president, and under his leadership the company entered a period of great growth. Lee M. Clegg, stock chaser in 1919, became vice president; and A. T. Colwell, valve salesman in 1922, later advanced to the position of vice president in charge of engineering. During years of peace, a nationwide organization was built. Plants in six cities in the United States and Canada were making precision parts for producers of practically every automobile, truck, bus, tractor, and aircraft engine in the country. Markets expanded, engineering and research were given fresh impetus, bringing forth numerous products, improved and diversified. A progressive personnel division was established to foster teamwork between management and labor, under the direction of Raymond S. Livingstone, who won national prestige for the company.

Conservators were named for two closed banks on April 7: a California banker, Oscar L. Cox, for the Union Trust, and the city's manager of the Reconstruction Finance Corporation, Sidney B. Congdon, for the Guardian. The Ohio bank probe began on April 9, when inquiry was demanded by Auxiliary Bishop McFadden, who asked for complete facts concerning the Union and Guardian collapse. The Guardian Bank's unsecured loans were estimated at $3,396,916. The statement also listed notes and bills, probably unsecured, at $14,144,625. A new First National Bank was planned to take over the assets of the Union and Guardian banks, and it had the approval of major depositors on April 18. Large subscriptions for the proposed First National were made immediately, but the plan did not materialize. The directors of the National City Bank then persuaded the First National Bank group to turn in their subscriptions for what amounted to $2,700,000 of common stock in the National City, and sold to the RFC a $4,000,000 issue of preferred stock, bringing the capital stock in common shares—$20 par value—to $4,700,000 and preferred shares to $4,000,000.

The community's greatest period of unemployment came in April, when 219,000 persons in Cuyahoga County were out of work. Relief agencies on April 26 were thronged with unfortunate city workers awaiting pay day.

It was not until May 4 that payments began, the first in thirty-four days. A survey disclosed that approximately four thousand Clevelanders were homeless, and a rise in transients was reported. There was a touch of irony in the fact that Wayfarers Lodge opened early in March at 1705 Lakeside Avenue, on the site of Clinton Park, the first recreational area in Cleveland.

The Cleveland Medal for Public Service was awarded in April by the Chamber of Commerce to William G. Mather, "eminent industrialist and philanthropist, who had been a leader in the movement to group Cleveland's public buildings around a central mall." The medal was also given to Alfred Clum, "lawyer, administrator and unusually efficient public servant."

The Cleveland Typothetae Association was founded this year, but under the name of the Fellowcraft Club it had its modest beginning in 1902. The members of the printer's association later formed the Cleveland Graphic Arts Club and broadened their field of activities. In 1911 the Ben Franklin Club was formed and this was merged with the Cleveland Graphic Arts Club in 1918. Fifteen years later the name was changed to Cleveland Typothetae, which was related to the national Typothetae. In 1921 the Cleveland Club of Printing House Craftsmen was formed by ambitious workers devoted to their trade. Among the publishing houses in the 1930s were: The Penton Publishing Company, one of the nation's largest producers of trade magazines: *Steel, The Foundry, Machine Design, New Equipment Digest, Revista Industrial,* and technical books; The World Publishing Company, the largest publisher of *Bibles* in the United States and one of the largest reprint publishers; The American Greeting Card Company, one of the leading firms in its field; *The National Petroleum News; The Midwest Purchasing Agent;* The William Feather Company, widely known for house organs and institutional publications, with the writer and philosopher for whom the company was named as its head; *The Ohio Farmer; Church Management;* the *Daily Legal News;* Banks-Baldwin Law Publishing Company; Huebner Publications, and The Dan S. Wertheimer Company. Among other publications and publishers were: American Home Publishing Company; American Jugoslav Printing & Publishing Company; *American Roumanian News; Catholic Universe Bulletin;* The Cleveland Call & Post Company; Cleveland Citizen Publishing Company; *Cleveland Herald; Cleveland Union Leader; Hungarian Daily Szabadsag;* Jewish Independent Publishing Company; *Jewish Review & Observer; Jewish World;* L'Araldo Publishing Company; Polish Daily News, Inc.; *Svet Bohemian Daily; Waechter & Anzeiger.* The Foreign Newspaper Advertising Service represented in the Cleveland area the foreign-language newspapers of the country.

The Museum of Modern Art Exhibit on Housing stimulated the public-housing movement in Cleveland. Wide citizen interest helped the city to lead the nation in establishing the first project to be undertaken by the Public Works Administration. Ernest J. Bohn, student of the national housing situation, helped inspire the State of Ohio to adopt the first public-housing law in the country. This legislation recognized the public responsibility of giving to all families an opportunity to live in clean, safe housing of minimum standards, at rentals that they could afford to pay. The law provided that those families whom private enterprise could not be expected to house because of their "low-rent paying ability" must be assisted with public funds, part to come from the Federal Government.

Many Clevelanders attended the opening of the Century of Progress Exposition in Chicago on May 27, where a number of impressive Cleveland industrial exhibits were on display.

The Brookpark Bridge, 1,919 feet long and 120 feet high, cost $382,800 and carried Brookpark Road over the picturesque Rocky River Valley.

The Lithuanian Cultural Garden in Rockefeller Park was dedicated, June 11, with the unveiling of a bust of Dr. Jonas Basanavicius, scholar and liberator. The bust and garden plan were presented by Lithuanian army officers to the City of Cleveland as a token of good will. In October, 1938, a monument was unveiled, honoring Dr. Vincas Kudirka, writer, poet, and author of the Lithuanian national anthem. The garden, constructed in the form of a lyre, was marked by beautiful stonework and lovely landscaping. In 1936, the Biruta fountain, named for the first queen of Lithuania, was unveiled. The Lithuanian minister to the United States said of the garden: "It is an encouraging sight to see a great municipality actually demonstrating that its citizens may speak many different tongues, may have many different customs, may be partisans of various political or religious beliefs and still be peacefully united in a common purpose, for a common and noble achievement. Aside from being a picturesque lesson on the origins of the diverse population of this city, the cultural garden development offers also an excellent course in international relations."

Harry F. Payer, widely known Cleveland lawyer, was named assistant secretary of state by President Roosevelt. He resigned in November to become special counsel to the Reconstruction Finance Corporation.

The first cub pack of Boy Scouts of America, Greater Cleveland Council, was organized in June at Lomond School, with George McCourt as cubmaster.

A statue of Conrad Mizer, who begged donations to establish music in the parks, was erected in Edgewater Park by people who loved outdoor music.

Mayor Ray T. Miller and his associates scanned the public-works legislation passed by Congress and announced that federal aid would be sought for a number of projects in the city, county, and ten suburbs amounting to $27,925,000. The projects included Cuyahoga River straightening, harbor dredging, grade-crossing eliminations, paving, construction of two sewage plants, and completion of Huron Road Hospital and John Carroll University.

The National Industrial Recovery Act was signed, June 16. Local firms numbering 4,410 signed pledges to support the NRA. It proved a shortsighted venture that brought much adverse criticism, and it was voided by the Supreme Court on May 27, 1935.

Jesse Owens set three world scholastic records in Chicago, June 18, running 100 yards in 9.4 seconds; 220 yards in 20.7; and making a broad jump of 24 feet and 9⅝ inches.

Checks were mailed to 300,000 depositors in closed banks on July 21, as a

$57,047,000 bank payoff began. Awaited for five months, the plan was facilitated by RFC loans. A month later, the Federal Banking Department was authorized to participate in the investigation of the closed Guardian and Union Trust banks.

The Cuyahoga County Relief Administration, which took over from the Cleveland Associated Charities the bulk of local relief, including unemployment relief, was set up with Stockton Raymond as director. In 1934, Helen W. Hanchette was appointed general secretary of the Associated Charities, the first woman executive to hold this position in Cleveland.

The Society of Collectors was organized in August to foster and promote an interest in collections of early Americana, and to restore and maintain Dunham Tavern.

In its attractive new home on the second floor of the Bulkley Building, the Women's City Club continued to sustain its original purposes of interpreting the needs of the community to its members and promoting the welfare of the City of Cleveland. It gave valuable assistance to the establishment of the Blossom Hill School for Girls, instituted forum sessions on controversial subjects, stimulated a slum-clearance movement, launched a crusade for new equipment at City Hospital, and brought distinguished visitors and speakers to the city. Through its many committees, the club played an active part in the city's development; and, guided by Virda L. Stewart, president in 1946, and Grace D. Treat, executive secretary, it continued its challenging task of civic housekeeping. Miss Stewart was succeeded by Mrs. Henry Friede and Miss Treat by Polly Prescott.

James R. Weddell won the Thompson Trophy Race in the National Air Races at Los Angeles with an average speed of 237.95 m.p.h.

Upper downtown shops were hosts to seventy-five thousand spectators of a style parade in which century-old styles were revived in a mile-long procession on September 8.

Track stars and sports enthusiasts cheered Cleveland's Stella Walasiewicz —or Walsh—as she broke records by running 60 meters in 7.3 seconds at Lemberg, Poland. On June 9, 1935, she established the world's record for the 220-yard dash in 24.3 seconds in Cleveland. On August 15, she ran 200 meters in 23.6 seconds in her native city, Warsaw. In 1946, she held sixty-five world and national track and field records, and had won thirty-three women's national AAU championships. She owned more than a thousand medals and trophies won in Japan, China, Africa, Canada, every country in Europe, and in the United States. She was also a star player in softball and basketball. Her records seemed to justify the statement that, among women, Stella Walsh was the world's outstanding all-round athlete.

Wesley Ferrell of the Indians was the only pitcher to win 20 or more games in each of his first four years in the major leagues—21, 25, 22, and 23, a total of 91 games.

Charles E. Adams, Community Fund leader, died at Charity Hospital on November 5. He had been chairman of the Community Fund since its birth in 1919, and was one of Cleveland's most forceful leaders. As president of the Cleveland Hardware Company from 1891 until his death, he had built the organization into one of the largest institutions in its field. He was also a director of The Cleveland Trust Company and had other business and financial interests. It was as general chairman of the Community Fund that Adams became known nationally for his genial and efficient leadership. He was a trustee of both the YMCA and the YWCA, and his efforts in their behalf and in furthering the Red Cross were outstanding.

Harry L. Davis defeated Ray T. Miller for mayor by 14,446 votes, November 8, the total of 280,000 votes establishing a record for a municipal election.

The campaign goal set for the Community Fund was $3,585,000. The amount raised was $2,968,002.39, with 426,844 subscribers.

Thirteen years of constant debate on the subject of the Eighteenth Amendment resulted in the Twenty-first Amendment which went into effect on December 5. The rise of intolerable graft and violence during the prohibition era had been a leading factor in bringing about repeal. Despite expensive attempts at law enforcement, smugglers and bootleggers were piling up fortunes in the unlawful manufacture and sale of potent, poisonous liquors. There was a growing contempt for laws, and the criminal population was swelled by racketeers and outlaw gangs who dared to supply liquor at the cost of crime or even murder. Reformers cited statistics, the reports of life-insurance companies relating to health, and social-science research in the claim that alcoholism is perhaps more often a result than a cause of bad social conditions. However, many people believed the prohibition law to be unwise and unfair. National prohibition ended, but the dry-wet battle continued, as government regulations were imposed.

In a two-car, sheet-metal garage near East 61st and Waterman streets, the Pump Engineering Service Corporation was launched by William S. "Bill" Jack, general manager, and James Johnson, chief engineer. They manufactured fuel pumps for airplanes. Six years later, the Borg-Warner Corporation purchased the concern. The enlarged plant of the Pesco Products Company, 11610 Euclid Avenue, was known as its twenty-first division. In World War II, Pesco produced a substantial part of the pumps used by American planes. Expansion after the war provided for production of special pumps for rocket propulsion and ram jet projects. Pesco later became a major producer of hydraulic equipment for agricultural tractors and machinery for road-building, earth-moving, and material-handling. Future planning included a laboratory in which to test aircraft fuel systems, and a huge new plant in Bedford Township. R. J. Minshall, awarded the Musick Memorial Trophy for his contribution to the safety of transoceanic travel, was made president of the Pesco Division in 1941.

All debts had been paid by the congregation of the First United Presbyterian Church of Greater Cleveland, and more than $110,000 had been contributed to mission enterprises, which included the founding of six United Presbyterian churches in and near Cleveland. A merger of the Fourth and Heights churches in 1942 resulted in the Washington Boulevard United Presbyterian Church, located in the building of the latter that had been erected in 1922 at Washington Boulevard and Lee Road in Cleveland Heights. This church, in turn, joined the First Church in 1943, then in its centennial year, and the Rev. J. Paul Graham became pastor. His successor, the Rev. Virgil McComb Cosby, announced plans for a new house of worship to be erected on the same site in 1948.

Experiments in business and labor co-operatin were under way by the end of 1933, as the Government attacked the industrial-recovery problem, armed with an increasing number of codes and regulations. Cleveland industry had been hit hard in the national crisis. Bank clearings had tumbled to $2,531,000,000 by the end of 1933. The slow upward climb had begun, however, led by textiles and steel, and there was a glimmer of progress in the figures at the end of the year: 1,803 establishments, employing 95,189 wage earners, reported products valued at $471,324,205. Relief of the unemployed burdened welfare agencies and the city administration. Almost 31 per cent of the estimated labor force of 500,541 in Cleveland were jobless.

1934

Leonard P. Ayres, Cleveland economist, said on January 2 that "he saw Uncle Sam at the throttle, while private capital watched." Ayres hoped public works would advance and improve national conditions. W. J. Austin, president of the Austin Company, stated that "lack of credit retards many improvements at sound plants." Local realtors asked for federal financing to help develop real-estate opportunities. Financial Editor Guy T. Rockwell of the *Plain Dealer* on January 1 predicted improvement in 1934, but suggested as the watchword, "Be alert!"

The city government faced serious financial difficulties as the new year started. Mayor Davis and his associates wanted the same budget as the year before, but realized that increasing public revenues would be essential. Finance Director Louis West stated that the city must reduce expenditures and cut payrolls. In April it became necessary to issue scrip to city workers in lieu of currency; but in July, the Finance Department began canceling the $495,000 issued in scrip. Late in the year there was a further issuance of scrip, which was canceled during the first half of 1935.

Andrew Squire, distinguished for his astute knowledge of corporation law, practicing attorney in Cleveland for more than half a century, and one of the oldest as well as one of the ablest among the legal minds, died January 5. His father, Dr. Andrew Jackson Squire, a practicing physician, became a resident of Ohio in 1810. Andrew was sent to the Western Reserve Eclectic Institute at Hiram, Ohio, in 1866, then to Cleveland to begin a medical career. Instead, *Blackstone's Commentaries* captured his interest, and he began his study of law in the office of Cadwell & Marvin in 1873. Seventeen years later, he organized the law partnership of Squire, Sanders, & Dempsey. His precept was, "The harder the conflict, the greater the triumph." He carried this thought like a banner in all his legal battles. As a contestant he had the faculty of presenting the facts in a case with such obvious conviction and force that the jury generally became convinced. His

Typical crowd of 10,000 at an ice hockey game. The Cleveland Barons ranked high in the nation for years.

A capacity audience of more than 13,000 ready to enjoy a basketball game.
ARENA—HOME OF SPORTING EVENTS

Looking west on the south side of Euclid Avenue from East 14th Street: Halle Bros. Company, the CAC Building and other buildings with fine shops.

Playhouse Square—looking east on Euclid Avenue from East 12th Street. On the right is the Hanna Building at the corner of East 14th Street. PERRY CRAGG, CLEVELAND NEWS.

Upper Downtown

specialization in corporation law led him to handle the affairs of many of Cleveland's largest and most important businesses. He was a member of the executive committee of the Union Carbide & Carbon Corporation and Union Trust Company. He was a director of Case Library and was on the boards of Hiram College and Western Reserve University.

"Radical as the New Deal," was the estimate of the new 1934 automobiles at the impressive Auto Show, January 14. The third annual show luncheon, sponsored by the *News,* in co-operation with the city's civic and business organizations, was held in the Public Auditorium on January 13, with Postmaster General James A. Farley and Harry G. Moock of the Plymouth Motor Car Company as principal speakers. The leading American cars were shown in attractive settings.

John Sherwin, who started his banking career as messenger boy for The National City Bank in 1888 and later became prominent in Cleveland's financial and industrial life, died on January 16. In 1895, Sherwin organized the Park National Bank, and was made cashier and director before its merger with the Euclid Avenue National Bank, of which he became vice president and executive officer. The assets of two other banks were acquired and, in 1904, the Euclid-Park Bank had become the largest national institution in Cleveland. The following year, it merged with the First National Bank, with Sherwin as president; and in 1920, the First National and many other banks formed the Union Trust Company with Sherwin as chairman of the board until his retirement in 1929. His business acumen and compelling personality led to many important achievements contributing to Cleveland's industrial growth. He was a director of the Ohio Bell Telephone Company, Cleveland Railway Company, Otis Steel Company, Kelley Island Lime & Transport Company, and United States Security & Investment Company of New York. He married a Clevelander in 1893, Frances McIntosh, daughter of H. P. McIntosh. His son, John Sherwin, Jr., became an industrial and financial leader. The Fine Arts Garden Endowment Fund of $250,000 was established by Mr. and Mrs. Sherwin.

Dr. Frank P. Corrigan, who had been chief surgeon of St. Alexis Hospital, began his diplomatic career as minister to El Salvador. Appointed on February 17, he was the first Ohioan to be placed in a diplomatic post by President Roosevelt. In 1937 he became minister to Panama, and in 1938, the first American ambassador to Venezuela.

County Jail officials stated on February 26 that the prison population was 206, the lowest in fifteen years.

Army pilots took over the flying of the air mail on February 26, and within a week six were killed and six injured. Accidents were blamed on bad weather, inadequate planes, and unfamiliarity with routes. All air mail was halted by army order on March 12, the action resulting from ten recent deaths. The Government withdrew from the service.

The late Mrs. Marion C. Tyler willed most of her estate of $3,398,000 to worthy institutions, 75 per cent of the income to be paid to Lakeside Hospital, and the other 25 per cent to Western Reserve University for the benefit of Flora Stone Mather College.

Conventions had brought 42,157 delegates to Cleveland in 1933, leaving $1,203,540 in the city's cash registers. This volume entitled the Convention Board of the Cleveland Chamber of Commerce to stand on its own feet, and in February, 1934, the Cleveland Convention & Visitors Bureau, Inc. was organized. F. J. Andre was the first president. A. J. Kennedy, secretary, 1923-32, ably managed the Bureau until July, 1935, when enthusiastic Mark Egan became executive secretary and manager.

The National Education Association, meeting in Cleveland on March 1, asked Congress to aid the schools. To provide equal education for all was declared a state duty.

The Dog Show, March 11, was said to be the best in the city's history. The Kennel Club won praise when the exhibition was pronounced the third largest in the United States.

Living costs rose 23 per cent in the past year, according to a survey concluded March 23. The number of homes owned in Cuyahoga County was 121,088; 41 per cent were owned by occupants, a large percentage for a big city. Nine per cent of the families in Metropolitan Cleveland lacked bathtubs or shower baths, and 25 per cent central heating, according to the Real Property Inventory. Forty-four per cent did not own automobiles, and 62 per cent were without telephones.

Chardon celebrated its Maple Sugar Festival, April 6, with a crowd of eight thousand, the greatest in its history. It was the ninth in the interesting series.

A group of Clevelanders formed The Sight Saving Council of Cleveland, knowing that the sight of the average person becomes defective all too soon, and appreciating that "one's eyes are his most valuable possessions." The Council selected two purposes: "to find ways and means of furthering the preservation of eyesight, and to disseminate these findings, thus advancing human welfare." Two hundred representative men and women were appointed as members of the general committee, headed by Professor H. B. Dates of Case School of Applied Science, and it was decided to concentrate the Council's early efforts in the schools.

The Cleveland Medal for Public Service was awarded in April by The Cleveland Chamber of Commerce to Francis F. Prentiss, "an outstanding citizen of Cleveland, whose public charities and unselfish and distinguished work . . . have endeared him to the entire community." The medal was also given to Eckstein Case in recognition of "his devotion to Case School of Applied Science and his generous sponsorship of scientific research."

A religious event of world importance was the merging on June 26 of the Evangelical Synod of North America and the Reformed Church in the United States, uniting them into one denomination, known as the Evangelical and Reformed Church. This historic meeting was held in Cleveland's old Zion Church, founded in 1867 at Branch and West 14th streets. In 1817, in Germany, the Reformed and Lutheran churches had been united to form the Evangelical Church. Early in the Nineteenth Century, many members of this church came to America and organized the Evangelical Synod of North America. The Reformed Church, which had spread through-

out Central and Eastern Europe, established The Reformed Church in the
United States in Pennsylvania in 1725. The merged churches had a combined membership of approximately one million followers. The united
church embraced 2,937 individual churches and foreign-mission work in
British East India, Honduras, China, and Iraq. On November 1, 1939,
women delegates and visitors representing the Evangelical Synod of North
America and the Reformed Church in the United States met at the old
Zion Church in Cleveland to merge the women's work of the united Evangelical and Reformed churches. So it was that two historic meetings were
held at the old Zion church in Cleveland, the delegates to both gatherings
being welcomed by the city's fourteen thousand members of the twenty-
seven Evangelical and Reformed churches.

The city honored St. Alexis Hospital's fifty years of usefulness, July 18,
and civic leaders praised Sister Leonarda, the founder, at a jubilee banquet.
The hospital had treated forty-four thousand people of all faiths.

The British housing expert, Sir Raymond Unwin, visited the city on
August 31 with European housing authorities. He praised Cleveland's spirit
of enterprise, and called the city's slum-clearance plan the "most hopeful"
in the United States.

For years it had been claimed, but never proved, that slum areas were an
economic liability to a city. At the request of the Cleveland Metropolitan
Housing Authority, the Rev. R. B. Navin, dean of Sisters College, Catholic
Diocese of Cleveland, with the counsel of Howard Whipple Green, director
of the Real Property Inventory of Metropolitan Cleveland, made an analysis
establishing this fact. The section of Cleveland selected for study was between Central Avenue and Woodland Avenue from East 22nd Street to
East 55th Street. This area had deteriorated until it was pronounced "an
actual social menace." It was shown that this section, with 2.5 per cent of
the population, was characterized by shocking social conditions. In it 21.3
per cent of the city's murders were committed, and 26.3 per cent of the
houses of prostitution were located. Illegitimate births numbered 10.4 per
cent of the city's total, and tuberculosis deaths 12.5 per cent. The community was putting $1,750,000 into the cost of maintaining the section in
excess of the money that it received from real-estate taxes from the section.
The appraised value of land and buildings in the area was $8,153,470, prov-
ing that the cost of maintaining the section was 21 per cent of the appraised
value of land and buildings upon which taxes were levied. The cost of police
protection per family was $57.60 as compared with the cost of $18.12 for
Cleveland. The Navin survey proved conclusively that the rebuilding of the
section would be sound, economically as well as socially.

Famous flyers arrived in Cleveland for the National Air Races, and Navy
and Marine squadrons attracted record crowds. Approximately a hundred
thousand people were drawn to the giant spectacle, and a German ace,
flying upside down in a blaze of searchlights, thrilled the spectators at night.
Harold Neumann won the Greve trophy race, and Doug Davis was presented with the Bendix trophy, his speed averaging 216.24 m.p.h. On
September 4, Davis was killed in a trophy-race crash. Roscoe Turner was

the winner of the Thompson Trophy, his speed being 248.13 m.p.h. The races were a financial success, with attendance the second largest on record.

Approximately six thousand Welsh folk on September 4 took part in the sixth annual National Gymanfa Ganu Festival, and hymns of Wales rang throughout the Public Auditorium.

The United States Post Office was dedicated, September 10. The last building of the Terminal Group, it was a great monumental structure designed by Walker & Weeks. J. A. Greitzer's murals, and Frank Jirouch's marble reliefs decorated the interior of the five-million-dollar structure. The Federal Building on the Public Square continued to house the Bureau of Customs, the federal courts, and government agencies. The postal department became known as the Public Square Branch. Michael F. O'Donnell, appointed postmaster in September, 1933, had come up from the ranks in the Cleveland office. Upon retirement in 1943, he was succeeded by James L. Collins, who continued in office for one year. In January, 1945, Guy R. Lucas became postmaster. Forty-three years earlier, he had been a letter carrier, advancing through all departments until he was appointed assistant superintendent of mails in 1944. Like O'Donnell, he was civic-minded and an able administrator. Postal receipts for the year 1934 totaled $7,634,000.

Superintendent Charles H. Lake reported that a greater emphasis would be placed on social studies and current events in the schools, as a result of the citizenship study made by a committee headed by Harold H. Burton.

The Elbert H. Baker Fellowship Hall was dedicated at the YMCA, Prospect Avenue and East 22nd Street. It was a formal memorial to Baker's allegiance to the "Y."

A. V. Cannon, outstanding figure in the administration of relief and one of the city's most prominent lawyers and businessmen, died suddenly at a rally of social workers, September 28.

Clocks were turned back an hour on September 30 to gain the hour lost on April 29 in the daylight-saving venture.

Colorful rites at St. John's Cathedral marked the elevation of the Rev. Stanislaus Gmuca of the Order of St. Benedict to the office of abbot, October 2. Church dignitaries and hundreds of devout people were present when he became Ohio's first abbot, the world's youngest living abbot, and the only Slovak abbot.

The Slovak Garden in the Cultural Garden chain was dedicated this year. Two years later, busts of Stephen Furdek, Slovak priest, writer, and cultural leader, and Jan Kollar, Lutheran pastor and poet, were unveiled. John Tenkacs of Cleveland was the sculptor. The garden was modern in spirit with a raised terrace from which the design opened into a large oval lawn to accommodate gatherings at celebrations.

City Council unwillingly played host to 1,500 Communists who insisted on presenting demands for relief on October 28. Police kept the crowds from invading City Hall, while a committee of the Council met with representatives of the Communists. During World War I, the Communists, called Bolshevists or Reds, had found allies in extreme "left wing" Socialists and a large number of members of the deteriorating IWW. Radical agitators had been sent out to gain control of labor unions by inciting revolutionary violence in vital industries and opposing peaceful arbitration of differences. There was a growing consciousness of the Red menace, inspired by Moscow. Boring from within, the Communists aimed to breed intolerance, crime, and oppression, and eventually to overthrow the United States government.

The Polish Cultural Garden was dedicated in Rockefeller Park to Frederic Chopin on October 28. A bust of the famous creator and exponent of classical music was unveiled at a later date. Judge Frank Pickarski of Pittsburgh gave the dedicatory address. The garden was constructed in the form of a hexagonal sunken court with a pool and fountain in the center. To acquaint visitors with the quality of Polish culture was the purpose of the planners.

A. Vic Donahey for United States Senate, Martin L. Davey for governor, and John M. Sulzmann for sheriff, won by a landslide on November 7. All were Democrats.

The campaign goal set for the Community Fund was $3,500,000. The amount raised was $3,037,696.87 with 445,295 subscribers. The chairman was Randolph Eide, and the Community Fund dinner had Bishop Charles H. LeBlond as its speaker.

The May Company provided a massive Christmas tree for the Public Square. It was so enthusiastically greeted that the store continued the custom every year, its trees standing majestically on the northeast sector of the Public Square as sentinels of good cheer.

The greatest quantity of snow in eight winters covered the city on December 10. The heaviest fall was six inches in six hours.

The number of starlings living in the Public Square district was estimated on December 12 at thirty-five thousand by Herbert C. Shamo of the Society for the Prevention of Cruelty to Animals. It was recommended that the pests be eradicated by the use of a poisonous gas, but the plan was never carried out and the population continued to grow.

1935

The Sherwin-Williams Company took a practical interest in encouraging young singers by establishing the Metropolitan Auditions radio program. George A. Martin, president of the company, was also a member of the board of the Ohio Opera Association. During ten years on the air, twenty-five contestants each won a $1,000 prize, five won $500 scholarships, and several were given contracts with the Metropolitan Opera Company. The close tie between Cleveland and the Metropolitan was thus strengthened. Winners of the auditions appeared in a pre-opera concert in Cleveland.

The Great Lakes Exposition was suggested as an appropriate event to mark Cleveland's Centennial as a city, the incorporation dating back to 1836. Meetings to discuss plans were held, an organization was formed, and a general program was outlined. The prospectus stated that "Cleveland has for several years been so depressed by adverse circumstances that a forward-looking enterprise is needed to revive the spirit of civic pride that formerly characterized the city. Cleveland has resources equaled by few industrial centers, a location ideal for future development, and a civic leadership on the part of men who have expressed the feeling that a revival of co-ordinated action for community advancement is a pressing necessity." This exposition would not be confined to local interests nor would it make pretensions as a world's fair, but it would relate itself to the most important industrial and commercial district in America. Committees were appointed, money was raised, and Cleveland's greatest exposition project was assured.

Mickey Mouse won many new friends when his creator, Walt Disney, exhibited his pictures at the Cleveland Museum of Art on January 3.

Saluting the nation's automobile industry, the fourth annual *News* luncheon was held, January 12, in the banquet hall of the Public Auditorium. Among the speakers were Governor Paul V. McNutt of Indiana; Colonel Edward V. Rickenbacker, "ace of fliers and talkers"; Congressman Martin L. Sweeney, representing Governor George S. White; Harry J. Klingler, president of the Pontiac Motor Company; Governor-elect Martin L. Davey; and Allen L. Billingsley, representing the Cleveland Advertising Club. The Automobile Show was pronounced the most beautiful in the city's history, and the announcement was made that more than 100,000 Clevelanders were directly identified with the automobile business.

The Ohio Sales Tax became effective January 27, and under the direction of R. P. Barthalow, chief of the sales-tax section of the State Tax Commission, and Frank W. Koval, Cuyahoga County district manager, the first day in Cleveland's collection went smoothly. According to the law in Ohio, the customer paid three cents on the dollar. This system of taxation in the state was a source of bitter disputes, many feeling that it was an unfair burden on the taxpayer. Clevelanders moaned and paid, receiving colorful receipts in return.

The Ajax Building on St. Clair Avenue was torn down in March to make way for the Mall development, and the old Court House on the Square was razed to provide a much-needed parking space.

The Cleveland Medal for Public Service was awarded in April by the Chamber of Commerce to the late Austin Victor Cannon, "leader of profound learning of the law which he practised with high distinction; a man who counted no cost above the call of public duty."

East Technical High School students spent the entire week of April 12 studying the automobile. Principal Pliny W. Powers believed transportation was so important to modern life that every student in every class, shop, or academic subject should study some aspect of the motor car.

The Memorial Day Association was incorporated, April 12, to perpetuate the memory of ex-servicemen and women. Membership consisted of units of the Grand Army of the Republic, Spanish-American War, World War, and auxiliary veteran units. The president was Adrian G. Newcomb.

The Cleveland Restaurant Association on April 19 ordered apple pies sent to Congress to prove the superiority of Ohio apples.

The Cleveland Council of Girl Scouts, Inc., was formed, April 30, to

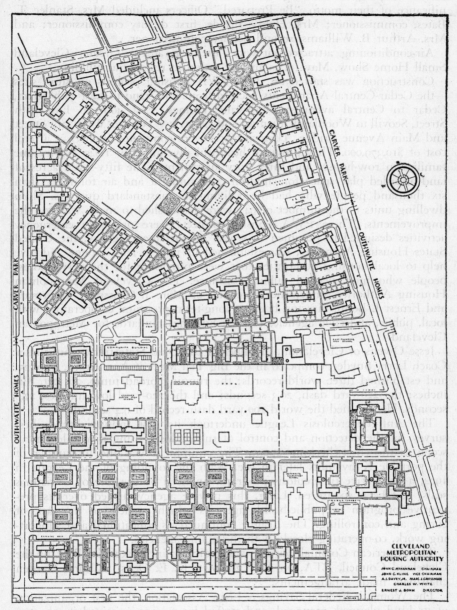

Carver Park and Outhwaite Homes housing projects as they appeared in 1943.

further its program teaching resourcefulness, good citizenship, and the significance of their motto, "Be Prepared." Officers included Mrs. Stanlee T. Bates, commissioner; Mrs. Henry Friede, first deputy commissioner; and Mrs. Arthur B. Williams, second deputy commissioner.

Air-conditioning attracted citywide attention at the Greater Cleveland Small Home Show, May 12, as an innovation in residential building.

Construction was started on three PWA housing projects on slum sites —the Cedar-Central Apartments, located from East 22nd to East 30th Street, Cedar to Central avenues; Outhwaite Homes, East 40th to East 46th Street, Scovill to Woodland Avenue; and Lakeview Terrace, West 28th Street and Main Avenue Bridge. These projects were completed in 1937 at a total cost of $10,379,000. They provided healthful dwellings for 1,849 low-income families in row-houses and three-story apartments. The fifty-seven acres of land afforded play space for children, and sunlight and air for more than six thousand people who had been living in substandard quarters. Slum dwelling units to the number of 943 were demolished to make way for the improvements. These PWA housing projects were primarily emergency activities designed to put men to work. A permanent agency, the United States Housing Authority, was established in 1937 to lend money and give help to local housing authorities that were providing for the very poorest people who most needed public assistance. The Cleveland Metropolitan Housing Authority, under the leadership of Marc J. Grossman, chairman, and Ernest J. Bohn, director, began a long-term program, co-operating with local, public, and civic agencies to raise housing standards for Metropolitan Cleveland.

Jesse Owens of Cleveland, a member of the Ohio State track team under Coach Larry Snyder, competed in the Big Ten Meet at Ann Arbor, May 25, and established three world records: the running broad jump, 26 feet, 8¼ inches; the 220-yard dash, 20.3 seconds; and the 220-yard low hurdles, 22.6 seconds. He also tied the world 100-yard dash record of 9.4 seconds.

The Anti-Tuberculosis League undertook its first industrial-type chest survey for the detection and control of tuberculosis, using a mobile fluoroscope as the chest-checking agent. The equipment was the forerunner of the portable X-ray units later in use. With the founding of the League in 1904, a preventive tuberculosis program, financed by the sale of Christmas seals, had been sponsored. Later, this private agency turned over its preventive program to public-health agencies which carried on the task of curing and controlling. The League continued its educational and supporting work, co-operating closely with the public agencies.

The American Colonial Garden was dedicated in Rockefeller Park by the Cleveland Council, PTA, on May 26. Mrs. K. E. Ochs, Cultural Garden chairman, made arrangements.

The Women's Federal Savings & Loan Association, the first organization of its kind planned, managed, and staffed by women, received its charter. It was founded by Judge Lillian M. Westropp and Clara E. Westropp. The association was launched in the Colonial Arcade in 1935, and opened its doors in the Superior Building, formerly the Crocker Block, at 320 Superior

Entering the inner harbor, the United States Coast Guard Station at right. PERRY CRAGG, CLEVELAND NEWS.

Ships from foreign nations in increasing numbers call at Cleveland, a world port. CARL McDOW.

Main Avenue Bridge, with Lakeview Terrace, a Government housing project, left in foreground. PERRY CRAGG, CLEVELAND NEWS.

Avenue, N. E., January 1, 1937. The building and site were purchased in 1944.

The Ohio State Skating Association, organized for the purpose of speed skating, included 180 active members and 100 non-skaters in its six member clubs: Brookside, Edgewater, Shaker, Sovereign, Lakewood, and Woodhill.

Janis Carter, who was graduated from Flora Stone Mather College in June, became a choir singer and attracted attention through her beauty, acting ability, and pleasing voice. She entered her Hollywood career in 1938 and soon became a star. Alan Baxter of East Cleveland was embarking on his theatrical career. His appearance in the *Fugitive* was followed by *The Trail of the Lonesome Pine,* and outstanding productions that led to stardom. Burgess Meredith, born in Cleveland, started a successful stage career in summer stock in 1929. His experience in the movies began in 1936 with his appearance in *Winterset.* Eleanor Parker was soon to prove her histrionic ability in important parts in Hollywood productions. She attended Shaw High School in East Cleveland and soon afterward was given a film contract by Warner Brothers.

Albert G. Dalton became the president of the Cleveland Federation of Labor, July 4.

The third All-Star Baseball Game was played in the Cleveland Stadium, July 8, the Americans defeating the Nationals by 4-1. The paid attendance was 69,812 and the receipts were $82,179.12.

Cleveland saw the moon's big show on July 16. Crowds watched the shadow of the earth on Luna, the first total eclipse of the moon visible to the United States since 1927, and the longest eclipse in a half century.

Old Home Week was observed July 22-27, with a program of interesting civic events, and many former Clevelanders returned to celebrate the city's birthday. The opening luncheon featured the introduction of the descendants of founders, the presentation of those living the greatest number of years in Cleveland, the singing of the Orpheus Male Chorus, and an address by Dr. Charles F. Thwing. The screen star, Colleen Moore, was a glamorous guest. A summer festival was given at the Stadium with a revival of *The Last Days of Pompeii,* accompanied by fireworks.

Economic conditions had delayed the erection of the new Huron Road Hospital building, but on August 13, it opened at the corner of Belmore and Terrace roads in East Cleveland. In 1946 it had a capacity of 350 beds, and an additional wing was planned.

President Roosevelt signed the Social Security Act on August 14. Designed to "give some measure of protection to the average citizen and his family against the loss of a job and against poverty-ridden old age," it was a major step in the administration's long-term "security" program.

All America and much of the world read with genuine grief of the death of Will Rogers and Wiley Post, killed on August 15 when their airplane fell in a fog fifteen miles from Point Barrow, Alaska. Rogers occupied a unique place in American history. He was a practical ambassador of good will for the United States when he traveled abroad; he was an honest interpreter of national and international affairs; he was a comedian on the stage and off, but his humor served to educate millions, while brightening life's serious pathway. Cleveland recalled the many visits to the city of this outstanding American.

The longest scoreless period in the history of the American League was witnessed, August 24, Willis Hudlin shutting out Philadelphia for fifteen innings and allowing but nine hits. The Indians in the fifteenth inning, with two out and one on base, won the game when Earl Averill drove the ball over the right-field wall at League Park. The game ended at 6:20 P.M., and five thousand fans were willing to accept late dinners.

Thousands of visitors were attracted to Cleveland by the National Air Races. Women flyers, including Amelia Earhart Putnam, entered several events. Leland Hayward led the field in the transcontinental derby, and Ben O. Howard won the Bendix trophy. The Ford tri-motor was the most spectacular plane at the races. Among other features, the Army's Flying Trapeze stunts thrilled spectators, and eighty-five thousand saw Harold Neumann win the Thompson Trophy race.

Citizenship training in the Cleveland public schools was studied by the committee on education of the Cleveland Chamber of Commerce. As a result, Chairman William E. Wickenden, president of Case School of Applied Science, delivered a prepared statement to the committee on citizenship training of the Board of Education, from which the following is quoted: "It is recommended that public education contribute as largely as possible to a citizenship that is informed, discriminating, and constructive in matters affecting the economic welfare of the community." With this idea in mind, the Cleveland Teachers' Federation arranged with the Cleveland Engineering Society to permit teachers of the sciences in the Cleveland schools to attend illustrated lectures by engineering experts and to go on inspection trips through some of Cleveland's leading industrial plants, thus witnessing the practical application of the theories they were teaching.

The Government was helping needy pupils in the city under the plan of the emergency educational program of the WPA. Pupils were to work twenty hours a month at useful jobs and to receive thirty cents an hour or a minimum of six dollars to balance their educational budgets.

The National Amateur Golf Championship was held at the Country Club, Lawson Little winning with brilliant play. In doing so, he set a record of thirty-one match-play victories in a row, capturing four consecutive major titles, two British and two American. The match was over when Little made an eagle-three on the sixteenth hole, defeating Walter Emery for the title. In his matches, he had scored thirty-six birdies and two eagles.

The seventh annual Eucharistic Congress met in Cleveland on September 21, the first to be held in the United States in half a decade. Assembled for four days, 500,000 Catholics from all walks of life honored the Sacrament. Alfred E. Smith of New York, Patrick Cardinal Hayes, and Bishop Joseph Schrembs were prominent in the significant event. The bishop was national director of the Eucharistic Congresses in the United States, and to him and to Auxiliary Bishop James A. McFadden was due the credit for bringing the Congress to the city. Cleveland had grown from a community of but eight or ten Catholic families in 1835 to a city which embraced more than a hundred Catholic churches with a vast number of communicants in 1935. The crowds that thronged Cleveland made it necessary to close the Public Auditorium after it was filled to capacity by successive programs. This meeting, probably the largest assembly of Catholics in the country, covered a week of ceremonies dedicated to worship and devotion. On September 26, nearly 125,000 worshipers met at the Stadium for midnight mass, the greatest crowd in the history of the amphitheater.

The first of the infamous Kingsbury Run torso murders was made public on September 23, and for three years similar murders followed until twelve were supposed to have been the work of the same individual. A decade later, the mystery of the murderer or murderers was still unsolved.

The Cleveland Osteopathic Hospital and Clinic were established in the remodeled Hall residence, East 32nd Street and Euclid Avenue, in October, 1935. Dr. C. V. Kerr was president of the Clinic and Dr. Richard A. Sheppard, chief of staff.

The Czech Garden, one of the largest in Rockefeller Park, was dedicated on October 6. Facing on a formal lawn were busts of Frantisek Palacky, historian; Jindrich Baar, author; Karel Havlicek, journalist; and the two great composers, Dvorak and Smetana. A large frieze, completed for the back wall of the garden, contained sixty figures depicting the progress of the Czech arts and sciences. On two great pillars, a dedicatory inscription, in English and in Czech, read, ". . . to our beloved Czech parents who by their teachings and by precept and example have established for us a high ideal of American citizenship."

The Cleveland Bloomer Girls became the softball champions of the nation on October 22. The team was sponsored by Gene and Glenn, popular comedians who enjoyed remarkable success in radio and on the stage in Cleveland.

Harold Hitz Burton, running as an Independent, defeated Harry L. Davis, Republican, and Ray T. Miller, Democrat, to become mayor. He selected cabinet members with little regard for politics. Alfred Clum as law director, G. A. Gesell, finance director, and Elliot Ness, safety director, met with immediate public approval. Miller continued to direct the activities of the local Democratic organization.

The Great Lakes Exposition Committee, which had been developing the many plans for the city's largest undertaking in the field of exhibitions, announced that the financing of the project had been assured by Cleveland business interests; that the Cleveland Building Trades Council volunteered wholehearted support; and that Cleveland architects pledged their full assistance in design and construction. In the phenomenal time of eighty days, beginning early in 1936, the ground was cleared; roads, bridges, and buildings were erected; and landscaping was completed.

A Cleveland safari was to aid science when Dr. George W. Crile and party started on November 15 for Africa. They brought back with them the brains, glands, and hearts of many animals for important research work. Some of the animals were later included in the interesting exhibit in the

Clinic Museum, known as the Sarah Tod McBride Museum. It was named for Mrs. Crile's niece, daughter of Herbert McBride.

The civic Automotive Luncheon, sponsored by the *News,* was held on November 23 in the Public Auditorium ballroom with a capacity attendance. Among the speakers were Melvin H. Purvis, the G-man who planned the capture of Dillinger, the gangster; Charles West of the United States Department of the Interior; and A. van Der Zee, general sales manager of the Dodge Brothers Corporation. The enthusiastic gathering opened one of the city's most successful automobile shows.

Mayor Harold H. Burton appointed Edward J. Schweid as traction commissioner on November 16, and together they undertook a study of the Cleveland Railway Company and Cleveland's transit problems. Transit in Cleveland had for many years been the subject of public criticism. The Van Sweringen interests controlled the Cleveland railway system through stock-voting agreements, and, after analysis by Commissioner Schweid, it was disclosed that the Metropolitan Utilities, Inc., top holding company of the Van Sweringens, was unable to insure the payment of 6 per cent as required by the stock-voting agreements. Thereupon, Mayor Burton issued an ultimatum to the Metropolitan Utilities, Inc., that unless control of the railway system was returned to the stockholders, so that the city could deal with the stockholders directly on a new franchise, it would no longer negotiate and would consider a public-ownership program. The Van Sweringen holding company then surrendered its control of the system and returned it to the stockholders. The company's negotiator was a well-known Cleveland attorney, Joseph C. Hostetler, who had plenipotentiary powers to work out a franchise for the company, subject to the directors' approval. Mayor Burton reposed full power in Commissioner Schweid to represent the city, and the City Council approved this designation, subject to approval of any final decision by the Council and the mayor. For five months these negotiators worked on the problem; and in May, 1941, they presented a plan for a new franchise under private ownership, subject to adequate public control.

The proposed settlement of the street-railway problem encompassed a plan designed to give low-cost transportation to Metropolitan Cleveland. Mayor Burton pronounced the plan extremely fair to stockholders, affording them an opportunity to salvage their investment while receiving a fair return on it. Most city officials accepted the proposal as the solution to thirty years of transit warfare. However, a minority group of company interests refused to accept the plan in principle, and, in an effort to be fair, the majority group in the company permitted three company directors to attempt to renegotiate the matter. The renegotiations ended without success, and service became chaotic. Finally, Commissioner Schweid recommended a plan for public ownership that would give to the shareholders the highest amount reasonably possible for their stock investment. This became an issue in the ensuing mayoralty campaign. Frank J. Lausche, who became mayor in 1942, requested Schweid to continue in office in order to complete the transaction. The commissioner remained until the intricate details of financing the acquisition of the system were completed, but later resigned and, in doing so, criticized the charter conditions under which municipal ownership was established. It was his view that the new administration's provisions for public control were wholly inadequate to insure satisfactory, low-cost transportation for Cleveland and to meet future requirements.

The campaign goal set for the Community Fund was $3,250,000. The amount raised was $3,097,620.04 with 466,680 subscribers. Ellwood H. Fisher was chairman. Dr. George E. Vincent and Dr. Royal S. Copeland were speakers at the organization dinner.

A bust of Mark Twain was unveiled in the American Garden of the Cultural Gardens on December 6, the pennies of the school children in the Cuyahoga County system making the statue possible. This first bust of an American in the gardens was the work of the Cleveland sculptor Frank L. Jirouch. The ceremonies closed a week of celebration of the one hundredth anniversary of Samuel L. Clemens' birth. A statue of John Hay was presented on the one hundredth anniversary of the great statesman's birth by B'nai B'rith in 1938.

From December 9 to December 24, the Finnish Industrial Art Exhibition, sponsored by the Finnish Government, was held at the Higbee Company. The collection consisted of fifteen thousand pieces of glass, pewter, ceramics, and textiles.

The series of *Press* Christmas Charity Shows was launched, December 12, in the Public Auditorium before a great audience. Each annual event was to be a revue of local talent—mostly young singers, dancers, and instrumentalists —with a famed Hollywood or radio star as headliner. The purpose of the undertaking was to raise money to provide food, clothing, and toys for needy children at Christmas-time. Among stars later presented were Jack Benny, Bob Hope, Frank Sinatra, Walter Pidgeon, Errol Flynn, Pat O'Brien, Abbott and Costello, and Danny Kaye. Each show drew capacity audiences and earned large sums for the worthy purpose of the newspaper.

1936

On New Year's Day, Cleveland began to observe its one hundredth anniversary as an incorporated city, with satisfaction over past glories and confidence in the future. Cleveland looked forward to several spectacular events, the Great Lakes Exposition, the Republican National Convention, the American Legion Convention, and the National Air Races.

The Board of Education "five-man bloc"—Ray C. Miller, Thomas J. Martin, John E. O'Donnell, Edwin J. Bradley, and Frank T. Jamieson—took control, January 10, and elected Miller president. Their domination of school policies was the subject of much public criticism. The electorate finally awoke to the realization that representation of partisan and selfish groups was contrary to the best interests of the pupils of the public schools and the community. From that time, the effort was made to elect school-board members for their ability, broad vision, and sincere purpose.

The big bass drum was pressed into emergency service on the stage of the Roxy burlesque house, 1882 East 9th Street, where it proudly told the audience in bold red letters that it belonged to "Cleveland, O., Kirk's Military Band." Howard Beaufait of the *News,* in recovering its time-honored past, found that back in 1873 it belonged to the Oriental Concert Band, organized "by a bunch of undisciplined youngsters." It was taken over about two years later by William Kirk, formerly with Dan Rice's Circus. He changed the name to Knights of Pythias Band, and later to Kirk's Military Band, which was in great demand for dances, at race tracks, in parks, and at public functions. It was the first band to march across the Superior Viaduct and the Detroit-Superior High Level Bridge. It was playing at the Pan-American Exposition in Buffalo when President McKinley was assassinated, and it opened Euclid Beach Park. Kirk died in 1922 and was succeeded by Henry Pfizenmayer as leader, but the organization disbanded, as old-time players passed on. Instruments disappeared with their owners, but one drum that had boomed for its first bandmaster was preserved by Pfizenmayer in the Musicians' Union headquarters on East 22nd Street. The emergency assignment became permanent, and the big drum continued to punctuate exits and entrances of spangled chorus girls and funny men.

While Cleveland business felt keenly the loss of John Long Severance, who died January 16, humanity and the youth of many lands had lost a friend and benefactor. He came of a distinguished Cleveland family, and was born in 1863, the son of Louis H. Severance. After he was graduated from Oberlin College in 1885, he entered the employ of the Standard Oil Company, where he pyramided his father's success pattern. He was an executive of the Cleveland Linseed Oil Company and an organizer of the American Linseed Oil Company, its successor. He was also the organizer and president of the Colonial Salt Company, a founder of the Linde Air Products Company, and a director of banks and industrial companies. Ever prominent in Cleveland's cultural development, he was president of the Cleveland Museum of Art and The Musical Arts Association supporting the Cleveland Orchestra. His interests in educational work extended to Presbyterian-mission endeavors in China, while in this country he was a trustee of Oberlin College, Auburn Seminary, and Western Reserve University. Projects that had been fostered by the father to advance the Christian church were supported by the son. Severance Hall, the most beautiful and practical of symphony homes, was a memorial to Elizabeth DeWitt Severance, his wife, and a reminder of a benevolent Cleveland family, traditionally devoted to purposeful giving.

With the opening of the second term, February 3, Cleveland College of Western Reserve University offered a plan of co-operative education for men and women taking the business-administration course. Students were to divide their time between paid jobs in business and college study.

Trackless trolleys went into operation on the Payne Avenue line.

Municipally controlled and supervised beaches included Gordon, Edgewater, Perkins, and East 140th Street or White City. Municipal recreational activities were arranged in the form of baseball, softball, and soccer. Approximately ten thousand players participated in the first two classifications. A representative soccer team was sent to Germany in August to compete in the Olympics, and the score was Berlin 1, Cleveland 0. The Works Progress Administration and government aid supplemented the depleted force administering municipal recreation, and many improvements were achieved that a lean city budget could not have accomplished. Eleven of seventeen recommended parcels of land suitable for use as emergency playgrounds were opened and operated. Taxpayers felt it was time to count the cost.

Cleveland ended the coldest twenty-nine-day period in the city's history on February 20, with an average of 13.17 degrees above zero. The Chagrin River then went on a rampage and inundated Horseshoe Glen. Dynamite broke the ice jam and saved homes.

The history of park-protection clubs, which exist in many Cleveland schools, began this year, when a group of students at Doan School, under the guidance of Ann Burgess, organized the first club. A creed was adopted and later meetings were held at the Cleveland Museum of Natural History. Arbor Day celebrations became annual events.

The James F. Lincoln Arc Welding Foundation was established to stimulate scientific interest, research, and study in furtherance of the arc-welding industry. The breadth of its achievement is indicated by the founding of welding reference libraries in 235 colleges and universities throughout the world. New products and new developments contributed not only to the industry, but to metal-working in general.

The exhibition of the Dutch artist, Vincent Van Gogh, was shown at the Cleveland Museum of Art from March 25 to April 19. The paintings, which filled several galleries, were shown under the auspices of the New York Museum of Modern Art. Brilliantly colored pictures of the Dutch painter, who had come under the influence of French impressionism in the latter part of the Nineteenth Century, were the subject of many vigorous discussions among Clevelanders.

The first public announcement of "fluorescent lighting" was made by engineers of the Nela Park laboratories in East Cleveland on March 26.

The participation of the United States Government in the Great Lakes Exposition was assured by the passage on April 21 of a bill authorizing the expenditure of $275,000. Shortly after, President Roosevelt invited Canada to have a part in the exposition.

The Cleveland Medal for Public Service was awarded, April 21, by the Chamber of Commerce to Harris Creech for many public services rendered over a long period of years; and to Major General Dudley J. Hard for distinguished military service, resulting in many essential improvements in the organization and discipline of the National Guard of Ohio.

Gala features of the Great Lakes Exposition were nearing completion. The Parade of the Years, the impressive railroad show, was under construction by Producer Edward Hungerford; the S. S. Moses Cleaveland, anchored at the shore, was to be the home of officials and a club for sponsors; the Streets of the World were being laid out as a colorful feature for nationality presentations, with a great outdoor stage where shows were to be given day and night. The Globe Theater, which would feature early-day English dramas, and other popular attractions were taking form.

The first twelve-block strip of the Lakeland Freeway was opened from East 9th Street, and the demand grew for further east-and-west highway improvements along Lake Erie.

Erie C. Hopwood was admitted to the journalistic Hall of Fame at Ohio State University in May, eight years after his death. Two other *Plain Dealer* men were also elected: Artemus Ward in 1931, and Elbert H. Baker in 1938.

Lawnfield, home of President James A. Garfield at Mentor, twenty-five miles east of Public Square, became the property of the Western Reserve Historical Society on May 20, by deed of the heirs. Through the efforts of the Lake County Chapter of the society, a ten-thousand-dollar fund was provided by act of the Legislature to renovate the property. Other financial help was given by the Garfield heirs, the society, and friends to preserve the home as a shrine and museum. Behind the house was erected a replica of the log cabin in which President Garfield was born. The original cabin, located at the southwest corner of what became SOM Center Road and Jackson Street, Orange Township, Cuyahoga County, had burned about 1850.

The silver jubilee of the founding of Cleveland polo witnessed many tournament matches and title-defense games between May 24 and September 13. Weekend games were attended by large crowds at Hunting Valley and Halfred Farm. Popularity of the game brought into use Walter C. White's beautiful field at Circle W Farms, John Sherwin's Waite Hill Farm, and two fields at Kirtland. Among the ranking players were Henry, Fred, Alexander (Sandy), and Lewis Baldwin, Tom and Mike White, John and Francis Sherwin, Courtney Burton, David S. Ingalls, Otto Knutsen, Dan Ford, Dan R. Hanna, Severance A. Millikin, and the Firestones of Akron.

The Municipal Collection of Cleveland Art, comprising nearly three hundred pictures displayed in the Music Hall of the Public Auditorium and in the City Hall, was dedicated. Established by an advisory board on Cleveland art, composed of prominent local artists and citizens with Edward C. Daoust as chairman, the collection, owned by the City of Cleveland, was limited to pictures that depicted Greater Cleveland and its activities. The plan was initiated by Hugo E. Varga, director of parks and public property.

The last GAR member to ride a horse as grand marshal of the Memorial Day parade in Cleveland, Nicholas Weidenkopf, remained in the saddle for more than an hour and a half, reviewing the marchers. The ninety-four-year-old veteran was astride the well-behaved police horse, Sambo; and although riding was difficult, Weidenkopf's pride and determination won the battle.

The Republican Party came to Cleveland early in June, and nominated Governor Alfred M. Landon of Kansas for President and Colonel Frank Knox for Vice President. On June 10, Senator Frederick Steiwer delivered the keynote speech, and, later, former President Herbert Hoover made a vigorous attack on the New Deal. John Hamilton placed Landon's name before the undemonstrative convention.

William G. Bahner succeeded Earl J. Bryan as Cuyahoga County superintendent of schools and Bryan became assistant superintendent of Cleveland public schools.

The Great Lakes Exposition opened on June 28 when Marguerite Bacon, direct descendant of Moses Cleaveland, cut the ribbon at the main entrance while bands played, choruses sang, barkers barked, swimmers splashed, and hundreds of exhibits and shows welcomed 61,206 visitors. Among the speakers at the opening were Secretary of Commerce Daniel C. Roper, Mayor Burton and Senator Robert J. Bulkley.

Early in July, the Great Lakes Exposition was in full swing. William M. Milliken, director of the Cleveland Museum of Art, brought famous art collections for exhibition, including the International Exhibit of the Carnegie Institute. A twelve-million-dollar collection of masterpieces, also shown in connection with the exposition, was known as the Twentieth Anniversary Exhibit of the museum. Special exposition attractions followed one another in rapid succession. The Horticultural Building and its lovely Horticultural Gardens, designed by A. Donald Gray and conducted under the auspices of the Garden Center of Greater Cleveland, attracted gardeners from distant points; the industrial exhibits drew many buyers; the Streets of the World contributed an international flavor; and celebrities came to Cleveland every day of the week. Visitors were impressed with the seven stately pylons marking the main entrance, the mammoth Sherwin-Williams shell with its symphony concerts and other attractions, Radioland and Hall of the Great Lakes in the Public Auditorium. Inspiration blended with education in the attractive Ohio Building, Garfield Memorial Cabin, County Civic Exhibits Building, Model Homes, Court of Presidents, Marine Plaza, Western Reserve University Building, the spacious Hall of Progress housing the Government exhibit and industrial displays, the huge Automotive Building with cars of the past and present; and the building of the *Christian Science Monitor.* Visitors returned again and again to the spectacular open-air Marine Theater with its swimming exhibitions and style shows, Porcelain Enamel Hall, Newspaper Headquarters Building, Firestone Building with its fountains and farm, Higbee Tower, Florida National Exhibits Building, and the Open Air Exhibits Building. The Amusement Zone featured exhibits, restaurants, and promenades. Byrd's South Pole ship, the submarine *S-49,* and a comprehensive midway were popular attractions, and a great fireworks display closed each day's events. Cleveland entertained as never before.

"America's most distinguished day train," the *Mercury,* made its inaugural run between Cleveland and Chicago, via Toledo and Detroit, July 15. From the tremendous high-speed locomotive to the "turtle back" observation car, this streamlined, air-conditioned addition to New York Central rolling stock provided smooth travel in an atmosphere suggestive of a luxurious club. Detroit was now only three hours away, and the trip from Detroit to Chicago was less than four hours.

Inspired by the desire to perpetuate an accurate record of life in Cleveland's early days, and to interest the people of the city in the pioneer background of their community, a group of civic-minded citizens organized Dunham Tavern, Inc., a subsidiary of the Society of Collectors, to preserve the famous inn, and on July 15 held a tea in honor of its restoration. Located at 6709 Euclid Avenue, the tavern was the oldest building in its original state on Cleveland's famous avenue. Among those most interested in maintaining the historic landmark were Mrs. Benjamin P. Bole, Laurence H. Norton, Abram Garfield, Mrs. Windsor T. White, Julia Raymond, A. Donald Gray, I. T. Frary, and Harold T. Clark. In the early 1930s, A. Donald Gray, landscape architect, had leased the tavern for business offices, and through his persistence, influenced others to save it from destruction.

The Townsend Old Age Pension followers—thousands of them—met in the Public Auditorium in July. Norman Thomas, a guest speaker, surprisingly called their efforts futile; but Dr. Francis E. Townsend bolstered the hope of the members that their ideals might eventually be achieved.

The Jewish Community Council, composed of 160 affiliated organizations devoted to community relations, was founded this year. Ezra Z. Shapiro was president and Harry I. Barron, executive director. The Council represented every Jewish viewpoint and was the official voice of the Jewish community. Religious, welfare, educational, fraternal, and social groups were represented in this unified effort to build a finer city.

Akron Day, August 2, witnessed a record crowd at the Great Lakes Exposition. There were many special features, and the Firestone Farm proved a particular drawing card. At night, two balloons representing Akron and Cleveland flew from the Stadium; and later, over northeastern Pennsylvania, the Akron Goodyear entry appropriately won the race with a flight of 297 miles.

After startling the world's athletic and sports fans a year before by making track history at Ann Arbor, the youthful Jesse Owens once again brought international fame to Cleveland when he captured three Olympic records in Berlin. He received his first medal for running the 100-meter dash in 10.3 seconds; the following day he leaped 26 feet, $5\frac{3}{4}$ inches, setting a broad-jump record; and he won the 200-meter race in 20.7 seconds. Owens became a four-event Olympic prize winner when he ran in the 400-meter relay race with Ralph Metcalfe, Foy Draper, and Frank Wyckoff to a world record of 39.8 seconds. Although the coveted Olympic trophies belonged to Owens, they were also a tribute to Charles Riley, Fairmount Junior High coach, who discovered the runner, gave him his fundamental training, and launched him on his famous career.

Ted Kara was captain of the United States boxing team in the 1936 Olympics. He reached the quarter finals in the featherweight class. Eight years later, as a lieutenant of the Army Air Forces, he was killed on his fifth mission from a base in the Admiralty Islands. Jackie Wilson reached the finals in the bantamweight boxing class in the 1936 Olympics, but lost the decision to Ulderico Sergo. He had won the AAU bantamweight crown and was victorious in his first four matches in the Olympic games.

Long-needed improvements planned for the Cuyahoga River were undertaken by the city and Federal Government. Based upon the estimate of army engineers, the plan called for an expenditure of $13,781,417. The following year, the program was inaugurated along lines recommended by the Chamber of Commerce through Vice President O. A. Reynolds, who had given expert study to the problem. The plan called for the widening, straightening, and deepening of the river channel, the replacement and repair of bridges, and the extension of the navigable channel as far as the New York Central high level viaduct. By the mid-1940s substantial progress had been made, and approval of the War Department and the Rivers and Harbors Committee of Congress ensured a more comprehensive program estimated to cost $23,000,000.

President Franklin D. Roosevelt visited the Great Lakes Exposition on August 14, and was given an enthusiastic reception.

At a spirited convention of the National Union for Social Justice in the Public Auditorium, Father Charles E. Coughlin was elected president.

Robert William "Bob" Feller, an Iowa high-school student, made his debut in baseball by striking out eight members of the St. Louis Cardinals in three innings in an exhibition game. He struck out fifteen members of the Browns on August 23, and seventeen of the Athletics on September 13, surpassing the American League record and equaling the National League mark established by the famous Dizzy Dean. The seventeen-year-old farm boy was the sensation of the year.

The opening feature of the National Air Races, held in Los Angeles, was the Bendix Trophy Race won by Louise Thaden in a Beechcraft plane. The Thompson Trophy Race was won by a Frenchman, Michel Detroyat, breaking Jimmie Doolittle's 1932 record by averaging 264.26 m.p.h.

A new attendance record was established at the Great Lakes Exposition on Labor Day when 125,192 visitors enjoyed the special features arranged for the holiday. Each Sunday vesper services were held in the great Sherwin-Williams shell, in which were presented America's leading symphony orchestras and other important musical events.

The American Legion came to Cleveland in national convention, played, had a few serious meetings, elected Harry W. Colmery national commander, and marched on September 20, 70,000 strong, for eleven and a half hours before 500,000 cheering citizens. The dedication of the American Legion Peace Garden of the Cultural Gardens was a feature of the convention. The garden included a Peace Monument unveiled by the Honorable Paul V. McNutt. One section of the garden was given over to the nation and the other to the states of the Union. The dedication was marked by the mingling of soil from foreign nations and from American shrines.

Charles A. Otis, William T. Higbee, and S. J. Kelly, three members of old Brooks School, were present, September 23, at the dedication of a tablet to the memory of General Clarence Ransom Edwards, the school's first major, who became a famous war hero. Mrs. Charles A. Otis, sister of General Edwards, was also present. The ceremony took place before the Ohio Building at the Great Lakes Exposition, and the memorial was presented by members of the Yankee Division of the American Expeditionary Forces, the famous body of soldiers he had commanded.

Mrs. Sophia Strong Taylor, individualist and prominent Clevelander, died at her home in Bratenahl, September 30. A dominant figure in the mercantile life of the city, she was also a leader in religious and philanthropic activities. Following her husband's death in 1892, she served as president of William Taylor Son & Company until 1935, when she became chairman of the board. She gave liberally to Presbyterian missions, the Community Fund, and other philanthropies. A large part of her estate in Bratenahl had been converted to homes for crippled and needy children.

The Great Lakes Exposition concluded its first season on October 8, when General Chairman Dudley S. Blossom presented a financial report, urging continuance of the project in 1937. The attendance had totaled four million, and General Manager Dickey announced to the trustees that educational features would be emphasized during the next year.

A man was elected for the first time as a Council chairman of the Cleveland PTA, October 11. He was Mark C. Schinnerer, chairman of school education, and later superintendent of Cleveland schools.

The Presidential candidates visited Cleveland in October. Alfred M. Landon came to the city on the 12th, filled the Public Auditorium and Music Hall, and told seventeen thousand followers about his political platform. Three days later, thousands of Clevelanders stood for more than an hour in a drizzling rain to hear President Roosevelt's political speech made from the rear platform of his train on the lakefront. In November the President was re-elected for a second term in a political landslide.

Eugenio Cardinal Pacelli, Papal Secretary of State, the highest Vatican official ever to visit the United States, was received at the Cleveland Airport by clergy and laity of the Catholic Church on October 25. Cardinal Pacelli was crossing the continent by plane. Among those honoring him during the stop of only a few minutes were Bishop Joseph Schrembs, Auxiliary Bishop James A. McFadden and others prominent in the clergy, the first Ohio brigade of the Knights of St. John and the brigade band, the ladies auxiliary of the brigade in costume, and Franciscan monks from Our Lady of Angels Monastery in their brown habits. The Cardinal was wearing the robes of his office as Bishop Schrembs greeted him with the kiss of peace.

A second Recreation Survey was completed by the Cleveland Foundation. It influenced better planning of additional facilities, better-selected and better-trained personnel for the city's recreation division, a more varied and interesting program, and a greater centralization of administration responsibility. The Foundation made gifts to the city for building and equipping certain model playgrounds, and recommended a constructive program to advance recreational services in the community.

Radio station WJAY was purchased, October 30, by the United Broadcasting Company and merged with WHK in the Terminal Tower. Call letters were changed to WCLE in 1937, when the station began carrying the programs of the Mutual Broadcasting System. In 1945 WCLE moved to Akron, where it became Station WHKK.

The opening of Cleveland's Automobile Show, November 21, was marked by the annual *News* luncheon held in the Statler ballroom. A capacity audience heard W. F. Hufstader, vice president of the Buick Motor Company, and Robert L. Ripley of "Believe-It-or-Not" fame. Donald Novis contributed vocal numbers. A feature of the automobile show was a great turntable upon which popular car models were shown.

O. P. Van Sweringen died in his sleep on November 23, at the age of fifty-seven years, while en route to New York, and the nation as well as Cleveland was stirred. Jesse Jones, RFC chairman, said that "O.P. owned America's most brilliant mind." A local newspaper, referring to the great scope of his operations, said that he worked with iron, steel, and concrete rather than with words. A short time earlier, his brother, M. J. Van Sweringen, had passed away. Their advance had been halted by adverse economic conditions, and with their associates they had suffered heavy financial losses. The lives of the two Van Sweringens conspicuously illustrated the fact that men reared in poor circumstances in America could achieve, within a few years, fabulous success.

The campaign goal set for the Community Fund was $3,300,000, and the amount raised was $3,333,669.72, with 496,653 subscribers.

The Cleveland public schools were attracting wide attention. The John Adams High School Orchestra gave a request program at the Metropolitan Opera House, New York City, before the Music Educators National Conference. West Technical High School was the first high school in the nation to conduct an auto-driving class. A citywide examination for tuberculosis was conducted in the schools, and twenty-five thousand pupils were examined.

Cleveland in 1936 won the reputation of having many excellent athletes. Jesse Owens, through his victories in the Berlin Olympics, gained the title of "the world's greatest living athlete." Jackie Wilson, Cleveland flyweight, made the Olympic team but was defeated in the finals by Sergo of Italy. Later he easily defeated his Olympic conqueror. Helen Perry, fifteen-year-old East High junior, representing the Women's Swimming Association, won the women's national junior backstroke championship in Buffalo. Joe Goudreau of the Central YMCA became the national junior handball champion, the fifth Clevelander to win the title. The national amateur women's softball championship was won by the team of the National Screw & Manufacturing Company, whose women's bowling team also won the championship. The Cleveland Fisher Foods gave the city its fourth National Baseball Federation championship in six years, finishing first in the tourney sponsored by the Great Lakes Exposition.

Ambrose Swasey, on his ninetieth birthday, December 19, went to New York to receive the Hoover Medal from the four engineering societies of America. Asked what he expected to see with the new two-hundred-inch telescope in which he had shown keen interest, he replied, "I can tell you one thing they will not see with it; they will not see over the edge."

During the past decade, a number of Clevelanders were winning attention for their writings. Everett Rhodes Castle, with his short stories based upon business and politics, was appearing in leading American periodicals. Textbooks written by Dr. Emile B. deSauze, director of the foreign-language department of the Cleveland Public Schools, were helping students of French throughout the United States; Dr. James Holly Hanford and Mrs. Hanford were attracting public interest, Dr. Hanford through his contributions to professional literature, and Mrs. Hanford through her short stories.

Dr. Matthew Luckiesh, physicist and director of the Lighting Research Laboratory of General Electric Company, was developing the "science of seeing," and, with the aid of Frank K. Moss, was giving the world new and valuable ideas concerning lighting and the use of eyes; and Dr. Dayton C. Miller, distinguished professor of physics at Case School of Applied Science, was giving to science his important findings with relation to sound. Charles S. Brooks took his place as a leading American essayist by adding several publications to his list of delightful books; Herman Fetzer, under the name of Jake Falstaff, was increasing the number of his followers with whimsical verse and appealing humor; Charles Alden Seltzer was adding to the list of his popular works of fiction; and Marie Emily Gilchrist's poems were becoming widely known.

Francis Hobart Herrick added to his list of books on bird life; Gary Cleveland Meyers was giving counsel on building personality in children; Clarence Stratton, English professor, was helping prospective writers with sound advice; Frank N. Wilcox, artist, graphically told the story of Ohio's Indian trails; Agnes B. Young, stage designer, described the recurring cycles of fashion; and Charles Abel made professional photography an interesting subject in an authoritative book.

1937

Fenn College acquired the twenty-one-story skyscraper at Euclid and East 24th Street. This beautiful new building, erected on the site of Rufus K. Winslow's stone residence for the ill-fated National Town and Country Club, became the main college building containing administrative offices, library, gymnasium, swimming pool, dormitories, and student social quarters, as well as many classrooms. Since the opening of the new home, Fenn enrollment jumped from 3,000 students to nearly 5,000 in the 1940s. Although the college pioneered in business administration, it offered many types of education, including co-operative programs in engineering, business administration, and arts and sciences. Research and study services were provided for industries and business and civic organizations. Much of the progress of the college was due to the high purposes and vision of its president and director, Dr. C. V. Thomas, who had been associated with the YMCA since 1916 and was president of Fenn College from 1930. Upon his death in 1947 Dr. Edward Hodnett was made president.

The Regional Association of Cleveland, a non-profit organization, was launched in January, concerning itself with "the development of comprehensive regional plans for land use in Cleveland and its environs; the promotion of better housing conditions for the people of Cuyahoga County, and the exercise of governmental powers in respect of land use and housing conditions." The association was non-political and non-partisan, and it co-operated with other organizations and with governmental agencies throughout the Cleveland region. It correlated research, surveys, and inventories by others; and instituted or conducted such additional or original studies as were required to develop regional planning of maximum permanent benefit to the community as a whole. From its launching, the association studied zoning revisions, housing problems, and ways and means of abating the smoke nuisance. It interested itself in problems relating to the lakefront, in making highway studies, in offering a consulting service to near-by cities and smaller communities, in public education relating to planning and in organizing a geodetic survey. The association established a planning and housing center on the Mall where a library of maps and literature was maintained and where other facilities were provided for interested agencies and organizations. Literature of educational character was published from time to time dealing with the planning problems of the region and how to solve them. Since its establishment, Abram Garfield was president; Leyton E. Carter and Paul L. Feiss, vice presidents; and Stanley M. Buckingham, treasurer. Ernest J. Bohn, director, headed the staff, with John T. Howard, city planner, as associate.

American and French dignitaries at Paris joined on February 11 in unveiling a memorial to Myron T. Herrick, famous United States ambassador to France. The bronze bust, mounted on a marble base, was appropriately located in the Place des États-Unis.

Thelma Votipka, graduate of South High School this year, was attracting favorable attention for the power and rich quality of her voice. She was later signed by the Metropolitan Opera Company and won national fame.

The Art Gravure Corporation of Ohio was founded in February at 1845 Superior Avenue, the Plain Dealer Publishing Company owning a majority interest. The plant was the only one of its kind between New York and Chicago, and in it were printed rotogravure sections of the *Plain Dealer, Buffalo Courier Express, Pittsburgh Press, Youngstown Vindicator, Akron Beacon Journal, Toledo Blade,* and *St. Paul Pioneer Press.*

Francis Fleury Prentiss, industrialist and philanthropist, died on April 1, and Cleveland lost one of its most useful citizens. He had given millions of dollars to worthy institutions; and, for three decades prior to his death, was a participant in important movements designed to further Cleveland's civic and cultural interests. Born in Vermont in 1858 and educated in Winona, Minnesota, he came to Cleveland to make his way in business. In 1880 he and Jacob D. Cox formed a partnership, forerunner of the Cleveland Twist Drill Company. There were ten men in the factory at the start, but the company grew until it was one of the largest in its field in the world, with a huge export business. Prentiss became president and general manager, and at the time of his death was chairman of the board. He served as president of the Chamber of Commerce, and his days were so full that he appeared at his desk sharply at seven every morning. He was chairman of the Cleveland Committee of the National Education Association Convention in 1908 and of the first Cleveland Industrial Exposition the following year. He gave leadership to many enterprises, including Hiram House, of which he was president for thirty years; and he served as trustee of both Western Reserve University and Case School of Applied Science, vice president of the Western Reserve Historical Society, president of the Cleveland School of Art, and trustee of Andrews School for Girls, Willoughby, while his business affiliations were many. His wife, Mrs. Elisabeth Severance Prentiss, joined him in numerous important activities.

Cleveland celebrated John P. Green Day on April 4 to commemorate the ninety-second birthday of John P. Green, son of a slave, able lawyer, state representative, and state senator from Cleveland. The distinguished citizen was killed on September 1, 1940, when he stumbled and fell under an automobile.

After a lapse of four years the Metropolitan Opera Company returned to Cleveland under the auspices of the Northern Ohio Opera Association, presenting on opening night *Le Coq d'Or* and *Cavalleria Rusticana.* It was said that New York never interested a greater assembly of stars, the casts including Helen Jepson, Lily Pons, Rosa Ponselle, Bruna Castagna, Irra Petina, Gladys Swarthout, Richard Crooks, Lauritz Melchior, Ezio Pinza, and many other talented artists. Among the productions were *Faust, Aïda, Lohengrin, Carmen,* and *Il Trovatore.* Thomas L. Sidlo had become general chairman of the Opera association.

The Cleveland Medal for Public Service was awarded by the Chamber of Commerce on April 20 to Dudley S. Blossom, "patron of musical arts and champion of humanitarian enterprises, for successful achievements in the civic and philanthropic undertakings of Cleveland." The medal was also given to William A. Stinchcomb as "a testimonial of the regard in which he is held by his fellow citizens for exemplifying to them the highest type of the career man in public service"; and to Dan Freeman Bradley, D.D., "in recognition of thirty-two years of distinguished leadership as a farsighted clergyman and public-spirited citizen of Cleveland."

An audience of 2,000 in the ballroom of the Public Auditorium on May 2 saw Cleveland's reception of 104 German school children who came in exchange for students from the city who went to Germany. The visiting boys and girls were greeted by the young people with whom they were to live for six weeks while attending school and studying life in America. The guest group arrived by bus from Buffalo, and Mayor Harold H. Burton voiced the city's welcome.

A memorial World War cannon was dedicated on May 3 at Superior and Payne avenues and East 12th Street, as a memorial to Casimir Pulaski, "father of the American Cavalry." One hundred thousand Clevelanders attended the ceremony. The liberty-loving Polish general, who died in 1779, served brilliantly in General Washington's army in command of the cavalry.

Inspired by the Toronto Skating Club Carnival, a small group of Clevelanders interested in the sport had formed the Cleveland Skating Club. Their numbers increased rapidly and outgrew the Elysium. In the spring of this year the organization expanded and purchased the property, clubhouse, and other facilities of the Cleveland Tennis and Racquet Club, 2500 Kemper Road. This was the first private figure-skating organization in the

United States to own its building. Most exciting of all events was the annual Carnival presented at the club in March. An elaborate and gala program featured current professional figure-skating champions and top-ranking amateurs, among them Richard Button, Barbara Scott, John Lettengarber, and Yvonne Sherman.

Cream-colored automobiles inscribed "Accident Prevention Squad" began patrolling Cleveland on May 10, manned by the first eighteen traffic graduates of the Cleveland Police Academy.

An impressive service honoring the memory of Francis Fleury Prentiss was held at Severance Hall on May 16. Newton D. Baker gave the principal eulogy, referring to Prentiss as "the splendidly helpful." Dr. William E. Wickenden and Dr. Winfred G. Leutner participated in the ceremony.

Quietly, on May 23, life ebbed away from the frail form of John D. Rockefeller, one of the world's richest men, at his winter home, "The Casements," Ormond Beach, Florida. He was born at Richford, New York, July 8, 1839, the son of thrifty and resourceful William A. Rockefeller. As a lad, young John D. learned the value of work, the wisdom of saving money, and the importance of practical trading. The family moved to Cleveland in 1853, and he entered the High School, later called Central. At the age of fifteen, he became a member of the Erie Street Baptist Church (later Euclid Avenue Baptist Church), thus forming an association that became deep-rooted and claimed his earnest support. Young Rockefeller financed a commercial course at E. G. Folsom's Commercial College (later Spencerian School) in the Rouse Block. Having graduated in August, 1855, he searched until late fall for a job, when Hewitt & Tuttle, commission merchants, hired him on trial as a bookkeeper. On the last day of December he was rewarded with the princely sum of fifty dollars for services to date. His business experience, although difficult and ill-paying, was of inestimable value to the young man who quickly demonstrated his ability and learned to deal skillfully with men. At the age of nineteen, his father ordered him to build a house. John D. drew the plans, found the materials and a builder, and the red-brick structure on Cheshire Street was the family home for many years. The Titusville oil rush in 1859 captured Rockefeller's interest, and he turned from the commission business to oil refining. Through efficient management, wise investments, and careful spending, he and his associates gradually bought up struggling competitors and stabilized the business. In 1870 the million-dollar Standard Oil Company was organized. His system of organization and his policy of strict economy proved immensely profitable, and soon the company was not only providing employment for thousands of workers, but Cleveland had become the capital of petroleum production. In his giving, John D. Rockefeller was as systematic and prudent as he was when his weekly wage as a clerk was $4.50. He investigated all requests for financial aid and dedicated his great ability for organization and his vast fortune to the most worthy projects. Among his greatest benevolent enterprises was the University of Chicago to which he ultimately gave thirty-five million dollars, firmly believing that his "co-operation" was the best way in which he could help men to help themselves. Constantly seeking to contribute to broad programs advancing the interests of humanity, he established the Rockefeller Institute for Medical Research in 1901 and the General Education Board in 1902. Of untold benefit to many organizations and to far-flung institutional programs was the great Rockefeller Foundation, chartered in 1913 "to promote the well being of mankind throughout the world." The Laura Spelman Rockefeller Memorial, in memory of his wife, was established in 1918 and later merged with the Rockefeller Foundation. Laura C. Spelman, daughter of H. B. Spelman, and John D. Rockefeller were married in 1864. For some years they made their home at Euclid and Case avenues, moving later to lovely Forest Hills, which became one of Greater Cleveland's beautiful parks. Although Rockefeller spent much of his later life in New York City, he enjoyed playing golf on his Cleveland estate, attending the Euclid Avenue Baptist Church, and contributing to its welfare. The name of John D. Rockefeller, one of the world's greatest philanthropists, endures in Rockefeller Park and in his many generous gifts to Cleveland, in the worldwide Standard Oil Company, and in benefactions totaling more than five hundred million dollars to colleges, churches, and humanitarian institutions that will advance the welfare of humanity over the years. His remains were brought to Cleveland, May 27, for quiet burial beside his wife and his mother, Eliza Davison Rockefeller, in Lake View Cemetery.

The Chamber of Commerce, under the direction of President A. C. Ernst, started a Cleveland Advancement Program by which ideas, men, and money were to be mobilized for the benefit of the businesses and the people of Cleveland. Many committees were formed, and suggestions were invited from businessmen, 1,300 being received. A membership campaign was launched, and a substantial fund was raised to carry out a broad program. Walter I. Beam was made executive vice president. Officers at this time included A. C. Ernst, president; Frederick C. Crawford, first vice president; F. J. Andre, second vice president; Sidney B. Congdon, treasurer; Munson Havens, secretary. New activities were undertaken, membership grew and business was stimulated as the long-range plan of advancement developed. Beam had a wide experience in management and financial matters in both governmental and private business fields. Parker Hill, vice president, who had long been an official of the Chamber, was staff executive for the Committee on Taxation and Bureau of Municipal Research and was also executive of the Military Committee. Oliver A. Reynolds, who had gained valuable experience as secretary of the Chamber of Commerce at Dubuque, Iowa, and through association with the United States Board of Engineers and the United States Shipping Board, was staff executive to the Committee on River and Harbor Development. Among other heads of departments were Clifford Gildersleeve, commissioner of Industrial Development; J. Jones Hudson, executive of the Education Committee; Spencer D. Corlett, manager of the Legislative Department; B. T. Franklin, manager of the Membership Department; William E. Tousley, manager of Municipal Research; J. W. Vanden Bosch, statistician of the Statistical Department, and Andrew H. Brown, commissioner of the Transportation Department.

St. Peter's Lutheran Church found new opportunities for service and expansion this year when it moved to Shaker Heights, where a beautiful sandstone edifice was erected at 18000 South Moreland Boulevard. Cemented in its wall were fragments taken from five of the world's famous churches: Martin Luther's historic St. Mary's in Wittenberg, the mother church of Lutheranism; Church of the Holy Sepulchre, Jerusalem; Church of the Annunciation, Nazareth; Constantine the Great's Church of St. John the Baptist, Sebaste; and the Crusader Church of Dominus Flevit on the Mount of Olives. The Rev. Arthur F. Katt began his long pastorate in 1925.

The Cleveland Industrial Union Council of the Committee for Industrial Organization was formed under the leadership of Beryl Peppercorn. The CIO had a membership of sixty-five thousand workers in the County. In a decade, the membership was said to approximate a hundred thousand.

The Great Lakes Exposition opened its second season on May 29, with the 150-acre fair grounds made even more interesting than in 1936. New features were destined to attract national attention. The Making of a Nation was the great central educational display, depicting the growth of America. Located in the Lakeside Exhibition Hall, it showed a vast topographical model of the Great Lakes district, while on the walls were colorful murals. Nearby were cultural, industrial, and scientific exhibits that indicated American progress. The Aquacade with its Billy Rose production thrilled audiences in the five-thousand-seat theater-restaurant. On a floating stage were given performances of rare beauty with the nation's leading swimmers participating. Winterland, a huge ice-skating spectacle, was a popular attraction.

Charles Lathrop Pack, internationally known forestry conservationist and first executive-committee chairman of The Cleveland Trust Company, died on June 14 in New York City at the age of eighty years. It was largely through his foresight that the bank secured land at the corner of Euclid Avenue and East 9th Street for its main office. From 1916 to 1922 he was president of the American Forestry Association. His books were widely read, 7,300,000 copies of his garden and forestry primers having been distributed free throughout the nation. He organized the National War Garden Commission which inspired the planting of three million gardens. Many honors were conferred upon him by colleges, societies, and nations.

Dr. Charles G. Abbot, one of the world's foremost scientists, installed a solar boiler at the Great Lakes Exposition in connection with indoor educational displays. He used incandescent lamps in place of the sun, and with them developed a high steam pressure in the solar boiler in about a minute's time. The eminent scientist's talks were a source of great interest for thousands of exposition visitors.

The Federal Music Project supplemented the city's free band concerts by presenting symphony performances of light and grand opera.

It was announced on August 10 that James H. Knight of Cleveland had led all air-mail pilots in hours and distance flown with 17,500 hours, the total distance being 2,250,000 miles.

Dr. Charles Franklin Thwing, president emeritus of Western Reserve

University, died on August 29, and Cleveland lost one of its foremost educators. Born in Maine in 1853, he had been graduated at Phillips Academy, Andover, Massachusetts, in 1871. He won high honors throughout his four years in Harvard, publishing his first book, *The American College,* while still a sophomore. He devoted his early years to the Congregational ministry and to writing articles and books. In 1890, when he was brought to Western Reserve University as the sixth president, there were 246 students in four buildings; but, through his leadership, the number of students grew to more than 5,000 and the number of buildings to more than thirty. When he retired, he continued to be one of the busiest men in Cleveland, writing, speaking, and helping constructive projects. Humor was one of the happy character-istics of Dr. Thwing, an attribute that remained with him always. Not many days before he died, Newton D. Baker called at his home. With his usual enthusiasm, he looked up and asked his visitor, "Tell me, Newton, what books are you reading these days?" Baker answered, giving the names of a history, a book of biography, and one of philosophy. "Excellent," cried Dr. Thwing. "Newton, if you keep on reading books like these, you will make a name for yourself some day." The great educator left upon Cleve-land the impress of one of the brilliant minds of his time, a noble character and a powerful personality. Dr. Thwing's numerous writings include *Edu-cation in the United States since the Civil War,* 1910; *American Colleges and Universities in the Great War,* 1920; *What Education Has the Most Worth?* 1924; *The American and the German Universities,* 1928; and *Friends of Men,* 1933.

The Rola Company, Inc., was organized as an Ohio corporation, taking over a portion of the assets of The Rola Company and becoming the operat-ing organization. In 1924 the parent company had been formed in Seattle, Washington, for the manufacture of radio loud speakers. When The Rola Company became a wholly owned subsidiary, Bernard A. Engholm, a pioneer in the radio industry, was elected president. Before his death in 1945, all of the capital stock of The Rola Company, Inc., was acquired by the Muter Company of Chicago, and Laurence A. King became president. Loud speakers made by the company in its plant at 2530 Superior Avenue were sold to manufacturers of radio and television sets.

The National Air Races drew record crowds to Cleveland for the Labor Day classic. The Bendix Derby, opening the meet, was won by Frank W. Fuller, Jr., who set a new record of 258 m.p.h. S. J. Wittman captured honors, and parachute events thrilled the spectators. Lee Miles of Fort Worth crashed to his death. Count von Hagenburg stunted before the enthusiastic crowds who were also attracted by the Navy Squadrons' formation maneu-vers. The principal event of the races was won by Rudy A. Kling when he captured the Thompson Trophy with an average speed of 256.91 m.p.h.

Fort Huntington Park, just west of the Court House, was dedicated as a memorial park on September 17 to commemorate the fort erected on the grounds in 1813. Walter P. Rice thanked the Board of County Commis-sioners on behalf of the Early Settlers Association of which he was president.

The one hundredth anniversary of the founding of the Cleveland public schools was celebrated in September. It was announced that a $42,600 grant was received from the General Education Board to help finance a school radio station and to purchase 150 receivers.

A tribute to the memory of Thomas G. Masaryk, founder and President of the Czechoslovak Republic, was paid on October 2 in a Cleveland radio broadcast through station WGAR. Dr. Jaroslav Gardavsky, Czechoslovak consul, was on the program. One speaker read from the Czechoslovak Declaration of Independence the sections written by Robert M. Calfee, Cleveland attorney, showing how President Masaryk and his country adopted American principles of democracy.

President Franklin Delano Roosevelt, returning from a seven-thousand-mile western tour, stopped for a half hour at the Cleveland Terminal, October 5, to give a radio address on a *New York Herald Tribune* forum.

It was estimated in October that Cleveland had been enriched by at least thirty million dollars because of the Great Lakes Exposition, of which Dudley S. Blossom was general chairman, and Lincoln G. Dickey general manager. Cleveland had received worldwide publicity as a progressive, productive city. Persons from every state in the Union came to the exposition, and there were visitors from Canada, Mexico, and other foreign countries. Mark Egan was manager of the Cleveland Convention and Visitors Bureau, which brought many gatherings to the city during the exposition years. From the inaugural noon, June 28, 1936, until the closing day, benefits were obtained for Cleveland which could not be measured in dollars and cents.

The annual *News* luncheon honoring the automotive industry, November 13, was given an international flavor, with the Right Honorable Arthur Meighen, twice Prime Minister of Canada, delivering the principal address. Other speakers included A. Edward Barit, president of the Hudson Motor Car Company; Charles F. McCahill, vice president and general manager of the *News;* Sterling E. Graham, president of the Advertising Club; and William Ganson Rose, toastmaster. In the Automobile Show, twenty-two motor-car exhibits, Dick Powell's songs, and a musical spectacle, *Brides of the Nation,* attracted large crowds. This was the last in the series sponsored by the *News,* beginning in 1932.

The greenhouse industry and its operations in and near Cleveland involved a ten-million-dollar capital investment, with 225 acres under glass. The largest concentrated area under glass in America, it centered around Schaaf Road and Olmsted Falls.

The Arena was opened in November. Located at 3737 Euclid Avenue on the old Brush estate, the $1,500,000 project provided 10,000 seats for hockey and 12,500 seats for boxing. Al Sutphin was president. Cleveland, with the Arena and the Shaker Heights rink of the Cleveland Skating Club, became ice-conscious as never before. The Arena was the home of the Barons, Cleveland's hockey team; and here were presented ice shows, boxing matches, six-day bicycle races, circuses, and important sports events that drew vast audiences.

By City Council ordinance, the area between the Cleveland Public Library and the *Plain Dealer* Building was designated a reading spot and named Linda A. Eastman Park, in honor of the woman who, in her forty years as librarian, brought worldwide distinction to the Public Library.

The Cleveland Child Health Association obtained permission from the Federal Housing Authority to set up a demonstration nursery in the Lakeview Terrace Housing Project. This project had the financial aid of the Cleveland Foundation.

The campaign goal set for the Community Fund was $3,450,000. The amount raised was $3,360,428.45 with 493,688 subscribers. The chairman was Ellwood H. Fisher. The National Community Chest figures proved that Cleveland, the pioneer Chest city, raised the largest total of contributions among 135 cities in the United States, Canada, and Hawaii.

Streetcars and motor coaches carried 328,410,000 passengers in 1937—almost one million "rides" per day—at a speed of 12.2 miles per hour, said to be the fastest surface-line record in the nation. The city's railway system consisted of 28 regular streetcar routes, 20 motor-coach routes, and 1 trackless-trolley route, equipped with 1,361 cars and coaches. Four thousand workers were employed.

The new *Cleveland City Directory*, the sixty-fifth edition, published by the Cleveland Directory Company, was one of the most complete in the world, according to the company's manager, A. E. Perlin. The population of Greater Cleveland, estimated at 1,204,799, and facts about the city, its business, and institutions required 1,158 pages. Hospitals numbered 18; there were more than 100 theaters and motion-picture houses, and 120 hotels. The city had 36 parks, valued at fifty million dollars. Cleveland's first directory had been issued just one hundred years earlier.

Newton Diehl Baker, eminent statesman, military leader, and citizen of the world, died on Christmas Day. Born in 1871 in Martinsburg, West Virginia, and educated at Johns Hopkins University and Washington and Lee University, he came to Cleveland at the turn of the century. He first drew attention in the office of city solicitor, serving from 1902 to 1912, when he was known as Mayor Tom L. Johnson's right-hand aide. He became mayor of Cleveland in 1912, and was re-elected, serving his second term before listening to President Wilson's urgent request to join his cabinet. He served as Secretary of War in the greatest struggle that the United States and the world had known. As mayor, he was co-author of the city's first home-rule charter, and he became one of the most eloquent and influential speakers of his time. In the War Department, his policy of training and sending to Europe the largest number of men in the shortest time, no matter what the cost, overwhelmed the enemy and contributed to the victory of the Allies. Baker returned to private life and refused many requests to run for the Presidency. He had been the mainstay of Wilson as he had been of Johnson, and throughout his life he seemed strongly influenced by these leaders. He gave much time and effort to the support of the League of Nations, foreseeing that the future safety of the world would depend upon an organization of all nations under high ideals. Newton D. Baker was one of the most modest and unassuming of men, democratic in heart and action.

Overwork on behalf of his fellow citizens undoubtedly hastened his death, which was mourned throughout the nation he served

1938

A group of talented colored singers, under the name of Wings Over Jordan, made its first appearance over a national network of the Columbia Broadcasting System on January 9. Having originated in 1935 as a choir in the Gethsemane Baptist Church at East 30th and Scovill Avenue, the group was organized by the Rev. Glenn T. Settle. Since that initial broadcast from Station WGAR, its fame grew steadily through a Sunday-morning program of spirituals. Worth Kramer, program director, became the director of the chorus, and in 1940 it toured the country. Five years later, in 1945, under the leadership of Hattie Easley, the group went on a concert tour of Europe.

Mrs. Francis Fleury Prentiss was elected president of St. Luke's Hospital Association and of its board of trustees on January 26, succeeding her late husband. The growth of the hospital and its prestige were due in large measure to the personal interest and financial gifts of Mr. and Mrs. Prentiss. He had given more than three million dollars and she added more than two million dollars. It was reported by Dr. C. S. Woods, superintendent, that the hospital had increased in the number of patients from fifth to second of the city's hospitals during the past five years. C. G. Watkins was made vice president to serve with Mrs. Prentiss.

The death of Alfred F. Arthur, composer and singing teacher, was a loss to Cleveland's music world, for through his great talent, initiative, and resourcefulness he had built up the Cleveland School of Music from its founding in 1884. Alfred F., Jr., had taken over management of the school several years before his father's passing. Frederick Williams, a graduate who became head of the department of piano and theory, was well known for his many compositions and books of studies. Upon his death in 1942, Andrew M. Setter succeeded him, bringing a wealth of experience. The building at 3101 Prospect Avenue, in which the school was located for forty years, was sold in 1942, and a new home was secured in Carnegie Hall. Well-known musicians received their training at the Cleveland School of Music. On recital and concert programs the names of Birdie Hale, Dora Hennings, Gustave Berneike, Carrie Bishop Searles, Mr. and Mrs. C. B. Ellinwood, Bernice Boest, Lotta Brewbaker, Walter Logan, Louis Rich, James D. Johnston, and Ernie Taylor appeared many times.

The Erie Railroad, encountering financial difficulties, and unable to negotiate a substantial loan, turned to the courts for protection. The United States District Court sitting in Cleveland appointed Charles E. Denney, Erie's president, and John A. Hadden, local attorney, as trustees of the railroad. These appointments were ratified the following May by the Interstate Commerce Commission. Multitudinous problems confronted the two trustees, involving the sale of eight ships of German registry, and finding money with which to pay the rentals on leased lines. Denney and Hadden purchased the capital stock of the Cleveland Mahoning Valley, resulting in a large annual saving for the Erie Railroad.

On February 14 the mercury reached 68 degrees, breaking the Weather Bureau record.

American Indian art was being taught to fifty thousand school children who yearly visited the Cleveland Museum of Art. William M. Milliken, museum director, originated the idea and converted little-used storage space into classrooms for the Indian collection.

Bishop T. C. O'Reilly died in Florida on March 26. The former Clevelander had headed the Scranton, Pennsylvania, Diocese for ten years.

The Cleveland Board of Education was authorized by the Federal Communications Commission on March 30 to proceed with plans for Station WBOE. This Cleveland station, which became one of the outstanding FM school stations in the nation, was an outgrowth of more than a decade of experimental teaching by radio. At first, scheduled programs of radio lessons were heard regularly in 117 elementary schools with 64,600 pupils as listeners. Later, the program expanded to include junior- and senior-high-school lessons; and by 1947, all grades in 250 public, private, and parochial schools were receiving instruction from this pioneer project. Two programs were presented weekly for parents' group meetings in various schools, subjects dealing with the child and the school. The transmitter room and broadcasting antenna were installed at Lafayette School, 12415 Abell Avenue. Under the supervision of Dr. William B. Levenson, who became director of the station in 1938, WBOE stimulated the progress of radio education throughout the nation.

Loss of the *City of Buffalo* on March 30 by fire was a death-dealing blow to the Cleveland & Buffalo Transit Company. Coupled with the effects of depression years and increasing motor-truck and railroad competition, this was more than C & B could withstand, and in 1939 liquidation began. The East 9th Street Pier lease was transferred to the Lederer Terminal Warehouse Company. The *Seeandbee,* pride of the fleet, was sold to Chicago interests, and in 1942 was converted by the Navy to the *U.S.S. Wolverine,* an aircraft-carrier training ship. Excursions and traditional "moonlight" rides came to an end when the *Goodtime* went for salvage in 1940. The *City of Erie,* last of the famous "honeymoon line" steamers, was sold for scrap. The Buffalo-terminal property was also eventually sold. The Cleveland & Buffalo Transit Company continued in name only, without a ship.

When the Federal Government invited smaller-business men to a conference in Washington to discuss their problems, more than a thousand attended, and planned a non-partisan, non-profit organization. The name adopted was Smaller Business of America, and the Greater Cleveland Council was the third group to be incorporated. Local members adopted a program of advancing the business of the Greater Cleveland area and of taking a firm position on public issues affecting the welfare of the community. Benjamin S. Hubbell was the first president. In 1946, the chief executive was George Bissett and the executive vice president was S. R. Christophersen. Bissett was succeeded by William J. Franz.

A world record was established in April when music lovers, 68,078 of them, attended the Metropolitan Opera in the Public Auditorium. Kirsten Flagstad and Lauritz Melchior appeared in *Tristan und Isolde* and *Tannhauser*, in response to public demand. Elizabeth Rethberg, Bruna Castagna, Giovanni Martinelli, Ezio Pinza, and Norman Cordon were in the cast of *Aida;* and Helen Jepson, John Charles Thomas, and Nino Martini sang the principal roles in *La Traviata.* Grace Moore, Jan Kiepura, Amri Galli-Campi, Carlo Tagliabue, Anna Kaskas, and Cleveland's Thelma Votipka and Donald Dickson were favorites in other operas.

Demands for services became so great that, through the generosity of Clevelanders, a new $150,000 building was erected this year on East 55th Street for the Association for Crippled and Disabled. The name was changed to the Cleveland Rehabilitation Center in 1943. The institution was considered outstanding, being one of the few furnishing under one roof a combination of highly specialized services vital to rehabilitation. Belle Greve had been the executive director since 1933. Her efficient leadership gave her an international reputation.

The subject of lakefront rights was brought to a head upon the building of the Lakeland Freeway from East 9th Street to Gordon Park, principally over submerged land. Certain shore-land owners asserted their right to compensation from the City of Cleveland because the road interfered with the claimed rights of access and to wharf out, and a suit was started this year asserting such rights. The city took issue. For technical reasons, the Common Pleas Court decided that the Fleming Act was unconstitutional, and, after so holding, held that in the absence of valid legislation, the shore owners did have the right of access and to wharf out and were entitled to compensation. The city appealed the case to the Court of Appeals in 1946. The court reversed the judgment of the Common Pleas Court and sustained the validity of the Fleming Act so far as it declared the public and private rights. The shore owners, however, carried the case to the Ohio Supreme Court, where the Fleming Act was upheld, except as it authorized carrying out the Union Depot Ordinance, which was declared unconstitutional. Judge Robert M. Morgan represented the city.

The Cleveland Medal for Public Service was awarded, April 19, by The Cleveland Chamber of Commerce to Henry G. Dalton in recognition of "the devotion of his constructive mind and his broad vision, to the charitable, educational and civic institutions of Cleveland."

The Cleveland Fashion Institute was established through the co-operation of the Apparel and Accessories Manufacturers and Wholesalers Committee of The Cleveland Chamber of Commerce. The Cleveland market was regarded highly throughout the country as a source of well-styled merchandise. There were 158 manufacturers and wholesalers in the industry, with payrolls totaling nearly fifteen million dollars.

The Real Property Inventory of Metropolitan Cleveland disclosed interesting facts in April. For five years, the average excess of families entering the Cleveland metropolitan district over families leaving was 1,245. In 1936, more than 7,800 families made room in their homes for another family.

Dave Albritton of Cleveland, representing Ohio State University, established a national high-jump record of 6 feet, 7¼ inches, indoors.

The Yugoslav Garden was dedicated on May 14, and, despite a downpour of rain, an estimated crowd of a hundred thousand was attracted to Rockefeller Park for the event. Adjacent to the Polish Garden, this cultural garden was designed about the central motif of a fountain. Hedged niches bordering the garden contained busts of poets. Ivan Cankar and the Rev. Simon Gregorcic were recognized, and the unity of Yugoslavs was symbolized by busts of Bishop Friderik Baraga, Peter H. Petrovich-Niegosh, and Archbishop Strossmayer, ardent apostles of this unity.

The doors of the Union Bank of Commerce opened in the former home of the Union Trust Company on May 16, and a distribution of $38,000,000 was made to depositors of the latter bank, materially helping the business of Cleveland. It was the largest release of frozen funds scheduled for any city in the country in 1938. The new bank, a reorganization of its predecessor, had capital of $8,000,000, and offered complete commercial banking facilities. The president was Oscar L. Cox; the executive vice president, Clare W. Banta; and other directors were Harry F. Affelder, Frederick C. Crawford, Randolph Eide, W. H. Gerhauser, Robert C. Norton, John B. Putnam, Henry S. Sherman, and Franklin G. Smith. The Union Bank of Commerce, which became one of Cleveland's major financial institutions, was incorporated, February 21. Evidence that it served the public well was found in deposit growth from $23,976,958 at the end of 1938 to $108,776,830 by April, 1946. John K. Thompson, widely known railroad executive, became president in 1944, and other officers in 1946 included Harry F. Burmester, senior vice president; Charles B. Anderson, Edward F. Meyers, and Ernest N. Wagley, vice presidents; and George R. Herzog, vice president and cashier.

The Cleveland Chamber of Commerce moved into its new home in the Union Commerce Building. The quarters were so complete, efficient, and attractive that they drew national attention.

West Technical High School won publicity for its advanced intra-mural broadcasting system, rated as one of the best in the country, and for the fact that it was the only regular city high school which pupils in any part of the city might attend by choice.

Munson Havens resigned as executive secretary of the Chamber of Commerce on May 27, four days after the fortieth anniversary of his valuable service. The board of directors accepted his resignation with expressions of appreciation and esteem. Havens contributed to the city's commercial and cultural advancement and attracted national attention for his civic endeavors.

A Dunham Tavern committee announced a program of restoration of the old stagecoach inn, 6709 Euclid, June 1. The taproom was completely furnished by Dr. and Mrs. G. E. Follansbee from their famous collection of Americana. The garden was maintained by the Little Garden Club of Cleveland Heights, and the early-day barn was converted into a primitive theater. Mrs. Benjamin P. Bole was president of Dunham Tavern, Inc.

Cain Park, an open-air community theater, was dedicated at Lee and Superior Avenue in Cleveland Heights, providing an outlet for local talent of many types. Programs were expertly directed by Dina Rees Evans, and choral singing, lectures, and orchestra recitals were presented out-of-doors. The project was named in honor of Mayor Frank C. Cain. Each year the park grew in popularity.

Joe Scott, Western Reserve track star, won the national decathlon title with 6,526 points.

Councilmen rejected plans for a lottery to provide city relief.

Two young Clevelanders, Jerry Siegel and Joe Shuster, after trying for six years to sell illustrated stories, were eventually rewarded when a publisher bought the first *Superman* story. Then followed one of the most phenomenal successes of its kind. *Superman* was syndicated in more than two hundred newspapers with a circulation reported to be twenty million. He appeared in several comic books regularly and was made the hero of radio programs.

The Grotto's Mardi Gras attracted 250,000, and cheers filled the Stadium as the "prophets" paraded on June 30.

Rio Rita was presented on the Aqua-stage by the Cleveland Summer Music Society on July 3. The lake theater had been a feature of the Great Lakes Exposition.

Twenty-five thousand people attended the formal dedication of the Hungarian Cultural Garden in Rockefeller Park on July 10. Nicholas Roosevelt, former minister to Hungary, was the speaker. The garden was dedicated to the composer Frank Liszt, whose bas-relief had been unveiled on October 21, 1934, the 123rd anniversary of his birth. The arched gateway was an excellent example of the Hungarian iron-worker's art. Traditional trees and shrubs of Hungary were planted, and a large reflecting pool was the central feature of the upper garden. A hillside garden and another formal garden completed the design.

During the first six months of 1938, Cleveland recorded a low death rate, according to the announcement made on July 20 by Health Commissioner Dr. Harold J. Knapp. Traffic fatalities were approximately one-half those of the previous six months, and infectious-disease mortality was also reduced. The death rate for the first six months was 10.5 for each thousand population. Cleveland was known as the national leader in the control of pulmonary tuberculosis. Infant mortality was reduced to 36.9 per thousand births, while the birth rate increased 16.5 per thousand.

The Lorenzo Carter Monument was dedicated at Erie Street Cemetery on July 22 by the Early Settlers Association. Restoration of the monument was made possible by Mrs. Jessie Carter Martin, direct descendant of Lorenzo and Rebecca Carter, pioneer residents at the mouth of the Cuyahoga River. Charles Martin Carter, great-great-grandson; Mrs. Jessie Carter Martin, great-granddaughter; and Mary Martin, great-great-great-granddaughter, participated in the ceremony.

Public attention was called in July to the fact that the East Cleveland

Cemetery at East 118th Street and the Nickel Plate Railroad, while located in the City of Cleveland, was owned and managed by the municipalities of East Cleveland and Cleveland Heights. The cemetery tract of 9.76 acres had been purchased on September 5, 1859, from Mr. and Mrs. Edwin Fuller by East Cleveland Township. The cemetery was then established, and the property later became officially known as the East Cleveland and Cleveland Heights Cemetery.

A plan to advance the business interests of the city, called The Cleveland Plan, was developed by The Cleveland Chamber of Commerce, at the suggestion of J. E. North on July 24. The purpose was to impress upon the nation Cleveland's advantages as a great market-place. The general chairman was North, president of the Electrical League of Cleveland; chairman of the executive committee was W. T. Holliday, president of the Standard Oil Company of Ohio; C. H. Handerson, director of the Chamber of Commerce Trade Expansion Program, was secretary. Surveys were made, confidence was strengthened, and business was given a new impetus. Many Cleveland industries spruced up their display cabinets and plants, and organizations polished their "showcases" as they prepared to greet Cleveland businessmen making an inspection trip, November 28-29. This tour was the culmination of a novel plan called "Cleveland on Parade," sponsored by The Cleveland Plan and designed to help citizens know their city and discover how its plants contributed to growth. More than fifty companies joined in this outstanding event which gained wide attention.

Josephine Forsyth, later Josephine Forsyth Meyers, composer of songs, appeared in a concert at Grays Armory on July 27. This Cleveland musician wrote an accompaniment to *The Lord's Prayer* and her musical setting for the immortal words became famous.

Dorothy Doan Henry, Cleveland's first policewoman, and superintendent of the Cuyahoga County Juvenile Detention Home, was given the important post of reorganizing the welfare program of Washington, D. C.

The following fleets of ore carriers had their headquarters in Cleveland: Pittsburgh Steamship Company, 79 vessels; Interlake Steamship Company, 45; Hutchinson & Company, 22; Cleveland-Cliffs Iron Company, 24; Great Lakes Steamship Company, 19; Wilson Transit Company, 13; Columbia Transportation Company, 14; The M. A. Hanna Company, 11; The Tomlinson Fleet, 10; Buckeye Steamship Company, 11; Midland Steamship Company, 7; Interstate Steamship Company, 4; Henry and G. M. Steinbrenner, 4; and Shenango Furnace Company, 3 vessels. Cleveland was maintaining its leadership by owning or controlling well over 75 per cent of the ore carriers on the lakes.

The altitude baseball-catch record was broken on Cleveland's Public Square on August 20 before ten thousand excited witnesses. Henry Helf and Frank Pytlak caught balls thrown from the top of Cleveland's Terminal Tower. On August 21, 1908, Charles E. "Gabby" Street, later manager of the St. Louis Browns, had caught a baseball thrown from the 555-foot Washington Monument in the national capital. The Terminal Tower, with a height of 708 feet, offered the opportunity of breaking the record catch by 153 feet. Cleveland scientists estimated that the ball would reach a speed of 202 feet per second. Catchers Helf and Pytlak stood on grass plots in the Square, with steel helmets on their heads, waiting for the opportunity to make record catches. The first few balls struck the pavement and bounced thirteen stories into the air. First Helf, and later Pytlak, made their catches and achieved a new world's record for a stunt that received national attention from newspapers, scientific journals, and other publications. Later, the New York World's Fair management planned to beat the record with a throw from the Trylon, but it was discovered that the shaft fell far short of the height of the Terminal Tower.

Sales Management magazine asked 207 leading sales and advertising executives what cities they would select as the best test cities for marketing goods. Cleveland ranked first, with Chicago, St. Louis, Columbus, and Hartford following.

Douglas "Wrong Way" Corrigan visited Cleveland, August 28, and was given remarkable receptions on the Public Square and at the Air Races. He flew to Cleveland in the old plane in which he made his New York-to-Dublin solo flight, when he claimed he thought he was headed for California.

Linda Anne Eastman retired from service on August 31 to rest and travel, after nearly twenty years of nationally recognized leadership in the Cleveland Public Library. She was given a civic reception on September 1 and was remembered with many gifts. A citizens' committee of five hundred, under the chairmanship of John C. McHannan, sponsored the testimonial. Charles E. Rush, formerly associate librarian at Yale University, became Cleveland's fifth public librarian on September 2.

Visitors poured into Cleveland to witness the National Air Races, a great Labor Day spectacle featuring daring demonstrations of endurance and speed. Jacqueline Cochran won the Bendix Trophy Race, with an average speed of 249.774 m.p.h. Roscoe Turner, who piloted a Laird Special, won the Thompson Trophy Race, beating the mark set by Detroyat in 1936 and setting a new record of 283.419 m.p.h.

The 125th anniversary of the Battle of Lake Erie was celebrated with an impressive parade and meetings on September 10. Put-in-Bay, Sandusky, and Erie held memorial programs simultaneously. The Cleveland procession featured many floats, and it was estimated that thirty thousand citizens were on hand to greet the five thousand marchers and attend ceremonies at Gordon Park and on the Public Square.

Clevelanders turned time backward for three days beginning September 14, as they "went to the fair" at Dunham Tavern. Sponsored by Dunham Tavern, Inc., for the development and continuance of the tavern, an Old-Fashioned County Fair was held under the direction of the executive committee: Mrs. Benjamin P. Bole, Mrs. Charles A. Otis, and Mrs. Windsor T. White. One hundred and thirteen descendants of Euclid Avenue families were named to the honorary committee. For three days "villagers" in hoopskirts and breeches sold wares and antiques. Quilting bees, farm contests, square dancing, and plays revived early-day spirit in the restored tavern, whose future was assured.

The Higbee Company presented a series of impressive advertisements during Cleveland Plan Week, September 18-24, concerning Cleveland and its future. The messages inspired pride and confidence in Cleveland, and backed their dramatic claims with facts.

Dudley S. Blossom, outstanding civic leader, died October 8, and charity shared in his estate. Among the institutions named were: Church of the Covenant, Cleveland Community Fund, Musical Arts Association, Cleveland Welfare Federation, Associated Charities, City Hospital, Blossom Hill Home for Girls, Cleveland Boys Farm, House of Correction, City Infirmary, and Sunny Acres County Tuberculosis Hospital. The benefactor had inspired community effort in advancing cultural, charitable, and business activities. Blossom, after his graduation from Yale University, worked his way up in the W. Bingham Co. to become a vice president. During World War I he went to France with a captain's commission in the service of the American Red Cross and became chief of the Bureau of Supplies. Returning to Cleveland he became director of public welfare for the city through appointment by Mayor Harry L. Davis. His philanthropic and business affiliations were many.

The Greater Cleveland Chapter of the American Red Cross moved its headquarters to the Andrew Squire mansion at 3443 Euclid Avenue through the co-operation of Western Reserve University, a major beneficiary under the wills of Mr. and Mrs. Squire. The twenty-seven-room home provided space for the different departments, and a large library was converted into a meeting room.

National Fire Prevention Week was observed in Cleveland with displays of new and old apparatus in the Public Square. One feature was the starting of a fire, Jesse Owens, "the fastest human," acting as spectator and speedily covering the hundred yards to turn in the alarm. The Fire Department arrived in a remarkably short time and extinguished the blaze. Another feature was the rescue of people from the old Morison Block, a supposedly burning building with smoke pouring from the windows. These events attracted national attention.

Thousands who wished to sit in Charles Dickens' editorial chair in the Daisy Hill farm home of the late O. P. and M. J. Van Sweringen were disappointed when it was roped off. Crowds circulated through the typically American estate where the contents were to be auctioned on October 25. The interior of the large home was characterized by an atmosphere of informality and comfort, the furniture and furnishings being selected with discriminating taste. Regret was expressed when the fine home of the famous brothers was dismantled. The mansion was sold in 1946 to Mr. and Mrs. Gordon Stouffer who renamed it "Stowood."

Important improvements were furthered in October: work started on the west approach to the Main Avenue Bridge; $1,700,000 was being expended on the Willow Cloverleaf; East 14th Street was widened from Euclid to Broadway at a cost of $1,100,000.

The Housing Center, first of its kind in the country, was established on the Mall. As the planning and housing headquarters in the Cleveland area, it provided space for the Regional Association of Cleveland, the Cleveland Metropolitan Housing Authority, and the Ohio State Planning Conference. Ernest J. Bohn, director of the Metropolitan Housing Authority, announced plans for additional projects, stating that the Cedar Apartments, the Lakeview Terrace, and the Outhwaite Homes, which were occupied in 1937, were fulfilling their purposes and leading to the demand for further low-rent housing projects. In 1940, Valleyview Homes, including 582 dwellings at 2543 West 7th Street and Starkweather Avenue, were occupied. Ball fields, playgrounds, and spray pools were among the healthful recreational facilities for children and adults, and it was a community center for meetings, indoor recreation, a nursery school, and craft shops. The total development cost of this undertaking was $3,503,539. In November, 1940, Woodhill Homes, including 568 dwellings at 2567 Woodhill Road and Woodland Avenue, were ready for occupancy. This project utilized the land formerly occupied by Luna Park, a well-known amusement resort. When the park closed, the gaiety of the area disappeared, and the property became dilapidated, two fires finally demolishing what was left of the run-down section. The vacant land was soon improved with attractive dwellings and landscaping, and more than 1,800 people were comfortably housed. The cost of this development was $2,870,761. Members of the Metropolitan Housing Authority Committee at this time were Marc J. Grossman, chairman; John C. McHannan, vice chairman; John C. Kline, Max S. Hayes, and Charles W. White, with Bohn serving as director.

At the death of the Rt. Rev. Warren L. Rogers, the able fifth bishop of Ohio, the Rt. Rev. Beverley Dandridge Tucker became the sixth bishop of the diocese. Born in Warsaw, Virginia, in 1882, he had served in the churches of his home state and as professor of practical theology in the Virginia Theological Seminary. In World War I, he was first lieutenant and chaplain, United States Army, 1918-19, attached to the 17th Engineers. When he became a leader in diocesan activities, he continued his relationship with several educational institutions.

The stirring overture to *Die Meistersinger* was the opening number played by the Cleveland Philharmonic Orchestra at its concert in Cleveland College on November 14. Organized by three Cleveland musicians— Robert Zupnik, Alfred Zetzer, and Irving Klein, and directed by Dr. F. Karl Grossman, the orchestra was formed to provide an opportunity for Cleveland instrumental students to acquire a professional type of orchestral experience. Forty former members were rewarded with positions in symphony orchestras.

When the voters elected Margaret A. Mahoney to the Ohio House of Representatives from Cuyahoga County this year, their approval represented victory for a young attorney who had overcome many obstacles. Her father died in her early teens, and Margaret Mahoney worked as a cash girl while attending high school. Believing that knowledge of certain phases of the law would help her in her work as a secretary, she began her studies and passed the bar examination in 1929. Her interests broadened and she became active in women's organizations. Miss Mahoney was defeated in her campaign for state representative in 1936; but in 1938 she won a seat, and again in 1940. Continuous service in the Ohio Senate began in 1942.

The Highway Department received reports on November 25 from the Lake Shore Route Association that more than three million passenger cars passed through Cleveland every twelve months in the flow of east- and west-bound traffic.

The campaign goal set for the Community Fund was $3,450,000. The amount raised was $3,108,972.32, with a total of 466,836 subscribers. J. H. Donahey, A. C. Ernst, Dr. George E. Follansbee, Marc J. Grossman, Bessie E. Hall, Felician Janowski, and Margaret O'Neill received distinguished-service awards for outstanding helpfulness to the Fund, no matter what the character of the service.

The twelfth annual national bridge championships began in Cleveland on November 28. Four hundred and four players participated, an all-time-high attendance record. At the conclusion of the tournament, December 5, it was announced that Frank E. Bubna and Mrs. H. E. Funk of Cleveland won the national open pair championship.

To impress the public with the need for traffic safety, rites were held on the Public Square on November 29 for 112 persons killed in traffic accidents during the year.

A Good Will Day program on December 13 was broadcast by Dr. Robert B. Whyte, Rabbi Barnett R. Brickner, and Auxiliary Bishop James A. McFadden to South American countries. Acting Secretary of State Sumner Welles sent a message which was included in the program. Recordings of the proceedings were forwarded to South American governments.

Nathan L. Dauby announced the gift of the world-famous painting, "La Danse Dans un Pavillon," by Jean Antoine Watteau, on December 18 to the Cleveland Museum of Art. The painting was valued at $110,000, and the donor was Commodore Louis D. Beaumont, president of The May Company. The masterpiece created by "the prince of court painters" had once hung in the palace of Frederick the Great at Potsdam.

A huge cross, 160 feet high and 80 feet wide, formed by red lights in windows of the Terminal Tower, attracted citywide attention. The bells of the Old Stone Church and the Christmas tree, erected annually by The May Company on the northeast section of the Square, brought holiday cheer to thousands.

Samuel Prentiss Baldwin, seventy, outstanding Cleveland ornithologist and pioneer in the banding of birds, died December 31. He was a lawyer by profession, and his avocation was ornithology. On his Gates Mills estate he erected the Baldwin Bird Laboratory, and scientifically studied birds, particularly the house wren, with unique equipment he built for the purpose. He wrote valuable books and reports, some published by the Cleveland Museum of Natural History of which he was a trustee.

Although Cleveland industrial production approximated $693,800,000 in volume, a new high of 101,094 relief cases was recorded on the rolls of 1938. Public-works projects and federal emergency programs, in full swing, provided work for 66,625 people and direct relief for 34,469. Relief expenditures,

Public Square, the heart of Cleveland, in the shadow of the lofty Terminal Tower. The Federal Building, Public Library, and Plain Dealer *Building border the north side of Superior Avenue, and the Cuyahoga and Williamson buildings flank the east side of the Public Square.* PERRY CRAGG, CLEVELAND NEWS.

Wade Park and the Medical Center. Cleveland Museum of Art, in foreground, in a setting of lovely gardens and a sparkling lake. Euclid Avenue divides the scene, and to its south are buildings of Western Reserve University and the University Hospitals Group. PERRY CRAGG, CLEVELAND NEWS.

excluding administration, totaled $59,366,000 for the year; and the staggering sum of $216,792,000 had been spent in the city since 1931. Planned economy and social reconstruction were proving to be gravely expensive. There was criticism that federal relief pampered the shiftless and weakened the nation's moral structure, and disheartened taxpayers saw little sign of a change in administration policy. Promises of a balanced budget and reduction in the cost of government had long since been forgotten, and the spending program lengthened at an alarming rate.

1939

As Cleveland entered the new year, the city's important problems seemed to be the following: concluding the impasse between the city and the Cleveland Railway Company; bringing more trunkline roads into the Union Terminal; securing state legislation that would enable Cleveland to improve its lakefront; developing rapid transit in the downtown area; and promoting co-operative relations between the city and its suburbs. Despite failure of the state government for the second successive year to provide adequate relief funds for Ohio municipalities, Cleveland finished 1938 with a balanced operating budget and with its net bonded indebtedness $400,000 less than on December 31, 1937.

The old Central Viaduct, which had been declared unsafe, was destroyed on January 6, by wreckers, who set off a hundred sticks of dynamite in the arch. The purpose was to widen the Cuyahoga River and broaden Cleveland's commercial opportunities. In 1943, the great central span found its way into plants to be made into implements of war.

Cleveland Boys Towns, which had been started the first of the year, held their initial elections in February. Organized and planned by Mayor Burton and Russell Thierbach, president of the Boys Town Foundation, they were developed when the Cleveland Police Department became motorized, and vacated police stations were used. Based on the merit system, six Boys Towns were located at East 105th and Nottingham, East 80th and Superior, West 83rd and Detroit, West 53rd and Clark, East 55th and Broadway, and East 79th and Woodland. These Boys Towns were set up under efficient supervision, the Safety Department, the Welfare Department, and the Park Department co-operating with the Boys Town Foundation. The influence for good inspired by these projects was proved in character building and in the effective combating of juvenile delinquency.

A thirty-day period of mourning began, February 10, in all Catholic churches in the city, when Pope Pius XI died at the age of eighty-one. His successor was Eugenio Cardinal Pacelli, Papal Secretary of State, who became Pius XII.

The Bender Body Company was achieving an annual production of three million dollars worth of automotive bodies. A specialty of the company was the Bender-Studebaker air-conditioned ambulance. School buses and city transportation buses were other products. Herman Bender was the president and general manager, and plants were located at West 62nd Street and Barberton Avenue, with a branch maintained in Elyria.

A four-alarm fire destroyed Charles F. Brush relics of historical value. Apparatus and original blueprints used by the inventor were lost at the Brush Laboratory, 3714 Chester Avenue, when the old warehouse burned on February 22.

Eldred Hall of Western Reserve University was dedicated with a performance of Strindberg's *Spook Sonata* in February. Recognizing the high quality of the university's work in drama, the Rockefeller Foundation had provided funds to establish the office of the National Theater Conference on the campus, and gave thirty-five thousand dollars to enlarge and rebuild the theater. The institution was named for the Rev. Henry B. Eldred, who donated much of the original cost of the building built in 1900. In the Eldred Theater were presented plays, revues, operas, and pageants by the Eldred Players, the Sock and Buskin Club, Television Club, University Players, and Curtain Players. Productions under the direction of Barclay Leathem attracted citywide attention.

The Cleveland Fire Department tested two of its new fifteen-thousand-dollar streamlined pumpers at East 9th Street Pier. They pumped 1,000 gallons of water at 150 pounds pressure every minute and could feed twice as many hose lines as previous pumps.

Ignace Jan Paderewski, the great Polish pianist, was forced on March 5 to suspend his tour because of an inflamed tendon sheath in the left wrist. He stayed in his private Pullman car at the Union Terminal where his practicing was enjoyed by fortunate office workers who stopped work to hear the "concert on the tracks." Paderewski's brilliant performance before millions of American music lovers had closed, and he went back to Europe never to return.

The Railway Express Agency celebrated its one hundredth anniversary on March 5 by having a pony-express rider, mounted on a speedy horse, dash through the streets of Cleveland from the Public Square to the Airport where he delivered a package to an airliner. One hundred homing pigeons were released in the Public Square to carry anniversary messages to the New York and San Francisco world fairs.

Bishop Joseph Schrembs was made Archbishop on March 25, and Cleveland was to remain his home. Sixty-five thousand Catholics acclaimed him at the Stadium on June 12. Fifty years earlier he had been made a priest.

Cleveland, unique in the country for its support of grand opera, welcomed a galaxy of stars to its Public Auditorium on March 27. Many tourists and visitors thronged the city for the week of magnificent music and pageantry, and the operas represented popular selections of patrons. Opening night starred Helen Jepson, Martinelli, Brownlee, and Tibbett in *Otello;* and the engagement ended with Lily Pons, Martinelli, Brownlee, and Pinza in *Lucia di Lammermoor.* Kirsten Flagstad, Marjorie Lawrence, Kerstin Thorborg, Lauritz Melchior, Friedrich Schorr, and Herbert Janssen headed the casts of Wagnerian operas. Grace Moore, Charles Kullman, Ezio Pinza, Jan Kiepura, and John Charles Thomas were other Cleveland favorites who thrilled opera audiences during the week.

Dr. Eduard Benes, co-founder and President of the lost Republic of Czechoslovakia, and Mayor Fiorello H. La Guardia of New York City, spoke before nine thousand persons at the Public Auditorium on April 3, giving assurance that the republic would rise again. The meeting followed the dissolving of the Republic of Czechoslovakia and the establishment of a "protectorate" by Germany.

"Know Your City" was the title of an exhibit that opened on April 5 in the lobby of the Terminal Tower. The Real Property Inventory map of Greater Cleveland was accompanied by an informative statement showing that "there were more than 250 shopping centers in the metropolitan area, and that 30 per cent of the homes in the metropolitan district were owned free from mortgage."

Twelve per cent of the population of Cuyahoga County lived outside of Cleveland in 1910; 27 per cent was reported in 1938. In 1930, 48 per cent of the city's gainful workers were employed in manufacturing and building industries as compared with 44 per cent in Philadelphia, 40 per cent in Chicago, and 35 per cent in New York. Detroit was the only other large American city having so high a percentage of gainful workers in these classifications. Three per cent of family units were vacant in 1938. It was claimed, however, that there were sufficient vacant sub-lots to provide for a half century of expansion.

The Wade Park line bowed to buses, the fifty-year streetcar service ending April 13.

The Cleveland Safety Council with its educational campaigns and the Cleveland police with their handling of traffic merited high praise. Chief George J. Matowitz, who had succeeded Chief Jacob Graul in 1931, enlisted able assistants in all departments related to traffic. The National Traffic Safety Committee of the National Safety Council gave Cleveland first place among the large cities in its traffic safety ratings in 1939, honorable mention in 1940, first place in 1943, second in 1944, third in 1945, third in 1946, and first in 1947. Furthermore, the American Automobile Association in its Pedestrian Protective Contest gave Cleveland first place among the large cities in 1939 and 1940, honorable mention in 1941, 1944, 1945, and 1946, a special citation in 1943, and second place in 1947. In safety education, through the efforts of the Cleveland Safety Council and the Cleveland Police Department, Cleveland stood particularly high. The city was known internationally for its mounted troops A, B, and C, which rated first in the country, year after year.

The Cleveland Barons won the American Hockey League Championship and the Calder Trophy for the season 1938-39. A year earlier the team won the Western Division Championship. Cleveland, with its beautiful Arena, became one of the nation's leading hockey cities, and President Al Sutphin and his associates secured players that insured excellent teams year after year. The Western Division Championship was awarded to Cleveland in

1941, 1944, and 1945. The American Hockey League championships after 1939 were awarded Cleveland in 1941 and 1945.

The new $300,000 Chemical Laboratory at Case School of Applied Science was dedicated on April 15.

On April 19, Cleveland became the nation's leading "Health City," winning the United States Chamber of Commerce 1938 contest based on community protection and upbuilding of health. Cleveland also was given the title of No. 1 Red Cross city, because it enrolled a greater percentage of its population than any other municipality, a total of 110,000 members. The local chapter again won first place in 1940.

WPA projects since 1935 added $4,800,000 worth of improvements to the Cleveland school system, according to a report made April 19. Every school building in the city benefited, the improvements including better grounds, heating facilities, and public-address systems. The board maintained a "pupil per teacher" ratio of 38.2 pupils for each elementary teacher, 33.6 for each junior-high teacher, and 34 for each senior-high teacher.

The east and west sides of the Main Avenue Bridge were linked together on April 25 by driving home a golden rivet. A great crowd witnessed this spectacular feature of the gigantic project.

The fifth annual meeting of the Sight Saving Council, April 25, was addressed by Dr. Morris Fishbein, secretary of the American Medical Association. A review of the Council's achievements was presented to the public: booklets and leaflets to the number of 1,175,000 had been issued; 170,000 pupils of the elementary schools had been entertained and instructed through puppet shows; radio presentations had been used to reach hundreds of thousands of listeners; and the total audience of those hearing the story directly in schools and general meetings had reached the number of 828,000. As a result, Cleveland had become known as the leading American city in the appreciation of eyesight.

Charles Francis Brush Day was celebrated, April 29, the sixtieth anniversary of the first practical outdoor light provided by his arc lamp. A large audience assembled at the Square, and the many program features included the Brush High School Band. The street lights were turned out, a replica of the first arc lamp was lighted, and a cannon salute was fired on the Mall. The Grays Band, under the direction of William J. Maloney, played appropriate music, and Clara Gaiser Linder sang *The New Electric Light,* written by Luke J. Grace in 1878 and sung at the lighting of the first arc. A verse and chorus follow:

> While strolling thru the park one eve
> I saw some funny sights
> That appeared to me beneath the glare
> Of the new electric lights.
> A nice young couple passed me
> And I heard a sly request,
> Will you take me for your husband
> And I heard her answer, yes.

The New Electric Light—
On any pleasant night;
You'll see some funny pictures
By the New Electric Light.

The Cleveland Medal for Public Service was awarded on May 31 by The Cleveland Chamber of Commerce to Alwin Charles Ernst, "Patron of arts and culture, whose career has been marked by notable civic accomplishments."

Control of William Taylor Son & Company went to Major Charles H. Strong, brother of the late Sophia Strong Taylor, its president. Departing from sixty-nine-year-old custom, the store's display windows were opened to public view on the Sabbath, and a policy of advertising in Sunday newspapers was inaugurated. Complete rehabilitation of the department store at 630 Euclid Avenue followed. Outstanding in Taylor's war-service record was its War Bond window, which sold five million dollars worth of bonds and stamps. A million-dollar expansion program was undertaken in 1945, to include construction of supports in the two-story annex, for the future addition of five stories to equalize the height with that of the main building.

The dedication of the new Ohio National Guard Armory at 1437 Wayne Avenue, Lakewood, for Battery B, 135th Field Artillery, marked the one-hundredth anniversary of the regiment. This was the oldest national-guard organization outside the thirteen original states, its history going back to a gun squad of the Cleveland Grays known as the Cleveland Light Artillery.

Dr. Albert Jay Nock, historian and biographer, named Artemus Ward and Dr. Dayton C. Miller, the distinguished physicist at Case School of Applied Science, as the two Clevelanders who had the best chance of being remembered by Americans after a hundred years. Dr. Nock delivered the Western Reserve Academy commencement address on June 10.

Ambrose Swasey, born December 19, 1846, learned the machinist's trade as a boy in his home town of Exeter, New Hampshire. He had become a man of many achievements when he died June 15, 1939. With Worcester R. Warner he established the Warner & Swasey Company, one of the outstanding machine-tool producers of the world. The French government decorated him in 1900 for his work on astronomical instruments. Case School of Applied Science and Denison University of Granville, Ohio, conferred degrees upon him. He was one of the organizers, vice president, and president of the American Society of Mechanical Engineers. He was also a member of the Institution of Mechanical Engineers in Great Britain, the British Astronomical Society, and a Fellow of the Royal Astronomical Society. Swasey was a solid man who believed that engineering was a practical means of helping mankind. He became interested in the establishment of the Engineering Foundation, and in 1914 made the initial gift toward this purpose. He circled the world twice, and his practical curiosity was alerted to gaining knowledge for himself, and to contributing his own talents toward engineering progress and education. For many years he was especially interested in promoting education among the Chinese, and visited the Orient three times during his life.

Robert N. Wilkin, lawyer, was appointed judge of the United States District Court in June, after winning distinction as a member of the Ohio bar. He was a trustee of Western Reserve University and Oberlin College, and his scholarly writings were widely read.

The Museum of Art honored Coralie Walker Hanna on June 19, when an art collection was established by her son, Leonard C. Hanna, Jr.

Rotary International convened in Cleveland in June. Growth of the idea, "Service above Self," was indicated by the attendance of fifteen thousand members from all over the world. More than thirty languages were spoken. The Cleveland Rotary Club with four hundred members was the second largest in an international organization of five thousand clubs.

Crown Prince Olaf and Crown Princess Martha of Norway visited Cleveland on June 24, and enjoyed a busy schedule of events in the city, where three thousand of their countrymen made their homes.

The Rusin Garden in the Cultural Garden chain was dedicated, June 25, at an impressive ceremony. Adjoining the Slovak Garden through the unification walk, the Rusin Garden was planned in the form of a cross, and was dedicated to the cultural advancement of the Rusin people. A sandstone terrace overlooking Doan Brook was a feature of the picturesque garden. Before World War I the Rusins, inhabitants of Ruthenia, were generally ruled by Austria-Hungary although considered by Russia as belonging to the Russian family.

Cleveland was introduced to night baseball in the Stadium on June 27, before a crowd of 53,305. Bob Feller pitched a one-hit game against Detroit, the Indians winning 5-0. Their star pitcher had struck out thirteen men. Feller won 24 games in 1939 and struck out 246 men, a total that boosted both his salary and gate receipts for the Cleveland Indians. He was the youngest pitcher to win 20 games a season and earn $20,000 a year for doing it.

For the sixth consecutive year, the commercial team of John Hay High School won, on June 28, the grand prize in the annual international commercial-school contests, held this year at the New York World's Fair.

The first Festival of Freedom was held at the Stadium under the auspices of the Come-to-Cleveland Committee of the Advertising Club on Independence Day. Rain interfered with the big production, but a large crowd assembled the following week to see the conclusion of the presentation. The Police Department was represented by its mounted division, the famous Troop A; by its iron-horse brigade—the motorcycle men of the traffic division; and by its radio-equipped automobile patrol. The Fire Department displayed its newest apparatus and demonstrated its ability with hook-and-ladder drills and the shooting of a life line. Bands, drill corps, Boy Scouts, a sham battle, and patriotic ceremonies contributed to a program that was so successful the public demanded a continuation of the celebration each Fourth of July.

Lakewood began a week of celebration on July 16, commemorating its Golden Anniversary. Historical exhibits at the library and a parade marked the event. *Wagons West,* a dramatic presentation of local history, was given nightly at the Lakewood High School Stadium. The interesting *History of Lakewood,* by E. George Lindstrom, gave a comprehensive account of the city's growth and development.

Cleveland held two celebrations of the city's 143rd birthday on July 22: the first in the Public Square, and the second in the New York World's Fair at the Court of Peace. Marguerite Bacon, direct descendant of Moses Cleaveland, and William Ganson Rose, chairman, participated in both events. Mayor Harold H. Burton was the principal speaker at the Fair. Reports from New York stated that the ceremony was the most impressive conducted by an American city. To dramatize Cleveland Day, the Come-to-Cleveland Committee of the Cleveland Advertising Club and the Convention and Visitors Bureau launched a round-the-world race by air mail. Two packets were sent from the Cleveland Day ceremony in the Public Square, one flown east to New York by the Come-to-Cleveland Committee, and the other flown to San Francisco by the Convention Bureau. Aboard east- and west-bound clippers, the packets were expected to pass each other over India or China. The east-bound packet arrived at the New York World's Fair in time for the Cleveland Day ceremony, the names of distinguished guests were signed, and it was rushed by messenger to the clipper. Mayor A. J. Rossi of San Francisco signed the west-bound packet and delivered it personally to the clipper. The air-mail packet sent west around the world arrived in Cleveland, completing the trip of 23,930 miles in 22 days, 5 hours, and 55 minutes, breaking the record held by the Kellogg Company by 3 days, 1 hour, and 5 minutes. The average speed was 1,075 miles per day during the 534 hours of the flight, approximately one mile every ninety seconds. The start and finish of the race was at the Moses Cleaveland Monument on Cleveland's Public Square. The contents of the winning packet included an American flag, the seal of the City of Cleveland, and a proclamation by Mayor Burton.

Cleveland welcomed the Seventh World's Poultry Congress on July 28 with a parade and reception. On one day, the attendance was 117,000, exceeding by 20,000 the attendance at the New York World's Fair on that day. The total attendance was 382,000, and the number of out-of-town visitors was 50,000, with delegates from forty-five nations. This international agricultural show continued for eleven days.

Forty-seven countries were represented, July 30, among the 35,000 persons who attended the mass dedication of the chain of Cleveland Cultural Gardens, which covered thirty-five acres in Rockefeller Park. Earth from twenty-eight nations was deposited in a vault in the American Colonial Garden. In honor of each nation, a tree was planted in native soil mingled with Cleveland soil.

The Thirty-Seventh International Convention of Christian Endeavor, the largest Protestant religious gathering in America in 1939, opened in the Public Auditorium on August 6. Former President Herbert Hoover, the first speaker, was given a Scroll of Achievement by Dr. Daniel A. Poling of Philadelphia, president of the International Society of Christian Endeavor. For six days, conferences, banquets, and devotional sessions constituted the program.

Citizens led by the Early Settlers Association gathered at the City Hall to urge preservation of the Erie Street Cemetery, the burial ground of Cleveland pioneers, long neglected and overlooked. Rehabilitation was assured those who championed the cause of the ancient graveyard, and a promise was made that it would be preserved as a shrine sacred to those who carved Cleveland out of a wilderness.

A new greenhouse, with modern buildings and grounds covering five acres, was completed by the City Bureau of Horticulture in Gordon Park. The bureau operated the greenhouse and city nursery, and cared for the Cultural Gardens, the Donald Gray Lakefront Garden, and trees bordering streets. During the past four years, the bureau planted more than thirteen thousand trees in parks with the aid of the WPA tree-and-park projects.

The public schools were introducing new features. Talking books were provided for blind pupils, an educational program in city planning was led by Allen Y. King, and John Adams High School was selected as one of fourteen schools in the State for a ten-year curriculum study.

Joe Scott, Western Reserve University's "one man track team," won the national decathlon title a second time with 6,671 points.

The eyes of the nation were focused on Cleveland, scene of the National Air Races during the Labor Day weekend. By this time, the races had become an American institution, demonstrating their value not only as a thrilling spectacle, but also as a proving ground for the nation's aircraft industries. Making aviation history with his Seversky plane, Frank Fuller, Jr., won the Bendix Trophy Race for the second time, his record of 282.098 surpassing all previous figures. Flying his Turner-Laird plane at a speed of 282.536 m.p.h., Roscoe Turner captured the Thompson Trophy Race for the third time, the only pilot to have scored this record.

W. A. Stinchcomb, director-secretary of the Metropolitan Park System, stated that parks and recreation were inextricably interwoven with richer, healthier, community living. Opportunities for outdoor recreation served to counteract the nervous tensions and strained influences of city life. In 1939, the Metropolitan Park System consisted of nine major reservations, containing 11,285 acres. Reservations west to east were: Huntington, Rocky River, Big Creek Parkway, Hinckley, Brecksville, Bedford, South Chagrin, North Chagrin, and Euclid Creek. Purchase price was $4,724,090, with permanent improvements costing $10,226,548, of which $7,836,616 was contributed by the United States emergency relief agencies. The Park System had 55 miles of auto roads, 60 miles of bridle paths, 53 miles of foot trails, 10 shelter houses, 3 trailside museums, 2 public golf courses, 33 picnic grounds, and 14 camping centers. In co-operation with the Cleveland Museum of Natural History, five nature trails were labeled, while three trailside museums, served by trained naturalists, were open to the public. More than eight

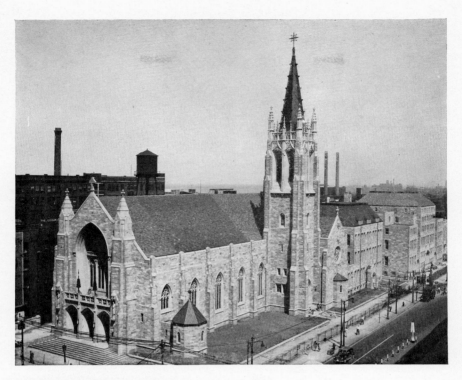

St. John's Cathedral and
Cathedral Square.

Old Stone Church. PERRY
CRAGG, CLEVELAND NEWS.

Trinity Cathedral

The Temple. PERRY CRAGG, CLEVELAND NEWS.

million people visited the parks annually, making an average of six visits for each person in the district.

The first American Congress on Obstetrics and Gynecology convened at Public Auditorium on September 16.

The priceless collections of the Western Reserve Historical Society were moved into a beautiful new home on East Boulevard—the McKinney house, built for Mrs. John Hay in 1908 by Abram Garfield, and for many years the residence of the Price McKinney family. Early in 1940, the society exchanged its University Circle building for the Leonard C. Hanna home, built by Harry Payne Bingham in 1918 and just west of the Hay-McKinney house. Here the extensive historical and genealogical library collections, consisting of valuable records, books, and manuscripts, were established. School children with their teachers visited the society every year for a realistic lesson in history and the social sciences. Classes in art, decorating, and crafts met for study. Research work was carried on in many fields with the aid of society specialists. Lecture rooms and the lovely grounds were available for group meetings. The society was supported by endowment income, and the subscriptions of more than five hundred public-spirited citizens. There was no admission charge to the buildings. Laurence H. Norton was president.

With the slogan "Cleveland has it and can ship it quick," Cleveland wholesalers and the Trade Expansion Department of the Chamber of Commerce welcomed in September thousands of out-of-town buyers. Evening meetings and daytime trips to wholesale houses made, the visiting retailers better acquainted with local jobbers, wholesalers, and distributors. Cleveland was an important wholesale and jobbing center, supplying a rich trading area that was steadily increasing in purchasing power. Sales of 2,287 wholesale business firms reporting in Cuyahoga County for the year 1939 totaled $959,724,000, giving employment to 23,958 wage earners. Retail business amounted to $506,426,000, as reported by 16,716 establishments employing 58,367 workers.

Ceremony marked the dedication on October 6 of the Main Avenue Bridge, the gigantic structure linking the Lakeland Freeway on the east with Bulkley Boulevard on the west. Ground was broken on May 12, 1938, for the project which cost $7,000,000. This Cuyahoga County undertaking was made possible by the authorization of $6,000,000 in bonds at the November, 1930, election, together with financial aid from the Public Works Administration. The six-lane, cantilever-truss structure was 8,000 feet long, including approaches. In the construction, 24,000 tons of steel and 16,000 gallons of paint were used. Girders across the railroad on the east approach were 270.8 feet long, the longest span girders built in America. More than a hundred thousand people attended the formal opening. In a parade were the workmen who participated in the erection of the bridge, military organizations, and fraternal bodies. The city, the county, and the nation were represented in the speaking program, and reference was made to the record-breaking time in which the bridge was constructed—less than one and a half years. The county commissioners at this time were Joseph F.

Gorman, John F. Curry, and James A. Reynolds. In charge of construction was John O. McWilliams, county engineer, whose associates were W. E. Blaser, F. L. Plummer, R. W. Deitrick, and C. M. Haake, with Dr. Wilbur J. Watson as consulting engineer.

The Santa Claus Club was formed, with Bert Elsbury as president and fifteen active members who represented Santa Claus for the city's department stores. This was said to be the first club of its kind in the country. Elsbury and his family for years had made their home with fourteen other families in the old Myron T. Herrick mansion at 2425 Euclid Avenue.

The National Museum of Baseball and Hall of Fame was dedicated in Cooperstown, New York, where the game of baseball was inaugurated by General Abner Doubleday. Among the immortals in the Hall of Fame are the following players who were members of Cleveland teams: Jesse Burkett, Walter Johnson, Napoleon Lajoie, Tris Speaker, and Denton T. "Cy" Young.

Work was started on October 17 on the cleaning of the Federal Building on the Public Square, the first bath this monumental structure had received since it opened in 1911.

The Cleveland Round Table of the National Conference of Christians and Jews came into being as part of the national program which had been launched eleven years before. Dr. Arthur J. Culler was local chairman. The first full-time professional staff worker was Dorothy Whitney, whose talents were valuable in carrying the program to cultural groups. She was succeeded by Reginald Kennedy in 1941, who expanded the groups' relations; and in 1945, James D. Nobel became regional director. One of the most notable efforts in educational co-operation was inaugurated on January 1, 1945, when intergroup education was projected in four American school systems, one of them Cleveland. Teacher scholarships were financed for research projects, and programs promoting the cause of intercultural relations were fostered. Under Nobel's guidance, the Conference had united the efforts of educational, religious, and community organizations in promoting better understanding of problems in human relationships.

The Stadium was filled with eighty-one thousand football fans who watched Notre Dame defeat Navy 14-7 on October 22.

The Irish Cultural Garden in Rockefeller Park was dedicated on October 29, Eamon de Valera, Prime Minister of Eire, attending the ceremonies. It was designed in the form of a Celtic cross, and featured a bed of Killarney roses planted in honor of Thomas Moore, the Irish poet. Two heroic symbolic figures were placed at the entranceway, and beautiful landscaping and walks contributed to the setting of the nationality shrine managed by the Irish Cultural Garden Association. The first ceremony had been held in 1933, when Msgr. Kirby of St. Cecelia's Parish had planted roses to symbolize "an Irishman's love for all nature."

Harold H. Burton was selected for his third successive term as mayor of Cleveland. He was the first man in twenty years to serve as chief executive for a continuous period of three terms. George H. Bender was elected to Congress, representing Ohio at large, an office he was holding in the 1940s. While a member of the Ohio Senate, 1920-30, he had become chairman of the Republican Central Committee of Cuyahoga County, bringing characteristic enthusiasm and resourcefulness to this important position.

Dr. Dan Freeman Bradley, eighty-two, pastor of Pilgrim Congregational Church from 1905 and chaplain of the Early Settlers Association, died suddenly on November 12. He had been a constructive civic leader as well as an inspiring spiritual guide.

Thanksgiving Day was celebrated on November 16, President Roosevelt having made the proclamation that the third Thursday in November instead of the fourth would be the national holiday. Since Civil War days, the fourth or last Thursday in the month had been observed, and the change to the New Deal holiday aroused much criticism. Some Clevelanders celebrated both Thursdays. On December 26, 1941, the President approved a joint resolution of Congress designating the fourth Thursday in November in each year.

The campaign goal set for the Community Fund was $3,350,000. The amount pledged was $3,237,476.46, with 492,747 subscribers. Those who received the distinguished-service award were Anthony Acierno, Rev. Frank M. Baker, Boy Scouts Troop 339 of Rainbow Hospital, Mary B. Gilbert, and Mrs. E. B. Palmer.

The Foreign Affairs Council was chosen by the Canadian Institute of National Relations to represent the United States in a series of international conferences for the purpose of exploring the future of Canadian-American relations. On December 9, Raymond Leslie Buell, round table editor of *Fortune,* addressed the council; and on December 16, Admiral Harry E. Yarnell, retired commander in chief of the Asiatic fleet, spoke on "The Protection of American Interests in the Far East."

Impressive ceremonies at Trinity Cathedral were held, December 17, when twenty-two new stained-glass windows were dedicated. These windows were arranged to depict a consecutive narrative in the life of Christ. Former members of the church, who had moved to other cities, returned for the memorial dedications which were in charge of Dean Chester B. Emerson. He had come to the Cathedral, January 1, 1933, as canon residentiary and became dean later in the year. His vital discourses in the pulpit, before civic groups, and over the radio reached great audiences who enjoyed his messages of hope and helpfulness.

The Public Square was given its most impressive holiday appearance the week before Christmas, with Mother Goose characters coming to life and organ chimes of the Old Stone Church playing carols. A Norway spruce with 1,200 colored lights was a feature.

A building transaction involving more than $4,500,000 was undertaken on lower Euclid Avenue by the W. T. Grant Company, which took over the Ames and Chandler sites at 240 Euclid Avenue on December 20.

Cleveland's Christmas-buying season established a new record with sales estimated at more than $15,000,000. On one day, the Post Office handled 4,769,359 pieces of mail.

Dr. Jason J. Nassau designed the optics of the first large Schmidt telescope this year. Built by the Warner & Swasey Company, it was installed in the Warner and Swasey Astronomical Observatory of Case School of Applied

Science. Dr. Nassau's telescope, with a lens two feet in diameter and three-tenths of an inch thick, made possible the photographing of several hundred thousand stars at one time. This new instrument enabled the designer to study the spectra of the stars and determine facts concerning their chemical composition and true brightness. Thus students of the heavens were able to intensify their quest for knowledge of the universe.

Dr. Ida Treat was writing literary and scientific reviews which were being published in France and the United States; Mary Margaret McBride became famous as a ghost-writer and as an able reporter; and Ruth McKenney, formerly an East Clevelander who was graduated from Shaw High School, won wide acclaim for her play, *My Sister Eileen,* produced on Broadway and later made into a motion picture. Arthur Charles Cole added to his list of interesting historical books; and David Dietz popularized science with books and newspaper stories, winning the Pulitzer Prize for Journalism in 1937. William Feather blended wit and philosophy in his own magazine and other publications; William M. Gregory made the study of geography interesting and popular; Dana Thomas Bowen told the *Lore of the Lakes* in story and pictures; and Mrs. Mary Cannon Whittaker, as president of the Cleveland Writers Club, was encouraging young authors.

At this time, the monthly deposit of soot was 46 tons per square mile in the metropolitan area, and 55 tons in the downtown area. An ordinance, enacted on December 18 as the result of many discussions and compromises, set up controls that were fair and acceptable to industry. While industry was sympathetic to the necessity of smoke abatement, it protested that with possible war in the offing the time was not propitious for strict enforcement.

A survey of Ohio coal properties indicated that thirty-four billion tons were still underground, enough to last two thousand years at the current rate of consumption.

Henry G. Dalton, industrialist, died on December 28. The Pickands Mather senior partner, aged seventy-seven, started work as a clerk in 1883 and became one of Cleveland's civic, business, and philanthropic leaders.

The University Hospitals Pharmacy Department filled 60,000 prescriptions in 1939, and approximately 170,000 patients were recorded in the outpatient department, sometimes 700 a day.

At the end of the year, Cleveland had six more telephones per hundred population than the average for the United States. The Ohio Bell Telephone Company was listed as the eighth largest subsidiary in the system in the total number of telephones, with 765,400 subscribers. In Greater Cleveland, as of December 31, there were 154,700 residential subscribers and 33,800 business subscribers.

The Cleveland Society for the Blind announced that its services were available to the thousand blind and nearly-blind persons in Cuyahoga County. Continuous efforts were being made to secure employment for which the blind were best fitted. Instruction was given in Braille and Moon types as well as in typewriting and shop work. Mrs. E. B. Palmer, executive secretary of the Society, had distinguished herself for more than a quarter-century as a leader in this important phase of the city's welfare work.

CHAPTER 17

Greatness Achieved

·1940·

CLEVELAND was "born great" in 1796. The strategic location selected by General Moses Cleaveland on the Great Lakes proved an ideal site for a community in which to live and work. One hundred and fifty years had passed since the founder predicted that the trading-post settlement would become as large as Old Windham, Connecticut.

At the natural gateway to the rich Ohio valley and the central plain of the flourishing Midwest, men of vision and stamina had built a great city, stretching along the southern shore of blue Lake Erie for a distance of thirty-five miles. The banks of the crooked Cuyahoga were lined with vast warehouses, immense mills, factories, and refineries. Downtown Cleveland, once a clearing with log cabins on the level above the lake, was a compact community of towering office structures, monumental public buildings, large department stores, smart shops, and theaters. Its streets were noisy and teeming with business and traffic. Gentle lake breezes tempered the extremes of summer and winter, and population figures had grown as people attracted by economic and cultural advantages decided to stay and make the city their home. Avenues of traffic and trade reached out to the boundaries of thriving cities and villages that nestled close to the sprawling, fan-shaped mother city, content in their municipal independence and the charm of their residential sections. This was Metropolitan Cleveland, a city that had achieved greatness in industry, commerce, education, culture, and philanthropic endeavor far beyond its founder's dreams.

The City of Cleveland held sixth place in population in the nation, according to the 1940 census. It was surpassed by New York, Chicago, Philadelphia, Detroit, and Los Angeles, and followed closely by Baltimore and St. Louis. Within an area of 73.35 square miles were 878,336 people, the total representing a small loss during the 1930s. Cuyahoga County showed a slight gain, however, with a population of 1,217,250 within its boundaries of 458.22 square miles. In the nation's ninth county in point of population there were 1,644 more women than men, and a breakdown of the county figures showed 74.5 per cent native white, 18.3 per cent foreign-born white, and 7.2 per cent Negro—87,145. The population of the city was 69.9 per cent native white, 20.4 foreign-born white, and 9.7 non-white. There were 609,125 persons aged twenty-one years or older, and 12,082 more than seventy-five years of age. In the city were 249,896 households, with 80,540 living in "dwelling units." The average renter paid $33.61 a month for his quarters.

The birth rate in the nation, which had been 27 per thousand persons in 1910, decreased to 17.9 in 1940. In the century from 1790 to 1890, the average increase of urban population between the decennial censuses was 60.7 per cent; but the increase in the 1920s was a little more than 27 per cent, and in the 1930s, 7.9 per cent. Laws governing immigration had become increasingly restrictive between 1930 and 1940, and, for the first time in the nation's history, immigrants were outnumbered by emigrants. So it was that the rate of population increase experienced by Cleveland in the early decades of the century became less and less as a result of decreased immigration and birth rate. The average family now represented 3.8 persons, indicating the steady downward trend toward a smaller family. An increase in births beginning in 1940, however, produced about 168,000 new citizens in Cuyahoga County by the end of 1946. Housing authorities, welfare workers, educators, and legislators faced with anxiety the mounting problems relating to the future of these young Clevelanders.

In the early years of the Twentieth Century, Cleveland was known as "the melting pot of nationalities." Waves of immigrants, attracted by the city's steady industrial growth, gradually submerged Old World characteristics into the habits and customs of the new. The proportion of foreign-born to native-born became less in the 1920s, and in the following decade the city was emerging from the melting-pot stage. Descendants of foreign-born parents took on American ways and caught the American spirit. Nevertheless, they remembered the countries of their forebears, finding fellowship in social and religious organizations and in developing the Cultural Gardens. On special occasions they wore colorful homeland costumes and indulged in traditional folk dances. Citizenship classes, "nationality nights" held at neighborhood schools, and co-operative movements helped to encourage understanding and dissolve prejudices in a city comprising more than forty nationality groups.

"Foreign" concentrations were based on culture rather than on language, and it was believed that in another decade there would be few persons in the area who could not speak intelligible English. Leading the foreign-born white groups in the county in 1940 were Poland, 27,960; Czechoslovakia, 26,040; Italy, 24,033; Hungary, 23,833; Germany, 21,042; Yugoslavia, 16,097; Russia (U.S.S.R.), 14,772; Austria, 12,080; England, 10,739; Canada and other, 8,691; Irish Free State (Eire), 6,399; Scotland, 5,542; Rumania, 4,782; Lithuania, 4,331; and other nationalities, making a total of 222,978, of which 142,733 had become naturalized by 1940, and an additional 22,686 had taken out first papers.

Although new housing construction had been retarded by the depression of the 1930s, the suburbs surrounding Cleveland made marked gains. There were fourteen cities, including Cleveland, in Cuyahoga County in 1940: Lakewood, with a population of 69,160; Cleveland Heights, 54,992; East Cleveland, 39,495; Shaker Heights, 23,393; Euclid, 17,866; Garfield Heights, 16,989; Parma, which had the greatest area, excepting Cleveland— 20.08 square miles—16,365; Rocky River, 8,291; Bedford, 7,390; Maple

Heights, 6,728; South Euclid, 6,146; Berea, 6,025; and University Heights, 5,981. Forty-one villages accounted for an area of 266.89 square miles: Bay, with a population of 3,356; Beachwood, 372; Bentleyville, 117; Bratenahl, 1,350; Brecksville, 1,900; Broadview Heights, 1,141; Brooklyn, 1,108; Brooklyn Heights, 496; Brook Park, 1,122; Chagrin Falls, 2,505; Cuyahoga Heights, 674; Fairview, 4,700; Gates Mills, 906; Glenwillow, 218; Highland Heights, 356; Hunting Valley, 336; Independence, 1,815; Linndale, 445; Lyndhurst, 2,391; Mayfield, 448; Mayfield Heights, 2,696; Middleburgh Heights, 1,225; Moreland Hills, 561; Newburgh Heights, 3,830; North Olmsted, 3,487; North Randall, 92; North Royalton, 2,559; Olmsted Falls, 754; Orange, 492; Parkview, 208; Parma Heights, 1,330; Pepper Pike, 423; Richmond Heights, 507; Seven Hills, 555; Solon, 1,508; Strongsville, 2,216; Valley View, 753; Warrensville Heights, 1,175; Westlake, 3,200; Westview, 407; and Woodmere, 277. Five townships—Bedford, Chagrin Falls, Olmsted, River Edge, and Warrensville—rounded out the Cleveland Metropolitan District. Over a period of fifteen years, on the basis of housing, the fastest-growing suburbs were University Heights, 244.2 per cent; Euclid, 143.3; Rocky River, 72.1; Fairview, 56.6; and Shaker Heights, 47.4.

The rapid growth of outlying suburbs was not surprising, and war years had accelerated the population shift from farms and small towns. Ohio and the Great Lakes States experienced population gains exceeded only by the West Coast and Florida.

Cleveland claimed distinction as "the best location in the nation"—at "the crossroads of industry." Within five hundred miles of the city lived more than half the people of the United States and Canada; and in this important trade empire were produced 71 per cent of the nation's manufactured products by 71 per cent of its wage earners, their earnings representing 75 per cent of the American payroll. Cleveland was the natural meeting place of iron ore, coal, copper, gypsum, stone, sand, lumber, wood pulp, hides, clay, wool, oils, and other vital raw materials that were transformed into a diversity of manufactured products supplying a great marketing area. Efficient transportation by rail, lake, highway, and air facilitated delivery and reduced costs.

Iron-and-steel output of steel works, rolling mills, and blast furnaces amounted to almost one-sixth of the dollar volume of manufacturing industries in the Cleveland Industrial Area—Cuyahoga and Lorain counties —in the census of manufacturers of 1939. Cleveland ranked high in the production of bolts and nuts, rivets and screws, forgings, hardware, and a vast number of iron-and-steel products that were channeled into foreign and domestic trade. It was the world center of the lighting industry, second in the production of machine tools, and leading producer and control center of paints and varnishes, motor fuel, trucks and buses, electrical goods, and metal products. It was claimed that every airplane and automobile made in America contained parts or accessories manufactured in Cleveland. The Cleveland district had pioneered in the development of aluminum, magnesium, copper, and brass products; and for many years the city had

Map of Cleveland Metropo

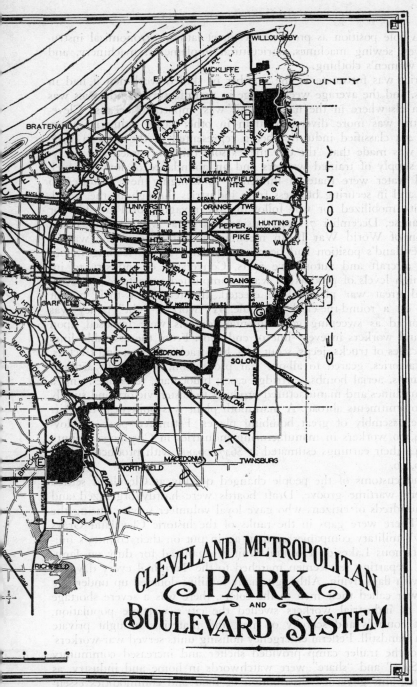

Cleveland Metropolitan Park and Boulevard System—1949

held an enviable position as producer of turret lathes, astronomical instruments, stoves, sewing machines, agricultural implements, machinery, and men's and women's clothing.

The district was fortunate in the number of skilled workmen it had in many fields, and the average weekly wage in manufacturing industries was higher than elsewhere in the nation. This was important, because Cleveland industry was more diversified than in other large industrial areas, 323 of the 454 classified industries being represented in the area in 1946. The claim was made that "the city makes something of practically everything." Its supply of trained workers and an abundance of low-cost fuel, power, and water were material influences in bringing new factories to the district and in securing business from industries throughout the world.

As the city mobilized for war following the ravaging of Pearl Harbor by the Japanese, December 7, 1941, business as usual was abandoned for the duration of World War II. In meeting the demands of the war in Europe, Cleveland's position had been strengthened as the leading manufacturer of aircraft and automotive parts. Conversion of industry to increasingly high levels of production was accomplished as factories were expanded and great war plants were erected, the tempo of their output quickening on a round-the-clock schedule. A "work-or-fight" policy was rigidly enforced as sweeping governmental controls were imposed upon employers and workers in every line of endeavor. From the assembly lines rolled cavalcades of trucks, jeeps, scout cars, half-tracks, trailers, and tractors. Cleveland factories, geared to all-out war production, turned out artillery and small arms, aerial bombs, cartridge cases, binoculars, telescopes, and a myriad of machines and manufactured products to hasten victory and supply lend-lease commitments abroad. A mammoth plant was built near the Airport for the assembly of great bombing planes. Estimated peak employment of 234,100 workers in manufacturing industries in Cuyahoga County came in 1944, their earnings estimated at $647,600,000 with products valued at $3,406,800,000.

Habits and customs of the people changed quickly as Cleveland settled into the stern wartime groove. Draft boards were hastily organized and staffed by hundreds of citizens who gave loyal volunteer service during the war years. There were gaps in the ranks of the historic Cleveland Grays and the city's military companies as men again put on their country's uniform. The famous Lakeside Hospital Unit reorganized for duty on January 4, 1942. Departing servicemen marched to the Terminal every day, led by a band with flags flying. Although many families doubled up under one roof when war called their men to the colors, there was a severe shortage of housing as industrial workers swelled the city's wartime population. Government controls and scarcity of men and materials brought private housing to a standstill. Federal emergency housing units served war-workers' families, and the trailer camp provided shelter and increased community problems. "Save" and "share" were watchwords in home and industry, as rationing programs governed distribution of food and commodities essential to victory.

United effort on the home front and curbs on travel encouraged community fellowship and strengthened the morale of Cleveland's fighting men. An army of bondadiers, working house-to-house, urged young and old to send their dollars to war in a series of highly successful War Bond campaigns. Stores promoted sales of bonds and stamps and established selling stations convenient to their large traffic lines of customers. The schools and youth organizations gave invaluable service in projects of practical helpfulness. Employers and employees relieved pressure on the over-taxed transit system, saved automobile wear and tear, tires, and fuel by co-operating in staggered-hours and share-the-ride plans. Progress of the war was reflected in continuous reminders in the form of manpower drives, dimouts, scrap drives, Block Plan and Civilian Defense developments, projects quartered in the War Service Center on the Public Square, and activities of the USO, servicemen's canteens, Red Cross, veterans' clubs, Blue Star Mothers, Gold Star Mothers, American Women's Voluntary Services, and hundreds of other patriotic and purposeful organizations.

World War I had been called the war to end war, and the people of the United States joined those of stricken countries in a firm declaration, "Never again!" World War II proved anew that every nation, victor and vanquished, loses as the result of war. When the surrender of Germany came in May, 1945, the distressed and hungry people of shattered countries sobbed, "Never again!" But even as they despaired, military men and those in high places were speculating as to how soon the lust for power would reassert itself.

The most devastating war in history was ended, and Cleveland celebrated the victory with thanksgiving. From Cuyahoga County had gone more than its quota of young men and women to join the service, and the war record at home was unsurpassed in the land. On the military roll of honor there were many gold stars representing "the last full measure of devotion" in the nation's defense. As men and women laid away the khaki and the blue to take up peacetime pursuits, others, sick and maimed, were striving to find health in veterans' hospitals. In the postwar era came pyramiding problems of rehabilitation—sending relief to the suffering in allied countries and helping peoples to re-establish order out of chaos. In characteristic neighborly fashion, Clevelanders campaigned in their behalf, sending vast shipments of food and clothing abroad to the needy in a war-torn world.

Cosmopolitan Cleveland followed with more than humanitarian interest the historic meeting in San Francisco on June 26, 1945, when representatives of fifty countries signed the United Nations Charter. While hoping for the maintenance of international peace through this great forward step, many remembered the fate of the League of Nations following World War I. Cleveland's Council on World Affairs was a leader in its field, interpreting international events to the people. As the year 1946 closed, the Council planned a series of meetings entitled "Report to the World," suggested and supported by Time, Inc., with internationally known leaders of several countries as speakers.

Postwar planning had taken practical form before the conclusion of the war, and Cleveland was prepared for the transition to peacetime production. Private enterprise began to take over the war plants; and, with a "know-how" improved by the experiences of the war years, immediately recorded an output far surpassing any known in prewar years. Wartime developments found peacetime uses that played important parts in world progress. Among the products that came out of the laboratories were new tubes for radar application, new steels to meet tough engineering problems, improved cutting and grinding oils, wire for recording purposes, rayon cord for heavy-duty tires, synthetic and plastic products by the thousands, new foods, drugs, and insecticides. Cleveland companies had been honored for their contributions to atomic-bomb development: the Harshaw Chemical Company, Victoreen Instrument Company, Brush Beryllium Company, McGean Chemical Company, and H. K. Ferguson Company. Now scientists were working diligently to harness atomic energy for peacetime use.

Reaction from war brought a period marked by high wages in industry, easy spending, labor upheavals, and price advances. Political factions battled over the power of unions, tax reduction, housing, and veterans' problems. Burdened with taxes, the people watched prices climb higher and higher. Black markets flourished, rackets were re-established, night clubs thrived, and there was a careless feeling that good times were here to stay. Inflation seemed inevitable as foreign loans and gifts of the Federal Government increased, unbalanced by imports. In some lines, wages trebled. Dividends reached new highs as the purchasing power of the dollar diminished. Expert opinion was divided, fearing on the one hand that out of a false economy would come a financial crash, on the other, an unprecedented boom.

To finance World War II, the nation borrowed billions of dollars, raising the national debt to an all-time high of $279,764,000,000, or $1,908 per person, in February, 1946—almost eleven times the figure after World War I! In all history, no people had owed so much money. Economists warned that the financial structure of the United States would collapse unless the brakes were applied to fantastic spending and the cost of government was reduced. Production must be expanded, they declared, responsibility for the poor and unemployed returned to the States, and restrictions imposed by government and other forces removed to permit the free-enterprise system to work.

Clergymen preached sermons emphasizing the growing need for parental responsibility and Christian living as fundamental to the preservation of the family in an era of broken marriages and mounting juvenile delinquency. Cleveland families were having maid troubles. Homemakers found it increasingly difficult to hire "live-in" domestics, even at the unprecedented offer of forty dollars a week, plus room, board, laundry, and more free time than they had ever enjoyed. "Baby sitting," a new occupation giving employment to youth and old age, was in demand at prices that jolted the family budget.

It was not until the early 1940s that comprehensive city planning, worthy of the name, was really undertaken. Amos Spafford and Seth Pease, Moses Cleaveland's surveyors, had laid out the Public Square and the orderly pattern of central streets with practical vision. Then came topsy-turvy development during years of rapid growth, when planning was considered an expense rather than an investment. The city was allowed to take haphazard form, resulting in inefficient street development, traffic bottlenecks, and a lack of north-and-south streets in the central city that became an increasingly serious shortcoming. Like its sister cities, Cleveland was suffering from the slow rot of decentralization as the decade opened, a destructive trend that had blighted districts around the central area. To combat decay, the City Planning Commission was making studies of land use and prescribing new housing districts, parks, and improvements in order to protect the heart of Cleveland and increase property values.

This was the period in which municipal ownership of the street-railway lines was being tested. The system was in serious need of new equipment and an extension of rapid-transit lines, and the Cleveland Transit Board found a critical citizenship calling for better service as fares increased. Engineers were employed to study rapid transit, to chart new routes that would reach greater numbers of people, and to recommend equipment that would carry riders with greater speed and safety. Major problems confronted the management in rising costs of operation and construction, and the need for new financing. Since the beginning of the century, the suburbs had been growing into cities in their own rights, most of them using common utilities and transportation systems. Although many residents shopped, visited, found entertainment, and earned their daily bread in Cleveland, they scarcely realized that, while enjoying its advantages, they did not share its responsibilities. As a result, the mother city's problems related to taxes, transit, finance, and decentralization were aggravated year by year to alarming proportions.

Practical attention was given to traffic congestion and mounting parking problems in Cleveland, the studies of the Transportation Panel of the Cleveland Automobile Club proving to be important in furthering progress. Winner of many safety records, due to police and Safety Council, Cleveland was known nationally as a "safe" city.

A long-range express-highway plan, calling for the expenditure of more than $240,000,000, was developed by the Express Highway Committee of the Regional Association, formulated by engineers representing the state, county, city, Regional Association, City Planning Commission, and Cleveland Transit System. The plan, designed to promote speed and safety, called for an inner belt surrounding the central area and an outer belt skirting the greater part of the city. The committee's ambitious plans were to be carried out over a period of years, a system of priorities indicating the order in which highway units were to be built. Cleveland had many plans on paper, and practical-minded, forward-looking citizens constantly called attention to the fact that too few were put into operation.

Cleveland schools continued to hold high rank in the nation, increasing the ability of youth to rise to the challenge of the tremendous problems of tomorrow's greater city. There was a growing appreciation that good teaching depends upon good teachers, that maintaining a good teaching staff depends upon adequate pay, and that adequate pay depends upon public interest continuously alert and informed. There was an increasing realization that citizenship and business depend upon schools and colleges to develop the minds and hands of the youth who shape the future.

The city's educational institutions struggled through the war period, many students and faculty members entering war service and industrial employment. At the conclusion of the war, student enrollment in public and private schools—day and night—reached record highs, as heroic efforts were made to take care of veterans who wisely sought to complete their education with the financial support of their country. Schools of higher and specialized education included Western Reserve University and its downtown institution—Cleveland College; Case School of Applied Science, a new and modern name—Case Institute of Technology—not yet having been adopted officially; John Carroll University, Fenn College, Notre Dame College, Ursuline College, John Huntington Polytechnic Institute, Cleveland Institute of Music, Cleveland School of Art, and in neighboring Berea, Baldwin-Wallace College.

The Cleveland Public Library, with more than two and a half million volumes on its shelves, led big-city libraries in per-capita circulation, and its Business Information department stood at the top in its field. A system of branch and school libraries and library stations served the metropolitan city.

Typical of the forward march in safeguarding public health was the Cleveland Health Museum, the first permanent health museum in the Western Hemisphere, which opened in 1940. This unique institution represented the achievement of the Academy of Medicine of Cleveland in cooperation with medical, dental, public-health, civic, and cultural organizations in portraying the advances made in medical and health science, and promoting personal and community hygiene.

Sport, recreation, and amusement could be found in many forms in 2,317 acres of parks provided for the people in the Cleveland Park System. Thousands enjoyed the wonders of the outdoors in the almost unbroken chain of parks in the Metropolitan Park System which began at Cahoon Creek and the lake on the west and ended with the Chagrin Reservation on the east. Nature was brought close to Clevelanders who visited the Cleveland Museum of Natural History and the Zoo in Brookside Park.

In the realm of music, Cleveland held a high place. The Cleveland Orchestra, one of the nation's finest symphonies, had carried the city's cultural fame to the world over the air waves, through recordings, and in concerts in this nation, in Cuba, and Canada. At the same time, it had enriched the lives of vast audiences in beautiful Severance Hall; and thousands of children found new appreciation of music in daytime concerts arranged in co-operation with the Board of Education. The Metropolitan Opera Company played each year before its largest audiences in the Public Auditorium. Love of art and interest in things historical brought a steady trek of visitors to see the famous treasures in the Cleveland Museum of Art and the priceless exhibitions in the Western Reserve Historical Society Museum and Library in the Wade Park cultural center.

Cleveland offered a variety of top-billing entertainment. The Cleveland

Indians, under the direction of "Bill" Veeck, master showman, drew the biggest baseball crowds the city had known; the Festival of Freedom proved America's leading Independence Day celebration on each succeeding Fourth of July; the Barons filled the Arena with cheering hockey fans; the Browns professional football team attracted the largest gate in its league; the Hanna Theater, Public Music Hall, and motion-picture houses testified to Cleveland's appreciation of varied and worthy entertainment. After a wartime lull, national expositions and conventions were again choosing Cleveland as host city.

Fast-moving radio shows, featuring big-name celebrities and music, sweet or blaring, characterized the 1940s, punctuated by quiz programs, hair-raising mysteries, and singing commercials. Contests pyramided fabulous prizes running into four figures. Old-timers hoped that television would bring back vaudeville. Although Fibber McGee and Molly, Allen, Hope, Crosby, Benny, and Bergen monopolized the top rungs of the radio ladder, it was rumored that they were studying television techniques against the time when their high-salaried crowns might be challenged by radio progress.

Boogie-woogie was popular as the decade opened. Swing was beginning to fade, and the rave over "scat singers" and barbershop harmony was growing. *Don't Sit Under the Apple Tree* was sweeping the country in 1942 when *Praise the Lord and Pass the Ammunition* came out of the war zone to inspire home-front workers with new win-the-war spirit. The immortal *Army Air Corps* song, "Off we go—into the wild blue yonder!" was composed by Robert M. "Bob" Crawford, Case School graduate, as he flew with the service. Toil and tension were drowned in crazy tunes called *Mairzy Doats* and *Pistol-Packin' Mama*.

The screen was finding that it paid to present in motion pictures the plays that were winning greatest success on the stage. Audiences enjoyed the quaint humor of *Life with Father*, the delightful satire of *The Man Who Came to Dinner*, the amusing situations of the *Philadelphia Story*, and the riotous chills of *Arsenic and Old Lace*.

The jitterbug cut his capers on the dance floor in a crazy creation of balloon-like trousers and baggy frock coat called the zoot suit, a fad that was nipped in the bud by Uncle Sam's wartime restriction of the use of clothing material.

When dress designers decreed that a "new look" in fashions would center in a return to Gibson-girl styles, millions of women raised their voices in protest. Dropping the hemline was a shock to "bobby soxers" who shouted that "slip-over sweaters, sloppy white shirts, and blue jeans shall not go," while irate office workers and homemakers declared they would not trade just-below-the-knee freedom for femininity at increased cost. Flashy costume jewelry was purchased riotously by women freed from war restrictions, and platform shoes were gaining favor.

Drug stores were hardly worthy of the name. Drugs had been relegated to obscure shelves in streamlined, fluorescent-lighted establishments, to make way for gleaming soda fountains and quick-lunch counters, glamorous displays of cosmetics, candies, and gift items, and counters laden with gadgets, toys, and housewares. Chain stores and "stupendous" serve-yourself supermarkets challenged the independent grocer's future. The cracker barrel had been replaced by potato-chip and pretzel racks, soft-drink coolers and juke boxes as the center of political forums at community meeting places. Short-order diners, used-car lots and filling stations flashing neon signs spotted historic Euclid Avenue. Mansions of massive architecture built by influential families around the turn of the century were filled with transient roomers who knew little if anything of their glorious past.

With an eye to the future, air-minded Clevelanders continued to strive to make Cleveland the aviation center of America. The city's stake in the industry had grown in proportion to giant strides made during World War II. Cleveland was the hub of the nation's air-transport system. It was the home of the Air Foundation and the gigantic aircraft engine research laboratory of the National Advisory Committee for Aeronautics, the largest in the world. The scope and importance of aviation to the progress, development, and defense of America were graphically demonstrated in the National Aircraft Show and at the Air Races, resumed in 1946.

Three major air lines served the city, providing passenger and cargo service to all parts of the nation from the Municipal Airport, the largest airport operated by a city. Increased air traffic required continuous enlarging of the port, the 1946 volume—86,530 ships cleared, 1,286,144 passengers—setting a new high. A lakefront airport was projected east of East 9th Street in downtown Cleveland. The metropolis was the center of a network of highways, bus, and truck routes connecting with all parts of the country. Excellent railroad facilities were provided by seven trunk lines radiating to east, west, and south.

Cleveland possessed one of the busiest and finest harbors on the Great Lakes, more than 80 per cent of the lake fleets being owned or controlled in the city. Limited to a seven-month shipping season, as great a total tonnage was handled as in Boston, Philadelphia, or Baltimore, cities enjoying a twelve-month season. No wonder Cleveland continuously sought the aid of the Federal Government in improving the inner harbor, handicapped by bends and curves. Engineers pointed out that there were 13 miles of dock space in a distance of 5½ miles from the heart of the city. Since the turn of the century, the channel had been widened and sharp bends cut back, so that by 1941 great freighters, 635 feet long and 70 feet wide, could navigate with safety, where a few years earlier boats half their size had been blocked. Still further improvements, to cost more than twenty million dollars, were planned for the future.

Lakefront developments were proceeding at a disappointingly slow rate, but plans were made for checking erosion and capitalizing on the shore line for business and pleasure.

Cuyahoga County's industrial record was well above the national average in 1946. Employment had climbed to within 2½ per cent of the V-J Day level. Payrolls of manufacturing industries had reached $500,000,000 as compared with half the figure in 1929, the best peacetime year prior to World War II. Four hundred and thirty-four new industrial companies had

The spacious Cleveland Municipal Airport.

Army Air Corps at the National Air Races. OFFICIAL PHOTOGRAPH, U. S. ARMY AIR CORPS.

A portion of the great Laboratory of the National Advisory Committee for Aeronautics at the Cleveland Airport.

A section of quaint Shaker Square, its New England architecture, broad lawns, and the spacious Moreland Courts, upper left. Below is Stouffer's attractive Shaker Tavern, flanked by fine shops.

been established since 1937, and, during the past ten years, two thousand plant expansions had been made at a cost of nearly $500,000,000.

The year 1946 showed an increase in the cost of living in Cleveland of about 51 per cent as compared with the autumn of 1939 when World War II was getting under way, according to Russell Weisman, *Plain Dealer* economist. However, increases in average weekly earnings in the manufacturing industries had grown approximately 91 per cent in the same period. In October, 1946, the average wage earner was receiving $45.83 weekly, or 76.3 per cent more than in 1926 when his weekly earnings were $26.

Eleven clearing-house banks, with resources of almost $2,300,000,000 in 1946, were operating 68 neighborhood branches, and providing for the business and industrial requirements of the Cleveland area. Bank debits of more than $16,907,000,000 had doubled since 1940. Thirty-nine building-and-loan associations were in business in 1945, their resources of $141,763,000 almost double those of 45 institutions in 1940. Cleveland was the home of more than 40 trade associations furthering the interests of manufacturing, distribution, and service.

Cleveland was said to have had more businessmen with international-trade experience than any other American city its size, and they were continuously studying ways and means to expand volume. Trade relations between Cleveland and the nation's neighbors to the south were resumed after the war and amounted to millions of dollars. Cleveland-made machinery, parts and equipment, paints and varnishes, tools and hardware, oils and greases, wire and wire products, chemicals and drugs, motor trucks and office machines were finding increasing export markets, while from South America came coffee, cocoa, oil-seed products, wool, hides and skins, fruits and edible nuts, basic medicinal products, bananas, liquors, wines, candy, jewelry, and precious stones. Steady trade expansion was reflected in increased attendance in foreign-language classes of public and private schools, particularly those of Spanish and Portuguese.

Believing that "research is the spearhead of progress," Cleveland laboratories and factories had discovered basic processes and developed products that commanded world attention. The city had become the center of research in aircraft engines, valves for internal-combustion engines, friction bearings, forgings and castings, induction hardening of steel, machine tools, medicine, and many other fields. Progress in electric lighting, home planning, and electrical development centered at Nela Park, that numbered among its thousands of pioneering achievements in a quarter century the tipless lamp, the inside frosted lamp, the photo-flash lamp for photography, the standard fluorescent tube, the ultra-violet sun lamp, and a 50,000-watt incandescent lamp, the largest in the world, used in the motion-picture industry.

The trade-union movement skyrocketed to a quarter-million membership in the Greater Cleveland area by 1946, but seemingly failed to make progress in its drive for political recognition. When the New Deal was at the height of its power in 1942, labor organizations in the district—AFL, CIO, MESA, and the powerful railroad brotherhoods—endeavored through political action to further the Roosevelt program. Economists believed that union demands were becoming excessive and that higher wages would mean higher prices, resulting in a wage spiral with inflation inevitable. The year 1946 witnessed nearly full employment, yet unsatisfactory industrial conditions were charged largely to strikes that slowed down production. It became evident that new labor legislation would be enacted by Congress in the near future. A political upset came in the November elections. The Democratic Party, in power since 1933, was decisively defeated, and significant changes in the country's economic program were expected to follow.

The city had bridged the transition from wartime, and was maintaining production levels far in excess of any peacetime period. New records were established in Sesquicentennial Year by wages, department-store sales, postal receipts, bank resources, bank clearings, postal savings, telephone subscribers, air traffic, and streetcar riders. Building construction reflected the pace of business and industry. In 1946, 6,503 building permits were issued in Cleveland. Building operations valued at $36,176,500 were 65 per cent greater than those in 1940.

The population continued to increase. Marriages rose from 11,945 in 1945 to 19,165 in 1946 in the county; births increased from 24,056 to an estimated 29,144. The housing problem had become more acute as government controls continued to hamper building progress. There was little evidence of a trend in the direction of normal living. Many immigrants admitted to the United States after the war, largely from Canada, Germany, England, and Italy, sought new homes in Cleveland. There were few skilled workmen among them, and their occupations were reported mostly as professional, semi-professional, clerical, and the like. A large part of the newcomers were women, children, elderly persons, and enthusiastic young people.

Merchant ships from foreign countries had been making irregular calls at the Cleveland port prior to World War II. Following the war, foreign lines began to operate regularly, and vessels flying the flags of Great Britain, the Netherlands, Norway, Sweden, Denmark, and Belgium mingled with those of American, Canadian, and Great Lakes ships, emphasizing international relations at the lake port.

Generation after generation, Cleveland families contributed to public welfare through generous giving. The Severances, Cases, Stones, and Mathers founded colleges and built chapels and cathedrals, laboratories and libraries. The Wade, Bolton, and Blossom families, along with those of Prentiss, Warner, Swasey, Drury, Rose, Squire, and Beaumont, left a heritage that would benefit humanity for decades to come. Philanthropies of the Harkness and Rockefeller families reached beyond Cleveland to the nation and the world. Through the Tyler, Norton, and Hanna bequests, welfare and cultural institutions expanded their services. Gifts from innumerable public-spirited citizens—great and small—to the Cleveland Foundation, Community Fund, and worthy civic agencies represented the unity of Clevelanders in purposeful giving.

The story of Cleveland's pride in 150 years of achievement is written in the pages of the chronology of 1946. As the Cleveland flag proudly caught the breeze under the American flag on New Year's Day morning, Sesquicentennial Year was inaugurated at the city's traditional meeting place, the Public Square. A parade of events, attracting national attention, continued until fall and honored past glories and celebrated accomplishments that had given the city leadership in important fields. More meetings were held in the city than ever before. Civic organizations, trade associations, luncheon clubs, and many groups of women and youth arranged special historical programs that inspired civic pride. In these friendly exchanges of ideas, horizons broadened and new and richer fields of endeavor opened.

During Cleveland's 150th Anniversary Year, distinguished journalists came to the city and reported to their publications gratifying reactions regarding the metropolis and its institutions. Leonard H. Robbins, well-known feature writer for the *New York Times,* paid tribute to the city's civic pride and enthusiasm in an article published in his paper on August 1. Of the Cleveland spirit, he said, "that is something to put heart into any American oppressed by the surface materialism of his generation. All Clevelanders agree on one thing, that their city, in this Sesquicentennial Year, as it salutes the past and builds for the future, is a swell city. And so it is." The *Baltimore Sun* sent Frank Henry to survey Cleveland, and the opening paragraph of his report was significant: "Cleveland's zeal for civic and cultural improvement is perhaps its greatest distinguishing mark among American cities. For nearly half a century, its business and political leaders have kept their eyes on one goal—making Cleveland the best possible place in which to live."

Cleveland had become known nationally for its fine spirit of co-operation. When a worthy cause involving the people's welfare was presented to the citizenship there was a wholehearted response. Campaigns in wartime and peacetime, Red Cross drives, and civic movements were furthered by characteristic teamwork. A local philosopher declared, "Cleveland is the campaign-ingest town on earth: first it campaigns for size, then for wealth, then for safety, then for health—but it's always campaigning."

Hard-working citizens, quiet and peace-loving, were proud of their steady march in the making of a city—Cleveland. Talented leadership and organized effort had made it a good place in which to live and to work. Wizards of engineering and mass production had geared its abundant yield to the needs of global industry. Masters of finance and planning had shaped its firm foundations. Unselfish men and women had given of time and talents to extend cultural and charitable opportunities to those who would share them. Democracy worked in Cleveland, a city of home owners, good government, and co-operative enterprise. A throbbing city of tremendous energy, it echoed the ring of foundry and forge and the whir of motors and machines, and its fiery furnaces lighted the night sky. With advantages of many kinds, Cleveland had indeed achieved greatness.

1940

Mayor Burton reported that during 1939 Cleveland enjoyed a 10 per cent gain in business volume, a 20 per cent reduction in crime, a material improvement in traffic safety, and in fire prevention. His plans for the new year included community effort to encourage industrial progress, securing of federal and state action to meet relief and unemployment needs, establishment of a sound financial program for the city, negotiation of a fair franchise agreement between the City of Cleveland and the Cleveland Railway Company, continued progress on the river-and-harbor program, installation of parking meters, co-operation with suburbs in the study of an annexation program for Greater Cleveland, and beautification of the Erie Street Cemetery.

A Lutheran Center was organized by a group of laymen who recognized the need for a central church office and a clearing house for information and publicity. Originally owned by the Walther League, the site at 4106 Franklin Avenue became the headquarters of denominational activities in Greater Cleveland.

The exhibition of masterpieces of art from the New York World's Fair drew great throngs to the Cleveland Museum of Art from February 7 through March 7. It was considered the most impressive traveling exhibit ever seen in Cleveland. Some of the most famous paintings of Rembrandt, Rubens, Hals, Watteau, and a score of other old masters were displayed, most of the noted works not having been seen before in this country until they were sent to the World's Fair.

Commemorating the 150th anniversary of the American patent system, fifteen Clevelanders were honored for their inventive genius, on February 7 in the Hotel Statler, by the Associated Industries of Cleveland, the Ohio Manufacturers Association, the National Association of Manufacturers, and the Cleveland Chamber of Commerce. "Modern Pioneers" selected for special recognition by a national committee of leading scientists included the following Clevelanders: Marvin Pipkin, of Nela Park, for his development of the inside frosting process for lamp bulbs; James B. Kirby, of the Apex Electrical Manufacturing Company, for "revolutionary" improvements in the vacuum cleaner and the washing machine; Dr. C. Baldwin Sawyer and B. R. Kjellgren, of the Brush Laboratories Company, for their development of crystals that became standard in radios, loud speakers, phonograph pick-ups, and the like; Arthur F. Case, consulting engineer for the Wellman Engineering Company, for machinery handling coal and bulk materials and other inventions; Joseph V. Emmons, of the Cleveland Twist Drill Company, for his part in developing alloy steels relying on molybdenum rather than tungsten; Alfred F. Harris, chairman of the board of the Harris-Seybold-Potter Company, for developing the method and machinery of the offset-lithographic method of printing; William J. Harshaw, president of Harshaw

Chemical Company, for a number of chemical contributions; Hayden B. Kline, vice president in charge of plant operations, Industrial Rayon Corporation, for a new continuous process by which viscose rayon yarn could be spun, after-treated, dried, and twisted in a single, integrated operating sequence; Samuel B. Kraut, of the Westinghouse Electric & Manufacturing Company, for sodium vapor lamps used in illumination of highways and bridges; John C. Lincoln, chairman of the board, and James F. Lincoln, president of Lincoln Electric Company, for pioneering achievements in electrical arc welding; Rex D. McDill, president of the Inspection Machinery Company, for a machine to wash, dry, polish, and wax citrus fruit in a single operation, for an instrument to determine density of materials such as tomato paste, and other inventions; Professor Carl F. Prutton, head of the chemistry department, Case School of Applied Science, for lubrication discoveries and developments that increased speed and horsepower in automotive engines and industrial machinery; and Dr. Harry F. Waite, president of Picker X-Ray Corporation, Waite Manufacturing Division, for the shockproof, oil-immersed X-ray tube and transformer protecting patients and operators. The dinner program featured a style show of clothing made from coal and coal tar, air, water, milk, glass, rubber, and moth balls.

Special ceremonies marked Lincoln's birthday. The visit of Lincoln to Cleveland was re-enacted at the Weddell House, a comprehensive exhibit was arranged in the Terminal, and a special radio broadcast was presented over Station WGAR.

Fewer cases of infant mortality, diphtheria, typhoid, and tuberculosis were recorded in 1939 than in any previous year. The first open-air, public-school classes in the country were conducted in Cleveland as a step in the war on tuberculosis.

Walter Logan, sixty-three, dean of Cleveland orchestra leaders, died in March. A gifted violinist and composer, his experiences and associations with leading musicians were numerous. He was musical director of Station WTAM and had been dean of the Music School Settlement.

On April 1, a crew of fifteen men under John B. Fitzgerald, stage manager, finished hanging one of the largest stage curtains in the world at the Public Auditorium. The wine-colored velour curtain, 84 feet wide and 43 feet high, cost $6,000.

The Cleveland Chamber of Commerce on April 1 welcomed the year-old Junior Association of Commerce as an affiliate, the purpose being to offer new opportunities to Cleveland's young men by opening unlimited fields of civic participation.

The John Adams High School Orchestra, under the leadership of Amos G. Wesler, appeared in the Los Angeles Philharmonic Auditorium on April 3, as the invited guest of the Music Educators National Conference. The fourteen-day trip was planned and directed by Dwight W. Lott, assistant principal and orchestra manager. It was the third guest appearance of this famous musical organization, the others being in the Metropolitan Opera House, New York City, in 1936, and in Detroit in 1939. This latest trip represented a unique co-operative achievement, as the students, the faculty, and the parents contributed $13,500 for necessary expenses—a dynamic expression of community loyalty!

The first opening-day no-hit game in modern major-league history was

"Give this Feller a great big hand!" (*Willard Combes in the Press.*)

pitched by Bob Feller on April 16. He fanned eight men and beat Chicago, 1-0. Bob Feller led the major leagues this year in victories with 27 games won against 11 defeats. He led in innings pitched with 320; in games pitched, 43; in strikeouts, 261. During World War II Feller spent thirty months in combat duty on the *U.S.S. Alabama,* after having won 107 major-league games at the age of twenty-two. His start toward fame thus surpassed the records of Cy Young, Walter Johnson, Christy Mathewson, and Grover Cleveland Alexander, generally accepted as the greatest pitchers in baseball history. Feller came back to the mound for the Indians late in 1945.

So successful had been the Metropolitan Opera performances in Cleveland that Manager Edward Johnson indicated this city was "the Metropolitan's second home." This year saw the fruition of the ingenious Sherwin-Williams auditions, when for the first time the winners of earlier years—John Carter, Annamary Dickey, and Leonard Warren—appeared in leading roles. As usual, the season was an artistic and financial success, maintaining Cleveland's prestige as an opera center.

The Cleveland Medal for Public Service was awarded in April by the Chamber of Commerce to Arthur Douglas Baldwin, "distinguished attorney, thoughtful civic leader, valuable citizen, who has given generously of time and effort to Cleveland's civic and philanthropic institutions"; to Edward Belden Greene, "distinguished banker, far-visioned industrialist, patron of the arts, who plays an important role in the financial and industrial life of the nation"; to Nathan G. Richman, "distinguished business man, wise humanitarian, generous philanthropist, and enlightened leader in employer-employee relationships."

Frederick C. Crawford was elected president of The Cleveland Chamber of Commerce. He was succeeded in the 1940s by Charles J. Stilwell, 1941; James F. Lincoln, 1942; W. T. Holliday, 1943; Sam W. Emerson, 1944; Herbert P. Ladds, 1945; Percy W. Brown, 1946; Elmer L. Lindseth, 1947, succeeded by John K. Thompson.

Sensational was the wartime story of Jack & Heintz, makers of precision parts for army and navy planes. The founders were William S. "Bill" Jack and Ralph Heintz, who had begun their association in a tool-shed at 17600 Broadway, Bedford, some time before. Jack had new ideas concerning employer-employee relations, and, before long, the whole nation watched his procedure with amazement. Frequent secret meetings in downtown hotels, the ballrooms packed with Jahco "associates," the sale of stock to workers, gifts of bonuses averaging $300 and of insurance policies, and vacations in Florida or Georgian Bay were among the many ideas designed to bring about a spirit of co-operation that would increase production. The novel plan seemed to obtain results during wartime. By 1944, personnel had skyrocketed from 46 to 8,700. Then came a slump which led to an amalgamation, the new name being Jack & Heintz Precision Industries, Inc., with Byron C. Foy as president. The new management substituted conservatism for sensationalism, and added to its list of aviation products, new lines of motors, bearings, magnets, refrigeration units, and other items, with Reber C. Stupp in charge of operations.

The Cleveland Yacht Club boasted the largest fleet of Comets in the world. Among the skippers of the thirty-five little sailboats were Richard MacHenry, Louise and Dorothy Davis, Armin Wagner, Gordon McIntosh, P. W. Wilson, R. W. Purcell, Harry Wirl, William Holland, and Fred Best. Skippers of the R fleet, six-ton boats carrying approximately 650 square feet of sail, were Frank Jontzen, Dr. R. M. Stecher, Lee Wilson, Al Edgerton, R. A. St. John, Bernard Ware, and Al Mastics. The twenty-three-foot Stars were proving great racing craft under their skippers, Gordon Beck, Robert Young, Arthur Wather, Robert McKinstry, Donald M. Weaver, and L. A. Lux. The Cleveland area along the lakeshore had become one of the leading yachting districts of the nation. In inter-lake contests, Cleveland was providing many winners year after year. There were long waiting lists for dockage at the Cleveland, Edgewater, Lakeside, and Mentor Harbor yacht clubs.

The Cleveland Automobile Club, fourth largest of its kind in the country, moved on May 13 from its Hollenden headquarters, where it had been since 1903, into the forty-five-room Samuel Mather mansion at 2605 Euclid Avenue. The club assisted 99,817 stranded motorists, free of charge, this year. A driver-training school was maintained, and many useful activities were included in its program. The club was affiliated with 118 local garages, 750 member clubs, and 78 clubs in foreign countries. In the 1940s, membership was more than 65,000. Under the continued leadership of R. J. Schmunk, president, and John L. Young, director, the organization was one of Cleveland's most alert and helpful institutions.

Announcement was made, May 15, that the $4,500,000 bond issue for major highways was carried, with a vote of 66 per cent in its favor. The issue covered six improvements: the Lakeland Freeway, the extension of Jennings Road, Rocky River Bridge, the Willow Freeway, continuation of Chester Avenue, and the Newburgh Freeway. The coming of World War II, the question of priorities with regard to carrying out public works, the preparation of an over-all plan for the county, and the shortage of funds for a comprehensive plan interfered with achievement. However, progress was made on the Lakeland Freeway, while the Willow Freeway was tediously extended northward from the cloverleaf to Dalton Street. After repeated efforts, harmony was secured among various factions so that Chester Avenue could be made a through street from Wade Park to the downtown area. Those living in homes in the path of the improvement opposed the new plans, and it was not until after the war that progress was made in buying the right-of-way.

The Cleveland Farmers Club, founded under the auspices of the Chamber of Commerce, was an attempt to bring city and country closer together. Country gentlemen and active farmers constituted the membership, whose interests embraced lectures by farm experts as well as livestock and agricultural exhibits.

Since the early days of German-Wallace College in 1866, a substantial brick building had served for the most part as student dormitory on the Baldwin-Wallace College campus. The period of World War I left it the worse for wear; but, this year, it found a friend in Mrs. Josephine B. Kohler of Cleveland, who gave $100,000 for reconstruction, and it emerged with a new name, Kohler Hall. The $120,000 gift of Mrs. Annie M. Pfeiffer of New York City, made possible Merner-Pfeiffer Hall, men's dormitory on South Campus, this year. Just before her death in 1946, Mrs. Pfeiffer gave

Western Reserve Historical Society Museum

Pioneer's log cabin

Pioneer room with John Brown's desk

Entrance hall

Capacity crowd in the Stadium at the Festival of Freedom, July 4, 1946.

Eighty thousand at a football game in the Cleveland Stadium.

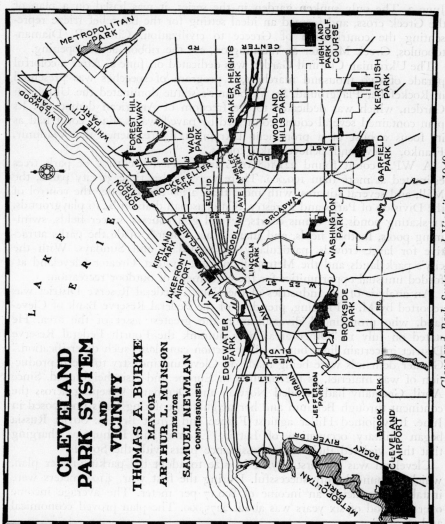

Cleveland Park System and Vicinity—1949

an additional $100,000 for the new Home Economics Building. She was the niece of the Rev. Jacob Ward, early minister of the Northern Ohio Methodist Conference.

The Grecian Garden, in the Cultural Garden chain, was dedicated on June 2. The only sunken garden in the series, it was based on a plan of the Greek cross, and formed an ideal setting for the bas-relief frieze representing the contribution of Greece to civilization. Cimon P. Diamantopoulos, Greek Minister at Washington, cut the ribbon at the opening.

The Ukrainian Cultural Garden was dedicated on June 2. After a colorful parade of two thousand marchers, a program of speeches was presented in Rockefeller Playground. St. Volodimir's statue dominated the Ukrainian Garden, which was dedicated to the freedom of American democracy. Its plan contained several courts connected by paved walks. Each court had as its focus a bust of a prominent Ukrainian figure, hence the Vladimir, Franko, Kiev, and Schevchenko courts.

A WPA count found 221,198 trees in the city, exclusive of park trees estimated at more than 100,000. There were at this time 32 city parks, the Mall, and several squares, with more than 2,300 acres, under the control of the Division of Parks and Forestry. Sixty baseball diamonds, 16 playgrounds, 11 skating ponds, 92 tennis courts, several golf courses, soccer fields, swimming pools, football fields, and many other features made the parks attractive for large crowds, particularly on Saturdays and Sundays. With the city's park lands and the Metropolitan Park System, Greater Cleveland afforded unusual opportunities for the enjoyment of outdoor recreation.

An analysis of the industries of the Fourth Federal Reserve District was reported by M. J. Fleming, president of the Federal Reserve Bank of Cleveland, who pronounced diversification the greatest asset of the area. He stated on July 1: "Other areas may outrank the Fourth Federal Reserve District in certain lines but no other section can claim such diversification." Greater demands were being made on Cleveland industry to speed production of war matériel, as the conflicts in Europe and Asia heightened. Since April, Germany had invaded Norway and Denmark, sweeping across the continent through Belgium and her neighbors, entering Paris unopposed in June. Italy joined Hitler against France and Great Britain. Soviet Russia began military occupation of Latvia, Estonia, and Lithuania, charging that they violated their mutual-assistance pacts with the Soviets.

Cleveland was the first city of its size to adopt the parking-meter plan, which it found highly successful. During the first year, 3,100 meters were installed, producing an income of $99.17 per meter. The average income over a period of six years was about $275,000. The plan proved economical and efficient.

The Festival of Freedom, held in the Stadium under the auspices of the Come-to-Cleveland Committee of the Cleveland Advertising Club and the American Legion Club, attracted nationwide attention. More than 75,000 people gathered in the Stadium on July 5, while nearly a third as many listened to the music and watched the fireworks from outside the great enclosure. The *Boston Post* commented: "The magnificent audience of Clevelanders included 2,500 new citizens who joined in a mighty tribute to this nation, its flag, and its Independence Day, so that even over the air, it made a man's heart swell with pride. The Festival lifted a fellow right out of his chair all the way back here in Boston." This was Cleveland's greatest patriotic celebration, and it led to the public demand that the Festival be made an annual event. Among the features were the inauguration of the "match stunt," when all spectators held lighted matches in front of their faces in the darkened Stadium, the singing of Donald Dickson and the Wings Over Jordan Choir, the playing of a great orchestra under the direction of Rudolph Ringwall, the marching of Boy Scouts and Girl Scouts carrying one of the largest of American flags, the presentation of a patriotic motion picture, and a mammoth fireworks display. William Ganson Rose, writer of the script, was master of ceremonies, with George F. Buehler and Judge Frank J. Merrick as co-chairmen.

The forty-first Triennial Conclave of the Grand Encampment, Knights Templar, was held July 12-14 with nearly twenty thousand members in attendance.

A new stone, erected by The Cleveland Chamber of Commerce, July 20, was dedicated in Erie Street Cemetery at the grave of Joseph L. Weatherly, founder and first president of the parent organization.

Cleveland Day at the New York World's Fair was celebrated, July 22, by 750 Clevelanders who took the *Plain Dealer* two-train excursion trip managed by John A. Crawford. At the Goodrich Arena, the Goodrich distinguished-service award was presented to Law Director Edward Blythin, who accepted the honor for Mayor Harold H. Burton. The Cathedral Latin High School Band drilled and played before large crowds.

One of the most tragic train wrecks in the history of Ohio occurred in Cuyahoga Falls on July 31 when forty-three persons were killed. It was said that the collision of a double-header freight train and a gas-electric locomotive was due to a failure in signal-reading.

At the mouth of the Cuyahoga River, the nation's most beautiful United States Coast Guard station had been erected on "made land." A dedication program on August 10, arranged by Commander Ephraim Zoole, chief of staff of the Cleveland District, in connection with the Coast Guard's 150th-anniversary observance, was attended by prominent guests. Life-saving demonstrations, boat races, and a regatta attracted many spectators to the lakefront. The $360,000 streamlined station, replacing the old station, was designed by J. Milton Dyer of Cleveland. It provided headquarters for commanding officer and crew, boats and equipment, and a lookout tower rose sixty feet above the dock level. The cutter *Tahoma* berthed at the East 9th Street Pier. The Coast Guard services included rescuing the shipwrecked and those endangered by flood or hurricane, carrying food and supplies to isolated communities, and eliminating navigation menaces.

Breaking a precedent of almost a century, the *Plain Dealer,* an independent Democratic paper, endorsed a Republican for President of the United States.

An editorial entitled "The *Plain Dealer* Supports Willkie," published in August, was reprinted widely and circulated by Wendell L. Willkie's campaigners throughout the nation.

Agitation against the old Central Market culminated in a special hearing at the City Hall on August 12. Representatives of various civic bodies testified that the market house was a health menace and a safety menace. It was informally agreed that a new market should be built for the tenants as soon as possible and that the old market should be torn down.

Benedict Crowell, former assistant secretary of war in World War I, was called to Washington to act as expert consultant to Secretary of War Stimson. For his outstanding service he was made a brigadier general in the Ordnance Department.

The Frederick W. and Henryett Slocum Judd Fund became effective as part of the Cleveland Foundation in August. This fund of $525,000 was designed to enable the Public Library "to extend its facilities to those who may be ill or incapacitated or unable to come personally to its Main Library or branches." More than sixteen thousand books were circulated during the first year, the readers' ages ranging from seven to ninety-one.

The Selective Service Act was signed, September 16, and the first United States peacetime compulsory military service was inaugurated. On September 15 the Battle of Britain began, the Germans loosing a deluge of deadly bombs from hundreds of planes. In November, Hungary, Rumania, and Slovakia joined the Axis powers.

Cleveland construction companies were busily engaged on war plants throughout this area. The Hunkin-Conkey Construction Company and Wilbur Watson & Associates were at work upon the new Ravenna munitions loading plant which was to cost nearly twelve million dollars. The Austin Company, Arthur G. McKee & Company, the H. K. Ferguson Company, the George A. Rutherford Company, and the Gillmore-Carmichael-Olson Company were all working to capacity.

Edwin A. Johnson, a grand old veteran of the Civil War, died on September 19, at the age of ninety-eight.

The Weather Bureau moved from the Society for Savings Building and consolidated with the Airport office in September.

Public schools inaugurated courses for adults in restaurant management and bake-shop decorating. Gardening courses were begun for adults in three schools. A preview of the results of a six-month survey of eighty-five American high schools on the teaching of democracy ranked Cleveland schools at the top, according to Dr. Howard E. Wilson, Harvard University. Three new buildings—Central, Kentucky, and William Dean Howells— were completed in a $4,600,000 PWA building program. Defense training programs were opened in technical high schools.

The Cleveland Bar Association was given the 1940 award of merit for outstanding public service by the American Bar Association. The Cleveland organization's investigation of "ambulance chasing" and its prosecution of a municipal judge were among the outstanding activities mentioned.

In October of this year, the administration of the Cleveland Zoo was entrusted to the Cleveland Museum of Natural History, thus ensuring continuous scientific guidance. Under its management the number of animals increased, rare species were added, and the collection was rated as one of the most valuable in the country. In February, 1942, Fletcher A. Reynolds, who had enjoyed wide experience as curator of several important zoological gardens and had participated in numerous expeditions, was selected as director of the Cleveland Zoological Park. Expansion then took place, and, in 1944, the portion of Brookside Park lying east of the Fulton Avenue Viaduct was designated for the purposes of a Zoological Park. The new Waterfowl Sanctuary was opened in the summer of 1946 as the home of more than three hundred waterfowl. The lake was constructed at a cost of thirty thousand dollars. A popular figure at the Zoo for many years had been Captain Curley Wilson, highly skilled animal trainer who had been superintendent since 1931. Harold T. Clark, president of the Cleveland Museum of Natural History and chairman of the Cleveland Zoological Society, had been the guiding spirit behind these progressive developments.

The Educational Policies Commission of the National Education Association issued a report praising the public schools of Cleveland and Shaker Heights for superior methods of teaching citizenship.

The $1,750,000 Willow Cloverleaf, which had been under construction for two years, was opened on October 21. It was the first step in the building of the important Willow Freeway, the north end of which would eventually lead to the center of Cleveland.

The National Metal Exposition and Congress opened in the Public Auditorium on October 21, and attracted more than thirty-three thousand representatives of the metal industries from all over the world.

Seven thousand physicians and medical specialists from points throughout North America came to Cleveland, October 25, to attend the twenty-fifth International Assembly of the Inter-State Post Graduate Medical Association. Wide attention was attracted to their sessions.

President Roosevelt spoke on November 2 in the Public Auditorium, giving his reasons for seeking a third term. His opponent, Wendell L. Willkie, had preceded him on a campaign tour. President Roosevelt was re-elected on November 5; no other holder of the office had served more than two four-year terms. The New Deal was the major issue, and the radio battle was bitter.

Edward Blythin, director of law, was called to fill the unexpired term of Mayor Burton, elected United States senator; Blythin served until the end of 1941. His early education was secured in Wales, and his legal education was obtained in the Cleveland Law School and Baldwin-Wallace College. After leaving the City Hall, he became financial vice president of Western Reserve University and was appointed a member of the Cleveland Transit Board.

"To teach people to use the blessings of medical science by making health visible" was the fundamental purpose of the Cleveland Health Museum, which was formally dedicated on November 12. The first of its kind in the

Western Hemisphere, the museum not only assisted individuals in finding methods of solving their health problems, but also co-operated with health-education organizations in the community. It was made possible by physicians, dentists, and public-spirited citizens who felt it was important to teach the public the basic facts about the human body. Four years earlier,

"There's that man again." (Willard Combes in the Press.)

representatives of twenty-three institutions had met at the invitation of the Academy of Medicine of Cleveland to discuss the possibilities of a permanent project. A health exhibit at the Great Lakes Exposition inspired the group to continue plans for the establishment of a central source for disseminating information; and on December 28, 1936, the Cleveland Health Museum was incorporated by Dr. Lester Taylor, Dr. Hubert C. King, Dr. James A. Doull, Howard Whipple Green, and H. Van Y. Caldwell. Dr. Taylor was elected president. The museum's first home, at 8811 Euclid Avenue, was the gift of Elisabeth S. Prentiss—Mrs. Francis F. Prentiss—who also established trust funds amounting to $420,000, said to be the largest endowment ever made to health education. Dr. Bruno Gebhard, eminent authority on hygiene, became first director. Realistic exhibits were presented, classes in health education were promoted, and group tours and special-film showings were organized. The museum became particularly proud of its counterparts in Dallas and Mexico City. In order to encourage health education as a profession, internships were planned for graduate students. The Elisabeth S. Prentiss National Award in Health Education was established in 1943. The museum moved into its new home at 8911 Euclid Avenue in 1946. The gift of James A. Bohannon, in memory of his mother, Mrs. Sallie C. M. Bohannon, it included full ownership of four buildings and several acres of land.

The planting of more than three hundred trees and flowering shrubs was begun on November 18 at Erie Street Cemetery, as an initial move in the restoration and beautification of the last resting place of many pioneers.

Cathedral Latin School defeated West Tech on November 23, in the *Plain Dealer* charity football game of 1940; Collinwood tied Lincoln, 1941; Lincoln defeated Collinwood, 1942; and Cathedral Latin won the next four years, defeating Lincoln in 1943 and 1944, St. Ignatius in 1945, and Holy Name in 1946. The 1946 game drew an attendance of 70,955, the largest crowd in the long series. These games were the crowning events of the annual high-school football season, and were made colorful by the playing and marching evolutions of many bands and by interesting contests.

The campaign goal set for the Community Fund was $3,350,000. The amount raised was $3,278,969.16, with 519,862 subscribers. The chairman was Dale Brown. Persons who received distinguished-service awards were: Mrs. Estelle Birkhold, Dr. James E. Cutler, Mrs. Julius Fryer, Victor L. Carfen, Hal H. Griswold, and E. F. Whitney.

Cleveland was now the second largest Slovene city in the world, surpassed only by Ljubljana in Yugoslavia. A closely knit community centering on St. Clair Avenue between East 55th and East 76th streets represented the hub of Slovene life in America. Early in the 1890s the Slovenians moved eastward from St. Clair and East 26th. At 6417 St. Clair they erected the Slovene National Home, a cultural center that eventually occupied a city block. St. Vitus Church, 6019 Glass Avenue, the heart of the neighborhood of home owners, was later rebuilt as one of the world's most beautiful Slovene Catholic churches. Anton Grdina, president of the North American Bank, had been influential in advancing the interests of his people for many years. Croatians constituted a part of the population of this neighborhood, their social and community activities centering at 6314 St. Clair Avenue.

Cleveland was selected as the site for the Government's new $8,400,000 engine research laboratory by the National Advisory Committee for Aeronautics, December 3. Seventy-two sites throughout the country had been considered, and Dr. Vannevar Bush, chairman of the NACA, announced the unanimous decision of the committee in favor of Cleveland. A modern administration building with complete research facilities was planned. Research activities began on May 8, and additions to the buildings advanced the cost to eighteen million dollars. A two-hundred-acre site was occupied at the edge of the Cleveland Municipal Airport. One important unit was the Engine Propeller Research Building where lubrication and air-cooling problems were studied. Other facilities were the Engine Research Building, Altitude Wind Tunnel, Flight Research Hangar, and Ice Tunnel. The wind tunnel was the largest in the world with a throat diameter of twenty-five feet. Here wind was created at three hundred miles per hour, sub-stratosphere density. The laboratory at all times consumed enough power to service a fair-sized city. The aim of engine research was to develop an engine giving more power for less weight. Edward R. Sharp was administrative officer in charge.

An important aid in dissolving prejudices in a city comprising more than forty different nationality groups was the practice of holding nationality nights at the neighborhood schools, where people of all races could experience the cultural significance of other groups.

The remains of the schooner *Porcupine,* which fought in Commodore Perry's fleet, were presented to Western Reserve Historical Society on December 19. Ravaged by the elements for over a century and stored in a sub-basement of the City Hall, only about twenty main timbers remained of the once gallant little ship.

The property of the telephone company at 2136 East 19th Street was acquired by The Cleveland Engineering Society this year, providing a beautiful permanent home with well-appointed facilities, including a fine auditorium given by Mrs. Worcester R. Warner. The growing society had been increasingly active in regional planning, building codes, standards, smoke abatement, and civic improvement. Student aid helped worthy Cleveland young people to complete technical education; and educational classes, conferences, discussions, inspection trips, recreational and social activities contributed to making Cleveland a better city, and enriched the membership that had reached nearly 1,500. Bert W. Charlton was president, and George C. A. Hantelman was secretary-manager.

Northern Ohio was the steel center of the nation. The geographical center of production located at a point near Harrisburg, Pennsylvania, in 1874, had moved westward almost in a straight line until in 1933 it was about thirteen miles west of Mansfield, Ohio. An eastward reversal came in 1936, however, when a point about a mile north of Mansfield was marked as the center of ingot-steel production. Authorities believed that the westward trend following the shifting population had halted, and Chicago's hopes to be the nation's steel capital would not be realized. Construction of new plants and expansion of operations, particularly in the Cleveland, Lorain, and Youngstown districts, had increased production in these areas. Likewise, northern Ohio was a flourishing center of large consumer industries of increasing importance. Cleveland businessmen were encouraged by the growing affinity between steel production and consumption that had checked the westward march of the industry.

The Cleveland Industrial Area—Cuyahoga and Lorain counties—led the nation's large industrial areas in diversity of manufacturing industries. Iron and steel and their products, except machinery, showed a product value of $311,050,770 as reported by the 1939 census of manufactures. Of this total, steel works and rolling mills represented $137,095,635; blast-furnace products, $40,428,290; stoves, ranges, water heaters, and hot-air furnaces, except electric, $23,298,984; bolts, nuts, washers, and rivets—made in plants not operated in connection with rolling mills, $18,816,467; gray-iron and semi-steel castings, $13,885,196; and screw-machine products and wood screws, $13,418,181. Products manufactured by 2,699 establishments in the area were valued at $1,123,146,504, and the payroll of 140,653 wage earners amounted to $200,153,593.

Cleveland maintained fifth position in the nation in 1939 in the value of manufactured products, 2,330 establishments with an output of $5,000 or more reporting $881,629,869, wages of $158,272,247 earned by 112,092 workers, and valuation of $433,737,418 added to manufacture. The output of iron and steel and their products, except machinery, was valued at $211,438,269, as reported by 270 establishments. The payroll for 30,688 wage earners was $44,801,908. Included in the product-value total were bolts, nuts, washers, rivets—made in plants not operated in connection with rolling mills, $18,048,657; forgings, iron and steel, $10,675,288; gray-iron and semi-steel castings, $9,139,193; screw-machine products, wood screws, $6,640,917; stamped and pressed metal products, except automobile stampings, $5,905,694; fabricated structural steel and ornamental metalwork, $5,276,578; steel works and rolling mills, blast-furnace products, castings, wire and wirework, hardware, plumbers' supplies and steam fittings, power boilers, oil burners, steam and hot-water heating apparatus, stoves, ranges, water heaters, hot-air furnaces, heating and cooking apparatus, automobile stampings, and a diversity of iron-and-steel products.

Machinery, except electrical, with products valued at $107,373,302, represented the city's second largest industrial classification, 247 establishments employing 15,917 workers with a payroll of $25,770,753. Included in the total were machine tools, product value of $21,281,767; machine-shop products, $17,402,151; and machine-tool and other metalworking-machinery accessories, metal-cutting and shaping tools, machinists' precision tools, $11,199,433.

Cleveland, the parts center of the nation, produced motor vehicles, motor-vehicle bodies, parts, and accessories valued at $89,642,863. Importance as a food center was increasing, the value of food and kindred products reported by 448 establishments amounting to $88,228,554. Included in this total were meat packing, wholesale, $29,831,671; bread and other bakery products, except biscuits, crackers, and pretzels, $20,484,061; malt liquors, $10,180,935; and confectionery and ice cream, $6,531,036. The product value of chemicals and allied products was $66,982,813, of which $26,473,528 represented paints, varnishes, and lacquers; and substantial amounts included production of insecticides and related compounds, fertilizers, drugs and medicines, plastic materials, explosives, printing ink, and the like. The manufacture of electrical machinery, including electrical appliances, automotive electrical and communication equipment, wiring devices, electric lamps, batteries, radios, phonographs, and allied products, showed a product valuation of $62,866,737, of which $19,775,870 represented generating, distributing, and industrial apparatus, and apparatus for incorporation in manufactured products, not elsewhere classified.

Men's and boys' suits, coats, and overcoats valued at $28,089,744 were included in the classification of apparel and other finished products, which had an output of $48,443,602. The product value of 369 establishments engaged in printing, publishing, and allied industries was $45,596,351, which included newspapers, $15,350,997; general commercial (job) printing, $9,186,599; and lithographing and photo-lithographing, $4,624,005. Textile-mill products and other fiber manufactures were valued at $18,633,377; nonferrous metal products, not elsewhere classified, $15,490,513; transportation equipment, except automobiles, $13,689,056, which included aircraft parts and engines, shipbuilding, ship repairing, and the like; furniture and finished lumber products, including store and office fixtures, $10,882,704; lighting fixtures, $9,707,800; paper and allied products, $9,433,635; and stone, clay, and glass products, $9,284,090.

Outside of Cleveland's boundaries, 246 establishments in Cuyahoga County boosted the value of manufactured products by $115,073,691. Combined volume of city and county had climbed to $996,703,560 in 1939, exceeding the 1930 figure. Wages of $178,521,574 paid to 125,876 Cleveland and Cuyahoga County workers surpassed those in the manufacturing industries of thirty-five individual states.

Workers in manufacturing industries were taking home larger pay envelopes. The rate for skilled labor averaged $.827 per hour; unskilled $.661. In the construction industry, skilled workers received $1.47 per hour; unskilled, $.699. The Cleveland labor force, reported by the 1940 census, totaled 545,406, of which 395,537 were men and 149,869 women. Industries related to manufacturing employed 142,280 men and 31,251 women; transportation, 32,394 men and 4,371 women; trade, 62,814 men and 29,570 women; professional service, 15,791 men and 21,438 women; domestic and personal service, 11,552 men and 26,993 women; and finance, 12,882 men and 6,202 women.

Cleveland was one of the chief ports on the Great Lakes. Increasing quantities of iron ore, automobiles, grain, and merchandise were shipped from the upper lakes to the Cleveland port, the clearing house for the nation. Iron ore received in Greater Cleveland in 1940 totaled 11,517,000 net tons; outbound coal tonnage, 1,331,000. Total tonnage at the Cleveland port amounted to 17,673,926; at Conneaut, 13,304,455; Ashtabula, 13,252,966; Sandusky, 10,190,681; and Lorain, 6,929,811. Ocean-going vessels transported Cleveland-made products to the countries of the world, and returned with imports resulting in well-balanced foreign trade.

Cleveland was an important financial center of the nation. Thirteen clearing-house banks with resources of $1,013,840,000 in 1940 were in a position to meet the business requirements of the area they served. Bank clearings for the year amounted to $5,734,000,000. Resources of forty-five building-and-loan associations were reported at $71,410,000. The construction of new buildings had been sharply curtailed by the depression years. No hotels and no large office buildings had been erected. Although a few side-by-side and two-family dwellings and apartment houses were built, no row houses or terraces were constructed other than government housing developments. Cleveland was known for its high percentage of home ownership, particularly by workers' families, who preferred the one- or two-family house. The census of 1940 showed that 39.1 per cent of Metropolitan Cleveland homes were owned by their occupants. Building construction in Cleveland in 1940 valued at $21,874,000 was only about two-thirds of the 1930 volume; 6,821 building permits were issued during the year. Tax-duplicate valuation of Cuyahoga County property was reported at $1,829,733,945 in 1940, of which $1,433,625,010 represented real estate.

1941

The Cleveland International Exposition, which brought to the city many of the finest foreign exhibits from the New York World's Fair, opened on January 4 with twenty-two nations represented. Each day the representatives of several nations took over the central stage and gave characteristic entertainments. Many prominent speakers, representing the nationalities, were on the programs and shared attention with the cultural, scientific, and industrial treasures shown in twenty-seven exhibits in Public Auditorium.

Telenews Theater, 241 Euclid Avenue, a $200,000 project, opened its doors on February 1. A continuously greater number of Clevelanders were soon reading the news on the picture screen.

The Health Exhibit in the Terminal Tower, under the auspices of the Cleveland Health Museum, displayed among its features a chart indicating how Cleveland's average family spent its money. It showed a percentage of 32.3 for food; 6.5 for welfare; 5.5 for recreation; 4.8 for furnishings and equipment; 4.1 for medical care; 10. for fuel and lighting; 10. for transportation; 15.6 for housing; and 11.2 for clothing. The average family income was $1,611.

The Builders Exchange of Cleveland opened its "Home Information Center" for home owners and prospective home owners, and those interested in the building of commercial units and apartments. The Exchange moved its headquarters from the Terminal buildings to 1737 Euclid Avenue, and expanded its services to the public. At this time, it was headed by Howard Pearse, president; Joseph M. Schultz, Jr., secretary, assisted by Muriele Reid. A comprehensive exhibit of building materials was presented, and private quarters, adjacent to the Exchange, were arranged for trade associations and member companies. A plan-room was a practical feature for estimators, and a meeting room accommodating two hundred was provided for Exchange meetings. The officials for 1946 were Warren Bicknell, Jr., president; Thomas Dougherty, vice president; H. R. Templeton, treasurer; and Charles W. Jauch, executive secretary. Dougherty succeeded Bicknell as president.

The Cleveland public schools were teaching history with motion pictures, lantern slides, newspapers, magazines, and the school radio system. Thus pupils better understood the significance of war influences.

Cleveland Camp Fire Girls, with a membership of 2,800 in 155 groups, helped celebrate the organization's birthday on March 20. Groups met weekly in churches, settlements, schools, and homes under guidance of guardians. The goals of Camp Fire Girls were "to worship God, seek beauty, give service, pursue knowledge, be trustworthy, hold on to health, glorify work, and be happy." Home, health, hand, camping, nature, business, and citizenship offered outlets for talent. The president of the executive board in 1946 was Mrs. Deming Bronson.

Mary Van Kirk, who studied music in Cleveland for four years, won the Metropolitan Opera Company audition on March 23. Her rich contralto voice was heard in important roles.

A seventy-two-foot, porcelain-enamel, steel mural, entitled "Man's Conquest of the Elemental Forces of Nature," was hung on the south wall of the Union Terminal by the Ferro Enamel Corporation after it attracted considerable attention at the New York World's Fair. It was the work of the ceramic artist, J. Scott Williams of New York City, and was fired in the kilns of the Ferro corporation.

The Cleveland Advertising Club on April 5 honored charter members A. H. Madigan, Clyde E. Horton, and Charles W. Mears. An evening banquet-dance, which celebrated the club's fortieth birthday, was addressed by Henry R. Luce, chairman of the board of Time, Inc. The club spanned the time between Theodore Roosevelt and Franklin D. Roosevelt, plug hat and snap-brim fedora, ragtime and boogie-woogie, Gibson Girl and Sweater Girl, crowned heads and blitzkriegs of Europe. But the Ad Club members, who forty years before wanted a place where they could talk about improving Cleveland in a practical way, still had the same motive in getting together during the presidency of George F. Buehler.

The last member of GAR Post 189, Commander George Cogswill, ninety-six, delivered a faded charter and other properties on April 12 to the Western Reserve Historical Society for safekeeping. The date was the eightieth anniversary of the beginning of hostilities of the Civil War. Representatives of more than two hundred patriotic organizations were at the Museum to mark the event.

All the traditional grandeur of Metropolitan Opera returned to Cleveland for another season of brilliant and colorful productions. Stars who came for the first time this year were Bidu Sayao, the Brazilian soprano; Rise Stevens, American mezzo-soprano; and Salvatore Baccaloni, famous basso. A visitor to Singers Club programs, Tito Schipa, sang in *The Barber of Seville*. Unqualified success again crowned opera week.

The Cleveland Medal for Public Service was awarded, April 15, by the Chamber of Commerce to Frederick Coolidge Crawford, "engineer, industrial leader, enthusiastic contributor to and participant in important undertakings for the advancement of Cleveland." The medal was also given to George Abraham Martin, "business administrator, humanitarian, patron of arts and culture, through whose efforts many talented persons have found an opportunity to become artists of the opera."

The *Press* and the Regional Association were hurling heavy statistical blasts at the smoke nuisance: "Smoke costs the city $20,000,000 annually. Every month, 50,000 tons of soot are washed off buildings, lawns and clothing. The average Clevelander inhales five pounds of soot a year. Extra laundry due to excessive smoke, costs $1,500,000 a year; extra dry cleaning of clothes, $750,000, and extra cleaning of clothes, curtains and upholstery, $400,000." But the smoke and fume nuisances ignored statistics.

The Red Cross enrollment in Cleveland for the third consecutive year was the largest in the nation. The city stood first in the total number of members regardless of population, 203,207 being entitled to wear the Red Cross emblem.

The formal opening of the Sarah Tod McBride Museum of Intelligence, Power and Personality at the Cleveland Clinic was celebrated on May 26. The museum represented a study of 3,694 animals, collected on expeditions during fourteen years, Dr. and Mrs. George W. Crile and Dr. Daniel P. Quiring having traveled 100,000 miles on their extraordinary research program. Careful studies indicated to medical experts that intelligence, power, and personality are determined by the size of the brain, the sympathetic system, the thyroid and adrenal glands, the heart, and the blood volume. It was proved that the brain is larger in civilized man than in native man, and larger in warm-blooded animals than in cold-blooded animals. In the museum were many mounted animals together with their energy-controlling organisms.

Nathan G., the last of the famous Richman brothers, passed on. The brothers were remembered for philanthropies, and, through the Richman Foundation, they left large holdings to ensure benefits to workers in the Richman Brothers Company. In 1946, when Frank C. Lewman was president, George H. Richman, vice president and general manager, and Richard H. Kohn, vice president, sixty Richman stores were operating in fifty-five cities.

The *U.S.S. Cleveland,* a new eighteen-million-dollar cruiser of ten thousand tons, was built in the New York Shipbuilding Company yards at Camden, New Jersey. Mrs. Harold H. Burton, wife of Senator Burton, christened the ship with a bottle of Ohio champagne. This was the first government ship to bear the name of Ohio's first city since the sale of the thirty-one-year-old *U.S.S. Cleveland* in 1930. The older ship saw duty in the North Atlantic in World War I.

Estimating the cost of noise in Cleveland at forty thousand dollars per day, civic leaders launched a new campaign toward its abatement in June. Principal offenders against quiet in the community were blaring auto horns, noisy streetcars, and rattling street-sweeping machines. More than fifty organizations were represented by prominent citizens at the meeting under the chairmanship of Allen J. Lowe, manager of Hotel Carter.

Dedication of the new million-dollar Veterans Administration Hospital, June 15, was marked with fanfare and martial music. Located in Brecksville at Broadview and Oakes roads on a hundred acres of land donated by Cleveland, the grouping of seven buildings constituted the ninety-first hospital of the Administration. This Brecksville institution had been in partial operation since November 1, and 1,600 ailing veterans had already been admitted. A capacity of 269 beds could be amplified by an emergency overflow arrangement with the United States Marine Hospital. Offices of the Veterans Administration were located here under Dr. N. M. Jeffrey, regional manager and chief executive of the hospital. The medical staff operated under the direction of Dr. William H. Bradford, chief medical officer. The hospital served forty-two counties in northern Ohio.

With the sale of property at 2725 Orange Avenue, Hiram House headquarters moved to 3054 Euclid Avenue, former brownstone rectory of the late Bishop William A. Leonard. Clubrooms were also established at East 22nd Street and Woodland Avenue, an old branch of the Cleveland Trust Company. Activities at Paul Revere School and the summer Hiram House Camp continued, and the University House at 2090 Abington Road was rented as a residence for college students studying at the social settlement during the summer. Later Hiram House turned over to the public schools its child-development program in which the schools had co-operated for years, but it continued its camp work for children.

Western Reserve University had the distinction of being the only privately owned and financed urban university in Ohio. The corporations of Western Reserve University and Adelbert College of Western Reserve University, together with The Cleveland School of Architecture and the Leonard Case Reference Library, were consolidated under the name of Western Reserve University on July 1. Cleveland College joined the corporation in May, 1942. The enlarged institution was progressing under the leadership of President Winfred George Leutner, who was installed in 1934. He was a graduate of the famous Class of 1901, Adelbert, professor of Greek and Latin, acting secretary-treasurer of the university, dean of Adelbert College and university administration, and acting president of Western Reserve, 1933-34. A major institution of instruction and a center of original research, the expanding university in the mid-1940s, enrolled in twelve schools and colleges more than ten thousand students.

The Festival of Freedom program in the Stadium on July 4 included many new features that were cheered by an audience of eighty thousand. *The Pageant of Freedom* told the story of the preservation of the nation's liberty, with a series of heroic floats.

Cleveland suffered a distressing epidemic of infantile paralysis beginning July 5. Eight deaths occurred among residents and ten among non-residents. Cases reported numbered 133. The Health Department, under the able direction of Dr. Harold J. Knapp, commissioner of health, publicized symptoms and precautions, efficiently suppressing the epidemic. Funds raised by the annual infantile-paralysis campaigns were ready to meet the situation.

The sale of the old *City of Erie* to the Otis Steel Company for scrap was announced by Alva Bradley, president of the liquidating Cleveland & Buffalo Transit Company, one of the lakes' popular steamship lines. The proud sidewheeler was one of the most famous ships that sailed the inland seas.

Cleveland Amateur Day, July 27, was marked by the participation of three of the greatest baseball players of all time, Babe Ruth, Ty Cobb, and Tris Speaker. Fans recalled the eventful day twelve years earlier when the Babe was scheduled to make his five hundredth home run. Thousands packed League Park and many stood on Lexington Avenue to see the ball come over the fence. Sure enough, in the second inning Willis Hudlin's first pitch was met solidly by the "Sultan of Swat," and the horsehide traveled over the wall. Jake Geiser of New Philadelphia, Ohio, recovered the sphere and received twenty dollars and two autographed balls for returning it to the mighty Babe.

When Margaret Wagner became director of the Benjamin Rose Institute in 1930, she began to make plans for the founding of recreational centers for the aged. The numbers of old folks were increasing constantly as science, education, and improved health measures contributed to lengthened life. As funds were made available, Miss Wagner put her ideas to work, and in 1941 her Golden Age Clubs became a reality. A chain of clubs began to spring up in Cleveland where aged members enjoyed programs of inspiration and entertainment suited to their environment and culture. Soon Hobby Clubs were organized, substituting interesting occupation for lonely years of idleness. When the hobbyists joined in 1945 to display their achievements in their first annual Golden Age Hobby Show, membership in sixteen Golden Age Clubs had reached 850. Recognizing its community responsibility, the Cleveland Welfare Federation organized the Committee on the Aged in 1944. A five-year plan was initiated, directed by Mrs. Lucia Bing, who inspired volunteer effort that would help to bring happiness and contentment into the lives of the aged and encourage workers to plan for a future of satisfying and enjoyable retirement. Again Cleveland pioneered in the nation.

Alarmed at the fall of nations before the German war machine, the United States had strengthened the Pan-American countries, fortified the Panama Canal, and stationed troops in Greenland and Iceland. The lend-lease plan had been put into effect, the Congress pledging billions to the Allies. The Atlantic Charter was announced to the world, August 14, after a meeting at sea between President Roosevelt and Prime Minister Winston Churchill to develop a program of peace aims. The Germans were pushing into Russia and captured Odessa in October.

The Cunningham Sanitarium, 18485 Lake Shore Boulevard, was purchased by the Cleveland Catholic Diocese for the Catholic Youth Organization on October 10. The million-dollar sanitarium was built in 1928 for Dr. Orval J. Cunningham of Kansas City for treatment of diabetic patients. A steel ball, 64 feet high with 38 rooms and 350 portholes in its 5 stories, treated patients under air pressure of from 5 to 30 pounds above normal. The institution changed hands in 1934 when James H. Rand III of the Remington-Rand Company, New York, headed the Ohio Institute of Oxygen Therapy. In 1935, the sanitarium was reorganized as a general hospital, with Rand in charge, and Dr. G. P. Tyler giving patients pressure and oxygen treatments. The steel ball went into disuse prior to its sale to the Catholic Diocese.

Robert E. Woodruff crowned thirty-six years of railroading with the Erie road by accepting office as its twenty-third president on October 23. Woodruff proved to be the only top officer of the Erie who had devoted his entire career to that company, rising from section laborer in 1905.

"They won their battle—let's win ours!" (*Willard Combes in the* Press.)

Cleveland manufacturers were worried when, on October 25, John L. Lewis called a strike on the "captive" coal mines of the seven largest steel companies, in defiance of the President of the United States. On November 22, Lewis accepted the proposal of the President for arbitration and called off the strike.

The first Catholic Labor School in the Diocese of Cleveland opened a six-week course devoted to instruction in the history of labor, ethics of labor relations, and the fundamentals of parliamentary law.

War was declared on rats when two Department of Interior agents went to work on a control program in Lakewood and East Cleveland. E. B. Buchanan, Cleveland food-and-drug inspector, and leaders in neighboring suburbs, joined the attack to cut down the estimated two-million-dollar yearly cost of destruction by rats in Greater Cleveland.

Frank J. Lausche was elected mayor of Cleveland. He was born in Cleveland in 1895 and educated in the city schools. He practiced law from 1920 to 1932, and served as judge of the Municipal Court and of the Court of Common Pleas. His facility for making friends, and his earnest administration as mayor for two terms led to his election as governor of Ohio on the Democratic ticket, serving in 1945-46.

Cleveland was chosen as one of the cities to set up a Red Cross blood-donor center for the purpose of securing blood to be processed into plasma for use of the Army and Navy. An average of 3,809 donations weekly was recorded for the year 1944, placing the Greater Cleveland Chapter among the leading units of thirty-one centers throughout the country.

The campaign goal set for the Community Fund was $3,350,000. The amount raised was $3,440,785.66, with 557,351 subscribers. The campaign chairman was Dale Brown. Persons who received distinguished-service awards from the Community Fund were: Harry F. Affelder, Arthur Douglas Baldwin, Hanna Buchanan, Jane E. Hunter, Fred W. Ramsey, and Joseph T. Sweeney.

On December 2, less than eight months after ground was broken, production started in the great wartime plant of the Thompson Aircraft Products Company. The largest addition to the production facilities of Thompson Products, Inc., it was a Defense Plant Corporation subsidiary, erected in Euclid, Ohio. A peaceful country vineyard had been speedily transformed into the 120-acre site for the thirty-million-dollar factory, which produced an increasing volume of turbine wheels, nozzle diaphragms, and components for jet-propulsion aircraft engines. In 1945 the plant was purchased by the company and continued mass production of automotive and aircraft parts in peacetime.

On Sunday morning, December 7, came the sudden Japanese attack on Pearl Harbor, forcing the United States into the war as a belligerent. Declarations of war came in rapid succession, the conflict quickly developing into world proportions. Raids on Singapore, Hong Kong, the Dutch East Indies, and other Pacific islands followed, and within ninety days the Japanese had added thousands of square miles to their empire. The tragedy at Pearl Harbor brought grief to Cleveland homes, and the lines of volunteers and draftees lengthened as they marched behind the colors to embark at the Union Terminal for military duty. Home-front workers in factory, office, and civilian endeavor went to work with new determination, as well as with fear and anxiety in their hearts.

Cleveland's peacetime living standard was indicated by a few graphic figures taken from the newspapers the week of December 7, the period memorialized by the attack on Pearl Harbor: men's shirts, $2 to $2.50; suits, $34.50; a modern eight-room house in Lakewood was offered for $6,850; and a six-room house in Cleveland Heights could be rented for $95 a month. There were more than 150 want ads for women and 160 for men. According to the employment-agency ads, stenographers' salaries ranged from $100 to $110 a month. Dealers asked $750 for a Chevrolet, $950 for an Oldsmobile, and $800 for a Plymouth.

Cleveland abandoned the rotary turn in favor of the inside left turn, which became standard under the new state traffic code. At this time, the county had 367,600 registered motor vehicles.

The Cleveland harbor was completing its busiest year, with an all-time-high average of 1,100 ships entering each month.

1942

Cleveland led the 147 trading areas of the nation in its percentage of increase in business activity, the city operating at a rate of 48 per cent above normal. The areas of Pittsburgh, Baltimore, Detroit, and Los Angeles followed in the order named.

Dr. C. Langdon White, head of the Department of Geology and Geography of Western Reserve University, was made director of the Cleveland Council on Inter-American Relations. In 1944 this Council, under the direction of Charles J. Ewald, was federated with the Council on World Affairs, later to become a division of that organization.

The Clifton Club, long a center of social activities in Clifton Park, Lakewood, burned to the ground on January 12.

George Ashley Tomlinson, shipping and industrial leader, died on January 26. He had been one of the most powerful figures in the business of the lakes. A former cowboy, captured and tortured by the Ute Indians; a rough rider and broncho buster in Buffalo Bill's Wild West Show; a member of the troupe which gave a private, wild-west performance before Queen Victoria and her friends; an enterprising, red-headed cub reporter who donned a frock suit and silk hat to approach the unapproachable railroad magnate, Lewis Cass Ledyard, by posing as his nephew; these events of Tomlinson's life could be woven into a yarn rivaling fiction. Entering the vessel brokerage business in Duluth, he soon built the Tomlinson fleet of steel ships. He established an office in Cleveland in 1917, and represented a large fleet of independently owned freighters sailing the Great Lakes. In addition to the operations which identified him as one of the shipping magnates of the United States, he was president of the Wade Park Manor, and a member of the executive committees of the Missouri Pacific Railroad Company, Goodyear Tire & Rubber Company, and Goodyear Zeppelin Company.

The Plain Dealer—One Hundred Years in Cleveland, written by Archer H. Shaw, long a member of the editorial staff, was the admirable story of one of America's great newspapers, published in the Plain Dealer's centennial year. It related in an informative and entertaining manner how the newspaper and the city grew up together.

The Cleveland Metropolitan Housing Authority was continuing to provide low-rent accommodations. Outhwaite Homes extension was now complete with 449 dwelling units, the total cost being $2,840,171. Carver Park, constructed during the year, was to include 1,287 dwelling units at 2382 Unwin Road near Central Avenue and East 43rd Street. There were 83 buildings in this project located on nearly 40 acres of land and housing 4,747 people. The development cost was $7,348,064. To meet the demand for housing in Euclid, which had enjoyed a large industrial expansion, Euclid Homes, a permanent war-housing project was built with 500 dwelling units at 20600 Shawnee Avenue, the cost being $2,210,970. Other war-housing projects under construction were to be opened in 1943. These included Lake Shore Village with 800 dwelling units at 24151 Briardale Avenue, and Brooklyn Acres with 600 dwelling units at 6301 Woburn Avenue. Lake Shore Village covered 118.7 acres, the development costing $4,825,745, and Brooklyn Acres covered 75 acres costing $3,634,579.

Nathaniel R. Howard, editor of the News since 1937, was appointed assistant director of the United States Office of Censorship. He served as a director of the American Society of Newspaper Editors from 1939 and was made president in 1947.

Teachers throughout the county were handling the ration books for sugar and were assuming many other responsibilities in an efficient manner, while the children of the public, parochial, and private schools were playing an important part in the war drives. Preparations for the conflict were being made in many fields besides that of manufacturing. By spring, the Office of Price Administration ordered ceilings on 75 per cent of food products, and restrictions included gasoline, tires, wearing apparel, and many other items in short supply by reason of war demand. OPA ordered ceilings on nearly all prices at the highest March levels. Virtually everything that the people wore and used and ate came under sweeping controls. The city, the schools, and the Cleveland Employment Center were developing a training program to supply workers who would be needed in war activities later in the year.

The Greater Cleveland Home and Flower Garden Show opened on February 21 at the Public Auditorium, emphasizing the importance of Victory Gardens. Throughout the county, preparations were made for back-yard gardens and community gardens in vacant lots.

General Frank Purdy Lahm came to Cleveland to live, after one of the most remarkable careers in aviation achieved by any man. A graduate of the United States Military Academy in 1901, he became the first balloon pilot in the Army. He made many experiments with balloons for war purposes, and won the James Gordon Bennett cup in the International Balloon Race from Paris in 1906. He organized aviation service in the Philippines and conducted training on airplanes and seaplanes in 1912. His services in the lighter-than-air field were many, particularly during the first World War when he was appointed brigadier general of the Air Corps Training Center,

1926-30. He retired in 1941 after having been awarded the Distinguished Service Medal.

Mayor Frank J. Lausche formed an advisory committee in the spring, with a view to reorganizing the City Plan Commission and making it more effective. The committee under the chairmanship of Walter L. Flory included G. Brooks Earnest, Randolph Eide, Abram Garfield, George B. Mayer, Leonard W. Mayo, C. M. Stedman, L. M. Toner, Leo Weidenthal, Paul J. Hurd, and John T. Howard. Before making recommendations, the committee consulted outstanding city planners, and then drafted a charter amendment. Voters of Cleveland approved on November 3 the amendment changing the name of the City Plan Commission to City Planning Commission, to denote a continuing function of planning rather than adherence to a static plan. The amendment provided for a citizens' advisory committee, a co-ordinating board of city, county, and state public officials, and a board of appeals. For a quarter century many citizens had given earnest and valuable service to the Commission, but, handicapped by lack of money and power, their efforts had not been adequately recognized. It was hoped that greater appropriations and an enlarged staff would mean achievements not possible in earlier years.

John Stanley won the singles title in the American Bowling Congress in Columbus with a score of 756.

The Metropolitan returned on April 6 for an outstanding season of Grand Opera. Helen Jepson, who called Akron and Cleveland "home," was enthusiastically greeted in *La Traviata,* and Rose Bampton, born in Cleveland, shared honors with Bidu Sayao. Grace Moore in *Tosca* and other popular favorites made the week memorable. Among the distinguished conductors were Bruno Walter, Sir Thomas Beecham, Paul Breisach, Ettore Panizza, Erich Leinsdorf, and Wilfred Pelletier. A five-year contract between the Northern Ohio Opera Association and the Metropolitan Opera Association was signed, ensuring the continuance of Cleveland's high place in the musical world. Thomas L. Sidlo was chairman of the local association, and the executive committee consisted of Sidlo, Percy W. Brown, Robert J. Bulkley, A. C. Ernst, Edgar A. Hahn, George A. Martin, Charles B. Merrill, John P. Murphy, and Harry R. Valentine.

The Cleveland Medal for Public Service was awarded on April 21 by The Cleveland Chamber of Commerce to Major John Berry, "internationally known airport builder and administrator, whose untiring efforts contributed to making Cleveland an outstanding aviation center."

The City of Cleveland acquired the Cleveland Railway Company on April 28, thus ending more than thirty years of operation by that company. Revenue bonds were issued by the city for the purchase, including provisions for the acquisition of new equipment. The city bought the 313,944 shares of stock at $45 per share for a total of $14,127,480. Cleveland thus became the owner and operator of a street-railway system with 4,400 employees, doing an annual business of $15,000,000 and serving a metropolitan area of 1,250,000 people. It seemed ironical that the day of purchase was the thirty-fourth anniversary of Tom Johnson's famous "Free Ride Day." The

Cleveland Transit System came under the supervision of the Public Utilities Department with William D. Young as director. Walter J. McCarter, who had been operating vice president of the company, became general manager for the city. In 1943 the Cleveland Transit Board was appointed by Mayor Lausche, with William C. Reed, chairman, Edward Blythin, and William C. Keough as members. McCarter was retained as general manager until December, 1946, when Donald C. Hyde succeeded him.

On April 30, a huge parade inspired the city to hasten preparations for war. The spotlight was on War Bonds' vital part in victory. Thirty thousand workers arranged to visit 340,000 homes in the county to promote the sale.

Thirty Hollywood stars appeared in the Public Hall, May 4, and staged the greatest variety show Cleveland had seen. Cleveland responded, paying $31,667 to the Army & Navy Relief Fund.

The Japanese had taken possession of vast resources in oil and rubber in their relentless drive to the south, and on May 6 Corregidor surrendered. Escaping in a PT boat, General Douglas MacArthur made his historic declaration, "I came through and I will return."

The price of newspapers rose to four cents on May 7. The Sunday *Plain Dealer* sold for twelve cents. Before the emergency was over, the dailies rose to five cents and the Sunday edition to fifteen cents.

A huge book, with pages the size of a desk top, was opened by the *Press* as Cleveland's Roll of Honor. Parents, wives, and relatives were invited to sign their servicemen's names in the book, as a permanent record of those servicemen from Cuyahoga County. Four hero-books were filled with ninety-five thousand names on the mammoth pages, and the volumes were turned over permanently to the Cleveland Public Library.

The first city dim-out, May 21, was pronounced a success. The threat of air-attack continued throughout the war. Four hundred doctors were sworn in as members of a defense-casualty team to serve twenty-nine areas of the city.

This America, a book designed to tell the world about the United States, was written by Allen Y. King, assistant superintendent of Cleveland schools, Dr. Howard E. Wilson of Harvard, and Nellie E. Bowman of Tulsa, Oklahoma. Published by the American Book Company, this informative volume was to be used as the basis of a program of education in the schools.

The Cleveland Ordnance district office was opened on May 28, and its record of business handled from the Terminal Tower headquarters was phenomenal. Within a few months the Cleveland district turned out more than a billion dollars worth of military equipment. Under the direction of Colonel H. M. Reedall, the staff grew to include 4,200 civilian workers. Contracts were let to nearly 800 privately owned plants in the 55 counties comprising the northern Ohio industrial area, and the office was responsible for the procurement of more than 5,000 of the 13,000 items making up war-matériel requirements. The war over, the great organization shrank until in 1946 there were less than 100 on the staff headed by Colonel Edison A. Lynn.

The Office of the Inspector of Naval Material had been opened in Cleveland in 1912 as a branch of the Pittsburgh District. This office became highly important in World War II as a supervisory office covering Ohio, Indiana, Kentucky, and the lower peninsula of Michigan. Eight hundred and five men and women were employed in 1944, and at this time the volume of business reached a peak of seventy million dollars per month. The office tested and inspected material procured in this area for the Navy, and expedited delivery while acting as liaison between private contractors and the Government in Washington.

The Blue Star Mothers Service, Inc., with the help of the *Plain Dealer*, was organized on May 28. Mrs. A. L. Eggleston was the first president. A lounge, where sewing was done and parties were given, was opened at 1831 East 13th Street for service men and women. The organization staffed the kitchen at the Stage Door Canteen and initiated many patriotic projects.

During the Russian invasion in 1940, Antanas Smetona, national hero and President of Lithuania, fled with his wife to America. They had come to Cleveland, and were making their home with their son, Julius, a factory worker, at 11596 Ablewhite Avenue. In his attic study, President Smetona wrote letters to his countrymen and contributed articles to Lithuanian newspapers. "Of all the towns I visited since coming to America," he said, "I like Cleveland best." He died in a Cleveland fire in 1944.

Seven persons were drowned on June 1 as a freak wave hit the shore from Bay Village to Geneva. A water wall, four to twenty feet high, struck with fury.

The last unit of the old Whitehall Hotels at Chester Avenue and East 107th Street, final home of Mayor Tom L. Johnson, was sentenced to demolition by Benjamin S. Hubbell, architect and owner.

The twenty-seventh annual Kiwanis International Convention was held in Cleveland, June 14-18. More than six thousand Kiwanians came from every state in the Union and every province in Canada. Addresses by Thurman W. Arnold, assistant attorney general of the United States, and Leonard W. Brockerman, K.C., British advisor on empire affairs, and other leaders urged membership and public to carry forward the programs of club and Government looking toward the successful conclusion of the war. The president of the Cleveland club in 1946 was Chalmer F. Lutz and the secretary was James B. Danaher.

The Stadium was filled on the Fourth of July, when the annual Festival of Freedom was presented under the auspices of the Come-to-Cleveland Committee of the Advertising Club and the American Legion Club. Again, the celebration was the largest in the nation. *The Pageant of Flags* brought into its patriotic pictures the Cleveland Grays, Cleveland's military company in its one-hundred-and-fifth year; the Veterans of Foreign Wars; contingents of the United States Army from Camp Custer and Camp Perry; the United States Marines; the Coast Guard; and inductees of Army, Navy, and Coast Guard. Among the notables introduced was Clevelander Josiah Williams Hill in his one-hundred-and-first year, scout for General Sherman in the Civil War, descendant of a soldier in the War of 1812, and grandson of one of Ethan Allen's Green Mountain Boys in the Revolutionary War.

The people of Cleveland purchased $325,000 worth of War Bonds and stamps as the result of a *News* campaign to buy a bomber for General MacArthur. The great plane was christened the *Spirit of Cleveland* on July 4.

Alexander Winton's pioneer automobile, a prized relic, was sold for scrap on July 24, bringing $7.80 to the Navy Relief Fund. The car had been made in 1896 when it attracted national attention.

The Court of Flags of the United Nations, provided by The Cleveland Chamber of Commerce, was dedicated on July 25 in the southwest section of the Square. With appropriate ceremony, the avenue of flags and flagpoles was presented to the City of Cleveland in the presence of Brigadier General Ulysses S. Grant III and Colonel H. M. Reedall, Ordnance Department, as a constant reminder of the feeling of good will and unity toward the nation's allies.

It was reported, July 27, that ninety-two labor controversies were settled in the city instead of being referred to Washington.

Fire destroyed a substantial part of Ringling Brothers Circus on August 4. Forty animals died on the lakefront grounds, east of East 9th Street.

The National Noise Abatement Council on August 8 gave Cleveland second place among five large cities for its successful efforts in "elimination of needless noise."

The War Service Center in the northwest section of the Public Square was dedicated, August 21, as a pledge to victory. More than twenty-five thousand Clevelanders attended the opening ceremonies which were marked by patriotic addresses and a parade. Joseph M. Schultz, manager of the Chamber of Commerce Construction Industries Department, supervised the activities and arranged exhibits. Women of the local Civilian Defense Office maintained a record of service men and women and provided public information. War-service organizations utilized the facilities of the building, among them the USO, Red Cross, War Bonds and Stamps Committee, Blood Donor, and Recruiting offices. The War Service Center building was for four years a practical headquarters for war agencies, and later for postwar services. Planned by William Ganson Rose and erected through the joint effort of the City of Cleveland, civic, and labor organizations, with Herman Kregelius as architect, it was the outstanding feature of its kind in the United States.

The united labor committee of twenty-four Cleveland leaders in the AFL, CIO, and railroad brotherhoods, appealed to labor in war industries to pledge the three-point program calling for increased production, decreased absenteeism, and increased War Bond purchases. Labor patriotically celebrated Labor Day, September 7, by working in Cleveland plants and pledging co-operation for victory.

Fast, trim, wooden ships were built in Cleveland at the Stadium Boat Works for war duty with the Navy. Sturdy and sleek, these twin-powered, Diesel-motor craft were 136 feet long, with a 24½ foot beam and an eight-foot draft. Oak timber used for keel and hull was found within sixty miles of Cleveland. The city was reviving the lost art of wooden shipbuilding on the Great Lakes.

A Navy bond show on September 13, featuring the Navy's Great Lakes

Band, drew thousands of persons who obtained admission to the Public Auditorium by buying bonds. This plan was followed in Cleveland from time to time and always with success.

The enrollment in the public schools was the lowest in more than a decade, due to participation of many pupils in the war effort. The schools were carrying on a war training program, teaching physical fitness and victory gardening while explaining rationing systems, economic problems, and other appropriate subjects.

The Army presented a spectacular demonstration of military might at the Stadium, drawing more than 43,000 to its first performance on September 19. The total attendance during the engagement was 340,000.

The Cleveland Museum of Art, already internationally famous for its significant accessions, announced that it had received the magnificent art collection of John L. Severance valued at three million dollars, which had been bequeathed by him in 1936. Director William M. Milliken indicated that the collection was the most important ever received, of "unqualifiedly high quality" and breadth of interest. The bequest included world-famous paintings, rare tapestries, period furniture, outstanding sculpture, priceless prints, and many other art masterpieces.

Commodore Louis D. Beaumont, merchant, traveler, philanthropist, and art connoisseur, died on October 1. Although he had lived in Cleveland only eight years of his busy life, he was particularly fond of the city, enjoyed close friendships with some of its citizens, and remembered its institutions with generous benefactions. He gave much of his time to the development of The May Company in Cleveland. He was succeeded by Nathan L. Dauby, under whose management the store became one of the largest in the nation. Commodore Beaumont survived the three other co-founders of the May Department Stores Company, established in Denver in 1888, and devoted the last thirty years of his life to travel, war service, and personal supervision of his ever-expanding philanthropies. To France, he gave a beautiful memorial in honor of Wilbur Wright, and the American Red Cross in France benefited substantially from his support. Members of the American Expeditionary Force found free accommodations in French clubs through the generous arrangements he made. Within seven months after his death, Cleveland was to have more practical evidence of his devotion to the city.

A war scrap pile in the Public Square, October 7, included the Brush dynamo that gave the city light in 1893. As the electric machine, patented by Brush on April 24, 1887, slid down planks from the Cleveland Electric Illuminating Company truck, tears moistened the eyes of John T. Kermode, assistant general manager of the company. He had started the operation of the dynamo in 1893 at the Brush plant on Lime Street. The little machine ran only three hundred forty-watt lamps, but it was a step toward the modern turbines which powered more than a million forty-watt lamps.

Effie Ellsler of the famous Ellsler theatrical family of Cleveland, died on October 9, and her stardom from 1870 to 1900 was recalled by many theatergoers. Her passing inspired fond recollections of her artistic acting at the Academy of Music, where her father, John A. Ellsler, was manager as well as actor; and where her mother, Mrs. Effie Ellsler, and her sister, Annie Ellsler, appeared in many fine stock productions.

Edward C. Daoust was selected as executive head of the Cleveland Clinic Foundation which owned the Cleveland Clinic and Hospital. He succeeded Henry S. Sherman, who became chairman of the board. The Clinic Foundation, chartered as a non-profit institution operated for charitable, scientific, and educational purposes, employed 656 persons including a staff of 69 physicians and surgeons. Endowment approximated $1,500,000.

A mammoth plant was constructed at the Municipal Airport, as one of the world's greatest war factories. It was popularly known as the Bomber Plant, although when opened the official title was Fisher Aircraft Assembly Plant No. 2. The construction had started shortly after the bombing at Pearl Harbor, and the floor space reached the astounding total of 2,500,000 square feet. The factory was built for the assembling of B-29's and later was also used for the construction of P-75's. After the war, the Bomber Plant was used mainly for the sale of surplus properties. One of its hangars housed an air-base unit of the Eleventh Air Force, and another hangar was occupied by the Ohio National Guard Air Squadron. Many thousands appreciated for the first time the colossal size of the structure when, in 1946, it was used for the huge National Aircraft Show with many of the largest types of planes on display in one room.

The United States Navy took over the former Higbee Building at Euclid Avenue and East 13th Street as its district headquarters. Here many activities were conducted during the war, and for some time after its conclusion.

John W. Bricker, Republican, was elected governor of Ohio, November 4, by a landslide. Mrs. Frances Payne Bolton was re-elected to the House of Representatives; and because of her fine record in the Congress, she was re-elected for successive terms in the 1940s. She was known for her breadth of interest and generous spirit in aiding local and national health and welfare institutions. She was a leader in projects benefiting women and children and in the study of practical foreign affairs. She had entered politics after the death of her husband, Chester C. Bolton, who had given able service in the Ohio Senate, 1923-28, and in the Congress, 1928-36, and 1938, until he died in 1939.

Mary Melrose, supervisor of elementary science in Cleveland schools, sent out a call early in November for trees which school children would plant as memorials to men in the armed services. H. C. Cook, assistant supervisor of the United States Forest Service in Ohio, participated with the children in thus honoring heroes of World Wars I and II. Hundreds of trees and tree seeds were planted in parks and ravines.

The largest Cleveland-built ship, the *Belle Isle,* left the American Ship Building yards, November 15, a 621-foot ore carrier constructed for the United States Merchant Maritime Commission. During the year, the steamer *Greater Buffalo,* of the D & C fleet, was taken over by the Navy and converted to the aircraft training carrier *U.S.S. Sable,* stationed at the Great Lakes Naval Training Station, Chicago. The great sea battle in the Solomon

Islands was at its height in the Pacific; and on November 23, the Allies gained control of Dakar and French Africa. Hundreds of Clevelanders in uniform were being sent overseas, and in Britain they were training for the invasion of Europe.

The campaign goal set for the Community Fund was $5,000,000. The amount raised was $5,109,558.88, with 605,853 subscribers. James R. Garfield, Helen W. Hanchette, and Paul Ryan received distinguished-service awards. Willis W. Clark was chairman of the fund and Dale Brown chairman of the campaign, known this year as the War Chest.

The lake barge *Cleveco* was sunk in a severe winter storm near Cleveland on December 3, when it separated from the tug *Admiral,* which also sank. A toll of thirty-two lives was taken.

Curtis R. Phillips, ninety-eight, of Lakewood, who served throughout the Civil War with Company B, 12th Ohio Volunteer Cavalry, was laid to rest on December 23 in Butternut Ridge Cemetery.

Cuyahoga County's first War Bond campaign was launched shortly after Pearl Harbor by the War Savings Committee, headed by Percy W. Brown and General Newell C. Bolton. Brown later became executive vice chairman of the Ohio War Finance Committee, and his inspirational leadership was praised throughout the State. A volunteer army, that at times numbered more than twenty thousand bondadiers, achieved a brilliant sales record in eight War Loan drives, concluding with the Victory Loan in December, 1945. Sales far exceeded quotas, those of E Bonds amounting to $600,736,000, or more than 25 per cent of the State total; and total bond sales reached the staggering sum of $2,584,132,000. Chairmen of the county campaigns were A. A. Stambaugh, William S. Goff, Harry B. Winsor, M. E. L. Cox, Allen C. Knowles, and Frank McFarlane. Workers were encouraged to continue to invest in Government bonds in peacetime, particularly through the payroll-savings program, as a thrift measure and to combat inflation.

1943

The War Manpower Commission on January 6 "froze" more than 300,000 people to their jobs in Cuyahoga County. The Post Office, because of manpower shortage, was forced to close twenty-five substations located in drug stores.

The City Council on January 7 approved an ordinance regulating the sale of horse meat for human consumption. "Dobbin" steaks did not become particularly popular.

Dr. George Washington Crile, one of the country's great surgeons and world famous for his outstanding medical research, died January 8 in Cleveland, content that he had made provision for his important work to go on. He was the son of Michael and Margaret Deeds Crile, born in 1864 in Coshocton County, Ohio. He attended Ohio Northern University and Wooster Medical School (School of Medicine of Western Reserve

University), and his thirst for scientific knowledge led him to study in Europe in the 1890s. He returned to Cleveland as lecturer and professor in the School of Medicine, and was visiting surgeon at Lakeside Hospital, where he eventually became professor emeritus of surgery. His most famous undertaking was the Cleveland Clinic Foundation, launched in 1921 with Drs. F. E. Bunts, William E. Lower, and John Phillips. The Cleveland Clinic Hospital was founded in 1924 and the Cleveland Clinic Research Building was built in 1928. Dr. Crile's brilliant military career in the Lakeside Unit during World War I brought out the genius of his surgical skill. He revolutionized accepted methods of treatment for preventing infections and surgical shock and saved countless lives in the carnage of war. Dr. Crile won many international prizes, was honored with a long list of fellowships in this country and Europe, and was on the membership roll of many associations for the advancement of science and research in America, in Europe, and in South America. His list of published works is as impressive as it is important. His son, George, Jr., became associated with the Cleveland Clinic. Three years after Dr. Crile passed away, Edward C. Daoust, chief executive of the Cleveland Clinic, was killed in an airplane disaster. Dr. William E. Lower, famed urological surgeon, the only surviving founder, led in planning new buildings that brought the total Clinic investment to approximately nine million dollars. Research went forward with the latest facilities and contributed to advance in the diagnosis and treatment of human ailments, keeping the Cleveland Clinic at the forefront in the medical field.

The Foreign Affairs Council was incorporated as the Council on World Affairs. The organization had been launched in 1923 as the Council for the Prevention of War, and, under the leadership of Newton D. Baker, it had made sound progress. Dr. Brooks Emeny was the director from 1934 to 1944, and during this period substantial gain was made in membership while the scope of its activities was broadened. When Dr. Emeny became president in 1944, Shepherd Whitman was named executive director of the Council, and membership in the mid-1940s exceeded 3,900. Purposes of the organization were two-fold: "to provide facts and figures concerning international life, and to develop thorough and effective methods for the peoples' own analysis and study of these facts."

The Stage Door Canteen at 1515 Euclid Avenue was opened on January 14. More than 250,000 service men and women enjoyed food and entertainment in this lively headquarters. Among the most popular visitors was Cleveland's Bob Hope.

Cleveland Boys Towns were reorganized in January by Safety Director Frank D. Celebrezze; Arthur L. Munson, director of public properties; Frank Moore, director of industrial arts of the Cleveland Board of Education; Boys Town Foundation; and the Cleveland Kiwanis Club. Captain Arthur Roth was director. Four headquarters were renovized and operated throughout the war with 1,500 boys, aged eight to fifteen years, enrolled.

Announcement was made on February 18 that the city would sponsor a downtown war garden to stimulate food production by education. Plans were immediately drawn, and the War Garden played a practical and picturesque role through the summer. The garden opened on March 22 in the south end of the Mall between the Board of Education Building and the Cleveland College Building.

Peter J. Diemer was the last member of the Grand Army of the Republic in Cuyahoga County. He died on February 23.

The Intercultural Library was opened on February 23 at East 55th Street and St. Clair Avenue. The idea of Public Librarian Clarence S. Metcalf, it was instituted to foster cross communication between groups. Frank T. Suhadolnik, Cleveland-born Slovene, was chosen as director, and Ruth Trattner as secretary. Exhibits in factories were arranged, and work was also carried on in public and parochial schools, churches, and women's clubs.

Councilmen were investigating the possibility and desirability of the acquisition of The Cleveland Electric Illuminating Company by the City of Cleveland. The excellent service provided over the years by the Illuminating Company and the strong sentiment expressed against the idea by representatives of private enterprise and civic and business institutions, led to the abandonment of the idea.

Music-loving Clevelanders and opera patrons of northern Ohio virtually demanded that the Metropolitan Opera Company return to the city during the wartime period. The company responded by offering a season of old favorites featuring its greatest singers. A special committee of leading industrialists, headed by Albert J. Weatherhead, Jr., sponsored an additional underwriting guarantee further to insure the season's success. Gladys Swarthout as Carmen, Helen Jepson as Marguerite, Norman Cordon as Mephistopheles, John Charles Thomas as Valentin, and Licia Albanese as Violetta were among the artists.

Prices in general were frozen on April 9. Most items contributing to the cost of living were placed under ceilings, and Manpower Commissioner Paul V. McNutt ruled against workers taking new jobs at higher pay. The Office of Price Administration ordered that price ceilings in restaurants conform with prices of April 4 to 10, 1943. Soon after, the Government declared commercial sports in general non-essential, although baseball was permitted to continue because of the interest of soldiers and sailors.

Richard E. Reisinger was elected head of the Cleveland Industrial Union Council on April 15. Later in the year, William M. Davy, secretary of the Cleveland Newspaper Guild, became executive secretary of the Cleveland Council, CIO, succeeding A. E. Stevenson, who was inducted into the army.

The Cleveland Medal for Public Service was awarded, April 20, by the Chamber of Commerce to Carl David Friebolin, "public-spirited citizen who works tirelessly for civic interests of a variety matched only by his versatility . . . a distinguished public servant." The medal was also given to James R. Garfield, "distinguished lawyer, statesman and civic leader, whose life has been an example of outstanding public-spirited citizenship."

It was announced on April 23 that bequests of the late Commodore Louis D. Beaumont, co-founder of the May Department Stores, totaled several million dollars, $565,000 of which was shared by eighteen Cleveland hospitals and educational and welfare institutions. The sum of $200,000 was designated for research by Western Reserve University in memory of his son, Dudley. Trustees of the fund were Nathan L. Dauby, vice president and general manager of The May Company; Morton J. May of St. Louis, president of the May Department Stores Company; and Nathan Loeser, Cleveland attorney and friend of the department-store founder. The remainder of the substantial fund was to be distributed annually under their guidance and direction for charitable and educational purposes.

Officials found on April 23 that 28 per cent of prospective members of the Army and Navy had to be rejected in the Cleveland draft, but the figure was more favorable than the United States average.

A severe twisting wind did considerable damage in northern Ohio on April 28, Cleveland's west and southeast areas suffering severely. Utility services were crippled, some homes were leveled, and more than a thousand workers were made idle.

The eighth strike in Cleveland's streetcar history was called on the anniversary of the transfer of the transit system to municipal ownership, April 29. No major change in working conditions had been made during the past year, and the employees were becoming impatient. A mass meeting was held in the Public Hall, and the mayor and officers of the Cleveland Federation of Labor asked the men to call off the strike and to return to work while resuming negotiations. This advice was followed, and mutually satisfactory arrangements were made between the system and the men.

The merchants of Cleveland on May 9 set a goal of eight million dollars in a special bond drive to equal the purchase price of a destroyer to be named the *U.S.S. Brush* for Cleveland's Charles Francis Brush, developer of the arc light and the storage battery. A town luncheon and the Navy's Great Lakes Band were two popular features of the campaign, which went over the top by a comfortable margin. Max Schwartz of the Bailey Company and Almeda B. Schindler of the Halle Bros. Company played leading parts in this and other campaigns.

The NACA Aircraft Engine Research Laboratory of Cleveland was formally dedicated on May 20. Originally designed as an eight-million-dollar project, it quickly expanded into a twenty-five-million-dollar undertaking, occupying twelve buildings. It was the research center for jet propulsion and was equipped with the greatest altitude wind tunnels, and with giant fans able to produce wind speeds of more than five hundred miles an hour. Full-scale aircraft engines could be studied at precise atmospheric conditions, fifty thousand feet above the earth, where temperatures are 67 degrees below zero.

Msgr. Joseph F. Smith of St. John's Cathedral died on May 25. The citizenship mourned his loss as a great religious leader and useful civic worker. He had been associated with this historic church since 1928.

The great war hospital, 7300 York Avenue, Parma Heights, Ohio, opened in May under Army auspices, and was directed by Major H. H. McCarrans, the area engineer. Covering 153 acres, there were 7 miles of corridors in the group of eighty-seven connected buildings. The institution was formally dedicated on March 31, 1944, as Crile General Hospital, named in honor of

Dr. George W. Crile, famous Cleveland surgeon and brigadier general in the United States Army. The first commanding officer was Colonel Robert D. Harden. The number of wartime patients approximated three thousand, which was double the original number. Plastic and orthopedic cases predominated, although a general medical and surgical division was maintained. A neuro-psychiatric service was also instituted. Four clinic buildings provided X-ray installations and extensive research facilities. Ward buildings provided space for 1,725 beds. The cost of the hospital exclusive of equipment was $4,500,000. The earliest convoy of patients, direct from the European theater of operations, arrived on April 8. On June 1, 1946, the hospital was taken over by the Veterans Administration and was headed by Colonel G. U. Emerson. Its manager was Dr. Harrison S. Collisi, and it was affiliated with the Western Reserve University School of Medicine on a training basis.

The Federation of Women's Clubs of Greater Cleveland during its 1942-43 season added many activities to its regular peacetime interests, such as furnishing the Army Induction Center and maintaining it. The granting of two scholarships to young women for nurses' training, co-operating with Red Cross, aiding the sale of war bonds and stamps, and making college scholarship loans indicated the varied interests to which the club women gave of themselves and their time. The far-reaching activities during the 1943-44 season touched these war or peacetime causes: furnishing of the lobby of the Red Cross Lounge at Crile Hospital, contributing to the purchase of a Red Cross mobile unit, co-operating with Friends of the Land, aiding the Easter Seal Campaign for Crippled Children, and giving help for the Russian War Relief. Mrs. Walter V. Magee, who had been vice president for several years, succeeded Mrs. W. P. Lander as president in 1944-45.

The ninety-fifth anniversary of the Lutheran schools of Cleveland came this year. From the first school, established by the Zion Lutheran Church in 1848, the system had developed until at this time there were sixteen Lutheran schools in Greater Cleveland, attended by 1,600 students. In the early days, religion, church history, and regular subjects were taught in the German language; but, in the 1930s, classes were conducted only in English. In recent years, arithmetic, history, English, geography, and the sciences were supplemented by church history, civics, civil government, hygiene, and music.

The City Council on June 8 took action to put black markets out of business by passing an ordinance providing severe penalties.

The grindingstones of the first grist mill, built in 1799, were placed in a permanent setting on the grounds of the Western Reserve Historical Society. The runner stone, which had disappeared many years before, was finally located by Thomas A. Knight of the Early Settlers Association on the lawn of Wilfred Caine's home, 9151 Broadway.

The Cuyahoga County schools had advanced through the enthusiastic direction of William G. Bahner, superintendent since 1936. He was succeeded this year by another able executive, William L. Shuman. In 1946, the county system consisted of fourteen districts with an enrollment of 6,363 pupils, and ten high schools—Brecksville, Brooklyn Village, Cuyahoga

Heights, Independence, Mayfield, North Royalton, Olmsted Falls, Orange, Solon, and Strongsville.

Outstanding civilian support of the war effort in Cleveland was due largely to the mobilization of neighborhood families in the Block Plan. Under the able direction of Albert I. Cornsweet of Shaker Heights, who originated the plan, it became generally accepted throughout Cleveland suburbs, and later was adopted as part of the national program under Civilian Defense. Each block unit, consisting of about thirty-five families, met regularly, and carried out many activities approved by a council of block leaders. Scrap and salvage drives, recruiting campaigns, blood donations, War Bond sales, and aid to other war programs were stimulated by this effective united effort.

Trunks belonging to Effie Ellsler, celebrated Cleveland actress of the gas-lit era, were opened, June 12, in a Lakewood storage house. Costumes in the trunks recalled her many roles when she was at the zenith of her career in the 1880s. Her last Cleveland appearance was in 1919. Many of the documents found within the old trunks were given to the Western Reserve Historical Museum. The famous actress died in 1942 at the age of eighty-eight.

A forty-five-acre tract of land on West 103rd Street was leased to the Government, June 24, as a site for five hundred trailer homes. Cleveland was meeting the housing shortage as best it could.

The *U.S.S. Huron* slid down the ways at the American Ship Building Company on June 30, the first American frigate launched on the Great Lakes since Commander Oliver Hazard Perry built the frigates *Lawrence* and *Niagara* in 1813 at Erie, Pennsylvania. The *Huron,* named for the City of Huron, South Dakota, which raised $2,500,000 in bonds to build her, was 303 feet long.

The pay-as-you-go income tax bill went into effect on July 1, with wage and salary earners subject to a 20 per cent withholding tax including a 3 per cent returnable Victory tax.

For the fifth consecutive year, Cleveland held the nation's greatest Fourth of July celebration, the Festival of Freedom, the Stadium being filled before the patriotic production was started. A colorful feature, entitled *Women at War,* was given by WAACS, WAVES, SPARS, the USO, Blue Star Mothers, Red Cross, Gold Star Mothers, Civil Air Patrol, women of volunteer services, factory workers, and forty-eight Daughters of America, each representing a state. The Akron Chorus, led by William Albert Hughes; the Festival of Freedom Orchestra, directed by Rudolph Ringwall; Miriam Berg, soloist; and community singing stirred the patriotic eighty thousand present. A picturesque pageant, introducing the nationalities that were represented in Cleveland, and a display of fireworks were among the other popular features. The Cleveland Grays Band, under the spirited direction of William J. Maloney, was given an ovation by the great assembly. The audience rose in silent tribute to the memory of those who had given their lives in World War II, and then repeated the pledge to the flag.

The Cleveland & Buffalo Transit Company, Inc., organized on July 10, successor to the Cleveland & Buffalo Transit Company, originated in a trucking business started by the former company in 1930. M. C. Portmann was president of the new organization.

Forty planes dropped paper bombs on the city, and County Defense Director William A. Stinchcomb praised the public for its prompt reaction to siren signals.

The Anti-Tuberculosis League of Cleveland continued its chest-survey campaign with portable X-ray equipment. Within four years, more than 300,000 persons had free examinations, and three high-speed mobile clinics were serving the county. Funds supporting this activity came from Christmas Seal sales. Frank J. Ryan and Dean Halliday were campaign leaders.

A War Bond luncheon featuring motion-picture stars was held with George A. Schneider, veteran campaign leader in both world wars, as auctioneer. The mammoth total of $83,702,000 in bonds was sold. Ohio, on September 25, was the first of the large states to reach its quota in the Third War Loan bond sale. Heartening reports were coming from the war zones. The Allies had invaded the mainland of Italy; and early in October, the Americans bombarded Jap-occupied Wake Island.

The Reed-McCarter plan, calling for rapid transit east and west with a downtown subway, was debated by the citizenship and then for several months by Council. It passed Council eventually, but, because of the rising cost, was abandoned.

Football was not forgotten in the war effort, and eighty-two thousand people crowded into the Stadium, October 31, to see Notre Dame defeat Navy, 33-6. Cleveland sports writers were keeping public interest alive in their vigorous columns. Ed Bang and Ed McAuley on the *News,* Gordon Cobbledick and James E. Doyle on the *Plain Dealer,* and Frank Gibbons and Franklin Lewis on the *Press* were among those whose reviews and forecasts were followed by a legion of readers.

The Cleveland Chapter of the American Red Cross moved into its new headquarters at 1227 Prospect Avenue. This ten-story building and its four-story annex housed the many services which comprised the Red Cross in Cuyahoga County.

Frank J. Lausche was re-elected mayor by a margin of sixty-five thousand, November 4, and he announced that he would retain his cabinet.

The Heroes Homecoming Fund was launched by the *Press* in a campaign designed to raise $100,000 to equip Crile General Hospital with a bedside radio system for the entertainment of convalescent servicemen. So great was the response of Clevelanders that the goal was met in thirty days, and money continued to arrive until $180,000 had been received. Another radio installation was made for servicemen patients at Fletcher General Hospital at Cambridge, Ohio, while other surplus money was used to beautify the grounds at Crile Hospital, to purchase athletic and gymnasium equipment, to provide a phonograph-record library, and to furnish the hospital chapel.

Appointment of the Most Rev. Edward Francis Hoban as coadjutor to Archbishop Joseph Schrembs was made on November 17. He was a graduate

Top:
Tomlinson Hall, Case Institute of Technology

Center:
Notre Dame College

Lower left:
Flora Stone Mather Memorial Building of Western Reserve University

Lower right:
Amasa Stone Chapel

Upper left:
Marting Hall,
Baldwin-Wallace College

Upper right:
Fenn College

Center left:
Cleveland Institute of Art

Lower right:
Grasselli Tower,
John Carroll University

of St. Mary's University, Baltimore; he took postgraduate work at Gregorian University, Rome; and was ordained priest in the Roman Catholic Church in 1903. He was sent to Chicago as chancellor of the archdiocese in 1909, consecrated bishop in 1921, named bishop of Rockford in 1928, and appointed assistant to the Pontifical Throne in 1937.

The Auto Album and Aviation Museum, the first industrial museum in Cleveland, was established by Thompson Products, Inc., at East 30th Street and Chester Avenue. It traced the evolution of the automobile and airplane from pioneer days.

By action of the distribution committee of the Cleveland Foundation, the Cleveland War Memorial Fund was dedicated on November 23 to the memory of the men and women who gave their lives in the service of their country. Gifts for the memorial were to contribute over the years to the well-being of those worthy of charitable aid or educational assistance.

John F. Patt, head of Radio Station WGAR, was chosen campaign chairman of the Community Fund. The goal set for the War Chest this year was $5,540,000, and the amount raised was $5,692,370.01, with 596,639 subscribers. Distinguished-service awards were received by Lieutenant Colonel Fletcher Reed Andrews, Mathew David Crackel, Albert Duprey, Mrs. Laurence Hamill, Mrs. Edward M. Williams, and Edward W. Palmer.

The largest crowd—14,241—in the history of the Arena attended the *News* boxing show on December 1, and, as usual, the proceeds were devoted to Christmas charity.

A series of lectures arranged by the Council on World Affairs as a memorial to the late Newton D. Baker was launched on December 3 with Walter Lippmann as the first speaker. The date selected was the seventy-second birthday of the eminent statesman, whose guiding influence had contributed in large measure to the organization's advance.

1944

During the past year, Pickands Mather & Company controlled twenty-two iron-ore mines and produced fourteen million tons of ore. The Interlake Steamship Company, which Pickands Mather had organized in 1913, was now managing thirty-six freighters. This was in contrast with one iron-ore mine and one Great Lakes bulk freighter in operation in 1883.

The Euclid Road Machinery Company, 1361 Chardon Road, announced that it would build trucks at three times its prewar rate. About 40 per cent of the big "off-the-highway" trucks built in the country for use in mines, quarries, and heavy construction, were made by Euclid. The company, which pioneered in "off-the-highway" trucks on rubber, was incorporated in 1931. R. Q. Armington was general manager in the 1940s.

The Cleveland Foundation Combined Fund, established on January 8, provided for the administration of gifts of varying amounts in a single trust fund at each trustee institution, namely, The Cleveland Trust Company, the National City Bank of Cleveland, and Central National Bank of Cleveland. Gifts to this fund, large and small, were combined for purposes of economy and efficiency.

Main Street, an adjunct to the Thompson Products Auto Album and Aviation Museum and a prototype of a typical small town of the Gay Nineties, was opened to the public on January 27.

A master freeway plan was completed, January 29, by a committee of engineers representing the Regional Association: Edward A. Fisher of the County Planning Commission; Antonio Cruz Kayanan, planning technician of the Regional Association; Ralph C. Chaney, State Highway regional planning engineer; Norman W. Willke, State Highway Department design engineer; William E. Blaser, chief deputy county engineer; Martin M. Friedman, county bridge engineer; John T. Howard, plan director, City Planning Commission; James M. Lister, assistant planner, City Planning Commission; Robert Hoffman, consulting engineer, City Division of Engineering; John Heffelfinger, city bridge engineer; Morse W. Rew, chief engineer, and Arthur F. Blaser, reserve engineer, Cleveland Transit System; and Vurnen Johnson, traffic engineer, Cleveland Safety Department. The plan called for a $240,000,000 integrated freeway system as the solution of the major traffic problems of the Cleveland area. It was recommended as the logical expansion of the freeway program endorsed by the voters four years before. Priorities were established to carry out this plan, and actual work proceeded.

Ohio, an Empire within an Empire was the title of a book presenting data about the "Buckeye State" in factual form. Valuable information had been gathered concerning the agricultural, historical, industrial, and recreational advantages of the State and was presented in an interesting manner by the Ohio Development and Publicity Commission, of which Homer H. Hampton, well-known railroad executive of Cleveland, was chairman.

Cleveland's metropolitan war-housing developments continued to attract national interest, and several new projects were ready for occupancy this year. Riverside Park at 17800 Parkmount Avenue, including 440 dwellings on six acres of land, conveniently located with regard to schools, churches, and stores, was developed at a cost of $2,428,157. Four temporary war-housing projects were completed this year. Berea Homes, 214 Arden Avenue, Berea, including 522 dwelling units, were built in the outskirts of that city. The dwellings provided accommodations for 1,960 people, and the development cost was $2,137,737. Seville Homes, 15515 Seville Road, provided dwelling units accommodating 2,039, the development cost being $1,623,166. Woodland Dwellings, 2572 East 79th Street, and Kinsman Homes, East 79th to 81st streets, south of Kinsman Road, were other temporary undertakings jointly accommodating 1,873 people, the development cost being $1,397,378.

The Cleveland Medal for Public Service was given on April 18 to Charles A. Otis "for invaluable and continuous contributions, over many years, to the civic life of Cleveland, and for the courage and patriotism which have distinguished his useful career and inspired the friendship of his fellow

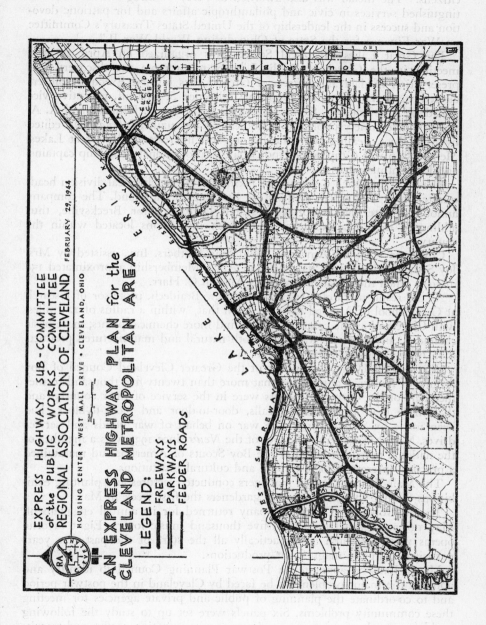

citizens." The medal was also awarded to Percy Whiting Brown "for distinguished services in civic and philanthropic affairs and for patriotic devotion and success in the leadership of the United States Treasury's Committee on War Finance for the State of Ohio during World War II."

The Great Lakes Historical Society was organized on April 27 at a meeting in the Cleveland Public Library to promote the discovery and preservation of data and objects of Great Lakes history. Executive officers elected were Alva Bradley, president; Clarence S. Metcalf, executive vice president; and Louis C. Sabin, Donna L. Root, Leo P. Johnson, and A. A. Mastics. The society published periodically a magazine, *Inland Seas,* edited by Miss Root, dealing with the history and interests of the Great Lakes. Membership was composed of industrialists, professional men, ship captains, and lake enthusiasts.

The B. F. Goodrich Company of Akron moved its chemical-division headquarters and sales offices to the Rose Building in Cleveland. The company announced later an important research laboratory for Brecksville, thus adding to the remarkable list of research institutions located within the county.

Cuyahoga Chapter, American Gold Star Mothers, Inc., assisted by Mrs. Joy Seth Hurd, received its charter in April. Membership approximated 150 in 1946, when the president was Mrs. Marion C. Harr.

As the result of careful research, Mathew Braidech, professor of research at Case School of Applied Science, stated that "within a radius of 220 miles, with Cleveland as the center, you will find more chemical plants, more basic chemicals, and a greater variety of both natural and manufactured products than in any section of the country."

Charles F. McCahill, president of the Greater Cleveland Council of Boy Scouts of America, announced that more than twenty-five thousand former members of the Cleveland Scouts were in the service of their country, and that more than three million calls, door-to-door and block-to-block, had been made by Scouts during the war on behalf of war bonds and service drives. McCahill, general manager of the *News* since 1933, was a member of the national executive board of the Boy Scouts of America, and maintained a practical interest in local welfare and cultural institutions.

The Mall Victory Garden managers conducted lectures and planting exhibitions for five thousand amateur gardeners the first week in May.

The Metropolitan Opera Company returned for its annual engagement, May 1-6, and played to seventy-five thousand music lovers. Eight favorite operas were presented and practically all the stars of the past few years participated in the magnificent productions.

Mayor Lausche appointed a Postwar Planning Council to identify and appraise the major problems to be faced by Cleveland in the postwar period and to co-ordinate the planning of public and private agencies for meeting these community problems. Six panels were set up to study the following problems: needs of returning servicemen; transportation, traffic, and transit; public finance and taxation; inter-racial relations; public works; and labor-management relations. S. Burns Weston served as executive director. The members of each panel diligently studied their problems and at the end of the first year made comprehensive reports that helped the city to meet the complicated conditions following the war. Constructive activities were carried on for another year; but after the major postwar problems had been studied, the citizenship lost interest in the greater part of the work and failed to give financial support, thus causing the abandonment of the Council. One panel, however, that of transportation, traffic, and transit, was continued as a special department of the Cleveland Automobile Club, which provided headquarters, secretarial help, and engineering facilities. This panel continued to study highway developments, transit problems, parking, and related subjects, making its influence felt throughout northern Ohio. William A. Stinchcomb was chairman, and Walter P. Greenwood, vice chairman. The membership included engineering representatives of state, county, and city, and citizens closely related to the problems studied.

In Cleveland's May Shows local talent was attracting wide attention. Among the artists whose work was winning special praise in painting were Henry G. Keller, Peter Paul Dubaniewicz, Dean Ellis, Hazel Teyral, John Teyral, James E. Peck, and Frank N. Wilcox; in sculpture, Walter Sinz, Sol A. Bauer, Katherine Gruener Lange, and Caroline Pickands Richard; in pottery, Viktor Schreckengost, Charles Masgo, Alice Ayars, Mrs. A. R. Dyer, Harry Schulke, and Charles J. Lakofsky; in enamel, Kenneth Francis Bates, Charles Bartley Jeffery, Mildred Watkins, and Edward Winter; in silver, Dominick Sylvester and Potter & Mellen; in weaving, Sara Mattson Anliot, Ruth Erickson, and Elsa Vic Shaw.

The city was sleeping when the news of D-Day—Invasion Day—was received in the early morning of June 6. Whistles, bells, and radio announced the good news. Thanksgiving services were held in the churches, and anxious families awaited word from loved ones in the European war zones.

The Cleveland Committee for Economic Development, with W. T. Holliday as chairman of the northeastern Ohio district, and Elmer L. Lindseth as Cleveland chairman, reported gratifying results after an aggressive program of postwar planning. The committee found that, of 1,679 manufacturers who had appointed postwar planners, 708 employed more than 50 workers. From the inception of the work, launched in 1943, the committee encouraged planning by individual companies, assisted trade associations to organize for postwar planning within their own industries, and established a clearing house for dissemination of postwar information.

The Cleveland Museum of Art, through the bequest of Elisabeth Severance Prentiss, received a priceless collection of fine and decorative arts. In addition to her many previous gifts, she presented a magnificent group of paintings, a collection of rare furniture and valuable sculptures, prints, and ceramics. Art critics and connoisseurs were impressed with the relativity of the many objects which she had assembled. A considerable fund, known as the Elisabeth Severance Prentiss Fund, was also bequeathed, without hampering restrictions, indicating a breadth of vision and generosity of purpose. Mrs. Prentiss had been a member of the advisory council since 1923, and a trustee from 1937 until the time of her death, January 4, 1944.

The Festival of Freedom, under the sponsorship of the Come-to-Cleveland Committee of the Cleveland Advertising Club and the American Legion Club, attracted sixty-eight thousand spectators to the Stadium on July 4, admission being granted only to War Bond purchasers.

The Standard Oil Company of Ohio built a new catalytic cracking unit, which was dedicated, July 15, on the site of Rockefeller's first crude refinery at Broadway and Independence roads. Cleveland's first aviation-gasoline "cat cracker," entirely automatic in operation, cost about ten million dollars and required two years to build. One of the latest marvels of petroleum engineering, it could process eighteen thousand barrels of petroleum a day in aviation base stock and other ingredients. Water was pumped from the river for steam and cooling purposes, thirty thousand gallons being used every minute.

The Cleveland Union Stock Yards Company was rebuilding after a fire in the spring. The new yards were to cover 360,000 square feet of covered pens, alleys, and scalehouses, and 40,000 square feet of open pens. The institution had become one of the largest livestock markets between Chicago and the Atlantic seaboard, serving Ohio, southern Michigan, eastern Indiana, and northwestern Pennsylvania. Approximately four thousand people were employed here.

In observing its fiftieth anniversary, The Cleveland Trust Company on September 2 was hailed as holding seventeenth place among the banks of the nation, its resources having passed the billion-dollar mark. About 1,800 employees were on its payrolls, and 46 branches were operating in Cuyahoga, Lake, and Lorain counties. I. F. Freiberger was chairman of the board, and George Gund was president.

The City of Shaker Heights took over the Moreland and Shaker rapid-transit lines on September 6, purchasing them from the banks in which ownership of the Cleveland Interurban Railroad Company had been vested. The city established by the Van Sweringens thus was assured of good service to and from the Cleveland Union Terminal. Mayor William J. Van Aken was in his twenty-seventh year as chief executive of Shaker Heights, known widely for its good government. Van Aken took the leadership in acquiring the rapid-transit lines.

Each month five hundred veterans were returning to Cuyahoga County to resume work. The Selective Training and Service Act of 1940 provided methods of putting these men back to work through the appointment of a re-employment committeeman. The responsibility of reinstating the veterans lay directly with the draft board under the law then on the books. Frank E. August was brought to Cleveland to organize the city's facilities in aiding returning veterans.

On October 20 Clevelanders witnessed "what seemed to be the breaking out of hell," when the East Ohio Gas Company explosion hurled liquid fire. The whole neighborhood was aflame in the vicinity of East 61st and East 62nd streets, north of St. Clair Avenue. Casualties numbered 130, and the district of homes and stores was reduced to ruins. Emergency aid was provided by the local chapter of the Red Cross for sufferers in the stricken area, which had an estimated population of 22,468. Relief and rehabilitation in the amount of $45,400 was rendered to 395 families. At this time, Common Pleas Judge Stanley L. Orr was chairman of the Cleveland Red Cross chapter, and he later received a certificate of merit for "outstanding leadership during the critical years, 1941-45, and for giving prompt relief to the gas disaster sufferers." Judge Orr was succeeded as chairman in 1945 by Albert M. Higley who also became known for outstanding service. Carlton L. Small, chairman of the gas-disaster committee, was made first vice chairman; and Mrs. A. A. Brewster, chairman of the Red Cross camp and hospital council, second vice chairman. Frederick L. Elder and Milton T. Daus were re-elected secretary and treasurer.

The Cleveland Hospital Service Association announced, November 5, that it had passed its tenth year with subscribers numbering more than 815,000 people located in Cuyahoga, Ashtabula, Geauga, Lake, and Lorain counties. The entire cost of operating the plan was slightly more than 7 per cent, the remainder being used either for direct benefits for subscribers or for a reserve against unusual conditions, such as epidemics.

To build postwar business and create jobs in the Cleveland area, The Cleveland Electric Illuminating Company launched an intensive campaign to bring new industries to Cleveland and to encourage the expansion of those already located here. By thorough research, the company had demonstrated the Cleveland-northeastern Ohio area to be the nation's most advantageous location for many industries. In a continuing national advertising campaign, conducted under the direction of Frank J. Ryan, assistant to the president, the company told and retold millions of magazine and newspaper readers why the 1,700-square-mile district which it served was "the best location in the nation." The company offered a free, confidential, location-engineering service to companies desiring to locate or expand here. As a result of these efforts, together with those of other civic and business groups, commitments were made for the spending of many millions of dollars to create in the district new manufacturing facilities employing many thousands of workers. Upon the death in 1945 of Eben G. Crawford, president of the Illuminating Company since 1933, Elmer L. Lindseth succeeded to the office. Crawford had maintained interest in civic activities and was a leader in postwar planning programs.

An excellent supply of high-grade labor was available to Cuyahoga County industry. Weekly earnings of workers in manufacturing industries were higher than in the rest of the United States. During the last quarter of 1944 they averaged $66.25 as compared with $46.68 for the nation. Skilled workmen in Cleveland factories were receiving $1.15 to $1.35 per hour; semi-skilled, $.95 to $1.15; common labor, $.75 to $.90. The starting rate for women was $.55; semi-skilled, $.70 to $.90; and $.90 and up for highly skilled.

For the fourth time, Franklin D. Roosevelt was elected President of the United States. Frank J. Lausche was elected governor of Ohio, Cuyahoga County giving him a record 190,000 majority. Cleveland's political writers were rated high in the Middle States for the news interest in their columns and the accuracy of their predictions. Jack Kennon of the *News* combined a thorough knowledge of political history with the ability to give interesting reports concerning political developments. Richard L. Maher of the *Press* and Alvin Silverman of the *Plain Dealer* were able reporters who proved capable forecasters. Walker S. Buel, veteran head of the *Plain Dealer* Washington Bureau, and his associate, Fletcher Knebel, were sending news of local interest from the nation's capital.

More than eighty-three thousand spectators filled the Stadium to watch the Ohio State-Illinois football game on November 18. The Buckeyes topped the Illini, 26-12.

The campaign goal set for the Community Fund was $5,750,000, and the amount raised was $5,751,011.92 with 606,404 subscribers. Dr. William Evans Bruner, Paul L. Feiss, John A. Greene, Mrs. Robert H. Jamison, Louis B. Seltzer, Dr. Charles I. Thomas, and Emma Unterberger received distinguished-service awards.

Collinwood Methodist Church, founded in 1894, celebrated its Golden Jubilee on December 3. In 1914, the congregation purchased a frame structure from the Lakewood Methodist Church and floated most of the building by barge on Lake Erie from Lakewood to Collinwood. It was hauled, section by section, to 15232 St. Clair Avenue, where it was reconstructed. A parsonage was moved alongside the church, and the congregation entered into community activities. The Rev. Paul R. Balliett, pastor, came to the church in 1943 and encouraged a co-operative spirit throughout the neighborhood without regard to creed. He soon established an industrial service which was held on Wednesday noons for the workers in near-by plants, and provided speakers of different creeds—Catholics, Jews, and Protestants. One company developed a fine choir for the services. A band and athletic events were included in the program of neighborhood activities. It was the purpose of the church "to serve Christ and country."

The attendance in the eighty-eight elementary parish schools in Cleveland was approximately fifty thousand pupils. The oldest Catholic seminary for the training of members of religious orders was Our Lady of Angels Seminary at 3644 Riverside Drive. It was conducted by the Order of Friars Minor, or Brown Franciscans. Classes were limited to philosophical studies. The sisters of the Cleveland community were conducting three academies: St. Joseph's at the motherhouse, 3430 Riverside Drive, and Our Lady of Lourdes Academy, 3398 East 55th Street, Cleveland; Rose-Mary Home for Crippled Children, Euclid; Mount Marie, Canton, Ohio; and three hospitals. At this time the Rev. Clarence E. Elwell was director of Catholic high schools. His educational training had been broad and thorough. He was graduated from St. Ignatius and St. Mary's Seminary in Cleveland; served four years on the theological faculty of the University of Innsbruck, Austria; and completed postgraduate work at Western Reserve University and Harvard University.

General Leonard P. Ayres described 1944 as a year when more than half of the nation's forty-four-billion-dollar industrial production had consisted of war goods, and more than half of the national income had originated in federal funds. "In a large measure," he said, "business has been serving one great customer who has known exactly what he wanted and who has had limitless purchasing power with which to back up his demands. Now we must begin to make the transition back to civilian production and do it in an economy dominated by war."

1945

It was reported that teachers and pupils of Cleveland public schools had purchased $9,800,000 worth of war stamps and bonds. A review of the past two years proved that Cleveland's public, private, and parochial schools and colleges had made invaluable contributions to the war effort. Alfred A. Benesch was beginning his twentieth year of constructive effort as a member of the Board of Education, his service as president having continued from 1932 through 1944, when he resigned to direct rent control in Cleveland for the Government. Norma F. Wulff succeeded Benesch as president of the board, of which Benesch remained a member.

The Standard Oil Company of Ohio issued an anniversary book on its seventy-fifth birthday and suggested as possibilities for the future "automobiles that can fly, and, conversely, airplanes that can take to the road." Standard Oil of Ohio was not limited to the Buckeye State in its activities, as it operated in Oklahoma, Missouri, Kansas, Michigan, and intervening states, with its own oil wells, pipe-line facilities, barge lines on the Mississippi and Ohio rivers and their tributaries, and with refineries primarily interested in marketing in Ohio. More than ten thousand Sohioans with their families attended the birthday party at the Public Auditorium and listened to a national broadcast, with Gladys Swarthout, Jan Peerce, Victor Borge, and the Cleveland Heights High School Choir conducted by George F. Strickling.

A vigorous educational campaign to recruit labor for the war effort and improve morale throughout the Cleveland district was conducted by the War Efforts Committee of the Cleveland Advertising Club under the direction of the War Manpower Commission. The three-month drive, beginning in January, resulted in large employment gains, and the Cleveland pattern of advertising was adopted in many cities.

February 3 marked the opening of the historic conference of the Big Three—United States, Great Britain, and Russia—in Yalta on the Black Sea. Agreement was reached by Roosevelt, Churchill and Stalin as to the progress of the war. On the same day, a thousand American planes began steady night bombing of Berlin. Campaigns on all fronts moved rapidly, but at an alarming cost of lives and material: February 15, United States carrier planes began bombing Tokyo; on the sixteenth, Bataan was captured; the Marines planted Old Glory on Mount Surabachi in Iwo Jima on February 23; and the flag was raised on Corregidor, March 2.

The development of new food products from the nutritional values of spent brewers' yeast was undertaken by the Brewing Corporation of America in Cleveland. A large appropriation was made for research.

The National Association of Home Builders awarded the first prize of $1,000 in war bonds to Hugh Selby of the Selby Construction Company for the home he had planned to build. The $12,000 home was designed by Architect Edward G. Conrad.

Case School of Applied Science announced a permanent research program to assist Cleveland industry after the war, while providing unusual opportunities for training Case students. This plan was based upon the large volume of wartime research carried on at the institution. The work involved twenty-four research projects for government agencies and twenty-five for private industry, costing $604,500, a sum almost equal to the 1944 regular college expenditures.

The number of wage earners in Cuyahoga County in 1944 was placed at 235,000 by J. W. Vanden Bosch, analyst of the Chamber of Commerce. Earnings approximated $600,000,000, which was about equal to the 1943 total. Department-store sales increased 5½ per cent over the preceding year, and 174 per cent over the 1935-39 average. The Transit System had a big year with revenue of $22,842,000; and, for the second consecutive year, the annual output of manufactured goods exceeded $3,000,000,000.

The city was attempting to relocate many Japanese living in America whose lives had been disrupted by war. These newcomers, encouraged by Cleveland churches, were proving earnest workers, ambitious to succeed in education and business.

When General Benedict Crowell was advanced from the presidency of the Central National Bank to become chairman of the executive committee in 1945, Loring L. Gelbach, who joined the bank as vice president in 1939, became president. Central had grown steadily until in 1946 it was the third largest bank in Ohio, with assets and liabilities in excess of $350,000,000 and eleven branch offices. As the year closed, forward planning was in process: to move the main office to the Midland Building banking quarters, the building at 308 Euclid Avenue having been sold to the F. W. Woolworth Company, which planned to raze it; to construct a new building at 509 Euclid, and to open a branch in the City of Euclid.

Many Cleveland families anxiously awaited news from the Pacific theater of war. After a fierce struggle American forces landed on Okinawa on April 1, and on April 16, MacArthur's men freed the Philippines. In Italy, the rule of Benito Mussolini, former Premier, came to an inglorious end on April 28.

Twenty-five years of constructive activity were reviewed by the League of Women Voters when they met for their anniversary celebration in Halle's Steinway Hall on April 10. Those who spoke were leaders who contributed to the early progress of the organization: Mrs. Malcolm L. McBride, who had twice served as president; Mrs. Ruth Feather, who had been a valuable worker for the suffrage cause; and Elizabeth J. Hauser of Warren, who helped organize the Woman Suffrage Party in northern Ohio in 1911. "Study precedes action" was the guiding motto of the organization, which was interested in both national and local issues and operated on a non-partisan basis. Like the National League, the Cuyahoga County group provided political education that contributed to the growth of the citizen and helped to assure the success of democracy. In 1946, five local leagues joined in establishing a new organization: the Cuyahoga County Council of the Leagues of Women Voters. Mrs. E. J. Kenealy served as president; with Mrs. Reed Rowley, vice president; Mrs. Louis Scher, secretary; and Mrs. Lowell Raymond, treasurer. The newly elected presidents of local leagues were Mrs. A. A. Treuhaft, Shaker; Mrs. Edmund Smercina, Cleveland; Mrs. R. A. Townsend, East Cleveland; Mrs. H. R. Davies, Lakewood; and Mrs. Andrew Meyer, Cleveland Heights. Mrs. Kenealy continued as president after the Council was established.

Franklin Delano Roosevelt died on April 12 of a cerebral hemorrhage, while serving his fourth term as President of the United States. He was succeeded by Harry S. Truman, thirty-second President. Radio and newspapers carried to the world descriptions of the impressive funeral rites.

Another season of the Metropolitan Opera was launched on April 16. An all-American cast appeared in the elaborate production of *The Golden Cockerel,* which was financed by the generous gifts of patrons and friends of the Northern Ohio Opera Association. In other productions, such outstanding stars as Pons, Bampton, Steber, Albanese, Sayao, Pinza, Baccaloni, Baum, Janssen, Peerce, Brownlee, Tibbett, and Melton thrilled Cleveland audiences, who were impressed by the fact that six conductors appeared, among them Erich Leinsdorf, conductor of the Cleveland Orchestra.

James "Jimmy" Lee, director of athletics for the Cleveland Athletic Club, was made chairman of the National AAU boxing committee for the 1948 Olympic games. His practical interest in sports had given him an international reputation. While in France during World War I he started the first baseball teams in the army and captained one of the nines; he organized the Northeastern Ohio Association of the AAU, and had a valuable part in most of the important athletic events held in Cleveland.

The Cleveland Medal for Public Service was awarded, April 17, by the Chamber of Commerce to Percy Whiting Brown, Sam W. Emerson, Alwin Charles Ernst, David L. Johnson, and Frank Augustus Scott, "in recognition of the highest type of unselfish public service resulting in widespread benefits to the community of Cleveland and elsewhere, in the orderly and successful liquidation of the properties of the former Union Trust Company." The medal was also given to Harold T. Clark "for his unselfish contribution of intelligent and effective public service to meet the material and educational needs of the unfortunate and underprivileged."

The end of the war in Europe came after a series of dramatic events. Germany's unconditional surrender to the United States, Great Britain, and Soviet Russia was signed, May 6, in a little red schoolhouse in Reims, France, headquarters of General Dwight D. Eisenhower. Two days later, the Act of Surrender was signed in Berlin, and V-E Day—victory in Europe—was proclaimed to a war-torn world.

The Festival of Freedom drew another huge Fourth of July crowd.

Among features arranged by John A. Crawford, who directed the spectacle, were a parade of guns and tanks from the Erie Proving Grounds; the Camp Perry Band; the WAVES Band; Lieutenant Commander Joseph T. O'Callahan, chaplain hero of the aircraft carrier *U.S.S. Franklin;* mock warfare; and fireworks.

The Cleveland Athletic Club and the Cleveland Chamber of Commerce united in a luncheon meeting for the purpose of selling bonds in the seventh War Loan Drive. Ed Wynn of stage-and-screen fame was a popular guest. With Auctioneer George A. Schneider inspiring the bidding, a record high of $153,128,875 in bonds was sold.

The Veterans Administration planned to occupy the Cuyahoga Building on August 1 as headquarters for its many activities in the area. A year later, the educational and training program was benefiting more than sixty-two thousand ex-servicemen and women, and disabled veterans receiving pensions had reached a total of approximately sixty-six thousand. Home loans for veterans by private agencies amounted to twenty-four million dollars.

Peace terms for Germany were determined by the Big Three—the United States, Great Britain, and Russia—at the historic Potsdam Conference ending August 2. Four days later, American fliers dropped an atomic bomb on Hiroshima, wiping out 60 per cent of the Japanese city of 343,000 population. Soviet Russia declared war on Japan on August 8, as Nagasaki crumbled under a deadly atomic bomb. Fear of the devastating power of the awful weapon brought Japan's unconditional surrender to the Allies on August 14; and on the battleship *Missouri,* the formal surrender to the Allies was signed. V-J Day—victory over Japan—was proclaimed on September 2, ending hostilities in the bloodiest and costliest conflict in the history of civilization.

These were historic days in the life of the nation and of Cleveland. As the momentous steps in bringing hostilities to a close were flashed into the city, floodgates of emotion burst wide open. Auto horns blared, whistles shrieked, bells rang, and thousands milled in the littered downtown streets, laughing and shouting, many with tears streaming down their faces. Rain on the evening of August 14 failed to dampen the enthusiasm of grateful people, and the raindrops blended with tears and cheers as the celebration went on. Men and women were soon coming home to lay aside their country's uniform; but for several thousand Greater Clevelanders, the grave was their reward.

During World War II, employment at Thompson Products, Inc., expanded from 6,000 to 21,000 workers, and the company became Cleveland's largest employer. Annual output rose from $25,255,000 to $120,000,000. Thompson factories were operating in Euclid, Cleveland, and Toledo, Ohio; Detroit, Michigan; Bell, California; and St. Catherines, Ontario. Efficient mass production of valves, engine parts, and accessories for automotive and aircraft manufacturers continued in peacetime. Engine and chassis replacement parts were being marketed in ninety-eight foreign countries. Postwar employment rose from 8,000 shortly after V-J Day to 12,800 at the end of 1946.

Harold Hitz Burton was appointed associate justice of the Supreme Court of the United States on October 1. He had engaged in private law practice until 1929, when his career of public service began as a member of the Ohio House of Representatives. He had given able service to the City of Cleveland, serving as mayor during the trying depression years, 1935-40. Burton represented Ohio in the United States Senate, 1941-45.

A gloom-chasing story-teller named Bob Hope ranked at the top in the business of comedy. Although his name was known around the world, he was devoted to Cleveland, his home. Leslie Townes Hope was a small child when his humble parents left England in the early 1900s to come to America and settle in Cleveland. As a boy, Leslie was mascot for the Cleveland Tigers, a semi-pro baseball team. He attended Fairmount Junior High School and East High School, and spent a year in the Western Reserve University School of Dentistry. Leslie Hope broke into vaudeville as a blackface song-and-dance man, playing houses in the Midwest. His wisecracking ability was recognized, and he formed his own company of performers. To test his talents in New York in 1927, he was given a part in *The Sidewalks of New York*. He succeeded on Broadway, and in 1932 he took the name Bob. The next year found him in an important role in *Roberta*. Fanny Brice shared the spotlight with him in *The Ziegfeld Follies* in 1936. Bob Hope's success as a top-flight radio comedian began in 1938. The hit tune of his first feature-length movie, *The Big Broadcast of 1938*, became his theme song on the air, *Thanks for the Memory*. Box-office figures mounted with screen successes beginning with *The Cat and the Canary*, 1939. Hope's riotous best sellers, including *I Never Left Home* and *So This Is Peace*, inspired good-natured ridicule of their author who never took himself seriously. He appeared frequently in Cleveland, at the *Press* Christmas Show, the Festival of Freedom, the Sesquicentennial, lending a helping hand as his time permitted. When war came, his ability to build morale at home and overseas was of inestimable value. He and his troupe made six perilous trips abroad, where they brought smiles to the grim faces of fighting men, the wounded, and the dying. The Medal of Merit awarded by the Army to two performers, Bob Hope and Irving Berlin, recognized their loyal and untiring service to their country. Hope, with his brother Ivor as partner, and his nephew Milton as vice president, established the Hope Metal Products Company, Ltd., in Cleveland in 1939. The business was the outgrowth of the Parbrook Manufacturing Company, founded about 1900. Bob Hope became a stockholder in the Cleveland Indians when Bill Veeck and his associates purchased the team in 1946.

Fifty thousand people swarmed through the palatial Prentiss mansion on Mayfield Road, Cleveland Heights, on October 4, in response to a public invitation to attend open house before wreckers tore it down. The thirty-room home was built in 1914 by the late Dr. Dudley P. Allen, Mrs. Prentiss' first husband.

A curriculum center in international affairs was opened at Lincoln High School. Veterans were returning to the classrooms both as students and teachers. The school had won a reputation as a leader in the nation for educational teaching programs that encouraged community service.

The World War over, city officials stepped up the battle against the smoke nuisance. It was estimated that in damage to property, depreciation of home furnishings and other losses, smoke was costing the people of the community twelve million dollars a year. The anti-smoke campaign was given a new impetus with gratifying results. Manufacturers were installing smoke-consuming devices, and their co-operation was manifested in a substantial reduction. In 1945, the total precipitation was 60 tons per square mile per month; while in 1946, it was cut to 52.5 tons. At the same time, the drive against fumes, particularly from plants in the "Flats," was being successfully carried on. The enemies of health and property were gradually being overcome.

WJW's 1945 contribution to "World Peace and Harmony" was recognized by the Radio Manufacturers' Association. Local and national organizations had presented the station with certificates for helpful service. Commendation was won in the United States and Canada for the station's organization and sponsorship of the first annual Junior Olympics, a summer play program for boys and girls from twelve to seventeen years. William M. O'Neil was president and manager in 1946, G. G. Rogers was chief engineer, and Charles Hunter was program director.

Upon the death of Archbishop Joseph Schrembs on November 2, Bishop Edward F. Hoban, former coadjutor, became the sixth ordinary of the Cleveland Catholic Diocese. Joseph Schrembs came to America at the age of eleven from his native Bavaria to find in this land the opportunity which made him Archbishop of the Roman Catholic Church. Because of his outstanding record in St. Mary's Church in Grand Rapids, Michigan, he was created a Domestic Prelate by Pope Pius X. In 1911 he received the honorary degree of D.D. in Rome, was named auxiliary bishop of Grand Rapids, and then was consecrated bishop of the Diocese of Toledo. Other honors came rapidly. He was named assistant to the Pontifical Throne in 1914 and was one of the four bishops elected to the National Catholic War Council of the United States during World War I. From 1919 until his death, he was a member of the administrative Board of Bishops of the National Catholic Welfare Conference, serving also as trustee and secretary of the board of trustees of the Catholic University of America. Cleveland first felt the influence of this gentle man of many honors in 1921 when he was appointed bishop of the Diocese of Cleveland. Bishop Schrembs was vested with the title of Archbishop in 1939. Monuments to his ecclesiastical achievements and useful life were the new St. Mary's Seminary, 1227 Ansel Road, John Carroll University, and Notre Dame and Ursuline colleges for women. His interest in children resulted in the building of Parmadale.

Thomas A. Burke, Democrat, was elected mayor of Cleveland. Son of a well-known doctor, Thomas A. Burke, Sr., he had proved himself an able lawyer and a leader with unusual personal popularity. He was admitted to the Ohio bar in 1923, and was director of law of the City of Cleveland, 1941-44.

WTAM was the first radio station to give a series of orchestra concerts in co-operation with high-school a cappella choirs. The first concert was on November 6.

Formation of an Air Foundation to carry on Cleveland's tradition of contributing to the advancement of aviation was announced on November 10. Incorporators of this non-profit organization which expected eventually to have $250,000 at its disposal, were four men whose names were linked with civic activities and aviation: Frederick C. Crawford of Thompson Products, Inc., Albert J. Weatherhead, Jr., of the Weatherhead Company, A. C. Ernst of Ernst & Ernst, and W. T. Holliday of the Standard Oil Company of Ohio. The specific purpose of the Air Foundation was "to promote, encourage, finance, and conduct, either alone or in conjunction with individuals or other organizations or institutions, scientific investigation and research relating to the science or art of aerial transportation and navigation, and the design of materials for, and processes and methods which may be used for, the construction and manufacture of all types of aircraft and parts."

The Associated Charities became The Family Service Association on November 14, continuing its primary function of family rehabilitation. A steady demand for its services emanated from many community sources; and postwar problems of family adjustments, bad-housing situations, and financial insecurity were increasing challenges to the staff. Since 1904, more than 132,000 families and 500,000 individuals received substantial assistance from the agency.

The campaign goal set for the Community Fund was $6,000,000. The amount raised was $5,436,548 with 552,901 subscribers. J. M. Berne, for nine years president of the Jewish Welfare Federation, was awarded a distinguished-service citation for his deep community interest and civic activities as well as his benevolent influence. Other service citations went to Elizabeth M. Folckemer for her courage, ability, and high purposes as director of the Visiting Nurse Association since 1919, and as chief nurse of the Lakeside Unit during World War I; to Thomas L. Sidlo, for his notable contribution to music in Cleveland and his participation in cultural and civic life; to Dale Brown, chairman of the Fund campaigns of 1940, 1941, and 1942; to George A. Bellamy, founder of Hiram House and executive director, "who has constantly broadened the horizon of social service"; and to Stanley and Stella Klonowski for outstanding work among citizens of Polish ancestry. Curtis Lee Smith was campaign chairman.

Station WGAR received the *Billboard* award for publicity and programs. The station had sent Carl George, assistant manager, to the Pacific war theater as correspondent.

The Cleveland Rams won the national professional football championship on December 16 by defeating the Washington Redskins, 15-14. More than thirty-two thousand fans saw the game in the Stadium despite the fact that the temperature was 6 degrees above zero. The Rams moved to Los Angeles in January to represent Los Angeles in professional football, and their place was taken by the Cleveland Browns.

Part of the dream of railroad empire of the Van Sweringen brothers of

Cleveland was being carried out by Robert R. Young, chairman of the board of the Alleghany Corporation and the Chesapeake & Ohio Railroad. After eight years of controversy and financial reorganization, Young planned a billion-dollar company with roads of about 7,500 miles, tapping some of the richest industrial sections of the nation. The four lines involved in this proposed merger were the Chesapeake & Ohio, Nickel Plate, Pere Marquette, and Wheeling & Lake Erie. Savings were to be effected through cutting of passenger routes and standardization of equipment.

The Greater Cleveland Safety Council recorded a gradual decline in yearly motor-vehicle deaths from a high figure of 275 in 1929 to 104 in 1945. In that period, child fatalities dropped from 141 in 1929 to 55 in 1945.

For the first time in Cleveland's public-health history, there were no deaths, in a year's time, from typhoid fever.

The navy cruiser *U.S.S. Cleveland* had participated in World War II in two surface battles, numerous air attacks, and nineteen shore bombardments from North Africa to the coast of China, according to her commander, Captain Charles J. Maguire. It had aided in capturing Emirau Island in the Pacific; played a part in the conquest of Saipan, Tunian, and Guam; and participated in the first battle of the Philippines Sea.

Americans had found air travel a safe and convenient means of going about their daily affairs. Peak traffic was reached in 1946, when 86,530 ships were reported with 1,286,144 passengers at the Cleveland port, one of the largest and finest in the world.

Cleveland was a leading graphic-arts center. The value of the products of the industry, excluding book and newspaper publishing, amounted to $29,658,736; 332 establishments employed 4,645 workers. In the general commercial printing business there were 191 companies, among them Brooks Company, The Buehler Printcraft Company, Caxton Company, The Corday & Gross Company, Edwards & Franklin Company, The William Feather Company, W. S. Gilkey Printing Company, A. S. Gilman, Inc., J. C. Hub Manufacturing Company, The Judson Company, The Lezius-Hiles Company, The Penton Press, Prompt Printing & Publishing Company, Stratford Press Company, and Tower Press, Inc. Among the companies engaged in lithography were Central Lithograph Company, Continental Lithograph Corporation, Copifyer Lithograph Corporation, The Crane Howard Lithograph Company, Great Lakes Lithograph Company, Morgan Lithograph Corporation, Reserve Lithograph & Printing Company, and Schmitz-Horning Company.

Cleveland concluded the year with its transit, market, and Pennsylvania Railroad station problems still unsolved, and with the need of finding employment for approximately fifty thousand people, made jobless in the conversion from war to peace. There was optimism, however, as the city made plans for the celebration of its Sesquicentennial.

The committees to assume charge of the Sesquicentennial Celebration were formed and a program of events to be launched on January 1, 1946, was outlined. In the spring of 1944, the Early Settlers Association of the Western Reserve had appointed a committee to develop the idea of holding a suitable celebration to commemorate Cleveland's 150th birthday. Later, representatives of the Cleveland Chamber of Commerce, the Cleveland Advertising Club, and the Western Reserve Historical Society were invited to join the preliminary organization.

In view of the fact that the nation was engaged in war, it was decided to defer development of the idea of the city's 150th birthday celebration until peace was declared. The City Council, in the meantime, requested Mayor Burke to appoint a commission that would prepare a municipal program. This led the pioneer committee to make a similar request of the mayor, so that a united organization would be effected. Mayor Burke selected William G. Mather and Charles A. Otis as co-chairmen in September, 1945, and the mayor was persuaded to serve as honorary chairman. In making his appointments, the mayor considered the records of his appointees:

William Gwinn Mather came of a family whose name had been associated with the growth and development of Cleveland from the formation of the Connecticut Land Company. His grandfather, Samuel Mather, Jr., original shareholder and prominent member of that company, rode on horseback to the wilderness of the Western Reserve in 1798 to inspect the vast tract that he had purchased; his father, Samuel Livingston Mather, came to Cleveland in 1843 to look after the Mather holdings, and industrial successes led to a career of outstanding public service. Two sons, Samuel and William Gwinn, in turn became leaders of the industrial and cultural life in the city. William Gwinn Mather was born in downtown Cleveland on September 22, 1857. He began his business career as a clerk in the Cleveland Iron Mining Company, worked his way to the top, and in 1890 was made president of the new Cleveland-Cliffs Iron Company, a merger of the Cleveland Iron Mining Company and the Iron Cliffs Mining Company. Since 1933 he had been board chairman, and other business affiliations were numerous and important. His outstanding contributions to culture, education, and civic betterment had continued for many years. He was president of the Cleveland Museum of Art, member of the board of trustees of Western Reserve University, Trinity College, Western Reserve Historical Society, Kenyon College, and Lakeside Hospital. He was a vestryman at Trinity Cathedral, and founder of the Episcopalian Church Club of Cleveland. Because of his diverse and useful activities, Mather was rewarded by The Cleveland Chamber of Commerce with the medal for distinguished service. In February of Sesquicentennial Year, he was honored by a civic testimonial dinner given by his fellow townsmen as a tribute to his remarkable record.

Charles Augustus Otis also came from a long line of able pioneers who played an important part in the development of New England and brought leadership to the Western Reserve. William A. Otis, his grandfather, arrived in Cleveland in 1836 and became a commission merchant of importance, serving in the Legislature. He became the pioneer ironmaster of Cleveland in 1840, and his business interests broadened to include railroad development and banking. His son, Charles Augustus Otis, succeeded his father in the iron business, set up the first forge in Cleveland, and introduced the Bessemer process of making steel. He found time to give admirable service as mayor of

Cleveland, and advanced many worthy enterprises. Charles Augustus Otis, Jr., was born on Wood Street, July 9, 1868. A Yale graduate, he spent three years in the cattle business in the West, after which he returned to Cleveland and formed the firm of Otis & Hough, agents in iron and steel and later stock brokers. He helped to organize the Cleveland Stock Exchange, and was the first Clevelander to hold a seat on the New York Stock Exchange. As president of The Cleveland Chamber of Commerce, Otis brought to the organization new enthusiasm that resulted in greatly increased membership. He purchased the *World,* the *Evening Plain Dealer,* and the *News and Herald,* thus developing the *News.* For several years he served as president of William Edwards & Company, the wholesale grocery business founded by his father-in-law; and later he became vice president of the Brewing Corporation of America. As a dollar-a-year man in World War I, he gave distinguished service to the War Industries Board, and his city profited over the years by his service on business, civic, and social committees. His love for all that entertained and improved his fellowman, his affection for horses and dogs, his fondness for sports and the theater, made him popular at home and beyond the city's borders. For nearly a half century, his wit and humor, good fellowship, personal enthusiasm, and genuine friendliness won for Otis the title of Cleveland's "best-known citizen."

After the co-chairmen were named, the mayor's Sesquicentennial Commission was appointed and the organization was completed. Laurence H. Norton was elected president. He was a member of a prominent family that contributed to the city's industrial, commercial, and cultural advance. His wide acquaintanceship, many business and social affiliations, and leadership of the Western Reserve Historical Society were helpful to the celebration in many ways. Other officers were John F. Curry, John F. Patt, Thomas L. Sidlo, and A. J. Weatherhead, Jr., vice presidents; Robert F. Bingham, secretary; L. M. Harter, assistant secretary; John K. Thompson, treasurer; and Ernest N. Wagley, assistant treasurer. William Ganson Rose was director of cultural and civic events, Seward A. Covert was director of publicity, and Benjamin T. Franklin was business manager.

The executive committee included the officers and the following members: Harold J. Barber, Walter I. Beam, Paul Bellamy, J. A. Bohannon, George F. Buehler, T. J. Conway, Fred C. Crawford, N. L. Dauby, Joseph Eaton, William H. Gray, George Gund, K. K. Hackathorn, Samuel H. Halle, Clifford F. Hood, N. R. Howard, Elton Hoyt II, George M. Humphrey, Herbert P. Ladds, Edward D. Landers, Elmer L. Lindseth, Frederic S. McConnell, J. C. McHannan, J. P. Murphy, Vernon Pribble, Louis B. Seltzer, A. A. Stambaugh, Charles J. Stilwell, Robert A. Weaver, and L. B. Williams.

Among the committee chairmen were William M. Milliken, Art Committee; W. R. "Russ" Jack, Aviation Committee; Mrs. Rob Roy Alexander, Central High School Centennial Committee; Mrs. Joseph H. Thompson, City Beautification Committee of The Garden Center of Greater Cleveland; Donald F. Lybarger, Cuyahoga County Committee; Leo Weidenthal, Dramatic Committee; Benjamin P. Forbes, Early Settlers Sesquicentennial Committee; Charles A. Otis, Founder's Day Committee; Edward H. Scanlon, Grove of Stars Committee; Donald F. Lybarger, chairman after the death of Dr. E. J. Benton, Historical Committee; E. D. Landers, Junior Chamber of Commerce Slogan Contest Committee; William H. Gerhauser, Marine Committee; Arthur B. Williams, Moses Cleaveland Trees Committee; Mrs. Lewis W. Phillips, Mother's Day Committee; Russell V. Morgan, Music Committee; Dr. Herbert C. Hunsaker, National Folk Festival Committee; Charles J. Wolfram, One World Day Committee; Clarence S. Metcalf, Public Library Committee; Paul Bellamy, N. R. Howard, and Louis B. Seltzer, co-chairmen, Publicity Committee; Allen James Lowe, Reception and Entertainment Committee; A. J. Salzer, Regatta Committee; Stanley B. Cofall, Sports Committee; Mrs. John B. Dempsey, chairman, and Mrs. Robert H. Jamison and Mrs. Ervin C. Pope, vice chairmen, Sesquicentennial Women's Committee.

It was decided that the four foundations upon which the Sesquicentennial celebration should be built were history, education, culture, and business. The purposes announced were as follows: to impress upon the citizenship the history, the traditions, and the sound foundations upon which our city had been built; to inspire in the children of Greater Cleveland faith in the future of the city as an ideal place in which to live and earn a living; to launch ideas and projects that would continue to benefit the city in future years; to advertise and publicize Cleveland to the nation as an outstanding center of industry and commerce, and as an ideal center of culture and civic pride; to advance the interests of Cleveland business by attracting a vast number of visitors throughout the observance period; to hasten the completion of plans and projects of the city, county, and individual institutions with the goal of building a finer city; to attract worthy exhibits and gatherings throughout the celebration period, and stimulate the securing of future expositions and conventions; to celebrate in suitable manner Cleveland's magnificent contributions to World War victory; to instill in the citizenship a newborn confidence in Greater Cleveland and its opportunities; and to inspire co-operative effort in fostering the city's advance.

Early in the campaign, a contest to select a slogan was conducted by the Junior Chamber of Commerce. The winning slogan, "Saluting the past, Cleveland builds for the future," submitted by Donald W. Athearn, was used in many ways throughout the year.

1946

The celebration of Cleveland's Sesquicentennial Year was ushered in, New Year's Day, at a ceremony on the Public Square. Mayor Thomas A. Burke, Co-chairman Charles A. Otis, and President Laurence H. Norton of the Sesquicentennial Commission, and Marguerite Bacon, direct descendant of Moses Cleaveland, city's founder, raised the Cleveland flag while the wind blew a gale and the thermometer registered 14 degrees above zero. Nearly every week of the year witnessed one or more Sesquicentennial events, and new records were made in the number of conventions and expositions held in the 150-year-old city.

Ruth Seid, whose pen name was Jo Sinclair, was declared winner of the ten-thousand-dollar Harper novel prize contest with her first novel, *Wasteland*. Miss Seid, a Clevelander, contributed short stories to national magazines.

A comprehensive plan for parking in the central area of the city was submitted to the City Planning Commission by its Parking Advisory Committee on January 6. It called attention to the serious congestion of automobiles that was obstructing Cleveland business. The report was approved in principle, and city-planning engineers then developed the project further, with two major goals: to make a complete survey, and to establish a parking authority to carry out detailed plans resulting from the survey. Late in the year, a comprehensive survey was assured through the co-operation of the Federal and State governments. Members of the City Planning Commission at the end of 1946 were Ernest J. Bohn, chairman; Walter L. Flory, vice chairman; M. C. Clarke, Alfred C. Grisanti, George B. Mayer, Mrs. Malcolm L. McBride, Peter J. Slach, with John T. Howard, planning director. It had a staff of twenty-eight and a budget of $105,000. Advisory sub-committees were active in the subjects of downtown parking, truck terminals, fine arts, recreation, highways, and urban rehabilitation.

The Lake Carriers Association members controlled 318 vessels, engaged primarily in the transportation of iron ore, coal, grain, and limestone, with a gross register of 2,000,000 tons. These ships comprised 90 per cent of the entire cargo-carrying fleet under United States registry in transportation on the Great Lakes. Vessels comprising 85 per cent of the association membership were operated by companies with offices in Cleveland. During the years 1940 through 1945, the Great Lakes fleet transported more than 1,035,000,000 tons of iron ore, coal, grain, and limestone. By comparison, the United States ocean merchant marine transported 200,000,000 tons of cargo and supplies. Under the chairmanship of John Sherwin, the Education and Public Relations Committee obtained a greater national recognition for the importance of lake transportation and extended the educational activities of the Association. Officials of the Lake Carriers Association at this time were Alexander T. Wood, president; L. C. Sabin and Lyndon Spencer, vice presidents; Oliver T. Burnham, secretary; F. J. Hollman, treasurer; and Gilbert R. Johnson, counsel. Sabin, veteran association official, was honored in September, 1946, for "his knowledge of and advice in the analysis of navigation needs" on the Great Lakes. A lock in the Soo Canal bore his name.

The "greatest aviation show in history," the National Aircraft Show, was held in the Public Auditorium, January 11-20, under the auspices of Cleveland's new Air Foundation. One of the first of many impressive Sesquicentennial events, it demonstrated that air-minded Clevelanders were interested in planes, the marvels of equipment, and devices used by the Army and private companies. A Boeing B-29 dominated the display, surrounded by army planes and exhibits of war and postwar uses of radio, radar, photography, and weather equipment. Albert J. Weatherhead, Jr., was president of the show which was attended by 200,000, despite a newspaper strike that handicapped publicity. Ben T. Franklin was executive vice president, and Lieutenant Colonel J. J. Spatz directed the Army Air Force display.

The East Ohio Gas Company planned a $12,000,000 expansion program, and the gas-transmission capacity was to be increased from 355,000,000 cubic feet daily to 474,000,000 cubic feet. A 144-mile transmission pipe line from the Ohio River to Cleveland was a major item in the program. For cooking, water heating, and refrigeration, the cost of gas service in Cleveland was the second lowest among the twenty-five largest cities. Other companies planning large industrial expansions were General Motors Corporation, $27,000,-000 for two automobile plants; Westinghouse Electric Corporation, $1,000,000; Eaton Manufacturing Company, $1,500,000; Gabriel Company, $1,250,000; Fisher Body Division of General Motors Corporation, $10,000,-000; Republic Steel Corporation, several million dollars; White Sewing Machine Company, approximately $1,000,000; while a score of companies were planning improvements and expansions, each to cost $100,000 or more.

Brigadier General Woods King of Cleveland was presented the Distinguished Service Medal on February 23 by Major General R. S. Beightler, commander of the famed 37th Infantry Division. General King was cited for his work in training and organizing Chinese troops in South China while connected with the 4th Army Group Command, Chinese Combat Command.

Case School of Applied Science filed a petition in Common Pleas Court, asking that the institution's name be changed to Case Institute of Technology. The name "school" was given to Case by its founder, Leonard Case, Jr., but in time the term came to be used generally to indicate a school below college level. The new title was to become official on July 1, 1947. Plans for new buildings costing a million dollars were launched in the spring. Construction began this year on Tomlinson Hall, a three-story student union, with cafeteria, assembly hall, and quarters for alumni activities. The $750,-000 building was made possible through the generosity of Mrs. George Ashley Tomlinson, widow of the Great Lakes shipping and industrial leader. Mrs. Tomlinson was known for her educational philanthropies. Death claimed Dr. William E. Wickenden, president of Case, in 1947. For years he had been a leader in community development. He was succeeded by T. Keith Glennan, business executive and electrical engineer.

The Cleveland Bar Association on March 5 honored nine lawyers ranging from seventy-six to ninety-one years of age in a ceremony presided over by President Thomas H. Jones. The veterans were Joseph C. Bloch, Homer H. Johnson, Charles S. Reed, William H. Boyd, James R. Garfield, Frank A. Quail, Frederick A. Henry, and D. M. Bader. They had contributed to Cleveland's advance in many ways.

The Child Program Plan for adapting primary children to organized education with maximum consideration for the children themselves, was attracting national attention. The plan, introduced as an experiment in 1928, was adopted by the Board of Education as a policy, and applied to more than forty thousand children classified as the first, second, and third grades.

These pupils were progressing from one level to another, and the length of time spent on any one level depended upon the individual pupil's capabilities. The result was better training, with failures negligible. "The Cleveland Plan has built its success on education of children around their strengths instead of their weaknesses," was the claim. The members of the Board of Education in 1946 were: Norma F. Wulff, president; Carl F. Shuler, vice president; Alfred A. Benesch, Joseph M. Gallagher, Robert H. Jamison, Charles A. Mooney, and Franklin A. Polk. Mark C. Schinnerer became superintendent of schools in 1947, succeeding Charles H. Lake, who became consultant to the Board. The assistant superintendents were E. E. Butterfield, John E. Fintz, William B. Levenson, and Harry E. Ritchie. There were 150 buildings in the public-school system, and 101,024 pupils were enrolled under 3,186 teachers. The total number of public, parochial, and private schools in the county was 401 with an enrollment of 194,939.

John A. Zangerle began his thirty-fourth year as county auditor on March 11, at the age of eighty. Born on the West Side in 1866, he practiced law for ten years and served as a member of the Board of Education in 1893.

An elaborate pageant in observance of the Sesquicentennial was presented as a feature of the Music Educators National Conference, held in Cleveland from March 26 to April 3. Seven thousand music teachers from all over the country attended this meeting and the convention of the National Catholic Music Educators Association. The central theme was "Music Education Looks and Plans Ahead." Besides the Cleveland pageant, beginning with 1796 and ending with the contemporary scene, events included International Night with delegates from all countries, and an Ohio Day Festival on March 30, with musical groups from the eighty-eight counties of the State participating. The Sesquicentennial Night Committee included Russell V. Morgan, Harriet Fitchpatrick, Alfred Howell, Allen Y. King, William B. Levenson, Dwight W. Lott, William R. Mason, Harry E. Ritchie, and Mark C. Schinnerer.

The *Cleveland Book, A Buyer's Guide to Cleveland's Postwar Products and Services,* was distributed throughout the world by the Chamber of Commerce. Thirty-five thousand copies were designed to bring business to the Cleveland area, the book listing the products and services of 5,300 Cleveland companies and containing fifty illustrated articles dealing with the city's industrial, cultural, civic, and governmental activities. Industry's ability to produce a wide diversity of products was presented graphically.

In the past forty-four years, the Cleveland Council of PTA had accomplished much in youth service. The 1946 membership was 28,000 with 124 units, and the officers included Mrs. Charles Bill, president; Mrs. E. E. Bubb, vice president; Mrs. G. D. Russell, recording secretary; Mrs. G. H. Selig, corresponding secretary; Mrs. C. E. Dickman, treasurer; and Mrs. Clyde L. Downs, historian. The Council's aims were to promote the welfare of children in home, school, church, and community; to raise the standards of home life; to secure adequate laws for the care and protection of youth; to bring into closer relation the home and the school; to develop between educators and the public such united efforts as will secure for every child the highest advantages.

Dr. Elbert J. Benton, director of the Western Reserve Historical Society and chairman of the Sesquicentennial Historical Committee, died on March 28. Formerly head of the Graduate School of Western Reserve University, he had served the institution since 1942. Three concise volumes of his *Cultural Story of an American City—Cleveland* represented a brief story of the early-day city and its people. Some months later, the trustees of the Society appointed Dr. Russell H. Anderson as director. Dr. Benton's successor had been curator of the Museum of Science and Industry in Chicago and previously had taught history at the University of Illinois. The Historical Society, founded in 1867, was achieving admirably its objective of discovering and preserving "whatever relates to the history, biography, genealogy," and statistics connected with Cleveland and the Western Reserve. The Historical Society library contained approximately 20,000 books, 20,000 volumes of newspapers, 1,000 rolls of microfilm, and a collection of maps, atlases, and valuable manuscripts. Its collection of broken-bank currency was said to be the best in the United States, and the genealogical section of the library was sixth in rank, including 13,000 family histories. The Napoleonic exhibit collected by David Z. Norton and given to the museum by his children; the notable Shaker collection assembled by Wallace H. Cathcart, former director; the Washington collection presented to the Society by George William Bierce; the comprehensive World War collection presented by Franklin S. Terry, were among the priceless treasures on display. The museum and the library were open daily, free to the public.

April 11 marked the visit to Cleveland of General Dwight D. Eisenhower, who led the Allied forces to victory in Europe in World War II. Cheering citizens packed the Public Square to welcome him, and he was honored at a civic banquet sponsored by the Cleveland Aviation Club.

For fifty-two months and ten days, it was reported on April 19, "a home away from home" had been provided efficiently and graciously by the Cleveland United Service Organizations Council for thousands of service men and women. From the modest beginning of a refreshment stand in the East 9th Street Bus Station to the Easter Sunday when it officially closed, the USO had expanded its activities to seventeen different projects, and its reputation for successful planning and effective operation had become nationwide. Since the autumn of 1941, when Mrs. Robert H. Jamison and Mrs. Neal G. Gray launched the local unit, the organization established and maintained at various times the following activities: a snack bar and recreation lounge in the Terminal concourse; the famous USO Service Club at 620 Prospect Avenue under the direction of Mrs. Frank L. Hornickel; a lounge in Hotel Cleveland for officers with Mrs. John Sherwin in charge; Camp Cheerful for Crile Hospital, supervised by Mrs. James M. Osborne; donations of magazines, food, cigarettes, and thousands of personal services given voluntarily through many channels. Clevelanders were particularly proud of the record established by the USO, recalling that all the outstanding work was contributed by hundreds of volunteers, that unsolicited contributions totaled $104,920.72, that the value of food donated was estimated at $15,500, and that the city exceeded its share of the national campaign drive in 1941 by $14,843. The USO represented the combined war efforts of the YWCA, YMCA, Travelers Aid Association, National Catholic Welfare Conference, Jewish Welfare Federation, and Salvation Army. Among the many citizens who gave of their time and energies were Mrs. Robert H. Jamison, chairman; Fred W. Ramsey, honorary chairman; Mrs. Neal G. Gray, vice chairman; Herman L. Vail, treasurer; Mrs. Robert Evans, secretary; Mrs. Theodore Willis, Mrs. F. Carlisle Foster, and Mrs. George Binkley.

The Cleveland Medal for Public Service was presented by The Cleveland Chamber of Commerce in April to Nathan L. Dauby, "distinguished businessman, wise humanitarian and civic leader who has built a great business enterprise for the community on the foundation that business, as a part of the community, must assume its full responsibility in civic, humanitarian and philanthropic endeavors for the common good." The medal was also awarded to Robert Fry Bingham, "distinguished attorney and thoughtful civic leader for having given generously of his time and effort to the administration and support of Cleveland's civic and philanthropic organizations."

Metropolitan Opera in Cleveland set an attendance record during the week's season ending April 29. Seventy-seven thousand opera lovers had attended the eight regular performances. A Sunday matinee was added, featuring Puccini's *La Bohème,* honoring Cleveland's Sesquicentennial celebration, which brought the total attendance to eighty-five thousand. Thomas L. Sidlo was chairman of the Northern Ohio Opera Association, which had sponsored the annual event, and H. J. Miskell was general manager for Cleveland.

Bob Feller hurled a no-hit game against New York on April 30, striking out eleven men, Cleveland winning, 1-0. He pitched a one-hit game against Boston on July 31, striking out nine, Cleveland winning, 4-1. On August 8, Feller held Chicago to one hit and Cleveland won, 5-0. He was hailed as the greatest pitcher of his time. His speed was measured, the ball traveling 98.6 miles per hour, and his judgment in changing pace and plans to suit each batter was considered remarkable. Best of all, in the minds of many, was the fact that the plaudits of the crowd and the fabulous salary never seemed to have the slightest destructive effect upon his character and conduct. When the 1946 season closed, Feller's record showed 26 games won, including 10 shutouts. For the fifth time he led the major leagues, with 348 strikeouts, breaking Rube Waddell's record that had stood for forty-two years.

Msgr. John R. Hagan, diocesan superintendent of the Catholic schools, was appointed titular bishop of Limata and designated as auxiliary to Bishop Edward F. Hoban in the Cleveland Diocese on April 30. He had been ordained in 1914; served as assistant at St. Augustine's and St. Patrick's churches, Cleveland; had been pastor of St. Mary's, Bedford; and superintendent of diocesan schools since January 1, 1923. Honors were conferred upon him for able service. He had been elevated to the office of bishop before his outstanding career came to an abrupt end on September 27, 1946. Mourned by the church and the citizenship of Cleveland, he was laid to rest in St. John's Cathedral. The Rev. Clarence E. Elwell became superintendent of Catholic schools succeeding Msgr. Hagan.

The Federation of Women's Clubs of Greater Cleveland announced it had actively participated in many welfare projects and civic enterprises during the 1944-45 season. The club's co-operation was given the Crime Commission, Welfare Federation, Radio Council, Library Program Planning Conferences, and Crile Hospital. Attention to outside problems came through the Mental Health Program for Ohio, living Memorial Forests to honor Ohio war casualties, and nationwide campaigns, such as the clothing drive for Czechoslovakia. To concentrate thought and effort on specific phases of community life, the Federation separated its interests and activities into six departments: education, including formal education, radio, motion pictures, and safety; American home, including consumer interest, spiritual values, youth conservation, and women in the home; civics and legislation, covering conservation, courts, citizenship, council, and legislation; fine arts, including creative art, drama, literature, and music; health and welfare, with particular attention to Blossom Hill, thrifty teens, health and hygiene, and recreation; and international relations. The Federation had expanded into a membership of 13,500 in 101 clubs. Officers were Mrs. Louis B. Seltzer, president; Mrs. Gaylord P. Kurtz, first vice president; Mrs. Guy T. Rockwell, second vice president; Mrs. Homer H. Geiger, recording secretary; Mrs. G. C. Frank, corresponding secretary; Mrs. A. E. Griffith, treasurer; and Mrs. Harry Carter, department treasurer. Mrs. Seltzer was succeeded as president by Mrs. Guy T. Rockwell, active in many organizations.

The membership in the Academy of Medicine of Cleveland and the Cuyahoga County Medical Society had risen from 459 in 1902 to 1,600 in 1946, when Dr. R. B. Crawford was president; Dr. D. M. Keating, vice president; Dr. Robert F. Parker, secretary-treasurer; and H. Van Y. Caldwell, executive secretary. That Cleveland was one of the healthiest cities in America was due in large measure to the able members of the medical profession in hospitals and clinics, schools and colleges, laboratories and private practice. Physicians, surgeons, and nurses gave valiant service in wartime as in peacetime, and helped to make Cleveland a medical center of the nation. There was a growing appreciation of the contributions to the advancement of medicine and science made by Clevelanders in the past half century. Outstanding because of general application and practical importance were the researches of Drs. David Marine and O. P. Kimball in causation and prevention of goitre, George W. Crile in surgical shock, Henry Gerstenberger in infant feeding, and Harry Goldblatt in hypertension.

Members of the Academy of Medicine of Cleveland were leaders in national and international organizations. Dr. Clyde L. Cummer, who had served as president of the Ohio State Medical Association, was to become president of the American Academy of Dermatology and Syphilology. Dr. John A. Toomey, professor of clinical pediatrics and contagious diseases of the School of Medicine of Western Reserve University and physician in charge of City Hospital's contagious-disease division, was made president of the American Academy of Pediatrics. Dr. Edgar P. McNamee, past president of the Ohio State Medical Association, who gained experience in the X-ray department of the 3rd Division during the first World War, was in line for the presidency of the Radiological Society of North America. Dr. Charles C. Higgins was named for the presidency of the American Urological Association; and Dr. Roy W. Scott, professor of clinical medicine of the School of Medicine and physician-in-chief at City Hospital, was president of the American Heart Association.

For the first time in ninety-four years, the sanctuary light before the main altar of the historic St. John's Cathedral, at the northeast corner of Superior and East 9th Street, was extinguished on May 6, when the cathedral was closed preparatory to construction work. Bishop Edward F. Hoban, head of the Catholic Diocese, had won the esteem of his people and the citizens of Cleveland when he announced that from the historic landmark would rise a new cathedral upon the walls of the old. Beautiful and awe-inspiring in architecture, Cathedral Square, the heart of Cleveland Catholicism, was the symbol of a people's faith. The building plan was designed to transform the early-day structure and the adjoining buildings into an architectural group which would rank among the finest church groups in the nation. Extending on Superior to East 12th Street, it included a reconstructed cathedral with a complete new sanctuary, two additional transepts, rectory, diocesan office known as the chancery, St. John College—formerly known as Sisters College, and an auditorium annexed to the school unit. The interior of the cathedral, designed along French Gothic lines, was planned as a blending of beautiful imported marble altars, rare wood carvings, and unique architectural fixtures. During renovation, the auditorium of St. John's old parochial school became the temporary cathedral.

The Diocese of Cleveland had influenced almost a century of religious growth since it was created in 1847, when one Catholic priest served 34 Ohio counties. Now there were three dioceses within the territory, the Cleveland Diocese embracing eight counties in which there were more than two hundred parishes. The earthly remains of six bishops lay entombed within hallowed St. John's Cathedral in the projected Cathedral Square. Five bishops were trained here—Bishop James A. McFadden of Youngstown, Ohio; Bishop John P. Treacy of LaCrosse, Wisconsin; Coadjutor Bishop John F. Dearden of Pittsburgh; Bishop Joseph Hurley of St. Augustine, Florida; and Auxiliary Bishop Floyd L. Begin of Cleveland. Twelve Clevelanders went forth as bishops. Edward Cardinal Mooney of Detroit; Bishop Charles H. LeBlond of St. Joseph, Missouri; and Bishop Michael Ready of Columbus, Ohio, were Clevelanders.

Cleveland citizens thoroughly demonstrated their faith and confidence in the future of their city by voting in the primary election, May 7, for the twenty-four proposals providing for future betterment of all. One of the largest improvement programs adopted at one time by any city of comparable size, it called for public improvements to cost fifty-seven million dollars. A citizens committee headed by Harold T. Clark, chairman, and Howard

Whipple Green, executive secretary, promoted the passage of the proposals, and the vote carrying each proposal ranged from 72.5 per cent to 84.9 per cent of all the votes cast. There were five Cuyahoga County bond issues, eighteen City of Cleveland bond issues, and one Board of Education levy. The list of improvements included hospitals, schools, a new viaduct, a county administration building, a new Central Market, recreation centers, park improvements, airport expansion, and many other projects affecting the health, welfare, safety, public service, and industrial expansion of Greater Cleveland.

The Cleveland Museum of Art on May 8 reported a total of 9,453,039 visitors since its inception in 1916. May shows had exhibited work of local artists to more than a million people and sold well over $200,000 worth of art. Director William M. Milliken stated that Saturday and summer classes implanted interest in tens of thousands of children, and that adults enjoyed lectures, film showings, and art courses. Music had become a regular attraction, the fine organ, given in memory of P. J. McMyler, having been the first to be placed in any museum of art.

Frank A. Quail, who became a member of the Cleveland Bar Association in 1894 and was active for fifty-two years, was elected president in May. Over a period of seventy-three years, the original membership of fifty-three had increased to 1,700. The American Bar Association Award of Merit was won by the Cleveland Bar Association for the second time in 1945.

Mother's Day was observed, May 12, with an interesting program under the auspices of the Mother's Day Committee of the Sesquicentennial Women's Committee. Among the speakers were Mrs. Joy Seth Hurd, chosen by the Women's Forum as the Ohio Mother of the year; Mrs. Harold H. Burton, who had been chosen as Mother for the Nation's Capital; and Mrs. Benjamin Levine, a distinguished Cleveland mother. Tabitha Stiles, Cleveland's first mother, was impersonated by Marguerite Bacon, direct descendant of Moses Cleaveland. Music was provided by the Collinwood High School Band and the Flora Stone Mather College Glee Club. Among the honored guests at the Sesquicentennial bandstand on the Mall were Gold Star Mothers, Blue Star Mothers, and Daughters of the American Revolution. The arrangements were made by Mrs. L. W. Phillips, chairman of the committee. In the morning, a memorial service was held in Lake View Cemetery at the grave of Ernest Ball, who had written the most popular of America's mother songs, *Mother Machree*.

The City Council approved the twenty-five-million-dollar De Leuw transit-modernization plan on May 20 by the vote of 21 to 12. Shortly afterward, the Cleveland Transit System announced that inflation of construction costs would delay the rapid-transit features indefinitely. Subsequently, new plans were studied. The Cleveland Transit System announced a new passenger record in 1946, the total being nearly 494,000,000. Walking was becoming a lost art.

The Mid-America Exposition, held in the Public Auditorium from May 23 to June 2, provided Cleveland's first opportunity to show its postwar ideas, products, and methods to the public. A large number of interesting exhibits representing the Cleveland district, and unique entertainment features attracted many visitors from other cities as well as the Cleveland public. It was decided to repeat the exposition the following year. The president was Norris J. Clarke of the Republic Steel Corporation, and the managing director was John A. Crawford of the *Plain Dealer*.

Stella Jajunas, twenty-five-year-old Cleveland typist, became the first contestant to win four world championships when she competed in the tenth annual world typewriting speed contests at Chicago, June 20. A graduate of John Hay High School, she was given a rousing welcome by her classmates when she returned.

William "Bill" Veeck and associates became owners of the Cleveland Indians on June 22. The thirty-two-year-old Milwaukee war veteran named Harry Grabiner, Robert Goldstein, Bob Hope, Philip R. Clarke, Lester Armour, T. Philip Swift, Sidney K. Schiff, Newton P. Frye, and A. C. Allyn as stockholders. Plans were made immediately to purchase new players and develop a leading team for Cleveland. Incidentally, it was decided to add show business to night baseball, with bands, vaudeville, and fireworks. Lou Boudreau of the Indians, "greatest of shortstops," was made manager.

The Cleveland Metropolitan Housing Authority steadily met new demands for veterans' housing and in 1946 opened several temporary projects. These were constructed for in-migrant war workers and were available to veterans of World War II in need of housing. They included Berea Homes Extension, Navy Park, Bedford Dwellings, Memorial Park, and Seville Homes Extension. By the end of 1946, the cost of public low-rent housing in Cuyahoga County, representing seven estates erected by the Metropolitan Housing Authority, had been $26,596,962, including land, buildings, and facilities. Dwelling units totaled 4,739. The investment in four permanent war-housing estates had been $13,099,451; in three temporary war-housing estates, $5,158,281. There were under construction veterans' temporary housing, eight estates, providing 1,051 dwelling units. The combined total of dwelling units in twenty-two estates was 9,537. At this time, the officials of the Metropolitan Housing Authority were Charles W. White, chairman; A. I. Davey, Jr., vice chairman; John C. McHannan, Colonel Marc J. Grossman, L. D. McDonald, and Ernest J. Bohn. Director Bohn had achieved national fame for his work in Cleveland's housing projects. The American Design Award of $1,000 was given to him by Lord & Taylor of New York City for improving housing conditions of the poor and clearing the slums.

The Sesquicentennial Regatta, a great lake spectacle, was staged on the lakefront on June 29-30 by the Sesquicentennial Commission and the Cleveland Boating Association. More than a quarter of a million shoreline spectators saw eighty Navy planes demonstrate breathtaking speed, precision flying, and lightning bombing. Nearly five hundred water craft took part in the regatta, the outstanding event on the Great Lakes during the year.

The two-masted schooner *Bowdoin,* skippered by the well-known explorer, Commander Donald B. MacMillan, set out from Boothbay Harbor, Maine, June 29, on a five-week expedition of research to Baffin Island and Frobisher Bay. Accompanying MacMillan on this, his twenty-fifth trip to Arctic waters, were Elmer L. Lindseth, president of the Cleveland Electric Illuminating Company; A. R. Horr, vice president of the Cleveland Trust Company; and Harold S. Wood, vice president of Oberlin College. The *Log of the Schooner Bowdoin* was published by The World Publishing Company, Cleveland and New York.

The Youth Bureau of the Welfare Federation, during the past year, provided help for more than a thousand boys and girls. Problems of work, home, and school were solved. Dr. David J. Wiens was president of the agency's board of trustees, and Mrs. Prudence Payne Kwiecien was director.

The National City Bank, trustee of the Elisabeth Severance Prentiss Foundation, created for the improvement of public health, announced assets amounting to $5,680,000. Gifts from the foundation during the year included St. Luke's Hospital, $110,073; department of biochemistry, Western Reserve University Medical School, $50,000; Greater Cleveland Hospital Fund, $30,-000; Visiting Nurse Association, $10,000. The foundation was established in 1939 and became operative on the death of Mrs. Prentiss in 1944.

The Central Mall in the Group Plan was popularized by band concerts given throughout the summer by the Cleveland Sesquicentennial Band and school bands. A stand with sound equipment was provided, and the Cleveland Band, under the direction of J. Leon Ruddick, proved so popular that demands were made for a permanent organization. Guest conductors were Angelo Vitale, Al Russo, and August Caputo.

The Cleveland Baseball Federation held its twenty-fifth anniversary celebration at the Stadium on July 14. This was a Sesquicentennial event with baseball games, bands, and pageants honoring the twenty-five thousand Cleveland boys of the sandlots who served the country during the war. As usual, Max Rosenblum was general chairman, while officers of the Federation included William T. "Bill" Duggan, W. R. "Pete" Johns, Frank P. "Doik" Novario, Irving S. "Nig" Rose, and Dr. C. J. Sterling, Clevelanders who had worked a quarter-century to provide hospital and medical care and free equipment for the boys. Amateur Day had been suggested by Duggan in 1923; and his associates joined him to make a great success of the day every July, keeping Cleveland the leader of cities in amateur baseball. The Federation now boasted a membership of eight hundred teams.

Sesquicentennial Women's Day was celebrated in the Public Music Hall on July 16, where an inspiring program was presented under the direction of the Women's Committee. Mrs. John B. Dempsey, chairman, presided, and, after an organ prelude by Vincent Percy, the Cleveland Women's Symphony Orchestra of eighty pieces, under the direction of Hyman Schandler, contributed several artistic numbers. Mrs. B. F. McQuate, because of distinguished service to her city, was chosen to discuss "Cleveland Women— Past, Present and Future"; Mrs. George Ford Russell told of the activities of the women's organization in 1896 and introduced several of the Centennial women; and Mrs. Robert H. Jamison, who had for years given constructive leadership to worthy Cleveland projects, presented Sesquicentennial certificates and souvenir plates to the five women chosen to represent Cleveland women in their fields. These leaders were Lillian Baldwin, in the field of fine arts; Mrs. Frances Payne Bolton, humanities; Lena Ebeling, business and industry; Marion G. Howell, science; Mrs. Norma F. Wulff, education. Musical features included piano solos by Eunice Podis, Cleveland's talented young pianist; and the Women's Fortnightly Chorus, under the leadership of Mrs. Anne B. Hisey, wearing the costumes of 1846, and delightfully re-enacting a scene in an old-time singing school. The Early Settlers Association presented Cleveland's first wedding, under the direction of Ben P. Forbes of the Association. A style show was given with silhouette models wearing the pioneer dress of 1800, the empire dress of 1815, the hoopskirt of 1850, the bustle of 1880, the fashions of Cleveland Centennial Year, the Gibson girl of 1900, the hobble skirt of 1914, the flaming-youth dress of 1925, the evening gown of 1928, and the modern dress of 1946. At the conclusion of the program, a great birthday cake appeared on the stage, and the company, chorus, and audience joined in singing *Auld Lang Syne,* as thousands of rose petals dropped from the ceiling.

Cleveland's most colorful parade was the Sesquicentennial feature on July 21, dedicated to One World Day. Forming in the Mall and surrounding streets, the parade moved out Euclid Avenue to University Circle, thence to the reviewing stand on the lower boulevard in the Cultural Garden area. The first of the many floats was entitled "One World," presenting a massive globe and the "Sesqui" Queens Mary Dublin and Eileen Kelly. The City of Cleveland float featured the famous Cleveland Grays Band, while the Early Settlers in appropriate costumes appeared in a Conestoga wagon. Cowboys and Indians on horseback led the covered wagons filled with pioneers, and then followed Cleveland's nationalities represented by many beautiful floats. The participants of this section of the parade included Chinese, Czechs, English, Finns, French, Germans, Greeks, Hebrews, Hungarians, Irish, Italians, Lithuanians, Poles, Scotch, Slovaks, Slovenians, Spanish, Swiss, and Ukrainians. There were numerous educational, historical, and cultural floats, including those of the Cleveland Museum of Art, Boy Scouts, John Carroll University, Sons of the American Revolution, Hiram House, Cleveland Public Library, American Legion, Fenn College, Karamu House, St. Stanislaus School, Garden Center, James Ford Rhodes High School, Western Reserve Historical Society, and Red Cross. There were singing and instrumental groups on nearly all of the floats, making the parade unique and impressive. The Fire Department, Police Department, and a parade of old-time automobiles were among the other features. One hundred and fifty thousand people gathered along the line of march to cheer the participants.

One of Cleveland's greatest celebrations came on the city's 150th birthday, July 22, with a continuous program from morning to midnight. The arrival of Moses Cleaveland's party was enacted by the Early Settlers Association in the forenoon, boats provided by the Coast Guard bringing those impersonating the first pioneers to the foot of St. Clair Avenue where they were met by Indians and escorted to the Public Square. Here a brief ceremony was held at the Moses Cleaveland monument before a large audience. At noon, a luncheon was given in the Hotel Carter ballroom with Co-chairman Charles A. Otis of the Sesquicentennial Commission as chairman, and with

Mayor Burke and Janice Carter, East Cleveland screen star, as speakers. The Early Settlers, dressed in the costumes of 1800, were presented, and a Floradora sextet of singers of the Fortnightly Club, and a Gay Nineties quartet provided other entertainment. In the afternoon, the Early Settlers held a Sesquicentennial service in the Erie Street Cemetery, where Mrs. Jessie Carter Martin, direct descendant of Lorenzo Carter, placed a wreath on a monument erected to the unknown early settlers. In the evening, 200,-000 people visited the Mall to witness a wealth of entertainment. Thousands of multi-colored lights turned the Mall into a fairyland; and on four stages were presented simultaneously programs of music and dancing for three hours with ever-changing bands, orchestras, and singing groups. The Army Air Forces sent many planes in a stirring show of military power; and when the stage shows were completed, a mammoth fireworks exhibition in the lake and on the shore was presented east of East 9th Street. A parade of illuminated boats was another feature of the evening's entertainment.

Membership in the Cleveland Council of Girl Scouts, Inc., August 7, totaled 8,878, including 6,776 girls, seven to eighteen years, and 2,102 adults. The principal goals of scouting were to help girls "to become healthier, happier individuals, more successful homemakers, and intelligent, active citizens of the world." Officers included Mrs. Josephine Hallock, commissioner, Mrs. Neil Mathews, Mrs. H. F. Tielke, Mrs. Victor Lawrence, Mrs. Stanley L. Orr, and Mrs. Roy E. Bowers, deputy commissioners.

The Cleveland World Trade Organization was established as an affiliate of the Chamber of Commerce. Its purposes were to provide Cleveland business interests with information on foreign trade, promote knowledge of Cleveland products abroad, acquaint local business with opportunities for export and import, and assist foreign business representatives when they visited Cleveland.

A new Cleveland Press Club was formed by those in the newspaper profession and others closely related to newspaper work. The officers were Milton J. Lapine, president; Jack Gamble, vice president; Ralph G. Platt, secretary; and Glenn W. Dietrich, treasurer. Plans called for attractive headquarters in Hotel Olmsted, including a spacious lounge and dining facilities. Efforts were made to place the new organization upon a firmer basis than its predecessors, and the early months saw the membership grow rapidly.

Cleveland's newspapers were nationally known for their talented columnists. On the *Plain Dealer* were William F. McDermott, whose stories of the stage, his travels, interesting personalities, and unusual conditions at home and abroad commanded a large audience; Russell Weisman, widely read editorial writer on economics and business; Guy T. Rockwell, veteran financial editor; Philip W. Porter, whose comments on people and events were given in a keen and interesting manner; Roelif Loveland, who reported local happenings entertainingly in prose and verse; Richard T. F. Harding, who gave lively comments on business matters under the heading of "The By-Product"; Claire MacMurray, who combined humor and heart interest in her stories of personalities; and Eleanor Clarage, who for years had made a legion of readers laugh through her witty and whimsical columns. Sterling E. Graham was general manager and John A. Van Buren business manager. The editor of the Sunday paper was W. G. Vorpe, veteran newspaperman whose stories of Cleveland's earlier days commanded wide attention; and a particularly popular feature was the series of colorful historical articles written by Grace Goulder Izant on the cities and towns of Ohio.

On the *Press,* Carlton K. Matson was making interesting editorial comments on a variety of themes; John W. Love was giving valuable interpretations of happenings in the business world; Milton Widder and Winsor French were dealing with personalities and entertaining events; Frederic Sterbenz was analyzing international affairs; Robert Seltzer was providing informative financial columns; David Dietz was popularizing science; and George Davis was sharing entertaining and informative historical recollections of Cleveland with his readers. Norman Shaw was managing editor and James A. Foltz had succeeded John G. Meilink as business manager.

On the *News,* N. R. Howard, editor, combined information and inspiration in his distinctive column; J. B. Mullaney handled important happenings in forceful editorials; Howard Beaufait and Severino P. Severino wrote impressive feature stories; F. F. Duncan graphically reported financial happenings; and Howard Preston and Maurice Van Metre blended fun with interest in their daily columns. Hugh Kane, veteran newspaper man and a leader in City Club activities, was the managing editor.

Cecil B. Whitcomb was commissioned brigadier general after reverting to the Ohio National Guard as assistant division commander of the 37th Infantry Division. At the outbreak of World War II, he had commanded the First Battalion of the 145th Infantry, remaining in command for three years. In the Pacific theater, his was the first regiment to reach the heart of Manila. He received the Oak Leaf Cluster to be added to his previously won Distinguished Service Cross, Legion of Merit, Bronze Star, Oak Leaf Cluster to Purple Heart, and Combat Infantry Badge. He was also awarded the War Department's Citation Ribbon, and was the only man in Ohio to receive the Distinguished Service Cross in both wars.

Walter M. Halle became president of the Halle Bros. Company, succeeding his father, Samuel H. Halle, who became chairman of the board. Jay Iglauer, identified with the store for many years, was executive vice president and treasurer. As part of the company's expansion program, executives were planning a large branch store to be built on Shaker Boulevard near Shaker Square. Plans were also under way for an eleven-story building to replace the Halle Annex.

The Cleveland Public Library received from James A. Bohannon on August 12 the Peerless Collection of Early Automotive Literature. The collection included 770 volumes dating back to 1896 when the "horseless age" began. Books and magazines had been gathered by Bohannon and the Peerless Motor Car Company, of which he had been president; and presentation to the library was a feature of the 50th anniversary of the motor car and the 150th anniversary of the founding of Cleveland. The Library was continuing to circulate more books per capita than any library serving a

Co-chairmen *William G. Mather and Charles A. Otis.*

Mayor *Thomas A. Burke, the honorary chairman.*

Cleveland's Bob Hope and Chairman Otis.

Spectacular finale of Cleveland Day.

Members of the Early Settlers Association re-enacted the first Cleveland wedding. Marguerite Bacon, great-great-great-great-granddaughter of Moses Cleaveland, third from left, portrayed Chloe Inches, the bride.

CLEVELAND'S SESQUICENTENNIAL CELEBRATION

*General Dwight D. Eisenhower was welcomed at Public Square by a hundred
thousand admirers.*

*The Sesquicentennial Regatta and Navy Air Show were enjoyed by two hundred
thousand lakefront spectators.*

population of more than 500,000. Cleveland's circulation was 6.86 per capita, the total number of books lent for home use being 5,675,976. Of these, 3,232,-259 went to adult readers, while 2,443,717 went to juvenile readers. Ten thousand films dealing with many subjects were lent to the public. An inventory showed nearly 2,500,000 volumes in the library. The Library Board in 1946 consisted of John H. Rohrich, president; Louis H .Weber, first vice president; William J. Corrigan, second vice president; Dr. Charles H. Garvin, Charles A. Vanik, Mrs. Winifred Fryer, and Mrs. Robert H. Jamison. Clarence S. Metcalf, appointed in 1941, continued as librarian.

The Native Forests of Cuyahoga County, Ohio by Dr. Arthur B. Williams, curator of education of The Cleveland Museum of Natural History, appeared as an attractively illustrated scientific publication of the Museum. It told of the location, topography, soils, drainage, and climate of Cuyahoga County and discussed the native forests in a manner interesting to both scientist and layman. One chapter dealt with the "Moses Cleaveland Trees" which had been marked during the Sesquicentennial celebration. One hundred and fifty trees, one for each year of the city's life, and each more than 150 years old, were labeled during suitable ceremonies. Each metallic label described its tree and concluded, "Let us preserve it as a living memorial of the first settlers of the Western Reserve." Dr. Williams was chairman of the committee and selected the trees from all parts of the county in places where they might easily be seen and appreciated by the public.

There were five Rotary clubs in Metropolitan Cleveland that numbered 850 members. The downtown club, second largest unit in the world, had 540 members. Famous Cleveland Rotarians of the past included Myron T. Herrick, former ambassador to France; Newton D. Baker, Secretary of War under President Wilson; Harold H. Burton, associate justice, United States Supreme Court. Headquarters of the Cleveland Rotary Club had been in Hotel Statler since 1921. Officers in 1946 were Frederick T. McGuire, Jr., president; Ernest Dowd, vice president; Ernest Caldwell, Jr., treasurer; Fred Sowers, veteran secretary of national fame. Dowd succeeded McGuire as president.

Robert R. Young, board chairman of the Alleghany Corporation, with headquarters in Cleveland, was attracting national attention for his comprehensive transportation plans and his criticisms of what he termed old-fashioned methods in the railroad business. He was given credit for cutting the debts of the corporation and putting it on its feet. He had obtained control from George A. Ball, successor to the Van Sweringens who did not live to see their Alleghany dreams realized. Young was also credited with paying off substantial debts of the Chesapeake & Ohio, Pere Marquette, and Nickel Plate railroads, and improving equipment and services of the lines in which he was interested. These lines he withdrew from the Association of American Railroads, severely criticizing that organization while inaugurating a new organization based upon his own ideals. His future plans envisioned a nationwide development of the railroad-transportation systems, and his aggressive program was being watched by the American public.

The glamour of aviation crystallized in the National Air Races, which returned to Cleveland for the Labor Day weekend after having been discontinued during the war years. A new corporation, Cleveland National Air Races, Inc., with Frederick C. Crawford, president, directed the group operating the affairs of the races under the sponsorship and underwriting of the Air Foundation. Ben T. Franklin was manager of the great event, the post formerly occupied by Cliff and Phil Henderson. The opening classic, the Bendix Trophy Race, flown from Van Nuys, California, featured jet participation and offered competition for United States military jet planes and reciprocating engine planes. Paul Mantz of Burbank, California, took first place with an average speed of 435.501 m.p.h. The Army's jet-propelled P-80 Shooting Stars displayed high speed and low-level stunting; and a jet-propelled P-80 Lockheed, piloted by Colonel Leon Gray, maintained an average speed of 494.779 m.p.h. Jet-propelled flying was further stimulated by the Weatherhead Trophy Race, established by the Weatherhead Company as the first measured-distance speed run for jets flown before the public. The race was open to Army Air Force pilots, as the Government was the sole possessor of jet planes. The speed dash was won by First Lieutenant William J. Reilly with an average speed of 578.360 m.p.h. Many Army, Navy, and Marine Corps servicemen gathered to see and participate in the demonstration of military might. Exhibitions of air power, including high-speed and low-level stunting and acrobatics, thrilled the many visitors, who watched the precision combat flying tactics and the massed-formation flying. The "classic" Thompson Trophy Race, the international championship speed event over ten laps of a thirty-mile quadrangular course, was won by Alvin Johnston with a speed of 373.908 m.p.h. in the "R" division, planned for reciprocating engine airplanes. The Thompson "J" division race for jet planes called for seven laps of the thirty-mile quadrangular course and was won by Major Gus Lundquist of Wright Field with a speed of 515.853 m.p.h. The Sohio Trophy Race, sponsored by the Standard Oil Company of Ohio in honor of Cleveland's Sesquicentennial, was a free-for-all, open to engines of unlimited cubic-inch displacement. The distance was 240 miles, eight laps around the thirty-mile quadrangular course, and the victor was Dale Fulton with a speed of 352.781 m.p.h. The Halle Trophy Race, sponsored by Halle Bros. Company, was the first closed-course race for women pilots and was won by Margaret Hurlbert of Painesville with an average speed of 200.588 m.p.h.

The Cleveland Browns played their first game in the Stadium with the Miami Seahawks as opponent, September 6. The local team romped to a 44-0 victory. Arthur B. "Mickey" McBride had acquired the Cleveland professional football franchise in the All-America Football Conference in 1944. He first came to Cleveland in 1913 as circulation director of the *News,* where he remained until 1931, when he went into business for himself. He acquired large real-estate holdings in Cleveland, Chicago, Miami, and other cities and entered the taxicab business in Cleveland, Akron, and Canton. Deciding to promote football, he secured as coach and manager, Paul E. Brown, well known for his football successes in Massillon, Ohio State, and the Navy.

McBride and Brown soon proved the outstanding combination in the business and gave Cleveland the champion team of the Conference.

The General Electric Company opened its newly equipped Lighting Institute at Nela Park, the "lighting headquarters of the world," on September 9. Nearly 500,000 people had visited the Institute since 1920. Educational programs and dynamic displays acquainted the public with the newest developments in the field of lighting, under the direction of L. C. Kent. Among the many distinguished guests at the re-dedication was Mrs. Thomas A. Edison.

The anniversary of Perry's Victory was celebrated by the Early Settlers Association on September 10, after the custom inaugurated many years earlier. The meeting was held in the Western Reserve Historical Society, and among the features was the presentation to the Early Settlers of an American flag by Mr. and Mrs. Daniel B. Sommers. Attention was called to the fact that the members included Marguerite Bacon, great-great-great-great-granddaughter of Moses Cleaveland; Mrs. Carrie Kingsbury Easton, only living granddaughter of Judge James Kingsbury; and Mrs. Jessie Carter Martin, great-granddaughter of Lorenzo Carter. It was agreed that October 29, 1947, the ninetieth anniversary of the arrival of Artemus Ward in Cleveland, would be marked with suitable ceremonies.

A Cleveland pilot who had distinguished himself in both World Wars, Errol H. "Zip" Zistel, was placed in command of the 55th Wing of the Air National Guard as brigadier general. In World War I, he had been a pursuit pilot in the Royal Flying Corps and then was transferred to the American 148th Air Squadron. Wounded in action in 1918, he was awarded the Purple Heart. His advancement in World War II was rapid, and he became chief-of-staff and deputy chief-of-staff of the 4th Air Force. He was awarded the Legion of Merit and the Army Commendation Ribbon.

WGAR, now a fifty-thousand-watt station, received the Award of Merit presented by the City College of New York for "the most effective direct-selling sponsored radio program developed by a clear channel station." At this time, George A. Richards was president of WGAR, and John F. Patt, who had come to the station when it started in 1930, was vice president and general manager. Other names that became familiar to Cleveland listeners were Carl E. George, for years program manager and later assistant general manager; Wayne Mack, production manager, who had participated in many programs; Henry Pildner, musical director; and Ralph Worden, news director.

The Cleveland Chamber of Commerce, through Executive Vice President Walter I. Beam, announced it had more than four thousand members, an increase in membership of 139 per cent in the past decade. Civic improvements in which the Chamber played a part during that period included establishment of 434 new industries, adding nearly $60,000,000 to the area's annual payroll; securing the world's largest aircraft-engine research laboratory, maintained by the National Advisory Committee for Aeronautics, a total investment estimated at $40,000,000; launching of a $15,000,000 lakeshore-improvement program; expenditure of $15,000,000 for improvements to the Cuyahoga River; bringing the National Air Races to Cleveland as a permanent feature; and establishment of the Air Foundation to aid in all phases of research and development of aviation.

The faculty and students of James Ford Rhodes High School made a valuable contribution to the Sesquicentennial celebration in the form of a book entitled *South Brooklyn,* a brief history of that part of the City of Cleveland, lying south of Big Creek and west of the Cuyahoga River. Careful research, well-written copy, and many maps and photographs made the work a permanent and valuable reference volume for the students of history. The publication was appropriate, because the school, which opened in 1932, was named in honor of the Cleveland historian, James Ford Rhodes.

Starting its fifty-third year of service on September 20, The Cleveland Trust Company reported fifty banking offices in operation in Cuyahoga, Lake, and Lorain counties, and more were in prospect. Deposits exceeded a billion dollars, capital funds were more than fifty-one million dollars, and deposit accounts numbered more than 700,000. It was the sixteenth largest bank in the nation, and sixth largest in volume of savings deposits. Few, if any, of the country's banking institutions with offices confined to a single metropolitan community had as large a number of depositors. I. F. Freiberger had served as chairman of the board, and George Gund had been president since 1941, when President Harris Creech died.

A Memorial Fountain on Cleveland's Mall was suggested by the *Press,* and the newspaper launched a campaign to raise $100,000 for the project. When the total was exceeded, Marshall M. Fredericks, a young sculptor who had served in the United States Air Forces in the Pacific and Far East as a lieutenant colonel, was commissioned to plan the memorial. "Eternal Life" was selected as the title of the fountain, the center figure of which was to stand forty-five feet high in the center of a mirror pool of water.

Wreckers started moving tons of ornamental wrought iron and Italian marble from the former Western Reserve Historical Society Building, overlooking University Circle. The National City Bank purchased the building and site from Leonard C. Hanna, Jr., for ninety thousand dollars and planned to erect a branch bank.

A milestone in Cleveland's newspaper-publishing history was marked in the fall when the *News* added a weekly tabloid book section to its Saturday paper, known as the *News* Week-End Review of Books. In only three other cities—New York, Chicago, and Philadelphia—were weekly sections published successfully. At this time the well-known conductors of book departments of Cleveland newspapers were Frank O'Neill of the *News,* Robert I. Snajdr of the *Plain Dealer,* and Emerson Price of the *Press.*

The old "steamers" made their last run on the South Shore Belt Line, operated by the Newburgh & South Shore Railway. New Diesel locomotives were introduced on this seven-mile line, with eighty miles of switch tracks and sidings connecting railroads and industrial plants in the Cuyahoga Valley. It was the first Ohio railroad to discard steam completely as its motive power.

Director Arthur L. Munson of the department of public properties stated that the Lakefront Airport, under construction between East 12th and East 26th streets, would provide two runways, each 3,500 feet long, anchorage for seaplanes, and beaching facilities for amphibious planes.

Canada-United States Day was a feature of the Sesquicentennial. A large delegation of the Ontario Provincial Command, the Legion of Frontiersmen, and attracted attention on September 28, with their inspiring music, military drills, and colorful uniforms. At noon, in a beautiful ceremony, they laid a wreath at the base of the Moses Cleaveland monument, and in the evening attended the banquet arranged by the Sesquicentennial committee and the Canadian Club of Cleveland. Among those speaking at the banquet were Mayor Burke; Co-chairman Otis of the Sesquicentennial Commission; Paul J. J. Martin, Secretary of State of Canada; Judge Carl V. Weygandt, chief justice of Ohio; and Lieutenant Colonel G. R. N. Collins, commanding officer of the Canadian Legion of Frontiersmen. Expressions of good will between Canada and the United States were cheered by the large audience.

The Garden Center of Greater Cleveland was called "the hub of public interest in all matters relating to horticulture, conservation and civic landscape." Situated in Wade Park, it served as a center for cultural activities, and promoted and sponsored such community projects as the Mall Victory Garden, the Crile Hospital planting program, Japanese-beetle control, the Wade Park horticultural garden, flower shows, and the improvement of parking places. On April 1, 1945, the Center had appointed Arnold M. Davis, nationally known expert on horticulture, as director of its activities; and since that time, its dynamic program, carried out under his stimulating leadership, was an inspiration to Cleveland citizens. One of the most colorful activities included an annual White Elephant Sale which helped materially to finance the Center's constructive plans. It was ably directed by Mrs. Charles A. Otis and her associates. Mrs. Kelvin Smith was president of the Center in 1946, and other officers included Mrs. John A. Hadden, Mrs. Joseph H. Thompson, Mrs. Charles B. Gleason, Helen Grant Wilson, and Mrs. Fayette Brown.

Plans were being made for the presentation of the Frances McIntosh Sherwin Garden Center awards to four prominent Cleveland women who had given unselfishly of their time and effort for civic advance. They were Mrs. William G. Mather, Mrs. Thomas P. Howell, Mrs. Charles A. Otis, and Mrs. Windsor T. White, co-founders of The Garden Center of Greater Cleveland, and the awards for distinguished service would honor their part in making Cleveland a more beautiful and healthful city.

A survey by Raymond T. Cragin, president of the Cuyahoga County Regional Planning Commission, indicated the serious need of regional planning. Of the fifty-five cities and villages in Cuyahoga County, forty-seven had their own planning commissions, and only one had a full-time staff. Public improvements were being seriously delayed because of the lack of a planning agency to study the over-all problems. The recommendation was made that a regional planning commission should be composed of representatives of the county and of as many of the seventy-or-more communities within the region as would care to participate. It was hoped that a constructive, unified agency would supplant the confused multi-government structure that had proved cumbersome and inefficient.

Nearly a thousand residents of the neighborhoods seared by the East Ohio Gas Company fire of 1944 gathered at the explosion site, where ground was broken for Grdina Avenue. Named for Anton Grdina, president of the St. Clair-Norwood Community Rehabilitation Corporation, the street connected East 61st and East 62nd streets, scene of the disaster. Nearly twenty-four thousand dollars was given by neighborhood merchants to begin the building program.

A million-dollar gift came from the Hanna family, the M. A. Hanna Company and its employees of Cleveland, to the Greater Cleveland Hospital Fund. The gift was made in memory of Howard M. Hanna, to provide plant and scientific equipment for the Psychiatric Institute of the University Hospitals. The Howard M. Hanna Memorial Building joined two other important hospital units bearing the Hanna name.

The Community Fund goal was $4,880,000, and 576,657 contributors pledged $4,755,675.52. Hal H. Griswold was chairman of the campaign and Curtis Lee Smith became president of the Community Fund following the sudden death of Walter Klie. Smith, who was a leader in several important philanthropic campaigns, continued to serve as president, and Griswold, who had advanced numerous charitable projects in the city, remained as campaign chairman for another year when he was succeeded by William I. Ong. Kenneth Sturges, able general manager of the Community Chest for nearly three decades, presented in Sesquicentennial Year interesting facts concerning the consistent success of the pioneer Community Chest. In thirty-one years the total money raised was $123,214,160.95, the contributions coming from people of more than forty different nationalities in support of 101 welfare agencies.

The Cleveland Church Federation sponsored a Festival of Faith, October 27, in Public Auditorium, which was attended by thirteen thousand Christian citizens as a testimony to United Protestantism. At this time there were more than six hundred Protestant churches in Greater Cleveland.

General Jonathan M. Wainwright, hero of Bataan in World War II, was entertained on October 27 by Sesquicentennial officials. More than seventy thousand football fans greeted him at the Cleveland Browns-San Francisco game in the Stadium, when he was presented with a saddle horse by Patrolman James Matowitz.

It was announced on October 28 that a new church, the Forest Hill Presbyterian, would rise from John D. Rockefeller's historic Forest Hills lawn. The church, established by the Cleveland Heights Presbyterian Church, was to be endowed with "durability and substance," according to Rockefeller's wishes.

Brigadier General Leonard P. Ayres, famed economist and statistician, died on October 29. Thoroughness characterized this eminent analyst, whose counsel and reports were of great value to The Cleveland Trust Company, of which he was vice president, and to the Van Sweringens to whom he gave valued assistance. He served for a time as secretary of the Cleveland Foundation for which he conducted surveys on education, recreation, and the administration of criminal justice. He was a director of the Russell Sage Foundation and a trustee of the American Bankers Association Education Foundation. Boston University conferred upon him the degree of Doctor of Commercial Finance. In the first and second World Wars, he gave the Government outstanding aid through his statistical knowledge, and was made brigadier general.

Thomas J. Herbert, Republican, was elected governor of Ohio, November 6, defeating Frank J. Lausche, Democrat, who had served in 1945-46. Herbert, who was born in Cleveland in 1894, enjoyed a successful career in the law, and was elected attorney general of Ohio in 1938, 1940, and 1942. In World War I, he earned high British and American honors for his distinguished service in the Air Force. The political battle preceding the election had been a vigorous one, and the governor-elect offered a platform of sound and progressive policies.

The silver jubilee of Bishop Edward F. Hoban's consecration was celebrated on November 11. The occasion marked the first time that three cardinals had visited the city simultaneously. They were Edward Cardinal Mooney, Francis Cardinal Spellman, and Samuel Cardinal Stritch, archbishops of Detroit, New York, and Chicago, respectively. Priests of the Cleveland Catholic Diocese made a gift of $150,000 to Bishop Hoban for a Laymen's Retreat League building.

The Joint Veterans Commission of Cuyahoga County included in its membership the United Spanish War Veterans, Veterans of Foreign Wars, American Legion, Disabled American Veterans, Polish Legion of American Veterans, Jewish War Veterans, Army & Navy Union, and Military Order of the Purple Heart. Plans were made for the admission of the Amvets in 1947. The officers of the Commission were John H. Price, president; Morris Morganstern, vice president; and Chester J. Koch, secretary-treasurer. The organization interested itself in the work of the Veterans Information Center, the veterans housing program, the planning of a memorial building, the effort to secure larger hospital facilities for veterans, vocational and educational programs of the Veterans Administration, work on programs of the United States Employment Service, and many other activities. Facts had been assembled to show there were more than 200,000 war veterans living in the county after the conclusion of World War II.

Plans were being made to bring to Cleveland the Eighty-first National Encampment of the Grand Army of the Republic in 1947. There were but sixty-six living members in the nation. Arrangements were in charge of John H. Grate of Atwater, Ohio, the national commander whose one-hundred-and-second birthday would occur before the opening of the convention on August 10. Many Clevelanders remembered the Encampment held in the city in September, 1901, when nearly thirty thousand members of the GAR came for their reunion, most of them participating in one of the greatest military parades Cleveland has known.

The Municipal Airport, with 1,020 acres of drained and graded land, served five airlines. For several years, American Airlines, Pennsylvania-Central, and United were the only ones operating through Cleveland; but in November, 1945, Eastern Airlines began their Great Lakes-to-Miami service; and in August, 1946, Trans-Canada Airlines gave Cleveland its first international service from Toronto to Cleveland.

The comprehensive National Aircraft Show opened November 15 and attracted more than 165,000 spectators during the ten-day exhibition at the mammoth Bomber Plant. Great war bombers, transport planes, the latest radar equipment, personal airplanes, and plans for future aircraft fascinated the visitors. The exhibition was brought to Cleveland through the invitation of the Air Foundation and The Cleveland Chamber of Commerce.

The Occupational Planning Committee reported the results of its County Survey, November 15. Co-sponsored by civic, service, labor, and educational groups, the survey showed that, of about thirty thousand specific forms of employment in the United States, approximately ten thousand were found in the 210 fields of work in the county. Out of a total employment of 560,000 persons, as of July 15, 1945, four industrial groups stood out: machinery (not electrical) with 66,122 workers; iron and steel, 50,332; transportation equipment, 33,823; electrical machinery, 26,412. These groups accounted for about 177,000 employees at the time the survey was made. One notable fact was that federal, state, and local governments were employing a total of 31,600 persons on their payrolls. Construction groups showed a total of 26,000 workers; retail food and liquor stores, 19,798; retail general merchandise, 19,257; interstate railroads, 17,000; manufacturing managerial tasks, 12,144; routine clerical tasks, 27,544; selling jobs, 21,439. The occupational pattern of the area was believed to be of importance to business and industry, vocational-guidance agencies, schools and colleges, labor unions, community government, and city planners. No other large community in the nation had obtained the type and quantity of information contained in the Cuyahoga County study. More than a thousand citizens gave time to the production of the report.

The trend toward merger of Protestant churches strengthened with the union on November 16 of the Evangelical and United Brethren denominations, to be known as The Evangelical United Brethren Church, for the purpose of developing greater influence. A number of Cleveland churchmen attended the historic meeting in Johnstown, Pennsylvania. Another move to promote fellowship was under way, pointing toward a proposed merger of Congregational and Christian churches, united in 1931, and Evangelical and Reformed churches which joined forces in 1934 in Cleveland. There were 37 churches in the Cleveland Congregational Union with a membership of 16,500, and 27 Evangelical and Reformed churches with 11,500 members, making a total of 28,000. If consummated, the denomination, to be known as the United Church of Christ, would represent one of the largest in the Cleveland area from the standpoint of the number of churches. The national chairman of the Congregational commission on inter-church unity was Dr. F. Q. Blanchard, pastor of the Euclid Avenue Congregational Church.

New-made land north of the Stadium was designed to halt erosion and provide for an extension of Erieside Avenue along the Donald Gray Gardens from east of the Stadium to West 3rd Street. The new street was to bypass the Stadium and give to many thousands the opportunity of enjoying the gardens.

Traditions of the Old World were made colorful by the pageantry and ceremonies marking the golden jubilee of St. Theodosius Russian Orthodox Cathedral. The head of the Russian Orthodox Church in America, Metropolitan Theophilus, officiated, and seven archbishops and bishops participated. In 1896, the church had been established by a small group who fervently desired to keep alive the faith of their fathers. The building rose majestically with its rounded oriental towers and lofty spires. Influence spread far beyond the neighborhood of the cathedral at 733 Starkweather Avenue. In 1946 the Rev. Jason R. Kappanadze was completing his thirtieth year as pastor, and the congregation was made up of 1,250 families. A mixed choir of singers of all ages was formed, and its fame spread throughout northern Ohio, when people of many different denominations attended the picturesque Christmas and Easter services.

The YMCA membership in 1946 totaled 55,000, and there were seventeen branches. Attendance at activities in association programs in all branches averaged almost 14,000 per day. Fifty-two professional secretaries and 4,800 volunteers directed the work. Officers were Joseph W. Meriam, president; Louis D. Cull, first vice president; Dudley S. Blossom, Jr., Alfred E. Gibson, and Homer M. Jewitt, vice presidents; John S. Crider, treasurer; and Dr. C. V. Thomas, general secretary, succeeded by Elwood V. Rasmussen.

Judge Lee E. Skeel was re-elected president of the Greater Cleveland Safety Council this year, with Carl L. Smith as vice president and secretary. Cleveland received first prize in the Ohio Traffic Safety Contest and third prize in the National Safety Contest. The two officials were re-elected year after year.

The National Council of Catholic Women met in Cleveland, with Mrs. Michael C. Geraci as president, and adopted an extensive program designed to awaken the laity in the church militant.

Three new radio stations were being planned for Cleveland: WJMO, headed by Wentworth J. Marshall and David M. Baylor, manager, who had enjoyed successful experience as manager of WGAR; WSRS, planned for Cleveland Heights by S. R. Sague; and WEWS, which was to pioneer in television.

The spirit of the founders of St. John's Episcopal Church was revived when loyal churchmen, under the leadership of William G. Mather, made possible the restoration of the century-old landmark at 2600 Church Avenue, N.W. At a home-coming service on November 24, the well-worn pews were filled, as the Rev. Arthur J. Rantz and his congregation celebrated the re-creation of Historic St. John's, Cleveland's oldest house of worship.

The Ohio Poetry Society elected as state president Gertrude Gouvy, who succeeded Frances B. Mehlek. Membership included Cleveland poets and students of poetry: Dr. E. M. "Ted" Robinson, *Plain Dealer* Philosopher of

Folly; Dr. Clarence Stratton, head of the English Department, Cleveland Board of Education; Dr. Frederick H. Adler, Dr. Joseph Remenyi, Rev. Lionel Carron, Dr. Linda A. Eastman, Dr. James Holly Hanford, John French Wilson, Joseph S. Newman, and Carr Liggett.

The West Side Savings & Loan Association, the oldest in Cleveland, celebrated its sixtieth birthday anniversary, December 6.

Investment in plants and properties of The Cleveland Electric Illuminating Company now exceeded $180,000,000, and a new $65,000,000 expansion program was under way. From 1,400 customers at the beginning of the century, the number had increased to 370,000 by 1946. The company's electric-service system was among the largest in the world, serving 1,500,000 people in 132 communities in northeastern Ohio. Three power plants—on Cleveland's lakeshore, at Avon, and at Ashtabula—were interconnected to assure economy and continuity of service. The company's main offices occupied the entire fifteen-story Illuminating Building on the Public Square and the near-by Illuminating-St. Clair Building. Unexcelled service, with low power rates, gave industries in the district an important advantage over competitors located elsewhere, and was a prime factor in encouraging industries to locate in the area. Officers of the company included Elmer L. Lindseth, president, and Dean C. Ober, executive vice president.

The Cleveland Convention & Visitors Bureau, Inc., reported 202 conventions bringing 152,185 visitors to Cleveland during the year, and the business value to the city was estimated at $8,674,545. Louis B. Seltzer, editor-in-chief of the Scripps-Howard Newspapers of Ohio since 1937, headed the Board, and Edward C. Brennan was executive vice president. Brennan had succeeded S. A. Weissenburger in 1942. Seltzer's administration was so successful that he was re-elected.

Plans were being made for the laying of the cornerstone of the new million-dollar nurses' residence at St. Luke's Hospital. Fred E. Watkins was chairman of the building committee.

Walter Johnson, popularly known as "Big Train," died December 10 and was mourned by baseball fans throughout the nation. He had concluded his career as manager of the Cleveland Indians, 1933-1935, after a notable success as a pitcher. For six years he headed the American League in the greatest number of games won, and for twelve years he led in the number of strikeouts, winning a place in the Hall of Fame. Johnson was succeeded as manager by Steve O'Neill, popular catcher of the 1920 World Champion Indians. Oscar Vitt was manager, 1938-40, a period of serious dissension among the players.

The M. A. Hanna Company closed its year with a balance sheet of seventy-seven million dollars of assets, and through its investments in other companies was exerting an important influence on iron and steel, bituminous coal, rayon, and natural gas. It was conducting research in the fields of iron and coal, particularly for the purpose of making available lower grades of Lake Superior ore. Furthermore, it was exploring mineral deposits in North and South America. The company owned and operated three Pennsylvania collieries with combined capacity of twelve thousand tons daily; managed the largest coal business on the Great Lakes, in the Northwestern States, and in Canada, as well as a lake fleet and mammoth docks. It operated twenty Lake Superior ore mines, a mine in Missouri, and one in northern New York. A major investment had been made in the Pittsburgh Consolidation Coal Company, formed in 1945.

The Cleveland-Cliffs Iron Company, oldest of the city's great iron-ore firms, was operating nine iron-ore mines in Michigan and seven in Minnesota, and its reserves of unmined ore were among the largest in the industry. A fleet of twenty-two freighters, with a total carrying capacity exceeding 200,000 tons of ore per trip, was being operated. Much of this ore was loaded from the dock of a subsidiary, The Lake Superior & Ishpeming Railway Company at Marquette, 200 pockets having a capacity of 250 tons each. Acting as sales agent for many producers, the company operated coal docks at Duluth, Escanaba, Green Bay, and Port Huron. Edward B. Greene had served as president of Cleveland-Cliffs since 1933, when he succeeded William G. Mather who became chairman of the board. Mather resigned in 1947 and Greene became board chairman, with Alexander C. Brown, president.

Announcements were made that two new government hospitals would be constructed in Cleveland. A second veterans hospital, to cost $12,500,000, specializing in the treatment of neuropsychiatric cases, was approved by President Truman on December 12. A general medical and surgical institution for veterans, costing between ten and fifteen million dollars, was also projected, but details were not announced. It was believed that the psychiatric hospital would be built adjacent to Crile Hospital, and the general medical hospital would be erected north of Wade Park and east of East 105th Street.

The new chimes of Old Stone Church rang out across the Public Square on the evening of December 20. Placed in the main tower, the carillon and a clock were the gifts of Margaret Rusk Griffiths (Mrs. Edwin S.) "as an expression of her love for this church and her native city." Dr. Robert B. Whyte, pastor, formally accepted the chimes at the annual candlelight service. A historic eighty-one-year-old bell had been removed to make way for the beautiful gift which brought daily inspiration to those in the vicinity of the Square. Old Stone Church, rich in historical heritage, was "home" to 1,900 members of the cosmopolitan community it served.

The Cleveland Browns defeated the New York Yankees, 14-9, to win the national football championship on December 22. More than forty thousand watched the concluding game of the season on a half-frozen, half-muddy turf, and saw the victorious Coach Paul Brown carried off the field on the shoulders of his champions. The Browns continued their successes the two following years.

Statistics proved that Cleveland, in proportion to population, took a greater interest in sports than any other city in the country. The Cleveland Indians drew 1,057,289 spectators to the local baseball games in 1946; the Cleveland Browns drew 648,924 fans to fourteen games; the National Open Golf Championship at the Canterbury Golf Club attracted more than 40,000 people who paid admission of approximately $70,000. The world's outstanding track star in 1946 was Harrison Dillard of Baldwin-Wallace College, who won the high and low hurdles in the National Intercollegiate games and the National Amateur Athletic Union games. The following records made by Dillard were approved by the Union: 23 seconds for the 220-yard low hurdles around a turn, a new American record; 23.3 seconds for the 200-meter low hurdles around a turn, a new national senior mark; and 22.5 for the 220-yard low hurdles, equaling the American record.

Postwar living costs had soared to an all-time high, and the price of the family's Christmas dinner, according to newspaper advertisements of December 24, was something to remember: turkey, from 55 to 72 cents a pound; ham, 62; butter, 83; sugar, 9; coffee, 39; eggs, 65 cents a dozen; bread, 16 cents a loaf. A dollar bought a thin little Christmas tree. Despite high prices, store counters had been emptied of the biggest display of merchandise in the city's history. Men's suits were offered at $42.50, but shirts were not advertised. The housing shortage continued to be critical. "House Wanted" ads far outnumbered "For Rent" ads. The home situation presented a grim picture to veterans and displaced families seeking shelter. Blame for high prices went the rounds, while people dipped deeper in their pockets and their savings. Although breadwinners earned big money, it bought less; but spending was free and easy, and night clubs, theaters, and sports events drew capacity crowds. The hoped-for downward trend of prices failed to come and instead new high levels were met in succeeding months.

The Cleveland Foundation announced that it had distributed $315,186 during the year for charitable and educational purposes, and seventy institutions benefited. Endowment was increased in 1946 by $615,203, making a total of $10,222,846. Many institutions and organizations were enabled to carry on their work of serving humanity through the generosity of donors, who adopted the sound and economical Foundation plan for giving. The trustees' committee consisted of George Gund, chairman, Sidney B. Congdon, and Benedict Crowell. The distribution committee included Fred S. McConnell, chairman, Mrs. Benjamin Patterson Bole, Nap H. Boynton, Harold T. Clark, and William E. Wickenden. The director and secretary was Leyton E. Carter, and the counsel, James R. Garfield.

The Society for Savings, oldest and largest mutual savings bank west of the Allegheny Mountains, was the sixteenth largest in the nation. As of December 31, the bank was serving 177,393 depositors, deposits amounting to $201,-263,270.54. Henry S. Sherman, who had served as president since 1933, was succeeded by Mervin B. France, who joined the institution in 1934. Sherman became board chairman. Samuel Scovil was made honorary chairman, having served as trustee since 1909 and chairman of the board since 1938.

According to estimates reported by the Real Property Inventory, the value of manufactured products produced in Cuyahoga County industries in 1946 was $2,673,300,000, exceeding the volume of 1942 and almost 2.7 times the value of manufactures in 1939. The payroll of 201,500 wage earners amounted to $508,100,000. The labor force had increased 1.6 times since 1939, but the industrial payroll had increased more than 2.8 times during this period. Average weekly earnings in the manufacturing industry were

$54.09 as compared with $29.54 in December, 1939. Common labor was receiving $.899 per hour on the average. Although employed persons, estimated at 613,693 in Cuyahoga County in December, 1946, reached the highest of record and exceeded the war years, there were 5,228 in the ranks of the jobless.

As 1946 came to a close, it was estimated that more than 150 Cleveland companies were planning investments in expansions and facilities totaling $200,000,000. It was expected that these developments would create thirty-two thousand jobs in the Cleveland area. These plans indicated industry's faith in the future of Cleveland.

While people enjoyed postwar prosperity in the late 1940s, they wrestled with the high cost of living and watched taxes climb with wages. Business competition was keen as depleted stocks were replenished. President Truman's surprising election vote in 1948 revealed the unpredictable state of party politics, and socialistic trends in government were viewed with alarm by many thoughtful citizens.

The future was threatening as the cold war between the Soviet and world powers continued. Strife-ridden foreign countries struggled for survival, and reserves at home were strained dangerously as billions in American money and relief were poured into Europe to stimulate recovery and oppose Communism.

Clevelanders continued to campaign with their characteristic spirit of co-operation for an efficient transit system, a more comprehensive highway plan, and other improvements that would make their city an ever-better place in which to live and work and find gratification.

CHAPTER 18

The Western Reserve

THE AREA in northeastern Ohio encompassing the Western Reserve was a district so rich in natural advantages that in the 1940s it was frequently called "The Best Location in the Nation." Extending from the Pennsylvania boundary 120 miles westward to the westerly border of Huron County, and southward from Lake Erie to an imaginary straight line marked by the southerly border of the county, the Western Reserve was called "the heavy end of the State of Ohio" because of its leadership in agriculture and industry. Cleveland, the "capital" city, located midway on the lakeshore, owed much of its growth and progress to its environment.

Within five hundred miles were 55 per cent of the people of the nation, and here 71 per cent of the country's products were manufactured. Easily available were coal, iron ore, limestone, oil, salt, silica, soybeans, dolomite, wood, wood pulp, and other vital materials. Electric power was furnished at low rates with excellent service, natural gas was provided economically, and water for industry was plentiful. Five principal ports of the Great Lakes, located in the Reserve, unloaded thirty-six million of the fifty-three million gross tons of iron ore sent from the head of the lakes to Lake Erie in 1945. Resources of large banks met increasing financial requirements.

Despite its relatively small size, Ohio ranked fourth among the States in wealth, fourth in population, and fourth in manufacturing. With only 13 per cent of Ohio's land area—2 per cent of that of Texas, the Western Reserve in the mid-1940s produced 15 per cent of Ohio's farm crops by value, 21 per cent of the dairy products, 37 per cent of the retail trade, 44 per cent of the wholesale trade, and 45 per cent of the manufactured products. Exceptional transportation facilities by land, air, and water brought the richest markets of the world within easy reach.

Retail sales of the Western Reserve approximated a billion dollars annually, or more than the volume in each of thirty-five states; and the wholesale business was greater than that in each of thirty-eight states. As for manufactured products, only nine states produced more goods by value.

The population approximated 2,450,000; twenty-eight states had smaller populations. An army of workers included skilled men and women who had the advantages of specialized training in educational institutions, laboratories, and factories. The Western Reserve was the birthplace of two great Presidents, Garfield and McKinley, and here lived Wade, Giddings, Rockefeller, Hay, Hanna, Burton, Baker, and many other national figures. It was the home of some of the world's greatest inventors, including Edison, Brush,

Goodrich, Goodyear, Brown, Hall, Wellman, and Hulett. Known for educational and cultural leadership, the Western Reserve boasted a number of leading colleges and universities, as well as excellent school systems, libraries, museums, churches, and organizations of every kind.

Considered an ideal location in which to live, work, and operate a business, the Western Reserve was measured by the growth and achievement of its many enterprising cities and towns. Brief sketches tell stories of the rise and development of the principal industrial and agricultural centers in the district.

Akron

The location of the Ohio Canal led General Simon Perkins to establish the site for Akron in 1825. Dr. Eliakim Crosby built a rival town as part of an ingenious water-power scheme, the raceway starting at Middlebury (East Akron) and supplying water for industry. When the Pennsylvania & Ohio Canal opened in 1840, Akron stood at the strategic intersection of two important waterways.

The canal market made Akron an industrial center and attracted Dr. Benjamin F. Goodrich, who started a factory in 1870 and began making the first rubber fire hose and belting. The Goodyear Tire & Rubber Company, organized in 1898; Firestone, 1900; General, 1915; Seiberling, 1921; and subsequent companies multiplied the output of tires and rubber products marketed universally, earning for the city the title of "The Rubber Center of the World." Before the era of rubber manufacture, however, Akron-made sewer pipe was known around the world; and farm implements patented by John F. Seiberling formed the nucleus of the farm-machinery industry that grew up with the city.

From his pioneer mill, Ferdinand Schumacher introduced breakfast food to the nation in 1851 by manufacturing rolled oats. Oatmeal became an important product of the Quaker Oats Company, and was produced in one of the world's largest cereal mills. George Barber began the manufacture of matches in his barn in 1847. With his son, Ohio C., in 1864, he organized the Barber Match Company, forerunner of the Diamond Match Company.

The *Summit County Beacon,* which fathered the *Akron Beacon Journal,* was launched in 1839. Charles Landon Knight, editor and guiding spirit of the *Journal* for many years, was succeeded by his son, John S., who became head of the influential Knight Newspapers, Inc.

Free admission of pupils and support of schools by general taxation were basic principles embodied in a plan for public-school education that was adopted by Akron in 1846 and became a pattern for the nation. From Buchtel College, founded by John R. Buchtel in 1870, developed the University of Akron, which played an ever-greater part in educational and industrial advance.

The population grew steadily until it totaled 69,067 in 1910. Through rapid growth and expansion, it had tripled a decade later, and in the mid-1940s had reached 265,000, when Akron factories were producing more than 50 per cent of the tire output. Probably the most diversified manufacturer in the rubber industry was the B. F. Goodrich Company. Goodyear, considered the largest rubber company in the world, developed the lighter-than-air industry. In the mammoth Goodyear Airdock, the world's largest structure, without interior supports, for the building and housing of dirigibles, the giant *Akron* and *Macon* were built for the Navy. The Goodyear Aircraft Company, a subsidiary, produced large numbers of Corsair planes for the Navy during World War II. Akron was leading the world in research in rubber, synthetics, and lighter-than-air aviation, and all types of aircraft were being tested in the Guggenheim Airship Institute, division of the University of Akron. One of Ohio's first commercial airports was built in Akron in 1922. The Rubber Bowl, a municipal stadium seating forty thousand people, was erected in the mid-1940s.

The annual All-American Soap Box Derby for boys, sponsored by newspapers and Chevrolet dealers, originated in an experimental race of home-made "soap-box" creations on wheels run in Akron in 1934. Inspired by Myron E. Scott, *Dayton News* photographer, the local event soon reached national proportions.

The city's industry also included a leading publisher of children's books, the world's largest producer of fishing tackle, one of the largest automobile-rim plants, machine shops and foundries, and producers of airplane parts, clay, wood, and chemical products, salt and foods, dies, molds, and storage batteries. A transportation center of increasing importance, Akron was called the "capital of the trucking industry."

The city, county seat of Summit County, operated under the charter form of government. City officials in 1946-47 were Charles E. Slusser, mayor; Roy E. Browne, director of law; Marvin L. Davis, director of public service; and John D. Currie, director of finance. Robert M. Sanderson was president of the Council, and Charles M. Kelly served as presiding judge of the Municipal Court.

Amherst

One of the pioneers of Amherst, founded in about 1845, was Jonas Stratton, who named the settlement for his home town of Amherst, New Hampshire. Deposits of superior-quality sandstone were discovered near the village, and the product was soon in wide demand as building material. Operations of the Cleveland Stone Company dated from 1886, with the merger of small quarries; the name Cleveland Quarries Company was adopted in 1929. Production increased and Amherst became the world's sandstone center. East of the village was "Gray Canyon," said to be the world's largest worked deposit. The best-known citizen of Amherst was Frank H. Hitchcock, Postmaster-General under President Taft. The census reported Amherst's population as 2,896 in 1940. Henry J. Kane was mayor in 1946-47.

Ashtabula

Ashtabula, an Algonquin Indian name pronounced "Hash-tah-buh-lah" and meaning "river of many fish," was first applied to the river east of the Pennsylvania boundary, said to have been the dividing line between the hunting grounds of tribes from the east and from the west. Here the clans fished peacefully until the War of 1812. Thomas Hamilton built the first white-man's cabin on the west side of the river in 1801; but Matthew Hubbard was the first permanent white settler, and George Beckwith erected the first family residence in 1802.

When Ashtabula Township was organized on April 4, 1808, the settlement located on the east side of the river was known as East Village. On the west side, the Borough of Ashtabula, incorporated in 1831, became the Incorporated Village of Ashtabula in 1853, and later the City of Ashtabula.

It is said that the Battle of Gettysburg was planned in the home of Assistant Secretary of War Peter H. Watson on Park Street, to which Secretary of War Edwin M. Stanton had retired incognito for two weeks while he sought respite from strenuous war duties, and here he and his generals planned military strategy. The building, later known as the Hotel James, was remodeled as the Smith Home for Aged Women.

The first cargo of ore, arriving in Ashtabula on the schooner *Emma Mays,* was unloaded on June 10, 1873. Progress was slow and conservative, and the lake city became the focal point of a rich farm-industrial area, favorably located with regard to lake, rail, and highway transportation. Its harbor developed into one of the finest on the Great Lakes, equipped with modern machinery for the handling of coal and iron.

Principal industries of the city and surrounding territory in the 1940s were manufacturing, agriculture, dairying, fishing, coal and iron-ore shipping, and the growing of fruits and vegetables. Chief manufactured products were automobile forgings, farm tools, leather goods, corrugated boxes, ships, rubber products, and dresses. Ashtabula County was the second largest dairy district in the nation. Ashtabula's population of 21,405 persons in 1940 represented 89 per cent native white, and approximately 70 per cent of the residents owned their own homes.

The Council-Manager Plan of city government was inaugurated in 1906. City officials in 1946-47 were R. M. Hoisington, city manager; Clifford R. Kadon, president of City Council; Julius Lukkarila, treasurer; J. H. Shaw, auditor; and F. R. Hogue, solicitor. The population approached 25,000.

Barberton

Ohio C. Barber, founder of the Diamond Match Company, and his associates acquired a section of land south of Akron for the purpose of manufacturing soda ash, of which salt was the basic part; but it was learned after drilling several wells that a newer and cheaper process of extracting pure salt had been discovered, making Barber's surface-evaporation plan commercially unprofitable.

A dispute with the City of Akron over the collection of back taxes on his small Akron match factory incited Barber, and not wishing to give up his options on the newly acquired land, he moved his operations and founded Barberton, planned as an ideal industrial city. He entered the city plat in the Summit County records on March 23, 1891. Eastern industries were attracted to the city which grew so rapidly that it became known as the "Magic City."

Barberton was a city of 24,028 people in 1940. Its products had become highly diversified, including marine boilers, matches, chemicals, high-tension insulators, aluminum flakes, sewer pipe, iron and metal products, reclaimed rubber, rubber soles and heels, plastics, tools, brass and pattern designs, tires, rubber products, valves and fittings, insulation and furnace equipment, window conditioning materials, soap products, and metal alloys.

The mayor of Barberton in 1946-47 was Roy K. Dobbs, and other city officials were John McNamara, president of City Council; Stanley R. Shaw, safety director; Daniel Stevenson, service director; Harold J. Eckroate, solicitor; C. E. Duncan, auditor; and Edna Culbertson, treasurer. The population approximated 30,000.

Bay Village

Joseph Cahoon, Vermonter, drew his team to a halt, climbed down from his covered wagon and claimed lot No. 95 in Dover Township on the lakeshore west of Cleveland, October 10, 1810. On the east bank of the creek that was to bear his name (north side of West Lake Road), he and his sons built their cabin home in four days, and immediately planted apple and peach trees. Reuben Osborn, Nathan Bassett, and Aaron Aldrich followed soon afterward with their families. With the help of his neighbors, Cahoon raised the frame of the first grist-mill west of the Cuyahoga on September 10, 1813, the day of Perry's victory on Lake Erie. The millstones were quarried from the creek at North Dover by the pioneer and his son, Joel. Cahoon built the ancestral home in 1818, on a gentle slope overlooking the stream.

The trend toward suburban home building began to encroach upon the farming district, and the Village of Bay was organized in 1904. A closely knit residential community took form, its people keenly interested in civic betterment, education, social and cultural advance. The early-day home of the Cahoons was willed by the last heir to become the village library, and the early-day millstones were placed on the lawn in the shadow of the tall trees that passed the century-mark with them. The Cahoon barn was converted into a community hall. By will of Ida Maria Cahoon, who died in

1917, the village received land which became Cahoon Park. A condition of the gift banned boating, bathing, games, and sports on Sunday. A stepping-stone bearing the name "Huntington" marked the entrance to the mansion of pioneer John Huntington, whose estate became Huntington Park in the Metropolitan Park System.

Descendants of the early settlers continued to till their small farms in 1940, when the population of Bay Village had grown to 3,356. In 1946-47, when Edward C. Knoll was mayor, there was only one manufacturing concern in the village, a producer of syrups, fruit extracts, and flavorings. The community of homes had not been blighted by industry.

Bedford

Tradition gives 1786 as the beginning of Bedford, when a few Moravian missionaries settled Pilgerruh—or Pilgrim's Rest—near the junction of the Cuyahoga River and Tinker's Creek. Named for Joseph Tinker, one of Moses Cleaveland's surveyors, the creek became famous for its wild beauty and scenic gorge, called Bedford Glens. Button Road, laid out in 1801, was one of the first trailways in northern Ohio. The first white settler on the stream was Elijah Nobles, who arrived in 1813 and erected a tavern that was preserved through the years as a dwelling.

In the early 1820s, the Marble family, New England chairmakers, established the pioneer industry in Bedford, laying the foundation for thriving concerns that greatly expanded with the demand for office furniture.

Bedford Township, named by Daniel Benedict in honor of his home—Bedford, Connecticut, was organized in 1823. Bedford's first charter, granted in 1837, lapsed and was re-issued in 1852. Authentic records of the village were destroyed by fire in 1860, so that a complete history was not preserved.

A distinguished son was Archibald M. Willard, painter of the famous "Spirit of '76." Dr. Theodatus D. Garlick, eminent surgeon and scientist, chose Bedford as home for his family in 1874.

The population in 1940 had reached 7,390, many of the citizens finding employment in local industries manufacturing chairs, china, precision instruments, whisky, and rubber specialties. The mayor in 1946-47 was George W. Nichols, and O. E. Hutchinson was city manager.

Bellevue

An early-day railroad influenced the founding of Bellevue on the western boundary of the Western Reserve in 1839. The town was named by James Bell, who was then building the Mad River & Lake Erie Railroad from Sandusky.

The first settlers in the district had come from New York State in 1815.

The first election in Lyme Township was held in 1820 in a log schoolhouse on the ridge. Members of the Lyme Township Congregational Church, founded in 1836, raised a frame meeting house that year, and it was revered by the congregation more than a century later. Incorporated in 1851, Bellevue grew as a commercial and railroad center, and attracted a few industrial plants important to the area.

The slow action of water working on limestone strata through the centuries formed the Seneca Caverns near Bellevue—eight caves on different levels attracting a steady stream of sight-seers. In the lowest depth, 165 feet underground, a stream flowed to the famous Blue Hole, a spring at Castalia.

Bellevue was a city of 6,127 people, according to the 1940 census. Located in an important fruit-growing district, Ohio's largest cherry orchard was two miles west of the city. In 1946-47, J. F. Shannon was serving as mayor.

Berea

The low swamp land in township 6, range 14, in the Western Reserve survey, purchased by Gideon Granger, Postmaster General under President Thomas Jefferson, could hardly have been considered a wise investment. Settlement was slow. An offer of fifty acres induced Jared Hickox, kin of Cleveland's pioneer blacksmith, to accept the gift of land in 1809 (on Bagley Road between Berea and the old turnpike), and he became the first settler. The Vaughn family came in 1810, followed by the Fowls, Beckets, and Meekers. A civil township called Middleburgh was organized in 1820.

The coming of John Baldwin in 1827 marked the real beginning of the community's uphill struggle for survival. Baldwin was born on October 13, 1799, of humble parents in Branford, Connecticut. His meager education was broadened by diligent study, and he became a teacher with deep religious conviction. Berea, a monument to his passion for righteous and intellectual living, was founded in 1836. The name chosen to supplant Middleburgh was decided by the toss of a coin.

Baldwin's discovery of a wealth in sandstone under his property eased heavy financial burdens brought about by the Panic of 1837 and an unfortunate lyceum venture with Josiah Holbrook. That project was designed to bring self-improvement to the earnest settlers, to "assist in spreading knowledge and holiness over our globe; and to redeem men from ignorance and vice." To attract people of character, Baldwin donated a church site and seventy acres of land to the Methodists, who predominated in the village.

The products of Baldwin's quarries provided industry for the "Grindstone City" and found their way into major building projects in many parts of the nation. The world's largest sandstone operations gave Cuyahoga County its first college in Baldwin Institute. The institution flourished as a Christian influence and became widely known as Baldwin-Wallace College. The yawning pits were gradually silenced as the supply became exhausted; and in 1946, when John J. Baesel was mayor of Berea, the last stone was turned in the grindstone and curbing factory of the Cleveland Quarries Company, and men and machinery were moved to Amherst, then the world's sandstone center. A thriving community of 6,025 people in 1940, Berea shared in the prosperity of large neighboring industries.

Campbell

With the opening of the Youngstown Sheet & Tube Company in East Youngstown, the population grew quickly from a few hundred inhabitants to more than 3,000. In 1908, the people, largely foreign-born, voted to incorporate. To strengthen its position as a separate municipality, the city took the name of Campbell in 1926, honoring J. A. Campbell, who was executive head of the tube company for many years. The population of 13,785 in 1940 included more than thirty nationalities. City officials in 1946-47 were Anthony F. Pacella, mayor; Patsy M. Buccilli, president of City Council; William Glass, auditor; Joseph Sirilla, treasurer; Joseph E. Julius, solicitor; and John Grdic, director of public service and safety.

Cleveland Heights

Trustees of the hamlet of Cleveland Heights held their first meeting on April 9, 1901, those present being J. M. Spence, president, J. G. W. Cowles, and William Quilliams. Incorporation as a village was effected on May 3, 1903. In the earlier days, when wild turkeys were plentiful, the district was known as Turkey Ridge in East Cleveland Township.

One of the first large tracts of land was purchased by Dr. Jason Streator for $40,000. Patrick Calhoun laid out the first allotment on "Heathen Ridge," an enterprise founded on high community standards that became the basis for future city growth. In three years, Calhoun initiated improvements costing $5,000,000, and there were those who called him a dreamer. He developed Euclid Heights and became a power in many projects. Real-estate development was also promoted by M. M. Brown, who laid out Mayfield Heights; the Walter brothers, who planned Cedar Heights; and Will Ambler, who gave Ambler Heights its start.

The Euclid Club, organized in 1900, with its golf course led to the building of fine residences, and rapid growth followed. Forest Hills, the widely known estate of John D. Rockefeller, later became a model residential section; and among prominent residents of the Heights were Myron T. Herrick, W. D. B. Alexander, F. F. Prentiss, John L. Severance, John Sherwin, and Howard P. Eells. The population mounted from 15,396 in 1920 to 50,945 in 1930, and 54,992 in 1940.

Cleveland Heights became a city in February, 1921. Frank C. Cain, elected mayor in 1914, retired in 1945, and a bronze plaque at the Lee Road entrance to the Cain Park Theater was a tribute to his long and efficient administration. The City-Manager Plan of government became effective on January 1, 1922. Harry H. Canfield, who became city manager, served until 1946, when he was succeeded by Henry M. Kimpel, who had been finance director for fourteen years. City officials in 1946-47 included William C. Dunlap, mayor; R. F. Denison, vice mayor; Ray Martin, director of finance; G. E. Hartshorn, director of law and vice manager; Dr. E. P. Edwards, director of health; and Wiley C. Davis, commissioner. The population was estimated at 60,000.

A city of homes and shady streets, Cleveland Heights ranked high in the nation in the quality of its government, schools, libraries, and churches. A unified public-park system embraced about 135 acres of land, the municipally operated Cain Park outdoor theater, and modern recreational facilities. John D. Rockefeller, Jr., added by gift as a public park 70 acres of the former Forest Hills home of his late father.

Conneaut

Originally called Salem, Conneaut took its name in 1845 from Conneaut Creek—a Seneca Indian word meaning "river of many fish." The first white settler was a hermit named Halstead who had come from Massachusetts. After defeating General St. Clair on the Miami River, the victorious Senecas brought to the district two white prisoners, Edmund FitzJeralds and a soldier companion.

On July 4, 1796, Moses Cleaveland and his surveying party stopped at the creek on their way to establish Cleveland, "capital" city of the Western Reserve. They built a large cabin and called it Port Independence, honoring the historic day. The cabin, nicknamed "Stow's Castle" for Joshua Stow, one of its builders, was occupied during the winter by the James Kingsbury family, which subsequently settled at Newburgh near Cleveland. The first permanent white settlers arrived in the spring of 1798: Aaron Wright, Levi and John Montgomery, Nathan and John King, Robert Montgomery, and Samuel Bemus.

Conneaut benefited early from the stimulus of two major railroads, the Lake Shore & Michigan Southern (New York Central) and the Nickel Plate, and it became an important railroad terminal. Its position on Lake Erie brought it fame as an iron-ore receiving port, the first shipment of 1,130 tons being unloaded on November 6, 1892. In 1944, Conneaut was one of the world's leading ore ports, unloading 11,737,110 tons; and a record shipment of 18,593 tons was unloaded from the steamer Benjamin Fairless, on July 3, 1945. A spur line of the Pittsburgh, Bessemer & Lake Erie Railroad, from Conneaut to Pittsburgh, was hauling more iron ore than any other line in the world.

The hub of a rich agricultural area, Conneaut had a population of 9,355 in 1940. Leading industries included lake and railroad transportation, steamship and railroad shops, metal fabrication, production of farm implements, and electrical goods, fishing, and canning. Within easy reach were vast resources of coal, salt, silica, and vital raw materials contributing to its increasing importance as an industrial center. Arthur J. Picard was mayor in 1946-47.

Cuyahoga Falls

Before the coming of the white man, Cuyahoga Falls was known among the Indians as "Coppacaw," signifying the shedding of tears. Pioneers from the East seeing the possibilities of unlimited water power from the Cuyahoga River, established in 1812 a settlement called Manchester, later known as Cuyahoga Falls. They built a dam across the "crooked river" and set up the first industry, a sawmill from which came lumber to build their homes and to supply the navy yard at Old Portage, the frontier military camp of General Wadsworth in the valley. Joshua Stow, owner of the township that bore his name, never took up residence.

Primitive industry was flourishing when Henry Newberry claimed the lands of his father, General Roger Newberry, in the early 1820s. The first coal used by Lake Erie steamers was mined near the Falls and shipped by canal boat. Stow and the sons of his land-and-business agent, Judge William Wetmore, launched a paper mill in 1830. The first temperance society in Ohio was founded, and the first band formed in the district in 1834 helped Cleveland to celebrate Independence Day.

Aspiring to become the Lowell of the West, Cuyahoga Falls lost its industrial leadership when elaborate plans of Dr. Eliakim Crosby and others to divert water power to supply an ingenious manufacturing venture resulted in financial ruin and ultimate abandonment. Incorporated as a village in 1868, created from four townships—Tallmadge, Stow, Northampton, and Portage, Cuyahoga Falls was a well-known summer resort. Nearby was Silver Lake, the "Coney Island of the West" founded by Ralph H. Lodge, and river craft plied the stream to Gaylord's Grove.

Senator Elisha N. Sill came to the Falls in 1829; and his nephew, Edward R. Sill, early poet known as "the Shelley of America," lived in the village for years. Cuyahoga Falls produced several leading lawyers—Samuel H. McClure, Virgil P. Kline, and Henry McKinney. Orlando Wilcox helped Theodore Roosevelt organize his Rough Riders. T. F. Walsh built the first electric line from Akron through Cuyahoga Falls to Ravenna in 1893.

Cuyahoga Falls soon became a picturesque community of modern homes and civic improvements, reaching the stature of a city in 1922. Its population of 20,546 in 1940 had doubled twice in two decades. City officials in 1946-47 were Joseph W. Harding, mayor; Harvey O. Bolich, auditor; Lloyd Ellsworth, solicitor; Lawrence F. Paul, treasurer; Henry B. Graham, director of public service; and William Hobday, director of public safety.

East Cleveland

The name East Cleveland is woven into the fabric of early-day Euclid and Cleveland, as related earlier in this volume. As many as five political entities in Cuyahoga County bore the name.

East Cleveland Township was formed in 1847 largely from portions of the townships of Cleveland and Euclid and fragments of Newburgh and Warrensville. At a town meeting on June 26, boundaries were fixed at Willson Avenue on the west, the site of the Windermere car barns on the east, and the Newburgh line on the south. At the next meeting, in June, 1848, the western part of Euclid and a small part of Warrensville were annexed, thus extending the eastern limits.

When East Cleveland Village was organized in 1866, its streets were unpaved and unlighted. Doan's Corners had flourished, however, and Cleveland proposed annexation of the property outlined roughly by Willson Avenue, Quincy Avenue, a line east of Doan, and another north of Superior Avenue. East Cleveland voters gave approval after feverish debate, and on October 24, 1872, this valuable piece of land was added to the city. The remaining portion of East Cleveland, chartered soon afterward, was abandoned as a village in 1879 and absorbed by East Cleveland Township. In 1892, Cleveland annexed another township tract, bounded roughly by University Circle, Lakeview Avenue, Cedar Avenue, and a line north of Superior.

The hamlet of East Cleveland was organized in the early nineties, with W. H. Gaylord as the first president. In 1895, East Cleveland Village was formed, and Dr. E. D. Burton was the first mayor. East Cleveland was a residential community of ten thousand people in 1911 when it became a city. The commission-manager form of government was adopted on January 1, 1918. C. H. Osborne, the first city manager, was succeeded in 1923 by Charles A. Carran, former finance director.

The best-known industry in East Cleveland, the Lamp Department of the General Electric Company, located in Nela Park, became the "lighting headquarters of the world." During World War II, zoning laws were relaxed to permit erection of war plants.

Forest Hills, a beautiful residential area, was developed on the estate of John D. Rockefeller, who spent his summers in East Cleveland for many years. Progressive and well-managed, East Cleveland had reason to be proud of its high-ranking public-school system, Huron Road Hospital, its churches, and its general-welfare institutions. It was a city of 39,495 people in 1940.

Guiding the administration of East Cleveland in 1946-47 were Charles A. Carran, city manager; G. T. Apthorp, director of finance; E. A. Binyon, director of law; and G. W. Stober, director of health. Richard S. Horan was president of the Commission and Stanton Addams, municipal judge.

Elyria

Justin Ely, of the Connecticut Land Company, acquired a large tract in the township that was given his name. His son, Heman, who settled it, was attracted by the Black River falls, the scenic beauty of the wild country, and the fact that two branches of the river provided protection from the Indians. Here he founded Elyria in 1817. The industrious settlers showed an early interest in education, and one of the first high schools west of the Alleghenies was opened in 1830. Elyria was incorporated as a city in 1833.

Arthur L. Garford was a leading manufacturer of bicycles during the boom of the nineties, and some of the small plants that he founded developed into large industries.

A streetcar accident on Memorial Day in 1907 brought tragedy to the home of E. F. "Daddy" Allen, prominent businessman. His efforts inspired a worldwide movement for the care of crippled children. The movement was later endorsed by Rotary Clubs, and led to the founding of Elyria Memorial Hospital and Gates Hospital for Crippled Children. The International and Ohio Societies for Crippled Children established headquarters in Elyria.

Efficient city government and well-managed financial and business institutions contributed to Elyria's steady advance. As the county seat of Lorain County, it served a wide trading area and was the center of an important dairying, fruit, and truck-gardening district. Its population in 1940 was 25,120.

Sixty-two plants were operating in Elyria in the mid-1940s, and General Motors was building a four-million-dollar enterprise. The city's diverse manufactured products included automotive air brakes, motors, bar steel, wire, steel tubing, bicycles, building materials, castings and stampings, chemicals, furnaces and heaters, golf balls, industrial trucks and hoisting machinery, paint, plastic products, pumps, rubber heels, screw-machine products, tools, machinery, invalid chairs, and lace.

Wise planning had resulted in wide, well-paved streets and spacious residential sections, abounding in tall trees. The natural beauty of rocks, caves, waterfalls, and forests was preserved in Cascade Park, in the heart of the city. Elywood Park, adjoining, also attracted many visitors annually.

The mayor of Elyria in 1946-47 was A. R. Agate; Henry Ault, president of City Council; I. D. Faxon, director of safety-service; Richard S. Horan, solicitor; Ellsworth J. Alheit, auditor; and W. H. Gaston, treasurer.

Euclid

The early history of Euclid Township, named for the mathematician, was closely identified with that of Cleveland. In the late summer of 1796, General Moses Cleaveland appeased his dissatisfied surveyors by making an informal agreement with them to divide land east of Cleveland among forty-one men at a cost of a dollar an acre. Upon stated terms of colonization, Seth Pease, Moses Warren, and Amos Spafford became responsible for the settlement of families and the sowing of wheat. One of the first settlers was David Dille, who built a cabin in 1797 in the vicinity of Dille Road. Timothy Doan, brother of Nathaniel Doan of Doan's Corners, settled in 1801. An early industry was the "salt-works," a salt well located on a half-acre tract (east side of Lloyd Road, north of Lake Shore Boulevard). The Euclid Baptist Church, organized in 1820, was preceded in Cuyahoga County by the Chesterland Baptist Church, founded in 1819.

Euclid Township was incorporated in 1809. The original boundaries extended from the lake southward approximately one-half mile from the line later established between Cuyahoga and Lake counties for a distance of 7.8 miles (to Cedar Road), thence westward for five miles, and northward (at approximately East 140th Street) to the lake. In later years, much of the territory became the municipalities of East Cleveland, Cleveland Heights, South Euclid, Lyndhurst, and Richmond Heights.

The first recorded census of the farming community of Euclid was taken in 1880 and totaled five hundred. In the nineties, crop failures were widespread, and many farms were sold to Clevelanders seeking suburban homes and property. Euclid had been a grape-growing center for more than thirty years, when it was incorporated as a village in 1903. Henry S. Pickands was elected the first mayor at a salary of ten dollars per year, and a modern city was soon in the making.

Industry began to gain a foothold in about 1914. Progressive plans related to public improvements, industry, and housing were introduced during the administration of Mayor Charles R. Ely, 1926-37, and in ten years the population increased nearly five times. When Euclid reached city stature in 1930, it was known as the "fastest growing city in Ohio." Problems relating to its phenomenal growth multiplied as educational, cultural, and welfare opportunities increased; and in 1940 the reported population was 17,866. Large industrial plants were producing a diversity of manufactures, including metal products, business machines, stampings and castings, road machinery, hoisting and excavating machinery, tractors, and aircraft parts.

Kenneth J. Sims, elected mayor in 1938, continued to serve in 1946-47, when Harry J. Knuth was president of City Council; Paul H. Torbet, solicitor; William A. Abbott, auditor; Mrs. Glenna H. Clarke, treasurer; Michael A. Spino, director of public service; and William McMaster, director of public safety.

Fairport

In 1796 Moses Cleaveland and his party surveyed the lands that later became Fairport. First called Grandon, Fairport was founded by ex-Governor Samuel Huntington, Captain Abraham Skinner, and Seymour Austin. Laid out in 1812, it was incorporated as a village on March 14, 1836.

Fairport's importance in lake trade dated from 1825, and early-day shipyards produced many schooners from the headland forests. The steamer *Fairport,* 135 feet long, of native wood, was the first built in the port. A brick lighthouse, erected in 1825 by Jonathan Goldsmith at the mouth of the Grand River, was the eighth "tower light" on the Great Lakes. Trade multiplied, and a second beacon was raised in 1845. It is said both were havens on the Underground Railroad for slaves fleeing to Canada. A third guide to mariners, built in 1871, replaced its predecessors until 1925, when a modern lighthouse was constructed. In the dwelling quarters of the historic landmark, a marine museum was dedicated by the Fairport Harbor Historical Society in 1946.

Fairport's first mayor, Ralph Granger, promoted the Fairport, Painesville & Warren Railroad, chartered in 1835. It operated until 1841, as far as Painesville. Lake traffic suffered from the influence of the railroad era, and for three decades Fairport was scarcely more than a ghost town. New developments in iron manufacture and in the handling of iron ore and coal came in the eighties. The Pittsburgh & Lake Erie Dock Company bought river frontage and began to build docks, and railroad lines were broadened to carry heavy traffic to Youngstown mills. An ore-and-coal slip, 1,000 feet long and 300 feet wide, projected in 1890, provided for six vessels at one time, and was the forerunner of giant docking facilities in one of the busiest harbors on the lakes.

The village awoke with a start as a building boom endeavored to keep pace with the growing population. Painesville's proposed annexation of Fairport was refused, and village government was revived. Industrial workers crowded into the harbor town, many of them Finns who strongly opposed the saloon evils. Churches and the Temperance Society won a victory for the "drys" in the election of 1901.

Local industry consisted of farming, fishing, and lake shipping when the Diamond Alkali Company began to erect its first plant in 1910 to produce soda ash. Operations expanded until Diamond was the second largest alkali company in the country. Neighboring industries provided employment for many of Fairport's population, totaling 4,528 in 1940.

Dr. Amy Kaukonen, elected mayor in 1921, was the first woman mayor in the United States. Arthur J. Ritari, formerly solicitor of the Village of Fairport, also called Fairport Harbor, was serving as mayor in 1946-47.

The heirs of Samuel Huntington, co-founder, donated the land for Huntington Park, dedicated in 1946. "Riverside," the Skinner home, once a fashionable summer resort of the gay nineties, was a prominent landmark. For decades, the lure of buried treasure—fifty thousand dollars in gold bullion reputedly hidden by bank robbers near the west bank of the river in 1862—inspired periodic and futile searches.

Fairview

In the early 1800s, six families settled in the wilderness that became the Village of Fairview on December 1, 1910, with George Sweet as mayor. Four days before dedication, the pretentious Fairview Community Cabin, center of civic and social activities, was destroyed by fire. Co-operative, neighborly spirit rebuilt it, however, and within its friendly walls many plans for progress and improvement were furthered. A residential district known for its civic and cultural advance, Fairview had no post office, or manufacturing, or industrial business. Its population of 4,700 in 1940 increased to 6,500 six years later. Karl A. Bohlken was serving his second term as mayor in 1946-47.

Garfield Heights

A farming area detached itself from the Village of Newburgh in 1907 and became known as the Village of South Newburgh. In 1919 it became the Village of Garfield Heights.

According to some residents, the name Garfield Heights was chosen in 1919 because the town was adjacent to Garfield Park. Others contend that it honored President James A. Garfield, born on a farm just inside the Cleveland city limits (Connecticut Avenue and Warner Road). Still others believed that the dignity of the name would attract purchasers of real estate.

The village expanded greatly in the building boom of the 1920s and became a city in 1930. A few farms remained in the residential district in 1940, when the population was 16,989. The Poles were the most prominent of the various nationalities. There were several manufacturers in the mid-1940s, the General Chemical Company and the Round Chain Company being among the largest.

Raymond H. Ring, mayor in 1946, became ill and was succeeded by Grant K. Weber, acting mayor. Other officials were Joseph Klima, acting president of the Council; Harry Benson, auditor; Haydn Rees, treasurer; Robert L. Ross, solicitor; John Gulick, director of public service; and Carl O. Dettman, director of public safety, serving in 1946-47.

Geneva

Geneva was separated from Harpersfield on March 16, 1816, and incorporated. The first settler of the area was Theobolt Bartholomew, of Charlotte County, New York, who located on the west bank of the creek (South Ridge Road) in 1802. Then came young Elisha Wiard, of Connecticut, who died of fever in the winter of 1812-13.

The first railroad in the district, laid through Geneva in 1852, became an important link in the great New York Central System. Abraham Lincoln made a short speech from the station platform en route to his inaugural. One of the largest gatherings in early township history witnessed the dedication of the Soldiers and Sailors Monument on August 3, 1880, by President James A. Garfield.

Perhaps Geneva's greatest son was Platt R. Spencer, author and pioneer in the founding of commercial and business colleges, and "Father of the Spencerian System of Penmanship." Platt R. Spencer, Jr., became known as "the teacher of teachers of penmanship." Edith M. Thomas, the poetess, made her home in Geneva until 1888.

Located on heavily traveled highways in a rich agricultural district, Geneva had a population of 4,171 in 1940. Its industries included the American Fork & Hoe Company, Geneva Metal Wheel Company, Champion Hardware Company, and Lake Erie Milling Company. C. H. Gleason was mayor in 1946-47.

Girard

Mystery shrouds the origin of the name given to Girard, settled in 1807. It is believed that in a struggle with Warren, Niles, Youngstown, and Canfield over the location of the seat of Trumbull County, the settlement may have adopted the name honoring Stephen Girard, great American benefactor, hoping thus to gain an advantage.

The first known settlers were the Eckman party of Pennsylvania, which camped beside a spring, later the corner of State and Prospect streets. Ambrose Eckman, grandson of the leader, was Girard's first mayor in 1891. A town plat was completed by David Tod and associates in 1837. Jesse Baldwin and Abner Osborne opened a grist-mill in 1840 that continued in operation more than a century later.

Girard's steady growth was influenced by the Pennsylvania & Ohio Canal, the railroad, and the discovery of coal in the southern part of the county. Depleted supply produced a slump in coal mining about 1880 and retarded progress until 1908, when the A. M. Byers Company built the largest puddling mill furnace in the valley, producing a boom in Girard. Iron manufacture really began, however, in 1866, when Joseph G. Butler, David Tod, William Ward, and William Richard organized the Girard

Iron Company and set up "Old Mattie" from Wales blueprints, said to be the first brick bell-top blast furnace in the valley. The Corns Iron Company erected a rolling mill in 1872 that changed hands several times, and a strike resulted in dismantling of the plant by the Carnegie interests in 1905. Remodeled by the Byers Company, "Mattie" saw many years of operation. Expansion of company properties continued steadily, providing employment for a large number of Girard workers. The Ohio Leather Company, organized in 1901, became known as one of the world's finest plants.

The City of Girard was a flourishing community of 9,805 people in 1940. Its mayor in 1946-47 was Clyde V. Helman.

Hubbard

Acting as land agent for Nehemiah Hubbard, Jr., shareholder in the Connecticut Land Company, Samuel Tylee brought his family to the southeast section of the Western Reserve in the late 1790s. They were the first settlers in the township organized in 1806 and named for the original owner. The Village of Hubbard was incorporated on June 20, 1868. Its industrial future faded when local coal mines became exhausted about 1880, and progress was retarded until the steel industry revived the town in the early 1900s. Hubbard was an industrial community of 4,189 people in 1940. It had three steel mills in 1946-47, when Joseph J. Baldine was mayor.

Jefferson

Gideon Granger, Postmaster General of the United States, received the township of Jefferson as a part of his lands in the Western Reserve, purchased from the State of Connecticut. Platting a village, he called it Jefferson, honoring the third President, in whose administration he served. A map of "the Philadelphia of the West" was filed in 1805 at Burton, then county seat of Geauga County. Two years later, Ashtabula County was formed.

The village was incorporated in 1836. It was important politically in the early 1840s, when Whig and antislavery sentiment was so intense that Henry Clay, Whig candidate for President in 1844, contributed to the building fund of the Jefferson Congregational Church. It is well that the ambitious southerner was not present when Betsey Cowles led a meeting of woman-suffrage advocates, believed by some to be the first meeting of its kind in America, in that church. Clay favored gradual emancipation of the Negro, and he would have been incensed could he have heard the feverish speeches of Abolitionists delivered in this meeting house as the Civil War drew near. A portion of the historic building was still standing in the 1940s.

Joshua Reed Giddings, law partner with Benjamin F. Wade, Abolitionist leader, was elected to Congress by the Whigs in 1838, and for twenty years he was a leading Abolitionist in Washington. Giddings in 1856 wrote most of the platform for the Republican Party in a small, white law office on North Chestnut Street still in existence nine decades later. Here he met John Brown of Harpers Ferry fame in 1858 and 1859. Wagons loaded with arms and material were brought to Ashtabula County from Kansas in 1858, and moved at night to the canal near Wayne, Pennsylvania, for shipment to Maryland. Men who escaped from the Harpers Ferry raid came to the county and were protected by the Black Strings, a secret organization of about a thousand armed men. On the night of the day that John Brown was hung in Charles Town, West Virginia, December 2, 1859, his father, Owen Brown, and Barclay Coppic spoke from Jefferson's court house steps.

Jefferson numbered among its citizens men who gained wide recognition in state and national affairs. William Dean Howells, American novelist, editor, and critic, spent a few years in the office of his father's newspaper, *The Ashtabula County Sentinel,* sold to E. C. and R. D. Lampson, owners of *The Jefferson Gazette,* in 1909. The *Gazette,* founded in 1876, was bought in 1883 by E. L. Lampson, speaker and president pro tem of the Ohio Senate and for sixteen years a leader in Congress. The oldest newspaper in Ashtabula County, it continued to be operated by the Lampson family, with E. C. "Chet" Lampson, a historian of the Western Reserve, as its well-known editor in the 1940s.

Erie C. Hopwood, who attended high school in Jefferson, became editor of the *Cleveland Plain Dealer.* William C. Howells, Jefferson newspaperman, father of William Dean Howells, served as United States consul to Canada. John L. Hervey earned fame as top-flight writer and, for fifty years, as historian of the American trotting horse. Senator Theodore E. Burton was born here and Brigadier General Charles R. Howland, author of a military history of World War I, was closely identified with Jefferson. Major Douglass Steakley piloted the first airplane over Tokyo on a photographic mission.

The county seat of Ashtabula County, Jefferson had a population of 1,676 in 1940. The county was noted for cattle raising and dairy products, and for its production of fruit and vegetables. A small General Electric plant, a wholesale-lumber firm, and the Cozier Wood Package Company were the principal industries of Jefferson in 1946-47, when C. D. Utterback was mayor.

Kent

The Village of Franklin Mills, organized about 1805 by Jacob Haymaker, was a glass-manufacturing center in its early days. In 1864 the name was changed to Kent, honoring Marvin Kent, Atlantic & Great Western official, who was instrumental in locating railroad shops there.

Dr. John McGilvrey had a large part in locating and developing a normal school that became Kent State University, a state-supported institution founded in 1910.

The population of Kent in 1940 was 8,581. The principal products of industry included passenger buses, electric motors, nuts and bolts, flour, and machine-shop production. Alf C. Lovell was mayor in 1946-47.

Lakewood

The story of Rockport Township, created on February 24, 1819, in which Lakewood was located, is entwined with that of Cleveland, and many early-day facts have been recorded previously in this volume. The *History of Lakewood* by E. George Lindstrom and *The Lakewood Story* by Margaret Manor Butler were of great assistance in assembling historical data.

Pioneer James Nicholson, who settled west of the Cuyahoga River in 1812, became one of the community's most useful citizens. His son, Ezra, gained fame as the inventor of the Nicholson log, used by the United States Navy. Mars Wagar bought a tract adjoining Nicholson in 1820, and a close friendship began. Shrewd and well educated, Wagar realized admirable profits from his real-estate transactions. The Wagar homestead site at the "corners"—Warren Road and Detroit Avenue—became the home of The Bailey Company in 1930.

Dr. Jared P. Kirtland, famed naturalist, moved to Rockport in 1837. He introduced grape culture to the farmers, who transformed the district between Detroit Road and the lake into vineyards and orchards yielding abundantly. Township population was about four hundred when citizens proposed incorporation, the petition bearing the names of French, Hird, Edwards, Wagar, Hall, Nicholson, Coutant, Webb, Cook, Newman, Cannon, and others whose names were later perpetuated by streets. The petition was granted on December 19, 1885. The new hamlet was christened Lakewood, in keeping with its natural setting. Officers were not elected, however, until July 11, 1889, when I. E. Canfield, William Maile, and Noble Hotchkiss became trustees, Canfield being designated as mayor. Their first meeting was held on August 31.

Stirred by the splendor of electric light, Lakewood in 1896 built a municipal light plant that later became part of the Illuminating Company system. Clifton Boulevard was projected through farms, vineyards, and gardens in 1898, and property owners fought invasion of the streetcar, delaying completion of the line until 1903. Clifton Park, at the suburb's western limits on the lake, became an exclusive residential district.

The population was estimated at 3,500 when Lakewood became a village on May 4, 1903, with Joseph J. Rowe, mayor. As the horseless carriage was adopted, farms were quickly converted into real-estate developments at inflated prices, as high as $2,500 an acre. Lakewood City Hospital opened in 1907. By 1910, the population was 15,181. The village form of government was outmoded, and Lakewood was incorporated as a city on February 17, 1911. Nelson C. Cotabish was the first mayor. The Lakewood Chamber of Commerce, organized in 1911, led in fostering sound business and civic advance.

ONE WORLD DAY, SESQUICENTENNIAL CELEBRATION

NATIONALITY FEATURES OF THE SESQUICENTENNIAL

Fortunes in gas, discovered in 1911, faded within a few years when the field was exhausted, and the "city of homes" was safeguarded against industrial inroads. A second real-estate boom came with the opening of the Detroit-Superior High Level Bridge over the Cuyahoga River in 1917, and prices of lakefront property soared to as high as $15,000 an acre. The Lakewood Public Library opened in 1916. By 1920, the population had leaped to 41,732.

The Rhodes homestead, purchased by the city in 1918, became Lakewood Park. In 1920, city offices were moved from the old City Hall at Warren Road and Detroit Avenue, site of the old toll gate until 1901, and established in the Rhodes residence in the park. Wagar Park was given to the city by the Wagar estate in 1904, and Madison Park was purchased in 1917.

Lakewood in 1940 was a beautiful and enterprising city of 69,160 people, who earned their livelihood in Cleveland and neighboring communities. It was known nationally for its excellent school system, busy shopping centers, churches, and homes reflecting a proud citizenship. Lakewood's leadership in the nation in fire prevention began in 1928, and the city stood high, year after year, in safety competitions. Its outstanding health record was maintained through constant public co-operation with a vigilant health department.

Amos I. Kauffman, former finance director, became mayor in 1932, and continued to serve in 1946-47. Other city officials included William R. Fairgrieve, president of City Council; Henry A. Rees, director of finance; Charles F. Ross, director of law; Charles Foster, director of recreation; and Dr. W. J. Benner, health commissioner.

Leavittsburg

John Leavitt, Jr., became the owner of a western portion of Warren Township in about 1800, and a village site with a public square was dedicated. A farming community took form on the Mahoning River, slightly west of the location proposed for the original town, and became known as Leavittsburg. It gained strength with the building of a railroad that became part of the Erie system. Leavittsburg had a population of 2,535 people in 1940. It continued unincorporated in the 1940s, under township government. Mahoning Park, located on the river, was a popular pleasure resort.

Lorain

An Indian trading post preceded the settlement of Azariah Beebe and his family of Vermont at the mouth of the Black River in 1807. Augustus Jones and William Murdock were given land in 1818 to compensate for the burning of their shipyards on the Connecticut River by the British.

They started to build ships in 1820 on the bank of the river that gave the settlement its name, Black River.

Vessel owners formed the Black River Steamboat Association in 1836, and Black River became important as a lake port. The name Charleston was given to the settlement in 1837, the year that the first steamboat, the *Bunker Hill,* was launched. Here also was built the first merchant ship to sail Lake Superior.

The village took the name of Lorain in 1874. Railroad lines were projected in the seventies and eighties to the coal fields of southern Ohio and Pennsylvania, connecting Lorain on the lake with the Ohio River. At the Lorain harbor, coal met iron ore that came down from the lake regions to feed the Pennsylvania mills. Lorain thus became an increasingly important point of transshipment, also exporting large quantities of agricultural products.

A city of steel grew with the industry. It became a "tube city" in which one of the largest plants of the National Tube Company was located. A division of the American Stove Company opened in 1893, and here the American Ship Building Company and the Thew Shovel Company established large operations.

A devastating tornado leveled nearly a thousand homes and much of the business district on June 28, 1924. Three hundred were reported dead and the injured were estimated at 1,500. Through careful planning and rebuilding, the stricken city came back. Population gained steadily with industrial development, reaching 44,125 in 1940. The busy port became headquarters for some of the lake fisheries, and large railroad shops were maintained.

Lorain was the birthplace in 1878 of Admiral Ernest J. King, U. S. N., commander-in-chief of the United States Fleet and chief of naval operations during World War II.

Serving as city officials in 1946-47 were Patrick J. Flaherty, mayor; John C. Jaworski, president of City Council; Earl R. Frank, auditor; Maurice C. Brown, treasurer; John D. Pincura, Jr., solicitor; Wallace J. Chapla, director of public service; and James M. Ryan, director of public safety. The population of Lorain grew rapidly in the 1940s to keep pace with the expansion of National Tube Company activities.

Maple Heights

The people of the northern section of Bedford Township, eager to achieve independent development, incorporated the Village of Maple Heights in 1915. Through steady growth, status as a city was reached in 1930, when the charter form of government was adopted.

Maple Heights was a residential city of 6,728 people in 1940, with 95 per cent of the population home owners. Large industries, including Lempco Products Company, Cleveland Steel Erecting Company, plants of Jack &

Heintz, Aluminum Smelting & Refining Company, Automatic Die & Products Company, and the Cuyahoga Steel & Wire Company had located in the city. Plans were under way in the mid-1940s for new homes, a shopping district, and expanded park and recreational facilities. Fred E. Frehmeyer was mayor in 1946-47.

Medina

When shareholders in the Connecticut Land Company divided their holdings, Elijah Boardman of Connecticut drew a tract roughly five miles square in the heart of the Western Reserve.

Zenas Hamilton, his wife, and seven children, of Connecticut, the first permanent settlers, made their home in 1814 in the deserted cabin built by Al Hinman and his brother in 1812. The first of a steady stream of settlers was Rufus Ferris, Boardman's land agent, who came in 1816. By the winter of 1817, there were fifteen families in the settlement called Mecca, and several families had located in the 237-acre tract surveyed by Abraham Freese in 1810, in which a town site was designated.

A. G. Hickox and Captain Austin Badger opened an inn and trading post on the west side of the Public Square in 1817, and Captain Lathrop Seymour and Timothy Doan erected a sawmill and grist-mill on the river.

Medina County was organized in 1818, and the plat of the Village of Medina was registered on January 6, 1820. Medina became the county seat because it had made provision, gratis, for county-building sites. The forerunner of the *Medina County Gazette* appeared in 1832.

Important highways contributed to steady growth of the district. Of the essential primitive industry, that of A. I. Root, manufacturing jeweler, is perhaps the most interesting. Noticing a swarm of bees in 1865, he offered his workmen a dollar to capture it. Root studied the scant available information on bees and set up an apiary, inventing a rotary extractor to remove honey from the comb, and developing hives and special tools. The A. I. Root Company had become Medina's largest industry by 1880. Root's authority on bee culture achieved world renown, and his descendants maintained company leadership.

In 1871, the first railroad, the Lake Shore & Tuscarawas Valley Railway Company, was completed into the county, opening trade routes and encouraging a trend away from agriculture and cattle-raising to dairying and the raising of fruit and vegetables.

The challenge of city growth and progressive influences was met by alert businessmen and county farmers who geared development to sound, advanced policies and methods that safeguarded Medina's future. Retail-store sales per capita were second highest in Ohio in 1939. The population in 1940 was 4,359. Industry included bee culture, foundry products, pickle and food manufacture, and production of aluminum castings. Roy Kruggel was mayor in 1946-47.

Newburgh Heights

The Village of Newburgh Heights was organized in 1904, with E. S. Peck as the first mayor. The district was originally part of Newburgh Township, extending from Cleveland on the north to Independence on the south, and from Warrensville on the east to Brooklyn and the Cuyahoga River on the west. In the 1940s, the area of Newburgh Heights consisted of approximately one-half square mile.

A vital industrial community, with a population of 3,830 in 1940, it was inhabited largely by industrious Poles, some Bohemians, and a few Germans. In it were located major industries, including the United States Air Compressor Company, Varnish Products Company, Cleveland Co-Operative Stove Company, American Stove Company, McGean Chemical Company, and Aluminum Company of America. Frank Ptak, elected mayor in 1939, was serving in 1946-47.

Newton Falls

While traveling Duck Creek in his canoe, Jesse Halliday found the rapids that provided water power for a mill that he built, and soon a road opened to Warren. Founded in 1807, Newton Falls was a business rival of Warren, its neighbor in the early days. Years later, the Hydro-Electric & Gas Company purchased mill sites along the Mahoning River and built plants that furnished power to cities and villages in the valley. Thriving industries established during World War I were largely abandoned as depression casualties. The population of Newton Falls was 3,120 in 1940. Arthur Palmer was mayor in 1946-47.

Niles

The junction of the Mosquito and Meander creeks with the Mahoning River, which provided water transportation, and the health-giving waters of "salt springs" afforded a strategic location for a city. Coal, iron-ore, and limestone deposits attracted James Heaton, who founded a settlement in 1806 known as Heaton's Furnace. It was named for his forge which produced the first bar iron west of the Allegheny Mountains. Reconstructed on its original framework in 1839, Heaton's grist-mill, built in 1806, stood sturdy and strong in the 1940s.

William McKinley came to operate Heaton's plant in about 1830. The Village of Nilestown, organized in 1834, took the name Niles in 1843. This year, a son, William, Jr., was born in the humble McKinley home; he was to become governor of Ohio and President of the United States.

The first tin plate in the nation was rolled at Niles. Industry prospered and, in the early 1920s, the city's mills produced more sheet steel than Gary, Middletown, or Pittsburgh.

Far-sighted planning had shaped a beautiful city with a population of 16,273 in 1940. The McKinley Memorial, a fitting and useful tribute to an illustrious son, was dedicated in 1917. It housed the McKinley Library, mementoes, and an auditorium.

Sheet steel continued to be a leading product in the 1940s, when diversified manufacture included fire brick, chemicals, automobile parts, glass bulbs, steel drums, structural steel, machine parts, steel lath, electrolytic tin plate, stamping and steel products. Niles factory workers were English, Welsh, Irish, German, Italian, and some of Slavic descent.

City officials in 1946-47 were Elmer E. Fisher, mayor; Murray I. Wick, president of the Council; Homer Thomas, auditor; Paul B. Moritz, solicitor; Thomas R. Smith, treasurer; John F. McGlynn, director of public service; and Thomas H. Hall, director of public safety.

North Olmsted

James Greer was the first permanent settler in the southeast corner of township 6, range 15, in 1814. Elijah Stearns of Vermont and his large family came to the district, called Kingston, in 1815. Stearns purchased 1,002 acres on Butternut Ridge, and gave to his son, David Johnson Stearns, 150 acres. They were followed by Daniel Bunnel, Amos Briggs, Isaac Scales, Major Samuel Hoadley, and a wave of New Englanders who shaped the Village of Lenox, organized on April 14, 1823.

The large holdings of Aaron Olmstead, shareholder in the Connecticut Land Company, inherited by his son, Charles H., were located in the north part of the village. Young Olmstead's offer to give a library to the settlement if it would take the name Olmstead, honoring his father, was accepted in 1829. Covered wagons set out from New England with five hundred volumes. Some were lost on the way; but many books of the first library brought west of the Alleghenies were treasured in the village library in the 1940s.

In the late 1820s, Watrous Usher built a sawmill at the Rocky River falls, the first improvement in the village organized as Olmstead Falls, April 7, 1856, with Thomas Brown, mayor. Not ambitious industrially, it was content through the years as a small residential community.

In time, the "a" was dropped from the name Olmstead. The Village of North Olmsted was formed from portions of Olmsted and Dover townships in 1908, and George Willet was the first mayor. Until about the 1920s, North Olmsted was a farming district; then it began to flourish as a truck-gardening and greenhouse center.

Municipally owned bus service was introduced in the village in 1931, during the administration of Charles Alden Seltzer, mayor from 1926 to

1932. Seeking to solve the local transportation problem, Seltzer was opposed by some of the residents and certain public utilities; but with the sanction of the Ohio Supreme Court, North Olmsted established a precedent for the nation when it organized The North Olmsted Municipal Bus Line. Seltzer was a notable author of western stories that were translated into many languages.

North Olmsted, numbering 3,487 people in 1940, was proud of its heritage. It was a quaint, neighborly village reminiscent of New England, as characterized by the quiet simplicity of the little Universalist meeting house erected on Butternut Ridge in 1847. David L. Douglass, elected mayor in 1935, was serving in 1946-47.

North Royalton

Melzer Clark pioneered in 1811 in the settlement of township 5, range 13, in the Western Reserve, and the Engle, Francis, and Coates families were among the early newcomers to the district. Township government was under the jurisdiction of Brecksville until 1818, when Royalton Township was created. One of the early settlers was John Edgerton, who refused low, swamp land in central Cleveland at the same price in favor of Royalton.

Life in the peaceful farming community was accelerated by the move from Cleveland to the suburbs. City dwellers were attracted by scenic beauty and the grand view from one of the highest points in the Western Reserve, in the foothills of the Allegheny Mountains, 1,238 feet above sea level and about 735 feet above the Lake Erie level, according to a marker on the Disciples Church. One of the biggest population gains in Cuyahoga County was made by North Royalton in the 1930s, when the census of 1940 reported 2,559 people, an increase of 83 per cent. The incorporation of the village had been effected in 1927. Lester Edgerton, great-grandson of Royalton's early settler, was mayor in 1946-47 and one of the few residents making his living from the soil.

Norwalk

Norwalk was founded in 1816 by Platt Benedict, Elisha Whittlesey, and Frederic Fallig. Whittlesey, one of the best known and most beloved men of the Western Reserve, was a member of Congress for many years. The three-story, brick building that he erected in 1826 was occupied by the Norwalk Academy, for years the most popular institution of its kind in Ohio. Noted Americans were scholars here, among them James B. McPherson, who gained fame as a Civil War general; Rutherford B. Hayes, President of the United States; and Charles Foster, governor of Ohio and Secretary of the Treasury.

From its beginning, Norwalk was the industrial center of Huron County, and, except for a brief period, the county seat. Its growth was stimulated in 1882 by the railroad shops of the Wheeling & Lake Erie Railroad, and later by the great plant of the Huron Steel & Iron Company. The seven Fisher brothers, makers of automobile bodies, spent their early years in Norwalk; and, in 1927, they built the Memorial Shrine, a chapel in memory of their grandmother. Here also was located the Firelands Museum, housing collections of the famous Firelands Historical Society, organized in 1857.

Early American architecture, Anglo-Saxon names, and a general conservatism reflected the New England heritage of Norwalk, one of the most beautiful cities in northern Ohio. The population was 8,211 in 1940. Edgar L. Tucker was mayor in 1946-47.

Oberlin

From their founding, Oberlin, the village, and Oberlin, the college, were inseparable. In April, 1833, young Peter Pindar Pease built the first cabin, marked years later by a tablet on a revered campus elm. After him came Rev. John J. Shipherd and Philo Stewart, missionary-educators, who dared to establish a Christian school within a small supporting community in frontier country. To settlement and institution they gave the name Oberlin, honoring Jean Frederic Oberlin, Lutheran clergyman, whose system of education by manual labor in a community in France had attracted their interest.

Staunch New England Congregationalists were prominent in the early faculties of the Oberlin Collegiate Institute, forerunner of Oberlin College. In a day of heated debate on the right of women to enjoy education, Oberlin introduced co-education to the world, opening its doors in December, 1833, to twenty-nine men and fifteen women. The bachelor's degree, conferred upon three women in 1841, aroused stern antagonism. From the beginning, students were admitted without regard for race, creed, or color. Early emphasis on the importance of theology and music fathered the well-known Graduate School of Theology and the Conservatory of Music.

Oberlin leaders were idealists who put their ideas to work. Antislavery sentiment was firmly crystallized here before the Abolition movement gained momentum. Garrison's first support came from Oberlin when he began spreading *The Liberator* in 1831. The village was one of the principal stations on the Underground Railroad, and its influence was largely responsible for the attitude of the Middle West toward slavery. The anti-saloon movement originated in the First Congregational Church in Oberlin. In a college laboratory, Charles Martin Hall began research in aluminum that led to his discovery in 1886 of the electrolytic process of making aluminum, a discovery that transformed not only industry, but the architectural and domestic worlds. Dr. Robert A. Millikan, Nobel prize winner in physics, was a distinguished graduate and direct descendant of Pioneer Pease.

Oberlin, incorporated as a village in 1846, gained distinction as an educational, moral, and religious center in the midst of a rural district. In 1905, it installed one of the first municipal water-softening plants in the world. Educational advantages attracted an unusually high quality of citizens, who lived in comfortable homes sheltered under stately trees. Impressive campus buildings contributed to the beauty of the village, called "an ideal town in which to live." It had a population of 4,305 in 1940. Oberlin Inn, operated by the college, originated in a log tavern built on the site in 1833. H. V. Zahm became village manager in 1946.

The spirit of Oberlin went out to the ends of the earth over the years, interpreted in missionary effort in many lands, and in the lives of men and women motivated by the zeal of the founders and the principles of Christian living.

Painesville

John Walworth had lived in the Grand River district a month when General Edward Paine, Revolutionary soldier from Connecticut, arrived on May 1, 1800, with a party of sixty-six to establish a permanent settlement called "The Openings" between Lake Erie and the river. In August, Painesville Township was created. The name Champion was taken in 1807, honoring Henry Champion, owner of the land on which the future city was built. In 1816 it was changed to Painesville as a tribute to General Paine, in whose memory a monument was later erected in Charter Oak Park. Walworth had exchanged his property for a Cleveland home in 1805.

The village grew slowly, neither blessed with wealth nor burdened with poverty. Small industries developed. The Little Red Tavern, built by Josiah Brown about 1805, was believed to be the oldest frame building in Lake County in the 1940s. The famed Rider Tavern was expanded in 1818, from a log cabin that had been erected in 1810, by Jonathan Goldsmith, master builder of many fine homes in the Western Reserve. It was a station on the Underground Railroad in pre-Civil War days, and continued to serve the public a century later. The *Painesville Telegraph,* launched in 1822, was destined to enjoy an uninterrupted publication record. An academy opened in 1829.

When Lake County was organized in 1840, Painesville became the county seat. The Court House, erected this year, later became the City Hall. Its construction was financed by public subscription. The Cleveland, Painesville & Ashtabula Railroad (later New York Central) went into operation in 1852. The Coe Manufacturing Company, founded in 1852, became the world's largest manufacturer of veneer machinery. The Storrs & Harrison Company, organized in 1854, grew to be one of the nation's largest dealers in seeds and nursery stock. Thus Painesville became the center of a great nursery and fruit-growing district. Willoughby Female Seminary was moved to Painesville in 1856 after a destructive fire. It became Lake Erie Female Seminary, and later Lake Erie College, widely known school for girls.

Business blocks razed by the fires of 1857 and 1861 were restored with improved and safer structures.

Painesville became a city in 1902, and adopted the City-Manager Plan of government in 1919. It gained strength as new industries were attracted. The population, reported to be 12,235 in 1940, was estimated at 16,000 in the mid-1940s. The city's largest industrial plant was the Diamond Alkali Company, its buildings covering twelve acres. Nearby was the newest plant of the vast Industrial Rayon Corporation. The opening of a soybean processing plant introduced a new industry and stimulated the raising of soybeans in northern Ohio. In addition to harbor activity, Painesville industries produced metallic binding, aluminum castings, concrete building blocks, and baskets; and plants were under construction for the manufacture of venol resin and electrolytic iron powder.

City officials in 1946-47 included W. D. Toyne, city manager; H. A. Geldbaugh, chairman of the Council; C. V. Boudreaux, auditor and clerk; Seth Paulin, solicitor; and E. Burdett Talcott, treasurer.

Parma

Benjamin Fay, of Massachusetts, and his large family were the first settlers in 1816 in the area designated as Parma Township in 1826. The Emerson, Hodgman, Nicholas, Small, and Steel families were among those who opened up the rich agricultural district.

City folk seeking homes in the countryside increased the population, and in 1931 Parma was incorporated as a city. It was the seventh largest municipality in Ohio in point of area, more than twenty square miles. Much of the land represented farms, ravines, and woodlands in 1940, when the census reported 16,365 people.

The community won national recognition because of Parmadale, the model village of homes for orphan boys, operated by the Catholic Diocese. Growth quickened with the building of Crile Hospital in Parma Heights.

Parma's prosperity in 1946 was measured by an estimated population of twenty-six thousand. An industrial future seemed assured when plans were announced by General Motors Corporation for early construction of a large automobile plant which would employ about five thousand workers. City officials in 1946-47 included Roland E. Reichert, mayor; Lawrence Stary, president of the Council; George Weckerling, auditor; Josephine Baker, treasurer; and Richard de Nobel, solicitor.

Ravenna

Benjamin Tappan, of Massachusetts, purchased a sixteen-thousand-acre tract of land in the Western Reserve that included a ridge forming a watershed between the Cuyahoga and Mahoning rivers. His son, Benjamin, pioneered a settlement at a point about three miles southeast of the site of Ravenna in June, 1799, and he was joined by his brothers, John and William.

A township school opened in 1803. Dr. Joseph DeWolf, the first doctor, came in about 1804, and his fame as a surgeon became widely known. In 1807, Mrs. Benjamin Tappan urged her husband to clear an area as a proposed site for the county court house, in order to forestall the honor going to near-by Franklin Mills (Kent), which was competing with "Old Portage." In 1808, Benjamin, Jr., plotted a village called Tappanville or Tinnicum, an Indian name. Here the county seat of Portage County was established in 1810.

Benjamin Tappan, Jr., a lawyer, is said to have tried the first case in the Western Reserve at Warren in 1800. It involved the shooting of an Indian and a half-breed. Although he moved to Steubenville in 1809, he continued his law practice in Tappanville. He was a distinguished member of the first Ohio Legislature, headed the Ohio Canal Commission, and served in the United States Senate.

James Haslip opened the first general store in the village in 1812. In about 1815, Jesse Grant, father of Ulysses S. Grant, built a tannery on Chestnut Street. In 1850, the village name was changed to Ravenna, members of the Tappan family having been charmed by Ravenna, Italy, while touring Europe.

Ravenna was incorporated in 1853, and O. P. Brown was elected the first mayor. The little village was known for its lawyers who gained prominence, among them John C. Wright, L. V. Bierce, the three Ranneys, and Rufus P. Spalding. Also prominent in public affairs were Ezra B. Taylor, Congressman; Luther Day, justice of the Ohio Supreme Court; and W. R. Day, associate justice of the United States Supreme Court. Some of them later located in Akron and Cleveland. Henry P. Crowell, a revered resident of Ravenna, headed the local plant of the Quaker Oats Company before the turn of the century, and advanced to the helm of the giant industry.

A city of 8,538 people in 1940, Ravenna was a residential community surrounded by fine farms, with the scenic Portage Lakes near by. The county ranked high in the production of potatoes, dairy products, and maple sugar. In the mid-1940s Ravenna industry included a worsted mill, foundries, and plants producing machines, ceramics, toys, chrome furniture and fixtures, rubber and electrical products, and farm machinery. Walter N. Miller was serving as mayor in 1946-47.

Rocky River

Settlement of lands west of the Cuyahoga River, the organization of Rockport Township in 1819, and the development of the district that became Rocky River are so intimately woven with the history of Cleveland that many facts relating to the early-day community were recorded earlier in this volume.

The hamlet of Rocky River had a population of about seven hundred people when it was established on December 19, 1891, comprising "all that part of Rockport Township lying west of Rocky River." Fine farms flourished here until the early 1920s, when the automobile began to shorten distances. Then the transition to a suburban city of homes began, facilitated by the Rocky River Bridge, completed in 1910, the longest single-span, concrete bridge in existence.

Rocky River was incorporated as a city in 1930. Greenhouses and truck gardening provided profitable industry, but many citizens earned their livelihood in Cleveland. The population had reached 8,291 in 1940. Rocky River boasted of good schools, careful zoning and planning, the widely known Westwood Country Club, and the Westlake Hotel, located on a traditional tavern site overlooking the deep river valley. The Metropolitan Park System formed the city's easterly line and provided popular recreation, and semi-private beaches served the people in the Beach Cliff section. A clock tower, marking the boundary of the estate of Clifton B. Beach, Congressman, 1895-99, became a landmark at the union of West Lake Road and Avalon Drive. Beach Cliff took its name from the Beach property. At the mouth of Rocky River, in the snug refuge of the Clifton Park Lagoon and along its wooded banks, pleasure-boat owners moored their craft. Across the river was the Cleveland Yacht Club. A. R. Thomas was mayor of Rocky River in 1946-47.

Sandusky

Roger's Rangers, of "Northwest Passage" fame, were said to have camped on the site of Sandusky in 1760. Some of the earliest fighting of the War of 1812 took place in the vicinity, and Commodore Oliver Hazard Perry's victory over the British at near-by Put-in-Bay was commemorated a century later by the million-dollar Perry Monument.

The first permanent settlers, who arrived in 1816, founded the town of Portland in 1817, laid out by its "proprietor," Zalmon Wildman of Danbury, Connecticut. As the result of disputed ownership to certain land in 1818, Wildman and Isaac Mills of New Haven merged their interests and plotted the town of Sandusky City, which was incorporated as a village in 1824. The Indian name Sandousky meant cool, clear water.

The Marblehead Lighthouse, third oldest on the lakes, was built on Marblehead Peninsula in 1821. Construction of the Mad River Railroad, the second rail line in Ohio, later known as the Cincinnati, Sandusky & Cleveland Railroad, began in about 1832, connecting Sandusky with Dayton and points south.

Erie County was separated from Huron County in 1838, and Sandusky

City became the county seat. Incorporated as a city in 1845, the name was shortened to Sandusky in 1869. Cholera wiped out more than half the population in the epidemics of 1849 and 1852, and its victims were laid to rest in the historic Cholera Cemetery.

After the Civil War, Sandusky progressed steadily as one of the primary industrial and shipping points of the Great Lakes, gaining fame as a fishing and wine-producing center. The eighteen-mile Sandusky Bay, with the protective arms of Cedar Point and Marblehead peninsulas, afforded one of the finest natural harbors on Lake Erie. Cedar Point opened as a resort in 1882, inaugurating Sandusky's long career as a tourist center.

Called the "key city of the central Ohio lake region," the city grew in importance as a strategic shipping and receiving point for coal, lumber, and iron ore; and in the 1940s, the port was the second largest on the lakes in point of coal tonnage shipped. Sandusky was the largest fresh-water fishing port in the nation, and the Catawba vineyards and orchards had brought it fame. Vast stone quarries were operated on Kelley's Island, that was known for remarkable glacial grooves and unusual geological formations, and here was the prehistoric "Inscription Rock," a renowned example of Indian pictograph record.

Sandusky's population had reached 24,874 in 1940. Unusual balance characterized the city's industry, more than sixty plants producing a wide range of products. Besides fishing, shipping, and wine-making, manufactures included paper and paper products, crayons, chalk, water colors, washing machines, castings, chain, boats, fertilizer, rubber goods, radios, and farm machinery.

Sandusky was known as a beautiful and unusually picturesque city, and was the center of popular Lake Erie summer resorts. It was the gateway to the historic islands—Kelley's, the Bass group, and Canadian Pelee. Sportsmen and vacationers by the thousands were attracted annually to enjoy fishing, hunting, swimming, and boating, and to explore unique caves and caverns and the great wine cellars. Lakeside, on the north shore of Marblehead, became known as "the Chautauqua of the Great Lakes," the center of musical, educational, and religious activity in the summertime. To the south, the fabulous Blue Hole of Castalia, a mysterious, bottomless pool of ever-changing color, fed by an underground river, fascinated steady streams of visitors.

Sandusky's city officials in 1946-47 included Karl H. Kugel, city manager; Paul L. Heiberger, president of the commission; William H. Smith, solicitor; and Carl F. Breining, auditor and treasurer. Lewis L. Marquart was municipal judge and Dr. F. E. Mahla, health Commissioner.

Shaker Heights

Shaker Heights derived its name from the Shakers, a religious sect that established a colony called North Union, or "Valley of God's Pleasure," on the site in 1822. Prior to 1911, the main part of the territory which became Shaker Heights was included in the Village of Cleveland Heights. In that year, it was detached and identified as the Township of Shaker Heights. John L. Cannon, William J. Van Aken, and O. P. Van Sweringen were elected trustees in August. On October 27, the Village of Shaker Heights was incorporated. When John Mitchell was elected as the first mayor, the population was estimated at 250. City government under a charter became effective in 1931.

The Village of East View, with a population of about six hundred, was annexed in 1920. Lack of transportation facilities restricted growth until this year, when rapid-transit service to downtown Cleveland was inaugurated. The trend to the "Heights" quickened as city-dwellers sought home sites in the choice farm-land allotments, studded with the picturesque Shaker Lakes; and the 1930 census reported a population of 17,783. In 1929, a revolutionary shopping-center plan was introduced in the form of Shaker Square, a traditional English village of fine shops built in uniform Georgian architectural style. Following the lead of Moreland Courts, stately apartment houses began to rise around the Square. Beyond, tree-arched streets bordered with lovely homes carried out the residential pattern envisioned by the Van Sweringen brothers, the planners of Shaker Heights, recognized as one of the most beautiful small cities in the nation.

From its inception, the community remained distinctly a residential, suburban area, with the necessary provisions for retail-business centers, as originally planned. The Rapid Transit lines of the Cleveland Interurban Railroad Company were acquired by the City of Shaker Heights in 1944. The school system was outstanding in the educational world. Within the boundaries of six and a half square miles, was an estimated population of 28,000 in 1946. In 1940, it had been 23,393.

City officials in 1946-47 included William J. Van Aken, mayor, who had served since 1917; Carl Palmer, president of the Council; Rudolph Rife, director of public service; Edward P. Rudolph, director of finance; Ralph W. Jones, director of law; Dr. Paul M. Spurney, director of health; and Paul K. Jones, director of transportation.

South Euclid

The territory that became South Euclid was formed from what was originally Euclid Township. In his sawmill set up in 1830 (on Belvoir Boulevard), Thomas D. Webb cut the lumber from which pioneer homes were built.

The first important activity in the southern section of the township was the discovery in about 1852 of valuable blue sandstone by Duncan McFarland, who opened a quarry on Nine Mile Creek, giving the district the name Bluestone. With increased demand for stone, members of the McFarland family and others operated quarries that flourished until the turn of the century, when concrete began to displace stone as building material. The quarries then gave way to farming and real-estate development.

The Village of South Euclid was incorporated in 1917, with E. A. Foote as its first mayor. Its population had grown to 6,146 in 1940, meriting the status of city. Ninety per cent of families owned their homes. In 1946-47 when Lloyd N. Reynolds was mayor, a few stone quarries and a basket factory continued to operate. Industrial expansion of neighboring Euclid had greatly stimulated home-building in South Euclid, whose estimated population was nine thousand. A portion of the early-day quarries had been landscaped as picturesque Euclid Creek Reservation of the Metropolitan Park System.

Struthers

Captain John Struthers, of the Pennsylvania Militia, pursued a band of marauding Indians from Washington County, Pennsylvania, in August, 1798, following them up the Beaver River Valley to satisfy himself that they had left the territory. The beauty and fertility of a clearing at the mouth of Yellow Creek so impressed him that he purchased four hundred acres of land from Turhand Kirtland of Poland, agent for the Connecticut Land Company. Here he settled with his wife and sister in October, 1799, and the little village that took form bore his name.

Incorporation of the Youngstown Iron, Sheet & Tube Company in 1900 brought a boom to Struthers, and in 1902 it became a village. It increased in importance as industry flourished, reaching city stature in 1920; and by 1940 the population numbered 11,739. Located between high hills, its manufacturing possibilities were limited.

Officials of the industrial community in 1946-47 were Thomas H. Needham, mayor; Joseph Repasky, president of the Council; John F. Pearce, auditor; Nan H. Mayberry, treasurer; Theodore T. Macejko, solicitor; and William Harvey, director of public service and safety.

Tallmadge

The Rev. David Bacon's missionary work among the Indians around Sandusky Bay proved disappointing, and he was recalled by the Connecticut Missionary Society. At the request of David Hudson and two Western Reserve ministers, Bacon returned with his family to preach in the Hudson, Ohio, settlement. Believing, however, that he could contribute more to the settlers' moral and religious welfare by conspicuous example in a well-organized township, Bacon returned to Hartford and contracted for about twelve thousand acres of land south of Hudson in 1806. The name Tallmadge was given to the township, honoring Benjamin Tallmadge, a deeply religious man and former owner of a large portion. Bacon and his family settled on the village site in June, 1807. The Church of Christ, forerunner of the First Congregational Church, organized in January, 1809, in the Bacon cabin, became the nerve center of the community.

Lemuel Porter, of Waterbury, Connecticut, and David Hoadley were fellow apprentices while learning the joiner's trade. Hoadley designed and erected fine churches in the vicinity of New Haven; Colonel Lemuel Porter gained prominence in Ohio as a builder of residences and churches of architectural refinement, and as a maker of wooden-wheel clocks. Porter came to Tallmadge in 1818, and his skill was immediately in demand. He undertook the design and erection of the historic Congregational meeting house in 1821. Western Reserve College employed him to build its first building, and engaged him as carpenter and "joiner" for further construction. He moved to Hudson in the late 1820s and died soon afterward. His son, Simeon C., completed the contract. He later moved to Cleveland and became associated with Charles W. Heard, the famous architect.

Bacon, the pioneer, was the inspiration of a model village, including an academy and a district school on the Public Square, from which radiated eight roads bisected by crossroads, making for ease in attending church. A district school was planned for each corner of the town, the first school opening in 1810. To extend religious influence, purchasers of township land were obliged to join the church and subscribe to the confession of faith adopted by the Connecticut Legislature. To support the gospel, a tax of two dollars per year was levied on each hundred acres of land sold. Settlement was slow, and Bacon became unable to make payments on his land. Disillusioned, he gave up his work and moved his family to the East, where he preached and taught, but his spirit left a lasting impress upon the community he fathered. Simeon Woodruff of Connecticut, graduate of Yale College and Andover Theological Seminary, succeeded Rev. Bacon as pastor-missionary at Tallmadge, serving for nine years.

The Academy, built in 1815, was under the direction of Elizur Wright, Yale graduate, for a number of years. Fire leveled it, and on the Public Square site a church was dedicated in 1825, a subscription of $3,500 having been voted to be paid in wheat, wool, and labor. With the exception of an addition to the north side of the building, the exterior of the historic, classic edifice remained much the same in the 1940s.

Tallmadge had the first deaf-and-mute school in Ohio. When a school was started in Columbus in 1827, Tallmadge pupils were transferred there. The historical society, organized in 1858, survived the years, emphasizing the proud heritage founded upon religious and educational privilege.

Sereno P. Fenn, wealthy Cleveland manufacturer, was born in Tallmadge and gave generously to beautify the township cemetery. John Thomas rose from chemist at the Firestone Tire & Rubber Company to become its chief executive. Charles E. Ritchie inspired the move to incorporate the Village of Tallmadge in 1935, and was elected the first mayor, serving until his untimely death in his third term. Through his benefaction, the park was improved; and a tract of land which he gave as a memorial to those who served in World War II is known as Ritchie Park.

Although located on the canal and possessed of industrial advantages in its early years, Tallmadge became an agricultural community. Gradually it was allotted for real-estate development, and industries began to spring up. The population in 1940 was 3,452. The village was growing rapidly, but it retained much of its historic charm, and visitors were attracted from far and near. Vincent W. Ziegler was mayor in 1946-47.

University Heights

Some of the earliest settlers of the district that became University Heights were Manxmen who claimed Connecticut land grants. At one time a part of Warrensville, Idlewood Village was incorporated in 1908. John Carroll University sought expansion here, and the name University Heights was adopted in 1925.

Conversion from farm land to residential suburb began in 1914. From 26 voting families in the early 1920s, University Heights, covering less than two square miles, contained 5,981 people in 1940 when it became a city. Bellefaire, the Jewish orphan home for boys and girls, was an outstanding institution in its field. After twenty-three years of service as mayor of the rapidly growing city, John Howard retired from office and was succeeded by Earl W. Aurelius, who was mayor in 1946-47.

Wadsworth

General Elijah Wadsworth of Connecticut was the owner of large tracts of Western Reserve land, including most of the township that bore his name. He was one of the first United States postmasters appointed in the Western Reserve, and through his efforts the first mail route was blazed in the territory in 1801. His death in Canfield in 1817 was hastened by the loss of his wealth in the Revolutionary War and in the War of 1812, and by concern over a vast government debt assumed by him and not repaid until 1825.

Daniel Dean and Oliver Durham of Vermont, the first settlers, began clearing land in March, 1814, on the east line of Wadsworth, near the future site of Western Star. The first log house was built by Frederick Brown, ardent Congregationalist. Levi Blakeslee, tanner, built the first frame house. After him came Hiram C. Kingsbury, blacksmith. New Englanders followed, settling mostly north of the center road, while Pennsylvania pioneers of German ancestry moved into lands in the southern portion of the township. Differences in speech, customs, and religious beliefs were soon dissolved as citizens merged their interests in co-operative enterprise for the common welfare. Wadsworth had been attached to Norton Township for a year, when it was organized independently in 1817.

The arrival of Shubel Whitney, 1844-45, was significant, for in his large family was Asa Whitney, who envisioned a railroad across the Rocky Mountains. His plans, abandoned after cruel derision, were accomplished later by others.

Wadsworth developed as a community of farms and pioneer industry until 1865, when the location of the Atlantic & Great Western Railroad (later Erie) transformed it to a thriving coal-mining town. The village was incorporated in 1866, and Aaron Pardee was elected the first mayor. The mines had become almost exhausted in the 1890s, when industry began to gain a foothold, and to produce injectors, matches, and salt.

Citizens who gained prominence included Burke A. Hinsdale, born in Wadsworth Township, who became president of Hiram College, superintendent of the Cleveland Public Schools, and member of the faculty of the University of Michigan. His brother, Wilbert B., local physician, was for many years dean of the College of Homeopathy in the university. Don A. Pardee, judge of the United States Circuit Court, fifth district, was born in Wadsworth; Laura C. Spelman, born here, married John D. Rockefeller. Prominent residents were Captain Theodore D. Wolbach, soldier, photographer, and collector of relics; and Peter P. Cherry, historian of the section.

Wadsworth continued to grow industrially, attaining city status in 1931. The population was reported at 6,495 in 1940. Leading manufactures included matches, injectors and injector valves, salt, brick and tile, pipe-joint compounds, paint and varnish. B. G. Birkbeck was serving as mayor of the city in 1946-47.

Warren

The first sale of Western Reserve lands by Connecticut was a 25,000-acre tract in the Mahoning Valley purchased in 1788 by General Samuel H. Parsons, one of the three original judges of the Northwest Territory. Indian trails converged at the "Salt Springs Tract," as it was called, because of the saline waters of the extensive springs. Parsons' early death halted his plans to exploit the product. For several decades, settlers traveled long distances to supply their needs at high prices.

In the fall of 1798, Ephraim Quinby and Richard Storer, of Washington County, Pennsylvania, selected the timbered region along the Mahoning River as worthy of investment. Quinby arranged to purchase 441 acres from Ebenezer King, Jr. Quinby, Storer, William Fenton, and Francis Carlton and their families settled here in the spring of 1799, giving Warren its start. In 1800 Quinby plotted the town, named for Moses Warren, surveyor with the Moses Cleaveland party, reserving four acres in the center as the Public Square. Years later an acre of the tract became known as Monumental Park, and Quinby Park honored the founder.

Trumbull County, created on July 10, 1800, included the whole of the Western Reserve, with Warren as the county seat. Court convened between Quinby's corn cribs in Warren on August 25, 1800, representing the organization of government in the Western Reserve that continued until 1803, when Ohio was admitted to the Union. John Stark Edwards, who looked after the interests of his father, Pierpont Edwards, became the first county recorder. In 1807, he built a log house, later acquired by Thomas D. Webb, that gained renown as the famous Webb house, the oldest building in Warren in the 1940s.

Although the Rev. Henry Spears, Baptist, preached the first sermon in Warren in 1800, the congregation was not fully organized until 1822. A Presbyterian church, formed in 1803 by the Rev. Joseph Badger, became the historic First Presbyterian Church.

General Simon Perkins, who had been sales agent for the Connecticut Land Company, was appointed the first postmaster at Warren when the Pittsburgh-Cleveland postal route was laid out in 1801. Perkins Park perpetuated his name. A log schoolhouse, built this year on the river bank near the Square, was the first in the Reserve. Primitive mills were inaugurated by George Loveless in 1803, when he dammed the Mahoning to produce water-power.

The Western Reserve Bank, the first bank in the Reserve, opened in 1811. *The Trump of Fame,* the first newspaper in the Western Reserve, was launched by Thomas D. Webb, and it was the forerunner of the *Warren Tribune Chronicle.* A library of a thousand volumes opened in a cabinet shop in 1814.

Warren was incorporated as a village in 1834. Its iron industry originated in a foundry and blast furnace set up in Brookfield Township in 1836. The Pennsylvania & Ohio Canal brought unusual prosperity to the village in 1840, opening markets for farm products, coal, and iron. Railroads were projected, beginning in the 1850s, to serve the industrial valley.

Warren became a city in 1869. Culture was encouraged this year when William H. Dana and his father, Junius Dana, organized the Dana Musical Institute, whose influence broadened through the years. William studied with masters on the continent, became a well-known lecturer and author, and was one of the three founders of the National Music Teachers Association.

Accompanied by his wife and daughter, Stephen Collins Foster visited his sister, Mrs. Henrietta Thornton, in Warren from early April until the late fall of 1860. While here, he wrote *Under the Willows She's Sleeping, The Glendy Burk,* and *Jenny's Comin' o'er the Green.* Tradition says that moonlight on the Mahoning inspired *Come Where My Love Lies Dreaming.* D. Rhys Ford, local Welsh musician, became a noted composer of secular and religious works.

Earl Derr Biggers, born in Warren, rose to fame as author of *Seven Keys to Baldpate* and the Charlie Chan stories. Harriet Taylor Upton, born in Ravenna, was living in Warren when she gained prominence in the woman-suffrage campaign. Her *History of Trumbull County, History of the Western Reserve,* and other writings were important achievements.

J. Ward and William D. Packard, sons of Warren Packard, prominent industrialist, launched Warren's electrical industry in 1889. The Packard

Electric Company, organized in 1893, became one of the world's leading manufacturers of automotive cable. At one time Warren led the nation in lamp production, and it was the first to introduce complete Mazda tungsten street lighting.

J. Ward Packard's interest turned to the "horseless carriage," and on November 6, 1899, his first Packard car made its noisy debut in Warren. Finding financial backing in Detroit, the brothers moved to that city in 1903. Members of the Packard family gave Packard Park to Warren in 1911.

Citizens who found pride in the quiet town opposed invasion by the steel industry. Warren's location, midway between iron ore from the lakes and vast coal deposits in western Pennsylvania, inspired the founding of the Trumbull Steel Company which introduced steel-making to the city in 1913. Caught in the war era of industrial expansion, a steel empire rose in the "Flats," and into the mill district crowded workers of many nationalities. The tempo of Warren's industrial pace was geared to that of the nation in the coming years, and the "Little Steel" group of plants merged with the Republic Iron & Steel Company (later Republic Steel Corporation) in 1928.

With 42,837 people in 1940, Warren was one of the most highly industrialized cities of its size, producing electric lamps, motors and fans, transformers, railroad tools, fire-fighting equipment, tanks, steel barrels and hoops, welding machinery, and pressed-steel products. Warren served as the marketing center of a fertile agricultural district that led the State in dairy products and was increasing its truck-gardening and potato output.

The city officials of Warren in 1946-47 were Henry C. Wagner, mayor; Reynard Nill, president of the Council; B. M. Hillyer, auditor; Maurice E. Hillman, treasurer; Donald J. DelBene, solicitor; and Floyd E. Pardee, director of public service and safety.

Wellington

In the distribution of Western Reserve lands, Ephraim Root and James Ross, of Berkshire County, Massachusetts, became the original "proprietors" of township 3, range 18. Early in 1818, John Clifford, Charles Sweet, Ephraim Wilcox, and Joseph Wilson of Berkshire County were joined on their westward trek by William T. Welling of New York State. They cleared the site for a settlement called Wellington, and friends and relatives soon followed. Whether the name honored the Duke of Wellington or Pioneer Welling was never established.

Wellington Township, a part of Medina County, was organized in 1821. In 1855, the central portion became an incorporated village, with John M. Swift as the first mayor.

In the Tripp carriage factory, an early industrial enterprise, an ingenious painter named Archibald M. Willard found employment after the Civil

War. His gaudy decoration of wagons and circus vehicles and his humorous pictures attracted unusual attention, but his celebrated "Spirit of '76" won for him world fame. The artist died in 1918 and was buried in Wellington. Myron T. Herrick, statesman and ambassador to France, lived on a farm near Wellington when a boy. As a memorial to his parents, he presented the Herrick Public Library to the village.

The Lorain County Fair was launched in Wellington in 1855, and was held there continuously through the years. Dairying was an important industry in this flourishing farming district. Large quantities of cheese and butter were produced, and in the late 1870s there were more than forty cheese factories in operation. As transportation facilities improved, however, farmers were able to sell milk direct with greater profit, and the cheese business declined while that of milk increased rapidly.

There were 2,529 people in the Village of Wellington in 1940, many of them commuting to places of employment in Cleveland. Local industry was producing gray iron castings, hand trucks, glass cloth, screw-machine products, and implement parts in the 1940s. Franklin M. Jones was serving as mayor in 1946-47.

Westlake

Asahel Porter, his family and a nephew, young Leverett Johnson, halted their heavy wagons in the Dover Township forest near the lakeshore west of Rocky River on October 10, 1810, and decided to go no further. Later in the year, Moses Hall of Lee, Massachusetts, took up 2,163 acres in the vicinity as well as land in Ashtabula and Euclid. Hall gave a hundred acres of Dover land to each of his seven sons, and fifty acres to each of his five daughters. In 1811, eight devout New Englanders founded the Dover Congregational Church, the first of the denomination in Cuyahoga County.

The Dover settlement grew steadily as an agricultural community. Pioneer industry kept pace with aggressive neighbors, boasting mills, shops, two asheries for the making of potash, and a blast furnace producing pig iron.

Clague Park, a memorial to the Clague family, early settlers from the Isle of Man, was at one time a fine fruit farm. The Clague vineyards contributed largely to the position of Dover Township as the nation's second largest grape-producing district before the turn of the century.

Dover Village, incorporated in 1911, took the name Westlake in 1940 to avoid confusion with Dover in Tuscarawas County. The steady move from Cleveland increased the population to 3,200; but farms, truck gardens, and flower gardens continued to flourish in the village, and the growing of strawberries and grapes was a profitable industry. Hugh D. Price was mayor in 1946-47.

Wickliffe

Concluding that land in the vicinity of Cleveland's Public Square was too sandy for tillage, the Tarbell and Jones families, of Haddam, Connecticut, retraced their wagon trail eastward, locating on the site of Wickliffe in 1817. The settlement derived its name from Charles Wickliffe, who was Post-master General in President John Tyler's cabinet.

Harry Coulby, "Czar of the Great Lakes," was the first mayor of Wick-liffe, which was incorporated as a village in 1916. He was devoted to the cause of civic betterment and spent a vast sum on his Ridge Road estate in the southwest section of Wickliffe. Here also were the pretentious homes of the Devereux, McKinney, and Winslow families.

The fertile farming district was transformed to a suburban community as the outward move from the city gained momentum, and in 1940 Wickliffe's population was 3,155. Chief industries in the mid-1940s were the Cleveland Crane & Engineering Company, the Lubrizol Corporation, and the Euclid Shale Brick Company. Frank L. Fickel was mayor in 1946-47 of the rapidly growing residential village, with an estimated population of 4,800. Property along Euclid Avenue had been fairly well built up, while large suburban estates made up the southern section, and to the north there were developed but unoccupied allotments.

Willard

Chicago Junction was founded in January, 1874, when the Baltimore, Pittsburgh & Chicago Railway (later Baltimore & Ohio) began construc-tion of the Baltimore-to-Chicago western division. From that time forward, the railroad constituted the chief industry locally, the junction being the main terminal point between Pittsburgh and Chicago.

Confusion with Chicago, arising in the mails, inspired in 1917 a change in name to Willard, honoring Daniel Willard, president of the Baltimore & Ohio Railroad Company.

Willard was a pleasant and progressive municipality of 4,261 people in 1940. The Pioneer Rubber Company, the city's principal industrial plant, established in 1918, became one of the largest manufacturers of rubber gloves and toy and novelty balloons, with a worldwide market. From the fertile fields south of Willard, vegetables were being shipped to all parts of the nation. Corn, wheat, and oats were raised extensively on Huron County farms. The celery industry centered in a little village called Celery-ville, founded by Holland Dutch in 1896, and fostered by industrious descendants. Robert J. Vetter was mayor of Willard in 1946-47.

Willoughby

David Abbott, Peter French, Jacob West, Ebenezer Smith, and Elisha Graham were among the pioneers from Vermont and Maine who founded a settlement called Charlton, later changed to Chagrin, on Lake Erie at the mouth of the picturesque Chagrin River in 1799. A grist-mill built by Abbott in the fall of 1798 is believed to have been the first in the Reserve. In 1796, Charles Parker, surveyor, had built a cabin at the mouth of the river. It was probably the first in the district. He became a settler in 1802.

The first organized town meeting was held on April 3, 1815. Prominent leaders of the Western Reserve founded the ill-fated Willoughby University at Chagrin in 1834, and citizens adopted the proud name for the village.

On the edge of the forest, land was cleared by a clan of settlers who were indifferent to the church and loved their whisky. Resentful of their boisterous, drunken revels, the townsmen called them the "lost nation." A road fronting on the newcomers' farms carried on the Lost Nation name.

Although Willoughby gradually developed into a suburban, residential community, it retained the charm and dignity of a proud past. Impressive homes in spacious, well-kept lawns bordering tree-arched Euclid Avenue typified its wealth and conservatism. The lovely residence of Dr. Phrania Chesbrough, built in 1918, was converted to a home for the First Federal Savings & Loan Association, called the "handsomest savings and loan building in Ohio."

Through the wise planning of Mr. and Mrs. Wallace C. Andrews, the Andrews School for Girls was founded in 1910 to provide vocational education opportunities.

The family of Sidney S. Wilson, local historian, was one of the first to settle in the community. Wilson's retirement in 1936 concluded twenty years of service to Western Reserve University as secretary-treasurer.

Willoughby, incorporated as a village in 1835, had a population of 4,364 in 1940. Located in an important fruit-growing region, it served as a shopping center for communities in three counties. The Ohio Rubber Company was the largest of Willoughby's few industrial plants. C. B. Todd, elected mayor in 1935, was serving in 1946-47.

Youngstown

John Young, frontiersman, settled in the Mahoning Valley in 1797 and built his cabin home. With the help of Turhand Kirtland, Connecticut Land Company agent, he laid out the first plat in 1798 for a town bearing his name. Six years later, when the founder moved to New York, there were between two and three hundred settlers in fertile Youngstown Township.

The settlement's spiritual life had its beginning in the congregation organized by the Rev. William Wick on July 1, 1801. It became the First Presbyterian Church, the first church body on the Western Reserve.

Native iron ore was discovered in 1802, and about three years later the first blast furnace was built. Several booms and expansions in the industry came from 1855 to 1875, when railroads and rolling mills were first introduced in the Mahoning Valley; then came the Bessemer process, 1893-1900.

Youngstown was incorporated as a village in 1848, and in 1867 a population exceeding five thousand entitled it to become a city. It was declared the county seat of Mahoning County after a seventy-six-year contest with neighboring towns. A final decision was rendered by the United States Supreme Court, which heard the case brought in 1879 by the Village of Canfield —two years after a new court house had been built in Youngstown.

The Greater Youngstown area claimed famous sons, among them David Tod, governor of Ohio, 1862-64; Harold Bell Wright, author; Jesse Grant, father of President Ulysses S. Grant; Chauncey Andrews, railroad builder and banker; Major John A. Logan, organizer and head of the famed Logan Rifles, prominent Mahoning County military unit in the Spanish-American War; Edmond H. Moore, nationally known attorney and political organizer; John H. Clarke, associate justice of the United States Supreme Court, who resigned his high office to promote world peace; and John D. "Bonesetter" Reese, world-famous benefactor, whose gifted ability to adjust bones and muscles brought relief from suffering to rich and poor. In the realm of art, the citizens found pride in the works of Kenyon Cox and Tom J. Nicholl, and of Grant E. Hamilton, political cartoonist and creator of the famous "Full Dinner Pail" feature.

Youngstown College, founded in 1908, originated as part of the YMCA program. Fostered by public and private interest, it developed into a fully accredited institution of increasing importance. A new and beautiful college and campus on old residential Wick Avenue was designed as the focal point of plans for an impressive cultural center. In the locality was Butler Art Institute, given to the city in 1919 by Joseph G. Butler, pioneer producer of iron and steel. Stambaugh Auditorium was recognized as one of America's most beautiful public buildings. The Municipal Airport, built in 1941 at a cost of $2,250,000, was considered one of the most modern and efficient in the State. Mill Creek Park, famed for its natural beauty, stretched for seven miles through a winding valley in the south portion of the city.

Youngstown was made a Catholic Diocese in 1943, under the spiritual guidance of Bishop James A. McFadden. The city was the home of Edward Cardinal Mooney, later of Detroit, Michigan.

Workers of many nationalities swarmed into Youngstown as steel mills expanded during World War I. The population, influenced by the pace of industry, had reached 167,720 in 1940. Mammoth plants of the Youngstown Sheet & Tube Company, Republic Steel Corporation, Carnegie-Illinois Steel Corporation, and Truscon Steel Company were producing an output in the 1940s that gave Youngstown fourth place in the nation's steel production. In 1946-47, city officials were Ralph W. O'Neill, mayor; Fred G. Weimer, president of the Council; Forrest J. Cavalier, director of finance; and John W. Powers, director of law. Peter B. Mulholland, John Joseph Buckley, and Robert B. Nevin were municipal judges.

Appendices

GREATER CLEVELAND MANUFACTURERS

Employing 100 or More Persons

COMPILED BY THE MANUFACTURERS DEPARTMENT
THE CLEVELAND CHAMBER OF COMMERCE

Accurate Die Casting Co., The
Accurate Parts Mfg. Co.
Acme Foundry Corp.
Acorn Refining Co., The
Acro Electric Co.
Addressograph-Multigraph Corp.
Aetna Rubber Co., The
Aircraft Fitting Co., The
Air-Maze Corp.
Ajax Mfg. Co.
Allyne-Ryan Foundry Co.
Aluminum Company of America
American Agricultural Chemical Co.
American Bifocal Co., Inc.
American Box Co.
American Coach & Body Co.
American Fork & Hoe Co., The
American Greeting Publishers
American Magnesium Corp.
American Monorail Co.
American Ship Building Co.
American Steel & Wire Co.
American Stove Co.
Anchor Rubber Products, Inc.
Anderson, V. D., Co.
Apex Electrical Mfg. Co.
Apex Smelting Co.
Arco Company
Armour & Company
Arrow Aluminum Castings Co.
Art Gravure Corp. of Ohio
Art Metal Co.
Artisan Metal Works Co.
Astrup Company
Atlas Bolt & Screw Co.
Atlas Car & Mfg. Co.
Austin Company
Austin Powder Co.

Bailey Meter Co.
Baker-Raulang Co.
Bamberger-Reinthal Co.
Bardons & Oliver, Inc.
Barmatic Products Co.
Barth Stamping & Machine Works, Inc.
Bartlett, C. O., & Snow Co.
Bartunek Bros. Co., Inc.
Basic Refractories, Inc.
Beverages, Inc.
Bishop & Babcock Mfg. Co.
Black Boring & Machine Co.
Bliss, E. W., Co.
Bloomfield Co.
Bonnar-Vawter, Inc.
Bowler Foundry Co.
Brewing Corp. of America
Brown Fence & Wire Co.
Browning Crane & Shovel Co., The
Brush Development Co., The
Bryant Heater Co.
Buckeye Brass & Mfg. Co.
Buckeye Forging Co.
Bud Radio, Inc.
Builders Structural Steel Co., The
Bunell Machine & Tool Co.
Burdett Oxygen Co. of Cleveland, Inc.,
Canfield Oil Co.
Capper-Harman-Slocum, Inc.
Cashmere Corp. of America
Celotex Corp., The
Central Brass Mfg. Co., The
Champion Forge Co.
Champion Rivet Co.
Chandler & Price Co.
Chandler Products Corp.
Chase Brass & Copper Co., Inc.
Chicago Pneumatic Tool Co.

Chilcote Company, The
Chromium Corp. of America
City Ice & Fuel Co., The
Clark Controller Co.
Cleveland Brass Mfg. Co.
Cleveland Builders Supply Co.
Cleveland Cap Screw Co.
Cleveland Chain & Mfg. Co.
Cleveland City Forge Co.
Cleveland Coca-Cola Bottling Co.
Cleveland Container Co.
Cleveland Co-Operative Stove Co.
Cleveland Crane & Engineering Co.
Cleveland Dental Mfg. Co.
Cleveland Electric Illuminating Co.
Cleveland Electronics, Inc.
Cleveland Frog & Crossing Co.
Cleveland Fruit Juice Co., The
Cleveland Furniture Mfg. Co., The
Cleveland Graphite Bronze Co.
Cleveland Hardware & Forging Co.
Cleveland Heater Co., The
Cleveland Hobbing Machine Co.
Cleveland Home Brewing Co., The
Cleveland News
Cleveland Plain Dealer
Cleveland Pneumatic Tool Co.
Cleveland Press
Cleveland Provision Co.
Cleveland Punch & Shear Works Co.
Cleveland Quarries Co., The
Cleveland Refrigerator Co.
Cleveland Republic Tool Corp.
Cleveland-Sandusky Brewing Corp.
Cleveland Shopping News Co.
Cleveland Slag Co.
Cleveland Society for the Blind, The
Cleveland Steel Barrel Co.
Cleveland Steel Products Corp.
Cleveland Trencher Co., The
Cleveland Tucking & Pleating Co.
Cleveland Twist Drill Co.
Cleveland Welding Co.
Cleveland Wire Spring Co., The
Cleveland Worm & Gear Co.
Cleveland Worsted Mills Co.
Colonial Woolen Mills Co., The

Columbia Axle Co., The
Commercial Bookbinding Co.
Commercial Forgings Co., The
Consolidated Iron-Steel Mfg. Co.
Container Corp. of America
Continental Carbon, Inc.
Continental Lithograph Corp.
Copifyer Lithograph Corp.
Cowles Tool Co.
Crome-Rite Corp.
Crucible Steel Casting Co.
Curtis Lock & Key Co.
Cuyahoga Foundry Co.
Cuyahoga Spring Co.
Cuyahoga Stamping Co.
Dairymen's Ohio Farmers Milk Co.
Dandee Pretzel & Potato Chip Co.
Daniel, Edw. W., Co.
Darling & Co.
Davies Can Co., The
Dean, O. A., Dairy Co.
Dennison Sewer Pipe Corp.
Diamond Alkali Co.
Dickey-Grabler Co.
Dill Mfg. Co.
Di-Noc Mfg. Co.
Dobeckmun Co.
Donley Bros. Co.
Dougherty Lumber Co.
Dracco Corp.
Dresser Industries, Inc.
Dunham Co., The
du Pont, E. I., de Nemours & Co.,
    Grasselli Chemicals Department
East Shore Machine Products Co.
Eaton Mfg. Co.
Eberhard Mfg. Co., Div. of Eastern
    Malleable Iron Co.
Edwards, William, Co.
Electric Controller & Mfg. Co.
Electric Products Co.
Electroline Mfg. Co.
Elwell-Parker Electric Co.
Empire Plow Co.
Enamel Products Co., The
Erie Dyeing & Processing Co.
Euclid Road Machinery Co.

Excelsior Knitting Mill, Inc.
Exline, William, Inc.
Fairmont Foods Co.
Fairmount Tool & Forging Co.
Famous Dress Co., The
Fanner Mfg. Co.
Fawick Airflex Co.
Ferbert-Schorndorfer Co., Div. of American Marietta Co.
Ferro Enamel Corp.
Ferro Machine & Foundry Co.
Ferry Cap & Set Screw Co.
Ferry, E. W., Screw Products, Inc.
Fishel-Vierling Co.
Foote-Burt Co.
Forest City Foundries Co.
Forest City Products, Inc.
Foundry Equipment Co.
France Mfg. Co.
Fulton Foundry & Machine Co.
Gabriel Company, The
Gair, Robert, Co., Inc.
Garland Co.
Geier, P. A., Co.
General Aluminum Mfg. Co.
General Baking Co.
General Chemical Co., Div. of Allied Chemical & Dye Corp.
General Dry Batteries, Inc.
General Electric Co.
General Motors Corp., Cleveland Diesel Engine Div.
General Motors Corp., Fisher Body Cleveland Div.
Geometric Stamping Co., The
Gilkey, W. S., Printing Co.
Glascote Products, Inc.
Glidden Company, The
Gluntz Brass & Aluminum Foundry Co.
Goodman, H., Inc.
Goodrich, B. F. Chemical Co.
Gottfried Company
Grabler Mfg. Co.
Great Lakes Box Co., Div. of General Container Corp.
Greif Bros. Cooperage Corp.

Gross, L. N., Co.
Guarantee Specialty Mfg. Co.
Haber, D. C., Knitting Co.
Hall Baking Co. (Star Bakery)
Hankins Container Co.
Harris Calorific Co.
Harris-Seybold Co.
Harsch, John, Bronze & Foundry Co.
Harshaw Chemical Co., The
Hauserman, E. F., Co.
Hecker, A. W., Co.
Hertner Electric Co.
Hickok Electrical Instrument Co.
Hildebrandt Provision Co.
Hill Acme Co.
Hill, F. H., Co., Inc.
Hillside Dairy Co.
Hodell Chain Co., The
Hohlfelder, F., Co.
Horsburgh & Scott Co.
Hotstream Heater Co.
Hough Bakeries, Inc.
Hupp Corp., Globe Stamping Div.
Hydraulic Equipment Co.
Hygrade Food Products Corp.
Industrial Rayon Corp.
Inland Steel Products Co.
Interior Steel Equipment Co.
Interlake Chemical Corp. of Delaware
Interlake Iron Corp.
International Molded Plastics, Inc.
Iron Fireman Mfg. Co.
J & L Steel Barrel Co., Draper Div.
Jack & Heintz Precision Industries, Inc.
Jaite Co., The
Johnston & Jennings Co.
Jones & Laughlin Steel Corp. (Otis Wks.)
Joseph & Feiss Co.
Joy Mfg. Co., Breckenridge Div.
Kaase, Richard W., Co.
Kaynee Company, The
Keller-Kohn Co.
Kelley Island Lime & Transport Co.,
Kemet Laboratories Co., Unit of Union Carbide & Carbon Corp.

Kilby Mfg. Co.
Klausner Cooperage Co.
Kroehler Mfg. Co.
Lake City Malleable Co.
Lampl Fashions, Inc.
Lampl Sportswear Mfg. Co.
Lamson & Sessions Co.
Langenau Mfg. Co., The
Laub, Jacob, Baking Co.
Leece-Neville Co.
Lees-Bradner Co.
Leisy Brewing Co., The
Lempco Products, Inc.
Le Roi Co., Cleveland Div.
Lewis Knitting Mills
Lewis Welding & Engineering Corp.
Lincoln Electric Co.
Linderme Tube Co.
Lindsay Wire Weaving Co., The
Lion Knitting Mills Co., The
Lockwood, L. B., Co.
Lubrizol Corp., The
Lyon Tailoring Co.
M. & N. Cigar Mfg. Co., Inc.
Manufacturers Brush Co.
Marble, B. L., Chair Co., The
Marquette Metal Products Co., The,
    Div. of Curtiss-Wright Corp.
Master Builders Co., The
Master Products Co.
McGean Chemical Co.
McNally-Doyle Co., The
Medusa Portland Cement Co.
Meister Brothers
Mendelson's, S. N., Sons Co. (Sher-
    man's Clothes)
Meriam Instrument Co., The
Meyer Dairy Products Co.
Midland Steel Products Co.
Mid-West Forge Co.
Midwest Industries, Inc.
Mighton, S. E., Co., Ltd.
Miller-Becker Co., The
Mills Company, The
Modern Tool & Die Co.
Monarch Aluminum Mfg. Co.
Monmouth Products Co.

Montana Flour Mills Co., Cleveland
    Div.
Morgan Lithograph Corp.
Motch & Merryweather Machinery Co.
Murray Ohio Mfg. Co.
N.E.A. Service, Inc.
National Acme Co.
National Biscuit Co.
National Bronze & Aluminum Foundry
    Co.
National Carbon Co., Inc.
National Malleable & Steel Castings Co.
National Refining Co.
National Screw & Mfg. Co.
National Tool Co.
Nickel Plate Foundry Co., The
North American Mfg. Co.
North American Refractories Co.
Noss Pretzel & Cone Co., The
Ohio Carbon Co.
Ohio Chemical & Mfg. Co.
Ohio Crankshaft Co., The
Ohio Electric Mfg. Co.
Ohio Forge & Machine Corp.
Ohio Foundry Co.
Ohio Gear Co.
Ohio Knitting Mills, Inc.
Ohio Mattress Co.
Ohio Nut & Bolt Co., The
Ohio Piston Co.
Ohio Provision Co.
Ohio Public Service Co.
Ohio Rubber Co.
Ohio Tool Co.
Oliver Corp., The
Osborn Mfg. Co.
Oster Mfg. Co.
Park Drop Forge Co.
Parker Appliance Co., The
Parker-Street Castings Co.
Parsons Engineering Corp.
Paterson-Leitch Co.
Patterson-Sargent Co.
Penton Publishing Co.
Perfection Stove Co.
Pesco Products Co., Div. of Borg-War-
    ner Corp.

Phoenix Machine Co.
Picker X-Ray Corp., Waite Mfg. Div.,
Inc.
Pilsener Brewing Co.
Pipe Machinery Co.
Platzner Knitting Mills
Precision Castings Co., Inc.
Pressure Castings, Inc.
Printz-Biederman Co., The
Producers Milk Co.
R. B. Biscuit Co., The
Rackle, George, & Sons Co.
Radiart Corp.
Reliance Electric & Engineering Co.
Republic Brass Co.
Republic Steel Corp.
Republic Structural Iron Works Co.
Reserve Knitting Mills, Inc.
Restemeier H. T., Potato Chip Co.
Richman Bros. Co.
Ric-Wil Co.
Riester & Thesmacher Co.
Ritmor Sportswear Co., Inc.
Rola Company, Inc., Div. of The Muter
Co.
Russell, F. C., Co.
Safety Clothing & Equipment Co.
Sanymetal Products Co., Inc.
Schmeller Aluminum Foundry Co.,
Inc.
Schoenberger, W. J., Co.
Scott & Fetzer Co.
Sealy Mattress Co.
Serbin, Inc.
Sheffield Bronze Paint Corp.
Sherwin-Williams Co.
Shuler Company
Simon, M. & D., Co.
Simplex Piston Ring Mfg. Co.
Slavin Tailors
Sly, W. W., Mfg. Co.
Smayda's Home Bakery
Smith, Werner G., Co., Div. of Archer-
Daniels-Midland Co.
Snapout Forms Co., The
Sommer & Adams Co.
Spang, J., Baking Co.

Stadler Products Co.
Stalwart Rubber Co., The
Standard Alloy Co., The
Standard Brewing Co.
Standard Envelope Mfg. Co.
Standard Knitting Mills, Inc.
Standard Oil Co. (Ohio)
Standard Products Co., Reid Products
Div.
Standard Tool Co.
Steel Improvement & Forge Co.
Sterling Brass Co.
Strabley Baking Co.
Strong Cobb & Co., Inc.
Superior Die Casting Co.
Superior Foundry, Inc.
Swartwout Company
Swift & Company
Taylor & Boggis Foundry
Taylor Chair Co., The
Telling-Belle Vernon Co., Div. of Na-
tional Dairy Products Corp.
Theurer-Norton Provision Co.
Thompson Aircraft Products Co.
Thompson Products, Inc.
Tinnerman Products, Inc.
Titan Valve & Mfg. Co., The
Towmotor Corp., The
Tremco Mfg. Co., The
Triplex Screw Co.
Truck Engineering Corp.
Truscon Steel Co.
Tyler, W. S., Co., The
Uarco, Inc.
United Screw & Bolt Corp., Cleveland
Div.
United States Air Compressor Co.,
The
U. S. Steel Wire Spring Co.
Upson-Walton Co.
Valley Mould & Iron Corp.
Van Dorn Iron Works Co.
Victoreen Instrument Co.
Viking Air Conditioning Corp.
Virden, John C., Co.
Vlchek Tool Co.
Wade, Nicholas H., Inc.

Wagner Awning & Mfg. Co.
Wagner Baking Corp.
Walker China Co., The
Ward Baking Co.
Ward Products Corp., Div. of The
  Gabriel Co.
Warner & Swasey Co.
Wasmer Bolt & Screw Corp.
Wean Equipment Corp.
Weatherhead Co.
Weaver Wall Co.
Weideman Co., The
Weldon Tool Co., The

Wellman Bronze & Aluminum Co.
Wellman Engineering Co.
Wellman, S. K., Co.
West Steel Casting Co.
Westinghouse Electric Corp.
Wheeler Industries, Inc.
White, H. N., Co., The
White Motor Co., The
White Sewing Machine Corp.
Willard Storage Battery Co.
Wolf Envelope Co.
World Publishing Co., The
Yoder Company, The

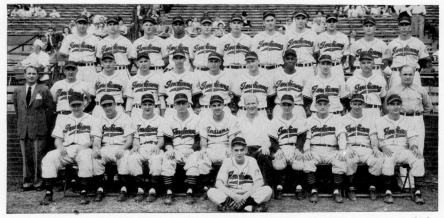

Cleveland Indians baseball team, winners of the American League Pennant and the World Series.
Front row: Eddie Robinson, Ken Keltner, Al Rosen, Mel Harder, Manager Lou Boudreau, President Bill Veeck, Muddy Ruel, Bill McKechnie, Joe Gordon, Johnny Berardino.
Second row: Traveling Secretary Spud Goldstein, Sam Zoldak, Ed Klieman, Steve Gromek, Russ Christopher, Gene Bearden, Bob Lemon, Satchel Paige, Bob Feller, Bob Muncrief, Trainer Lefty Weisman.
Back row: Walt Judnich, Allie Clark, Hal Peck, Larry Doby, Hank Edwards, Dale Mitchell, Bob Kennedy, Jim Hegan, Ray Boone, Joe Tipton, Thurman Tucker.
Seated in front: Batboy Billy Sheridan. Missing from picture: Don Black.

Cleveland Browns champion football team.
Front row: Trainer Wally Bock, Leonard Simonetti, Dean Sensanbaugher, Warren Lahr, George Terlep, Ed Ulinski, Tom James, Alex Agase, Trainer Morrie Kono.
Second row: Guard Coach Fritz Heisler, Ollie Cline, Ara Parseghian, Otto Graham, Cliff Lewis, Captain Lou Saban, Bob Gandio, Billy Boedeker, Bob Cowan, Edgar Jones, Backfield Coach John Brickels.
Third Row: Head Coach Paul Brown, Backfield Coach Blanton Collier, Dante Lavelli, Chubby Grigg, Tom Colella, Frank Kosikowski, Mel Maceau, Lin Houston, Tony Adamle, Weldon Humble, Marion Motley, Tackle Coach Bill Edwards, End Coach Dick Gallagher.
Back Row: Horace Gillom, George Young, Frank Gatski, Dub Jones, Lou Rymkus, John Yonakor, Mac Speedie, Ben Pucci, Lou Groza, Bill Willis, Chet Adams.

WORLD CHAMPIONS OF 1948

TERRITORIAL GROWTH
OF THE
CITY OF CLEVELAND

CITY OF CLEVELAND–
CITY PLAN COMMISSION

Annexations to the City of Cleveland

KEY TO ANNEXATIONS MAP

A. Original Village of Cleveland, incorporated by legislative act of Dec. 23, 1814.

B. Annexation by act of Dec. 31, 1829. Includes A.

C. Annexation by act of Feb. 18, 1834. Includes A and B.

D. Incorporated with A, B, and C as City of Cleveland by act of Mar. 5, 1836.

E. Remainder of Cleveland Township annexed by act of Mar. 22, 1850.

F. City of Ohio annexed by act of June 5, 1854.

G. Annexation of part of Brooklyn Township passed by legislative act of Feb. 16, 1864, and granted by county commissioners, Sept. 6, 1864.

HI. Portions of Brooklyn and Newburgh townships annexed by act of Feb. 28, 1867, and approval of county commissioners granted, Aug. 6, 1867.

K. Annexation of part of Newburgh Township granted by county commissioners, Mar. 9, 1870.

L. Ordinance to annex East Cleveland Village passed, Oct. 24, 1872.

MNO. Annexation of parts of Brooklyn, Newburgh, and East Cleveland townships granted by county commissioners, Feb. 8, 1873.

P. Annexation of portion of Newburgh Township granted by county commissioners, Dec. 8, 1873.

R. Annexation of part of Brooklyn Village granted by county commissioners, Nov. 10, 1890.

S. Annexation of portion of East Cleveland Township granted by county commissioners, Sept. 28, 1892.

T. Annexation of portion of Newburgh Township granted by county commissioners, Nov. 15, 1893.

U. Annexation of West Cleveland Village granted by county commissioners, Mar. 5, 1894.

V. Date of annexation of Brooklyn Village fixed by passage of ordinance by its council, June 15, 1894, after authorization passed, Apr. 30, 1894.

W. Portion of Village of Glenville annexed by grant of county commissioners, Feb. 26, 1898.

X. Annexation of portion of Glenville Village granted by county commissioners, Nov. 18, 1902.

Y. Annexation of portion of Linndale Village ordered by county commissioners, Dec. 19, 1903, and resolution adopted on Apr. 11, 1904, declaring said annexation as part of Cleveland.

Z. Ordinance to annex a portion of Brooklyn Township rejected, May 31, 1904.

AA. Annexation of portion of Brooklyn Township ordered by county commissioners, July 11, 1904.

BB. Annexation of portion of Newburgh Heights Village ordered by county commissioners, Sept. 25, 1905.

CC. Ordinance to annex Glenville City passed, June 19, 1905.

DD. Ordinance to annex Village of South Brooklyn passed, Dec. 11, 1905.

EE. Secretary of state notified of passage of ordinance to annex Corlett Village, Dec. 28, 1909.

FF. Secretary of state notified of passage of ordinance, annexing the Village of Collinwood, Jan. 21, 1910.

GG. Secretary of state notified of passage of ordinance annexing a portion of Shaker Township, June 22, 1912.

HH. Secretary of state notified of passage of ordinance annexing the Village of Nottingham, Jan. 14, 1913.

II. Secretary of state notified of passage of ordinance annexing the City of Newburgh, Feb. 10, 1913.

KK. Secretary of state notified of passage of ordinance annexing portion of Euclid Village, Aug. 27, 1914.

LL. Secretary of state notified of passage of ordinance annexing portion of East View Village, Dec. 1, 1914.

MM. Secretary of state notified of passage of ordinance annexing portion of Shaker Heights Village, Feb. 12, 1915.

NN. Secretary of state notified of passage of ordinance annexing portion of Brooklyn Township, Aug. 7, 1915.

OO. Secretary of state notified of passage of ordinances annexing portions of Brooklyn Township, Aug. 10, 1916, and Apr. 12, 1917, respectively.

PP.

QQ. Secretary of state notified of passage of ordinances annexing portions of East View Village and Warrensville Township, Sept. 15, 1917.

RR.

SS. Secretary of state notified of passage of ordinance annexing portion of East View Village, Feb. 10, 1919.

TT. Village of West Park recorded, Jan. 3, 1923. Record of village incorporations, county recorder's office.

UU. Annexation of portion of Euclid Village granted by county commissioners, Oct. 15, 1926.

VV. Annexation of portion of Warrensville Township granted by county commissioners, Mar. 9, 1927.

WW. Annexation of portion of Brooklyn Heights Village granted by county commissioners, June 6, 1927.

XX. Annexation of portion of Warrensville Township granted by county commissioners, May 25, 1927.

YY. Annexation of portion of Warrensville Township granted by county commissioners, July 21, 1927.

ZZ. Annexation of portion of Miles Heights Village granted by county commissioners, Apr. 25, 1928.

50. Annexation of Miles Heights Village ordered by county commissioners, Dec. 29, 1931. Annexation passed, Mar. 28, 1932.

51. Portion of old West Park Village detached from the City of Cleveland by Court of Common Pleas, Oct. 28, 1932.

52. Portion detached from the City of Cleveland to South Euclid by county commissioners, Mar. 12, 1943.

53. Annexation of portion of Brookpark Village granted by county commissioners, Mar. 28, 1946.

INDEX TO EARLY-DAY STREETS

A systematized plan of naming and numbering Cleveland streets was inaugurated in 1906 and it necessitated changes affecting many existing thoroughfares. The following streets are listed here with their modern equivalents, as their early-day identity was used in this volume prior to the transition.

PUBLIC OFFICIALS OF CLEVELAND, 1949

Thomas A. Burke   Mayor
Emil A. Bartunek   Secretary to Mayor
John P. Butler   Executive Assistant to Mayor

DEPARTMENT AND DIVISION HEADS

Law Department
Lee C. Howley, Director
Joseph H. Crowley, Chief Counsel
Joseph Stearns, Chief Police Prosecutor

Public Finance Department
Frank R. Hanrahan, Director
A. W. Akers, Commissioner of Accounts
Leonard S. Levy, City Treasurer
Stanley P. Nemec, Commissioner of Assessments and Licenses
Leo Weil, Acting Commissioner of Purchases and Supplies

Public Health and Welfare Department
Edward L. Worthington, Director
Harold J. Knapp, M.D., Commissioner of Health
Robert A. Burri, Commissioner of Welfare Institutions
Herbert G. Dyktor, Commissioner, Division of Air Pollution Control
Stanley A. Ferguson, Commissioner of City Hospital
John J. Pokorny, Commissioner of Relief

Public Utilities Department
Emil J. Crown, Director
George W. Hamlin, Acting Commissioner of Water and Heat
Joseph W. Ellms, Commissioner of Sewage Disposal
George C. Oxer, Commissioner of Light and Power
Stephen A. Ryan, Commissioner of Utilities Fiscal Control
Frank J. Schwemler, Commissioner of Utilities Engineering

Public Safety Department
William F. Smith, Director
Alvin J. Sutton, Assistant Director
George J. Matowitz, Chief of Police
James E. Nimmo, Acting Chief of Fire
William D. Guion, Commissioner, Division of Building and Housing
Al Rhoden, Acting Chief Dog Warden

Public Service Department
Samuel F. David, Director
Anthony Gattozzi, Commissioner of Architecture
John C. Wenrick, Commissioner of Engineering and Construction
Frank M. Cunningham, Commissioner of Motor Vehicle Maintenance
A. J. Preusser, Commissioner of Streets

Public Properties Department
Arthur L. Munson, Director
Samuel Newman, Commissioner of Parks and Forestry
Paul J. Hurd, Commissioner of Cleveland Auditorium and Stadium
John Berry, Commissioner of Municipal Airport
Axel M. Freed, Acting Commissioner of Cemeteries
James M. Lister, Commissioner of Design and Construction
F. C. Jeroski, Commissioner of Markets, Weights and Measures
John S. Nagy, Commissioner of Recreation
Edward H. Scanlon, Commissioner of Shade Trees
William T. Sojeba, Chief, Bureau of Street Lighting

PUBLIC OFFICIALS OF CUYAHOGA COUNTY, 1949

COUNTY COMMISSIONERS

John F. Curry   Joseph F. Gorman   Henry W. Speeth

ADMINISTRATIVE OFFICIALS

John A. Zangerle	County Auditor
Leonard F. Fuerst	County Clerk
Samuel R. Gerber, M.D.	County Coroner
Albert S. Porter	County Engineer
Frank T. Cullitan	County Prosecutor
Donald F. Lybarger	County Recorder
Joseph M. Sweeney	County Sheriff
Leslie R. Munroe	County Treasurer
E. R. Maher	County Purchasing Agent
John H. Puzinski	Sanitary Engineer
H. Leffingwell (Dog and Kennel)	Warden

BOARD OF ELECTIONS

Dan W. Duffy, Chairman   F. T. Matia
Albina R. Cermak   Daniel H. Wasserman
Ray C. Miller, Clerk

COUNTY BOARD OF CHILD WELFARE

Malcolm B. Vilas,   Winifred Fryer,
Chairman   Secretary
James E. Ewers, Executive Secretary

COUNTY BOARD OF EDUCATION

Gordon Mutersbaugh,   Clyde C. Hill,
President   Vice President
W. L. Shuman, Superintendent

COUNTY BOARD OF HEALTH

Marston Bergmann,   E. O. Klaas,
President   Vice President
Arthur J. Pearse, M.D., Commissioner

COUNTY LIBRARY BOARD

Raymond C. Linquist,   Arthur W. Fiske,
Librarian   President
John Hay, Secretary

COUNTY WELFARE DEPARTMENT

John J. Schaffer,   Clarence Yaeger,
Director   Assistant Director

METROPOLITAN PARK BOARD

S. H. Hazelwood, President   Oscar J. Horn
George R. Klein,   W. A. Stinchcomb,
Vice President   Director

SOLDIERS' RELIEF COMMISSION

William A. Sweeney,   James P. Mooney,
President   Secretary

CLEVELAND METROPOLITAN HOUSING AUTHORITY

L. D. McDonald,   A. I. Davey, Jr.,
Chairman   Vice Chairman
Ernest J. Bohn, Director

REGIONAL PLANNING COMMISSION

Raymond T. Cragin,   Clifford F. Hood,
President   Vice President
Proctor Noyes, Director

U. S. DISTRICT COURT

(Northern District of Ohio)

Paul Jones	Judge
Frank L. Kloeb (Toledo)	Judge
Emerich B. Freed	Judge
Robert N. Wilkin	Judge
Charles B. Watkins	Clerk
Herbert A. Horn	U. S. Commissioner
M. E. Patterson	Chief Probation Officer

U. S. REFEREES IN BANKRUPTCY

Carl D. Friebolin   William B. Woods

STATE

OHIO SUPREME COURT

Carl V. Weygandt, Chief Justice
William L. Hart   Kingsley A. Taft
Edward S. Matthias   Edward C. Turner
James G. Stewart   Charles B. Zimmerman
Seba H. Miller, Clerk

COUNTY
COURT OF APPEALS

Lee E. Skeel,   Joy Seth Hurd
Presiding Judge   Weldon L. Weber,
Charles J. McNamee   Bailiff

PROBATE COURT

Nelson J. Brewer   Judge
Philip Knowlton   Chief Clerk

JUVENILE COURT

Harry L. Eastman	Judge
William J. McDermott	Judge
John J. Mayar	Chief Probation Officer
Mary A. Neary	Supt., Detention Home
Lotti Biolosky	Girls' Referee
Milton F. Hay	Boys' Referee

COMMON PLEAS COURT

Samuel E. Kramer, Chief Justice

Joseph A. Artl	Frank J. Merrick
Edward Blythin	Adrian G. Newcomb
James C. Connell	Benjamin D. Nicola
Arthur H. Day	Homer G. Powell
Harry A. Hanna	Roy C. Scott
Julius M. Kovachy	Joseph H. Silbert
Charles J. McNamee	Samuel H. Silbert
Leonard F. Fuerst, Clerk	Simon W. Steenstra, Chief Bailiff

CITY

CLEVELAND MUNICIPAL COURT

John J. Busher, Chief Justice

James T. Cassidy	David C. Meck, Jr.
Frank D. Celebrezze	Louis Petrash
Lewis Drucker	John E. Sweeney
Edward F. Feighan	Charles A. Vanik
Mary B. Grossman	Lillian M. Westropp
P. B. Jackson	William J. Reichle, Clerk
A. M. Kovachy	Frank T. Kelly, Bailiff

OHIO GENERAL ASSEMBLY

STATE SENATE

Cuyahoga County Members

J. W. Bartunek	Howard M. Metzenbaum
William M. Boyd	Edwin F. Sawicki
Margaret A. Mahoney	Frank J. Svoboda

HOUSE OF REPRESENTATIVES

Cuyahoga County Members

Joseph H. Avellone	John J. Gallagher

Mrs. Marie Babka	Mrs. E. F. Gorman
Albert A. Benesch	William J. Hart
James M. Carney	B. V. Malikowski
Edward A. Cipra	Mark McElroy
Michael J. Crosser	J. J. McGettrick
John T. Duffy	John F. O'Brien
George E. Fedor	Francis D. Sullivan
Stephen A. Zona	

UNITED STATES CONGRESS

Michael A. Feighan (D)—20th District, Cleveland

Robert Crosser (D)—21st District, Cleveland

Frances P. Bolton (R)—22nd District, Cleveland

Stephen M. Young (D)—at large, Cleveland

Index